THE CAMBRIDGE
ANCIENT HISTORY

VOLUME XIV

THE CAMBRIDGE
ANCIENT HISTORY

VOLUME XIV

Late Antiquity: Empire and Successors,
A.D. 425–600

Edited by

AVERIL CAMERON
Warden of Keble College, Oxford

BRYAN WARD-PERKINS
Fellow of Trinity College, Oxford

MICHAEL WHITBY
Professor of Ancient History, University of Warwick

CAMBRIDGE
UNIVERSITY PRESS

PUBLISHED BY THE PRESS SYNDICATE OF THE UNIVERSITY OF CAMBRIDGE
The Pitt Building, Trumpington Street, Cambridge, United Kingdom

CAMBRIDGE UNIVERSITY PRESS
The Edinburgh Building, Cambridge CB2 2RU, UK
40 West 20th Street, New York NY 10011–4211, USA
10 Stamford Road, Oakleigh, VIC 3166, Australia
Ruiz de Alarcón 13, 28014 Madrid, Spain
Dock House, The Waterfront, Cape Town 8001, South Africa

http://www.cambridge.org

First published 2000

Printed in the United Kingdom at the University Press, Cambridge

Typeface Monotype Garamond 11/12pt   *System* QuarkXPress [SE]

A catalogue record for this book is available from the British Library

Library of Congress Catalogue card number: 75–85719

ISBN 0 521 32591 9 hardback

CONTENTS

v

PART II GOVERNMENT AND INSTITUTIONS

PART III EAST AND WEST: ECONOMY
AND SOCIETY

MAPS

TEXT-FIGURES

PREFACE

The decision to extend *The Cambridge Ancient History* to the end of the sixth century, from the closing date of A.D. 324 selected for the first edition of 1938, has already been explained in the Preface to Volume XIII. Scholarship in Britain lagged behind continental Europe in the discovery of 'late antiquity', which suffered (and to some extent still suffers) from the disadvantage of falling between the two stools of 'ancient history' and 'medieval history'. However, in 1964 the political and institutional parameters of the period were magisterially set out in English in A. H. M. Jones's *The Later Roman Empire 284–602. A Social, Economic and Administrative Survey*, which was followed seven years later by the very different picture presented in Peter Brown's *World of Late Antiquity* (1971).

Jones's evidence consisted primarily of legal texts, administrative documents and narrative political histories, from which he constructed a powerful, if undeniably bleak, image of the late Roman state; whereas Brown exploited mainly hagiography and the writings of pagan and Christian *literati* to reconstruct a world of vibrant (if somewhat anxious) spiritual and intellectual debate. More recently, in work pioneered by French and Italian scholars, the abundant and ever-increasing archaeological evidence for the period has also been brought into play. This material evidence proved conclusively that, in the eastern Mediterranean at least, late antiquity was no mere appendage to classical glories, but a period of spectacular prosperity and splendour.

It is our hope that *CAH* XIV mirrors and builds on earlier work on late antiquity; and that it provides an introduction to the richness of the different sources and different approaches that are now readily available for this period. As a multi-author work, it cannot have the crispness and sense of direction of the best single-author surveys, and we have not attempted as editors to iron out differences of opinion or of emphasis. On the other hand, there are obvious merits in multiple authorship. In particular, no single scholar can hope to be as much at home in sixth-century Britain as in Egypt, nor as comfortable with late antique saints as with barbarian warlords; so a wide range of expertise is needed to provide detailed introductions to specific fields of knowledge. Furthermore, multiplicity of opinion and approach characterizes modern scholarship; and this volume may rather be faulted as too single-minded in its overall shape than as too diverse.

The dates selected for the start and finish of the volume (*circa* 425 and *circa* 600) are, of course, primarily dates of convenience, in order to break 'history' into bite-size chunks and single, if door-stopper, volumes. The 420s are, however, a reasonable point for an historical break. In the west, the Vandal invasion of Africa in 429 brought about a decisive decline in imperial resources and influence; while, in the east, the growth of Hunnic power in the 430s was a very significant development. Historiographically, the now fragmentary *History* of Olympiodorus, which covered both western and eastern developments in some detail, concluded in 425, to be continued by the much more Constantinopolitan focus of Priscus' narrative; while the eastern ecclesiastical historians Socrates, Sozomen and Theodoret all avoided providing a thorough account of the Nestorian controversy and the 431 First Council of Ephesus, leaving this to their successors Liberatus and Evagrius. Our concluding date of *circa* 600 also needs some explanation, since it marks the end of the entire *Cambridge Ancient History*, and must therefore mark the approximate date when we think 'antiquity' ended. In the west, in politics, an earlier concluding date would probably be simpler: either towards the end of the fifth century, with the definitive fall of the western empire; or around 550, with the defeat of the Ostrogothic successor-state in Italy and the firm establishment in northern Europe of Frankish power. In the west, it is principally in terms of cultural and social continuities (in particular, in the survival of a recognizably 'Roman' episcopal and secular aristocracy) that our 'long' late antiquity, reaching up to A.D. 600, is justified. This is, indeed, close to what Henri Pirenne expounded in *Mahomet et Charlemagne* in 1937, though few scholars nowadays would agree with his argument for underlying economic continuity through the fifth and sixth centuries.

In the east, the choice of *circa* A.D. 600 as a concluding date for a history of antiquity is more straightforward (despite a recent fashion for extending late antiquity up to 750 and beyond), and received authoritative sanction in Jones's decision to draw his work to a close with the death of Maurice in A.D. 602. Scholars may debate whether the eastern empire had begun a process of serious decline at an earlier date (perhaps with the Great Plague of 541/2, or with the Slav and Avar invasions of the Balkans at the end of the century), but no one disputes that the Persian wars and Arab conquests of the earlier seventh century brought about dramatic and, as it turned out, irreversible shifts in the balance of power and political geography of the east, accompanied by a *bouleversement* of the political, social and economic order. Out of the dramatic events of the seventh century came eventually those changes in religious, cultural and ethnic identity that created the Arab and Islamic Near East and North Africa, and destroyed for ever the political and cultural unity of the ancient Mediterranean.

Although strong and valid arguments can be made for continuities in many fields of life up to around A.D. 600, it is also undeniably the case that the political and military upheavals of the fifth century in the west began a process whereby separate regions of the former empire went their separate ways and developed their own distinctive identities. Furthermore, in cultural and social life there was a great deal of diversity even within the politically united eastern empire. It is our hope that this volume brings out, particularly in its long regional section (Part IV), not only the ways in which the fifth- and sixth-century Roman world was still united and identifiable as 'ancient', but also the ways in which it was diverging from older patterns of life and fragmenting into separate units.

In contrast to earlier volumes that cover Roman history, the two volumes of the *CAH* that deal with late antiquity are probably more eastern than western Mediterranean in their focus. In part, this merely reflects the establishment of a specifically eastern polity during the fourth century, so that political 'events' now take place in the east as well as in the west. But it also reflects the way that the eastern empire came to dominate the political and mental worlds of the fifth and sixth centuries. The earliest barbarian successor-states in the west were, for the most part, in theory still part of a Roman empire, and after 476 this was an eastern-based power. Furthermore, the reality of eastern wealth and military muscle was brought home to the west very forcibly during the sixth century, when Justinian 'reconquered' Vandal Africa, Ostrogothic Italy and part of Visigothic Spain.

The centring of this volume on the Mediterranean and its leanings towards the east are in fact fortunate, given the decision, subsequent to the initial planning of *CAH*, to recommission the *Cambridge Medieval History* and to have a first, overlapping volume, running from A.D. 500 to 700. The *CMH*, inevitably and reasonably (from the perspective of later history), is essentially a history of what was to become Europe, and offers only partial coverage of events and developments in the Byzantine and Arab regions of the Mediterranean. By contrast, the *CAH*, including this volume, is equally correct (from the perspective of antiquity) to centre itself firmly on the Mediterranean, and to treat northern Europe as somewhat peripheral.

The work of editing *CAH* XIV was a genuinely collaborative venture, and, as a result, both pleasant and instructive. The three editors together were responsible for the overall shape of the book, and subject matter and length of the chapters, and their allocation to individual authors (aided at an early stage by John Matthews). All three editors subsequently read and commented on both first and second drafts of each chapter.

Our main debt of gratitude must be to the individual authors whose work is here presented: for being prepared to summarize their complex knowledge within a meagre allocation of words; and for their courtesy in responding to our promptings and suggestions. All of us have learnt a great deal from working with their chapters. We are particularly grateful to those authors who, for one reason or another, had to step into the breach at the last minute, and yet (without exception) produced full and stimulating chapters. We also must apologize to those who were prompt in submitting their work and then had to wait while other distinguished members of the camel-train were politely goaded into action.

Once again Barbara Hird has compiled the index. The editors are pleased to take this opportunity to acknowledge her enormous contribution to *The Cambridge Ancient History*. With the exception of Volume VII.1, and of Volume XII which is not yet in production, all of the volumes from V to XIV have been indexed by Barbara Hird. Her meticulously detailed and intelligent indexes draw together the scattered contents of these huge works and make them easily accessible to readers.

Both the editors and the individual contributors would also like to thank the many people and institutions who gave permission for their illustrative material to be reproduced.

Finally, it is a very pleasant duty to thank Pauline Hire at Cambridge University Press for all her help. She has seen the new *CAH* through from its very beginnings in 1970, and has been endlessly patient and helpful with us, despite our many academic twistings and turnings. Although this is not quite the last volume of the new *CAH* to appear, we are delighted to congratulate her on reaching the final date of A.D. 600, a long way from the 'Geological Ages' which opened Volume I. The commissioning and production of the new *Cambridge Ancient History* was a massive enterprise; that it succeeded is due to Pauline's efficiency, courtesy and perseverance.

A.C.
B.W.-P.
M.W.

CHAPTER 1

THE WESTERN EMPIRE, 425–76

PETER HEATHER

On 23 October 425 the emperor Valentinian III was installed as ruler of the western half of the Roman empire. The act was a triumph for the Theodosian dynasty, which had lost its grip on the west following the death of Valentinian's uncle, the emperor Honorius, on 15 August 423, and, at first sight, a remarkable demonstration of imperial unity. The young Valentinian (born on 2 July 419) had been taken to Constantinople by his mother Galla Placidia even before Honorius died. Valentinian's father, Flavius (Fl.) Constantius, had done much to reconstitute the western empire in the 410s. He then married Galla Placidia (Honorius' sister) on 1 January 417 at the start of his second consulship, and had himself declared co-emperor of the west in February 421. He died the following September, before he could extract recognition of his self-promotion from Constantinople. His death let loose an extended power struggle in the west, which at first centred on controlling the inactive Honorius.

Placidia and Valentinian had fled east in the course of these disputes in 422. When, after Honorius' death, power was seized by a high-ranking member of the western bureaucracy, the *notarius* John, the eastern emperor, Theodosius II, eventually decided to back Valentinian and the cause of dynastic unity. Hence, in spring 425, a large eastern force – combining fleet and field army – moved west, and despite the capture of its commander, Ardaburius, quickly put an end to the usurper. Imperial unity was sealed by the betrothal of Valentinian to the three-year-old Licinia Eudoxia, daughter of Theodosius II. The whole sequence of events was recorded in considerable detail by the historian Olympiodorus, who brought his story of a twenty-year period of crisis and reconstruction in the western empire to a happy conclusion with Valentinian's installation.

Thus Olympiodorus, writing from an eastern standpoint (he was, in fact, an eastern diplomat), might well have entitled his work 'How the West was Won'.[1] For the landowning Roman élites of the west, however, Valentinian's installation did little to address a series of problems, whose

---

[1] Although we know he liked to refer to the work as 'raw materials for a history' (ὕλη συγγραφῆς): Photius, *Bibl.* LXXX, trans. Blockley, p. 153.

I

causes were far-reaching indeed. A brief survey of the western empire at the end of 425 both makes clear the fact of imperial disarray and hints at its causes (cf. Fig. 1).

At the periphery, control had been lost altogether. Local Romano-British élites had declared themselves independent of Honorius in c. 410, relying, it seems, upon mercenaries from across the North Sea (Angles and Saxons) to assist in their defence. Across the Channel, a similar sequence of events had unfolded in Armorica (broadly speaking, modern Brittany) at more or less the same time (Zos. VI.5.3). Although central imperial control was in the process of being restored there by 417, north-western Gaul remained, as we shall see, a centre of separatist tendencies. In the south-west, the Goths whom we know as Visigoths had been settled by formal treaty in Aquitaine – the Garonne valley between Bordeaux and Toulouse – in 416 and/or 418.[2] They likewise remained assertive of their own interests, exploiting the central power-struggles of the mid 420s, for instance, to besiege Arles (see below). By this date, Arles had replaced Trier as the main seat of imperial power north of the Alps.

Elsewhere, the situation was no less problematic. In eastern Gaul, along the Rhine frontier, while there is no record during 425 of any actual Frankish, Alamannic or Burgundian activity, the ambitions of these peoples (either as whole confederations or by way of their constituent parts) posed a constant threat which would develop in intensity. In 413, for instance, they had supported the Gallic usurper Jovinus against Honorius' regime,[3] and, as we shall see, the crisis of the mid 420s was exploited by all three.

In the Iberian peninsula, likewise, central imperial control was under threat. Groups of Vandals, Alans and Sueves had crossed the Pyrenees in 409. As the chronicler Hydatius put it, 'some say September 28th, others October 12th, but it was definitely a Tuesday' (34[42]). They had subsequently divided the Hispanic provinces between them, and, although one group of Vandals and many Alans had been destroyed by joint Romano-Gothic campaigns in the second half of the 410s, the Hasding Vandal coalition (which also now included many Alans) and the Sueves remained unsubdued in Baetica and Gallaecia respectively. The death of Honorius and its aftermath provided the Vandals, at least, with an opportunity for expansion which they cheerfully accepted. In and around 425, they captured Seville, the capital of Baetica, moved into Carthaginiensis, took the Balearic islands, and even made a first move into Mauretania in North Africa (Hydat. *Chron.* 77[86]).

Thus, of the western empire's traditional territories, only the Italian peninsula and its rich and strategically vital North African provinces were

---

[2] See e.g. Wolfram (1988) 170–4 or Heather, *Goths and Romans* 220–1.
[3] Matthews (1975) ch. 12.

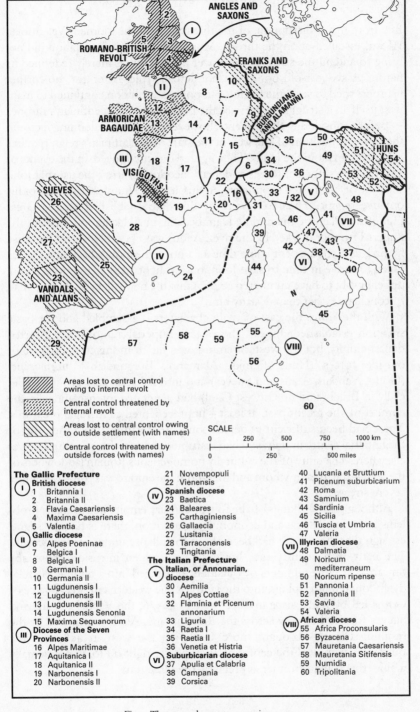

ANGLES AND SAXONS

ROMANO-BRITISH REVOLT

FRANKS AND SAXONS

BURGUNDIANS AND ALAMANNI

HUNS

ARMORICAN BAGAUDAE

VISIGOTHS

SUEVES

VANDALS AND ALANS

N

SCALE
0   250   500   750   1000 km
0   250   500 miles

Areas lost to central control owing to internal revolt

Central control threatened by internal revolt

Areas lost to central control owing to outside settlement (with names)

Central control threatened by outside forces (with names)

The Gallic Prefecture
(I) British diocese
1 Britannia I
2 Britannia II
3 Flavia Caesariensis
4 Maxima Caesariensis
5 Valentia
(II) Gallic diocese
6 Alpes Poeninae
7 Belgica I
8 Belgica II
9 Germania I
10 Germania II
11 Lugdunensis I
12 Lugdunensis II
13 Lugdunensis III
14 Lugdunensis Senonia
15 Maxima Sequanorum
(III) Diocese of the Seven Provinces
16 Alpes Maritimae
17 Aquitanica I
18 Aquitanica II
19 Narbonensis I
20 Narbonensis II

21 Novempopuli
22 Viennensis
(IV) Spanish diocese
23 Baetica
24 Baleares
25 Carthaginiensis
26 Gallaecia
27 Lusitania
28 Tarraconensis
29 Tingitania
The Italian Prefecture
(V) Italian, or Annonarian, diocese
30 Aemilia
31 Alpes Cottiae
32 Flaminia et Picenum annonarium
33 Liguria
34 Raetia I
35 Raetia II
36 Venetia et Histria
(VI) Suburbicarian diocese
37 Apulia et Calabria
38 Campania
39 Corsica

40 Lucania et Bruttium
41 Picenum suburbicarium
42 Roma
43 Samnium
44 Sardinia
45 Sicilia
46 Tuscia et Umbria
47 Valeria
(VII) Illyrican diocese
48 Dalmatia
49 Noricum mediterraneum
50 Noricum ripense
51 Pannonia I
52 Pannonia II
53 Savia
54 Valeria
(VIII) African diocese
55 Africa Proconsularis
56 Byzacena
57 Mauretania Caesariensis
58 Mauretania Sitifensis
59 Numidia
60 Tripolitania

Fig. 1 Threats to the western empire, c. 425

free from major disruption, or the threat of it, at the moment Valentinian III was installed upon the throne. More than that, his installation did not bring to an end the struggle for power in the west; it merely redefined its nature. A six-year-old boy could not actually rule. After 425, no further usurpers tried to seize the throne, but political ambition continued to manifest itself in a struggle to exercise the power behind Valentinian's throne.

Before considering these events, however, one further defining factor in the strategic position of the west at the start of Valentinian's reign requires brief examination: the Huns. They figured directly, indeed, in the events of 425. Lacking sufficient forces to defeat Theodosius' army, the usurper John sent one of his trusted supporters, Aetius, to seek Hunnic assistance for his putative regime. The Huns were by this date established on the Great Hungarian Plain of the middle Danube, still, in all likelihood, beyond the imperial frontier marked by the river. Aetius was chosen, it seems, because he had, as a child, spent some time as a hostage among the Huns. Aetius failed to arrive in time to save John, but brought such a large force (said, unbelievably, to have numbered 60,000) that the new rulers of the west had to conciliate rather than destroy him.[4]

With the Huns, the cast of main characters is assembled and the basic situation established. In 425, the eastern imperial authorities reasserted dynastic unity, but the western empire was far from intact. A mixture of outside forces (Huns, Franks, Alamanni, Burgundians), immigrants (Goths, Vandals, Alans and Sueves) and internal separatist groups (especially in Britain and north-west Gaul) had generated intense and – in the context of the recent past, at least – unprecedented centrifugal pressures. These had been sufficient to detach some areas entirely from the orbit of the imperial centre in Italy, and had disrupted the exercise of central power elsewhere. The unity of the culturally homogeneous Roman landowners of the west – the men by whom and for whom the empire was run – was under severe stress.

Although the workings of the fourth-century empire betray many problems in socio-political and economic organization, there is not the slightest sign that the empire had been about to collapse under its own weight. The early fifth century saw, however, the sudden intrusion, from 405 onwards, of large numbers of outsiders, organized into a number of relatively coherent groupings, into the lands of the western empire. A force of Goths led by Radagaisus invaded Italy in 405/6, the Vandals, Alans and Sueves forced their way across the Rhine in 406, Alaric – attracted by the resulting chaos – brought more Goths to the west in 408, and the Burgundians moved the centre of their power right on to, if not actually within, the Roman frontier at precisely the same time.

[4] Refs. as *PLRE* II.22.

Why this should have happened has occasioned much debate. To my mind, however, the key to these events is provided by the activities of the Huns. It is well known that their western movements had pushed some of the Goths later led by Alaric across the Danube in 376. What is less well understood is that, as late as the 390s, the centre of Hunnic power still lay north of the Black Sea, well to the east of the Carpathian mountains. By 425, as we have seen, they had moved in force into Hungary, and it was almost certainly in response to this second wave of western Hunnic expansion that Goths, Vandals, Alans, Sueves and Burgundians fled across the Roman frontier during the first decade of the fifth century.[5] By 425, these intrusions had caused, as we have seen, enormous difficulties for the western empire, which the installation of Valentinian III in 425 did nothing in itself to solve.

I. THE ERA OF AETIUS 425–54

The half-century of imperial history covered by this chapter can be divided into two roughly equal parts, the watershed marked by the death of Aetius. This is no artificial divide. The nearly thirty years of Aetius' prominence were characterized by a very different mode of political operation from the last two decades of the western empire's existence after his death. Broadly speaking, Aetius was able to pursue a more traditional line of policy towards the immigrant groups who had forced their way into the western empire than was possible in the circumstances faced by his successors.

1. *The struggle for power 425–33*

The main contenders for power in the years after 425 were the leaders of three of the main army groups in the west: Felix, senior *magister militum praesentalis* and commander in Italy, Boniface, commander in Africa, and Aetius, commander in Gaul. The latter post was Aetius' pay-off for not using his Hunnic army against Valentinian's eastern forces in 425. Felix, it seems, made the first move. Accusing Boniface of disloyalty, he ordered the latter to return to Italy in 427. When Boniface refused, Felix sent a force to North Africa, but it was defeated. Then Aetius stepped in. On the back of military success against both Visigoths (426) and Franks (428), Aetius felt confident enough to move against Felix. Perhaps these successes had attracted political support from Valentinian's mother, Galla Placidia, and other key members of the court. They certainly secured for Aetius a transfer to Italy and promotion to the post of junior *magister militum praesentalis*. The surviving sources are too thin for us to be certain of the exact course

[5] Heather (1995) 5–19.

of events, but in May 430 Aetius had Felix and his wife arrested for plotting against him. They were quickly executed at Ravenna.

A decisive encounter with Boniface was not long delayed. As the struggle between Aetius and Felix played itself out, Boniface was attempting to deal with the Vandals who had crossed from Spain to North Africa in 429. Although Aetius had successfully undermined Felix, he clearly lost ground at court in the early 430s. Perhaps other court politicians, such as Galla Placidia, did not want to fall entirely under Aetius' control. Thus Boniface was recalled to Rome in 432, seemingly in Aetius' absence, and promoted *magister militum praesentalis*. Aetius was quick to respond. Marching to Italy with an army, he met Boniface in battle near Rimini. Boniface was victorious, forcing Aetius to flee, but was himself mortally wounded in the action and died soon afterwards. The post of *magister militum praesentalis* passed to his son-in-law Sebastianus.

Aetius, however, had other resources upon which to draw. He first retreated to his country estates but, after an attempt was made on his life, he turned (as he did in 425) to the Huns. In 433, he returned to Italy with sufficiently large Hunnic reinforcements to cause Sebastianus to flee to Constantinople, where he remained until 444. Aetius became senior *magister militum praesentalis*. By the end of 433, therefore, both of Aetius' main rivals had been defeated, and his position in the west was unchallenged. On 5 September 435, he adopted the title *Patricius* to express his pre-eminence. Valentinian, perhaps wisely, continued to take no active part in the struggles going on around him. By a combination of assassination, battle and luck, Aetius had gained control of the western empire.

Fierce struggles, with death the likely price of failure, were hardly a new phenomenon in imperial politics. Once semi-autonomous outside groups had established themselves on imperial territory, however, the paralysis that such struggles caused at the centre resulted in other dangers too. In the era of Aetius, most of the immigrants were content to operate within a political and ideological framework which accepted the existence of the Roman empire. According to circumstance, they sought Roman commands and dignities, married into the imperial family (Galla Placidia's first husband was Alaric's successor, Athaulf), or sponsored usurpations, rather than attempting to carve out their own entirely independent states.[6] Ostensible respect for *romanitas* never prevented the immigrants, however, from looking to extend their own particular niche within the empire. Hence the struggle of the three generals between 425 and 433 further loosened the bonds of central control.

---

[6] Cf. Athaulf's famous remark that he had first thought to replace *Romania* with *Gothia*, but then decided to use Gothic military power to sustain the empire: Oros. VII.43.2–3. On the ambitions of Alaric and Athaulf, see Heather, *Goths and Romans* 215–17, 219–24. Burgundians and Alans supported the usurpation of Jovinus (p. 2 above), and the Vandal Gunderic seems to have supported a usurpation in Spain (*PLRE* II.745).

As we have seen, the Goths of Aquitaine threatened Arles, the second city of the empire, in 426. A second revolt against Roman power led by a Gothic noble, Anaolsus, unfolded in 430, but this was perhaps the unsanctioned, independent action of an autonomous sub-leader. The Vandals were even more active. In the mid 420s, they first dramatically expanded their range of action in the Iberian peninsula, and then in 429 took the decisive step of crossing *en masse* to Mauretania in North Africa. With their departure, the Sueves were free to extend their attacks on the Roman population of Gallaecia in both 430 and 431 (Hydat. *Chron.* 81[91], 86[96]). Rhenish groups, likewise, exploited the power vacuum. Counterattacks are recorded against the Franks in 428 and 432, and, in 430 and 431, the Alamanni raided across the frontier.

All this directly threatened the empire's survival. To put it simply, the Roman state taxed the agricultural production of its dependent territories to pay for a powerful army and a political-cum-administrative establishment.[7] Any loss of territory through permanent annexation or temporary damage in warfare thus meant loss of revenue and a weakening of the state machine. The pragmatic realization on the part of immigrant leaders that, in the early fifth century, the Roman state was still the most powerful political and military force of its day, and hence demanded some show of deference, did not make them any less assertive of independent political interests, nor those interests any less inimical to the Roman state.[8]

Moreover, any weakening of the Roman state (permanent or temporary) had the more insidious effect of breaking down ties between local Roman élites and the imperial centre. Again reducing the matter to basics, it can be said that the late Roman élite consisted of a geographically widespread class of local landowners, who also participated in imperial institutions. They did so because the Roman state offered protection and legitimation of their position at home and, via imperial careers, substantial additional opportunities for making money and acquiring influence. This extra wealth and power, together with the lifelong rights and privileges which were part and parcel of an imperial career, further strengthened the landowners' position within their local societies.[9]

When, because of the appearance of outside military forces, the Roman state was no longer in a position to sustain local élites (and hence to constrain their loyalties, either), the whole point of their attachment to the empire disappeared. As a result, they had to look elsewhere for props to their position, notably to whichever barbarian immigrant group was currently most powerful in their own locality. For some, perhaps those with most invested in the imperial system, the process of psychological adjustment to the decline of

---

[7] On its workings: Jones *LRE* ch. 13. Structural importance: Wickham (1984).

[8] For a different view, Goffart (1981) 295ff. and Goffart (1989) 93ff.

[9] On careers, Matthews, (1975) ch. 1 and *passim*; Heather (1994) 25ff.

imperial power was naturally slow (see further pp. 29–30 below); for others, such switches of loyalty could happen quickly. In Gaul in the early 410s, for instance, Athaulf attracted considerable support from local landowning élites. They saw good relations with the militarily powerful Goths as the best means, in changed circumstances, of preserving the essential fabric of their lives – above all, their property.[10] An alternative response to the same problem, and equally damaging to the interests of the imperial centre, was self-assertion. As we have seen, in Britain and Armorica local élites of a more determined and martial character had attempted to take responsibility for their own defence as early as the 410s,[11] and there may have been similar separatist movements in Vindelicia and Noricum in 430.[12] The central power vacuum of the 420s and early 430s thus gave complete freedom to a whole range of forces which posed a direct threat to the Roman state.

2. *Years of hope 434–9*

Once his position was secure, Aetius was able to take direct action to restore the situation. As we have seen, even during his struggles with Felix and Boniface, he had won some victories over the Franks and Goths. After 434, he pushed the policy forward with greater vigour. Defeating Roman rivals before tackling the barbarian threat might seem the wrong order of priorities. But political crisis does not suspend personal ambition; in fact, it often provides a genuine pretext for a quarrel. And to combat the grave threats now facing the empire, any leader needed to deploy the full range of imperial resources – particularly, of course, on the military front.

Aetius' main military successes again came in Gaul. In 436, the Goths revolted again and, moving south and east, laid siege to Narbonne. This was no small-scale raid, and it took Aetius three years to restore some order. His main commander in the region was the *dux* Litorius, who operated with an army primarily of Huns. The Goths suffered considerable losses in 437/8, but in 439 Litorius was himself defeated, captured and killed near Toulouse. There followed a renewal of the treaty of 418. Despite the loss of Litorius, Aetius had prevented the Goths from making any further gains. More successes came against the Franks (among whom unrest had broken out in 432). Perhaps more worrying was the extensive revolt of so-called bagaudae led by one Tibatto in 435. It began in Armorica (where, as we have seen, there had been trouble before) and spread more widely through Gaul. In 437, however, Tibatto was captured and the revolt suppressed. Aetius also enjoyed great success against the Burgundians. Since the first decade of the fifth century, they had been established right on the Roman frontier. They

---

[10] The best illustration of the fundamental importance of secure property is Priscus, ed. Blockley fr. 11.2, p. 72.504–7.   [11] See e.g. Wood (1984); Van Dam, *Leadership and Community* pt 1.
[12] *Chron. Min.* 11.22 s.a. 430; Sid. Ap. *Carm.* VII.233–4; cf. Thompson (1956) 35.

are recorded in different sources as suffering heavy defeats in both 436 and 437. The first occasion was explicitly at Aetius' hands, the second at the hands of the Huns. As we shall see, Aetius may well have organized the Hunnic attack too (if both were not part of one and the same campaign).[13] In the Iberian peninsula, Aetius' approach was less direct, but not, it seems, unsuccessful. The Sueves were still harassing the Gallaecians, and Aetius responded to requests for help by sending embassies in 433 and 438 (Hydat. *Chron.* 88[98]; 91[100]; 105[113]). A panegyric of Aetius does record a military intervention in Spain by one of his subordinates, but there is no record of this in the writings of the Hispano-Roman chronicler Hydatius.[14] Whatever the case, the second embassy seems to have persuaded the Sueves to make peace, not least, one presumes, because by the latter date Aetius had already enjoyed considerable military success in Gaul.

Apart from the indigenous resources of the western empire, Aetius drew on two outside sources of assistance in these years. The first was the eastern empire. In 431, initially in support of Boniface (whom the east may have backed in the struggle with Aetius), an eastern army under Aspar came to North Africa to combat the Vandals. According to Procopius (*Wars* III.3.36), Aspar left North Africa for Constantinople after being defeated by the Vandals, and before Boniface's death in battle against Aetius (432). He was still in Carthage on 1 January 434, however, by which time Aetius was securely established in power in Italy, so that a working relationship was probably established between Aspar and Aetius. It also seems likely that Aspar brokered the peace treaty with the Vandals in 435, which saw them settled in relatively poor areas of Mauretania and the Numidian coast (Fig. 2).[15] Constantinople thus continued to take an active interest in western affairs, and, if eastern forces were unable to defeat the Vandals, they did enough to exclude them from the richest North African provinces of Proconsularis and Byzacena.

Second, Aetius drew very heavily on Hunnic military manpower, which he presumably paid for in hard cash. The Huns had been his trump card in internal imperial political disputes in both 425 and 433.[16] From the mid 430s onwards, Aetius also used them extensively in Gaul, where they were responsible both for crushing the Armorican bagaudae and for much of the campaign against the Visigoths.[17] The Huns also savaged the Burgundians in 437, an event organized – according to some of our sources, at least – by Aetius, and which preceded a resettlement of the survivors within the Roman frontier.[18]

---

[13] Refs. as *PLRE* II.24–5. Secondary accounts: Mommsen, (1901) 523; Stein (1959) 322ff.; Zecchini (1983) ch. 9.   [14] Merobaud. *Pan.* fr. IIA 22–3; Jord. *Get.* 176; cf. *PLRE* II.25.
[15] Sources: *PLRE* II.166; cf. Courtois (1955) 155–71.   [16] Refs. as *PLRE* II.23–4.
[17] Refs. as *PLRE* II.684–5.
[18] Refs. as *PLRE* II.523. On Aetius' role: Stein (1959) 323; O'Flynn (1983) 89 n. 4.

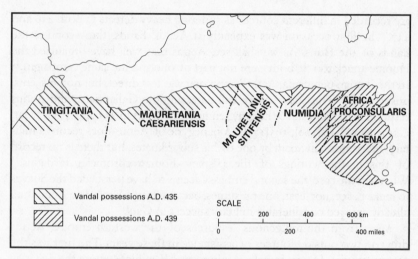

Fig. 2 Vandal and Alan settlements in North Africa

In the later 430s, therefore, Aetius restored some order to the western empire. Britain did not return to the fold, although substantial contacts of a more informal nature clearly continued between Romano-Britons and their continental counterparts. The two famous visits to the island of bishop Germanus of Auxerre in 429 and (probably) the early 440s are likely to be no more than the tip of a substantial iceberg. Otherwise, indigenous and immigrant revolts in Gaul were suppressed, and Rhine frontier groups defeated. The Sueves were kept within reasonable bounds in north-western Spain and, with eastern help, the Vandals confined to the poorer North African provinces. This last point is worth stressing, for Aetius has been criticized in modern times for concentrating on Gaul at the expense of the richer and strategically more defensible provinces of North Africa. Ties between Italian and southern Gallic élites were very strong, however, and Aetius had made his name in Gaul. Abandoning the latter would have been politically impossible, therefore, and it was far from an unreasoanble line of policy to rely on eastern help to retain the most valuable African provinces. In many ways, the most striking aspect of Aetius' success is the role played by the Huns. Not only did they rescue him from political defeat in both 425 and 432, but were also central to his military success in Gaul. With Hunnic and eastern imperial assistance, therefore, Aetius succeeded in creating a precarious balance of power in the 430s, which, at least to some extent, checked the process of political fragmentation in the west.

3. The loss of Africa and after, 439–49

An already difficult situation was pushed into acute crisis, however, when in 439 the Vandals marched into Carthage to take possession of the richest provinces of North Africa.[19] These lands were crucial to the empire, not least in feeding the population of Rome. The Vandals also followed up this success by exploiting to full effect the maritime expertise available in the city. Early in 440 a large Vandal fleet left Carthage, and landed on, and devastated, large parts of another major revenue centre of the western empire: Sicily. Both east and west reacted swiftly to the Vandals' new capacities. The maritime defences of Rome and Constantinople were immediately strengthened,[20] and plans were laid to restore the situation. That eastern help was on its way was announced by Aetius as early as June 440, but, given all the logistic problems (cf. *CJ* XII.8.2; 50.21), a counter-expedition could not be ready before the campaigning season of 441. At the start of the year, a combined force from east and west gathered in Sicily, the eastern troops, under the command of Areobindus, having been drawn from the Danube frontier.[21] In many ways, this crisis was the acid test of whether Aetius' efforts could really hold the line against political fragmentation in the west or were merely slowing it down. Unfortunately for the western empire, the expedition went no further than Sicily. A critical change had occurred in the political stance of the Huns.

By *c.* 440, the Hunnic empire was approaching the apogee of its power, under Attila and (at first) his brother Bleda. This was the end result, it seems, of related processes, which saw both the increasing centralization of power among the Huns and continuing conquests of other tribes. Between them, these transformations brought unprecedented numbers of different subjects under the direct control of individual Hunnic leaders.[22] Because of this greater strength, Hunnic leaders could widen the scope of their ambitions, and Aetius' old policy of using them against unwanted immigrants on Roman soil collapsed.[23] As the joint east–west Vandal expedition gathered in Sicily, Attila and Bleda launched their first major invasion across the Danube. Exploiting a variety of pretexts, the Huns crossed the river in force, capturing the cities of Viminacium and Margus. Smaller-scale raiding extended over a wider area.[24]

One direct result of this sequence of events was that North Africa was secured for the Vandals. Many of the eastern troops in Sicily had been drafted from the Danube frontier and, because of the Huns, had to return. In consequence, Aetius was forced in 442 to acknowledge by treaty the

---

[19] Courtois (1955) 171ff.   [20] *Nov. Val.* 5.3; *Chron. Pasch.* ad a. 439 = *Chron. Min.* 11.80.

[21] Best account: Maenchen-Helfen (1973) 108ff.; cf. Stein (1959) 324–5; Zecchini (1983) 171ff.

[22] See further Mommsen (1901) 524–6; Thompson (1996) 26ff.; Harmatta (1952) 292ff.; Maenchen-Helfen (1973) 94ff.; cf. ch. 23 (Whitby), pp. 704–8 below.

[23] Cf. amongst others Mommsen (1901) 526; Stein (1959) 334–5. This has perhaps also been the policy of Fl. Constantius: Heather (1995) 26.

[24] The sources for Attila's campaigns of the 440s have prompted two alternative chronological reconstructions. In general, I prefer Maenchen-Helfen (1973) 108ff. to Thompson (1996) 86ff. The question turns on the reliability of a notice provided by the Byzantine chronicler Theophanes; cf. Heather (1996) 252.

Fig. 3 Suevic expansion in Spain, c. 440-4

Vandals' latest conquests. In this agreement, Aetius recognized their control over Proconsular Africa, Byzacena and western Numidia. He received back the poorer and now devastated provinces previously ceded to the Vandals in 435.[25]

In the meantime, imperial control had suffered further setbacks in Spain. In the wake of Geiseric's seizure of Carthage, the Sueves, under a new king, Rechila, took advantage of Aetius' preoccupation with North Africa to expand their dominion. In 439, they moved out of Gallaecia to take the main city of Lusitania, Mérida. In 440, they captured Censurius, Aetius' commander and main representative in the peninsula. In 441, they took Seville and extended their control over the whole of Baetica and Carthaginiensis (Fig. 3).[26] Imperial control was further undermined by a series of bagaudic uprisings, particularly in Tarraconensis, the one province

[25] Maenchen-Helfen (1973) 108ff.; Courtois (1955) 173ff. Taxes in the returned provinces were reduced to an eighth: *Nov. Val.* 13.

[26] Hydat. *Chron.* 119 (capture of Merida: A.D. 439), 121-3 (fall of Seville, Baetica and Carthaginiensis: A.D. 440-1), *Chron. Min.* 11.23-4.

still under direct imperial control from the centre. As in Gaul, these uprisings would seem to have represented assertions of local against central imperial power. At least one of the revolts, that led by Basilius in Tyriaso (Tirasona) in 449, seems to have favoured a Suevic take-over of the province.[27] After Censurius' capture, a succession of imperial commanders were sent to the region: Asturius in 442, Merobaudes in 443 and Vitus in 446. Asturius and Merobaudes had to concentrate on defeating bagaudae, presumably to maintain imperial control in Tarraconensis (Hydat. *Chron.* 117[125]; 120[128]). Vitus' brief was more ambitious. Repeating the strategy of the 410s, he led a combined Roman and Gothic force into Carthaginiensis and Baetica to restore broader imperial control in the peninsula. Hydatius complains bitterly about the logistic demands the army made upon local Hispano-Romans, but this complaint was perhaps dictated by the expedition's outcome. When Vitus' force met the Sueves in battle, it was routed (Hydat. *Chron.* 126[134]). After 446, Hydatius records no further imperial military initiatives in the peninsula, and, in alliance with local groups, the Sueves began to make headway even in Tarraconensis.

Of Gaul in the 440s we know comparatively little. In the south-west, at least, Aetius' successes of the 430s were enough to keep the Goths quiet. No revolt of any kind is mentioned, and they contributed to Vitus' Spanish venture of 446. Elsewhere, imperial control did not go unchallenged. Armorica continued to present particular difficulties. Aetius seems to have established a group of Alans, under Goar, in the region in 442 to discourage rebellion. This did not prevent trouble from breaking out again in 448 – apparently because of the Alanic settlement – but, once again, the bagaudae were suppressed.[28] Whether the same reasoning underlay Aetius' decision to settle Burgundians in Savoy, in south-eastern Gaul, is unclear. This has sometimes been argued, but it is also possible that the Burgundians, heavily defeated by combined Romano-Hunnic action in the mid 430s, were refugees from the power of Bleda and Attila (repeating the pattern of earlier frontier penetrations in 376 and 406). Whatever the case, Aetius supervised their installation in Savoy in 443 (Chron. Gall. 452 no. 128 = *Chron. Min.* 11). On the Rhine frontier, we hear only of a Frankish attack on Arras which Aetius himself beat off, probably in 448. Control was thus substantially maintained in Gaul, but the loss of North Africa had plunged the western empire into acute financial crisis.

Such a crisis had been in the offing since the first decade of the century. Any territory caught up in warfare, annexed outright by ambitious barbarian kings or turned independent, involved temporary or permanent losses of revenue to the central Roman state. No more revenues came from

---

[27] Hydat. *Chron.* 133–4 [142], where Basilius firsts acts independently, and then helps the Suevic king Rechiarius to plunder Saragossa (Caesaraugusta).   [28] Refs. as *PLRE* II.26–7.

Britain after *c.* 410, and Spanish revenues must have been entirely lost for most of the 410s and were only partially restored thereafter. Parts of Gallaecia remained in Suevic hands throughout the fifth century, and the Vandals remained very active (sometimes attacking the Sueves, sometimes pillaging the Hispano-Romans) until they left Spain in 429.[29] It is also unlikely that much tax was raised in war-torn Gaul either in the 410s or the 430s. Moreover, substantial tax remissions had sometimes to be granted to areas caught up in fighting. After Alaric's Goths left Italy, Honorius reduced the land-tax of the eight Suburbicarian provinces to one-fifth of their normal level in 413, and, after a further five years, the taxes of Picenum and Tuscia to one-seventh, and those of Campania to one-ninth.[30]

The western empire's tax base had thus suffered substantial losses – both temporary and permanent – even before 439. Not surprisingly, tax-payers in those areas which did remain under central control seem to have faced ever-increasing burdens. It has been argued, for instance, that in 440 western tax rates were twice as high as those prevailing in the east even a century later.[31] When, in addition, the west lost control of its richest assets to the Vandals, and of other worthwhile ones to the Sueves, a bad situation was made incomparably worse. The legislation of Aetius' regime from the 440s shows unmistakable signs of the consequent financial stress. In 444, an imperial law claimed that plans for a larger army were being frustrated by revenues which were not large enough even to feed and clothe the existing troops. This statement was used to justify the introduction of the *siliquaticum*, a new sales-tax of about four per cent.[32] Just a few months previously, many bureaucrats had lost their exemptions from the recruitment tax (*Nov. Val.* 6.3 of 14 July 444), and other efforts had been made in 440 and 441 to cut back on tax privileges and corruption. The regime was thus desperate enough for cash to increase taxes for the landowning, bureaucratic classes on which it depended for political support.[33] The precarious balance of power established by Aetius in the 430s had been undermined, primarily because of the Huns' expansionary ambitions. Further twists in the Hunnic saga, in the late 440s and early 450s, would totally destroy it, and with it Aetius himself.

4. *Attila and after, 449–54*

Although unable to reverse the situation in Africa or the gains made by the Sueves in Spain, for most of the 440s the west did not, at least, have to deal

[29] E.g. Hydat. *Chron.* 71, 75, 86, 89–90, *Chron. Min.* II.20–1; cf. Thompson (1977).
[30] *C.Th.* XI.28.7, 12. After Vandal attacks, the taxes of Sicily were similarly reduced to a seventh: *Nov. Val.* 1.2 (440).   [31] Jones, *LRE* 464 n. 128, deduced from *Nov. Val.* 5.4.
[32] *Nov. Val.* 15 of September 444 to January 445; cf. *Nov. Val.* 24 of 447.
[33] Privileges: *Nov. Val.* 10.1 (A.D. 441), 10.1.3. Corruption: *Nov. Val.* 7.1–2 (A.D. 440 and 442). Unjustified exemptions: *Nov. Val.* 4 and 10 (440 and 441). Stein (1959) 337–8 argued from these laws that Aetius conspired with leading landowners to keep the land-tax down against the interests of the state. On this point, see Twyman (1970); Zecchini (1983) ch. 10; and, more generally, Weber (1989).

directly with Attila's ambitions. Sometime before 449, presumably under duress, Aetius had ceded the Pannonian province of Savia to the Huns (Priscus fr. 7; Blockley fr. 11.1). By the same date, Attila was also enjoying the rank of honorary *magister militum* of the western empire, with its attendant salary (Priscus fr. 8; Blockley fr. 11.2, p. 278.627–31). The circumstances of these concessions are unknown. In the meantime, Attila had concentrated on the Balkan possessions of the eastern empire, where he won huge victories in 441/2 and (probably) 447.[34] In the late 440s, however, Attila turned his attention westward.

Scandals within the royal family provided him with a pretext. The emperor Valentinian's sister, Honoria, conceived a child, we are told, as the result of an unsuitable love affair with one Eugenius, the manager of her estates. Eugenius was executed and Honoria placed in custody. To prevent further scandal she was subsequently betrothed to a trustworthy senator called Herculanus. At this point, she seems to have written to Attila offering him half the western empire as a dowry if he would rescue and marry her. In 449 or 450, consequently, Attila made a formal demand, based on the letter, and threatened war. What we should make of this is hard to know. The story appears in a wide variety of sources, and the fact of Honoria's disgrace seems securely enough established.[35] The likelihood is, however, that Attila (having probably exhausted the possibilities of immediate gains in the east) was in any case planning a western campaign, or series of campaigns.

Indeed, Attila carefully prepared the ground for a major western move, and Honoria was not his only pretext. In the summer of 449, western ambassadors were sent to Attila to answer his charge that a Roman banker called Silvanus was in possession of gold plate which was Attila's by right. The issue was trivial, but Attila threatened war if it was not settled as he wished (Priscus fr. 8; Blockley fr. 11.2, pp. 263, 265, 277). This might have been an autocrat's megalomania, but, given its context, I would take it as another sign that Attila wanted to press a quarrel with the west. Diplomatically, too, the ground was carefully prepared. In the summer of 450, outstanding issues in Attila's relations with Constantinople were settled on terms which the historian Priscus regarded as favourable to the eastern empire (frr. 13–14; Blockley fr. 15.3–4). Attila's generosity suggests that he was keen to secure his eastern front, presumably with a western campaign in mind.[36] At the same time, he was interfering in the west, not least in an attempt to sow discord among its different constituent powers. There are vague records of some kind of contact between Attila and Geiseric, who is said to have bribed Attila to turn his armies westwards. One of the leaders of the recently defeated bagaudae, the doctor Eudoxius, had fled to the Huns in 448. His reception may suggest that Attila foresaw

---

[34] I would generally follow Maenchen-Helfen (1973) 108ff. (cf. p. 11 above, n. 24). For details, see ch. 2 (Lee), pp. 41–2, and ch. 23 (Whitby), pp. 704–12 below.
[35] For further details with refs., Thompson (1996) 145–6.   [36] Cf. Thompson (1996) 143.

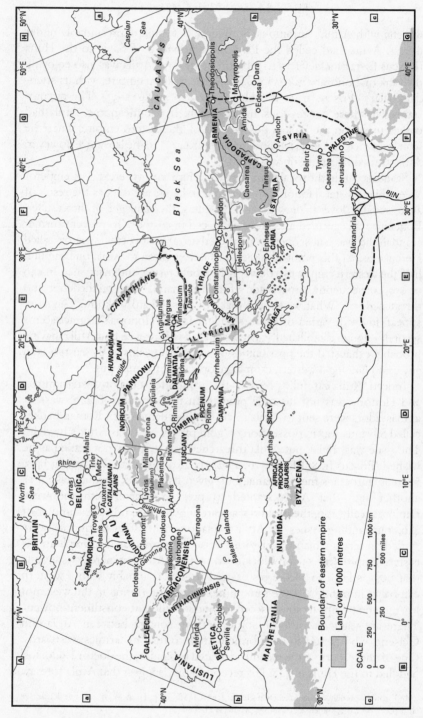

Map 1 The Roman world of the fifth and sixth century

a possible use for him in fomenting a revolt to ease the path of any Hunnic army operating in the west. Late in 450, likewise, Aetius and Attila backed different candidates for the recently vacant kingship of the Ripuarian Franks. Every possible opening was thus being exploited by Attila, first, to provoke a quarrel, and, second, to prevent the creation of any united front against him in the west. The diplomatic offensive reached a climax in 451, when, as his forces finally began to march, Attila sent letters both to the western court at Ravenna and to the Visigothic king Theoderic I in Toulouse. To Ravenna, Attila proclaimed that he had come to attack the Visigoths on their behalf. Theoderic was told that the Huns' quarrel was with Ravenna and he was urged to bring the Goths over to Attila's side.[37] As Jordanes comments: 'Beneath his ferocity, [Attila] was a subtle man, and fought with craft before he made war' (*Get*. 36.185–6).

At the start of 451, Attila's expedition moved westwards along the left bank of the Danube. The Rhine was crossed around Mayence, the province of Belgica ravaged, and the city of Metz burned on 7 April. Towards the end of May, the Huns were encamped around Orleans, when Aetius finally appeared. His army was composed of Roman regulars and a series of detachments from allied peoples. Of these, the most important was Gothic, under the command of their king, Theoderic I. Jordanes also mentions the presence of Franks, Saxons and Burgundians (*Get*. 36.191). The western authorities, it seems, had been expecting an invasion of Italy, and Aetius had had to work extremely hard to make the Goths take the field. Attila's diplomatic manoeuvrings had nearly worked. On Aetius' appearance, Attila retreated towards the Champagne, where battle was joined on the so-called Catalaunian Plains (or *campus Mauriacus*) in late June or early July. In a bloody encounter, the Visigothic king was killed, but victory went to Aetius. Attila at first contemplated killing himself, but then withdrew to Pannonia to lick his wounds and prepare another effort.[38]

Attila's second western expedition followed in the next campaigning season, and this time did fall on Italy. Friuli was taken by storm – a victory followed in swift succession by the capture of, amongst others, Aquileia, Padua, Mantua, Verona and Brescia. It was after these successes that the famous encounter between Attila and pope Leo is supposed to have taken place on the river Mincius. Whether it ever occurred is doubtful, and it seems most unlikely that the pope's persuasion really saved Rome. Aetius has sometimes been criticized for not giving full-scale battle to the Huns, but without bringing the Goths to Italy – a very dangerous move – he lacked sufficient forces. Further, contrary to some interpretations, he does seem to have been harrying the Huns with the troops that were available to

---

[37] On these matters, see Thompson (1996) 143ff.; Clover (1972).
[38] Further details: Thompson (1996) 148ff.

him. The new eastern emperor Marcian also launched an attack on Attila's underprotected homelands, and disease was becoming rife in the invading army. In all probability, a combination of these factors, rather than papal intervention, led Attila to withdraw.[39]

On his return to Pannonia, the Hunnic king decided to take another wife. Precisely how many he had it is impossible to ascertain. The wedding took place early in 453, and, as is well known, the great conqueror burst a blood vessel and died in his sleep. His death let loose a vicious struggle for power among his sons, which culminated at the battle of the Nedao in 454 or 455, where his eldest son Ellac died in the conflict. This succession crisis was seized upon by many of the Huns' subject peoples as an opportunity to throw off the Hunnic yoke. The exact course of events is difficult to reconstruct, but, by the early 460s at the latest, Attila's composite empire had dissolved into its constituent parts; Gepids, Goths, Rugi, Heruls and Sueves had all asserted their independence. By the late 460s, the remnants of Attila's Huns were themselves seeking asylum inside the eastern empire.[40] This dramatic Hunnic collapse brought in its wake a final crisis for the Roman empire in western Europe.

II. THE FALL OF THE WESTERN EMPIRE

The most immediate effect of the collapse of the Huns was that the emperor Valentinian III, thirty-five years old in 454, felt no further need of Aetius. Aetius himself would seem to have sensed this, since in that year he pressed the emperor into a marriage alliance. Aetius' son Gaudentius was to marry Valentinian's daughter Placidia. Since Valentinian had no son, this would have reinforced Aetius' political pre-eminence by making his son Valentinian's likely successor. Valentinian, however, resented the move, and there were other western politicians who chafed under Aetius' long-standing predominance, not least the senator Petronius Maximus who encouraged the emperor to act. Valentinian assassinated Aetius personally, we are told, on 21 or 22 September 454. Valentinian himself was murdered the next March by two of Aetius' bodyguards.[41] The disappearance from the scene of Aetius, Valentinian and, above all, Attila marked the opening of a new (and final) era in the history of the Roman west.

1. *A new political order: Petronius Maximus, Avitus, and after, 455–7*

After the collapse of Attila's empire, it was no longer possible to use Hunnic troops to pursue a policy of military containment towards the

[39] Further details and full refs.: Thompson (1996) 156ff.; Maenchen-Helfen (1973) 129ff.
[40] Maenchen-Helfen (1973) 143ff.; Heather, *Goths and Romans* 228–9, 246–9; cf. Thompson (1996) ch. 6.   [41] Sources as *PLRE* II.28.

immigrants who had established themselves in the western empire since A.D. 400. This policy, though it was the basis of Aetius' success in the 430s, had broken down anyway in the 440s, when Hunnic ambitions increased. After 453, it ceased altogether to be relevant. Not only was Hunnic power in the process of being extinguished, but the western empire, as we have seen, was itself chronically short of funds and could perhaps no longer have afforded to pay for its assistance. It would probably also have raised political difficulties to re-employ the Huns after the devastation they had so recently caused. As a result, a fundamental change followed in the nature of power politics in the western half of the empire.

The traditional players of the power game – at least at first – remained. The eastern empire continued to play a significant political role; so too did the western Roman military. The Gallic army was prominent, particularly under Aegidius in the 460s,[42] the Italian army underlay the influence of Ricimer, and the forces of Dalmatia provided a solid power base between 450 and 480 for Marcellinus and his nephew Julius Nepos.[43] These western army groups had all to be reconciled individually to imperial regimes. In the same way, leading members of the Roman landed élite, especially the senators of Italy and southern Gaul, remained politically important. In contrast to fourth-century career patterns, the fifth century was marked by an unprecedented tendency for Gallic senators to hold the top jobs in Gaul, and Italian senators those in Italy. Each group also had its own institutional focus. The senate of Rome and the imperial court at Ravenna continued to function as centres for élite political activity in Italy. From 418, the refounded Gallic council did the same for Gallic senatorial élites.[44] There was thus a greater tendency towards the emergence of regional solidarities in the fifth century, though this should not be overstressed. Major families north and south of the Alps remained interrelated,[45] and there is quite as much, if not more, evidence for dispute within the ranks of Gallic and Italian senators as between them. Very immediate interests tended to surface, indeed, at moments of crisis. Sidonius' resentment that his native Clermont was traded by the emperor Nepos to the Goths in return for Provence is a famous example.[46] Both the Roman senate and the Gallic council remained as much gatherings of rich, interrelated and politically powerful landowners as forums through which genuinely regional views were expressed.[47]

From c. 450, however, the major autonomous barbarian groups on Roman territory also began to demand and play an increasingly active role

---

[42] The *comites* Nepotianus, Paul and Arbogast also commanded elements of this force between the 450s and the 470s.   [43] Cf. Wozniak (1981) 353–63.

[44] Jobs: Sundwall (1915) 8–9, 21–2; cf. Matthews (1975) esp. 331ff., 356ff.

[45] Matthews (1975) 338ff.; Barnish (1988) 134–5; Mommaerts and Kelly (1992).

[46] Sid. Ap. *Ep.* 7.7: cf. Harries (1995) 236ff.

[47] E.g. Max (1979) 225–31; Weber (1989) 491–3. The case for a Gallic–Italian divide as a fundamental factor in political activity has been made by several: e.g. Twyman (1970) 484–7; Mathisen (1981).

in western affairs. This was true, in the first instance, of the Goths and
Burgundians of southern Gaul, and the Vandals of North Africa. By the
470s and 480s, however, they had been joined by groups of Franks, particularly those led by Clovis' father, Childeric. Previously, Hunnic power was
used by Aetius to contain these groups within designated physical boundaries, and to minimize their political influence. When Hunnic power collapsed, the only viable alternative was to include all – or some – of them
within the western empire's body politic. Such a move was already
prefigured, indeed, in the great alliance Aetius put together in 451 to defeat
Attila on the Catalaunian Plains. The old strategic order was reversed.
Instead of the western Roman state using Hunnic power to control the
immigrant barbarians, in 451 it allied itself with the immigrants against the
Huns.[48]

Western imperial politicians clearly understood the new realities. The
first move of Petronius Maximus, for instance – the immediate and self-
proclaimed successor of Valentinian III – was to win Gothic support. His
close associate Avitus was despatched to Toulouse to court the Visigothic
king, Theoderic II.[49] Perhaps the best example of the sea change in western
politics, however, is Avitus himself. While he was still in Toulouse, news
came through that Maximus had been killed in the Vandal sack of Rome
(May 455). Avitus took his place, being proclaimed emperor first by the
Goths and then by Gallo-Roman senators at Arles on 9 July 455. The writings of Sidonius Apollinaris provide us with a fascinating document from
these tumultuous months of political reordering. As we have seen, some
members of the Roman landowning élite had in the 410s quickly allied
themselves to the Goths. Many, however, remained to be convinced that
this was an acceptable strategy. Around the time of Avitus' accession,
Sidonius wrote a detailed account of life at the Gothic court. In it, he
records Theoderic's natural physical perfection, the ordered, rational procedure of daily business, and the moderation and virtuous nature of the
food, drink and entertainment on offer there. Given that the traditional
images of 'barbarians' in Graeco-Roman ideology were irrationality and
sensuality, the letter carries a clear ideological message. Its tone would still
appear to be patronizing in places (particularly in its account of the king's
willingness to grant requests if you let him win at board games), but its
central theme still rings out clearly. Theoderic was a king close enough to
Roman ways of doing things for him to be properly included within the
Roman order.

Avitus' regime quickly took off in Gaul, where it combined Goths, Gallo-
Romans and Burgundians, but failed to establish itself in Italy, whose army,

[48] A similar analysis: Clover (1978) 171.
[49] Valentinian III was murdered on 16 March, Petronius Maximus proclaimed on 17 March: *PLRE*
II.751. Avitus' mission: Sid. Ap. *Carm.* VII.392ff.

under Ricimer and Majorian, remained implacably hostile. The eastern empire also withheld its recognition, although it did not go so far as to condemn Avitus as a usurper.[50] And in practice, when Avitus advanced into Italy in 456, Ricimer's forces were powerful enough to defeat him, at the battle of Placentia on 17 October. In the aftermath, Avitus resigned to become bishop of Placentia, and died soon after. The manner of his defeat is indicative. Most subsequent western imperial regimes took the form of Ricimer plus a variety of frontmen; Ricimer himself never sought the throne. This would suggest that the Italian army he commanded was too powerful for any western regime to function without it as a central player. Nevertheless, Ricimer's army was not by itself sufficient to control areas outside Italy, and every imperial regime after Valentinian III also attempted to include other Roman army groups, senators (Gallo-Roman and Italian) and, from among the barbarians, at least the Goths and Burgundians.

Regimes largely independent of the immigrant groups, of the kind which had prevailed earlier in the century, thus gave way, after 450, to regimes which included them. This fundamental change in the nature of political activity had important consequences. No group of supporters was ready (nor previously had any of the more traditional power blocs ever been ready) to back a regime without some kind of pay-off. One effect of including immigrants in governing coalitions, therefore, was to increase the numbers of those expecting rewards.

The most obvious reward sought by, and given to, the leaders of immigrant groups was involvement in the running of the empire. Burgundian kings took Roman titles, for instance, while the Visigoth Theoderic II attempted to order affairs in Spain.[51] The Vandals' intervention in Italy in 455 should also be read as an attempt to stake a claim in the new political order. That they sacked the city of Rome has naturally received most attention, but Geiseric, the Vandal leader, also took back to North Africa with him Eudoxia and Eudocia – respectively, the widow and daughter of Valentinian III. Geiseric subsequently married the daughter to his son and heir, Huneric. The two had been betrothed, but not married, under the treaty of 442 (see p. 11 above), but, on assuming the throne in 455, Petronius Maximus married Eudocia to his son, the Caesar Palladius, instead. Thus Geiseric intervened in Italy at least partly because a match which should have cemented the Vandals' place in the new political order of the west appeared to have been thwarted. Subsequently, Geiseric would also attempt to forward the imperial claims of Olybrius who married Placidia, the younger daughter of Valentinian, and was thus his relative by marriage.[52]

[50] Refs. as *PLRE* II.198; cf. Mathisen (1981) 233–4.
[51] The Burgundian kings Gundioc and Gundobad were both *magister militum per Gallias*: *PLRE* II.523–4. Goths in Spain: p. 22 below, n. 54.
[52] Clover (1978) 193ff.; cf. generally Clover (1989a), (1989b).

Involvement in imperial affairs carried great prestige, and had been sought by immigrant leaders since the time of Alaric and Athaulf. The western empire only had this prestige, however, because it was, and was perceived to be, the most powerful institution of its day. Prestige certainly incorporates abstract qualities, but the attraction of the living empire for immigrant leaders was firmly based upon its military might and overall wealth. They wished to avoid potentially dangerous military confrontations with it, while its wealth, when distributed as patronage, could greatly strengthen a leader's position. By the 450s, however, the reality of power behind the western imperial façade was already slipping. Britain, parts of Gaul and Spain (at different times) and, above all, North Africa had removed themselves, or been removed, from central imperial control. The rewards – wealth in the form of money or land, wealth being the basis of power[53] – given after 454 to new allies from among the barbarian immigrants were granted, therefore, from an already shrunken base. And, of course, the very process of rewarding caused further shrinkage.

Take, for example, Avitus. Under him, the Goths were sent to Spain to bring the Sueves to heel. In contrast to the position in the 410s, however, Theoderic II's troops seem to have operated by themselves and, by Hydatius' account, basically ransacked northern Spain, including its loyal Hispano-Romans, of all the wealth they could force their victims to produce.[54] This benefited the Goths, but not the western Roman state. There is no indication that Roman administration and taxation were restored by their actions to any lost territories. Likewise the Burgundians: after participating in the Spanish campaign (Jord. *Get.* 44.231), they received new and better lands in Savoy. An enigmatic chronicle entry tells us that they divided them with local senators. Another prosperous agricultural area no longer formed part of central imperial resources.[55]

After 454, there thus built up a vicious circle within the western empire: too many groups squabbling over a shrinking financial base. With every change of regime, there had to be further gifts. Having been granted a free hand in Spain under Avitus, the Goths then received the city of Narbonne and its territory (presumably especially its tax revenues) as the price of their support for Libius Severus in the early 460s (see below).[56] Even worse, this concentration on the internal relations of established power blocs allowed the rise of other, more peripheral forces, such as the Franks. In previous eras, this would have been prevented by direct military and diplomatic

[53] The point is unaffected by whether the Roman state granted these groups land or tax proceeds, a subject of recent debate. Some major contributions are Goffart, *Barbarians and Romans*, and Durliat (1988) (both arguing, with slight differences, in favour of allocations of tax revenue); Barnish (1986) and Wood (1990) (arguing the case for a land settlement in, respectively, Italy and Savoy).

[54] Hydat. *Chron.* 170, 172–5, 186, *Chron. Min.* 11.28–9.

[55] Mar. Avent. ad a. 456.2, *Chron. Min.* 11.232; cf. *Auct. Prosp. Haun.* s.a. 457, *Chron. Min.* 1.305; cf. Wood (1990) 65–9.   [56] Hydat. *Chron.* 217, *Chron. Min.* 11.33.

action. The activities of Franks and other parvenus took still more territory out of central control. Particularly ominous in this respect was the expansion of the Armoricans and, above all, the Franks in northern Gaul from the 460s.[57] The dangers inherent in the new political order were thus profound. Centrifugal forces could not be transformed into centripetal ones merely by throwing around a few Roman titles.

2. Attempts at equilibrium, 457–68

The deposition of Avitus in October 456 was followed by an interregnum. It was not until 28 December 457 that Majorian was declared Augustus at Ravenna. The new emperor had served under Aetius and was brought back from retirement by Valentinian III, after Aetius' murder, to help reconcile the latter's troops. As early as 455 he was being talked of as a potential emperor, and, although he worked closely with Ricimer against Avitus, Majorian was clearly no mere puppet of the Italian army's generalissimo (unlike many of his successors). The delay between Avitus' deposition and Majorian's election was taken up with delicate negotiations, winning support for his candidacy not only in the west but also from Marcellinus, the army commander in Dalmatia, and from Constantinople. Majorian eventually took the throne with the backing of the eastern emperor Leo I.[58]

Majorian's four-year reign is marked by determined efforts to restore order in the west. In the letters of Sidonius, considerable evidence survives of the efforts he made to woo Gallic aristocrats. In 458, Majorian progressed through southern Gaul and, employing a mixture of force and generosity, attempted to heal the divisions created by Avitus' defeat.[59] Sidonius, at least, was won over. He composed and delivered a panegyric in the new emperor's favour, receiving in return a minor official post. Majorian's military forces were also active outside Italy. Of his commanders' activities, we know that Aegidius in Gaul fought both Franks and Goths. The latter engagement, at least, would seem to have been successful, since Gothic forces later assisted Nepotianus, another of Majorian's commanders, to curb Suevic activities in north-western Spain.[60] In 461, however, Majorian attempted to invade Vandal Africa via Spain and was heavily defeated (see below). This provided Ricimer with an opportunity which he was quick to take. He formally deposed Majorian on 2 August 461, and had him executed five days later.

[57] Franks: James (1988a) 64ff. Armorica may have seen substantial immigration from Britain (e.g. Riothamus: PLRE II.945), on top of an indigenous population which had already shown separatist tendencies: p. 8 above.

[58] Stein (1959) 374–5; Max (1979) 234–6; O'Flynn (1983) 185–6 n. 18. Marcellinus took part in Majorian's Vandal expedition (PLRE II.709).   [59] Mathisen (1979).

[60] Refs. PLRE II.12 and 778, cf. O'Flynn (1983) 106ff.

The next western emperor, Libius Severus, was much more Ricimer's puppet. He was proclaimed emperor on 19 November 461, and, once again, determined efforts were made to win support for him throughout the remaining Roman west. The Goths, for instance, were granted Narbonne in return for their support, and Ricimer had close relations with the Burgundian royal house, which guaranteed their adherence to the new regime. The murder of Majorian and the ceding of Narbonne, however, prompted a major revolt from elements of the Gallo-Roman military under Aegidius. The year 463 thus saw the interesting, if confusing, spectacle of a western emperor employing Goths to attack part of the Roman army in Gaul. When battle was joined at Orleans, Aegidius was victorious. His revolt was only contained in the autumn of 465, when he was assassinated. At the time, he was engaged in negotiations with the Vandal king Geiseric, trying to construct an alternative balance of western forces to challenge Ricimer's domination. Severus' regime also failed to win eastern approval; he was never recognized by the emperor Leo. Ricimer may eventually have poisoned Severus (he died on 14 November 465).[61] If so, it was presumably because Severus had become an obstacle to Ricimer's continued negotiations with the east. It is perhaps significant that major developments in the east–west relations followed Severus' death.

The next western imperial regime, for instance, was clearly the product of careful negotiation between Ricimer and Leo. In spring 467, again following an interregnum, a successful eastern general by the name of Anthemius advanced into Italy with Leo's support. He brought with him military forces which probably consisted, in large measure, of the Dalmatian troops of Marcellinus. Ricimer too was ready to accept Anthemius, and even married his daughter, Alypia. Gallic landowners, as in the time of Majorian, were carefully courted, and Goths and Burgundians, at least in the first instance, were ready to defer to him.[62] On 12 April 467, therefore, Anthemius was proclaimed western emperor. The central plank of his policy was revealed the next year, and turned out to be exactly the same as that pursued earlier by Majorian. Having obtained the support or acquiescence of the major power blocs in Italy and southern Gaul, Anthemius, like Majorian, turned on the Vandals. In 468, a very large expedition was put together, comprising both forces from the western empire and a vast eastern fleet commanded by Basiliscus. On its approach to North Africa, however, Vandal fire ships destroyed the bulk of the fleet, and with it sank any hope of Roman victory (Procop. *Wars* 3.6.10–26).

[61] Cass. *Chron.* s.a. 465; cf. Sid. Ap. *Carm.* 11.317–18.
[62] Anthemius himself: *PLRE* 11.96–8. Marcellinus accompanied him to Italy in 467 and was named Patrician in 468 (*PLRE* 11.709–10). Ricimer: O'Flynn (1983) 115ff. On Anthemius in Gaul, Stein (1959) 389–90; O'Flynn (1983) 118.

The policy of attacking the Vandals makes very considerable sense. There were only two possible ways of breaking the vicious circle affecting the western empire after the collapse of Hunnic power, whereby too many political participants were bankrupting the entity to which they were looking for rewards. Either the number of political participants had to be reduced, or central financial resources increased. This clarifies the logic, it seems to me, behind attacking the Vandals, the policy pursued by both Majorian and Anthemius. Victory over the Vandals would have renewed imperial prestige, but, more important, it would have removed from the political game one of its major players. Perhaps above all, it would have restored to the rump western empire the richest of its original territories. Both Vandal expeditions failed (and as a result both regimes fell apart),[63] but what if either had succeeded? Particularly in 468, the expedition was a very serious effort,[64] and the later success of Belisarius shows that reconquering North Africa was not inherently impossible.

Buoyed up by victory and the promise of African revenues, a victorious western emperor could certainly have re-established his political hold on the landowners of southern Gaul and Spain. Many of them would have instinctively supported an imperial revival. Sidonius, and the other Gallic aristocrats who would later organize resistance to Euric the Goth, for instance (see below), would have been only too happy to reassert their ties to the centre.[65] Burgundians, Goths and Sueves would have had to be faced in due course, but victory would have considerably extended the active life of the western empire.

3. The end of empire, 468–76

As events turned out, the expeditions failed, and with them disappeared any possibility of escaping the cycle of decline. As the Franks in particular grew in importance, the number of players increased rather than diminished. Since the empire's financial base was simultaneously decreasing, the idea of empire quickly became meaningless. The centre no longer controlled anything anyone wanted. In consequence, the late 460s and 470s saw one group after another coming to the realization that the western empire was no longer a prize worth fighting for. It must have been an extraordinary moment as the realization dawned on the leaders of individual interest groups, and upon members of local Roman landowning élites, that, after hundreds of years of existence, the Roman state in western Europe was now an anachronism.

---

[63] Majorian was deposed by Ricimer after his defeat (p. 23 above); Anthemius' defeat allowed Ricimer to assassinate his main supporter, Marcellinus: O'Flynn (1983) 117.

[64] Refs. as *PLRE* II.213; cf. Courtois (1955) 199ff.

[65] Sidonius: pp. 29–30 below. So, too, men in Spain such as Hydatius who had previously looked to the centre for help: see pp. 9, 13 above.

The first to grasp the point was Euric, king of the Visigoths. After the Vandals defeated Anthemius, he immediately launched a series of wars which, by 475, had brought under his control much of Gaul and Spain (see ch. 5 (Collins), pp. 121–2 below). There is a striking description of his decision to launch these campaigns in the *Getica* of Jordanes:

Becoming aware of the frequent changes of [western] Roman emperor, Euric, king of the Visigoths, pressed forward to seize Gaul on his own authority.

This snippet captures rather well what it must have been like suddenly to realize that the time had come to pursue one's own aims with total independence.[66] Euric's lead was soon followed by the other interested parties. The eastern empire, for instance, abandoned any hope in the west when it made peace with the Vandals, probably in 474.[67] As we have seen, Constantinople had previously viewed the conquest of North Africa as a means of reinvigorating the western empire, giving its support both to Majorian's and especially to Anthemius' efforts in this direction. Making peace with the Vandals was thus a move of huge significance, signalling the end of substantial attempts to sustain the west. Diplomatic recognition as western emperor was subsequently granted to Julius Nepos, but he never received any practical military assistance.[68]

That the western empire had ceased to mean anything dawned on the Burgundians at more or less the same time. Gundobad, one of the heirs to the throne, played a major role in central politics in the early 470s. A close ally of Ricimer, he helped him defeat Anthemius. Relations between Ricimer and Anthemius had turned sour soon after the collapse of the Vandal expedition. A first quarrel, in 470, was healed by negotiation in 471, but in 472 relations deteriorated to the point of war, and it was Gundobad who captured and killed Anthemius on 11 July. Gundobad also supported the subsequent regime of Olybrius, whom Ricimer proclaimed emperor in April 472, and even took over the role of kingmaker after Ricimer's death. Ricimer died on 18 August 472, closely followed to the grave by the last of his imperial nominees, Olybrius, on 2 November. Gundobad subsequently persuaded Glycerius to accept the western throne, to which he was elevated on 3 March 473.[69] Sometime in late 473 or early 474, however, Gundobad 'suddenly' (as one chronicler put it) left Rome.[70] Possibly this was due to his father's death, or perhaps he just gave up the struggle. Either way, he

---

[66] Jord. *Get.* 45.237; cf. Wolfram (1988) 181ff.

[67] Malchus, ed. Blockley fr. 5, dating between February 474 and Zeno's exile in January 475, therefore most likely mid 474; cf. Courtois (1955) 204. The treaty is misdated to 'probably 476' at *PLRE* II.499.

[68] Leo supported Nepos in 473/4 before the latter seized the western throne: John of Antioch fr. 209. But cf. Malchus, ed. Blockley fr. 14: Nepos got no practical help between his retreat from Italy in 475 and his death in 480.   [69] Refs. as *PLRE* II.524; cf. Stein (1959) 395; O'Flynn (1983) 121ff.

[70] Malalas, ed. Bonn, 374–5; otherwise *PLRE* II.524.

never bothered to return. Events at home were now much more important to Gundobad than those at the centre.

The army of Dalmatia made one more attempt to sponsor a regime, when Julius Nepos marched into Italy in 474. Glycerius was deposed without a struggle and ordained bishop of Salona. One year later, however, Nepos left again – definitively – in the face of the hostility of Orestes and the army of Italy.[71] Fittingly, it was the army of Italy which was the last to give up. In 475, its commander Orestes proclaimed his own son Romulus emperor, but within a year lost control of his soldiers. Not surprisingly, given all the resources which had by now been seized by others, it was shortage of money which caused the unrest. A subordinate commander, Odoacer, organized a putsch, murdered Orestes, and deposed Romulus, derisively titled Augustulus, on or around 4 September 476.[72] He then sent an embassy to Constantinople which did no more than state the obvious. There was no longer any need for an emperor in the west.[73]

4. Romans and barbarians

Alongside, and often as part of, the great power blocs, many millions of individuals found themselves caught up in the events which brought about the end of the Roman empire in western Europe. Of these, the surviving sources allow us to say most about the experiences and reactions of local landowning élites. As much as the imperial court at Ravenna, the provincial landowning élites of the west were the Roman empire, in that it was run by them and for them. Their adherence to it, or lack of it, is thus as good a measure of the prevalence of empire as are the activities of the court. The variety of reactions to fifth-century events among even this élite is very striking, and, thanks to the correspondence of Sidonius Apollinaris, particularly well documented in the case of Gallo-Roman landowners.

Some local landowning groups throughout the west (outside, perhaps, Italy) responded quickly to temporary or permanent power vacuums created by the intrusion of armed immigrants into the western empire. In Britain, independence was asserted as early as 410, although, as the Saxon threat grew, some seem to have regretted the decision and wrote to Aetius (probably in 446) requesting his assistance (Gildas 20). Likewise, in northern, and particularly north-western, Gaul, many of the groups labelled bagaudae should probably be understood as representing a similar kind of phenomenon, rather than, as has sometimes been argued, outright peasant

[71] Refs. as *PLRE* II.777.

[72] Refs. as *PLRE* II.811–12. Cf. Procop. *Wars* v.1.5–8; the troops demanded 'one-third of the lands of Italy'; what this means is debated: p. 22 above, n. 53.

[73] Malchus, ed. Blockley fr. 14; despite the opening sentence, the rest makes clear Odoacer's responsibility for the initiative.

revolt. In Armorica, the disturbances aimed at independence or some degree of autonomy. In Spain, at least some of the groups operating in Tarraconensis in the 440s were advocating accommodation with the Sueves as opposed to continued allegiance to the empire (see p. 13 above).

Not dissimilar processes had begun to unfold even in southern Gaul in the 410s. In the early years of the decade, some members of the Gallo-Roman élite rallied to usurpers sponsored by the Goths and Burgundians. Such alliances of immigrants and Roman landowners represented as great a danger to the unity of the empire as declarations of independence. For local power-brokers to see political entities other than the imperial court as the main force in their lives presaged imperial collapse. Moreover, after the Gothic settlement in Aquitaine in 418, economic reasons dictated that any Gallo-Roman with estates in the Garonne had to enter into relations with the Goths or leave. Much of Paulinus of Pella's patrimony, for instance, inherited from Ausonius, was situated in areas around Bordeaux that were now dominated by the Goths. This was perhaps the primary reason why his sons migrated to the Visigothic court.[74] The sources provide us with no evidence between *c.* 415 and 450, however, of further close political alliances between Roman and Goth. In this I suspect that the re-establishment and continued operation of the Gallic council probably played a part. The council was re-established in 418, the year of the Gothic settlement in Aquitaine. This is unlikely to have been mere chronological coincidence. Giving Gallic landowners a designated forum established firm lines of communication between these men and Ravenna.[75] Aetius' campaigns and the council can be seen as two reflections of one policy which contained within very strict limits the ability of Goths and other immigrants to exercise influence within the empire.

After 450, circumstances changed dramatically. Sidonius' writings illustrate the ways in which an ever wider cross-section of the political classes of southern Gaul were drawn particularly into a Gothic orbit, as Goths participated ever more centrally in imperial politics. From the early 460s, we find Romans holding military offices to which they were appointed by Gothic kings. The first was probably Arborius,[76] and others quickly followed. Vincentius was perhaps an imperial general in 465, but by 477 he was Euric's *dux Hispaniae.* Others were Victorius, Calminius and Namatius.[77] At the same time, similarly, disaffected Roman officials entered into negotiations with the Gothic king. In 468, the newly reappointed prefect of Gaul, Arvandus, wrote to Euric telling him to throw off the rule of Anthemius – the 'Greekling' who had just taken the throne – and divide up the provinces

[74] *Euch.* 499ff.; cf. 570ff., 514f.; Salvian, *De Gub. Dei* v.5ff.
[75] On the council, see Matthews (1975) 333ff.; Heather (1992).
[76] Hydat. *Chron.* 213 s.a. 461; cf. Harries (1995) 97.
[77] On these men, see respectively: *PLRE* II.1168; *PLRE* II.1162–4; Sid. Ap. *Epp.* 5.12; 8.6.

of Gaul with the Burgundians (Sid. Ap. *Ep.* 1.7.5). Shortly afterwards, another high civilian imperial official, Seronatus, possibly *vicarius* to the Gallic prefect, visited Euric on several occasions and encouraged him in the same direction. Seronatus was brought to trial and executed before 475 (*PLRE* 11.995f.). By the mid 470s, Romans were holding high civilian appointments under Gothic kings. The first known example is Leo of Narbonne, who became Euric's chief civilian adviser (*PLRE* 11.662f.).

As Gothic influence increased, more Romans took up service among the Goths, prompted by a wide variety of motives. Some probably did think that accommodation with the Goths and others was the best way to maintain order in a changing political climate (cf. Paulinus of Pella, *Euch.* 290ff.). Others were probably more personally ambitious. Sidonius is perhaps being ironic in commenting, in a letter to Namatius, on how sensible it is of him to follow 'the standards of a victorious people' (*Ep.* 8.6.16). In addition, recent studies have stressed how competitive were the lives of Gallo-Roman aristocrats. They were constantly in dispute with one another for prestige and financial gain.[78] In circumstances where Gothic power was increasing, it became only natural to look to the Goths for assistance in both climbing to the top and staying there.

This whole process of accommodation between immigrants and Roman élites was, however, far from smooth. In the fifth century, as we have seen, western imperial authorities conducted a whole series of major campaigns and fought countless minor engagements to maintain their control. Local assertions of independence and the so-called bagaudic movements also involved violence and disruption on a very considerable scale. Even relatively peaceful transfers of loyalty among the landowners of southern Gaul could be traumatic. A good case in point is that of Arvandus, the Gallic prefect toppled for plotting with the Goths. He was taken before the senate in Rome, where his accusers were fellow Gallic aristocrats. All were related to, or associates of, Sidonius, whose letter describing the trial is strongly critical of Arvandus. Yet, despite being sentenced to death, Arvandus was eventually spared, partly because Sidonius and his friends appealed for his life (Sid. Ap. *Ep.* 1.7.4ff.). The rise of Gothic power thus split opinion in southern Gaul. Nor is Arvandus an isolated example. Calminius, correspondent of Sidonius, fought for the Goths at Clermont, at the same time as Sidonius was busy conducting its defence (Sid. Ap. *Ep.* 5.12).

While some were willing to work with Gothic kings, therefore, others were not, especially when the Goths threw off their allegiance to the empire. Sidonius himself is representative of this strand of opinion. He was happy to work with, and even praise, the Goths when they were a plank of Avitus' regime (see p. 20 above). He was also willing to accept Gothic

---

[78] Van Dam, *Leadership and Community* 57ff.; Brown (1982); Harries (1995) ch. 1.

territorial extensions, such as the ceding of Narbonne, if they were legitimized by the empire. But when the Goths took over southern Gaul without authorization, he resisted, his chief collaborators being Ecdicius, son of Avitus, and Eucherius.[79] For these men, and others like them, the Goths may have been acceptable allies in the creation of imperial regimes. They were entirely unacceptable, however, as a complete alternative to the continued existence of the western empire.

In the course of the fifth century, then, we witness a process of psychological adjustment, among local Roman landowning élites, to the fact of imperial disintegration. That different local situations prompted different local strategies for survival and self-advancement is hardly surprising. We can perhaps venture to say more. Local landowners represent that class of men who had prospered (to different degrees) under the established political order: the Roman empire. As a group, they had potentially the most to lose from the political revolution represented by its collapse. Some, however, had more to lose than others. A fair rule of thumb would seem to be that those who had gained most from the old order clung to it the longest. This would explain why élites in peripheral areas, who did not participate as fully in the benefits of empire, were quicker to cast in their lot with barbarians or to declare independence. For them, presumably, the benefits of empire (assessed in terms of personal rewards and collective defence) did not outweigh its costs (above all, taxation). For others such as Sidonius, however, relatives of emperors, or would-be emperors, and holders of high imperial office, life without the empire was a much more intimidating proposition. But in the end, continued tenure of their landed possessions would demand that even this group mend its fences, in so far as it could, with the new powers in the land. It was either that or lose everything. Thus Sidonius eventually wrote verses in praise of the glories of his erstwhile enemy, Euric (Sid. Ap. *Ep.* 8.9.5). He did it, however, to effect his own release from exile, and another letter makes clear his hatred of old Gothic women 'quarrelling, drinking and vomiting' outside his window (Sid. Ap. *Ep.* 8.3.2).

III. CONCLUSION

Seventy years separated the deposition of Romulus Augustulus in 476 from the invasions and population movements of the first decade of the fifth century (themselves prompted by the intrusion of the Huns into central Europe). None the less, the two are intimately linked. The regular political crises for the empire in intervening years represent no more than the slow working out of the full political consequences of the earlier invasions. The

[79] *PLRE* II.384; cf. Sid. Ap. *Ep.* 3.8, Harries (1995) 185–7.

loss of territory to the invaders – sometimes sanctioned by treaty, sometimes not – meant a loss of revenue and a consequent loss of power. As
the state lost power, and was perceived to have done so, local Roman landowning élites came to the realization that their interests would best be
served by making political accommodations with the outsiders or, in a
minority of cases, by taking independent responsibility for their own
defence. Given that the empire had existed for four hundred years, and that
the east continued to prop up the west, it is perhaps not surprising that
these processes took between two and three generations to work themselves out in the old empire's heartlands: southern Gaul, Italy and Spain
(even if élites in other areas, such as Britain, were quicker off the mark).
Despite the time-lag, the well-documented nature of these processes sub-
stantiates a direct link between the invasions and the collapse of empire.
There was no separate additional crisis.

The nature of this crisis has been much debated and, in some ways, does
not now appear so cataclysmic as it did to older generations of historians.[80]
The appearance of barbarian powers actually within the western empire's
borders in the fifth century, for instance, can legitimately be seen as having
opened up a pre-existing fault line in the relationship between imperial
centre and local Roman landowning élites. The centre relied on a mixture
of constraint and reward to focus the loyalties of landowners, some of
them many hundreds of miles distant, upon the empire: never an easy balancing act.[81] Moreover, at least in some areas – particularly southern Gaul,
Italy and Spain – there was a considerable degree of survival among Roman
landowning élites, many choosing to cast in their lot with the new powers
in the land, and so survive as élite landowners into the post-Roman political era. In recent years, likewise, the peaceful nature particularly of the final
stage of the process – when Roman élites actually jumped from Roman
imperial to barbarian royal courts – has received considerable and due
attention. And it has also been pointed out – again correctly – that many
of the intruders (Goths, Burgundians, Franks, etc.) were not unknown outsiders, but peoples who had been established on the frontier for many
years. Indeed, the Roman state had previously enjoyed, with all or most of
them, a whole range of close diplomatic, economic and social contacts.[82]

None of this means, however, that the fall of the Roman empire was
anything other than a revolution. In political terms, a unitary state in
western Europe fragmented into a whole series of mutually antagonistic
successors. As we have seen, the process of fragmentation was protracted
and violent. Likewise, the immigrant groups, even if tied to the empire, had

---

[80] Just in English, for instance, one might compare Bury (1928) with Brown (1971).

[81] One case study is Heather (1994).

[82] See, for instance, the works of Walter Goffart cited in the Bibliography, and, for a broader perspective over time, Whittaker (1994).

previously been its subordinate satellites. Now they became its masters. And Roman landowning élites had, in the end, no choice but to make their accommodations with the immigrants, or lose the very lands on which their élite status was based. The end of the empire was thus not the result of free choice. In making their way to the courts of barbarian kings, Roman élites (at least in the inner core of empire) were merely struggling to ensure that political revolution should not be accompanied by social and economic cataclysm.

CHAPTER 2

THE EASTERN EMPIRE: THEODOSIUS TO ANASTASIUS

A. D. LEE

When he assumed sole rulership of the eastern half of the Roman empire in 408, Theodosius II became head of a state which during the short reign of his father Arcadius (395–408) had experienced an extraordinary array of crises. Gothic troops in Roman employ had risen in revolt under the leadership of Alaric in 395 and spent much time during the following years freely plundering the Balkan provinces until Alaric eventually decided to move westwards (401).[1] Also in 395, nomadic Huns had invaded the empire through the Caucasus, bringing widespread destruction to Syria and eastern Asia Minor until 397.[2] Another Goth named Gainas, who held a command in the Roman army, instigated a revolt which was only suppressed in 400 with much bloodshed in and around Constantinople.[3] Within a few years there was further turmoil in the capital over the bitterly contested deposition and exile of the bishop John Chrysostom (403–4),[4] while eastern Asia Minor suffered a prolonged bout of raiding by Isaurian brigands (403–6).[5] In addition to all this, relations with the western half of the empire throughout Arcadius' reign were characterized by antagonism and mutual suspicion, the result of the ambitions and rivalries of dominant individuals, such as Eutropius and Stilicho, at the courts of Arcadius in Constantinople and his younger brother Honorius in the west.[6]

Against this background, one might justifiably have wondered about the prospects for the eastern half of the empire – even more so when one adds into the equation the fact that Theodosius was a mere seven years old in 408. Contrary to expectation, however, Theodosius' reign was a long one (408–50),[7] and although he and his successors down to the early sixth century were to experience numerous crises of a gravity comparable to those of Arcadius' reign, the eastern empire proved able to survive this critical period, during which its western counterpart succumbed. Why this

[1] Liebeschuetz, *Barbarians and Bishops* ch. 5; Heather, *Goths and Romans* ch. 6.
[2] Maenchen-Helfen (1973) 51–9.
[3] Liebeschuetz, *Barbarians and Bishops* chs. 9–11; Cameron and Long (1993) chs. 5–6, 8.
[4] Liebeschuetz, *Barbarians and Bishops* chs. 15–21; Kelly (1995) chs. 16–18.   [5] Shaw (1990) 249.
[6] Cameron, Alan (1970); Matthews (1975) ch. 10; Liebeschuetz, *Barbarians and Bishops* chs. 6, 8.
[7] Arcadius had elevated him to the status of co-emperor in January 402 while still a baby, so the formal length of his reign was actually forty-eight years – the longest of any Roman emperor.

should have happened is not easy to account for, particularly because it is generally more difficult to explain why something did *not* happen. Nevertheless, it remains a question of fundamental importance, to which this chapter will endeavour to suggest some answers.

I. THEODOSIUS II

1. *Political life*

There was obviously no question of the seven-year-old Theodosius having any real involvement in government affairs for some years, so it should occasion no surprise that during his minority power lay in the hands of various officials at court, notably the praetorian prefect Anthemius.[8] Even once he reached adulthood, however, Theodosius appears rarely to have attempted to exercise power in his own right, showing greater interest in theological and scholarly pursuits. One consequence of this was that his court gained a reputation for patronage of literary and educational endeavours,[9] reflected, among other things, in reforms of university teaching in the capital (425)[10] and the production of the Theodosian Code (429–37).[11]

Another consequence, however, was that the initiative in political life by and large lay with individuals other than the emperor himself, making it difficult to determine the extent to which Theodosius deserves credit or blame for particular decisions or policies. Female members of the imperial family feature prominently in this respect, notably Theodosius' sister Pulcheria and his wife Eudocia, whom he married in 421, although the extent of their power has probably been exaggerated.[12] Helion's long tenure of the important office of *magister officiorum* (414–27) marks him out as a man with influence, while the praetorian prefect Cyrus was important during the 430s, until displaced by Theodosius' chamberlain, the eunuch Chrysaphius, who was pre-eminent throughout the 440s.[13] Although less conspicuous, certain military figures are also worthy of note: the way in which the Alan general Flavius Ardabur and members of his family, especially his son Aspar, held high commands throughout much of Theodosius' reign must be significant,[14] while during the emperor's final years, the Isaurian general Flavius Zeno (not to be confused with the later

---

[8] On the early years of Theodosius' reign, see Lippold (1973) 964–6, *CAH*[2] XIII, ch. 4 (Blockley).

[9] Momigliano (1972) 12–17.   [10] Cameron, Alan (1982) 285–7.

[11] Harries and Wood (1993) 1–6.

[12] See Holum (1977) and Holum, *Empresses* for this emphasis, Liebeschuetz, *Barbarians and Bishops* 134 and Harries (1994) 35–6 for reservations.

[13] See *PLRE* II, *s.v.* Helion 1, Cyrus 7, Chrysaphius, with emendations on points of detail (especially on Cyrus) in Cameron, Alan (1982).

[14] Family solidarity is epitomized in the silver *missorium* celebrating Aspar's consulship in 434: *CIL* XI.2637 (= *ILS* 1299) with Painter (1991). For details of careers, see *PLRE* II, *s.v.* Fl. Ardabur 3, Fl.

emperor) emerged as a powerful enemy of Chrysaphius and someone whom Theodosius is said to have feared as a potential usurper.[15]

The important role of these individuals in the political life of Theodosius' reign can be explained partly in personal terms, as a result of Theodosius' own apparent lack of inclination to exercise power (a tendency no doubt encouraged by his advisers and tutors during his formative years). But it also reflects an important structural change in the character of the imperial office which began during the reign of his father – namely, the way in which first Arcadius and then Theodosius abandoned leading the army on campaign in person and indeed rarely travelled far beyond the environs of Constantinople, instead spending virtually the whole of their reigns in the capital.[16] The permanent residence of emperors in Constantinople enhanced the opportunities for those at court to exercise influence because the emperor was now constantly in contact with them and was also less exposed to the outside views and influences that would have been one of the incidental benefits of a more itinerant lifestyle.[17] To be sure, the adherence of subsequent emperors of the fifth and sixth century to this pattern did not prevent them from taking more active roles in political life, but they had experienced substantial portions of their lives beyond the confines of the palace before they assumed the imperial purple. Theodosius, on the other hand, had known nothing else and was therefore that much more susceptible to the limiting effects of this regime.

Despite all this, however, Theodosius was not overthrown, nor did the imperial office come to be seen as something which could be dispensed with.[18] For one thing, Theodosius' formal claim to the throne, unlike that of most of his fifth-century successors, was not open to question: he was the son of the deceased emperor, and had already been elevated to the status of co-emperor with his father some years earlier.[19] For another, the very prominence of influential courtiers and advisers is likely to have had

---

Ardabur Aspar (though he was probably not *magister* in the final years of the 440s: Zuckerman (1994) 170–2), Fl. Plinta (though he was probably still *magister* in 439/40: Zuckerman (1994) 160–3).

[15] *PLRE* II, *s.v.* Fl. Zeno 6.

[16] Presumably it was anxieties about this development, coming as it did after more than a century of military emperors, which spawned the story that Theodosius I had forbidden his sons to campaign: Joh. Lyd. *De Mag.* II.11, III.41. For Theodosius' known movements outside Constantinople, see Dagron, *Naissance* 85–6, with Roueché (1986).

[17] Hopkins (1978) ch. 4, valuable though it is on the power of eunuchs, does not take sufficient account of this fundamental change in imperial behaviour in the fifth century. On eunuchs, see also Patterson (1982) 299–333.

[18] Reports of potential usurpers (Priscus fr. 16) show that Theodosius' position was sometimes perceived to be under threat. Cf. the popular anger expressed against Theodosius himself during a grain shortage in the capital (Marcell. *Chron.* s.a. 431).

[19] This is not to deny that the months immediately following Arcadius' death were nervous ones in Constantinople, since Theodosius was still vulnerable on account of his extreme youth: see Zos. v.31.3–4, Soz. *HE* IX.4 (Stilicho's plans), Lippold (1973) 963–4, Blockley (1992) 51–2 (for the problematic sources on possible Persian interference); threats from these quarters, however, soon dissipated.

the effect of deflecting criticism from the emperor.[20] Similarly, although his non-involvement in military campaigning curtailed his contact with the army and risked leaving him more vulnerable to military usurpation, it also had the important benefit of shielding him from the political (and possible physical) consequences of military defeat, and so played its part in his survival and that of his office.[21]

At the same time Theodosius was quick to capitalize on anything which could be presented as a success on the part of his armies. The Persian war of 421–2, which may in part have been embraced anyway for its potential political benefits for the unmilitary Theodosius,[22] quickly became the subject of a flurry of celebratory poetry even though the war itself ended in stalemate, while news of the success of eastern troops against the western usurper John in 425 was the occasion for the emperor to lead an impromptu procession of thanksgiving through the capital.[23] Theodosius' participation in hunting is surely also significant in this context: in earlier centuries, hunting, as the sport most closely allied to warfare, had been a way for unwarlike emperors to offset any stigma arising from their lack of involvement in military affairs.[24]

But though victory had always been an important element in the projection of a strong image by emperors, it was, fortunately, not the only imperial virtue available for exploitation.[25] *Philanthropia* was another which Theodosius could be seen exercising,[26] while his renowned reluctance to impose capital punishment secured his claim to *clementia*.[27] But it was *pietas*, an attribute with a respectable pedigree going back to Augustus,[28] and given fresh significance more recently by Christianity, which through the influence of the devout Pulcheria and in the hands of contemporary writers became the keynote of the Theodosian court. There is no reason to doubt Theodosius' personal sincerity in this area, but in a society where asceticism was accorded great respect there were also clear political advantages to be gained from advertising this aspect of the emperor's behaviour – his regular fasting, self-denial of comforts, daily devotions and memorizing of the scriptures – and the stories which circulated concerning the role of the emperor's prayers in achieving military success served to confirm that such piety was an attribute of real consequence.[29] It was to

---

[20] Cf. Hopkins (1978) 196.   [21] Cf. Whitby (1992).

[22] Liebeschuetz, *Barbarians and Bishops* 129.

[23] Soc. *HE* VII.21.7–10, 23.11–12; John Ant. fr. 195 (= *FHG* IV.613). Cf. *Chron. Pasch.* p. 579 which reports the formal announcement in the capital of a Roman success during the Persian war of 421–2.

[24] Theodosius' hunting: John Ant. fr. 194 (= *FHG* IV.612); Theodore Lector, *HE* 353 (Hansen p. 100.4); earlier centuries: Charlesworth (1943) 4.

[25] Charlesworth (1937), with Wallace-Hadrill (1981).

[26] Notably in subventions towards the costs of public building projects in provincial cities: *Nov. Th.* 23 (443) (Heraclea Salbake, Caria: see Roueché (1986)); cf. Marcell. *Chron.* s.a. 436 (Cyzicus).

[27] Soc. *HE* VII.22.9–11.   [28] Charlesworth (1943).

[29] Soc. *HE* VII.22.4–7, 23.9; Harries (1994).

play a role of continuing and increasing importance in preserving the integrity of the imperial office through the vicissitudes of the fifth century and beyond.

2. Religious affairs

'Give me the earth undefiled by heretics, and in return I will give you heaven. Help me to destroy the heretics, and I will help you to destroy the Persians.' This blunt appeal, reportedly made to Theodosius by a bishop of Constantinople, provides a telling insight into how it was believed the emperor could enhance his piety – and the practical benefits that would ensue.[30] Certainly, Theodosius' reign witnessed the proclamation of a number of measures aimed at penalizing heretics, as well as pagans and adherents of other religious groups in the eastern empire.[31] The confident rhetoric of these laws, however, often belied their effectiveness. Despite Theodosius' assumption to the contrary in 423, pagan practices continued, as the very repetition of the laws, together with other evidence, shows.[32] Indeed, it cannot in practice have been a straightforward task to enforce such laws consistently anyway, and a significant element of pragmatism is also apparent in their application. Known pagans and Arians continued to hold high military rank throughout Theodosius' reign,[33] and the significant numbers of Arian Goths serving in the army must have acted as a powerful disincentive against strict implementation of the relevant laws, let alone the introduction of more severe ones.[34] But perhaps for a regime concerned to promote the idea of imperial piety, it was the pronouncement of the laws, rather than their enforcement, which was ultimately of primary importance. At the same time, it is worth remembering that, even if the extent of official enforcement was variable, some clergy had no hesitation about taking matters into their own hands.[35]

Another important dimension of imperial piety, first articulated by Constantine, was concern for harmony within the church, and Theodosius' reign was not short of opportunities for its exercise. The latent potential for conflict between the theological traditions of Antioch and Alexandria over the seemingly rarefied issue of the relationship between the human and the divine in Christ was realized when the renowned Antiochene preacher, Nestorius, was chosen by Theodosius to be bishop of Constantinople (428) and proceeded to use his position to insist that the appropriate epithet for

[30] Soc. *HE* vii.29.5 (the bishop in question was Nestorius).
[31] Heretics: *C.Th.* xvi.6.65 (428), *Nov.Th.* 8.9 (438); pagans: *C.Th.* xvi.10.21 (415), 22 (423), 25 (435), *Nov.Th.* 3.8 (438); Jews and Samaritans: *C.Th.* xvi.8.25 (423), 27 (23), *Nov.Th.* 3.2–5 (438), with discussion in Linder (1987) (see also Millar (1992) 117–21).   [32] Harl (1990); Trombley, *Hellenic Religion*.
[33] *PLRE* ii, *s.v.* Apollonius 3, Fl. Zeno 6 (pagans); Fl. Plinta, Fl. Ardabur Aspar, Ardabur 1 (Arians).
[34] Liebeschuetz, *Barbarians and Bishops* 148.   [35] E.g. Soc. *HE* vii.29, 31; Gregory (1979) 143.

the Virgin Mary was *Christotokos* ('Mother of Christ') rather than the traditional title of *Theotokos* ('Mother of God') with its implicit emphasis on
Christ's divinity. In an attempt to resolve the ensuing controversy which this
aroused with Cyril, patriarch of Alexandria (412–44), Theodosius intervened and called a council at Ephesus (431), in the expectation that it would
uphold Nestorius, for whose abilities Theodosius had great respect. In fact,
the council took the view that his teaching effectively proposed the existence
of a human Christ and a separate divine Christ, and condemned Nestorius.
Despite the council's serious procedural irregularities, Theodosius executed
a volte-face and approved the verdict.

The controversy did not, however, go away. In the late 440s a prominent
Constantinopolitan monk, Eutyches, who had been teaching his version of
Cyril's views in the capital, was condemned for denying Christ's humanity
by a local council convened by the bishop, Flavian (448). Cyril's successor
at Alexandria, Dioscorus (444–51), was outraged and induced Theodosius
to convene a second council at Ephesus (449), at which the condemnation
of Eutyches was reversed and Flavian and other supposed Nestorian sympathizers were condemned. The proceedings were, however, accompanied
by intimidation and violence on the part of Dioscorus' supporters,
prompting pope Leo to denounce the whole occasion as 'brigandage' and
demand a fresh gathering under his own presidency. Theodosius, however,
was not at all enthusiastic about this proposal.[36]

Although these disagreements were in the first instance doctrinal in character, the vehemence of the feelings and behaviour they aroused betrays the
existence of important non-theological dimensions as well. For example, it
was difficult for Antioch, Alexandria and Constantinople to disentangle the
debate about orthodoxy from questions of ecclesiastical rivalry and prestige,[37] and the support of some western Anatolian bishops for Cyril's condemnation of Nestorius was motivated by resentment at encroachments on
their independence by the patriarchate of Constantinople.[38] Imperial
actions were likewise swayed by political considerations. Theodosius initially resisted the idea of calling a council in 430 until public disturbances in
Constantinople persuaded him otherwise; his reluctant abandonment of
Nestorius in 431 seems to have been induced by his realization of the extent
of popular opposition to the bishop; and his behaviour in the late 440s
reflected the loyalty of Chrysaphius, then the key figure at court, to
Eutyches, who happened to be his godfather.[39] This goes a long way
towards explaining Theodosius' cool response to Leo's demand for a fresh

---

[36] For a succinct but magisterial exposition of the theological issues and historical context of the
events outlined in this and the preceding paragraph, see Chadwick (1983). For more detailed discussions, see Gregory (1979) chs. 4–5; Young (1983) 229–89; Frend, *Monophysite Movement* ch. 1 (to be read
with Wickham (1973)).   [37] Baynes (1955).   [38] Gregory (1979) 102.
[39] Gregory (1979) 100–1, 108–14, 134–41.

council, a response which looked set to create an impasse until Theodosius' unexpected death the following year reopened the possibility of new developments.

3. Foreign relations

For much of the fourth century, relations with Sasanian Persia had been the most taxing external problem confronting the eastern half of the Roman empire. In the final decades of that century, however, the focus of attention had shifted elsewhere, and this pattern continued during Theodosius' reign. The empire did fight two wars against Persia in the first half of the fifth century, but these conflicts – the first in 421–2, the second in 440[40] – were of short duration and constituted brief interruptions to otherwise quiescent relations between the two powers, both of whom had other, more pressing preoccupations. In the case of Persia, this took the form primarily of nomads from Central Asia troubling its north-eastern frontier.[41] In the case of Constantinople, there were two pre-eminent areas of concern – developments in the western Mediterranean, and relations with the Huns in the lower Danube basin.

Eastern forces were despatched westwards on four occasions during Theodosius' reign. In 410, 4,000 men were sent to Ravenna to assist in the defence of the western emperor Honorius against Alaric and the Goths, while in 424 an army commanded by Ardabur and Aspar intervened in the upheaval that followed Honorius' death, eventually defeating the usurper John and overseeing the installation on the western throne of Honorius' nephew, Valeninian III (425). The third occasion was in 431, when eastern units under Aspar went to North Africa to aid western forces struggling to hold back the eastward advance of the Vandals towards Carthage. Although Aspar's forces enjoyed limited success in the ensuing campaign, this involvement none the less contributed to achieving the settlement of 435 which preserved, albeit only temporarily, Roman control of the more valuable eastern provinces of the region. Finally, when the Vandals subsequently broke the treaty and captured Carthage itself (439), another expedition – probably the largest of the four – was organized to act in concert with western forces (441).[42]

Constantinople's willingness to commit substantial forces to the western Mediterranean in this way may initially appear somewhat surprising. On the first three occasions, eastern interests were not threatened in any obvious or direct manner, so that intervention is best understood as an expression of dynastic solidarity with members of the Theodosian family, mingled

---

[40] Blockley (1992) 56–61.   [41] Frye (1984) 320–1.
[42] For further detail on these events, see ch. 1 (Heather), pp. 9–12 above.

with an element of self-interest.[43] However, the Vandal capture of Carthage with its docks and shipping introduced a dramatic new element into the equation. The western empire promptly undertook hurried defensive measures in anticipation of sea-borne attacks on Italy,[44] and an imperial order to extend the mural defences of Constantinople along the seaward sides of the city has often been interpreted in the same light.[45] The Vandal invasion of Sicily in 440 showed that there was genuine cause for apprehension, and concern about its potential ramifications for the security of the eastern Mediterranean must have influenced Constantinople's decision to commit substantial forces to the expedition of 441.

In the event, the expedition never progressed beyond Sicily because a Hun offensive in the Balkans forced Constantinople to recall its troops. Not for the first time during Theodosius' reign, Hunnic moves dictated eastern policy. The Huns had of course impinged on Roman horizons well before Theodosius' accession, having first made their presence felt indirectly as far back as the 370s, when their movements across the steppe regions north of the Caspian and Black Seas induced Gothic tribes adjacent to the lower Danube to seek admission to the empire. However, it was probably not until the early years of Theodosius' reign that the Huns themselves reached the Danube in significant numbers,[46] or were in a position to pose a serious threat to the heartlands of the eastern empire. Throughout history, the general socio-economic character of nomadic pastoralist peoples such as the Huns has never been conducive to the emergence of centralized political power – dispersal in small groups over large areas, absence of permanent settlements, and minimal social differentiation have tended to militate against any such development. However, where they are able to establish dominance over a sedentary population and exploit their produce and manpower, such a development can occur.[47] By the early fifth century, the Huns had achieved hegemony over various settled peoples living north of the Danube – Goths, Gepids, Heruls and others – and Constaninople found itself having to deal with rulers such as Rua and Attila who could command significant human and material resources.

The consequences were felt for the first time in 422 when Rua took advantage of imperial preoccupation with war against Persia to launch an invasion of Thrace, and the empire had to buy him off by agreeing to an annual payment of 350 pounds of gold.[48] Rua employed a similar strategy in 434, making further demands when significant numbers of eastern troops were absent defending Carthage against the Vandals. Negotiations

[43] Kaegi (1968) ch. 1; Matthews (1975) 378–82.   [44] *Nov. Val.* 5 (March 440), 9 (June 440).
[45] *Chron. Pasch.* p. 583 with Whitby and Whitby (1989) 72 n. 243.   [46] Heather (1995) 5–19.
[47] Anderson (1974) 219–26; Khazanov (1984) ch. 5.
[48] Croke (1977) with Zuckerman (1994) 162 n. 12.

evidently broke down and war ensued, but the sudden death of Rua (apparently struck by lightning) threw the Hun forces into disarray. He was succeeded by his nephews Attila and Bleda, who took time to consolidate their position internally, before the empire's concern to ensure peace on the Danube in preparation for its second expedition against the Vandals presented them with the opportunity in 439/40 to extract further significant concessions, including an increase in the annual payments to 700 pounds of gold.[49]

Once the expedition for North Africa had departed, however, the Huns found a pretext for reneging on their agreement and attacked the empire, capturing a number of Danubian cities and plundering widely in Illyricum and Thrace (441–2). The crack imperial troops bound for Africa were recalled from Sicily, and, faced by this threat, Hunnic forces withdrew. The empire then discontinued its annual payments to the Huns until, in 447, Attila – now sole ruler after the murder of Bleda (445) – took advantage of a concatenation of natural disasters – earthquake, famine and plague – to renew the offensive, this time with devastating effect.[50] Eastern forces were comprehensively defeated, there was widespread destruction in Thrace, the city of Constantinople itself was threatened, and the eastern empire was forced to make its most serious concessions yet. In addition to the now customary requirement that Hunnic fugitives be returned, Attila claimed all territory five days' journey south of the lower Danube, and stipulated an annual payment of 2,100 pounds of gold (together with arrears of 6,000 pounds).[51]

One immediate result of this disaster was the need to increase taxation, from which not even senatorial families escaped.[52] Priscus' account may well engage in rhetorical exaggeration about the burden this entailed for senators, but the fact that everyone was obliged to contribute suggests strongly that Attila's new demands did impose a strain on the empire's resources.[53] Another probable consequence was the construction of the Long Walls in Thrace, designed to afford greater protection to Constantinople and its immediate hinterland.[54] Yet another, indicative of the nadir to which Roman fortunes had sunk, was Chrysaphius' scheme to assassinate Attila, a 'solution' to which the empire had had recourse a

[49] For the events of the 430s, I follow the persuasive reconstruction of Zuckerman ((1994) 160–3), who revises the older accounts of Thompson ((1948) 70–8) and Maenchen-Helfen ((1973) 81–94) in significant respects. The other concessions comprised the return of Hunnic fugitives, a (high) fixed rate of ransom for Roman prisoners, agreement not to enter an alliance with any enemy of the Huns, and establishment of safe markets (Priscus fr. 2.29–38).

[50] Again, I follow Zuckerman's ((1994) 164–8) reinterpretation of the events of 441–7. See also ch. 23 (Whitby), pp. 704–8 below.   [51] Blockley (1992) 63–4.   [52] Priscus fr. 9. 3.22–33.

[53] Priscus' rhetoric: Thompson (1948) 191–7; Jones, LRE 206–7. Jones's minimizing of the burden seems to take no account of Priscus' statement that all had to contribute.

[54] Whitby, Michael (1985), contra Croke (1982). Crow (1995) adds nothing to the debate about the date.

number of times over the past century when confronted by particularly intransigent barbarian leaders.[55] On this occasion, the plan became known to Attila and failed, and the empire was fortunate to escape the consequences of his wrath relatively lightly, probably owing to the fact that his attention was now turning westwards.[56]

There can be no doubt that the Huns, and Attila in particular, caused the eastern empire considerable damage and discomfort during Theodosius' reign, whether in terms of the loss of productivity and revenue caused by Hunnic devastation of the Balkans,[57] the financial drain of annual treaty payments, or the way in which the timing of Hunnic demands and invasions limited Constantinople's freedom of action elsewhere. But while the situation was often grim, particularly for the inhabitants of the Balkans and particularly in 447, the period as a whole was not one of unremitting disaster in which the eastern empire was utterly helpless in the face of the Hunnic threat. Eastern armies undoubtedly suffered decisive defeats in 447, but they had also been able to force a Hunnic withdrawal a few years earlier.[58] The very fact that the Huns did so often time their diplomatic and military offensives to take advantage of temporary Roman handicaps or the absence of troops implies a healthy respect for Roman arms on the part of the Huns and helps to keep Hunnic successes in perspective. Attila's death in 453 was to reveal just how fragile the foundations of his empire were, though Theodosius' own demise in 450 meant that it was his successor who savoured the relief occasioned by that fortuitous turn of events – and who had also to cope with the first phase of its momentous consequences.

II. THE SUCCESSORS OF THEODOSIUS

1. *Marcian*

Theodosius died on 28 July 450 from injuries sustained in a fall from his horse while hunting. His marriage to Eudocia had produced no male offspring,[59] and perhaps excusably, given the sudden and unexpected nature of his death, he had not made public any choice of successor. Nearly a month later, on 25 August, a new emperor was at last proclaimed in the person of an unknown fifty-eight-year-old former army officer of Balkan origin named Marcian. The long delay between Theodosius' death and Marcian's accession belies the reports, no doubt initiated by Marcian's supporters, that the new emperor was Theodosius' deathbed choice. But if Theodosius did not promote Marcian, then someone else must have. The western emperor Valentinian III was the one individual with an obvious claim to arbitrate in this matter, but

---

[55] Lee (forthcoming).   [56] Blockley (1992) 66–7.
[57] On which see ch. 23 (Whitby), pp. 709–12 below.   [58] Zuckerman (1994) 167–8.
[59] On the spurious 'Arcadius 1' of *PLRE* ii, see Holum, *Empresses* 178 n. 14.

Marcian was certainly not his selection, since Valentinian pointedly refused to acknowledge his accession until March 452.[60] Some sources attribute the choice to Pulcheria, a possibility rendered plausible by her subsequent marriage to Marcian, but one which there are in fact strong reasons to doubt.[61] Aspar is more credible as kingmaker in 450: Marcian had served as aide to Aspar and his father for fifteen years, and Aspar's son Ardabur was promoted to a high military command soon after Marcian's accession. Yet Aspar himself was not in a strong position during Theodosius' final years – unlike Flavius Zeno, who also benefited from Marcian's rise. Strange though the notion of co-operation between Aspar and Zeno may seem, Marcian may in fact have been their joint candidate.[62]

Whatever the solution to this conundrum, there can be no doubt that Marcian's accession signalled significant change. Chrysaphius was quickly eliminated, and with him went the major policies with which he had been identified: Marcian refused to make any further annual payments to Attila and soon took steps to overturn the results of the recent second council of Ephesus. If Zeno played a key role in Marcian's promotion, then this would help to explain the reversal of policy towards Attila, Zeno having been a staunch critic of the payments during Theodosius' final years. It is less likely, however, to account for the change in ecclesiastical policy, for Zeno was a pagan.[63] Pulcheria, however, had a deep interest in the latter area, and undoing the second council of Ephesus may have been her *quid pro quo* for agreeing to marry Marcian, an essential step towards legitimating his rule.[64]

Marriage to Pulcheria did not, however, solve all his problems on this front. His undistinguished background was an impediment to winning senatorial support, and Valentinian's refusal to acknowledge his accession left a worrying question mark over his right to rule. His changes of policy can also be seen as strategies for overcoming these immediate political handicaps. A tough line towards Attila as he moved to invade Gaul was a good way of expressing solidarity with the west and, hopefully, of earning the gratitude and recognition of Valentinian,[65] while the termination of payments to Attila permitted tax concessions and so stood to gain the new emperor much-needed domestic support, particularly from the senatorial

---

[60] Burgess (1993–4) 63. One source (John Ant. *Excerpta de insidiis* (de Boor) 85) even suggests that Valentinian would have taken steps to remove Marcian had he not been opposed in this by Aetius.

[61] Burgess (1993–4).

[62] This is the proposal of Zuckerman (1994) 169–76, who argues that Aspar had been removed from his command after the defeats of 447, whereas Zeno had effective control of the only two eastern field armies not damaged in that débâcle and was therefore the most powerful general at the time of Theodosius' death. Moreover, Zeno's elevation to the distinction of *patricius* must date to the beginning of Marcian's reign (174 n. 56), and Marcian's reversal of policy on subsidies to Attila coincides with Zeno's views on this issue.

[63] Zuckerman (1994) 176 observes the irony of this. Of course, Zeno's hostility towards Chrysaphius may have inclined him to overturn as many as possible of the latter's policies, irrespective of where Zeno's personal sympathies lay.   [64] Cf. Burgess (1993–4) 65.   [65] Hohlfelder (1984) 60.

aristocracy,[66] whose good will was further courted by the abolition of the tax on senatorial land known as the *collatio glebalis* or *follis*.[67] The senatorial aristocracy also appears to have resented the direction of ecclesiastical policy in Theodosius' final years, so that a reversal on this front might be expected further to increase their sympathy for the new regime,[68] as well as winning the favour of pope Leo who in turn had influence with Valentinian's court at Ravenna.[69]

The embodiment of Marcian's ecclesiastical policy was the oecumenical council held at Chalcedon in 451, a watershed in the history of the church. Dioscorus of Alexandria, the instigator of the Second Council of Ephesus, was condemned and deposed; those in whose condemnation he had been instrumental in 449 – Flavian of Constantinople and other supposed Nestorian sympathizers – were rehabilitated; and a formula was sanctioned which aimed to find common ground between the Antiochene and Alexandrian positions on the relationship of the human and the divine in Christ. The council brought immediate benefits for Marcian – he was hailed as a new Constantine and relations between Constantinople and the pope were much improved – but the Chalcedonian formula failed to reunite the warring factions and, if anything, served to harden divergent tendencies. In the eyes of supporters of the Alexandrian school of thought, it still made too many concessions to unacceptable Antiochene ideas, and the rejection of Chalcedon became a rallying-cry which strengthened their sense of sep-arate identity and gave rise during the ensuing decades to the so-called Monophysite movement. Moreover, although the Chalcedonian definition was compatible with Antiochene teaching, the council also reaffirmed Nestorius' condemnation as a heretic, prompting some adherents of the Antiochene tradition also to reject Chalcedon and furthering the process through which an independent Nestorian church eventually emerged.

The strength of popular feelings aroused by Chalcedon may be gauged from the fact that Marcian was obliged to use military force to maintain pro-Chalcedonian bishops in office in Alexandria and Jerusalem, and when news of Marcian's death reached the former city in 457, the incumbent was lynched and replaced by an anti-Chalcedonian candidate whom Marcian's successor was in turn only able to replace by deploying troops. Of course, incidents of this sort simply served to reinforce popular antagonism towards Chalcedon and strengthen support for Monophysite theology in Egypt and Palestine, and increasingly even in Syria.[70]

[66] Jones, *LRE* 219.

[67] *CJ* XII.2.2 (450–5). Barnish (1989) discusses the evidence for how significant a source of income this was for the government.   [68] Gregory (1979) 141–2, 166.

[69] Stein (1959) 1.312; Jones, *LRE* 219.

[70] Frend, *Monophysite Movement* 148–69; Gray, *Defence of Chalcedon* 17–25; Meyendorff, *Imperial Unity* 187–90.

Marcian enjoyed more enduring success in foreign relations. His policy towards the Huns enraged Attila, but preoccupation with his campaigns in Gaul and Italy during 451–2 meant that he was unable to make good his dire threats. No doubt Attila's lack of success in the west and Valentinian's eventual recognition of Marcian in 452 strengthened Marcian's resolve in pursuing this course, but it is not difficult to understand why he should have been regarded as fortunate when Attila unexpectedly died in 453.[71] The importance of Attila's personal authority in maintaining the coherence of the Hunnic empire soon became apparent as his sons fell to fighting over their inheritance and the various subject peoples seized the opportunity to assert their independence, culminating in the battle at the river Nedao (454).[72] The consequences of all this were to be a continuing anxiety for Constantinople for most of the remainder of the century, but Attila's death certainly marked the beginning of the end of Hunnic power.

The early years of Marcian's reign also witnessed other successes on the military/diplomatic front: Arab attacks in the east were repulsed in late 451/early 452,[73] while offensives into Egypt by Nobades and Blemmyes, tribesmen from the south, were defeated in 453.[74] At the time of his death Marcian was planning an expedition against Carthage, an understandable reaction to the Vandal sack of Rome in 455 and the abduction of the western empress Eudoxia and her daughters,[75] but though he had himself portrayed as a conquering hero,[76] his regime otherwise avoided unnecessary foreign commitments, which, together with the ending of payments to Attila, must go a long way towards explaining the healthy reserve of more than 100,000 lbs of gold which he had accumulated by the end of his reign.[77]

2. Leo

Marcian died on 27 January 457 at the age of 65.[78] There was never any prospect of his marriage to Pulcheria producing an heir: Marcian had agreed to respect her vow of chastity and she was already beyond child-bearing age anyway. Marcian may have hoped that the succession would pass to his son-in-law Anthemius, who had received rapid promotion

---

[71] Jord. *Rom.* 333.   [72] Thompson (1948) 152–4; Maenchen-Helfen (1973) 143–52.
[73] Priscus fr. 26; Nicephorus xv.9; Shahîd (1989) 55–7.
[74] Priscus fr. 27,1 with Zuckerman (1994) 176–9.   [75] Mathisen (1981) 242–3.
[76] *Anth. Pal.* ix.802 (statue of Marcian on horseback trampling on a defeated enemy).
[77] John. Lyd. *De Mag.* iii.44 for the figure. Marcian's rapid creation of this surplus has been taken as proof that payments to the Huns cannot have been that serious a problem and that the reserve must already have been building up under Theodosius: Thompson (1948) 194; Hendy, *Studies* 264. But if Theodosius already had a reserve of any substance in place by 447, then surely he would have avoided imposing new and obviously unpopular taxes to meet Attila's demand. Moreover, it can be argued that the growth of the surplus during the years after the termination of the payments in 450 shows just how serious a burden they had previously been.   [78] For the details, see Croke (1978).

during the mid 450s,[79] but, if so, those hopes were not realized. An element of uncertainty remains concerning the manoeuvrings behind Marcian's own assumption of the purple, but the sources are explicit in stating that the succession in 457 was determined by Aspar, who preferred another candidate.[80] His choice was similar to Marcian in many respects – a relative nonentity of Balkan origin, in his mid fifties and from a military background, named Leo.[81] Formal legitimation was a more serious problem this time: recognition from the west was not an issue (Valentinian had been assassinated in 455 and the ensuing chaos was still unresolved), but there was no female member of the Theodosian household available to provide a convenient dynastic link through marriage.[82] The character of the ceremonial accompanying Leo's accession – much more elaborate than what is known of previous such occasions and, interestingly, displaying an apparently novel 'liturgical' dimension – is highly significant in the light of this.[83]

Aspar no doubt promoted the unknown Leo in the expectation of being able to exercise a predominant influence in the affairs of state, and the way in which his sons and kinsmen monopolized the consulship during Leo's early years is one measure of his success.[84] By the mid 460s, however, Leo showed himself prepared to follow his own mind. Sources refer to disagreements between the two over certain high officials and over a foreign policy decision, and in the latter case Leo certainly prevailed.[85] It must also have been in the mid 460s that he began pursuing a longer-term plan designed to free himself completely from dependence on the Alan general. Aspar's strength lay particularly in the support of the Goths serving in the army, but from the mid 460s Leo sought to counterbalance this by drawing on manpower from Isauria, a rugged, mountainous region in south-western Anatolia whose inhabitants had a reputation for brigandage and savagery on a par with foreign barbarians but who were also, for this very

[79] Anthemius, grandson of the powerful praetorian prefect of Theodosius II's early years, married Marcian's daughter (from a previous marriage) in 453/4; for further details, see *PLRE* II, *s.v.* Anthemius 3. If Anthemius did have such aspirations in 457, Leo's choice of him for the western throne in 467 might in part be explained by a concern to mollify an aggrieved party, while also conveniently removing him from the eastern scene.

[80] Priscus fr. 19; Candidus fr. 1.4, 25–6. Aspar's power in 457 is confirmed by pope Leo effectively treating him as co-ruler: Leo, *Epp.* 149.2, 150, 153 (= *PL* LIV.1120, 1121, 1123). Flavius Zeno had died during Marcian's reign, possibly as early as late 451 (Zuckerman (1994) 175).

[81] Two sources, but both late (Theophanes p. 116.7–8, Zonaras XIII.25), also report that Leo had once been in the service of Aspar.

[82] Pulcheria had died in 453, predeceased by Theodosius' other three sisters; Theodosius' second daughter Flacilla had died in 431, while his first, Eudoxia, widow of Valentinian III, was a prisoner in Carthage.   [83] *De Caer.* I.91, with Nelson (1976), MacCormack (1981) 240–7.

[84] His second son, Patricius, was consul in 459, his third, Herminericus, in 465 (his eldest, Ardabur, had already held it in 447), and Dagalaifus, husband of his granddaughter, held the consulship in 461. They also held various military or administrative posts of importance.

[85] Foreign policy: Priscus fr. 45 (dated to *c.* 466 in *PLRE* II, *s.v.* Fl. Ardabur Aspar); officials: Candidus fr. 1.28–30, who places this after the great fire of 464, though he does not explain the point at issue or the outcome.

reason, excellent fighters.[86] Isaurians were drafted into the army on an increased scale, and probably also into the new élite bodyguard of the *excubitores* which Leo established as a further way of trying to ensure his independence.[87]

A necessary part of this strategy was Leo's advancement to high military rank of a leading Isaurian chieftain, Tarasicodissa, who changed his barbaric-sounding name to Zeno, hoping by its Greekness and the reputation which his fellow countryman of that name had enjoyed in the late 440s and early 450s to mitigate the prejudice which attached to his Isaurian origins.[88] He discredited Aspar's son Ardabur on charges of treasonable communication with Persia (466), secured marriage to Leo's elder daughter Ariadne (466/7),[89] and held the consulship (469). Although Aspar was in turn able to pressure Leo into not only marrying his younger daughter Leontia to another of his sons, Patricius, but also declaring that son emperor-designate, Zeno steadily eclipsed Aspar as the leading influence in the state, to the point where Leo finally had Aspar and Ardabur murdered (471),[90] winning him the epithet 'the butcher' and leaving the way clear for Zeno effectively to succeed him in 474.

There was a significant degree of continuity of policy between the reigns of Marcian and Leo. Leo was a supporter of Chalcedonian orthodoxy and also initiated further measures against pagans and heretics, including a blanket exclusion from the legal profession of anyone not an orthodox Christian.[91] For the first decade of his reign, he also sought diplomatic solutions to foreign-policy issues. In one area, however – the lower Danube – he faced increasing problems arising from the break-up of Attila's empire, while in a second area – relations with the Vandals – he eventually abandoned a cautious approach for a more aggressive one – with disastrous consequences.

Some of Attila's sons remained a disruptive presence along the Danube during the 460s – Dengizich's abortive invasion of 468 is the best-documented example[92] – but more problematic were the peoples previously subject to the Huns who gained their independence during the years

---

[86] For the Isaurians' reputation, see e.g. Philostorg. *HE* xi.8, Theodoret, *Ep.* 40 (Azéma), Joshua Styl. *Chron.* 12. For the region and its history: Matthews (1989) 355–67; Hopwood (1986), (1989); Shaw (1990). [87] Leo and the Isaurians: Brooks (1893) 211–15; *excubitores*: Haldon (1984) 136–8.

[88] For the name, see Feissel (1984) 564 n. 105, *contra* Harrison (1981); for his career to 474, see *PLRE* II, *s.v.* Fl. Zeno 7.

[89] The suggestion of Pingree ((1976) 146–7) that Zeno was engaged to Ariadne as early as 463 is doubtful; cf. Dagron (1982) 275.

[90] For the fates of Patricius and Herminericus, see *PLRE* II, *s.v.* Iulius Patricius 15, Herminericus.

[91] *CJ* 1.4.15 (468), 1.11.8 (472?). Cf. *CJ* 1.5.9–10. (For Marcian's anti-pagan legislation, see *CJ* 1.11.7 (451).) Leo's *quaestor* Isocasius was accused of being a pagan, stripped of office and forced to undergo baptism (*PLRE* II, *s.v.* Isocasius), and Leo is also reported as enforcing anti-heretical legislation against one group of Arians (Malal. p. 372.3–5) – perhaps to spite the Arian Aspar?

[92] Thompson (1948) 154–60; Maenchen-Helfen (1973) 152–68.

following Attila's death, the most important of whom were the Goths (though they were certainly not a unified people at this stage). During the late 450s and 460s, various groups of Goths are found in Pannonia (effectively no longer imperial territory since the 440s), while a second cluster was located within the empire in Thrace.[93] Some of the latter had, by the 460s, acquired formal status as federate troops within the eastern empire with particular ties of loyalty to Aspar. Predictably, his assassination by Leo in 471 provoked a revolt, which Leo was only able to end (473) by making various concessions to their leader Theoderic Strabo – an annual payment of 2,000 pounds of gold, an imperial generalship for Strabo and recognition of him as the only Gothic leader with whom Constantinople would deal – but not before a substantial portion of the Pannonian Goths had seized the chance presented by Leo's preoccupation with the revolt to invade the eastern empire, advance as far as Macedonia and extract concessions of their own in the form of land.[94] At Leo's death, therefore, the situation in the Balkans was one fraught with difficulties.

As for relations with the Vandals, during the decades following the abortive expedition against Carthage in 441, Vandal raiding had concentrated on the western Mediterranean, but had also increasingly impinged on the east,[95] to the extent that by the mid 460s there were fears of a Vandal attack on Alexandria[96] – an ominous prospect in the context of the grain supply. The Vandal abduction of the western empress Eudoxia and her daughters following the sack of Rome (455) had clearly provoked alarm and outrage in Constantinople, and was a continuing vexation so long as the imperial womenfolk remained prisoners in Carthage,[97] while the persecution of orthodox African Christians by the Arian Vandals must have been a further cause for concern in the east.[98]

These varied circumstances help to explain why Leo eventually abandoned diplomacy and took the fateful step of organizing another expedition against Carthage. In preparation, he arranged in 467 for Marcian's son-in-law Anthemius to occupy the then vacant imperial throne in the west, so that the following year a formidable eastern armada was able to

---

[93] Marcian is often given responsibility for their entry to the empire (on the basis of Jordanes), but there is good reason to think that at least some of the Pannonian Goths were placed there by Attila, and that at least some of the Thracian Goths had been settled there by the imperial authorities during the 420s (Heather, *Goths and Romans* 242–4, 259–63).   [94] Heather, *Goths and Romans* ch. 7.

[95] Raiding in the east in the late 440s and early 450s: Priscus fr. 10.12–13 (with Croke (1983a) for the date), Jord. *Rom.* 333; attacks on Illyricum and Greece in the late 450s and 460s: Vict. Vit. *Hist. Pers.* 1.51, Procop. *Wars* III.5.22–6.1, 22.16–18.   [96] *V. Dan. Styl.* 56.

[97] All but Eudocia were finally released *c.* 462; the soures are contradictory concerning the eventual fate of Eudocia, who was forced to marry Geiseric's son, but it is likely she was still in Carthage in 468: see *PLRE* II, *s.v.* Eudocia 1.

[98] Courtois ((1955) 292–3) is sceptical about Geiseric as a persecutor on the basis of a lack of martyrs during his reign, but persecution can entail other forms of discrimination, which are certainly in evidence in this period: Moorhead (1992b) xi–xii.

combine with western forces, while an eastern army also advanced towards Carthage along the coast from Egypt.[99] The difficulties of co-ordination inherent in such a strategy no doubt go far towards explaining the subsequent débâcle, though Geiseric's skilful use first of diplomatic delay and then of fireships was also clearly important. It is less easy to determine whether the odium which fell on the eastern commander, Basiliscus, resulted from the need for a scapegoat or was genuinely deserved.[100] The ensuing disaster cost Constantinople dearly in terms of military and financial resources. The sources differ about the precise sums involved, but the most conservative estimate is still in excess of 64,000 pounds of gold – 'a sum that probably exceeded a whole year's revenue'.[101] It is hardly surprising that one source talks of the entire state being shipwrecked – a particularly apposite metaphor in the context.[102] In this respect, Leo left his successor a most unwelcome legacy.[103]

3. Zeno

Leo's wife Verina had given birth to a son of unknown name in 463, but he died when only five months old,[104] and when Leo himself succumbed to the effects of dysentery on 18 January 474 he was succeeded by his seven-year-old grandson Leo, son of Zeno and Ariadne, whom he had made co-emperor shortly before his death. Leo II, however, died ten months later, but not before having in turn raised his father to the rank of co-emperor.[105] By thus gaining the throne, Zeno has a strong claim to be regarded as the most politically successful general in the fifth-century east. Once emperor, however, he had to channel most of his energies into clinging on to power, for his reign was overshadowed by a succession of revolts and usurpations – that of Basiliscus (who actually controlled Constantinople for twenty months during 475–6), of Marcian (who almost gained control of the capital in 479), and of Illus and Leontius (former supporters of Zeno's

---

[99] Courtois ((1955) 202–4) gives priority to Theophanes' version, whereby the army from Egypt becomes a quite separate campaign in 470, but this view has found little support (cf. Blockley (1992) 75–6, 212).

[100] Accounts of Basiliscus' less than glorious role in the expedition may have been coloured by the unpopularity he had earned by the end of his later usurpation (475–6).

[101] Convenient summary of figures and quote in Hendy, *Studies* 221, 223. Courtois ((1955) 202–4) downplays the size and cost of the expedition, arguing that they were inflated by sixth-century writers concerned to enhance the significance of Belisarius' expedition (533). This is plausible in principle, but some of the relevant sources pre-date Justinian's reign, his strictures against Priscus are unpersuasive, and the evidence of Candidus does not receive due consideration. [102] Joh. Lyd. *De Mag.* III.44.

[103] *Suda* E 3100 refers to the treasury being empty during Zeno's reign, but its attribution to the alleged failings of Zeno is suspect (Cameron (1965) 505–6), and the financial repercussions of the disaster of 468 are a more plausible explanation (cf. Malchus fr. 3).

[104] Pingree (1976) 146–7 with the important qualifications of Dagron (1982) 275.

[105] The sources do not even hint at any suspicious circumstances surrounding young Leo's death (Croke (1983b) 82 n. 5), a silence of considerable import given Zeno's subsequent unpopularity.

regime who raised a revolt against him in Isauria itself during 484–8).[106] Those of Basiliscus and Marcian were inspired partly by resentment on the part of some of Leo's relatives at their displacement by Zeno's rise – Basiliscus was Leo's brother-in-law, Marcian his son-in-law – and partly by public prejudice against uncouth Isaurians. Even before Zeno's accession, this prejudice had manifested itself against the Isaurians increasingly resident in Constantinople, many of whom were killed in a hippodrome riot in 473.[107] Antagonism was heightened by Zeno's promotion of fellow countrymen to positions of importance in the state, and when Basiliscus seized the throne in 475, large numbers of them were massacred in the capital.[108] Zeno's struggle with his fellow countrymen Illus and Leontius, on the other hand, was much more of a power struggle between rival Isaurian chieftains, on this occasion played out on a far larger stage and for much higher stakes than usual.[109]

Zeno's domestic political difficulties were compounded by the situation in the Balkans which he inherited from Leo, where there were now two rival groups of Goths in close proximity to the imperial capital, one of which (that of Theoderic Strabo) was hostile towards the new emperor, who had been no friend of their patron Aspar and was the chief beneficiary of his fall. This hostility soon found opportunity for expression, with the Thracian Goths lending their support to Basiliscus' usurpation in 475.[110] It was not sufficient, however, to prevent Basiliscus' downfall the following year, and upon Zeno's return, the Thracian Goths found themselves displaced from their position of favour by the Pannonian Goths, with whom Zeno had established links during his enforced absence from Constantinople. The annual payments were now to go to the latter, and their leader, Theoderic the Amal, was given the generalship formerly held by Theoderic Strabo. In return for these favours, Zeno expected the Pannonian Goths to act against the Thracian Goths, but Theoderic the Amal soon came to believe (no doubt with some justice) that Zeno was actually trying to engineer the mutual destruction of the rival groups and he in turn revolted, leaving Zeno to patch up a fresh agreement with Strabo in 478.[111]

---

[106] For narrative of these complex events, see Brooks (1893); Stein (1959) 1.363–4; Stein, *Bas-Empire* II.15–20, 28–31. The part played in these events by Leo's widow Verina is noteworthy in the context of influential imperial women.   [107] Marcell. *Chron.* s.a. 473 with Croke (1995) 100.

[108] Joshua Styl. *Chron.* 12; Candidus fr. 1.57.

[109] There appears also to have been a religious dimension to this struggle. Although Illus was a Christian, one of his leading supporters was the pagan Pamprepius and it is apparent that Illus' revolt inspired hopes of a pagan revival among sections of the urban élite of the eastern empire (*PLRE* II, *s.v.* Pamprepius; Zacharias Rhetor, *V. Severus* (*PO* II (1907)) 40). However, the attempt to place certain anti-pagan measures in this context (Trombley, *Hellenic Religion* 1.81–3 on *CJ* 1.11.9–10) overlooks *P.Oxy.* 1814 (line 16) which shows that the first of these laws is from Anastasius' reign, in turn making it probable that the second is also later than Zeno.

[110] Malchus fr. 15.20–2; *V. Dan. Styl.* 75; Heather, *Goths and Romans* 273–5.

[111] Heather, *Goths and Romans* 275–93.

This already complicated sequence of developments then took yet another tortuous turn in 479 when Strabo's backing of another usurper – on this occasion the unsuccessful Marcian – once more alienated him from Zeno. However, Strabo's subsequent attempts to capture Constantinople (480) failed, and in the course of withdrawing into Greece the following year he fortuitously died. This simplified Zeno's problem, but in the face of the growing challenge from Illus and Leontius, Zeno now sought a new *rapprochement* with Theoderic the Amal, as a result of which the latter gained land for his people and a generalship and prestigious consulship for himself. He further consolidated his position by organizing the elimination of Strabo's son and successor Recitach, thereby opening the way for the amalgamation of the Thracian Goths with his own. Although Theoderic provided Zeno with help in his campaign against Illus, Zeno continued to harbour doubts about Theoderic's intentions and loyalty, and only arrived at a definitive solution to this problem, greatly protracted by the instability of Zeno's own position, through the time-honoured tactic of setting one barbarian against another, in this case persuading Theoderic to lead his people to Italy (489) and challenge the Scirian general Odoacer who had been ruling the peninsula since deposing the last western emperor in 476.[112]

In the sphere of religious policy, Zeno's reign was chiefly notable for his attempt to resolve the controversies arising from Chalcedon. The usurper Basiliscus had tried to win support for his regime in Egypt and Palestine by issuing an edict condemning Chalcedon, but this had the effect of provoking riots in the capital – Constantinople and the Balkans were for the most part staunchly pro-Chalcedonian. These riots, which had much more direct implications for the viability of his regime, forced Basiliscus to retract the edict, but the damage was already done.[113] Zeno showed a keen appreciation of the lessons to be learned from Basiliscus' failure when in 482 he issued his famous juggling-act known as the *Henotikon* or 'formula of union', through which he hoped to please everyone. It affirmed the condemnation of both Nestorius and Eutyches, approved one of Cyril's most important formulations (the so-called Twelve Anathemas), spoke of the one Christ without mentioning 'natures' or other terminology which had been a stumbling block in the past, and denounced any who had advanced different views at Chalcedon or any other council.

Zeno's interest in establishing ecclesiastical harmony in the east is not hard to understand: his hold on power had been tenuous from the start and a breakthrough here offered the prospect of consolidating much-needed support for his regime. The *Henotikon* did not in fact meet with a rapturous reception in all quarters, but it achieved short-term success where it mattered

[112] Heather, *Goths and Romans* ch. 9; Moorhead (1984) 261–3. For Constantinople's sometimes troubled relations with Theoderic as ruler of Italy, see Moorhead (1992a) ch. 6.
[113] *V. Dan. Styl.* 70–85; Evagr. *HE* III.7.

most for Zeno. Although extreme Monophysites were unhappy at its failure to condemn Chalcedon, others, including the patriarchs of Alexandria and Antioch, were willing to endorse it, as was the patriarch of Constantinople, Acacius (471–89), who rather surprisingly (given his see) was unenthusiastic about Chalcedon. In the west, the pope was incensed by its ambivalent attitude to Chalcedon and by Zeno and Acacius associating themselves with the Monophysite patriarchs, and threatened to excommunicate them (484). However, Zeno evidently judged that the benefits to be derived from a greater degree of harmony within the east outweighed the disadvantages of poor relations with the west. So began the so-called Acacian schism between Rome and Constantinople which was to last until Anastasius' death.[114]

Zeno was also responsible for the final closing of the school at Edessa (489) which had been an important centre for Antiochene theology in its Nestorian guise – another way of trying to win the support of both Monophysites and Chalcedonians. The closure was in fact largely symbolic, since the majority of the teachers had some time before realized that the tide of opinion in the eastern empire was increasingly against them and had therefore established themselves afresh across the border at Nisibis in Persia, from where they had long drawn many students anyway and where Nestorian Christianity was to have an enduring future.[115]

III. ANASTASIUS

1. *Politics and administration*

Zeno died from dysentery (or perhaps epilepsy) on 9 April 491. His marriage to Ariadne had produced no further male offspring after young Leo, another son from a previous marriage had also predeceased him,[116] and Zeno had nominated no successor. His brother Longinus believed that he had a good claim to the throne, but after the turmoil of Zeno's reign there was little enthusiasm for another emperor of Isaurian origin. Court officials and senators promptly met to discuss the succession and, perhaps unable to agree on a suitable candidate themselves, they accepted the proposal of the chief chamberlain Urbicius that Zeno's widow Ariadne be invited to nominate the successor. This surprising move must have been due not so much to Ariadne's status as the widow of the unpopular Zeno, as to her being the daughter of Leo and the last surviving member of the imperial family previous to Zeno's reign. It is another interesting, if unusual, example of the opportunities that both imperial eunuchs and imperial women sometimes had to influence political life during the fifth century, in

---

[114] Frend, *Monophysite Movement* 174–83; Gray, *Defence of Chalcedon* 28–34; Meyendorff, *Imperial Unity* 194–202.   [115] Meyendorff, *Imperial Unity* 98–9.   [116] *PLRE* II, *s.v.* Zeno 4.

the tradition of Chrysaphius on the one hand and Pulcheria, Eudocia and Verina on the other.[117]

If the decision to give Ariadne the choice was surprising, then the outcome of her deliberations was even more unexpected, for she selected a palace official named Anastasius, who was already sixty years of age and held heterodox theological views. Though this last characteristic became the cause of difficulties in the final years of his reign, he nevertheless proved to be in other respects a good choice, for he was to display a degree of political and administrative competence superior to that of any of his fifth-century predecessors. Once again, the lack of any dynastic link was a potential problem, but another elaborate accession ceremony (11 April 491) helped to offset this handicap,[118] while a month later Ariadne strengthened his position immeasurably by marrying him.

Anastasius' most pressing problem upon his accession was Isaurian resentment at the fact that Zeno had not been succeeded by his brother Longinus, which rapidly provoked a revolt in Isauria. Anastasius seized the initiative in Constantinople by despatching Longinus into exile and using the pretext of a hippodrome riot to expel all Isaurians from the capital. Rebel forces advancing against Constantinople from Isauria were defeated in late 492, though it took six years to reduce the various rebel strongholds in Isauria itself.[119] Although this should not be equated with the pacification of Isauria,[120] it did mark the end of the Isaurian factor in political life at the centre, and Anastasius was not slow to capitalize, via victory ceremonial, panegyric and architecture, on the kudos to be gained from this success.[121]

In addition to the Isaurian revolt, the early years of Anastasius' reign were also troubled by frequent outbreaks of unrest in Constantinople and Antioch, some of it very pointedly directed at the emperor himself.[122] The violence regularly manifested itself at places of public entertainment, though why there should have been a sudden upsurge of such incidents in the 490s is not easy to determine.[123] Anastasius responded initially by sending in troops, with much resultant bloodshed, and then by banning

---

[117] Ariadne does not, however, appear to have exercised any sustained influence; it is known, for example, that Anastasius turned down her request for the promotion of a particular individual to the praetorian prefectship (Joh. Lyd. *De Mag.* III.50). Urbicius was a man of vast experience, having already served most eastern emperors during the fifth century: *PLRE* II, *s.v.* Vrbicius 1.

[118] *De Caer.* 1.92 with Nelson (1976), MacCormack (1981) 240–7.

[119] Brooks (1893) 231–7; Stein, *Bas-Empire* II.82–4.

[120] Shaw (1990) 255–9, *contra* Jones, *LRE* 230–1.

[121] Victory ceremonial: McCormick, *Eternal Victory* 61; panegyric: Procopius of Gaza, *Panegyric* 9–10; Priscian, *De laude Anast.* 15–139; *Suda s.v.* Christodorus (a six-book epic entitled *Isaurika*; cf. Colluthus' *Persika* a decade later); architecture: *Anth. Pal.* IX.656 (a palace built to commemorate his victory). The abolition of the *chrysargyron* (see p. 54 below) was also timed to coincide with celebrations of the Isaurian victory: Chauvot (1986) 154; McCormick, *Eternal Victory* 61.

[122] Cameron (1973) 233–4 lists the incidents with references; see esp. John Ant. fr. 214b (= *FHG* v.29–30) and Marcell. *Chron.* s.a. 493 with Croke (1995) 107, when statues of the emperor were pulled down. [123] For discussion of possible causes, see Cameron (1973) 234–40.

wild-beast shows (498) and pantomimes (502).[124] His decision to abolish the highly unpopular tax known as the *collatio lustralis* or *chrysargyron* (498) should perhaps also be understood in this context, as a more positive response to this problem. The *chrysargyron* was a tax on urban traders and craftsmen, and its abolition may have been an attempt to counteract popular hostility in the cities by gaining good will towards the emperor from at least one important sector of the urban community.

Despite his abolition of this tax[125] and his granting of tax remissions in areas of the empire adversely affected by natural disasters or warfare,[126] and despite other significant expenses incurred during this reign – major building projects[127] and war against the Isaurians and, later, the Persians (see pp. 58–9 below) – Anastasius nevertheless managed over the course of his reign to accumulate a massive reserve of 320,000 pounds of gold.[128] This figure is testimony to Anastasius' skill in financial management, or at the very least to his skill in selecting officials with the requisite abilities in this area. Three policies seem to have played particularly important parts in achieving this astonishing result. The first, evident in Anastasius' laws, was a concerted effort on the part of the emperor and his officials to minimize waste and unnecessary expenditure through such measures as increased use of *adaeratio* (commutation of the land-tax in kind to gold). The second was the creation by one of Anastasius' praetorian prefects, Marinus, of a new category of officials, the *vindices*, who assumed responsibility for overseeing the collection of the land-tax in place of city councillors, a move which is likely to have reduced the scope for abuses on the part of the latter.[129] The third, perhaps less obviously, was Anastasius' currency reform, modelled, interestingly, on recent changes in Vandalic Africa and the new Gothic regime of Theoderic in Italy.[130]

Although fourth-century emperors had managed to keep the value of the gold *solidus* stable, attempts to do the same for the copper *nummus* had been unsuccessful, and its steady loss of value encouraged the continuation of inflationary trends. Anastasius' reform of 498 created a new set of copper coins valued at forty, twenty and ten *nummi*. They had specified weights which fixed their relationship with the *solidus*; these weights were later doubled (512), at which time an additional five *nummi* denomination was added.[131] A number of significant consequences ensued. The initial issuing of the new coins in 498 slowed inflationary trends, while their doubling in

---

[124] Bans: Joshua Styl. *Chron.* 34, 46; cf. Procopius of Gaza, *Panegyric* 15–16, Priscian, *De laude Anast.* 223–8; Cameron (1973) 228–32.

[125] In spite of its unpopularity, its abolition may not, in any case, have represented that great a loss to the government: Bagnall, *Egypt* 153–4.   [126] Jones, *LRE* 237.

[127] Malal. p. 409; Capizzi (1969) ch. 6.   [128] Procop. *SH* 19.7.

[129] Jones, *LRE* 235–6; Chrysos (1971); Chauvot (1987).

[130] Metcalf (1969); Hendy, *Studies* 478–90.

[131] Hendy, *Studies* 475–8, *contra* Jones, *LRE* 443 (who associates the five *nummi* coin with the initial reform of 498).

weight in turn began to reverse those trends; the new coins made life easier for ordinary consumers by reducing the quantity of low-value *nummi* they needed to carry around; and because the specified value of the copper coins in relation to the gold *solidus* was greater than the actual cost of the copper used in their production, it is likely that the imperial treasury made a profit from selling them to the public in return for *solidi*.[132]

Despite the rejoicing occasioned by his abolition of the *chrysargyron* and the benefits of the currency reform for ordinary people, Anastasius' accumulation of a surplus and some of the means by which this was achieved earned him an unwarranted reputation for avarice.[133] In fact his competence, and that of senior officials, in the unspectacular but crucial area of imperial finance made a significant contribution to the recovery of the eastern empire's fortunes, and constituted one of the major achievements of his reign.

2. Religious affairs

As a native of Dyrrhachium in the Balkans, Anastasius might reasonably have been expected to be an unequivocal supporter of Chalcedon, but this did not prove to be the case. Like Justinian, he had aspirations to be a theologian, and the result of his deliberations was considerable sympathy with the Monophysite cause.[134] This was already known at the time of his accession, so that the pro-Chalcedonian patriarch of Constantinople, Euphemius (490–5), at first opposed his nomination and then, when overruled by Ariadne and the senate, demanded that he sign a declaration that he would not abrogate Chalcedon.[135] Anastasius' initial policy – to continue trying to maintain a degree of ecclesiastical stability in the east on the basis of the *Henotikon* – was not incompatible with this, but Euphemius' subsequent attempts to achieve reconciliation with Rome by effectively abandoning the *Henotikon* threatened the success of that policy and eventually led Anastasius to have Euphemius deposed on charges of Nestorianism (495). His successor was Macedonius (495–511), who initially supported Anastasius' approach.

Antioch also posed problems for Anastasius. The patriarch Flavian (498–512), while personally sympathetic to Chalcedon, referred only to his adherence to the *Henotikon* in official pronouncements, thereby accommodating himself to Anastasius' aims. Some Syrian Monophysites, however,

---

132 Jones, *LRE* 444; Metcalf (1969) (though he questions whether the reform contributed anything to Anastasius' surplus (p. 12)).

133 E.g. Malal. p. 408; Joh. Lyd. *De Mag.* III.46; *Anth. Pal.* XI.271; John Ant. fr. 215 (= *FHG* IV.621).

134 The heterodox theological views of his mother and an uncle may also have played a part: see *PLRE* II, *s.v.* Anastasius 4 for references.

135 Evagr. *HE* III.32; Theodore Lector, *HE* 446 (Hansen pp. 125.25–126.15); Vict. Tunn. *Chron.* s.a. 491.

were unhappy with Flavian's failure to condemn Chalcedon and began a concerted propaganda and diplomatic campaign to persuade Anastasius to remove him. Meanwhile, in Constantinople itself, Macedonius began reverting to the capital's more usual uncompromising adherence to Chalcedon, while the highly articulate Monophysite theologian Severus, also present in the capital (508–11), brought further pressure to bear on Anastasius from the anti-Chalcedonian side.[136]

It is against this background of increasing polarization that Anastasius' adoption of a less neutral stance from 511 onwards must be understood. Like Zeno, Anastasius understandably viewed stability in the east as a more important priority than reconciliation with the west, and accordingly took various steps to ensure that he retained the support of Monophysites – first through the deposition of Macedonius at Constantinople, then through the deposition of Flavian at Antioch (in favour of Severus), and finally through decreeing the inclusion of controversial Monophysite phraseology in the liturgy of the capital's churches. The reaction to this last move was more extreme than Anastasius can have anticipated. There were several days of serious rioting (November 512), during which much blood was shed and parts of the city were burnt, but most worrying was the overthrow of statues of Anastasius accompanied by calls for a new emperor. Anastasius' response was to appear in the hippodrome without his diadem and to offer his abdication – a course of action which quelled the unrest.[137] While this may seem an idiosyncratic way of dealing with such a crisis, it is perhaps better viewed as a remarkable demonstration of the susceptibility of the capital's populace to a calculated display of imperial piety.

It did not, however, mark the end of religious turmoil, for Anastasius' actions of 511–12 provoked a further serious challenge to his position, a revolt orchestrated by an army officer, Vitalian, who commanded units of barbarian federates in Thrace.[138] The failure of their supplies to arrive in 513 and dissatisfaction among the regular troops with the *magister militum* for Thrace, Hypatius,[139] enabled Vitalian to win their support,[140] but the real issue for him – as indeed for many inhabitants of the Balkans – was Anastasius' stance on Chalcedon. That this was not a mere pretext for Vitalian's personal ambitions is indicated by the way he was prepared, on the first two occasions when he advanced against Constantinople (513 and 514), to withdraw after Anastasius agreed to take steps which offered the hope of resolving the religious issue. His willingness to do so, particularly

---

[136] Frend, *Monophysite Movement* ch. 5; Gray, *Defence of Chalcedon* 34–40; Meyendorff, *Imperial Unity* 202–6.

[137] Evagr. *HE* III.44; Malal. pp. 407–8; Marcell. *Chron.* s.a. 511–12 with Croke (1995) 114–16.

[138] For full details, see Stein, *Bas-Empire* II.178–85; Capizzi (1969) 123–7; *PLRE* II, *s.v.* Fl. Vitalianus 2; Croke (1995) 117–19.   [139] Probably not the nephew of Anastasius: Cameron (1974) 313–14.

[140] John Ant. fr. 214e (= *FHG* v.32).

the second time after Anastasius' original promises of 513 had proven empty, is strong evidence for this being his genuine motivation. When Anastasius once more failed to fulfil his side of the bargain, Vitalian advanced a third time (515), but on this occasion suffered a military defeat sufficiently serious for him to have to abandon any further attempts to capture the capital, and it was only after Anastasius' death and the accession of the Illyrian Justin that a resolution of the issue acceptable to Vitalian became possible. Anastasius survived this crisis, but his reign showed that the *Henotikon* was not a satisfactory basis for attaining an enduring settlement of the east's ecclesiastical difficulties. In acknowledging Anastasius' failure in this area, however, it is worth remembering that his Chalcedonian successors were not to find it any easier to achieve a solution to this intractable problem.

3. Foreign relations

Anastasius' priorities in foreign relations proved to be rather different from those of his predecessors. Although the failure of Leo's expedition in 468 had left the eastern Mediterranean vulnerable to further Vandal depredations,[141] the death of the long-lived Geiseric in 477 and growing domestic problems with Moorish tribesmen led to a less confrontational stance on the part of Geiseric's successors and much more stable relations between Constantinople and the Vandals over the next half-century[142] – a stability reflected in the archaeological and numismatic evidence for a substantial increase in trade between the eastern Mediterranean and Carthage during the last quarter of the fifth and first quarter of the sixth century.[143] The Danube frontier was rather more problematic, in part because of the way the empire's defensive infrastructure in that region had suffered extended neglect during Zeno's reign. So long as the various Gothic groups were active in Illyricum and Thrace, they effectively cushioned the empire from the consequences of this neglect, but soon after Theoderic's departure for Italy, the empire began to feel the effects in the form of invasions by peoples referred to in contemporary sources as Bulgars, generally taken to be descendants of the Huns who survived north of the Danube after the break-up of Attila's empire. Between 493 and 502, they are known to have made three significant thrusts into the Balkans.[144] Anastasius took various steps to try to remedy the deficiencies of fortifications in the region,

---

[141] Of which there were some in the early 470s: Courtois (1955) 197.

[142] Stein, *Bas-Empire* II.59–60.   [143] Fulford (1980).

[144] Marcell. *Chron.* s.a. 493, 499, 502 with Croke (1995) 108, 110, 111. The first record of involvement with the empire is Zeno's attempt to use them against Strabo in 480 (John Ant. fr. 211 (4) (= *FHG* IV.619)). The observations in *CJ* x.27.2.10 (491/505) on the debilitated economic state of Thrace perhaps reflect the impact of the Bulgars in addition to that of the Goths.

including, probably, repair of the Long Walls in Thrace which had been damaged by the great earthquake of 479,[145] and nothing further is heard of depredations across the Danube until the final years of his reign.[146]

The major foreign policy issue during Anastasius' reign, however, was Persia, with whom relations had been relatively untroubled throughout the fifth century. Tensions had undoubtedly existed, notably over the treatment of religious minorities within both empires[147] and over Persian demands for Roman financial assistance with the defence of the Caucasian passes, from which, the Persians argued, the Romans derived as much benefit as Persia.[148] These tensions, however, had only escalated into warfare on the two brief occasions already noted during Theodosius' reign, for Persia also faced many other problems comparable in gravity to those confronting the Romans during this period. In the second half of the fifth century, the Persians had to deal with another nomadic people, the Hephthalites, who captured the Persian king Peroz in one campaign and killed him in a second. Succession crises and Armenian revolts at various points created further distractions, and then in the final decade of the century, Kavadh's radical social reforms, probably designed to weaken the power of the Persian aristocracy, resulted in social upheaval and his temporary deposition (496–8).[149]

It was Kavadh who initiated war with the Romans in 502, ostensibly over the issue of Roman subsidies for the defence of the Caucasian passes, but probably as much because such a campaign offered the hope of uniting a recently strife-torn state against a common enemy. The Romans were slow to react to Kavadh's invasion – perhaps partly because of preoccupation with the Bulgar invasion of that year and a major Arab raid[150] – and his forces quickly captured Armenian Theodosiopolis, Martyropolis and Amida. That Kavadh's invasion created considerable uncertainty and insecurity in the empire's eastern provinces is indicated by the contemporary piece of apocalyptic literature emanating from the region known as the 'Oracle of Baalbek'.[151] It took Roman forces until 505 to effect the recovery of Amida, by which time Kavadh found himself having to deal with another Hephthalite invasion and was therefore amenable to a seven-year truce (which in practice lasted until 527).[152] The deficiencies of Roman

[145] Long Walls: Whitby (1985); generally: Capizzi (1969) 204–6.
[146] Marcell. *Chron.* s.a. 517 (it is unclear whether the *Getae* referred to here are Bulgars or Slavs: cf. Bury, *LRE* 1.436 n. 2; Stein, *Bas-Empire* 11.105–6; Croke (1995) 120).
[147] E.g. Soc. *HE* VII.18.1–7 (persecution of Persian Christians); Priscus fr. 41.1 (persecution of Zoroastrians living in the Roman empire).   [148] Blockley (1985).
[149] Frye (1984) 321–4. For a different interpretation of some aspects of Kavadh's reforms, see Crone (1991), with corrections of detail by Whitby (1994) 249 n. 72.
[150] Marcell. *Chron.* s.a. 502; Theophanes p. 143.20–7.   [151] Alexander (1967).
[152] The most important source for this war is the contemporary *Chronicle* attributed to Joshua Stylites. For modern accounts, see Bury, *LRE* 11.10–15; Capizzi (1969) 180–5; Blockley (1992) 89–91.

defences in the region revealed by the war resulted in action to repair and strengthen them and in the construction of a new frontier fortress at Dara, the aim of which was to provide a forward base for Roman troops.[153] This last move provoked strong protests from the Persians, since a fifth-century settlement had prohibited any new forts close to the frontier, but by the time Kavadh had dealt with the Hephthalites and was in a position to translate protest into action, he was confronted by a Roman *fait accompli*. Anastasius' judicious use of diplomacy and money apparently dissuaded him from pursuing the issue further,[154] and relations between the two empires thereafter remained stable until the reign of Anastasius' successor.

4. Epilogue

Anastasius died on 9 July 518. Given his age and the availability of suitable candidates among his relatives,[155] his failure to nominate a successor represents an uncharacteristic oversight on the part of an emperor who had, in most areas of government, shown himself to be energetic and intelligent, and had done much to ensure the continuing viability of the eastern empire. That continuing viability, of course, stands in marked contrast to the demise of the western empire, and prompts reflection on the question posed in the introduction to this chapter as to why the fate of the east during the fifth century diverged from that of the west. Needless to say, the following observations make no claim to comprehensive coverage of all the major issues which bear on this subject. In keeping with the focus of the chapter, they concentrate primarily on the emperor and his policies in key areas.

One feature of imperial behaviour in the fifth century which distinguishes it sharply from that in the third and fourth centuries is the way in which it became rare for the emperor to participate personally in military campaigning. This development arose in the first instance out of the youth and inexperience of Arcadius and Honorius, and then of Theodosius II and Valentinian III (whose collective reigns, it is worth recalling, account for the first half of the fifth century). However, the way in which it remained the pattern thereafter until the early seventh century, in spite of the military experience of many subsequent incumbents, suggests that a more fundamental consideration was also at work – namely, concern to protect the emperor from the political and physical consequences of military defeat, which the fates of Julian and Valens in the latter half of the fourth century had particularly highlighted.[156] The corresponding disadvantage of this change was that it limited the emperor's contact with the

---

[153] Dara: Whitby (1986b); other sites: Capizzi (1969) 206–7, 214-28; Whitby (1986a) 726.
[154] Procop. *Wars* I.10.13–19.   [155] For the relatives, see Cameron, Alan (1978).
[156] Cf. Whitby (1992).

army and increased the potential for ambitious generals to exert a dominating influence on political life – a potential realized in the careers of Stilicho, Aetius and Ricimer in the west. That this trend was less evident in the east can be attributed in large part to differences in the military command structure in the two halves of the empire. In the early-fifth-century west (probably as a result of Stilicho's actions) all forces were ultimately under the authority of one general, whereas in the east the field armies were throughout the fifth century divided amongst five generals.[157] This arrangement not only acted as a safeguard against the concentration of military power in the hands of one individual, it also diverted commanders' energies into rivalries between themselves. Moreover, it enlarged the scope for others – civilian officials, prominent courtiers, female members of the imperial family – to compete for power and counterbalance the political weight of the military.[158]

In the middle of the fifth century, to be sure, Aspar came to exercise influence analogous to that of the western 'generalissimos', yet when Leo began to assert his independence, Aspar never gave any sign of contemplating his removal in the way that Ricimer eliminated Majorian and Anthemius, thereby seriously devaluing the authority of the imperial office in the west. Whether from choice or necessity, Aspar pursued the much less destructive strategy of establishing a marital alliance with Leo in the expectation that his son would succeed to the throne in due course. In the event, Aspar lost out to another general of ambition and ability. Unencumbered by Aspar's dual handicap of barbarian origin and religious heterodoxy, Zeno was able to assume the imperial purple himself via the same strategy of marriage into the imperial family, so preserving the integrity of the imperial office in the east and helping to ensure that it never came to be viewed as an irrelevancy or an anachronism. Granted Zeno did not prove to be a popular emperor and the political turmoil of his reign raised the spectre of the eastern empire disintegrating into anarchy, yet it is noteworthy that, of those who challenged him for power, Basiliscus and Marcian had dynastic links, while Illus and Leontius came from the same provincial background as Zeno himself. Even if any of them had succeeded in removing Zeno permanently, therefore, there was never any question of the imperial office itself being done away with.[159] Had the reign of his successor been as tumultuous as Zeno's, then perhaps questions might have been asked. As it was, Anastasius proved to be a very capable

---

[157] Jones, *LRE* 609–10.

[158] Through their marriages, the two most important imperial females – Pulcheria and Ariadne – also played a crucial role in maintaining a high degree of dynastic continuity during the fifth century (Leo's accession marks the only break), and the significance of that continuity for preserving the integrity of the imperial office ought not to be underestimated.

[159] Basiliscus, of course, actually adopted the title of emperor during his twenty-month occupation of Constantinople.

ruler whose policies by and large served to stabilize the empire, which at his death was in most respects in a stronger position than it had been for more than a century.

Religious policy also played a part in preserving the emperor's position. Regular pronouncements throughout the century against pagans, Jews or heterodox Christian groups served to re-emphasize imperial piety, a virtue which helped to offset the less martial character of imperial life in the fifth century. Like non-campaigning, however, religious policy could be two-edged in its potential consequences. Chalcedon undoubtedly brought Marcian immediate political benefits in certain vital quarters, but it was also the catalyst for a polarization of opinion within the eastern church which caused increasing difficulties for his successors. Arguably the most important success of Zeno's reign was his holding of the resultant tensions in balance, albeit temporarily, through the *Henotikon*; arguably the most important failure of Anastasius' reign was his inability to sustain that balance, though as we have seen he was to a considerable extent at the mercy of pressures beyond his control. Interestingly, this was one area where western emperors had far less to worry about, but recognition of that serves only to pose the basic question all the more acutely.

In foreign relations, the east undoubtedly faced some serious tests, particularly in the Balkan provinces, whose security and economy were placed under severe strain by the Huns during the first half of the century and then by the Goths in the second half. Against these difficulties, however, must be set the experience of Asia Minor, Syria, Palestine and Egypt, which remained securely under government control and suffered only occasional disruption, if any. This situation owed much to the geographical configuration of the region – Asia Minor and Egypt were both well insulated from serious external threat – and to the overall stability of relations with the empire's most powerful neighbour, Persia, despite the existence of the tensions discussed earlier. In addition to circumstances specific to the fifth century such as the preoccupation of both powers with dangers on other fronts, this stability may also in part be attributed to the general constraint imposed by the sheer difficulty both powers faced in mounting a major invasion without its being anticipated by the other.[160]

It is in their implications for the area of imperial finances that these considerations have their greatest significance: compared with the west, the eastern empire suffered only limited erosion of its tax base. Above all, the revenues of Egypt, whose importance in the eastern economy paralleled that of North Africa in the western, remained at the uninterrupted disposal of Constantinople. Thus even when financial crises occurred, such as those precipitated by Attila's demands in the late 440s or by the failure of

---

[160] Cf. Lee (1993b) 18–20, 112–20, 139–42.

Leo's expedition against the Vandals in 468, imperial finances never lapsed into the downward spiral they did in the west, and the eastern government and its armies were able to continue functioning with a sufficient degree of effectiveness. This underlying economic strength of the eastern empire is further highlighted by Anastasius' demonstration of what could be achieved through prudent management of the treasury. By the end of his reign, therefore, although continuing ecclesiastical controversy gave cause for concern, the eastern empire was in most other respects in a position to face the future with considerable optimism.

CHAPTER 3

JUSTIN I AND JUSTINIAN

AVERIL CAMERON

1. JUSTIN I (518–27)

For understandable reasons the reign of Justin I tends to be eclipsed by that of Justinian, his nephew and successor (527–65). Not only was Justinian already a powerful figure during his uncle's reign, but Procopius of Caesarea, the leading historian of Justinian, regarded his rule as effectively including that period.[1] In view of their common background and the continuity of imperial policy in certain areas, Justin's reign is often associated with that of Justinian in modern accounts.[2] Although Anastasius had three nephews, Hypatius, Pompeius and Probus, there was no designated successor when he died in 518. As *magister militum per Orientem*, Hypatius was away from Constantinople, and Justin, then the head of the excubitors (the palace guard), is said to have used cash destined for the support of another candidate to bribe his troops to support his own name; as a result, on 10 July 518 he was proclaimed by the senate, army and people and then crowned by the patriarch.[3]

The new emperor was already elderly and his background was humble. He originated from Latin-speaking Illyricum, having been born at Bederiana, near Naissus (Nis), and he owed his success to his career in the guard. According to Procopius he was illiterate,[4] and in his religious views he was staunchly Chalcedonian. Other contemporaries recorded the arrival of this backward provincial in Constantinople in about 470 and his subsequent success as something at which to marvel, and the story was depicted in art.[5] Though the family of Anastasius was to continue to have an influential role,[6] the new regime was bound to be very different; Justin lost no time in giving the title of *comes* to his nephew Justinian, who was a *candidatus*, and seems also to have formally adopted him.[7] Justinian was

---

[1] See Cameron, *Procopius* 9. However, Justin's reputation suffers in that the evidence comes from the *Secret History*, where in his intent to blacken Justinian Procopius exaggerates the rusticity of Justin and the ruthlessness of both uncle and nephew.

[2] E.g. Evans (1996) 96–115; see, however, Stein, *Bas-Empire* 11.219–73; Vasiliev (1950).

[3] Marcell. *Chron.* s.a. 519; Malal. p. 410; Evagr. *HE* iv.1; further, *PLRE* ii, *s.v.* Iustinus 4.

[4] *SH* 6.11; see *PLRE* ii, *s.v.* [5] Zach. Rhet. *HE* viii.1. [6] See Cameron, Alan (1978).

[7] See *PLRE* ii, *s.v.* Iustinianus 7.

involved, according to Procopius and others, in the murders in 518 of the
pro-Monophysite eunuch Amantius and in 520 of Vitalian, his own closest
rival and the consul of the year.[8] In 519 he was already building a basilica
to Sts Peter and Paul in the palace of Hormisdas, and requesting relics from
Rome.[9] The fall of Vitalian was followed by Justinian's consulship in A.D.
521, inaugurated by brilliant consular games and from which three sets of
diptychs survive;[10] he was now *magister militum praesentalis*, also an office held
by Vitalian. Also in the reign of his uncle, and before April 527, he married
the Hippodrome performer Theodora, whose early career and exploits
Procopius recounts in prurient detail in the *Secret History* (*SH* 9.1–30); the
marriage was made possible only after the death of Justin's wife Euphemia,
who was strongly opposed to it, and by the passage of a special law allowing retired and reformed actresses to petition the emperor for the right to
marry even into the highest rank.[11] Theodora is praised in the Monophysite
tradition for her piety; however, it is not denied there that she was originally
a prostitute.[12]

Both Justin I and Justinian were supporters of Chalcedon. Under
popular pressure, within days of Justin's accession, the patriarch John of
Constantinople recognized Chalcedon and condemned Severus of
Antioch, while a series of eastern synods sought to overturn the religious
measures taken by Anastasius. Justin reopened relations with Rome;
Theoderic's son-in-law Eutharic became western consul for 519 with Justin
himself as his eastern colleague, and the ending of the Acacian schism
between Constantinople and the papacy was announced in Constantinople
in terms favourable to Rome at the end of March, 519.[13] Predictably, this
led to discontent among eastern Christians, which was met by repression;
this was to cause difficulties for Justinian later,[14] and the 520s also saw the
appearance of other doctrinal issues, with which he had to struggle as
emperor.[15] In Africa Hilderic, king of the Vandals from 523 to 530, developed a warm relationship with Justinian and lifted the persecution of
Catholics in his kingdom, but the alliance with Theoderic in Italy did not
prove straightforward; in 524, suspicious of possible plots with
Constantinople, the aged king turned on members of the Roman senatorial class, and when the philosopher Boethius, whose sons had both been

---

[8] *SH* 6.27–8; Zach. Rhet. *HE* VIII.1–2; Vict. Tunn. *Chron.* s.a. 523; *PLRE* II, *s.v.* Amantius 4;
Vitalianus 2.   [9] Procop. *Buildings* 1.4.

[10] Procop. *SH* 18.33; 23.1; 24.29; Cyril of Scythopolis, *V. Sabae* 68. Procop. *SH* 6.27–28; career of
Justinian: *PLRE* II.645–8; Bagnall *et al.*, *Consuls* 576–7.

[11] *CJ* v.4.23, 1–4 (A.D. 520–3); Procop. *SH* 9.51; *PLRE* III, *s.v.* Theodora 1. The name Euphemia was
given to the empress on Justin's accession in preference to the unsuitable Lupicina; Procopius alleges
that she had originally been bought by Justin as a slave (*SH* 6.17; see *PLRE* II, *s.v.* Euphemia 5).

[12] For John of Ephesus' *Lives of the Eastern Saints*, an important source for Theodora, see Harvey,
Asceticism and Society in Crisis.   [13] Stein, *Bas-Empire* II.224–8.

[14] *Ibid.*, 228–325; Egypt escaped the persecution and was able to offer haven to Monophysite exiles.
[15] See below and ch. 27, p. 811 below.

consuls in 522, attempted to intervene he was tried and executed himself; his death was followed in the next year by that of his father-in-law Symmachus, the leader of the senate.[16] The king's own death in 526, leaving his young grandson Athalaric as heir under the guardianship of his mother Amalasuintha, soon provided Justinian with an excuse for intervention in Italy.

In the east, Justin's government followed the traditional policy of using diplomacy and alliances to maintain Byzantine interests, supporting an Axumite (Ethiopian) expedition against the Jewish regime of Himyar in south Arabia (A.D. 524–5) and adopting a long-term policy of utilizing the Monophysite Ghassanids as federates to balance the pro-Persian Lakhmids.[17] Christianity and Byzantine influence likewise went hand-in-hand in the Caucasus, but here the highly political baptism and marriage to a Christian wife of Tzath, the king of Lazica, in Constantinople led to retaliatory moves by Kavadh of Persia and to the flight of the Iberian royal family to Constantinople. In Justin's last year, the generals Belisarius and Sittas raided Persarmenia; as *dux Mesopotamiae*, Belisarius' base was the fortress at Dara, and Procopius the historian now became his aide.[18]

II. JUSTINIAN'S EARLY YEARS (527–32)

Before he died on 1 August 527, Justin had made his nephew Justinian co-emperor, and the latter now succeeded.[19] He is perhaps best known from his depiction in the famous mosaic in the church of San Vitale, Ravenna. The contemporary chronicle of Malalas describes him as 'short, with a good chest, a good nose, fair-skinned, curly-haired, round-faced, handsome, with receding hair, a florid complexion, with his hair and beard greying'.[20] The formula is conventional, but at least the description lacks the sheer malice of that given by Procopius in the *Secret History*, where Justinian's appearance is slyly compared with that of the tyrant and persecutor Domitian.[21]

The importance of Justinian's reign has been recognized by contemporaries and modern historians alike. It is seen as a time of triumph, marking the re-establishment of strong imperial rule, or the transmission of an ideal of Catholic government to the western Middle Ages and the Renaissance. Equally, it has been seen as an autocracy, marked by persecution and ending in failure. The early successes of Justinian's 'reconquest' of the western

---

[16] See *PLRE* II, *s.v.* Boethius 5 and Symmachus 9, and see ch. 19, p. 525 below.

[17] See Evans (1996) 86–90, 112–14; Fowden (1993); ch. 22c, p. 678 below; Shahîd (1995) I.1 and 2.

[18] For the diplomatic aspects and the idea of a Byzantine 'commonwealth' see Fowden (1993); the subsequent activities of Belisarius are known in detail from Procopius, and are given in detail in *PLRE* III, Belisarius 1.   [19] Malal. 422.9–21; 424.14–425.9; *Chron. Pasch.* 616 Bonn.

[20] Malal. 425, 1–9, trans. Jeffreys *et al.*; on the 'portraits' in Malalas, see Elizabeth and Michael Jeffreys, in Jeffreys *et al.*, *Studies* 231–44.   [21] *SH* 8.12–21.

empire were accompanied and followed by profound difficulties; his much-vaunted aim of restoration, realized in the great codification of Roman law which took place in his early years, sat awkwardly with the harsh measures taken against teachers and the effective closure of the academy at Athens; the great church of St Sophia, perhaps his finest achievement, owed its very existence to a serious riot which almost led to the emperor's own fall. Bitterly opposed, but also eulogized as a Christian monarch, Justinian forced his own compromises on an unwilling church, only to fall into heresy on his deathbed. Edward Gibbon, in his *History of the Decline and Fall of the Roman Empire*, had some difficulty in deciding whether to place Justinian's reign in the context of Roman success or Greek decline, and indeed it is still an open question whether the emperor's policies over-stretched the empire's resources to a dangerous level, as the propaganda of his successor suggests.[22]

Much of the problem is to be traced to the contradictions to be found between the contemporary sources. Procopius of Caesarea began as the emperor's ardent supporter, but in the course of the composition of his *History of the Wars* in eight books (finished A.D. 550/1–553/4) turned into his bitter opponent. Procopius' vituperative pamphlet, the so-called *Secret History*, seems to have been composed while the *Wars* was still in progress (A.D. 550/1), and was followed soon afterwards (A.D. 554/5) by a panegyrical account of Justinian's *Buildings*.[23] No reliable biographical data about Procopius exist to provide us with an explanation for this change.[24] But a similar ambivalence can also be detected in the work *On Magistracies* by his contemporary John Lydus, a former official in the praetorian prefecture,[25] and in the work of the North African Latin poet Corippus, who wrote a hexameter poem in praise of the accession of Justinian's successor Justin II (565–78); like his own contemporary, the historian and poet Agathias, Corippus accords Justinian the respect due to a major emperor while at the same time criticizing him.[26] The contemporary *Chronicle* of John Malalas records the reign in detail and from a different and specifically Christian

[22] For this see Corippus, *In laudem Iustini minoris* 1.250–71; with notes in Cameron, *Corippus*; Agathias, *Hist.* v.14; Menander Protector, ed. and trans. Blockley 1985: fr. 8. There is also a hostile portrayal of the reign in the work of the Chalcedonian church historian Evagrius Scholasticus, *HE* iv.30f., on which see Allen, *Evagrius* 171–208. For Gibbon's view of Justinian see Cameron, Averil (1997). The extent to which Justinian's military ventures resulted in a weakening of Roman resources (Jones, *LRE* 298–302) is questioned by Whitby, ch. 11, p. 288 below.

[23] The traditional dates have recently been defended again by Greatrex (1994). The discovery of a single manuscript of the *Secret History* in the Vatican Library (published by Alemanni, 1623) upset the then prevailing favourable opinion of Justinian and led to Procopius' authorship being denied.

[24] See Cameron, *Procopius* for the argument that the works are more similar than would at first appear, and that Procopius' 'change of view' is explicable in relation to the developing circumstances in which he wrote.   [25] See Maas, *John Lydus*.

[26] Cameron, *Corippus*; cf. Agathias, *Hist.* v.14, with Cameron, Averil (1970) 124–30. Evagrius' criticisms (see n. 22 above) are combined with a neutral account of Justinian's wars drawn from Procopius' *Wars*, but Evagrius apparently used neither the *Buildings* nor the *Secret History*. On the hostility to Justinian expressed here and elsewhere, see Carile (1978) 81–4.

perspective;[27] other important chronicle sources are the Latin *Chronicle* of Marcellinus Comes[28] and the early-seventh-century Greek *Chronicon Paschale*, which is dependent on Malalas only for the early years.[29] Naturally, there were always poets and writers ready to render the conventional praises to Justinian, just as there were artists ready to commemorate his victories.[30] Since antiquity, many have wanted to claim Justinian as the prototype for their own ideal, whether legal, religious or political.[31]

Theodora had been crowned Augusta with Justinian while Justin was still alive, and her forceful character soon revealed itself, although she did not formally share the imperial power. In the mosaics in San Vitale she is depicted in parallel with her husband, and she was also shown on the ceiling of the Chalke entrance to the imperial palace, standing beside him to receive the triumphal homage of Belisarius.[32]

The new emperor was ambitious. His second consulship, in 528, was remarkable for its lavish display and largess,[33] and significantly, after 541 the consulship was reserved for emperors alone.[34] Less than a year had passed since his accession when on 13 February 528 Justinian appointed a commission to produce a new code of imperial law which would revise the existing ones and add laws passed subsequently; by 7 April 529 the task was complete and the *Codex Justinianus* was formally promulgated.[35] Excited by this success, Justinian went further and set up a commission to codify the writings of the Roman jurists (15 December 530), again meeting with astonishing success. Only three years later its members, led by Tribonian, had completed their apparently impossible task, which involved reading some three million lines of Latin contained in two thousand books. Their compilation, known as the 'Digest', appeared on 16 December 533.[36] A month earlier, Tribonian and others had produced the *Institutes*, a handbook for law students, and Justinian issued a law reforming the structure of legal studies; finally, the *Code* itself was issued in a revised edition, bringing it up to date, at the end of 534.[37] The achievement was extraordinary, and much

---

[27] See Jeffreys *et al.*, *Chronicle*; Jeffreys *et al.*, *Studies* (here especially Scott, *ibid.*, at 69–71).

[28] See Croke (1995).   [29] Trans. with detailed notes by Whitby and Whitby (1989).

[30] See Paul the Silentiary's hexameter poem on the restoration of St Sophia, delivered in January 563: ed. Friendländer 1912, see Whitby, Mary (1985); Magdalino and Macrides (1988); for the 'Mirror for Princes' of the deacon Agapitus see Henry (1967). Little of Justinian's triumphal art has actually survived, but see Cameron, *Corippus* 140–1, 184; McCormick, *Eternal Victory* 67–8.

[31] Capizzi, *Giustiniano* 17–23; Justinian the Catholic legislator: Biondi (1936); Justinian as tyrant: Honoré (1978) ch. 1.

[32] See Barber (1990); the lost Chalke mosaic is described by Procop. *Buildings* 1.10.16–19; for the Chalke see Mango (1959).

[33] Marcell. *Chron.* s.a., with Croke (1995) 124; *Chron. Pasch.* 617; Bagnall *et al.*, *Consuls* 590–1.

[34] On this see Cameron and Schauer (1982).

[35] Const. *Haec* and *Summa*, *Corp. Iur. Civ.* II.1–3. The Code was revised and reissued in 534: *Chron. Pasch.* 633–4; Const. *Cordi. Corp. Iur. Civ.* II.4.

[36] Const. *Deo auctore*, *ibid.* I, Dig. 8 (= *CJ* 1.17.1); *Tanta, ibid.* 13–14 (= *CJ* 1.17.2).

[37] *Institutes*: Const. *Imperatoriam, Corp. Iur. Civ.* I, Inst. xxi); legal education: Const. *Omnem, ibid.* Dig. 10–12.

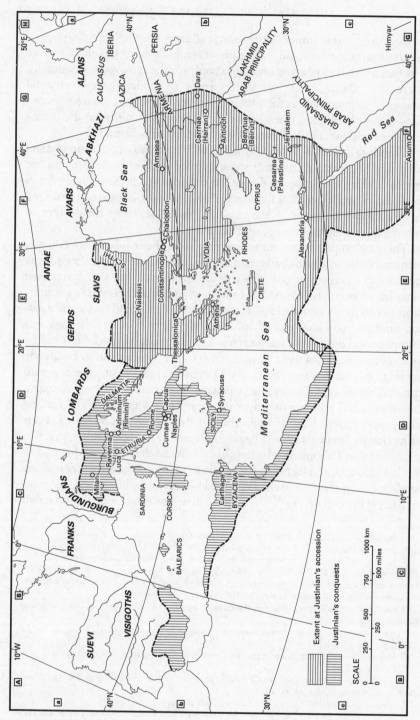

Map 2 Justinian's empire in 565

SCALE

Extent at Justinian's accession

Justinian's conquests

0   250   500   750   1000 km

0   250   500 miles

of the credit must go to Justinian's *quaestor*, Tribonian, of whose learning both Procopius and John Lydus write with respect, though the former, typically, also accuses him of being avaricious and a flatterer.[38] Tribonian held the post of *quaestor sacri palatii* twice, being dismissed by Justinian during the Nika revolt in order to pacify the crowd, but later reinstated. The great compilations were all issued in Latin, but, like John Lydus, Tribonian could function in both Latin and Greek, and Justinian's later laws, known as *Novels*, because new, were issued mainly in Greek.[39]

Justinian's activity as codifier of imperial Roman law was of immense importance in its later transmission and adoption in western Europe. But he was also an energetic legislator himself – indeed, restless innovation is one of Procopius' charges against him. Vehement against homosexuals, his legislation on family matters gives more rights to mothers and recognizes women as being in need of protection, also allowing them to initiate divorce, even if on restricted grounds.[40] Justinian was severe in his measures against pagans, and indeed all who deviated from the orthodox norm. Pagans, heretics, Manichaeans, Samaritans and Jews were the targets of a series of laws beginning very early in his reign; property and other rights were severely curtailed; Manichaeans and renegade Christians were liable to death; pagans were forbidden to teach, and ordered to convert on pain of exile and confiscation of property.[41] A harsh law directed against the Samaritans led in A.D. 529 to the first of two serious revolts which broke out during Justinian's reign, both put down amid much bloodshed.[42] Among those singled out for investigation as a pagan was the patrician Phocas, who as praetorian prefect was later in charge of the construction of St Sophia and who is praised for his integrity by John Lydus.[43]

Something of the milieu shared by many of those who came under attack now and later in the reign can be sensed from an anonymous dialogue on political knowledge preserved in palimpsest, in which the speakers are a certain Menas, *patricius*, and Thomas, *referendarius*;[44] like John Lydus, the author uses Platonic categories to put forward a critique of contemporary monarchy. The legislation forbidding pagans to teach effectively put an end to the existence of the Academy at Athens, where Platonic philosophy had

---

[38] Procop. *Wars* I.24.16, with I.25.2, *SH* 13.12; Joh. Lyd. *De Mag.* III.20; for Tribonian, see *PLRE* III, *s.v.* Tribonianus I; Honoré (1978), especially ch. 2.

[39] The *Novels* on ecclesiastical and religious matters were soon collected and issued together with collections of church canons: van der Wal and Stolte (1994).

[40] Beaucamp (1990, 1992). Justinian's laws: Malal. 430.12–17; 436.3–16; 437.3–18; 439.8–440.13. Procop. *SH* gives much detailed information, even if from a hostile point of view.

[41] Stein, *Bas-Empire* II.370–5; Pertusi (1978) 185–7; Lemerle, *Byzantine Humanism* 73–9; for Justinian's measures against Samaritans and Jews see Rabello (1987).

[42] Procop. *Wars* I.13.10; Malal. 445.19–447.21; *Chron. Pasch.* 619, with Whitby and Whitby (1989) 111 n.; second Samaritan revolt (555): Malal. 487; not mentioned in Procop. *Buildings*, see Cameron, *Procopius* 92. [43] See Maas, *John Lydus* 78–82; Phocas committed suicide after a similar purge in 546, *ibid.* 71.

[44] Ed. Mazzucchi (1982); cf. Phot. *Bibl.* cod. 37.

been taught for a thousand years. Fifty years later, Agathias told a romantic story of the flight of seven Athenian philosophers, including Damascius, the head of the school, to seek a philosopher king in Persia; disappointed in the young Khusro I, they nevertheless secured special treatment under the terms of the treaty of 531 between Byzantium and Persia and were able to return to Byzantine territory. Simplicius, at least, continued to write important commentaries on Aristotle, possibly establishing himself at Harran (Carrhae) in Mesopotamia; but organized philosophical teaching at Athens had come to an end.[45]

At the same time as initiating these measures against non-orthodox minorities, Justinian built churches and secular buildings[46] and involved himself in religious affairs. The rededication between 524 and 527 of the massive and ostentatious church of St Polyeuktos by the patrician Anicia Juliana, daughter of the western emperor Olybrius (*Anth. Pal.* 1.10), had clearly rankled with him, and, while on a far smaller scale, the domed octagon-in-square church of Sts Sergius and Bacchus (A.D. 527–36), built alongside Justinian's basilica of Sts Peter and Paul in the palace of Hormisdas, and with a long inscription honouring himself and Theodora, pointed forward to the innovative masterpiece which St Sophia was soon to represent.[47] In 532–3 public disputations were held under imperial auspices between Chalcedonians and Monophysites in the palace of Hormisdas, and it was also here that Theodora sheltered Monophysite monks and clergy until her death in 548.

As in religious matters, so in matters of foreign policy and external relations, Justinian was faced with the need to perform a balancing act. Mundo achieved a success against Goths and Bulgars already threatening Thrace in 529–30 and claimed a victory procession.[48] In the east, Justinian continued to attempt by a mixture of diplomacy and mission to create a strategic buffer between the rival states of Byzantium and Persia, extending from Transcaucasia and the Caucasus in the north to Ethiopia/Axum in the south – a task complicated by the religious divide between Constantinople and some of the churches in this large area.[49] In the war against Persia which occupied the years 528–31 the Byzantines had considerable difficulty in holding their own, despite the favourable light in which the activities of Belisarius are presented by Procopius, who was

---

[45] Malal. *Chron.* 451; Agathias, *Hist.* II.23–31. On Simplicius and Harran see Tardieu (1990); on the closing of the Academy: Chuvin, *Chronicle* 135–41.

[46] For the latter, see, besides Procopius' *Buildings*, *Chron. Pasch.* 618.

[47] The basilical church of St Polyeuktos (Saraçhane), with its elaborately carved capitals, was one of the most lavish and influential of early Byzantine churches: see Harrison (1989); Sts Sergius and Bacchus: Mango (1972), (1975); Rodley (1994) 69–71. [48] Marcell. *Chron.* s.a.

[49] Fowden, *Empire to Commonwealth* ch. 5; Stein, *Bas-Empire* II.296–305; the range of Justinian's policies in the east is shown clearly in Malal. 427–36. For a good statement of some of these problems see Brock (1995), and see p. 79 below, n. 100.

present with him;[50] the latter's account shows little interest in the attempts of Justin I and Justinian to strengthen Byzantine military and diplomatic interests in the east.[51] The terms of the 'eternal' peace concluded in the autumn of 532 and pushed through by Kavadh's son and successor, Khusro I, nullified whatever had been gained by the Romans while at the same time imposing on them a payment of 11,000 pounds of gold; it was under this treaty that the Athenian philosophers were granted safe return.[52]

In January of the same year Justinian had faced the most serious crisis of his reign, in the so-called Nika ('Victory') revolt, so named after the rallying-cry of the rioters.[53] The trouble began at the chariot races in the Hippodrome on 13 January, and its immediate cause was the mishandling by the city prefect of the execution of Blue and Green malefactors. During 13 and 14 January the praetorium of the city prefect, the seating in the Hippodrome and parts of the portico as far as the baths of Zeuxippos were destroyed by fire. The damage soon extended to the Chalke entrance to the imperial palace, the portico of the *scholae*, the senate house and Augustaion, and the church of St Sophia, and thus to the ceremonial heart of Constantinople. According to Procopius, Justinian would have turned to flight and was only restrained by the proud and defiant words of Theodora: 'Empire is a fair winding sheet.'[54] The Blue and Green factions chanted slogans and demanded the removal of Justinian's ministers, including the praetorian prefect John the Cappadocian, Tribonian the *quaestor* and the city prefect Eudaimon. But the rioting continued after the emperor had complied with these demands and went on for some days even after Belisarius had been sent into the Hippodrome to put it down with force; more of the city was destroyed in the ensuing violence between rioters and soldiers. Justinian himself appeared to the people in the Hippodrome on Sunday, 18 January; some rioters were won over by bribery, but others were inflamed into an attempt to crown the patrician Hypatius in his stead. At last Justinian was able to stage a counter-coup with his loyal supporters, including Belisarius and the eunuch Narses the *cubicularius* and *spatharius*,[55]

---

[50] Stein, *Bas-Empire* II.283–93; Lazica; Malal. 427.1–13; on the Persian war the narrative of Malalas, perhaps based on reports of the *magister* Hermogenes, provides a corrective to the narrative in Procopius, *Wars*.   [51] See Shahîd (1995) I.1, 139–143.   [52] Stein, *Bas-Empire* II.294–95.

[53] Differing accounts are given in the sources: Procop. *Wars* II.24, with *SH* 12.12 and *Buildings* I.20f., attributes the riots to political factors, especially dislike of Justinian's ministers and his attacks on the senate, or to the excitability of the factions or 'the rabble'; Marcell. *Chron.* s.a. 532 blames an attempt on the throne by the nephews of Anastasius; further accounts in Malal. 473–7; *Chron. Pasch.* 620–9, based on Malalas, with lacuna at the start of the account (detailed discussion in Whitby and Whitby (1989) 112–27; see also Croke (1995) 125–6); Theophanes, *Chron.* pp. 181–3 de Boor, also based on Malalas, but less reliably. See Bury (1897); Stein, *Bas-Empire* II.449–56; Cameron, Alan (1976) 278–80; *PLRE* III, *s.v.* Calapodius 1; Greatrex (1994).

[54] *Wars* I.24.33–7; see Cameron, *Procopius* 69, pointing out the literary tone of the speech.

[55] *PLRE* III, *s.v.* Narses 1.

and managed with difficulty to break into the imperial box, seizing Hypatius and the patrician Pompeius, who were executed on the next day, 19 January. Many thousands of people were killed in the fray.[56]

It is difficult to establish either the chronology of the rioting or the reasons for it. Procopius ascribes it in the main to the irrationality of the Blues and Greens, though admitting that the people had real grievances and that the senators were divided.[57] The 'revolt' must indeed be seen in the context of the high level of urban violence that characterized the cities of the eastern empire in the early sixth century;[58] but its effects were far more serious than most, and the call for the removal of unpopular ministers was to be a recurring feature of the reign. The career and eventual fall of John the Cappadocian, in particular, the bad effects of whose rule John Lydus catalogues in relation to his own provincial region,[59] are treated extensively by Procopius as a major element in the network of power and intrigue which he sees as characteristic of Justinian's rule.[60] Understandably, Justinian himself claimed the suppression of the Nika revolt as a major victory, issuing a public announcement in the course of which he promised to make good all the damage that had been done.

III. ST SOPHIA, THE 'RECONQUEST' AND THE MIDDLE YEARS (c. 532–54)

The Nika revolt not only made peace with Persia even more desirable but also provided the need and the opportunity to rebuild St Sophia on a grander scale than before. Described in detail by Procopius (*Buildings* 1.1.20–77) and again on the restoration of the dome in January 563 in a lengthy verse encomium by the poet Paul the Silentiary,[61] Justinian's 'Great Church' remains extraordinary today for its size, its innovative design and, even though most of its internal fittings have long since disappeared, for the interplay of its coloured marbles and the light of its many windows (Fig. 34, p. 904 below). Work began on the new church almost at once and it was dedicated on 27 December 537. Again Justinian was well served by those he had put in charge of the task, this time the architects Anthemius of Tralles and Isidore of Miletus. Justinian's great building, together with the square situated between St Sophia and the palace, and known as the Augustaion, where an equestrian statue of Justinian himself (now lost) was erected, the huge Basilica cistern and the Chalke entrance to the imperial palace (see above) formed an impressive imperial centre for the city, whose impact can still be felt today.

---

[56] 35,000: *Chron. Pasch.* 627; 30,000: Procop. *Wars* 1.24.54; 50,000: Joh. Lyd. *De Mag.* III.70; see Whitby and Whitby (1989) 125, n. 366.

[57] See Cameron, *Procopius* 166–7; analysis of the sources in Bury (1897), and see Greatrex (1998).

[58] Cameron, *Mediterranean World* 171–4.   [59] *De Mag.* III.58, 61.   [60] Cameron, *Procopius* 69–70.

[61] *H. Soph.* ed. Friedländer; see Whitby, Mary (1985); Magdalino and Macrides (1988). Cf. also the much later *Narratio de S. Sophia* ed. Preger, with Dagron (1984) 191–314. The church: Mainstone (1988).

Equally active in religious affairs, the emperor was anxious to find a doctrinal formula that could reconcile east with west, and in 533 he issued a lengthy decree, for which he later obtained papal approval, affirming Chalcedon while at the same time seeking to meet Monophysite concerns.[62] Meanwhile it was believed that Theodora was seeking to promote Monophysite interests – for instance, in achieving the appointments of Anthimus and Theodosius as patriarchs of Constantinople and Alexandria in 535, and in engineering a visit to the capital by Severus of Antioch and lodging him in her own palace. Procopius was not the only one who suspected, rightly or wrongly (*SH* 10.13f.), that the emperor and empress followed opposing religious policies in order to divide and rule.[63] However, Justinian was soon persuaded by a visit from pope Agapitus (536) to remove Anthimus and Severus alike, deposing Theodosius also in 537.

Long before the completion of St Sophia in A.D. 537, and indeed very shortly after the Nika revolt, the emperor had launched the first stage in the enterprise for which he is probably best known, the so-called 'reconquest' of the west. The scheme may have developed in stages, the first being the despatch of Belisarius against Vandal Africa in the summer of 533, with 15,000 troops in addition to *bucellarii*. According to Procopius, many were doubtful of the prospects of success, but the emperor's determination was increased by a vision conveniently vouchsafed to one of his bishops (*Wars* III.10.1–21). Procopius took part in this expedition himself in the entourage of Belisarius' wife Antonina. Having sailed via Sicily, the fleet landed on the coast of Byzacena, and the expedition met with extraordinary success, defeating the Vandal army at Ad Decimum and entering Carthage, where Belisarius occupied the palace and took possession of the throne of the Vandal king Gelimer on 14 September. He was rewarded with the exceptional honour of a triumph in Constantinople in 534, during which he marched into the Hippodrome at the head of a procession of Vandal prisoners and spoils and with Gelimer himself walking in chains. The spoils included the treasures originally taken by Titus from the Temple at Jerusalem in the Jewish war and captured from Rome by the Vandal king Geiseric. Belisarius presented all this to Justinian and Theodora in state as they occupied the imperial box in the Hippodrome, only two years after the scenes of carnage which had taken place there during the Nika revolt, while the noble Gelimer neither wept nor lamented, but only repeated the verse from the Book of Ecclesiastes: 'Vanity of vanities, all is vanity.'[64] This great occasion was echoed soon afterwards when on 1 January 535 Belisarius celebrated his

---

[62] *CJ* 1.i.6; cf. Amelotti and Zingale (1977) 31–5; the decree is also preserved with some differences in *Chron. Pasch.* 630–3.

[63] Cf. Evagr. *HE* IV.10, 30, 32; Zonaras, *Epit.* XIV.6, 9; Stein, *Bas-Empire* II.377–86.

[64] Procop. *Wars* IV.9.1–12, see *PLRE* III, *s.v.* Belisarius, 193; Marcell. *Chron.* s.a. 534, the end of the *Chronicle*, with Croke (1995) 126–7; McCormick, *Eternal Victory* 125–9.

consulship by leading Vandal captives in another triumphal procession and distributing Vandal spoils.[65]

The ease of the success over the Vandals inspired further initiatives. In 535 Belisarius was again despatched to the west, this time to Italy; in this case, however, reconquest was to prove a far more difficult and lengthy business. The conquest of Sicily was the first and easy step, and Belisarius was able to celebrate the ending of his consular year there with yet another procession at Syracuse.[66] Interrupted by a diversion to Africa to put down a serious military revolt which had broken out there, Belisarius proceeded on Justinian's orders to invade Italy and make war on the Goths. Naples fell to him in 536 and he entered Rome on 9 December in the same year,[67] preparing the city for a siege by Vitigis and the Goths, which began early in 537 and lasted for over a year.

From now on, problems became apparent: reinforcements were urgently needed; Belisarius became involved in necessary dealings with the Roman church, replacing pope Silverius with Vigilius; and he had to resort to diversionary ploys in order to allow the passage into the city of army pay sent from Constantinople. The siege ended after a year, in March 538, when the Goths too ran short of provisions and heard that Ariminum had fallen and that Byzantine troops were threatening Ravenna; however, Belisarius and Narses (recently arrived with a new army) together foiled the Gothic attempt to recapture Ariminum. Division between Belisarius and Narses led to a Gothic entry into Milan and the massacre of its male citizens early in 539,[68] and Narses was recalled on Belisarius' request. But Justinian's uncertainty undermined Belisarius' attempts to achieve total victory. In 540 the Goths of Ravenna, discontented with Vitigis and unwilling to make a treaty with Justinian as the latter's envoys proposed, invited Belisarius to become emperor of the west; his loyal refusal seems to have been a turning-point for the historian Procopius, who became increasingly critical of him thereafter.[69] Belisarius was able to carry the other Roman generals with him, enter Ravenna and place Vitigis under guard (540), but the emperor, whether influenced by Belisarius' detractors or because he wanted to send him to Persia, now recalled him to Constantinople.

The return of Belisarius with Vitigis and his wife and the Gothic treasures should have been a great moment in the reign, but this time the general was denied the glory of a triumph, and spent the winter in Constantinople as a private citizen.[70] His career illustrates the uncertainties of Justinian's conduct of the wars in both east and west. Though Belisarius seemed to

---

[65] Procop. *Wars* IV.9.15–16.

[66] Procop. *Wars* V.5.17–19; there is also a fairly detailed account of the Gothic war in the continuation of Marcellinus' *Chronicle*, on which see also the notes by Croke (1995).

[67] *Wars* IV.15; V.7.26; see *PLRE* III.196.   [68] *Wars* VI.22.1.

[69] *Wars* VI.29.17–18; for the change in Procopius' view see Cameron, *Procopius* 189; Procopius and Antonina were also present at these events.   [70] *PLRE* III.207–8.

have snatched victory in Italy despite the emperor's readiness to make terms with the Goths, his success was achieved only at the price of Justinian's suspicion. Belisarius was now sent to the east, hostilities having been renewed by Khusro I, and had some success there, but was again recalled in winter 541–2 and, despite further success against Khusro in 542, he came under suspicion at the end of this year and (according to Procopius) was dismissed and his property seized through the agency of Theodora.[71] The second Persian war of the 540s coincided with the onslaught of plague in the Byzantine east, and lack of Byzantine manpower exposed the cities of Mesopotamia and led them to make ignominious and expensive treaties of surrender to the Persians, while Byzantine achievements were inglorious at best.[72] Procopius' narrative reveals that the Byzantine presence in the east was dangerously weak. Set battles were avoided, and Khusro was able to extort treasure from the cities almost at will. Furthermore, Belisarius' expedition followed the sack of Antioch in 540, one of the worst disasters that occurred in Justinian's reign.[73] Similar conditions prevailed in Italy when Belisarius returned there on his second expedition in 544; this was made far more difficult than the first through the lack of necessary troops and resources; it is recounted unsympathetically by Procopius.[74] Belisarius had a difficult time, and even when he succeeded in reoccupying Rome (547), which had fallen to Goths under Totila after a terrible siege, he had to keep writing to Justinian for reinforcements, and sent Antonina to Constantinople on the same mission in 548. Procopius did not accompany him on this expedition, and describes it as ignominious for Belisarius.[75] The latter was recalled again in 549, possibly through the intervention of his wife, after the death of Theodora in 548, and was sent neither to the east nor back to Italy when the newly appointed Germanus died in 550.

It is difficult to gauge the truth about Justinian's military policies from the tendentious and personalized account given by Procopius; indeed, Evagrius' version has a rather different emphasis. In the event, it was not Belisarius who ended the long and difficult Italian war but his rival Narses, with victories at Busta Gallorum and Mons Lactarius in which, respectively, the Gothic leaders Totila and Teias were killed (552).[76] Nevertheless, the war in Italy was not yet over, for Narses had still to recover Cumae and the cities of Etruria, and to face the army of Franks and Alamanni under Butilinus and Leutharis which had invaded Italy from the north; the siege of Cumae lasted a year, that of Luca three months. Narses spent the winter of 553–4 in Ravenna and Rome, and defeated Butilinus and the Franks, who had a much larger army, near the river Casilinum in the vicinity of

[71] *Wars* II.19.49; cf. *SH* 2.21–5; 4.13–17; see *PLRE* III.211.   [72] See Cameron, *Procopius* 159–65.
[73] Procop. *Wars* II.10.4.   [74] *PLRE* III.212–16, see especially *Wars* VII.35.1, *SH* 4.42–5, 5.1–3.
[75] See Cameron, *Procopius* 189.   [76] Procop. *Wars* VIII.32.6–21; 35.16–32.

Capua in the summer of 554.[77] Justinian's so-called Pragmatic Sanction of 13 August 554, regulating matters in Italy, was addressed to Narses; the latter was still in Italy when pope Vigilius died while *en route* from Constantinople (555), and present at the consecration of his successor Pelagius (April 556).

Though technically it resulted in victory for Justinian and certainly achieved its aim of defeating the Goths, the long war in Italy destroyed the very structures it had sought to rescue.[78] Procopius movingly describes the sufferings of the Roman aristocrats during the Gothic war; among them was Rusticiana, the widow of Boethius, who with other Roman ladies was reduced to begging for food during the siege of the city in 546, and was rescued only by the intervention of Totila.[79] A number of the Italian aristocrats went to the east in the 540s, where they put pressure on the court as to the conduct of the final stages of the war, and contributed to a circle of Latin letters in Constantinople. For the Byzantines, the Gothic war had also been difficult: the attitude of the Romans in Italy was by no means straightforwardly pro-Byzantine, and the Byzantine armies were often outnumbered by those fielded by the Goths, while personal rivalries complicated relations between the commanders in Italy and the government in Constantinople.[80]

During the 540s Justinian had to juggle the needs of the Italian front against those caused by renewed hostilities in the east, while simultaneously attempting a religious policy that produced as many anatagonisms as it hoped to cure. Nor had the situation in Africa after the early victories been straightforward: the conquest required a heavy investment of men and resources, and the adverse effects first of mutiny in the Byzantine army and then of Berber hostilities were only made good with difficulty by John Troglita in 546–9, as Procopius admits. By the end of the sixth century Africa seems to have recovered some of its old prosperity, but Corippus' panegyric on the accession of Justin II in 565 laments the bad state of affairs there, which John's campaigns had not in themselves been enough to reverse.[81]

Justinian's difficulties were increased by a severe outbreak of bubonic plague, beginning in Egypt late in 541 and spreading in the following year to the capital and the eastern provinces, from where it also passed to the west. Repeated outbreaks were still being felt in places as far apart as Syria and Britain in the seventh century, and the church historian Evagrius, a

[77] These events are told by Agathias, *Histories*, Procopius' narrative having ended with winter 553–4; see *PLRE* III, *s.v.* Narses 1, 920–2, with Cameron, Averil (1970).

[78] See ch. 19 (Humphries), pp. 544–8 below.   [79] *Wars* VII.20.27f., with Cameron, *Procopius* 192.

[80] For these issues see Thompson (1982) chs. 5 and 6; Moorhead (1983).

[81] *Wars* VIII.17.22, cf. the exaggeratedly hostile picture at *SH* 18.4f. John Troglita's campaigns are described in the *Iohannis*, eight books of Latin hexameters by Corippus (ed. Goodyear and Diggle, 1970); see also Cor. *In laudem Iustini, Pan. Anast.* 37. See further ch. 20, p. 552 below.

native of Antioch, vividly describes their effects on different generations of his own family (*HE* IV.29). Procopius has left a description of the plague's impact in Constantinople (*Wars* II.22f.) which remains moving and credible even when allowance is made for literary allusions to the famous plague description in Thucydides, and the Syriac writer John of Ephesus has recorded the devastation it caused in rural Asia Minor.[82] It is of course dangerous to rely on impressionistic accounts in literary sources, and the outbreaks have left few clear traces in the archaeological record in the east. However, Justinian's legislation immediately after the outbreak in the capital demonstrates the government's concern for the effect on revenues when so many tax-payers were dying; prices rose, and had to be controlled by a law of 544.[83] The emperor fell ill himself, but foiled those who were plotting about the succession by recovering. There were other disasters, notably earthquakes, one of which destroyed the famous law school at Berytus,[84] and in June 548 the empress Theodora died;[85] her death was a severe blow to her husband, who never remarried.

Theodora's influence, like that of Justinian's favourite ministers, was clearly a major factor in the internal politics of the reign. While Monophysites had good reason to be grateful for her support and cast her in the role of repentant sinner turned virtuous protectress, Procopius saw her as an unprincipled schemer who would stop at little to advance her favourites. Theodora remained conscious of her powers of sexual attraction; she took care of herself well and knew how to exploit her beauty.[86] According to Procopius, she attended meetings of the imperial consistory and effectively ruled in partnership with her husband; the two together were like a pair of bloodthirsty demons or furies in human form such as one can read about in the ancient poets. This portrayal, however, which manifestly depends on misogynistic prejudice, may also arise from personal resentment.[87] It is clear enough that Theodora protected Monophysite monks and clergy, though apparently with Justinian's knowledge, for he would also join her in personal visits to and discussions with those who had taken refuge in the palace. But Procopius also claims that she brought about the downfall of her enemies, chief among them Justinian's minister John the Cappadocian, who had been quickly reinstated after his dismissal from the praetorian prefecture during the Nika revolt; Procopius, John Lydus and the church historian Zachariah of Mytilene are all highly critical of his administration, but it was Theodora, Procopius claims, who brought about John's fall in A.D. 541.[88] Justinian was reluctant to carry the policy through, and despite enforced ordination, John was able to recover some of his property and apparently to

[82] Full references: Stein, *Bas-Empire* II.758–61; Allen (1979); see Durliat (1989) for a minimizing view, and against this, Whitby (1995).   [83] Edict 7, pref.; *Nov.* 122.   [84] Stein, *Bas-Empire* II.756–8.
[85] *PLRE* III.1241.   [86] Procop. *SH* 10.11f., 15.6f.   [87] *SH* 12.14; see Cameron, *Procopius* 67–83.
[88] *PLRE* III.627–35, *s.v.* Ioannes 11.

continue scheming; thus Theodora was not fully successful, and after her death Justinian brought John back from exile. Another key figure in the reign was the Syrian Peter Barsymes, twice *comes sacrarum largitionum* and twice praetorian prefect; unlike John, Peter was protected by the empress, who shortly before her death prevailed on Justinian to reappoint him to office after he had removed him.[89] Tribonian, *quaestor sacri palatii* and the master mind behind Justinian's legal codification, himself fell during the Nika revolt, only to be subsequently restored; unlike John the Cappadocian and Peter Barsymes, he does not seem to have been either a particular favourite or a victim of Theodora, but like them he was the object of critical attack, including such stock abuse as charges of paganism.[90]

Procopius is by no means the only hostile witness to Justinian's reign. In John Lydus' work on Roman magistracies, he contrives to be critical of Justinian while superficially praising him.[91] Justinian posed as a restorer of tradition, and at one level these criticisms are the reactions of conservatives disappointed that the emperor had not been successful in that aim. But at a deeper level, the apparent contradictions in contemporary political comment, and in artistic and literary expression,[92] are indicative of a mismatch between actual social and economic change and the persistence of an administrative structure still recognizably similar to that established in the fourth century. In the face of these internal tensions and the impact of external threats and increased military demands, Justinian himself adopted a rhetoric of strong government,.[93] but his critics attacked him from an even more conservative and traditionalist stance. Procopius paints a picture in the *Secret History* of a deliberate onslaught on the wealth of the senatorial class, fuelled by greed and combined with religious bigotry and caprice. He further viewed the emperor's legislative activity, which seems to have been aimed predominantly at checking abuses and raising revenue,[94] as a sign of restless meddling, and was equally ready to blame 'the rabble' for the instability which was a structural feature of urban life in the sixth century.[95] The best Procopius could do by the early 550s in summing up the results of the African campaigns was to ascribe them to Justinian's desire for bloodshed and human slaughter.[96] Much of the contemporary and later criticism of Justinian, by secular and ecclesiastical historians alike, rests on traditional accusations against a 'bad' emperor who is not seen to be sufficiently amenable to the aspirations and wishes of the élite.[97]

[89] *PLRE* III.999–1002, *s.v.* Petrus 9.

[90] *PLRE* III.1335–9, *s.v.* Tribonianus 1; Justinian's ministers: Stein, *Bas-Empire* II.433–9, 463–83, 761–9.   [91] Maas, *John Lydus* 83–96.   [92] Cameron, *Procopius* 19–32; Carile (1978).

[93] For Justinian as a ruthless autocrat see Honoré (1978) 1–39.   [94] Stein, *Bas-Empire* II.437–49.

[95] Cameron, *Mediterranean World* 171–5; Justinian is blamed for using the factions to foment trouble by Evagr. *HE* v.32, as well as by Procopius.

[96] *SH* 18; signs of this critique in the later parts of the *Wars*: Cameron, *Procopius* 186.

[97] See Allen, *Evagrius* 194–6, on Evagr. *HE* IV.30 and Zonaras, *Epit.* XIV.6.1–9.

IV. RELIGIOUS POLICY: THE THREE CHAPTERS AND THE FIFTH
OECUMENICAL COUNCIL

During the 540s Justinian continued his attempts to keep the eastern and western churches in balance, a task now complicated by the fact that on the one hand North Africa had been officially restored to the empire and its church hierarchy released from the Arian rule of the Vandals, while on the other the fluctuating fortunes of the war against the Goths in Italy put new problems in the way of relations between Constantinople and the papacy at the same time as it added urgency to Justinian's desire for union. Religious policy was still complicated by the apparently conflicting aims of Justinian and Theodora. Monophysite ordinations were already being performed by John of Tella, and a Monophysite monk from Amida, later to be created titular bishop of Ephesus and well known as the Syriac church historian John of Ephesus, was allowed to proselytize widely in Asia Minor; he claimed 80,000 conversions between 535 and the end of the reign, as well as taking credit for ninety-six churches and twelve monasteries.[98] John of Tella died in prison in 538, just before Severus.

In 542 Theodora responded to a request for clergy from the Ghassanid allies of Byzantium, who were Monophysite in sympathy, and Justinian was persuaded to allow the consecration of two 'flying bishops', Theodore as bishop of the nomadic Ghassanids, and Jacob Bar'Addai (Baradaeus) as titular bishop of Edessa.[99] Of these, Theodore, also a Monophysite, had come from a monastery in Constantinople; their activity was spread all over the east, and John of Ephesus claims that Jacob ordained more than 100,000 clergy, as well as nearly thirty bishops. Whether this is true or not, the long-term effects were important: the ordinations gave the Monophysites not only a rival identity but also a rival ecclesiastical structure in the east, and Jacob's influence extended to the consecration of a Monophysite patriarch of Antioch. While the initiative helped to retain the loyalty of the Ghassanids, whose military support was essential for the defence of the east, it made religious unity in the empire even harder to achieve.

As before, Justinian continued to search for a formula which could bring east and west together.[100] He now evolved a policy which he was to push through with great determination, but which was to be no more successful in the longer term than his earlier efforts. In a long edict published in 542–3 he had taken sides with pope Pelagius in a dispute which was proving

---

[98] The numbers are variously given by John himself: Mitchell, *Anatolia* II.118–19.

[99] See Harvey, *Asceticism and Society in Crisis* 105–6; Stein, *Bas-Empire* II.624–2; Shahîd (1995) I.2, 755–92.

[100] For what follows see ch. 27, p. 811 below; there is an authoritative treatment of Justinian's religious policy in Grillmeier, *Christ in the Christian Tradition* II.2, and of doctrinal division in the east in the sixth century in *ibid.* II.4.

deeply divisive in Palestine, and formally condemned Origen and Origenism. Immediately afterwards he published an edict known as the Three Chapters which formally condemned certain writings by the fifth-century theologians Theodore of Mopsuestia, Theodoret of Cyrrhus and Ibas of Edessa which were held to be Nestorian.[101] The emperor hoped thereby to conciliate the Monophysites and hold ecclesiastical interests in balance but only found himself in deeper trouble. The Monophysites were unimpressed, and the edict aroused passionate opposition among Latin-speaking Catholics in North Africa and Italy, who considered that it went too far in a Monophysite direction. Holding a balance was next to impossible: the African Junillus, for instance, who had recently been appointed imperial *quaestor*, was himself the translator and adapter of a work clearly inspired by Theodore of Mopsuestia. The imperial decision incensed the African church, and bishop Facundus of Hermiane in Byzacena at once started work on a treatise in twelve books defending the authorities condemned in the edict.[102]

Stung, the emperor summoned pope Vigilius to Constantinople and pressurized him to accept. Vigilius arrived in Constantinople early in 547,[103] under equal pressure from the Roman and African clergy to refuse (the deacon Ferrandus of Carthage had categorically denied the emperor's right to impose his own views in this way). At length Vigilius reluctantly acceded to the edict in his *Iudicatum* of 548, but this document was forthwith rejected in Dalmatia, Scythia and Gaul,[104] and provoked Vigilius' formal condemnation at a council held at Carthage in 550. Having been received by the emperor with a great show of ecclesiastical pomp in 547, he now found his name formally erased from the diptychs (formal lists) of orthodox bishops.[105] Justinian next issued a summons to the recalcitrant African bishops to come to Constantinople. When they arrived, Reparatus of Carthage and others were deposed and exiled, and the rest kept under arrest. Among the African bishops who took refuge at the church of St Euphemia at Chalcedon, where Verecundus of Iunci died, was the chronicler Victor of Tunnuna.[106] There were also difficulties in the east, and the patriarchs Menas of Constantinople, Zoilus of Alexandria, Ephraem of Antioch and Peter of Jerusalem agreed to sign the edict only under the greatest pressure.

Faced with such a level of unrest, the emperor determined to refer the matter to a council of the whole church. Meanwhile, however, he himself

---

[101] Capizzi, *Giustiniano* ch. 3; Stein, *Bas-Empire* II.392–5; 632–8.

[102] Junillus, *Instituta regularia divinae legis*, *PL* LXVIII.15–42; Facundus, *Pro defensione*, ed. Clément and Vander-Plaetse, *CCSL* 90 A, 1974, 1–398; see further O'Donnell (1979) 169ff.; Cameron, Averil (1982) 46–8.   [103] Procop. *Wars* VII.16.1; Malal. 483.3–5; Marcell. *Cont.* s.a.

[104] Stein, *Bas-Empire* II.638–46.   [105] Malal. 484.11–13; 485.4–7; cf. Theoph. *Chron.* 225.21–5.

[106] Vict. Tunn. *Chron.* s.a. 551, 552.

issued a second document of the same import as the first,[107] which so much enraged Vigilius that notwithstanding his recent experience he decided to oppose it formally. Imperial officers had already succeeded in forcing him to leave his place of sanctuary at the church of Sts Peter and Paul, and now troops would have dragged him with his supporters from the altar of the church of St Euphemia, where he next sought sanctuary. Justinian sent a high-level delegation, which included Belisarius, to guarantee Vigilius' safety if he returned to the palace of Placidia, but the pope refused to leave and succeeded in publicizing his ill-treatment.[108] Before the council began, the patriarch Menas of Constantinople died, and was quickly replaced, late in 552, by Eutychius of Amasea, who had distinguished himself as a supporter of Justinian's policy, and who could be relied upon to guide the council in the right way.[109]

If the preliminaries made a sorry story, the council and its aftermath were no better. The Fifth Oecumenical Council opened in Constantinople on 5 May 553, attended by 166 bishops, of whom only nine came from Illyria and none from Italy outside Milan and Rome.[110] Eustochius, the patriarch of Jerusalem, was not present, and, though he was still in the city, Vigilius refused to attend, responding to delegations from the council with a document of his own which led to the council's removing his name from the diptychs. At last, however, he gave way, and in February 554 published a second *Constitutum* and was formally reconciled with the emperor and council. The unfortunate Vigilius died on the way back to Rome in June 555.

While scrupulously refraining from attending the council in person, Justinian had pushed his views through, but without achieving any of his objectives. Pelagius, Vigilius' successor, was resisted by his own bishops, while the Illyrian opposition spread into north Italy; in the east the Monophysites were not reconciled, and the church of Persia reaffirmed its attachment to Nestorianism.[111] In seventh-century Spain, Isidore of Seville effectively denied the authority of the council, which was thus remembered as either illegitimate or a failure; only Eustratius the deacon, apologist for the patriarch Eutychius on the latter's death some three decades later, could bring himself to praise it as a major achievement. The Italian church had been alienated just as Italy itself had been officially 'recovered', while the growing Monophysite self-identity in the east had received encouragement.

The events leading up to the council and its outcome were also felt sharply in North Africa. Victor of Tunnuna, who shared the experiences

---

[107] Known as the *Expositio rectae fidei*, ed. Schwartz (1939), 73–111 (Greek and Latin); cf. *Chron. Pasch.*, 636–84 (not translated by Whitby and Whitby (1989)).   [108] Stein, *Bas-Empire* II.649–50.

[109] Evagr. *HE* IV.38, *V. Eutych.*, *PG* LXXXVI.3. 2300, with Allen, *Evagrius* 203.

[110] *ACO* IV.I; numbers: Chrysos (1966); cf. Stein, *Bas-Empire* II.654–69; Capizzi, *Giustiniano* 118–31; Herrin, *Formation of Christendom* 119–25; Meyendorff, *Imperial Unity* 241–5. An account highly flattering to Eutychius is given in Eustratius' *Life* of the patriarch Eutychius, ed. Laga 1994: see Cameron (1988), and see also Evagr. *HE* IV.38.   [111] See Guillaumont (1969/70) 54–62.

of the African bishops summoned to Constantinople and effectively held under arrest there, finished his sharply worded *Chronicle* in 565/6, a few years after Liberatus of Carthage's *Breviarium*. In effect, the African bishops, who had traditionally looked to Rome but who may have allowed themselves to nurture hopes that Belisarius' 'reconquest' would allow a real restoration of Catholicity, found themselves instead subjected to a new and equally unwelcome domination. The late 540s, with the death of Theodora in 548, were a difficult period for Justinian, and it was now that Procopius' disappointment seems to have reached its height; the *Secret History* and the highly critical seventh book of the *Wars* were both finished in 550–1, as the author witnessed the spectacle of an emperor apparently obsessed with forcing his own dogmas on an unwilling church. He did not include the Fifth Council when he updated the *History of the Wars* by adding an eighth book in 553/4; it lay strictly outside his scope, but one may also imagine that he found the subject distasteful.

Following a historiographical tradition whose origins can be traced back to the Reformation, modern scholarship still devotes a good deal of attention to the question of whether Justinian can be termed 'Caesaropapist' – that is, whether he can be seen as an emperor who controlled the church.[112] This debate has usually, however, been conducted from a western perspective, and the position in Byzantium was more complex than is suggested.[113] Justinian's dealings with the church lay at one end of a wide spectrum of differing kinds of negotiation. He was prepared to use force as well as intimidation in his desire to achieve and maintain unity, but there was little that was new about this, not even the degree to which he would go.

V. THE LAST DECADE (c. 554–65)

By now the great achievements of Justinian's early years were proving difficult to emulate or sustain. The Gothic war ended in A.D. 554 with the settlement known as the Pragmatic Sanction (13 August 554), following a similar ordinance issued to regulate affairs in North Africa some twenty years earlier.[114] But the mood now was very different and no official celebration followed.[115] The Pragmatic Sanction sought to turn back the clock to the days before Ostrogothic rule, but the restoration of civil administration which it promised soon gave way to a military hierarchy.[116] By the late sixth century the establishment of a Lombard kingdom had forced the Byzantines back into pockets of influence centred round Ravenna, Rome

---

[112] Against: Biondi (1936); Amelotti (1978); discussion: Capizzi, *Giustiniano* 151–64 ('objective Caesaropapism').   [113] See Dagron (1996), especially 290–322; Ducellier, *L'Église byzantine*.

[114] *Nov.*, app. 7; for the terms, Stein, *Bas-Empire* II.613–22; Africa: *CJ* 1.27.

[115] See ch. 19 (Humphries), p. 525 below, and cf. Wickham (1981) 26: 'the wars devastated Italy . . . The Goths disappeared as a nation.'   [116] Brown, *Gentlemen and Officers*, and ch. 19, p. 525 below.

and Naples; again, the effects of war were severe.[117] A series of Greek popes and a strong eastern monastic presence in Sicily and south Italy kept religious and cultural ties with the east alive in the seventh century; but after the Gothic war there was no long-standing Byzantine investment in Italy such as happened in the case of North Africa.

The northern frontiers in the Balkans and Thrace came under attack in the later part of the reign, and Justinian's fortifications did not serve to keep these raiders out, though they did preserve Roman control of the main centres. In 550 Sclavenes crossed the Danube, not for the first time, reaching the Adriatic coast and threatening Thessalonica. Justinian's plans for dealing with them, like his intentions for the final stages of the war in Italy, were upset by the death of his cousin, the general Germanus,[118] recently married to the Ostrogothic princess Matasuintha, and the Sclavenes remained within Roman territory. The Balkans and the Danube area received much attention in Justinian's programme of fortification, causing Procopius to make extravagant claims,[119] yet Kotrigurs were permitted to settle in Thrace in the 550s and in 559 a dangerous invasionary force of Kotrigurs and Sclavenes crossed the Danube, and eventually even threatened Constantinople, undeterred by Justinian's Long Walls. Agathias gives a colourful account of the panic that set in and the emergency measures which had to be taken.[120] Palace guards, more used to ceremonial than to fighting, were mobilized, and finally the aged Belisarius was summoned to take charge. But despite an extraordinary success at the head of an army allegedly consisting of peasants and civilians, he was once again slandered and recalled, leaving the young Germanus, the son of Dorotheus, a fellow countryman of the emperor, to defend the wall which protected the Chersonese. In this task he had considerable success, but the Kotrigurs retreated and returned Roman captives only after a large payment from the emperor.[121] The threats from the north were to continue. The first Avar embassy arrived in Constantinople in 558, and another in 561; their haughty dismissal by Justin II was an ominous prelude to future danger.[122]

Following the classic pattern of the last years of a great ruler, plots and suspicion darkened Justinian's final years.[123] The dome of St Sophia was cracked in an earthquake in 557 and, while under repair, partially collapsed during further tremors in 558. In the following year it was rumoured that the emperor had died;[124] the people's agitation was successfully calmed, but

[117] Wickham (1981) 64.   [118] Procop. *Wars* VII.40.1–9; cf. *PLRE* II.507, *s.v.* Germanus 4.
[119] *Buildings* 4.1.14; 11.20.   [120] *Hist.* V.11–20.
[121] *Ibid.* 21–3; Agathias' defence of Justinian's subsidy policy, which his successor made a great show of ending: V.24.1–2.
[122] Malal. 489.11–12; Theoph. *Chron.* 232.6–14. Justin II: Corippus, *Laud. Iust.* III.151–401, cf. *Praef.* 4–9; Men. Prot. fr. 8 Blockley; John Eph. *HE* VI.24.
[123] See Malal. 493–5, supplemented by Theoph. *Chron.* 232–41.
[124] Theoph. *Chron.* 234.20–235.15.

a plot was suspected. In 560 Justinian had to order action against factional violence in the Hippodrome and again in 561 his nephew and successor, Justin the *curopalatus*, was able to put an end to rioting and arson by the factions in the centre of the city only with considerable difficulty.[125] The dedication of the restored dome of St Sophia took place during the festival of Christmas and Epiphany, A.D. 562–3; emperor and patriarch were lauded together in Paul the Silentiary's poem, and the people sang Psalm 23, but the memory of the serious plot of 562, as a result of which Belisarius had been stripped of his household and assets, was fresh in their minds. One of those involved was Sergius, nephew of the Aetherius who was himself to be executed for treason in the first months of the reign of Justin II.[126] Sergius was dragged from his place of sanctuary at the church of the Theotokos at Blachernae and his information led to the arrest of two men, one of whom was a retainer in Belisarius' household who in turn informed against his master. More disturbances took place in Justinian's last year, when both Blues and Greens engaged with imperial troops; after the rioting had ended, members of the factions, especially the Greens, were castrated, burned, impaled or dismembered.[127]

Peace with Persia was brought during these years at a very high price. Whereas the Romans could defeat enemies such as the Vandals and, eventually, the Goths, the Persians were different; it had been clear for three centuries that the military strength of the two empires was evenly balanced, and neither side expected to inflict permanent defeat on the other. War with Persia was the reality of early Byzantine experience, and ceased only in 628 when a powerful counter-strike by Heraclius ended the Sasanian dynasty on the very eve of the Arab conquest. In 561–2, however, the master of offices, Peter the Patrician, met the Persian envoys at Dara and negotiated a peace treaty whose terms are given in full by Menander Protector.[128] Both empires were ready to negotiate, Byzantium after recent events in Lazica and Armenia, and Persia in the light of developments in the north Caucasus. The peace was made for fifty years; the Persians renounced all claim to Lazica, while the Romans agreed to pay a heavy annual tribute consisting of 30,000 gold nomismata, payment for the first seven years to be due immediately. Most of the detailed provisions sought to regulate border trade and communication. The peace did not last: it made no official provision for the treatment of the Christians of Persia, which had been a point at issue between the two powers since the days of Constantine, this matter, which continued to be a matter of tension, being dealt with separately. Nevertheless, the negotiations were accompanied by great pomp and formality, and the reception of the Persian ambassador at Constantinople a

[125] *Ibid.* 235.26–237.1; Malal. 490.16–492.2.   [126] Malal. 493.1–495.5.
[127] Malal. *De Insid.* fr. 51.   [128] Fr. 6 Blockley, with notes: Stein, *Bas-Empire* II.516–21.

few years before is probably reflected in the protocol for such a diplomatic visit still extant in the tenth-century *Book of Ceremonies* and taken from the records of Peter the Patrician himself.[129]

Like Agathias, Menander Protector describes Justinian in these years as tired and growing feeble with age.[130] But he had not given up his passion for theology, and one of his last actions was to depose the patriarch Eutychius of Constantinople when the latter refused to support the emperor's desire for all bishops to subscribe to a decree confirming the incorruptibility of the body of Christ; Anastasius of Antioch, who also refused and convened a synod against the emperor's decree at Antioch, was also threatened with deposition.[131] For the first time Justinian had clearly departed from the traditions of Chalcedon. Naturally, also, the move to depose Eutychius was exploited by the latter's personal enemies.[132] The patriarch went into exile at Amasea and was replaced by John Scholasticus, a canon lawyer and *apocrisarius* from Antioch, who was soon to prove highly influential in bringing about the succession of Justin II.

Justinian died on 14 November 565, allegedly expressing on his death-bed his wish for his nephew Justin to succeed him and his promise to those of his associates who supported Justin that they would be rewarded and his enemies punished.[133] The emperor lay in state in the palace, his bier covered by a magnificent pall on which he was depicted in the symbolism of victory, trampling the defeated Gelimer beneath his feet, flanked by the personifications of Africa and Rome and by rows of conquered kings and vanquished peoples.[134]

---

[129] Cameron (1987).

[130] Menander fr. 5 Blockley; Corippus, *In laudem Iustini* II.260–3; cf. Agathias, *Hist.* v.14: 'in his declining years when old age came upon him he seemed to have wearied of vigorous policies' (trans. Frendo).

[131] Evagr. *HE* IV 39–40; Eustratius, *V. Eutych.*, *PG* LXXXVI.3.2313–24 (both very hostile to Justinian); Theoph. *Chron.* 240.24–241.5.   [132] Stein, *Bas-Empire* II.685–8.

[133] Corippus, *In laudem Iustini* IV.339–50, with notes of Cameron *ad loc.* and pp. 126, 130–1.

[134] Corippus, *In laudem Iustini* I.276–90, with notes; cf. III.1–27 for the funeral. The triumphal scene here described is classic, see McCormick, *Eternal Victory*; the pall has perished, but many embroidered or woven textiles with figural decoration survive from the period.

CHAPTER 4

THE SUCCESSORS OF JUSTINIAN

MICHAEL WHITBY

I. JUSTIN II

Imperial succession

Despite his age and the conspiracies of his latter years, Justinian took no steps to designate a successor. Whether he could not decide between the merits of various relatives, or stubbornly preferred to allow the traditional constituencies of senate, army and people to select a suitable candidate, is unknown, but as a result the succession was presented to the man on the spot, his nephew Justin, son of his sister Vigilantia and husband of Sophia, the ambitious and competent niece of Theodora. Since at least the early 550s Justin had been *curopalatus*, a position of modest significance but central to palace life, and had shown resolution in quelling faction rioting in 562, but his career does not appear as distinguished as that of his main rival within the extended imperial family, his cousin Justin, son of Germanus, who had won victories in the Balkans and was currently serving as *magister militum* on the Danube. Justin the *curopalatus*, however, was in Constantinople and was well supported: the *comes excubitorum*, Tiberius, was a protégé, and his presence in command of the imperial bodyguard indicates that Justin had been planning ahead; other supporters included the *quaestor* Anastasius, and the newly-appointed patriarch of Constantinople, John Scholasticus, who had transmitted the prediction of Justin's succession made by Symeon Stylites at Antioch, and who now performed the coronation; Callinicus, a leading senator, invited Justin to accept the succession, while his brother Marcellus and son-in-law Baduarius were both patricians. Sophia, too, was a powerful lady and will have had her own network of friends.[1]

But no chances were taken. Before news of Justinian's death could spread, Justin was hurriedly crowned on the same day (14 November) within the Great Palace so that the populace, which had rioted in 560 at a rumour of Justinian's demise, was presented with a *fait accompli* when Justin entered the Hippodrome. Justin may also have feared that his cousin, Justin

---

[1] For details on these individuals, see *PLRE* III.

the general, might attract support. In 566 the latter was recalled from his Danubian command and despatched to Alexandria, where he was murdered, and in the same year two prominent senators, Addaeus, a former city prefect, and Aetherius, *curator* of the palace of Antiochus, were executed for alleged conspiracy. Imprecisions and distortions in the evidence make it impossible to prove that there really were moves to topple Justin II, perhaps in favour of his cousin, and it is significant that the closest connections of Addaeus and Aetherius are with known supporters of Justin II – namely, the *quaestor* Anastasius and the patriarch John; thus they might have been removed as over-mighty kingmakers.[2]

Whatever the reason, Justin was quick to consolidate his hold on power. His son-in-law, Baduarius, replaced him as *curopalatus*, the post's importance now enhanced by Justin's own career. Elaborate celebration of Justinian's funeral allowed Justin to demonstrate his closeness to his uncle, perhaps providing scope for stories of a deathbed declaration in his favour, while in other respects he emphasized the significance of the change in ruler. On first entering the Hippodrome he won instant popularity by repaying out of his own pocket compulsory loans to Justinian; the redeemed contracts were joyfully burnt in a powerful display of imperial generosity. The ecclesiastical turmoil of Justinian's last months was also countered by an edict that permitted most exiled bishops to return to their sees. Reception of foreign embassies gave scope for further demonstration of the new forceful emperor: Avars on a routine mission to receive gifts from Justinian were dismissed empty-handed, after enduring a harangue on the grandeur of the Roman empire, and Persian envoys soon experienced a similar tough stance in negotiations about frontier disputes. Justin, actively encouraging perceptions of a renewed empire under younger and more dynamic control, assumed the consulship on 1 January 566 as the culmination of his inaugural image-building: the consulship had been in abeyance for twenty-five years, but the sequence of costly ceremonies allowed Justin to present himself to the people of his capital city with a lavish display that bought popularity and rewarded his supporters. These different initiatives are recorded in Corippus' contemporary panegyric.[3]

2. *Internal affairs*

This initial generosity was reinforced by an edict in 566 which remitted tax arrears, though not exactions in kind or revenues from certain categories of military land. But despite this, and comparable behaviour by Sophia who in 567/8, according to Theophanes, won praise for taking debt pledges from bankers and returning them to the borrowers, Justin was to achieve a

---

[2] Evagr. *HE* v.3; *Life* of Eutychius 76–7.   [3] Discussion in Cameron, *Corippus*.

widespread reputation for avarice. His cautious attitude is evident from the inaugural speech credited to him in Corippus: 'Let no one seize what belongs to the treasury. Know that the treasury has the position of the stomach, by which all the limbs are fed. If the stomach should be empty, everything fails ... Let the benefits of the holy treasury be enough for all ... Let the treasury be protected without any of the just suffering harm: let it take what is its own, and leave alone what belongs to private individuals.'[4] Justin stressed the weakened position of state finances under his predecessor, and this official rhetoric underlies assessments that Justinian bequeathed his successors an empire that was internally exhausted and completely ruined financially and economically.[5] But by the end of Justin's reign the position had been reversed, and a considerable surplus was available to Tiberius for charitable distributions, which might suggest that Justinian's difficulties had been cyclical rather than structural.

Precisely how Justin achieved this is unclear: a short-term reduction in external payments would have helped, but Justin did have to send 90,000 *solidi* to the Persians in 568, and payments were made to the Avars from the early 570s, perhaps as much as 80,000 *solidi* each year, and to the Persians again from 574 after warfare in the east had restarted. Another area where expenditure may have been reduced is buildings: Justin showed concern for the state of urban defences in the east, and attempted to impose a new imperial image on Constantinople through various family monuments;[6] but even cumulatively these and his various religious benefactions will not have matched the costly repair works that Justinian had to undertake in his last decade after earthquake damage in Constantinople and tribal invasions in the Balkans.

One factor in the empire's apparent financial recovery may have been that the personal wealth of Justin, and of his relations as they died (Germanus' sons Justin in 566, for example, and Justinian in 577) or were disgraced (Marcian, 573; Baduarius, 575), was incorporated into the imperial treasuries: this seems to have happened in the case of Justin's brother Marcellus, whose considerable wealth was subsequently available for Maurice to bestow on his father and brother, and Justin's personal wealth had been sufficient to repay public debts, admittedly of unknown size, at his inauguration. In this way some of the considerable benefactions of Justinian's reign to his own and Theodora's relatives will have returned to the state. Another factor may have been a gradual recovery in the prosperity of important provinces, and hence of imperial revenues: the great plague was now a generation in the past, and rural life might not have been particularly affected by subsequent recurrences of the disease, which will

---

[4] *Nov.* 148; Theophanes 242.21–7; Cor. *In laudem* ii.249–57 with Cameron, *Corippus* 70.
[5] Ostrogorsky (1956) 78.   [6] Menander fr. 9.16–19; Cameron (1980).

always have struck hardest in densely populated cities but more lightly in the countryside. Recent survey and other archaeological work in Syria and Palestine suggests that there was no appreciable decline in population before the seventh century.[7]

Justin was certainly interested in provincial stability, and in a law of 569 he attempted to ensure that governors were appointed without payments (*suffragia*) and on the nomination of local interest groups, though an edict of Tiberius from 574 may indicate that the law was ineffectual. Justin also acted quickly to stop urban violence in Constantinople, warning the Blue faction that their patron Justinian was dead but threatening the rival Greens that they would find Justinian still alive.[8] One factor in the rioting of Justinian's last years was undoubtedly the general awareness of the emperor's extreme age and the lack of a clear successor, whereas an appearance of stability, coupled with decisive leadership and an occasional show of force, was normally enough to contain urban unrest.

The church benefited from Justin's determination to reverse some of Justinian's policies. Aphthartodocetism was renounced, and it was ruled that the creed of Constantinople should be read in churches before the Lord's Prayer, a move that both demonstrated Justin's orthodoxy and sidestepped the contentious question of the status of Chalcedon (since the Constantinople creed antedated that of Chalcedon). Justin's objective was doctrinal unity, but this meant being seen to act differently in different parts of the empire. In the west the schism caused by Justinian's Three Chapters edict dragged on, and Justin could only bring peace by appearing a staunch upholder of Chalcedon: he seems to have achieved this by means of a statement of intent that was perhaps reinforced by strategic gifts such as the silver-gilt cross and the reliquary of the Cross that were sent respectively to Rome and the monastery of Radegund at Poitiers. In the east the opposite behaviour was required, and Justin initiated discussions with leading Monophysites in an attempt to find a neo-Chalcedonian formula on which reconciliation could be based.[9]

It is difficult to follow these ecclesiastical developments because our sources were all interested parties, but it is clear that at an intellectual level compromise could be reached by emphasizing the single nature of God the Word incarnate. Monophysite confidence was further attracted by the honourable treatment accorded the patriarch Theodosius of Alexandria, who died in 566, and by Justin's willingness to have the name of Severus of Antioch included in the diptychs. In the east, however, Monophysite monks reacted angrily to proposals agreed by their leaders, while back in Constantinople Justin's attempts to rescue discussions failed when

---

[7] Whittow (1990) 13–20; Whitby (1995).   [8] *Nov.* 149, 161; Theophanes 243.4–9.
[9] Cameron (1976); Allen (1980).

Monophysite bishops found that an otherwise acceptable agreement was not accompanied by an explicit condemnation of Chalcedon. Justin's doctrinal edict, probably to be dated to 571, proclaimed his compromise formula, with Chalcedon neither mentioned nor condemned and a provision that disputes over the persons of the Trinity and over terminology should be avoided. Monophysite sources record that, after six years of toleration, Justin then resorted to pressure and persecution in an attempt to coerce them into agreement, with the Constantinopolitan patriarch, John Scholasticus, being a prime mover. Justin and Sophia apparently visited monasteries in their attempts to win over Monophysites, and John of Ephesus, our main source, records the harsh treatment which he suffered.[10] Perhaps Justin's patience had snapped, but it is unsafe to talk of forced conversions and mass persecutions, since John's testimony lacks precision and corroboration: John had compromised himself by twice accepting communion with Chalcedonian 'heretics' during negotiations, and so may have exaggerated the pressures applied to himself and other Monophysites at Constantinople.

Pressing secular concerns supervened, and doctrinal unity was relegated. This, however, did not amount to religious neglect. Justin was an active patron in the religious field, and was alert to the benefits to be derived from official involvement in the cult of the Virgin at Constantinople and the acquisition of famous relics: the Chalkoprateia church which housed the Virgin's girdle was repaired after earthquake damage, while the Camuliana icon, one of the images of Christ 'not made by human hand' (*acheiropoietos*), was conveyed to the capital in 574. Justin communicated with Symeon Stylites the Younger outside Antioch, and the saint, who had prophesied Justin's accession through the intermediary of John Scholasticus, cured Justin's daughter of demoniac possession by a letter; he might have saved Justin himself from madness if Sophia had not already consulted a sorcerer before approaching Symeon.[11]

3. *External affairs*

Justin is traditionally judged, and condemned, as a ruler mainly because of his handling of the empire's external problems. In the Balkans he achieved initial success. After the diplomatic rebuff at Justin's accession, the Avars concentrated on westward expansion at the expense of the Franks, while the two dominant tribal groups occupying Pannonia, the Gepids and the Lombards, struggled for supremacy. Gepid victories persuaded the Lombards to summon the Avars as allies on very favourable terms, and

[10] Evagr. *HE* v.4; John Eph. *HE* 1.23–30; 11.9, 25.

[11] *Patria* III.32; Cedrenus 1.685; *Life* of Symeon 208; Cameron (1976) 65–7 and (1980) 77–9.

after the Gepids, who had been unreliable allies of the Romans for much of Justinian's reign, failed to obtain support from Justin, Avar participation proved decisive. The Lombards migrated to Italy, wary of the enhanced power of their erstwhile supporters; the Avars now occupied Pannonia; and the Romans contented themselves with the recovery from the Gepids of the fortress of Sirmium, which controlled an important crossing of the river Sava. This prompted hostilities between Avars and Romans, Avars claiming their right to all former Gepid possessions, the Romans relying on their prior claim to Sirmium and the advantages of possession. There was fighting in 570/1, with the Romans under the command of the *comes excubitorum* Tiberius perhaps winning an initial victory but then being seriously defeated. Justin did not concede Sirmium, but was probably forced to resume diplomatic payments to the Avars.[12]

The consequences of these events were felt most immediately in Italy, where the Lombards, already familiar with the province from service during the Byzantine reconquest, arrived in 568. In parts of northern Italy Roman control had only recently been restored with the removal of Frankish garrisons from certain Alpine forts and the submission of the last Gothic resistance in 561, and elsewhere eastern administration was proving unpopular: Justin was apparently told that Gothic rule was preferable. There is an implausible story that Narses, who still controlled Italy as commander-in-chief, was dismissed by Justin and retaliated by summoning the Lombards.[13] Old age (Narses died, probably in 573/4, aged ninety-five) and lack of resources meant that the Lombards could not be prevented from overrunning much of the Po plain, where they installed dukes and garrisons in the major cities, and establishing themselves further south at Spoleto and Beneventum. The struggle may have been complicated by the fact that significant contingents of Lombards were still serving in the Roman armies and might switch sides as their fellow tribesmen were successful. The main Roman achievement was to procure the assassination of Lombard rulers – in 572 Alboin, who had led the invasion, and then in 574 his son Cleph. Thereafter there was a ten-year interregnum when the Lombards were controlled by local dukes, a situation that should have favoured the divisive operations of Roman diplomacy.[14]

In the east Justin attempted to present the same bold front. The fifty-years' peace treaty of 561/2 had left some minor issues outstanding, notably the status of the sub-Caucasian region of Suania. In negotiations about this, Justin's ambassador, John son of Comentiolus, was upstaged at the Persian court and in return Justin snubbed a Persian ambassador and haughtily rejected a request for subsidies from the pro-Persian Lakhmid

---

[12] Menander frr. 8, 11–12, 15; Whitby, *Maurice* 86–7. [13] Discussion in *PLRE* III.925–6.
[14] Wickham (1981) 28–32.

Arabs: Persian and Roman rulers were locked into a competition over status. Tension between the two great kingdoms was raised by the installation of a Persian governor in the Homerite kingdom in south Arabia, and further increased as a result of Roman diplomatic contacts with the Turkish federation in central Asia, whose sphere of influence extended up to the Persian north-east frontier. The Turks had approached the Romans in order to sell silk, whose overland passage from China they could now control, and to co-ordinate action against the Avars, whom the Turks regarded as fugitive subjects, but a common interest in Persia soon emerged. Roman and Persian envoys argued at the Turkish court, the Roman envoy Zemarchus was invited by his Turkish hosts to participate in a raid into Persia, and the Persians then tried to ambush the Roman embassy as it returned through the Caucasus. The upshot was a proposal from the Turkish Chagan for a joint attack on Persia from opposite sides.[15]

This tempting offer coincided with two other factors conducive to war in 572: in Persian Armenia the local nobility had been in contact with the Romans for some time, since they objected to Persian efforts to extend fire-worship in this region; the murder of the regional Persian commander in February prompted leading Armenians to flee to Roman protection. Furthermore in 572 the first annual payment under the fifty-years' peace fell due: this would initiate a regular yearly transfer to Persia of money scarcely distinguishable from tribute, and hence an offence against the strong image that Justin had been constructing. Khusro realized that the moment was sensitive, and despatched as ambassador a Persian Christian, Sebukht, to dissuade Justin from war, but the chance to exploit Persian troubles along their northern frontiers seemed too good to be missed; Justin rudely rejected Sebukht's mollifications and request for the promised payment.[16]

Neither side was particularly ready for war, and Justin is roundly criticized for this by Evagrius, but in reality events moved fast and Justin had to decide quickly whether, like Khusro in 540, he should break a recent treaty to take advantage of his enemy's temporary weakness. Justin's cousin Marcian was appointed to command in the east, and in the latter part of 572 he mounted a minor raid into Arzanene; he may also have begun preparations to besiege Nisibis, whose recapture after two centuries in Persian possession seems to have been an objective for Justin. In Armenia the Romans and their local allies made some headway against Persian supporters and occupied the capital, Dwin.

In 573 Marcian operated around Nisibis; unfavourable reports on his siege operations were secretly sent by the city's Nestorian bishop to Gregory of Antioch,[17] but these may have been distortions characteristic of an

[15] Menander frr. 9–10, 13.5; Whitby, *Maurice* 217–18.   [16] Menander fr. 16; Whitby, *Maurice* 250–4.
[17] Lee (1993a) 571–5.

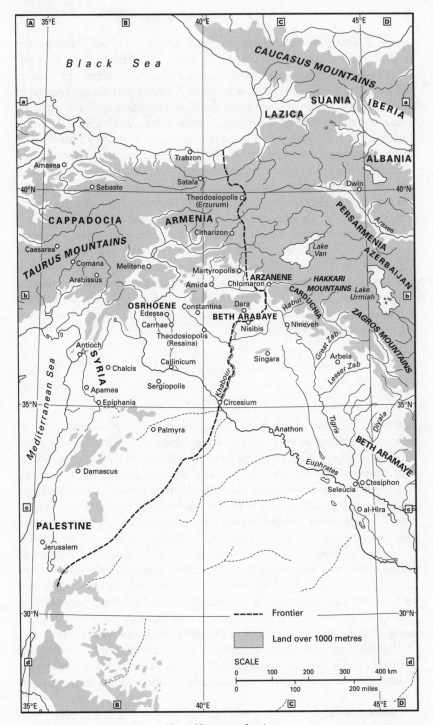

Map 3 The eastern frontier

over-enthusiastic amateur observer of military preparations. Whatever the truth, Justin's patience snapped and he dismissed Marcian, but this coincided with the appearance of a Persian relief army led in person by Khusro, who had been believed to be close to death. Khusro's preparations and rapid march up the Euphrates surprised the Romans, who may have expected some warning from their Arab allies, but the Ghassanid leader al-Mundhir claimed to have been insulted, or even betrayed, by Justin and had withdrawn from the conflict. Part of the Persian army ravaged Syria and sacked Apamea, while Khusro's contingent invested Dara. After six months the city fell, and the great bastion of the Roman frontier was in Persian hands for the first time.[18] Justin's sanity may already have shown signs of instability, if there is truth in Theophanes' story about the row with his son-in-law Baduarius, but the loss of Dara, capping a sequence of disasters, finally turned his mind. In desperation, the empress Sophia sent the physician Zacharias to Persia to negotiate, on the grounds that it would demean Khusro to fight a defenceless woman: at a cost of 45,000 *solidi* a one-year truce was arranged to permit more substantive negotiations, though the Persians insisted that fighting could continue in Armenia, where they wanted to restore control.[19]

II. TIBERIUS

1. *Succession*

Justin's failure to regain his sanity during 574 forced the proclamation of an imperial colleague. Sophia, keen to remain influential, identified the *comes excubitorum* Tiberius as a loyal aide to Justin who would also serve her interests. Rumour held that she saw him as a replacement spouse, apparently unaware that Tiberius was married with children, but our source, John of Ephesus, was basically hostile to Sophia and the story might have been generated by jealousy at Tiberius' newly-imperial family and by Sophia's reluctance to be ousted from the comforts and opportunities of the palace. Whatever her intentions, Tiberius was proclaimed Caesar on 6 December when Justin, in a brief moment of lucidity, gave a simple but moving speech that encapsulated his ideas about imperial rule and the supremacy of God. For almost four years Tiberius functioned as junior but operative colleague to Justin, until the latter's death on 4 October 578, when Tiberius succeeded as Augustus. Sophia was still loath to relinquish her power: John of Ephesus records ructions between the imperial women inside the palace, while Gregory of Tours preserves stories about attempts by Sophia to have Justinian, the cousin of Justin, proclaimed – even if the precise

---

[18] Whitby, *Maurice* 254–8.   [19] Theophanes 246.11–27; Menander fr. 18; Whitby, *Maurice* 258–9.

details must be untrue, since Justinian was already dead, they illustrate the widespread perception of tensions in the imperial family. Tiberius' declaration that he would regard Sophia as a mother might have been a politely calculated insult. Later Syriac tradition described Tiberius as the first Greek emperor, which may simply reflect the fact that after a succession of emperors from Latin-speaking Illyricum (Anastasius from Dyrrachium, the family of Justin from Bederiacum) Tiberius as a Thracian was probably a native Greek-speaker, as the Cappadocian Maurice would also have been.[20]

2. The Persian war

Tiberius, who must already have been influential in the councils of the 'interregnum', acted decisively to stabilize the Roman position. Ambassadors were despatched to Khusro to announce his proclamation and extend the truce, while large numbers of Germanic tribesmen in the Balkans were recruited to replenish Roman ranks. Both initiatives succeeded: the envoys Trajan and Zacharias secured a prolongation of the true for three years, although Armenia was still excluded (contrary to Tiberius' hopes), while the recruits were formed into a corps called *Tiberiani*, 15,000 strong, and allocated to the new eastern commander, the patrician Justinian, son of Germanus, another of Justin's cousins. To mark his accession Tiberius announced in April 575 the remission of one year's monetary taxes, to be spread in instalments over four years, but payments in kind were maintained and specific mention was made of military needs in Osrhoene and Mesopotamia.[21]

In 575 there was probably little major action on the eastern front, but in 576 Khusro attempted to combine aggression in Armenia with discussion of a permanent peace: with a large army that included elephants, he reasserted Persian authority in Persarmenia but then failed to capture Theodosiopolis. Negotiations began while Khusro pushed west towards Sebaste and then Caesarea in Cappadocia, but Roman forces harassed his unwieldy army into retreat and after a confrontation near Melitene the Persian royal baggage was captured; there were severe Persian losses, either in set battle, as the Romans claimed, or during a disorganized flight over the Euphrates. Khusro retired across Arzanene, having to cut a path for his elephant through the Hakkari mountains. These failures, coupled with energetic Roman ravaging that reached as far as the Caspian Sea, stimulated Persian interest in negotiations, with the Romans arguing for peace on equal terms and the exchange of Dara for Persarmenia and Iberia. In 577, however, Persian confidence revived when Tamkhusro defeated Justinian in

---

[20] John Eph. *HE* III.5–10; Greg. Tur. *Hist.* v.30; Gregory Barhebraeus IX p. 81 (Budge).
[21] *Nov.* 163.

Armenia, where Roman actions had alienated local inhabitants. Discussions stumbled on through the winter of 577/8, but the main objective was now to observe, or deter, the opposition's military preparations.[22]

Maurice, *comes excubitorum*, who had been involved in secret aspects of these negotiations at Constantinople, was now appointed supreme eastern commander, since Justinian had died and his former subordinates were wrangling. Maurice recruited troops in his native Cappadocia, Anzitene and Syria, before positioning himself at Citharizon, suitably located to react to Persian moves in both Armenia and Upper Mesopotamia when the truce ended. The Persians Mahbodh and Tamkhusro anticipated this, at least on the Roman interpretation of the agreement, and ravaged Constantina and Theodosiopolis-Resaina and then Amida, but throughout most of summer 578 the initiative lay with the Romans: Maurice attacked Arzanene, captured Aphum and closely besieged the region's main city, Chlomaron; ravaging was sufficiently extensive to be visible to Khusro in his summer retreat in Carduchia, and the Romans took thousands of prisoners whom they resettled on Cyprus.

Roman successes again prompted the Persians to negotiate, but talks were disrupted, this time by Khusro's death and the accession of his son Hormizd, who was reluctant to start his reign with a surrender of territory. Diplomatic delays prevented serious fighting during 579, though the two sides probably attempted to consolidate their positions in Arzanene. In 580 Maurice returned to the offensive, with extensive raids across the Tigris, and for 581 he planned an even more ambitious enterprise, an expedition down the Euphrates towards Ctesiphon with the Ghassanid leader al-Mundhir, while other Roman troops occupied the Persians in Armenia. His grand plan failed, for reasons that are not clearly recorded in the sources; Maurice extricated his forces from a position that might have been as desperate as Julian's in 363, but the commanders quarrelled and accusations of treachery were levelled against al-Mundhir. The justification for these is uncertain, but the Ghassanids withdrew from the fighting and their king was subsequently arrested. In 582 the Persians tried to exploit the Roman discomfiture, and Tamkhusro once again advanced towards Constantina, but was defeated and killed. By now Maurice had his eye on events in Constantinople, and at some point, perhaps even before the victory at Constantina, he left the eastern army to pursue imperial ambitions.[23]

3. *The west and the Balkans*

In the west Tiberius' main preoccupation was to restore the Roman position in Italy; a major expedition under Justin's son-in-law, Baduarius, was

---

[22] Whitby, *Maurice* 262–8.   [23] *Ibid.* 268–74.

despatched in 575, but he was severely defeated and killed. This encouraged the Lombards to further expansion, in spite of their lack of an overall leader, and in 578 Faroald, duke of Spoleto, even captured Classis, Ravenna's port, and besieged Rome. An embassy from the Roman senate, led by the patrician Pamphronius, begged for practical help and presented 3,000 pounds of gold, perhaps the senate's traditional coronation offering to a new ruler. But Tiberius had no troops to spare; he returned the money and advised that it be used to purchase support from Lombard leaders or secure alliances with the Franks.

The orthodox Franks of Austrasia were incited to oppose the Arian Lombards, and the new pope, Pelagius II, who had been consecrated during the Lombard pressure on Rome, wrote to the bishop of Auxerre to urge him to persuade the Burgundians to assist. Guntram of Burgundy, however, was already allied with the Lombards, and the first goal of Roman diplomacy now became an alliance of Austrasia and Neustria against the uncooperative Guntram. Tiberius sent gold, and the size and decoration of his coins or medallions are said by Gregory of Tours to have impressed the Gallic nobility. Pelagius also renewed appeals to Constantinople for help, but without success. The problems of controlling the remaining Roman territories in the west may have prompted Tiberius to initiate significant administrative reforms: an exarch, a local commander who combined civilian and military authority, is first attested in Italy in 584, and in Africa in 591, but greater local independence in the production of gold coin in Africa and Sicily between 581 and 583 suggests that fiscal and administrative reform was already under way.[24]

In the Balkans the Roman position deteriorated significantly under Tiberius: troops had probably been removed for service with Baduarius in Italy as well as for the east, and numerous recruits were siphoned off for eastern service after the disasters of 573. The empire could only afford a major war in one area at a time, and the east took priority. Initially the Avars were quiet, content with an annual payment of 80,000 *solidi*, and the main threat was posed by the various Slav tribes who crossed the lower Danube to ravage Thrace and other regions. But once the Avars appreciated the full extent of Roman weakness, they quickly exploited this by renewing their attempts on Sirmium, which dominated the Balkans during Tiberius' sole rule, since possession of the city would provide a foothold south of the Sava and so facilitate attacks on Roman territory. The Avars, exploiting the technical expertise of some Roman engineers, isolated Sirmium by building bridges over the Sava both upstream and downstream, to cut it off from relief by water, though in negotiations the Chagan asserted his loyalty, saying that Slavs rather than Romans were his intended target. In spite of

---

[24] Menander fr. 22; Greg. Tur. *Hist.* VI.2; Goffart (1957); Brown, *Gentlemen and Officers* 49–53.

their suspicions, the Romans could not prevent the bridge construction, even though Tiberius, pretending to accept Avar protestations, warned them that their dreaded former overlords, the Turks, had reached Cherson on the Black Sea and might exploit the absence of the Avar army from Pannonia.

The Roman problem is bluntly presented in Menander: the Persian war had completely drained the Balkans of troops, and no thought had been given to laying in supplies to resist sieges, since the Avars had seemed well-disposed. Relief proved impossible and Sirmium was eventually forced to surrender after a blockade of three years. While Roman attention was focused on the north, elsewhere in the Balkans Slavs roamed with little apparent restraint. Brigands, referred to as Scamareis, interfered with travel even by official embassies on the main highways. Scamareis, perhaps to be considered the eastern equivalent of the bagaudae, had similarly appeared in Noricum as central control evaporated. Coin hoards, probably to be dated to Tiberius' reign, have been found from the foothills of the Stara Planina in northern Bulgaria as far south as Porto Cheli and Olympia in the Peloponnese, illustrating the extent of disruption. Even at Constantinople Tiberius is alleged to have erected a fortification to protect shipping in one of the harbours. The Slavs were no longer content to ravage, but were thought to have begun to settle.[25]

4. *Internal affairs*

Such lack of success did little to dent Tiberius' popular reputation. In contrast to Justin, who had come to be regarded as stingy, Tiberius retained an image of conspicuous generosity: the contrast of regimes is made in the stories of disagreements between Sophia and Tiberius about the level of his charitable expenditure, with Tiberius expressing the laudable but quite impractical attitude, at least for an emperor, that gold in the treasury was of little use when the world was suffering from hunger.[26] Quite apart from charity, warfare and diplomacy in west and east cost Tiberius dear, at a time when state income was reduced by almost 25 per cent because of the tax remission of 575: in his first year as emperor John of Ephesus alleges that he spent 7,500 pounds of gold, 540,000 *solidi*, as well as quantities of silver and silks – his expenses would have included a consulship, in imitation of Justin, and an accession donative for the armies, but the outlay is still impressive. Western rumour had it that he had benefited from the discovery of the fabulous treasure of Narses, the former duke of Italy, but it is not surprising that the empire was impoverished at his death.[27]

[25] Menander frr. 15.6, 25, 27; John Eph. *HE* VI.24–5, 30–2; Whitby, *Maurice* 86–9.
[26] Cameron (1977).   [27] John Eph. *HE* v.20; Greg. Tur. *Hist.* v.19.

Tiberius attempted to avoid being drawn into religious disputes. He achieved a good reputation with Monophysites even though persecution was allowed to continue, since blame was ascribed to Eutychius, who had returned as patriarch of Constantinople in 577. Tiberius was believed to have asserted that he could see nothing wrong with Monophysites, and that it was senseless to contemplate persecution at a time of external crisis; he also invited the Monophysite Ghassanid leader al-Mundhir to Constantinople in an unsuccessful attempt to promote unity between splintered Monophysite groups, and gave him an honourable reception. He appears to have favoured inaction in two other religious disputes, first when the people of Constantinople rioted against concessions supposedly made to Arian Germans recruited for military service, and second when an embarrassing scandal implicated imperial administrators and even the patriarch of Antioch, Gregory, in pagan worship. Such toleration could give rise to accusations of being too passive.[28]

In August 582, Tiberius fell ill, allegedly after eating a dish of poisoned mulberries. His first intention was to appoint two successors: the *comes excubitorum* Maurice and Germanus, son of the Ostrogoth princess Matasuintha and Justinian's cousin Germanus, were proclaimed Caesars on 5 August and betrothed to Tiberius' two daughters, Constantina and Charito. One source, hostile to Maurice, alleges that Germanus was Tiberius' real preference, although another claims that the dowager empress Sophia was consulted and declared support for Maurice. In retrospect Maurice's accession attracted the usual predictions from contemporary holy men, predictions which boosted the reputations of both the saint involved and the secular beneficiary: Symeon Stylites outside Antioch, who had already prophesied the rise of Justin II and Tiberius, identified Maurice as the next emperor, as did Theodore of Sykeon in central Anatolia. Whatever the truth, Tiberius' health deteriorated; on 13 August Maurice alone was proclaimed Augustus and successor in a ceremony at the palace at the Hebdomon, and on the next day Tiberius died, his corpse being escorted into Constantinople for burial in the Holy Apostles.[29]

III. MAURICE

1. *Internal affairs*

Finance was the key problem throughout Maurice's reign: Tiberius' generosity had apparently exhausted the central treasuries, so that Maurice had to tackle the various external threats to the empire while struggling at the

---

[28] John Eph. *HE* III.17–22; IV.39–43; III.26, 29–32. Cameron (1977) 13.
[29] Whitby, *Maurice* 5–9.

same time to acquire the necessary resources: 'I do not scatter and disperse, but amass and store away so that I may pay for the peace of the state' is a statement of policy attributed to him by John of Ephesus. When Maurice, like his two predecessors, held the consulship at the start of his reign, he entered office on Christmas Day 583, which probably enabled him to avoid some of the expenditure associated with the post. A significant change in financial administration may be represented by the appearance of a logothete, and the first known holder of this senior financial post, Constantine Lardys, shared Maurice's unpopularity and fate in 602.[30]

Financial stringency generated accusations of avarice. When Maurice attempted in 588 to reduce military expenditure on the eastern army, the soldiers mutinied and castigated him as a 'shopkeeper'. The Balkan army was equally hostile when Maurice imposed analogous changes in pay and conditions in the winter of 593/4, and in Egypt Maurice was believed to have greedily sold Constantinople's grain for gold; in the capital itself during a food shortage in 602 Maurice was heckled as a Marcianist, an adherent of a heresy which rejected normal standards of charity. The imperial family, however, had money to spend on building projects in Constantinople. Even if many of the constructions were of a charitable or more broadly religious nature, expenditure on palaces, on statues of the imperial family at prominent places such as the façade of the Chalke, the ceremonial entry to the Great Palace, and even on private monasteries would not win sympathy from ordinary people faced by famine.[31]

The contrast with Tiberius' munificence was bound to cause problems, but Maurice made matters worse by showing generosity to his relatives, who in common with members of other new dynasties received titles, high office and property. His father Paul became head of the senate, Philippicus, husband of his sister Gordia, was appointed *comes excubitorum* and commander of the eastern armies, his brother Peter was made *curopalatus* and became a general in the Balkans, and another relative, Domitian, for whom Maurice had obtained the bishopric of Melitene in 577/8, was an influential adviser. Such patronage was no greater than that bestowed on Justin's relatives, and indeed Maurice could economize to some extent by 'recycling' the property of Justin's brother Marcellus, but Tiberius had not had an extensive family on which to lavish gifts, so that the new direction of patronage would be more obvious. Prominent individuals from outside the family included Comentiolus, who progressed from being a *scribon*, an officer in the *excubitores*, to one of Maurice's most regular if not successful generals, and Priscus, another frequent commander. Of these relatives and favourites only Priscus remained prominent under Phocas; most of the chosen clique were executed in the coup of 602.[32]

[30] John Eph. *HE* v.20; Hendy, *Studies* 193; Haldon (1979) 33–4; Whitby, *Maurice* 17.
[31] Whitby, *Maurice* 286–7, 166–7, 19–21.   [32] *Ibid.* 14–17.

Maurice was faced with the same religious problems as his predecessors. With regard to the Monophysites, the contemporary John of Ephesus praised him for resisting moves to stimulate persecution, and in this Maurice was supported by the patriarch John Nesteutes, but later Syriac writers criticized him for allowing Domitian of Melitene to punish Monophysites in the east towards the end of his reign; four hundred monks are said to have been slain outside the walls of Edessa. Maurice was also inclined to be tolerant towards lapses into pagan practices: Paulinus, a 'magician' discovered at Constantinople, was only executed after strong insistence by John Nesteutes, and Gregory, patriarch of Antioch, was acquitted on various obscure charges that probably included paganism.[33]

A new source of trouble was an increasingly heated argument with pope Gregory: a significant factor was the Constantinopolitan patriarchs' use of the title 'oecumenical', to whose alleged universalist claim Gregory took exception, misguidedly, but questions of ecclesiastical control in the Balkans and imperial policy in Italy also played their part. Maurice contin- ued the imperial practice of associating himself with the acquisition of relics, and with popular cults, such as that of the Virgin: the weekly Friday feast of the Virgin at Blachernae was developed, and the commemoration of the Virgin's Assumption on 15 August was instituted as a feast; the holy man Theodore of Sykeon was invited to Constantinople to bless the impe- rial family. Maurice was deeply religious, spending the night in church before a major expedition, marking victory with religious celebrations, and apparently showing concern for the need to justify his worldly actions before the eternal throne of judgement.[34]

Maurice's rule has been characterized as both negligent and unpopular, but the evidence is insufficient to justify such an assessment.[35] Most emper- ors experienced bouts of unpopularity, especially when famine or other misfortune disrupted normal patterns of life, and attempts to change long- standing arrangements in financial or military matters were bound to provoke opposition. In many respects, perhaps, Maurice was an interven- tionist or reformer, as might be suggested by his reputation as a military commander in the east. He was also, directly or indirectly, associated with the *Strategikon* that bears his name, a military manual that shows good knowledge of contemporary Balkan warfare and overall is less attached to the traditions of this genre than most such texts. He attempted to tackle the key financial problem of the late Roman empire, the cost of the army, and the appearance of a logothete suggests there may have been some redefinition of duties in civilian administration. His quarrels with pope Gregory sprang, in part, from his willingness to interfere in areas that the western church regarded as its traditional prerogative. His unpopularity,

[33] John Eph. *HE* v.15–17; Michael the Syrian x.23, vol. II pp. 372–3; Theophylact 1.11.
[34] Whitby, *Maurice* 20–4.   [35] Olster (1993) 49.

perhaps, was the typical fate of a reformer who was unable to complete his intended changes.

2. *Eastern warfare*

As his replacement in charge of the eastern armies, Maurice initially appointed his former subordinate, John Mystacon, who continued operations in Arzanene in autumn 582 and then through 583 with mixed success.[36] Arzanene was a vulnerable salient of Persian territory, control of which would allow the Romans to consolidate their hold on Armenia to the north. For 584 Maurice appointed a new general, his brother-in-law Philippicus; negotiations occupied the first part of the year, possibly another Persian delaying tactic, but in autumn 584 and through 585 Philippicus ravaged the plains of Beth Arabaye near Nisibis and continued operations in Arzanene, though progress slowed when Philippicus fell ill. Raiding into Syria by Rome's former allies, the Ghassanid Arabs, who had been alienated by the arrest and punishment of their king, al-Mundhir, may also have caused disruption.

In 586 activity seems to have been on a different scale. Philippicus thwarted a Persian invasion of Upper Mesopotamia with victory in a pitched battle at Solachon in the plains south of Mardin, and thereafter returned his attentions to Arzanene. Although unsuccessful in an attack on the main city, Chlomaron, which Maurice had also failed to capture in 578, the Romans maintained the initiative during the rest of the year, building or capturing strategic forts and raiding deep into Persia; Philippicus' ill health meant that much of this activity was conducted by Heraclius, the father of the future emperor, and other subordinate commanders.

During winter 587/8 there were two developments: Priscus was appointed to replace Philippicus, and he was ordered to introduce a reduction in military pay, a move whose unpopularity may have been offset by improvements in conditions of service. Priscus' arrival at the camp at Monocarton was unhappy, and the army mutinied during the Easter festival: Priscus was forced to retire to Edessa, his attempts to reconcile the troops were rebuffed, and the mutineers chose as leader Germanus, duke of Phoenicia. The mutiny persisted for a whole year, until Easter 589, but the Persians were surprisingly unable to exploit this opportunity, which may reveal the extent of Roman successes in recent years. Germanus indeed defeated the Persians near Martyropolis and sent 3,000 captives to Constantinople as a gesture of allegiance to Maurice. The troops were finally won back through a combination of imperial emissaries, who disbursed normal payments, and exhortations from Gregory, patriarch of

[36] For discussion of these years, see Whitby, *Maurice* 276–92.

Antioch; Philippicus was now reinstated as commander, but this return to
normality in fact prompted a reverse for the Romans when the frontier city
of Martyropolis was betrayed to the Persians. Philippicus quickly invested
the city, but was unable to prevent Persian reinforcements from entering;
as a result he was superseded by Comentiolus, who persevered with the
blockade of Martyropolis but also moved south to threaten Nisibis and
defeated the Persians nearby at Sisarbanon.

Dramatic developments in Persia now affected the course of the frontier war.[37] The king Hormizd had not commanded military expeditions in
person, perhaps obedient to advice given by his father after the mishap in
Armenia in 576, which meant that he was out of touch with his troops. His
leading general, Vahram Tchobin, recently returned from the north-east
where victories against the Turks had stabilized the frontier, had then campaigned against Roman supporters in the Caucasian principalities. But here
he was routed. Hormizd saw this as an opportunity to humble an over-
mighty commander, and publicly insulted Vahram with a gift of female
clothing. Vahram persuaded his army to revolt and marched south on
Ctesiphon; Hormizd's support evaporated, and in February 590 he was
overthrown in a palace coup that placed his son, Khusro II, on the throne;
this did not mollify Vahram, and after a confrontation north of Ctesiphon,
Khusro fled across the Tigris towards the Roman empire.

The rest of 590 was occupied by negotiations, Khusro eager to secure
Roman support for his reinstatement, Vahram wanting to persuade
Maurice that he was the man to deal with. Although some of his advisers,
including the patriarch John Nesteutes, thought the Persians should be
allowed to weaken themselves through internal conflict, Maurice decided
that legitimate sovereigns had a duty to support each other, accepting the
argument that the Roman and Persian empires, even if antagonists, had
considerable self-interest in mutual stability. Khusro's careful professions
of interest in Christianity seem also to have been a significant factor, and
the two leading clerics in the east, Domitian of Melitene and Gregory of
Antioch, were sent to supervise his stay on Roman territory and to co-ordinate action; subsequently pope Gregory commiserated with Domitian on
his failure to win over Khusro.[38]

Preparations were made for a grand campaign to restore Khusro, with
support being canvassed in the frontier areas. By 591 everything was ready
and Vahram was too weak to oppose a three-pronged attack against
Azerbaijan, Upper Mesopotamia and Ctesiphon; he was defeated near
Canzak in Azerbaijan, and Khusro resumed his throne. The Roman reward
for their assistance was the return of Dara and Martyropolis and the acquisition of Iberia and much of Persarmenia. Twenty years of war initiated by

---

[37] For discussion, see *ibid.* 292–304.   [38] Greg. *Reg.* iii.62.

Justin had been brought to a surprisingly successful conclusion, and during the last decade of Maurice's reign relations on the eastern frontier were generally good: Arab tribes and local arguments might raise tension, but in 602 Maurice was sufficiently confident of Khusro's good faith to contemplate sending his son Theodosius to appeal for Persian support against Phocas.

3. *The west and the Balkans*

Comparable success eluded Maurice in the west. In Italy he continued the policies of Tiberius, attempting to engage the Franks as allies against the Lombards, but two invasions in 584 and 585 achieved little; as a result, in 586 the exarch Smaragdus made a three-year truce with the Lombards. Meanwhile in Gaul financial support was given to Gundovald, an illegitimate member of the Merovingian royal house, in attempts to gain the throne of Burgundy or Neustria; these had failed by the end of 585. In Spain Roman possessions had been whittled away by the Visigoths, but small enclaves based on Seville and Cartagena remained, and the fortuitous capture of the Merovingian princess Ingund, daughter-in-law of king Leovigild, and her son Athanagild gave Maurice considerable influence at the Austrasian court. In Africa Moorish raids had troubled the province under Justin II and Tiberius, but it was peaceful throughout most of Maurice's reign, and tribal threats were dealt with by the exarch Gennadius.[39]

During the 590s the Roman position in Italy remained weak. The exarch Romanus maintained pressure on the Lombards and managed to secure communications across the Apennines between Ravenna and Rome, but his belligerence was not favoured by the new pope, Gregory (590–604); Gregory, more concerned by the isolation of Rome and the city's lack of troops, preferred to establish links with the Lombards and in this he was successful after Romanus' death in 596, with the orthodox queen Theodelinda as an important contact. Policy towards the Lombards remained a contentious issue between Gregory and Maurice, and relations were complicated by the row over the Constantinopolitan patriarch's use of the oecumenical title, disputes about jurisdiction in Illyricum, a diocese under papal control but geographically orientated more closely with Constantinople, and Gregory's desire to prevent secular interference with church estates in the west. By 602 relations were sufficiently bad for Gregory to react warmly to the news of Phocas' accession and the death of Maurice's supporter, Comentiolus, whose involvement in a dispute about church property in Spain had displeased Gregory.[40]

---

[39] Goffart (1957); Goubert (1951–65) II.   [40] Richards (1980) chs. 11, 13.

At Maurice's accession the Roman position in the Balkans appeared per-
ilous, with Slavs overrunning much of the countryside and the Avars controlling a bridgehead across the Sava at Sirmium.[41] The Avars tried to
exploit the change of emperor by demanding diplomatic gifts, and then an
increase in annual payments from 80,000 to 100,000 *solidi*. The extra tribute
was conceded after an Avar invasion reached Anchialus on the Black Sea.
This purchased two years' peace from the Avars, but all the time the Slavs
were on the move, ravaging and restricting the areas of Roman control: in
584 they approached the Long Walls of Constantinople, and then in 585
had to be driven from the Thracian plain. Such Roman actions prompted
Slav bands to wander towards less protected areas, and the lower city of
Athens was sacked, followed by Corinth in 586, and in the same year
Thessalonica, the second city of the Balkans, was briefly besieged. In
autumn 586 the Avars found a suitable excuse to renounce their treaty, and
again they swept from Pannonia to the eastern foothills of the Stara Planina
near the Black Sea. Maurice raised a scratch army through harsh conscription, but 40 per cent of the 10,000 troops were apparently unsuitable for
battle, and their commander, Comentiolus, seems to have restricted his
aims to curbing Avar depredations and keeping them north of the Stara
Planina. In this he failed, partly perhaps because of his troops' inexperience, and he was pursued across the mountains. In the Thracian plain,
however, the Avars were less successful, in that the major cities withstood
their attacks and a force of Lombards inflicted a tactical defeat on them.

At this point the chronology of Balkan events becomes uncertain,
because our main source, Theophylact Simocatta, who was writing a generation later, did not fully understand events. The detailed solution adopted
here is no more than a possibility, although the contrast of severe crisis in
the late 580s followed by considerable recovery in the 590s should be
right.[42] In 588 Priscus, recently returned from the mutinous eastern army,
was given command with the task of attempting to defend the Stara Planina
again. He was no more successful than Comentiolus, since Roman garrisons were too small to defend key passes. The Avars managed to capture
Anchialus, and the Chagan donned imperial robes, which the empress
Anastasia had dedicated in a church there, and blatantly challenged
Maurice's authority as emperor. The Avars then pushed south to Heracleia
on the Sea of Marmara, where they ravaged the shrine of the martyr
Glyceria, but eventually withdrew after receiving a payment from the
Romans, and perhaps also influenced by rumours of a Turkish threat to
their homeland in Pannonia.[43]

After this catastrophe for Roman control, Maurice himself took the field
and marched across Thrace to Anchialus in autumn 590, perhaps to

---

[41] Whitby, *Maurice* 140–51.   [42] See *ibid.* 151–3.   [43] *Ibid.* 153–5.

counter the Chagan's assertion there of imperial pretensions. Thereafter Roman operations were greatly assisted by the termination of the Persian war and the transfer of resources and eastern troops to the Balkans.[44] Between 593 and 595 Priscus and Peter gradually reasserted Roman control of the eastern Balkans, driving scattered Slav groups back to the Danube, campaigning across the river to deter further incursions, and reopening contacts with those Roman outposts that had survived the invasions of the 580s. This sequence of imperial collapse followed by recovery provides a context for the story of Maurice's achievement in winning over a brigand chief:[45] 'brigands' was a convenient term to apply to local self-help groups that appeared as central authority collapsed, but in many cases their priority was efficient protection for their own territory and so they were prepared to show deference to an emperor who appeared to be capable of providing this.

The Avar Chagan, though concerned about these actions, was unable to intervene: Singidunum was protected by a Roman fleet, and the Avars were forced to turn their attentions west to Illyria and the Frankish kingdoms. In autumn 597 the Avars again raided eastwards and reached Tomi on the Black Sea; in 598 a Roman attempt, perhaps too ambitious, to trap the Avars there failed, and the Avars were able to burst across the mountains to ravage the Thracian plain, but disease and diplomacy persuaded them to withdraw. A new treaty established the Danube as the frontier, but the Romans were specifically allowed to cross the river to attack Slavs, a recognition of the considerable Roman recovery that had been achieved. This time it was the Romans who were on the offensive and had no intention of preserving the treaty; in 599 there was a successful campaign into Pannonia itself, in 601 Roman control of the Danube Cataracts was safeguarded, and in 602 there were further successes against the Slavs. Constant campaigning, much of which is probably reported inadequately by Theophylact, had reasserted Roman authority in the Balkans: the Danube was now a real frontier, Slavs beyond the frontier were becoming cowed, while Slavs south of the river might be turned into Roman subjects.

This achievement, however, was the product of hard toil, and fighting perhaps became less lucrative for the Romans. Concern about Maurice's desire for financial economies, which had already prompted sedition in winter 593/94, culminated again in late 602 when Maurice ordered the troops to spend the winter north of the Danube.[46] There were good military reasons for this, expounded in the contemporary *Strategikon*, but the soldiers mutinied, chose Phocas as leader and marched on Constantinople. In the capital Maurice's unpopularity had been demonstrated in rioting over a food shortage in February; there were insufficient troops to defend the city, and

[44] *Ibid.* 153–65.   [45] Farka (1993/4).   [46] Whitby, *Maurice* 165–9.

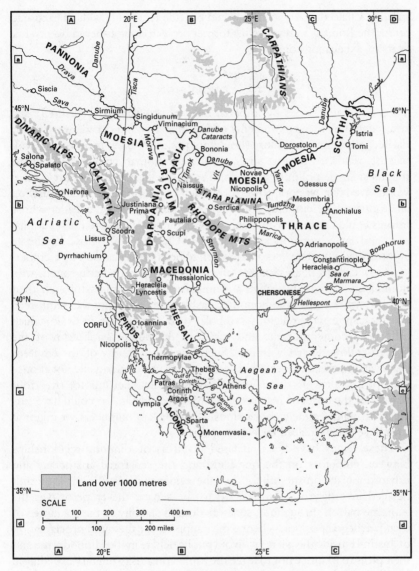

Map 4 The Balkan frontier

Maurice's position was undermined when he quarrelled with Germanus, the other son-in-law of Tiberius, who is noticeably absent from most events of Maurice's reign but whose daughter had recently married Maurice's eldest son Theodosius. On 22 November Maurice fled across the Bosphorus after a night of rioting, and the next day Phocas was proclaimed emperor at the Hebdomon; on 27 November Maurice and most of his male relatives were killed at Chalcedon, an act that would provide Khusro II with an excuse to attack the Romans to revenge his former protector and usher in twenty-five years of exhausting conflict.[47]

IV. CONCLUSION

Thus the grand hopes of imperial renewal proclaimed by Justin II and resuscitated by the achievements of Maurice's second decade were finally dashed, but long-term failure should not prejudice assessments of individuals or trends. In the late sixth century the Roman empire was still the mightiest single political institution in the Mediterranean or near eastern world, even if it was not powerful enough to dominate simultaneously on all frontiers. The emperor controlled this great machine, a leader whose images could excite envy in Gaul, whose grandeur prompted first submission and later imitation from the Avar Chagan, and whose legitimate authority led a fugitive Persian monarch to beg for assistance. These emperors were civilian figures, palace officials or notaries by background, who dominated the administrative and military infrastructures through their secular authority. In time-honoured fashion this authority was reinforced by association with religious symbols, such as relics or festivals, which influenced contemporaries and sustained the potent symbolism of the heaven-endowed earthly empire. Such was the authority of the emperor that even imperial madness or severe personal unpopularity did not at once prompt a change of ruler: Justin remained sole Augustus for over four years after the onset of insanity, while Maurice even in 602 could have survived by making timely concessions to the Balkan mutineers, or might at least have been replaced by a close relative.

These reigns have been analysed in terms of differing relationships between emperors on the one hand and the senatorial aristocracy and urban populace on the other,[48] but the evidence is insufficient to permit detailed investigation. With regard to the senate, the emperor was the supreme patron throughout; senators desired stability as the guarantee of their privileged position – hence their support for the rapid proclamation of Justin II inside the palace to avoid public debate in the Hippodrome and their pleas to Maurice not to leave the capital on a risky military expedition. Undoubtedly there were tensions in this relationship, but there was also a fundamental community of interest. With regard to the populace, emperors seem to have managed to achieve a more secure control over the circus factions, the most prominent or vocal representatives of public opinion: in 602 for the first time demarchs, official controllers, of the Blues and Greens are mentioned, and these now maintained lists of registered followers who

---

[47] *Ibid.* 24–7.   [48] Bury, *LRE* 11.92–4; Ostrogorsky (1956) 82–3.

could then be summoned for military action. The factions were prominent in imperial ceremonial outside as well as inside the Hippodrome, the original focus of their activities, and the closeness of their connection with the emperor persuaded both Maurice in 602 and Phocas in 610 that they might support an unpopular ruler in a crisis.[49]

During this period the frontiers of the empire contracted, except in the east, where Roman authority was re-established as far as the Caucasus. Justinian's western reconquests ceded priority to the defence of the east, so that Lombards in Italy and Visigoths in Spain took over Roman territory, but this might have been a temporary phenomenon: Maurice's friendly relations with Khusro and reassertion of Roman control in the Balkans could have permitted the transfer of attention and resources to the far west again, and the division of the empire between his sons proposed in his will of 597 suggests a traditional Roman view of the Mediterranean world. If peaceful co-existence had continued on the eastern frontier, it is arguable that the Islamic raids and attacks of the 630s would not have achieved the dramatic success which they did. Maurice had acted timeously in curbing the power of the Ghassanid federation at a point when it threatened, like any oversuccessful quasi-client neighbour, to become too powerful for the good of its supposed patron.

The usurper Phocas was a convenient scapegoat for the misfortunes that befell the empire in the early seventh century, and some of the blame should certainly be allocated to the considerable disruption that attended the coup of Heraclius' family in 609–10,[50] but Phocas' seizure of power does mark a break. Previous emperors – Zeno when briefly ousted by Basiliscus, Anastasius when faced by religious rioting and the challenge of Vitalian, or Justinian during the Nika riot – had been seriously threatened, but in 602 for the very first time a Constantinopolitan emperor had been overthrown and killed, and his corpse displayed for public humiliation. A precedent had been created. Furthermore, the new emperor was a man with no obvious experience of court life or administration at Constantinople. It is true that the empire was a military monarchy, and that military ability was about to become important again as an imperial quality after a lapse of two centuries, but the secular machinery of rule had to be regulated and, when necessary, dominated. Phocas seems to have been insensitive to the niceties of the emperor's ceremonial existence within the capital, and this caused tension, plotting and hence further misfortunes for the empire.

Heraclius' coup generated conflicts within many of the empire's major cities, with rival supporters appropriating the confrontation of the circus partisans – Greens for Heraclius, Blues for Phocas – even in places with no immediate access to a hippodrome. It took time for Heraclius to assert his

---

[49] Theophylact VIII.7.10–11; Cameron, *Circus Factions* 120–2.   [50] Olster (1993) ch. 7.

authority completely, and this hiatus permitted the Persians to extend their conquests across the Euphrates and on to the Anatolian plateau. A Roman counter-offensive failed, and major disasters ensued: in 614 Jerusalem was captured and the True Cross taken into captivity; Egypt, the granary of Constantinople, was invaded in 616 and Alexandria fell in 619. To face this onslaught Heraclius transferred troops from the Balkans, where peace with the Avars had to be purchased at a rapidly increasing price; the less orga- nized Slavs ravaged extensively throughout the peninsula and the Aegean islands. Heraclius himself was almost taken prisoner while attempting to negotiate an agreement with the Avar Chagan at Heracleia in 623, and it is clear that the emperor's authority scarcely stretched beyond the Long Walls of Constantinople. In this crisis Heraclius took personal charge of the armies, and energetic campaigning in the 620s gradually turned the military balance in Anatolia, even though the Persians remained in control of the whole of the near east and occupied Chalcedon on the Bosphorus. The year 626 was critical for Roman survival. Constantinople withstood a short but fierce attack co-ordinated by the Avars; this failure was a serious blow to the Chagan's prestige, and contributed to the fragmentation of his fed- eration. By 627 Heraclius was ravaging Azerbaijan, the spiritual heart of Persia; victory at Nineveh and an advance on Ctesiphon led to a coup against Khusro II, and Heraclius was able to arrange a favourable peace with his successor Shiroe. Thereafter the Sasanid dynasty lapsed into dynastic chaos.

This triumph, like that of Maurice in 591, could have been the cue for a determined recovery of Roman affairs in other parts of the empire. Heraclius made a start. The restoration of the relic of the True Cross to Jerusalem was a major ceremonial triumph, and he attempted to translate his divinely achieved military success into a resolution of the long-stand- ing divide between Monophysites and Chalcedonians. Here, however, his compromise formulae, the Monergist and Monothelete doctrines, achieved no more success than similar initiatives by Zeno in the fifth century and by Justinian and Justin II in the sixth: any move towards the Monophysite position was regarded as heresy by Chalcedonian traditionalists, especially in the west. In the Balkans Heraclius may have taken advantage of the col- lapse of Avar power to make agreements with some of the emerging smaller tribal groups, such as the Croats and Serbs, but our evidence for events here is extremely sketchy. Constantinople itself had suffered a con- siderable loss of population: a major aqueduct destroyed during the Avar siege in 626 was not repaired for 150 years. Further west, if Africa appears to have remained relatively peaceful, much of Italy was firmly under Lombard control. The potential for recovery was shattered by the Arab attacks on Palestine which began in 633. Three years later at the Yarmuk a large imperial army was defeated, and Heraclius then withdrew Roman troops north of the Taurus. At his death in 640 Roman control in Egypt was virtually confined to Alexandria. In his later years Heraclius had been seriously ill, and between 638 and 641 dynastic rivalries within the imperial family again distracted attention from external events at a crucial time. The world of east Rome, which had united the Balkans and Asia Minor with the Levant and Egypt, was conclusively destroyed; the near east adopted its Byzantine shape, with the Anatolian plateau as the frontier between Christian and Islamic worlds.

Justinian has been described as the last Roman emperor to occupy the throne,[51] but his immediate successors in their different ways strove to uphold Roman authority along the important frontiers and to preserve efficient administration internally. Difficult decisions were repeatedly required, and Justin II, Tiberius and Maurice took these when necessary, with a reasonable measure of success. Phocas, however, lacked the authority, and perhaps also the ability and inclination, to sustain these efforts. In 610 Phocas, on the point of being executed, had responded to Heraclius' question, 'Is this how you have governed the state?' with the challenge, 'Will you be able to do better?' In spite of the transient victories of the 620s, Heraclius failed the test; the year 602, adopted by Jones,[52] is an appropriate terminus for the Roman empire in the east.

[51] Ostrogorsky (1956) 77.   [52] Jones, *LRE*.

CHAPTER 5

THE WESTERN KINGDOMS

ROGER COLLINS

I. GAUL: VISIGOTHIC KINGDOM, 418–507

In 418 the patrician Constantius concluded a peace treaty with the Visigothic king Wallia (415–18), giving him and his following the province of Aquitania Secunda and some adjacent territories to occupy. This completed a process initiated in 416 when Wallia returned his predecessor's widow, Galla Placidia, to her brother, the emperor Honorius. He had subsequently campaigned for the emperor in Spain, destroying the kingdoms of the Alans and of the Siling Vandals. The nature of the Visigothic presence established in Aquitaine by the treaty of 418 remains controversial. The argument concerns the nature of the process known as *hospitalitas*. Traditionally, this has been interpreted as involving a major change in land ownership, with the Visigothic 'guests' receiving two-thirds of all Roman estates within the designated regions. More recent arguments have seen it as involving not a physical redistribution of land, which would involve large-scale expropriation by the empire of aristocratic property, but a revision of tax obligations, with the Roman landowners having to pay the fiscal burden on two-thirds of their property directly to the designated Visigothic recipients rather than to the imperial administration.[1] According to the view adopted, the Visigoths can be seen in the aftermath of the treaty either as being settled on the land and widely distributed throughout southern Aquitaine or as forming a purely military presence, based on a limited number of urban garrisons.

The next thirty years saw several fluctuations in relations between the newly established Visigothic kingdom, with its centre in Toulouse, and the western imperial government. Under Theoderic I (418–51), who was not a descendant of the previous kings but may have married a daughter of Alaric I (395–410), the area of southern Gaul under Visigothic control was expanded whenever Roman authority was too weak to prevent it. Thus, unsuccessful attempts were made to seize Arles in both 425 and 430. More general warfare broke out in 436 when the Visigoths tried to take Narbonne. The use of Hun mercenaries, a practice espoused by Aetius as

---

[1] Goffart, *Barbarians and Romans*. Durliat (1988). Heather, *Goths and Romans* 220–4.

a means of controlling the Burgundians and the bagaudae, enabled the imperial government to take the offensive. In 438 Aetius defeated Theoderic in battle, and in 439 his deputy Litorius was able to besiege Toulouse. Here, though, the latter was defeated, captured and subsequently executed. A new peace treaty was made later in the same year.

The abrupt change in imperial policy brought about by the Hun invasion of Gaul in 451 led to a new military alliance with the Visigoths, resulting in the defeat of Attila at the battle of the Catalaunian Plains. Theoderic I was killed in the battle, and his eldest son Thorismund (451–3) was persuaded by Aetius not to pursue the Huns. In 452/3 he renewed his father's attempts to capture Arles. His reign proved brief in that he was soon murdered, for reasons that are not known, by his brothers Theoderic II (453–66) and Frederic. The end of Aetius' regime in 454 and the Vandal sack of Rome in 455 provided new opportunities for the Visigothic kingdom to enlarge itself. The threat from Vandal Africa now replaced that of the Visigoths as the prime concern of the Roman senate. In consequence Avitus, a Gallic aristocrat and former tutor of the new Visigothic king, was chosen as emperor. Theoderic II was ordered by Avitus to invade Spain to counter the expansion of the Suevic power in the peninsula.[2] This objective was achieved by the defeat and subsequent killing of Theoderic's brother-in-law, the Suevic king Rechiarius, at the battle on the river Orbigo in 456. The Suevic kingdom rapidly broke up, and Visigothic control was established over most of the south and the east of Spain.

Avitus did not last long as emperor, not least because the Visigoths failed to provide him with adequate military assistance, and under his successor Majorian (457–61) there was renewed confrontation between the Visigoths and the imperial government. The Visigothic king made another unsuccessful attempt to take Arles in 458 and was defeated by the new emperor in 459. Theoderic's hold on much of Spain was, however, enhanced by the failure of Majorian's attempt to invade Africa in 460 and by the ensuing fragmentation of Roman imperial authority in the west. The Visigothic kingdom also extended itself in Gaul at this time. Thus, Narbonne was taken in 461, but the Visigoths encountered competitors in the north on the Loire, where they came in conflict with the former Roman general Aegidius. Theoderic's brother Frederic was killed in a battle against Aegidius in 463. Theoderic himself was murdered in 466 in a conspiracy led by his younger brother Euric. Sidonius Apollinaris provides in one of his letters (*Ep.* 1.2) both a pen portrait of Theoderic and a somewhat rhetorical account of daily life at his court.

Euric (466–84) took advantage of the disintegration of the power of the western emperors in the 470s to occupy the Auvergne in 474/5, and to

---

[2] Hydat. *Chron.* 173, ed. Tranoy *SChrét.* 218, p. 154. For dating see Muhlberger (1990) 279–311.

capture Arles and Marseilles in 476. In the same year, a Roman general in his service carried out an unsuccessful invasion of Italy. In Spain the remaining areas still under direct imperial rule, notably the province of Tarraconensis, were brought under Visigothic control by campaigns in the same decade.[3] Thus, by the end of Euric's reign the Visigothic kingdom extended from the Rhône to the Loire and also encompassed all but the north-western corner of the Iberian peninsula. Euric is recorded by Isidore of Seville as having issued laws, but it is not certain that the extant fragmentary code that is called the *Codex Euricanus* is his work or that of his son.[4] He is also reported by Gregory of Tours to have been a persecutor of his Catholic subjects, being, like most of the Visigoths, an Arian.[5] However, there is no contemporary evidence for such a view. Sidonius merely confirms that he was strongly committed to Arian theology.[6]

Further territorial expansion came to an end under Euric's son Alaric II (484–507), but considerable advances were made in the establishment of a stable Romano-Gothic state. These culminated in the holding of a major council of the Catholic church in the kingdom at Agde in 506, and the issuing in the same year of an abbreviated corpus of imperial laws and juristic writings that came to be known as *The Breviary of Alaric*.[7] Under this king, as under his father, a number of Gallo-Roman and Hispano-Roman landowners are found in royal service, and there are no real indications that the religious divide between Arians and Catholics served to undermine political loyalty to the Visigothic monarchy. Where Alaric II did face a problem was in the rising power of the Franks to the north of his kingdom. One consequence of this was the making of close ties with the Ostrogothic monarchy in Italy, symbolized not least by Alaric's marriage to Theodegotha, daughter of its ruler Theoderic (493–526). An alliance between the Frankish king Clovis and the Burgundian ruler Gundobad led to a joint attack on the Visigothic kingdom in 507. Alaric II was killed in battle against the Franks at Vouillé near Poitiers, and Toulouse was sacked. In the course of 507/8 all of the Visigothic kingdom north of the Pyrenees, other than the coastal region of Septimania, passed into Frankish control. In Spain, where Visigothic settlement may have been increasing since the 490s, what was effectively a new kingdom came into being in the aftermath of the battle of Vouillé.

II. THE BURGUNDIAN KINGDOM, 412–534

Following the collapse of the Rhine frontier in the winter of 406 and the migration across Gaul of the Vandal–Sueve–Alan confederacy, the

[3] *Chron. Gall. A* DXI, nos. 651–3, ed. Mommsen pp. 664–5.
[4] *Historia Gothorum* 35, ed. Rodríguez Alonso (1975) 228.
[5] *Historiae* 11.25, ed. Krusch and Levison, *MGH SRM* 1.70.1.   [6] Sid. Ap. *Ep.* 7.6.6.
[7] See ch. 10 (Charles-Edwards), p. 285 below.

Burgundians crossed the river and established a kingdom in the vicinity of Mainz. In the political vacuum that followed they gave their backing to the short-lived Gallic imperial regime of Iovinus (411–13) and Sebastianus (412–13). Little is known of the Burgundians after the destruction of these usurpers by the Visigoths. In 435 they negotiated a treaty with the Roman *magister militum*, Aetius, following some conflict, but soon after they were attacked by the Huns (436/7). The latter may have been in the employ of Aetius, as he used them against other groups in Gaul at this time. The Burgundian king Gundichar was killed and many of his followers massacred.[8] In 442 the survivors were established in Savoy, probably on the orders of Aetius. According to the *Chronicle of 452* this involved a division of lands, implying the application of the system of *hospitalitas*.[9] As in the case of the Visigoths, argument continues as to whether this should be taken to mean a physical division of estates or a fiscal procedure.

The Burgundians next appear, now under the rule of two kings, Gundioc and Chilperic I, as allies of the Visigoths. In 456 they accompanied Theoderic II on his campaign against the Suevic ruler Rechiarius, and in consequence were given more extensive lands to occupy, probably in the central Rhône valley and to the east of it. By 463 Gundioc had received the Roman military office of *magister militum*, possibly from his brother-in-law Ricimer, who dominated the imperial government in Italy at this time.[10] Nothing more is known of Chilperic I. Gundioc probably died in 473/4, and the kingdom was divided between his four sons. One of these, Gundobad, had succeeded his uncle Ricimer as *magister militum* in Italy in 472 and had provided the main military prop for the imperial regime of Glycerius (473–4). He abandoned Italy to go and contend with his brothers Godigisel, Chilperic II and Godomar for part of the Burgundian kingdom.

The settlement reached in 474 was unstable, and conflicts between the brothers continued. Chilperic II, who controlled Lyons and Geneva, was murdered by Gundobad at some unspecified date. In 500 Godigisel obtained the help of the Frankish king Clovis and was able to expel Gundobad from his kingdom, forcing him to take refuge in Avignon. However, after the Franks left, Gundobad besieged and captured Godigisel at Vienne and tortured him to death.[11] As nothing more is known of Godomar, it seems that Gundobad thereby reunited all the parts of the Burgundian kingdom under his own rule. He was an Arian, but was willing to receive theological treatises from Avitus, the Catholic bishop of Vienne. Various of the laws that he issued have survived in the code that was promulgated in the reign of his son.[12]

[8] Prosper, *Epit. Chron.* 1322, ed. Mommsen *MGH AA* 9, p. 475; *Chron. Gall. A* CCCCLII 118, ed. Mommsen p. 660.   [9] *Chron. Gall. A* CCCCLII 128, ed. Mommsen p. 660.   [10] *PLRE* II.523–4.

[11] *Marii Episcopi Aventicensis Chronica* s.a. 500, ed. Mommsen *MGH AA* 11, p. 234. On Chilperic II see Greg. Tur. *Hist.* II.28, ed. Krusch and Levison pp. 73–4.   [12] See ch. 10, pp. 284–6 below.

Gundobad's son Sigismund seems to have shared the kingdom prior to his father's death in 516, and during this joint reign he converted to Catholicism. He subsequently founded the monastery of Saint-Maurice at Agaune. His marriage to Ostrogotho, the daughter of Theoderic the Ostrogoth, was part of the complex web of diplomatic ties that the latter created for the defence of Italy. In 522 Sigismund, who had by this time remarried, executed his son Sigeric for his possible involvement in a conspiracy. This was certainly regarded by some as unjust, and may have contributed to the subsequent political weakness of the kingdom. In 523, in the course of a Frankish invasion, Sigismund and his family were surrendered by their own followers to the Frankish king Chlodomer, who subsequently had them thrown down a well near Orleans. Sigismund's brother Godomar (524–32) took over the kingdom, and held off a renewed Frankish attack in 524 in which Chlodomer was killed. Godomar was less lucky when they tried again in 532. He was defeated, captured and imprisoned, and in 534 the Burgundian kingdom was divided up between the Frankish monarchs.[13]

III. FRANKISH GAUL, 481–596

A Frankish presence was established in the far north-east of Gaul in the mid fourth century in the time of Magnentius (350–3), and the Franks were never thereafter dislodged. Other Franks remained east of the Rhine, and the limited nature of the evidence makes it impossible to delineate the cultural and political differences between the various groups. The breakdown of imperial administration and of the Roman military presence in the second half of the fifth century provided opportunities for some of the Frankish leaders to aggrandize themselves and build up powerful followings, in the way that various other Germanic military commanders were doing at this time.[14] The most successful of these was Childeric, whose probable tomb was discovered at Tournai in 1653. His power was built up partly on the basis of alliance with some of the competing Roman commanders jockeying for control of parts of northern Gaul in the 460s and possibly also on some support from his wife's people, the Thuringians. He may have helped Aegidius defeat the Visigoths on the Loire in 463. In 469 in alliance with a Roman count, Paul, he defeated Odoacer and an army of Saxons at Angers. In the late 470s he was discussing, probably with the same Odoacer, now established as king in Italy, a possible joint campaign against the Alamans.

On his death, usually dated by the implications of Gregory of Tours' narrative to 481, his son Clovis (481?–511?) took over the kingdom. Clovis

[13] In general the *Chronicle of Marius of Avenches* has here been followed in preference to Greg. Tur. *Hist.* III.5–6, ed. Krusch and Levison pp. 100–3. See also *PLRE* II: Gundobadus 1, Sigismund, Godomarus 2.   [14] Collins (1991) 94–108.

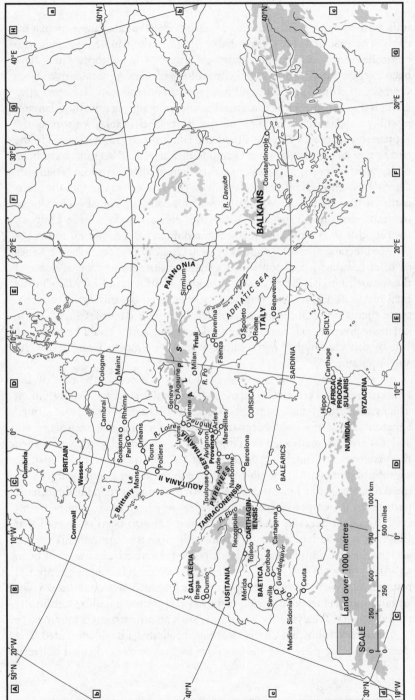

Map 5 The post-Roman west (places mentioned in chapter 5)

transformed its size and scale in a series of effective campaigns against his rivals. The first of these was probably Syagrius, the son of Aegidius, who controlled Soissons, though the wider extent of his authority may have been exaggerated.[15] The general chronology of Clovis' wars derives from Gregory of Tours' account, and has proved contentious.[16] It seems clear enough that in the 490s he undertook some campaign against the Alamans, possibly in alliance with some of the Rhineland Franks, known as the Ripuarians. In 500 he was the ally of the Burgundian king Godigisel in the latter's war against his brother Gundobad. This would seem to have been undertaken in return for payment rather than further territorial expansion. Clovis' best-known conflict was that with the Visigoths in 507. In the aftermath of the battle of Vouillé he and his Burgundian ally Gundobad overran virtually all of the Visigothic territories in Gaul. Only an Ostrogothic intervention in 508 prevented them from acquiring control of the Mediterranean coastal regions as well. Gregory of Tours places a series of brief campaigns and conspiracies leading to the elimination of some of the minor Frankish kings around Cologne, Cambrai and Le Mans in the final phase of Clovis' life, but he may have been organizing his material more thematically than chronologically. The exact date of Clovis' death, normally given as 511, is not easy to determine, and it could be as late as 513. By this time he had made himself master of most of northern Gaul and Aquitaine.

As well as for his military exploits, Clovis is noted as the first of the Frankish rulers to accept Christianity – though it is arguable that his father, usually thought of as a pagan, had been a Christian. Gregory of Tours' apparent dating of Clovis' baptism to the later 490s has not been accepted, and it is now normally seen as taking place in 508, linked to the war against the Visigoths. Although it is unlikely that his conversion led to an upsurge of support for him on the part of the Catholic Gallo-Roman subjects of the Arian Visigothic king, it did make Clovis a more acceptable diplomatic partner for the emperor Anastasius I, who awarded him an honorary consulship in 508. Recently and persuasively, it has also been suggested that Clovis may have had some flirtation with Arianism prior to his formal acceptance of Catholicism.[17] Indeed, it is possible that he had actually been an Arian. Equally plagued by later myth-making is Clovis' supposed responsibility for the first version of the Frankish law code, *Lex Salica*. Although this is frequently said to have been promulgated by him in the period 507–11, the evidence to support such an affirmation is minimal.[18]

The decade following Clovis' death is peculiarly badly documented. It is clear that by the early 520s his kingdom had come to be divided between

---

[15] James (1988b).   [16] Van de Vyver (1936, 1937, 1938).   [17] Wood (1985).
[18] See ch. 10 (Charles-Edwards), pp. 271–8 below.

his four sons: Theuderic I (511?–533), the product of a first marriage, and Chlodomer (511?–524), Childebert I (511?–558) and Chlothar I (511?–561) who came from his marriage to Chlothild, daughter of the Burgundian king Chilperic II. Like their father, these kings had to build up their own personal followings by effective war leadership to be able to acquire the land and treasure with which to reward their supporters. In this respect each presented a threat to the other, and such rivalries between members of the ruling house became a standard feature of the political life of sixth-century Gaul. Initially, however, a number of vulnerable neighbours presented the best opportunities for territorial aggrandizement. In 523 and 524 the three younger rulers combined against the Burgundian kingdom with some success at first. The death in battle of Chlodomer in 524 put an end to this, but provided alternative rewards: Childebert and Chlothar murdered his children and divided his kingdom up between them.

The best opportunities for building up a powerful realm probably existed along the eastern frontiers of Francia. This area was dominated by the senior branch of the descendants of Clovis in the persons of Theuderic I (c. 511–33) and his son Theudebert I (533–48). They built up a hegemony over most of the peoples living immediately to the east of the Rhine, notably the Frisians, the Jutes, the Saxons and the Thuringians. The outbreak of war between the emperor Justinian and the Ostrogothic kingdom in 535 provided fresh ways of expansion. Theudebert in a series of extant letters presented himself to Justinian as a powerful potential Catholic ally against the Arian Goths.[19] At the same time he negotiated with the Ostrogoths, who sought, if not his active help, then at least his neutrality. Their king Vitigis ceded Provence to Theudebert in 536 with just such a hope. In the outcome, Theudebert deceived both sides and in 539 invaded Italy to try to annex more territory. Although, after taking Milan, his expedition was forced to retreat by the outbreak of disease, Frankish control was established over several regions in the north of Italy. These were eventually regained by the empire in the time of his son Theudebald (548–55). It is possible that Theudebert aspired to even greater things, and Justinian ceded northern Pannonia to the Lombards not least to block the perceived threat of a Frankish move into the Balkans, possibly aimed at Constantinople.

The early death of Theudebald brought this branch of the Merovingian dynasty (so named from Clovis' possible grandfather Merovech) to an end. The kingdom built up by these monarchs was taken over by Chlothar I, but the Frankish position east of the Rhine began to weaken immediately, with successful Saxon revolts. This shrinking of the eastern territories did not immediately matter in that, on the death without heirs of his brother

---

[19] *Epist. Austras.* 18–20, ed. Gundlach *MGH SRM* III, pp. 131–3.

Childebert I in 558, Chlothar was able to unite all of the Frankish kingdoms under himself. However, Chlothar faced problems within his own immediate family through the ambitions of his eldest son Chramn, who had conspired with Childebert, perhaps hoping to succeed to the latter's kingdom, and who rebelled in 560 in Brittany. He was defeated and burnt to death along with his family.

The death of Chlothar I led to a new partition of the Frankish territories amongst his four surviving sons: Charibert I (561–7), Sigebert I (561–75), Chilperic I (561–84) and Guntramn (561–92). Each had a primary residence – Paris, Rheims, Soissons and Orleans respectively – but, as in the division following the death of Clovis, compact territorial kingdoms were not created. Each brother had an interest in most parts of Francia, and enclaves of one kingdom might be found in territory largely belonging to another. Such apparent anomalies are probably explained by the pattern of personal adherence to the various monarchs on the part of the leading Frankish and Gallo-Roman (a distinction that was becoming harder to make in most parts of Gaul) landowners. Changes in allegiance could have considerable impact on the strength of the individual kingdoms, and competition between the monarchs was intensified by the increasing difficulties to be faced in trying to expand their territories. The Frankish hegemony over peoples east of the Rhine became increasingly tenuous at this time and was threatened by Avar pressure. The Lombards established a kingdom in Italy after 568, and Visigothic resistance to Frankish raids across the Pyrenees became more effective in the reign of Reccared (586–601).

The death of Charibert I in 567 enabled his brothers to divide his kingdom, but open conflict between them soon followed. Chilperic tried to take Tours and Poitiers, which were in that part of Charibert's former kingdom claimed by Sigebert, and civil war ensued. Guntramn, who had a territorial dispute of his own with Sigebert, was persuaded to join Chilperic. Although forced to make peace in 574, Chilperic and Guntramn resumed the fighting in 575. Following the defeat of Chilperic near Rheims, Guntramn made a separate peace. Chilperic's kingdom was only saved from being overrun when, thanks probably to his wife Fredegund, hired assassins murdered Sigebert. Sigebert's kingdom passed to his son Childebert II (575–96), who was still a minor. The same occurred after the murder of Chilperic in 584, when his kingdom passed to his young son Chlothar II (584–629). In both cases the presence of an under-age king exacerbated factional conflicts amongst the aristocracy, jockeying for power and the prospects of enhanced rewards, either at a local level or in the royal courts. The premature death of his sons had left Guntramn with no male heirs, and in 585 he came to an agreement with Childebert II, who thereby inherited his uncle's kingdom on his death in 592. This left Childebert as by far the more powerful of the two surviving Merovingian monarchs, but on his own death when aged only twenty-five, his realm was redivided between his two young sons, Theudebert II (596–612) and Theuderic II (596–613).

IV. SPAIN: THE SUEVIC KINGDOMS, 425–584

The Sueves who entered the Iberian peninsula in 409 benefited from the elimination by the Visigoths of two of the other components of their confederacy, the Siling Vandals and the Alans, in 417/18, and then from the removal of the other remaining ally, the Hasding Vandals, into Africa in 429. This left them free to expand their authority from the north-west of the peninsula, where they had first established themselves, over most of the south and the centre as well. Under their king Rechila (438–48) the provinces of Baetica and Lusitania were conquered by 441, and from 439 Mérida became the Suevic capital. A last imperial attempt to regain these regions was defeated in 446. Rechila's son Rechiarius (448–56) was the first Germanic king to become a Catholic Christian, and his decision would suggest that the Sueves, previously noted for their plundering of the Galician civilians, were looking towards better relations with their new Hispano-Roman subjects and with the vestigial imperial government. After conducting raids in the Ebro valley in 448 and 449 Rechiarius made a treaty with Rome in 452, which was renewed in 454. However, when in 455 Rechiarius invaded the province of Tarraconensis, the last portion of the peninsula to remain under rule from Rome, his brother-in-law, the Visigothic king Theoderic II, was sent against him by the emperor Avitus (455–7). In 456 Rechiarius was defeated in a battle on the river Orbigo, captured and executed (see p. 113 above). In the aftermath the Visigoths established their rule over much of the former Suevic kingdom in the south and the east, leaving a series of rival Suevic leaders to fight for dominance in the north-west. One of these, Rechimund (459–61), may have been related to the previous royal dynasty, but the other competitors – Maldras (456–60), Framtano (457–8), Frumarius (460–5) and Remismund (464–?) – probably were not.[20] Under the last of these the Sueves were once more united, and Remismund is recorded as opening diplomatic links with the emperor Leo I when faced with renewed conflict with the Visigoths.

The termination of the *Chronicle* of Hydatius in 469 marks a caesura in information on the Sueves, and it is not until the mid sixth century that they re-emerge into historiographical light. Confined to the north-west, in more or less the boundaries of the province of Gallaecia, the Suevic kingdom was now surrounded by that of the Visigoths, under whose influence a

---

[20] Chronology followed is that of Muhlberger (1990) 308–11; that in the entries in *PLRE* II can be erroneous.

conversion to Arian Christianity had taken place at some unknown period. However, communications were maintained by sea with the west coast of France and the Loire valley. Contacts with Tours, including the despatch from there of some relics of St Martin, played a part in the conversion of the Sueves from Arian to Catholic belief. Another important participant in this poorly reported process was the Pannonian ascetic Martin, who established a monastery at Dumio (Guimarães) and subsequently became bishop of Braga. The dating of these events is uncertain but must have preceded the holding of the first council of the Catholic bishops in the Suevic kingdom at Braga in 561. This was in the third year of the reign of a king Ariamir. By the time of the holding of a second council in 572 the monarch was Miro (570–83). Politically the Suevic kingdom was still overshadowed by that of the Visigoths, and Miro died while aiding the Visigothic king Leovigild in the latter's civil war with his son Hermenegild. When Miro's son Eboric (583–4) was overthrown by a certain Audeca, Leovigild invaded the kingdom in 585. As the *Chronicle* of John of Biclar describes it, he 'placed the people of the Sueves, their treasure and their homeland under his power, making it a province of the Goths'.[21] It was never re-established.

V. VISIGOTHIC SPAIN, 456–601

The permanent extension of Visigothic power into the Iberian peninsula resulted from the campaign undertaken by Theoderic II (453–66) against the Sueves in 456. Much of Baetica, Carthaginiensis and southern Lusitania came under Visigothic rule as a consequence, and Tarraconensis was added as the result of campaigns carried out by the generals of the next Visigothic king, Euric (466–84) in 474/6. Only northern Lusitania and Gallaecia then remained outside the kingdom, which continued to be centred on Toulouse. References in the marginalia to two manuscripts of the *Chronicle* of Victor of Tunnuna, which have been ascribed to an otherwise lost 'Chronicle of Zaragoza', suggest that a more intensive Visigothic settlement of Spain took place in the 490s. This may have facilitated the survival of the kingdom in the aftermath of the battle of Vouillé in 507. While most of the Visigothic territories in Gaul were then overrun by the Franks and the Burgundians, Spain was retained and Narbonne and then Barcelona replaced Toulouse as the royal centre.

After Alaric II's death at Vouillé the kingship was taken by his illegitimate son Gesalic (507–11), but he was subsequently ejected by Ostrogothic forces sent by Theoderic to install his grandson Amalaric (511–31). This king, the son of Alaric II by his marriage to Theoderic's daughter Theodegotha, was still a child, and effective power seems to have remained

---

[21] *Chronicon* anno III Mauricii, 2, ed. J. Campos (1960) 93.

in the hands of Ostrogothic regents appointed by Theoderic. Only on the latter's death in 526 did Amalaric exercise personal rule. In 531 he was defeated by the Franks near Narbonne and was murdered at Barcelona while in flight. He was replaced by the Ostrogothic general Theoderic, also known as Theudis (531–48), who had previously served as regent during the minority of Amalaric. Little is known of his reign, but in his time the Catholic church in Spain was able to hold a number of provincial councils. An attempt to extend the kingdom into North Africa proved abortive. Ceuta was occupied by a Visigothic army, but they were rapidly expelled by eastern Roman forces. Theudis was murdered in consequence of an obscure personal vendetta, a fate that also befell his successor, Theudisclus (548–9).

A period of weakness for the monarchy ensued. The next king, Agila (549–54), provoked a revolt in Córdoba and, in trying to suppress it, was defeated, lost his treasure and had his son killed. Another Visigothic noble called Athanagild (552–68) soon after rebelled against him in Seville. In 552, during the course of the ensuing civil war, the emperor Justinian sent an army to assist one of the parties, which then succeeded in establishing an imperial enclave along the south-east coast of the peninsula from Cartagena to Medina Sidonia, though not extending into the Guadalquivir valley as is sometimes assumed.[22] Although this hostile presence never developed into the full-scale attempt at imperial reconquest that had taken place in Africa and Italy, this territory was not finally recovered by the Visigothic kingdom until the mid 620s. After Justinian's expedition, led by Liberius, had established itself, the unsuccessful Agila was murdered by his own men in Mérida. Athanagild, having reunited the kingdom and established a new capital at Toledo, failed to make headway against the imperial forces in the south-east. Since he lacked male heirs, another Visigothic noble, Liuva I (568–73), was chosen as king on his death.

Faced with Frankish threats on the Pyrenees and in Septimania, the new king established his brother Leovigild (569–86) as joint ruler, initially with responsibility for the south. This new monarch was by far the most effective Visigothic ruler since the fifth century. In a series of campaigns in the 570s he regained some of the imperial territory in the south, reconquered Córdoba, which had been lost by Agila, and suppressed various independent local authorities that had come into being in the north of the peninsula. He also fought against the Basques, and established a new town in the middle of Spain, which he called Reccopolis after his second son Reccared. In 579 he set up his elder son Hermenegild as joint ruler in the south, but in 580 the latter broke free of his father's control. When Hermenegild began to negotiate with the emperor and, probably in 582,

---

[22] Thompson (1969) 320–34.

became the first Visigothic king to convert from Arianism to Catholicism, Leovigild invaded his kingdom. Mérida was taken in 582, Seville in 583 and Córdoba in 584. Hermenegild, sent into internal exile, was subsequently killed.

This conflict should not be regarded as a religious war, but it did make clear the need to resolve the religious divide. Leovigild had reunited virtually all of the peninsula, a process that culminated in his conquest of the Suevic kingdom in 585, and had rebuilt the power and prestige of the Visigothic monarchy. However, the Catholic church, whose bishops were often the most influential local notables and whose interests were best served by a strengthened central government, could not rally to the cause of an uncompromisingly Arian king. Although there were rumours that Leovigild contemplated conversion in the last phase of his reign, it was left to his son Reccared (586–601) to take this step. Following the king's own personal conversion in 587, most of the Arian clergy followed suit, and in 589 a great ecclesiastical council was held in Toledo to celebrate the formal conversion of the Visigoths, and to settle any outstanding practical problems. Some local Visigothic potentates and some of the Arian metropolitan bishops, who stood to lose their regional authority, tried to resist this process, and a number of unsuccessful revolts occurred in the years 587–90. From this point on, however, the issue became a dead one.

VI. VANDAL AFRICA, 429–533

Of the four components of the loose confederacy of peoples that crossed the Rhine in the winter of 406/7 and entered Spain in 409, the Alans and the Siling Vandals were perhaps the most powerful, and they established themselves in the richest parts of the Iberian peninsula. However, they were destroyed as coherent units by the Visigoths in 416/17, and the survivors merged with the Hasding Vandals under their king Gunderic (406–28). They were subjected to attack by imperial armies in 422, and it may have been their inability to achieve a treaty with the Roman government that drove them into moving to the potentially greater safety of North Africa in 429. On the other hand, there may be some truth in the report of Procopius that they were invited to cross into Africa by its military ruler Boniface, who was then in conflict with Felix, *magister militum* in Italy.[23]

Following the crossing of the straits the Vandals, now led by Gunderic's half-brother Geiseric (428–77), moved eastwards along the coast, and took Hippo following a siege in 430. In 435 a treaty was made with the imperial government, giving them control of coastal Numidia. In 439 Geiseric

[23] Procop. *Wars* III.3.23–4.

broke this by invading the province of Africa Proconsularis and capturing Carthage. In 440 a Vandal fleet raided Sicily. Under Aetius the western empire was too involved in conflict with the Visigoths in Gaul to undertake any punitive measures. An eastern expedition sent by Theodosius II in 441 only proceeded as far as Sicily, and in 442 the western government made a new treaty with the Vandals. This placed the provinces of Proconsularis, Byzacena and eastern Numidia under their control. A future marriage between Geiseric's son Huneric and Eudocia, the daughter of Valentinian III, may have been an element in this treaty, and this justified Geiseric's despatch of a fleet to Rome in 455 when Valentinian was overthrown by Petronius Maximus, and Eudocia forcibly married to the new emperor's son. Rome was subjected to a second and perhaps more vigorous sack, and Valentinian III's widow and daughters were taken back to Carthage. At the same time Corsica and the Balearic islands were subjected to Vandal rule, and Sardinia was added in 468.

The Vandal attack on Rome, and the wider damage inflicted around the western Mediterranean littoral by Vandal sea-power, made the elimination of their kingdom in Africa a primary aim of imperial policy over the next few decades. In 460 and 468 naval expeditions were planned against the kingdom. In the first case, the western fleet was captured near Cartagena, and the second fleet, sent by Leo I, was destroyed by fire ships on the African coast. In 472 the western regime controlled by Ricimer came to terms with Geiseric, making his son's brother-in-law, Olybrius, emperor. A treaty was made subsequently with the eastern emperor Zeno, probably in 476. Despite this high degree of success in repelling imperial attempts at the reconquest of Africa and in making themselves masters of all the larger islands in the western Mediterranean, the Vandals were less successful militarily in Africa in combating the growing pressure of the Berbers. The former imperial *limes* in the south could not be maintained, and the Vandal army suffered a major defeat by the Berbers in the reign of Thrasamund (496–523) and another under Hilderic (523–30).[24]

Geiseric and the Vandals had regarded the African provincials, especially the Roman nobility, with considerable suspicion. Members of many leading families were exiled and had their lands expropriated. Similarly, the religious conflict between Arian Vandals and Catholic Romans was unusually savage. Many Catholic bishops and priests were subjected to internal exile, and their churches and landed endowments given to Arians instead. A highly coloured account of their suffering was presented in Victor of Vita's *History of the Persecution of the African Province* of c. 484. Both of these phenomena appear symptomatic of considerable unease on the part of the Vandal rulers, and it is very probable that there was no significant settlement of the

[24] Procop. *Wars* III.8.14–29; 9.3.

Germanic population on the land. The ill-treatment of the Catholic clergy, which had begun under Geiseric, intensified under Huneric (477–84). His brother Gunthamund (484–96) reversed this policy and permitted the Catholic clergy and others to return from exile. In the reign of Thrasamund (496–523), another of the sons of Geiseric, bishops once more were exiled, this time primarily to Sardinia. However, this monarch allowed some of the exiled bishops to return, and even permitted Arian–Catholic theological debates. His successor Hilderic (523–30), the son of Huneric, was also, through his mother Eudocia, a grandson of Valentinian III and perhaps in consequence the most Romanophile of the Vandal kings. He finally put an end to the exile of the Catholic bishops, which had been reimposed in the last years of Thrasamund, and made amicable diplomatic advances to the empire. This reversed a previous policy of closer ties with the Ostrogothic kingdom in Italy, symbolized by his predecessor Thrasamund's marriage to Amalafrida, the sister of Theoderic.

These moves on the part of Hilderic led to his overthrow by his nephew Gailamir in 530, and this in turn proved to be the diplomatic *casus belli* that led in 533 to the emperor Justinian I sending an expedition, ostensibly to restore Hilderic. A rebellion was fomented in Sardinia, which led to the despatch there of an army and fleet under Gailamir's brother Tzazo, and this enabled the imperial expedition led by Belisarius to reach Africa and disembark unchallenged. Landing ten miles from Carthage, Belisarius advanced on the city and defeated Gailamir and a hastily assembled army. When Tzazo and his forces had been recalled from Sardinia, Gailaimir attempted to retake Carthage but was convincingly defeated. His brother was killed and he and his remaining followers retreated into Numidia. They were blockaded in the mountains, and forced to surrender in 534. The remaining Vandals were then shipped back to Constantinople to be absorbed into the imperial army. As a distinct ethnic unit they disappeared.

VII. OSTROGOTHIC ITALY, 493–535

The Ostrogothic invasion of Italy that followed from the agreement made in 488 between their king Theoderic and the emperor Zeno helped to give this people a new identity. For the previous forty years a very mixed Germanic population had maintained itself precariously in the eastern Balkans under a variety of rival leaders. In the later historiographical tradition of the Italian Ostrogothic kingdom, this was presented as a conflict between a legitimate and supposedly ancient Amal dynasty and such *parvenus* as Theoderic Strabo (d. 481) and his son Recitach (d. 484). It was only on the murder of the latter, which Theoderic the Amal arranged for Zeno, that the various rival groups were first united under a single leader. Failing to obtain a secure position in imperial service, Theoderic was persuaded to take his confederacy to Italy to dispossess Odoacer (476–93). The ensuing migration and four years of fighting began the process of uniting these disparate Germanic elements into a more coherent and ethnically self-conscious people.[25]

The Ostrogothic conquest of Italy was initially hard-fought. Moving westwards, they had to defeat the Gepids around Sirmium in 488 before forcing their way into Italy in August 489. Odoacer was defeated in battle twice that year and again in 490, after he had for a while besieged Theoderic in Pavia. After a battle near the Addua in August, Odoacer fled to Ravenna, which the Ostrogoths proved unable to take. The blockade of the city lasted until 493, when an agreement was finally made whereby Theoderic and Odoacer undertook joint rule of Italy. This proved meaningless, as, once admitted to the city, Theoderic rapidly secured the murder of Odoacer and his family. Such an outcome may have been prompted by the attitude of some of the leading Roman office-holders who refused to enter Theoderic's service while their former master still lived. This was the position of Liberius, who became praetorian prefect of Italy immediately following Odoacer's death.[26] In general, the seizure of power by Theoderic was marked by remarkable continuity as far as the Roman aristocracy was concerned. Families and individuals who had served Odoacer continued to hold office under the Ostrogoths. Despite some initial hesitation, and following three embassies to Constantinople, the new eastern emperor Anastasius I (492–518) finally recognized Theoderic as ruler of Italy around 497.

The Roman landowners had already found the regime of Odoacer an improvement on the political instability and military disorder of the last twenty years of western imperial rule, and they were to benefit even more from the government of Theoderic.[27] In particular, the external security of Italy attained a level previously unmatched in the fifth century. The defeats of the Alamans at the hands of the Franks in the 490s led a significant body of them to put themselves under Theoderic's protection. They were then settled in the Alps to defend the northern passes into Italy. Further north, the defence of Italy and a wider stability in the region were augmented by an alliance with the Thuringians. In 510 the Thuringian king Herminafrid married Theoderic's niece Amalaberga. The eastern approaches were secured by the conquest of Pannonia in 504–5. Theoderic's general Pitzia took Sirmium from the Gepids and defeated a Bulgar army sent by the emperor. The Heruls on the Danube were also at this time brought into the Ostrogothic political orbit – a change marked by Theoderic's adoption of their king Rodulf as his 'son by arms'. To the south, good relations were

---

[25] Heather, *Goths and Romans* 227–308.   [26] *PLRE* II, *s.v.* Liberius 3, 677–81.
[27] See ch. 19 (Humphries), pp. 544–8 below.

achieved with Vandal Africa; this new concord was again symbolized by a marriage, that of Theoderic's sister to the Vandal king Thrasamund (496–523). To the west, the dominance in southern Gaul of the Visigoths, who had sent help to Theoderic in 490, was assured by family ties and sentiments of common ethnicity.

This western Mediterranean 'co-prosperity sphere' that Theoderic and his advisers created was to prove fragile. The empire, initially grudgingly tolerant of Theoderic's position, became hostile after the Ostrogothic seizure of Pannonia. An imperial fleet was despatched to the Adriatic in 508 and carried out some raids on the Italian coast, but the troubled internal politics of the empire in the second half of the reign of Anastasius prevented the outbreak of more extensive hostilities. Anastasius turned instead to the use of diplomatic means to try to undermine the Ostrogothic kingdom. This was well matched by the territorial ambitions of the Frankish king Clovis, whose hopes of expansion southwards were blocked by the Gothic presence. In the aftermath of the defeat of the Visigoths at Vouillé in 507, Theoderic was forced to intervene directly in Gaul and annex Provence to secure the western approaches to Italy. In 511 he brought the whole Visigothic kingdom under his hegemony, by sending an army to expel Gesalic and to install his grandson Amalaric (511–31) as king. Frankish aggression, abetted by imperial diplomacy, was held in check, but the Herul kingdom was destroyed in 510 by the Lombards. The Thuringians at least remained secure until after Theoderic's death in 526. Only in 534 was their kingdom overrun by the Franks and Herminafrid killed. In the south, Vandal friendship with the Ostrogothic kingdom survived until Hilderic succeeded Thrasamund in 523, when the new king's *rapprochement* with Constantinople led Theoderic to order the building of a fleet in 526 against the possibility of attacks from Africa.

Internally, Theoderic's achievements were potentially longer-lasting. His programme of public works, involving the building or restoring of aqueducts, baths, defensive walls and palaces in many of the principal cities of Italy, conferred immediate benefits and gave a sense of patronage that was imperial in character, as was his formal *adventus* into the city of Rome in 500. Public entertainments and charities were also supported, including a restoration of the corn dole to the poor of Rome. This emphasis on the revival of traditional features of public life, together with the use made of senators in the administration, seems to have endeared Theoderic's regime to many of the Roman aristocracy. Others were less willing to see the rule of an Arian Germanic soldier as a permanent replacement for imperial government, and such sentiments surfaced in the accusations made against Boethius, the former consul and *magister officiorum*. He was accused by some fellow senators, late in 523, of shielding traitors in the senate. After trial by the *praefectus urbis*, he was condemned and executed in 524. Despite his later reputation and the propagandistic use of the episode in subsequent imperial historiography, there is no evidence that this and the parallel execution of his father-in-law Symmachus led to any alienation of the Roman aristocracy from the regime of Theoderic.

The Ostrogothic king was faced with problems over his succession. Lacking a son of his own, in 515 he married his daughter Amalasuintha to Eutharic, a member of a collateral branch of the Amal dynasty living in Spain. The emperor Justin I (518–27), who was initially less hostile to the Ostrogothic kingdom than his predecessor, adopted Eutharic as his 'son by arms' and shared the consulship with him in 519. However, Eutharic predeceased Theoderic, who left the throne to his ten-year-old grandson Athalaric (526–34) under the tutelage of Amalasuintha. The problems of a minority were always acute in Germanic military societies, and Amalasuintha apparently resorted to violent measures to maintain her authority. She is said to have had several of her opponents murdered. The death of her son in 534 left her unable to rule in her own right, and she was forced to concede the crown to the senior male member of the family, Theodahad (534–6), a nephew of Theoderic. Her attempts to continue to exercise influence led him to have her imprisoned on an island, where she was murdered, apparently by the relatives of those she herself had had killed.[28]

This, following the precedent used to justify the imperial invasion of the Vandal kingdom in 533, was made the excuse for the despatch of Belisarius' army from Africa to Sicily in 535 and then on to Italy in 536. Theodahad failed to take any effective action against the imperial forces, and after Naples fell to Belisarius the leading Gothic nobles deposed him. He was subsequently murdered on the orders of his successor while trying to escape to Ravenna. Under the new king Vitigis (536–9), who was not a member of the Amal dynasty but who married Athalaric's sister Matasuintha, more energetic measures were taken to try to stem the imperial advance. However, Belisarius was allowed to occupy Rome and a subsequent siege failed to dislodge him. When a second imperial army took Rimini, threatening to cut Vitigis off from his capital, he was forced to retreat to Ravenna. Blockaded there, he submitted in 539, having allowed himself to be persuaded that Belisarius would proclaim himself emperor if admitted to Ravenna. In 540 Vitigis and those Ostrogoths with him in Ravenna, despite the existence of an earlier plan to establish a reduced Ostrogothic kingdom north of the Po as a buffer for Italy, were shipped off to Constantinople and incorporated into the imperial forces. This was due to the acute military needs of the empire, resulting from the Persian invasion of the eastern provinces, something that Vitigis is said to have tried to persuade the shah Khusro I to undertake in the final stages of the war in Italy.

---

[28] Procop. *Wars* v.4.25–7, in preference to Jord. *Get.* 306.

Despite the loss of Ravenna, many other major towns of northern Italy were still in the hands of Ostrogothic garrisons, and in 540 fighting was renewed when it was clear that Belisarius was not going to honour his secret pledges to make himself western emperor. A new king was chosen in the person of Ildibad (540–1). After his murder, the crown passed rapidly to his nephew Baduila or Totila (541–52), who won a significant victory over imperial forces at Faenza in 542. The scale of the renewed war was such that Belisarius had to be sent back to Italy in 544, but he failed to achieve the same dramatic results. Baduila took Rome in December 546, was forced to abandon it in 547 and regained it in 550. Belisarius was recalled in 548 and eventually replaced by the emperor Justinian's cousin Germanus, who had married Vitigis' widow Matasuintha. On Germanus' unexpected death *en route* for Italy in 550, the eunuch and former treasurer Narses was given command, and he inflicted a crucial defeat on Baduila in the battle of Busta Gallorum in June/July 552. Baduila died from wounds received there and was succeeded briefly by Teias (552), former commander in Verona. He too fell in battle against Narses, at Mons Lactarius in October. Some of the northern towns continued to resist, and the last of these, Verona, only fell in 562, but no Ostrogothic king was chosen after Teias.

VIII. ITALY: THE LOMBARDS, 568–90

It appears ironic that the restoration of imperial rule over Italy, that was so long and hard fought for, should have proved so short-lived. Within six years of the extinguishing of the last Ostrogothic resistance in 562, Italy was subjected to a new invasion, that of the Lombards. This people had been one of those who had moved into the vacuum north of the Danube caused by Odoacer's elimination of the Rugi in 488. They had fallen into subjection to the Heruls, but defeated them in 510, killing their king Rodulf. In the 540s they were encouraged by Justinian to cross the Danube into western Pannonia as a counter to possible Frankish aspirations in the Balkans. They shared this role with the Gepids, who were again given control of Sirmium, which they had lost to the Ostrogoths in 504, and, with the Heruls, were established around Singidunum. Justin II reversed his predecessor's policy of generally favouring the Lombards in their periodic conflicts with the Gepids, and in consequence the Lombards allied themselves with the rising power of the Avars, north of the Danube. The destruction of the Gepid kingdom of Sirmium by the Avars in 567 seems to have led the Lombards to decide to put a greater distance between themselves and their quondam allies. In later traditions, their move into Italy was presented as the result of treasonable negotiation on the part of

Narses, who had been dismissed from his Italian command by the new emperor.[29]

The Lombards were unable to achieve the unifying conquest of all Italy that had been possible for the Ostrogoths. This was because they failed to take either Rome or Ravenna, and were faced with unremitting imperial hostility. Some cities, such as Milan, capitulated without a fight; others; such as Pavia, which held out for three years, offered spirited resistance. The murder of king Alboin at Verona in 572 weakened the already stretched political cohesion of the invaders. His murderers, who favoured a *rapprochement* with the empire, fled with the royal treasure to the imperial governor or exarch at Ravenna. Although a new king, unrelated to the previous dynasty, was elected in the person of Cleph (572–3/4), his subsequent murder undermined centralized authority amongst the Lombards entirely. No new king was chosen for ten years, while regional potentates emerged in the persons of the dukes (*duces*). Although initially royal appointees as local military commanders, these men were able to establish themselves as effectively independent rulers in the absence of a monarchy. Only when the Frankish threat grew too great in the early 580s did the Lombard magnates accept the need to recreate a central leadership, and thus to choose a new king in the person of Authari (584–90), the son of Cleph. To reconstruct the economic basis for the monarchy the dukes agreed to surrender a fixed proportion of their assets to endow the revived royal house. In practice the more numerous and territorially smaller northern duchies co-operated more closely with the monarchy than the two large central and southern Italian duchies of Spoleto and Benevento, which may first have come into being during the interregnum, and were physically much further removed from the royal capital of Pavia. Not until the reign of Authari's successor Agilulf (590–616) was royal authority firmly imposed over the south.

The Frankish threat that had led to the recreation of the Lombard monarchy was the product partly of the expansionary ambitions of king Childebert II (575–96) and partly the product of imperial diplomacy. The military and economic problems of the empire in the 580s meant that large-scale intervention in Italy could not be undertaken from Constantinople. However, the Franks, who had suffered from Lombard raids across the Alps in the chaotic period of 568–70, were willing to act for the emperor in return for subsidies.[30] Although Childebert II was prone to take the imperial money and then fail to act, he did launch an expedition in 585 and again in 590. In both cases Authari negotiated a withdrawal in return for a formal submission and, doubtless, the payment of tribute.

---

[29] Isidore of Seville, *Chronica* 402, ed. Mommsen *MGH AA* 11, p. 476; Fredegar, *Chronica* III.65, ed. Kusternig, p. 134; Paul. Diac. *Hist. Lang.* II.5, *MGH SRG*, pp. 87–8.

[30] *Epist. Austras.* 25, 31–48, ed. Gundlach, pp. 138–9, 141–52.

Under his successor the Frankish threat receded, and the Lombard kingdom became more securely established.

The collapse of Roman provincial administration in Britain following the usurper Constantine III's departure from the island in 407 seems to have been followed fairly rapidly by the fragmentation of political authority. The principal problem to be faced in trying to understand these processes is the almost total lack of reliable evidence.[31] The testimony of the early-ninth-century *Historia Britonum*, also known from its supposed author as 'Nennius', is now largely discredited. There are no good evidential grounds for believing in the existence of a king Vortigern, let alone of an Arthur, but rulers of a still more or less united Britain may have existed for some decades after the end of imperial control. It is at least clear from the testimony of the *De Excidio Britonum* of Gildas (520/40) that a certain Ambrosius Aurelianus served at least as military leader of the Britons in the later fifth century.[32] By the time Gildas himself was writing there existed, certainly in western Britain from Cornwall through the Severn valley and up to Gwynedd, a series of small kingdoms ruled by dynasties whose members had Celtic names.

The military problems that the public authorities in Britain, whatever their character might have been, had to face came firstly in the form of sea-borne raiding by the Picts and by the Irish (the Scotti). An appeal to Aetius, probably in the period 446–54, failed to provide imperial assistance, and it seems, on the basis of Gildas' narrative, that increasing recourse had to be made to the Saxons for defence against these attacks. Although much debated, the dating of the start of this process cannot be given more precisely than *c.* 410–42.[33] The Saxons who came to settle, probably under some form of treaty of federation, in turn became a problem in their own right, demanding increased *annona*, in other words pay for their services. This led to a revolt and fighting between the Saxons and the British provincials, before a victory, probably of the latter, at the siege of Mons Badonius (*c.* 490) led to a peace that had still not been broken when Gildas was writing forty-four years later.

Just as the history of the British has been obscured by later legendary traditions, so too was that of the Anglo-Saxons affected by subsequent distortion and rationalization. By the middle of the seventh century a series of distinct, and in some cases quite substantial, kingdoms had come into

[31] Dumville (1977) 173–92.   [32] *De Excidio* 25.3, ed. M. Winterbottom (Chichester 1978) p. 98.
[33] *Chron. Gall.* A CCCCLII 126, ed. Mommsen, p. 660.

being throughout most of Britain. The origins of these were in several cases, through genealogical fabrication or historiographical invention, pushed back into earlier periods, and distinct ethnic identities were accorded them. However, the reality of conditions in the later fifth and sixth centuries was rather different. The picture that should emerge is one not of Germanic Saxons or Angles fighting against Celtic Britons and gradually squeezing them back into what would become Wales, Cumbria and Cornwall, so much as an entrepreneurial mêlée in which individual rulers and dynasties emerged in many different localities, depending on warfare against their neighbours to build up military followings. The population for such fluctuating kingdoms was ethnically mixed, consisting of Germanic and Celtic elements. Inevitably, because of the initial establishment of the Germanic federates in the east of the island, the cultural and ultimately linguistic mix took the form of a spectrum, with Germanic elements predominant in the east and Celtic ones in the west, and complex intermixtures of the two in the centre, notably the areas of the later kingdoms of Wessex, Mercia and Northumbria.

Evidential problems also abound with respect to the history of the Celtic kingdoms to the north of Hadrian's Wall, of the Pictish ones beyond them and of Ireland. In the case of the British ones in the north, some continuities can be traced between them and some of the Celtic tribes that existed in these regions in the early Roman period, though some of the tribes had clearly disappeared entirely. By the end of the sixth century the most powerful of these was probably the kingdom of Gododdin (the former Votadini), centred on Edinburgh, whose king's disastrous military expedition against the Anglian kingdom of Northumbria is recorded in the elusive verses ascribed to the poet Aneirin and known as *Y Gododdin*.[34] Another British kingdom, that of Strathclyde, existed around the Firth of Clyde, with its capital at Dumbarton, and to the south of it lay the kingdom of Rheged in Cumbria. Culturally distinct from these were the kingdom(s) of the Picts. Only references concerning the fifth-century missionary ventures of Nynia, based in Whithorn in Galloway, and of the Irish monk Columba (d. 597), founder of the monastery of Iona, have led to the deduction that two separate Pictish kingdoms or tribal confederacies, a northern and a southern one, existed at this time.

Similarly in Ireland, which was a pre-literate society until the beginning of Christian missionary activity there in the fifth century, it is only the letters of Patrick that give any reliable clue as to political organization. Later materials, notably the various *Lives* of Patrick and the annals which probably did not start being kept until the mid eighth century, cannot be relied upon to provide objective records of the earlier period.[35] In particular, the

---

[34] Jarman (ed.) (1988).   [35] Hughes (1972) 97–159, 219–32, but cf. Smyth (1972).

growth of the claims of the church of Armagh and its manipulation of its Patrician foundation led to the fabrication of complex historical myths. What relationship the political organization of Ireland in the fifth century had to that in the seventh or the ninth is not as easy to say as has sometimes been believed.

In general, the fifth and sixth centuries in the former provinces of the western Roman empire saw the fragmentation and rapid disappearance of the imperial administrative structures, and their replacement by the new Germanic kingdoms. These were, however, dependent on Roman traditions of government, and in many cases benefited from the close involvement in the administration of leading members of Roman provincial society. Initially, some of these realms had the character of little more than a military occupation, with most of the civil administration remaining in Roman hands. The law codes of the German rulers were also largely Roman in content and in the forms that they took. In some cases, such as that of the Vandals, no real *rapprochement* ever seems to have taken place between the German garrisoning forces and the Roman civil population, even though many of the invaders appear to have become increasingly Romanized in their lifestyles. This left their kingdom peculiarly vulnerable once an eastern army was able to land in Africa in 533. Wars, largely motivated by the expansionary needs of first the Visigothic and then the Frankish kingdoms could also lead to the elimination of some of the minor regional powers, such as those of the Burgundians in 534 and of the Sueves in 585. For those kingdoms that were able to survive and to expand, the sixth century was marked by an increasing integration between the indigenous population and the conquerors, a process that was not completed in either Gaul or Spain before the seventh century. However, in both the Frankish and Visigothic kingdoms the elimination of religious conflicts between the two elements of the population, symbolic not least of wider cultural cleavages, opened the way to the disappearance of the division between Roman and German. In the case of Spain the Arab conquest of 711 aborted this process, but it led in Gaul to the absorption of much of the indigenous population into a new Frankish ethnic identity. In Britain, where political fragmentation had been more intensive and the development of alternative structures of power more localized, cultural and governmental unity could not be re-established at more than a regional level. In Italy, where imperial authority, however much diminished, had survived longest, the Ostrogothic kingdom had offered the best example of the kind of Roman administrative and cultural continuity that could be established under a dynasty of German kings. However, Justinian's protracted war of reconquest wrought so much damage that the peninsula was not to regain political unity for well over a millennium.

CHAPTER 6

EMPEROR AND COURT

MICHAEL McCORMICK

The figure of the late Roman emperor dominated his society as few rulers before or since. To convey what it would be like to die and meet God, a contemporary evoked the emperor emerging from his palace, and an age obsessed with religion constantly linked emperor and God: 'God needs nothing; the emperor needs only God.' The emperor's body was human, but his imperial power made him 'like God'. Yet the all-powerful 'Master of Earth and Sea and Every People' never appeared alone: he was always accompanied by others, who bathed in the reflected glory of his splendour. Onlookers envied the luck of his closest attendants and companions, despite the realization that exalted rank at court was precarious.[1]

The concept of court conveniently encapsulates the convergence of people and structures at the pinnacle of late Roman society around this awesome figure. The remarkable social group surrounding the emperor encompassed but transcended the chief institutions of government and now assumed more elaborate forms. The recent and definitive establishment of imperial residences in the new capitals of Constantinople and Ravenna helped precipitate this change. A travelling monarchy yielded permanently to a sedentary one, and stable palace milieux began to drive roots into capital cities. This occurred in both halves of the empire and affected all other developments, although the evidence is much richer for the eastern empire.

Obvious components like the government and kinship ties constituted and shaped this milieu. Broader social factors were at work, too: friendship, shared religious enthusiasms and hostilities, gender, common ethnicity and professional experiences bound together and distinguished elements within the court. On a linguistic level, the eastern court formed an enclave of Latin or Latin–Greek bilingualism in a polyglot but Hellenized city: though Greek ultimately prevailed, court jargon remained studded with Latin loan words. The uniforms and insignia of government service visually assigned to courtiers their social and institutional rank. The laws, too,

---

[1] John Chrys. *Ad Theod. laps.* I, XI and XII; Agapetus, *Capitula admonitoria* LXIII and XXI; *ACO* 2.1. p. 417.

set the emperor's entourage off from the rest of the population: a draco-
nian law of treason governing the repression of conspiracies had been
extended to protect the prince's advisers, and palatine service usually
brought tax exemptions as well as special palace jurisdiction. Thus, even
menial posts in the palace were swamped with ambitious aspirants.[2] But
first and foremost, members of the late Roman court were distinguished
by their physical location, near the emperor and within the palace.

I. THE PHYSICAL CONTEXT OF POWER

Whereas the fourth century had favoured the vocabulary of a human
group on the move (*comitatus*) or, in striking Greek, 'the army camp' (*strato-
pedon*) for the itinerant imperial headquarters of its day, the new fact of the
fifth and sixth centuries may be summed up with the word for a building,
the palace (*palatium*, παλάτιον). Thus Justin I informed the pope that he
had been elected by 'the most splendid grandees of our sacred palace and
of the most holy senate'.[3] Insiders like Peter the Patrician, Justinian's *magister officiorum*, might think in terms of *archontes* ('officials' or 'leaders'), and in
the east *synkletos*, 'senate', and its derivatives seem sometimes to refer
loosely to élite court society as well as designating the institution which
attempted to replicate in Constantinople the senate of old Rome. But to
outsiders, the emperors' associates were simply *palatini*, even though over
time the term narrowed to mean the palace people most exposed to the
population at large, the financial bureaucrats based there.[4] The concept of
palace stretched beyond the physical buildings to encompass the entire
imperial establishment – for instance, in the public prayers Christian
churches offered for the state. Nevertheless, the physical context both
reflected and shaped the life of the emperor and his court, and it is there
that we begin.

By about 425 the east's new capital of Constantinople had expanded into
one of the empire's greatest cities, whereas Ravenna resembled rather a
glorified military base. Constantine I had established the original core of
Constantinople's main palace at the south-east end of the peninsula on
which the capital was built, in the city's monumental centre.[5] The massive
Hippodrome shielded much of the palace's western perimeter from riots
and fires. The size and importance of this palace warranted it the epithet
'Great'. From the site now occupied by the Blue Mosque, some thirty
metres above sea level, it spread down the slope towards the shore,
affording splendid sea views and breezes and dominating the view of the

---

[2] *C.Th.* IX.14.3; cf. *CJ* IX.8.5; Jones, *LRE* I.586 and 571.   [3] *Coll. Avell.* CXLI.2.
[4] Ensslin (1942).
[5] Janin (1964); Guilland (1969) (both to be used with caution); Dagron, *Naissance* 92–7; Müller-
Wiener (1977); Mango, *Développement*.

city for sea-borne travellers. It was impressively suited to the tasks of governance and providing comfort for its residents. Contemporaries imagined heaven as a palace,[6] and surviving remains confirm its grandeur. The complex expanded considerably in the fifth and sixth centuries. By the shore, the future Boukoleon palace was begun, possibly in the time of Theodosius II, and the north-east area of the palace was lavishly rebuilt by Justinian. Justin II and Tiberius added further ambitious buildings, gardens and monuments, until the rhythm slackened under Maurice as imperial resources declined.

The western empire's palace occupied the south-eastern quadrant of Ravenna. The government buildings into which Honorius moved and which have been uncovered so far underwent only superficial remodelling. Valentinian III added a new palace 'Ad Laureta'. However, excavation suggests – and it is symbolic of the west's straitened circumstances – that the western residence approached eastern standards of luxury and magnificence only under the Ostrogoths.[7] Though sparse, the archaeological and literary record from Ravenna is not contaminated by the living medieval tradition that so colours our data from Constantinople.

A number of lesser palaces and residences also served the emperors and their families in Constantinople and its environs. In addition to the Great Palace and four other nearby imperial establishments, the *Notitia* of Constantinople mentions at least five more mansions associated with the imperial family to the west and north.[8] During the Nika revolt, in fact, the usurpers gave some thought to establishing the rebel government in one of these secondary palaces.[9] Suburban palaces catered for the imperial family's enjoyment of the aristocracy's *villeggiatura* lifestyle. In some seasons, the emperor retired to a country residence and slowed the rhythm of court life: thus laborious negotiations aimed at unifying dissident church factions were suspended for thirty days when Justin II left the city to relax in the Asian suburbs.[10] The accompanying procession explains why these excursions became known as *prokensa* in the multilingual jargon of the court, reflecting a popular Latin pronunciation of *processus*.

In the European suburbs, the imperial family frequented the great military complex on the Via Egnatia at the Hebdomon (*Septimum*), the seventh milestone from central Constantinople, on the shore of the Sea of Marmara. There, near the present-day airport, the army assembled on a great parade ground, the *Kampos*. At its southern end, the Tribunal, a large platform adorned with statues, rose five metres above the field, whence the emperor and his entourage could be seen by the troops in relative security. Here the army acclaimed new emperors down to 457.[11] The Asian shore

---

[6] Nil. *Ep.* II.170.   [7] Deichmann (1976–89) II.3.58–70.   [8] *Notitia* II, IV, X–XI, XV.
[9] Procop. *Wars* I.24.30.   [10] John Eph. *HE* III.1.26–7.   [11] Demangel (1949).

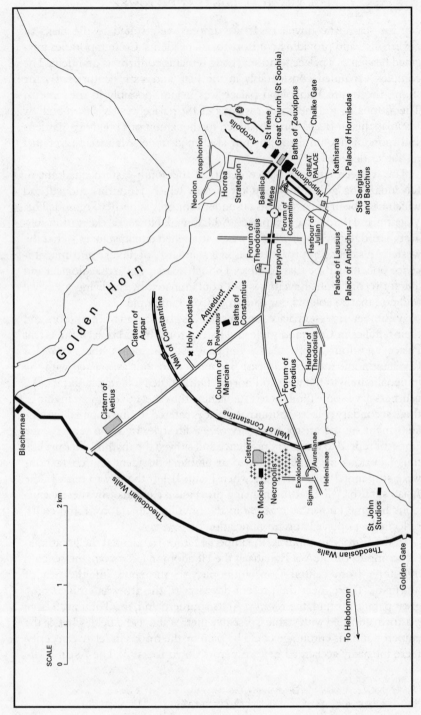

Fig. 4 The city of Constantinople (based on Mango, *Développement* plan II

attracted Theodosius II's sisters, who sometimes stayed at the palace of Rufinianae.[12] By 541 Belisarius and his wife had acquired this estate, presumably a sign of imperial favour.[13] Justinian and especially Theodora preferred the Hiereia palace, built on a peninsula just across the bay from Chalcedon and equipped with a splendid artificial harbour.[14] Farther north, the villa on the Bosphorus used by Justin II before his accession became the Sophianae palace, named for his powerful wife.[15] The emperor and empress did not relax in these suburban palaces by themselves. The crowd that accompanied Theodora on her lengthy stays in Hiereia required abundant provisions, which explains Justinian's construction of markets there. Justin II and Sophia travelled to the baths in the Asian suburbs accompanied by the 'senate'.[16]

In the capital, courtiers' mansions congregated in the Great Palace's immediate vicinity. Just south-west of it lay the palace of Hormisdas.[17] After 518 the increasingly powerful Justinian made his residence there seem palatial even before he assumed the purple, adorning it with the churches of Sts Peter and Paul and of Sts Sergius and Bacchus (the modern Küçük Ayasofia Cami);[18] this palace–monastery was subsequently connected to the Great Palace, and housed Monophysite monks under Theodora's protection, while the Caesar Tiberius resided there with his family in the last years of Justin II's reign.[19] Immediately west of the Hippodrome were the grandiose mansions of two imperial eunuchs that rivalled one another in splendour: the grand semi-circular entrance portico to Lausus' palace measured over twenty-five metres in diameter, while Antiochus' was double that.[20] Nearby lived consuls like the empress Verina's brother Basiliscus and Anastasius' nephew Pompeius, while Probus, another nephew and consul, dwelled within a few hundred metres.[21]

The prince's security was vital. Like contemporary town houses, the Great Palace was probably never an open structure; a perimeter wall has been detected at Ravenna.[22] The Mese, the main thoroughfare of Constantinople, brought visitors to the monumental square at the Milion or Golden Milestone, from where they would have walked through the Royal Colonnade or Regia to the Chalke or Brazen House, the palace's main entrance, which had been lavishly rebuilt by Justinian.[23] Beyond it lay a series of military quarters that housed various units of palace guards and

[12] Callin. *V. Hypatii* xxxvii.3; cf. xli.13 and Janin (1964) 152.   [13] Procop. *Wars* i.25.21.
[14] Procop. *Buildings* i.11.16–22.   [15] Cameron (1967).
[16] Procop. *Secret History* 15.36–7; cf. *Buildings* i.11.21; John Eph. *HE* iii.2.46.
[17] Guilland (1969) 1.294.
[18] Procop. *Buildings* i.4.1–3; cf. Müller-Wiener (1977) 177–83 and Mango in Kazhdan (1991) iii.1879.
[19] John Eph. *V.SS.Or.* xlvii; *HE* iii.3.8.   [20] Naumann and Belting (1966); Naumann (1965).
[21] Janin (1964) 123, 319–20; cf. Berger (1988) 434–5, also 282–4. Marc. Com. s.a. 512; Theoph. *AM* 6024, with Mango, *Développement* 38–9.   [22] Deichmann (1976–89) ii.3.60.
[23] Mango (1959); cf. Müller-Wiener (1977) 230 with pl. 263.

barred the way to the heart of the palace. The Ravenna palace probably displayed similar features, as the medieval place-names 'Ad Chalci' and 'Scubitum' (from Excubitum) suggest.[24]

The warren of buildings which housed the court's functions are most fully described by the tenth-century *Book of Ceremonies*, but that work rarely documents the late antique situation unequivocally. Excavation, medieval descriptions and general Roman practice suggest that rectangular peristyle porticoes constituted the palace's main building blocks. Some featured luxurious gardens adorned with statuary and fountains, or they dazzled with magnificent mosaics like the one still visible today.[25] Constantinople's climate encouraged the court to congregate out of doors, at least in good weather. For instance, during the deliberations preceding Anastasius' accession in spring 491, the most powerful men at court discussed the situation as they sat on benches in the portico in front of the Triclinium of the Nineteen Couches.[26]

The buildings in which the court lived and worked lined these porticoes. The palatine ministries must have occupied many rooms: the smaller palatine bureaucracy and court at Ravenna has recently been estimated at about 1,500 people, but the details escape us.[27] The *schola* or office of the *magister officiorum* was near the hall known as the Consistorium, since western ambassadors waited there immediately before an imperial audience.[28] At Ravenna the mint controlled by the *comes sacrarum largitionum* has been convincingly located near the palace's main entrance, while there are similar indications for the Great Palace.[29]

Large halls served as settings for the court's ceremonial business. Typically, access was through a triple set of doors and an antechamber which was perhaps identical with the silentiaries' station (*Silentiarikion*), where a final screening of participants occurred. A raised platform for the emperor seems to have closed one end; large curtains and inlays in the floor helped guide those entering the hall.[30] The Great Palace had both a Great or Summer Consistorium and a Small Consistorium. There the court assembled for the audiences granted to Roman legations and foreign ambassadors, promotions, or the reading of laws. Another type of large structure, the *triclinium*, was intended primarily for state banquets. The main banquet hall, the Triclinium of the Nineteen Couches – the old-fashioned style of dining while reclining survived at state banquets – could accommodate 228 guests in addition to the emperor, and may

[24] Deichmann (1976–89) 11.3.53–4; 56.

[25] Deichmann (1976–89) 11.3.65; John Eph. *HE* 111.3.23; Talbot Rice (1958).

[26] Const. Porph. *De Cer.* 1.92.   [27] Deichmann (1976–89) 11.3.114–15.

[28] Const. Porph. *De Cer.* 1.87.   [29] Deichmann (1976–89) 11.3.54–6; Hendy (1972) 131 n. 2.

[30] Deichmann (1976–89) 11.3.67; Cyr. Scyth. *V. Sabae* LI, and for an excavated hall: Talbot Rice (1958) 25. Const. Porph. *De Cer.* 1.89; cf. Deichmann (1976–89) 11.3.69, and Guilland (1969) 1.56–9.

have had a distinctive design.[31] Justin II added an octagonal and domed Chrysotriklinos or Golden Banquet Hall. To judge from banqueting arrangements from later centuries, this magnificent structure seated only 102 guests and so catered to particularly select gatherings.[32]

Churches inside the palace met the imperial family's normal religious needs. The oldest, the Kyrios or Church of the Lord, lay in the Constantinian part of the palace. The empress Pulcheria added the church of St Stephen to house the relics of the first martyr. As already noted, Justinian built two churches in connection with the Hormisdas palace.[33] The seclusion of the imperial chambers or *cubiculum* was nearly complete: curiosity about their appearance consumed even a prominent general and consul, and he incurred the emperor's wrath in finding out.[34] Normally, only court eunuchs, domestic servants and the occasional doctor or privileged holy man might set foot there. The empress occupied separate quarters that expressed physically the segregation of men and women. Her chambers admitted privileged visitors, perhaps because they functioned as her main reception space.[35] Who resided in the palace beyond the imperial family, their domestic servants and the security forces is an open question. The imperial family might well span generations: Zeno's mother-in-law, the dowager empress Verina, certainly continued to live within the palace, as did, apparently, his mother, Lallis.[36] Unable to dislodge his predecessor's widow, Tiberius expanded the northern part of the palace for his own family.[37] Foreign hostages also lived there, and Theodora supposedly sheltered five hundred Monophysites in the palace of Hormisdas. If they indeed occupied 'every chamber and room' and had to subdivide larger rooms to fit, then this secondary palace normally housed far fewer people.[38] Each high-ranking resident of the palace apparently constituted a kind of organizational cell, since he lived with his own personal domestic staff, including slaves, bodyguards and a cellarer, which in turn suggests separate arrangements for food storage.[39]

The infrastructure which supported the imperial household included stables and baths. The sixth-century palace's multiple cisterns made good sense, given the city's perennial problems of water supply, while Justinian's experience of the Nika revolt encouraged greater self-sufficiency for the palace, which was now furnished with granaries and bakeries.[40] Nothing is known about kitchens, workshops, storerooms, or sanitary installations.

The emperor's duties exposed him to his people in the Hippodrome, where he watched the races and patriotic displays from the *kathisma*, or

---

[31] Oikonomides (1972) 164 n. 136; cf. Krautheimer (1966).

[32] Oikonomides (1972) 196 n. 209; Deichmann (1976–89) III.2.53, 64–9.

[33] Mathews (1974) and Mathews (1971) 48–50; also Mango (1975).   [34] Priscus fr. 63.

[35] Marc. Diac. *V. Porph.* XLV; cf. Procop. *Secret History* 15.27.

[36] *Chron. Pasch.* s.a. 477; John Ant. fr. 94 (*Exc. de Insid.* De Boor).   [37] John Eph. *HE* III.3.23.

[38] *V. Petr. Iber.* pp. 24 and 28–9; John Eph. *V.SS.Or.* XLVII.   [39] *V. Petr. Iber.* pp. 25 and 27.

[40] John Eph. *HE* III.3.23; Janin (1964) 211; *Chron. Pasch.* s.a. 532.

imperial box. This was not easily accessible to other spectators but was directly and securely connected to the palace. Even when rioting factions acclaimed a usurper seated in the *kathisma*, Justinian and his loyal followers could approach from behind and listen to developments.[41] Arrangements to protect the emperors when they joined the people for services in the Great Church are unclear; in this period, their place was somewhere in the south aisle of the Justinianic church, at ground level. Typically for this society, the empress watched the service separately from the gallery.[42] Then, as now, boats allowed easy movement around Constantinople and afforded additional security. The emperor's private harbour by the Boukoleon palace provided direct access to suburban palaces or other seaside locations, and a secure escape route in emergencies. This was probably how Zeno and his followers escaped to Chalcedon during Basiliscus' usurpation.[43]

II. THE EMPEROR

Theoretical discussion about the imperial office and its Christianization intensified in the sixth century with works like the *Dialogue on Political Science*, the *Treatise on Strategy* and the writings of Agapetus, not to mention the reflections in the prefaces to Justinian's *Novels*. The visual symbolism of power fascinated contemporaries as the court's rituals themselves became the subject of panegyric and the meaning of the imperial insignia attracted new attention.[44]

The emperor's official titles remained substantially the same as before. In the Greek-speaking east, the official translation of *imperator* as *autokrator* persisted, with its connotations of autonomous power and monarchy. The last shreds of republican ideology were vanishing, however, as *basileus*, which originally meant 'king', prevailed in informal usage. The emergence of tribal kingdoms in the west imposed a distinction between the universalist monarchy of the Romans and the upstart western rulers, whose Latin title *rex* was transliterated into Greek. Even within the palace an increasing identification of *basileus* and 'emperor' – the *magister officiorum*'s private records already use *basileus* under Justinian – facilitated the adoption of *basileus* as the emperor's official title a century later. The empress, too, asserted her regal status ever more sharply, as an embittered Procopius testifies.[45]

---

[41] *Chron. Pasch.* s.a. 532; cf. in general Guilland (1969) 1.462–98.
[42] Paul Sil. *Descr.* 580–5; Evagr. *HE* IV.31.
[43] John Ant. fr. 94 (*Exc. de Insid.* De Boor); cf. Theoph. *AM* 6094; also *AM* 6003; Procop. *Wars* 1.24.32–7. Müller-Wiener (1977) 60.   [44] MacCormack (1981).
[45] Const. Porph. *De Cer.* 1.89; Theodora: Procop. *Secret History* 10.7, 15.13–17.

The emperor's activities varied according to the individual character and abilities of the ruler. Some appear to have been little more than figureheads, for whom officials, empresses and eunuchs guided the fortunes of state, while others, none more so than Justinian, worked day and night to achieve astonishing ambitions. Emperors did not leave the palace to direct affairs of state as they had in earlier days. They no longer led the Roman army into battle. A Justinianic civil servant claimed that Theodosius I had forbidden this to future emperors; Maurice's attempt to do so was met, we are told, with a flock of sinister portents.[46] In an age of great bureaucracies, emperors governed with the bureaucrat's tools of meetings and the pen.

We often see emperors performing symbolic acts of governance: inspecting granaries, celebrating triumphs, holding audiences. This was serious and time-consuming business. For reasons we shall see, questions of ceremonial and precedence sometimes required the emperor's personal attention.[47] Ceremonial catered to the institutions which translated imperial decisions into policy. An impatient Justinian could try to gain time only by shifting some obligatory ceremonies to odd hours of the day or night, or by performing them on the side as he proceeded to a public appearance in the Hippodrome.[48] But the seclusion and security which shielded the emperor make it difficult to see behind the ceremonial scenes into the emperors' daily routine of running the empire. We catch a glimpse of Marcian in the senate, discussing a wealthy widow's contested will.[49] Exception or routine? We cannot tell.

The emperor's purple ink fuelled the engines of bureaucracy. He will have spent many hours reviewing and subscribing documents; a child who could not write could not rule.[50] The emperor listened: to endless panegyrics and petitions in public, to proposals and reports in private, the responses to which are preserved in the laws and historians of the age. But Justinian's personal drafting of laws, which once would have epitomized an ideal emperor, was resented in the sixth century.[51] So far had the central institutions of the empire evolved towards autonomous activity. The parallel and competing organs of the central government jealously guarded their territory. John Lydus was acutely aware that every diminution of his beloved praetorian prefecture meant another bureau's increase, and vice versa.[52] The emperor must often have intervened to arbitrate among bureaucratic rivals.

Though the circumstances are unusual, the emperor occasionally appears at work in less secluded settings – for instance, when Justin II hammered out an edict of religious union. The emperor or his advisers first drew up a draft. The emperor's personal physician, a seeming sympathizer,

[46] McCormick, *Eternal Victory* 47.   [47] E.g. Const. Porph. *De Cer.* 1.86 and 87.
[48] Const. Porph. *De Cer.* 1.84 and 86.   [49] Marcian, *Nov.* 5, *praef.*
[50] Justin I needed a stencil: *PLRE* II *s.v.* Iustinus 4; *V. Dan. Styl.* 67; Classen (1977c) 60–7.
[51] Procop. *Secret History* 14.2–3.   [52] John Lyd. *De Mag.* II.11; cf. III.41.

conveyed it to one of the two main factions, representative Monophysites who had been confined in the patriarch's palace. The doctor invited them to propose amendments. Their list of revisions went to the other faction, which immediately began to lobby prominent court figures, and especially the *quaestor*, against the proposed changes. Both factions were convened in an imperial audience. Justin listened, approved the changes and commanded that they be entered into the edict's final text. The opposing faction of Dyophysite clergy and senators exploded in a raucous outcry, protesting against the political consequences of accepting the revisions. Justin II made a show of his wrath, threatened the protesters and commanded silence. He then ordered the *quaestor* to produce twenty fair copies of the revised edict by nightfall or lose his head. The Dyophysites began buzzing like angry bees. They entreated the emperor, despite his command for silence, to consider the disruptive consequences they foresaw. Finally Justin relented and left the protesters to draw up a compromise formula. The result was twenty official copies of an edict which, despite pressure and persecution, failed to achieve the desired union.[53]

The give and take, the efforts to persuade, apply pressure and terrorize, the emperor's limited success in imposing his will, the sheer noise – these surprise us after the choreographed silence of more formal ritual appearances. But even emperors had sometimes to persuade as they arbitrated among powerful subordinates and subjects. Thus, at a critical juncture which surely required a consensus among the ruling élite, Leo I presented incriminating evidence of treachery to the senate and elicited the response he wished for by skilful questioning.[54] Though we cannot distinguish their voices, we can hear the dissonance among the emperor's advisers in the dramatic scene when Theodora spoke up as the Nika riot engulfed the capital, urging death rather than escape by sea.[55] Though doubtless atypical, these incidents hint at how, in concrete terms, emperors made decisions and ruled their subjects.

Loyalty to the emperor was constantly forced on subjects' minds in capital cities and provinces alike. Across the empire's cities, his portraits enjoyed the sacred status accorded to his person, Roman citizens prayed publicly for his health and success, and they acclaimed his name when messengers read communiqués announcing his victories or new laws.[56] Holidays commemorating imperial accessions, victories or *adventus* had long punctuated the Roman months, but now, as regnal years increasingly organized public time, the emperor even began to supplant the old consular years and compete with the indictional system of dating documents.[57]

Though similar public gestures of loyalty persisted in both parts of the empire, broad regnal patterns point to a separation even before Odoacer

[53] John Eph. *HE* III.1.19–29. Text of Edict: Evagr. *HE* v.4.   [54] *V. Dan. Styl.* LV.
[55] Procop. *Wars* 1.24.32–9.   [56] McCormick, *Eternal Victory* 232–44.
[57] *C.Th.* VI.30.21; Justinian, *Nov.* 47. McCormick, *Eternal Victory* 73–4; cf. 2nd edn xiii–xiv.

deposed Romulus. After 425 the western empire would last only a half-century, but its instability produced nearly as many emperors as exercised power in Constantinople from 425 to 602, corresponding to average reigns of about five and sixteen years respectively. After Theodosius II, no son inherited his father's throne, whence great diversity among emperors. Where emperors came from suggests that the imperial élite, too, was fissuring along regional lines. Of the seven western emperors whose backgrounds are known, six certainly came from families based in the west or were born there. One was born in Constantinople, and Anthemius is the exception that proves the rule, since he owed power to the eastern empire's intervention in Italy. Conversely, nine or ten of the eleven men who actually wielded power at Constantinople certainly came from families established in the eastern empire.[58] The Balkan peninsula alone supplied nearly half the eastern emperors, while Constantinople or its environs apparently gave birth to only one western (Anthemius) and two eastern emperors (Theodosius II and Justin II).

The geographic pattern is closely connected with emperors' professional backgrounds, since the army recruited heavily in the Balkans. In fact, military careers or families supplied at least half of the emperors, whereas fewer than a fifth had significant backgrounds in the civilian bureaucracy.[59] The details of emperors' military careers, however, underscore the prominence of the court. Six out of ten or eleven military emperors had accomplished part or all of their military careers in palatine units and, even more significantly, Tiberius and Maurice both shifted from civilian careers as notaries to the palace guard, the excubitors.[60] In other words, until Maurice was overthrown by a field army, physical presence at court was an asset in competing for the purple. Indeed, as Justin II's success against his cousin and rival Justin, son of Germanus, shows, a field command was a liability. Finally, regardless of professional background, over one-third of all emperors owed their position to some sort of kinship with the imperial family.[61] The court had become more than the centre of power: it was also the best avenue to power.

III. THE COURT: THE HUMAN ELEMENT

Besides the emperor himself, who really wielded power at court? Efforts to lobby the imperial entourage show that contemporaries naturally valued

---

[58] Unless otherwise noted, this section is based on data in *PLRE* II and III; Basiliscus appears to be non-Roman, but his origin is unclear: Krautschick (1986) 350.

[59] Petronius Maximus, Anastasius; Tiberius and Maurice both started out as notaries.

[60] Whitby, *Maurice* 6.

[61] Valentinian III; Anthemius, who married Euphemia; Olybrius; Theodosius II; Zeno; Basiliscus; Justinian and Justin II.

the support of civil servants who headed the great imperial bureaux and worked closely with the ruler, especially the *magister officiorum*, the praetorian prefect of the east, and the *quaestor*.[62] Down to the 470s, extraordinary power lay also with the powerful professional and social group of the *magistri militum*. Though they were often barbarians and Arians by religion, like Ricimer in the west or the Ardaburs in the east, they acted as powers behind the throne, established marriage alliances with Roman families and claimed the ceremonial perquisites befitting their position in public life.[63] But the court comprised more than just the key bureaucrats and generals. One figure late antique lobbyists rarely neglected as much as modern historians was the empress.

The prominence and political significance of empresses advanced markedly: they gained control of their own *cubiculum*, which paralleled the emperor's, and efforts to influence the court regularly targeted them.[64] Justinian required his officials to swear a religious oath of allegiance to 'Our most divine and most pious Lords Justinian and Theodora', and from Justin II – whose wife's statue often flanked his own even as her portrait joined his on the bronze coinage – the Augustae always figured next to their husbands in legal oaths confirming citizens' public business.[65] The fourteen empresses known from 425 to 600 derived their emperor-like legal status from the emperor.[66] The Augusta issued coinage – or at least some coins were issued in her name – authenticated documents with lead seals,[67] wore imperial insignia, and disposed of dedicated revenues and the appropriate staff. With two exceptions (Pulcheria and Honoria), her title was linked to marriage to an emperor.[68] The cases of Eudocia in 423 and Eudoxia in 439 suggest a link between the birth of a child and the granting of the title.

The place that family ties held at court is underscored by the fact that the majority of Augustae themselves stemmed from the imperial family: seven were emperors' children (Pulcheria, Placidia, Honoria, Licinia Eudoxia, Euphemia, Ariadne and Constantina) and one, Sophia, a niece.[69] Thus, women supplied a family continuity that the emperors generally lacked. Unlike their husbands, moreover, many empresses grew up in an imperial capital or even, like the girls from the imperial family, at the heart of palace society. Once a woman rose to the purple, she tended to stay there, for the Augustae outlasted emperors, averaging over twenty years in their position (see Table 1 below). Background and longevity enabled empresses to help

---

[62] *ACO* 1.4. pp. 224–5; *Epist. Austras.* XXXIV–XXXV.
[63] Demandt (1970), (1986); McCormick (1989).
[64] *CJ* XII.5.3 and 5. *ACO* 1.4. pp. 224–5; *Epist. Austras.* XXIX–XXX and XLIV; Greg. I, *Reg.* V.38.
[65] *Nov.* VIII.1; Cameron (1980) 70–1; Morrisson (1970) 124–5, also 166 and 179; Worp (1982).
[66] *Digest* 1.3.31.　　[67] Licinia Eudoxia: Zacos, Veglery and Nesbitt (1972–84) no. 2759.
[68] Bury (1919).
[69] Also, perhaps, Nepos' anonymous wife, a relative of Verina: *PLRE* II *s.v.* Nepos 3.

Table 1. *List of empresses A.D. 425–600*

Aelia Pulcheria	414–53
Aelia Galla Placidia	421–50
Aelia Eudocia	423–60
Iusta Grata Honoria	?437–c. 450
Licinia Eudoxia	439–c. 462
Aelia Marcia Euphemia	?467–?472
Aelia Verina	?457–c. 484
Aelia Ariadne	474–515
Aelia Zenonis	475–6
Euphemia (Lupicina)	?518–c. 527
Theodora	527–48
Aelia Sophia	565–after March 601
Aelia Anastasia	?578–593/4
Aelia Constantina	582–?604/5

transmit an imperial tradition within an emerging court society: Pulcheria was credited with personally preparing Theodosius II for his ceremonial duties, while an anecdote reveals that Sophia and Constantina jointly procured a new crown for Maurice and suggests that imperial women contributed to the development of the symbols of power which is so prominent in this period.[70]

Did they actually wield power? After all, they operated in a society which severely limited their field of action. Sexual segregation restricted their contacts with men: empresses are noticeably absent from many, if not most, public ceremonies involving the emperor, and they apparently had their own female court, consisting chiefly of the wives of leading men in the emperor's entourage.[71] Yet modern historians have credited Galla Placidia and Pulcheria with decisive political roles. Between them, the mother and daughter Verina and Ariadne maintained a pivotal role at court for over half a century, notwithstanding coups and civil wars, while the diadem passed through the male hands of four biological families, including their own. Empresses' political importance is most obvious at times of transition – for instance, when, like Pulcheria or Ariadne, they married newly elected emperors. But their role went beyond merely legitimizing someone else's choice for emperor. Ariadne is reliably reported to have selected Anastasius as emperor, while her mother proclaimed the usurpers Basiliscus and Leontius.[72] Sophia attempted to exploit the transition at her husband's death and, as we saw, Tiberius had difficulty dislodging her from the Great Palace.

---

[70] Soz. IX.1.6; Theoph. *AM* 6093.   [71] Cf. John Eph. *HE* III.3.8.
[72] Const. Porph. *De Cer.* 1.92; *Chron. Pasch.* s.a. 477; Joh. Mal. (slav.) xv.

Her correspondence with the Persian king fits this pattern, since it was motivated by her husband's declining health. Theodora, on the other hand, may
have intervened in diplomacy with Ostrogothic Italy and Persia on her own
account.[73] According to Procopius, Theodora's religious differences with
her husband were consciously manipulated to capture the political loyalty of
her fellow Monophysites. In any event, her co-religionists treasured her
memory.[74]

But the empresses' greatest influence may have come from the links
between kinship and imperial politics, for Augustae had a voice in marriages involving the imperial family. According to one tradition, Pulcheria
was responsible for finding a wife for her brother; as long as she lived,
Lupicina Euphemia bitterly and successfully opposed her nephew's desire
to marry Theodora. And Theodora herself arranged or vetoed marriages
involving the imperial family, most of which, like Artabanes' plan to marry
Justinian's niece Praeiecta, had clear political implications.[75]

Household and the central institutions of government meshed within
the palace and so magnified the significance of family connections.
Whatever the constitutional mythology of the period, imperial children
enjoyed presumptive claims on the purple. Thus, Zeno's homonymous son
was expected to succeed his father, who promoted both his career and his
physical fitness to that end, even while anonymous members of the court
schemed against him.[76] The birth of a son to Maurice and Constantina was
hailed as the first male heir born to the purple since Theodosius II; he was
therefore baptized Theodosius.[77] Marriage into the imperial family was a
highly advantageous affair, and marriage to an emperor's daughter allowed
the son-in-law to hope for the purple, an expectation that in fact materialized for Maurice after his engagement to Tiberius' daughter.

One individual's promotion was a boon for the whole family. After his
accession, Anastasius' relatives received consulates and high offices and
concluded marriages with illustrious families: nine relatives obtained the
consulate between 500 and 518, a niece married into the blue-blooded
Anicii, creating connections with the Valentinian and Theodosian houses,
while two other nieces wed leading generals and thereby coupled the
emperor's family to the social group of the *magistri militum*.[78] Nor was this
an isolated phenomenon. Even disregarding Justinian's career, Justin I's
peasant kin rapidly experienced high office, wealth, and brilliant marriages
to the capital's great families: Justinian's cousin Boraides was enriched, and
his sister Vigilantia, whom one poet took the liberty of calling a queen, saw
her children make brilliant matches, while her son became Justin II.

---

[73] Menander fr. 18.1–2; Procop. *Secret History* 16.1–5; 2.32–6.   [74] E.g. John Eph. *V.SS. Or.* XLVII.
[75] Pulcheria: Malalas 352; Cameron, Alan (1981) 275–7, *contra* Holum, *Empresses* 115; *PLRE* II *s.v.*
Euphemia 5; Procop. *Wars* VII.31.2–14, esp. 5 and 14.   [76] Malchus, fr. 8.
[77] John Eph. *HE* III.5.14.   [78] Cameron, Alan (1978); cf., however, *PLRE* II.

Theodora's family was not left far behind. Her daughter by an earlier liaison probably married Anastasius' grand-nephew; the empress managed to marry the grandson that resulted from that union to Belisarius' daughter, and so attached the great general's family to her own. Another relative occupied a lucrative post in the palace administration and earned his keep when he uncovered a potential conspiracy.[79] In similar fashion, Maurice's accession brought new wealth to his family.[80]

Once these families reached the top, most showed remarkable staying power, especially in the light of the upheavals that wracked the broader society and economy of the sixth century. None of Anastasius' relatives followed him to the throne, but his descendants have been tracked in positions of prominence and power over the next five generations. It is interesting that the aristocratic eighth-century patriarch of Constantinople who dared oppose imperial iconoclasm bore the name Germanus, so well attested in Justinian's family, and was himself the son of a seventh-century patrician Justinian.

What we have been discussing so far looks like family patronage, the parcelling out of wealth and position on the basis of kinship. In fact, kinship meant more within the imperial palace. Family links functioned as a tool of governance as well as a key component of court society. Thus, between 468 and 476, the generals Basiliscus, Armatus and Nepos were related to the empress Verina by blood or marriage, while another two, Zeno and Marcianus, married her daughters. Indeed, Odoacer may have been Verina's nephew, and the coincidence of the *coup d'état* in Ravenna and Basiliscus' usurpation takes on new meaning.[81] In any event, Julius Nepos, who had seized the western throne with Leo I's support, was certainly married to a relative of Verina, which helps explain why she pressured Zeno not to abandon Nepos.

Zeno's own kin in turn supplemented and perhaps counterbalanced his mother-in-law's relations: we have already seen that his son by an earlier marriage had been groomed for the succession, but he died young. Zeno's brother Longinus was *magister militum praesentalis* and twice ordinary consul, granting the Isaurian highlander honour and a chance to gain favour in Constantinople through consular largess. Malalas identifies the Isaurian general Illus, *magister officiorum*, patrician and consul, as Zeno's uncle,[82] which suggests that the Isaurian emperor reached beyond the military bureaucracy to control the key post of *magister officiorum* through kinship or, at the least, ethnic solidarity. The same holds for another Illus or two, who were praetorian prefects of the east in this period.[83]

---

[79] Procop. *Wars* VII.32.17; *Anth. Gr.* VII.590 with Cameron, Alan (1978) 268; Theoph. *AM* 6055.
[80] John Eph. *HE* III.5.18.   [81] Krautschick (1986).
[82] Demandt (1989) 188 n. 29, *contra PLRE* II *s.v.* Illus 1.
[83] *PLRE* II *s.v.* Fl. Illus Pusaeus D. . .; Illus 2.

When Anastasius took over, Longinus was pushed aside. Anastasius' brother-in-law, Secundinus, was soon made city prefect, clearly to control public order. A nephew, Hypatius, who may have fought against the Isaurian rebels, certainly became *magister militum praesentalis* and occupied several other commands, even returning to prominence, after his uncle's death, until he was swept away by the Nika uprising. His brother Pompeius, who met the same fate, commanded an army in Thrace late in Anastasius' reign. Similar patterns obtain for Justin I's family. The extreme case is Maurice: the emperor's brother Peter was both *magister officiorum* and *curopalatus*, his brother-in-law Philippicus became *comes excubitorum* and commanded numerous campaigns, while a cousin or nephew, bishop Domitian, remained Maurice's closest confidant and adviser. Here the emperor's relatives indubitably spread through different segments of government. The empire had become so much a family affair that, in unprecedented fashion, Maurice's father and Domitian entered the imperial pantheon at the church of the Holy Apostles; indeed, the latter received a state funeral on an imperial scale.[84]

From Verina on, most high-ranking generals were family appointments, which surely reflects a threat emperors perceived in the armed forces. For all his power, the emperor's control was constantly jeopardized by conspiracies, usurpations and riots. By keeping the armies largely in relatives' hands, the emperor gained an added degree of loyalty. When other structures of imperial power cracked in crisis, as in the Nika riot, Justinian fell back on his kin. His wife alone urged him to keep fighting and she turned the tide when other advisers panicked. To his cousins Boraides, not otherwise known to have played a political role, and Justus, he entrusted the dangerous mission of arresting Anastasius' nephews who had turned the riot into a usurpation.

Another factor, too, may have figured in this conspicuous overlay of family on the institutions of late-Roman government, where power was partitioned among competing and compartmentalized bureaucracies. These stretched vertically through society, but lacked much horizontal integration below the emperor, since the normal bureaucratic career was advancement by seniority within one organization, whereas transfers seem to have been rare and resented.[85] This pattern also applied to the court. Thus the empress's court was distinct from the emperor's in its gender, location, organization and finances. Palace security and its personnel were split among the *magister officiorum*, another corps headed by the *comes excubitorum*, and, thirdly, the eunuch *spatharius*. Triply redundant security systems created countervailing pressures which enhanced the emperor's safety. Yet such pronounced corporate identity and rivalry also engendered inefficiency or

---

[84] John Eph. *HE* III.5.18; Whitby, *Maurice* 14–15; Theoph. *AM* 6085 and 6094.
[85] Jones, *LRE* I.602.

worse. By weaving together disparate organizational strands with the thread of kinship, the emperor could attempt to unite safely what earlier emperors and custom had set apart. The value of reliable kinship ties across professional divisions was obvious. For example, in 518 young Justinian was a *candidatus*, one of the emperor's personal bodyguards, in the palatine *scholae* commanded by the *magister officiorum*, while his uncle was *comes* of the rival excubitors. So Justinian was able to save one imperial candidate proposed by his *scholarii* from being massacred by his uncle's unit, and perhaps helped to persuade some *scholarii* to back his uncle, who of course enjoyed his own corps' support. The rivalry between the two groups was in fact so intense that some *scholarii* assaulted Justin.[86]

Within the palace, the imperial family's influence was consistently rivalled by one group which was both intimately linked with them and often kinless: the eunuch chamberlains, who staffed the imperial apartments.[87] Corippus aptly describes the essential duties of this 'crowd of chaste men': they enjoyed full trust and authority within the emperor's household, served his table, prepared his bed and garments, and locked the emperor and themselves in his bedroom every night. Their responsibility for access to the imperial couple, and for carrying and keeping the imperial insignia, created both visibility and the power that flowed from proximity.[88] The eunuch *castrensis* or major-domo oversaw the lower palatine staff, whence the latter's collective designation as *castrensiani*. In this capacity he ran much of the daily routine of the palace. Eunuchs were also influential in raising the imperial children: Antiochus tutored Theodosius II and the pope admonished Maurice's sister to see that the eunuchs set a proper example for the emperor's children.[89]

Their power reached into the highest affairs of state. Chrysaphius arranged an assassination attempt against Attila and had a patriarch deposed. Urbicius made the suggestion that led to his subordinate Anastasius' imperial election, and Amantius came close to imposing his own assistant in 518. The schedule of bribes paid by Cyril of Alexandria furnishes a rough scale of the value of the support of some dozen leading figures at court. Even leaving aside the luxury goods, the grand chamberlain or *praepositus sacri cubiculi* who headed the eunuch establishment leads the list with two hundred pounds of gold. Though a second grand chamberlain – one of the two is certainly the empress's – received only fifty pounds, the other chamberlains each received a hundred pounds. That is, their power was equated with that of the *magister officiorum, quaestor* and praetorian prefect, who each received the same amount.[90] But it was power of a very peculiar sort.

---

[86] Const. Porph. *De Cer.* 1.93.   [87] Hopkins (1978) 172–96; Clauss (1984).

[88] Coripp. *Iust.* III.214–19; care of insignia: Claud. *In Eutrop.* 1.417–23; Const. Porph. *De Cer.* 1.91 and 93; Theoph. *AM* 6041.   [89] Jones, *LRE* I.571; Malalas 361; Greg. *Reg.* VII.23.

[90] *ACO* 1.4, pp. 224–5.

Most eunuchs were foreigners from the empire's north-eastern frontiers. Though their condition almost implied slave status, they gained freedom on entering imperial service and their status rose in the fifth century. In fact, the grand chamberlain received precedence equal to prefects or generals by a decree of 422.[91] Yet unlike others at court, the foreign and kinless eunuchs lacked the ordinary late Roman social bases of power. Paradoxically, this very weakness fed their strength. Near-total dependence on the emperor and constant proximity to him could create an unparalleled degree of confidence between servant and master. Indeed, their fate was sometimes so closely tied to his that some, like Chrysaphius or Amantius, outlived their emperor by only a few days, though these were exceptional cases. Such utter dependence meant that they could be counted on for deeds which others might shun, whether it was the murder of Stilicho's son or Zeno's purported attempt to assassinate Illus. So too their dependency and physical disqualification from the purple made them safe choices as generals, an innovation probably intended for the same purpose as the generalships for the emperor's family. Thus, Zeno used a eunuch as co-commander during the civil war against his compatriot and possible relative, Illus. Justinian had Narses share Belisarius' command in Italy and ultimately turned the Italian war over to him, after the death of his cousin Germanus terminated the emperor's plans for keeping the Italian front under family control.

Another source of power lay in the eunuchs' unparalleled knowledge of the court itself. Combined with the fact that some long-serving eunuchs first appear in vital positions scarcely appropriate for newcomers, the length of some careers suggests that chamberlains often grew up in the palace, as we know was true of Justinian's trusted Narses.[92]

The careers of Urbicius, Misael and the earlier Narses (1) span virtually the entire period from Theodosius II to Tiberius' promotion to Caesar. Furthermore, palace links normally did not cease on retirement: many years after he retreated to a monastery, Misael copied a treatise in large letters for an apparently near-sighted Theodora.[93] In other words, the eunuchs provided an essential ingredient to the emergence of enduring court traditions, a kind of institutional memory. In particular, their duties meant that they contributed to the flowering of court ceremonial which occurs in this period. Eunuchs practised the corporate solidarity that typifies court organizations. For instance, two western eunuchs owned an estate outside Rome together. When a bishop refused to make an appointment sought by one chamberlain, he naturally turned to another chamberlain to intercede and explain his action. Links among fellow eunuchs extended even to a shared tomb.[94]

---

[91] *C.Th.* VI.8.1; cf. *CJ* XII.5.   [92] Agathias 1.16.1.   [93] Severus Ant. *Ep. Sel.* 1.63.
[94] *CIL* VI.31946 = XV.7131; Severus Ant. *Ep. Sel.* 1.17; John Eph. *V.SS.Or.* LVII.

Table 2. *Some prominent eunuch careers*

Eunuch	First attestation	Last attestation	Years of activity
Michael–Misael[95]	470	537	67
Urbicius PSC	434/449	505/6	57+
Narses 1 PSC	530 (*sacellarius*)	573/4	43+
Lauricius PSC	before 423	443/4	21+
Romanus 3	431	451	20
Narses 4 *spath.*	565 (*spatharius*)	about 581	16+
Lausus PSC	420 (PSC)	436	16+
Antiochus	before 408	about 421	13+
Artaxes	442 (PSC)	451	9+
Chrysaphius	about 441	450	9
Scholasticius	422	431	9

Note:
N.B.: the dignity in parentheses is that held at the earliest attestation; the last attestation may include retirement.

As Cyril of Alexandria's bribes suggest, chamberlains acquired fabulous wealth, some of which flowed into spectacular palaces like those of Lausus and Antiochus and some into religious enterprises. The eunuchs' religious zeal created privileged links between the court and the new urban or sub-urban monastic movements, and they constantly crop up in the Lives of holy men associated with the court. Lacking the progeny to whom other late Romans might turn, the eunuchs were early and active in founding or endowing monasteries which provided for their retirement, burial and per-petual prayer. Thus, Valentinian III's chamberlain Lauricius constructed a splendid tomb for himself in a monastery attached to the church of St Laurence, about six hundred metres outside the main gate to the palace quarter of Ravenna. Narses constructed a monastery in Bithynia for his eventual retirement: though he died on duty in Italy, his body was returned home and buried in his monastery by the sovereigns themselves.[96]

The grand chamberlain was in charge of the court ushers, the thirty silen-tiaries, who wielded golden wands to ensure quiet and order during the cer-emonies which constituted court routine. Their status and visibility were fairly high: they entered the imperial senate on retirement, and if Anastasius is any example, tall stature and dignified mien may have been part of the requirements for this post. In any case, personal association with the throne favoured chamberlains and silentiaries alike as personal emissaries who could forcefully represent an emperor's interest in problems arising in the

[95] *PLRE* II *s.v.* Michael 1; III *s.v.* Misael.
[96] Deichmann (1976–89) II.2.336–40; John Eph. *HE* III.1.39.

provinces. Thus Leo I sent the silentiary Diomedes along with a disapproving papal letter to the newly elected patriarch of Alexandria, Timothy Aelurus.[97] The women whom the sources call *cubiculariae* are more shadowy. Their name implies that they were the eunuchs' female counterparts, and Zeno explicitly included them in his blanket manumission of chamberlains. Like four specially selected silentiaries, they seem to have served the empress.[98]

Other members of the imperial entourage owed less to institutions or kinship. They range from Zenonis' nurse, who shared the secrets of the empress's heart, to old friends who experienced a meteoric rise in government, like Theodosius II's school friend Paulinus, who became *magister officiorum* before falling from favour, or the brothers who had cared for an ill Marcian long before he ascended the throne.[99] While the story that the brothers owed their fortune to their having predicted Marcian's imperial destiny may be fiction, there is no doubt that soothsayers and astrologers received high status at court in return for their services. Thus, Zeno's friend Maurianus, who foretold the next reign, held the rank of *comes*. Pamprepius' spectacular rise and fall in the household of Illus and the governments of Zeno and the usurper Leontius owed much to his prophecies. Proclus, an interpreter of dreams, was Anastasius' 'very close friend'.[100]

Court doctors occupied an enviable position in their profession and the palace. Retirement brought them membership of the senate and, judging from the laws, it was not unusual for them to reach the rank of *comes*. Their prestige could be considerable. The pagan *comes* Jacob, who dared to breach imperial etiquette when examining an afflicted Leo I, had statues raised to him in the public baths adjoining the Great Palace. When the pope needed to bring his views on a controversial issue to Maurice's attention, his method was to request the court doctor Theodore, not his own ambassador, to deliver his brief to Maurice's attention at a propitious moment, out of the public eye.[101]

Perhaps the least noticed of the socially prominent people at court must have been a powerful force for transmitting late Roman cultural values to foreign élites. These were the political hostages who were sent to the palace to be raised under imperial tutelage. For instance, when aged twelve, Nabarnugios, scion of the royal family of Iberia, was sent to Theodosius II's court and spent about a decade there. He received a royal education and held military rank, but became obsessed with ascetic practices. The veneration of martyrs' relics in his private chamber won friends among the palace eunuchs and other zealous Christians, including an architect and his brother,

[97] Evagr. *HE* II.10.   [98] *CJ* XII.5.4; Const. Porph. *De Cer.* 1.86; Holum, *Empresses* 132 n. 87.
[99] *PLRE* II *s.v.* Maria, Paulinus, Tatian 1.
[100] *PLRE* II *s.v.* Maurianus 2, Pamprepius; Proclus, cf. Malalas 409.
[101] *PLRE* II *s.v.* Iacobus 3; Greg. *Reg.* III.64, cf. *PLRE* III *s.v.* Theodorus 44.

a manager of imperial estates. Simultaneously – and most revealingly – it earned him the hatred of his Byzantine staff: his cellarer refused to supply oil for his devotions, and his bodyguards and slaves tried to kill him. Their grievance shows how the hostage system, beyond its geopolitical intent, was supposed to function. Nabarnugios had been sent from Georgia to achieve glory among the Romans but, instead of sharing in his worldly success as their master was assimilated into court society, his Roman household was being dragged down by his monkish desires. To escape from his gilded captivity required the miraculous intervention of the martyrs of Sebasteia, who guided the young man and his eunuch friend through the watch-posts that protected the sleeping palace.[102] This story parallels our limited evidence for the young Theoderic's decade at the court of Leo I and suggests the roots of the Ostrogothic king's later emulation of imperial ways at Ravenna.

One final group added their voice to the sometimes cacophonic chorus of court life. Although it may not have changed the structures of social access to the emperors, Christianization helped transform the kind of people who used them. Leaders of the institutional church clamoured for the emperor's ear and the bishops of Constantinople became a regular presence at court, routinely introducing visiting prelates to the emperor, for instance, or participating in the discussions surrounding an emperor's election, as well as performing the sacred functions court life demanded.[103] Not to be left on the sidelines, the pope established a permanent ambassador or *apocrisarius* to the emperor, whose inclusion among the influential figures targeted by a Merovingian diplomatic mission reveals his perceived value in lobbying the court.[104]

Even more novel was the access granted to holy men. Through their feats of asceticism and putative proximity to the supreme emperor in heaven, these rugged and malodorous individuals supposedly escaped the court's networks of power and pressure groups, conquering a significant position on its fringes like their prototypes on the edges of Syrian villages. Thus Hypatius established himself near the suburban palace of Rufinianae. Daniel the Stylite climbed a column overlooking the Bosphorus and was soon enjoying imperial patronage. Like other Syrian holy men, Daniel arbitrated between conflicting factions, and made predictions for courtiers and emperors alike; his biography opens a fine window on court life.[105] The concerted opposition of Justinian's chief financial officials and generals delayed his risky plan to invade Africa until an eastern holy man's vision supported the war.[106] We have already seen Theodora's role in housing the schismatic Monophysites she favoured right under her orthodox husband's nose in the palace of Hormisdas.

---

[102] *V. Petr. Iber.* pp. 25–35; cf. *PLRE* II *s.v.* Petrus 13, Proclus 3.
[103] *Coll. Avell.* CXVI.25; Const. Porph. *De Cer.* I.92.   [104] *Epist. Austras.* XXXII.
[105] Brown, *Society* 132–9; Callin. *V. Hypatii* VIII.1–7.   [106] Procop. *Wars* III.10.18–21.

Diversity, then, characterized the social groups that constituted the court. Differing religious enthusiasms, languages, social statuses, kinship networks and rival organizations included, excluded and collided with one another inside the Great Palace. And we have barely hinted at the ethnic underlay implied by the tribesmen – Goths, Lombards or Isaurians – serving in the palatine guards or the ethnic variety, ranging from Italians to Mesopotamians, which was concealed under the all-embracing Roman citizenship. United by service to the emperor, their corporate groups, and themselves, the people of the court shared proximity and the precariousness of their power and position. Today's all-powerful courtier who enjoyed free speech or 'outspokenness' (*parrhesia*) might be exiled or even executed tomorrow, whether he was the ruler's boyhood friend, like Theodosius II's *magister officiorum*, or his trusted physician, like Justinian's doctor.[107] This heterogeneous and dynamic human mass needed structure, and ceremony helped meet that need.

IV. COURT AND CEREMONY

In its zest for elaborate symbolic gestures, the palace reflected broader society, for imperial ceremonial capped a pyramid of rituals in late Roman society and government. The recurring dilemmas of choreographing the court's public movements in a stable landscape naturally encouraged court officials to codify ritual solutions once they had been devised. The durable empresses, and eunuchs who spent their entire lives in the palace acquiring or caring for the symbols of power, helped foster a growing ceremonial tradition, as the insignia of power, like ceremonies, began to accumulate: the Great Palace still boasted splendid thrones commissioned by Arcadius and Maurice five centuries later.[108] It is a token of the new situation that the palace tradition of ceremonial treatises begins in the fifth century.[109]

The interplay of the multiple elements we have sketched meant that their configuration within court society changed. The main scale for gauging one's importance was precedence. Accordingly, quarrels among competing bureaucratic élites explain much of the Theodosian Code, as law after law tinkered with the minutiae of official rank, and an imperial decision enhancing an official's precedence was a sure sign that he and his corporate compartment had arrived. Revealingly, precedence attained its definitive statement when members of the court adored the emperor at solemn audiences – for example, the *consistorium*. So long as a member of court held a governmental title – and virtually all significant figures within the palace received one – the senatorial order provided the general framework for these

---

[107] *PLRE* II *s.v.* Paulinus 8; *Chron. Pasch.* s.a. 532.
[108] Oikonomides (1972) 275.10; Const. Porph. *De Cer.* II.15.   [109] McCormick (1985) 4.

distinctions. Senate and *consistorium* had changed from earlier days: once they had been institutions where important decisions were made, but now they had become places where decisions were manifested. The connection between precedence and emperor was intimate. Indeed, when western dignitaries arrived at the eastern court to obtain recognition for their emperor – or, later, king – their ranks were studiously ignored during their initial audience, since recognizing their precedence meant recognizing their ruler.[110]

'Leva!' 'Raise the curtain!' With these words began the central act of the most solemn imperial audiences. As the great curtain (*velum*) rose in the *consistorium* to reveal the Roman emperor seated on an elevated throne beneath a golden baldaquin, the subject prostrated himself on a porphyry marker and adored him (*proskynesis*). After a final screening in the antechamber, each person or group was summoned to the adoration when their names and ranks had been read aloud (*citatio*). Precedence governed admission: the highest-ranking person entered last, and the silentiaries and ushers had to guard against people entering out of rank and usurping undue precedence. After adoring the emperor – and, in privileged circumstances, kissing his feet – each person joined his peers. He stood in the spot fixed for his personal rank, as determined by his office, his dignities and their seniority, and watched while the higher ranks repeated the procedure. When all had entered and adored the emperor in this way, the main ceremonial transactions began – audiences of ambassadors, reading out of new laws, promotions, retirements, etc. Afterwards the court was dismissed and exited by precedence, the highest-ranking individuals first.[111]

Eating with the emperor created a bond, and the growing significance of state banquets in court life can be seen in Justin II's Chrysotriklinos and Justinian's gold tableware depicting his victories. Here, too, the most powerful men at court were easily identified: they shared the emperor's couch; when the emperor sent part of his own meal to the Persian ambassador, this could only signify perfect concord between the two great powers.[112] The prominence of banquets explains why Justinian could signal the court's profound and public mourning at a catastrophic earthquake by cancelling one. By the time Maurice celebrated his marriage to the late Tiberius' daughter, state banquets figured on a par with comedy shows and circus races as elements of public rejoicing in the capital.[113]

When the emperor returned from excursions, the court was convoked to meet him at various places designated by his wishes and itinerary. Even if he sailed quietly to the Great Palace, key officials were expected to assemble to welcome him on the landing.[114] Alternatively, the emperor's travels

---

[110] Const. Porph. *De Cer.* 1.87–8.
[111] Coripp. *Iust.* III.191–256; Cyr. Scyth. *V. Sabae* x, John Lyd. *De Mag.* II.9, Const. Porph. *De Cer.* 1.84–8; Jones, *LRE* 1.528–35.   [112] Theoph. *AM* 6065; Const. Porph. *De Cer.* 1.90–1.
[113] McCormick, *Eternal Victory* 105 n. 109.   [114] Const. Porph. *De Cer.* Append. 497.

to the country could be inflated into a full-scale procession through the city, and these ceremonies outside the palace precincts projected different facets of imperial rule to a broader public. The emperor might ride through the streets in a gilded carriage pulled by snow-white mules, escorted by the imperial standards and heavily-armed, brawny men with long hair. He was preceded by the senate through cleaned and repaired streets where, at various locations, choruses saluted him.[115]

Some secular urban processions dramatized the emperor's role as civic benefactor – for instance, when he inspected the city's granaries – and onlookers could divine the political stature of leading figures by their proximity to the imperial carriage.[116] The visual symbolism of these elaborate displays was verbalized – and actively incorporated onlookers – by the acclamations chanted by the crowd or, increasingly, by semi-professional performers. Their simple, rhythmical formulae trumpeted the emperor's felicity, victory and piety and might also salute important figures in the power structure. Though street processions persisted, imperial ceremonies geared to broader audiences shifted increasingly to the circus. Emperors still braved the streets when necessary, but their security might be jeopardized, as Theodosius II discovered when a famished crowd stoned his procession to inspect the granaries.[117]

The army's role as audience and participant in these public ceremonies seems to diminish in this era. Thus, the great accession ceremony had remained closely linked with the Roman army so long as coronations followed the precedent established by Valens in 364. Down to the time of Leo I, emperors were proclaimed by the troops outside the city, on the parade ground at the Hebdomon, a place clearly identified with the army by the city's inhabitants.[118] But the pattern changed thereafter, perhaps in connection with Leo I's murder of his former patrons, the generals Aspar and Ardabur, which ended that military family's dominance at court. Leo I had his grandson proclaimed emperor in the Hippodrome, and Zeno's investiture followed suit shortly thereafter.[119] This new civilian setting for imperial accession kept the soldiers who symbolized the army's participation safely down in the arena. It geared the emperor's assumption of power to the urban crowd, as he appeared in the *kathisma* surrounded by leading figures of his court to receive the troops' Latin acclamations and his people's Greek ones. The first accession celebrated inside the city set a pattern which prevailed until the seventh century and affected other ceremonies – for example, triumphs.[120]

---

[115] Proclus of Constantinople, *Hom.* IX.1–2.
[116] Const. Porph. *De Cer.* II.51; cf. Mango, *Développement* 40.
[117] Marc. Com. s.a. 431; cf. McCormick, *Eternal Victory* 94 n. 61.   [118] Dagron, *Naissance* 100–1.
[119] Const. Porph. *De Cer.* I.94; Theoph. *AM* 5966.
[120] Beck (1966) 10–22; McCormick, *Eternal Victory* 60–9 and 93–100.

Though doubtless reflecting a shift in the structure of power that benefited the civilian bureaucracies to the detriment of the army, the move towards the circus probably responded to other factors as well. By linking great ceremonies to the empire's most popular sport, imperial ceremonial managers guaranteed a huge audience – the Hippodrome held perhaps 300,000 spectators[121] – for the key symbolic moments in the life of the state, at the same time that the *kathisma* guaranteed imperial security. Races had, in any case, long celebrated anniversaries or important events, while the cult of sporting victory came, in the emperor's presence, to be confused and fused with the all-pervasive cult of the emperor as the military victor *par excellence*. Now, however, the circus became not only a means of celebrating political realities, but the place in which those political realities were publicly acted out. In some sense, the move of imperial accessions from the suburban parade ground to the urban Hippodrome represents a final acknowledgement that the court was part of a great capital city.

As the ceremonial importance of the Hippodrome grew, so did that of the factions in the life of the city and, ultimately, the court. These associations of partisans of the colours which identified racing teams may have been inspired by late Roman theatre claques and grew out of the organizations which staged circus games. Though formally enrolled members would have been a small minority of Constantinople's population – 900 Blues and 1,500 Greens in 602[122] – they were young, energetic and well organized, they tended to come from comfortable backgrounds, and they were vociferous. They sat in special sections at the races and became amazingly adept at chanting the acclamations which, however carefully stage-managed by the authorities, were persistently regarded as the people's voice, with the capacity both to reassure and terrify men of power. The factions' skill at performing these indispensable tokens of public approval encouraged the court to build political bridges to this emerging pressure group.[123]

The emperor's scrupulous and flamboyant performance of Christian rites reassured all concerned that God was on the side of the Roman empire. Although the palace's churches allowed the emperor to discharge his Christian duties in seclusion, there was clear advantage to be gained by publicly worshipping with the people. By the reign of Theodosius II, the seasonal celebrations of the new religion permeated the social life of the court: the aristocracy customarily visited each other and the emperor on feasts like Epiphany.[124] Though emperors normally attended religious services in the Great Church only on great feast days, the stational nature of Constantinople's liturgy opened the way for new imperial processions to

[121] Müller-Wiener (1977) 64.   [122] Theophyl. Sim. *Hist.* VIII.7.10–11.
[123] Cameron, *Circus Factions*; cf. ch. 8 (Liebeschuetz), pp. 224–9 below.   [124] *V. Petr. Iber.* p. 25.

other shrines on other great feasts, again exposing the ruler to the populace's admiration or wrath, as during Maurice's procession to Blachernae.[125] Indeed, the emperor himself founded liturgical feasts and processions to honour the Virgin, who was emerging as the heavenly patron of the eastern capital.[126] Elaborate hymns, of which the most famous were composed by Romanos, enhanced these grand ceremonial occasions.

The connection between religion and political ideology became explicit when the forms of Christian worship were attached to specific events in the life of the state. The patriarch's blessing lent religious resonance to imperial accessions from the fifth century, and interaction between liturgy and public ritual steadily intensified.[127] Theodosius II interrupted a circus show and improvised a liturgical procession of thanksgiving when news of a usurper's defeat reached the eastern capital. By the reign of Maurice, purely liturgical forms had emerged to herald the success of Roman arms against the Persians.[128]

The ceremonial patterns which governed the adoration of the emperor also shaped the court's public devotions. The convergence of religion, ceremony and imperial ideology stands out clearly in the cult of the relic of the True Cross, which had become the simultaneous symbol of the new religion's victory over death and of the regenerated empire's victory over its enemies. So, when the relic was exposed to the city's veneration in the Great Church, Justin II's court assembled and proceeded in ranks of precedence to adore the cross, just as they adored the emperor.[129] The court also stimulated the cult of relics: Pulcheria obtained the supposed remains of St Stephen Protomartyr from Jerusalem and had them deposited in the palace church built especially for the purpose, and it has been argued that one of the exceedingly rare depictions of the imperial court shows precisely this procession. Leo I arranged for relics of St Symeon Stylites to be translated to the capital and lent his imperial carriage for the ceremony.[130]

V. COURT AND CULTURE

Court patronage helped promote new religious fashions, while its ceremonies and language prompted imitation within and beyond the empire's borders.[131] The court's influence extended into late Roman élite culture. The situation was propitious. The court, we have seen, comprised a polyglot mass of foreigners and Romans from throughout the empire drawn to the prestigious rewards of imperial service. Like the former hostage

---

[125] Theophyl. Sim. *Hist.* VIII.4.11–5.3; Baldovin (1987).
[126] Theoph. *AM* 6080; cf. Cameron, Averil (1978).
[127] Const. Porph. *De Cer.* 1.94; Winkelmann (1978b).   [128] McCormick, *Eternal Victory* 60; 69–70.
[129] Gagé (1933); John Eph. *HE* III.23.29.   [130] Holum and Vikan (1979); *V. Dan. Styl.* 58.
[131] McCormick (1989).

Theoderic, even the founders of post-Roman kingdoms might be intimately familiar with it. Their descendants, like the Vandal king Hilderic, might well have spent time and formed friendships there. Within the empire, constant emphasis on the emperor's omnipotence encouraged a stream of suppliants from the provinces who lobbied for various privileges or policies, whence, inevitably, wider exposure for the latest court trends among local élites. The court's lifestyle and its high fashion reverberated far afield, to judge from the inspiration detected in a Merovingian queen's burial gown long after direct contacts with foreign élites had decreased.[132]

In the capital, competition for visibility among the élite fuelled the demand for prestigious expenditure, as even the shreds of surviving evidence show. The general Ardabur and his Roman wife commissioned liturgical silver to satisfy a vow, and an emperor's daughter, Anicia Juliana, to whom a pope might turn when negotiating a *rapprochement* with the court, rivalled Justin I himself with her opulent shrine to St Polyeuctus. Justinian's lavish expenditure in the capital was followed by the remarkably extensive artistic patronage of his nephew. It is characteristic of the age that the balance of munificence shifts from the old civil projects of baths and theatres to religious buildings. These conditions fostered powerful cultural currents which spurred imitation in distant élites, as links between innovative sculptural decoration at St Polyeuctus and projects in the Ostrogothic kingdom indicate.[133]

Political practice dictated that the court have easy access to metalworkers and artists. As soon as Anastasius emerged as Zeno's successor, the future emperor was sequestered with engravers and painters, surely to publicize his accession throughout the empire by coinage and official portraits whose arrival stimulated so many provincial rituals.[134] Standard governmental procedure thus diffused art to the provinces, as did the direct imperial patronage of distant shrines and sites practised by Justinian: Constantinopolitan influence has been detected in the spectacular mosaics he commissioned at Sinai in the monastery of St Catherine.[135] Justinian's construction of churches in Africa dedicated to the Virgin lent impetus to a cult of Mary which mirrored developments in the capital, while the charateristically Constantinopolitan saints' cults that took root at Ravenna from the fifth century have been ascribed to the court.[136]

The links between court and culture are especially clear in literature. Some Latin manuscripts connected to Constantinople testify to that court's

---

[132] Viereck (1981) 90–2.
[133] Demandt (1986); Cameron (1980); Mango, *Développement* 52; Harrison (1986) 415 and 420; cf. Deichmann (1976–89) II.3.273–6. [134] Const. Porph. *De Cer.* 1.92, cf. 1.87; Kruse (1934).
[135] Forsyth and Weitzmann (1966) 16.
[136] Procop. *Buildings* VI.2.20, 4.4, 5.9, 7.16, cf. Cameron, Averil (1978) for Gaul; Deichmann (1976–89) II.3.176–7.

bilingual culture.[137] Emperors who, like Justinian, actually composed learned theological treatises, or empresses like Eudocia who versified scripture, hagiography and her husband's victory over the Persians, were exceptions. But the political dimension of religious orthodoxy required the palace to marshal theologians in the search for harmony, just as emperors deployed considerable resources for codifying Roman law. Theodosius II, in particular, was noted for his scholarly bent, discernible in the theological library and a geographical project that he sponsored.[138]

Dedications of literary works to the emperor or courtiers suggest another aspect of the palace's cultural role. Sozomen and Olympiodorus addressed their histories to Theodosius II, and Palladius' *Lausiac History* owes its title to Lausus, Theodosius II's chamberlain, a dedication which surely contributed to its remarkable success in publicizing ascetic practices. Panegyrics are a special case. These command performances were often solicited from figures with court connections and were well remunerated. For the élite privileged to hear them and penetrate their glittering complexity, elegant panegyrics accompanied important ceremonies. So Paul the Silentiary recited his famous paean on God's 'colleague' Justinian and his magnificent church during the rededication of the Great Church, while the city prefect praised the prince in an ambassadorial audience granted by Leo I in 467. John Lydus, who had served in the palace before joining the bureau of the praetorian prefect of the east, performed a similar service for Justinian – in return for which he was rewarded both with cash and promotion.[139] Corippus ascribes the initiative for his Latin epic on Justin II's accession chiefly to his master, the *quaestor*, while his claim only to furnish the tongue for the words of Justin II's mother and the Augusta is tantalizing indeed.[140]

The recurring professional connection of panegyrists and palace points to a more invidious aspect of the court's role in late Roman literary life, for there is a repeated pattern among the histories from this period. Sozomen may well be identical with the personal assistant of a praetorian prefect of the east; Olympiodorus served Theodosius II as ambassador; Priscus was a trusted assistant to the same emperor's close personal friend; Candidus was notary for some leading Isaurians, whose rise at court his lost history chronicled. Marcellinus controlled access to the young patrician Justinian and apparently won the title *comes* and a place in the court hierarchy thanks to his chronicle. Procopius, of course, served as assistant to Justinian's top general, and the stress of composing acceptable history left its mark in the *Secret History*. Menander's dignity as *protector* and his references to Maurice's generosity and fascination with history at least suggest a connection

[137] Cavallo (1984) 629–30.   [138] Soc. *HE* VII.22; Traube (1891) 406–9.
[139] Paul Sil. *Descr.* 6; Const. Porph. *De Cer.* 1.87; John Lydus, *De Mag.* III.28–9.
[140] *Iust.* I.15–24; 7–11. Cf. *PLRE* III *s.v.* Corippus.

between the two.[141] Over and over, the pattern is the same: obscure but trusted assistants to key players at court took up their pens to write histories that interpreted recent events for contemporaries. While these names do not exhaust the historical record of the period, they surely dominate it. Just as the emperor and his court permeated the conditions of these works' production and readership, so, through them, the court continues implicitly to influence our understanding of their era.

[141] Fr. 1.

CHAPTER 7

GOVERNMENT AND ADMINISTRATION

SAM BARNISH, A.D. LEE AND MICHAEL WHITBY

The late Roman period saw the development, for the first time in the Roman world, of complex bureaucratic structures which permitted emperors, who had now abandoned the campaigning or peripatetic style of most of their predecessors during the first four centuries of imperial history, to retain their authority. The emperor and his court with its glittering ceremonies in Constantinople was the focus for the eastern empire, and from there issued the laws which announced imperial wishes. The armies, though no longer directly commanded by emperors, strove to preserve the frontiers and maintain law and order inside them.[1] But the smooth functioning of this system required administrative structures which had to become more complex and intrusive as the curial élites in individual cities, who had traditionally performed many vital tasks in the areas of revenue generation, dissemination of imperial wishes and preservation of local order, slowly declined in authority or surrendered control of some of these duties; here was a cyclical process, with administrative developments responding to, but also encouraging, a weakening of the curial class. The impact of administration is reflected in a story from the *Life* of Theodore of Sykeon: devils being exorcized cried out: 'Oh violence! Why have you come here, you iron-eater, why have you quitted Galatia and come into Gordiane? There was no need for you to cross the frontier. We know you have come, but we shall not obey you as did the demons of Galatia, for we are much tougher than they, and not milder.' It is telling that the author of the *Life* should have seen the power of governors to cross provincial boundaries in pursuit of bandits as an analogy for Theodore's dealings with demons.[2] Active emperors, such as Anastasius and Justinian, could attempt to dominate and reform the administration, but their interference raised hackles; passive emperors might be treated with contempt for their laziness and neglect of their subjects. Overall, the fifth and sixth centuries are a time of gradual development in the key processes which permitted the empire to function.

---

[1] See ch. 6 (McCormick), pp. 142–56 above, and ch. 9 (Liebs) and ch. 11 (Whitby), pp. 242–4 and 308–14 below.

[2] See ch. 8 (Liebeschuetz), pp. 219–22 below. *Life* of Theodore 43, with which cf. Justinian, *Nov.* 145; *Edict* 8; Jones, *LRE* 294.

I. SOURCES

The range of different types of source for government and administration
in the fifth to sixth centuries is extensive, and these can be exploited to yield
a wide range of conclusions (often, though, highly conjectural) on the
structures and methods of government, on its personnel, and on their
values and attitudes. The sources, however, are also tantalizingly patchy, too
often restricted to narrow areas of space and time. The range indicates the
pervasiveness of government, at least at literate levels of society, and the
role of emperors and their administration in defining social and economic
structures and ways of thought; the restrictions indicate the infrequency of
major change – people take special notice of institutions when they are in
peril.

The men who tell us most about the system are those who sat at its centre,
the emperors. Their laws, however, express not only the imperial will, but the
wishes both of the ministers who will in most cases have influenced, or
determined, the drafting of laws, and of other ministers and subjects whose
complaints, reports and recommendations evoked them, and without whose
active and passive co-operation the system could not work. When, in 438, the
emperor Theodosius II published the sixteen books of his Code, compiling
legislation from the time of Constantine onwards, four books were devoted
to laws concerning civil and military administrative duties, privileges and
precedence, four to taxation and the imperial fisc, and another to the administration of Rome and Constantinople.[3] Of the Code of Justinian (529,
revised in 534) which superseded it, three out of twelve books are largely
devoted to these themes. In addition, we have a number of imperial laws
(*Novels*) published after the Codes, especially from Justinian, which also
handle administrative matters. Setting aside the content of individual laws,
this legislation tells us much about the interrelations of politics and government. The Theodosian Code was compiled by a bureaucracy which had been
firmly established at Constantinople for a generation, and seems modestly
professional in its approach to the problems of running systems of government and law that had both grown up haphazardly over centuries: indeed,
one aspect of this professionalism is the very process of identification and
collection of laws from provincial archives, in order to provide information
that had not been preserved at Constantinople in the period before it became
the settled capital of the eastern empire. The authorities were tidiers, rather
than innovators; it is notable that the volume of legislation included diminishes markedly in the early fifth century.

The Code also, however, reflects insecurity: the fact that the control of the
Theodosian dynasty over the western parts of the empire was dwindling,

---

[3] In general on the Theodosian Code, see the papers in Harries and Wood (1993).

through barbarian occupation of the provinces, while emperors had increasing difficulty in collecting taxes and enforcing their will in their own territories. The Code (published when a marriage alliance drew together the eastern and western branches of the dynasty) symbolically reaffirmed imperial unity and central control; it legitimated emperors by stressing their role as founts of law; not surprisingly, it was used or imitated by barbarian kings in the west, who, on a smaller scale, faced similar problems.[4] Justinian's Code and his subsequent *Novels* reflect the problems of an emperor whose relationship with the senatorial élite was often tense, and who (arguably) had grandiose long-term ambitions for the restoration of the empire as a single administrative unit. Unlike his fifth-century predecessors, Justinian was a legislative and administrative innovator, ruling an empire undergoing increasing social, economic and religious change, and aware that his world was in a state of flux. The rhetorical preambles to his earlier *Novels* (laws when included in the Codes omit this standard form) emphasize continuity and tradition, even in major administrative reforms.[5]

The overall picture of government given by the Codes is, then, as much symbolic as practical, and needs to be treated with some suspicion, when we ask not what emperors ideally expected from their servants and subjects, and their servants and subjects from them, but what they actually achieved. This principle also applies to individual laws. Thus, the 192 constitutions of Theodosian Code XII.1, in which emperors from Constantine to Theodosius II repeatedly tried to force men of the curial class to stay in their cities and do their duties in the imperial system, are often used to highlight the contrast between aspirations and effectiveness. We should not, however, be too sceptical. The curial system probably continued to function in a reasonably effective way over much of the empire during that period. Such laws may be seen as a repeated symbolic beating of the parish bounds, allied with the very practical purpose of forcible reminding. At the same time, however, they acted as a sluice gate by which emperors, and the *curiae* which, directly or indirectly, raised these problems and pressed emperors to legislate, controlled the level of the pool of literate, upper-class citizens who were needed in both the central and the local administrations.[6]

Our other main official source for the system at work in this period is the *Variae*.[7] This is the compilation of letters written by Cassiodorus on behalf of the Ostrogothic kings of Italy between *c.* 506 and 537, and in his own

---

[4] See ch. 10 (Charles-Edwards), pp. 284–7 below; also Barnwell (1992); Rousseau (1996) 10.

[5] Maas (1986).

[6] Repetition of laws may also be a consequence of requests by officials and subjects for clarification of the law: Harries in Harries and Wood (1993) 15. On the *curiales*, see Heather in *CAH* XIII.204–9.

[7] See Mommsen (1910); also the introduction to his edition in *MGH Auct. Ant.* XII (Berlin, 1894), and Barnish (1992), introduction.

right as praetorian prefect of Italy from 533 to 536. Since his masters preserved most Roman institutions, and depicted their realm as an imitation of the empire, the *Variae* tell us as much about imperial as about barbarian government. However, they must be handled as cautiously as the laws, and for similar reasons. Individually, they were written not just to promulgate decisions, but to legitimate Gothic rule by showing it as effective in practice, and imperial in style and structures. As a compilation, they probably served in part as an apology for the author and other Romans who had served the barbarians, and as a model for future administrators of Italy appointed by Justinian. Hence, we must be alert for institutional anachronisms, and for an over-flattering portrait of government. However, the *Variae* are a valuable supplement to the laws, both for the institutions, techniques and principles of administration, and also for its discourse, in which it responded to the presumed aspirations of its subjects. They have the ring of a government liturgy, a note absent from the bulk of the laws through the loss of their preambles. In the appended treatise *On the Soul*, Cassiodorus gave this liturgy a foundation in semi-theological reflections on morality and social history. Moreover, by using, in some cases, the form of private letters between cultivated upper-class gentlemen (in this, Cassiodorus may have been an innovator), the *Variae* highlight the important bond between ruler and subject of a shared literary culture. All government depends on the formation of such bonds, and it may be more important to the historian to understand them than the minutiae of administrative institutions.

Both laws and *Variae*, moreover, are a prime source of information on the leading ministers of state, assisting the prosopographical exploration of social mobility, family ties, politics and career paths. In particular, the *Variae* give us not just names and offices, but, in their numerous letters of appointment to high office, sketches of characters, backgrounds and careers. These conventional eulogies should be treated with the usual caution, but are at least evidence for what monarchs and senators expected of the top administrators. If the Codes affirm the dignity of the monarch as a fount of laws, the *Variae* affirm him as a fount of honours.

A variety of unofficial or semi-official sources help us to build up an image of the establishment classes and their ideas about government. Procopius' *Secret History*, with its scurrilous attacks on Justinian as the great innovator, tells us both something about his administrative practices and a great deal about the alienation of men on whom his government depended. The well-rehearsed invective *topoi* of the *Secret History* are the mirror image of the laudatory presentations of Cassiodorus' *Variae* and other more direct panegyrics such as those of Anastasius by Procopius of Gaza and Priscian, or of Justinian by Procopius of Caesarea (*Buildings*) and Paul the Silentiary.[8]

---

[8] Scott (1985) argues that Malalas' *Chronicle* is another mirror to the *Secret History*.

The contents of all such works require close but sceptical attention, though they can serve to reveal the aspirations of the educated élite. The expectations of a pious Christian are encapsulated in the deacon Agapetus' treatise of advice to the emperor Justinian. John Lydus' *On Magistracies*, primarily a highly informative, if often fictional, history of the praetorian prefecture by a middle-ranking official in its legal department, includes some illuminating autobiography, a Procopian attack on Justinian's great reforming prefect John the Cappadocian, and a general critique of changes which had affected the prefecture since the reign of Constantine.[9] John's history was not unique; it had a partial parallel, now lost, in the work of Peter the Patrician, master of the offices, who wrote a history of his bureau from Constantine to Justinian; the sixth-century *Liber Pontificalis* may likewise be seen as an in-house history of papal administration.[10] An anonymous and fragmentary dialogue on political science, probably from senatorial circles in the reign of Justinian, may supplement Procopius and John with its approval of a non-interventionist emperor. Like the works of John, Cassiodorus and Agapetus, this dialogue exemplifies a marked and significant sixth-century fashion for thinking about government.[11]

More conventional historiography gives only incidental information on administration, but, in its techniques, seems, like bureau-histories, to suggest the increasing penetration of late antique culture by a bureaucratic mentality. Historians seem willing to delve into archives, and to cite original documents at length, to an extent foreign to the classical tradition: not only church historians like Socrates, Sozomen and Evagrius, following the Eusebian tradition, but the chronicler John Malalas, probably an official in the bureau of the count of the east, and Menander Protector, on the fringe of official circles in Constantinople; the continuator of the *Anonymus Valesianus* at Ravenna provides a picture of Theoderic's administration comparable to the representation of Justinian's in Malalas.[12] As in the early empire, history continues to be largely the work of members of the classes from which governors and imperial officials were recruited, but also to show, at times, a latent or overt tension between their values and those of the emperor and his immediate circle: the alienation from government of a Procopius was hardly a novelty in the Roman world.

Upper-class circles – their cultural bonds, their political values and their relations with officialdom – can also be illuminated by other types of literary activity. This is a valuable corrective to the world of official documents:

---

[9] Maas, *John Lydus*.   [10] Noble (1990).

[11] Cameron, *Procopius* ch. 14; the dialogue is edited by C. Mazzucchi, *Menae Patricii cum Thoma Referendario, De Scientia Politica Dialogus* (Milan, 1982).

[12] Scott (1985); Jeffreys, *Studies* 204–11; Blockley (1985) 18–20. Note too the hypothesis of Howard-Johnston (1995) 166 n. 13 that behind the accounts of the Persian campaign of 503–4 in Theophanes and Joshua the Stylite there lies an official report circulated as propaganda.

it reminds us that a man's power depended as much on contacts, relatives and cultural prestige as on the posts he did or did not hold; prosopographies dominated by office-holders give a misleading picture of the establishment by ignoring the important gift-exchange relationships of praise and honour which produced their own parallel system.[13] From Constantinople, we have the poetry exchanged or collected among lawyers and civil servants like Agathias, and preserved in the *Palatine Anthology*; from Egypt, the poems which Dioscorus of Aphrodito addressed to local bigwigs; from Ostrogothic Italy, the letters and poems of bishop Ennodius of Pavia, or the account of Theoderic's activity as judge and builder preserved in the continuation of the *Anonymus Valesianus*; from Gaul at the end of the empire, the letters and poems of Sidonius Apollinaris.[14] Boethius' *Consolation of Philosophy* gives a brief attack on Theoderic's administration which balances Cassiodorus and stands in the ancient tradition of senatorial opposition to bad emperors. Papal correspondence – for example, the letters preserved in the *Collectio Avellana* – illumines the increasingly important role of popes in maintaining relations between Rome and Constantinople; the voluminous correspondence of Gregory the Great, in particular, tells us much about Byzantine Italy at a period when the pope was closely involved with imperial administration and diplomacy.[15]

Papyri continue to be a source, not only for the running of Egypt, but also of Palestine, and for the administrative personnel of Ostrogothic and Byzantine Ravenna;[16] unlike most literary texts, they can sometimes yield information about the lowest, almost invisible levels of the bureaucracy. Well down into the sixth century, inscriptions, especially those from Aphrodisias (Caria), continue to tell us much about the running of eastern cities and their relations with provincial governors.[17] Archaeology, too, casts light on the bureaucracy, specifically on archive storage (see below), while in the sixth century, seals emerge as a useful source for offices and office-holders.[18] New discoveries will produce more evidence, as for example the collection of sixth-century papyri discovered at Petra in 1992 which, among other details of local life, refer to a Ghassanid leader in the context of a dispute about water rights.[19]

Perhaps the most serious deficiency of our sources is the near invisibility of the minor civil servants referred to above. We seldom know even the

[13] Cf., in general, Lendon (1997) ch. 3–4.

[14] Anthology: see Cameron and Cameron (1966); McCail (1969). Dioscorus: MacCoull, *Dioscorus*. Ennodius: Cesa (1988); Rohr (1997). Sidonius: Harries (1994b).

[15] For interesting use of Gregory's letters, see Brown, *Gentlemen and Officers*.

[16] For a recent survey of eastern papyri found outside of Egypt: Cotton, Cockle and Millar (1995); Ravenna: Tjäder (1955–82), with discussion in Brown, *Gentlemen and Officers*.

[17] Roueché, *Aphrodisias*; Roueché, *Performers and Partisans*.

[18] The most accessible collection of this information is in the *fasti* at the back of *PLRE* III.

[19] Daniel (1996).

names of the more lowly staff of prefects or governors; of their competence, culture or official values, if any, almost nothing. Even at the top levels
of the administration, we are informed of only a tiny percentage of office-
holders (especially during the fifth century, with its dearth of legislation),
and know all too little about their careers (especially any lesser posts they
may have held) and their achievements;[20] this means that general assessments of competence, promotions and power are bound to be conjectural.

II. THE STRUCTURES OF GOVERNMENT

The structures of civil administration in the east when Justinian came to
power, or in contemporary Ostrogothic Italy, had, at least in outward
appearance, altered very little from the days of Valentinian I at the end of
the fourth century. However, following the reign of Maurice (582–602),
change (very ill documented) seems to have been radical: from a complex
and essentially civilian system of a few multi-tiered departments, subject to
great ministers, there evolved a number of simpler departments (*sekreta*),
as listed in the *Kleterologion* of Philotheos (899); these were directly subor-
dinated to the emperor, and integrated with a militarized system of provincial government.[21] As we shall see, however, it is possible to detect changes
beneath the surface of the fifth- and sixth-century system which prepared
the ground for the empire which fought off the Arabs.

The fundamental purpose of the administrative system remained the
delivery of the resources upon which the empire's existence depended.
This entailed the control of a complex system of apportionment, extraction, transport and redistribution, and the judicial supervision of the problems and complaints which this process inevitably generated. When
studying the administration, it is important to remember that state service
extended far outside the official hierarchies. Thanks in part to the classical
tradition of personal, liturgic service of the community, there was no clear
division between public and private: it is significant that ancient languages
have no word for the concept of the state as something distinct from, and
superior to, its citizens.[22] Any man of standing in the empire was, or might
easily become, an unsalaried civil servant, administering his city (the basic
unit of the empire) or an imperial estate, collecting taxes on his estates,
organizing corvée labour on the roads or finding transport for military or
civil supplies. Conversely, it was easy for him to treat any paid office he
might hold as a kind of private property. A regular civil servant might wield

---

[20] The best lists of known office-holders are provided in the *fasti* in *PLRE* II and III.

[21] Philotheos: Bury (1911). Bureaucratic change: Haldon, *Byzantium in the Seventh Century*;
Winkelmann (1976).

[22] Note, too, that the verb πολιτεύεσθαι, 'to be a citizen', came to mean 'to hold public office':
Cameron, *Circus Factions* 288–9.

his office as in the case of the praetorian prefect Cyrus of Panopolis (simultaneously prefect of Constantinople), like a great private benefactor, or even like an emperor: this point was lost neither on the Hippodrome crowd in Constantinople, which compared Cyrus' building achievements with those of Constantine, nor on the emperor Theodosius II, who promptly relegated Cyrus to the bishopric of Cotyaeum. No description of the administration can really do justice to its pervasiveness and complexity.[23]

Among those at the top in the fifth and sixth centuries, the men whose offices gave them the rank of *illustris* and membership of the senate of Rome or Constantinople, were the two great palatine heads of department, members of the emperor's personal entourage (*comitatus*) with the title of count (*comes* or companion of the emperor).[24] These were the *comes sacrarum largitionum* (count of the sacred largesses), who collected the revenues due in the form of precious or semi-precious metals and textiles, and disbursed it in coin, plate and uniforms, and the *comes rerum privatarum* (count of the private estates), who saw to the incorporation and administration of estates accruing to the emperor by confiscation or bequest, and as abandoned or heirless property (*bona vacantia* or *caduca*).[25] The former headed a large and elaborate department, with ten sub-departments (*scrinia*) at the imperial court; in each diocesan group of provinces, he controlled an administrator with a large staff, and jurisdiction in fiscal cases; he also controlled provincial depots, customs offices, mines, certain state factories and a departmental transport service. The latter's organization was similar, but on a smaller scale: five sub-departments at court, administrators at diocesan and provincial level, and officials in charge of individual estates or groupings of estates (*domus divinae*). Both ministers supervised the work of their provincial subordinates, principally the collection of revenue, by annually despatching staff (*palatini*) from their central *scrinia*.

In the west, some of the functions of the *comes rerum privatarum* were eventually hived off to a new *illustris* minister, the *comes patrimonii*, perhaps first attested under the emperor Glycerius (473–4).[26] He seems to have been in charge of imperial estates directly administered, while the *comes rerum privatarum* took in new accessions and collected revenues from those estates which had been rented out. This reform was imitated in the east by the emperor Anastasius in the 490s, although it is uncertain whether the responsibilities of the two counts were identical to those of their western counterparts; it may be that the *patrimonium* was dedicated to the emperor's public, fiscal expenditure, his 'largesses', the *res privata* to the expenses of the court. This may reflect a distinction between public and private property which had accrued to the crown, the former including confiscated civic or temple lands,

---

[23] In general, for description see Jones, *LRE* chs. 12–16.   [24] Cf. Kelly in *CAH* xiii.162–9.
[25] Delmaire (1989).   [26] Hänel (1857) 260.

and old Roman *ager publicus*. The *comes rerum privatarum* also tended to lose control of the *domus divinae*: by 414, the administration of the vast Cappadocian *domus divina* had been taken over by the emperor's head eunuch chamberlain, the *praepositus sacri cubiculi*, presumably as the man chiefly responsible for the court; under Justinian, other *domus divinae* came under high-ranking curators, who probably worked independently from the *privata*.[27] Theoderic seems to have earmarked the revenues of Visigothic Spain for his *cubiculum*, perhaps on the legal excuse that they were due to him personally as guardian of the Visigothic king Amalaric.[28] This fissiparous tendency of the *privata* may reflect the difficulties of administering enormous and far-flung estates through one department. It may also show attempts to clarify the blurred distinction, which dates back to the overlapping competences of *aerarium* and *fiscus* under the first emperor Augustus, and which will continue into the medieval west with the interlocking roles of royal exchequer and wardrobe, between the wealth of the state and of the emperor as an individual. The growing power of the *cubiculum* also reflects the reality that rulers were always interested in direct control of cash.

The third great palatine ministry – and politically, perhaps, the most important – was that of the *magister officiorum* (master of the offices),[29] who was titular superior to a range of palace staffs, including the *sacra scrinia* of the chancellery (which handled legal affairs, as well as general imperial communications) and the *scholae* of imperial bodyguards; how far, if at all, he actually controlled their operations, is obscure. The *magister officiorum* also ran the politically sensitive arms factories. His power lay mainly in his dominance of communications with the emperor. He organized audiences, provided interpreters for foreign envoys, and controlled the corps of couriers and public post inspectors, the *agentes in rebus* or *magistriani*. The *agentes* sometimes acted as spies and informers in the provinces, and the senior members of their corps were appointed to head the staffs of prefects, diocesan vicars, and certain provincial governors and generals. In this capacity, they countersigned all orders issuing from their offices, but remained under the control of the *magister*, who was thereby well placed to get information on a wide range of official activity.[30] When Arvandus, praetorian prefect of Gaul, was suspected of treason in 468, his correspondence was intercepted and his secretary arrested;[31] in this the *agens* may have assisted.

The *magister*'s control of the palace was balanced, to some extent, by an independent corps of socially and politically prestigious notaries.[32] Their original duty of acting as secretaries to the imperial *consistorium* (council) was taken over during the fifth century by the *agentes*, but they came to supply the emperor with an important group of law officers, the referendaries;

[27] Kaplan (1976) 10–16.   [28] Cass. *Variae* v.39.13.   [29] Clauss (1980); Delmaire (1995) ch. 6.
[30] Giardina (1977) part 1; Sinnigen (1964); Morosi (1981).   [31] Sid. Ap. *Ep.* 1.7.5.
[32] Teitler (1985).

these enjoyed frequent access to him, presenting legal appeals and transmitting his responses. Cyprian, who served as referendary to the Ostrogoth Theoderic and rose to high office, presented appeals to the king when they were out riding for relaxation; he was able to challenge the *magister* Boethius in the presentation of a treason case and bring about his downfall.[33] Petrus, a *magister* of the *sacra scrinia* (*magister epistularum*) under Majorian, commanded armies and conducted diplomatic negotiations; politically, he probably outweighed the *magister officiorum*, his nominal superior.[34]

Another top palatine minister was the *quaestor* of the sacred palace.[35] He was the emperor's mouthpiece, drafting letters, proclamations, responses, rescripts and laws, and transmitting petitions to the emperor; consequently, he was often a legal expert. He headed no department, administered nothing, and borrowed his staff from the chancellery *scrinia*.[36] His duties, those of the chancellery heads and those of the referendary overlapped each other; in Merovingian Gaul, the royal referendary seems to have been the principal law officer and secretary; in Ostrogothic Italy, the *quaestor* probably took over the role of the *magistri scriniorum*, who became honorary officials, while the *quaestor*, 'the mother of all honours', 'the gate of royal favours', issued letters of appointment to major offices.[37] Since suggestions for reforms in the system of government came from the relevant ministers and departments, the *quaestor* had little power over the system; he merely put into legal shape what others had originated. However, his influence over non-administrative legislation was great, and he presumably had constant access to the emperor. His chancellery role probably meant that he had to work closely with the *magister*, and was presumably another counterbalance to his power (and vice versa): Boethius, as *magister*, was temporarily able to block the appointment of an objectionable *quaestor*, Tribonian alternated between the two offices, and even combined them in 535, while under Justin II Anastasius also held these concurrently.[38] In the east, the *quaestor* gradually developed a role as judge of appeal, in which he outlasted the praetorian prefect (another example of administrative balancing). From 440, he sat with the prefect to hear appeals from *spectabiles iudices*, and under Justinian he heard appeals from Sicily and the provinces of the *quaestura exercitus*. This reflected his close association with the emperor: 'For we think it not improper that the *quaestor* should take under his jurisdiction Sicily, which is established as, so to speak, our personal estate.'[39]

[33] Bury (1910); Cass. *Variae* v.41.3; *Anon. Valesianus* 85.   [34] See *PLRE* II *s.v.* Petrus 10.
[35] Guilland (1971); Tribonian: Honoré (1978) 8–9; Harries (1988).
[36] However, the preface to Justinian, *Nov.* 35 may indicate that he came to control the *scrinia memoriae et epistularum*; cf. also Cass. *Variae* VIII.18.3.
[37] Cass. *Variae* VI.5.5; VIII.13.5–7; Justinian, *Nov.* 17 (*CJC* III.117, 33) indicates that the *quaestor* is issuing codicils to new provincial governors, an extension of his involvement in appointments.
[38] *Cons. Phil.* 3, prose 4; cf. Cass. *Variae* v.3–4.
[39] *CJ* VII.62.32; *Nov.* 20, 41; 104; quotation from 104.3

The praetorian prefects stood, in theory, and sometimes in practice, outside the palatine system: they were imperial deputies, and their judicial functions, their right to issue edicts and the honours paid to them paralleled and mimicked those of the emperors: 'On his entry to the palace, he is adored as I [the monarch] am, by large numbers, and so high an office permits a practice which would mean a treason charge for others.'[40] Post-Roman monarchs in the west may have adopted something of their legislative role from the prefects.[41] However, an informal distinction grew up between the prefects of Italy and the east (*Oriens*), who resided in the imperial capitals and were *de facto* members of the *comitatus*, and the prefects of Gaul and Illyricum, who were usually based far from the court and enjoyed less wealth, prestige and influence on the court and emperor. From commanding the praetorian guard of the early empire, the prefects developed into something like ministers of war, deputizing for the emperor as head of the army, even though operational command of troops was taken from them by Constantine I. They remained the army's chief purveyors, drawing up the empire's annual budget, calculating the needs of the empire and the corresponding taxes or special levies, and seeing to military recruitment and supply; hence they controlled the systems of taxation and communications – namely, the roads and the *cursus publicus* (public post) – on which these were based, supervising the lower administrative tiers, the diocesan vicars, the provincial governors and even the town councils. It should be noted that the *cursus publicus* was 'probably second only to the army in its command of manpower and resources – certainly it must have been superior in this respect to the civil bureaucracy'.[42] Praetorian duties of military supply seem also to have been gradually extended into the food supply of the imperial capitals and of lesser cities.[43] This formidable accumulation of responsibilities highlights the degree to which the Roman empire was an institution organized for war; the fourth-century separation of military and civilian powers, important politically, seems, in this light, an artificial and vulnerable distinction. Aided by tax changes (discussed below), these mighty prefectures increasingly overshadowed the financial ministries, but their powers were also exposed to encroachment by generals and warlords, and to reforms that aided the army's needs, notably Justinian's creation of the *quaestura exercitus*.

The staffs of the prefectures (we know most about the prefectures of the east) were divided into two sections, judicial and financial. In the latter, one *scrinium* was allocated to the tax affairs and administrative expenses of

---

[40] Cass. *Variae* VI.3.4. Cf. Eunap. *VS* 490 ('an office which, while lacking the imperial purple, exercises imperial power'); Soc. *HE* II.16 ('second in power after the emperor').

[41] Barnwell (1992) 74; though note the criticism of Sirks (1996a) 154–5.

[42] Hendy, *Studies* 605; though cf. n. 168 below for the *magister officiorum* sharing control of the *cursus*.

[43] Cass. *Variae praef.* 5; XI.2.2–4, 5, 11, 15, 39; XII.11.26–8. Durliat (1990a) 67, 234, 245.

each diocese; others dealt with outgoing payments or levies of money or commodities for public works, and for the state arms factories. Another looked after the treasury, and thereby apparently channelled the prefecture's holdings in gold to the other *scrinia*; the eastern treasury was divided into the General Bank and the Special Bank (the *Genike* and the *Idike Trapeza*), the separate duties of which are virtually unknown. There were also departments without the title of *scrinium*, one for army rations and one (formed under Justinian) for the corn supply of Constantinople. The judicial sections had a smaller range of *scrinia*, concerned with legal records, management of trials and the general secretarial work of the prefectures. The staffs of diocesan *vicarii* (also those of the quasi-vicarial augustal prefect and count of the east) and of provincial governors replicated the judicial/financial division, and many of the official grades of the prefectures above them; how far the formal *scrinium* organization was also reproduced is unknown, although some elaboration must have been necessary in the larger diocesan staffs. All departmental staffs had a large administrative penumbra of supernumeraries, assessors, advisers, and men recruited from the households of their heads, or assigned by them to special duties. They also had many low-ranking sub-clerical personnel officially on the strength.[44]

In addition to the great ministries, staffed at the upper levels by men from the landed aristocracies of the empire, the emperors maintained large numbers of *cubicularii* (chamberlains), usually eunuch slaves or freedmen. In addition to potentially vast influence in politics and patronage (reflected in the rise of the *praepositi sacri cubiculi*, by the early fifth century, to *illustris* rank), these had important administrative roles. Their control of the *domus divina per Cappadociam* has been noted; in addition, the eunuch *sacellarius* managed the privy purse. Presumably dedicated initially to court expenses, under Justinian, if not earlier, it was used to fund warfare and fortifications; hence, *sacellarii* emerge as generals and army paymasters. The distinction between public and private imperial resources seems to have proved hard to maintain, and emperors probably received nearly as much wealth from crown properties as from taxes: in 431, Valentinian III, an emperor whose tax revenues were very inadequate, boasted of his public expenditure from the *res privata*.[45] It may be that emperors were, in fact, making themselves increasingly independent of the traditional state hierarchies and the ruling class of the empire. Procopius describes at length and with bitterness Justinian's methods of enriching the crown; there may be more in this than just a standard attack on a bad emperor. The counts of the various parts of the *domus divina* were already important people by the end of Justinian's reign, a reflection of the emperor's determination to secure direct control

[44] Jones, *LRE* 586–96.   [45] *C.Th.* XI.1.36.

of financial matters.[46] In the seventh century, the *sacellarius* grew further in importance, and came eventually to supervise the small departments of the new Byzantine system: the land survey and tax reassessment conducted by the *sacellarius* Philagrius in the late 630s illustrates this growing domination.[47]

Offices were not just bureaucratic posts; they were also highly-prized dignities: the source which provides our best evidence on official structures at the end of the fourth century, the *Notitia Dignitatum*,[48] is, as the title suggests, a register of dignities: offices, civil and military, are defined in terms of insignia and subordinates far more than of duties. Precedence mattered, and was controlled and demonstrated, in the eastern empire, through the organization of imperial ceremonies at Constantinople.[49] Much administrative legislation of the late empire is devoted to problems of precedence, and in eleventh-century Byzantium Anna Comnena saw the emperor Alexius' skill in devising new and splendid titles for his supporters as decisive evidence of his political talent.[50] The distinction between service and honour was blurred. Moreover, the practice of short-term appointments at the higher levels of the system both enlarged the emperor's patronage and confirmed the preference of his more prominent subjects for honoured leisure. Not surprisingly, then, outside the departmental structures but within the late Roman establishment stood large numbers of *honorati*: retired officials, or men with honorary titles. Such titles were not sought only for prestige and influence; they freed their holders from the duties of service on the town councils, although they might still involve them in local or civic administrative tasks: checking of accounts, revision of the census, and supervision of buildings or the corn supply. One effect of the multiplication of *honorati* was to create a class in each province which might rival, or outweigh the authority of, the provincial governor,[51] though in some areas governors came to be drawn from this class.[52] The gradual replacement of civic by imperial service as the prime source of honour may often have tied the provinces more closely to the centre, though to offset their declining importance one finds surviving *curiales* usurping the title of *clarissimus* by the late fifth century.[53] At a higher level, the emperors, especially in the east, might grant honorary *illustris* offices to serving officials to lift them to senatorial status, or to men called in for special tasks: thus, jurists

---

[46] Theophanes 235.1–7; 237.1–4.   [47] Kaegi (1992) 256–8.

[48] On the *Notitia*, see Kelly in *CAH* XIII.163–5.

[49] See ch. 6 (McCormick), p. 157 above. Haldon, *Byzantium in the Seventh Century* 387–94.

[50] *Alexiad* III.4; cf. Eusebius, *Life of Constantine* IV.1: 'For the emperor devised new dignities, that he might give tokens of his favour to a larger number of people.' For the combined process of development of new ranks and titles and devaluation of existing ones, see Brown, *Gentlemen and Officers* 130–43; Haldon (1990) 389–91.

[51] Lendon (1997) 223–35; cf. Van Dam (1996) 80 for bishops and governors.

[52] Cass. *Variae* 1.3.5; 1.4.13; XI.39.5; Greatrex (1996); Roueché, *Aphrodisias* 66; Barnish (1988) 131–3.

[53] Barnish (1988) 121 n. 9.

working on the Theodosian Code might be honorary *quaestor*, or men charged with supplying an army for a campaign might rank as praetorian prefects. Some of those so honoured were *vacantes*, without specific duties, but still (presumably) enjoying the official salary of their rank.

Recruitment to the corps of notaries might also be a way of honouring high-flyers with a sinecure post, but many notaries withdrew entirely from their nominal duties at court. In the sixth century, in particular under Justinian, the number of high honorary officials, especially prefects, proliferated enormously, as did the more formally honorific titles of patrician and honorary consul, far beyond the capacity of the emperors to find occasional employment for them. The emperors were enlarging the pool of gentry who were bound more directly to them than those associated with the traditions of town councils or state departments; like politicians at other periods, they also increased their revenues through the sale of honours (see further below). The practice testifies to the integration of the imperial system and its wealthier subjects, who pressed for admission; it may also reflect Justinian's problems with the established aristocracy, especially during the 520s when he was desperate to ensure his succession to the throne. In the long run, this tendency to separate power and status from imperial service must have weakened emperors and devalued the active offices on which status was ultimately based.[54]

Another potential challenge to imperial domination might be provided by the senates of Rome and Constantinople, which embodied the traditions of Rome even more than did imperial office. Constantine I and Valentinian I had made senatorial membership the highest reward for service; senatorial approval still legitimated emperors or actively aided their accessions, as it did for Anastasius and Justin II; the senate at Rome may have played a part in the rise of Theodahad to the Gothic kingship.[55] Senators were also capable of passive resistance, and even active opposition to rulers. Justin I and Justinian, for example, both submitted controversial plans to the senate and faced strong opposition, led on one occasion by the *quaestor* Proclus and on another by the praetorian prefect John the Cappadocian.[56] Phocas seems to have encountered determined opposition from the administrative and social élite in Constantinople. The elimination of Boethius reflects Theoderic's justified anxiety about the behaviour of the Roman senate.

Again outside the administrative structures, but loosely associated with them by function, and by imperial honours, payments and supervision, stood the professional groups of lawyers, doctors and teachers. The judicial functions of Roman magistrates and emperors, and the engagement in litigation

---

[54] The *fasti* in *PLRE* III provide lists of honorary offices and ranks.
[55] For this speculation, see Barnish (1990) 28–30.
[56] Theophanes 168.2–6; Procop. *Wars* 1.11.10–18; 3.10.

of the imperial treasury, had long intertwined lawyers and government; 'more and more of the law, in the late Roman empire, was administrative'.[57] In 469, Leo described the legal profession as a *militia* as important to the empire as the army.[58] The empire conventionally defined itself, over against the barbarians, as the domain of law. Every official with judicial duties (including generals) had his own bar of registered advocates, the most senior of whom briefly served, with a high salary and with retirement honours, as *advocatus fisci*, presenting cases for the emperor. Magistrates also picked out advocates to serve as their judicial assessors, with salaries from the state, and many lawyers passed on to government office. The emperors did much to regulate the career structures and rewards of lawyers at the official bars: from 460 onwards they even demanded of them some measure of formal professional qualifications, a requirement probably unique in the ancient world. Even high-ranking officials used the title *scholasticus*, which denoted their legal qualifications, though for the advocate the skills of jurisprudence never quite seem to have outclassed those of rhetoric.[59]

From the time of the Hellenistic monarchies onwards it had been seen as a ruler's duty to foster scholars and teachers. In the sources for the late empire, this duty becomes so conspicuous that it is possible to speak of an *étatisation* of higher (but not of primary) education. When appointed to the chair of rhetoric at Autun by Constantius I in 298, Eumenius likened his promotion to a military command (compare Leo on the lawyers' *militia*) and acclaimed his role in teaching potential imperial barristers and secretaries; in about 310 a panegyrist from Autun described as sons his ex-pupils who had moved on to such service.[60] Gratian increased the number of endowed chairs of grammar and rhetoric in the provincial capitals of the Gallic prefecture, Theodosius II those of grammar, rhetoric, philosophy and law in Constantinople; in both Rome and Constantinople, public teachers and students were regulated by the emperors and supervised by the urban prefects. In 370 Gratian ordered the prefect of Rome to despatch annual registers of students to the imperial *scrinia* 'in order that we may learn of the merits and education of the various students and may judge whether they may ever be necessary to us'.[61] In 533 king Athalaric described the teachers of Rome as 'those through whom good morals are advanced and the talent of rhetoric is nurtured to serve my palace'.[62]

All the same, education was never fully a function of the central authorities. No bureau was specifically dedicated to its supervision; control was exercised mainly by the cities which had endowed the majority of the

---

[57] Crook (1995) 192.   [58] *CJ* 11.7.14.
[59] Roueché, *Aphrodisias* 76–7; Crook (1995) 188–94. In the fifth century, *scholastici* were usually described as 'most eloquent'.
[60] *Pan. Lat.* 9.5.4; 6.23.2. See further Cameron in *CAH* XIII.673–9, and ch. 29 (Browning), pp. 871–2 below.   [61] *C.Th.* XIV.9.1 (trans. C. Pharr).   [62] Cass. *Variae* IX.21.8.

chairs; imperial grants of appointment and salaries seem to have been rather unsystematic, exemplifying patronage of individuals and cities rather than any long-term educational policy. Julian, in decreeing that town councils should appoint their own teachers, remarked, 'I cannot be present in person in all the municipalities.'[63] The expectation that rhetorical training would supply the empire with lawyers and civil servants seems genuine (though Gratian's registers may never have proved workable), but it is less prominent in the sources than a more generalized concern for literary skills and the upper-class moral values which that training was supposed to inculcate. The extensive involvement of emperors in the education of the aristocracy may illustrate the extent to which the imperial system and the empire's ruling class were identical, with no division between state and individual; then, as now, education was a public utility, which the state was prepared to fund in return for perceived benefits. The most consistent and important form of teachers' pay was indirect – namely, immunities from curial and other burdens – which demonstrates that education was seen as one form of the liturgic duties which citizens in general owed to their cities and the empire. Education was interwoven with the traditions of civic life, with the winning of praise among one's peers in the forum, so that the transformation of the classical city would affect both education and imperial administration.[64]

Other professions appear in the same light. Public doctors were similarly maintained in the cities by a mixture of civic and imperial funding and immunities. There were also, however, court doctors who were granted official rank as counts, with duties of supervision and technical advice for the medical profession, whereas teachers do not seem to have been attached to the palace in this regular fashion. Emperors likewise, though more spasmodically, used immunities to encourage the teaching and practice of architecture, and even of crafts and fine arts.[65]

Office in the church was increasingly supervised by emperors, and exploited for local administration and as a channel for benefactions – to such an extent that, by the reign of Justinian, the church seems almost a government *militia*, while Gregory the Great looks, at times, like a second exarch in Maurice's Italy; in the 630s patriarch Cyrus of Alexandria was simultaneously governor of Egypt.[66] Yet the church was never formally a department, but, like the other professions, experienced grants of immunities, privileges, occasional subventions, and spasmodic regulation of appointments; the church could be seen as another alternative to liturgic service of the community. Significantly, pope Gregory usually refers

---

[63] *C.Th.* XIII.3.5.   [64] Cass. *Variae* VIII.31.4–6.   [65] Cass. *Variae* VI.19.3–7; Jones, *LRE* 1012–13.

[66] On bishops, urban corn supplies and taxation, see Durliat (1990a) 131–56, 316–17 (perhaps overstated). Benefactions: M. Sartre in *IGLS* XIII.1.210–11, discussing Justinian and the archbishop of Arabia.

to ecclesiastical functions as a *dignitas* or *honos*, even though the competitive culture of honour was deeply offensive to his ideal of the priesthood. With the church's increasing administrative role should be linked the partial replacement of the classical and civic by Christian and ecclesiastical education, the decline of the *curiales* and other changes in civic life, and Justinian's purging of highly educated pagans from the government.[67]

This overview of the structures of government has focused, justifiably, on personnel and their organization. However, such a survey would be incomplete without some consideration of that other quintessential element integral to bureaucracies and their ethos – paperwork (i.e. records on papyri, for which we have some local examples from Egypt and Palestine). The evident increase in the number of bureaucrats during the late Roman period compared with the principate would seem logically to imply, first, an increase in the volume of administrative paperwork and, second, the need to organize such material more effectively than is assumed to have been the case in previous centuries.[68] The first proposition has in fact been disputed on the basis of the papyrological evidence,[69] but it is a view which fails to give due weight to the evidence of the laws contained in the Codes and collections of *Novels* from the fifth and sixth centuries. In their mode of promulgation and in much of their substantive content, these imply the generation of significant quantities of official documentation. The second proposition is a logical corollary not only of greater amounts of paperwork, but also of the more sedentary lifestyle of emperors during the fifth and sixth centuries. As a result of their active involvement in military campaigning, the governmental apparatus of the tetrarchs and their fourth-century successors had to be relatively mobile, which must have retarded the development of centralized imperial archives to any great extent. The new pattern, initiated under the sons of Theodosius I, of non-campaigning emperors who rarely travelled far from the imperial capital will, by contrast, have favoured such a development. Records could function as a symbol of government, but also as weapons whose control gave power and wealth to the bureaucrats who understood their language and had access to long-forgotten receipts. John the Cappadocian earned great unpopularity in the praetorian prefecture by a determined effort to reduce its paperwork and, ultimately perhaps, the number of officials who handled it.[70]

Repositories for a variety of records are attested in Constantinople during our period – the judicial records of the office of the praetorian

---

[67] Marrou (1956) ch. 10; Mango (1980) ch. 10; Haldon, *Byzantium in the Seventh Century* 425–35; Cameron, *Rhetoric of Empire* ch. 6.

[68] John Lydus, *De Mag.* III.11–13, 19–20, 68. Cf. Millar (1977) 259–68.   [69] Harris (1989) 290, 317.

[70] Symbols: John Lydus, *De Mag.* III.14; Cass. *Variae* XI.38; weapons: *Nov. Val.* 1.3; cf. 7.1–2, and *Nov. Maj.* 2.1; John the Cappadocian: John Lydus, *De Mag.* III.11–19, 66, 68.

prefect of the east,[71] the archives of the city prefect,[72] tax registers[73] and the texts of treaties with foreign states.[74] It is apparent that archives of official documents were also maintained in provincial capitals,[75] and one of Justinian's reforms extended this further by requiring the *defensor civitatis* in every city to establish a building for the deposit and consultation of documentation associated with his duties, under the care of a designated guardian.[76] Some of the physical structures for the storage of official documents have even been identified in the archaeological record, in both metropolitan and provincial contexts. The archive rooms of the praetorian prefect have been located under the Hippodrome in Constantinople, while recent excavations in Caesarea Maritima (Palestine) have revealed a late Roman building (18×15 metres) described in a mosaic inscription set into its floor as an office (*skrinion*) staffed by *chartularii* and a *numerarius*, presumed to be part of the provincial governor's administrative apparatus; comprising seven rooms facing on to a courtyard, it includes a further inscription (appropriately, in duplicate), which quotes St Paul, to urge their duty on tax-payers and officials.[77] Of course, one should not assume too high a level of efficiency in the maintenance of such collections: the need for the compilers of the Theodosian Code to resort to provincial archives to locate copies of some imperial laws provides a salutary warning in this respect.[78] On the other hand, this particular episode dates from early in our period and in fact more likely serves to confirm the limited character of central archives in the fourth century; as already noted, Constantinople had not long been the settled capital of the eastern empire.

III. ADMINISTRATION IN OPERATION

Assessing the operational effectiveness of these administrative structures is no easy task, and requires attention to a number of different issues. One is the responsiveness of the administration to the problems and grievances of the administered, another its impact on the financial well-being of the empire – its cost-effectiveness. The first issue involves consideration of the modes of communication between ruler and ruled. The emperor communicated a variety of messages, both explicit and subliminal, to the inhabitants of his empire through media ranging from official proclamations to

---

[71] John Lydus, *De Mag.* III.19, with discussion in Kelly (1994) 261.

[72] *Chron. Pasch.* p. 622 (destruction during Nika riot); Theophanes p. 297 (destruction during riot in 608).   [73] Evagr. *HE* III.39 (discussed below).

[74] Menander fr. 6,1; Greg. *Reg.* IX.229, with discussion of further possibilities in Lee (1993) 33–40.

[75] Jeffreys, *Studies* 203–9; Evagr. *HE* III.39.

[76] *Nov.* 15.5.2. How far this law was implemented by *defensores* is another matter, but it certainly demonstrates an appreciation of the value of storage of records.

[77] Kelly (1994) 161–3; *SEG* 32.1498 (the *skrinion* inscription); Holum (1988) 169–71; Stern (1993) 1.285. Further discussion in Holum (1995).   [78] Matthews in Harries and Wood (1993) 19–45.

architecture and coinage, but, within the context of administration and government, the primary form of communication from centre to subject was imperial legislation, usually circulated to provincial officials and then, as appropriate, conveyed to the upper classes in provincial assemblies and to the populace by the display of laws on boards in public areas, such as the market-place or at the doors of churches[79] – though officials might sometimes prove obstructive in their implementation.[80] The system worked partly through exhortation and persuasion, partly also through the fear induced by the prospect of savage punishment, something of which loyal officials like Malalas thoroughly approved.[81]

The emperor's subjects in turn communicated their views and grievances to the centre by a variety of methods. At the individual level, those with the resources might travel to Constantinople to seek legal redress from the emperor or senior officials, or they might send written petitions. Communities sent similar embassies: at Aphrodisias the *pater civitatis* and the *possessores* bypassed the governor of Caria to approach Justinian directly about the regulation of civic funds.[82] An individual willing to undertake such communal business might well also have private matters to transact, as, for example, Dioscorus of Aphrodito. In spite of the danger that orchestrated chanting might present unrepresentative opinions, acclamations were an important form of administrative feedback; although the term has positive connotations in English, acclamations in the late Roman empire were often negative in import. Constantine had actually urged gatherings of provincials to express approval or criticism of governors, and later in the fourth century the public post was made available for their transmission to the emperor.[83] An inscription from Ephesus, recording a letter from the praetorian prefects in response to acclamations in favour of the proconsul of Asia, shows that the system was continuing to function in the mid fifth century; Constantine's law was retained in Justinian's Code, and it has been argued that acclamations became increasingly prominent and important as expressions of popular opinion during the fifth and sixth centuries. The grievances of Thracian farmers were not submitted to Justinian in an official report, but may well have been brought to his attention by chanting.[84]

---

[79] Assemblies: Sid. Ap. *Ep.* VIII.6.5. Display: e.g. Malalas pp. 470–1; Justinian, *Nov.* 8 (preface to the edict: p. 79.15–17 (Schöll-Kroll)), 128.1; Cass. *Variae* VIII.33.8; IX.16.2, 20.2. This practice raises important questions with respect to the issue of literacy, which cannot, however, be pursued here.

[80] *ACO* 1.4, 155 (432/3: the praetorian prefect Flavius Taurus advises against publication of an imperial letter which he believes will result in disorder in Cilicia and interrupt the flow of taxes); Theod. II *Nov.* 3.8–9 (438: inaction of officials with regard to legislation against heretics, Jews and pagans).

[81] Scott (1985) 103–4.

[82] Justinian, *Nov.* 160; cf. also Liebeschuetz (1985) 150–8 discussing Syn. *Ep.* 95.

[83] *C.Th.* 1.16.6 (331); VIII.5.32 (371).

[84] *Inscr. Ephes.* 44 (439/42); *CJ* 1.40.3; Rou--é (1984), who also argues that the dangers of manipulation of acclamations have been overemphasized. *Nov.* 32, 34; cf. also Cass. *Variae* IV.10 (contrast II.24 for a report by a governor).

The church provided another means of access to the emperor: imperial attendance at major church festivals offered an especially good opportunity for the submission, sometimes with tumult and outcries, of petitions, and the *quaestor sacri palatii* was delegated to receive and pass these on; petitioners deterred by fear of a powerful individual were authorized to approach the emperor with the help of the patriarch or of ecclesiastical *defensores*.[85] In the provinces, the clergy could act as a channel for reports back to the centre, as is illustrated by the commending of Stephen, governor of Palestina Prima, to Justinian by a delegation of clergy; assemblies of bishops regularly demanded that their acclamations be transmitted to the emperor. Justinian explicitly sought to exploit the clergy to monitor judicial abuses in the provinces; by contrast, his complaint about the shortage of information from Egypt might reflect his lack of contact with the Monophysite church which dominated the province.[86] Another linkage was provided by high officials themselves, who might well lend a sympathetic ear to petitions from their home provinces.[87] Overall, the role of curial élites in sustaining links between the imperial centre and its subjects was diminishing as other channels took over. A determined official, however, was likely to override local opposition, regardless of who was articulating it: at Philadelphia in Lydia John Maxilloplumacius, a relative of John the Cappadocian, for whom he acted as a local agent in securing tax revenues, is alleged to have forced the bishop and clergy to perform a mock eucharist in the theatre after they had tried to rescue an upper-class citizen from a scourging over taxation.[88]

A crucial question is whether the laws issued by the emperor and the central administration represented, to any significant degree, responses to the concerns of the empire's inhabitants communicated via these channels. As one might expect, explicit indications in the surviving evidence of such causal links are elusive, but some imperial legislation can clearly be characterized in these terms. Perhaps the most striking instance relates to the office of *quaestor exercitus*, effectively an additional praetorian prefect created by Justinian to provide more efficient logistical support to the armed forces on the lower Danube; in the same way as any praetorian prefect, the *quaestor* exercised both fiscal and judicial authority over the provinces under his responsibility – in this case, Moesia II and Scythia (where the troops were stationed), and Caria, Cyprus and the (Aegean) Islands (from where army supplies were to be gathered). This institutional arrangement was established on 18 May 536, but soon proved problematic, though not on the logistical front: in order to gain legal redress from the *quaestor's* court, the inhabitants of Caria, Cyprus and the Islands had to travel all the way to Odessus on the Black Sea coast, where the *quaestor* was

---

[85] *CJ* 1.12.8.   [86] *PLRE* III.1184–5, *s.v.* Stephanus 7; *Nov.* 86.1; *Edict* 13 (preface).
[87] Cass. *Variae* XI.39; XII.5, 13–15.   [88] John Lydus, *De Mag.* III.59.

based, and clearly did not appreciate the opportunity to broaden their horizons. Justinian therefore issued an edict allowing them to come instead to Constantinople, where a representative of the *quaestor* would hear their cases. What is of particular interest in all this is, first, the fact that Justinian ascribes his revision of arrangements to the appeals of those inconvenienced, while, secondly, the law implementing the revision was issued on 1 September 537 – little more than fifteen months after the office of *quaestor* was first established.[89] It is unusual to be able to determine the speed of reaction in such an exact manner, but Justinian's legislation does offer further examples of laws being issued in response to the difficulties or complaints of individuals.[90] We are, however, prevented from going further by the nature of the evidence: we only know of these cases from Justinian's reign because his *Novels* retain their prefaces, in which the background prompting legislation is sometimes alluded to, but these prefaces have usually been excised by the compilers of the Codes, on which we rely for our knowledge of most of the legislation of his predecessors. Justinian, with his interventionist approach to government, may not be typical: his accessibility, which might be regarded as a token of a conscientious ruler, was criticized by Procopius, while Evagrius praised Maurice precisely for not being too readily available.[91]

The other issue highlighted at the start of this section was that of cost. The later Roman empire is often described as a bureaucratic state whose substantial running costs, compounded by the role of corrupt practices such as bribery, contributed to its ultimate demise by placing an excessive burden on the agricultural base.[92] There is evidence for resistance to taxation: Salvian, notoriously, speaks of harassed provincials fleeing to the barbarians or the bagaudae, or putting themselves under the *patrocinium* of local *potentes*. Inhabitants of remote regions might stay put and resist, provoking protestations of lawlessness from emperors. Emperors were aware that unpopular activities – for example, warfare in remote areas – might prompt resistance to the taxation needed to fund it; Arcadius was even reluctant to harass loyal pagan tax-payers in Gaza in case they abandoned their city. Paulinus of Pella prided himself on his timely and willing payment of taxes, through which he attempted to purchase peaceful repose, but his self-congratulation is contrasted with the behaviour of others who found the surrender of their wealth especially bitter.[93] It has

---

[89] *Nov.* 41 and 50, with Stein, *Bas-Empire* II.474–5.

[90] E.g. *Nov.* 32, 34, which responded to complaints of Thracian farmers; further details in Jones, *LRE* 349 n. 59, 350 n. 63.   [91] Procop. *Secret History* 13.1–2; 15.11–12; Evagr. *HE* v.19.

[92] Jones, *LRE* 563; 469, 819–20; Brown *Gentlemen and Officers* 113. MacMullen (1988) is an extreme case.

[93] Salvian, *De Gub. Dei* v.5–9; cf. *CJ* xi.54 (law of Leo, A.D. 468) for *patrocinium* in the east. Justinian, *Nov.* 24, 25; Sidonius, *Pan. Maj.* 441–69 (taxation of Gaul for use against Vandals); Justinian, *Nov.* 8.10.2; Marc. Diac. *V. Porph.* 41; Paulinus of Pella, *Euch.* 194–201.

been argued that Africa after the Justinianic reconquest was so peaceful that its inhabitants saw no advantage in paying taxes which would be used to finance the defence of other parts of the empire, an attitude which ultimately resulted in a lack of resistance to the Arabs in the late seventh century.[94]

However, generalizations about the quality and financial impact of late Roman administration are dangerous – administration generates complaints more often then praise, and complaints had to be extravagant to have any chance of success, as in this appeal composed by Dioscorus for his village of Aphrodito: 'we are suffering more than places afflicted by barbarians, with our minds constantly on exactions of *diagraphai* ... abnormal demands, and all surcharges of that type'.[95] A more appropriate starting-point is the survival of the eastern empire throughout this period: its fiscal structures were able to produce surpluses under Marcian, Anastasius and Justin II, and, even if with difficulty, to cater for the Vandal expedition of Leo, Justinian's heavy expenditure, and the liberality of Tiberius.[96] There may have been tax rises under Justinian, but the evidence is complex and contentious, since the indications for a rise in taxation in gold in Egypt may reflect an increasing use of *adaeratio*, not an increase in overall tax levels. Natural disasters and warfare caused problems which provoked demands for remissions or cancellations, but the rhetoric of such requests does not provide evidence for structural over-taxation.[97] Campaigns which extended over several years, or even decades, as in the Balkans, created local problems and a *de facto* rise in taxation: thus under Anastasius *coemptiones* were a permanent element of the tax system in Thrace, whereas elsewhere they were only to be levied in special circumstances, and in 575 the need for payments in kind to be maintained in Mesopotamia and Osrhoene is specifically mentioned in the context of Tiberius' remission of taxation in gold.[98]

The best tax regime was one which was stable and predictable, since both rises and ultimately remissions in tax proved counter-productive: although Basil of Caesarea could defend tax immunities for the clergy on the grounds that the benefits could be passed on to the disadvantaged, a law of Theodosius II asserted that 'some men appear to have converted to their own gain and booty the remission of taxes ... so that what had been public

---

[94] Durliat (1981) 526–31.   [95] *P. Lond.* 1674, 21–4; MacCoull, *Dioscorus* 47.

[96] Though for problems caused to the prefectural treasury, see John Lydus, *De Mag.* III.43–4, 54, 56.

[97] *Life* of Theodore of Sykeon 73; Joshua the Stylite 39, 82, 92–3. Johnson and West (1949) 62 claim overall stability for Egyptian tenants during 600 years of Roman rule, but contrast Rémondon (1965), whose argument is accepted by Liebeschuetz (1974) (using this as proof of increasing peculation) and Banaji (1992) 124. Jones, *LRE* 820–1 bases his argument for a substantial rise in state demands on evidence from Ravenna and Antaeopolis, but for greater caution see the discussions of Whittaker (1980) 8–9, 13, and Bagnall (1985) 302–6. Cf. also more generally MacMullen (1987).

[98] *CJ* x.27.5–6; *Nov.* 163.

debts became private debts'.[99] The eastern empire achieved this stability, at least until Justinian's reign: the tax burden was heavy, but in most places for most of the time it continued to be met and was probably even increased during the seventh century in the provinces under Arab control.[100] By contrast, the western empire suffered a spiralling financial crisis during the fifth century as its fiscal base was drastically reduced, especially by the loss of Africa, while special levies greatly increased the tax burden on surviving territories. Constant warfare required money, and may also have facilitated tax evasion: Ostrogothic Italy achieved a reputation for prosperity partly because Theoderic did not indulge in regular major campaigning, but the return to insecurity during and after the Justinianic reconquest ensured that Italy in the late sixth century mirrored the state of Salvian's Gaul: as the inhabitants complained to Justin II and Sophia in 566/7, 'It would be better for the Romans to serve the Goths than the Greeks when the eunuch Narses is a ruler who subjects us to slavery and our most pious prince does not know it. Either deliver us from his hand or we and the Roman citizenry will serve the barbarians.'[101]

After the provincial and administrative reforms of the tetrarchy, the number of imperial employees engaged in administrative duties far exceeded those of the early empire, when many tasks were handled centrally by the imperial household and in the provinces by the curial élite and by governors attended by their small staffs.[102] Thus the official salary bill will have grown substantially, though whether the overall cost of administration had grown in proportion is a much harder question to answer, since the hidden costs of maintaining the imperial household and the whole curial class during the principate cannot be quantified. A few figures are available for the size and salary costs of late Roman offices. When Justinian reconstituted the office of the praetorian prefect of Africa, he was allocated 396 staff, of whom three-quarters were paid at the modest level of an ordinary soldier (nine *solidi* per year); admittedly, this office will have been smaller than the other prefectures, but the pay scale is likely to have been representative.[103] A standard size for the staff of provincial governors was 100, with average rates of pay substantially lower, at a 'miserable' three–four *solidi*, than for the more privileged praetorian staff.[104] Such levels of pay meant that staff depended heavily for their overall income on the fees and perquisites to which their positions gave them access, so that, in certain respects, those who made use of the imperial administration had to pay for the privilege of doing so. Whereas it might seem reasonable for those with judicial business to have to contribute to the costs of their

[99] Basil, *Letter* 104; *C.Th.* XI.28.10; cf. Amm. Marc. XVI.5.14–15; XVI.2.10 on Julian's financial administration in Gaul.   [100] Reinink (1988); Drijvers (1992) 204–8.   [101] *Lib. Pont.* John III.
[102] For an estimate of numbers, see Heather (1994) 18–20.
[103] Jones, *LRE* 590–1; Hendy *Studies* 164–73.   [104] Jones, *LRE* 592–4.

action, it is less clear that tax-payers benefited from having to supplement their regular payments by a variety of fees (*sportulae*): in the western empire, these might amount to over a third of the total sum collected, though in the east the amounts were very substantially lower.[105] It would, however, be possible to interpret these customary exactions as a substitute for higher official salaries, and hence higher taxes, with correspondingly larger opportunities for graft, which was harder to control than the recognized *sportulae*; they might almost be regarded as a form of indirect taxation, with the subjects contributing directly towards the salaries of officials, who in turn contributed to the income of their superiors and ultimately to that of the emperor. In response to such indirect taxation, *autopragium*, the right to pay directly to a representative of the central administration, was a valuable privilege which cut out profiteering middlemen.[106]

These perquisites are categorized as one aspect of the endemic corruption which has been canvassed as an explanation for the empire's demise.[107] It is, however, impossible to prove that the situation in late antiquity was any worse than in preceding centuries, and payment for securing a post was accepted, indeed on occasions regulated by emperors. Thus office-holders, like the magistrates of republican Rome who had bribed the electorate, had to recoup their costs: the first permanent court in Rome had been established to deal with the issue of recuperation of wealth wrongly acquired by Romans in the provinces, while 750 years later a governor of Sardinia was, to pope Gregory's disgust, prepared to accept protection money to permit the continuation of polytheist practices since he had to repay his *sportula*.[108] But, to an extent, corruption is in the eye of the beholder, or dependent on circumstances.[109] Justinian legislated against the sale of offices and appears to have made a determined attempt to eradicate the practice – for example, by providing compensation for lost income to those who had traditionally controlled the disposal of the office; on the other hand, although Procopius' allegation that Justinian was himself selling offices again only a year after this legislation is open to doubt, both Justin II and Tiberius also legislated on the subject; John the Lydian both condemns and accepts the custom, and the upright Gregory was prepared to give bribes to ensure that Leontius' financial investigation in Sicily was speedily ended.[110] Sale of offices was regarded as a sign of personal greed, and is a stock accusation against unpopular ministers or rulers, but its overall impact on the administration is unclear: the practice seems usually to have been restricted to provincial offices and rarely to have extended to the most powerful positions at

---

[105] Jones, *LRE* 467–8; this calculation is based on the consolidation of fees under Majorian in 458.
[106] Cass. *Variae* XII.8.2.   [107] MacMullen (1988).   [108] Greg. *Reg.* V.38.
[109] Heidenheimer, Johnstone and Levine (1979) 21; 88–90.
[110] *Nov.* 8; Procop. *Secret History* 21.4; 24.6; *Nov.* 149, 161; John Lydus, *De Mag.* III.66–7; Greg. *Reg.* IX.130. Cf. Kelly in *CAH* XIII.171–80.

court,[111] which the emperor tended to rotate quite rapidly among the interested nobility. Anastasius is criticized by John of Antioch for transforming the entire empire into an aristocracy through his sale of office; Justin II's anti-corruption measure to have provincial governors chosen by local grandees, clerical and secular, will presumably have resulted in the selection of similarly wealthy individuals.[112] In each case imperial action may have encouraged family traditions of public service; some minor offices became quasi-hereditary, with sons having the reversion right of precedence in purchasing their fathers' posts, whose value might be included in the inherited estate.[113]

Bribery or gift-giving was an integral part of the late Roman patronage system, but there is also evidence for more extreme abuse of official position. In Egypt, the pagarch Menas' attempts to annex the right to collect the taxes of Aphrodito involved the exploitation of a group of violent shepherds, damage to irrigation works and threats to Christian women. In southern Italy, the misdeeds of a tribune at Otranto and a duke of Campania each prompted part of the local population to desert to the Lombards.[114] In all these instances we never have more than one side of the case, and it is possible that self-interest has distorted the presentation: at Aphrodito Dioscorus had to whip up official sympathy against a member of the administrative structure, the pagarch, and so might have exploited traditional complaints, while pope Gregory was attempting to persuade officials to behave in ways that better suited the interests of the church. Feuding between higher and lower, central and provincial officials might add to administrative disorder, and the ruler might find it hard to protect the party of lower status: Theoderic was often forced to give special protection, usually enforced by a Goth, to subjects, even of high status, who were being harassed by great men, and the church of Ravenna offered protection against violent attacks, in return for the grant of estates.[115]

Abuses there certainly were, but attempts to investigate and regulate them would not necessarily be welcomed: Gregory's keenness to restrict Leontius' activities in Sicily has already been noted, while the unpopular activities of Justinian's emissary, the logothete Alexander 'the Scissors', whose cost-cutting achieved notoriety through Procopius' account in the *Secret History*, can be regarded as an attempt to overhaul an administrative system in which a decade of warfare, as well as a long period of Ostrogothic rule, had permitted abuses to arise. Alexander's mission is one

---

[111] Cass. *Variae* IX.24.6; XI.1.18 imply bribery was used in competition for the *magisterium officiorum*.

[112] John of Antioch fr. 215, though note Theophanes 143.18; *Nov.* 149; important discussion in Jones, *LRE* 391–6.

[113] *CJ* III.28.30.2–3; Jones, *LRE* 577, 581. For a comparative discussion, see Doyle (1996).

[114] MacCoull, *Dioscorus* 23–8; Greg. *Reg.* IX.205; X.5.

[115] Feuding: Cass. *Variae* III.27; John Lydus, *De Mag.* III.50. Protection: Cass. *Variae* I.15, 37; III.27; IV.27; VII.39; *P. Ital.* 13.

example of methods of controlling regional officials, by the despatch or assignation from the centre of a special officer, such as the *cancellarii* and *canonicarii* appointed to provinces by Cassiodorus when praetorian prefect.[116] Other methods were the encouragement of reports by junior staff on superiors, and the public apportionment of praise and blame, as for example in the letters of appointment which were read out in the senate.[117] Imperial concern for fairness is also evident in Zeno's law which stipulated that governors must wait in their provinces for fifty days after the end of their term of office in order to be available to answer complaints. It had never been easy for provincials to gain access to their former governors, and this law refers to the means of circumventing its good intentions: the former governors were to be present in the public places of major towns, not hiding in sanctuaries or the houses of powerful friends. By contrast, Justinian expounded on the glory which honest governors might win from himself and provincials.[118] Distance from the court, the source of redress and centre of supervision, increased the chances of corruption, as Cassiodorus was well aware. It also enhanced provincial discontent: embittered plaintiffs and refugees fleeing the exactions of John the Cappadocian's agents seem to have contributed to the Nika riot in 532; in 410 the inhabitants of remote Britain and Armorica had thrown out the imperial administration altogether.[119]

The system had numerous imperfections, and human nature ensured that many opportunities for enrichment and advancement were exploited, but blanket condemnation is inappropriate. At Edessa in 497 the governor Alexander placed a complaints box in front of his residence, and every Friday he gave judgement free of charge in the church of John the Baptist and Addai; the governor Demosthenes organized charitable relief during the Edessa famine of 502, and after the Antioch earthquake of 526 the effectiveness of count Ephrem's actions prompted the inhabitants to select him as their next bishop.[120] It might, however, be significant that these examples of responsive government occur in provincial or metropolitan capitals, whereas in smaller cities and more remote areas it may have been harder for the central government to have an impact on local practices; implementation of the imperial will now required the presence of a representative of the administration, since the inclination or ability of local councillors to act had diminished along with their status. It is also the case that evidence for good conduct by officials has to be treated with the same degree of scepticism as for complaints: it would be misguided to rely on

---

[116] Brown, *Gentlemen and Officers* 152–3; Cass. *Variae* XI.10; XII.1; Morosi (1978).
[117] Blockley (1969); Lendon (1997) 191–201; Cass. *Variae* VIII.13.1; 20.1–2; cf. 1.25; III.20; IV.29; IX.12. [118] *CJ* 1.49.1; *Nov.* 8; 10.
[119] Cass. *Variae* VI.22.1–2; IX.12.4; John Lydus, *De Mag.* III.70; Justinian, *Nov.* 8; Zos. VI.5.
[120] Joshua 29; 42–3; Malalas 423–4.

evidence for public-spirited officials to imply that the system regularly worked well. When pope Gregory praised the public conduct of particular officials, his reasons cannot be reconstructed,[121] but are unlikely to have been simple – there are instances of governors being praised by one group of provincials and attacked by another.[122]

John Lydus' *On Magistracies* provides a glimpse of the operation of one particular bureau of the praetorian prefecture as seen through the eyes of a loyal and talented, but also embittered, member; he was proud of his own unit's skills and talents, and jealous of the prestige of the financial branch of the prefecture – though his overall loyalty to the prefecture ensured that he took an intelligent and sympathetic interest in its fiscal health and the differing impact on it of high-spending or frugal emperors.[123] According to John, not surprisingly, patronage was of crucial importance in securing advancement; much attention was devoted to increasing the official remuneration and constructing a healthy cash balance on which to retire; members of the bureau were jealous of their own positions within the bureau, but also of the position of their bureau relative to other parts of the administrative machine; the dull routine of quotidian duties was alleviated by the shared literary interests of many of the officials. Many elements of John's picture would be quite familiar to the inhabitants of modern administrative units, with their concern for mutual back-scratching, departmental gossip, inter-office rivalries and the diversion of crosswords. Above all, administrators always know better than their political masters: an anonymous sixth-century dialogue regarded a good emperor as one who left the administration to run itself.[124]

The bilingual Greek and Coptic archive of Dioscorus casts light on administration at a much lower, provincial level. Learning was still important, and Dioscorus is representative of the educated lawyers whose shared literary and professional interests provided some coherence to the disparate bureaucratic structure. Favourable decisions required the interest of the local governor, and Dioscorus used his talents to attract attention: strong metaphors presented the governor with the qualities which his petitioners hoped he would display; grandiloquent poetry showed him, and influential members of his or the prefect's staff, the rewards that favourable decisions might bring, while enemies would be publicly shamed by Dioscorus' vituperation.[125] Dioscorus represented the intertwined interests of his family (including a monastery founded by his father) and local community in the

---

[121] Greg. *Reg.* VII.3; XI.4; Brown, *Gentlemen and Officers* 122–3 with n. 25 for other references.

[122] Amm. Marc. XXVIII.6.21, the Romanus affair, where complaints from the *curiales* of Tripolis in Africa were discredited by their fellow citizens. There were clearly divergent attitudes among leading inhabitants of Gaul to the prefect Arvandus: Sid. Ap. *Ep.* 1.7.

[123] John Lydus, *De Mag.* III.43–5, 51, 54, 56.   [124] Anon. *Peri politikes epistemes* 5.

[125] MacCoull, *Dioscorus* ch. 2; and cf. pp. 168–9 above on sources.

manner characteristic of late Roman society: infringements of the rights of Aphrodito might well have entailed extra taxes for the family of Dioscorus (see above). For Dioscorus, public duties and private interests naturally interlocked.

The careers of John and Dioscorus provide evidence for the type of person who joined the administration. Anyone who had completed all stages of the educational system was likely to possess the resources to purchase a position, though education might have raised expectations above what the individual could realistically hope to obtain: for many it was necessary to wait in the unsalaried ranks of the *supernumerarii* attached to the *officia*, or of lawyers waiting for registration at the bar.[126] Personal contacts also mattered, whether through kinship, regional solidarity, shared factional allegiance or the favour which a timely panegyric might procure: John Lydus was lucky, whereas Augustine, for example, was less fortunate, until his Manichee connections at Rome helped him secure his position at Milan. An unlikely potential recruit to the administration was the future holy man, Theodore of Sykeon: his father was a Hippodrome entertainer, who performed acrobatics on camels, and so was undoubtedly attached to one of the factions; he also had official connections, since he had met Theodore's mother, the prostitute Mary, while travelling through Galatia on imperial orders; when Theodore was still only six, his mother decided to journey to Constantinople to secure his entry into imperial service and so kitted him out with a gold belt and expensive clothing.[127] Granted the long queues of supernumeraries attached to all desirable administrative posts, Mary was probably starting her employment drive none too soon. Advancement up the career structure was, in many cases, achieved through seniority, with progression being so slow that senior officials might be too ancient to perform their duties properly. There are, however, examples of exceptional abilities being rewarded: the reforming praetorian prefects Polycarp, Marinus, John the Cappadocian and Peter Barsymes. These individuals had experience in subordinate financial positions or in related areas (Peter was a banker), and in each case it was probably their administrative talent which brought them to imperial attention and resulted in exalted office.[128] Another example of such apparently rare professionalism is John the Paphlagonian, a former *tractator* in the *scrinium Orientis*, who, as *comes sacrarum largitionum*, conducted Anastasius' currency reform (see below); the careers of Basilides in the first decade of Justinian's reign and of Magnus under Justin II might also suggest that hierarchy and precedence were no longer of supreme importance in the choice of major ministers.

---

[126] For these, see Jones, *LRE* 510, 585, 598, 604.   [127] *Life* 5.
[128] Note John Lydus, *De Mag.* III.57 on John's appointment as logothete 'because he had promised to do things beyond belief on behalf of the government'; Procop. *Secret History* 22.1 on the intensive search before Peter's appointment. Epinicus (see *PLRE* II) is another example.

Inevitably, the men who emerged from the ranks and thought innovatively about administrative issues had their detractors: to a traditionalist like John Lydus, however, their excessive professionalism was as unwelcome as the literary talents of Cyrus of Panopolis – John might have been expected to appreciate the latter's cultural sophistication, but instead criticized him as an amateur. John Lydus, of course, represented the ideal balance between these inappropriate extremes, but we should be cautious about accepting his judgements at face value. It would be wrong to assume a lack of fiscal, as distinct from legal or rhetorical, professionalism among all aristocrats and littérateurs: Cyrus in fact seems to have been an effective administrator. The classical education, if pursued beyond rhetoric and law, might be of value: Boethius' mathematical talents were summoned to reform Theoderic's gold currency, and a high level of mathematical skill was expected of the emperor's chief architect, as demonstrated by Anthemius of Tralles whose family also produced doctors, a lawyer and a grammarian.[129] The men who inherited and ran great estates in Egypt, whose organization might be modelled on that of the empire, may often have had substantial skills – for example, Apion, whom Anastasius appointed to manage the food supply of the eastern army. Good estate management earned praise for Roman nobles under the Ostrogoths, and, as with the Cassiodori, who provided remounts for the army, their activity might be integrated with the state system. Many landowners had experience of that system: Justinian encouraged the praetorian prefect to promote to governorships *curiales* and other *honestiores* knowledgeable in taxation.[130] In spite of the usually short terms of aristocratic office, when state service ran in families experience might be transmitted down the generations by combinations of personal advice and the tenure of minor posts: Cassiodorus began his career as *consiliarius* to his father when the latter was prefect of Italy. There was a tendency for the *comes sacrarum largitionum* and the *comes rerum privatarum* to be recruited from families linked to imperial service rather than from intellectual circles; these recruits had often held relevant offices earlier in their careers, and they tended to move on either to the other financial countship, or to an urban or praetorian prefecture. Youth spent at a monarch's court might also give training to educated gentry, as well as to palace eunuchs like Narses. Within departments, the in-house histories noted above should be associated with an induction into bureaucratic values – though the training provided by the prefect Zoticus to his young protégé John Lydus was apparently more concerned with personal profit than administrative competence.[131] In general, Cassiodorus' letters of

[129] Cass. *Variae* i.10; vii.5, and cf. *Inst.* 1.30.4–5; Agathias v.6.3–6 with *PLRE* iii *s.v.* Stephanus 1.

[130] Hardy (1968) 29; Banaji (1992) 164, 179. Cass. *Variae* i.4.17; ii.1.3–4; iii.6.6. Justinian, *Nov.* 8.8.

[131] *Ordo Generis Cassiodorum*; cf. *Variae* viii.16.3; 20.5–6; 31.1. Education at court: *Variae* iv.4.3; viii.10.3; John Lydus, *De Mag.* iii.27; Delmaire (1989) 94–118.

appointment, while usually stressing the nominee's noble birth and rhetorical skills (both linked with personal integrity), also emphasize his or his family's record of service and the close attention paid by the monarch to performance, in and out of office. The system, especially at the top, was still far from professional, but was probably less amateurish than that of the early empire.[132]

IV. ADMINISTRATIVE CHANGE

The difficulty involved in effecting permanent change to administrative arrangements is well illustrated by Anastasius' abolition of the *chrysargyron* tax. Once the emperor had decided that the tax should no longer be collected – whether for moral reasons, as asserted by Evagrius, or because the empire's finances were sufficiently healthy to do without the relatively small return – he instructed his reluctant officials to destroy the relevant paperwork. This stage removed the records stored in central archives, but Anastasius surmised that there would be enough information in provincial archives to reconstruct the tax precept if a future emperor decided, or was persuaded by grasping officials, to do so. Hence, Anastasius played a trick on his administrators by persuading them to assemble all surviving paperwork relevant to the tax, on the grounds that he had realized his mistake and now wanted to reinstate the *chrysargyron*; the officials gladly obliged, only to find that their endeavours resulted in another bonfire of their precious records. Even if embroidered in the telling, Evagrius' story,[133] besides providing an intriguing glimpse of the extent of official archives, including the existence of parallel record systems in Constantinople and provincial centres, illustrates how administration was a collaborative process: the emperor was all-powerful, but the exercise of that power depended on numerous individual officers who transmitted information into, and orders out from, the imperial centre. Abolition of the *chrysargyron* had significant consequences quite unconnected with the motivation for the change: the *sacrae largitiones* lost a sizeable chunk of revenue and, even though Anastasius replaced it by allocating to a special fund imperial estates which generated the same income, this ensured that the *comes sacrarum largitionum* was now, to an extent, beholden to the administrators of those estates. The appointment to the post of *comes sacrarum largitionum* of John the Paphlagonian, a *tractator* in the praetorian prefecture, may have been intended to help secure the reform.[134]

Any change was bound to tread on vested interests, as in the case of the *chrysargyron*, and it was more common for processes and structures to

---

[132] Cass. *Variae* I.42.2; v.40–1; VIII.16–17, 21–2. Goffart (1970); Barnes (1974).
[133] Evagr. *HE* III.39.   [134] Stein, *Bas-Empire* II.204.

evolve gradually, through the introduction of a new official or procedure which ran alongside existing arrangements until the innovation either demonstrated its effectiveness by marginalizing its predecessor or proved unequal to the task. Such an approach is illustrated by the introduction by Anastasius of *vindices* to supervise the collection of taxes by town councils: though they began as monitors of local arrangements, their superior authority contributed to undermining that of the local *curiae* (as Evagrius complained), which consequently declined further in power and attractiveness.[135] This tendency for change to be gradual could also explain some of the apparent administrative anomalies of the seventh century, when the praetorian prefecture and elements of provincial administration under its authority persisted long after the appearance of the systems that would replace them.

Major administrative change might creep up on the empire for a variety of reasons, and it is difficult to be specific about causes and effects. A good example is the question of *adaeratio*, the practice of commuting into gold coin taxes and payments which were assessed in kind. This habit emerged in the western empire during the fifth century, but rather more gradually in the east, where commutation of the land-tax into gold remained restricted until Anastasius switched most into gold, while leaving sufficient to be collected in kind for the needs of the field armies. It is interesting that *adaeratio* was regarded as a privilege, since the most obvious beneficiary of the practice would appear to be the state: it could obtain the gold which it needed to pay troops, especially non-Roman mercenaries,[136] and also save on the expense and labour of the *cursus clabularis* and corvées; the state could then, in theory, choose where to purchase the goods and services which it needed, hence permitting armies to move rapidly to respond to crises, though in practice this flexibility will have been constrained by the facts of supply and demand. Benefits for taxpayers are less clear: the combined consequences of demands for tax payments in coin and the removal in Asiana of the state post, which had provided the means for injecting coinage into local economies, are reported, in similar terms, by Procopius and John Lydus;[137] both reports are tendentious and may exaggerate a transitional local crisis. If Asiana failed to adjust to the new tax regime in the medium term, it may have been exceptional: the emperor Leo had already introduced a similar change in the Oriens diocese in 467/8, while the picture of rural life in Galatia in the late sixth century in the *Life* of Theodore of Sykeon suggests a moderately prosperous and tax-paying peasant economy – these

[135] Evagr. *HE* III.42; Priscian, *Pan. Anast.* 193 presented the panegyrical claim that the *vindices* protected the farmers from the rapacity of the *curiales*. For further discussion of the fate of the *curiales*, see ch. 8 (Liebeschuetz), pp. 219–22 below.   [136] Carrié (1995) 35–9.
[137] Procop. *Secret History* 30; John Lydus, *De Mag.* III.61; Hendy, *Studies* 294–9.

areas undoubtedly still benefited from the presence of coin-using soldiers and official travellers.[138]

If *adaeratio* in the absence of coin posed problems, it is unclear why it was adopted sooner in the less monetized and controlled west than in the east. Vera's proposal – that *adaeratio* was no more than a monetary valuation of tax which was still paid in kind – is not demonstrated by his questionable interpretation of pope Gregory's reference to the gold *pensiones* of Sicilian church *coloni* (*c.* 600).[139] It is at variance with earlier evidence from the east for payments nominally calculated in kind actually being made in gold, and with the problems in Asiana recorded by Procopius and John Lydus. Further, the payment of taxes in three instalments, *trina illatio*, though made in kind in the 360s, was strongly linked by Majorian in 458 with the sale of produce to raise cash for taxes.[140] An alternative solution is that *adaeratio* was favoured in particular by the larger landowners, the people who had greatest access to cash reserves to see them through phases of low prices and to the facilities for transporting surpluses to markets or using commercial agents to dispose of produce as means to acquire coin. A good harvest might, paradoxically, be a special disadvantage to peasants, who would be forced to make hurried sales in a glutted market in order to raise money for their taxes.[141] In such situations, *adaeratio* might mean the slippage of land from the tax system, and ultimately from state control, into the hands of the grand proprietors who could sustain their weaker neighbours through periods of crisis: the dominance of gold within the state economy ensured the pre-eminence in society of those with ready access to gold, namely soldiers, senior officials and those with extensive connections.[142]

One further consequence of *adaeratio*, undoubtedly unintended but of vital importance in administrative terms, was the eclipse of the finance ministries, the *res privata* and *sacrae largitiones*, by the praetorian prefectures which now controlled greater monetary resources than all other departments; this led in turn to an increase in the size of the prefectures, especially that of the east, which became so unwieldy that some of its financial functions were transferred to special logothetes who would eventually, in the seventh century, overshadow the prefect. Logothetes tend to have the same terminology applied to them by Justinian as the *comes sacrarum largitionum* had done, and to perform similar roles in dispensing payments and imperial largess; they were drawn from the prefecture, but were assigned

---

[138] *CJ* XII.50.22; Mitchell, *Anatolia* II ch. 19. [139] Vera (1986).

[140] Liebeschuetz (1972) 88–90; *Nov. Maj.* 2.3; cf. *C.Th.* XI.1.15–16; 19.3; XII.6.15; V.15.20; but note that the Breviary of Alaric's *interpretatio* to XI.1.15 speaks only of payment in kind.

[141] E.g. Sid. Ap. *Ep.* VI.12.6, and on tied trade in general, Whittaker (1983); Liebeschuetz (1987) 463 on possible disadvantages to the state. Banaji (1992) 113. Transport: Mitchell, *Anatolia* I.233, 247–8.

[142] *Anon. De Rebus Bellicis* 2; Theodoret, *Ep.* 37; Barnish (1987) 166–8, arguing the case of the pig-based economy of San Giovanni di Ruoti; Banaji (1992) ch. 6.

their tasks by the emperor himself.[143] It is notable that the dominance of the prefecture in the east is associated with the careers of a series of astute financial officials: Polycarp and Marinus under Anastasius, John the Cappadocian and Peter Barsymes under Justinian. These reforming administrators are precisely the professional appointees identified above: emperors who wanted to introduce change knew that they had to sideline the aristocratic amateurs and promote lower-ranking bureaucrats, even if they lacked the liberal *paideia* prized by the cultured élite.[144] Marinus was responsible for the introduction of *vindices*, officials charged with the supervision of local collection of taxes. John was admitted, even by his enemies, to be capable at identifying problems and devising solutions to them, while it was his efficiency in securing revenues to meet Justinian's considerable expenditures, by improving the efficiency of the collection system, eliminating abuses, reducing delays in judicial appeals and challenging the established practices of career civil servants, which earned him the wrath of 'victims' like John Lydus. John, in fact, appears to have been a prudent controller of imperial resources, and like any canny financier he was reluctant to endorse major new commitments: he opposed Justinian's plans for the Vandal expedition, partly on financial grounds, and he may have been responsible for ensuring that the experienced Archelaus was appointed to oversee the logistical side of the campaign.[145] Peter Barsymes has a similarly unscrupulous reputation, but two Justinianic laws addressed to him suggest that his concern for the interests of the treasury extended to protection of the rights of tax-payers, i.e. the people who were ultimately responsible for the health of the treasury.[146] In part, such reformers were the victims of Justinian's determination to tighten up the whole tax-collecting system: the same law which abolished *suffragia* gave governors considerable authority in the rigorous exaction of taxes to support the wars of reconquest – unless there was actually theft, provincials were forbidden, under pain of the most severe penalty, to complain of their exactions and punishments.[147]

Understanding the mechanics of *adaeratio* is complicated by the practice of *coemptio*, the purchase of produce, often compulsory[148] and usually for military needs. The development of *coemptio* was an inevitable consequence of *adaeratio*: the state had to purchase the supplies which had formerly been brought in as tax. In theory, it could be used to benefit the tax-payer, since the state could adjust its demands to accord with local fluctuations in harvests and trade, and could finance the storage of surplus

---

[143] Millet (1925); *CJ* x.30.4.

[144] Procop. *Wars* 1.24.12 for the alleged illiteracy of John the Cappadocian.

[145] Since the mid fifth century, there had developed the practice of appointing a special deputy praetorian prefect to oversee the logistical arrangements for major campaigns: Jones, *LRE* 627–8, 673–4.

[146] *PLRE* II *s.v.* Marinus 7; *PLRE* III *s.v.* Johannes 11; *PLRE* II *s.v.* Archelaus 5; *PLRE* III *s.v.* Peter 9; *Nov.* 128, 130.   [147] Justinian, *Nov.* 8.

[148] *C.Th.* XI.15.2 (A.D. 384) indicates that it was not always compulsory.

produce.[149] In this case, gold coin would be recycled through the tax system, though if payment was arranged by the allocation of a notional credit to the individual's tax account, the effect of *coemptio* would be to demonetize local economies by removing the need for tax-payers to obtain coinage, thus reversing the impact of *adaeratio*. This conflict of effects indicates that the imperial administration focused on certain specific objectives – a need for coin in one area at one time, a reserve of supplies at another – and that planning at a macroeconomic level was, not surprisingly, beyond the capacity of officials and the information available to them.

Economic theory has rarely matched practical reality. Because *adaeratio* entailed greater reliance on *coemptiones*, there was a danger that the latter could merge into a permanent supplement to the annual tax levy, a super-indiction: Anastasius, who permitted the extension of *adaeratio*, had to decree that *coemptiones* were not a regular part of the tax system.[150] The estates of the *potentiores* were particularly liable to *coemptio*, presumably because these could deliver the necessary surpluses, and there was a prohibition on exactions from those with no surplus, but there were still alleged cases of *coemptiones* being levied on regions which could not supply the produce locally.[151] The practice of *coemptio* required the state to take greater heed of fluctuating harvests and the need to move produce around the empire: instead of extracting the regular tax indiction in kind, the state obtained money with which it could purchase its necessities from the most suitable places. Customs dues had always been an important source of imperial revenue, and even in the fourth century provincial governors had exploited the grain market to profit from public stocks,[152] but there are signs of tighter control from the centre in the sixth century. Anastasius created important customs posts at the Bosphorus and Hellespont, whose lucrative operation was overhauled by Justinian, and recaptured Iotabe, an island in the Red Sea which had housed a customs post; Justinian established state monopolies in various goods which he then licensed to individuals, with the result that prefects of Alexandria and governors of Lazica could be accused of behaving like merchants in their operation of these.[153] Even Anastasius' abolition of the *chrysargyron* could contribute to this picture, since by forgoing the modest gold revenues derived from taxing

---

[149] Cass. *Variae* XII.22.1–2; cf. also *CJ* appendix 7 (Pragmatic Sanction 22). State storage: Amm. Marc. XXVIII.1.7 with Vanags (1979); Procop. *Secret History* 22.14–18.

[150] *CJ* Appendix 7 (Pragmatic Sanction 26) might suggest that the landowners of Apulia and Calabria regarded regular *coemptio* and superindictions as similar; *CJ* X.27 (Anastasius).

[151] *C.Th.* XI.15.2; *CJ* X.27.2.4 (Anastasius); Cass. *Variae* XII.14.6. Other examples of corrupt practices: Agathias, *Hist.* IV.21–2 for the activities of John the Libyan; Cass. *Variae* II.26.2; *CJ* Appendix 7 (Pragmatic Sanction 18); Procop. *Secret History* 23.11–14.

[152] *De Rebus Bellicis* 4.1; cf. Peter Barsymes: Procop. *Secret History* 22.14–22; perhaps also Maurice and the Egyptian grain: John of Nikiu 95.21.

[153] Stein, *Bas-Empire* II.196–7; Procop. *Secret History* 25.1–10; 20.4; 25.13–26; 26.36–9. Leo and Zeno had prohibited the licensing of monopolies by palace officials: *CJ* IV.59.1–2.

commercial production in towns, the emperor perhaps hoped to gain more from the closer supervision of an increased movement of goods.

Another indication of greater official interest in trade is the growing number, from the time of Anastasius, of lead seals which belonged to individuals entitled *commerciarius*: it is disputed whether these should be regarded as customs collectors, who developed into controllers of state warehouses, or as the farmers of the more lucrative monopolies, but in the sixth and early seventh century they included men of high status who sometimes moved into, or even from, major office. In the latter years of Justinian, the bankers of Constantinople were capable of underwriting substantial imperial expenditure, even if somewhat reluctantly; they were also attached to, and politically involved with, leading courtiers and soldiers.[154] These developments were not confined to the east: in the west Valentinian III had met military needs through the creation of the *siliquaticum* tax on sales and purchases; in Spain and Italy the Ostrogoths sold monopolies to merchants, perhaps – as conjectured by Jones – to ease collection of the *siliquaticum*; at Ravenna the wealth of the banker Julianus Argentarius rivalled that of his Constantinopolitan contemporaries; in Merovingian Gaul, customs dues sustained royal revenues while the return from the land-tax declined; in Anglo-Saxon Britain, royal control was maintained over centres of commerce and production, and resources were allocated to the upkeep of the Roman road system over considerable distances.[155] The involvement of the state in such economic matters is paralleled by that of major bishops – for example, John the Almsgiver at Alexandria or pope Gregory at Rome – and big secular landowners, such as the Apions.

The problem of distinguishing between civilian and military competences supports the impression that aspects of administration were haphazard rather than the product of systematic design.[156] Separation of military command from provincial administration is accepted as an important element in the stability of the empire in the fourth century, a separation achieved through Diocletian's initiation of the process whereby *duces* assumed the military responsibilities of provincial governors, through Constantine's completion of that process and his removal of military duties from praetorian prefects, and by the insistence of conscientious emperors, like Constantius II, on preserving the divide.[157] In Ostrogothic Italy, this separation of powers (to which there were some exceptions) was displayed as a balance between Goths who fought and Romans who paid and administered

---

[154] Hendy, *Studies* 626–9; Nesbitt (1977); Oikonomides (1986); Dunn (1993). Bankers: Coripp. *Iust.* ii.361–406, with the notes of Cameron, *Corippus*; Barnish (1985) 35.

[155] *Nov. Val.* 15, 24. Ostrogoths: Cass. *Variae* ii.4; ii.26.4; ii.30.3 with Jones, *LRE* 826. Iulius: Barnish (1985). Gaul: Pirenne (1939). Britain: Sawyer and Wood (1977) 143–8; Rackham (1986) 257.

[156] Tomlin (1976).   [157] Amm. Marc. xxi.16.1.

the taxes which supported their masters and defenders.[158] This separation was probably vital to the fiscal structure of the state; if Romans were allowed to become warriors in the Gothic army, they would tend to remove themselves from the ranks of tax-payers, as seems to have happened in Merovingian Gaul, and was effectively the case at the ending of Roman rule in Britain.

The distinction, however, was difficult to maintain and may often have been unrealistic. Powerful generals naturally had an interest in the business of the praetorian prefects, if only to ensure supplies for their troops: the patrician Aetius engaged in tax supervision and reform, and his murder was accompanied by that of the prefect Boethius and the purging of *honorati*;[159] successful commanders often acquired control of civilian affairs – for example, the sequence in Italy of Stilicho, Aetius, Ricimer, Odoacer, Theoderic, Narses and finally the institution of the exarchate of Ravenna; the exarchate of Africa is a parallel case where the resources of a particular area had to be placed under a unitary authority to cope with local military threats. The case of Sabinianus Magnus, *magister militum per Illyricum* in the late fifth century, who acted to prop up local councils and the tax register which were under threat, indicates that administrative blurring was not confined to the west. Military problems were a factor in this merging of responsibilities, and security considerations, which were in part sharpened by the waning authority of the curial élites, also led to Justinian uniting civil and military authority in various provinces of the Asianic diocese and in Egypt: there were administrative precedents for the western exarchates of the late sixth century.[160]

Sabinianus was a soldier who undertook civilian tasks, which might appear to be the natural process: Vegetius remarked on the superiority of the army's bureaucratic procedures to those of the civilian administration.[161] In areas of the empire where the urban infrastructure was weak and hence educational levels probably relatively low, there may have been a problem with the supply of civilians to undertake minor routine tasks. Justinian assigned command over troops in Arabia and Phoenicia Libanensis to the local governors precisely to keep the army out of civilian affairs and to repair the impoverished state of the fisc, and a similar move in Thrace was explained because of the need for 'a man who is good for both civilian and military affairs'.[162] Most administrators were recruited from the peaceful and educated provinces of Asia, Syria, Palestine and Egypt, whereas from Justinian onwards natives of warlike Armenia became prominent as governors or exarchs of frontier regions.

The military may have been keen to encroach on civilian responsibilities, but there are also numerous instances of civilians who took on military

---

[158] Cass. *Variae* IX.14.8; XII.5.4.   [159] *Nov. Val.* 1.4; Priscus fr. 30; Hydat. *Chron.* s.a. 453/4.
[160] Marc. Com. s.a. 479. Just. *Nov.* 145; *Edict* 13.2; Haldon, *Byzantium in the Seventh Century* 35–6.
[161] Vegetius II.19.   [162] Justinian, *Nov.* 102; *Edict* 4; *Nov.* 26.

command: the *sacellarius* Rusticus acted as paymaster for Justinian's army in Lazica, transmitted information between the emperor and his troops, and participated in tactical debates; John the Armenian, treasurer in Belisarius' household, was also one of his trusted commanders, and Alexander the logothete also led an army;[163] Narses and the exarchs Smaragdus and Eleutherius were all eunuchs with some financial experience within the palace before their appointment to Italian commands; the future emperor Maurice was an imperial notary before becoming count of the excubitors and then *magister militum per Orientem*. The assumption of responsibility for oversight of the *limitanei* in the eastern half of the empire by the *magister officiorum* from 443 is analogous.[164] These appointments and rearrange-ments might be seen as politically motivated, with the intention of keeping generals under control, but administrative efficiency is an equally plausible explanation. The empire was organized for war, and military expenditures consumed the majority of tax revenues, so that the appointment of prae-torian prefects – for example, Apion and Calliopius for the Persian war under Anastasius – to co-ordinate the supply of particular armies is not surprising, since the costs of military disaster were high – for example, Leo's expedition against the Vandals in 468, which cost over seven million *solidi*, of which the prefectural reserve provided almost half.[165] John Lydus bitterly lamented the loss by the prefecture of its military role,[166] and may well have wished to see it restored. The necessities of internal security, external threats or the enforcement of tax collection might dictate the inte-gration of military and civilian duties, but the reversals of Justinian's legis-lation on the provincial powers indicate that there was no overall policy:[167] what mattered was what worked in a specific area at a particular time; emperors were prepared to change their minds in the light of experience.

One interpretation of the shifting balances between military and civilian interests, and between the different elements in the civilian administrative structure, is to see the late Roman empire as a polycracy of competing and overlapping powers, with the emperor as the ultimate arbitrator.[168] This enabled the emperor, at least in the east, to avoid being dominated by his mil-itary commanders and to ensure that no single office controlled the state: emperors were able to intervene in administration at any level, by-passing senior ministers to communicate directly with governors and other local agents on even the most trivial matters. Emperors undoubtedly perceived the benefits of a balance, and sometimes acted to eliminate individuals who had

---

[163] Agathias, *Hist.* III.2–5 (Rusticus), and cf. IV.17.2–3 (Martin); Procop. *Wars* III.17 (John); *Wars* VII.3.4 (Alexander); see also *PLRE* III.   [164] Theod. II, *Nov.* 24.

[165] Hendy, *Studies* 221 for the various figures.   [166] John Lydus, *De Mag.* III.10–11.

[167] E.g. *Nov.* 145.

[168] Jones, *LRE* 341–7; Tomlin (1976); Kelly in *CAH* XIII.169–75. John Lydus, *De Mag.* II.10; III.22, 40 for the claim that the prefecture lost control of the *fabricae* to the master of offices, and had to share control of the *cursus publicus*.

become too powerful – for example, Valentinian III and Aetius or Leo and the family of Aspar – but the balance was probably more accidental than planned. Prominence of a particular individual in one post was often followed by the pre-eminence of someone in a different position, as if emperors spontaneously reacted against the dominance of one office: thus, after Anthemius held the praetorian prefecture for nine years (405–14), Helion emerged as the most prominent individual in the east, as master of offices for thirteen years (414–27); Cyrus of Panopolis, who occupied both urban and praetorian prefectures for two years (439–41) and had probably held the urban prefecture for longer (as well as a previous stint as praetorian prefect), was followed as the power at court by the eunuch Chrysaphius, the *sacellarius*, and Nomus, master of offices 443–6 and subsequently an influential patrician; when Chrysaphius was executed after the death of his patron, Theodosius II, in 450, Palladius occupied the praetorian prefecture for five years (450–5).[169] Although the prefecture was gaining power during the fifth and sixth centuries, it would not appear that emperors had a policy of relying on this or any other particular office, at least until the long tenures of the prefecture by John the Cappadocian (531–2, 532–41) and Peter Barsymes (543–6, 555–62) under Justinian – and even this development was followed by a reaction under his successors, when the posts of *curopalatus* and count of the excubitors became the most important at court. Normally, emperors will have been surrounded by a variety of influential individuals, as suggested by the schedule of bribes deployed by the patriarch Cyril of Alexandria to ensure the acceptance of his Christological views at Theodosius II's court in the 430s: the master of offices, the *quaestor*, the wife and assessor of the praetorian prefect and numerous eunuchs from the bedchambers of both Theodosius and his sister Pulcheria, as well as two of Pulcheria's ladies of the bedchamber, received gifts of varying size.[170] Powerful offices were usually held for short terms, to avoid the development of local power bases;[171] much of the jockeying for power may have been played out through ceremonies and individual precedence, privileges and immunities, rather than the transfer of departmental functions, although competition is not unknown.[172]

Overlapping structures probably enhanced imperial control, but emperors did not favour disruptive competition: the existence of diversity in the provinces could cause confusion, and an exasperated Justinian terminated

---

[169] References in *PLRE* ii. Note that Nomus as master of offices was given joint management with the praetorian prefect of the East of civic lands, and took over from the praetorian prefect of the East management of *agri limitanei*: *Nov. Theod.* 23–4. [170] *ACO* i.4.2, 224–5.

[171] An exception is the Lycian Tatianus: after his fall from power in 392, his fellow provincials were banned from the administration for some years (*C.Th.* ix.38.9). John the Cappadocian counteracted his unpopularity in the prefecture by relying on his own household.

[172] Lendon (1997) 135–6, 153; *CJ* xii.8.2; *C.Th.* vi.6–19, 21–3, 27. Competition: *Nov. Val.* 8.1–2 for rivalry over tax collection in the western empire between the praetorian prefect of Italy and the *comes sacrarum largitionum* and the *comes rerum privatarum*; Lendon (1997) 177–85.

military–civilian disputes in Pisidia and Thrace by uniting powers.[173] The
archive of Dioscorus of Aphrodito illustrates the problems caused by
conflict between a community's traditional right of *autopragia*, the right to
pay its taxes direct to the provincial governor, and the desire of the governor's tax-collector, in this case the pagarch Menas, to have all local taxes
gathered under his authority (with consequent opportunities for graft).
Dioscorus' reports of the violence inflicted on Aphrodito may well be
exaggerated (see pp. 185 and 188 above), but his plea appears to have been
upheld, and he was able to obtain an injunction from the duke of the
Thebaid that ordered the pagarch to behave properly, and confirmation for
Aphrodito's special tax position from the imperial court after an appeal to
the empress Theodora. From Dioscorus' perspective, the actions of Menas
were an unwarranted encroachment on Aphrodito's long-standing privileges, but from a broader perspective this competition to extract tax revenues might have been seen as a means of ensuring the full payment of fiscal
dues.[174]

A final area of change deserving comment is the linguistic dimension of
government. Latin had always been the official language of administration
and continued to be so in the various barbarian successor states of the west.
In the surviving eastern half of the empire, however, our period sees its
gradual displacement by Greek – one aspect of the broader transformation
of the Roman empire into the Byzantine. Although during the principate
the imperial government had generally communicated with Greek-speaking communities in their own language, this was a practical concession on
the part of emperors drawn almost uniformly from Latin-speaking parts
of the empire, who issued their legislation in Latin (even if it was then
sometimes translated into Greek) and who communicated in Latin with
their officials, most of whom were from the same background. Indeed, the
advent of the military emperors of the late third and fourth centuries,
accustomed as they also were to Latin as the language of the army, seems
to have resulted in a renewed emphasis on Latin as the language of administration even in the Greek east, while the opportunities offered by an
enlarged bureaucracy and the emergence of Constantinople as an administrative centre created a demand in the fourth-century east for education
in Latin, much to the chagrin of Libanius.[175] This heightened profile for
Latin, however, proved relatively short-lived. Concessions to the predominant language in the east began to appear from the turn of the fourth
century onwards – a law of 397 allowed judges to give their decisions in
Latin or Greek, another of 439 accepted the legal validity of wills in Greek,
while the contemporary praetorian prefect of the east, Cyrus (439–41),

---

[173] *Nov.* 24.1; 26.   [174] MacCoull, *Dioscorus* 10–11, 23–8.
[175] Dagron (1969) 38–40; Liebeschuetz (1972) 242–55, esp. 251–2.

earned the contempt of John Lydus for having initiated the practice of issuing prefectural edicts in Greek.[176] The second half of the fifth century saw a steady increase in the proportion of imperial laws issued in Greek, and the erosion of Roman civilization in the Latinate north-western parts of the Balkans will have reduced the availability in the east of native Latin-speakers.[177] The fifth and sixth centuries did witness the great codifications of Roman law, in Latin, under Thedosius II and Justinian, but these were as much grand exercises in asserting the continuity of the eastern empire with increasingly distant Roman traditions as they were projects of practical administrative import. Greek translations of Justinian's Code, Digest and Institutes were soon available,[178] and although Justinian's great jurist Tribonian appears to have tried to resist the trend, Justinian's own subsequent legislation was increasingly issued in Greek alone, unless specifically directed to one of the Latin-speaking provinces of the west.[179] These changes were not completely one-sided, for in the process Greek absorbed a wide range of Latin administrative terminology, but by the end of the sixth century, Gregory the Great could complain of the difficulties of finding anyone in Constantinople competent to translate from Greek into Latin,[180] while soon after, in a highly significant move, Heraclius began using the term *basileus* in his official titulature.[181]

V. FROM ROME TO BYZANTIUM

The seventh century was a time of major administrative change, when the structure of civilian provinces which could trace its origins back to the days of the Roman republic began to be replaced by the middle Byzantine system of themes, whose primary function was the maintenance of the major army groups, initially the Anatolic, Armeniac, Thrakesian and Opsikion. Just as military needs in the mid third century contributed to the emergence of the 'new' Diocletianic tax system, so now the location of army groups led to the development of administrative structures to support them. The sequence and chronology of these developments have been much disputed, partly because of misguided attempts to establish the identity of the grand reformer who devised such an administrative revolution, but there is now a substantial consensus that the process was gradual, a set of responses to the fundamental changes which overtook the eastern Roman world during the seventh century.[182] The Persian war which dominated the first quarter of the century played its part, since the empire successively lost control of

---

[176] *CJ* VII.45.12; Theod. II, *Nov.* 16.8; John Lydus, *De Mag.* II.12.   [177] Honoré (1978) 39.
[178] Jolowicz and Nicholas (1972) 481–2, 500–1.   [179] Dagron (1969) 44–5; Honoré (1978) 58–9.
[180] Greg. *Reg.* VII.27.   [181] Dagron (1969) 38.
[182] An illustration of this process is the gradual emergence of a militarized society in the exarchate of Ravenna: on this, see Brown, *Gentlemen and Officers*.

all its major revenue-generating regions, with the result that Heraclius was forced to rely on emergency measures, such as the annexation of church treasures; since the emperor was far removed from Constantinople, temporary mints had to be created to service his needs. The capture of most provincial cities by Persians, Avars or Slavs effectively destroyed much of the administrative network, with an inevitable increase in the role and power of administrative elements attached to the court.

But military disaster did not occasion a complete break in organization; perhaps rather it accelerated tendencies already apparent in the sixth century, such as the declining importance of provincial cities and of the curial class which had upheld the liturgical principle on which much of the administration of the empire had formerly depended. Some important administrative developments also had their antecedents in practices of the preceding century. A case in point is the emergence of *coemptio* (*synone* in Greek), i.e. a reversion to taxation in kind, as the basis for imperial finances. In the early sixth century Anastasius had increased the monetary element in imperial taxation through commutation of the land-tax, *adaeratio*, and arguably also through changes to the collection of customs dues; even if *adaeratio* benefited rich landowners, who might control the local provision and collection of the necessary gold, Anastasius' reforms appear to have increased the resources available to the emperor. In the late sixth century, Maurice was still interested in commutation, since he converted the Egyptian grain-tax into gold, and the process was also attractive to major landowners such as pope Gregory, who commuted for gold the rents from papal estates which had been registered in produce by pope Gelasius in the fifth century.[183] But Maurice was also desperately short of money, and twice attempted to reduce the cash element in military pay by a return to issues in kind. The regularity of warfare in the Balkans and the east must have increased the need for *coemptiones*, and these were probably levied as tax credits so that in certain areas the tax cycle was being demonetized: the empire, and more especially its armies, were living from hand to mouth, so that financial problems might rapidly assume critical proportions. If this was true under Maurice, it was even more so during the three decades of constant turmoil under Heraclius.

Heraclius' triumph over the Persians (628) might have enabled a restoration of traditional arrangements, but almost immediately the Arab invasions of the 630s ensured that there could be no return to normality. The richest areas of the empire were lost for good, the major army units had to regroup on the Anatolian plateau and the coastline of Asia Minor became vulnerable to sea-borne raiding. By the mid seventh century, endemic warfare had led the empire to revert to a tax system based on levies in kind,

---

[183] John of Nikiu 95.21; John the Deacon, *Life of Gregory*.

as had happened in similar circumstances in the late third century: *coemptiones* were now the backbone of taxation, to the extent that regular land-taxes on property might be referred to as the *extraordina* of the public fisc.[184]

Survival for the impoverished empire, parts of which were demonetized and decommercialized, took the form of the attachment of troops to specific regions and the concentration of administrative structures in the only city of any substance to survive, namely Constantinople.[185] Authority in threatened cities tended to be given to military governors of proven loyalty, who were less likely than local figures of authority such as bishops to negotiate surrenders, thereby ensuring that imperial interests were sustained in each particular locality.[186] This development resembles the appointment of *comites civitatis* in the west, a practice which probably emerged during the military crises of the fifth century: as in other matters, the east follows western practices, after a considerable time-lag. The governors of themes have been interpreted as a regularization of the sixth-century practice of appointing extraordinary praetorian prefects to oversee the supply of major armies (see p. 200 above);[187] even if the precise link cannot be proved, the similarity of powers is evident. Another element of continuity with the empire of the fifth and sixth centuries is that, despite the greater overall militarization of administration, financial and military matters were largely kept separate.[188] In this respect there is a significant divergence from the western empire, where simplified, patrimonial administration tended to follow the collapse of imperial authority, with real power held by landowning soldiers, whose support had to be courted by the rulers of the different successor states.

With the disappearance of intermediary provinces and cities, the state came to relate more directly to its tax-paying subjects. It has been argued that the tax system shifted from the late Roman distributive model, in which the state fixed its total requirements and then distributed these among the contributing regions, to the contributive model of middle Byzantium, in which assessments might vary according to the resources of tax-payers as well as the needs of the state.[189] This development would have been facilitated by the increased use of *coemptio* in the sixth century, since this process was supposed to be geared to the ability to provide the requisite produce; there is also evidence from the sixth century for increasingly frequent reassessment of taxes and of rents on great estates, which would point to greater flexibility within the system.[190] A contributive system

---

[184] Farmers' Law 19; Haldon, *Byzantium in the Seventh Century* 146–53.
[185] Haldon, *Byzantium in the Seventh Century* ch. 5; Dunn (1993); note Whittow (1996) 104–6 for reservations about demonetization.   [186] Kaegi (1992) 167–9.
[187] Haldon, *Byzantium in the Seventh Century* 203–7, 223.
[188] Whittow (1996) 105–6; Haldon, *Byzantium in the Seventh Century* 101.
[189] Haldon, *Byzantium in the Seventh Century* 150; following Oikonomides (1987).
[190] Goffart (1989) ch. 5.

required the regular updating of information. It has also been suggested that the unsettled conditions forced the state to adjust its procedures to recognize the facts of demographic mobility: the agricultural population could no longer be tied to the land by imperial legislation, and so methods of attracting population to underexploited land had to emerge, with a consequent increase in the numbers of peasant smallholders and the emergence of the village as a key intermediary between the state and the tax-payer; also the household came to replace the individual as the basic tax unit, which would also help the state to avoid the disappearance of mobile tax-payers.[191]

The late Roman state was bureaucratic, certainly in comparison to the administrative structures of the earlier empire, but, as the foregoing discussion shows it, it was not a monolithic or petrified structure. There were competing elements within the administrative structure, for which the emperor acted as the ultimate umpire, while the balance between the imperial centre and its local operators and the base of tax-payers also shifted. The administration provided the eastern empire with at least a century of significant prosperity, and then proved itself capable of reshaping its structures to respond to the disruption of its world in the early seventh century.

---

[191] Haldon, *Byzantium in the Seventh Century* 150–2.

CHAPTER 8

ADMINISTRATION AND POLITICS IN THE CITIES OF THE FIFTH TO THE MID SEVENTH CENTURY: 425–640

J. H. W. G. LIEBESCHUETZ

I. EAST AND WEST: COMMON TRENDS

This chapter is concerned with the political evolution of the ancient city – that is, of a political unit comprising an urban core serving as administrative centre of a rural territory – in a period of great change. As the western empire broke up, the relatively uniform environment that had been provided by the imperial administration was replaced by a great variety of conditions. In view of this, it is perhaps surprising that the evolution of cities in different regions continued to a large extent to follow parallel lines and that comparable developments can be observed in the new barbarian kingdoms and in areas which remained under imperial control, regional differences often being a matter of timing rather than substance.[1]

Taking the city of the second century as a standard of comparison, the type survived better in the east[2] than in the west,[3] but not uniformly well even there. The classical city with an urban population, monumental buildings, games and a highly literate upper class continued in at least the provincial capitals[4] of western and southern Asia Minor,[5] in Syria, Arabia, Palestine[6] and Egypt[7] right up to the Arab invasions,[8] and in the areas under Arab rule even beyond that. In the west the Roman version of the classical ideal survived best in North Africa – but only up to the Vandal conquest[9] – in southern Spain,[10] in Provence[11] and in much of Italy, especially the north.[12] In much of Spain, Gaul and the Balkans, cities had contracted within a reduced circuit of walls. The late fifth century saw signs of revival, first in the east,[13] then in the west, mainly in church building. It is first

---

[1] General surveys: Rich (1992), Dölger (1959).   [2] Claude (1969); Brandes (1989); Kirsten (1958).
[3] There is no general survey to compare with Claude's, but see Février (1980) on Gaul.
[4] For the qualification see Roueché (1989) 218–20 and Roueché, *Aphrodisias* 34.
[5] Brandes (1989); writings of Foss cited in Bibliography.
[6] Kennedy (1985b); Whittow (1990) 13–20.   [7] Bagnall, *Egypt* – much, but mainly fourth century.
[8] So Foss, see Bibliography; but much evidence suggests some 'decline' from *c.* 550: see Cameron, *Mediterranean World* 158–66; Kennedy (1985b); Kennedy (1992).   [9] Lepelley, *Cités*.
[10] Cordoba, Mérida, Italica and Hispala seem to have been independent and active in the sixth century; see Keay (1988).   [11] Vittinghoff (1958).
[12] Ward-Perkins (1978); Wickham (1981); Eck and Galsterer (1991); also p. 234 below.
[13] E.g. at Aphrodisias, Gerasa, Bostra, Caesarea; see p. 215 below.

observed in Ostrogothic Italy,[14] then, in the second half of the sixth century, in Merovingian Gaul,[15] and last of all in Visigothic Spain.[16]

Meanwhile, the cities were changing. On the negative side, self-government by legally defined bodies (the *curiae*) in accordance with constitutional procedures – that is, politics in the classical sense – was perishing everywhere. Cities came to be run by groups of powerful individuals who are described in various ways without our ever being told the criteria which qualified a man for membership of this ruling group.[17] A plausible explanation of this development was given by Libanius towards the end of the fourth century. The maintenance of curial strength depended essentially on the *curiales* themselves. If they did not keep their colleagues to their duties, nobody could. But the most powerful councillors did not mind their colleagues' departure, for it meant that they could concentrate power in their own hands.[18] The consideration that they would also have to bear a larger share of the financial burdens ceased to carry much weight as the civic services which councillors had paid to provide – that is, public buildings, banquets, spectacles and competitions – came to be valued less or were financed in different ways. On the other hand, there was little reason why an ordinary decurion should want to remain in his council. If he was well connected, he was likely to win more wealth and esteem in the imperial service or the church. In any case, he was likely to enjoy a more carefree life outside the council. Councillors were at risk of being beaten or bankrupted, and this risk was no longer compensated for by the prospect of high esteem in the city. So they left.

The government did its utmost, right up to the reign of Justinian, to stop this trend through legislation,[19] but to little effect. In the east, the notables were in control by the reign of Anastasius. The government recognized the situation, and new legislation took account of this fact. This may well have been an important factor in the Justinianic revival.[20] In the west, the process may have taken a little longer but the outcome was the same: the government had to find ways of raising the resources it needed in peace or war through agencies other than decurions,[21] and perhaps in the seventh century gave up collecting the basic land-tax altogether.[22]

The helplessness of the government in face of the relentless decline of the councils was related to another empire-wide development: the decline in the effectiveness of the provincial governor, the key figure in the administration of the late empire as organized by Diocletian. In various areas of

---

[14] La Rocca (1992).
[15] Rouche (1979) table p. 295; also Claude (1960); Dhondt (1957); Cüppers (1977); Février (1980).
[16] Part of a remarkable cultural revival after the union of Goths and Romans: Collins (1983) 51–5.
[17] See pp. 219–22 below.   [18] Lib. *Or.* XLIX.8–11, cf. XLVIII.37–41.   [19] Schubert (1969).
[20] See p. 220 below.
[21] Merovingian Gaul: Greg. Tur. *Hist.* IV.2, V.34, IX.30; Visigothic Spain: *De fisco Barcinonensi* in *SCNAC* x.473f.; see also Vives (1963) 54.   [22] Goffart (1982).

the east, civil provincial governors proved unable to keep order, and Justinian saw himself obliged to combine military and civilian administration.[23] Soon after, provincial notables were given a voice in the appointment of the men who were to govern them; in other words, the office was localized.[24] In the barbarian west, the provincial system disappeared altogether, and the rulers attempted to control cities directly by appointing counts over at least the most important of them.[25] It is doubtful whether barbarian rulers were in fact able to exercise stronger control than the emperors. Many of the counts, too, were local magnates. It is likely that many cities enjoyed greater independence in the sixth century than they had done since the reign of Diocletian. Independence was greater in proportion to a city's distance from the centres of imperial or royal power, and particularly in situations where city authorities had to decide whether or not to resist an invader,[26] or to support one or the other contender in a civil war.[27]

A positive development in east and west was the growth of the power of the bishop. The importance of the church became increasingly conspicuous in the structure of the town. There had, of course, been a significant amount of church building in some towns since the early fourth century, but the building of monumental churches only became general towards the end of the fourth and the beginning of the fifth century. In many parts of the empire, and particularly in the west, church building was interrupted by the military crises of the mid fifth century. It resumed in the late fifth and sixth century and continued to the end of our period and beyond. Ecclesiastical buildings became particularly prominent in the reduced fortress cities of the west, which became centres of prayer dominated by an episcopal complex of sometimes two cathedrals, a bishop's palace and a baptistery, with nunneries and smaller churches within the walls, and cemetery basilicas and monasteries in suburbs beyond the fortifications.[28] The east did not see the development of church- or monastery-centred suburbs, but the periods of high activity in church building in towns and villages were earlier than corresponding periods in the west, and the donors seem to have come from a much wider social range.[29] Of course, the whole process came to a stop with the Muslim conquest and subsequent raids all over Asia Minor.

Another development which had a strong impact on cities everywhere was the growth of monasticism, though in this case the effect was, at least

---

[23] Just. *Nov.* 24–5, 27–31; on the reorganization, Jones, *LRE* 280–1.
[24] In reconquered Italy: Just. *Nov.* App. vii (Const. Pragm.) 12 (552), for east *Nov.* (Justin II) 149 (569).
[25] Claude (1964); Spandel (1957); Declareuil (1910); Lewis (1976); Murray (1986); Thompson (1969) 139–43; Ewig (1976) 451–62.
[26] Many examples in Procopius' accounts of the wars in the east and in Italy.
[27] E.g. Greg. Tur. *Hist.* vii.24 (Poitiers), 26 (Périgueux), 27 (Toulouse), 31 (Bordeaux).
[28] Testini *et al.* (1989) – Italy; J.-P. Sodini (1989) – Asia Minor; N. Duval (1989) – North Africa.
[29] Dagron (1989).

at first, different in east and west. In the west, the first stages of the spread of monasteries were controlled by bishops, so that the number and wealth of monasteries actually strengthened the power of the bishop over city and suburb. It was only later, in the seventh and eighth centuries, that the establishment of rural monasteries in northern and north-eastern Gaul by members of the Frankish aristocracy was one of the factors contributing to the break-up of the classical *civitas* as a political unit in that area.[30] In the east, monasteries were generally founded well outside cities and without the participation of the bishop. Abbots and holy men established a close relationship with the population of neighbouring villages and became their patrons *vis-à-vis* the authorities of city or empire.[31]

One of the attractions of the classical city was that it was the centre of literary culture, whose continuity was ensured by the availability of teachers, with the higher rhetorical education only being provided at regional centres. Cassiodorus explained that to be able to get one's children educated, and so to ensure the continuance of the cultural tradition, was a strong reason for keeping one's main residence in a city (*Variae* VIII.31). So the survival of cities, or rather their continuing to be the centre where the leaders of a region lived, was linked with the continued prestige of secular literary culture. But this was under pressure during the whole of our period. The Bible was steadily taking over more of the ground that had been occupied by classical authors, and the ascetic ideal had no place for secular literature at all, and could be pursued quite without book knowledge.[32] Now this development had very different consequences in east and west in our period. In many cities of the east, literary culture and Christianity continued to coexist through the sixth century.[33] The poems of Dioscorus of Aphrodito and the speeches of Choricius of Gaza are evidence of this. During this period in the west, literary education came to be restricted to an ever narrowing group of leading families at a few centres of government. Cities ceased to have schools, and the transmission of higher literary culture was left to private tutors and ultimately to the church.[34] But in the seventh century the same trend became conspicuous in the east as well. Books became scarce, and learning was increasingly restricted to clergy and Constantinople.[35]

II. THE CITIES OF THE EAST

The written material for the study of the political and administrative development of the late Roman city in the east comes principally from three

---

[30] Prinz (1965), particularly chs. IV and V; Wood, *Merovingian Kingdoms* 193–4.
[31] Well illustrated in Ševčenko (1984) and Mitchell, *Anatolia* II.122–50. See also p. 217 below.
[32] Markus (1990) 199–211.
[33] Mid-fifth-century Seleucia: Dagron (1978); sixth-century: Bowersock, *Hellenism*; MacCoull, *Dioscorus*.   [34] Riché (1973).   [35] Wilson (1983) 58–9; Lemerle (1971) 74–85; Mango (1980) 130–7.

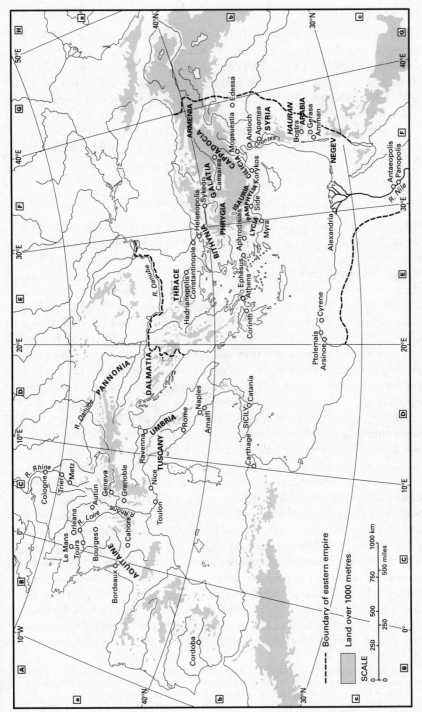

Map 6 Cities of the fifth and sixth century (places mentioned in chapter 8)

kinds of evidence: inscriptions, laws and, in Egypt, papyri. For each kind of evidence, the material is relatively abundant for the fourth century, scarce in the middle of the fifth century, and again becomes more abundant from the last quarter of the fifth century to at least the middle of the sixth.[36] It will be seen that the revival of the late fifth century corresponds to a transformation of civic government. The decline from the mid sixth century probably reflects the changes which were to bring about the 'collapse' of the ancient city in Asia Minor which became manifest after the Arab invasions.

1. Cities of the Greek east: pattern I

What general conclusions can be drawn about the political condition of these cities in the fifth and sixth centuries? The fading out of monuments commemorating local politicians suggests that by the beginning of the fifth century the competitive civic politics of the early empire were dead or dying nearly everywhere. In the smaller cities, it had already disappeared early in the fourth century; in the larger cities and provincial capitals, it had for practical purposes come to an end towards the end of the century. Decurions, from being the political élite, had become a group of hereditary functionaries whose position was nothing to boast about – certainly no longer worth publicizing on an expensive monument. In the case of provincial capitals, imperial officials remained concerned to maintain the classical and monumental appearance of the cities and took epigraphic credit for such public work as occurred.[37] It looks as if the administration was coming to regard provinces rather than cities as the basic administrative units of the empire.[38] Provincial assemblies, meeting at the capital, could be attended by decurions and *honorati* of all the cities in the province, and expressions of either praise or discontent, included in the acclamations of the provincial assembly, were sent to the emperor. Imperial legislation was now often addressed to the inhabitants of a particular province, and it would be logical if it was first promulgated to the provincial assembly, and subsequently placed on permanent public record in the provincial capital.[39] The traditional diplomacy by embassy and panegyric seems to have ceased to operate between ordinary provincial cities and the emperor, and even between the provincial governor and the ordinary cities of his province. At any rate, such cities seem first to have stopped putting up inscribed monuments to emperors, and then to provincial governors as well. It becomes rare for an imperial decree to be inscribed in a provincial city. Imperial

---

[36] Examples of temporal distribution of inscriptions: Roueché, *Aphrodisias passim*; Sartre (1982) (Bostra). Laws: Seeck (1919) lists laws year by year. Papyri: Rémondon (1966); Bagnall and Worp (1980).
[37] Robert (1948).   [38] Roueché, *Aphrodisias* 33–4; Roueché (1989) 218–21.
[39] Notably the provincial reforms of Justinian: see above, n. 23.

statues, statues of governors and inscribed imperial decrees continued to be displayed in provincial capitals, at least – certainly at Ephesus. After some resistance, the imperial government sanctioned the transfer of civic funds, statues and even building materials from ordinary cities to the provincial capital.[40]

Great centres like Ephesus or Antioch, and provincial capitals like Corinth or Aphrodisias, retained their classical monumentality into the mid sixth century and beyond.[41] But it seems that in places which were not centres of government the decay of buildings characteristic of classical city life often began much earlier. Gymnasia went out of use, and were built over or fell into ruin. Public spaces such as theatres or colonnaded streets were invaded by shoddy structures. The agora might be built over, and sometimes even aqueducts were allowed to decay, although it appears that, of the classical amenities, baths were maintained, and even new ones built, when other monumental public buildings had been abandoned.[42] In central and northern Asia Minor especially, where the emergence of classical cities had been closely linked with Roman rule under the early empire,[43] there is very little evidence, whether inscriptions or remains of buildings or indeed objects of any kind, that suggests conspicuously urban activity after, say, the early fourth century. If such places continued to have bishops, as is suggested by their continuing to figure on bishops' lists, it is likely that the bishops presided over what were little more than large fortified villages.[44]

The imperial government was aware of the development and tried to maintain the monumental appearance of cities,[45] not, in the long run, successfully. Unfortunately, it is not yet possible to tell the story of the decline of classical urbanism in detail or even, except in a few cases, to provide a chronology. Of the excavations that have taken place, too few have been concerned to answer this kind of question. The decline of classical urbanism did not, in any case, necessarily mean that cities ceased to be centres of population. Indeed, the building on previously open spaces implies that there was a need for more houses and shops. In some towns there may well have been a shift in the location of population. Early churches were sited on the periphery of cities, and it is quite conceivable that the population sometimes tended to group round churches on the edge of the cities, leaving the centres empty – a development which was common in the western provinces.

[40] C.Th. xv.1.18 of 374, 26 of 390, 37 of 398.

[41] The evidence for undiminished secular monumentality and continued secular building in the writings of Foss (see Bibliography) is derived mainly from cities like these, which are the cities which in the sixth century had a financial official entitled 'father of the city'; see Roueché (1979).

[42] Scott (1987), Crawford (1990) 6 – Sardis; Brandes (1989) 88 – Priene, 95 – Hierapolis, 108 – Caesarea in Cappadocia, 110 – Pergamum – 115 Cycicus, 120 – Anemurion (for Anemurion see also Russell in Hohlfelder (1982) 133–4). [43] Mitchell, Anatolia I.81–98.

[44] Mitchell, Anatolia II.120–1. [45] C.Th. xv.1.1 (357), 14 (365), 37 (398); xv.5.1 (372), 3 (409).

2. The Greek east: pattern II

There is a second pattern of evidence, epigraphic and other, bearing on the condition of the cities which is found in eastern areas of the Hellenistic classical world. Starting perhaps at Side in Pamphylia,[46] further east in Cilicia-Isauria,[47] then at Apamea[48] and other sites in eastern Syria, in Palestine and in Arabia,[49] where Gerasa and Bostra[50] are the most notable of a number of sites, there is an abundance of fifth- and sixth-century evidence of activity in cities. The pattern is found not only in cities, but also in the villages in their territories and in areas where villages predominate: inland Cilicia, eastern Phrygia, western Galatia, the Hauran, the Negev.[51] A feature of this area is that the inscriptional habit came relatively late, and that late Roman inscriptions form a much higher proportion of surviving inscriptions than in the core areas of classical civilization. In these areas, the epigraphic habit seems to remain strong through most of the sixth century.

Among Cilician-Isaurian inscriptions those of the small port of Korykus are outstanding. They are overwhelmingly funereal and a high proportion are late imperial and Christian (fourth–sixth centuries). They seem to provide a social profile of a small late Roman town.[52] Among 591 inscriptions no fewer than 408 commemorate craftsmen, with the great majority working in trades providing for the subsistence of their fellow townsmen. There are 74 members of the clergy or employees of the church. The town had at least nine ecclesiastical institutions for looking after the poor. In format, the inscriptions are remarkably egalitarian. The higher ranks of society did not receive significantly more elaborate epitaphs than craftsmen. There are five members of the council, one *illustris*, two *comites*, one *protector*, five *privatarii*, a *censitor*, a *censualis*. These were the élite of the place. They were not numerous or particularly prominent, but they were no doubt among the *ktetores* who together with clergy and bishop elected the *defensor* and the *curator*.[53] The procedure for election was laid down in an edict of Anastasius, issued in reply to a petition by bishop, clergy, landowners and inhabitants, who were concerned that elections should not be fixed in advance by members of the provincial *officium*. So this little town had a council, but its role was subordinate. It was no longer the voice of the city.

To the east of Cilicia, in Syria and Arabia, villages have produced a very large number of late inscriptions.[54] Of the major cities, Emesa, and Edessa have few epigraphic remains, perhaps because their sites remained densely

---

[46] Robert (1958) (=*OMS* v (1989) 155–93).   [47] *MAMA* III, Dagron and Feissel (1987).

[48] Balty (1980), (1989).   [49] *IGLS* XI, *Inscriptions de la Jordanie*, X, *Inscriptions de Bostra*; Dentzer (1985).

[50] Kraeling (1938); Sartre (1985).

[51] Summary: Patlagean, *Pauvreté* 307–13; Dentzer (1985); Mitchell, *Anatolia* II.122–34; Wilkinson (1990) 120; Tchalenko, *Villages*; Tate (1992); Dauphin and Schonfield (1983); Evenari (1971); also n. 66 below.   [52] *MAMA* III.197–788; Patlagean, *Pauvreté* 158–69; Trombley (1987).

[53] *MAMA* III 197A.   [54] Published in the series *IGLS*.

built up. Late Roman Antioch is very deeply buried. But Bostra[55] and Gerasa[56] have left many late inscriptions, confirming considerable building activity on both sites, in each case with a peak in the first half of the sixth century. At Bostra, most of the building was military or ecclesiastical. The walls were maintained, and many churches built, some with interesting plans, but using *spolia* rather than stone cut for the purpose. Political life shows the same trends as elsewhere. The civic magistrates are last mentioned, in connection with building projects, in 320 and 325.[57] The council does not figure in late inscriptions at all, but there is reference to a decurion supervising work on the governor's palace as late as 490.[58] Around the same time, some building work was carried out by individuals who were neither decurions nor officials. Goldsmiths and silversmiths are mentioned as taking part in the administration of building. Most secular work was ordered by the military governor, who often doubled his post with that of civil governor. Some work was ordered by the *magister militum per Orientem*. The emperor Justinian provided financial support for a great deal of building at Bostra – for restoration of an aqueduct, for work on fortifications, for at least one church and for an almshouse. It is significant that the bishop is involved in the administration not only of the building of churches but also of secular and military work: the subsidy for the fortification had been urged on the emperor by the bishop.[59]

The pattern of activities evidenced by inscriptions at Gerasa is very similar to that at Bostra. There was a considerable amount of building in the later fifth and early sixth century. This included work on walls, on the orders of a military commander, but also some secular building, a bathhouse at the expense of an *agens in rebus*, a portico, a small baths complex paid for by bishop Placcus in 454/7, and, most conspicuously, no fewer than seven churches, three of them in 529–33.[60] No doubt the church made a major contribution to the expense of building, but individual donors, lay and clerical, are mentioned too. So much activity, in what was not a provincial capital, bears witness to the flourishing condition of cities in this area well into the sixth century.[61] But the apparent cessation of building at Bostra around the middle of the century may also be significant.[62] There is evidence which may suggest that the cities of northern Syria were weakened before the last and most destructive Persian war (602–29).[63] Yet the seventh century did not see a permanent collapse of urbanism in Syria comparable to that in Asia Minor.[64]

---

[55] Sartre (1982), (1985).   [56] Kraeling (1938).   [57] Sartre (1982) nos. 9111–12.
[58] *Ibid.* no. 9123.   [59] *Ibid.* nos. 9128–36.
[60] But building is recorded until 629: Zayadine (1986) 16–18, 137–62, 303–41.
[61] Whittow (1990) 14–18; Kennedy (1985b).
[62] The latest inscriptions: Sartre (1982) 540–1, but Bostra has not been excavated.
[63] Kennedy (1985b); Conrad (1986).   [64] Kennedy (1992) 196–7.

3. Greater prominence of villages and the ascetic movement

In many areas of the Greek provinces of the empire, there are remains of solid stone-built villages dating from late antiquity. They are found in Galatia, Cappadocia, Pisidia and Isauria in Asia Minor,[65] east of the Orontes in Syria, in the Hauran, in Galilee, Judaea and the Negev in Palestine,[66] and around Bostra and Amman in Arabia.[67] They have also been found in Libya and Tripolitania.[68] Most of the remains are in areas that have been scantily inhabited in later times. It remains an open question whether similar villages once existed in areas like western Syria or the coastal territories of Asia Minor, which have continued to be densely inhabited. Naturally, no such villages have left remains in Egypt, but papyrus documents show that large villages with village councils and elders, craftsmen and prosperous peasants did exist there.[69] Aphrodito in the territory of Antaiopolis was probably larger than its city, and it certainly had many characteristics of a city, including some highly literate inhabitants.[70] So large and, in many areas, stone-built villages, with considerable churches with mosaic pavements and cemeteries with inscribed tombstones, are a feature of late antiquity. It needs to be explained.

The high empire, which saw monumental classical building in so many cities, did not as a rule produce buildings of this kind in villages. The late empire saw much less activity in cities, and it is therefore tempting to suggest that the late Roman villages grew at the expense of the city in whose territory they lay. This might well have been the case in central and northern Asia Minor where, as we have seen, city sites show few signs of activity in this period. But it cannot be the whole explanation, since in Arabia and eastern Syria villages and the cities in whose admittedly large territory they were situated seem to have prospered together.

A development which must have strengthened the village *vis-à-vis* the city was the ascetic movement. Monasteries were established largely in the countryside and around villages,[71] and in some areas – for instance, the villages of northern Syria – they were very numerous indeed. At and around Aphrodito in Egypt there were no fewer than forty monasteries.[72] These institutions benefited from donations and legacies,[73] and could afford buildings of a quality not previously seen in villages. Their existence must have diverted resources from towns. Heads of monasteries, particularly if they acquired a reputation for holiness, were men of influence and power

---

[65] Mitchell, *Anatolia* ii.100–8.   [66] See above, n. 51; also Tate and Sodini (1980).
[67] Donceel-Voûte (1988); building goes on longer than in cities: Sartre (1985) 136–8.
[68] Sjöström (1993); Barker (1985).   [69] Bagnall, *Egypt* 115–19, 127–30, 138; Rathbone (1990).
[70] MacCoull, *Dioscorus* 5–9.
[71] Vööbus (1958–60); Tchalenko, *Villages* iii.63–106; Brown, 'Holy man'; Hirschfeld (1992); Palmer
(1990).   [72] MacCoull, *Dioscorus* 7.   [73] Wipszychka (1972) 37, 75–7).

whose connections might reach far beyond the neighbourhood of their monastery and, in a few cases, to the emperor himself. Such a one was Theodore of Sykeon, head of a monastery in north-western Galatia, who was called in to solve problems in other villages and was evidently revered over a very wide area. Theodore frequently and successfully interceded for villagers with threatening potentates from the city: landlords lay and ecclesiastical, tax-collectors, and the provincial governor himself. Theodore several times visited Constantinople and was in communication with the emperor Maurice.[74] Nicholas of Sion, in the neighbourhood of Myra in Lycia, had a widespread practice as a miraculous healer in the hill villages of Lycia. He rarely, if ever, used his powers in the city. But the authorities in the city knew about him. After the outbreak of plague in 541–2 it was thought that he had organized a boycott of Myra among the peasants who normally supplied the city with its food. Men were sent to arrest him. But the villagers rallied on his behalf and prevented the arrest. Subsequently Nicholas set out on a tour of the villages, slaughtering oxen and feasting with the villagers.[75] More formidable than Theodore and Nicholas was Shenoute of Atripe, abbot of the White Monastery near to Panopolis in Egypt, who ruled over hundreds of monks, suppressed pagan shrines in his neighbourhood, championed the poor and acted as spokesman for the region to imperial officials.[76] A celebrated hermit might play a comparable role. Symeon Stylites was the most celebrated of many. We know about these men from Lives which usually, but not always, celebrate their hero from his own village-centred point of view.[77] All the names mentioned were 'orthodox', but it is part of the same trend that the Monophysite movement[78] was centred on monasteries and villages[79] and developed liturgy and theology in Syriac or Coptic, the languages spoken by the majority of villagers in Syria and Egypt. All this amounted to a major cultural and political change, and a challenge to the age-long cultural and political monopoly of the towns.

4. The rise of the bishop

By the time of Justinian, the bishop had a very special position in the cities of the east. This emerged most clearly in times of emergency, like the Persian invasion[80] and later the Arab invasions.[81] For it was inevitably the bishop who negotiated the surrender of his city to the invaders. The development of this position was recognized and consolidated by the emperors,

[74] Mitchell, *Anatolia* II.122–50; A.-J. Festugière, *La vie de Théodore de Sykéon*, Subsid. Hag. 48 (1970) 36–8, 58, 76, 78–9, 82, 97.   [75] Ševčenko (1984).   [76] Leipoldt (1903); Van der Vliet (1993).
[77] Brown, 'Holy man'; Festugière (1959).   [78] Frend, *Monophysite Movement* 136–41.
[79] Liebeschuetz and Kennedy (1988) 81ff.; Tchalenko, *Villages* III.63–83.
[80] Procop. *Wars* II.5.13ff., 6.13ff., 11.20ff.; Claude (1969) 124–36.   [81] Donner (1981).

notably by Anastasius, who got the bishop formally involved in urban administration by giving him a part – inevitably a very influential part – in the election of *curator* and *defensor*, and *sitona*.[82] Subsequently, Justinian assigned the bishop a supervisory role in important aspects of urban administration.[83]

That emperors tried to base urban administration on the bishop is not surprising. Over the years the bishop must have become the most powerful individual in many, if not most, cities.[84] He was elected with at least the consent of the citizen body. Once consecrated, he held the office for life, as no secular civic functionary did. As the church grew in wealth, the bishop came to control greater financial resources than all but the wealthiest inhabitants, and these enabled him to fulfil his claim to be the guardian of the poor and the sick. The bishop settled disputes between members of his community more quickly than any public official and without any charge. Cases involving church business and church personnel were normally reserved for the jurisdiction of the bishop.[85] The religious character of his office gave weight to the bishop's intercession on behalf of individuals with imperial officials. It also afforded him some protection from violence at the hands of the provincial governor, something which even men of standing in the city had to fear. So Synesius, bishop of Ptolemais, was able to excommunicate and bring about the dismissal of Andronicus, governor of Libya.[86] The bishop was in a better position than almost anybody else to start a demonstration or a riot, or to appease it.

That a bishop might have, or be well on the way to having, such power did not mean that he automatically became an integral part of the city's government. In fact, it is safe to say that, up to the end of the fourth century at least, the church and its head stood outside the machinery and ceremony of civic government. Indeed, it represented a rival ideology, in that the competitive giving for public entertainment and display which was the essence of traditional civic politics was condemned as vanity and seeking after vain glory by Christian preachers, while the calendar of civic festivals was deeply suspect because of its pagan origin. Lepelley has shown that this was the situation in the already strongly Christian cities of Africa in the age of Augustine, and the situation was no different in Christian Antioch.[87] It may well be that in 387, at the time of the riot of the statues, bishop Flavian emerged as the natural spokesman of the city, and the one most capable of winning a pardon from the emperor.[88] But very few laws were actually addressed to bishops. It is clear that the bishop did not play a

---

[82] See p. 220 below.   [83] See p. 221 below.
[84] Brown (1992) 46–158 is a brilliant reconstruction of the 'rise of the bishop', though the development was probably slower and more sporadic.   [85] Jaeger (1960); Hunt (1993) 151–4.
[86] Syn. *Ep.* 57–8, 72–3, 79.   [87] Lepelley, *Cités* i.391–42; Liebeschuetz (1972) 239–42.
[88] *Or.* xix.28; John Chrys. *Hom. de Statuis.* 21; cf. Van de Paverd (1991); Brown (1992) 105–8.

part in routine civic affairs except as far as he considered that they affected his church, especially the exercise of Christian compassion and charity or the suppression of paganism and, more consistently, heresy.[89]

In the fifth century, the bishops' power generally increased as the councils grew weaker, and as the leaders of the cities became more thoroughly Christianized. As far as the administration of the cities was concerned, there was a power vacuum into which the bishop was naturally drawn. But the extent to which the bishop was drawn into routine civic affairs varied very greatly from city to city and in accordance with the character of the individual bishop. No doubt Justinian wanted the bishop to act as the chairman of the notables. In some cities – for instance, at Gerasa – the bishop may well have played that role. But even so, he did not simply become part of the civic or imperial executive. The church had its own sense of priorities and its own growing financial resources, which were quite separate from those of the city and from those of the empire.[90] Some churches received imperial subsidies, but that was always a special favour. We do hear of bishops who undertook secular civic tasks, like paying for public works or going on an embassy to Constantinople or even presenting chariot races. But that was a matter of their individual choice. It was not part of their regular job.[91] Bishops became prominent in emergencies, in war and famine. Normally, most bishops seem to have been fully occupied running their church. Papyri provide us with a relatively detailed view of the administration of the towns of Egypt. It is remarkable how rarely the documents mention the bishops in connection with secular affairs. The bishop of Alexandria, is, of course, an exception.

5. Government by notables

When we look at the laws dealing with the administration of cities, we must not be misled by the fact that the Code of Justinian includes a lot of laws aimed at compelling decurions and their property to remain in the service of their councils and so at the disposal of their cities, and generally gives the impression that the councils remained essential for running the internal affairs of cities, as well as for the collection of the taxes of the empire.[92] The *Novels* – that is, Justinian's own legislation – and even such of Justinian's laws as were early enough to be included in the Code show that this was no longer so. We read of certain officers or magistrates who might be responsible for administration of a city. Generally the most important

[89] Lib. *Or.* xxx.11; cf. Lieu (1985) 160–4.
[90] See Gaudemet (1958) 288–310. Durliat (1984) and Durliat (1990b) 58–63 are unconvincing.
[91] Avramea (1989); Dagron (1977) 19–23; Feissel (1989). Considering the influence and resources of bishops, references to their intervention in routine administration are surprisingly few.
[92] Jones, *LRE* 741–8.

was the *defensor*.[93] There was also the *sitona*, responsible for the buying of corn,[94] and the *pater*, responsible for local finance, who probably did not have the same functions as the old *curator*.[95] Anastasius appears to have tried to transfer the organization of tax-collecting to the somewhat mysterious *vindices*. This experiment was evidently soon abandoned except in a few cities, including Alexandria.[96] Elsewhere in Egypt we find the pagarch directing the collection of taxes.[97] Above all, the laws seek to give the bishop a leading part in civic affairs.[98] Bishops are instructed to intervene on behalf of cities and their inhabitants in cases of abuse of power by imperial officials.[99] Justin II went as far as to give bishops, jointly with notables, the right to nominate the governor of the province.[100] Bishops were even given the right to check the genuineness of newly arrived documents claimed to be orders of the emperor, and an inscription from Hadrianopolis in Bithynia tells us how an official ordered to suppress banditry in the neighbourhood presented his imperial letter of instructions to the bishop and notables of Hadrianopolis in the court of the bishop.[101]

The laws suggest that the old uniformity of civic administration had broken down, and that there now existed considerable variation in how cities were run.[102] But a point to note is that none of the men in charge of civic business was a curial official. They were not as a rule *curiales* themselves and they received their appointment not from the *curia* but, formally at least, from the emperor through the praetorian prefect.[103] The *defensor*, the *curator*, the corn-buyer and the *pater* were actually elected by bishop, clergy and principal landowners.[104] In the Justinianic laws, decurions are no longer mentioned separately, although some will certainly still have been included among the principal landowners.

When it came to supervising and controlling civic officials, obviously the provincial governor or the military commander, if he was on the spot and interested, would play a key role. Otherwise, supervision was assigned to 'leading citizens'. For example, bishop, clergy and 'leading citizens' audit the accounts of magistrates once a year. The bishop and three men 'of good repute and in every respect outstanding citizens' are to audit the accounts of anybody responsible for spending civic revenues.[105] It is the bishop who is to take steps against imperial officials who have demanded an excessive gratuity for publishing an imperial proclamation.[106] Maintenance of public

[93] Jones, *LRE* 726–7, 758–9.   [94] *CJ* x.27.3; Just. *Nov.* 128.16.   [95] Roueché (1979).
[96] Chauvot (1987); Chrysos (1971).   [97] Gascou (1972); Liebeschuetz (1973), (1974).
[98] Esp. laws of *CJ* 1.4.26.   [99] Just. *Nov.* 86.1, 2, 4 (539); 134.3 (566).
[100] Just. *Nov.* App. vii.12 (Prag. Sanct. of 554); *Nov.* (Just. II) 149 (569).
[101] Feissel and Kaygusuz (1985).
[102] A variety of arrangements for tax collection suggested by: Just. *Nov.* 128.8; 134.2; 163.2.
[103] *CJ* 1.55.8; *Nov.* 8 notitia 36 (535); *Nov.* 15.6.
[104] *CJ* 1.55.8, 11; 1.4.19 (505); *MAMA* iii.197A; Just. *Nov.* 15. epilog.
[105] *CJ* 1.4.26 prol.; *Nov.* 128.16.   [106] *CJ* 1.4.26.7.

buildings and the enforcement of building regulations is the responsibility of bishop, *pater* and *possessores*.[107] In short, the duty of protecting the interests of the city and its citizens from the abuses of local as well as imperial functionaries is assigned to the bishop[108] and to semi-imperial officials like the *defensor* or *pater* and to 'leading citizens' or *possessores*. Decurions as such have no function. Contrary to what is stated as a general fact by some literary sources,[109] the *curiae*, and certainly the decurions, have not disappeared.[110] But their status has become subordinate, almost contemptible. So Justinian ordered clergy caught taking part in an illegal game of dice to be enrolled in the city council.[111]

Who then were these notables who played so prominent a part in running the city and in safeguarding its interests? It is striking that they are never defined. They are regularly described by a rather indefinite general term like *proteuontes, andres dokimoi* or *primates*, though not incidentally *principales*,[112] or sometimes by a more comprehensive description, as, for instance, *possessores et habitatores*. The lack of formal definition and the coexistence of narrower and wider descriptions suggest that we are not dealing with permanent constitutional bodies of fixed composition, but with a *de facto* oligarchical group, who in practice decided for themselves who was to be one of themselves and who was not. (The five *primates* of Alexandria may have been an exception.)[113] Most cities will have included among their inhabitants a number of individuals who would have been recognized as outstanding in wealth and influence – above all, the men holding titles real, honorary or assumed, from 'most glorious' and 'illustrious' downwards, leading members of the provincial *officium*, *principales* of the council, and men of outstanding wealth who did not fall into any of these categories. Some of these will have had the right to sit with the provincial governor during sessions of his court, others will have attended regularly by invitation.[114] Such men were self-evidently the leading citizens and they will have made the decisions needed for the administration of the city. Who convened these men and thus also decided who was to be invited and who not presumably depended on the particular circumstances of each city. In a provincial capital the initiative might most often have been taken by the provincial governor. Elsewhere, the convenor may often have been the bishop, or else the *defensor* or the *pater* or another of the principal magistrates. In Egypt, about which we have by far the most information, the bishops of cities other than Alexandria seem to have played a comparatively small part in municipal affairs.[115]

---

[107] *CJ* 1.4.26.9–10; *Nov.* 17.4 (535); *Nov.* 25.4. [108] Just. *Nov.* 86.1–4 (539); 134.3 (556), 128.17.

[109] John Lydus, *De Mag.* 1.28, III.46, III.49; Evagr. *HE* III.42.

[110] Just. *Nov.* 38 pr.; *Ed.* XIII.15 (538/9); *Nov.* 128.7; 163.2 (575). [111] *CJ* 1.4.33.12.

[112] References to *principales* in *C.Th.* (Jones, *LRE* III.230 n. 41) have generally not been taken over into *CJ*. [113] *CJ* X.32.57 (436). [114] Lib. *Or.* LI, LII.

[115] Individuals simultaneously holding three principal offices *logisteia, proedria* and *pateria*: *P.Oxy.* 2780 (553); *SB* XII.11079.7–8; Sijpesteijn (1986).

I know only one account of an episode that involved the assembly of notables. This was the occasion when a jury of sixteen laymen was summoned at Mopsuestia in A.D. 550; together with the same number of clerics, they were to confirm that Theodore of Mopsuestia had never been entered on the diptychs of the church of that city.[116] This list starts with two *clarissimi* and includes altogether seven men with imperial rank. Only one is described as a decurion and a *principalis*. Some or all of the remaining six could, I suppose, have been decurions, but they are not described as such. Members of this particular group had been presumably selected from the more elderly notables because they were being asked to give evidence about the past. So this composition was probably not typical. Other meetings of *possessores* and *habitatores* were no doubt chosen by other criteria, as were appropriate to the occasion. In the case of the Mopsuestia group, the summons came from the bishop. Selection of the laymen had been made by the *defensor*. That such informal and irregularly constituted groups should play a leading role in the government of cities of the late fifth and sixth centuries marks a great change from the well-defined constitutional bodies that governed Greek and Roman cities in earlier time.

But such arrangements were not confined to the government of cities. They were a characteristic of the time. Bishops were elected by clergy and laity. It was laid down that a bishop was needed to consecrate a bishop. But it was nowhere defined what bishops or what members of the clergy precisely, or what laymen, were entitled to have a say in the election of a bishop.[117] In practice the election was normally made by the archbishop, with a group of local clergy, and approved by acclamation of the local laity.[118] Sometimes, no doubt, lay opinion or, in the case of an important see, the voice of the emperor would have a decisive say.

6. *The internal administration of cities*

For a detailed picture of how cities were run by the notables we have to look to Egypt, which alone has left us administrative documents. The picture is, however, still far from complete. Taxation and provision for the needs of the imperial administration and army continued to be organized through cities. Duties were to a considerable extent assigned to blocks of property or monasteries[119] and even guilds, rather than to individuals. The blocks of property were known as 'houses'. Presumably a share of the duties attached to a particular house would pass to whoever inherited or

---

[116] *ACO* IV.i, pp. 116–17; Dagron (1984b) VI.19–26; Wickham (1995).
[117] *CJ* 1.3.41 *praef.* (528); *Nov.* 123.1 (546).
[118] Cf. the election of St Augustine's successor: Aug. *Ep.* 213, *CSEL* 57.372; see also Jones, *LRE* III.314 n. 119.   [119] Rémondon (1971); Gascou (1976a).

purchased part of the land.[120] The houses differed greatly in size, from what were no more than large peasant holdings to the estates of the Apions, which were large even by senatorial standards.[121] The Apions were not the only landowners on a grand scale,[122] but it is not clear how important these very large landowners were in the economy and politics of Egypt as a whole. Gascou argues that large estates had come into existence in the course of the fifth century as a result of an arrangement between landowners and the government precisely for the purpose of making it possible for the taxes to be collected by them. Alternatively, estates may have grown through patronage, as more and more peasants agreed to pay their taxes through patrons powerful enough to protect them from the rapacity or the officiousness of tax-collectors.

The administration of taxation continued to be city-based. Every city had a financial office to keep the register up to date and to administer collection. The accounting was presumably done by professionals. The director of taxation was known as the pagarch.[123] This office was held by the biggest families of the city in turn, sometimes by a woman, sometimes by one of the family's administrators. At Oxyrhynchus and Arsinoe the office was split into several parts, each of which seems to have been run by one of the great houses.[124] A pagarch had at his disposal considerable coercive power.[125] In the actual collection, the 'houses' were once more prominent, for a large part of the revenue, whether in gold or in kind, was actually paid in by them. Some of it they paid in their own name, some on behalf of others. It is not clear whether only tenants in the strict sense paid 'through' the great houses, or whether, as Gascou thinks, each of the houses had been assigned responsibility for collecting the taxes of a certain number of independent peasants.[126] Surviving accounts show that landowners collected both tax and rent from peasants without clearly distinguishing which was which.

Civic duties, too, were assigned to 'houses'. A consortium of them contributed to the painting of the baths.[127] The *riparius* or police officer was supplied by the principal 'houses' in turn in accordance with a rota drawn up for many years in advance.[128] Similar rotas may have existed for other civic functions too. Justinian ordered the notables to hold the office of *defensor* in turn.[129] But the 'house' of Timagenes seems to have provided staff for a taxation office for part of Oxyrhnchus over many years.[130] The individuals representing the 'houses', and even the administrators of the greatest of them, used high imperial titles. It looks as if the imperial administration had lost control of the use of titles of rank. Many of the users of

---

[120] Gascou (1985) is fundamental but not definitive.
[121] For houses and their contributions: *P.Oxy.* 2020, 2040.   [122] Johnson and West (1949) 49–65.
[123] *PLRE* III.2.1498–9.   [124] Gascou (1972).   [125] MacCoull, *Dioscorus* 24–8, 48–9.
[126] Gascou (1985) 48–52 – controversial.   [127] *P.Oxy.* 2040.   [128] *P. Oxy.* 2039.
[129] *Nov.* 15.1.   [130] *P. Warren* 3 (*c.* 500); *P.Oxy.* 1887 (538); cf. *P.Oxy.* 125, house of Theon (572).

lofty senatorial titles surely were the descendants of decurions or owners of curial land. But there still were individuals described as decurions (i.e. *bouleutai, politeuomenoi*) who continued to play some public role, even if it is not clear how they fitted into the system.[131]

In spite of a seeming abundance of material, the picture of civic government remains extremely fragmentary. How were the various appointments made, and how were the various activities co-ordinated? It may be that assignement to 'houses' rather than individuals meant that fewer elections and appointments were needed. But somebody must have drawn up the rotas and supervised the working of the administration. At Antaiopolis,[132] and at Arsinoe, Herakleopolis and Oxyrhynchus, politics seem to have been dominated by the heads of a handful of great houses. These families, of whom the Apions are much the best known, regularly filled not only the pagarchate but also the civic executive offices of *logistes, pater* or *proedros*.[133] Sometimes the same individual held all three.[134] It is likely that if any serious problem arose at Oxyrhynchus or Arsinoe, the Apions would have had the last word.

7. *The factions and the games*

It will be seen that the 'late late Roman' arrangements for municipal government had no constitutional procedure for compelling the oligarchy of notables to admit colleagues whom they did not want to admit – unless the imperial administration could be induced to intervene, or the oligarchs could be impressed with the strength of public opinion. Both objectives were achieved most effectively by demonstrations. The best-documented example of a campaign of demonstrations against a local magnate is that orchestrated against bishop Ibas of Edessa by a group of mainly clerical or monastic opponents, who were successful in winning the emperor's support for the deposition of the bishop.[135] We hear of a comparable but unsuccessful campaign waged against the patriarch Gregory of Antioch.[136] We have no information about any comparable campaign against a secular urban magnate. But then the historical sources at no period concern themselves with the municipal politics of provincial cities. However, the role of the factions in the troubles in Egypt in the reign of Phocas suggests that these organizations, whose duty it was to lead acclamations in theatre and hippodrome, had become deeply involved in local conflicts.[137] This is precisely what one would expect in a political situation where demonstrations, more or less violent, were the only procedure for bringing about change. In late antiquity, civic shows underwent important changes. There were

---

[131] Geremek (1981), (1990).   [132] E.g. *PLRE* III.830: the various Fl. Mariani . . . Gabrielii . . .
[133] Gascou (1985) 61–71.   [134] *P.Oxy.* 2780.7–11; *SB* XII.11079.7–8; Sijpesteijn (1986) 113–7.
[135] Flemming and Hoffmann (1917) 15–55.   [136] Evagr. *HE* VI.7.   [137] See p. 228 below.

fewer of them and there was less variety. Athletic games and gladiatorial shows came to an end. Theatrical shows continued, and chariot racing of the Roman type – that is, as a professional spectator sport – became more widespread. It seems to have become the principal entertainment in larger cities, perhaps in most provincial capitals – and not only in capitals.[138]

Organization of shows was fundamentally affected by the decline of the councils and the passing of power to the notables. Under curial government games were paid for and administered by decurions, who took turns to perform these duties. There must have been some permanent organizational infrastructure to maintain the buildings and equipment, and endowments to pay for them. There were also guilds of performers, with the help of which the decurions would be able to engage actors, hunters, gladiators, charioteers or whatever they needed for their particular show. This system of course depended on decurions and could not survive the loss of power and resources of the councils. Reorganization was inevitable. It seems that in the course of the fifth century the liturgical organization was replaced in very many, if not all, cities of the east by an organization ultimately modelled on that of the games at Rome and Constantinople. This gave a principal part in the production of shows to the 'factions', the Greens and the Blues. These were large organizations that provided all the personnel, animals and equipment needed for the show, and as there were two of them (in a sense, four), they provided the competition as well.[139] They thus took over the role of the decurions as well as of the guilds of performers,[140] and they were paid largely, but not entirely, out of taxation – that is, by the emperor. So the new organization involved a kind of 'imperialization'. Subsequently the emperor paid, and his representative, the provincial governor, or at Constantinople the emperor himself, presided.

What had been celebrations of the city-community became occasions of celebration of the emperor. For the factions not only produced the games, but also had the duty of leading the spectators in formal acclamations[141] of the emperor and his representative, and not only in the theatre or the hippodrome but on other ceremonial occasions as well. For this purpose each faction paid a chorus, which had the double duty of leading applause for the emperor and of rousing the fans to enthusiasm on behalf of the competitors of one colour or the other. The choruses were large and included not only the unemployed and the rootless, but also young men of good family with money to spend.

Once the factions had come into existence, they attracted the permanent loyalty of very large numbers of fans. Cities became divided into supporters of the Greens and supporters of the Blues. The relationship of the fans

[138] Cameron, Alan, *Factions* 210–14, 314–17; Gascou (1976a).
[139] Cameron, Alan, *Factions* 214–21.   [140] Roueché, *Performers and Partisans* 44–7.
[141] Roueché (1984) 181–99.

to their faction bears some similarity to that of modern football fans to the club they support. Football fans are sometimes destructive but hardly ever political. But the ancient games had a very considerable political significance, so that the activities of the factions could not avoid having a significant political aspect. The acclamations which it was the duty of the Greens and Blues to lead played an important part in two highly political activities: the making of an emperor and the voicing of popular grievances. Acclamation led by the factions was an essential stage in the making of a legitimate emperor; and whenever the succession to the throne was not universally agreed, their indispensability gave the factions power. Both – or at least one – had to agree to lead the acclamation for the new ruler. A coronation would have to be preceded by bargaining with the factions.[142]

The second source of the factions' political power resulted from the privileged character of demonstrations at the games. Since the time of Augustus, the games had been treated by the emperors as occasions for their subjects to publicize grievances.[143] In the later empire this applied not only to games in the capitals but also to those in provincial cities, and reports of provincial acclamations were taken down in writing and sent to the capital, so that the emperor could learn how his subjects felt about his officials, and reward or punish them accordingly. It is evident that acclamations were expected to include criticism and complaints as well as praise. In fact, surviving texts show that there was a fixed order for these demonstrations. They began with praise of God. This was followed by acclamations of the high officers of state, perhaps the patriarch or the bishop, then of the individual who was being honoured on that particular occasion and then at the end, and interrupted by more shouts of praise, petitions, requests or grievances.[144] Civic life offered many occasions for acclamations: the setting up of imperial statues, the arrival or departure of the provincial governor or some visiting high official, the honouring of a civic benefactor, but most regularly the shows in the theatre or hippodrome. While acclamations could be spontaneous, or organized without the help of one or both factions by some powerful, probably ecclesiastical, pressure group, the participation of one or both factions with their large choruses of professional supporters, whether open or covert, would have been an enormous advantage. Clearly it would have been difficult to get a particular grievance included in the acclamations without the co-operation of at least one of the factions.

Given the fact that the factions had a political role, it was inevitable that they should be manipulated by interested parties. By far the best-documented cases of manipulation involve emperors. Most emperors publicized

---

[142] Examples; Const. Porph. *De Cer.* 1.92–3 (Justin I); Theophylact VIII.9–10 (Phocas).
[143] Cameron, Alan, *Factions* 156–83.   [144] Roueché (1984) 186–7.

their support for one or the other of the colours,[145] and in this way made sure that one of the factions at least would support him through thick and thin. An emperor disposed of a wide range of favours by which to demonstrate his partisanship: gifts in money or in kind, posts in the administration and positive discrimination in the law courts.

The favour of the factions was sought by a wide range of people. Rich and powerful men acted as patrons of the factions, and wealthy young men figured among the organized fans.[146] At least one faction's support was clearly essential for anybody with the ambition to become emperor, as emperors were well aware. When the emperor Phocas heard that the factions had put up statues of his recently married son-in-law and daughter, he had the leaders of the factions displayed naked in the Hippodrome, and was only with great difficulty dissuaded from having them executed.[147] When the praetorian prefect John the Cappadocian flaunted his support for the Greens, this was taken as an indication that he had imperial ambitions.[148] When Germanus decided to claim the empire from Phocas, he offered money to the Greens.[149] The means by which the wealthy and powerful could manipulate the factions were similar to those at the disposal of the emperor, if on a smaller scale. They could offer money, or wine or horses, or dancers, over and above those provided out of taxation. So the accounts of the great Apion family of Oxyrhynchus in Egypt regularly show payments in wine or in money to employees of the Blue faction[150] – and even at least one to the Greens.[151]

It was not only the great who looked to the factions to represent their interests. This is suggested by the way minor disturbances escalated into great riots. Often a riot started over a relatively trivial incident – typically, fighting between fans of the two factions or the refusal of the authorities to release a few members of one of the factions arrested for some misdemeanour. But then attempts by the authorities to check the disturbance and to punish breakers of the peace produced escalation, until great crowds were roaming the streets and setting fire to buildings, and the situation was completely out of control.[152] So it would seem that a large number of people who did not take part in the street battles of the fans were prepared to go into the street when they saw the activists being disciplined. It was evidently a situation where a limited number of violent activists had the passive support of a large part of the population, who identified with the faction members when they saw them under pressure.

Alan Cameron has demonstrated that membership of factions, and the division between them, was not based on either geographical or administrative divisions of the city. It does, however, seem to have been the case

---

[145] Cameron, Alan, *Factions* 127–9.   [146] E.g. young Menander Protector: *FHG* IV.201–2.
[147] Theoph. 294 *AM* 6099 (A.D. 606/7).   [148] John Lydus, *De Mag.* III.36.
[149] Theoph. 293 *AM* 6098 (A.D. 605/6).   [150] *P.Oxy.* 152; 2480.28, 82, 82–3 etc.; *PSI* 953.49, 77.
[151] *P.Oxy.* 145.   [152] E.g. the development of Nika riot: Procop. *Wars* I.24ff.; Malalas XVIII.474–7.

that certain organized collectives – for instance, tanners, gardeners, gold-workers, young men, Jews and also old Jews – sat together and on the side of one of the factions or the other. The Jews regularly sat with the Blues. Presumably these groups supported the faction with whom they sat.[153] The question remains whether their faction allegiance was an accidental conse-quence of the position of their seats in theatre, odeon or hippodrome, or whether they had chosen to sit in a particular sector precisely because of their preference for the faction that sat there. It is unlikely that the location of seats is sufficient to account for the huge numbers that were ready to support one or both factions when they got into trouble. It is much more likely that what rallied people on behalf of one or even both factions was awareness that they had publicized grievances in the past and would be needed to do so again in the future. We do have information about a number of political episodes in which the active participation by the fac-tions is either explicitly stated or at least probable. The years 579–80 saw a large-scale anti-pagan witch hunt. The political background was certainly complicated. It involved political and religious antagonisms, both in Syria and at Constantinople.[154] Certainly the spectators in the hippodromes at Antioch and at Constantinople were manipulated to put pressure on the authorities, and were promised favours by lay and ecclesiastical authorities trying to restore order. The colours are not mentioned in connection with these demonstrations, but it is difficult to believe that they were not involved. The reason could well be that in this episode they were on the same side – as they were in a subsequent wave of demonstrations against bishop Gregory of Antioch in 588–9.[155]

In the violent local dispute between some of the cities of the Nile delta known as the Aykela revolt, the factions were active participants, though their allegiance was not consistent. This was in the 590s.[156] When the Persians besieged Jerusalem in 614, the factions were united in pressing for resistance when the patriarch advocated surrendering the city.[157] When the Roman generals Menas and Domentianus quarrelled in Alexandria at the time of the Arab invasion (641), one was supported by the Greens and the other by the Blues, and in this case Monophysitism was an issue.[158]

There is one feature of the urban troubles of the later sixth century which is not found earlier: they were regional rather than confined to a single town. This was certainly the case with the anti-pagan witch hunt of 579–80, the Aykela revolt of the late 590s, and the support for Heraclius'

[153] Roueché, *Performers and Partisans* 83–128.
[154] Evagr. *HE* v.18; John Eph. *HE* iii.29, 31–2. Rochow (1976).
[155] Evagr. *HE* vi.7.   [156] J. Niciu 97.1–30, tr. Charles 157–60.
[157] Strategius Monachus, *La Prise de Jerusalem* v.10, ed J. Garitte, *CSCO* 202, Louvain 1960.
[158] J. Niciu 119.5–17, tr. Charles 189–90.

revolt against Phocas.[159] One factor which helped to bring about this development is probably the fact mentioned earlier, that provincial governors were now appointed by the emperor on the advice of bishops and outstanding landowners and inhabitants of the province. This meant that the province rather than the city had become the important political unit, and that political groupings, and consequently also political conflicts, tended to be on a provincial or regional scale.

III. ADMINISTRATION AND POLITICS IN THE WEST

In the fifth century and after, many western cities continued to exist as centres of civil and/or ecclesiastical administration, refuges for the country population and bases for defending troops in time of war. The degree of contraction varied. It had gone furthest in Britain, where cities, together with Christianity, seem practically to have disappeared,[160] and had gone very far in the invasion-harassed Balkans[161] – though even in exposed Noricum, resistance to invaders seems to have been organized on a city basis, as it is not known to have been in Britain.[162] On the lower Danube, cities received a severe blow from the raids of the Huns. If Nicopolis ad Istrum is typical, rebuilding took the form of a powerful circuit of walls enclosing military buildings and churches.[163] The cities of Aquitaine[164] and of central Gaul, roughly south of a line from Avranches to Geneva,[165] were much reduced in area and population, but retained more of their urban character than the cities of northern France and the Rhineland.[166] The latter suffered heavily during the invasions of the fifth century; Franks settled in much of their territories and their bishops' lists have wide gaps, but habitation seems to have continued on most urban sites.[167] A few became the residence of a Germanic king. Among the latter the most outstanding were Trier,[168] Metz,[169] Soissons and Paris. In southern Spain,[170] city life seems to have continued much as in the fourth century. In the north, Tarraco lost its monumental centre but kept a large population.[171] In northern Italy and Tuscany, of some hundred Roman *municipia* three-quarters still survived in A.D. 1000. Of those abandoned, the majority had never had a bishop. By contrast, less than half of the cities of southern Italy, with their small and infertile hill territories, survived the troubles of the sixth and seventh centuries.[172] The decline of classical monumental

---

[159] J. Niciu 107–9.17, tr. Charles 167–75.
[160] Frere (1977); Hobley (1986); Brooks (1986); Dixon (1992); Reece (1992); Millett (1990).
[161] Poulter (1992a); Dagron (1984a).   [162] Noll (1963); Lotter (1971).
[163] Poulter (1992a), (1992b).   [164] Rouche (1979), Sivan (1992), Loseby (1992).
[165] Ewig (1976) 231–4, 430–4.
[166] Wightman (1978); Wightman (1985) 219–42, 305–8; Horn (1987) 105–9; Pirling (1986); Frézouls (1988).   [167] Brühl (1975); Duchesne (1907) on individual cities.   [168] Cüppers (1977).
[169] Weidemann (1970).   [170] Taradell (1977).   [171] Keay (1991).   [172] Wickham (1981) 80.

urbanism which had taken place in most areas of the west more than a century earlier seems to have come to North Africa in the fifth century. A shortage of evidence makes it difficult to trace.[173]

In the fifth century, bishops had generally achieved a position of at least potential leadership in the cities of the west. Urban populations were now, at any rate nominally, Christian. The effect was profound. Many cities acquired a new Christian identity founded on the cult of relics of a saint or saints, whose presence provided an ever-effective source of supernatural patronage and protection to those who worshipped at their shrine.[174] The saint brought glory to the city and prestige to the bishop. The church made provision for pilgrims, and these, together with clerics travelling on church business, maintained communications in a world which in the west tended towards greater regional self-sufficiency.[175] As temples were destroyed or fell into decay,[176] churches came to be the most prominent buildings in their cities. The prestige of the episcopal office gave territorial magnates who had freed themselves from institutionalized civic responsibilities an incentive for returning to the service of their city.[177] Bishops were less involved in the regular secular administration of their cities under the Visigothic kings than under the eastern emperors.[178] However, wherever secular administration, whether urban or imperial, broke down, we find bishops left in charge. It was in the guise of the ecclesiastical diocese that the unity of city and territory, which was the essence of the Graeco-Roman city, survived longest. So the territory of the *civitas Agrippinensium* long survived as the diocese of Cologne.[179] Such survivals were particularly numerous in Italy[180] and southern Gaul.

Very extensive *civitates* were liable to break up into smaller ecclesiastical units. In the south of France, between 400 and 450, Nice, Carpentras, Toulon and Lizés were taken (or took themselves) out of the control of their *civitas* capital to receive a bishop of their own.[181] Thus we observe in the sphere of ecclesiastical administration the continuation of a secular trend which had promoted secondary centres like Geneva, Grenoble, Gap and Sisteron. The phenomenon can also be seen in North Africa.

The rise of the bishop was not paralleled by the elimination of secular institutions of city self-government. Certainly the mere fact of the establishment of kingdoms by Goths and Vandals seems to have made little difference to the condition of cities in areas under their rule.[182] In 506 the Visigothic king Alaric II published a law book, the *Lex Romana Visigotorum*

---

[173] Cameron, Averil (1982); Duval and Caillet (1992); Modéran (1993).
[174] Van Dam, *Leadership and Community* 230–300; Harries (1992a).   [175] Mathisen (1992).
[176] Ward-Perkins, *Public Building* 85–91.   [177] E.g. Prinz (1973); Kopecek (1974); Mathisen (1984).
[178] The same contrast between Lombard and Byzantine Italy: Wickham (1981) 77–8.
[179] Ennen (1975) 38–9.   [180] Dilcher (1964).   [181] Loseby (1992).
[182] Humphrey (1980); Clover (1982).

or *Breviarium Alarici*. This essentially consists of extracts from earlier Roman collections of laws, especially the *Codex Theodosianus* and the *Novels* of Theodosius and his immediate successors. Most of the extracts are accompanied by an *interpretatio* which is not simply a paraphrase of the legal text but introduces modifications adjusting the law to changes in society.[183] As a source for the social history of Visigothic Gaul, the *Breviarium* of Alaric has the serious disadvantage that, while we are provided with information about surviving Roman institutions and, thanks to the *interpretationes*, about the modifications which they have undergone, we are not informed about institutions introduced by the Gothic kings themselves. It is nevertheless possible to recognize some important developments. There has been a reduction in the administrative importance of the province and its governor, and a corresponding increase in that of city-based officials. Vicars and dioceses have disappeared. The Visigothic kings did not appoint a praetorian prefect. Provincial governors survive. They continue to exercise jurisdiction and are closely associated with the collection of taxes. But the ruler now has a representative in the city itself, the *comes civitatis*,[184] who also acts as a judge.[185] In Visigothic Gaul, *comites* were appointed by the Visigothic king but were not necessarily Goths.[186]

In the city decurions still had an essential role. The *Breviarium* retains many laws designed to prevent decurions from evading their duties. That decurions might escape into the imperial – or now the royal – service has become much less of a problem, but decurions might go into hiding, move to another city,[187] marry their daughters to non-decurions,[188] refuse to have legitimate children,[189] or enter the service of a magnate.[190] It seems that all decurions now had the rank of *honorati* and enjoyed the associated privilege of sitting with the judge when he was hearing a case.[191] The proliferation and devaluation of official titles was, of course, a characteristic of late Roman society. Since the rank of an *honoratus* recognized service to the empire, it had become meaningless in the territory of a Gothic king. But the use of senatorial titles by men who were not senators and lived in a provincial city was introduced in the east, too, sometime after 450[192] – yet another example of parallel development in the east and west of the divided empire.

---

[183] The *interpretationes* are cited below by page references to Conrat (1903) and then by the laws as numbered in Mommsen's edition of the Theodosian Code and the associated *Novellae*.

[184] Declareuil (1910); Spandel (1957); Claude (1964).

[185] It is often not clear whether a *iudex* mentioned in the *interpretatio* of a law is a governor (*iudex ordinarius*) or a civic judge (*iudex civitatis*), who might be the *comes* or the *defensor*.

[186] E.g. Attalus, *comes* of Autun: Sid. Ap. *Ep.* v.18.   [187] Conrat (1903) 736: *C.Th.* XII.1.2.

[188] Conrat (1903) 737: *C.Th.* XII.1.7.   [189] Conrat (1903) 737: *Novellae* of Theodosius XI.1.5–9.

[190] Conrat (1903) 239–40: *Novellae* of Majorian I.1.4–5.

[191] Conrat (1903) 773–4: I.15.1; I.71; on the privilege, see Liebeschuetz (1972) 190.

[192] Roueché, *Aphrodisias* 131; Jones, *LRE* 528–9. Both east Roman and Visigothic governments were anxious that lower-ranking *honorati* should return to the service of their city (*C.Th.* XII.1.187 (436); *CJ* XII.1.15 (426–42)).

The Code makes clear that apart from decurions there also existed a class of powerful landowners who were not liable to curial duties but available as patrons and protectors of fugitive decurions. These presumably included Goths but also descendants of the great senatorial families who had built up large estates in the last century of imperial rule, and were now consolidating their position in the service of Visigothic kings.[193] These men might still have town houses, but this does not mean that the city was still their principal place of residence. On the other hand, they did not continue to inhabit the spectacular late Roman villas. In Gaul as well as Spain, most of the villas seem to have been abandoned quite early in the fifth century.[194]

Under the Visigoths the late Roman tax system survived, and, as long as it continued, it was necessary that the tax, which was after all a land-tax, should be collected not only from the built-up area, but from the whole city territory. In this way, the system of taxation preserved the unity of urban core and surrounding agricultural territory. There must have been great difficulties. The greatest landowners were presumably no longer able to claim privileges as members of the imperial senate – certainly, these privileges have not been taken into the *Breviarium* – but their land-based power of obstruction and resistance was undoubtedly greater than ever: they were on the way to becoming medieval barons, even if landholding in return for military service was still centuries away. So the public revenue diminished. There is no reference to collection other than by *curiales* in Visigothic Gaul,[195] but collection by officials eventually became the rule in Visigothic Spain.[196]

It is not surprising to find evidence that amenities provided by cities have shrunk. Some laws of Book XI of the Theodosian Code, dealing with public works, aqueducts and public shows, have been included in the *Breviarium*. The one law about public buildings shows that some public buildings might be repaired, with the public fisc contributing a third of the cost, but it also permits persons who have built homes on public land to keep them. Some aqueducts are still functioning, since existing water rights are confirmed, but the Code includes no provision for maintenance of aqueducts. In fact, the most active form of secular building was the building or maintenance of walls. The games have come to an end. The *Breviarium* has no regulations for teachers or doctors or actors. Such literary education as survived was evidently provided by private tutors in senatorial houses.[197] The closing of schools and the declining prestige of

---

[193] Rouche (1979) 327–32; Mathisen (1993).   [194] Percival (1992); Gorges (1979).
[195] Rouche (1979) 338–46.
[196] Edict of Erwig of 683: Zeumer (1902) 479ff.; cf. Thompson (1969) 215.
[197] A late-fifth-century private (?) teacher at Arles: Pomerius, *PLRE* ii.896. The end of secular rhetorical culture as experienced by Gregory of Tours: Van Dam, *Leadership and Community* 221–6.

literary culture removed a strong incentive for landowners to reside in cities.[198] In this respect the situation in the cities of fifth-century Gaul was totally different from that of contemporary provincial cities in the east. In Gaul, Spain and Italy, the transmission of literary education was well on the way to becoming a matter for clergy and monks.[199] But even in the early seventh century some aristocratic bishops still displayed a rhetorical education.[200] A lower level of literacy survived much more widely. Administration and jurisdiction in Visigothic Gaul and Spain, and even in Merovingian Gaul, required a significant amount of lay literacy.[201] One function of the council has become very much more prominent: the witnessing and recording in the municipal *gesta* of legal transactions such as wills, gifts, emancipation of slaves, adoptions, oaths and sales of property. Perhaps this development reflects a reduction in the keeping of written records by landowners in the civic territory.

Under the Visigoths the principal civic magistrate in Gaul, as elsewhere in the empire, was the *defensor*. This office had been created by the imperial government, and, in the empire, appointments were still, at least formally, made by the praetorian prefect. Since one of his original functions had been to protect both *plebs* and decurions from wrong at the hands of the powerful,[202] it is likely that he was normally chosen from among the powerful himself. For all practical purposes, in most parts of the empire – perhaps North Africa was an exception – the *defensor*, often together with the *curator*, replaced the traditional curial magistrates.[203]

In Visigothic Gaul the *defensor* was elected by all citizens (*consensus civium, subscriptio universorum*). This procedure would seem to have been more popular than that followed in the east, where appointment was by bishop, clergy, *honorati, possessores* and *curiales*.[204] In cities which were inhabited principally by the bishop and a few magnates, the participation of the people is likely to have been a formality. But Aquitaine, the area for which the *Breviarium* was principally designed, included cities with a considerable plebeian population,[205] so that the people's role – probably acclamation or vilification of a candidate proposed by the notables – may well have been significant. In the north Italian cities, the people retained a genuine voice in the election of bishops, which thus did not become the exclusive concern of the clergy.

The *defensor* of Visigothic Gaul seems to have wider powers of jurisdiction than civic officials of the fourth century. He judges criminal actions involving offences against mobile or immobile property, and civil actions too can be started in his court.[206] Guardians are required to make an inventory

---

[198] Cass. *Var.* VIII.31.   [199] Riché (1973); Kaster (1988).
[200] Wood, *Merovingian Kingdoms* 239–42.   [201] Wood (1990).
[202] Conrat (1903) 728: *C.Th.* 1.10.2.   [203] Liebeschuetz (1972) 167–70.   [204] *CJ* 1.55.8.
[205] Sivan (1992).   [206] Conrat (1903) 729: *C.Th.* 11.1.8, 4.2.

of their ward's property in the *defensor*'s presence.[207] The *defensor* is to assure punishment of robbers irrespective of who the robbers' patrons are,[208] and he is allowed to order a whipping – but not of the innocent.[209] The enhanced position of the *defensor* in Visigothic Gaul resembles that of the same office as defined by Justinian in seemingly quite different circumstances in the east.[210]

The administration of cities in Ostrogothic Italy seems to have resembled that in Visigothic Gaul and Spain. The *defensor* was the local head of the city, whose inhabitants were his clients.[211] Theoderic was delighted when the *defensor* and the *curiales* of Catania in Sicily took the initiative of asking permission to restore the city walls using material from the ruined amphitheatre.[212] It was the *defensor* and *curiales* that Theoderic addressed when he made demands on cities.[213] The *defensor* was particularly responsible for fixing prices.[214] Besides the *defensor*, most – perhaps all – cities had a *comes civitatis*, appointed by the Ostrogothic king for supervision, and above all to exercise jurisdiction.[215]

We are once more allowed a relatively detailed view of cities in the west in the last quarter of the sixth century, when we have the *Letters* of Gregory the Great for Italy, the contemporary *History* of Gregory of Tours for Gaul, and the Visigothic Code for Spain, together with a varied assortment of supporting sources. It is clear that there has been a significant reduction in the classical institutions. Lay power in cities seems to be wielded by the royal representative, the *comes* and notables (*cives*) and their leaders (*maiores* or *seniores*) and of course the bishop, who will normally have been the most powerful and influential individual in the town. Bishops are recorded to have acted as judges, to have rebuilt walls, to have pleaded with the representatives of the king on the city's behalf for remission of taxation and to have negotiated with threatening commanders in war, civil or otherwise. Bishops provided poor relief for individuals on the church's register (*matricula*).[216] They built hospitals and ransomed prisoners. They received donations on behalf of the church and could afford to build churches and found monasteries, even in disturbed times.[217] As far as the cities were concerned, the competition for authority between royal count and bishop seems to have been won by the bishop. It must, however, be remembered that our principal sources are Gregory's *History* and the Lives of saints, which almost certainly exaggerate the importance of bishops relative to that of lay magnates.

Curiae and decurions and even the *defensor* seem to have ceased to play any part in the decision-making and administration of the city. They did,

---

[207] Conrat (1903) 730: *C.Th.* III.17.3.   [208] Conrat (1903) 731: *C.Th.* I.10.3.
[209] Conrat (1903) 732: *C.Th.* II.1.10–12.   [210] *Nov.* 15 (534).   [211] Cass. *Var.* VII.11.
[212] *Var.* III.49.   [213] *Var.* IV.45, transport; V.14, tax collecting; III.9, building material.
[214] *Var.* VII.11.   [215] *Var.* VI.23, 26.   [216] Rouche (1974).
[217] Wood, *Merovingian Kingdoms* 71–87; James (1988) 183–4; Pietri (1983).

however, continue to perform a function of great importance. They kept the *gesta municipalia*, which provided a written record of all property transactions in the *civitas*. This notarial role of the city council is attested by surviving formulae from Aquitaine (Bordeaux, Bourges, Cahors and Poitiers), Burgundy and northern Gaul (Sens, Orleans, Tours, Le Mans, Paris),[218] and also from Italy and Dalmatia, but scarcely from Spain. These documents show that city councils, sometimes with *curatores* and *defensores*, survived in some places well into the eighth century. In Italy *gesta municipalia* disappear around 800. At Naples the council survived to the tenth century.[219] Significantly, in some cities, such as Naples and Amalfi, the professional notaries, who took on this work, assumed the title of *curiales*.[220]

Under the Merovingians, *curiales* no longer seem to have been responsible for the land-tax, which appears to have been collected by agents of the *comes*.[221] In fact, the tax was no longer self-evidently essential for the maintenance of government. Gregory of Tours refers to the royal tax revenue as a luxury. He exaggerates. The kings had to reward their followers and to show generosity towards the church. They seem regularly to have done this not by paying salaries but through grants of estates or of 'immunity'. This meant that the 'immune' landowner kept the tax which, in the west as in the east, he had received from the tenant together with the rent, instead of passing it on to royal representatives.[222] The development severed an important link between the city and its territory.

The Germanic kings could afford to be extravagantly generous with their revenue only because they employed comparatively few civil servants, and above all did not have to pay a large professional army. They fought their wars with levies of peasants. The countryside was becoming militarized. This was partly a result of the settlement on the land of Franks in the north of Gaul and of Visigoths in Spain. But, in addition, the great landowners of Gaul and Spain were themselves acquiring armed followings. The process can be observed in the case of one Ecdicius,[223] who around 471 raised first a small troop and later on an army to resist the Visigoths.[224] The Visigoths themselves made use of this capability and compelled Roman aristocrats and their men to fight for them.[225] This was a development of fundamental importance.[226] In the independent city state, the peasants

---

[218] Zeumer (1886).   [219] Wickham (1981) 75.   [220] Schmidt (1957) 122–4.
[221] Greg. Tur. *Hist.* iv.2, v.34, ix.30.
[222] Goffart (1982), Kaiser (1979) – the traditional view – rather than Durliat (1990b).
[223] *PLRE* ii *s.v.* Ecdicius 3.   [224] Sid. Ap. *Ep.* iii.3.7–8.
[225] Sid. Ap. *Ep.* v.12; Greg. Tur. *Hist.* ii.3.
[226] Bachrach (1971); Rouche (1979) 350–2. In general on militarization in the west, see Krause (1987) 131ff., who supplies a comprehensive survey of the evidence but tends to underestimate the scale of the development. On fortified hill-fort refuges, frequent in frontier zones, and fortified villas, for which there is some but not abundant evidence, see Johnson (1983) 226–44. In Italy, militarization occurred, both under the Lombards and Byzantines, without ruralization (Wickham (1981) 72, 76–7).

were the army, and they were called up by the city. Under the empire, peasants might be individually conscripted into the imperial army, and in the late empire landowners provided recruits as a tax, while themselves remaining civilians. That landowners should join the army at the head of their own armed tenantry is a fundamental departure both from the principle of the city state and from the practice of the empire. But that was the way of the future.[227] Even the clergy became militarized.[228] The gradual militarization of the landed aristocracy, together with the equally gradual breakdown of the Roman city-organized system of taxation, did much to end the integration of urban centre and territory which had been a principal characteristic of the ancient city.

So power moved to the countryside. In the sixth century, bishop Nicetius of Trier had a castle on the Moselle in addition to his residence near the cathedral.[229] Not much later, the Frankish *comites civitatis* and their families seem normally to have lived outside the fortifications of their city.[230] Meanwhile, city centres emptied of inhabitants, and clusters of settlements grew up around churches and monasteries on the periphery. Timber or wattle and clay replaced stone as building material for houses, even in north Italian cities.[231] The Carolingians abandoned the Roman system of taxation, and ceased to use city organization as a basis of their administrative system. Kings and nobles founded monasteries deep in the countryside which became centres of agriculture, craftsmanship and trade.[232] The degree of physical and indeed demographic continuity between ancient and medieval cities of the former western Roman empire varies greatly from area to area.[233] It was strongest around the Mediterranean coast, and above all in Andalusia under the Arabs,[234] and in northern Italy,[235] and weak to the point of insignificance in Britain and along the Danube.

IV. CONCLUSION

The development of the late Roman city in east and west is a story of infinite variety. Nevertheless, we are dealing with a single cultural institution liable to the same vicissitudes. Even if these did not affect cities everywhere at the same time, the unity was manifest to the end. The eastern urban revival of the late fifth and early sixth century, of which there is evidence in the form of striking buildings at, say, Gerasa or Apamea, and of a rich munificent city-based upper class at Aphrodisias

[227] *Leges Visigothorum* IX.2.8–9; cf. Thompson (1969) 262–6.   [228] Prinz (1971).
[229] Venantius Fortunatus 3.12.   [230] Claude (1964).   [231] Bavand (1989).
[232] Prinz (1965) 121ff., 152ff.; Wood, *Merovingian Kingdoms* 183–94.
[233] Ennen (1975) 27–45; Wolff (1991).   [234] Ennen (1975) 70–1.
[235] Eck and Galsterer (1991); Picard (1988).

and Athens, is paralleled in Ostrogothic Ravenna[236] and – if on a more modest scale and some decades later in time – by abundant church building in remote western Aquitaine,[237] and as far north as Trier and Cologne.[238] In a sense the golden age of Visigothic Spain following the conversion of the Goths to Catholicism in 589 represents the last flowering of that revival.[239] But in the east the plague of 542[240] inaugurated a period of deepening crisis, which in due course spread to the whole area of the old empire: repeated visitations of plague, first Persian, then Arab invasions of the east, Slav invasions of the Balkans and Greece,[241] Lombard advances into Italy. Byzantine Italy was 'militarized',[242] and the Arabs conquered Spain. The chaos of the internecine wars among the Franks in the mid seventh century may have been exaggerated by Carolingian propaganda.[243] Nevertheless, when order was restored, Gaul and Italy had moved significantly further from their classical condition. This was the starting-point of Pirenne's famous theory that, without Muhammad, Charlemagne would have been inconceivable.[244] Pirenne was probably wrong about the importance of the Arab conquest's effect on Mediterranean trade. But it remains true that the economic and political centre of the western Christian world moved to the much more weakly Romanized north of Gaul and the Rhineland. The latest mention of a city council and a *defensor* in Gaul occurs on a formula from Poitiers of 805. In Italy most councils seem to have disappeared by 700, leaving the bishop, now by far the greatest landowner, supreme in the city.[245] Leo VI (A.D. 886–912) formally abolished city councils in the Byzantine empire.[246] By then, surviving councils had long become an anachronism. When the restoration of stability was begun by Charles Martel (A.D. 719–41) in the west and by Leo III (A.D. 717–41) in the east,[247] administration in neither area was any longer based on the ancient city units, and cities no longer functioned as centres of secular administration for an attached rural territory. In both east and west the history of the ancient city might be said to have come to an end with the emancipation of the countryside, even if the emancipation took very different organizational forms in what had been the eastern and western halves of the old empire.[248]

---

[236] Deichmann (1976–89).   [237] Rouche (1979).

[238] Kempf (1968); Oswald, Schaefer, Sennhauer (1966) 140, 150, 154.

[239] Palol (1968); Fontaine (1959).

[240] Conrad (1986); Durliat (1989) argues that the immediate impact was rather less.

[241] Huxley (1977); Wiseman (1984); Spieser (1984).   [242] Brown, *Gentlemen and Officers*.

[243] Wood, *Merovingian Kingdoms* 255–9.

[244] Pirenne (1939) 234; cf. Hodges and Whitehouse (1983); Barnish (1989).

[245] Wickham (1981) 19.   [246] Leo VI, *Nov.* 46–8.

[247] Haldon, *Byzantium in the Seventh Century* 84–91.

[248] Haldon, *Byzantium in the Seventh Century* 180–207 on 'themes'.

CHAPTER 9

ROMAN LAW

DETLEF LIEBS

I. INTRODUCTION: LAW IN THE LATE ROMAN EMPIRE

Law was central to the social structure of the Roman empire in the fifth and sixth centuries A.D., more so than in the principate and in the neighbouring barbarian kingdoms. The administration of justice, and of finance, had been strengthened by the reduction in the size of provinces and by the reforms which both relieved governors of military responsibilities and provided them with a substructure of bureaucratic support. The legislative machine had also become more energetic. The legislative functions of the senate in Rome had been transferred to the imperial *consistorium* in Constantinople and Ravenna, which worked with more expedition and produced incomparably more enactments. The number was especially high at the beginning and towards the end of our period – that is, A.D. 425–60 and, even more so, 527–46. Tradition had by this time built up a vast store of legal literature, impressive alike in its volume, antiquity and quality. A civilized state, based on the rule of law, seemed on the surface of things to be assured, and this must have enhanced Roman pride. With the exception of the Vandals, one nation of Germanic barbarians after another sought to emulate this Roman ideal (see pp. 260–87 below).

However, the aspiration was also a burden which was difficult even for the Roman state to sustain. The sources of law were remote from the ordinary inhabitants of the empire, since the personal contacts entailed by legal practice in the first centuries A.D. had now been displaced by bureaucratic structures. The jurists who used to give *responsa* and who, with the emperor's endorsement, made the development of law their personal responsibility had given way to career professionals with a technical command of a huge but ever more unwieldy body of enacted law, as well as other texts. Further, the social position of the numerous lawyers of late antiquity was now such that they seldom reached the top positions in the state. For financial reward,[1] they had for the most part to content themselves with more modest posts than the few who preceded them in the years before A.D. 212. The central bureaucracy was inclined to extend its

[1] Chastagnol (1979) 230f.

competence at the expense of the local officials nearer to the citizens. Jurisdiction over weighty matters, as for example capital punishment or the imposition of special levies, was transferred to the centre or made dependent on lodging a report and obtaining central assent. Even such an important official as the city prefect tended to prefer to report to the centre rather than decide matters himself.[2]

The substantive law of the principate was developed – with, for example, more sensitive differentiation in relation to succession on intestacy – and was adapted to changed circumstances. The most important change was the transformation of the dominant ideology, since the adoption of Christianity and imperial responsibility for enforcing orthodoxy produced a substantial body of legislation. Changes to the tax system under Diocletian and Constantine generated a huge mass of laws intended to tighten its efficiency and ensure that the state's increasing financial needs were promptly satisfied by all subjects. To ensure regularity of supplies, various posts and professions were peremptorily made subject to legal burdens on a hereditary basis. In particular, membership of town councils, which had become less attractive, relatively, in comparison to service in the imperial bureaucracy, and perhaps also absolutely, because of the demands of tax collection, had to be defended by a sequence of laws.[3]

Tenant farmers were another area of particular legislative concern. In the course of the fourth century they were gradually turned from a free smallholder into a serf with scarcely more rights than a slave, though with regional exceptions and differences, so that landowners' objectives were not universally achieved. There was also an important change in family law. The hitherto dominant rule had been that children followed the status of their mother if for any reason their parents' union did not amount to a fully valid marriage. Step by step this *regula iuris gentium* was displaced by the principle that such children must follow the parent with the lower status.[4] Penal statutes with grisly punishments aimed at life and limb multiplied for people of all ranks,[5] and free status no longer gave immunity from torture. For embezzlement in the public sphere, money penalties at hitherto unimaginable levels were introduced. However, corruption was to an extent legalized, in that payments for procuring position or office or securing performance of an official act, which had become customary, were generalized and had their amounts fixed.[6] There was also legislation which turned with new emphasis to the task of providing for public welfare.[7]

The texts give the impression that these laws reached out to their victims like the tentacles of an octopus, but the reality was different. The

[2] E.g. Symmachus, *Relat.*; Liebs (1983) 220–3; Dazert (1986) 157f.
[3] *C.Th.* XII; cf. Liebs (1986) 276f.   [4] Voss (1985).   [5] Liebs (1985).
[6] Merkel (1888); Veyne (1981); Noethlichs (1981); MacMullen (1988).
[7] Vogt (1945) 141–2; Biondi (1952–4).

effectiveness of the law against the rich was less than it had ever been,[8] and this weakness was well known. Every official act was prone to corruption, while the differences between rich and poor had grown so vast that the rich could defy local authorities and achieve their ends by applying sufficient pressure.[9] This did not mean that the legal system was entirely subverted, simply that it lacked authority. Those without money or influence had no choice but to rely on the law, and the majority of the people accepted it. Indeed, most people usually accept even thoroughly unsatisfactory laws, as being better than no law at all. Sometimes legal process and punishment were brought to bear even on the arrogant rich,[10] but neither reliably nor expeditiously.

II. THE JURISDICTION[11]

The subject matter of legal proceedings was diverse: civil litigation over property and debt, criminal prosecutions of dangerous offenders, administrative and tax cases concerning public duties and levies, military cases concerning both disciplinary infringements and the proprietary and other affairs of soldiers which in a civilian would have belonged to the ordinary private law. The regular judge for civil, criminal, administrative and tax cases was the governor of the province (*praeses, iudex*) or, where geographically appropriate, the city prefect of Rome or Constantinople (*praefectus urbis*). For minor matters there were town courts. The court of the governor sat in the capital of the province, the former practice whereby the governor took his court on circuit (*conventus*) having become a rarity. A frequent practice was for the governor, as for the prefect and the emperor himself, to delegate ordinary civil cases to lower judges (*iudices pedanei, iudices delegati*), so as to retain for himself the more important class of business, especially criminal cases and cases involving status, wardship and public finance.

There were also special courts for special categories of people: for criminal cases involving senators, there was the imperial consistory, the praetorian prefect or, in the west, the Roman city prefect together with five senators chosen by lot (*quinquevirale iudicium*); for the officials of the palace (*palatini*), the court of the *magister officiorum*; for the officials of the financial administration, the local *comes largitionum* or, where appropriate, the central *comes sacrarum largitionum*; for imperial tenants, the local *rationalis rei privatae* or, where appropriate, the *comes rei privatae* at the centre; for soldiers, the local *dux* or, where appropriate, the *magister militum*.

The jurisdiction of the town courts extended only to matters of small value and non-contentious items. They were presided over by the local

[8] Wieacker (1983b).   [9] E.g. Aug. *Ep.* 10*.2–8.
[10] Arvandus in 469: Stevens (1993) 103–7; Harries (1992b); Teitler (1992).
[11] von Bethmann-Hollweg (1866); Kaser and Hackl (1966) 517–644.

magistrates, the *duumviri*. Still lower down, the *defensor civitatis* exercised a summary arbitral jurisdiction over the small claims of ordinary folk. In the two capital cities, jurisdiction over both small claims and public order, as also over the personnel directly responsible for public order, was exercised by the *praefectus vigilum* (called the *praetor plebis* in Constantinople from A.D. 535). Similarly, disputes to do with the food supply to the capitals or involving the personnel concerned with it fell within the jurisdiction of the *praefectus annonae*. The praetors by this time were chiefly occupied in the planning and financing of the public games. They had retained jurisdiction only in some particular matters.[12]

Jurisdiction at first instance, albeit only in exceptional cases, was also exercised by the twelve to fifteen regional *vicarii* so long as they existed and by the equivalent authorities at the intermediate level, the *comes Orientis* in Antioch and the *praefectus Augustalis* in Alexandria, as also the higher authorities, such as the two to four *praefecti praetorio*. Normally, like the senates of both capitals and the emperor himself, these jurisdictions functioned as courts of appeal, of second or third instance. But their powers were of course larger, since in the Roman political system judicial functions were regularly associated with other governmental responsibilities: judicial, legislative and executive powers were not separated.

All governmental judges – provincial governors, vicars, and prefects – sat with an *assessor*, who was paid by the state and was, if possible, a professional lawyer. He had a decisive voice on questions of law.[13] Every court was permitted a fixed number of advocates, who had their own corporate organization. Thus, the courts of governors had thirty, of vicars and their equivalents fifty (sixty in Egypt), of city prefects eighty, and of praetorian prefects 150. However, in the west these numbers were not maintained after the early fifth century. The advocates' remuneration was fixed; they could only claim modest fees compared to the honoraria paid in the first centuries of the principate. They were now required to have had a legal education: anyone applying to practise in the court of the praetorian prefect had to produce certificates sworn by the professor of law who had taught him.[14]

From the delegated judges an appeal could be made to the delegating, and from the courts of towns to the governor of the province. There was then no further appeal. A case begun before the governor could be appealed to the vicar or, if he was nearer, to the praetorian prefect. From the latter there was no further appeal. However, from the vicar, as from the city prefects, it was possible to appeal again to the emperor himself. In that case the emperor acted as a court of third instance.

---

[12] *C.Th.* VI.4.16.   [13] E.g. Aug. *Conf.* VI.10.   [14] *CJ* II.7.11.2.

III. SOURCES OF LAW AND LAW MAKING[15]

Once the monarchical principal of government had been fully established in the fourth century, the emperor or, as it might be, the central bureaucracy acting in his name was in sole control of the machinery of legislation. To a greater or lesser extent he also dominated all other law-making organs – namely, the senate, the regional magistrates and local authorities, especially the towns and other communities, whose finances had gradually been brought under imperial control.

Imperial legislation adhered to the diverse forms handed down from the earlier period, above all resolutions of the senate and magistral edicts. In this spirit the fundamental pronouncement on the sources of law for the whole epoch, enacted on 7 November 426,[16] recognized as universally binding statutes only the so-called resolutions of the senate (imperial legislative proposals communicated to the senate, *orationes ad venerabilem coetum missae*) and imperial edicts. The term 'edict' must be understood as including not only pronouncements which expressly so describe themselves but also all others which were published throughout the empire by the governors and claimed to have general application. In short, pronouncements took effect according to their own tenor – to apply to everybody, the text had only to speak as a *lex generalis*. From A.D. 446, a new statute required the assent of the imperial *consistorium* and the senate.[17]

The mass of law handed down from the past continued in force so far as it had not been changed by more recent legislation. It remained the principal source of rules for contemporary application. The law was thus to be found in the standard legal literature, now known in the west simply as *ius* in contradistinction to *leges*,[18] which was used of imperial pronouncements. The A.D. 426 enactment concerning the sources of law gave instructions about handling conflicts of opinions in the canonical books:[19] these should be resolved by counting heads, while in a tie Papinian had the casting vote. In the west the only books easily available were those of Gaius, Papinian, Paul, Ulpian and Modestinus. Even in the case of Julian and Marcellus there were evidently problems so that their opinions were only to count when the relevant text could be corroborated from more than one manuscript.

Theodosius II entertained a plan to overcome all the uncertainties in relation to the law gathered from the writings of the old private jurists. He intended that the part of the old literature which was to remain in use should be issued in one authoritative edition of excerpted works. He did

---

[15] Gaudemet (1979a); Liebs (1992).
[16] Five pieces survive: *CJ* 1.14.3; 1.14.2; 1.19.7; 1.22.5; *C.Th.* 1.4.3.
[17] *CJ* 1.14.8; Wetzler (1997) esp. 127–31 and 197–9. [18] Gaudemet (1979b).
[19] *C.Th.* 1.4.3; see Volterra (1983).

not, however, accomplish this plan, but a century later it was taken up by Justinian and carried through. The result is the *Digest* (see p. 249 below).

Law-making utterances of the emperor were not confined to the enactment of *leges generales*. The absolute monarchy increased the tendency to accord legislative authority to his other pronouncements in the fields of both law and administration. These took many forms: official interpretations of legislation (*scripta ad edictum*), instructions to imperial officials (*mandata*), judgements of the emperor's court (*decreta, sententiae*), imperial answers (*rescripta*) to individual supplications (*preces*) or to questions from office-holders engaged in some legal process (*consultatio*). Rescripts to individuals (*rescripta personalia*) usually contained merely a ruling on the law and did nothing but apply the existing law (*rescripta simplicia*). Frequently the petitioner requested some special privilege, which, if granted to an individual, was called an *adnotatio* or an *adnotatio specialis* (a marginal note, or a special marginal note). They could only be granted by the emperor personally, and the grant was originally made in the form of an entry on the margin of the petition. A privilege for a province, town or other corporate body was called a *pragmaticum* or *pragmatica sanctio*. Examples were remissions of taxation, moratoria, immunities from compulsory labour and charters for the Catholic church. The same term included *ad hoc* disqualifications, such as the disabilities imposed on the Donatists in Africa.

Even oral utterances of the emperor (*interlocutiones*) could acquire statutory authority, as for instance where he declared a principle during a session of his court, or at a meeting of his *consistorium*, or indeed in any other imperial speech. Although the absolute conception of the imperial office simplified the business of legislation, it also entailed the danger that the legal system would be subverted from within, for grants of imperial graces and favours such as exemptions from a statute, or immunities, whether from the emperor himself or in his name, claimed the same status as general legislation. The system therefore had to cope not only with the ruler's policy of granting genuine graces and favours, but also with the corrupt multiplication of such dispensations. For the emperor's closest ministers knew every means of procuring the imperial signature, and petitioners sought to obtain privileges not only by laying out money but also by misrepresenting the facts.

Emperors made repeated assaults on abuse, especially of rescripts. Rescripts contradictory to the general law were to be treated as invalid; privileges were only to take effect if a petitioner had expressly applied to be exempted from the force of a particular statute; imperial favours must not encroach on the private rights of third parties. Further, rescripts were to be used only in the case for which they had been issued, a rule which Justinian abandoned, reverting to the earlier position.[20] Shortly afterwards Justinian

[20] *CJ* 1.14.12; VII.45.13.

also enacted that judges must disregard imperial rescripts or mandates which encroached on their jurisdiction, whether adduced by imperial *referendarii* in writing or by word of mouth. This law included all private rescripts, pragmatic sanctions, official rescripts and imperial instructions to public servants (*mandata*) and applied whether they had been obtained before or during the case. Further, the law was to be recited at the start of the record of every case.[21]

Hardly any records of law making by magistrates below the emperor have survived – essentially only a collection of abbreviated edicts emanating from the praetorian prefect of the east between 490 and 563 in Greek.[22] Three of these, in part preserved unabbreviated, were appended to the comprehensive collection of Justinianic *Novels*.[23] Documents relating to private transactions survive in large numbers. Of those in Latin the most important are the papyri from Ravenna dating from the fifth century.[24] Copious Greek papyri come from sixth-century Egypt.

IV. CODIFICATION

In 429 Theodosius II decided to have all imperial constitutions since Constantine brought into an official order on the model of the private collections made under Diocletian, the *Codex Gregorianus* and *Codex Hermogenianus*.[25] The flood of imperial pronouncements had become so great that no professional lawyer could pretend to master them all.[26] The first phase of the project was to be the collection of all constitutions since Constantine which had general validity: the resolutions of the senate (in reality, imperial communications to the senate), imperial edicts and other *leges generales* even where applicable only in particular regions. All were to be shorn of their legally superfluous outworks, especially the high-flown rhetorical introductions, distributed under titles according to subject matter and, within those titles, set out in chronological order. The resulting collection was intended to be no more than the foundation for a more far-reaching project: there was to be a volume of all contemporarily valid legal materials, purged of all that was obsolete, ambiguous or contradictory. This definitive work was to be assembled from what would, with the new addition, be the three extant collections of constitutions and from the private juristic literature. According to the plan, it was this work which was to bear the emperor's name.

However, the larger ambitions were not destined to be realized. After nearly seven years' work assembling the constitutions, the emperor ordered

---

[21] Just. *Nov.* 82.13 (A.D. 539); 113 (541), now confined to encroachments contrary to the law.
[22] Ed. by Zachariae von Lingenthal (1843b).   [23] Just. *Nov.* 166–8.   [24] Tjäder (1955–82).
[25] *C.Th.* 1.1.5; Albanese (1991a); Falchi (1989) 13–17; Honoré (1998).
[26] *Nov. Theod.* 1.1; cf. Anon. *De reb. bell.* 21, with Brandt (1988) 125ff.

his commissioners to bring the third codex to completion on the basis of what had originally been planned as only the first phase. He widened the scope of the commission's work on the constitutions which they had collected, and enlarged its membership. The commissioners were now to take on the tasks *necessaria adicere*, *ambigua demutare* and *incongrua emendare*. And the originally intermediate volume was now itself to be called the *Codex Theodosianus*.[27]

It was promulgated in Constantinople for the eastern empire on 15 February 438, to come into effect on 1 January 439,[28] and during 438 it was also brought into operation in the west through Valentinian III. The senate in Rome welcomed its introduction at its meeting on 25 December 438, when most careful attention was paid to ensuring reliable dissemination of the *Codex* throughout the empire; the senate also recognized the danger that privileges, surreptitiously obtained, would undermine the legal order, especially the holding of property.[29]

The work of assembling the constitutions had been difficult and only partly successful. In Mommsen's view the presence of a constitution in the *Codex* was determined more by chance than choice.[30] Only the more recent enactments, since Arcadius, could be taken from the imperial archives in Constantinople. The commissioners had to find the vast majority of the earlier ones from other sources in the capital or in the provinces. In the west many areas had fallen into the hands of the barbarians, and at Rome in 410 there had been widespread destruction. Nevertheless, it was possible to find many constitutions, even for instance in the records of cases, which had to set out such constitutions as had been adduced. The archives of the numerous lower courts would obviously be the source. It was still possible to obtain many from Carthage, which fell to the Vandals only in 439; also Beirut, where there was a famous law school (see pp. 253–4 below), contributed a good deal.

The collection was not accurate in every detail: many dates were incorrect, and it was not comprehensive. The prohibition which accompanied the promulgation forbade recourse to any enactment from the relevant period if it had not been included in the codex, but, typically, exceptions had to be admitted in the case of the specially sensitive areas of military law and state finance.[31] On the other hand, the fact that the collection was originally conceived as a stepping stone to a more perfect volume meant that it had not been purged of much obsolete material. With the help of the chronological arrangement it was for the user himself to decide what was still valid and what had been overtaken by later developments. Unfortunately the insertion of some enactments in the wrong place (*leges fugitivae*) made this task difficult.

---

[27] *C.Th.* 1.1.6.   [28] *Nov. Theod.* 1.
[29] *Gesta senatus Romani de Theodosiano publicando*, *C.Th.* ed. Mommsen, pp. 1ff., esp. 3, lines 8–12; 16; 20–4; 33.   [30] Mommsen (1905) 384; also Seeck (1919) 1–18.   [31] *Nov. Theod.* 1.6.

The *Codex Theodosianus* consists of sixteen books, each of which is sub-divided into between eleven and forty-eight titles systematically ordered according to subject matter. In every title the laws or the excerpts thereof follow each other in chronological order. The first book concerns the sources of law and the higher offices of state, hence the constitution gen-erally, though omitting the emperor himself. The second book deals with civil procedure and begins to address private law, which occupies the next three books as well. Book 6 is then directed to the law relating to the upper classes and the higher office-holders; book 7 to military law; book 8 to the law relating to lower officials and some supplementary private law matters. Book 9 turns to crime and criminal procedure; 10 to the *ius fisci*; 11 to tax-ation and appeals, together with evidence; 12 to local government. Book 13 governs the public duties of those engaged in business and the liberal pro-fessions; 14 the food supply to the towns, especially to the two capital cities; 15 public entertainments; and 16 ecclesiastical law.

In contrast to the *Codex Gregorianus*, of whose fourteen or possibly fifteen books thirteen had been devoted to private law, in the *Theodosianus* private law occupied only four out of sixteen. The reason for this difference lies partly in the materials which were in play, in that, while the earlier *Codex* gathered mainly rescripts to individual petitioners, Theodosius' commis-sioners collected only *leges generales*, even though this did not exclude many that were ephemeral in nature, such as the annual amnesties at Easter.[32] Nevertheless, the changed emphasis reflects the greater importance of public law in the later period and its inclination towards bureaucratic solu-tions – or perhaps simply the dominance of the bureaucracy. It is not to be forgotten that the bureaucracy itself was the force behind the entire project, while the *Codex Gregorianus* and the *Codex Hermogenianus* had been works of private enterprise. The *Codex Theodosianus* is thus an invaluable source for our understanding of the state and administration in the late Roman empire, though in private law it leaves much to be desired. Quite apart from the *Codex*'s initial imbalance, it is perhaps no coincidence that books 2 to 5 on private law survive only in part (about one-third of what was originally included), while the public law books have come down in full and in remarkably good manuscripts.[33]

The preparation and publication of the *Codex* did not bring the momen-tum of the legislative machine to a halt. Even in the late 430s in the east, and in the west chiefly in the 440s and 450s, *Novels* were issued in large numbers. Immediately valid in the legislator's own half of the empire, these took effect in the other half only if ratified.[34] That happened only once. On 3 June 448 Valentinian III ratified a series of thirty-five *Novels*,[35] which his

---

[32] *C.Th.* IX.38.3–8.   [33] Siems (1984) 51f.; Viden (1984).   [34] *Nov. Theod.* 1.6f.
[35] *Nov. Valent.* 26.

cousin and father-in-law in Constantinople had sent him with a letter dated
1 October 447.[36] A collection of *Novels* which was made in Italy in 460 or
461 contained these thirty-five from Theodosius II, thirty-nine from
Valentinian himself and at least twelve from Majorian. Later western collections made occasional additions to this 460/1 collection, including five
from the eastern emperor Marcian (450–7). In total we have from western
sources 102 post-Theodosian *Novels* dating from between 438 and 468. In
the east the story is hidden behind the *Codex Justinianus*, which prohibited
recourse to all earlier collections of constitutions.[37] Whether collected privately or officially in the manner of Theodosius II, the *Novels* surviving
from the western empire retain the outworks cut away in the codices. They
still have the preambles reciting their cause and purpose, and on occasion
an epilogue and particular instructions about promulgation. In addition,
the subject matter of individual constitutions, sometimes of several
together, is identified in a short title.

Half a year after his sole reign began, Justinian revived the project
mooted by Theodosius II for a codification of the whole law. He proposed
to achieve it in a rather simpler manner. On 13 February 528 he set up a
commission of ten, consisting of high-ranking public servants with two
generals, one professor of law and two advocates. He charged them to take
the three existing codices, the Gregorian, Hermogenian and Theodosian,
together with all eastern *Novels* issued since, to select all the constitutions
which remained in operation, to excerpt and simplify them and to purge
them of everything that was out of date, repetitive or contradictory. The
powers of the commission extended not only to deletions and alterations
but also to supplementation and to consolidation of diverse constitutions
on the same subject matter. And yet, since the constitutions were then to
be arranged in chronological order within titles and each with its proper
inscription (author and recipient) and subscription (place and date), the
edited texts would still bear attributions to the emperor who originally
issued them or, in the case of a consolidation of several constitutions, to
the emperor who issued the earliest.[38] Justinian thus gave his commissioners wider powers than had Theodosius in 429 and 435. He had also learned
by the earlier commission's experience that a professor of law was essential to its purpose. In the intervening period the archives in the capital had
also been put in a more satisfactory condition.

The commissioners were able to complete their work in just over a year.
They arranged the material in an intelligible order, easy to survey. And they
managed to bring the number of books down to twelve. Previously, if one
adds together those of the *Gregorianus*, *Hermogenianus* and *Theodosianus* and
the subsequent *Novels*, there had been more than thirty. Admittedly each

---

[36] *Nov. Theod.* 2.   [37] *CJ Const. Summa* 3.   [38] *CJ Const. Haec*; cf. Honoré (1978) 212–14.

book was now a good deal longer than before. On 7 April 529 Justinian promulgated the new codex, for use from Easter (16 April).[39] In fact the *Codex Justinianus* which survives is not this but a second edition, the *Codex Justinianus repetitae praelectionis*, dated 16 November 534, when it was promulgated to take exclusive effect from 29 December 534. The use or even citation of constitutions from other sources thereafter incurred the penalties of forgery. An exception was made for privileges expressly granted as a matter of grace and favour. All other privileges were in future to be exercised only so far as compatible with the laws generally applicable. No special allowance was any longer made for military matters.[40] However, the law contained in the old imperial constitutions relating to the state economy and financial administration retained independent validity.

The twelve books of the *Codex Justinianus* are each divided between forty-four and seventy-eight titles. Book 1 begins with ecclesiastical law and proceeds to sources of law and constitutional matters, again omitting the monarch himself. Books 2 to 8 deal fully with civil procedure and private law. Book 9 covers crime and criminal procedure; 10 the *ius fisci*, taxation and local government with particular reference to local taxes; 11 corporations with tied membership, state industries and estates. Finally, book 12 covers the law relating to rank and the holding of offices. Private law thus receives substantially more space than in the *Theodosianus*, albeit linked in with the law relating to control of the economy and status.

The manuscript tradition of the *Codex Justinianus* causes particularly awkward problems.[41] In the early Middle Ages the last three books were jettisoned and the first nine were reduced to about a quarter of their original size. When, from the late Middle Ages, interest in more complete texts revived, multiple copies were not made of any of the surviving full manuscripts. Instead, there was a process of gradual supplementation by the use of extracts from the fuller manuscripts. But this did not serve to achieve a complete restoration of the comprehensive range of the original work. We have lost in particular most of the constitutions which were issued in Greek, for which we have to make do with Byzantine paraphrases. The tradition has, however, preserved by way of introductory texts the constitutions by which Justinian first commissioned the work (*Const. Haec*), promulgated it (*Const. Summa*) and then again promulgated the new edition (*Const. Cordi*).

The second edition of the *Codex Justinianus* had been necessitated by the issue of numerous *Novels*. These had in turn been occasioned by the fact

---

[39] *CJ Const. Summa.*

[40] *CJ Const. Cordi.* Of the first edition of *CJ* there survives an index to the rubrics of Book 1, titles 11–16: *P.Oxy.* 1814.

[41] Krüger, *Praefatio* (pp. v–xxxxi) to *Cod. Iust.* (ed. maior); Krüger (1912) 425–8; Dolezalek (1985); Tort-Martorell (1989).

that in the meantime the juristic literature had been reviewed and excerpted with an eye to saving whatever was still useful, and the excerpts thus selected had been put together to produce the fifty books of the *Digest*. The emperor was fond of the number fifty, which symbolizes perfection in the Bible and the Early Fathers.[42] The number of books of classical legal writing still surviving had been 1,508 (Justinian maintains it was nearly 2,000), which suggests that only about a thirtieth of the material was retained. However, the proportion is nearer a twentieth, since more than three million lines of text were compressed into fifty books with almost 150,000 lines:[43] the average length of earlier books was 2,100 lines, whereas the comparable figure for the fifty books of the *Digest* is 2,800. The figure for the *Codex* is much larger, 5,000.

The books of the *Digest* contain between two and thirty-two titles (though books 30 to 32 exceptionally constitute only one title between them). Within the titles, the individual texts ('fragments') are for the most part set out in the order in which the old books were excerpted. In that exercise the work had been divided into four separate assignments, the so-called 'masses', whose contributions follow each other but not always in the same order. The masses are the Sabinian, named after the commentaries on Masurius Sabinus' *ius civile*; the edictal, named from the commentaries *ad edictum*; the Papinian, dominated by the writings of that jurist; and the appendix, a small additional group brought in after the beginning of the work, evidently because they were only acquired after the operation had begun. Every fragment retained in the *Digest* is preceded by an 'inscription' which sets out its provenance – the author, the work and the number of the book from which it was taken. However, where excerpts were taken from one book they are put together as a single fragment. Many fragments run to several pages, some to only a few words. The longer ones were divided into paragraphs, something which had already proved necessary in a few cases in the *Codex*.

The overall order is roughly the same as that of the *Codex*, although in many cases the different structure of the books which were excerpted was followed. Ecclesiastical law was of course not present in the materials. Private law and civil procedure filled books 2 to 47, eleven-twelfths of the whole. This compares with a quarter in the *Codex Theodosianus* and a good half in the *Justinianus*. There was minimal interference with the individual fragments. Changes chiefly took the form of abbreviation, even within passages selected for retention, especially if a path had to be cut through conflicting opinions. In addition, in order to adjust them to fit developments which had taken place in the law, the texts were modernized by

---

[42] Knütel (1996) 427–8; Scheltema (1975) 233; Schminck (1989) 81.
[43] *CJ* 1.17.2.1 (= *Digest Const. Tanta* 1).

'interpolations' and supplemented with *emblemata*. Nevertheless it is clear
that much obsolete material survived. Even reduced to a bare twentieth of
the extant corpus, the volume was enormous. That sufficiently shows that
the commissioners found it impossible to submit to the discipline of selecting only what was essential and that, quite to the contrary, they allowed
themselves to be carried along by their fascination with the classical legal
literature.

The work was not confined to the books of the five jurists approved by
the Law of Citations (see p. 242 above, n. 19) but took into consideration
all that were still obtainable, even the critical commentaries on Papinian
which Constantine had outlawed. Moreover, conflicts were to be resolved
by following the line which seemed most reasonable; there was no question
of counting heads or following an artificial structure of authority in the
manner of the Law of Citations. That law itself, though included in the first
edition of 529, was omitted from the 534 *Codex*. Only authors who had
achieved no recognition at all were excluded. The instruction to eliminate
all contradictions did not prevent the survival of much evidence for divergent opinions and unresolved discussions of difficult points.

The driving force was Tribonian. In the commission to compile the
Codex he had been sixth in seniority, and it was now he who put together
the team which Justinian commissioned to undertake the work on the
Digest. He included the four leading professors of law. It is also clear that it
was Tribonian's thinking that underlay the idea and scope of the project as
authorized by Justinian's constitution of 15 December 530, when in fact the
work had already begun.[44] On 16 December 533 the emperor was able to
publish the complete work.[45] The purpose which it served was not so much
the work of the courts and legal practice but rather the very demanding
programme of legal education. A fine manuscript from the sixth century
survives in Florence.[46]

From 529 the emperor had started on the business of resolving by legislation the outstanding controversies in the standard legal literatures.
These decisions were collected under the title *Quinquaginta decisiones* and
published at the earliest in late 531, more probably in 532. This collection
has not survived. Further interventions were necessitated as the work progressed, and more reforming constitutions were therefore enacted. A wide-
ranging law of this kind was issued on 17 November 533.[47] Apart from this,
the commissioners were left in peace from the time of the Nika riot in
January 532, which cost Tribonian all his offices except his chairmanship of

---

[44] *Digest Const. Deo auctore* = *CJ* 1.17.1; on Tribonian and his work, see Honoré (1978).
[45] *Digest Const. Tanta* (= *CJ* 1.17.2) or, in its Greek form, Δέδωκεν.
[46] Mommsen, *Praefatio* (pp. V–LXXVIII) to *Digest* (ed. maior); Krüger (1912) 428–33; Spagnesi (1986);
Mantovani (1987) with Kaiser (1991).
[47] *CJ* 1.3.53; V.17.11; VII.24.1; IX.13.1; XI.48.24, all from the same law.

the commission. Justinian was then busy with the rebuilding of S. Sophia. The commissioners made many changes on their own initiative.

A further project was the production, alongside the *Digest*, of a text for those embarking on the study of law. This was achieved in the form of a compilation in four books, averaging 2,200 standard lines, drawn from the introductory works (*Institutiones*) currently available. The new text, Justinian's *Institutes*, chose not to disclose the provenance of the excerpts of which it is composed.[48] They mostly come from Gaius' *Institutes* but also from his *Res Cottidianae* and from the *Institutes* of Florentinus, Marcianus and Ulpian. In addition some passages were borrowed from the already completed *Digest*, and summaries were added of the most important imperial reforms.[49] Once the principal task of compiling the *Digest* had been completed, the work of compiling the *Institutes* was undertaken by Tribonian and two famous professors of law, Theophilus of Constantinople and Dorotheus of Beirut. It was quickly done. By 21 November 533 it was possible to bring the *Institutes* into use.[50] On 16 December, together with the promulgation of the *Digest*, Justinian established a new legal curriculum.[51] In Constantinople and Beirut the course of study lasted five years. Instead of the customary diet of classical legal authors, it was now ordained that it should proceed from the *Institutes* through the first thirty-six books of the *Digest*, arriving in the fifth year at the study of the *Codex*.

Once again the legislative machinery was not brought to a halt by the completion of the three parts of the codification. On the contrary, the effect of the study in depth of the legal literature of the past was to precipitate numerous reforms even after the work of compilation had been concluded. These now came in the form of *Novels* which were, with a few exceptions, always in Greek. Between January and August 535 alone there were thirty-two, and down to 546 another 115. Their effect was to render obsolete many provisions in the codification. After 546 the rate of legislation fell back to a more normal level. In 534 Justinian was still planning an official collection of *Novels*,[52] and in 554 he proposed to promulgate for the new western provinces all those issued up to that date, presumably with appropriate deletions and translations.[53] Neither of these projects came to fruition. However, many private collections of *Novels* were made. They once again retain the outworks of the legislation and add a short descriptive title. Most *Novels*, short ones excepted, were divided into chapters.

We know of four such collections.[54] The second of these is built on the first, which itself had been slightly enlarged four times. It originally reached to 544 and numbered 111 *Novels*, but actually contained only 110, since one occurred twice. Thereafter it was extended in 548 to include four

---

[48] In general, see Stein and Lewis (1983).   [49] Zocco-Rosa (1908–10).
[50] *Inst. Iust., Const. Imperatoriam.*   [51] *Digest Const. Omnem.*   [52] *CJ Const. Cordi* 4 fin.
[53] *Nov. Iust.* App. 7.11.   [54] Noailles (1912–14); van der Wal (1964).

later constitutions. It was then extended another three times, adding two more *Novels* each time, but three on the last occasion, which had previously been omitted from those of the period 535–45. The third extension involved another duplication. Here the individual *Novels* stood in a numbered series, but the subdivisions, the chapters, were also numbered, in such a way that the numbering of the chapters overrode the boundaries between the individual *Novels*. The collection itself does not survive, but we have evidence of it in five documents emanating from Julian's contemporary teaching of law in Constantinople (see below). The most important is a Latin index, a summary of the contents of all 124 items by Julian himself, which survives as the so-called *Epitome Juliani*.[55] It is the textbook of his course on the *Novels* given in the academic year 556–7 in Latin, evidently for refugees from Italy. It met with success in the west and was almost exclusively relied upon in the early Middle Ages.[56] The second collection of Justinianic *Novels* originally reached to 556. It sought to put the late additions to the first collection into their proper chronological places, which it carried through with some minor mistakes, and to add some more recent pronouncements. It was later extended at least to 566.[57] The original edition survives only in fragments of a Greek course on the *Novels* given by Julian in 557–8.[58] The extended edition can likewise be seen only through the fragments of an anonymous writer of about 600. The third collection reached at first to 556 and contained 127 items. Here again we lack direct evidence, but most of the items were in Greek and we do have a word by word Latin translation of those (κατὰ πόδας), and we also have Latin texts of a few of those which were issued either in Latin or in both languages. The translation was made to back up a course on the *Novels* in Rome in 557–8 and was bit by bit extended by the addition of further Latin *Novels* reaching up to 563, till it included 134 items. It acquired the name *Authenticum* and in the west displaced the *Epitome Juliani* in the late Middle Ages.[59] Only the fourth and last collection of *Novels* has come down to us directly.[60] It reaches to 575 and includes 168 items. The last three, edicts of praetorian prefects from the early or mid sixth century, are clearly later additions. In 572 Athanasius of Emesa made a Greek epitome of the *Novels* and put them into a systematic order;[61] in 580–90 Theodorus Scholasticus of Hermopolis produced a Greek abridgement of the collection of 168 *Novels*.[62]

---

[55] Scheltema (1970) 47–50. On the four remaining pieces of Byzantine evidence see Liebs (1987) 220–44.   [56] Liebs (1987) 246–66, 269–76.

[57] van der Wal (1964) 164ff.; Liebs (1987) 223, 232–4.

[58] Simon *et al.* (1977) 1–29, supplemented by Liebs (1987) 223, 232–4.

[59] *Authenticum*, also in the sequence of the fourth collection: *CIC* III, but only the upper Latin text, if identified as *Authenticum* and supplied with its original numbering.   [60] *CIC* III.

[61] Simon and Troianos (1989).   [62] See p. 258 below, n. 113.

V. LAW SCHOOLS

Roman law was taught outside Rome and Italy even from the second or third century A.D. However, until the early fifth century Rome remained pre-eminent and, if they could, law students made their way there from all parts of the empire, even from the east. However, from the middle of the fifth century their preference was for Beirut or Constantinople. We know rather little about law teaching in Rome in late antiquity, although there is some evidence reaching into the seventh century.[63] It would seem that it was maintained even beyond that period, albeit at a modest level, and that in the eleventh century it was possible for scholars in Bologna to perceive a continuity between their school and that of Rome, perhaps through a connection via Ravenna. There were certainly professors paid by the state in Rome in the sixth century,[64] and probably long before. From the early third century law students in Rome were exempted from *liturgia* so long as their studies lasted. This exemption did not then apply elsewhere,[65] but about 286 it was extended to Beirut, though limited to those under twenty-five.[66] From 370 all students at Rome were obliged to complete their study by the age of twenty.[67] The exemption from liturgies also applied to law teachers in Rome from the early third century, though not elsewhere.[68] An inscription survives from the grave in Rome of the law teacher Floridus, who died in 427, aged sixty-two.[69] The teaching proceeded on the basis of the classical legal literature and the collections of imperial constitutions, but until the middle of the sixth century we do not have precise information. Justinian sent the *Institutes*, the *Digest* and the *Codex* to Rome without delay, and from the 540s onwards there is good evidence of teaching based on those books and the *Novels*, on the same system as in Constantinople.[70]

The law school of Beirut must be mentioned next. Roman law was taught there at a high level from the second century.[71] In the fifth century it overtook Rome. In the fifth and sixth centuries there were two chairs liberally maintained by the state;[72] and in addition to the two *antecessores* there were perhaps other law teachers since *Digest, Const. Omnem* is addressed to eight law teachers. After a devastating earthquake in 551 the law school found a home for a while in Sidon and later evidently in Antioch, where Athanasius taught.[73] Known figures from the fifth century are Cyrillus, Domninus the Younger, Demosthenes, Eudoxius, Patricius and Leontius.[74]

---

[63] Liebs (1987) 195–220, 246–82.   [64] Cass. *Var.* IX.21.5 (A.D. 533); *Nov. Iust.* App. 7.22 (554).

[65] *Fragmenta iuris Vaticana* 204 (in Krüger *et al.* (1890) 1–106): Ulpian referring to Caracalla.

[66] *Cf* X.50.1; for the exact dating see Honoré (1994) 150 n. 74; 181 n. 555.   [67] *C.Th.* XIV.9.1.

[68] *Digest* XXVII.1.6 12 (Modestinus, about A.D. 230); others: *Fragmenta iuris Vaticana* 150 (Ulpian, about 210).   [69] *CIL* VI 31 992 = *Carm. Epigr.* 686.

[70] *Digest Const. Omnem* 7 init.; cf. Liebs (1987) 124f., 195–220, 246–82.

[71] Collinet (1925); cf. Liebs (1976) 356f., Waldstein (1980) 251f. n. 64.   [72] Collinet (1925) 167–83.

[73] Agathias, *Hist.* II.15.2–4; Scheltema (1970) 61f.   [74] Huschke *et al.* (1927) 515–43; Berger (1958a).

The leading jurists of the sixth century called them ἥρωες, οἱ τῆος οἰκουμένης διδάσκαλοι or οἱ ἐπιφανέστατοι διδάσκαλοι. This shows that they looked up to them and claimed less importance for themselves. In Beirut in that period there were Leontius, Dorotheus, Anatolius, Thalelaeus, Julian (until he moved to Constantinople) and Stephanus.[75]

The course of study lasted five years, the academic year running from early autumn to early summer. The first year was based on the *Institutes* of Gaius together with four *libri singulares* (in fact, parts of longer works of Ulpian or Paul) on dowry, guardianship, wills and legacies. The students were called *dupondii*. In the second year they became *edictales*, and they then dealt with sources of law and the structure of the courts, together with some civil procedure, property, delict and, above all, contract. This study was based on the high classical commentaries on the edict, especially that of Ulpian. In the third year property, delict and contract were studied in great depth, using a selection (eight out of nineteen books) of the opinions of Papinian (*Digesta responsa*). The year began with the celebration of a feast in honour of Papinian, and the third-year students were called *Papinianistae*. In the fourth year, in which the students were called λύται, the *responsa* of Paul served as the foundation for the analysis of complex cases.[76] In the fifth year the imperial constitutions were read.

Law teaching in Constantinople began later. Professors paid from the public purse were established only in 425. As in Beirut, there were then two chairs, which were confirmed in 529 and 534.[77] The restructuring of legal education in 533 was directed to eight teachers of law, but that does not mean that the establishment in both schools had been doubled, since the codification perhaps required assistants, or here too there may have been *supernumerarii*.[78] From the fifth century we know of Leontius and Erotius and, from the sixth, Theophilus, Cratinus and Julian.[79] The curriculum was the same as in Beirut. After Justinian's death in 565 the overstretched exchequer was compelled to make many reductions in its commitments. As a result the expensive professoriate was abolished, and legal education was simplified and put in the hands of practitioners on a part-time basis.[80]

Private teaching of law was carried on in the east until 533 in Athens, Caesarea in Palestine and in Alexandria, but was then forbidden by Justinian.[81] In the west it is evidenced in fifth-century Narbonne. The fact that the town was incorporated into the Visigothic kingdom in 462 evidently

---

[75] *Anthologia Graeca* XVI.32b; *CJ* 1.17.2.9; cf. Krüger (1912) 408, 410 n. 26; van der Wal and Lokin (1985) 41–2; Berger (1958); *PLRE* III 773 *s.v.* Leontius 1, and *PLRE* II 772 *s.v.* Leontius 22 (confusing different people). [76] *Digest Const. Omnem* 1–5; cf. *Inst. Const. Imperatoriam* 3; Zach. *Life of Severus* intro.
[77] *C.Th.* XIV.9.3.1 = *CJ* XI.19.1.4. [78] Scheltema (1970) 3f.
[79] *C.Th.* VI.21.1 (A.D. 425); I.1.6.2 (A.D. 435); *CJ* 1.17.2.9; *Anthologia Graeca* XVI.32b; Hänel (1873) pp. XXXVII, XXXIXf.; Liebs (1987) 220–46; *PLRE* II 669 *s.v.* Leontius 7.
[80] Scheltema (1970) 8f.; Pieler (1978) 429f.; van der Wal and Lokin (1985) 55–8.
[81] *Digest Const. Omnem* 7. Athens: Malalas p. 451.

did not have any adverse effect.[82] Law teaching presumably survived even the fateful year 507. In Lyons law may also have been taught, at least in the Burgundian period:[83] legal manuscripts suggest significant activity, since a fifth- or sixth-century copy of the *Codex Theodosianus*, a late-sixth- or early-seventh-century Theodosian manuscript, and the seventh-century manuscript, now divided between St Petersburg and Berlin, which contains decisions of a Gallic council, the *Notitia Galliarum*, a papal letter and the *Constitutiones Sirmondianae*, all probably originated in Lyons.[84] In Carthage, too, it is probable that law was taught in the third and fourth centuries. Presumably there was one paid teacher endowed by the town itself, his post perhaps surviving into the period of the Vandals.[85]

VI. LEGAL LITERATURE

In the fifth and sixth centuries there was a modest output of legal writing, mostly in Greek.[86] In 430 there appeared a private collection of imperial enactments relating to ecclesiastical law, the so-called *Constitutiones Sirmondianae*. This probably emanated from Gaul.[87] Also from Gaul, in 445, comes the so-called *Consultatio veteris cuiusdam iurisconsulti*, a collection of authorities on the theme of settlement from the pseudo-Pauline *Sententiae* and from the *codices* of imperial constitutions, which was put together for use in a lawsuit.[88] A papyrus of the fifth or possibly the fourth century contains the remains of a Greek collection of Latin technical terms, the so-called *Collectio definitionum*. The Beirut teacher Anatolius also composed a dialogue with a student in the sixth century.[89] To the fifth or sixth century or even later belongs *The Laws and Customs of Palestine* of Julian of Ascalon, a collection of authorities relating to the law of building in Palestine. It survives only in fragments.[90] Of similar provenance is *The Laws of the Christian and Just Kings*, the so-called *Sententiae Syriacae*, which is an unsystematic collection of 102 short propositions on diverse subjects taken by their unknown author mostly from constitutions of Diocletian, but also from the *Pauli Sententiae*, occasionally from constitutions of Constantine and at

---

[82] Sid. Ap. *Carm.* XXIII.446–54, 464–74; *Ep.* II.13.1.

[83] Sid. Ap. *Ep.* V.5 to Syagrius A.D. 469; also 1.3; V.17.2 for Filimatius. Liebs (1987) 161f. for legal work at Lyons.

[84] Parisinus 9643, *CLA* 591; Vaticanus reginae 886, *CLA* 110; Berolinensis Philipps 1745, formerly the Cathedral Library of Lyons, *CLA* 1061.

[85] Liebs (1993) 19f., 119; Halban (1899) II.71–7; Wolff (1936) 398–420, esp. 417.

[86] Heimbach (1868); Krüger (1912) 361–5, 406–15; Wenger (1953) 549–53, 681–92; Scheltema (1970); Pieler (1978) 341–428; van der Wal and Lokin (1985) 20–62, 121–30.

[87] Ed. by Mommsen, in *Cod. Theod.* pp. 907–21; cf. Liebs (1993) 109–14.

[88] Ed. by Krüger (1890) 199–220; Huschke *et al.* (1927) 485–514; cf. Schindler (1962); Wieacker (1955) 92, 110–14; Gaudemet (1979a) 84. On the dating: Liebs (1993) 142 n. 52.

[89] Pieler (1978) 390. *Collectio definitionum*, ed. Arangio-Ruiz, *PSI* 1348. Cf. Schulz (1953) 308; Liebs (1971) 87–8. [90] Cf. Nicole (1893) 65–75; Ferrini (1929); Saliou (1996).

least twice, towards the end, from constitutions of Leo. There survives only a Syriac translation of what was evidently in origin a Greek text.

Similarly, it is only through Syriac, Arab, Armenian and Coptic translations of the Greek original that we know the so-called *Syro-Romano Law Book*, a supposed collection of constitutions of Constantine, Theodosius and Leo. The author is unknown. It contained a comprehensive collection of constitutions of the fourth and fifth centuries up to 472, matched up with short extracts from juristic writing too – 130 items in all, covering various subjects. It also belongs to the late fifth or early sixth century.[91] The *De actionibus*, a small book in Greek, similarly anonymous, collects forty-three short opinions concerning the claims that could be made on different facts. It dates at the earliest from Justinian's time and, like the other items already mentioned, was undoubtedly directed at the practitioner.[92]

There were also teaching materials which for the most part were not intended for publication. (The *Consultatio* was also probably not so intended.) Among these are the many commentaries on the texts studied in the curriculum, from juristic writings, collections of constitutions or the volumes of Justinian's *corpus iuris*. Our knowledge of this class of literature is sparse and comes mostly from schools in the west teaching in Latin. Thus the *Lex Romana Visigothorum* contains a much abbreviated paraphrase of the *Institutes* of Gaius, the *Liber Gaii*.[93] It stems from teaching-activity in about 460, presumably in Narbonne. Roughly to the same time and place belong the *Interpretationes* to the pseudo-Pauline *Pauli Sententiae*, also preserved in the Visigothic *Lex Romana*.[94] With these also stand the commentaries on an extract from the *Codex Gregorianus* and a very short piece of the *Hermogenianus*,[95] and, most important, that on the *Theodosianus*[96] and the post-Theodosian *Novels*.[97]

By contrast, from Sicily or northern Italy come the so-called *Antiqua summaria*, a thin work on the full *Theodosianus* from the later fifth century. The second half survives.[98] From the school in Rome in 545 some observations on Justinian's *Institutes* for a first-year course, the so-called Turin gloss.[99] From the same source come, about 560, the so-called *Paratitla* to Julian's epitome of the *Novels*, giving short accounts of the changes which Justinian's novels introduced. This comes from a course on the *Novels* based

---

[91] Bruns and Sachau (1880) (the German translation is no longer satisfactory); Sachau (1907). Cf. Selb (1964), (1965); Kaufhold (1966); Vööbus (1972), (1975); Memmer (1990). Sent. Syr.: Selb (1990).

[92] Sitzia (1973), with Simon's review (1975).

[93] Ed. Hänel (1849) 314–37; Kübler in Huschke *et al.* (1927) 395–431. Cf. Archi (1937), with Nelson (1995), review of Archi.

[94] Ed. Hänel (1849) 338–444; Kaser and Schwarz (1956); cf. Schellenberg (1965).

[95] Ed. Hänel (1849) 444–51; Krüger *et al.* (1890) 221–35; cf. Kreuter (1993).

[96] Ed. Mommsen, in *Cod. Theod.*   [97] Ed. Meyer (1905).

[98] Ed. Manenti (1887) 257–88; (1888) 141–57; (1889) 203–311. New edn Sirks (1996b). Cf. Liebs (1987) 177–88; Sirks (1991) 247–50, 345–50, 380f., 416–20; Sirks (1996c).

[99] Ed. Krüger (1868) 44–78; Alberti (1933); cf. Liebs (1987) 195–220.

on the *Epitome Juliani*.[100] Finally from late-sixth-century Rome come the
Glossae, which are later summaries of Julian's *Epitome* giving brief accounts
of the contents of his chapters.[101]

A first-year course in Alexandria based on the *Institutes* of Gaius may
have been the source of the Greek marginal comments on the fourth-
century *Florentine fragments of the Institutes* found in Antinoe in Egypt.[102] And
a second-semester course in Alexandria or Beirut on dowry and guardianship based on Ulpian's *Ad Sabinum libri* (books 31–6A on dowry, 36B–40A
on guardianship) is the source of the *Sinaitic scholia* from the middle of the
fifth century. These form part of a detailed and learned exposition of
books 35–9 of Ulpian's work by an unknown teacher and another called
Sab . . .[103] This Sab . . . had also discussed legacies, which were studied at
the end of the first year.[104] A third-year course based on Papinian's *responsa*
in Alexandria in about 500 accounts for the scholia to the Berlin and Paris
fragments of book 5 discovered in Egypt.[105]

Justinian's reformed curriculum yields, from courses in Constantinople:
the paraphrase of the *Institutes* by Theophilus, which was aimed at beginners in their first year and survives in full;[106] expositions of the first nineteen books of the *Digest* by Theophilus and presumably similar expositions
of the *Digest* by Kobidas,[107] aimed at the courses for the end of the first
year and the two following years of the curriculum; Julian's *Collectio*, a
unique text from teaching based on the *Codex*, and the Veronese scholia to
the *Codex*, both directed to the fifth year;[108] to the courses at the close of
the fifth year belong Julian's Latin and Greek explanations of Justinian's
Novels and his *De Consiliariis Dictatum*, which offers advice to those completing their studies.[109] From the corresponding activity in Beirut come the
diverse expositions of *Digest* texts from Dorotheus (soon after 542), Isidore
and Stephanus,[110] from whom we have also the meagre remains of his lectures on the *Codex*, supplemented with rather more from Thalelaeus,
Isidore and Anatolius.[111] To one or other of these leading schools must also

[100] Ed. van der Wal (1985) 102–37; Liebs (1987) 246–59; and cf. *ibid.* 259–64.
[101] Hänel (1873) 208–17. Cf. Liebs (1987) 269–73.
[102] Ed. Arangio-Ruiz, *PSI* 1182 (*CLA* 292) 6–17; Levy (1934) 262–4, in the footnotes. Cf. Nelson (1981) 63f. and Nelson and Manthe (1999) 7–9 and 547–9.
[103] Ed. Krüger *et al.* (1890) 265–82; Huschke *et al.* (1927) 461–84. Cf. Schulz (1953) 325–6.
[104] *P.Ryl.* 475, I. 16. Cf. Wenger (1953) 627–8.
[105] Ed. Krüger *et al.* (1890) 288–91, in the footnotes; *CLA* 1037.
[106] Ed. Ferrini (1884–97). Cf. Scheltema (1970) 17–21; Nelson (1981) 267–93; van der Wal and Lokin (1985) 40f., 125.   [107] Cf. Scheltema (1970) 30f.; Scheltema (1966).
[108] Ed. Zachariae von Lingenthal (1873) 313–55; cf. Scheltema (1962) 252f.; *CLA* 513. *Collectio* ed. Hänel 1873: 201f.; cf. Liebs 1987: 244–6.
[109] *Dictatum* ed. Hänel (1873) 198–201; cf. Liebs (1987) 235–44. Greek course, ed. Simon *et al.* (1977). Latin courses, ed. Hänel (1873) 21–177, 69–146 earlier footnotes (*lemmata*), 178–84; cf. Scheltema (1970) 47–60; Liebs (1987) 220–34.
[110] Wenger (1953) 686; Pieler (1978) 422. Scheltema (1970) 24–30; Simon *et al.* (1979).
[111] Scheltema (1970) 32–42; van der Wal and Lokin (1985) 42–4, 125f. Pieler (1978) 423–4.

belong the lectures on the *Digest* by Cyrillus and an earlier anonymous writer.[112] Theodorus Scholasticus from Hermopolis, who was a leading advocate, left comments on the *Codex* and *Novels* in the post-Justinianic period. He probably lectured in Constantinople on a part-time basis.[113]

All these texts on Justinian's *corpus*, presumably dictated to students by the lecturer, were short and modest, some of them very short. They do not compare with the wealth of learning in the *Sinaitic scholia*, which make many citations of classical juristic literature and imperial constitutions. Justinian had indeed forbidden recourse to the earlier materials, as well as criticism of his own. In particular he had outlawed commentaries and allowed only literal translations (κατὰ πόδας), brief surveys of contents (*indices*) and observations on passages relevant to a given title (παράτιτλα) or a given text (παραπομπαί or παραγραφαί). The Byzantine lawyers did not keep strictly within these constraints. Many indices are free restatements of the texts, and numerous expositions, especially those of Stephanus, are nothing if not commentaries based on the familiar blend of doctrine and exegesis.

VII. CONTINUITY, VULGARIZATION, CLASSICISM

The development of the law in the Roman empire between 425 and 600 did not follow a simple linear path. At the beginning of the period there was a phase in which the main task was to unite the law inherited from the classical past with the more recent imperial law. This phase is represented in the west by the enactment relating to the sources of law and in the east by the *Codex Theodosianus*, and it reflects the presence once again of increasing numbers of jurists in the administration. That then leads to a remarkable improvement in the level of legal science, especially in Beirut but also in Constantinople, Rome and Narbonne.

The level of legal scholarship finally presented Justinian with the opportunity to overhaul and restore the law in all its aspects. And that mighty project was in turn bound to enhance the role of law in social life. The finds of papyri in Egypt show that documents recording legal transactions were few and far between in the fifth century but that the number once again increased greatly in the sixth, especially from the beginning of Justinian's reign. After his death the evidence of dynamic legal science falls back, as also of the further advancement of the law and of individuals having recourse to law to resolve their disputes.

Between the 1920s and the 1960s the view was taken, especially among German scholars, that long before the collapse of the western empire into

---

[112] Sontis (1937). New evidence ed. Burgmann (1986).
[113] Pieler (1978) 436; van der Wal and Lokin (1985) 57f., 128f.

competing barbarian kingdoms the law had become vulgarized, i.e. simplified and popularized by local practice without positive enactment. On this view, the process of vulgarization went back to the early fourth or even to the late third century, ran throughout the empire and infected even the central administration and legal pronouncements emanating from the emperor. Only the east was able in the fifth century to free itself from this deterioration by a classicizing return to the law and legal science of the principate.[114] Not everyone was convinced by this diagnosis: Italian Romanists especially resisted it. But in the meantime it seemed as though Ernst Levy and Max Kaser had looked for and found vulgarization in every quarter.[115] Vulgarization therefore became a convenient means of explaining every imaginable difficulty.

It is undeniable that there were some breaches with received tradition. For example, in the early fourth century Constantine broke with many legal principles long regarded as sacrosanct. Nevertheless, the received legal tradition proved to be very strong, and the necessity of keeping in contact with it and developing the law from it could not be denied. Even under Constantine and in the middle and late fourth century, and also in the fifth, this is so evident that it is no longer possible to speak of a collapse of the legal tradition. This is true even in the west throughout the period in which the emperor remained at the head of the legal system, continually developing the law by interpretative and legislative pronouncements. Such utterances still had authority for Romans now living under federated Germanic kingdoms such as the Visigothic and Burgundian kingdoms, and even for those under the wholly independent Vandal rulers. As this control at the top first weakened in the 460s and 470s and then fell away altogether, provincial peculiarities and simplifications, already numerous, began to dominate. The communities of Romans were now thrown back on themselves, and the application of Roman law was invaded by vulgarizing tendencies.[116] However, even in the sixth century the aspiration of the Roman population throughout the west to continue in the inherited tradition of Roman law was not extinguished.

---

[114] Levy (1963a) 1.161–320; Levy (1945), (1951), (1956); Wieacker (1955), (1964); Kaser (1967) 1283–304; Kaser (1975) 11.
[115] Critical: Wieacker (1983b) 232–8; Wieacker (1955) 241–54; Simon (1978) 154–74; Voss (1982); Kreuter (1993).   [116] Vandals: Courtois et al. (1952); cf. Wolff (1936) 398–420; Wessel (2000).

CHAPTER 10

LAW IN THE WESTERN KINGDOMS BETWEEN THE FIFTH AND THE SEVENTH CENTURY

T. M. CHARLES-EDWARDS

Anyone seeking to write an account of law in the western kingdoms labours under two great difficulties.[1] The student of Roman law can find comfort in the knowledge that his legal tradition was the creation of a political élite which prided itself upon its literary accomplishments. It was both a tool of government and one of the proudest manifestations of a literate culture.[2] In the post- and non-Roman kingdoms, such comfortable assurance is only forthcoming in modest portions. The study of Roman law rests upon rich materials that have been analysed by some of the best minds of every generation since, in the eleventh century, Irnerius set out to teach the law of Justinian at Bologna. The written materials for a history of law in the western kingdoms are, however, much patchier and their relationship to the practice of law more uncertain.[3]

The second great difficulty is partly a consequence of the first: the almost irresistible temptation to judge all other laws in late antiquity by their relationship to Roman law. Moreover, this temptation may take a particularly pernicious form if one is induced to think of Roman law as, in some sense, 'modern' in outlook, so that the other laws can then be judged as relatively modern or primitive according to how closely they resembled Roman law. One form of this dangerous preoccupation is the ancient conception – already well expressed, for his own purposes, by Cassiodorus – of the culture of Europe as a fruitful mixture of Roman and Germanic (or Gothic). This imposes upon the subject an over-simple dichotomy: the scholar is prompted to scrutinize the texts for manifestations either of Roman or of Germanic legal tradition. According to his particular preference, or those of his political masters, he may be prone to exaggerate either the one or the other.

Although this traditional approach has considerable elements of truth – more, perhaps, than its opponents allow – it ignores several crucial

---

[1] In this chapter 'Law' with an upper-case initial letter will refer to a text of law; thus Salic law is the law of the Salian Franks whether written or unwritten, but Salic Law is the text known as *Pactus Legis Salicae*. I have been much stimulated, not always in directions of which they would approve, by the conversation and the written work of Ian Wood and Patrick Wormald.
[2] When the slave Andarchius of Greg. Tur. *Hist.* iv.46 is encouraged by his senatorial master, Felix, in their joint literary pursuits, these are specified as 'the works of Virgil, the books of the Theodosian Law and arithmetic'. [3] Wormald (1977); Nehlsen (1977).

considerations. One assumption which needs to be questioned is that the Roman empire desired or, if it did desire, was able to impose its law in a complete and thoroughgoing fashion upon all its provinces. In the west we do not have the evidence provided by Egyptian papyri to demonstrate that provincial law might take a form very different from that prescribed by Roman jurists and emperors.[4] The last fifty years have seen notable studies showing that late Roman law was not identical with that taught by the great jurists, but this has been done by developing the notion of a vulgar as opposed to a classical Roman law. Moreover, the vulgarisms have not been revealed by an examination of legal practice in remote regions of the empire but by a close reading of the Theodosian Code. Emperors, rather than mere provincials, were the prime vulgarizers.[5] It is, no doubt, very uncertain how much weight one can put on evidence from a much later period, but one body of evidence does at least raise serious questions about what went on among those remote western provincials. Welsh (earlier called British) law is mainly known from texts of the twelfth and thirteenth centuries;[6] yet it was the law of a people whose ancestors had formed part of the population of a Roman province, and a people, moreover, which had escaped being subsumed into a kingdom founded by barbarians from beyond the Roman frontier. Admittedly Gildas remarks that they superficially accepted Roman law, harbouring inner resentment, but he implies that they accepted it none the less.[7] One might suppose that the law inherited by the Britons should have been a debased descendant of Roman law; moreover, there are reasons for thinking that elements of Roman law did indeed survive the end of Roman power in Britain;[8] yet by the twelfth century its resemblances to Irish law were far more obvious than was any debt to Rome; they underline what Gildas described as the superficial nature of their adherence to Roman law.[9] If we allow that legal traditions may endure for centuries – so that they are not simply remade with each generation – Welsh medieval law can be used to give weight to the suggestion that, at least in one part of one western province, what survived Rome was remarkably un-Roman. Already in the sixth century Venantius Fortunatus could contrast the *iura Britannica* imported to Armorica from Britain with *publica iura*.[10] A study of law in the western kingdoms must, therefore, extend all the way from Theoderic's Ravenna to the western parts of Britain and over the Irish

[4] On Egypt, Jolowicz and Nicholas (1972) 405–6.

[5] Levy (1951) 29–34 on Constantine and the distinction between *dominium* and *possessio*; but see above, pp. 258–9, for a critique of Levy's views.

[6] Jenkins (1986) provides an excellent translation and commentary on some Welsh legal texts; Charles-Edwards (1989) gives a brief survey of the texts.   [7] Gildas, *De Excidio Britanniae* c. 5.

[8] Davies (1982).   [9] For some examples, see Binchy (1956).

[10] Venantius Fortunatus, *Opera Poetica* ed. Leo, *MGH AA* iv.1 (Berlin, 1881), iii.5, praising Felix, bishop of Nantes.

Sea. The variations in degrees of *romanitas* prevailing before a single barbarian king established his throne on the soil of the empire must not be forgotten.

1. LAW AND ETHNIC IDENTITY

The notion that a law may endure as a distinct tradition within, and long after, the empire, from the Iron Age to the late Middle Ages, runs counter to one strong tendency in contemporary scholarship. As a reaction against the notion of a single 'Germanic' cultural tradition, analogous to the family of Germanic languages, scholars have argued that the peoples of early medieval Europe were political entities created out of varied elements by particular historical circumstances. A people, *gens*, of this period was, paradoxically, often most obviously revealed to be a political creation by the origin-legends that traced it back into the remote past. Moreover, as the Lombard king Rothari's Prologue to his Edict illustrates, a conception of a legal tradition could be entwined with just such an origin-legend: he brought together a conception of Lombard legal tradition, a king-list extending back long before the migration into Italy, his own genealogy and a brief note on the Lombard occupation of Italian land.[11] In the shorter Prologue to the Salic Law, usually dated to the last third of the sixth century, we even have a specifically legal origin-legend, a story to show what Salic law should be by telling how it came into existence. Just as the origin-legend of a people might need to pay heed to the disparate elements that made up its population, so also, to take one example, Burgundian law might be much less purely Burgundian than a first reading might lead one to suppose.[12]

There is, then, a possible gap between perception and reality arising from two truths – namely, that laws were often conceived as the laws of distinct peoples and that ethnic identity was especially fluid during the migration period. There is a further problem in that it was possible for the written law of one people to borrow extensively from that of another. An extreme example, from after our period, is the wholesale borrowing from the fifth-century Code of Euric into the eighth-century Law of the Bavarians, the Bavarians being a leading example of an ethnic identity constructed in our period.[13]

The link between ethnic identity and the possession of a distinct law varied greatly in strength. From the end of our period, both from within and from the periphery of the Frankish kingdoms, come examples of laws which did not claim to be the laws of a *gens*. The Ribuarian Law is the law of a duchy

---

[11] *Edictus Rothari* Pref. (ed. Beyerle (1962) 16–17).

[12] For example, *Liber Constitutionum* 2.1 (ed. de Salis, *Leg. Burg., MGH* Leg. 1, 11.1 (Hanover, 1892), p. 42): 'Si quis hominem ingenuum ex populo nostro cuiuslibet nationis aut servum regis, natione duntaxat barbarum, occidere damnabili ausu praesumpserit . . .'   [13] See esp. Zeumer (1898).

within Austrasia, one division of one Frankish *Regnum*.[14] Æthelberht's Law became the first document of Kentish law, but the Cantware were the people of Kent, the land of a former British *civitas*, the Cantii; for some purposes they might be anxious to assert their kinship with the Jutes of the Isle of Wight and Hampshire, but they called their law Kentish, not Jutish.[15] It is approximately true that the further south we go in western Europe the more the *Laws* are Roman in construction and language but ethnic in scope.

Although the effects of migration upon conceptions and formulations of law might be considerable, there are cases in which they appear to have had no effect whatsoever. In Ireland we have a legal tradition from outside the empire: although some Irish had settled in Britain, their first written laws did not come from the colonies but from the homeland.[16] In this case, law was central to the conception of the Irish as one people, but in a quite different way from the relationship of law and ethnic identity in southern Europe, for the law transcended the limits of any one kingdom. Admittedly, the sense of Irish national identity was probably strengthened by the process of migration and conquest. Yet the results are seen in the homeland rather than in Irish colonies in Britain.

For Rothari, however, the Lombards' entry into Italy may have recalled the people of Israel entering the Promised Land; as that migration saw the foundation of the Law of Moses, so Rothari considered it his duty to correct current legal practice just as all previous kings had done in their day, including Alboin, who led the Lombards into Italy 'by divine power' just as Rothari led them into Liguria in the very year in which he promulgated his edict.[17] There was, then, great variety in the historical context of law in the period between the fifth and the seventh century. Some laws may indeed have undergone a major reshaping; yet the tradition was not necessarily always broken, as illustrated by the law of one people, some of whom were settled in the west and whose ancient traditions were, as we have seen, of peculiar interest to migrating peoples: the Jews.[18]

II. EDICTS AND JUDGEMENTS

In order to grasp the wide variety of law, it is helpful to extend the scope of the enquiry into the seventh century; in that way one can include the earliest European laws preserved in the vernacular, those from England and Ireland. A broad classification of the material (leaving aside such texts as

[14] Ewig (1976) 1.462–71.

[15] Bede, *HE* 1.15; IV.16/14. For examples of Cantware in the laws, see Hlothhere and Eadric, Prologue, 16; Wihtred, Prol. For Æthelberht's Law see now Wormald (1995).

[16] Cf. the preoccupation with Tara and Patrick shown by *Córus Béscnai*, ed. Binchy (1979) 527.14–28; cf. Charles-Edwards and Kelly (1983) §§31–3 and *Di Chetharslicht Athgabála*, ed. Binchy (1979) 356.5–6. Kelly (1988) surveys the contents of the early Irish laws.   [17] *Edictus Rothari* Prologue.

[18] Cf. *Edictum Theodorici* c. 143, ed. Baviera II.708.

the *Formulae* and the *Edictum Theodorici*) will give us provisional guidance. There are four main types:

1 Manuals of instruction written in the vernacular by judges for aspirant judges. This category is characteristic of Ireland.
2 Collections of decrees written in the vernacular, without any overt sub-divisions marked by 'titles' – i.e. headings that group together a series of decrees. This type is found in Kent, and later elsewhere in England.
3 Collections of decrees written in Latin and with titles, but with numer-ous vernacular glosses, and also vernacular terms given Latin inflexions. This type is exemplified by the *Pactus Legis Salicae*.
4 Collections of decrees written in Latin with titles, with some vernacular terms but without vernacular glosses. This category is exemplified by the *Liber Constitutionum* of the Burgundians, promulgated in 517 by king Sigismund.

As can easily be seen, these types are largely progressive – for example, in the amount of vernacular allowed into the text; and they also show varia-tion from north to south. They suggest, as we shall see, that the influence of Roman models declined as one moved away from the Mediterranean. I shall follow this suggestion by organizing my account of the different Laws geographically, beginning in the north and proceeding southwards towards the Mediterranean. One reason why this is the best approach is that the date of some crucial texts is debatable. For that reason a chronological approach will tend to make too many assumptions.

In order to understand a law from the inside, it is necessary to grasp the central ideas used by legislator, judge and litigant alike. It is here, rather than in the details of any given rule, that it may be possible to make the connec-tion between lawbook and law as it functioned in society. A good place to begin is with the construction of the individual decree in the Frankish sphere of influence. That will make it possible both to analyse the structure of texts and also to gain some notion of the way the law was used in court. Here it is particularly appropriate to proceed from north to south: since Æthelberht's Law and those of his seventh-century successors as kings of Kent were in the vernacular, they offer a better insight into the terms used in court and council than can be gained by analysing only Latin texts.[19] Bede also offers an interesting account of Æthelberht's Law, while the Law of Hlothhere and Eadric (673–85) has a prologue which exhibits the legislators' stance towards their predecessors. Bede represents Æthelberht's law-making as a royal activ-ity on behalf of his people, the Cantware, by whom the laws were observed, Bede says, up to the time at which he was writing.[20] The laws themselves are

---

[19] For the inclusion of Æthelberth's Kent within the Frankish sphere, see Wood (1983) and (1992).
[20] Bede, *HE* II.5.

called, in a difficult phrase, *decreta iudiciorum*, literally 'decrees of judgements'. What Bede seems to be doing is combining two ideas which we would expect to be kept quite separate: the edict of the lawgiver, the *decretum*, and the judgement of the court, *iudicium*. Plummer observed that Bede had Old English *dōmas*, 'dooms', in mind when he used the word *iudicia*, but this still leaves unexplained the link with the other term, *decreta*.[21] A clue is offered by the prologue to Hlothhere and Eadric, which declares that the two kings added to the law (*ǣ*) that their forefathers made 'these *dōmas* that follow hereafter'.[22] A *dōm* is, therefore, as much a decree promulgated by a king as a judgement which a judge, *dēma*, might judge, *dēman*.[23] What Bede was doing with his odd phrase, *decreta iudiciorum*, was to render the two aspects of the one English word, *dōm*, both royal decree and judge's verdict. One may compare the way in which Gregory of Tours writes of 'the judges' promulgating an 'edict' concerning a fine for late appearance on a military expedition.[24]

Much later, in the early tenth century, it would also be possible to use the word *dōmbōc* – 'doom-book' – for Alfred's lawbook, which provided the fundamental text to which later kings added further decrees, very much as Æthelberht's Law seems to have been the fundamental text for seventh-century Kent. Such notions of a royal lawbook – a book of *dōmas* which might be compared on the one hand with the Burgundian *Liber Constitutionum*, 'The Book of Decrees', and on the other with the Visigothic *Liber Iudiciorum*, 'The Book of Judgements' – cannot, however, be imported into seventh-century Kent without severe qualification, for Wihtred, at the end of the century, could speak of *bōca dōm*, without further qualification, to refer to a rule in books of church law.[25] Wihtred's law was carefully dated and situated in a place, with its authority buttressed by a list of great men who had met together on that occasion – all this going to show that it was primarily the law promulgated in a royal assembly. The same contrast between oral and written is part of contemporary perceptions of Irish law: the 'law of the written word' is a term for ecclesiastical law.[26]

Bede's *decreta iudiciorum* may therefore be compared with the notion, implicit in Hlothhere and Eadric's Law, that they were promulgating *dōmas* which were also to be the *dōmas* pronounced by judges, *dēman*. Both suggest an intimate relationship between royal legislator and local judge. Yet Bede also says, in a much-discussed phrase, that Æthelberht was legislating

---

[21] In the comment on this passage in his edn, *Baedae Opera Historica* II.87.

[22] Liebermann, *Gesetze*, p. 9. *Æ*, like *riht*, is collective, 'law as a whole', and thus entirely distinct from *dōm*, 'decree, judgement, fame'. The derived sense of 'fame', namely the judgement of contemporaries and later generations upon a person, is already attested in Gothic *doms*; *Skeireins*, ed. W. Streitberg, *Die Gotische Bibel*, 4th edn (Heidelberg, 1965) 459, 467 (II.17, VI.16).

[23] Cf. *Cantwara dēeman*, Hlothhere and Eadric, c. 8, ed. Liebermann, *Gesetze* p. 10.

[24] Greg. Tur. *Hist.* VII.42.   [25] Wihtred, c. 5, ed. Liebermann, *Gesetze*, I.12.

[26] *Corpus Iuris Hibernici* ed. Binchy, p. 346; also ed. and trans. R. Thurneysen, 'Aus dem irischen Recht, IV', *Zeitschrift für celtische Philologie* 16 (1927) 175.

'according to *exempla* of the Romans', and this has suggested to some that the conception of the king as legislator was not already traditional in Æthelberht's time; on this view, Æthelberht's Law was a conscious attempt to adopt, on a small scale, the legislative role of an emperor. According to Wallace-Hadrill, Æthelberht was putting into writing 'just that fraction of custom that seemed enough to satisfy royal pride in legislation'.[27] What was promulgated, on this view, was not so much the particular *dōm* – that was already customary – but an image of a royal lawgiver.

This is certainly not what Bede meant to convey, for he declares that Æthelberht promulgated his laws for the sake of his people and also that the laws were observed by them up to Bede's own day. It is also rendered unlikely by the particular situation that Bede has in mind. According to him, Æthelberht's laws were enacted with the advice of his wise men. This term, *sapientes*, recurs in Bede's account of the Northumbrian royal council at which Edwin and his *sapientes* debated whether or not the king and his councillors should, all together, accept the Christian faith. What Bede had in mind was the situation also implied by the late-seventh-century pro- logues to the laws of Wihtred and of Ine.[28] Although in the former the council is said to make the laws, while in the latter the king makes them with the advice of his wise men, both are probably alternative descriptions of the one process: the king took the advice of his councillors and then made a declaration, more or less formal, of his decision, to which they gave their assent.[29] The same process of decision-making lies behind early English charters and explains why they could be described by Bede both as *cartae* and as royal decrees promulgated in a council.[30]

The process of legislation was, therefore, oral. For kings to satisfy royal pride in legislation it was not necessary that those laws should be commit- ted to writing.[31] What did matter was that the political élite should put their collective weight behind legislation promulgated by the king with their advice and in their presence. Writing the law down, if it happened at all, was an entirely secondary matter; for precisely the same reason, writing a charter was a secondary matter. This pattern of legislative action provides a context in which the concept of a *dōm*, at once edict and judicial verdict, makes complete sense. As edict, the *dōm* is a decree promulgated by the king in his council; as judgement, it is the decision promulgated by judge or judges in the court.

The same pattern is exemplified among the Franks by the decrees of Childebert II, promulgated at the annual assembly on 1 March.[32] The extant

---

[27] Wallace-Hadrill (1971) 37.   [28] Ed. Liebermann, *Gesetze* 1.12, 88.
[29] Cf. Ganshof (1961) 35–40, 52–62.
[30] Bede, *Epistola ad Ecgberhtum* cc. 12, 13, 17, ed. Plummer, *Baedae Opera Historica* 1.415–21.
[31] The legislation of Earconberht, mentioned by Bede, *HE* 111.8, may never have been written.
[32] *Pactus Legis Salicae* ed. Eckhardt (1962) 267–9.

decrees only begin nearly twenty years after Childebert's accession – that is, after the death of Guntram in 593, when Childebert had succeeded his uncle as the dominant ruler of the Franks.[33] From then until his own death in 596, every spring saw legislation which is not only precisely dated but situated in a place within Childebert's kingdom: 594 at Andernach, 595 at Maastricht and 596 at Cologne. Childebert also makes it clear both that he has discussed the issues with his nobles and that he himself is promulgating the outcome. So the second decree at Andernach in 594 begins with an awkward combination of the two elements, noble counsel and royal promulgation:

Subsequently, however, it is agreed with our *leudes*: we have decreed . . .

The same pattern is also attested among the Burgundians.[34]

It may even be behind full-scale codes. Rothari's Edict was promulgated in 643, and the elaborate dating clause which opens the text places the promulgation at the royal palace in Pavia.[35] The year 643 saw a major Lombard campaign which resulted in the conquest of Liguria, hitherto a Roman province;[36] and it has very plausibly been suggested that Rothari's great legislative achievement, with its reminder of the divinely providential entry into Italy seventy-six years before, was intended as an assertion of Lombard identity. This was coupled with royal concern for the poorer element among the Lombards, before the campaign got under way.[37] What may have mattered most in 643 was the way in which Rothari's Edict was set before the Lombard army as an expression of their solidarity as a people, their identification with their kings and their claims to rule in Italy. Even when it came to the practical effectiveness of individual rules of law, royal legislation was likely to be sensitive to the political context: in the end, it rested on the combined strength exerted by the authority of the king and the consensus of his great men.

It is also possible to grasp how contemporaries understood the internal structure of individual decrees. Title 57 of the Frankish *Pactus Legis Salicae* is devoted to the *rachinburgii*, the sworn panel of men required to declare the Salic law in judgement. They are depicted as discussing the *causa* which divides the parties; and the *Pactus* is concerned lest the *rachinburgii* should refuse to declare the law. They may, therefore, be solemnly requested by a disputant 'that you declare the law according to the Salic law'. The particular verdict should thus be according to the law as a whole. This suggests

---

[33] For this reason the judgement of Eckhardt (1954) 139, that the *Decretio Childeberti* was solely a territorial law for Austrasia, is open to question. [34] *Constitutiones Extravagantes*, XXI, ed. de Salis, *Leg. Burg.* 119. [35] Beyerle (1962) 16.

[36] Paul. Diac. *Hist. Lang.* IV.45, ed. L. Bethmann and G. Waitz, *MGH, Scriptores rerum Langobardicarum et Italicarum, saec. VI–IX* (Hanover 1878), p. 135. On the date of the campaign, see Bognetti (1966–8c) II.313 n. [37] Bognetti (1966–8b).

the same binding together of law and judicial verdict that was implied by the Old English word *dōm*, but also its distinction between the individual *dōm* and the collective *ǣ* or *riht*, law in general.[38] Further hints are given by the origin-legend of Frankish Law contained in the Shorter Prologue (usually dated to the late sixth century).[39] Four wise men are said 'to have met together in three courts, *malli*, and to have earnestly discussed all the starting-points of *causae*, and to have decreed a judgement about each, as follows' (and then begins the text). This tale elevates the wise men to the exclusion of the king whom they might have counselled; but, again, it combines decree and judgement in one: they decree a judgement. Apparently, then, the individual Frankish judge is expected to follow the judgement already decreed by the wise men – a conception which agrees with the disputant's demand that the *rachinburgii* declare a law (corresponding to Old English *dōm*) in accordance with the Salic law (Old English *ǣ* or *riht*). In effect, the wise men of the Shorter Prologue are a legendary embodiment of all that *rachinburgii* ought to be, but within a conception of judgement determined by decree.

The *causa* is both the dispute and the complaint that brings one party to court. A plaintiff may '*mallare* his *causa* according to the laws'.[40] In this sense of pleading a case, *mallare* corresponds well to its cognate, Old English *mathelian*, derived from *mæthl*, a court.[41] The verb, *mathelian*, is used in *Beowulf* for making a solemn speech, and similarly *mæthl* itself may mean 'speech'. The pattern of derivation (*mallus → mallare*, *mæthl → mathelian*) and the semantic development ('court' → 'speech appropriate to a court or assembly') are thus closely similar in Frankish and English, though what we have in the Frankish cases are Latinized forms. What this range of usage suggests is that a particular linguistic register was expected in court, and that the verb for this style of grave pleading was extended to any weighty speech before an assembly. A *causa*, then, is what a disputant tries to *mallare* and the *rachinburgii* are expected to judge.[42]

The language used to describe the pleading and judgement of cases is echoed in the structure of the individual decree. The commonest form of a decree in the Salic Law consists of a conditional sentence:

If anyone should have done X, let him be judged liable to pay Y.

The first clause, 'If anyone should have done X' is a generalized form of a *causa*, the statement of what has happened which forms the basis of the

[38] Cf. Schmidt-Wiegand (1987).

[39] *PLS* Prologue (pp. 2–3); Eckhardt (1954) 170–2, but Wood, *Merovingian Kingdoms* 108 is inclined to date it to the seventh century.   [40] *Pactus Legis Salicae* ed. Eckhardt (1962) 105.2 (p. 261).

[41] Cf. *mæþlfriþ* in Æthelberht, c. 1, an medle oþþe þinge, Hlothhere and Eadric, c. 8. Gothic *maþl* is likewise used in Mark 7.4 to translate *agorá* (Latin *forum*).

[42] *Causa* may render *sace* in *sacebarones* etc. (cf. OE *sacu*).

plaintiff's case. The second clause is the judgement upon the *causa*. The logic of pleading and judgement implied by the principal concepts used at the time may be simply stated (assuming that the identity of the offender is known):

1 The plaintiff comes with a narrative of his *causa*.
2 The narrative is understood as an instance of a general category: 'If anyone does X'.
3 The *rachinburgii* then state the Salic law: 'If anyone does X, then let him pay Y', which immediately leads to the individual liability of the defendant. The general *dōm* gives the particular verdict.

There is no reason to suppose that a typical case proceeded in quite so expeditious a manner as this scheme suggests. What it implies, rather, is that this process was the central thread around which argument might develop.

The standard form of decree in *Lex Salica* is, however, slightly different from the last step (no. 3). The second clause goes, not 'let him pay Y', but 'let him be judged liable to pay Y'. 'Let him pay' is the judges' *dōm*, addressed to the disputants and to the court; 'let him be judged liable to pay' is the legislator's *dōm* addressed to the judges and purporting to determine their verdict. What we have, therefore, in the Salic Law is the legislator's *dōm*, addressed to the judge, as opposed to the judge's *dōm* addressed to the disputants. Yet the important thing is how close they are. We may take a straightforward example:[43]

If someone has killed a Roman required to pay tribute (for the *malloberg* [= court-hill] they are *walaleodi* [= Roman people]), let him be judged liable to pay 2,500 *denarii* which make 62½ *solidi*.

The only change we need in order to make this legislator's *dōm* into a judge's *dōm* is to replace 'let him be judged' by 'he is'. Moreover, in a case such as this one there ought to be no need to prove who killed the Roman: unless it is the much more serious offence of secret killing, dealt with elsewhere, the killer should have admitted publicly to his action.[44] True, once guilt is acknowledged and the court has delivered its verdict, the business of securing a settlement may only just be beginning, but such issues are not clarified by the wording of individual decrees and will be discussed later.[45]

III. LAWBOOKS AND CODES

In principle, then, there is a close link between decree and judgement: the decree prescribes the judgement; and it does so by closely echoing the

---

[43] *PLS* 41.10.
[44] Compare the way in which Chramnesind placed Sichar's body on a fence-post and set off to plead his case before the king: Greg. Tur. *Hist.* IX.19. [45] Cf. Wood (1986).

standard form of judgement. Matters begin to be a little more complicated, however, when we turn from the individual decree to the way in
which decrees are combined into 'titles'. Up to now the consideration of
decrees has not presumed that such decrees were written down: the texts
have been scrutinized in order to understand what men thought law was,
and this has been done on the assumption that most law was oral and
remained oral.[46] Once units larger than the decree come into play, we have
to confront the difficult issue of written law.

In their organization of decrees into larger units, Frankish and Kentish
law part company. There are groups of related decrees in Æthelberht's Law,
but they are not marked as such by being put under separate titles. The Salic
Law, however, follows the model of the Theodosian Code; and decrees are
therefore put under titles. So, for example, the decree about the killing of a
Roman *tributarius* is the tenth decree under Title 41, 'Concerning killings of
free men'.

The issue of larger textual units is all the more important because there
is nothing inherently necessary in the grouping of decrees of the kind discussed hitherto. If they were perceived as individual legislative acts,
responses at a particular place and time to circumstances of which we know
nothing, such an origin would not naturally engender any systematic organization of the material. Once such decrees had been put into written form,
they might be expected to constitute a series of separate unordered decrees.
This expectation might then lead to a further claim – namely, that just as the
titles of the Salic or the Burgundian Laws were a device borrowed from the
Theodosian Code, so too any ordering of these decrees would probably
have been a habit of mind introduced via the participation of Romans in
the compilation of barbarian laws. Such figures are indeed well attested,
notably in a letter from Sidonius Apollinaris, written about 469, mocking an
aristocrat of consular descent, Syagrius, for his cultural collaboration with
the Burgundians.[47] Syagrius had gone so far as to learn Burgundian, to play
the three-stringed lyre and to astonish the Burgundian elders by acting as a
judge, with the result that he was acclaimed by the barbarians as a new Solon
in the discussion of their laws. Similarly, it has been observed that
Childebert II's last edict is attested by Asclepiodotus, previously a referendary to Guntram, and clearly, to judge by his name, a Gallo-Roman.[48]

This argument – that Roman participation was necessary before decrees
could be grouped together – is, however, difficult to reconcile with
Æthelberht's Law, where, in spite of the absence of titles, there is consid-

[46] I would not accept Wormald's definition – (1977) 107 – of legislation as meaning 'written decrees
by secular authority with ostensibly general application'; Nehlsen (1977) 456–65 argues against the previously widely held view that references in the texts to *Lex Salica* were always to a written text of Salic
Law.   [47] Sid. Ap. *Ep*. v.5; Syagrius 3 in *PLRE* II.1042.
[48] See Asclepiodotus 3 and 4, *PLRE* III.134.

erable evidence of ordering.[49] This is achieved in three ways, in addition to simple collocation. First, there are decrees which themselves act as virtual titles: thus, c. 8, 'The king's *mundbyrd* [= protection] of fifty shillings', provides a basis for cc. 9–12. Secondly, the use of the definite article and of personal pronouns is normally to refer from one *dōm* to another within such a group.[50] Finally, groups of decrees may be marked by syntactical variation, especially a change from the dominant conditional sentence to another construction.[51] More elaborate ordering – of one group of decrees with another – could be achieved by ellipsis. Thus, in a series of groups depending on decrees which act as virtual titles ('The king's *mundbyrd* . . .'; 'the *eorl*'s *mundbyrd* . . .', 'the *ceorl*'s *mundbyrd*'), the middle one, specifying the *eorl*'s *mundbyrd*, is omitted but can be automatically supplied by anyone who appreciates the structure of the text. Æthelberht's Law is exceptionally terse but also both subtle and consistent. It is, therefore, unlikely that the Gregorian missionaries, with their recently acquired knowledge of the language, could be responsible for the way in which the text is organized. Later Kentish legislation is more varied in syntax; also, individual decrees are longer and more complex – a development which may plausibly be seen as symptomatic of a shift from oral to written modes of expression.

IV. THE EVOLUTION OF FRANKISH WRITTEN LAW

The history of the Salic Law is long and complex and, for that very reason, instructive. Indeed, it has recently become longer and more difficult because of the convincing argument put forward by Grierson and Blackburn that the monetary equivalence of forty *denarii* to one *solidus* asserted throughout the main text, but not in most of the capitularies added at the end, is only appropriate to the early fifth century.[52] This conclusion creates an immediate difficulty for those who would ascribe the main text in its original form to Clovis. The general, though not universal, opinion has been that the earliest version, the A Recension, of the *Pactus Legis Salicae* was compiled after the battle of Vouillé in 507, when Clovis defeated and killed Alaric, king of the Visigoths, and probably before Clovis' own death in 511.[53]

Apart from the coinage, there are three main considerations which must form any judgement on the date of the Salic Law. First, the main text is part

---

[49] An analysis is proposed by Wormald (1995) 971–2.

[50] So *hio* and *sio* in c. 11; similarly, 16, 25, 46 etc.

[51] The series of decrees in c. 1 are distinguished by being nominal sentences and by the instrumental use of *XIIgylde* etc.; the pairs cc. 70–1 and 72–3 are marked by the combination of a conditional sentence and a simple sentence, the latter with a prepositional phrase doing duty for the protasis of the conditional.

[52] Grierson and Blackburn (1986) 102–6. Capitulary V is the only one to share this equivalence.

[53] Eckhard (1954) 206–7, following Brunner (1906, 1928) 1.440.

of a collection including, in most manuscripts, the *Pactus pro Tenore Pacis* of Childebert I and Chlothar I, sons of Clovis, and sometimes the *Decretio Childeberti*, which we have already met, a series of three annual decrees promulgated in the last three years of Childebert II's reign. By then he had succeeded his uncle Guntram as the leading king of the Franks. The collection does not include legislation by Guntram, nor that of Chlothar II.[54] Part, at least, of the textual tradition was Austrasian and bears comparison with the Austrasian Letter Collection, which stretches from the time of Clovis to the Austrasia of Childebert II. Its emphasis is on legislation affecting all the Salian Franks, whether by the authority of a leading king or by an agreement between two, as with the *Pactus pro Tenore Pacis*, an agreement between Childebert I and Chlothar I on measures to keep the peace. Moreover, the collection is laid out chronologically, as what has aptly been called code and coda:[55] in other words, the original text is initially added to rather than revised, so that the coda is chronologically subsequent to the code and is itself chronologically organized. Leaving aside the capitularies in the coda, which do not bear indications of date, the entire collection, in its Austrasian form, is as follows: (1) *Pactus Legis Salicae* (the code); (2) the *Pactus pro Tenore Pacis* (probably between 548 and 558, when Childebert I and Chlothar I ruled the Franks between them); (3) the *Decretio Childeberti* (594–6).

Secondly, there is a clear difference between the code and the coda in their religious standpoints. Legal protection is given to pagan worship in the code, but no corresponding protection to Christianity.[56] Admittedly, the 'sacred gelded boar' which is the subject of the Salic Law's attention is still there in the K Recension, revised after Charlemagne's imperial coronation.[57] But that must attest an extreme reluctance to abandon any portion of the old law, however outdated; the attitude is consistent with the preference shown by most sixth-century kings for adding to rather than revising the text of Salic Law. They were ready to change the substance of a rule in practice, but left the old text where it was.

The problem of how pagan elements survived is not, therefore, the same as the problem of how they were included in the first place. On the face of it, the original A Recension was the work of a pagan. Admittedly, it has been argued that Title 35.1 (about what is to happen when one slave kills another) is an application of an idea derived from Exodus 21.35.[58] Even if

---

[54] The *Edictus Chilperici* is extant only in one MS (K17 = A17 for the capitularies) but was in the exemplar of its sister MS (A1) since it occurs in the table of titles. But, since they are sister manuscripts, the textual tradition cannot confirm that Chilperic's edict was in the archetype. The *Decretio Childeberti* is in those MSS and also in C6 and the D, E and K-Recensions.   [55] Daube (1947) ch. 2.

[56] The C Recension is a clear contrast: it has a few Christian decrees, notably *PLS* 55.6–7.

[57] *PLS* 2.16 = K Recension, 2.14 (ed. Eckhardt (1956) 474). Brunner (1906, 1928) 1.435 n. 39 argues on the basis of Greg. Tur. *De Passione et Virtutibus S. Iuliani* c. 31 that this reference may be Christian, but Gregory refers simply to animals given to the church of Brioude.   [58] Nehlsen (1972) 280–3.

this is true, the rule has no specifically Christian content – nothing which might offend the most fervent pagan. It may perhaps be taken as suggesting the influence on the text of a Christian Roman, who applied Exodus' rule about one ox killing another to the situation when one slave kills another, but it does not weaken the argument derived from the total absence from the A Recension of any Christian content, such as we find even in Æthelberht's Law.

The third argument stems from Title 47. The issue is the procedure to be followed when one person claims to recognize his property in the possession of another, who may, of course, have bought it, or received it as a gift, in good faith. The parties are to fix a date at which all those involved in any relevant exchange of the property in question may come together. If the parties live within limits defined by the forest known as the *Carbonaria* (near Brussels) and the Loire, the meeting is to occur after forty nights; if one party lives beyond those limits, the meeting is postponed so that it occurs after eighty nights.[59]

This text has been read in two quite different ways. On the one hand, it is argued that only after Clovis' defeat of Alaric in 507 and the subsequent conquest of Aquitaine would Franks live beyond the Loire; hence the usual date for the Salic Law of 507 to 511.[60] On the other hand, it is also pointed out that those boundaries were crucial for Clovis before his defeat of Alaric and before, at some time after 507, he took over the kingdom of Sigibert the Lame, centred at Cologne.[61] At that stage, the *silva Carbonaria* separated Clovis' Salian kingdom from Sigibert's eastern domain, which included most at least of the other Frankish peoples, the Chamavi, Bructeri and Ampsivarii. Moreover, the presence of Franks beyond the Loire before 507 is not impossible: they had been active in the Loire valley for fifty years before 507 and had even briefly taken Bordeaux in 498.[62] Nevertheless, it is difficult to reconcile the numismatic evidence as interpreted by Grierson and Blackburn with Title 47; if the former is held to rule out a date after *c.* 450, it may be necessary to ask whether Title 47's reference to the Loire may not be a later insertion.

The difficulties over the date of the Salic Law arise in part from uncertainty about its character. Thus Ewig is inclined to date it between Clovis' destruction of the other Salian kings – Ragnachar, Rignomer and Chararic – and his taking of power over the Rhineland Franks.[63] For him this explains why it is a law for all the Salians but not for the other Frankish

[59] *PLS* 47.1, 3.   [60] Eckhardt (1954) 202–3.   [61] Wood, *Merovingian Kingdoms* 112.

[62] Greg. Tur. *Hist.* II.18–19; *Continuatio Havniensis Prosperi* s.a. 498, ed. Mommsen, *Chronica Minora* 1.331: Ann. XIIII 'Alarici Franci Burdigalem obtinuerunt et a potestate Gothorum in possessionem sui redegerunt capto Suatrio Gothorum duce.'

[63] Ewig (1988) 30; this involves a major revision to Gregory of Tours' chronology, since he placed the acquisition of Sigibert the Lame's kingdom east of the Carbonaria before the conquest of the Salian kings.

peoples. If one sees the Salic Law as a code promulgated by royal authority, this view has a great deal to be said for it, particularly if the other Salian
kings had been disposed of before Clovis' conversion. This would then
explain both the pagan character and the geographical scope of the law.[64]
Yet, working still on the assumption that the Salic Law was promulgated
by royal authority, there are objections arising from the letter in which
Remigius, bishop of Rheims, welcomed Clovis' accession to power.[65] In it
he implies that Clovis' authority, and that of his father before him,
extended over the whole of the Roman province of Belgica Secunda. This
province included Cambrai, which is where Gregory of Tours placed
Ragnachar. Moreover, one element in Clovis' authority, inherited from
Childeric, was his role as judge, which Remigius perceives in completely
Roman terms.[66] The Angers material used by Gregory of Tours also
shows that Childeric's activities were on a much larger scale than one
would expect from a mere king of Tournai.[67] Childeric appears to have
been in close collaboration for part of his career with Aegidius, *magister
militum*, while Remigius' letter suggests that he had found it possible to
work well with the bishops. It is not therefore necessary to assume that
Clovis must have disposed of the other Salian kings before the promulgation of the Salic Law.

On these grounds and on the basis of the numismatic evidence, the possibility remains that the Salic Law belongs to the time not of Clovis but of
Childeric. Childeric would then have promulgated the law as principal king
of the Salian Franks; its Roman characteristics – principally its organization into titles – would be explained by his connections with men such as
Aegidius and Remigius, while its complete lack of any support for
Christianity would pose no problem at all. On the other hand, it is difficult
to see how an earlier dating than Childeric's reign could be reconciled with
Title 47's implied reference to Salian Franks who lived beyond the Loire. In
the reign of Chlodio in the second quarter of the fifth century – a date
which would fit perfectly the numismatic evidence as interpreted by
Grierson and Blackburn – the Salian Franks had only just established a permanent presence west of the *silva Carbonaria*. One must therefore assume
that the equation of forty *denarii* with one *solidus* was still accepted among
the Salian Franks in the third quarter of the fifth century. The implication
is that both the Salic Law and the Code of Euric, to which we shall come
later, belong to about a generation after the Theodosian Code and were
perhaps, in some sense, local responses to that great compilation.
Furthermore, there is no reason to suppose, as has been the near-universal

[64] This is not Ewig's view; he retains the date given to the conversion by Gregory of Tours.
[65] *Epist. Austras.* ed. Gundlach, no. 2, in *Epistolae Merowingici et Karolini Aevi, MGH* (Berlin, 1892),
p. 113.   [66] 'Iustitia ex ore vestro procedat . . . praetorium tuum omnibus pateatur.'
[67] Greg. Tur. *Hist.* II.18–19.

opinion, that Germanic written law began with Euric and the Visigoths. Frankish written law may be just as old.

It is also worth asking the fundamental question, however, whether Salic Law was indeed promulgated on royal authority. The Shorter Prologue was added when the C Recension was made.[68] It presents an account of the genesis of *Lex Salica*, which, while it is plainly legendary, conceives it as being the creation of men learned in the law and fails to mention any royal involvement. If we compare it with the Burgundian *Liber Constitutionum* of 517 the differences are very obvious. In the latter case, not only is there a prologue declaring the text to have been promulgated by Sigismund in the second year of his reign, there are also several other royal decrees, dated and often also located.[69] Moreover, the concerns of the king are regularly proclaimed. To give only one notable example, judges are firmly said to be royal appointees.[70] There are no laws within the text of *Lex Salica* itself which are, in the same fashion as the Burgundian decrees, overtly royal. Yet there are several in the texts attached to *Lex Salica* in one or more manuscripts: the *Pactus pro Tenore Pacis* of Childebert I and Chlothar I, the edicts of Chilperic I and of Childebert II. The contrast becomes all the more striking when we look at the texts of these royal decrees and compare them with *Lex Salica*. None of them follows the standard form of the main law: 'If anyone has done X, let him be judged liable to pay Y.'

There are indeed texts attached to *Lex Salica* which normally follow this form, but they are as innocent of overt royal features as is *Lex Salica* itself. The earliest is the one called Capitulary V by Eckhardt (though placed last in his edition, it is the only one frequently to give penalties in *denarii* as well as *solidi* and to use the equivalence of forty *denarii* to one *solidus*); there are numerous parallels between its contents and those of *Lex Salica*; it has not a single reference to the king. If we go outside the *Lex Salica* and its appended texts to Frankish royal legislation preserved elsewhere, the contrast remains: overtly royal texts are not dominated by the *dōm* type of decree.[71] The Frankish pattern is thus quite different from the Kentish. The difference is underlined by comparison with the church councils. In the

---

[68] A probable *terminus post quem* for the C Recension is the link with c. 22 of the Council of Tours, 567. This cites not just the Old Testament but also the *Interpretatio* to the *Codex Theodosianus* on incestuous unions. The same passage is cited in *PLS* 13.11: see Eckhardt (1954) 216–17. The *terminus ante quem* proposed by Eckhardt, namely the somewhat different treatment of incest in the *Decretio Childeberti* 1.2, is hardly compelling, since, in its general command to the bishops to reform by their preaching the remaining incestuous unions, it may simply be referring back to the Council of Tours.

[69] *Liber Constitutionum* ed. de Salis, *Leg. Burg.*, *MGH* Leg. 1, 11.1 (Hanover, 1892), or ed. F. Beyerle, Germanenrechte, x (Weimar, 1936), XLII, XLV, LII, LXII (date only), LXXVI, LXXIX. On the ascriptions to Sigismund and Gundobad, see Beyerle (1954) 24–7.

[70] *Liber Constitutionum* XC, ed. de Salis, *Leg. Burg.* 110.

[71] *Capitularia Regum Francorum* 1.i, ed. A. Boretius, *MGH*, Capit. (Hanover, 1881), no. 2, *Childeberti I Regis Praeceptum* (pp. 2–3); no. 5, *Guntchramni Regis Edictum* (pp. 10–12); no. 8, *Chlotharii II Praeceptio* (pp. 18–19); no. 9, *Chlotharii II Edictum* (pp. 20–3).

very period in which most scholars would place *Lex Salica* there is ecclesiastical legislation which is as open in its acknowledgement of royal authority as one could wish, the first council of Orleans in 511.[72]

There are, however, arguments in favour of seeing *Lex Salica* as royal legislation. The text begins with a decree about persons who neglect a summons to the court, the *mallus*. The summons in question is said to be *legibus dominicis*, 'according to the king's laws'.[73] It has also been argued that the very construction of a title may show whether it is a collection of royal decrees or of customary maxims.[74] There are, moreover, some turns of phrase which suggest legislation: thus *quae lex . . . conuenit obseruari*[75] and *hoc conuenit obseruare*[76] are reminiscent of the *Decretio Childeberti*'s repeated use of *conuenit* and likewise its *ita iussimus obseruari* and *placuit obseruari*.[77]

The difficulty with this argument is that there are two senses in which a rule can be said to be royal in character. On the one hand, the king may promulgate a traditional and customary rule, whether because he wishes to assert his authority over the law or because the rule in question is being flouted. The king gives his authority to the rule, but it does not originate with him. On the other hand, the rule may be royal in a stronger sense – namely, that the royal promulgation made something law when it had not previously been law; in other words, the rule originated with the king. Title 55, on spoliations of corpses, offers a good example of new law alongside old. In the C Recension of the Salic Law, rules were introduced into this title in order to protect Christian tombs and churches; but they naturally followed the pattern of the old laws in the title and are thus indistinguishable in form. Similarly, in the Law of Æthelberht, which was certainly royal in the sense of being promulgated by a king, there are new rules at the beginning to protect the church; yet, the rule protecting the peace of a church, *ciricfrith*, follows exactly the form of the rule protecting the peace of the court, *mæthlfrith*.[78] Things become still more problematic when it is a question, not of a single rule, but of an entire text. One might well admit that some of the rules in *Lex Salica* appear to be royal in form without thereby being committed to regarding the entire code as a royal promulgation.[79]

The difficulty is to strike a just balance. On the one hand, Salic Law contains *leges dominicae*; the king's authority stands behind the law, for they are his laws whatever their origin. On the other hand, the relationship between

---

[72] *Concilia Galliae, A. 511–A. 695*, ed. C. de Clercq, *CCSL* 148A, p. 4.

[73] Unsurprisingly, this title is seen as royal law by Brunner (1906, 1928) 1.432 n. 1.

[74] Beyerle (1924).   [75] *PLS* 42.1.   [76] *PLS* 46.1.

[77] *Decretio Childeberti*: for *conuenit, passim; ita iussimus obseruari*, 11.3; *decreuimus obseruari*, 11.5; *placuit obseruari*, 111.7. Similarly, *Edictus Chilperici, passim*.   [78] The Law of Æthelberht, c. 1.

[79] There is a difficulty in Beyerle's distinction (1924) between two types of *dōm* (both dominated by the conditional clause), one of which he regards as a royal decree, namely that texts such as the Edicts of Chilperic and Childebert II are not dominated by the conditional clause at all, but by the form *conuenit ut . . .*

king and law is evidently variable, strong in the case of such edicts as those of Chilperic I or Childebert II, more distant in most of *Lex Salica* itself. Moreover, the king could show his authority in other ways than by insisting on his role as promulgator of the law. The *rachinburgii* are said to proclaim the law;[80] but some cases will be heard 'before the king (*theuda*) or the *thunginus*'.[81] In Francia, then, putting law into writing did not entail making it overtly royal; moreover, the *Pactus Legis Salicae* is notably less royal than either the early English laws to the north or Burgundian law to the south.

Since the numismatic evidence now argues for a very early date, it is tempting to date *Lex Salica* before Clovis' destruction of the other Salian kings, such as Ragnachar of Cambrai. With divided kingship, no one king controls the law, although all support it and preside over legal processes. When, later, there is overtly royal legislation, it seems to come, as in the case of Childebert II, when a single king is clearly dominant or two kings made a treaty. Written law in Francia was still presumably the outcome of a collaboration between barbarian and Roman, but it also reflected the authority of men recognized for their knowledge of the law.[82] Their expertise in Salic law, only partly embodied in the text of *Lex Salica*, was mainly couched in rules of the *dōm* style; the king, perhaps Childeric using an authority exalted over other kings of the Salian Franks by his acceptance as ruler of Belgica Secunda, seems at most to have taken over a body of material assembled by experts, added some further decrees, and ordered it to be put into writing in a form imitating the Theodosian Code. But it is also possible that the absence of any parade of authority by a single king is because there were at the time several Salian kings, no one of whom had the power to promulgate law for all the Salians.

The question whether the Salic Law was promulgated by a king as a written text should not be confused with a quite separate question, whether kings played a major role in legal processes. Gregory of Tours provides several examples both of people who were prepared to travel considerable distances to seek royal justice and of local cases which were remitted to the king.[83] Remigius of Rheims emphasized, in very Roman terms, the judicial role expected of the king.[84] One cannot avoid the recently much-discussed question whether written law had any role in the Frankish court – whether, to use Peter Classen's question, 'one should imagine a Frankish judge of the

---

[80] *PLS* 57.

[81] The *thunginus* is likely to be the Frankish counterpart to the *gebungen wita* of Ine, c. 6.2, *pace* Wenskus (1964), who would see him as a minor king; he is coupled with the *centenarius* in 44.1, 46.1, 4, but with the *theoda* in 46.6 (reading *ante theuda* rather than *anttheoda*, which is only supported among the A and C MSS by A2's *anteuda*, itself a mechanical error, *ante(te)uda*). *Theuda* for the expected *theudan* is probably a West Frankish form influenced by the loss of final –*n* in Latin.

[82] Even in Burgundy Syagrius talked law with the *curua senectus*, not with the king: Sid. Ap. *Ep.* v.5.

[83] Greg. Tur. *Hist.* VI.11, 37; VII.232; IX.19.

[84] *Epist. Austras.* ed. Gundlach, no. 1 (*MGH, Epistolae Merowingici et Karolini Aevi*, pp. 112–13).

sixth or the eighth century presiding over a judicial assembly with a copy of *Lex Salica* under his arm'.[85] Yet this is not to be confused with the question whether, when kings (or wise men) promulgated law orally, such promulgation had any effect on the court. The content of a lawbook might influence court proceedings even when the book itself did not.

V. FROM NORTH-WEST EUROPE TO THE MEDITERRANEAN

As will be clear already, when we leave northern Gaul for the south we enter a very different legal world. It is worth, however, making a detour westwards to the Loire valley and to the Breton frontier. The first stop on this journey will be the region west and south of Paris, including Chartres, Châteaudun, Orleans and Blois, the setting of one of Gregory of Tours' tales of violence. Gregory's story may be compared with the *Pactus pro Tenore Pacis* promulgated by two sons of Clovis, Childebert I and Chlothar I, a text which was added, as we have seen, to *Lex Salica*.[86] The *Pactus* consists of four sections: first there are two brief introductory sentences, followed by an edict of Childebert; then comes Chlothar's edict, and, finally, a concluding statement, from both kings, permitting, in particular, pursuit of thieves across the boundary between their *regna*. The concluding section of the *Pactus* assumes an organized enforcement of the law based upon the *trustis*, the king's *comitatus*, and upon the *centena*, the hundred.[87] Chlothar's edict expected these *centenae* to prevent collusion between thieves and those charged with the night-watch. His scheme was that the *centena* to which the victim of the theft belonged had the responsibility of securing restitution. The victim's *centena* might itself find the stolen property by following tracks (livestock was presumably intended, especially perhaps cattle-rustling); it could also follow the tracks across the boundaries of its own territory into that of another *centena*, whereupon it would give formal notice to the other *centena* of what it had found and of the consequent duty of the other *centena* to find the stolen goods. This second *centena* might subsequently do the same to a third. There is, therefore, a framework of law-enforcement and clear provisions to determine where responsibility lay.

It is odd that Childebert's edict contains nothing as remarkable as the provisions in the name of his younger brother, even though Childebert's role as chief among the Merovingian kings of his generation seems so clear in the legislation of the church councils. There is a clear reference to a canon of the first council of Orleans (which itself refers back to the Theodosian Code), yet even this is part of Chlothar's edict.[88] The most interesting rule in Childebert's section of the text is one declaring that the

---

[85] In a letter to H. Nehlsen quoted in Nehlsen (1977) 451.   [86] *PLS* 79–93 (pp. 250–2).
[87] For a discussion of the origins of the *centena* and Chlothar's use of it, see Murray (1988) esp. 75–93.
[88] *PLS* 90.1; council of Orleans, 511, c. 1 (ed. de Clercq, *Concilia Galliae*, pp. 4–5).

victim of theft is not to be party to a private reconciliation with the thief, and, if he does attempt such a private settlement, the victim is to be considered as much a thief as the initial wrongdoer.

The *Pactus pro Tenore Pacis*, therefore, attempts to buttress the legal defences against theft by ensuring that the victim should always have someone from whom he can secure restitution. In particular, it charges the *centena* of the victim with his indemnification if it should fail to secure restitution from elsewhere, either the thief or another *centena* . The *trustis* was given an interest in catching the thief by being offered a share in his ransom. Finally, this method of securing both the welfare of the victim and a communal interest in apprehending the thief was not to be hampered by political boundaries; and here, of course, both kings had to agree to put their authority behind the whole process. Not only could the pursuit move from the territory of one *centena* to another, it could also move from one *regnum* to another.

Gregory of Tours' story about the minor war in 585 between the people of Châteaudun and Chartres, on the one side, and those of Orleans and Blois on the other, illustrates some of the issues that had earlier preoccupied Childebert I and Chlothar I.[89] The immediate context was the death of Chilperic in 584, but also relevant, in all probability, was the war between Chilperic and Guntram two years earlier in 583. Chilperic had become the most powerful of the Frankish kings and had taken possession of Clovis' *cathedra regni*, Paris; with Paris came Châteaudun, the possession of his brother Sigibert I until he was murdered in 575, and therefore claimed by Sigibert's son, Childebert II. Chilperic's hegemony had been threatened, first by defeat at the hands of Guntram in 583, and secondly by the forging of a new alliance in 584 between Guntram and Childebert. Orleans and Blois belonged to Guntram's *regnum* but were particularly exposed to attack by Chilperic's forces and had probably suffered considerably during his attack on Guntram in 583.

When Chilperic was, in his turn, murdered, the men of Orleans and Blois descended upon the territory of Châteaudun, removed everything that could move and burnt the rest. The tracks of the invading force were, however, followed by the men of Châteaudun and Chartres; yet the pursuers were not content to remove their stolen property but inflicted the same thoroughgoing harrying on the men of Orleans and Blois as the latter had meted out to them. They 'left nothing in the houses or outside the houses or of the houses'. On the other hand, Gregory, who was not normally restrained in his descriptions of riot and bloodshed, does not say that anyone lost his life as these Gallo-Roman *civitates* proceeded to inflict so much hard exercise on each other's livestock. Violence did, however,

---

[89] Greg. Tur. *Hist.* VII.2.

threaten when the men of Orleans took up arms to wreak vengeance upon
their attackers; but then the counts on both sides intervened and imposed
a peace 'until the hearing, that is, so that, on the day on which judgement
should be given, the side that had unjustly resorted to force against the
other should pay compensation, justice mediating between them. And thus
there was an end of the war.'

This, then, was a little war, not the night-time thief envisaged by the
Pactus pro Tenore Pacis but whole *civitates* resorting to plundering their neighbours' goods. And, since whole *civitates* were in action, the counts of those
civitates rather than any mere *centenarii* were required to put an end to the
trouble. Yet it is in many respects the same world as the *Pactus*. Men follow
the tracks of the livestock, not just across *civitas* boundaries but out of what
had been Chiliperic's kingdom into Guntram's. More strikingly still, the
death of a king and the uncertainty about who would succeed to his authority around Paris permitted a major outbreak of violence which had been
repressed while he was alive. The king might be killed by the assassins'
knives at Chelles, but while Chilperic still lived his capacity to repress violence was a very real social force. Nor was it treated simply as an outbreak
of vengeance by the dead king's victims on those who had been his subjects: both counts took the line that the men of Orleans and Blois, who had
started the affair, should pay compensation, and yet they were Guntram's
subjects who had, in 583, probably suffered from the men of Châteaudun.
Peace had been re-established after the war of 583 and the men of Orleans
and Blois were not entitled to stir up old grievances.

From further west, in Brittany, comes a short text in two recensions,
plausibly dated by Fleuriot to the sixth century but which could be of the
seventh or even perhaps the eighth century.[90] One of the recensions is entitled 'Excerpts from Laws of the Romans and the Franks'; the authenticity
of this title and the truth of the claim it embodies are both difficult to sub-
stantiate; but in form it is much closer to the additions to *Lex Salica* (other
than the overtly royal *Pactus pro Tenore Pacis* and *Decretio Childeberti*) than it
is to Irish or, later, Welsh law. It looks as though it may be the product of
some local assembly which took upon itself legislative authority; it is a valuable reminder of what might be happening in an independently-minded
province under intermittent Frankish hegemony.

The *Formulae Andegavenses* of *c.* 600 similarly give a clue, of a rather
different kind, to what was happening on the ground.[91] In many ways this
was a very Roman world, a *civitas* still retaining its *Gesta*, the record of
official transactions. Legal acts were not just remembered by a court, as

---

[90] The so-called *Canones Wallici*, ed. Bieler (1963) 136–59; Fleuriot (1971); Dumville (1984) is sceptical about the sixth-century dating.
[91] Zeumer (1886) 4–25; on pp. 2–3 Zeumer shows that real documents were used as models for this
collection.

they would be further north for centuries to come, but written in the record. The *Formulae* were thus directly useful in a local context, for they told the notary how he should write the documents that would then be recorded in the *Gesta*. In a legal context, Angers remained the focus of Anjou; there one would find both court and notary, and there would be the record of past legal acts. The court, however, seems to have a large element of communal self-help about it: it may be presided over by the abbot of the monastery or by another important figure – perhaps this helps to explain why *Lex Salica* uses the general term *thunginus*, 'eminent man', for a president of the court.[92] Finally, even here, on the edge of Aquitaine, which would in the seventh century emerge as Romania and a land of Roman law, we meet *rachinburgii*.[93] Significantly, they appear in a document about homicide and the threat of feud. Many of the formulae in the collection may be as early as the reign of Childebert II;[94] this one is probably a somewhat later addition and may be an instance of growing Frankish influence on the legal practices of the Loire region.

In the neighbouring Tours, Gregory himself was involved in attempting to settle a feud between natives of the Touraine; and, moreover, he acted together with the count and the other *iudices*, the latter perhaps *rachinburgii*.[95] While, however, Gregory's problem was to bring peace to a feud in which everyone knew who the killers were, in the Angers document the homicide was the much more serious secret killing – that is, murder. The person accused of the offence in Angers is said to have denied it 'absolutely and with vigour'. Faced with uncertainty, the public court of Angers did not resort to the ordeal, beloved of the Franks,[96] but to Gregory's own favoured answer to cruel uncertainty, the power of the holy dead conjoined with that of his neighbours. The accused man was to swear an oath with twelve others as compurgators that he was as innocent as he claimed. The formula for the official notification of the oath prescribed the following declaration:

By this holy place and all the divine powers of patronage (*patrocinia*) of the saints who rest here, inasmuch as the man . . . and his brothers . . . have accused me of killing or asking to be killed on some occasion their kinsman . . ., I have not killed him, nor have I asked anyone to kill him, nor was I in the know, nor was I ever a consenting party to his death, and I owe nothing in respect of this claim, except that I have undergone, in accordance with the laws, this appropriate oath, which has been assigned to me in judgement.

The accusers were not always content to accept such oaths,[97] which may explain why the formula seems to resonate with fear, not just of the powers

---

[92] For the abbot, see *Formulae Andegavenses* ed. Zeumer, nos. 7, 10 etc; for the *agens*, apparently of the church, nos. 11, 28; for the *prepositus*, no. 24.   [93] *Formulae Andegavenses* ed. Zeumer, no. 50.
[94] Buchner (1953) 50.   [95] Greg. Tur. *Hist.* VII.47.   [96] Bartlett (1986) 4–5.
[97] Greg. Tur. *Hist.* VII.23, where procedure corresponds closely to the Angers document, but the accusers remain unconvinced; and v.32, where the father's oath also fails to convince.

of those who live with God, but of the vengeance of men who could not in honour be satisfied until they had found the killer of their kinsman.

VI. BARBARIAN AND ROMAN LAW

The combination in the *Formulae Andegavenses* of elements from different sources raises, in a usefully sharp form, the old question of the relationship between barbarian and Roman laws. In Tours Gregory, the bishop, paid many of the church's *solidi* to heal a blood-feud, in the context of desperate efforts within and without the court, by judges and by the bishop himself, to make peace.[98] For the sake of the peace of the *civitas*, therefore, the bishop became the friend of the killer and paid *wergild* on his behalf. Gregory in the role of go-between was, although a bishop of proud senatorial descent, working in a legal world closer in some respects to that of *Lex Salica* than to the Theodosian Code. Romans feuded among themselves; so did Jews; Romans feuded with Saxons.[99] Yet the will of Remigius, bishop of Rheims, who died *c.* 532, reveals something different: the document itself rests directly on a particular provision in the Theodosian Code.[100] Similarly, the bishops assembled by order of Clovis at Orleans in 511 appealed in their first canon to secular law as well as to the authority of earlier councils, but the secular law to which they appealed was the Theodosian Code.[101] In the early sixth century the Theodosian Code was in use throughout Gaul.[102]

There is a scatter of general pronouncements on the legal relationship of barbarian to Roman, the upshot of which is that cases between Romans were settled by Roman law, while cases between barbarians or between barbarian and Roman were settled by barbarian law.[103] More complex, however, is the rule – plainly a royal *constitutio* – in *Lex Ribuaria*:[104]

We also decree the following, that Franks, Burgundians, Alamans or of whatever nation someone is who has taken up residence within the Ribuarian province and is impleaded at law, he should give answer according to the law of the place (*locus*) where he was born.

This passage explains why the common inclusion in a single manuscript of different national laws might be useful, but it also raises problems, first by its

---

[98] Greg. Tur. *Hist.* VII.47; Wallace-Hadrill (1962); James (1983).

[99] Greg. Tur. *Hist.* III.33, VI.17, VII.3.

[100] *Testamentum Remigii* ed. B. Krusch, *MGH SRM* III.336–47 and *CCSL* 117/1, 473–9, appeals to *C.Th.* IV.4.7; Jones, Grierson and Crook (1957); for the date of Remigius' death see *PLRE* II.938; Wood (1993).   [101] *Concilia Galliae* ed. de Clercq, p. 4.

[102] The legal knowledge of the ex-slave Andarchius, *legis Theodosianae libris eruditus*, helped to recommend him to King Sigibert: Greg. Tur. *Hist.* IV.46.

[103] *Lib. Const.* Pref. 3, 8; cf. 22 and 55, *Constitutiones Extravagantes* 20 (ed. de Salis, *Leg. Burg.* 31, 32, 90, 119); *Preceptio* of Chlothar II, c. 4: 'Inter Romanus negutia causarum romanis legebus praecepemus terminari': *Capitularia Regum Francorum* ed. Boretius, 1.1, *MGH*, Leg. II (Hanover, 1881) 1.19.

[104] *Lex Ribuaria* 35.3, ed. Beyerle and Buchner, *MGH*, Leg. I, III.2 (Hanover, 1954), p. 87.

use of the phrase 'the law of the place', *lex loci*, and secondly by its implication that the law under which a case is judged depends on the nationality of the defendant. The first suggests that legal nationality had come to depend on a version of the Roman concept of *origo*: as one belonged to a given *civitas* by having been born there, whatever the origin of one's parents, so here a defendant born in Burgundy (apparently whether or not he would have been regarded as a Burgundian according to Burgundian law) is to plead according to Burgundian law, but his children, if they were born in Ribuaria, would plead according to Ribuarian law. The second implication of this passage is that a case between, say, a Burgundian plaintiff and a Roman defendant would be judged by Roman law; this contradicts the provisions of the Burgundian *Liber Constitutionum*.[105] It may well be that the rule in *Lex Ribuaria* represents a crucial stage in the process of the territorialization of national identity in Francia: by the eighth century, natives of the lands north of the Loire, apart from the Bretons, were Franks, while those to the south were Romans (Aquitanians). While in the fifth and sixth centuries Remigius could live and die a Roman in one of the Frankish capitals, this was increasingly difficult for his successors in the seventh century and impossible by the mid eighth.[106]

The rule distinguishing between the jurisdictions of Roman and Burgundian law applies to cases in which two parties are in dispute. Disputes, however, are only one part of the law; another component consists of those devices which people may use to give legal effect to their wishes, such as gifts or sales. These legal acts are mostly never the subject of a dispute. Here there seems to be more room for manoeuvre. Thus the Burgundian *Liber Constitutionum* allows a barbarian who wishes to make a donation to confirm it either according to Roman custom, by a written document, or in the barbarians fashion, by witnesses.[107] Such a liberty to choose would likewise make perfect sense of the Frankish *Formulae* which contain model texts for all sorts of legal acts, very probably available just as much to Franks as to Romans.

Some law promulgated by barbarian kings was intended to apply as much to Romans as to barbarians: this is evident, for example, from the preface to the *Edictum Theodorici* where it is made clear that the edict does not abrogate from the *leges* and *ius publicum* – that is, Roman law – and that the edict's provisions are to be followed by Roman and barbarian alike.[108] The same is true of the Edict of Athalaric.[109] The identity of those subject

---

[105] *Prima Constitutio* 3, where the *leges nostrae* which have been *emendatae* would appear to be the *Liber Constitutionum* itself, since c. 8 refers to cases between Romans being judged by Roman law as if the latter was quite distinct from *leges nostrae*.   [106] Ewig (1958).

[107] *Liber Constitutionum* 50.2 (ed. de Salis, *Leg. Burg.* 92).

[108] *Edictum Theodorici Regis* ed. Baviera, p. 684. The identity of the Theodoric who promulgated the Edict is disputed: see Vismara (1967), who favours Theoderic, king of the Visigoths; in favour of Theoderic the Ostrogoth is Nehlsen (1972) 120–7; Nehlsen (1969).

[109] Ed. Mommsen, *Cassiodori Senatoris Variae*, *MGH AA* xii, ix.18.

to a law cannot, however, be inferred from the occurrence of the word 'edict' in the title: Chilperic's Edict appears to apply to Franks living to the south of the Garonne.[110] Like the *Pactus pro Tenore Pacis* of Childebert I and Chlothar I, it refers expressly to *Lex Salica*. The Edict of Rothari contained *lex*.[111] For the Franks and the Lombards, therefore, the Roman distinction between *lex* and *edictum* did not persist in the same way as it did under the Ostrogoths.

An essential distinction when discussing the question of who was subject to a particular law is between primary and secondary rules – that is, between rules that apply directly to the population in question and rules directed at judges and other officials concerned with the administration of the law. Burgundian law has, as we have seen, a particularly clear statement of the respective jurisdictions of Roman and barbarian law; Burgundy also provides us with a text of Roman law, the *Lex Romana Burgundionum*, which makes no such appeal to royal authority as does the *Liber Constitutionum*.[112] Yet the Burgundian kings naturally had no hesitation in making secondary rules which applied as much to Roman officials as to Burgundians.[113] The distinction between primary and secondary rules is therefore valuable for overtly royal legislation. It must, however, be handled with care when dealing with Frankish law. The normal rule in *Lex Salica* was, as we have seen, of the form, 'If anyone has done X, let him be judged liable to Y'; it is therefore a rule addressed to judges. Yet it is not secondary in the same sense as a royal decree directed at officials. The standard secondary rule is a normal part of a bureaucratic state with a central authority seeking to direct a body of officials. *Lex Salica* is mainly a set of instructions from men admitted to be wise in the law addressed to those who need training in knowledge of the law. It is not so much a part of a bureaucratic state as a partial written expression of the way in which a legal tradition is handed on.

VII. BURGUNDIAN AND GOTHIC LAW

Among the southern barbarian kingdoms, the law of the Burgundians made the most overt challenge to the imperial monopoly of law. In form and style, and also in its perception of itself, it aped the imperial constitutions collected together in the Theodosian Code.[114] The legislator refers to

---

[110] Beyerle (1961).   [111] *Edictus Rothari* Prol.; cc. 12, 171, 386.

[112] Thus the evidence for royal responsibility for the *Lex Romana* is to be found in the Pref. (c. 8, ed. de Salis, *Leg. Burg.* 32) to the *Liber Constitutionum* rather than in the *Lex Romana* itself.

[113] *Constitutiones Extravagantes* XIX (in the form of a letter from Gundobad to all counts), XXI.11 (*ut omnes comites, tam Burgundionum quam Romanorum*).

[114] *Liber Constitutionum* is the original name of the code: Pref. ed. de Salis, *Leg. Burg.* 30.

himself and is even liable to offer lofty justifications for particular decrees.[115] He has no doubt that his decrees have the status of *lex*; they were not mere edicts.[116]

The laws ascribed to the Visigothic king Euric, and by modern scholars called after him the *Codex Euricianus*, are preserved only in part.[117] Enough survives, however, to show that they have a very different character from the Burgundian *Liber Constitutionum*. They consist of a series of numbered sections broken up by titles which are, however, not themselves numbered.[118] The title thus has a less central position then it does in the structure of the Theodosian Code and the *Liber Constitutionum*. There is little self-referential language and no lofty justifications.[119] In formal terms the *Codex Euricianus* is closer to the Ostrogothic *Edictum Theodorici* than to the Burgundian *Liber Constitutionum*. On the other hand, it does seem to conceive of itself as *lex* rather than as edict.[120] This is not surprising: Theoderic the Ostrogoth needed to take up an ambiguous stance allowing him to appear to be part of the empire; for that reason it was politic for him to issue an edict like a magistrate of the past. The Visigoths, on other hand, had not been formally attached to the empire since the beginning of Euric's reign in 466.[121] The promulgation of the *Breviarium Alarici* at the end of the reign of Euric's son, Alaric II, demonstrates that Roman law had remained in force for the Roman subjects of the Visigoths. Euric's legislation thus served to give Gothic law the dignity of a written form in good legal Latin, while it also expressed the authority of an independent monarch. According to Levy, 'it may safely be called the best legislative work of the fifth century . . . superior to the Code of Theodosius, which was a mere anthology, superior to the contemporary imperial decrees with their obscure verbosity'.[122]

Yet although Euric intended his rules to have the full status and title of law, the substance of the law holds a balance between Roman and barbarian. We have already seen that, when it comes to confirmation of a donation, the

---

[115] *Liber Constitutionum* 52.2; 53.1; 54.1; 74.1; 75.1.

[116] For example, *Liber Constitutionum* Pref. cc. 9–11; Sigismund talks of *nostra lex* as well as of *praesentia edicta* in *Constitutiones Extravagantes* 20 (ed. de Salis, *Leg. Burg.* 119).

[117] *Codex Euricianus* ed. d'Ors (1960), and in Zeumer (1902) 3–32. Nehlsen (1972) 155–6 n. 18 places it between 469 and 476/7 on the basis of Sid. Ap. *Epp.* II.1.3; VIII.3.2. A useful survey with bibliography is Nehlsen (1984). I do not understand H. Wolfram's argument in favour of attributing the *Codex* to Alaric: Wolfram (1988) 196. [118] Thus *Tit. De Venditionibus* is prefixed to CCLXXXVI.

[119] In CCLXXVII Euric refers to himself and to his father: 'Antiquos vero terminos [*sic*] stare iubemus, sicut et bonae mem[ori]ae pater noster in alia lege praecepi[t].' Cf. Levy (1963b).

[120] CCLXXVII, CCCXXVII (ed. Zeumer (1902) pp. 5, 6, 25).

[121] Sid. Ap. *Ep.* VIII.3, to Leo of Narbonne, associating military prowess and legal achievement: 'Sepone pauxillulum conclamatissimas declamationes, quas oris regii uice conficis, quibus ipse rex inclitus . . . modo per promotae limitem sortis ut populos sub armis, sic frenat arma sub legibus.' This passage has given rise to the suggestion that Leo participated in the redaction of the *Codex Euricianus*.

[122] Levy (1963b) 209.

Burgundian *Liber Constitutionum* perceives written evidence as the Roman custom, while witnesses are characteristic of barbarian tradition. It is to be noted that this is a matter of distinctive customs as to how a transaction may be guarded against the possibility of subsequent dispute, not an issue about the validity of a gift or a sale: Roman law required neither documentary confirmation nor witnesses in order to make a gift or sale of movables valid.[123] In the Ostrogothic *Edictum Theodorici* it is declared that a donation of movable wealth may be confirmed by written evidence while a donation of immovable property, whether urban or rural, required to be confirmed by a document containing the subscriptions of witnesses – in other words, a charter – and that it was to be recorded in the *gesta municipalia*.[124] Euric, treating of a sale rather than a donation, allows confirmation either by written document or by witnesses without any observation as to whether one was Roman and the other barbarian.[125]

The end of the empire in the west brought about the extension of written law to the barbarian settlers. Initially, Roman law itself remained in force, alongside the laws of the various nations, even as far north as Cologne. Only in Britain did Roman law virtually disappear; to judge by the later Welsh law, as well as by Gallic attitudes to Bretons in the fifth and sixth centuries, that may have been because of its weak hold on the Britons. In Gaul, there is a marked contrast between the Roman pretensions of the Burgundians, perhaps derived from the political ambitions of Gundobad in the earlier part of his reign, and the Frankish tradition of law. Among the Franks, the legal tradition remained attached to the constituent peoples of the Frankish federation, to the Salians rather than to the Franks as a whole. This was associated with a less overt role for the king in lawmaking: until some date in Clovis' reign the Salians had more than one king. Among the Burgundians, however, a kingship that was much more assertive in the legal sphere also ensured that one law prevailed for all the Burgundians and any other barbarians within their kingdom. At the level of Frankish or Burgundian identity, rather than, say, Salian identity, Burgundian law is more ethnic precisely because it is more Roman and more royal. Gregory of Tours says that Gundobad made laws for the Burgundians, although he never says as much about any Frankish king.[126] When rulers such as Gundobad asserted their independence as legislators *vis-à-vis* the empire, they did so as kings of their own peoples; hence the less overtly royal character of the *Lex Romana Burgundionum* as compared with the *Liber Constitutionum*. Barbarian kings were most anxious to pro-

---

[123] Cf. *Lex Romana Burgundionum* 35.2.   [124] *Edictum Theodorici* cc. 51–2, ed. J. Baviera, p. 692.
[125] *Codex Euricianus* CCLXXXVI, ed. Zeumer (1902) p. 11. Cf. Classen (1977b) 20–5; Zeumer (1899) 20.   [126] Greg. Tur. *Hist.* 11.33.

claim their role as legislators for their own peoples when their kingdoms lay in the more Romanized south: they, much more than Franks and Anglo-Saxons, needed to assert a political independence of the empire; and, in the legal sphere, they asserted that independence by opposing a king's law for his *gens* to the law of an empire.

CHAPTER 11

THE ARMY, *c.* 420–602

MICHAEL WHITBY

The late Roman armies of the fourth and early fifth century are relatively well documented: Ammianus and other narrative historians describe them at work in their main theatres of operations on the Rhine, Danube and Persian frontiers, as well as in Britain and North Africa; the Theodosian Code preserves a range of laws pertaining to their creation, sustenance and functioning; the *Notitia Dignitatum* offers a view, albeit complicated by partial revision, of the structure and disposition of forces in both east and west.[1] The year 420 marks a convenient break: between then and the Persian wars of Anastasius' reign (502–7), recorded by Procopius and Joshua the Stylite, there is little reliable narrative of Roman military action, and no *Notitia*; also, there are few relevant laws, since only seven of the 175 titles in Theodosian Code VII, the book devoted to military matters, date from after 420, though eleven laws among the *Novels* of Theodosius II and four of Valentinian III can be added. During these years the western Roman army ceased to exist as a state institution, being superseded by the military forces of the successor kingdoms in Gaul, Spain, Africa and finally Italy, none of which maintained a standing army. In the east, however, the army, and hence the empire, survived in a recognizable form through to the early seventh century. The nature and causes of these distinct developments require explanation; but first, an overview of the late Roman army.

I. TROOPS: CATEGORIES, CONDITIONS OF SERVICE, NUMBERS

The Roman element in the late imperial army was divided into garrison or territorial units and mobile troops, a distinction that broadly accords with that between *limitanei* and *comitatenses*: the former were assigned to frontier regions, the latter notionally to the company of the emperor. The distinction was not absolute, since units might be transferred without necessarily being recategorized, but it does reflect ways in which armies were perceived and functioned. The *limitanei* were under the immediate command of *duces*, in charge of a sector of the frontier, but for operational purposes they could

---

[1] For discussion see, Jones, *LRE* 607–54; Hoffmann (1969); Tomlin (1987).

be incorporated into the mobile armies led by *magistri militum*. The relatively static *limitanei* naturally dug themselves in to their localities. Service in the imperial army gave influence and a desirable status in places where the military risk was slight: units at Syene in Egypt and Nessana in Palestine in the sixth century reveal considerable family continuity among their members,[2] and, though this can be explained by the legal requirement for veterans' sons to enlist in place of their fathers, enrolment was a privilege for which a fee was payable, like entrance to a club. On some frontiers, if not on all (the evidence is eastern), *limitanei* were assigned lands to ensure their maintenance, and such properties were sufficiently desirable to be coveted by outsiders.[3]

The quality of *limitanei* was open to criticism, particularly by observers eager to accuse an emperor of inadequate attention to provincial safety; stationary units might be allocated the weaker members of a draft of conscripts and were accorded less advantageous tax exemptions for their families. On the other hand, they guaranteed an imperial presence in frontier regions, thereby helping to protect local security and communications and to define the sphere of Roman authority. The cost was moderate, since the soldiers were partly supported by the territories they directly protected, and eastern emperors sensibly took steps to maintain the *limitanei*: Theodosius II legislated in 443 that numbers and training be kept up, various abuses eradicated, and an annual report submitted by the *magister officiorum* in the imperial consistory; Justinian re-established them in Africa to protect the frontiers of the newly reconquered provinces. When Attila wished to secure his authority over the Huns, he demanded that an uncultivated no-man's-land five days' journey in width should be created south of the Danube: Roman presence at frontiers mattered, since this helped to control all cross-border movement, whether hostile, commercial or transhumant.[4]

The *comitatenses* can be divided into two broad categories, those in the central or palatine forces that were based in the vicinity of the imperial capitals, Ravenna and Constantinople, and were commanded by a *magister militum praesentalis*, and those in regional armies commanded by *magistri militum* with a geographic specification. At Constantinople there were two praesental armies, probably billeted on either side of the Bosphorus; there were three regional commands in the east (Illyricum, Thrace and Oriens) and one in the west (Gaul); there was still a smaller, but significant, group of *comitatenses* in Africa commanded by a *comes*, although comparable units in Spain, Britain and the western Balkans had probably ceased to exist by 420. When not on active campaign, units of mobile armies were often billeted in cities, a procedure open to considerable exploitation in spite of the legislation intended to regulate abuses. Units stationed closest to the imperial

[2] Keenan (1990); Rémondon (1961); Kraemer (1958).   [3] Theodosius II, *Nov.* 5.3; 24.
[4] Theodosius II, *Nov.* 24; *CJ* 1.27.2.8; Priscus fr. 11.1.11–14 (Blockley).

centre were naturally more prestigious than regional units, but there were no legal distinctions within the *comitatenses*, in contrast to indications of their superiority to *limitanei*.

Both categories of troops were recruited through a mixture of the obligation to hereditary service imposed on veterans' sons and traditional conscription applied on the basis of provincial tax registers. Conscription was, not surprisingly, unpopular both with landowners who might lose essential farm labour and with potential conscripts threatened by service at a remote location. Monetary commutation of recruits (*aurum tironicum*) offered an escape from the burden, and was accepted at the government's discretion, especially when there was no desperate need for manpower and from areas whose inhabitants did not have a military reputation. All recruits received a certificate of enrolment and were assigned to a particular regiment, after which they became subject to military law: desertion during the conscription process could be excused, but not thereafter.[5]

Mobile armies were stiffened by the recruitment of non-Roman troops to meet particular military demands, and palatine forces also benefited from the presence of imperial guards. Non-Romans served in the army under various arrangements: some were volunteers, for whom imperial service offered regular pay and relative security and prosperity; others came from tribes defeated by the Romans or constrained by other circumstances to surrender, who had accepted a military obligation as part of their peace settlement. In the latter case, lands might be granted to provide support during military inactivity and stabilize the tribesmen in an accessible location. Both methods of acquiring non-Roman soldiers continued in operation, but the most prominent way of employing tribesmen during the fifth century was as federate units. These functioned as ethnic contingents under the leadership of their own chief – basically a tribal, or quasi-tribal, war-band which might vary in size from a few hundred to the 10,000 or so controlled by each of the Theoderics in the Balkans in the 470s. The commander received a Roman title – *magister militum* for the powerful and successful, with the consulship as the ultimate accolade – and this gave the tribesmen access to Roman salaries and provisions. Roman traditionalists like Vegetius, or those with an axe to grind like Synesius, viewed the employment of 'barbarians' as a disgraceful weakening of the army. In reality, exploitation of the military potential of neighbours had been an accepted strategy from the Republic onwards, as a method of annexing external resources and defusing potential hostility. Roman reliance on federates, however, had disadvantages in that the mechanics of the agreements served to increase the independent power of non-Roman leaders: their strength as patrons grew through disbursement of Roman resources, while

---

[5] Jones, *LRE* 614–19; Carrié (1986); Whitby (1995) sec. 4.

they remained outside the institutional structures and discipline of the state army. In the west in the fifth century independent action by federates on various occasions contributed significantly to the collapse of central authority.[6]

The main units in the imperial guard were the *scholae*, five regiments in the west, seven in the east, each 500 strong under Justinian. In the east there was also a small unit of *candidati*, forty in total, who served as a personal bodyguard for emperors, a duty which they ceded to the *excubitores*, a corps of 300 formed by the emperor Leo to protect the palace entrances. Close attendance upon the emperor was a privilege, so that individuals might pay to enlist in the *scholae* for social rather than military reasons, a tendency that Justinian exploited by enrolling four supernumerary regiments. The *candidati* acquired an important ceremonial role at imperial receptions and processions in Constantinople, but this does not mean that they, or the *scholae*, lost all military competence as Procopius and Agathias allege in criticizing Justinian, since individuals are attested on active service. The *excubitores*, however, remained the élite guards into the seventh century, and their commander, the *comes excubitorum*, became one of the most important men at court, a virtual heir presumptive or close member of the imperial family from Justin II to Heraclius.[7]

Remuneration for soldiers was provided in a mixture of money and kind, the proportions of which might vary according to availability or the needs of the army. Donatives at imperial accessions and quinquennial anniversaries, at least until allegedly abolished by Justinian, constituted an important part of the cash element: eastern emperors from Leo to Justin I paid an accession donative of five *solidi* plus a pound of silver, and this was clearly a standard amount, since the nine *solidi* paid by Tiberius represent this sum (with the silver commuted to gold).[8] Ration allocations (*annonae*) formed the basis for the calculation of salaries, with officers and those with special responsibilities being accorded multiple units. *Annonae* could either be supplied in kind or commuted into cash, a flexibility which probably improved the theoretical efficiency of the army by ensuring that soldiers received what they needed; but this also introduced the possibility of military exploitation of producers/tax-payers, since prices, and hence possible commutation tariffs, were bound to vary throughout the year. Clothing, financed by a special tax levy, was provided from the production of state clothing factories, though commutation of five-sixths of this distribution too was sanctioned by a law of 423. Military equipment, including the provision of cavalry horses, was

---

[6] Jones, *LRE* 611–12; Liebeschuetz, *Barbarians and Bishops* chs. 2–4; Vegetius 1.28; Syn. *De Regno* 22–6; Cameron, *Mediterranean World* ch. 4; cf. ch. 18 (Wood), pp. 505–6 below.

[7] Frank (1969); Procop. *Secret History* 24.15–23; Agathias, *Hist.* v.15.2–6, with Mary Whitby (1987) 465–6. For the *fasti* of *comites excubitorum*, see *PLRE* iii.1510.

[8] Durliat (1990b) 46–9; Hendy, *Studies* 175–8, 481; John Eph. *HE* iii.11.

the state's responsibility in the fifth century, but commutation was permitted at some stage. Cash substitution clearly benefited soldiers, since Maurice's attempt in 594 to reintroduce state provision contributed to a mutiny in the Balkan army.[9] Overall, supplying the army, and especially an army on campaign, represented by far the largest, costliest and most complex single element in the administration of the empire, and so would be the first to falter at times of crisis or dislocation.

Calculation of numbers in the late Roman army is a game with enough variables to make a definite solution impossible. John Lydus in the sixth century offers a global figure for the Diocletianic establishment two centuries previously: 389,704 in the armies, 45,562 in the fleets, a total of 435,266. Precision may lend credibility. Writing slightly later, Agathias offers 645,000 as the total military establishment at an unspecified date, which he contrasts with the effective Justinianic fighting force of only 150,000, but he had an axe to grind about Justinian's supposed military neglect.[10] Justification of, or extrapolation from, these figures on the basis of details of types of units recorded in the *Notitia* is circular, since the sizes of individual units are not recorded. The detailed calculations of Jones, however, produce a plausible balance, with the eastern establishment outnumbering the western in a ratio of 7:5. *Limitanei* constituted about two-thirds of eastern forces, but only a half of western, and here the *Notitia*'s record of Gallic and African *limitanei* drafted into the mobile armies reveals the impact of the collapse of the Rhine and Danube frontiers after 406. But precise numbers are less certain.[11]

Global figures, if known, might help to determine the cost of the military establishment,[12] but do not reveal the empire's disposable military strength, which depended on its ability to concentrate and provision troops in particular locations. The largest armament attested for the fifth or sixth century is the naval expedition mounted by Leo against Vandal Africa in 468, supposedly 100,000 strong, an unsuccessful outlay of men and money from which the east took time to recover: the cost is recorded as over seven million, or nine million, *solidi*.[13] On land, the rebel Vitalian is said by Marcellinus to have led more than 60,000 men, while the eastern army of 52,000 in 503 is described by Procopius as the largest before or after. The extraordinary nature of this army is suggested also by the special measures needed to ensure provisions: a praetorian prefect, Apion, supervised supplies, the inhabitants of Edessa received wheat to be baked for the troops, and finally Apion returned to Alexandria to organize further supplies, while a replacement prefect, Calliopus, controlled arrangements on the frontier.

[9] Jones, *LRE* 623–30; Carrié (1995) sec. 2; Theophylact VII.1.
[10] John Lydus, *De Mensibus* 1.27; Agathias, *Hist.* V.13.7–8.
[11] Jones, *LRE* 683–4; Whitby (1995) sec. 3.   [12] Calculations in Hendy, *Studies* 175–8.
[13] Procop. *Wars* III.6.1, with Hendy, *Studies* 221.

This massive army could only move slowly, and the scope of military oper-
tions was severely curtailed by logistical problems: this was one reason why
Anastasius' generals demanded the construction of Dara on the eastern
frontier as an accessible base from which to move against Nisibis.[14] A more
normal size for a large army on the eastern front was 20,000, as at
Callinicum in 530; 10,000–15,000 was perhaps a normal maximum in the
Balkans, where repeated invasions had undermined the administrative substructures for large-scale deployment away from the Danube, which the
Roman fleet controlled.[15]

Campaigns away from normal lines of supply required careful preparations. For Belisarius' expedition against the Vandals, supplies of *bucellum*,
biscuit, were prepared, but inadequate firing caused this to deteriorate and
when the fleet reached the Peloponnese, Belisarius requisitioned supplies
from local inhabitants to avert starvation and disease: receipts must have
been issued, to be offset against future tax demands, part of the bureaucratic palaver of the late Roman army on the move.[16] Movement by land
was harder and slower, and expeditions would have been supported by
extended wagon-trains: against the Bulgars in 499, Aristus' army of 15,000
campaigned from Constantinople with 520 wagons, while the vulnerability
of such transport is illustrated by the Roman ambush in 479 which captured 2,000 wagons from a Gothic column that must have stretched over
five miles or more.[17]

II. NAVIES

Relatively little is known about Roman fleets in the fifth and sixth century,
partly because there were few major sea battles. Vandal naval dominance
after their arrival in Carthage, a surprising achievement for a Germanic
group, posed a threat with which the western empire could not cope;
Sicilian and Italian coasts were regularly raided, which contributed
significantly to western collapse. In 455 the proximity of Geiseric's large
fleet encouraged the overthrow of Petronius Maximus, and the Vandals
then thoroughly pillaged Rome. In 456 Ricimer defeated Vandal raiders on
the plains of Agrigento in Sicily, and on Corsica, but each time he seems
only to have achieved a land victory: these perhaps resembled the success
in Campania under Majorian when the Vandals, though prevented from
ravaging, could flee to the safety of their ships. In 456 the Vandals deployed
sixty ships and, in spite of reverses, retained control of the sea and interrupted the food supply of Rome, which contributed to the unpopularity

---

[14] Marc. Com. s.a. 514; Procop. *Wars* 1.8.1–5 (Marc. Com. s.a. 503 records 15,000 men, but this perhaps relates to only part of the overall force); Joshua 54, 70, 77; Zachariah VII.6.

[15] Procop. *Wars* 1.18.5; Marc. Com. s.a. 499, 505. Whitby (1995) sec. 6.

[16] Procop. *Wars* III.13.12–20.   [17] Marc. Com. s.a. 499; Malchus fr. 20.226–48.

and subsequent overthrow of Avitus.[18] At some point a storm in the straits of Messina overwhelmed some ships along with their crews, presumably a naval squadron; if these were Romans it would help to explain their incapacity at sea.[19]

Majorian is praised for initiating a massive ship-building programme in Italy, but in 460 he still chose to campaign against the Vandals by the land route through Spain, partly perhaps as a means of asserting his authority along the Mediterranean fringes of Gaul and Spain, but partly because of the difficulty of confronting the Vandals on the open sea. A fleet of 300 ships was assembled for the crossing to Africa, but Geiseric managed to capture or destroy enough to thwart the invasion; Majorian was soon deposed, the third imperial victim of Vandal naval power.[20] When Sidonius praised Anthemius in 468 he referred to the enormous Vandal navy that annually threatened destruction, but hoped that the new emperor would at last activate the unused fleets – to no avail; without substantial naval help from the east, nothing could be achieved.[21] A Roman fleet survived at Classis, the port of Ravenna, down to Ostrogothic times, and this could be mobilized against fears of attack from the east, but the Vandals dominated the western Mediterranean: in 533 Gelimer could despatch 120 ships to recover Sardinia.[22] In the English Channel and down the Atlantic coast of Gaul, Saxon pirates were the major threat, but the Visigoths maintained a fleet in the Garonne to deter them; we hear of this under the command of the Aquitanian Namatius.[23]

The eastern Mediterranean was dominated by the Roman fleet, which from its dockyards on the Golden Horn ensured the safety of Constantinople and prevented problems in Europe spilling over into Asia, and vice versa. In 515 the rebel Vitalian gathered 200 ships from Thracian ports, but these were dispersed in the Bosphorus when the praetorian prefect Marinus attacked them with some sort of chemical incendiary agent. In 626 the professionalism of the Roman fleet saved Constantinople during the Avar siege, since naval patrols prevented the Slav *monoxyla* from transporting Shahvaraz's Persian army to the European side and from outflanking the capital's mighty land walls by attacking down the Golden Horn.[24] The Hellespont was similarly protected: in 400 Fravitta with a squadron of light *liburnae* overturned the rafts on which Gainas was attempting to ferry his men to Asia, and in a similar operation Germanus

---

[18] Priscus fr. 31.1; Hydat. *Chron.* 177, 176; Sid. Ap. *Carm.* 11.367–70, v.388–440.

[19] Priscus fr. 31.2.

[20] Sid. Ap. *Carm.* v.441–8; Priscus fr. 36.1; John of Antioch fr. 203; Mar. Avent. s.a. 460.

[21] Sid. Ap. *Carm.* 11.348–50, 384–6; Priscus fr. 39.   [22] Procop. *Wars* 111.11.23.

[23] Sid. Ap. *Ep.* viii.6.13–17.

[24] Malalas 403.3–405.20; Evagr. *HE* 111.43 (515). *Chron. Pasch.* 722.14–725.1; Theodore Syncellus 307–8, 310–12; George of Pisidia, *Bell. Avar.* 441–74 (626).

prevented the Kotrigurs in 558 from outflanking the Long Walls across the neck of the Gallipoli peninsula.[25]

The eastern empire could also despatch large naval expeditionary forces to the west: against Africa Leo allegedly sent 1,100 ships, while in 533 Belisarius' expedition consisted of 92 *dromons*, warships with single banks of oars rowed by men from Constantinople, which escorted 500 troop-transports crewed by sailors from Egypt, Ionia and Cilicia; Anastasius sent 100 *dromons* plus 100 other ships to ravage southern Italy in 507/8.[26] The navy preserved links with armies in Italy when, at the height of the Gothic counter-offensive in the 540s, the Roman hold was restricted to the coastal fringes where sea-power allowed isolated garrisons to hang on. Its most regular military duty, however, was probably in the Balkans, where control of the Danube was vital for the maintenance of frontier outposts. Sirmium, briefly recovered by the Romans in the 570s, could resist the Avars until access up the Danube and Sava was blocked by the construction of bridges, and Singidunum was similarly threatened in the early 590s until the Roman navy arrived. Naval superiority also facilitated Roman assaults against Slavs and Avars, and Maurice's *Strategikon* includes recommendations for the conduct of amphibious operations beyond the Danube.[27] The Avars had no maritime skill, and relied on Slavs or Lombards to produce their boats, but they appreciated the role of the Roman fleet, since they attempted to control the Danube Cataracts: here occupation of the river banks could prevent ships from being towed against the strong current, which would thwart naval operations further upstream.[28] The eastern navy may receive little attention in the sources, but it was clearly well organized and contributed importantly to the empire's security.

III. WESTERN COLLAPSE

In the western empire the cohesion of imperial armies was progressively undermined by a combination of tribal invasions and civil wars. At the start of Honorius' reign western armies appeared to be sufficiently strong to defend their traditional Rhine and Danube frontiers,[29] but the massive movement across the Rhine in December 406 changed the picture. Honorius' inability to protect his territories prompted local commanders or governors to assert their own power, often in combination with one of

---

[25] Zos. v.20.3–21.4; Agathias, *Hist.* v.21.7–23.1.
[26] Procop. *Wars* III.6.1 with Theophanes 115.21–30; Procop. *Wars* III.10–11; Marc. Com. s.a. 508.
[27] John Eph. *HE* vi.24, 30–2; Theophylact vi.4.1–2, vii.10–11; Maurice, *Strat.* xii.b.21.
[28] Paul. Diac. *Hist. Lang.* iv.20; Theophylact viii.5.5–7; Whitby, *Maurice* 87–8, 153–4.
[29] Elton (1992) 168.

the tribal groupings whose military success had contributed to the destruction of confidence in the emperor. These revolts could only be suppressed with the assistance of other tribes, whose loyalty had to be purchased with grants of territory – in effect, recognition of their squatters' rights. Units of *limitanei* were drafted into the mobile armies and most military action now occurred well within the nominal Roman frontiers, thereby placing further strains on the economic and military system, as imperial forces in Gaul and Spain desperately tried to limit the extent of tribal control.

In Italy Honorius' death in 423 revealed the weakness of the armed forces available to an emperor. The usurper John, supported by the *magister militum* Castinus, had to confront an eastern army marching to install Honorius' sister Placidia and her young son Valentinian III. John failed to rally western provincial armies, and his only hope of safety was the despatch of Aetius to the Huns to collect allies. These arrived just too late, and for the third time in a generation the eastern army overthrew a western usurper, but this time there was no need for a grand battle: Aspar indeed succeeded in spite of bad weather that disrupted his naval forces and led to the capture of his father Ardabur.[30]

Over the next two decades the demise of western armies as a public institution was hastened by the clash of local military interests, and by the personal ambitions of individual commanders. Initially, the ultimate prize for generals was the post of *magister militum praesentalis*, which gave predominance at the Ravenna court, but a reasonable substitute was a secure local power base. In this competition remnants of the Roman mobile and garrison armies played their part, but the allegiance of tribal groups was crucial: Aetius' influence was based on his ability to recruit Huns, while Boniface defended his control of Africa by summoning the Vandals as supporters, with a share of the African provinces as reward.[31] Boniface and Aetius could produce armies to fight for control of Italy while the Vandals overran Africa and Visigoths and Burgundians consolidated their positions in Gaul, but neither the emperor nor his ministers could easily deploy reinforcements across regional boundaries to uphold imperial interests. The administrative problem is expounded in a *Novel* of Valentinian III in late 444: the empire desperately needed an army, but this required regular supplies which could not be squeezed from the western economy – the serene mind of the emperor was in turmoil over the remedy required by the crises.[32] The western emperor no longer commanded a mobile army.

Valentinian's problem was that the state no longer controlled sufficient resources: in 415–16 the Visigoths in Spain had been starved into submission, and then bribed with food to enter Roman service. Such experiences,

---

[30] *PLRE* II *s.v.* Aetius 7, at p. 22; Bury, *LRE* I.221–5.   [31] *PLRE* II *s.v.* Bonifatius 3.
[32] Valentinian III, *Nov.* 15 pref.; also *Nov.* 6.2–3, for contemporary recruitment problems.

however, showed migrating tribes that the key to safety was the occupation of land, which they might hope to secure through successful participation in Roman civil strife.[33] Although it has been argued that tribes were allocated no more than the tax revenues for certain territories, it is much more likely that they took possession physically of land: the tribesmen needed somewhere to live and so would take up residence in the areas which sustained them. The difference between a grant of tax income and of real estate was perhaps not significant, since, whatever the legal arrangement, the individual tribal warriors supported themselves as a military élite through the labours of others. The impact on imperial administration would also have been similar: control over the land and tax wealth of a specific area was lost, either directly through the cession of land or indirectly through allocation of tax revenues whose extraction the tribesmen would have to supervise in the absence of effective imperial control.[34]

The result of this process was that by the 440s only Italy and southern Gaul were under imperial control, and even in these areas it was difficult to exploit human or economic resources without the consent of local élites. A military challenge could be met only by the construction of a coalition of local interest groups – for example, the alliance of Gallic military resources, tribal as well as Gallo-Roman, brought together by Aetius to oppose the common challenge of Attila's Huns, or on a smaller scale the grouping organized by Anthemius to fight the Visigoths under Euric.[35] The aristocracy of Rome was long accustomed to being protected by the efforts of others, and so was reluctant to take the actions or make the concessions that might have preserved a western emperor at Ravenna. Outside Italy, however, local aristocrats, including in some cases bishops, could organize effective armed forces, such as Ecdicius, the brother-in-law of Sidonius Apollinaris, in the Auvergne, Syagrius at Soissons, or the élite of Saragossa in Spain, but their range of action was limited:[36] it was not that all western Romans had lost the ability or will to fight, but that the state could not deploy this military potential, since the complex system for raising, paying, supplying and moving armies no longer functioned.

Valentinian attempted to assert imperial authority by personally killing Aetius with the help of the chamberlain Heraclius, but participation in military affairs removed him from the safety of the palace and he was assassinated by two of Aetius' former retainers on the Campus Martius.[37] Thereafter the army of Italy was controlled by its *magister militum* Ricimer,

---

[33] Heather, *Goths and Romans* 220–1.

[34] Allocation of tax revenues: Goffart, *Barbarians and Romans*, though he accepts that tribesmen soon became landowners (*ibid.* ch. VIII); Barnish (1986); Heather, *Goths and Romans* 220–3.

[35] *PLRE* II *s.v.* Aetius 7, at pp. 27–8; also Elton (1992) 171–3.

[36] Sid. Ap. *Ep.* III.3.7–8 with Elton (1992) 173–4, and Harries (1992b); Greg. Tur. *Hist.* II.27.

[37] Moss (1973) 729–30; Marc. Com. s.a. 455.

who made and unmade a succession of emperors until his death in 472; as the fate of Majorian showed, active campaigning by an emperor might not receive the full support of his main general. The army of Italy was composed largely of non-Roman federal units, off-shoots from the tribal groups dominant in Gaul and Spain or elements who preferred imperial money to Hunnic dominion on the Danube. These troops, like the armies of the emerging post-Roman tribal kingdoms, wanted the stability that only land ownership could afford in times of financial shortage. When their demands were refused in 476 by the patrician Orestes, father of the emperor Romulus Augustulus, they disposed of the last western emperor and elected as king the Scirian officer Odoacer.[38]

Odoacer's career reveals the problems of war-band leaders in the migration period: the loyalty of a military following depended on success in exploiting the Roman need for soldiers and/or in rivalries with the leaders of other war-bands. Odoacer was proclaimed king to satisfy his soldiers' demands, but the arrival in Italy of a more powerful leader, Theoderic the Amal, brought defeat and death.[39] The formation of post-Roman kingdoms reflected the success of certain leaders in institutionalizing their transient military authority: the ability to grant land to their followers, and then to dispense patronage through the successful exploitation and defence of resources, created new military structures that revolved around a dynasty, as opposed to a succession of chiefs elected by the assembly of armed men. Theoderic the Amal's career illustrates the process, and its limitations. In the Balkans in the 470s Theoderic led one of two Gothic war-bands that competed for imperial patronage, with the relative strength of the bands fluctuating according to their leaders' personal success – thus Theoderic Strabo could seduce followers from Theoderic the Amal, while in due course the latter annexed the followers of Strabo's son Recitach. In Italy Theoderic appeared to have established a stable Amal dynasty which also controlled the Visigothic kingdom in Spain and could challenge the Franks in Gaul. Lack of a son, dissension within the family and then failure against Belisarius' invasion caused the Goths to return to military election in an attempt to find a victorious leader.[40]

The Goths in Italy and the Vandals in Africa created kingdoms based on armed forces that were purely tribal – the war-band established on conquered territory and then campaigning when required by their king. In neither province had the native Romans, and especially their aristocracy, developed a tradition of participation in warfare, so that there could be no military fusion of Romans and war-band. As a result the tribal army remained an occupying force that could be supplanted by an alternative

[38] Moorhead (1992) 6–11.   [39] PLRE II s.v. Odovacer; Moorhead (1992) ch. 1.
[40] Heather, Goths and Romans chs. 8–9; Heather (1995); Moorhead (1992) ch. 2.

army: military forces were external to society, and fought for the control of a passive population.[41] In Italy the situation only began to change during the protracted wars of reconquest: in 546/7 a powerful local landowner, Tullianus, enrolled Lucanian peasants, whom he commanded in the defence of their province – though they were reinforced by the presence of 300 Antae.[42]

By contrast, in Frankish Gaul, and perhaps too in Visigothic Spain, though evidence is lacking there, the founders of post-Roman kingdoms managed to combine the strengths of the war-band with the military potential of the surviving Roman population: in these areas constant insecurity had stimulated local military initiatives in ways that had not been necessary in Italy or Africa. The resulting Roman–tribal blend may have contributed to the greater stability of the Frankish and Visigothic states, which were better able to survive military defeat, incompetent leadership or a dynastic minority. In Gaul both Frankish chiefs, who will have included a number of non-Franks assimilated into the war-band, and Gallo-Roman magnates gave oaths of allegiance to their king and organized their localities to provide troops on demand, so that the Merovingian kingdom was protected by a combination of strong local loyalties and duties to the central power. Clovis and his Merovingian successors managed to exploit the resources and public institutions of their part of the Roman world more effectively than any other tribal leader.[43] Their armies were, however, very different animals from their Roman predecessors: there was no standing army, the component units were territorially based, and allocation of land rather than disbursement of pay was the mechanism for attracting service. These changes entailed, or reflected, complementary changes in the nature of the state.

In the west the empire's military institutions failed to survive the tribal challenge. Distinctions between *limitanei* and *comitatenses* became irrelevant when frontier conditions prevailed throughout all provinces; the authority of the centre evaporated together with its ability to provide pay and organize supplies, while military force was provided either by the tribal war-bands whose federate status became increasingly nominal or by local leaders with the capacity to marshal the military potential of their particular region. If Merovingian Gaul represents the successful realignment of Roman military structures around a new provincial leader, the fate of Noricum Ripense in the 460s and 470s as revealed in the *Life* of St Severinus illustrates the processes of Roman decline. Here the frontier population struggled to exist in the face of constant tribal raiding. Town walls only provided temporary protection since there were few troops to

[41] Wickham (1981) 25.
[42] Procop. *Wars* VII.22; Brown, *Gentlemen and Officers* 78 for other examples of this development.
[43] James (1982) ch. 5.

offer resistance and these were demoralized by lack of pay – part of the garrison of Pessau set out for Italy to collect arrears of pay, but were killed in an ambush *en route*. Severinus gave spiritual leadership, made defences as efficient as possible, and arranged relief for refugees from sacked towns or starving inhabitants who had watched their fields being ravaged. Such measures, however, only delayed the end. In 488, six years after Severinus' death, Odoacer ordered the surviving Roman population to abandon their homeland and migrate to Italy; they obeyed the command of their non-Roman overlord and retreated south with Severinus' relics in the lead.[44]

IV. THE EASTERN ARMY: MEN AND RESOURCES

By contrast, the east managed to survive with its military institutions relatively intact, although in the Balkans it experienced many of the same problems and developments. There, Hunnic destruction of cities in the 440s had undermined the basis for Roman control, and for the next half-century the countryside was dominated by Gothic tribal bands. On occasions these notionally constituted the Roman army, but their presence still inspired terror in the inhabitants of surviving cities such as Thessalonica or Dyrrachium. Arrangements for local defence might be efficient, as at Asemus, but these could cause conflicts of interest with the emperor: the men of Asemus captured Huns whom Theodosius wanted to surrender to make peace with Attila, whereas the Asemites were determined to retain them as hostages for the return of some of their own people from the Huns.[45] The key to Roman authority lay in the control of supplies: the warbands of the two Theoderics lacked secure territory to make them self-sufficient, and so food and agricultural land were powerful bargaining counters for Roman commanders. The emperor, safe inside Constantinople, could control the distribution of food supplies by sea, and divert resources from other areas to support administrative reorganization when this became practical.[46]

The eastern army of the sixth century in theory preserved the traditional distinction between *limitanei* and *comitatenses*; the latter could be referred to under the generic term *stratiotai*, soldiers,[47] although this does not indicate that the former had no military function or status. Indeed, in reconquered Africa Justinian acted to re-establish *limitanei*: he sent one unit of *limitanei* from the east and ordered Belisarius to enrol other units from among suitable provincials. These were to receive lands, and so contribute to the cultivation of frontier districts and ensure their security; the *comitatenses* stationed in Africa were available as a reserve force. The same complementary roles

[44] Alföldy (1974) ch. 12; Thompson (1982) ch. 7; cf. ch. 18 (Wood), pp. 506, 513, 524 below.
[45] Malchus fr. 20.5–19, 63–87; Priscus fr. 9.3.39–80.
[46] Heather, *Goths and Romans* ch. 8; cf. ch. 23 (Whitby), pp. 713–14 below.   [47] Justinian, *Nov.* 103.3.

can be seen in Libya Pentapolis, for which Anastasius' regulations survive: the provincial garrison contained five units of *comitatenses*, but supervision of movements across the frontier and security along the roads were entrused to the *castrensiani* or garrison forces. At Palmyra, however, where Justinian established a regiment of *comitatenses* alongside the garrison of *limitanei*, the distinction may have become less clear, since *comitatenses* at a stable posting acquired the same range of social and economic connections with local society that *limitanei* naturally had.[48]

The *comitatenses* were grouped into units known as *numeri* or *arithmoi*, 'numbers', sometimes loosely referred to as *katalogos*, 'list'; in due course *tagmata*, 'formation', or *bandon*, 'flag', became current. Where evidence is available, the basic unit on active service numbered between 250 and 500 soldiers, who were grouped into larger *moirai*, units of 2,000–3,000 men, which might then be brigaded into *mere*, contingents of 6,000–7,000 men. Eastern Roman armies were raised from a variety of sources, which ensured that no single group could dominate, as the tribal war-bands could in the west.[49] The most effective Roman soldiers were drawn from the bellicose inhabitants of various mountainous regions of the eastern empire, notably the central Balkans, the Taurus range in southern Anatolia (Isauria and Pisidia) and the Armenian highlands. It was the emperors' ability to control and exploit this manpower which permitted the survival of the eastern army as a Roman institution. For leading Isaurians Tarasicodissa, the future emperor Zeno, showed the way to prominent positions at court, while their followers entered the guards units and the regular army, a development that was unpopular with those who regarded the Isaurians as more barbarian than the Germans or saw threats to their own power base.[50] After Zeno's death the Isaurians might have reverted to their lawless ways, but Anastasius' repression of Isaurian revolts ensured that central authority was upheld. An analogous development can be traced in Armenia, where the personal advance of men like Narses and Sittas was accompanied by widespread recruitment into the armies. At the same time local administration was reformed to increase direct Roman authority at the expense of semi-independent princes.[51]

The best elements in the eastern armies were the federates and various other units of non-Roman peoples. In contrast to the west, where federates eventually supplanted Romans, in the east federates came to be recruited from Romans as well as non-Romans. Procopius alludes to this

---

[48] *CJ* 1.27.2.8; *SEG* ix.356; Malalas 426.1–5; Jones, *LRE* 661–2.

[49] Jones, *LRE* 659–60; for use of terminology, see for example Maurice, *Strategikon* (consult index) to the Dennis/Gamillscheg edn (1981) for the different terms.

[50] Malchus fr. 22; cf. ch. 17 (Whitby), p. 477 below.

[51] *PLRE* iii *s.v.* Narses 1 and Sittas 1; Malalas 429.16–430.8; Justinian, *Nov.* 31; Jones, *LRE* 280–1; Whitby (1995) sec. 7.

change in the context of the Vandal expedition of 533, but the precise significance of the development is uncertain. Large numbers of tribesmen were now settled within the empire,[52] and it is possible that federates were soldiers of recognizably Germanic or Gothic origin, drawn from internal as well as external sources. Their quality remained superior to that of standard Roman units, since they were marshalled less deeply in the battle line,[53] and the availability within the empire of such recruits contributed to the eastern emperors' success in dominating a potentially autonomous, non-Roman element. Justinian in particular was quick to exploit the military potential of regions brought under his control. The Tzani, neighbours of Armenia, and the remnants of the Vandal army were both incorporated into the regular structure of the Roman army: the emperor increased the resources under his direct control, while the potential for local revolt was reduced.[54] By the end of the sixth century, a new 'foreign legion', the *optimates*, had been constituted alongside the federates: the *optimates*, as their Latin name might suggest, were the best unit in the army, drawn up only five or seven deep and accompanied by armed retainers who were themselves worthy of inclusion in the battle line.[55]

In addition to federates and *optimates*, there were allied units from outside the frontiers, Saracens organized under a Ghassanid phylarch who patrolled the Syrian and Arabian desert fringes,[56] Huns, Bulgars and Lombards recruited on the Danube for service elsewhere in the empire.[57] Many of the best non-Romans found their way into the *bucellarii*, the private bodyguards of individual generals, who were enlisted from men conspicuous for bravery or other talents.[58] Armies on campaign were composed of a mixture of units: garrison troops might be requisitioned for field service, though their officers would be mindful of their local responsibilities; higher-grade Roman units drawn from Isauria or Illyricum would share the burden of fighting with federates, who had the responsibility of holding the centre of the battle line; other allied contingents might be in attendance, depending on the area of operations and sometimes – for example, in the case of the Saracens in 573 and 581 – on the mood of their leader. The general was accompanied by his personal bodyguard, ready to impress enemy ambassadors with their discipline, to protect their commander in battle, and to execute his personal orders.[59]

The standard scholarly view is that Justinianic armies differed from their late Roman predecessors in being composed of volunteers rather than

[52] Jones, *LRE* 663–6; Haldon (1984) ch. 1, 96–118; Procop. *Wars* III.11.3–4.
[53] Maurice, *Strat.* 11.6.17–29.   [54] Procop. *Wars* 1.15.25; IV.14.17–18; Malalas 427.17–428.4.
[55] Maurice, *Strat.* 11.6.29–40.
[56] Isaac, *Limits of Empire* 235–49; Shahîd (1957); Parker (1987) 822–3.
[57] E.g. Procop. *Wars* V.27.1–2; VIII.26.11–13.
[58] Gascou (1976a); Liebeschuetz, *Barbarians and Bishops* 43–7; Whitby (1995) sec. 9.
[59] Whitby (1995) sec. 7 and 9.

conscripts, at least for the mobile units.[60] Closer examination, however, of the military provisions in the Justinianic Code reveals that the traditional *dilectus* or compulsory levy was still operated, and that recruits could still be furnished by units of tax-paying landowners (*temones* or *capitula*); the collective responsibility for providing the recruit was delegated in turn to a president, an onerous burden (*protostasia, prototypia*), from which exemptions were sought. Monetary commutation of this obligation was allowed for imperial lands.[61] This system represents a degree of imperial control that was signally lacking in the western empire in the early fifth century, when landowners had been able to demand concessions and emperors forced to entice volunteers with bribes whose fulfilment was uncertain. Of course, volunteers were not rejected from eastern armies, and on occasions when it was necessary to raise troops quickly for a particular campaign a commander would have to travel round, cash in hand, to attract the men he needed, rather than wait for the slower procedures of the provincial *dilectus*.[62]

In addition to conscription there was an element of hereditary service in all Roman parts of the army. This is demonstrable in the case of *limitanei* and static units of *comitatenses* in Egypt, Palestine and the exarchate of north Italy, where papyri attest family succession; it probably also applied to the mobile army, since in 594 Maurice proposed to give preferential enrolment to sons of deceased veterans, and this was regarded as a welcome aspect of an unpopular package of reforms.[63] Recruitment was supervised by the imperial bureaucracy, which would issue instructions about the numbers needed to bring units up to strength, and then individual approvals would be sent to the particular regiments to sanction the inclusion of a new name on their regimental muster. Such a complex system was obviously open to abuse, but energetic emperors like Anastasius and Justinian were prepared to risk unpopularity by legislating against corruption and arranging detailed inspections of regimental strengths and effectiveness.[64]

It is difficult to quantify the advantages of soldiering in terms of pay and conditions of service, since much depended on the nature of the military action to be undertaken. Membership of a unit of *limitanei* in upper Egypt was sufficiently attractive to merit payment of an entry fee, at least by those who could not claim a hereditary place; for such men, guard duty beyond the Danube represented a severe punishment, exile to active service in a distant and dangerous land.[65] In the static units automatic promotion through

---

[60] Jones, *LRE* 668–70; Haldon (1979) 20.   [61] Whitby (1995) sec. 4; *CJ* x.42.8; 62.3; xi.75.3.
[62] Procop. *Wars* vii.10.1–3.
[63] Haldon (1979) 21; Keenan (1990); Brown, *Gentlemen and Officers* 85–6. Theophylact vii.1.
[64] *P.Ryl.* 609; *SEG* ix.356; Procop. *Secret History* 24.5–11; Procop. *Wars* vii.1.28–33; Agathias, *Hist.* v.14; Jones, *LRE* 661–2.
[65] *P. Monac.* 1, with Keenan (1990) 144; Justinian, *Edict* 13.11.1 = *CJ* iii.785.

length of service provided pay increases, and Anastasius was prepared to tolerate the retention for life on military rolls of a proportion of each unit; Justinian was criticized for abolishing this concession to military inefficiency, but his expectation was that a combination of graduated pay plus some tax benefits for veterans constituted sufficient provision for retirement. In mobile units, life must have been less comfortable, but on successful campaigns these men could benefit from booty: its attraction tended to lead to undisciplined looting and disputes about proper apportionment.[66] For the majority of recruits, even the bellicose Armenians, service far from home was unpopular and might occasion dissent. The process of conscription was disliked, and legislation against poltroons was required. On the other hand, the right general in the right place could find volunteers through personal connections and disbursement of money, as Belisarius in Thrace in 544, Narses in the Balkans in 551/2, or Maurice in Cappadocia in 578.[67]

Justinian is alleged to have deprived *limitanei* of their pay, and declassified them from the status of soldiers, but this criticism in Procopius' *Secret History* probably misrepresents his actions. He may have instituted a system of payment only for active service, or service away from a unit's particular area, whereas normal sustenance was provided by the estates attached to each unit. The experience of an Illyrian contingent in Italy points to the importance of estates in terms of remuneration: the men returned to the Balkans after suffering serious arrears of pay, presumably in the belief that they could support themselves there.[68] On the other hand, mobile troops continued to receive annual cash payments which represented the monetary commutations for their *annona* or ration allowance, if this had not been supplied in kind, and for their uniform and arms. This was probably paid when the troops were in winter quarters, or on the point of marshalling for the next season's campaign, to provide a stimulus for prompt reporting and enthusiastic service. Although arms, horses and uniforms were not issued, soldiers were probably expected to acquire them ultimately from the state factories or stud farms. In spite of regulations that officers had to supervise the proper equipping of their men, with severe penalties for failure, allowances were not spent fully on their intended objects: when Maurice in 594 attempted to reintroduce issues in kind, the Balkan army mutinied. There was certainly a reluctance to expose precious possessions to extra danger, as concern for their horses was one reason why the mutinous army in 602 refused to spend the winter north of the Danube.[69]

The eastern army was underpinned by a massive administrative system that ensured the collection and distribution of money and supplies as

---

[66] Jones, *LRE* 675; Procop. *Secret History* 24.8; Maurice, *Strat.* v; Theophylact II.4.1–3, VI.7.6–8.3.
[67] Sebeos ch. 10; *Digest* 49.16.4.12; Procop. *Wars* VII.10.1–3, VIII.26.5–17; John Eph. *HE* VI.14.
[68] Procop. *Secret History* 24.12–14; *Wars* VII.11.13–16; Whitby (1995) sec. 8.
[69] Jones, *LRE* 670–2; Maurice, *Strat.* 1.2; Theophylact VII.1, VIII.6.2 with Whitby, *Maurice* 166–7.

needed. The empire's logistical organization was certainly capable of supporting the army in peacetime, mainly because troops were dispersed to
individual towns and cities from which they had to be reassembled for
service in a mobile army. Large-scale military campaigns required advance
preparations and on occasions, as at Edessa in 503, special measures, but
the fact that through into the seventh century imperial commanders were
capable of marshalling and manoeuvring very big armies is a tribute to the
overall functioning of the system. Availability of supplies was an important
criterion in the selection of sites for winter quarters, when officers were
responsible for ensuring adequate provisions. Eastern armies – for
example, in 503 – tended to break up into their constituent elements and
return to their provinces or the individual cities where they were billeted,
although in the 580s, after the development of Monocarton near
Constantina (Viranshehir), a large part of the army might remain there.[70]

In the Balkans the poverty of the countryside provided extra problems,
and in the 580s and 590s it seems that armies retired south-east for the
winter, to the Black Sea towns of Tomi or Odessus or towards the Sea of
Marmara to Drizipera, Tzurullon or even Heracleia, where the shipment of
essential supplies must have been easiest. At the same time, armies might
deliberately be sent to winter in dangerous places, since overwinter billeting
was a method of imposing control on recalcitrant subjects, as the Avars did
to the Slavs.[71] The process of reconstituting an army from scattered elements presupposed the existence of an efficient system of mustering the
troops. In Italy in the seventh century, and Dalmatia in the eighth, there is
evidence for the gathering of scattered local garrisons and militias to form
a mobile army, and the sequence of the Balkan campaigns in the 590s suggests that, not surprisingly, proper arrangements existed there, too; on the
eastern front it is possible that a general would instruct his troops to reas-
semble for a communal celebration of Easter.[72] Problems could occur, as
when the fugitive Lombard Ildigisal was able to defeat disorganized forces
in the Balkans, or when the commanders of contingents from Lebanon in
Belisarius' eastern army in 542 imposed a time limit on their co-operation.
The success of Khusro's march to Antioch in 540 can be attributed to the
difficulty of assembling an army very rapidly to respond to an unexpected
attack: in such a crisis, local Roman commanders might pay more attention
to the interests of their garrison towns and ignore, or affect ignorance of,
commands from the centre. The military machine moved too slowly to
respond in such circumstances. But overall, the system generally worked and
there are few signs of armies being immobilized by bureaucratic failures.[73]

---

[70] Joshua 65; Theophylact III.1.1–3.
[71] Brown, *Gentlemen and Officers* 89 n. 17; Theophylact VI.6.3; Fredegar IV.48.
[72] Brown, *Gentlemen and Officers* 92; Theophylact VII.1.3, 7.1.
[73] Procop. *Wars* VIII.27.1–18; II.16.16–19.

One indication of the underlying strength of eastern arrangements was the empire's ability, at least in the short term, to surmount the ravages of the Great Plague, which struck first in 541/2 and then flared up in various parts of the empire throughout the rest of the century. Mortality was certainly highest in the large cities, which were of limited relevance to the recruitment or supply of armies, but there were also deaths among farmers and disruption to agriculture, and concentrations of soldiers must also have been liable to high casualties. Thus, although the overall severity of the plague may be debated, it would have destabilized a system that was already insecure. In fact, however, it is difficult to detect any direct or immediate impact.[74] There is no apparent decline in the size of eastern armies after the 540s: few precise figures are available, but in the *Strategikon* of Maurice a force of between 5,000 and 15,000 is considered to be well proportioned, which accords with the sizes of Justinianic expeditionary forces for the west in the 530s. Complaints about shortages of soldiers under Tiberius and Maurice were caused in part by simultaneous campaigns on two or more frontiers: diversion of resources to the east left the Balkans and Italy vulnerable, but this problem of juggling available manpower to meet different commitments had existed since the reign of Augustus.[75]

There is also no clear increase in the proportion of non-Roman troops serving in the armies, another possible sign of a decline in available Roman manpower. Here definitions are important, since Roman armies had traditionally contained a large number of soldiers whom a blue-blooded aristocrat in Rome would have regarded as uncivilized, but who nevertheless originated from within the empire – and it is this which is the crucial consideration for an emperor's ability to control and organize military recruitment, whereas subjective judgements on barbarization are less relevant. Thus, soldiers might be Goth or Armenian by racial origin, but be subject to the Roman emperor as tax-paying inhabitants. Emperors recruited from outside their frontiers when necessary, but such foreigners were merely one element within an army that was already heterogeneous.[76] The largest single foreign recruitment was probably that initiated by Tiberius in 574, when it was essential to rebuild the eastern armies very quickly and a new force of Tiberiani, numbering perhaps 15,000, was raised.[77] Otherwise, emperors continued a pragmatic policy of exploiting the military potential of available tribes or war-bands but without creating a non-Roman army: enlistment of Lombards, Goths and even Anglo-Saxons in the late sixth century was balanced by recruitment from Cappadocia or Mesopotamia, as carried out by Maurice in 578 and Philippicus in 584.

---

[74] Whitby (1995) sec. 6.
[75] Maurice *Strat.* III.8, 10; Menander frr. 21, 22; for problems in the early fifth century, cf. Liebeschuetz, *Barbarians and Bishops* 129.   [76] Whitby (1995) sec. 7.
[77] Evagr. *HE* v.14 with Theophanes 251.24–8.

Emperors were not desperate for manpower, but they naturally acted to control human resources that might be useful in the future. The Herul king Grepes was told to return home after his baptism at Constantinople and await the imperial call. Subsequently, Justinian gave the remnant of this bellicose, but rather barbaric, tribe territory in the vicinity of Singidunum, from where they could be enrolled when needed; descendants of these Heruls were perhaps among the inhabitants of Singidunum who were saved from resettlement by the Avars in the 590s (an example of the Avars trying to annex Roman population resources). Justinian permitted the Lombards to dwell in Noricum and Pannonia, provinces so remote that his acquiescence was a formality, but the establishment of Bulgar Kotrigurs or the Lombard group led by Ildigisal in Thrace were definite acts of patronage, and anticipated a large settlement of Bulgars by Maurice. A final example of this policy was being contemplated in 602 when Maurice, in order to create an army of 30,000 Armenians in the Balkans, apparently ordered the resettlement of the same number of families in Europe.[78] Such actions reveal a continuity of imperial concern, which can be traced throughout late antiquity (e.g. Gothic settlements in the Balkans in the fourth century), not a new development consequent on the plague. In the east, land was used constructively at different levels to sustain an imperial army: *limitanei* received plots of land which contributed to their maintenance, while potential members of élite units also had properties on which they resided when not required for active service – the military strength of the empire was supported at a reasonable cost.[79]

Finance was the key constraint. It has been claimed that in the early fifth century the east kept its armed forces relatively small as a solution to problems in financing and controlling troops.[80] This assertion cannot be corroborated, and in fact the relative lack of problems may indicate that rising prosperity in Asia Minor, Syria and Egypt allowed emperors to avoid serious arrears of pay, and hence indiscipline. Under Anastasius a substantial financial reserve was created, which undoubtedly facilitated Justinian's expansive diplomatic and military activity. This, coupled with expensive building works in Justinian's last decade, caused a crisis of liquidity, but unpopular retrenchment under Justin II again created a surplus for his successor to exploit. Tiberius was notorious for generosity, and lavish spending allowed him to create an army in 574/5. The see-saw progress of imperial finances meant that Maurice was faced by a severe shortage of cash: he seems to have built up his armies in the 580s through determined conscription, carried out by *scribones*, but as soon as he had to pay a large army in the Balkans in addition to the eastern field army, he was forced to

[78] Procop. *Wars* VII.33.10–13; VIII.19.3–5; 27.8; Michael the Syrian x.21, vol. II pp. 363–4; Sebeos ch. 20.   [79] Whitby (1995) sec. 8.   [80] Liebeschuetz, *Barbarians and Bishops* 94–5.

attempt a highly unpopular reduction in military pay in 588.[81] It is possible
that the empire's economic resilience, which in tax-producing terms meant
its agricultural base, was gradually declining towards the end of the century,
as repeated visitations of plague, extensive invasions in the Balkans and
protracted campaigning in the east combined to take their toll. But, if so,
the trend was gradual, since in the seventh century Phocas – and Heraclius,
down to the loss of the major revenue-generating provinces of Syria and
Egypt – had funds to give bribes to the Avars and finance field armies in
the east.

V. EASTERN SURVIVAL

Eastern emperors controlled the commanders and officers in their armies,
not just the manpower, and here too the contrast with the west is
significant: the army remained an institution under imperial authority, not
an independent force capable of dictating to its nominal masters. The
eastern counterparts of Ricimer and Odoacer were the *magistri militum*
Aspar and his sons Ardabur and Patricius, Armatus and his son Basiliscus,
and Illus: these generals dominated emperors and attempted to manipulate
the imperial succession by placing protégés on the throne or by insinuating
their families into the imperial house (both Patricius and Basiliscus were
proclaimed Caesar). But, whereas Ricimer killed Majorian, Leo disposed of
Aspar's family inside the palace, while Zeno had Armatus killed when
leaving the palace to enter the Hippodrome and overcame Illus in civil
war.[82] Other powerful military families, like that of the Goth Areobindus,
married into the aristocracy: the younger Areobindus fled Constantinople
rather than accede to popular requests that he champion orthodoxy and
supplant the Monophysite Anastasius, perhaps to the disgust of his wife
Anicia Juliana, daughter of the western emperor Olybrius.[83] In the sixth
century, generals were often imperial relatives or members of the palatine
staff. Military unrest tended to be generated from the lower ranks disgruntled about lack of pay or other specific grievances, and was led by junior or
middle-ranking officers, Stotzas in Africa in the late 530s, Germanus in the
east in 588 or Phocas on the Danube in 602. The salient exception, the
sequence of revolts against Anastasius led by Vitalian, *comes* and then *magister militum*, had a religious motivation and in any case ultimately failed.[84]

Another aspect of the survival of the eastern army as a public institution is the emperors' ability to keep control of soldiers in private service.
Prominent Romans had always possessed retinues with a capacity to act as

---

[81] Evagr. *HE* v.14; Michael the Syrian x.21; Theophylact III.1.2 with Evagr. *HE* vi.4.
[82] For career details, see *PLRE* II.   [83] *PLRE* II.143–4 *s.v.* Areobindus 1; Malalas 406.22–408.11.
[84] Career details in *PLRE* III; discussion in Kaegi (1981) chs. 3–4, esp. 60–2. Cf. ch. 17 (Whitby),
pp. 473–5 below.

bodyguards, and imperial legislation prohibiting private citizens from carrying arms had been directed against such personal militias.[85] The contin-
utation of such arrangements into the late empire is no surprise, but
whereas in the west there was a tendency towards the privatization of military resources, in the east the private capabilities were kept accessible to
the state.[86] In part this was achieved by direct legislation against the maintenance of private guards in cities and on estates: a law of Leo from 468
was incorporated into the Justinianic Code, while Justinian himself legislated in 542.[87] But the inevitability of such guards could also be exploited.
In 528 Justinian had despatched senators 'with their forces' to defend
various eastern cities, and at the climax of the Nika riot Justinian ordered
those senators who had gathered in the palace to return to their own homes
and guard them, since the mopping up of rioters would be much easier if
they were denied access to the massive semi-fortified mansions of the
élite.[88] In Egypt some large landowners, like the Apion family, had *bucellarii* who appear to have received a public salary and could be used for official
administrative purposes.[89]

Within the armies individual commanders might build up large retinues
of *bucellarii*: Belisarius is credited with 7,000 retainers, probably an exaggeration, but even a less distinguished figure, Valerian, could command 1,000.[90]
But these men owed allegiance to the emperor as well as their commander,
and they might not follow their general through all the vicissitudes of his
career: thus some of Belisarius' retinue stayed behind in Africa in the 530s,
and when in 544 he was moved from the eastern frontier to Italy he was not
permitted to transfer his bodyguards, as he subsequently complained to
Justinian. Prospects for better employment could also outweigh loyalty to an
individual general: thus in 550 Germanus, possible heir to the throne and well
equipped with money, could attract guards from less advantaged patrons
when preparing to march to Italy.[91] *Bucellarii* made a significant contribution
to the performance of eastern armies: they might be used for special missions, or assigned to a place of danger in battle, or expected to help maintain
discipline, but it is misleading to regard this as a dangerous and inevitable
tendency towards semi-private armies. Rather, they could have a beneficial
impact on the mass of ordinary troops, by establishing higher standards of
appearance and conduct, and by dangling the rewards of preferential treatment to stimulate others to bravery. It was for this reason that an official
manual such as the *Strategikon* of Maurice paid attention to their existence.[92]

[85] Cameron and Long (1993) 211 n. 62.
[86] Whitby (1995) sec. 9; Liebeschuetz, *Barbarians and Bishops* 43–7.
[87] *CJ* IX.12.10; *Nov.* 116; cf. also Feissel and Kaygusuz (1985).   [88] Malalas 442.8–16.
[89] Gascou (1976a).   [90] Procop. *Wars* VII.1.18–20; 27.3.
[91] Procop. *Wars* IV.10.4; VII.10.1, 12.10; 39.17.
[92] Procop. *Wars* III.17.1; 19.23–4; Maurice, *Strat.* 1.2.10; 9.29–35.

The eastern armies preserved the Roman military reputation through to the end of the sixth century by capitalizing on available resources and showing a capacity to adapt to a variety of challenges. Not all battles were won, but two successful tribal kingdoms in the west (Vandals, Ostrogoths) were destroyed; Persian aggression in the east was contained and a substantial increase in Roman territory achieved on the north-eastern frontier; the Danube, which Hunnic attacks appeared to have removed from Roman control, was re-established as a frontier and held in spite of Bulgar, Avar and Slav incursions. Correct tactics played their part, since the Romans were sufficiently professional to realize that different opponents had different strengths and weaknesses to be encountered or exploited: these were observed and carefully listed in Maurice's *Strategikon* xi under four headings: Persians; Scythians – namely, Avars, Turks and comparable Hunnic tribes; the fair-haired races such as the Franks and Lombards; and finally the Slavs and Antes. Guidance was offered on the best tactics for use against each. The Romans also noticed military ideas that could be adopted from their enemies, with the Avars being the most influential example in the sixth century: their bows, tents and body and horse armour were highly regarded, and their flexible battle array was thought to be superior to the traditional single lines favoured by the Romans.[93]

The best individual soldiers in the Roman army were undoubtedly cavalrymen: Procopius, in the introduction to his *Wars*, selected the mounted archer as the epitome of the modern warrior, perhaps in part because this was such a contrast to the traditional Roman legionary equipped with shield and sword. The archer's skill as a horseman and the power of his heavy bow may have been borrowed from the fifth-century Huns, and Huns continued to serve throughout the sixth century, but training in archery was also recommended for all recruits.[94] But the army possessed a variety of skills: in conflicts with Persians the Romans were advised to rely on the superiority of their charge, which points to the existence of high-quality heavy cavalry armed with lances; against the Avars infantry were needed to lend stability to the battle line in its severest test, an indication that good foot soldiers were also available. Undoubtedly the heterogeneous origins of soldiers contributed to the range of their specialities, but it was intended that these abilities be taught to the internal Roman elements in the armies.

An important contribution to Roman superiority, at least over enemies in Europe, was their ability to construct and defend powerful fortifications. Roman torsion-powered siege engines were sufficiently complex to be beyond the skills of most tribal groups, unless like the Huns they managed to acquire assistance from Roman captives or deserters. Apart from the Huns, the only tribal group with an effective siege technology were the

---

[93] Maurice, *Strat.* 1.2, 11.1.   [94] Procop. *Wars* 1.1.8–16; Maurice, *Strat.* 1.2.28–30.

Avars, who should probably be credited with introducing into European warfare a simple type of siege engine, a counter-weighted stone thrower, that was propelled by human muscle power. But even the Huns and Avars also had to rely on human waves to overcome defences, and the ability of their leaders to force subject populations to suffer the enormous casualties of such assaults was a significant demonstration of their authority. These mass attacks involved the assembly of very large numbers of men, and it is perhaps not surprising that the Avars were incapable of maintaining a long siege outside Thessalonica or Constantinople, where the defenders could exploit their control of the sea to supply themselves.[95] Other tribal groups had to rely on protracted blockade, inducements to treachery, or the luck of a surprise assault, as is revealed in the numerous sieges during the Roman reconquest of Italy or in the Slav migrations into the Balkans.[96]

In Europe strong defences coupled with a determined garrison tended to thwart attackers: Roman armies were reluctant to risk heavy losses in frontal assaults, while their tribal enemies could usually find easier sources of booty. In Africa after the Justinianic reconquest the importance of defences is revealed by the attention devoted to the construction and repair of forts: from these bases a relatively small garrison could hope to withstand Moorish raids, and hence retain control of the province.[97] On the eastern frontier the balance of power and skills was much more even. The Persians had the technical capacity and logistical organization to sustain long and active sieges of fortresses and walled cities: in 502/3 Amida fell after three months, while in 573 it took six months to capture Dara. Here the solution for the Romans was to keep all defences in good order since, as the fall of Antioch in 540 demonstrated, the Persians were quick to exploit any weakness. It is not surprising that Anastasius and Justinian, but particularly the latter, achieved reputations for constructing major fortifications, since both had to react to successful Persian aggression.[98]

Discipline was a recurrent problem, and there was a sequence of mutinies in eastern armies which culminated in the military revolt that toppled Maurice and placed the officer Phocas on the throne in 602.[99] Part of the problem was caused by the variety of allied contingents present. Belisarius *en route* to Africa executed two Huns at Abydus, a punishment that nearly provoked their compatriots to mutiny; Narses in Italy in 552 found his Lombard allies a mixed blessing, and immediately after the defeat of Totila he paid them off and sent them back to their Balkan homes. Roman recruits, however, were far from perfect: Belisarius complained of the inexperience

[95] Whitby, *Maurice* 172–3; *Chron. Pasch.* 717.1–726.10; *Miracula S. Demetrii* 1.156–60, 11.212–13.

[96] Procop. *Wars* vii is dominated by accounts of sieges; see Thompson (1982) 82–6.

[97] Pringle (1981) 89–120; Procop. *Buildings* vi.5–7.

[98] Procop. *Wars* 1.7.29; John Eph. *HE* vi.5; Procop. *Wars* 11.8; Procop. *Buildings* ii–iii.

[99] Discussion in Kaegi (1981) chs. 3–5.

of his new Thracian recruits in 544, and in the 570s both Justinian and Maurice acquired reputations as disciplinarians after having to cope with significant influxes of new troops.[100] But accusations of declining standards are a familiar theme in Roman, indeed in all, military history, and criticism needs to be assessed in the light of the armies' performance in the field.

The main causes of poor morale and indiscipline in the sixth century were, unsurprisingly, lack of pay or supplies and military defeat. The army was such a complex and expensive institution to support that the existence of some problems was inevitable, especially at times of financial stringency. Armies serving in areas that could not locally support the troops were particularly liable to suffer, hence the difficulties in the expeditionary armies in Africa and Italy when counter-offensives prevented the organized exploitation of local resources, and in the Balkans, an area renowned for impoverishment but with a large military establishment. Mutineers were treated with the same mixture of exemplary harshness and general pardon as in previous centuries: soldiers had always been too valuable to squander if they could be cowed into obedience. There is no evidence that Roman traditions in this respect had been forgotten in the sixth-century army, whether because of difficulties over manpower or creeping 'barbarization' of the military.[101]

Eastern armies fulfilled their defensive functions through to the end of the sixth century. It seems unlikely that the late Roman army was ever organized in accordance with some grand 'scientific' strategy for protecting the empire: frontiers did not operate as rigid exclusion zones, and field armies tended to be marshalled after the appearance of a threat (as in 540) rather than maintained, at much greater cost, in a state of permanent readiness. But the protection of the empire was not as amateurish as might be concluded either from the lack of good maps and regular intelligence about threatening neighbours, or from the absence of discussions of strategic matters in Graeco-Roman literature, especially in the tradition of military handbooks. Generations of observation and experience ensured that Roman armies, officers and emperors, part of whose duty it was to protect the empire, were aware of the likely origin, nature and direction of threats.[102] Most military forces – obviously, Hunnic or Avar cavalry or a Persian grand army under the king's command, but also a Slav war-band when accompanied by wagons – were constrained to move along recognized routes where travel was easy and supplies available.

The Romans organized their defences as particular needs emerged. Problems of campaigning on the eastern front stimulated the construction of Dara by Anastasius, and after the loss of Dara in 573 the same logic

---

[100] Procop. *Wars* III.12.8–22; VIII.33.2–3; Theophylact III.12.7; Menander fr. 23.3.
[101] Maurice, *Strat.* 1.6.19–22; Whitby (1995) sec. 6, *contra* Kaegi (1981) 72.
[102] Contrasting views in Luttwak (1976), Isaac, *Limits of Empire* ch. IX and Lee (1993) esp. ch. 4.

dictated the development of Monocarton. The need to increase the security of the Armenian frontier led Justinian to strengthen Martyropolis and construct a new fortress at Citharizon: these eastern forts were focal points for future campaigns, an indication of their strategic impact.[103] In the Balkans, the Danube had a number of known crossing points which Roman garrisons could observe, and south of the frontier there were relatively few passes over the Haemus, Rhodope and Pindus ranges, so that Roman defenders, if well prepared, could anticipate the movements of raiding parties and attack when appropriate.[104] No emperor could afford to neglect his armies for long, and although it might make good propaganda to blame problems on a predecessor's mistakes or inaction, such accusations need to be treated cautiously.

Diplomacy was an essential element in the structure of Roman defences, its efficacy depending on the availability of military force to back up promises, and its operations often being conducted by, or at least in conjunction with, military commanders. Relations with Persia were organized sysematically, as befitted long-standing neighbours who were bound by a number of common interests as much as antagonized by points of dispute. Diplomatic exchanges were structured, with minor embassies following major missions and envoys travelling according to a schedule and being welcomed in Constantinople in set form.[105]

Throughout most of the fifth and sixth centuries the Romans remained on the defensive in the east: emperors had pressing concerns in the Balkans and the west and little expectation of territorial gain in Mesopotamia or Armenia, so that the combined objective of diplomacy and military defences was to deter Persian aggression, or terminate a war quickly once fighting had begun. The exception was Justin II's aggression in 572, when Persian difficulties with Armenians and Turks appeared to offer the Romans an escape from having to begin annual cash payments to Persia, the concession they fought hardest to avoid, since it could imply an acceptance of inferior tributary status.[106] Both empires accepted that local squabbles between clients could involve their patrons in wider conflict, willingly or unwillingly; the peace-time ideal – enshrined, for example, in the Fifty Years' Peace of 561/2 – was for the military authorities on both sides of the frontier to co-operate in the rapid elimination of such aggravations.[107] Diplomatic contacts across European frontiers were less governed by long traditions, but had the same basic objectives of protecting Roman interests and defusing threats without resort to the uncertainty and expense of war. Here there was always a danger that reluctance to fight would be interpreted as weakness, and hence merely act as an incitement to

[103] Zachariah VII.6; Procop. *Buildings* III.2–3; Whitby, *Maurice* 209–13.   [104] Whitby, *Maurice* 70–9.
[105] Whitby, *Maurice* 215–18; Lee (1993) 166–70; Blockley (1992) 151–63.
[106] Whitby, *Maurice* 250–3.   [107] Details in Menander fr. 6.1.

further demands, as happened with the Huns in the 440s and the Avars in the 570s and 580s. Selective patronage of tribes or war-bands had to be accompanied by visible strength in the vicinity of the frontier, so that invasion of Roman territory did not become an easy option for those under threat in their own lands.

'I know that war is a great evil, and worse than evils' is part of the preamble to a discussion on strategy that should probably be dated to Justinian's reign, but attention to the army was an essential part of an emperor's work, as the deranged Justin advised Tiberius at the latter's proclamation as Caesar.[108] The army had always been the most expensive element within the Roman empire, but without an efficient military system an emperor would quickly be seen to be naked, as occurred in the west in the early fifth century. Even in the wealthier east, constant attention and adaptation were required to maintain arrangements for recruitment, supply and training without the distortions that inevitably crept in as customary practice became petrified or abused. 'A general must not have to confess, "I did not expect it"' is one of the maxims in Maurice's *Strategikon*, a work that itself demonstrates the close attention that was devoted to military organization.[109]

In the sixth century the eastern empire had managed, not without difficulty, to maintain its basic integrity and even regain territory in the western Mediterranean. Luck played its part, as with the departure to Sardinia of the Vandal fleet in 533 or the Persian civil war of 590–1, but the Roman army remained an effective fighting force. In the seventh century civil war, the traditional threat to imperial prosperity, shattered the balance: in 602 and 610 coups at Constantinople distracted the armies on the eastern frontier and permitted the Persians to make significant gains, while in 641 a further bout of imperial strife helped the Arabs to consolidate their control over newly-won territories. During these decades, however, a succession of Roman armies was raised and manoeuvred by emperors and their commanders. The result was often defeat, but the sheer ability of the Roman military machine to function through a series of catastrophes greater than anything experienced since the Hannibalic War of the third century B.C. is impressive. By the mid seventh century, however, the permanent loss of the major revenue-producing provinces of Egypt and Syria necessitated a fundamental change in the nature of military organization, and the impoverished empire had to exploit its greatest remaining asset, land, in order to fund its defence forces. The result was the theme system of territorial organization which defined the nature of the middle Byzantine army.[110]

---

[108] Anon. *Peri Strat.* 4.9; Theophylact III.11.11.   [109] Maurice, *Strat.* VIII.1.26.
[110] Cf. ch. 7 (Barnish, Lee, Whitby), pp. 203–6 above, and ch. 17 (Whitby), pp. 494–5 below.

CHAPTER 12

LAND, LABOUR AND SETTLEMENT

BRYAN WARD-PERKINS

I. THE ISSUES AND THE EVIDENCE

The vast majority of the population of the Roman empire, as in all pre-modern societies, worked on the land. There is a great deal we would like to know about these people: exactly how many they were; how many others they fed (whether artisans, soldiers and clergy, or idle rich); which areas they cultivated, and with what crops and which methods; to what extent their agriculture was specialized and tied into commercial networks of exchange; what types of settlement they lived in; and how tightly their labour was controlled – how many agricultural workers were free peasants cultivating their own plots, and how many dependent tenants of great landlords, wage labourers, or even slaves?

In looking at these questions for the fifth and sixth century we are often moving from a period in which the data are severely restricted into one in which they are almost completely absent. However, by combining written and archaeological evidence, and with the aid of some informed guess-work, we can sometimes at least refine the questions, even if we cannot honestly provide any very firm answers to them.[1]

Over the last thirty to forty years, our picture of the Roman and late Roman countryside has been greatly enhanced, and in some areas transformed, by archaeology. When, in 1964, Jones published his magisterial account of the late Roman empire, he was still able largely to ignore archaeological evidence when discussing rural life.[2] Nowadays one is more likely to find accounts that bypass the contemporary written texts, or dismiss them as hopelessly unreliable.

Archaeology has contributed to our understanding of the ancient landscape partly through the excavation of individual sites, but mainly through

---

[1] Some of the questions I have raised (e.g. specialization and commerce in agricultural production) are discussed in the next chapter; others (e.g. choice of crops and methods of cultivation) I have had to mention only in passing, for reasons of space and because it is impossible to generalize across the Roman world. There is an excellent account of agricultural methods in Byzantium in Kaplan (1992) 5–87, nothing as wide-ranging or recent for the west. In both chapters 12 and 13 I have kept references to a minimum, citing wherever possible recent surveys that give access to further literature.

[2] Jones, *LRE* 767–823: archaeology makes a belated appearance on p. 823.

regional surveys of standing remains (where they survive), and through the practice of field-walking, which involves the systematic plotting and dating of lost settlement sites by the recovery on the surface of pottery and other datable items. Surveys of this kind have filled out the map of the Roman world with thousands of villages and scattered rural settlements, whereas before only the larger and more spectacular sites were generally known to scholarship. However, there are still vast areas of the empire where systematic survey has never been carried out (for instance, in the whole of Asia Minor, modern Turkey); and even amongst those surveys that have been published there are enormous differences in the sophistication of the work and in the consequent quality of the results. For example, surveys in the near east seldom discuss the way the data have been collected, and generally brand all 'late' sites as 'Byzantine', without any attempt to subdivide the huge date range from A.D. 300 to 700+, and they give little consideration to the size of individual settlements. On the other hand, state-of-the-art surveys, such as that carried out in Boeotia in Greece, discuss these important matters in exhaustive detail.[3]

Field-survey is a very good tool for charting the distribution and even the size of settlement in periods, such as the Roman, when material goods are both abundant and often readily datable. However, as we shall see, it is less successful in providing a clear picture of rural settlement in periods when material objects are much scarcer. It is also, of course, only indirectly informative about the fields that were cultivated from these settlements and about what was grown on them – though some reasonable inferences can always be made on the basis of the possibilities and limitations dictated by soil, climate and prevalent market-conditions within the surrounding territory. However, only rarely do we get more direct and detailed information about agricultural methods and products – where ancient field-systems have survived and been studied, as on the moors of south-west England or in the wadis of the Libyan pre-desert; or where careful modern excavation and subsequent analysis have produced evidence from a site in the form of bones and carbonized or waterlogged vegetable material, of the particular plants and animals consumed on it.

Archaeology finds 'things', and from these things it is often possible to reconstruct the human processes and structures that brought them about. However, some aspects of human life can only be very tentatively and insecurely explored from material evidence. In particular, the social structures that bind people together, willingly or unwillingly, are not normally revealed very explicitly in their houses and rubbish-dumps. For instance, there is as

---

[3] Throughout this and the following chapter I use 'near east' to describe the eastern provinces between Egypt to the south and Asia Minor to the north. For Boeotia: Bintliff (1985).

yet no satisfactory way of telling whether a small house in the countryside with an array of local and imported pottery was inhabited by a free peasant, a tied tenant or a slave. Here, in dealing with social relations, documentary evidence becomes essential. Unfortunately, such evidence is very limited from our period. The law codes of both the Roman empire and the barbarian successor states do provide some vital information on the ties that bound together the rural population. However, as we shall see, it is impossible to tell how generally and successfully such prescriptions from above were applied in practice on the ground.

For detailed local information on the organization of estates and on the status of agricultural labourers, we rely (except in Egypt) on very patchy and scattered written information which, even when it is roughly contemporary, tends to derive from very different types of document. What we lack are sequences of similar data, which would allow us to make reliable comparisons, either through time or across the Roman world at any one moment. For instance, from the years around 600, we have an important will from Gaul, listing the estates and tenants of a single great private landowner (Bertram of Le Mans, who died in 616); a smattering of letters relating to papal estates, primarily in Italy and Sicily (preserved in the Register of Gregory the Great, 590–604); and some passing references to villagers in a saint's *Life* from central Anatolia (in the *Life of Theodore of Sykeon*).[4] Only the documents on papyrus excavated in Egypt provide an extensive and varied corpus of material relating to a single region of the empire; but even here the survival of documents is necessarily haphazard, and the data do not compare to the articulated and complementary information that we might expect, say, from manorial and taxation records in late medieval western Europe.

Archaeology can provide important information on broad economic structures affecting the countryside, which will be explored in the next chapter (in particular, on the import of goods into rural contexts and on the export of rural products). But the available archaeological and documentary evidence cannot provide much information on the all-important local economic structures within which agricultural work was performed. For instance, we would like to know whether some peasants had a small specialized sideline in the rearing of, say, chickens, exchanging their surplus eggs with a neighbour who perhaps had a similar local specialization in the making and repair of basic agricultural implements. Equally, we would like to know whether some smallholders supplemented the produce of their own land by selling their labour to the owners of larger holdings at times of high demand, such as the harvest and the vintage. Even in Egypt we

---

[4] Bertram will: discussed in Jones, *LRE* 782–3, and in Wood *Merovingian Kingdoms* 207–10. Greg. *Reg.* ed. D. Norberg, 1982 (= *CCSL* 140). *Life of Theodore of Sykeon*, ed. and French trans. Festugière (1970), partial English trans. in Dawes and Baynes (1948); discussion in Mitchell, *Anatolia* II.122–50.

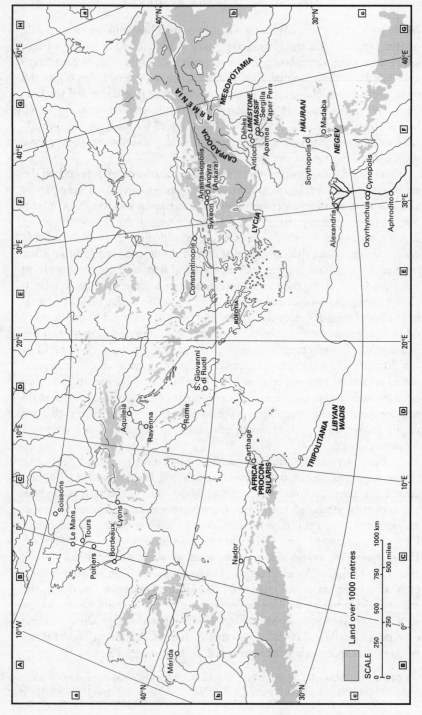

Map 7 Settlements of the fifth and sixth century (sites and regions discussed in chapter 12)

cannot tell, because these types of small transaction, vital though they might be to the well-being of peasant households and to the smooth running of the agricultural economy, do not show up archaeologically, and are 'below' the level of information that is habitually recorded in documents.[5]

In examining the life of the countryside with the scattered and partial information available to us, the best we can do, then, is work with the constant awareness that the data may be deceiving us, and in the certain knowledge that new evidence and new theories will soon alter what we at present believe. In 1953 Georges Tchalenko published a justly famous survey of the late Roman villages of northern Syria, whose limestone buildings are wonderfully preserved, and sometimes dated by inscriptions. On the basis of these inscriptions, Tchalenko assumed, very reasonably, that the villages were abandoned in the seventh century; and, inspired by the Pirenne thesis, he constructed a hypothesis that they had depended on the production of olive oil for the Mediterranean market (a trade supposedly halted by the Arab invasion of the region in the 630s and 640s). However, subsequent excavation in one of these villages, Déhès, has shown that although no new dated houses were constructed, the buildings that were sampled continued to be inhabited right into the ninth century. What is more, they were being used by people with enough copper coins and pottery to suggest that they were still actively involved in a vibrant regional economy.[6]

Written evidence is also, as we have seen, very patchy, and may well be equally deceptive. Until recently it was argued that the papyri from Egypt supported the view (derived from the law codes) that late antique rural society was dominated by the estates of the great and powerful, who used their public and private might to hold their tenants in rigid subjection. However, this impression was heavily dependent on the survival and study of the estate documents of a single great family's holdings around Oxyrhynchus. Recently, attention has been drawn to the very different picture that papyri from Aphrodito provide: here there was no single great landlord, but rather a fiercely independent group of small and medium landholders.[7] There is no way of knowing exactly how prevalent these two very different situations were in late antique Egypt. But without the chance survival and subsequent study of both these archives, we would naturally jump to a single conclusion that was, in fact, incorrect.

---

[5] We do, however, know that Egyptian monks earned money, for charity and for their institutions, by working at the harvest, because several of their recorded sayings refer to this: *The Sayings of the Desert Fathers* (*Apophthegmata Patrum*) (trans. B. Ward, 1975), 'John the Dwarf' nos. 35 & 47; 'Isaac of the Cells' 7; 'Lucius' 1; 'Macarius' 7; 'Pior' 1.　　[6] Tchalenko, *Villages*; Sodini *et al.* (1980) for Déhès.

[7] Apion estates around Oxyrhynchus: Hardy (1931); Gascou (1985). Aphrodito: Keenan (1993) and ch. 21*c* (Keenan), pp. 633–6 below.

II. POPULATION; THE SPREAD OF SETTLEMENT; DEMOGRAPHIC DECLINE?

It would greatly help our understanding of the economy, and indeed of the whole society of the late Roman world, if we could come up with even rough estimates of total population. These would give us figures to compare with later and better-documented periods, and thereby allow us to form a more accurate impression of the scale of operations within the Roman period. They would also help us to put into context some of the late Roman institutions to which it has been possible to attach rough estimates of numbers of people. For instance, estimates for the size of the Roman army at the end of the fourth century can rise as high as 600,000 men.[8] This is indubitably a very large figure, and certainly points to the existence of a heavy state structure. But exactly how large and how heavy depends very much on what one thinks the total Roman population was – if it was 20 million, then perhaps more than one in forty of the total population (around one in ten of adult males) was maintained under arms by the state; but, if the population was 200 million, the proportions drop to a less impressive one in 400 of the total population and one in a hundred of adult males. Similarly, a very rough estimate for the size of the population of Constantinople in around A.D. 450 is 300,000–400,000 souls[9] – a very large number of people, involving a massive system of supply. But quite how heavily this weighed on the eastern empire depends very much on how large one thinks its total population was at this time.

However, in the absence of census or tax returns, we unfortunately have no overall recorded figure for the total population of the empire in any period. Few have yet ventured even regional estimates on the basis of the ever-increasing archaeological evidence. The main imponderables are whether all sites (even if identified with confidence and shown to be roughly contemporary on pottery dating) were in reality all occupied at exactly the same time, and, more seriously, how to estimate from surface finds the numbers of households present on a site, and how then to decide the correct multiplier to use for individuals per household.

In the one province, Britain, where a number of archaeologists have recently been bold enough (or foolhardy enough) to attempt independent estimates, the suggested figures for Roman population are high, and have tended to rise over the last decades, as more archaeological data emerge. The estimates range between two and six million people, which are very different figures, but are none the less roughly within the same order of magnitude as estimates for the population of England in the period around and after the Domesday survey of 1086.[10] It seems possible that the land

[8] Treadgold (1995) 43–59.   [9] Mango, *Développement* 51.   [10] Millett (1990) 181–6.

of Roman Britain supported the same order of population as it did in the later Middle Ages.

In other provinces, estimates of population are rarer; but, wherever intensive field-survey has been carried out, extensive and dense rural settlement patterns, similar to those discovered in Britain, have always been found in at least part of the Roman period. However, recent work has revealed striking differences between the various regions of the empire when it comes to the precise period of the greatest spread of Roman settlement.

In the northern and western provinces, the clearest evidence for large rural populations comes from before the beginning of our period in 425: in Italy apparently under the early empire; in Gaul and Spain perhaps in the late first and second century; in Britain and Africa possibly in the fourth. By contrast, in both modern Greece and the near east, which are the only two east Mediterranean regions where a large number of field-surveys have been carried out, it is within our period, in the fifth and sixth century, that the highest number of sites and the greatest geographical spread of settlement are recorded.[11]

Indeed, in the late antique near east, some areas were densely settled which are very marginal for conventional agricultural exploitation and which for the most part have never subsequently been as intensively used again – in particular, the limestone uplands of northern Syria and the basalt region of the Hauran around ancient Bostra, both rocky landscapes in which the areas of arable soil are severely restricted (see Fig. 5) and, even more striking, the wadis of the Negev in southern Israel, where the surrounding landscape is bare rock, and where the rainfall is both very seasonal and very low.[12] In Egypt, evidence from the papyri of an increasing number of water-lifting devices from the fourth century onwards suggests a similar late antique spread of agriculture into less readily cultivable areas, and a similar rise in population.[13]

In the east, therefore, it seems certain that the fifth and sixth centuries were the period of both the greatest spread of settlement in Roman times and of the highest population density and overall numbers. Furthermore, in these regions population levels were almost certainly unmatched until very recent times (perhaps not until this century).

The spread and intensification of settlement in the eastern provinces, and the growth of the population until at least A.D. 500, seem clear and are not disputed. What is much more open to both doubt and dispute is what

---

[11] General surveys of the evidence, with further bibliography: Greene (1986) 98–141; Lewit (1991) 27–36. Greece: Alcock (1993) 33–92 (though focused on the earlier Roman period). Near east: Dauphin (1980).

[12] Northern Syria and Negev: useful review article of recent literature in Foss (1995). Hauran: Dentzer (1985) and Sartre (1985).   [13] Bagnall, *Egypt* 17–18.

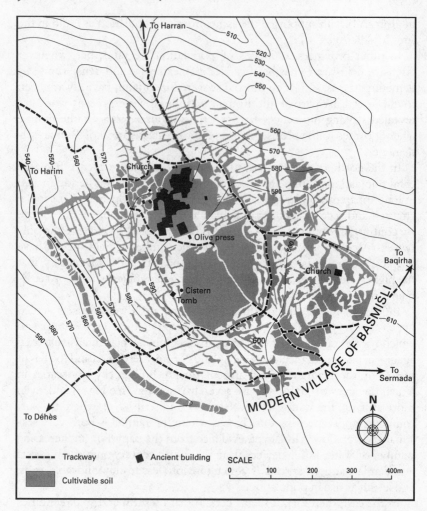

Fig. 5 The late antique village site of Bamuqqa in the north Syrian limestone massif. Ancient
buildings are in black; areas of cultivable soil, in pockets surrounded by bare rock, are in grey.
(After Tchalenko, *Villages* II, pl. XCII)

happened after the early sixth century. In 541/2 a dreadful plague hit the
east, subsequently spreading to the west and also recurring intermittently
through the sixth and seventh centuries. The impact of this disease on
Constantinople was graphically described by the historian Procopius, who
witnessed it there and claimed that at its peak it killed over 10,000 people a
day, while for Antioch the local historian Evagrius provides not only the
detailed information that it had recurred four times in the city by the time
of his writing in 594, but also the irrefutably circumstantial evidence that it

had hit his own family very hard. He himself survived the plague as a child, but his wife and 'many' (*pollous*) of his relatives had died of it, most recently a daughter, along with her own child.[14]

There is no doubt that this plague was harsh, nor is there any doubting the degree of personal tragedy that it wrought on many like Evagrius. But it is harder to be confident about its broad demographic impact.[15] The problem is that there are two possible models for the impact of such an epidemic, and both could be applied to the sixth-century plague on the basis of the limited information available to us. In the absence of fuller evidence, which model one accepts will depend largely on how far one prefers to explain demographic change in terms of random 'acts of God', or to play these down in favour of slower changes brought about by human agency.

Either the sixth-century plagues were a series of demographic hammer-blows comparable to the Black Death of 1348–9 (which probably killed at least a third of the population of fourteenth-century Europe), or their impact was more closely comparable to that of the epidemics that hit Europe in the sixteenth and seventeenth century (most famously, London in 1665). These were devastating locally, and wiped out entire families, but they did not affect all regions and settlements concurrently. Even within affected towns and communities, outbreaks hit some parishes and some families very much harder than others. Despite the death in England from plague of perhaps three-quarters of a million people between 1470 and 1670, over the same period the population of the country probably doubled.[16] Perhaps, like Samuel Pepys, Procopius saw plague at its very worst in the crowded metropolis of Constantinople, where rats and human beings were densely packed together. And perhaps Evagrius' family was one of the very unfortunate ones. Indeed, he himself tells us in some detail that the impact of individual outbreaks of plague varied a great deal, between cities, between urban districts, and even between individual households.

Uncertainty over the impact of plague on population levels in the sixth-century east is but one aspect of the central and knotty problem of how to detect population decline. It is generally assumed that the population of the west, or at least of most of its provinces, declined under the later empire (in the third and fourth century), and then fell markedly in the immediately post-Roman centuries (the fifth to seventh). In the Byzantine east, as we have

---

[14] Procop. *Wars* II.22–3; Evagr. *HE* IV.29. It was also witnessed, in the near east, by John of Ephesus, whose description survives in fragmentary form (it is published only in the original Syriac, but is used and discussed by Conrad (1986) 144–7). There is a good general discussion of the plague in the east in Patlagean, *Pauvreté* 87–91. For the plague in the west: Biraben and Le Goff (1969).

[15] As questioned by Durliat (1989). For a general discussion of sixth-century eastern demographic change: Whitby (1996) 92–103.   [16] Black Death: Hatcher (1977). Later plagues: Slack (1990) 53–195.

seen, demographic decline is presumed to have begun much later; but here too, after 542 or at the latest in the seventh century, it is normally thought that the population dropped considerably, perhaps even dramatically.

In the absence of good written records, we are basically dependent on the archaeological evidence for these impressions of a falling population. However, this evidence is deeply problematic. Archaeology, and field-survey in particular, finds people through their durable material objects. If people owned abundant and readily recognizable things that survive well in the soil (as they did in the Roman west, and in the fifth- and sixth-century east), then the population shows up well in the modern landscape, as scatters of tile and pottery, or even as mosaics, silver treasures and standing ruins.

However, excavation has shown that both fifth- and sixth-century westerners and seventh-century Byzantines generally lived in much less imposing and more 'biodegradable' surroundings than their Roman predecessors: with pottery that is less abundant and more difficult to identify than that of the preceding periods; in houses that were often of perishable materials; and with the public buildings and churches of former ages, rather than with new ones. All this means that post-Roman people can easily escape surface-detection.[17] For instance, the great sixth/seventh-century royal estate-centre and rural palace at Yeavering in Northumbria (termed by Bede a *villa regia*) was a settlement from the very top of the social pyramid and was home to perhaps hundreds of people; but it was built entirely of wood and other perishable materials and, despite full and meticulous excavation, produced only small quantities of pottery, all of it friable and close in colour to the soil.[18] The site of Yeavering was discovered through the good fortune that its post-holes and ditches showed up well in air-photography. It is a sobering but important realization for those interested in the history of post-Roman population levels that, without this, Yeavering might well have escaped even careful field-survey. By contrast, a tiny Roman farmstead, home to perhaps only ten individuals from much lower down the social ladder, will normally be readily spotted, dated and plotted on the archaeological map from the evidence of its pottery. There is no constant correlation between the number of archaeological sites detected and the number of sites that once existed; rather, the discovery-rate of sites will vary according to the nature of each period's material culture.

Nor, even when we have detected the sites, is there a constant multiplier that can be applied in order to move from identified dwellings to the number of people who lived in them. Modern experience shows that in

---

[17] For the details: ch. 13, pp. 350–62 below. For discussion of this archaeological problem: Lewit (1991) 37–46; Millett (1991).   [18] Hope-Taylor (1977) 170–200 and plates 3 and 4.

complex, prosperous societies, people use wealth in the pursuit of greater living space and in the purchase of more than one house; while in strait-ened circumstances, they retrench, housing, for example, elderly parents and young adult offspring within the family home. Similar variables may well have applied in antiquity and the early Middle Ages. Indeed, there is some archaeological evidence to support this, in the Roman dwellings found to have been crudely subdivided in post-Roman times (see, for example, that in Fig. 6).[19] Some of these remains, often dismissed in the past as 'squatter occupation', may show the descendants of the original owners living in a more densely packed and less comfortable way than their ancestors. Charting such subtle but important shifts in the practices of society is essential if we are to document demographic change at all reli-ably from the archaeological evidence; but they will certainly not show up in field-survey, and they may well be missed even in excavation.

The very real problem with the evidence is readily demonstrated from the example of Italy. Large parts of the peninsula have been surveyed in intensive and often sophisticated field-surveys over the last forty years, and many of the recent surveys have been specifically interested in discovering early medieval settlements – but, for the most part, they have drawn a com-plete, or almost complete, blank for the late sixth to the eighth century. If the archaeological record was straightforward, there would be no one living in huge tracts of early medieval Italy. This is self-evidently nonsense: there must have been people living in these areas, and we just cannot find them. And since this is so, we are scarcely in a strong position to begin speculat-ing as to how many of them there were.

It is not only a close examination of the archaeological evidence that urges caution before producing too confident an account of post-Roman demographic collapse. When (for the first time in the Middle Ages) we have documents that allow local population estimates to be made, the so-called polyptychs of ninth-century Carolingian church estates (most famously that of 806/29 from the abbey of Saint-Germain-des-Prés in the Île de France), these reveal remarkably large rural populations.[20] The tradition amongst economic historians of the Middle Ages has been to play this down by describing these ecclesiastical estates as exceptional pockets of dense population within a much emptier and undocumented landscape. But this argument smacks a bit of preconceptions and special pleading (designed perhaps to highlight a later, eleventh- and twelfth-century eco-nomic and demographic upturn). If instead we accept that both Roman and Carolingian Europe supported large rural populations, there is less room left for the traditional model of what happened to population in

[19] Nador: Anselmino et al. (1989). For other examples (at Carthage, Ptolemais and Déhès): Ellis (1985); Ward-Perkins et al. (1986); Sodini et al. (1980).

[20] Lot (1921); and, for further discussion and bibliography: Doehaerd (1971) 85–113; Rouche (1983).

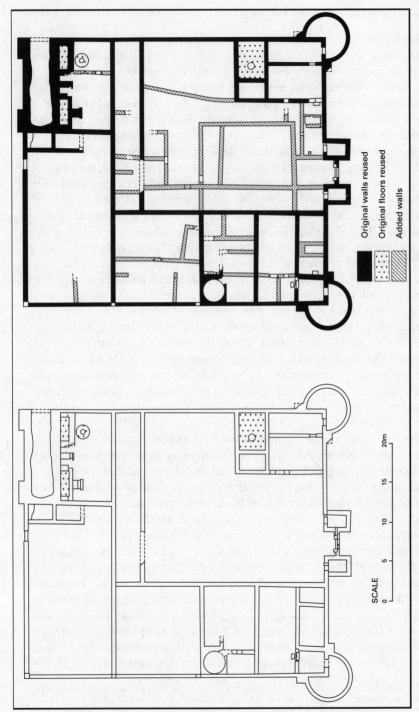

Fig 6 The fortified farmstead of Nador in Mauretania. On the left, as originally built in the fourth century; on the right, with the additional subdivisions of fifth- and early-sixth-century date. The defences seem to have been conceived of as partly functional, partly decorative, since the façade received much more attention than the equally vulnerable sides and rear. (After Anselmino et al. (1989) 228, fig 50)

Original walls reused

Original floors reused

Added walls

SCALE

0   5   10   15   20m

post-Roman times: cataclysmic collapse, followed by painfully slow recovery up to around 1,000 (when real economic and demographic growth, as well as decent documentation, begin).

The archaeological evidence available at present, therefore, cannot prove dramatic demographic decline, while the Carolingian evidence shows that the rural population could well have been large in the ninth century. However, there is still plenty of room within the archaeological record and within the four centuries between 400 and 800 for a substantial fall in population in post-Roman times. Indeed, on balance I believe that the population did drop, perhaps even dramatically (i.e. to half – or even less – of its previous, Roman levels). My reasons for thinking this have got less to do with the evidence directly relevant to population levels (whose unreliability I have stressed) than with my understanding of the workings of the Roman and post-Roman economies, as set out in the next chapter. There I argue that many Roman and late Roman farmers were involved in commercialized and specialized production, and that this both opened up marginal land for exploitation and settlement and allowed other land to be exploited in a more specialized and efficient way. If so, the land in the Roman period is likely to have produced more, and in consequence the population is likely to have risen. Equally, if, as I believe, these conditions did not persist into post-Roman times, then the population supported by the land is very likely to have dropped substantially.

III. RURAL SETTLEMENT (VILLAGES, FARMSTEADS AND VILLAS)

Both the archaeological and the documentary evidence are rather fuller when it comes to another fundamental aspect of rural life: the pattern of settlement. But even here the evidence is by no means entirely satisfactory. The written record consists mainly of incidental references to settlements, sometimes very obscure because we no longer know precisely what contemporaries meant by some of the terms they used. Did 'villa' in sixth-century Frankish usage, for instance, mean an estate, a luxurious country dwelling, a farmstead, a village or any one of the four in different contexts?[21] Meanwhile, the archaeological record, at least until recently, has been heavily weighted towards sites that are likely to produce beautiful and impressive results. Fortunately, in the near east this weighting has included the magnificent mosaic pavements of village churches in modern Israel and Jordan, and the wonderfully preserved stone village churches and village houses of regions like the Negev, the Hauran and the north Syrian limestone uplands.[22] But in most of the empire, archaeological interest has

[21] See, for instance, Heinzelmann (1993).
[22] See p. 321 above, n. 12. For the mosaics and churches of Jordan and Israel: Piccirillo (1985) and (1993); Ovadiah (1970).

focused away from villages, either towards towns or towards the luxurious and isolated rural dwellings of the rich.

Despite gaps in the available evidence, it seems clear that there was something of a contrast between rural settlement in the east and in the west. In the east, settlement appears to have been dominated by the compact village, with little evidence of dispersed farmsteads through the countryside, including little evidence for luxurious country dwellings of the aristocracy, while in the west dispersed settlement was common, and there is considerable written and archaeological evidence for aristocratic rural houses.

The papyri of Egypt show conclusively that country life in the Nile valley revolved around the village. A similar picture emerges from saints' *Lives* from Asia Minor, such as the *Life of Nicholas of Sion*, describing events in south-western coastal Lycia in the mid sixth century, and that of Theodore of Sykeon, from central Anatolia near Ankara, covering the period around A.D. 600.[23] Villages, not dispersed settlements, are the backdrop to both saints' lives, and both men deal with people who are very often described as being from a particular village.

Archaeological work in the eastern Mediterranean, particularly in the provinces of the near east, has revealed hundreds of late antique villages (see Fig. 7), with large and elaborately decorated churches of the fifth and sixth century, and with fine houses that suggest that not only peasants but also the owners of sizeable (but not immense) estates preferred to live within village communities rather than in isolation on their land.[24] Eastern surveys have also failed to reveal much evidence for luxurious rural dwellings, whether in villages or isolated in the countryside. This suggests that landlords of very large estates in the eastern Mediterranean, who certainly existed and who in the west would have maintained both an urban and a rural residence, preferred to live within the cities or in suburban houses, like the spectacular villas of Daphne just outside Antioch, with their rich mosaic floors.[25]

Villages in the eastern provinces, of course, varied greatly in size and importance, from tiny settlements to large agglomerations which are technically 'villages' only because they did not have the administrative status to make them Roman *civitates* or *poleis*.[26] Modern scholars have, indeed, sometimes been both confused and confusing in writing of these villages as the 'cities' of the Negev or the 'villes mortes' of Syria. The confusion is, however, an understandable one. Some of these villages were sizeable, like Kaper Pera, north of Apamea, which boasted five churches (see Fig. 8) and

---

[23] Egypt: Bagnall, *Egypt* 110–47; Keenan (1984). For Theodore, see p. 317 above, n. 4; for Nicholas: *The Life of Saint Nicholas of Sion* ed. and trans. I. Ševčenko and N. Patterson Ševčenko, 1984.

[24] Villages are, however, much less apparent in the surveys carried out in Greece, where dispersed settlement seems to have been common. For larger houses in (or just outside) villages: several examples in the north Syrian uplands, Tchalenko, *Villages* pl. cxxv–cxli; and in the Hauran, Villeneuve (1985) 113–16.   [25] Levi (1947).   [26] Dagron (1979); Kaplan (1992) 90–5.

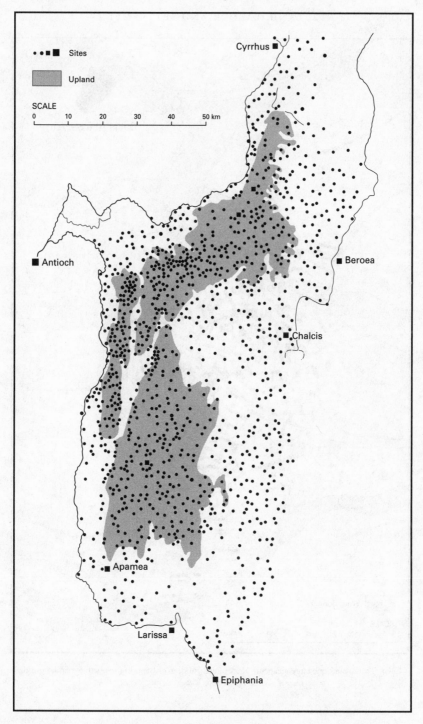

Fig. 7 Ancient sites in the north Syrian uplands, of which the greater part are villages.
(After Tchalenko, *Villages* ii, pl. xxxv)

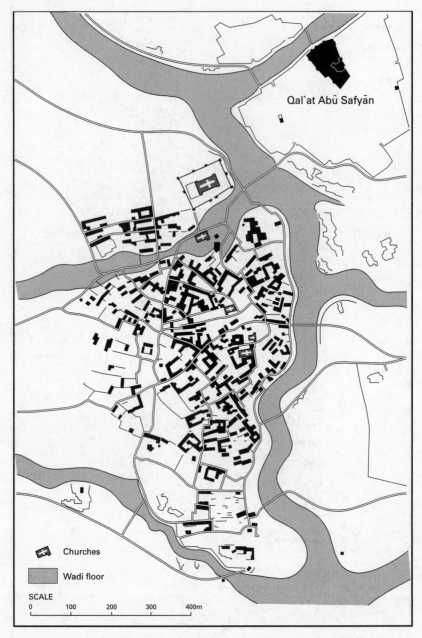

Fig. 8 The late antique large village of Kaper Pera (modern el-Bâra) in the north Syrian limestone massif. (After Tchalenko, *Villages* II, pl. CXXXIX)

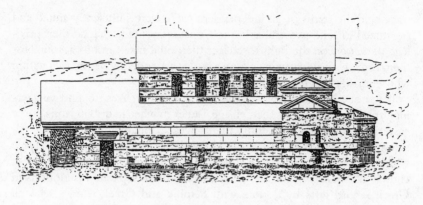

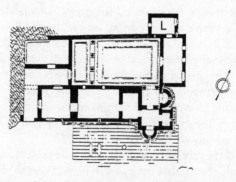

Fig. 9 South elevation and plan of the baths built in 473 by Julianos and his wife at the village of Sergilla, in the Syrian Jabal Zawiye. The plan shows the cistern and raised water conduit to the south. (L = latrine; after Butler (1920) ill. 134)

probably exceeded in size and splendour many 'true' *civitates* in the interior of central North Africa, where the Romans had established their local administration in a large number of very small centres. Villagers in the east could also act corporately to enhance their village environment and to defend their interests, in ways that we would more normally associate with the classical city, and that can rarely be documented in the contemporary west. A mosaic inscription of 473, for instance, excavated in the small public baths of the village of Sergilla in Syria (see Fig. 9), tells us that they were built in honour of his home village (*patrē*) by a certain Julianos, in conjunction with his wife Domna, and records the gratitude of the village (*kōmē*) towards its benefactor.[27] Almost a century later, in 547 and 550, the villagers of Aphrodito, a large Egyptian settlement (which, admittedly, had

[27] *Inscriptions* (1929–) IV, no. 1490. There is a recent discussion of this bath in Charpentier (1994). For the plan of another Syrian village, with three churches, see Fig. 42, p. 925 below.

once held the status of an independent *polis*), were sufficiently united and organized to send two embassies to Constantinople to defend their privilege of *autopragia*, the right to collect their own taxes and to account for them directly to the provincial governor, independently of the *polis* within whose jurisdiction they now fell.[28]

It is not surprising in local sources, like saints' lives, to find villagers identified by the name of their village. But even when in distant lands, some easterners still chose to identify themselves as inhabitants of specific villages, rather than as inhabitants of the wider and much better-known *polis* which contained them. We see this in the fifth-century mosaic floor of a church at Aquileia in northern Italy, where three separate inscriptions in Greek record gifts by donors with Semitic and Greek names, who all describe themselves as being of particular villages (*apo kōmēs...*).[29] Eastern villagers associated themselves with their home villages in ways that in the west can only be readily documented for cities. Such pride is also shown (admittedly, some time after our period) on the mosaic floor of an eighth-century church at Um-er-Rasas (ancient Kastron Mephaa), near Madaba. Here a number of important local cities were depicted, all identified by name; but also very prominently illustrated (opposite the Holy City of Jerusalem) is a representation of the village of Kastron Mephaa itself. Except for its name (*Kastron*, fortress) this representation is indistinguishable from those of the great cities of the region – indeed, it is larger and more splendid than any of them.[30]

In the west, villages seem to have played a lesser role. In some areas, this was for the simple reason that they were rare, and that the basic pattern of settlement was of scattered farmsteads. For instance, an extensive survey of the countryside north of the city of Rome revealed very few villages in the Roman period and large numbers of farmsteads, and a similar picture emerges for the region around Ravenna from the private documents that survive from the sixth century onwards.[31] Even where they did exist, western villages seem to have carried less social and political weight than their eastern counterparts. Certainly, they show up far less in the epigraphic, literary and excavation records. This lack of prominence may be because middling landowners, even in regions where there were villages, preferred to live in isolated farmsteads, and because parts of the countryside were also dominated by the great houses of the very rich.

However, that villages existed in parts of the Roman west is gradually becoming clear from detailed archaeological work, and has long been

---

[28] Jones, *LRE* 407–8; MacCoull, *Dioscorus* 5–11.   [29] Caillet (1993) 167–72, nos. 6, 7 and 13.
[30] Piccirillo (1993) 218–31 and 238–9.
[31] South Etruria survey (area north of Rome): Ward-Perkins (1968) (at some point in the early Middle Ages nucleated villages replaced these scattered farmsteads; but at present this is believed to have happened primarily from the tenth century onwards). Ravenna: Castagnetti (1979) 169–79.

apparent in some areas where written accounts survive. Gregory, bishop of Tours, writing at the end of the sixth century, mainly about the Auvergne and the Touraine, happens to mention in his works of history and hagiography seventy different villages (*vici*): they were clearly a standard feature of the countryside. From Gregory we also learn that at least thirty-six of these *vici* had their own church, some of them dedicated by Gregory himself.[32] As in the east, where the evidence lies in the survival and excavation of so many village churches, villages in the west were also clearly emerging as one important element in the organization of Christian life – an element which from the ninth century onwards was to develop into the fully-fledged parish system.

The countryside of the western provinces in Roman times had always also contained the houses of landowners, which, if they reveal some decorative features in the Roman style, modern scholars have tended to call 'villas'. The fate of the villas in the disturbed circumstances of the fifth- and sixth-century west remains somewhat mysterious, despite considerable archaeological attention. The most complete archaeological evidence is from the far north, Britain and northern Gaul, where it seems that villas in the Roman style disappeared early in the fifth century, though there is sometimes continued use of the same sites with buildings of much humbler materials.[33]

Further south, some impressive late villas have now been excavated and published (see Fig. 10), but we still rely heavily on literary references for evidence of the widespread survival in the fifth and sixth century of an aristocratic lifestyle centred on comfortable and marbled villas in the antique manner. For example, the poems and narrative sources from Vandal Africa clearly demonstrate that the new Vandal landlords readily adapted to this way of life; and, from southern Gaul as late as the second half of the sixth century, the poems of Venantius Fortunatus testify to building-works on three separate villas by a rich Gallo-Roman bishop of Bordeaux.[34]

Probably in the fifth and sixth century there emerged a cultural difference between the northern and southern regions of the west, with the division running roughly along the line of the Loire: to the north, archaeology demonstrates that Roman-style villa buildings had already disappeared; to the south, the literary evidence, even allowing for some rosy-tinted exaggeration in the poetic descriptions, makes it quite clear that

---

[32] Touraine and Auvergne: Longnon (1878) 16–19; Pietri (1983) 793–6 (for the rural churches). Similar evidence for villages in Maine, and in south-west Gaul in general: Latouche (1967) 64–72; Rouche (1979) 221. I and others are here making the assumption that *vicus* = 'village', which may prove over-optimistic.   [33] Lewit (1991) 37–46; Van Ossel (1992) 79–84.

[34] Africa: Rossiter (1990). Gaul: Venantius Fortunatus, *Carm.* 1.18–20; and the discussion of the late Gallic villa in Percival (1992).

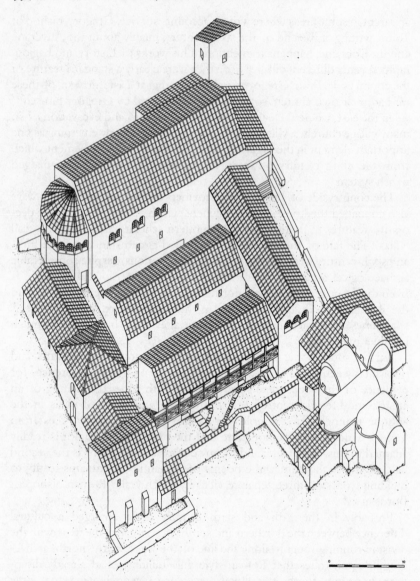

Fig. 10 The villa at San Giovanni di Ruoti as it might have appeared in the late fifth century.
(Reconstruction drawing by E. Haldenby, from Small and Buck (1994) fig. 133)

they persisted. In the seventh century, the history of rural settlement in the two regions again merges, with the disappearance of the 'villa' as a traditional style of building even in the southern provinces, and the persistence of the word in contemporary usage only to describe estates or villages.

Many questions about late villas, however, still remain, to which it would be very nice to have clear archaeological answers. Quite how large, sumptuous and classical were the villa buildings so lovingly described by Venantius Fortunatus in the sixth century (or indeed those similarly described by Sidonius Apollinaris a century earlier)? And what exactly did a sixth-century royal 'villa' in northern Francia look like, such as the one at Berny-Rivière near Soissons, where Gregory of Tours was tried in 580? Was it a recognizably 'Roman' building, or something that we might term 'sub-Roman'; or was it perhaps principally a great series of timbered halls, like the roughly contemporary Northumbrian *villa regia* at Yeavering?[35]

IV. RURAL FORTIFICATIONS

One feature of settlement in the countryside, which affected most of the late antique world, was an increase in the number of fortified sites. The third century had, of course, introduced war to many previously peaceful areas, and frontier-zones remained exposed to attack through the following centuries. The collapse of the frontiers in the west at the beginning of the fifth century, and the emergence here of new and often unstable political groupings, meant that in much of the former empire warfare became endemic. Unsurprisingly, these changes are reflected in the emergence of fortified rural sites.

Once again, the evidence is both documentary and archaeological. The documentary evidence is still very useful: for instance, from Gaul it provides us with information about rural fortifications sponsored by aristocrats, which seem to have combined the luxurious living-quarters of the traditional villa with the security of strong walls and towers.[36] But this literary evidence consists of individual snippets of information, which cannot on their own be fitted into a broad pattern of settlement. For this we must again rely on archaeological survey and excavation.

The archaeological record reveals a wide variety of different types of fortified rural site in the fifth and sixth century, with considerable regional variation in the precise type used: farmsteads and villages surrounded by a

---

[35] Gregory gives few clues, though *Hist.* v.50 refers to an *atrium*, and to a new *supertegulum*, presumably the apex of a tiled roof. On the archaeological and literary evidence for late rural settlement in Gaul, including 'villas', see also Samson (1987).

[36] Sid. Ap. *Carm.* XXII (on the *burgus* of Pontius Leontius on the Garonne, written probably in the 460s); Venantius Fortunatus, *Carm.* III.12 (on the *castellum* of Nicetius of Trier on the Moselle, written in the 560s).

ditch-and-bank; reoccupied and refortified Iron Age hill-forts; villas with towers and surrounding wall (see Fig. 6, p. 326 above); and settlements built around strongly fortified refuge-towers.[37] However, the prevalence of fortified sites in the late and post-Roman rural landscape should not be exaggerated: in some regions particularly exposed to raiding, like southern Tripolitania, it does seem as though rural fortresses were ubiquitous, but in most of the empire, even in the confused fifth- and sixth-century west, the vast majority of sites seem to have been only very lightly defended or not defended at all.[38]

The pattern of rural defence in our period is perhaps best understood in terms of the emergence of selected strongholds, leaving most settlements undefended, rather than as a widespread attempt to fortify every rural dwelling or to move people into enclosed defensible sites.[39] The fifth- and sixth-century countryside did contain fortifications that had certainly not existed before, but it did not yet resemble the landscape of, say, late medieval central Italy, dominated by fortified hill-villages. Even in the unstable world of seventh-century northern Britain, the kings of Bernicia did not site their *villa* at Yeavering within the security of the nearby late Iron Age *oppidum*, but seem to have preferred to retreat, in times of danger, to the impregnable fastness of their coastal fortress at Bamburgh, leaving Yeavering and their other rural estate-centres to be burnt to the ground.[40]

V. THE PATTERN OF LAND OWNERSHIP; THE STATUS OF PEASANTS

When looking at how the land was shared out, and at the legal and social ties that bound many at the lower levels of society to that land, we are dependent mainly on written sources for our information. Patterns of landholding and the status of rural dwellers can sometimes be revealed in the archaeological record: for instance, it is probably reasonable to infer that an excavated house which proves to have been expensively decorated was inhabited by an owner rather than a tenant. But often we are left guessing whether or not a small farmstead or a whole village, known only from archaeology, was part of a larger estate, and whether its inhabitants were free or tied to the land.

---

[37] For some examples of these types of fortification, and other variants: Van Ossel (1992) 163–4; Alcock (1972) 174–94; Démians d'Archimbaud (1994); Alföldy (1974) 214–20; Brogiolo (1994) 151–8; Anselmino *et al.* (1989); Mattingly and Hayes (1992); Mattingly (1995) 147–8 and 194–209.

[38] Tripolitania: Mattingly (1995) 147–8 and 194–209.

[39] The long list of (largely unknown) fortresses (*phrouria*) built or restored by Justinian in the Balkans, according to Procopius (*Buildings* iv.4), may be evidence of a different policy – of helping to provide or enhance defences for large numbers of villages and other settlements.

[40] Hope-Taylor (1977); Bede, *HE* iii.16 and 17.

The largest accumulations of land must have been in the hands of rulers, both in east and west; but better documented are the growing estates of the church, for which we have a fair smattering of information from most parts of the Roman and former Roman world. Except in Egypt, where the documentation is uniquely rich, it is the prinicipal churches and monasteries that happen to dominate the sources, rather than smaller landholding institutions.[41] The Great Church at Constantinople, unsurprisingly, held land throughout the east, and had separate departments in its estate-office for its different regional holdings. The church of Rome, lavishly and widely endowed already by Constantine after his capture of the city in 312, must have lost some of its outlying holdings during the troubles of the fifth century; but at the end of the sixth century it held land, administered by locally based rectors, not only in Italy, Sicily, Sardinia and Corsica, but also in Africa, Gaul and distant Dalmatia.[42] Some idea of the scale of this land-holding can be deduced from the annual figure of 25,200 *solidi*, which the emperor Leo III directed into his own treasury from the papal estates in Calabria and Sicily when in dispute with the papacy in the 730s.[43] For comparison, the huge and sumptuous church of S. Vitale at Ravenna cost 26,000 *solidi* to complete in the sixth century.

A bishop of one of the greatest sees might have very large sums of money under his control, much, though not all of it, derived from rural estates: the Life of John the Almsgiver, bishop of Alexandria at the beginning of the seventh century, tells us that at his accession John found a vast quantity of gold in the bishop's house, which he proceeded to spend on pious causes.[44] Lesser sees commanded lesser, but still substantial, incomes and estates: Sidonius Apollinaris tells how bishop Patiens of Lyons, during a famine in the second half of the fifth century, filled the roads and rivers with his transports bringing grain into the city; and Gregory of Tours records that one of his predecessors, in the mid sixth century, gave to the poor 20,000 *solidi* left by the previous bishop.[45] The desire and need to provide landed endowments for bishoprics could, on occasion, lead to dubious practices. Bishop Paul of Mérida, in the later sixth century, promised a massive legacy to his own church, but only if his nephew succeeded him as bishop.[46]

[41] Egypt: Wipszycka (1972).

[42] Jones, *LRE* 781–2; Kaplan (1992) 143–4 (for the church of Constantinople).

[43] Theophanes, *Chron.* a.m. 6224 (trans. C. Mango 1996). The passage is not crystal clear: although this is not stated, it seems reasonable to suppose that the sum mentioned was an annual payment; but it is less clear whether it was of rent or tax. For our purposes, either shows that the estates were massive.

[44] *Life of John the Almsgiver* 45 (trans. Dawes and Baynes (1948) 256). The exact figure mentioned is implausibly high: 8,000 pounds of gold, well over half a million *solidi* (enough to build more than twenty S. Vitales).

[45] Lyons: Sid. Ap. *Ep.* 6.12. Tours: Greg. Tur. *Hist.* ix.41 (the money was either saved from church income, or derived from the personal estate of the previous bishop).

[46] *Vita Sanctorum Patrum Emeretensium* iv.ii.14–18; iv.iv.4; iv.v.2–3.

By the fifth and sixth century, major monasteries were also accumulating sizeable and ever-increasing landed endowments. The monastery of the Holy Cross founded in Poitiers by Radegund apparently housed, at the time of her death in 587, some 200 nuns, many of whom were of high social status and so unquestionably in need of a substantial troop of servants. All this required a large endowment, and when in 589 the nun Chlothild ejected the rightful abbess, unsurprisingly she is recorded to have appointed her own *ordinatores* (presumably stewards) and to have seized the *villas monasterii*.[47]

It is clear that, as in later periods of history, church estates were vulnerable to encroachment from the great and powerful: Theodore of Sykeon, while bishop of Anastasiopolis, only managed to eject a local magnate from some of his church's estates with the help of villagers in armed revolt.[48] The insistence with which hagiographers like Gregory of Tours stressed that the saints would protect their own property and strike down intruders is only explicable in the context of a world where abuses of this kind happened all too often.

The boundaries between ecclesiastical and secular landholding may on occasion have become blurred. The man that Theodore expelled was not only a local aristocrat, but also held an official appointment as administrator of the episcopal estates. Was this a purely professional arrangement that Theodore now wished to undo, or had it been an act of patronage by the bishop of Anastasiopolis, wishing to buy the favour of a local magnate?

For monasteries in this period, we know remarkably little about any continuing relationship between them and the families of their aristocratic founders and benefactors. This may, however, only reflect the limitation of our sources for late antique monasticism (dominated by saints' *Lives* and Rules, rather than the land-deeds and books of commemoration that survive from later centuries). That they could serve as places of family commemoration and burial is shown by the mosaic inscriptions discovered in a small sixth-century monastery at Scythopolis (see Fig. 11). This was built for a monk, Elias, but was also intended as the burial place for one of its patrons, a certain Mary, and of any of her family 'at any time' who wished to rest there.[49] That families might not lose all control of the lands of one of their foundations is revealed in the exceptionally well-documented world of Egypt, where we learn of the small monastery of the 'Holy Christ-Bearing Apostles', founded by the entrepreneurial land-manager Apollos of Aphrodito. Here Apollos himself became a monk, without by any means fully retiring from business; and here his son Dioscorus served as guardian

---

[47] 200 nuns: Greg. Tur. *Gloria Confessorum* ch. 104. Chlothild: Greg. Tur. *Hist.* IX.41. For the lands of the great 'White Monastery' in Egypt, see ch. 21*c* (Keenan), p. 620 below.

[48] Theodore: *Life* ch. 76 (ed. Festugière (1970); English trans. Dawes and Baynes (1948) 139–40).

[49] Fitzgerald (1939). Another patron, John 'the ex-prefect', and two of his brothers were also commemorated in inscriptions (and an excavated tomb is thought to have been John's).

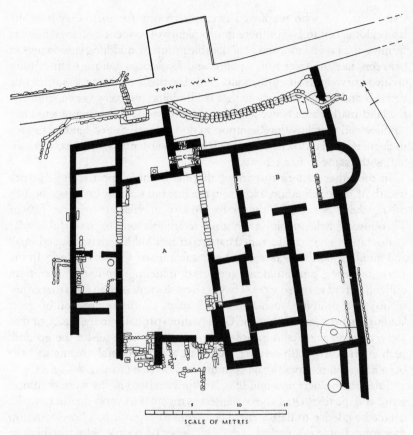

Fig. 11 The sixth-century monastery of a holy man, Elias, excavated at Scythopolis, in Palaestina II. A is a hall or perhaps an open courtyard; B is the chapel. Many of the rooms had fine mosaics, including inscriptions commemorating the patrons and asking for God's blessing on them. The intended tomb of one patron, 'Maria', was within the chapel (which she paid for); another patron, 'John the ex-prefect', is thought to have been buried in the small chamber C. (After Fitzgerald (1939) pl. 11)

(*phrontistēs*) and protector (*kouratōr*) long after his father's death.[50] This looks remarkably like a small aristocratic 'Eigenkloster', of a kind very familiar in the early medieval west, and designed to provide for both the spiritual and the material needs of a family.

For the estates of the secular landowning class, the information at our disposal is limited – except, again, in Egypt. Here, from the papyri, a rich and varied picture can be built up. There were some huge Egyptian estates, such as that of the Apion family, who perhaps held as much as two-fifths of all the land in the neighbouring districts (nomes) of Oxyrhynchus and

[50] Keenan in ch. 21c, pp. 633–4 below; Thomas (1987) 61 and 64.

Cynopolis, and who employed twenty stewards for their Oxyrhynchite lands alone. But in Egypt there is also plenty of evidence of smallholders farming their own land, and of a sizeable group of middling landowners in between, like the family of Apollos and Dioscorus, whose sixth-century archive survives from Aphrodito. The Egyptian evidence is sufficiently detailed and nuanced to show that landholding was very varied, and that the land market was active and fluid – with scope for entrepreneurs like Apollos and Aurelius Phoibammon to do very well out of lending money to farmers and landowners, leasing land from absentee landlords, and sub-letting the same to free tenants.[51]

In the other eastern provinces, there is nothing approaching Egypt's wealth of documentation. However, the fine but scarcely luxurious houses of northern Syria, and the active Anatolian villagers of the *Life* of Theodore of Sykeon (alongside some references here to powerful secular aristocrats), suggest that a varied pattern of landholding that included small and middling landowners was not just a feature of the Nile valley.[52] In the west, however, smallholders, and even middling landlords, are more difficult to find in the sources. They are best documented in texts that either record their undoing, such as Salvian's attack on the oppression by great landlords of the free farmers of Gaul (written probably in the 440s), or that are very generalized and impossible to illustrate in detail on the ground, such as the early-sixth-century Salic Law, which certainly seems to have been designed for small-scale communities of free farmers.[53]

Small freeholders and middling landlords existed in the west: common sense and the texts cited above suggest as much. We simply do not have the detailed evidence to detect them, let alone to begin to say how common they were. But in our period, lack of evidence of people below the highest reaches of society certainly is no proof of their absence. In the 1920s, forty-five written tablets of the late fifth century were discovered in the south of Africa Proconsularis, which revealed the presence of small-holders in Vandal Africa cultivating land on perpetual and alienable leases (by right of a centuries-old Roman law, the *Lex Manciana*). Without the chance survival and discovery of these tablets, we would have had no reason to suppose that such smallholders existed in fifth-century Africa, where surviving literary texts and mosaics point much more to a world of luxurious villas and rich landlords.[54]

---

[51] Egypt in general: Keenan in ch. 21*c*, pp. 629–36 below. Apion estates: p. 319 above, n. 7; Jones, *LRE* 780 and 784. Small and middling owners, and leasing: Keenan (1980); Keenan (1985); Bagnall, *Egypt* 114–21.

[52] Mitchell, *Anatolia* II 122–50. For powerful aristocrats at Anastasiopolis: *Life of Theodore* (ed. Festugière (1970) chs. 76 and 78 (English trans. Dawes and Baynes (1948)). For other evidence of (over)mighty landlords in late antique Asia Minor: Feissel and Kaygusuz (1985) 412–13.

[53] Salv. *De Gub. Dei* v.38–45; *Pactus Legis Salicae*; Wickham (1992) 233.

[54] Albertini tablets: Courtois *et al.* (1952). Villas: see p. 333 above, n. 34.

The only western landowners who are reasonably well documented in our period are those who held large quantities of land, whether ecclesiastical (who have been touched on above), royal or aristocratic. The properties of the latter are occasionally mentioned or alluded to in the narrative sources, as when Orosius and Olympiodorus tell us of the significant body of troops that two Spanish brothers were able to raise and finance in 409 just from their rural and domestic slaves, and as when Procopius records the huge estates, and even greater land-hunger, of the wealthy Ostrogoth Theodahad.[55] But our best evidence for the pattern of big estates comes from Gaul, where a number of wills detailing different aristocratic holdings survive from the end of the fifth century onwards. From these we learn that some individuals owned vast quantities of land, but that these large holdings were made up of scattered properties of very varied size, rather than concentrated blocks. Bertram of Le Mans, for instance, on his death in 616 disposed of about 300,000 hectares of land made up of more than 135 separate units (including sixty-two *villae* and thirteen groups of *villae*), dispersed through the territories of over fourteen *civitates*.[56]

Bertram's estates were widely spread (from Paris to Provence, and from Bordeaux to Burgundy), but they were all within Francia. In the west it is a feature of our period that, as political power fragmented, the even more widespread landholding, which had characterized the senatorial aristocracy of the fourth century, became impossible. Indeed, the scatter of Bertram's holdings throughout Francia was unusual for the sixth and seventh century, and the result of exceptional circumstances. Like all aristocrats, Bertram was compelled when necessary to take sides during the frequent wars between rival Merovingian kings, and earlier in his career he lost estates within hostile territory. In 616 he owned so many geographically scattered estates only through the great good fortune that he happened to have backed the right king, Chlothar II, and that Chlothar had (quite anomalously) come to rule an undivided Francia. Even in supposedly 'friendly' territories, the papacy found it very difficult to hold estates outside the borders of the empire. Gregory the Great (590–604) and his predecessors had enormous problems in getting adequate revenue out of the Roman church's southern Gallic estates (by then under Frankish control), and indeed after 613 the Gallic patrimony is never heard of again.[57]

Although the evidence is very patchy, and therefore unreliable, it is none the less possible that there was something of a contrast between the late antique east and west, with large landowners playing a more prominent role in the latter. It is tempting to draw a connection between this possibility and the evidence, which we will explore in chapter 13 (pp. 350–61 below), of

---

[55] Spanish brothers: Olympiod. *Frag.* 13.2 (ed. and trans. R. C. Blockley (1983) 172–3); Oros. VII.40. Theodahad: Procop. *Goth.* I.3.2 (see also Cass. *Var.* IV.39, V.12 and X.5). [56] See p. 317 above, n. 4.
[57] Papal estates: Richards (1979) 310 and 316.

greater eastern prosperity in the fifth and sixth century. Did small freeholders more readily seize economic opportunities than great landowners?
Unfortunately, the data are such that we really cannot tell. That smaller
landholders could create and take advantage of economic growth is, I
think, clear from their evident presence in the east, and from the equally
evident and growing prosperity of the region. It is also supported by scraps
of written evidence, such as a passing reference in the fifth century by
Theodoret of Cyrrhus to a village in the Lebanon of small freeholders
(they are described as farmer-proprietors, *kai geōrgoi kai despotai*), who specialized in growing nuts which they sold to merchants.[58]

However, there is no reason to suppose that large landowners were any
the less aware of economic opportunities than their smaller brethren.
There are indeed suggestions in the scanty documentary evidence that
owners of large estates might sometimes be better placed to exploit opportunities because of their greater access to the capital and labour necessary
for investment and innovation. In Egypt it is on the large estates (such as
those of the Apion family) that complex and extensive water-lifting devices
are most commonly recorded;[59] and, roughly contemporaneously (in the
later sixth century) but at different ends of the ancient world (the region
around Trier, and Mesopotamia where it borders on Armenia), two ecclesiastics are recorded to have laid out new vineyards. The vineyard in the east
is known to have soon attracted wine-merchants (from Cappadocia), and
it, at least, must have been planted with the potential profits of commerce
firmly in mind.[60]

If there really was a difference between east and west in the average size
of estates, the effect is perhaps more likely to have been fiscal, and felt by
the state, than economic, with an impact on regional standards of living.
Although it is difficult to prove, and although small landowners could club
together to buy a powerful patron in order to defend their interests, it is
nonetheless almost certainly true that the great in late antiquity were those
best able to escape or mitigate the fiscal demands of the state.[61] If so, the
western empire in the fourth and fifth century, and the barbarian successor states of the fifth and sixth, may not have been as well equipped to
exploit their tax base, on which so much of their power depended, as the

---

[58] Theodoret of Cyrrhus, *Hist. Mon.* (ed. and French trans. P. Canivet and A. Leroy-Molinghen
1977–9) XVII.2. The holy man (Abrahamēs) came to the village disguised as a merchant wanting to buy
nuts, and rented a house there in order to ply his business.   [59] Bonneau (1970) 49–50.

[60] Trier: Venantius Fortunatus, *Carm.* III.12, lines 39–40 (the bishop, Nicetius of Trier, also built a
watermill on the estate). Borders of Armenia: John Eph. *Lives of the Eastern Saints*, Syriac text and
English trans. E. W. Brooks, 3 vols. 1923–5 (= *PO* XVII.1, XVIII.4, XIX.2), 1.129–30 (on Addai).

[61] For villagers acquiring powerful patrons, the classic text is Lib. *Or.* XLVII (esp. XLVII.4). Here the
protection was given by military commanders against the villagers' landlords. Theodoret of Cyrrhus,
Hist. Mon. XVII.3, however, reveals a village of freeholders in the fifth-century Lebanon, brutalized and
powerless in the face of a tax demand (until saved by an advance secured by a well-connected holy man).

rulers of the east. In the west there were perhaps more great landlords standing between the state and the resources of the land which it wished to tax.[62]

The texts, particularly the surviving wills, also give some indication of the status of the labourers who worked the estates of both east and west. Slaves had probably never been very common on the land in the east (by contrast with their ubiquitous role in domestic service), and they do not feature in large numbers in the late antique papyri from Egypt.[63] In the west they appear much more frequently as agricultural labourers.[64] However, in contrast to the situation in some parts of the early empire, by late and post-Roman times there seems to be no evidence of great centralized troops of slaves, housed together in barrack-blocks. Rather, the slaves we meet in the documents seem to be in small groups on scattered, medium-sized farms, or even settled individually on single plots of land. Just possibly this was an improvement in their lot. It is hard to say, and certainly slaves could, as always, be terribly abused: in sixth-century Francia, one sadistic master buried alive two household slaves who had contracted a sexual union against his will, and regularly used boys in his house as living candlesticks, insisting that they hold the candles between their bare legs until they burnt themselves out.[65]

Coloni also feature frequently in the sources: agricultural workers whom a series of imperial laws, beginning in 332, tied (or at least tried to tie) to the land, in order to facilitate the process of raising both the land-tax and the poll-tax.[66] The evidence of the laws shows that the status of *coloni* continued to decline during our period, until in a law of Justinian one category of *colonus* is said to be very much on a par with slaves. *Coloni* were certainly a sizeable and oppressed group, and their oppression undoubtedly contributed to the powers of their masters. But exactly how significant they were in late antique society is open to dispute, since we lack both the information to tell us what proportion of all agricultural labour were *coloni*, and the detail of how a master–*colonus* relationship worked out on the ground. That modern scholarship has used quite so much ink on them may be for reasons of its own. *Coloni* have attracted two particular groups of scholars: those who wish to see the late empire as a dinosaur, brought down by the increasing inflexibility of its own social skeleton; and those who see in the *colonus* the ancestor of the tied serf of the Middle Ages, and hence evidence for Marx's theory of a direct transition from a 'slave' to a 'feudal' mode of production.

---

[62] A suggestion made by Jones, *LRE* 1066–7.   [63] Bagnall (1993).

[64] MacMullen (1987); Vera (1995) 346–56; Brown, *Gentlemen and Officers* 202–4 (for sixth-century Italy); Bonnassie (1991) 71–4 and 93–6 (for Visigothic Spain).

[65] Greg. Tur. *Hist.* v.3 (the human candlesticks are termed *pueri*, who may not have been slaves). For a general discussion of brutality to slaves: Bonnassie (1991) 19–21.

[66] Useful recent discussions: Whittaker and Garnsey in *CAH* xiii, ch. 9, pp. 287–94; Vera (1995) 353–4; Garnsey (1996).

In the west *coloni* may have been common: they certainly appear frequently in the surviving wills. It is also possible that their numbers were on the increase: Salvian states that many free persons were driven to become *coloni* during the troubles of the fifth century – though he also states that other peasants were able to escape oppression, by fleeing to the greater freedom of bagaudic or barbarian rule.[67] But the apparent prevalence of *coloni* in the west may partly be because western sources are focused so heavily on large estates. In Egypt, *coloni* also appear on the great estates, but balanced by considerable evidence of a free peasantry elsewhere. Is this fuller Egyptian evidence representative of the whole of Egypt, representative of the east in general, or even perhaps representative of the entire empire?

As with the possible connection between different patterns of landholding and different economic fortunes, it is tempting to link the apparently greater freedom of the east with the undoubted greater prevalence there of villages. Were villagers perhaps better placed for collective action, in order to fend off the claims of the aristocracy on their lands and their liberties? But again, when looked at in any detail, this possible connection is not readily sustainable. Libanius, in later-fourth-century Antioch, provides good evidence that there was no necessary correlation between types of settlement on the one hand, and the size of estates and the level of dependence of the peasantry on the other. He writes of villages with many owners (each with a small holding), but also of other villages under the control of a single proprietor.[68] Indeed, while it is easy to see that the community of the village could provide the focus for collective resistance to outside forces, it is also perfectly possible to suggest that, in different circumstances, it might provide the ideal context for centralized repression.[69]

In both patterns of land ownership, and in the social bonds that tied many people to the land and to their landlords, there may have been important differences between east and west; but it is much more difficult to detect changes and developments through time in either geographical region. It is possible that, in its social organization, country life really did alter very little, even in the west, which saw the collapse of Roman power and the advent of new barbarian masters and landlords. It is certainly remarkable to discover farmers in late-fifth-century Africa holding their land under a centuries-old, and very Roman, local form of land-tenure, and to find the Gallic wills of *c.* A.D. 600 populated by *servi* and *coloni*. As far as we can tell, these people (and the documents that describe them) would fit happily into the world of some three centuries earlier. Such

---

[67] Salv. *De Gub. Dei* v.43–5 and 21–6.   [68] Lib. *Or.* xlvii.11.

[69] As in parts of the medieval west, like Latium, where the appearance of nucleated villages, replacing dispersed settlement, is currently explained as a manifestation of the rising power of territorial lordship from the tenth century onwards: Toubert (1973).

apparent stability is striking testimony to the way that the barbarian invasions, although bringing new political masters and a Germanic aristocracy demanding a share of the land, by no means necessarily upset the social apple-cart.

However, as so often, a word of caution is also needed. It is always possible that the terminology of the formal documents that we rely on for evidence was highly conservative, and that this gives an exaggerated impression of lack of change. Even if there really was considerable stability in the social structures of the late antique countryside, this fact should certainly not lead us to embrace a view of rural life and rural dwellers in our period as entirely conservative, passive and unchanging. As we shall see in the next chapter, such a view will not fit the archaeological evidence that we now have for the broad nature of the economy, including the rural economy. Cultivators in the fifth and sixth century had to accommodate to a rapidly changing economic world, which, indeed, they themselves were often responsible for shaping.

CHAPTER 13

SPECIALIZED PRODUCTION AND EXCHANGE

BRYAN WARD-PERKINS

I. DIFFICULTIES AND EVIDENCE

Writing about complexity within the economy of the fifth to the seventh century will never be straightforward, partly because there has been so much debate about the nature of the 'classical' Roman economy that preceded it. Was the 'Roman economy' really a series of local economies, linked into a broader structure only by the demands of the state and by some limited trade in luxury products? Or was it a unified system in which even quite basic goods were produced by specialists, and traded by merchants across long distances? In examining economic activity in the late Roman and post-Roman period, we are inevitably measuring it against the classical economy that preceded it; but the measuring-stick itself is constantly being altered.[1]

As with evidence for the exploitation of the land examined in the last chapter, much of our information on economic specialization now derives from archaeology. However, the written record can also produce isolated but very valuable nuggets of information. For example, just before our period, Gregory of Nazianzus happens to tell us, in a poem on the events of his own life, that one of his enemies in Constantinople in 379/80 was a priest who had come to the city from Thasos, with money supplied by his church in order to buy 'Proconnesian slabs' (*prokonēsias plachas*). These must have been slabs for a chancel-screen in the marble of the island of Proconnesos (very close to Constantinople), of a type which was widely diffused in late antiquity (see Fig. 15, p. 359 below).

This tiny scrap of information, which entered the written record only by chance, is very useful. It confirms what we can infer from archaeology: that the Proconnesian quarries were engaged in commercial activity (alongside work for the state). But it also shows us, which we could not at present demonstrate any other way, that one buyer (admittedly from a town not too far distant in the northern Aegean) purchased his marble by the rather laborious process of visiting the region of the quarries, rather than doing it all from home via a middleman. There is much that we would

[1] See p. 369 below, nn. 38–40.

still like to know: after reaching Constantinople, did the priest have to travel out to the quarries themselves, or could he find what he needed within the city? Did he buy direct from an agent of the quarry, or from an independent trader? Did he purchase from stock, or did he have to place an order? And did he travel back with his new chancel-screen, or have it shipped? Our source, Gregory, was writing an apologia of his own life, not an economic analysis of the late antique marble trade. So we should not expect too much of him, but rather thank him for the useful information that he does provide.[2]

Such occasional references in the written sources provide details of human motivation and behaviour that can only be inferred from the material evidence that archaeology uncovers. However, for our purposes, the archaeological evidence is often more useful than the literary. It consists of clusters of information, which are not only ever growing in number, but which can also often be compared one with another. This ready comparability is precisely what is so difficult to achieve with small chunks of written evidence derived from very different types of source, and is an essential basis for any broad picture of developments and of regional differences within the Roman world of *c.* 425–600.

In looking at agricultural specialization and exchange, we have to note that some very important products (like wheat and wool) rarely survive in the soil and, even when found, generally give no clue as to their place of origin. But other things have left much better and much clearer archaeological traces. It is our particular good fortune that the ancients transported two of the most important products of the Mediterranean, oil and wine, in amphorae, and that the broken sherds of these vessels, which survive well in the soil, can often be attributed to a specific period and a specific region of production.[3] An individual amphora fragment will not tell us why it was transported across the Mediterranean nor how precisely it was moved. But, as the overall picture becomes clearer, revealing patterns of distribution that change through time, it even becomes increasingly possible to speculate intelligently about why and how these products came to be on the move.

As with the products of the land, artisan production can also only be documented archaeologically for those (comparatively few) items that have left material traces. Pottery, in particular, is found in vast quantities in excavation and field-survey, since pots are easily broken and yet the individual sherds are then virtually indestructible in the soil. Furthermore, the broken fragments are rarely affected by human intervention, since they can neither be melted down (like metal and glass) nor reworked

[2] Greg. Naz. *Carmen de Vita Sua* lines 875–7 (*PG* xxxvii.1089). For the priest travelling to Contantinople for his purchase, compare the buying of silverware in *Life of Theodore of Sykeon* 42 (ed. Festugière (1970); English trans. Dawes and Baynes (1948)). [3] Peacock and Williams (1986).

(like stone). Fortunately, pottery not only survives well, but also offers the economic historian enormous benefits. It can generally be dated and assigned to a particular manufacturing centre, and its quality and finish themselves tell us something of the level of sophistication that went into its production.

The pottery trade, within the wider economy, was never of great importance, but the considerable evidence we have for it can perhaps be used as an indicator of broader economic trends. Since pots are everyday products in universal use (whether cooking-pots, storage-jars or tableware), rather than rare or luxury items, it is, I believe, reasonable to use the pottery trade as an index of the wider role of specialization and exchange within the economy. If pottery was being produced by sophisticated potting industries and was being traded widely, reaching even distant and inland rural areas, then it is highly likely that other comparable industries, that have left few or no archaeological traces (making tools, clothing, farming equipment, etc.), were equally sophisticated. Conversely, if all pottery was poorly made and local in manufacture, then other products too are likely to have been of a similar lack of sophistication. Furthermore, shipwreck evidence shows that no pots, except amphorae, ever travelled alone in single shipments; so it is also possible to use finds of imported pottery as a trace-element of the shipment of goods that have themselves left no mark in the soil.

A major problem with the archaeological evidence of pottery and other products is that higher-quality goods and long-distance exchange have (not unnaturally) attracted far more archaeological attention than less spectacular regional industries, even though these were almost certainly of as great, if not far greater, economic significance. It is, for example, now possible to study in some detail the distribution within the Mediterranean of the fine marble and high-quality tablewares which were fashionable in late antiquity, but it is not yet possible to study the local and regional industries that produced the bulk building-materials (stone, brick, tile, mortar, etc.) nor the industries that produced the myriad different types of local cooking-wares.[4]

One further area of archaeological evidence – the quantities of coin found on different sites – sheds some light on the intensity of local exchange but is difficult to use in detail. There is good evidence from the Roman period of the widespread and frequent use of coins in everyday life, so their presence or absence can be an index of commercial exchange. However, coins were not primarily produced by the state in order to facilitate private economic activity. Rather, they were minted in order to ease the process of raising taxation and of paying imperial servants (in particular, the military). So, in their production and diffusion (and hence in patterns of discovery in

---

[4] Marble: Dodge and Ward-Perkins (1992). Tablewares: Hayes (1972); Hayes (1980); *Atlante* (1981).

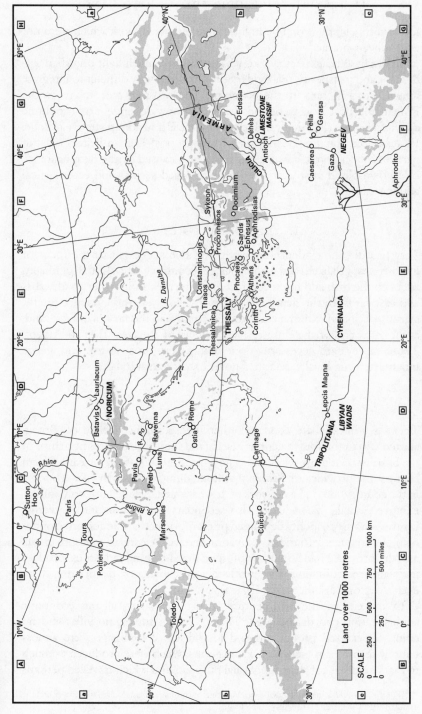

Map 8 Specialized production and exchange (sites and regions discussed in chapter 13)

modern times), there were administrative factors at work which were not primarily economic.[5]

Similarly, although archaeology has now shed much light on urban settlement and prosperity, this evidence too is often very difficult to integrate into a broad picture of the economy. The prosperity of towns in the Roman and post-Roman periods was not simply dependent on economic activity, but was also highly influenced by social and administrative change. For example, the disappearance of towns in post-Roman Britain must in part reflect economic change; but it was also caused by the disappearance of a town-based aristocracy and a town-based secular and ecclesiastical administration.[6]

II. THE GENERAL PICTURE

Very broadly, the evidence currently available suggests that the focus of intensive, specialized and sophisticated economic life shifted gradually, between the fifth and the seventh century, further and further southwards and eastwards. In the next few pages we will review this evidence briefly, starting with two extreme case studies: Britain, in the far north-west, and, at the other end of the empire, the provinces of the Near East and Egypt. These surveys are necessarily done with a very broad brush and ignore much detail and local variation, a point I shall return to later.

Britain

There is some debate about whether the economic decline of Britain started within the fourth century itself (and therefore before the arrival of the Saxons). But most scholars would agree that, at least in the early fourth century, the province of Britain was flourishing, with a rich villa economy in the countryside, and a network of towns which included not only administrative capitals (*civitates*), but also secondary production and marketing centres whose prosperity depended primarily on economic activity. Copper coins are frequently found in excavation and were clearly in widespread use, and the province had a number of specialized potting industries, producing standardized high-quality products, and capable of distributing them even over long distances (see Fig. 12).

By the end of the fifth century (at the vest latest) all this economic sophistication had disappeared. There were no towns, no villas and no coins. Specialized production and long-distance exchange were almost entirely restricted to very high-value goods which were produced as much to mark status as for their functional purpose, and which travelled perhaps

---

[5] For the state and coinage: Hendy, *Studies*. For coins in commercial use: Millar (1981) 72–4; and the useful overview in Greene (1986) 44–57 and 61–3.

[6] See Durliat (1990a) for an extreme view of the essentially 'artificial' nature of Roman cities.

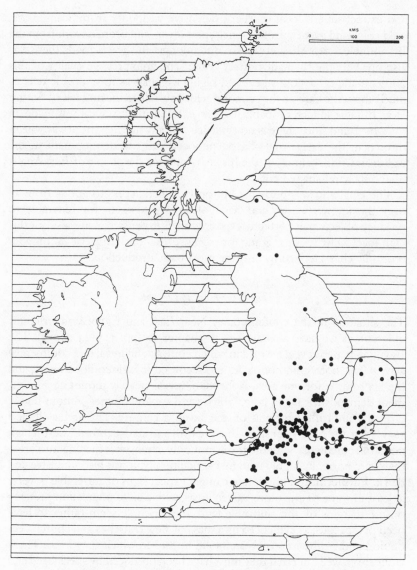

Fig. 12 The distribution of one type of pot (Form C51) produced by the third/fourth-century Roman potteries located in the area of modern Oxford. (From Peacock (1982) fig. 56)

more commonly as gifts and objects of political exchange than as objects of commerce.[7]

The nature of the early Anglo-Saxon economy is well reflected in the Sutton Hoo ship-burial of *c.* A.D. 625. This contained items both wonderful

[7] Esmonde Cleary (1989); Millett (1990) 157–230.

and exotic: superb local jewellery, defensive weaponry from Scandinavia, gold coins and garnets from Francia, and silver- and bronze-work from the Byzantine eastern Mediterranean. But amongst the grave-goods there was also one very poorly made pottery bottle. The unimpressive quality of this bottle, made on a slow wheel and highly irregular as it is, already tells us much about the base of the economy which sustained the marvels of Sutton Hoo. But it is, in fact, probably itself an exotic import, since it was made on the wheel, and since there is no evidence that any native pottery was wheel-thrown in the early Anglo-Saxon period. Until the development in the eighth and ninth century of the Ipswich potteries, the people of East Anglia used only hand-shaped pots.[8]

The king who was buried at Sutton Hoo had access to goods from all over the known world, and had goldsmiths working for him able to produce objects that perfectly exploited their expensive materials. But this high-level activity was going on against the backdrop of a broader economy characterized by only the most basic production.

The Near East and Egypt

The situation in the contemporary Near East and Egypt was strikingly different, as we have already seen in chapter 12 (pp. 315–45 above). The Egyptian papyri reveal a world in which complex financial and commercial activity was both commonplace, and recorded in written documents; and the tax returns for one area, Aphrodito, reveal steadily mounting govern-ment demands for tax in coin, which were apparently met without undue difficulty until the very end of the seventh century. The archaeological surveys of the Near East show that the fifth and sixth centuries were a high point in settlement. Settlement was not only extensive, reaching into areas that were normally highly marginal agriculturally; it was also intensive and dense. Furthermore, although one might expect signs of miserable poverty at least in some of the more barren areas, with a large population pressing on the margins of the cultivable land, these people seem rather to have been prosperous, as evidenced by a mass of new churches and church dec-oration and by the imposing and solid houses in which they lived. These latter are so well built that they must have been produced by specialized and paid craftsmen (see Fig. 13 and p. 954, Fig. 54).[9]

The inhabitants of the late antique Near East were involved in the long-distance exchange of agricultural goods (a subject to which we will return later). They were also at the centre of thriving local and regional exchange networks, testified to by the existence of abundant and diverse pottery and

---

[8] Bruce-Mitford (1975–83) (vol. 3. II.597–607 for the pottery bottle).

[9] See ch. 12, pp. 321 and 340 above, nn. 12 and 51. Aphrodito tax: Rémondon (1965). However, using different evidence, Bagnall (1985) argues for stable levels of taxation in Roman Egypt.

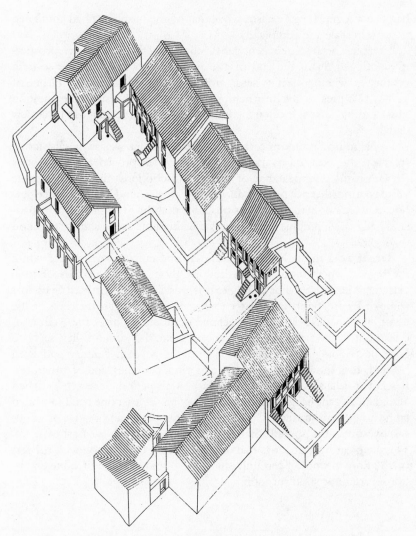

Fig. 13 A group of stone houses in the late antique Syrian village of Déhès. (From Sodini *et al.* (1980) 181, fig. 243)

by the presence of numerous copper coins, even on rural sites (see Fig. 14).[10] In *c.* A.D. 500 the contrast between the economies of the Near East and Britain was enormous, and much more marked than it had been in *c.* 350. Since the fourth century two things had occurred: the economy of Britain

---

[10] See, for example, the finds of pottery and coin from the village-site of Déhès: Sodini *et al.* (1980) 234–87; Orssaud (1992). Or from the town-site of Pella: Walmsley (1988) 152–5; Watson (1992).

had become much more basic, while that of the Near East had continued to grow in scale and complexity.

There has been some recent debate about whether this eastern prosperity continued up to the end of the sixth century and into the seventh century, or whether decline set in around the time of the Great Plague of 541–3.[11] At present the information available cannot resolve the question satisfactorily, since it is often incomplete and very little of it can be closely dated.

Partial information can certainly be deceptive. As we saw in chapter 12 (p. 319), the excavations at Déhès have now disproved earlier theories (based on the disappearance of building inscriptions) that the limestone villages of northern Syria were abandoned after around A.D. 600. Since new houses were not being built, it is probable that the great period of expansion had ended, but this is not necessarily the same as the start of a period of decline.[12]

Recent work in the Near East also tends to emphasize diversity within the region, which makes generalizations about specific periods of time extremely hazardous. For example, it is possible that northern Syria lost some of its prosperity in the later sixth century and that some cities of the coast, like Caesarea Maritima, declined quite rapidly after the Arab conquest; but in the same period other areas, like the Jordan valley, seem to have been doing very well indeed into the seventh century and even beyond, as is shown by the evidence of rural churches, and of urban settlement at Pella and Gerasa. For instance, Arab-period Gerasa (Jerash) had abundant Byzantine and Islamic copper coins, at least one solid mortared stone house, and substantial potting industries producing a range of good-quality wares. It is possible that, in comparison to the Near East of c. A.D. 550, the Near East of c. 650 had declined; but in comparison with the rest of the Roman world it certainly still stood out as a region of quite exceptional economic sophistication.[13]

Italy

Britain and the Near East are extreme cases, and the economic history of the regions that lay between them geographically is also somewhere between them in character. For the provinces to the north of the Mediterranean, I am best qualified to write about Italy, but the economic histories of Gaul and Spain are probably broadly similar.

[11] As argued by Kennedy (1985).

[12] Abandonment: Kennedy (1985) 160–2. Déhès: Sodini et al. (1980).

[13] Caesarea: Holum et al. (1988) 201–15. Rural churches: Piccirillo (1985). Jerash: Zayadine (1986) 107–36 and 411–59; Bellinger (1938) (for the coins).

In Italy, the large number of field-surveys that have been conducted in the centre and south of the peninsula suggest that there was a gradual but fairly steady decline in rural prosperity through the third, fourth, fifth and sixth centuries, to a point where, in the seventh and eighth centuries, it is very difficult from field-survey and even from excavation to find any trace of settlement at all.[14] In chapter 12 (p. 325), I considered whether this apparent disappearance of people from the landscape was 'real', and caused by dramatic population decline, or 'archaeological', and caused by the disappearance of the material objects by which settlements are normally found and dated. But, even if the disappearance of the rural population is only archaeological, this would still suggest that rural dwellers were very impoverished, since they have not left the material remains that enable us to find them.

Specialized production and exchange certainly declined markedly. Late-sixth- and seventh-century sites in Italy have, in general, far fewer pots, drawn from a far narrower geographical and typological range, than sites of the earlier Roman period. But some specialized production and regional exchange in low-value goods did persist – something that did not happen in Britain. For example, different quarries and production centres in the Alps seem to have produced vessels in a soft soapstone (*pietra ollare*) throughout late antiquity and the early Middle Ages and to have traded them widely in the Po plain.[15]

There is other evidence to suggest that local and regional exchange was far less important than in the contemporary Near East. Fig. 14 compares the number of coins found on an urban site in northern Italy, ancient Luna, with those found on a small rural site in the limestone massif of northern Syria, Déhès. The comparison is made much more striking when we realize that the Luna coins derive from the excavation of a massive area of the town, much of it certainly still occupied into the sixth and seventh century, while those from Déhès derive only from a small number of trenches opened into a selection of houses. To form a real comparison, the Déhès figures would have to take account of the far smaller sample area, and would therefore need to be multiplied by a factor of at least one hundred. Coins were clearly common in sixth- and seventh-century rural Syria, while they had virtually disappeared even in an urban context at Luna.

Africa

To the south of the Mediterranean, in the central provinces of Roman North Africa (modern Tunisia and Algeria), the high point of sophistication

---

[14] Greene (1986) 103–9; Lewit (1991) especially 172–5 and 188–92.
[15] *La pietra ollare* (1987); Brogiolo and Gelichi (1996).

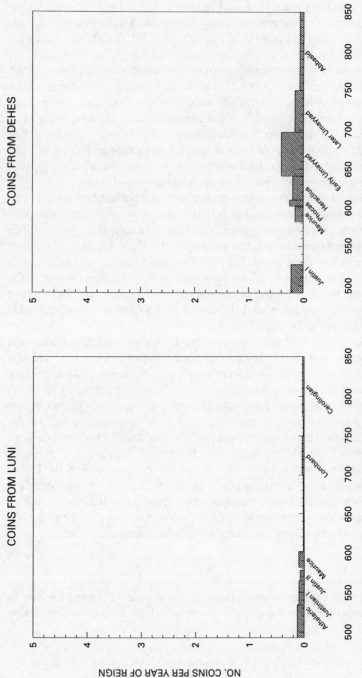

Fig 14 A comparison of the coin-finds from the town of Luna (modern Luni) in Liguria, Italy, and from the village of Déhès in the limestone massif of northern Syria. The coins derive from excavations on a very different scale (those at Luna were far more extensive than those at Déhès). The information is expressed as numbers of coins found from each possible year of the period of issue. (Based on the coins published in Frova (1973) and (1977), and in Sodini *et al.* (1980) 276–87)

and evident prosperity may have come just before our period, in the third and fourth century. The evidence for this is unfortunately rather impressionistic, since there are very few closely dated sites and surveys available for study. However, Carthage itself, which served as the administrative, political and cultural capital and as the principal port of central North Africa, has been the subject of a recent international research-project. Unlike some other great towns of this period, Carthage was never an imperial residence, and its prosperity must have depended heavily on the wealth of Africa, rather than on massive injections of cash from elsewhere in the empire (as in the case of imperial cities like Trier and Constantinople). The history of Carthage perhaps reflects reasonably accurately the history of its African hinterland.

In the fourth and early fifth century, the people of Carthage erected a large number of very substantial churches, and the recent excavations (many of them focused on the edge of the settlement) have shown that the city was at its largest at the time of the building of its great wall in the 420s, in the face of the Vandal threat.[16] Carthage was a very large and very rich fourth-century city, a phenomenon which in the contemporary western Mediterranean can otherwise only be found in the great aristocratic and imperial capitals of the empire (Trier, Milan and Rome).

Evidence from the interior, such as it is, confirms the picture from Carthage. Two dated and partially published surveys, though on a small scale, show rural settlement to have been at its densest and most extensive in the third and fourth century; and, although well-dated evidence is generally lacking, it seems that a number of the towns of the interior, such as Cuicul (Djemila), reached their greatest extent during the fourth century, when they were embellished with both churches and rich aristocratic housing.[17]

What happened after 400 is not yet clear, because there has been so little closely-dated archaeological work: many buildings are still dated on the very fluid chronology of mosaic style. But the two datable rural surveys and the excavations at Carthage suggest a gradual but steady loss of wealth and the abandonment of settlements through the fifth and sixth century, though the Vandal conquest in the 420s and 430s does not seem to have caused any sudden decline.[18]

This general picture of slow and steady decline is probably mirrored in the history of the two African exports which have left abundant archaeological traces: oil (documented through the amphorae in which it was carried) and the tableware known as African red-slip ware. African oil and African pottery dominated the western Mediterranean in the third

[16] Carthage: e.g. Carandini *et al.* (1983) 16–18.
[17] Segermes and Kasserine surveys: Mattingly and Hitchner (1995) 191–3. Djemila: Lepelley, *Cités* II.402–15. [18] Mattingly and Hitchner (1995) 209–13 for a useful account of recent work.

and fourth century, and also had some success in the east. The Vandal conquest seems to have caused some decline and some redirection of exports, but by no means ended the distribution overseas of African products: rather, they continued to be extremely important throughout the fifth- and sixth-century western Mediterranean. However, very slowly the areas reached by African amphorae and red-slip ware became more and more restricted, and the quantities involved diminished, so that, for instance, by the end of the sixth century, African red-slip ware, although still found on many sites in the western Mediterranean, now only appears on sites near the coast and generally in small quantities (see Fig. 16, p. 372 below).[19]

By 600, at the latest, the African provinces displayed far fewer evident signs of economic sophistication than they had done in the fourth century; and, although this cannot be stated with confidence (because of the difficulties of dating and of comparison), it may well have been the case that during the fifth century the provinces of the Near East had already overtaken Africa as the richest part of the empire.

The Aegean world

The period of the fourth, fifth and at least the early part of the sixth century seems to have been characterized by a flourishing and complex economy in the lands around the Aegean sea. Rural settlement in Greece, as revealed in a number of field-surveys, was far more extensive than in the early Roman period (the exact opposite of the situation documented in Italy). Towns, too, seemingly prospered in both Greece and western Asia Minor, as is shown by the building of some traditional public monuments, of churches and of aristocratic houses. However, the evidence from the towns presents a problem worth noting: we know far more about important centres (such as Corinth, Athens, Thessalonica, Ephesus, Aphrodisias and Sardis, as well as Constantinople itself) than we do about more 'ordinary' small towns, which have attracted far less archaeological attention. We also know much more at present about western Asia Minor, near the Aegean coast, then we do about the interior and the east.[20]

The Aegean region was, in the fourth to sixth century, involved in a wide overseas exchange network. For instance, the quarries of the island of Proconnesos in the Sea of Marmara (and, to a lesser extent, the other eastern quarries of Thasos, Thessaly and Docimium) came in late antiquity to dominate the production and trade of marble in the whole Mediterranean. Columns, capitals and bases in the grey-striped marble of Proconnesos, and in particular chancel-screens (because they weighed less

---

[19] Fentress and Perkins (1988); Reynolds (1995) 6–34 and 40–60.

[20] Rural surveys: Alcock (1985). Towns: Claude (1969); Spieser (1984); and particular studies such as Frantz (1988) on Athens and Foss (1979) 3–99 on Ephesus.

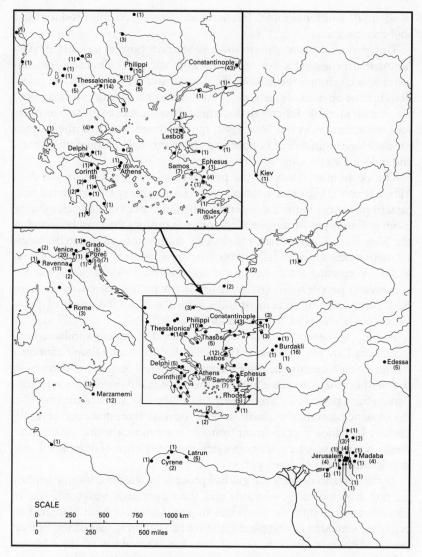

Fig. 15 Distribution of recorded finds of one type of late antique chancel-screen. The marble used is not always noted when the screens are published; but the vast majority were undoubtedly in the grey-streaked marble of Proconnesos, an island in the Sea of Marmara near Constantinople.
(After Sodini (1989) 184, fig. 11)

but made an immediate liturgical and visual impact), travelled widely, even reaching inland sites in the Negev desert, and churches in the western Mediterranean (where the marble of Luna had formerly dominated the market for white stone) (see Fig. 15). As we shall see later on, much of this marble was produced for the state's own ends (for instance, for the imperial buildings of Constantinople), but much was almost certainly produced and sold commercially.[21]

This period also saw the rise of a substantial potting industry in Asia Minor that produced a fine tableware now known as Phocaean red-slip ware, which is found throughout the Aegean and the Near East. As usual, despite their obvious importance, local and regional networks of exchange are at present more difficult to document than the more spectacular overseas trade; but, as in the Near East, the excavated towns of the Aegean produce large numbers of copper coins from throughout the sixth century, and indeed into the early seventh century.[22]

The economic history of the provinces of Aegean Greece and Asia Minor is very similar in the fourth to the sixth century to that of the near eastern provinces in the same period. The difference comes later, with far more evident signs of decline in the seventh century than can be found in the Near East. Rural settlements virtually disappear from the archaeological maps – perhaps, as in Italy, through a combination of falling population and the decreasing availability of the manufactured articles that reveal the presence of people to the archaeologist. In towns, too, there is evidence of both contraction of settlement and a loss of obvious indicators of prosperity (coins, churches, datable buildings, etc.).[23]

Possibly the seventh-century Byzantine world was not dissimilar to contemporary Italy, but, whereas in Italy the slide down to the simple economy of the seventh century had been slow and gradual (beginning perhaps in the third century, or even earlier), in the Aegean the drop came very suddenly, after a period of marked prosperity in the fifth and sixth century. On the evidence currently available, seventh-century Byzantium and seventh-century Italy look very different from the contemporary (and by this time Arab) Near East, where there is much more evidence of continued economic complexity and prosperity.

In the seventh century the gradual process by which economic sophistication had moved southwards and then eastwards was complete: in around A.D. 700 only the provinces of the Arab-held Near East had an economy similar in its complexity and sophistication to that of the Roman period. Although this is the end of one story, the subject of this volume, it is also, of course, the beginning of another. For by the late seventh century and the early eighth, we find the first signs of economic growth in some of the provinces that had been so badly hit earlier on – with, for

---

[21] Marble: Sodini (1989).

[22] Phocaean red-slip ware: Hayes (1972) 323–70; Hayes (1980) lix–lxi; Abadie-Reynal (1989). Coins: Morrison (1986).

[23] Rural settlement in Greece (there have been no extensive field-surveys in Turkey): Alcock (1985). Towns: Foss (1975); Foss (1979) 103–15; Müller-Wiener (1986); Frant (1988) 82–94; Brandes (1989). Coins: Morrison (1986). Unsurprisingly, there is much more early medieval coinage and sophisticated pottery in Constantinople than elsewhere: Harrison (1986); Hayes (1992).

instance, the appearance of new trading networks, and new towns, in both the North Sea area (as at Hamwic, Dorestad and Hedeby) and the western Mediterranean (as at Venice).

III. THE EXTENT OF THE CHANGE

Except in the Near East, the changes outlined above were remarkable. The phenomenon we are looking at is not a simple shrinkage, as if the economy of the seventh century were essentially similar to that of the fourth, but on a more restricted scale. Rather, there was a remarkable qualitative change in economic life, with whole areas of specialization and exchange disappearing and, in some regions, even very basic technology apparently ceasing to exist.

For example, in Britain a number of skills entirely disappeared, to be reintroduced from the continent only in the seventh and eighth century. Some of these, such as the art of building in mortared brick or stone, were perhaps particularly associated with Roman fashions of display, and so may have been peculiarly sensitive to political and cultural change. But at least one skill that disappeared, the art of making pottery on the wheel, is a very basic technique that speeds up considerably the production of good-quality pottery. It is hard to understand how such a simple tool as the potter's wheel could disappear, but presumably individual potters in the fifth and sixth century found the demand for pots was so low (because markets were so localized and so small in scale) that it was not worthwhile continuing its use (or borrowing it again from the continent).

The scale and impact of change was dramatic, as can be seen if it is placed in a broad historical perspective. Post-Roman Britain, of the fifth and sixth century, retained almost nothing of the sophistications of Roman economic life and, although this is a fact that is initially hard to credit, even sank to an economic level well below that reached in the pre-Roman Iron Age. In the pre-Roman period, southern Britain was importing quantities of Gallic wine and pottery, and sustained a number of native potting industries (some of them producing wheel-turned wares) whose products were distributed quite widely. It also had the beginnings of towns, some of which (like Hengistbury) were clearly dependent for their existence on commerce, as well as on their defensive and political importance; and it had a silver coinage, produced in such quantities that it was almost certainly used for economic as well as political transactions.[24]

Post-Roman Britain of the fifth and sixth century had none of these things, either in Anglo-Saxon or in British areas, with the single exception of a small-scale trade in Mediterranean pottery and wine amphorae that

---

[24] Iron Age Britain: see, for example, Cunliffe (1978) 157–9, 299–300 and 337–42.

reached the west of Britain. It was only long after the end of the Roman period, in the seventh and, in particular, in the eighth century that economic conditions in southern Britain again resemble those attained in the pre-Roman Iron Age, with the first Anglo-Saxon coins, the first coastal emporia, the first native pottery industries, and an evident growth of trade with the continent.[25]

The post-Roman economic regression is at its clearest and starkest in Britain (except possibly in the Balkans, where there has been less archaeological work to reveal it), but the same phenomenon can be seen widely, if in a less extreme form, right across the former Roman world. Two closely connected and striking features of early medieval people (whether in Turkey, Greece, Africa, Italy, France, Spain or Britain) are the unimpressive nature of their domestic material remains and the considerable difficulty archaeologists have in finding traces of their settlement (unless they had the decency to bury themselves with grave-goods or to leave good crop-marks). In the past, problems in finding early medieval people have undoubtedly been exacerbated by a lack of interest in their culture and a consequent ignorance about the nature of their material remains. But the example of countries like Britain and Italy, where a lot of sophisticated effort (much of it fruitless) has now been put into looking for post-Roman remains, shows quite clearly that the problem is no longer just the result of not knowing how to look.

Pre-Roman people in countries like Italy show up well in field-survey and in excavation, with scatters of recognizable pottery; and in areas like Greece and Asia Minor they of course left spectacular domestic and monumental remains. Roman people all over the empire broadcast their presence to the archaeologist with large quantities of pottery and, often, tile, brick and mortar. It is only early medieval people who seem to have owned so few material objects that they have often disappeared entirely from the archaeological map. Even in Italy, which had been the very heart of the empire, it is much easier to document local production, overseas trade, flourishing urbanism and extensive exploitation of the land in the Etruscan period than it is in the seventh century A.D.

IV. BEYOND THE FRONTIERS OF THE EMPIRE

The general picture of economic decline sketched out above – of a high point of sophistication sometime in the Roman period sinking to a low sometime between 400 and 700 – is based on work within the boundaries of the former empire. Interestingly, if we step beyond the old frontiers, things look rather different.

In Scandinavia, the first millennium A.D. is marked by steady exploitation and very slow economic growth throughout the period, without the dramatic

---

[25] Hodges (1989) 69–104.

Roman boom followed by the even more dramatic post-Roman crash seen, for example, in Britain. In Ireland it is the *post*-Roman period, the fifth century A.D. onwards, that produces evidence (through pollen-analysis, and in church buildings, metalwork and a huge number of fortified enclosures) of increasing exploitation of the land and of a rising complexity in economic life. Similarly, beyond the eastern frontier, in Armenia, although the only evidence we have so far comes from church building, the seventh century (the very period that saw the collapse of the Byzantine economy in neighbouring Asia Minor) is a high point in innovation and construction.[26]

The evidence from Ireland calls into question the model I have proposed so far, of a movement in economic complexity exclusively southwards and eastwards. Possibly a movement *outwards* in general is a more appropriate image: from a rich Italy in the first century B.C. and the first century A.D.; to Gaul and Spain in the second and third century; to Britain and Africa in the third and fourth; to the eastern provinces in the fifth and sixth; and finally, beyond the old frontiers, to Ireland and Armenia in the sixth and seventh century. As Randsborg has rightly pointed out, the slow and steady growth of the Scandinavian economy raises even more fundamental questions, about the long-term benefits of romanization.[27] Southern Britain, as we have seen, lost in the fifth century A.D. much more than its Roman economy: it reverted to a pattern of economic life simpler and more basic than that of the pre-Roman Iron Age. Without the Romans, might not Britain's economy have developed in a more sustained, if slower, way, like that of Scandinavia? Viewed in the very long term and with the benefit of a perspective from beyond the frontiers, the economic history of Roman Britain can be portrayed as a blind alley, before the population settled back to a pattern of steady growth comparable to that of the pre-Roman Iron Age.

V. REGIONAL AND LOCAL VARIATION

The surveys I have given above are very generalized, in order to bring out and illustrate the broadest underlying trends within the economic history of this period. For this purpose, it is, I hope, excusable to lump together vast areas, like the whole of Gaul, Spain and Italy, and to illustrate their economic history with a few choice examples drawn from Italy alone (indeed, primarily from the north of Italy). But it is also important to realize that the process of generalization and simplification necessarily ignores very important local variation.

In both Gaul and Spain, for instance, there was probably a major difference between the experiences of the south and of the north, where

---

[26] Scandinavia: Randsborg (1991) 72–81; Randsborg (1992). Ireland: Mitchell (1976) 136–7 and 159–71; Edwards (1990) 6–33; Mallory and McNeill (1991) 181–225. Armenia: Mango, *Byzantine Architecture* 180–91.   [27] Randsborg (1992).

dislocation was certainly greater politically, and probably also greater economically. But even within slightly more defined regions, like 'the north of Gaul', there were undoubtedly big differences between areas such as Brittany and traditionally more commercialized lands such as the Rhine valley, where, for instance, a pottery industry capable of producing good-quality wares survived from late Roman into early medieval times. Equally, within 'the south of Gaul', while most towns certainly stagnated and probably declined in this period, at least one centre, Marseilles, seems to have been flourishing, with large churches, close contacts with the Mediteranean, and its own sixth-century copper coinage.[28]

Even within the selected case study, Italy, the sketch I have produced is undoubtedly much too simple when subjected to closer examination. As in Gaul and Spain, there was in Italy probably a basic north–south divide, again in favour of the south. Although it is stated above that copper coins virtually disappear, the change is, in fact, much less dramatic in the south, where, for instance, the mints in Sicily issued large quantities of copper coins in the second half of the seventh century. Similarly, the decline in specialized artisan production is again less evident in the south than in the north. Mainland southern Italy, despite a relative dearth of archaeological work, is the region where it is at present easiest to document a continuity of production of decorated wares with a regional distribution right into the seventh century and beyond.[29]

Even within the north of Italy (the Po valley and Liguria), from which most of my knowledge and the bulk of my examples derive, there were, of course, important local differences of experience. Ravenna, for instance, as an important capital and port close to the mouth of the Po, kept its broad Mediterranean contacts (in the form of imported pottery and amphorae) and retained the use of copper coins until a much later date than did other northern Italian towns. In some cases, the difference of experience might be very localized indeed. In Liguria, for example, rural sites of the fifth and sixth century are generally characterized by buildings constructed of perishable materials and by tiny quantities of miserable pottery; but a walled site at S. Antonino near Finale Ligure has, by contrast, from the very same period produced imposing stone defensive walls and both imported pottery and copper coins.[30]

In Liguria and at S. Antonino we have evidence both for the broad regional picture and for an exception which stands out against it. This, of

---

[28] Loseby (1992).

[29] Coins: Grierson (1982) 129–38. Pottery: Arthur and Patterson (1994). Recent archaeological work on early medieval Rome has revealed (perhaps as we would expect) that it too had economic sophistications like coinage, and imported pottery and foodstuffs: Paroli and Delogu (1993).

[30] Ravenna: e.g. Bermond Montanari (1983). Liguria: Ward-Perkins, Mills, Gadd and Delano Smith (1986) 120. S. Antonino: Murialdo et al. (1997).

course, allows us to speculate that the experience of S. Antonino was a special one, due presumably to the stationing there of a Byzantine garrison supplied with coin and goods from the sea. Eventually, and ideally, it should be possible in all areas to know the broad picture, against which can then be set a mass of significant regional and local variation. But this state of knowledge is a very long way off at present.

It would, in fact, be strange if any broad pattern was entirely untouched by particular circumstance. In 'northern' lands there were certainly areas where economic complexity survived much longer than in contiguous regions: southern Italy and Sicily (perhaps because of their closer African and eastern links), Ravenna and Rome (because of their political and ecclesiastical importance), and the Marseilles–Rhône–Rhine corridor (because it was an obvious funnel for any surviving interregional trade, and perhaps because of the purchasing power of the new Frankish aristocracy).

Conversely, there were almost certainly areas in the southern and eastern Mediterranean which, for particular reasons, did not share in the prosperity of the fourth to the sixth century. One such area is the eastern North African littoral, Tripolitania and Cyrenaica, which suffered badly from barbarian raiding in late antiquity and which has produced much less evidence of fourth- to sixth-century prosperity than have the contemporary central North African provinces.[31]

In short, any model of economic movement southwards and eastwards needs to be loose enough to accommodate considerable local and regional variation. This meant, for instance, that, in A.D. 550, Marseilles, on the north-western shores of the Mediterranean, was probably a much larger and richer town than Lepcis Magna, in the south-east; something which had probably not been the case two hundred years earlier.

VI. 'PROSPERITY' AND 'SOPHISTICATION'

In the preceding pages, in describing different economies and economic processes, I have often used terms loaded with value judgement, like 'prosperous', 'poor' and 'economic decline'. Under the influence of anthropology (one of whose fundamental assumptions is that cultures are different, but *equal*), such terms have become profoundly unfashionable in historical writing. The various changes (including the economic) that took place at the end of the Roman empire, which were once happily described as symptoms of 'decline', are now generally seen as neutral 'transformations', or even as willed 'alternative strategies'.[32]

There are, indeed, problems with words that imply a generally 'better' or 'worse' state of the economy: they suggest that individuals were in every

---

[31] Mattingly (1995) 171–217. [32] E.g. Carver (1993) 46–61.

way materially better off (and maybe also happier) under one dispensation than under another. This was not necessarily the case, because, while archaeology gives us a good indication of the availability and diffusion of some consumer durables (bricks, pottery, etc.) and some cash-crops, it does not give us an accurate picture of individual diet, individual health or the amount of individual effort needed to sustain these. It is perfectly possible that peasants in sixth-century Britain, living in wooden huts and using only hand-shaped pottery, or nomads in seventh-century North Africa, living a pastoral life in tents, ate better, lived longer, worked less and perhaps felt better than did their Roman predecessors tied into a market-economy, despite their fine pottery, their solid houses and the coins jangling in their purses.

There is, at present, no satisfactory way of measuring these experiences against each other; and our view of them inevitably reflects the mixed feelings that we, from a position of great privilege, hold towards the extreme complexity and materialism of the modern world. If we did want to know more about individual physical well-being and longevity, we would have to put more effort into establishing the study of human bones on a sure footing and on recovering datable and well-preserved groups of skeletons. Perhaps we might then know who lived healthier and longer lives – though even then we would not know who had to work the hardest and who was 'happiest'.

It is therefore important to realize that in these pages 'poor' and 'rich' necessarily refer to 'poor' and 'rich' in those material objects which are readily identifiable archaeologically. Because these words are problematic, I have often tried to use more specific and less loaded terms to describe economic conditions: in particular, 'economic complexity' or 'sophistication' and its opposite, 'economic simplicity'. These terms do not imply that everyone was in every way 'better off' within a sophisticated economy, but merely that they were tied into a more complex network of economic activity, which allowed for more specialization of production and more exchange, both locally and over long distances.

There is, of course, a relationship between complexity and wealth, but it is a relationship that does not necessarily favour the individual, particularly the individual at the bottom of society. A complex economy, because it allows different areas and groups of people to specialize in producing crops or goods that they are perhaps particularly suited to grow or make, can undoubtedly support a larger population, give wider access to specialized products and produce more overall, than an economy in which each peasant community produces its own beer, its own tools, its own pots, etc. It will therefore make for a 'richer', more variegated and more specialized region. However, as we well know from nineteenth-century experience in Europe and twentieth-century experience elsewhere, this does not necessarily mean that all individuals within a complex system are 'better off'.

In order to imagine them more vividly, the complexity and sophistication of the Roman economy need to be placed in a very broad and comparative historical framework. In comparison to many other ancient and medieval economies, the Roman economy was highly developed. High-quality and exotic goods are probably available in all societies, as we have seen from the example of Sutton Hoo, but only for rulers and the very highest in the land. What is striking about the Roman period is the large-scale availability of standardized high-quality goods, many of them imported from afar, for a substantial middle and lower market well below this extreme upper-crust. The African pottery industry, for instance, produced literally millions of pots to a uniform high quality and to a range of standardized designs, and somehow distributed them to households of all sorts within much of the Mediterranean region and beyond. Such bulk and breadth of operation was characteristic of the Roman period, and not to be seen again for very many centuries.

However, it is also important to realize that, despite its undoubted sophistication, the Roman economy remained, from the perspective of modern prosperous nations, highly underdeveloped and very precarious. This is best seen by looking at agricultural production and at the agricultural labour needed to sustain it.

Mechanization of agriculture in the Roman and medieval worlds was extremely limited, and crops had, for the most part, to be laboriously coaxed from the soil by massive armies of agricultural labourers. For the Roman period there is no way of telling accurately what proportion of the population worked in the fields, but the overall balance between agriculture and 'industry' was probably not dissimilar to that of later medieval Europe. And, in later medieval Europe, figures from England (where we are fortunate to have the returns of both the 1086 Domesday and the 1377 poll-tax surveys) suggest that nine-tenths of the population lived in the countryside, of whom almost all were primarily engaged in agricultural work.

It is necessary to appreciate this basic economic pattern in order to understand the underlying nature of the Roman (and late medieval) economies. Their considerable sophistications, in terms of trade, specialization of artisan production and use of coin, which impress us when we visit museums, Roman sites and medieval cathedrals, were all achieved on the back of immensely laborious agricultural production which tied the vast majority of the population to the land. The agricultural surpluses that were needed to sustain the craftsmen, the aristocrats, the state and all the other sophistications that we associate with 'Rome' were only produced by enormous numbers of people working the land for returns that would seem paltry in a modern prosperous economy.

Furthermore, when we talk of Roman 'industries', such as those of the later Roman period that produced African red-slip ware or, on a much smaller scale, Oxford ware (see Fig. 12, p. 351 above), these were not, as far as we can tell from the archaeological record, centralized factory-based concerns of the modern type but, rather, collaborative ventures of groups of artisans. It may even be a mistake to imagine craftsmen as entirely dedicated to one specialized activity; potting, for instance, could have been seasonal, depending on the availability of fuel and on the availability of labour, freed during slack periods in the fields.[33]

The Roman economy was not only highly underdeveloped in modern terms, dependent as it was on a vast agricultural labour force; it was also precarious, since crops could and did fail, often with disastrous results. Cash-crops (oil and wine) and some artisan products (such as fine pottery for the table) seem to have moved widely around the empire, in what appear to have been large quantities; but it is not likely that there was much long-distance commerce in grain and other basic foodstuffs.

Probably the only regular large-scale shipments of grain over long distances were those organized by the state in order to provision its army and the major cities (in particular, Rome and Constantinople), and even these efforts were not always successful.[34] When a basic food-crop failed, transport and marketing structures were not in place to ensure that the gap was quickly and easily filled with the crop of another region, particularly if the area affected was inland.[35] Rather, people starved to death, and many of the debilitated survivors subsequently died of disease.

The so-called 'Chronicle of Joshua the Stylite' gives a graphic and harrowing picture of such a disaster in its account of the famine which affected the region of Edessa in 499–501, after a swarm of locusts had consumed the wheat harvest and a second havest, of millet, had failed. The cost of bread rose; people were forced to sell cheaply their other possessions in order to buy it; many fled the region altogether; others, particularly those too weak to travel far, flocked into the city to beg. Here disease killed many, but there was still far too little to eat (and not nearly enough to feed the crowds of beggars). Some were reduced to eating the flesh of the dead, and in the countryside people tried in vain to fill their bellies by eating the lees from the vintage. In the town, the poor ate leaves and roots, 'sleeping in the porticoes and squares, and day and night they howled from their hunger, and their bodies wasted away and grew thinner so that they came to look like corpses'. Many more died, particularly those who were sleeping rough during the cold nights of the winter, and the streets were filled with the dead. More disease followed.[36]

[33] Roman pottery production, with useful discussion of modern analogies: Peacock (1982). Some of the state-run *fabricae* may well have been more like modern factories.

[34] Garnsey and Saller (1987) 83–103; Durliat (1990a).

[35] Garnsey (1988) 22–3, quoting and discussing a passage by Gregory of Nazianzus.

[36] Joshua the Stylite: trans W. Wright 1882 (from the Syriac into English), 26–34; ed. and trans. (into Latin) J.-B. Chabot 1949, 193–9. Quoted in English, and discussed by Garnsey (1988) 3–6 and 20–37.

All this misery took place in Mesopotamia in a period when the near east seems to have enjoyed unprecedented prosperity. Edessa itself clearly benefited from this prosperity and was a very wealthy city, as can be seen from the amounts of tribute that it was (repeatedly) able to pay the Persians: 2,000 pounds weight (more than five times the cost of S. Vitale in Ravenna) promised in 503 soon after the end of the famine; 200 pounds paid in 540; and 500 pounds more in 544. All this gold did not spare the poor from misery and death in 499–501.[37]

VII. THE DISTRIBUTION OF GOODS AND WEALTH WITHIN THE LATE ANTIQUE ECONOMY: THE ROLE OF OVERSEAS COMMERCE

No one would or could dispute that wealth and goods travelled widely within the Roman empire. However, the relative importance of the state and of commerce in the distribution of goods and wealth has been much debated. Historians (taking written texts as their point of departure) have tended to emphasize non-commercial mechanisms to explain the move-ment of both goods and wealth. They have played down the role of a free market and stressed, above all, the role of the state, as a power that raised substantial taxes in both coin and kind and then spent these in selected parts of the empire. They have argued that, even when goods were trans-ported over a distance and sold, this happened only because they were able to travel at no cost (or at least at a heavily subsidized rate) in state-financed shipping.[38]

They have also pointed to private estate management as a means of dis-tributing goods between the scattered holdings of landlords with property in several different parts of the Mediterranean. According to this latter model, a dish in African red-slip ware or an African oil amphora found in Italy could have reached its destination at the command of a rich aristocrat who ordered the transfer of goods from one of his African estates to one of his Italian ones.[39]

Archaeologists, by contrast, tend to see things in more modern and more commercial terms, and talk blithely of 'trade' whenever they see an imported piece of pot. This difference of opinion has led to a lively debate between those who see the movement of goods in the Roman world as essentially commercial and those who emphasize non-commercial modes of distribution.[40]

[37] 503 promise (not in the end delivered): Joshua the Stylite, trans. Wright, 53, and trans. Chabot, 213. 540: Procop. *Wars* II.12.34. 544: Procop. *Wars* II.27.46.
[38] Finley (1973) 17–34; Jones, *LRE* 465 and 824–58.   [39] Whittaker (1985).
[40] The argument for trade as important, and for archaeological evidence as vital in revealing it, has been made most forcefully by a group of Italian archaeologists: see the papers by Carandini and others in Giardina, *Società romana* III.

In part, this is a debate born out of the nature of the evidence. Archaeologists find a mass of imported pottery and no indication of how it got there and, not unnaturally, think in terms of the obvious modern means of distribution: trade. The ancient texts, by contrast, tell us much about aristocrats and the state, but are notably silent about many of the products that archaeologists discover, so that we are often forced to make do with a cumbersome modern term ('Oxford ware', 'African red-slip ware', etc.) for a common archaeological find. Between the abundance of the archaeological evidence and the silence of the texts, there is obviously room for much debate.

In recent years there has been some convergence of the 'historical' and the 'archaeological' positions.[41] It does indeed seem likely that both mechanisms of distribution (commercial and non-commercial) were of great importance, probably to mutual advantage. For instance, in the fifth- and sixth-century east, it is not unreasonable to hypothesize that a great deal of the Phocaean red-slip ware that reached the near east was taken there commercially in empty ships returning to Egypt, whose main purpose had been to carry grain for the state to Constantinople.

Similarly, it must have been the building projects of the emperors that principally sustained the quarries of Proconnesos, in the Sea of Marmara near Constantinople, since Proconnesian marble was the main fine material used for both secular and ecclesiastical imperial projects throughout the fourth, fifth and earlier sixth century. It is also possible that some of the Proconnesian marble found in non-imperial buildings was a gift from the emperor to influential patrons whose good will was worth cultivating. Anicia Juliana for her church of St Polyeuktos in Constantinople, and Julianus Argentarius and Theoderic the Ostrogoth for their many buildings in Ravenna, perhaps received as gifts the large quantities of Proconnesian marble that they needed.[42]

However, it is equally possible that these rich patrons had to buy their marble from the imperial quarries. Certainly, at a humbler level, it is far easier to explain the very extensive distribution of basic architectural elements in Proconnesian marble, like capitals and chancel-screens, in terms of commerce rather than political favour, and, as we have seen at the beginning of this chapter, there is even a scrap of literary evidence to confirm this (see Fig. 15, p. 359 above). State production and distribution and commerce may indeed have been closely interlinked. The commercial sale of Proconnesian probably depended on a state-run quarry, and it was certainly the massive imperial projects which set the fashion for humbler patrons to emulate; yet the state quarries perhaps also needed sales to a wider private market in order to maintain large-scale production.

---

[41] E.g. Hopkins in Garnsey *et al.* (1983) ix–xxv; Garnsey and Saller (1987) 43–63; Peacock and Williams (1986) 54–63.

[42] St Polyeuktos: Harrison (1989) 77–124. Ravenna: Angiolini Martinelli *et al.* (1968–9).

The fifth and sixth century are particularly interesting in any debate about the relative importance of the state and of commerce in the distribution of goods overseas. In this period, the eastern Mediterranean remained under the control of a single political power (the Roman empire centred on Constantinople), but the former western empire broke up into entirely independent states and local aristocracies. The pattern of exports within the west, before and after the collapse of Roman power, should therefore tell us whether the existence of state mechanisms of distribution were essential for the distribution of goods over long distances.

The importance of the state in the distribution of goods does indeed show up in a sharp fall, around the time of the Vandal conquest, in the quantities of African red-slip ware reaching western sites (see Fig. 16).[43] Since red-slip ware may often have been carried 'pick-a-back' in grain ships financed by the state (at least in the early stages of its travels), such a fall could be expected with the ending of Rome's African *annona*. But what is also striking is that considerable amounts of African red-slip, as well as large quantities of African oil amphorae, continued to reach sites all over the western Mediterranean throughout the Vandal and early Byzantine periods. Quantities did gradually decline, and the area served did become more restricted. But this was a very slow change, which is more easily explained in terms of slowly declining purchasing-power in the north-western provinces than in terms of any Vandal-imposed changes to systems of production and distribution.

African amphorae and African red-slip ware, in the fifth and sixth century, must have travelled for commercial reasons – as must also have been the case for the eastern Mediterranean amphorae which appear on western sites in large quanties in the same period.[44] The impressive scale of this commerce and its persistence in the difficult times of the fifth and sixth century suggest very strongly that commerce and the lure of financial gain were important elements in the distribution of goods, not only in this period, when they are exposed by the disappearance of the unified state, but also in the earlier Roman period, when they were operating alongside, and were perhaps partly masked by, state-operated mechanisms of distribution.

As in all centuries before the advent of the railway, proximity to navigable waterways and, above all, to the sea were obviously essential for the long-distance trading of bulk goods. However, the evidence also suggests that 'proximity' needs to be understood quite widely, since it seems that the import and export of goods might spread remarkably far inland. For instance, the landlocked settlements of the Negev desert imported in this

[43] Fentress and Perkins (1988), which is a pioneering work, since it attempts to show changes in absolute quantities of imported pottery, rather than changing proportions of different imported wares.

[44] Eastern amphorae: Reynolds (1995) 70–83.

A

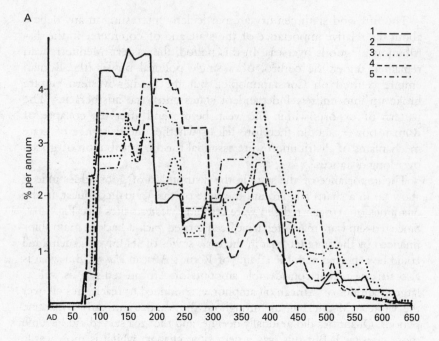

B

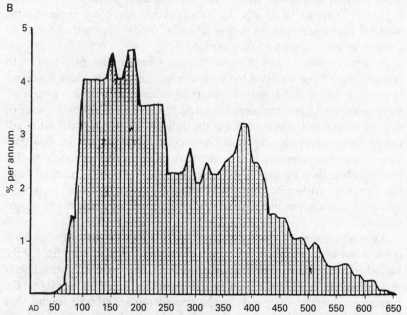

Fig. 16 Quantities of African red-slip ware recorded on five sites (or regional surveys) in the western Mediterranean. B is a consolidation into a single graph of all the data presented in A. (From Fentress and Perkins (1988) figs. 2 and 3)

period marble fittings from Proconnesos and probably exported at least some of their wine overseas through Gaza.[45]

But land transport undoubtedly added considerably to cost, and those who did not have reasonably good access to waterways undoubtedly stood at a disadvantage if they wished to sell their produce away from their home region. For instance, the landowners of central Asia Minor are described by John Lydus, in the time of Justinian, as unable to sell their crops because they were 'far removed from the sea'; while, by contrast, Agathias in the mid sixth century describes the Lazi, on the Black Sea coast of Asia Minor, as wealthy since 'they put out to sea whenever possible and carry on a thriving commerce'.[46] For many producers, commercial viability must have been dependent on their access to water transport.

Even if it is accepted that commerce, as well as imperial and aristocratic distribution, was one means whereby goods travelled overseas in the Roman world, it still remains to be seen how important this commerce was within the overall economy. Is it impressive only because archaeologists have concentrated their attention on it, since it both strikes the imagination and shows up so clearly in the archaeological record?

There is certainly much to be said for such scepticism, and there is no doubt that we now need detailed studies of regional and local industries and networks of exchange to set beside the work that has already been done on long-distance distribution. For fine tablewares, some of this research has already appeared. To set alongside the information on African red-slip ware, it is already possible to form some impression of more regional industries, producing pottery of comparable style and quality, such as the various types of south Gaulish *terre sigillée grise*.[47] On a humbler and more basic level, however, we know as yet very little about the plentiful buff-coloured and grey tablewares and cooking-wares of the Roman, late Roman and early medieval centuries, partly because they are often undecorated and difficult to distinguish.

Although regional and local economies undoubtedly deserve emphasis and more research, it would none the less be a mistake to dismiss long-distance trade as peripheral to the main base of the economy. For there is a very striking coincidence that cannot be avoided. Periods of rural prosperity in a particular region seem to coincide closely with periods in which the same region's products show up in the archaeological record as exports overseas.

This is true of Italy in the first century B.C. and the first century A.D., when Italian wine, pottery and marble were exported all over the western

[45] Gaza wine: Riley (1979) 219–22. See also ch. 12, p. 342 above, n. 60, for Cappadocian merchants travelling overland to northern Mesopotamia to buy wine.

[46] John Lydus: discussed by Hendy, *Studies* 295–6. Agathias *Hist.* III.5.3.

[47] Gaulish sigillata: *Atlante* (1981) 5–7; Reynolds (1995) 36–7.

Mediterranean, and when, from the evidence of field-survey, rural settlement was at its most extensive and prosperous. It is also true of southern Gaul and Mediterranean Spain at a slightly later date, at the end of the first century and through the second century. Moving closer to our period, the third and fourth century seem to have been the high point of wealthy rural and urban settlement in Africa, and they were also centuries when exports of African red-slip ware and African amphorae were very high. The fifth and sixth century then saw the gradual but distinct shrinkage of these exports, and also probably a gradual decline in rural and urban settlement in Africa itself.[48]

For the fifth and sixth century, it is very striking that Gaza wine amphorae appeared in quantity on eastern and even western sites at the very period that the small towns and villages of Gaza's desert hinterland, the Negev, reached their greatest size and displayed their most evident signs of prosperity. It is equally striking that the period of extensive and large-scale export of the amphorae known prosaically as Late Roman 1, which were produced in the region around Antioch (as well as in Cilicia and on Cyprus), coincides with the period of the best evidence for settlement and prosperity in the nearby Syrian limestone massif. Neither the Negev nor the limestone massif ever again sustained a large population, and yet in the late Roman period both were extensively settled by people who seem to have been well-off. Furthermore, in fifth- and sixth-century western texts Syrians are often referred to as traders, to the point that the very word 'Syrus' appears to have acquired the partial meaning of 'merchant': so that Sidonius Apollinaris, describing a topsy-turvy world in Ravenna in 468, could write 'the clergy lend money, while the Syrians sing psalms', confident that his audience would understand the paradox.[49]

If combined, the evidence from rural survey, amphora finds and texts strongly suggests that the prosperity of the fifth- and sixth-century near east was, at least in part, based on an ability to sell its products overseas, sometimes over very long distances. Overseas demand seems to have put cash and spending power into a region. It also probably encouraged, in the exporting regions, the development of specialization of production for those goods that could be sold. This is best seen in the opening up of marginal land. For instance, the Syrian limestone massif, though reasonably well watered, is very rocky, with soil restricted to basins of arable in the valley bottoms and to pockets of earth in the hill slopes (see Fig. 5, p. 322

---

[48] Overall summaries of the rural evidence: Lewit (1991); Mattingly and Hitchner (1995) 189–96 and 211 (for Africa). Summary of pottery and amphora evidence: Panella, in Giardina, *Società romana* III.431–59.

[49] Settlement in the Negev and limestone massif: see ch. 12, p. 321 above, n. 12. Amphorae: Reynolds (1995) 71–83 and figs. 155–60; Riley (1979) 219–22 (Gaza/*LRA*4); Empereur and Picon (1989) 236–43 (*LRA*1). Texts: Sid. Ap. *Ep.* 1.8; Lambrechts (1937); Pirenne (1939) ch. II pt 2; Ruggini (1959) (who rightly points out that by no means all easterners in the west were involved in trade).

above).[50] It is a region that can sustain a population engaged in mixed farming, but only in small numbers and at the margins of prosperity; and yet in the late Roman period the limestone massif was both densely settled (see Fig. 7, p. 329 above) and very prosperous. There is no way of proving how this exceptional state of affairs came about. But the known demand for Antiochene (Late Roman 1) amphorae, the presence of late antique olive-presses around the villages of the massif, and the possibility of planting trees in the tiny but numerous pockets of soil, together strongly suggest that increased demand opened up this region to the specialized cultivation of the olive.

This does not, of course, mean that all, or even the greater part, of the oil of the limestone massif was produced for an overseas market. Producers in all exporting regions must also have been growing to satisfy local and regional demand, as well as the needs of their own households. Long-distance trade, regional trade and local trade are indeed likely to have been closely interlinked and mutually sustaining. For instance, the growth of a regional trade in oil could create the structures to enable an overseas trade to develop; while conversely, if some oil went overseas, this might encourage the growth of a regional market in order to satisfy the regional need normally supplied by the exported product. Both overseas and regional trade might, in their turn, stimulate local demand, by helping to create a more prosperous and more numerous peasantry. The possible ramifications in the flow of goods and wealth are endless, and can never be thoroughly sorted out, if only because it is impossible to do so from the archaeological record. However, the archaeological record does suggest that overseas trade was one important element at work in the creation of regional wealth.

Just as we do not need to believe that every peasant in an exporting area worked directly for the overseas market, so we do not need to imagine specialized areas of production as massive zones of monoculture, in the manner of the modern American wheat-belt. The limestone massif, for instance, would never have been an area exclusively of olive trees, importing all other necessities from elsewhere. Rather, it was probably an area where there were many more olive trees than the local population needed, and where there were many more people living, at a higher level of prosperity, than the soil could possibly have maintained without extensive commerce and specialization. But, in amongst the olive trees, the peasants would certainly have kept up as mixed and extensive a range of cultivation as the landscape could support, with vegetable plots, fruit trees, small areas of arable, and as many animals as possible.

I have argued that overseas trade, on a scale large enough to enrich those who were exporting their goods, is the easiest way to explain the coincidence

---

[50] The discussion that follows is based on Tchalenko, *Villages*, and Tate (1992).

in time between the prosperity of certain regions of the ancient world and the spread of their products overseas. This does, however, raise a very basic question, to which there is no obvious answer, at least at present. Why did products like wine and oil, so long established in the Mediterranean and so widely produced there, come to be so favoured from particular provinces at particular times; and why, given the obvious additional costs of transport, did not local products compete successfully? If the peasants, landlords, marble-workers and potters of Italy lost out in the fourth and fifth century to those of Gaza, Antioch, Africa and Proconnesos, why did they not re-establish the extremely successful and widely exported Italian production of the first centuries B.C. and A.D.?

To answer these questions adequately would require more information than we will ever have. For instance, we would need to know about relative labour-costs across the empire and how they changed through time; about who organized and financed export-trades; and about consumer-perception of different goods and how these perceptions altered.

The archaeological evidence does suggest that a sophisticated Roman economy had produced a large market of discerning consumers; and if so, like supposedly discerning consumers today, they are likely to have been very much at the mercy of the dictates of fashion. Indeed, in the case of wines, we do know, from the written record, that some Italian wines were always prized and that some eastern wines (such as that of Gaza) became so in late antiquity.[51] But, as far as I am aware, there is no evidence specifically from late antiquity to show that consumers shared the modern perception of olive oil as of different qualities, with further potential as a status symbol; let alone whether (as with modern Tuscan 'estate-bottling') this was as much a question of historical perception, marketing and packaging, as of 'reality'.[52] Sadly, there is no information to tell us whether purchasers in the large and all-important Roman 'middle market' felt that a plate of real African red-slip ware was superior to a comparable local product in *terre sigillée grise* – let alone whether they prized their Gaza wine more highly if it was still in its original, and distinctive, amphora.[53]

An even more fundamental question will also never receive an answer: were there other products as important as wine, oil and pottery – perhaps even of greater importance – that were regularly exported overseas in large quantities, but which we have no knowledge of simply because they have the misfortune to be archaeologically invisible? For example, in the *Life of*

---

[51] Gaza wine: see the sources cited in Riley (1979) 219–22.

[52] From the earlier empire several texts discuss the quality of oil from different types of olive and from different regions: e.g. Columella, *Rust.* v.8.3–5; Pliny, *HN* iii.60 and xv.15–27; Athenaeus, *Deipnosophists* ii.66f–67b.

[53] However, see from the early empire Trimalchio's ostentatiously labelled, one-hundred-year-old Falernian: Petron. *Satyricon* 34.

Melania the Younger, the holy woman persuades her over-zealous and uncomfortable husband to abandon wearing sackcloth and to switch to unostentatious cheap Antiochene cloth.[54] The story is set in Rome at the beginning of the fifth century. Was Antiochene cloth perhaps the usual material for the mass-market of the city, chosen for her husband by Melania (and by the author of her life) because it was a clear and widely recognized item of lower-class dress? If it was common in Rome, was it also widely exported elsewhere, both within the regional economy of the Near East and within the broad Mediterranean economy? Unfortunately, we shall never know.

VIII. STATE AND ARISTOCRATIC DISTRIBUTION; THE EFFECTS OF TAXATION ON THE ECONOMY

To argue for the importance of commerce is not to argue that the role of the state (and to a lesser extent the aristocracy) in redistributing goods and wealth in the Roman world was negligible, nor to argue that there was no change here in the fifth and sixth century. The importance of state spending is, for instance, very clear just before our period, in the fourth century, when a large army and the presence of the emperors themselves in favoured residences near the frontier (such as Trier, Sirmium and Antioch) concentrated great wealth in the frontier regions, some of which were not by nature rich. Huge piles of gold, raised in the peaceful interior of the empire, were collected and spent along the Rhine and Danube, and along the eastern frontier. There is plenty of evidence – for instance, in the rich urban and rural houses of the fourth-century Trier region – to show how important this was as a mechanism for distributing wealth and encouraging local demand. Similarly, we have plenty of evidence, from the fourth and early fifth century, of the accumulation of widely scattered estates by wealthy aristocrats, which must have led to substantial transfers of wealth from region to region, and perhaps also to transfers of goods.[55]

A major change in the way that the state distributed its revenues, which took place just before our period, almost certainly had a marked and generalized effect on the Mediterranean economy. The establishment of Constantinople as an exceptionally privileged city in the fourth century, the diversion to it of the Egyptian *annona*, and its emergence at the end of the century as the pre-eminent eastern imperial residence, all helped create a new, stable and substantial focus of consumption in the east. Furthermore, the definitive break of the empire into two halves at the end of the fourth century undoubtedly spared the eastern provinces from pouring resources into the troubled fifth-century west. The creation of an autonomous

---

[54] Discussed by Jones, *LRE* 850.   [55] Trier: *Trier Kaiserresidenz* (1984). Estates: Jones, *LRE* 782.

eastern empire, with its own established capital at Constantinople (developments which were in place by the start of our period in 425), were probably essential foundations to the very different economic histories of the west and the east in late antiquity.

The other side to this same coin was the loss to Rome, and the western provinces in general, of the resources of the east. Any drop in imperial spending certainly had a negative effect on the regions that had formerly received the emperor's gold. We can see the consequences of this in the gradual abandonment of the paid army, first along the Rhine and upper Danube in the fifth century, and then along the lower Danube in the sixth century: from being areas with economies greatly enriched and stimulated by imperial pay and largess, they became peripheral zones, and, unless they had alternative sources of income, very poor ones.

The beneficial effects of state spending and the negative impact of its abolition are well illustrated in sixth-century Asia Minor, where two sources, John Lydus and Procopius, provide complementary accounts of the result of Justinian's cuts in the *cursus publicus* (the system of state-maintained transport) along the military road which linked Constantinople to the eastern frontier. The local effects of these cuts were apparently devastating. While the *cursus publicus* flourished, local landlords had supplied their taxes in kind to feed the grooms and horses of the *cursus*, and, by selling it additional food, had also been able to make money from the state. After the drastic curtailment of the *cursus*, the state no longer paid out gold, but rather demanded it in taxation, despite the fact that cash was extremely difficult to obtain in an inland region far from the commercial opportunities of the sea. While the state was spending money along the military road, all was well for the local landlords; but when that spending stopped and turned into a demand for cash, life became much more difficult.[56]

The great imperial residences of the empire were another obvious area where state spending had been concentrated, and they certainly suffered markedly in this period from a decline in state revenue. As provinces and their tax revenues were lost, so imperial cities inevitably declined in both wealth and splendour. Despite considerable imperial and Ostrogothic attempts to sustain it, Rome gradually shrank through the fifth and sixth century to a tiny proportion of its former size; not only was there no longer the government money to sustain it, but it also inevitably lost out from the shrinking overseas holdings of its senatorial aristocracy. Much later, at the end of the sixth century and in the seventh, Constantinople, which had increased in population, wealth and splendour in the very period that Rome declined, itself underwent a dramatic period of impoverishment and shrinkage.[57]

[56] Quoted and discussed by Hendy, *Studies* 294–6.
[57] Rome: Krautheimer (1980) 3–87; Ward-Perkins, *Public Building* 38–48. Constantinople: Mango, *Développement* 51–62.

The fragmentation of power in the west, of course, created in the fifth and sixth century a scattering of smaller political capitals within the territories of the former empire. Although we know very little about them archaeologically, these towns, such as Toulouse for the fifth-century Visigothic kingdom, Paris for the sixth-century Merovingians, and Toledo and Pavia for the sixth- and seventh-century Visigoths and Lombards, must have benefited from their new status. It is, however, notable that none of these new capitals (except Ostrogothic Ravenna) has so far produced the spectacular signs of wealth (imposing defensive walls, rulers' palaces, numbers of large churches, splendid aristocratic houses and secular monuments) that are so obvious in the new imperial residences of the fourth- and fifth-century empire (as at Milan, Trier, Ravenna, Thessalonica etc.). Indeed, the only new capital to have been extensively excavated in recent times, Carthage, seems to have declined in size, wealth and splendour through the fifth century, despite becoming in this very period the centre of a new Vandal kingdom which no longer needed to send the vast tax revenue of Africa to Rome. Perhaps Carthage and the other new capitals did gain from their new status, but only in relation to other, smaller centres; and perhaps this gain does not show up readily in the archaeological and monumental record because it was swallowed up in the massive overall decline in urban prosperity which took place in the fifth- and sixth-century west.

The areas that directly benefited from state spending in the Roman world were always limited. Unlike a modern state, which spends on a wide range of salaries and capital projects (for health-care, transport, etc.) and which often tries to share out the benefits of government money both geographically and socially, the late Roman state spent most of its wealth on one sector alone: the army. And much the greater part of the army was located in one – admittedly very large – region of the empire, the principal frontier zone which stretched from Antioch in the south-east to the Rhine mouths in the north-west. As we have seen in the case of land contiguous with the military road through Asia Minor, other restricted areas within the interior of the empire could also benefit from state spending; but, for the most part, the provinces at peace simply paid up and got little in return, except, of course, the all-important gift of peace.

Rates of taxation were high in the late Roman world. Land around Ravenna in A.D. 555 paid more to the state in tax than it did to its landlords in rent; and in the mid seventh century, the proportion paid to the state from the Sicilian lands of the Ravennate church was only slightly less: 15,000 *solidi* in tax were sent annually to Constantinople, and 16,000 in rent to the church treasury at Ravenna. It has, indeed, been argued that rates of taxation in late antiquity may have been responsible for pushing some land out of cultivation. The extensive archaeological evidence we have of an expanding and prosperous rural population in certain regions (particularly in the east) shows that this did not happen universally; but it is possible that heavy taxation was a real problem in poorer parts of the emire.[58]

Even if rates of taxation were perhaps not often so harsh as to ruin local economies, the decline of tax, which seems to have happened in many regions of the west during the fifth and sixth century, should have benefited all those areas that had been net-contributors to the Roman state's finances, just as it damaged those areas that had been net-beneficiaries.[59] However, strangely enough, in no case that I know of can the ending of taxation in a particular region be linked to any evident rise in that region's prosperity. The establishment of a Vandal kingdom in Africa in the early fifth century, for instance, must have meant that no taxes in gold and kind now went overseas to Rome, to Ravenna and to the armies north of the Alps, and that all the former tax revenue of the region was now being consumed locally. Yet, despite some evidence that goods once sent to Rome in tax were now sold elsewhere, the 'Vandal boom' that should have followed is apparent neither in the well-dated excavations at Carthage nor in the more impressionistic evidence from the interior.[60]

Similarly, the slow decline of taxation in Gaul through the sixth and seventh century is exceptionally well documented in Gregory of Tours' *Histories* and in hagiographical material.[61] In this case, the beneficiaries should have been the peasantry and the local towns, who previously had to forward their taxes to the various Merovingian kings. But, again, there is no trace in the evidence that towns like Tours and Poitiers boomed in the late sixth and seventh century as a result of the exemptions they had obtained, nor that this period was a golden age for the peasantry of Gaul. One suggested answer to this problem is that the new wealth of the untaxed regions was real, but is invisible to us, because it was consumed in ways that do not show up archaeologically: by peasants eating better, and by aristocrats displaying their wealth through perishable goods, such as clothing, and through items, like jewellery, which have not survived because they were later melted down.[62]

As argued above in discussing prosperity, that peasant diet improved is perfectly possible, though not at present demonstrable. However, I think it is very unlikely that the sixth- and seventh-century aristocracy had more perishable luxuries than their Roman predecessors, if only because we know that the Roman aristocracy revelled in every available luxury item

---

[58] Rates of taxation: Jones, *LRE* 819–21; Wickham (1984) 11–12; Agnellus, *Lib. Pont. Eccl. Rav.* cap. 111 (seventh-century Sicilian estates). Impact of taxation: Jones, *LRE* 819–23.

[59] Durliat (1990b) argues for continuing taxation and a continuing paid army in the early medieval west; but see Wickham (1993) for what I believe to be a convincing demolition of this thesis.

[60] Shift in direction of African exports: Reynolds (1995) 112–16; Fentress and Perkins (1988) 213.

[61] Lot (1928); Goffart (1982).   [62] Wickham (1988) 110 and 121–4.

(silks, gold-embroidered robes, ivories, silverware, jewellery, wasteful and exotic foods, the slaughter of imported wild animals, etc.). There were important shifts in modes of aristocratic display during our period; for instance, from the great silver dinner-services, so characteristic of late antique Roman hoards, to the gold- and garnet-encrusted weaponry of the highest-status Frankish graves. But I very much doubt that, within these shifts in kind, there were absolute shifts in quantity, in favour of the untaxed aristocrats of sixth- and seventh-century barbarian Europe.

The only solution I can think of to the very real problem of where the tax wealth went, once it was no longer collected and forwarded to the army and to the emperors, is to suggest that any obvious financial gains from the ending of tax were swallowed up in a more general decline of the economy. Perhaps there was more food per head, and perhaps people no longer had to work so hard; but perhaps, also, there were no longer the economic structures in place to convert surpluses of food into coins, into pots, into mortared walls, etc.

There may, in fact, be circumstances in which tax demands (particularly if in coin) can stimulate an economy rather than depress it: because they encourage producers to specialize and sell in order to raise their tax-money.[63] If demands for tax in coin can help awaken an economy, is it also possible that the ending of such demands can help it settle down into self-sufficient slumber? However, I would not like to argue very strongly in favour of this idea, since any suggestion that taxing in coin is necessarily a stimulant to economic growth is called into question by what happened at the beginning of the fifth century. At this date, the whole empire, both western and eastern, moved away from taxation in kind (favoured in the fourth century) towards taxation in coin, but with curiously divergent results. According to the model proposed above, the change should have stimulated economic complexity and growth throughout the empire. This did, indeed, occur in the eastern Mediterranean, at more or less the right time. But in the west, this same period saw widespread and generalized economic decline.[64] It may be that the model is not universally applicable, but only works when underlying economic conditions are favourable, as they were in the early-fifth-century east (but not in the west).

IX. CAUSES OF ECONOMIC DECLINE: A GENERAL CONSIDERATION

We have already encountered some possible causes of economic decline (heavy taxation, the ending of state spending, and the failure of some

---

[63] A model proposed by Hopkins (1980a) for an earlier period of Roman history.

[64] Wickham (1984) 10 n. 13. For the move to tax in coin: Jones, *LRE* 460.

regions to compete commercially); in the next few pages we shall meet some more. However, before we look further at individual causes, an important general point needs to be made. A central and essential prerequisite for understanding the decline of the Roman economy is, I believe, the acceptance that it was a closely interlocked structure in which commerce and regional specialization, as well as the redistributive power of the state, all had an important part to play. If we see the Roman economy in the way that, for instance, Finley did, as a series of essentially autonomous, very local economies, then it is extremely hard to understand the broad trends that seem to have swept through whole regions. But, if we accept that regional and overseas contacts mattered, it is then much easier to see how this complex network might slowly unravel.[65]

For instance, if Italy was important to Africa as a market for some of its oil and some of its pottery, then the impoverishment of Italy in the fifth century, through the loss of the revenues of empire and through the ravages of war (and perhaps also in part through its own failure to compete successfully in the Mediterranean market), will have markedly reduced demand for Africa's produce. This reduction would adversely affect both the direct producers of oil and African red-slip ware, and those Africans whose wealth depended, within the regional and local economies, on supplying these producers with African products, like grain, chickens, building-materials, etc.

This argument for interdependence does not necessarily require us to see the economic fortunes of *all* parts of the Mediterranean, let alone all parts of the empire, as tightly interlinked. As we have seen, the fifth century is a period of growing prosperity in the east and of marked economic decline in the west. Western proserity was clearly not an essential prerequisite for eastern growth. Rather, it looks as if one half of the Mediterranean could exist in great and growing prosperity, largely independently of the other. The Mediterranean in about A.D. 600 is indeed strikingly similar to the pre-Roman world of around 300 B.C. – with a highly evolved and commercial economy in the east that extended westwards into southern Italy, Sicily and the Carthage region, and which coexisted with a much more backwards north-west. The comparison even extends to the existence in both periods of important gateway communities (like Marseilles) between the two economic zones.

Though not quite on a Mediterranean-wide scale, multifarious but necessarily fragile links between different peoples and different economies were almost certainly very important in encouraging specialized production and in sustaining the great achievements of the Roman world. As we have seen earlier, there was no major technological, industrial or agricultural revolution

---

[65] See p. 369 above, n. 38.

in the Roman period. Rather, the methods of production used were essentially the same as those of the pre-Roman Iron Age and of the early Middle Ages. The achievements of the Roman economy depended on developing tiny surpluses and small-scale production into something much bigger, through complex and efficient structures. But these structures were fragile, and if they decayed or were disrupted, nothing of the impressive edifice was left.

To understand the far-reaching effects of the disappearance of this edifice, it also helps if we believe that the Roman economy had been able to encourage specialization of production to the point where consumers depended for very many of their goods on highly skilled and specialized producers (who in turn depended for their livelihood on sales over a wide area). Ironically, if (as in the modern world) economic complexity has accustomed us to getting what we need by purchase from specialized producers, when this supply is disrupted, we have no basic skills to fall back on. This may explain why, say, in fifth-century Britain, a province which had had highly specialized potting-industries in the third and fourth centuries reverted to the use of pottery that is technologically far less sophisticated than that produced by the regional industries of the Iron Age.

X. WAR, DISRUPTION AND ECONOMIC DECLINE

The period 400–650 is marked by the spread of war to almost all regions of the empire, which had previously (with a rude interruption in the third century) enjoyed peace for some four hundred years. The relationship between the arrival of war and the decline of the economy clearly requires detailed investigation.

Rather than conquest, it was probably war itself and the disruptions that it caused which brought about change for the worse. As we have seen in the cases of Vandal Africa and the Arab near east, the arrival of new peoples (even very different new peoples) did not necessarily cause rapid economic decline. This is, in fact, unsurprising, since, in all the cases we know about, the incoming barbarians came to enjoy, not to destroy, the benefits of Rome. In government and administration, they were certainly able and happy to employ local 'middlemen' to operate those systems of exploitation that they did not necessarily themselves immediately understand. Though this is not so well documented, it is likely that they did the same with the economy.

War and raiding, however, could certainly be very disruptive and damaging to local production, to systems of distribution and to demand. The *Life of Saint Severinus* provides detailed examples of such disruption from a frontier province on the upper Danube in the dark days of the late fifth century. At one moment the citizens of Batavis begged the saint to intercede with the king of the Rugi, who dominated the countryside around the town, to persuade him to allow them to trade. The market they wished to set up was probably to satisfy a purely local need: to exchange their own wares with the foodstuffs produced in the surrounding countryside. On another occasion, the saint intervened to fill a gap caused by the disruption of long-distance trade: he gave to the poor of Lauriacum a dole of oil, because merchants were now bringing so little to the region.[66]

In parts of the empire, the advent of war and the collapse or, at least, decline of a sophisticated economy do seem to have coincided quite closely. This is the case in fifth-century Britain, in late-sixth-century Greece and in seventh-century Asia Minor. It is, admittedly, possible that the coincidence of date between documented warfare and archaeologically-attested disruption was not always, in reality, quite as close as it now seems. In periods when datable archaeological materials (such as coins and fine tablewares) were disappearing or becoming very scarce, archaeological processes, which in fact took decades to occur, may all seem to have happened at one single moment (when the last datable object was deposited). However, there is no doubt that war and economic decline came at roughly the same time in all these three areas. And, conversely, it is equally striking that the period of the east's most evident economic prosperity (the fifth and early sixth century) is one of exceptional peace for the region (with the important exception of the Balkans).

In other parts of the empire, however, war and peace were probably more contributory than principal factors in their changing economic fortunes. For instance, in Italy and Africa there was no lack of trouble (from Visigoths, Vandals, Berbers, Ostrogoths, Byzantines, Franks and Lombards – to name only the principal protagonists); and there is sufficient documentary evidence to prove that warfare and raiding did harm the economy. There were also protracted periods of peace (for example, in Italy, forty years under the Ostrogoths). However, the underlying pattern in both Africa and Italy is more of slow and steady decline (in Italy probably starting well before the main period of invasion) than of marked downward and upward steps coinciding closely with known periods of insecurity and of peace. This is a pattern best explained in terms of longer-term changes.[67]

It is, indeed, worth wondering, even in the case of those regions whose economies do seem to have been knocked out by war, why they did not subsequently recover. Both in late antiquity and in other periods of history, other economies appear to have been more resilient. Greece, for example,

---

[66] *Vita S. Severini* ed. R. Noll (Berlin 1963), caps. 22 and 28 (English trans. L. Bieler, 79 and 83).

[67] Within the basic pattern of a downhill slope, there may also be some steps down (possibly attributable to known periods of insecurity, such as the Gothic and Lombard wars in Italy). At present the available data are insufficiently detailed to reveal them unambiguously.

was badly hit by violent destruction during the troubles of the third century, and yet in the fourth and fifth century the evidence from both town and countryside suggests a period of unprecedented prosperity. Europe in the ninth and early tenth century was devastated by Vikings, Hungarians and Saracens: trading-towns were deliberately targeted and destroyed, booty and tribute were extorted, and slaves were seized. Yet there is no sign that in the long term the underlying growth of the European economy was disrupted; indeed, the Vikings and Saracens were quite rapidly absorbed into a growing international network of exchange and commerce.

War and the disruption it brings will perhaps explain the precise moment of decline, but it is likely that underlying causes will also be at work if the decline persists. If not, why did western economic history in the fifth and sixth century not follow the pattern of the ninth and tenth centuries, especially given the remarkable cultural assimilation of the barbarians? And why did Asia Minor in the seventh century not follow the example of fourth-century Greece?

If we look again at the evidence of Noricum, we can note, as well as disruption, the resilience of the traders of Batavis, who were ready to set up their stalls once more, and the surprising fact that some oil was reaching the upper Danube despite the appalling conditions. Why, when Lauriacum and Batavis finally fell and perhaps found slightly improved political and military conditions, did not these economic links continue and perhaps grow? Probably because other factors were also at work and, in particular, because neighbouring regions which once might have helped in the regeneration of a devastated province were also going through hard times. We learn, for instance – once again from the *Life of Severinus* – that during the fifth century all pay from Italy stopped reaching the troops in Noricum: this was the end of Roman financial involvement in Noricum and the end of the redistributive power of the state, spreading the gold of interior regions into the frontier zone.[68] A more secure and prosperous Italy might have helped pull Noricum back into economic complexity and prosperity.

It may be wrong to view the relationship between military failure and economic decline as a simple, one-way process. The 'barbarians', both the Germans in the fifth- and sixth-century west and the Arabs in the seventh-century east, were unpaid part-time fighters, whereas the Roman army was made up of professionals, and so depended for its strength on taxed wealth and (ultimately) a healthy economy. Was the fall of the west in the fifth century a *consequence* (as well as a cause) of economic decline? Can Justinian's reconquest of the west in the first half of the sixth century be understood in part as the eastern Mediterranean flexing its new economic,

---

[68] *Vita S. Severini* ed. R. Noll (Berlin 1963), cap. 20 (English trans. L. Bieler, 78).

and hence also military, muscle? And did subsequent economic decline in the east help cause the military problems of later-sixth- and seventh-century Byzantium? It is important to bear these possibilities in mind and to continue to investigate them – even if, at present, the data (particularly relating to the western and later eastern military collapses) tend to be too hazy to provide any firm answers. For instance, it is not yet clear whether we can confidently identify widespread economic decline in the western provinces (which included a seemingly very rich Africa) *before* the great barbarian incursions of 406.

XI. CLIMATE, THE ENVIRONMENT AND THE ECONOMY

As well as warfare, climatic change or environmental change is sometimes blamed for the decline of the Roman economy. Climatic change at this date was an 'act of God', unaffected by man, while environmental change could be caused either by changes in the weather or by the human impact on the landscape.[69]

Strangely enough, despite its importance in present-day environmental debate, climatic change is not currently much favoured as an overall reason for Roman economic decline.[70] It would, indeed, be very difficult to find a change of climate that could explain the extraordinary and localized fluctuations of wealth visible between the fourth and the seventh century. What change in climate could have benefited Ireland, Armenia and the near east in the sixth and early seventh century, while at the same time devastating Britain, Italy and Asia Minor?

Even looking at highly marginal areas, which must be the first to be affected by any change in climate, changes in human activity, rather than broad changes in the weather, often provide more plausible reasons for fluctuations in settlement and wealth. The dry semi-desert of the Negev was, as we have seen, densely settled and prosperous in the fifth and sixth century, which might be explained in terms of a period of exceptional rainfall. However, in this same period, the closely comparable wadis of Tripolitania (in modern Libya), which were prosperous and densely settled at an earlier date (the later first and second centuries A.D.), seem to have been largely abandoned. Since the Libyan pre-desert and the Negev must share roughly the same climate, and since they were certainly exploited in very similar ways, their very different histories strongly suggest that it was human opportunity and human pressure that most influenced these two marginal regions, rather than some external change in the weather.[71]

---

[69] For a useful brief discussion of the issues raised in this section, with further references: Greene (1986) 81–6.

[70] The issue is, however, debated in relation to specific regions: see e.g. Rubin (1989) for the Negev.

[71] For Libya: Mattingly (1995) 144–53.

Environmental change is more current amongst the explanations recently proffered for the decline of the Roman economy, and for understandable reasons.[72] It is quite clear that, during the Roman period, farming was everywhere intense, and that in all regions it was extended into marginal areas that were previously uncultivated. In the process, a great deal of clearance must have taken place. Did this perhaps cause erosion and soil-loss in the higher lands, and the consequent dumping in the valley bottoms of enormous quantities of potentially damaging alluvium? Indeed, does the over-intense exploitation of the land explain the remarkable fluctuations in regional prosperity which I have outlined above, so that a new region took over the mantle of intense agricultural exploitation until it, in its turn, was ruined by the very process of wealth-creation?[73]

This picture is certainly not just a figment of the ecologically conscious imagination, since geomorphologists, studying the sequence of river sediments, have found widespread evidence of a post-Roman phase of alluviation, which dumped immense quantities of soil in the valley bottoms and left a number of formerly coastal cities, like Ephesus, landlocked (as they are today). However, it may be a mistake to see this evidence as conclusive proof of a late Roman and post-Roman environmental disaster that can be widely used to explain the period's economic problems. Firstly, it is normally impossible to establish, on the basis of the information currently available, exactly when and over how long a period, within the very wide 'late Roman and post-Roman' periods, such alluviation took place – or even whether the process had not begun earlier: Strabo, for instance, in the time of Augustus, already gives a detailed account of the problems of siltation in the harbour of Ephesus.[74] Sequences of alluvium are difficult to date, and many more closely-dated cases are needed before we can satisfactorily relate alluviation to economic decline.

Secondly, and more seriously, as with population decline, which we shall investigate next, on closer investigation the links between human activity, environmental decay and economic decline become complicated. Erosion (and consequent alluviation) may, for instance, have been caused less by the clearance of woodland cover to create fields and terraces than by the later abandonment of these terraces and field systems. If so, erosion and alluviation become as much a consequence as a cause of economic decay. Equally, even if alluviation did cause very real problems for settlements like Ostia and Ephesus, we need to question why, in late and post-Roman times, the inhabitants did not respond to the challenge more successfully. If the human resources of these settlements had been stronger, Ostia and Ephesus would surely have coped with environmental change (just as successful cities survive

---

[72] Greene (1986) 85–6. The pioneering Mediterranean-wide work was Vita-Finzi (1969).
[73] As argued by Randsborg (1992) 13–14.   [74] Strab. XIV.1.24.

earthquakes or great fires), and would perhaps even have improved their circumstances by draining the new alluvial plains for agriculture.

Attractive though it is at first sight, environmental disaster is also implausible as an explanation for the shifting prosperity, from region to region, of Roman agriculture. It is hard to envisage, in a period before mechanization, environmental devastation on a scale sufficient to destroy a province's entire agricultural prosperity – and certainly difficult to see how it could have extended into areas of activity (such as potting and marble-quarrying) which are only indirectly linked to agriculture, but which seem to have shared the same patterns of prosperity and decline as the countryside.

To argue against environmental decay as a simple and global explanation for late Roman economic decline is not to deny it any importance in the transformation of the economy in the fourth to the seventh century. The Romans made a dramatic impact on the landscape, and it is therefore likely that environmental changes ensued. When human resources were weakened for other reasons, many of these changes may well have had a marked negative effect.[75]

XII. POPULATION CHANGE AND ECONOMIC CHANGE

A major fall in population is often considered an important cause of economic decline in the late Roman and post-Roman worlds. Since rises and falls in population have an obvious effect on the availability of labour and on the size of overall demand, there is indeed little doubt that the number of people living within the empire would affect the economy. However, the relationship between population growth and economic growth, on the one hand, and population decline and economic decline, on the other, is not in fact as straightforward as is often suggested.[76]

Firstly, in certain circumstances, a fall in population, far from being a disaster, can even be an economic boon. In later medieval England the population may have been reduced by as much as a half between the outbreak of the Black Death in 1348 and the end of the century. But this does not seem to have brought about economic regression. Before 1348, high overall demand may have been diverted into producing miserable quantities of the most basic foodstuffs in order to feed a large population, and much of the labour force may have been tied down to extracting appalling returns from unsuitable land. After the period of mortality, the surviving peasants were almost certainly individually better off than before, since they were now able to abandon the cultivation of less productive land. In these circumstances, the overall scale of the economy shrank, since there were fewer

---

[75] See Hendy, *Studies* 58–68.   [76] For example, in Hodges and Whitehouse (1983) 20–53.

producers and fewer consumers around. But qualitatively the economy may even have improved, since individual peasants were able to produce greater surpluses and to convert them into more coins and into more specialized products.[77]

Precise circumstances in late antiquity were certainly different to those current in fourteenth-century England: for instance, the densely-settled marginal lands of the fifth- and sixth-century near east appear, at least from the archaeological record, to be characterized by prosperity rather than by the misery documented on marginal land in pre-plague England. However, if there was a marked fall in population in the sixth century (as there may have been in the plague of 541–3), whatever the detailed local circumstances, it should have been a relief to abandon some of the harsher lands (like the wadis of the Negev) and to concentrate on more productive and less difficult cultivation elsewhere. A substantial fall in population would certainly have led to a shrinkage of the total scale of the economy, and hence, for instance, to a fall in the profits of both the state and of landlords; but it should not have affected the base of the economy, except perhaps positively.

Another major problem in assuming that population growth caused economic growth (and, similarly, that population decline caused economic decline) is the probability that the causal relationship was often the other way round. Some population changes – in particular, the universal plague of 541–3 – cannot readily be related to specific economic circumstances, and were perhaps truly random acts of God. However, what seems to have been a much more gradual decline in the population of the west and north through the centuries of late antiquity is most simply explained as a consequence of the economic decline of these areas, just as the apparent rise in rural settlement and population through the fourth and fifth century in the east was perhaps the result of economic prosperity.

As argued earlier, some areas of the ancient world seem, in particular centuries, to have been much more prosperous and more commercialized than other areas. These same areas also produce evidence of both intensive and extensive settlement in the countryside. Conversely, periods of economic simplification correspond to periods of declining evidence of rural settlement. Prosperity and a rising population (and poverty and a falling population) do seem to have been related in our period; but it also seems likely that it was fluctuations in prosperity that were the prime movers in the relationship.[78]

[77] Hatcher (1977).
[78] Since, as I argued in ch. 12 (pp. 324–7 above), it is at present almost impossible to disentangle evidence for rural population numbers from evidence for changing rural prosperity, the apparently tight connection between the two may, however, be deceptive.

XIII. ECONOMIC DECLINE: SOME CONCLUSIONS

I hope I have shown that 'the decline of the Roman economy' was a very long process that took place with marked differences of effect and chronology between regions, and was, in fact, never 'completed'. Even during the post-Roman period of decline in the northern provinces, there are signs of growth just beyond the old frontiers; and long before the 'ancient economy' of the near east disappeared in the eighth century (if it did, since even this is controversial), there are clear signs of economic growth in the northern world and in the western Mediterranean.

But I hope I have also shown that economic decline, when it happened, was dramatic, leading to a drastic simplification in production and exchange, and to a remarkable regression in material culture. The large Roman middle and lower market for high-quality basic goods was substantially destroyed, and with it went most commercial activity and specialization.

No process so remarkable and so variegated can possibly be fully explained, let alone on the basis of the scanty evidence available to us. And certainly no simple monocausal explanations will ever do. Such explanations are intrinsically implausible, and, as I hope I have shown, they cannot be made to fit the varied and different histories of every region.

For myself, in order to begin to understand its decline, I find it necessary to believe, first, that the Roman economy (through both commerce and the state) linked local, regional and overseas networks of specialization and distribution into impressive but fragile overall structures. It is then possible to investigate a number of different factors that may have weakened these structures.

Individual 'causes' of economic decline were, probably, themselves closely interlinked. For example, the decline of state spending in Noricum was caused in the end by failure in war; but this military failure was itself perhaps caused in part by economic decline in the west (which made the taxation needed to support the soldiery more difficult to raise). The abandonment of state spending in Noricum then went on to cause further problems along the line, both in Noricum itself (which was devastated) and in other regions (because Noricum was no longer an attractive market for their goods). If we see both regions of the empire and causes of decline as closely interlinked, it becomes much easier to see how the Roman economy could have become caught in a general spiral of decay.

There are good reasons to continue to investigate the 'decline of the Roman economy'. It is a fascinating intellectual process, because we are much more used to looking at economic development and at the ways that different strands feed into growth than we are to investigating the progressive unravelling of such systems. It was also a dramatic change that had a marked effect on the material conditions of peasants and kings alike, and whose influence reached beyond the purely 'material' into all areas of life that are affected by levels of prosperity (as diverse as the size of the state or the scale of artistic production).[79] Furthermore, the unravelling of the centuries-old Roman (indeed, often pre-Roman) system raises the fundamental question of whether the complex material and economic world which we take for granted today could, in the right circumstances, also come unstuck.[80]

[79] For this reason I often find myself out of sympathy with modern historiography, which is fascinated by ideological and intellectual change, and often treats these as though they took place in an economic vacuum.

[80] Very many people have helped me with ideas, criticisms, comments and references, for both ch. 12 and ch. 13; but I must thank, for their particularly generous help, Jairus Banaji, Sam Barnish, Gian Pietro Brogiolo, Thomas Charles-Edwards, Ros Faith, Sauro Gelichi, Peter Heather, Simon Loseby, Peter Sarris, Michael Whitby, Chris Wickham and Greg Woolf.

CHAPTER 14

THE FAMILY IN THE LATE ROMAN WORLD*

ANDREA GIARDINA

I. CHRISTIANITY AND LAWS ON THE FAMILY

Before Constantine, no Roman emperor, not even Augustus, had displayed such a strong ambition to reshape family legislation and initiate thereby an extensive project of moral reconstruction: *pudor tutus, munita coniugia* was how a panegyrist pithily expressed it as early as 321.[1] In some respects, Constantinian legislation merely brought to completion tendencies that had been operative for some time; in others, it was more innovative. On the whole, it aimed at asserting principles of rigour, order and temperance in family relationships. Often it revealed a somewhat darker side, betraying both acute perception and ill-concealed pessimism, and alongside the wishful imperatives we also find realistic laws concerning concrete situations. The frequency and variety of these measures testify to the importance of political policy on these issues.

Constantine's laws had three principal aims, all closely interlinked: to safeguard celibacy, to encourage the *matrimonium iustum* and to protect infants and minors. The first was accomplished by repealing the Augustan marriage laws, which had penalized celibates and childless couples (by restricting their ability to receive inheritances and legacies) and provided incentives to matrimony and procreation. A variety of measures contributed towards achieving the second aim: socially mixed unions and concubinage were repressed; greater significance was attributed to the promise of marriage; abduction was severely punished; accusations of adultery could no longer be made by outsiders, but only by the husband or by the wife's close male relatives; adultery was punished by death. The third aim was the object of measures concerning the *patria potesta, tutores* and *curatores*, donations and inheritance, infant exposure and the cession of minors. Implementation of these policies reached its peak in the year 331, when the

---

* Editors' note: this chapter spans a wider period than that covered by the rest of the volume, in order to provide a broad thematic coverage of an important subject which is best treated on a wider chronological scale, and which was not specifically covered in *Cambridge Ancient History* volume XIII.

[1] *Pan. Lat.* 10.38.

most sensational measure was passed: the abrogation of the ancient law whereby a marriage ceased with the withdrawal of consent of just one of the spouses. *Repudium* was thus authorized only in cases of extreme gravity. Admittedly, there were other situations in which the bond could be dissolved, but the responsible party incurred heavy sanctions: the wife lost her dowry, relinquished all claim to her possessions in the marital house and suffered deportation; the husband, on the other hand, had to return the dowry and, if he remarried, his former wife could take possession of his second wife's dowry. Wives, moreover, were explicitly denied the right to repudiate their husbands on general grounds of immorality.[2]

In so far as the moral code of a minority group can be expected to influence the laws and ancient traditions of a large empire in a short space of time, this set of measures unequivocally shows the mark of Christianity.[3] Nevertheless, certain historians, even in recent times, have tended to deny that Christian morality had any influence on Constantine's family legislation, or at least to minimize its influence considerably; some have even extended their scepticism to cover much of late antique legislation. In so doing, however, they would appear to be conditioned not only by an abstract concept of 'Christian legislation' (i.e. one more or less consciously based on the twelfth- and thirteenth-century collections of canon law) but also by the relations between the papacy and the European states in the Middle Ages. In their search for symmetries, they claim that Christian influence is attested only where there is a 'perfect identity' between Christian doctrine and Roman law; they emphasize the deficiencies and excesses of imperial law; they suggest that a decisive contribution was made by pagan philosophical doctrine and that the imposition of a stricter morality reflected a revival of traditional Roman values; finally, they appeal to the independent evolution of the law.[4] None of these arguments are new, for, broadly speaking, the same ground was covered almost a century and half ago by the debate on Troplong's work.[5] And there are, in fact, two good reasons why the two conflicting opinions have been periodically confronting one another ever since then. The first, which in itself carries no negative implications, is that the subject itself inevitably leaves a wide margin for interpretation. The second, which is undeniably detrimental, is that the general terms of the problem are inadequately defined.

---

[2] *C.Th.* III.16.1.

[3] For a balanced account of the effects of Constantine's conversion on his legislation, see Liebeschuetz (1979) 277 (on the family, in particular p. 295).

[4] Among the more recent works, see, for example, with varying degrees of emphasis, Gaudemet (1978a); Castello (1983); Sargenti (1986); Bagnall (1987); Evans Grubbs (1995); for the position of women, see in particular Arjava (1996). [5] Troplong (1843).

Though useful in counterbalancing the exaggerated claim that Christianity systematically uprooted wide sectors of Roman law by virtue of its sheer independent strength,[6] the interpretations that deny, or significantly minimize, Christian influence on secular law have a common failing: that of excessive fragmentation. We observe this in two ways: firstly, the different issues on which the various emperors acted are analysed separately; secondly, the family laws are considered in isolation from the whole legislation in favour of the Christian religion. Such a splintered approach inevitably diminishes the validity of the overall evidence.

In order to play down the influence of Christianity on imperial legislation, historians sometimes resort to the argument of coincidence. In other words, the measures originated from specific needs that had nothing to do with, and just happened to be compatible with, Christian morals. For example, it is plausibly argued that the above-mentioned Constantinian measure abolishing the Augustan penalties on celibacy intended (in perfect agreement with Christian morality) to rehabilitate the condition of celibates, widows and divorcees who had not remarried; and also, perhaps, to encourage bequests in favour of clerics.[7] On the other hand, it is pointed out that the Augustan legislation had never been popular and had failed to achieve the intended results; quite the reverse, it had spread the phenomenon of informers, a problem considered as intolerable above all by the property-owning classes. According to this argument, therefore, Constantine was merely taking stock of a *de facto* situation and his law was principally aimed at restoring full rights of ownership and putting an end to the scourge of delation. Eusebius, Constantine's biographer, friend and adviser, held a very different opinion. He (as others after him) viewed this provision as proof of the emperor's Christian devotion.[8] But Eusebius, it is objected, at the time of writing the *Vita Constantini*, would have known nothing of Constantine's real intentions in the year 320 and simply gave, like many modern historians, a religious interpretation to a law that in fact had quite different motivations.[9] This reading, however, does not account for the likelihood that Eusebius' opinion dated to the time of Nicaea, when, both in the official assemblies and at the various meetings on the fringe of the council, Constantine had ample opportunity not only to tell the bishops about his Christian feelings but also to inform them of how such feelings had been officially and formally implemented. Even if (for the sake of argument) at the moment of repealing the Augustan laws, by a strange form of dissociation, the emperor had managed not to feel the

---

[6] As is well known, the key historical work representing this position is Biondi (1952–4).

[7] See in particular Humbert (1972) 360–73 and bibliography.

[8] Eus. *Vita Constantini* IV.26.2–4; see also Soz. *HE* I.9.3–4; Cass. *Hist. Tr.* I.9.

[9] Recently, Evans Grubbs (1995) 123ff. Spagnuolo Vigorita (1984) does not deny Christian influence but attributes more importance to the aspects of tax policy.

slightest concern for Christian values, we cannot escape the fact that the very same measures were susceptible to Christian interpretation only a very few years later. Thus, while we may deny Constantinian legislation the status of 'subjective' Christianity, we must at least grant it that of 'objective' Christianity. And, above all, we cannot forget that the morality of a man awaiting 'divine judgement' was something irremediably new, no matter how pervaded by traditional elements it may have been.

The affinity between certain traditional values and the inspiration of many late antique constitutions is, in fact, an argument often used to negate the influence of Christian ethics on secular law. This, however, does not place the phenomenon of historical continuity in its true context. In nearly every manifestation of late antique society, living survivals from the past are readily detected, and even its dead fossils. They appear in institutions, social relations, general behaviour, material culture, art and thought. And yet late antiquity was clearly a new age. Continuity may be displayed by individual details, but it is the discontinuity that shows up when we observe the system as a whole.

Another frequent means of negating the Christian influence on certain family laws is to accentuate the concrete, and not the spiritual, objectives of the legislators. We have already seen this in the case of the Augustan legislation on marriage. In the case of the Constantinian law punishing the unmotivated breach of betrothal, its Christian inspiration has been minimized by stressing the difference between the secular punishment and the religious sanction. Fines, it is claimed, were foreign to Christian prescriptions[10] – an argument that verges on the absurd, for it implies that in Constantine's day a secular power could impose religious sanctions and that a religious power could inflict material punishment.

A similar interpretation has even been advanced to explain the laws limiting unilateral repudiation and penalizing second marriages, laws that most people would quite rightly see as Christian-inspired. But since the emperors sometimes explicitly invoked the *favor liberorum* and not the respect of morals and religion, it has been inferred that the principal, if not sole, aim of such laws was to protect children from the property point of view.[11] But surely it is not at all surprising that a legislator should stress the aspects that bore upon *Realien*, or that he should highlight the argument to which most citizens could relate, regardless of their faith and the depth of their religious convictions. Indeed, such an approach was all the more necessary in matters like divorce and second marriage, for these were issues on which the imperial citizens were more traditionalist (as we shall see below). Besides, in the history of the family, questions of morality and property are

---

[10] Gaudemet (1978a) 196.
[11] Gaudemet (1950) 186; Bagnall (1987) 51 ff.; Arjava (1988); Brown (1988) 430.

bound to overlap and influence one another so closely that separate treatment is often not so much arbitrary as impossible.

Laws are like signifiers with numerous signifieds; in other words, the same law may respond to various needs, both moral and material. Naturally there can also be laws motivated by purely ethical needs. This, at least, seems to have been the case with Constantius II's measures confirming the ban on marriage between uncle and *filia fratris sororisve* (making it punishable by death) or Theodosius I's law prohibiting marriage between cousins-german.[12]

The relationship between Christian ethics and the laws restricting divorce must in any case have been very clear to the pagan Julian when he re-established the former conditions.[13] And if, as some believe, the document attesting Julian's nostalgic measures should prove unreliable, paradoxically this would actually enhance the value of the evidence, for it would suggest that the pagan Julian was widely expected to repeal the divorce law of the Christian Constantine. And it is surely no coincidence that Julian should fully revive the Claudian *senatus consultum*, which Constantine had modified in one important aspect.[14]

The crucial issue in the debate on Christian influence is the divorce legislation. According to one argument, the remoteness of divorce laws from the evangelical principle of indissolubility is proof that the secular legislators were deaf to the appeals of the church. Yet if Constantine's restrictions on divorce were distant from evangelical principle, they were even further removed from the sensibilities of the vast majority of his subjects. After all, he was the first to legislate against a practice that was taken for granted not only by the whole of contemporary society but also in all the societies of preceding ages. As in many other areas of his political activity – and as often happens in 'revolutionary' situations – he intervened too vigorously and too dramatically. And by doing so, he heavily conditioned the future. For a long time to come, divorce was the most important and troubled issue in the dialogue between human law and the evangelical message. Among the many problems tackled in the late antique imperial constitutions, perhaps none was the subject of so much rethinking, particularly in such fundamental aspects as the identification of sufficient motives for unilateral repudiation and the penalties for those who break the matrimonial bond without just cause.

Though unmotivated repudiation was punished by imperial legislation, this did not mean that a marriage broken without just cause remained valid before the law. Continuity was also preserved by admitting consensual divorce. For though the Council of Carthage of 407 had expressed the hope

---

[12] *C.Th.* III.12.1 (341); *Epit.* 48.10; Ambr. *Ep.* 60.8; see Shaw and Saller (1984) 440.

[13] Mention of Julian promulgating such a law is given in the so-called Ambrosiaster: *CSEL* L.322.

[14] *C.Th.* IV.12.5 (362).

that a *lex imperialis* would be promulgated against second marriages,[15] consensual divorce was a custom evidently taken for granted by a very high number of citizens (by pagans and Christians alike, including that broad frontier region linking and separating the two religions). It was Justinian who first declared the illegality of consensual divorce, except where chastity vows were involved. He also established the few causes justifying repudiation. The husband could divorce if his wife failed to inform him of a conspiracy against the emperor; if she made an attempt against her husband's life or failed to disclose plots schemed by others against him; if she committed adultery or behaved indecently in public. The wife could divorce if her husband conspired against the emperor or failed to disclose to her the plots of others; if he made an attempt against his wife's life or failed to disclose plots by others against her; if he falsely accused her of adultery; if he attempted to induce her to prostitution; if he brought another woman to live in the marital house or if he repeatedly frequented the house of another woman.[16] Once again, therefore, the law was aiming to constrain social habits, thereby creating a wide margin for disobedience. The inevitable result was that Justinian's immediate successor, Justin II, was obliged to resurrect the principle according to which the foundation of marriage was mutual affection and to re-establish legitimacy of consensual divorce.[17]

The uneven, syncopated development of the divorce legislation from the fourth to the sixth century perfectly expresses that tangle of concordances and discordances involving Christian doctrine, the conciliar canons, papal decretals, imperial legislation and social behaviour at large. The late antique emperors had no handy corpus of canon law to serve as a basis for reference. Though some of the local councils, notably that of Elvira, did emanate norms on sexuality, marriage and the family, and did establish appropriate religious sanctions for transgressors, their resolutions on specific points were often different, in spite of basic agreement on general orientation.[18] And as for the opinions of the church Fathers, again there were significant differences even on key issues, such as the consequences of the wife's adultery on the permanence of the bond.[19] Finally, since church legislation inflicted penalties on priests who blessed unlawful marriages, we deduce that such unions were not uncommon.

And when it came to actually imposing religious sanctions on the faithful, the bishops often availed themselves of their considerable discretionary powers, departing from the strict letter of the law to meet the needs of individuals. In celebrating the figure of Fabiola, a Roman noblewoman who had died in an aura of sanctity, Jerome could not help recollecting a youthful sin: she had left her first husband, whose dissolute life disgusted

---

[15] *CCSL* CIL.218.   [16] Just. *Nov.* 117.8–10 (542).   [17] Justin, *Nov.* 140 (566).   [18] Bagnall (1987) 50.
[19] In general, Crouzel (1971); for the long duration of the doctrinal uncertainties on the nature of the marriage bond, Gaudemet (1970) and (1978b).

her, and had remarried. This was a grave sin, Jerome admits, and rightly merited harsh expiation. But she had been forced into such action by necessity and had not been wrong in preferring a second marriage to a life of solitude full of uncertainties (echoing Paul's admonition 'it is better to marry than to burn').[20] The ladies of high society may well have enjoyed extenuating circumstances, but it would be a mistake to explain such leniency solely as a class issue. Rather it should be viewed in terms of the tormented relations between evangelical principle and the human factor: a real sociological constant not only in late antique society but also much later. And so, while Jerome himself contended that in Christian marriage 'certain are the laws of Caesar, others those of Christ' and that Christians were expected to obey the latter,[21] the vast majority of the faithful must have felt that there was no need to have harsher restrictions than those established by the moral code of their own class and by imperial legislation. The tensions between 'pastoral humanity', on the one hand, and decisions of 'an abstract, almost mathematical character', on the other, were destined to be an enduring trait even of Byzantine and medieval family history.[22]

The clarity of the religious prescriptions was also clouded by the existence of mixed marriages between pagans and Christians. Since such unions, which were still very common in Augustine's day, constituted an important vehicle for religious conversion, the church's attitude was stricter in theory than in actual practice. And inevitably, the presence of religious differences between married couples will have made it plain that absolute rigour in matrimonial affairs was beyond the reach of most Christians.

Finally, brief mention should be made of the *episcopalis audientia*, for historians have hitherto ignored this institution's role in the arduous process of adapting social behaviour to the prescriptions of Christian morality (as expressed in the writings of the Fathers, the sermons of preachers or the conciliar canons). In his capacity as *iudex*, the bishop was expected to ensure compliance with the *terrena iura*, the rules established by imperial legislation. Again, this was a field in which the Christian emperors of late antiquity had to temper the excesses of Constantine's enthusiasm, this time by reducing the scope of the bishops' jurisdiction. Nevertheless, the *episcopalis audientia* still commanded considerable authority on civil matters at the beginning of the fifth century.[23] To the majority of the faithful, the idea of a bishop judging cases involving family relationships in accordance with human (and not divine) laws must have seemed a legitimate

---

[20] Hier. *Ep.* 77.3.   [21] *Ibid.*

[22] For Byzantium, Karlin-Hayter (1992) 134; see also Vogel (1982). For the west, see for example Bishop (1985).

[23] As is shown in Augustine's new *Ep.* 24* (*CSEL* LXXXVIII.126f.): Lepelley (1983). On the relationship between marriage legislation and the *episcopalis audientia*, see for example *CJ* 1.4.16 (472) and 28 (530).

and feasible compromise between evangelical perfection and the hard realities of life.

It is incidentally worth noting that the difference between the religious and legal sanctions was not always a matter of the former being stricter than the latter. The formula certainly holds true for divorce, an area in which the secular legislators long evaded the aspirations of the church. On other issues, however, it was the imperial laws that applied unduly severe criteria, which the church preferred to avoid. For the crime of abduction, for example, an imperial law specified the death penalty,[24] while two Basilian 'canons' merely inflicted penances of a few years, not to mention the additional possibility of contracting a lawful marriage.[25] Such severity in the secular legislation must also have contributed (in the form of additional psychological pressure, if nothing else) to strengthening the bishop's role as a mediator, as a man who healed family conflicts and did his best to avoid the extreme consequences that would ensue if the interested parties became involved in the sphere of criminal law.

From today's perspective, centred as it is on our view of the modern state, the relationship between Christianity and the law is invested with an importance that the late antique church authorities would hardly have shared. To them, Christianization could take many forms, and there was nothing that made the collaboration of the secular legislator the most effective instrument or even, for that matter, an essential requisite.

It is unrealistic, therefore, to measure the Christianization of family legislation against the rigid criteria of doctrine. What the term 'Christianization' can – indeed, must – suggest is an extremely slow process accompanied by deviations, corrections, accelerations, delays and short-lived measures: in other words, all the elements we generally associate with the major phenomena of acculturation. It was not an already formed system that inexorably pervaded the whole of society, but a formative process. And to pose the problem of the coherent Christianization of family law in the fourth, fifth and sixth century is simply anachronistic. Even a half-millennium later, in both east and west, the process was anything but complete.

II. LAW AND SOCIETY

Dialogue between the two powers, the religious and the secular, was difficult, but was aided by the fact that both shared the same culture of control, one that extended from public life to the intimacy of the couple.

---

[24] *C.Th.* IX.4.1 (326); in *C.Th.* IX.4.22 (349) the *summum supplicium* inflicted by Constantine was replaced by the *capitalis poena*. The severity of the punishment has been used to deny the influence of Christian morality on these laws: Castello (1988); Evans Grubbs (1995) 191. The combination of repressive and protective aspects in Constantine's law has been rightly emphasized by Beaucamp (1990) 113.

[25] Bas. *Ep.* 199, *can.* 22 and 30; Karlin-Hayter (1992) 138; Laiou (1993) 134ff., with particular reference to the matter of the woman's consent.

Though late antiquity produced an extraordinary mass of laws, culminating in Justinian's formidable attempt at reducing them to order, what it did not do was to create a new juridical doctrine of marriage.[26] A large obstacle lying in the way of the authorities' efforts in this direction was the persistence of the ideas of marriage as consensual, along with a weak formalization of the wedding itself. The exchange of premarital gifts, the dowry, the signing of the *tabulae nuptiales* bearing a list of the bride's dowry and property clauses in the event of divorce, the religious ritual and the family festivities were all moments of social significance and by no means devoid of juridical implications. But they were not indispensable to the conclusion of a *matrimonium iustum*.[27] Informal marriages, such as were widely contracted among the poorer classes, were indistinguishable from concubinage, which made it difficult to stamp out practices such as bigamy, unjust breaking of the bond and adultery, and hence to establish the legitimacy of children with any certainty.

Increasing attention, therefore, was paid by both powers to the constitutive phases of the bond: betrothal and the wedding ceremony. As regards betrothal, imperial legislation inflicted economic penalties on defaulters, a measure that had the effect of making the promise of marriage more binding. At the same time, Christian preachers tried to endow the moment with a moral significance not unlike that of matrimony itself. This is well illustrated by the case of St Macrina, who proclaimed herself a widow after the death of her fiancé and refused to accept another man as husband.[28] Though her behaviour could be construed as a cunning ploy to avoid marriage, her justification does suggest that a new perception of betrothal was making slow inroads into contemporary culture. While for obvious biological reasons the minimum age for marriage remained generally stable (fourteen for the bridegroom, twelve for the bride), that of betrothal was lowered considerably. The Isaurian Code of 741 set the lower age-limit at seven years for both sexes, prescribing also the consent, or absence of dissent, of the two parties. In practice, however, such early betrothals and binding promises effectively reinforced parental control and emptied the notion of consent of all meaning, making it merely a tool for furthering matrimonial strategies.[29]

The wedding ceremony was the only moment in the couple's married life when the church exerted a solemn, public role. Even if matrimony was not yet a sacrament in the modern sense, various factors helped to establish the priest's elevated moral authority over the bond: the Christianization of the ancient pagan ritual, the blessing and, later, the matrimonial mass itself

---

[26] Wolff (1950). In the late antique period, the tendency to consider the various aspects of family legislation as distinct and separate fields persisted, and nothing comparable to a 'family law' emerged. For a different view, see Volterra (1967) 724.   [27] Treggiari (1991) ch. 5.

[28] Greg. Nyss. *Vita Macrinae* 4–5; see Giannarelli (1980) 40f.   [29] *Ecloga* 2.1; Patlagean (1973).

(attested for the first time in Rome in 432/40).[30] *Concordia pronuba*, the goddess traditionally invoked to foster the harmony of the couple, was replaced by *Iesus pronubus*.[31] The Christianization of the betrothal and wedding may also have had an impact on marriage in two other respects: by orienting the couple's subsequent behaviour; and by involving the community of the faithful, whose sentiments could in turn exert pressure on the couple. In reply to a query raised by a Spanish bishop, pope Siricius recommended taking every possible step to prevent betrothals from being dissolved: 'when the blessing given by the priest to her who is about to marry is violated by a transgression, the faithful feel that there is sacrilege'.[32] Siricius, however, was judging from a Roman point of view, and his opinion cannot be generalized. In fact, the persistence at a popular level of pagan ritual was such that it survived long after the full Christianization of the wedding ceremony. So while the bishops and councils of the fourth century inveighed against the faithful who celebrated their marriages according to lascivious pagan customs,[33] in the Carolingian age we still find a bishop cautioning his clergy against taking part in wedding festivities (which he likened to the frequenting of taverns and other base entertainments).[34]

As for written contracts, these could not exceed limits fixed by economic constraints. A law promulgated by Justinian in 538 laid down, among other things, the formal requisites for stipulating a legitimate marriage, which varied according to the social standing of the couple and the amount of property involved. Members of the higher ranks of society were expected to perform all the duties consonant with their position, particularly those regarding betrothal gifts and the dowry. Public officials, merchants and those engaged in respectable activities had the option of avoiding such complex procedures, but were required to sign a contract before the *ekdikos* of a church in the presence of at least three clerics. The document could be preserved in the church archives. Those who led very base lives and belonged to the lowest ranks of urban society (even if they may have been moderately well-off) were absolved from drawing up a written document. Also exempt were peasants and soldiers – a category

---

[30] The requisites indicated in 458/9 by pope Leo, *Ep.* 167.4, *PL* LIV.1204f. – i.e. the free condition of both spouses, the dowry and the public wedding – were not, as is usually assumed (see, for example, Orestano (1951) 297f.), needed for any legitimate marriage, but only to define the passage from concubinage with a woman of lower rank to legitimate matrimony. The dowry was indicated as a condition of legitimate matrimony by Majorian in 458 (*Nov.* 6.9), but the measure was short-lived (Sev. *Nov.* 1, of 463). For the later developments, see Lemaire (1929).

[31] Paul. Nol. *Carm.* 25.151f.; for the same transformation in Byzantine art, see Kantorowicz (1960) 7ff.

[32] Siricius, *Ep.* 4, *PL* LXXXIV.632; Siricius meant that the marriage blessing was contaminated because the *nuptura* had violated a former engagement: Anné (1941) 131; for later developments, with particular reference to the west, see now Vogel (1977).   [33] Ritzer (1981) 94ff., 130ff.

[34] *PL* CXIX.712f.; see Toubert (1977) 274.

the legislator describes as 'ignorant of civil affairs'. Families belonging to this group were defined solely by cohabitation, and the legitimacy of children depended on whether they lived under the same roof as their father.[35] It was social and economic classifications, therefore, that determined whether families were constituted by a formal act and by recourse to a written document or whether they came into being as a *fait accompli*, merely by mutual consent and cohabitation. From this we deduce that most families enjoyed a juridical existence only for as long as conditions of stability remained.

Over the centuries the traditional Roman notion of consent retained an important function. It appears strikingly in a famous document, the *Responsa ad consulta Bulgarorum*, a letter written by pope Nicholas I in the year 866 in reply to certain queries raised by the tsar of Bulgaria. After going through the *iura nuptiarum*, i.e. the various matrimonial duties and ceremonies generally performed in Rome at the time, the pope specified that these were not indispensable for establishing the legitimacy of the union. Bonds contracted outside the *iura nuptiarum* (mainly for economic reasons) were equally valid, and their validity was dependent solely on consent: *per hoc sufficiat secundum leges solus eorum consensus, de quorum coniunctionibus agitur.*[36] Here, therefore, the concept of *consensus*, the traditional foundation of the *matrimonium iustum* (i.e. the honourable union of respectable couples and free citizens), had been transfigured by Christian morality to legitimate above all the marriages of the underprivileged.

The history of the Roman family, it is often repeated, is inadequately explained if we merely tell the story of imperial legislation. It is equally poorly served, we might add, if we just narrate the history of the conciliar canons and papal decretals. In reconstructing the ways in which the culture of control manifested itself (in both the religious and secular spheres) historians are particularly bound to the ritual observance of posing the following question: to what extent did the laws actually influence general behaviour? For the question to be at all meaningful, we must remember that the law can also fulfil a function of concealment, which implies a certain margin of failed application (to a greater or lesser extent, as the case may be). As it is generally the law that follows social behaviour and values, and not vice versa, the gap between the law and custom tends to increase, slowly and gradually, until new laws are tailored to the new customs.[37] However, the law can also anticipate widespread social behaviour and values. This occurs especially when the ideology of a minority influences the decisions of government, even if only in certain fields. Late antique legislation on the family is a case in point. The relationship between the law

[35] Just. *Nov.* 74.4.1–3; see Patlagean, *Pauvreté* 116ff.
[36] *MGH, Epistolarum* VI, *Epistolae Karolini Aevi* IV, Berlin 1902, no. 99, 568ff., in particular §3; see, more recently, Laiou (1985).   [37] Saller (1991b) 29.

and society is thus a matter of particular significance in this specific area of research and in this historical period.

Even before beginning to assess his information, the historian knows very well that in most cases all he can do is to compare the legal texts with a few literary documents or papyri; and that the results of such comparisons are likely to offer a few tenuous confirmations, as many tenuous refutations and one or two fresh doubts. On the one hand, the imperial constitutions and religious prescriptions are, we suspect, proposing lists of desiderata rather than statements that can be translated into actual collective behaviour. On the other, the sources that really do talk about people and individual experiences have the annoying habit of being few in number, and those few not only refer almost exclusively to the upper classes but are also very widely scattered over a large geographical area and an extremely long time-span. As for the main Christian writers who tackle the family from the ethical and theological points of view, their approach is generally prescriptive. As with the legal sources, doubts are often raised, for again there is no satisfactory way of measuring the distance between the model and life itself. And so, while we may certainly agree that 'it is highly unlikely that the ascetic values so prominent in the apocryphal *Acts* and other Christian literature are separable from wider moral developments in society',[38] we are singularly ill-equipped to translate this statement into orders of magnitude – even very approximately.

Augustine's work, however, is of exceptional interest. Alongside his observations of a specifically doctrinal and theological cast, a large quantity of data on contemporary family life may also be gleaned from informative passages, allusions and oblique references. These unassuming, and apparently banal, data are of great value to the social historian, because they show the African family through the eyes of an exponent of the lower ranks of the regional upper class. The family emerges as a complex of relationships gravitating towards a central core, the nuclear group. The father – responsible for order, concord and the administration of the property – exerted his strong authority not only over the individual members of his *domus* (wife, children and slaves), but also over a much wider, contiguous yet external, social space. In the *domus* he would resort to corporal punishment, to the extent that the whip practically became the symbol of his authority. Such paternal severity – no matter how much it might have been offset by love and charity – tended to isolate the father emotionally from the rest of the family and to strengthen the affective bonds between mother and children or between siblings.[39]

There was nothing new about any of these features, either singly or in their various combinations. The behavioural, emotional and organizational

---

[38] Cameron, *Rheotoric of Empire* 116.
[39] Shaw (1987a); for family affectivity in the Roman west, see also ch. 15 (Wood), pp. 420–4 below.

aspects of the family reflected in Augustine's writings were in fact essentially traditional. Significantly, the environment described (Numidia) was
one where ancient customs survived strongest. Literary evidence for other
areas sometimes suggests that there also existed less oppressive situations,
in which tenderness played a more prominent role. But even these families,
ruled more by affection and respect than by fear and intimidation, were
essentially traditional. In other words, these sources do not give us the
impression that Christianity had substantially modified the existential conditions of women and children in late antiquity.[40] Where we do find the
display of new and subversive behaviour, among some of the more formidable figures of this period (for instance, certain women of the eastern
and western aristocracies), theirs was not so much a struggle in support of
a new family model as a struggle against the very notion of the family.[41]

But to explore the space separating the level of prescription (legal and
moral) from that of real life, we really need to consider evidence of a much
colder nature: those documents in which the specificity of the individual
dissolves into repetition and plurality. While the information from papyri
has been much scantier and less interesting than anticipated,[42] that from
funerary epigraphy has been sufficient to generate fundamental assessments. And though the data are fragmentary and poorly distributed (both
geographically and socially), the results of recent methods of investigation
cannot be underestimated.

Analysis of the family relationships attested in the inscriptions from
western sources in the first three centuries of the empire has shown that in
a clear majority of cases (c. 80 per cent) Roman society was characterized
by the nuclear family – Roman society being a 'peculiar nexus of urban
centres, whether village, town or city, and their rural territoria, that were
integrated into the political power structure of the Roman state'.[43] The
dominant relationship is that between husband and wife, whereas the
descending and ascending elements within the nuclear family are represented more or less equally; siblings, on the other hand, hardly feature.[44]

The same method, applied to western Christian epigraphy between the
fourth and the seventh century, shows certain changes in the family relationships, though within a framework of substantial continuity. First of all,
the nuclear family is further strengthened, now becoming practically the
sole focus of family life and affectivity (c. 97 per cent of cases). Secondly,
we find a larger number of commemorations between spouses and (to an

---

[40] Cameron (1993) 128ff.   [41] Recently, Giardina (1994), with bibliography.

[42] The lack of documents on divorce for this period is particularly significant: see Bagnall (1987),
who none the less claims there was a 'significant continuity, in substance and phraseology, from the
time before Constantine to the late sixth century, through numerous changes in imperial laws' (56); see
also Bagnall, *Egypt* 193f. For the patrimonial aspects, Beaucamp (1992b) 70ff. The private letters on
papyrus show no significant changes in family sentiment through Christian influence: Joxe (1959).

[43] Shaw (1984) 489.   [44] Saller and Shaw (1984).

even greater extent) in the descending line between parents and children. What is taking shape with increasing clarity, therefore, is the 'parent-to-child descending triad that is most typical of "modern" nuclear family structure'.[45] Finally, the inscriptions record a widespread collapse of interest in the memory of personal relationships. The sheer size of this phenomenon suggests that it was the result of deliberate, ideological choice: for in death even more than in life, the Christian devalues his earthly ties in favour of the heavenly bond. The same tendency is confirmed in the iconography, with a gradual disappearance of matrimonial scenes from sarcophagi.[46]

An examination of the inscriptions commemorating children who had died before the age of ten has shown significant differences. The percentage of such dedications reaches its highest levels in the cities of northern Italy and, above all, in Rome and Ostia; the lowest levels are found in the less urbanized regions. The tendency to commemorate children increases in the Christian inscriptions: in the areas where it was already high in early times, the percentage rise is less pronounced; elsewhere it is more substantial. Commemorations of the elderly (in their seventh decade of life), on the other hand, show an opposite trend: the highest percentages relate to the rural, non-Christian populations, the lowest to the urban, Christian areas. As regards the preference for male, as opposed to female, memorials, comparison among the urban populations shows a gradual tendency for the phenomenon to decline, if not disappear altogether. It has been rightly observed that, as a whole, these inscriptions reflect the sensibilities of the freedmen – that is, individuals who had no ascendant family tradition, but none the less wished to emphasize their status as Roman citizens who shared the stability of an affective and legal structure (the nuclear family). With respect to these tendencies, which had already existed for some time, Christianization seems to have had the effect of ideological strengthening – hence as a factor of continuity and reinforcement, not of novelty.[47]

In the past it has been held that Christian funerary inscriptions give evidence of a changed attitude to the correct marrying age for girls, raising it from its former, pagan levels. There would have been two reasons for this: as a means of championing virginity and to reduce the number of young girls dying in childbirth.[48] As it happens, however, the inscriptions taken as indicative of 'Christian' orientation (mainly from the city of Rome) were merely demonstrating that the lives of hitherto concealed strata of the population were beginning to be reflected in the documents.[49] And what

---

[45] Shaw (1984).   [46] Frugoni (1977).   [47] Shaw (1991); cf. Zanker (1975).

[48] Recently, Pietri (1979), on the basis of data collected and analysed by Carletti (1977).

[49] Shaw (1987b) 41 f.; for a reassessment of the data referring to the previous centuries, see Saller (1994) ch. 2.

they actually convey is that throughout the entire Roman imperial period there was a substantial continuity in the mode of family formation among the less affluent classes of the population.

The Christian epigraphy of Asia Minor also shows that Christianity did not, as has sometimes been held, make a significant contribution to demographic regression, at least as far as the fourth century is concerned. Using such material as demographic evidence has enormous, often insurmountable, limits, but what clearly emerges from a well-selected sample is that the birth rate of Christian families belonging to the middle strata of the population remained extremely high, very likely no lower than in the previous centuries.[50]

According to a recent theory, already in late antiquity Christianity played an epoch-making role in the history of the western family by imposing and spreading an exogamic model of matrimony, as opposed to the endogamic model traditional to the Mediterranean cultures. Within this tendency, the demands of morality combined with those of material expediency, for the interdiction of endogamy (along with restrictions on adoption, concubinage and second marriage) also favoured bequests of property to the church.[51] The evidence of western inscriptions, however, has shown a very strong prevalence and continuity of exogamy throughout the imperial period, among Christians and pagans alike. Besides, archaic Roman society had prohibited marriage up to the sixth degree inclusive,[52] and even after the lifting of the ban, parallel and cross-cousin marriages continued to be very rare in every rank of the pagan population. Hence the widening of the concept of incest (imposed by the Christian authorities and incorporated into imperial legislation) can hardly have had the devastating effect imagined.[53]

---

[50] Patlagean (1978) (the biggest weakness of this kind of enquiry is the lack of information on the marriage rate).   [51] Goody (1983) and (1990); for the traditional opinion, Weiss (1908).

[52] Bettini (1988).

[53] Shaw and Saller (1984); cf. Saller and Shaw (1984), Shaw (1984). The available evidence reveals marriages with a parallel cousin, either german or more distant, on the father's side; whereas those between cross-cousins or parallel cousins on the mother's side remain concealed (Shaw and Saller (1984) 435, 437). This fact has been pointed out by Moreau (1994) 67, in a brief criticism of Saller and Shaw's works. However, the quantity of data produced by these authors on the rarity (which doesn't necessarily mean absence) of marriages between parallel cousins in the pre-Christian west is decisive in one respect: it rules out the possibility that Roman marriages between parallel cousins on the father's side were very rare, while instead those between parallel cousins on the mother's side – or even other, closer, forms of endogamic marriage – were very frequent. In fact, the Roman rules of marriage either forbade or permitted marriages between cousins outright, without specifying further: 'Les différences de relation de cousinage ne constituent ni prétexte à un interdit, ni privilège préférential ou prescriptif, dans le champ matrimonial', a situation that is also perfectly reflected in the terminology (Bettini (1994) 234). Moreau (1994) 67 also argues that the legal interdiction of consanguineous marriages would be inexplicable if such marriages were very rare. Saller and Shaw, however, claim that they were rare in the west, while taking it for granted that they were widespread in the east. Reservations on the epigraphical analyses are also expressed in Corbier (1991).

III. NEGATIONS OF THE FAMILY

One of the most conspicuous factors of discontinuity between the earlier centuries and the late antique period concerns one particular aspect of family history: the negation of the family. The behaviour associated with this phenomenon can be classified into two broad categories. The first, which centres on the absolute primacy of virginity in the system of values, includes the rejection (expressed both before and after marriage) of the sexual act, of childbirth and of family life.[54] The second includes the following: the inability to form a new family through lack of economic resources; the practices of exclusion considered criminal, such as infanticide and the custom of the *ius vitae ac necis*, now (at least from 318) likened to *parricidium*;[55] and, finally, the actions deriving from the exercise of *patria potestas*, which principally meant the exposure and sale of infants, the temporary cession of grown-up children and the forced entry of daughters – and, to a lesser extent, sons – into monastic life. In the first category, moral motivations strongly prevailed over material conditioning; in the second, the opposite held true.

The lowering of the minimum age for entry into monastic life (and, though to a lesser extent, into anchoritism) was a development that paralleled the lowering of the minimum age for betrothal.[56] We learn, for example, that Symeon Stylites the Younger mounted his first pillar at the age of seven. Considered individually, this and other similar feats[57] could be taken as exaggerations aimed at establishing a heroic model: that of the saint who displayed a fully mature devotion to God in earliest childhood and an almost primordial purity in adulthood. Symeon, it is worth remembering, was still in his mother's womb when John the Baptist appeared to prescribe the ascetic diet on which the future child was to be raised.[58] But in fact such stories substantially agree with the data from the legal documents, which suggest that the phenomenon was widespread: a conciliar measure of 692 fixed the lower age-limit for entry into a monastery at ten years.[59] Significantly, the monastic world was strongly pervaded by family *lexis* (which was used to describe the system of relationships within the community) and the monastery itself often ended up by carrying out many of the functions of a nuclear or extended family.[60]

Unlike other practices, the exposure and sale of children, as well as the hiring-out of sons, was a type of negation of family that often implied entry into another family: as adopted children, as slaves or as hired labour. A small proportion of the exposed were either forced into prostitution or intro-

---

[54] See ch. 26 (Brown), pp. 791–5 below.   [55] Harris (1986) 92.

[56] See above, p. 400. Another problem concerns the imposition of monastic status for punitive reasons: Goria (1975) 131ff.   [57] *Vita Sym. Styl. Jun.* 15; Patlagean (1973).   [58] *Vita Sym. Styl. Jun.* 3.

[59] *Conc. in Trullo* 40.   [60] Talbot (1990).

duced to the harsher and more marginal sectors of slave exploitation; some were subsequently resold. The laws on these issues provide valuable evidence clarifying the general orientations of legislation and moral teaching on the family.

Evidence from the Severan period suggests that infant exposure had already, for quite some time, been provoking censure and unease in the pagan community (or at least among the classes that voiced their opinions in our documents).[61] But it was only with the Christian emperors that any attempt was made to discourage and, subsequently, stamp out the phenomenon. Alongside certain flimsy attempts at prevention in situations of emergency (in the form of aid to needy families), there were also some more realistic measures, which tried to limit the scourge of exposure by authorizing the cession of children while at the same time not excluding the possibility of recovery. This was an option already provided for in traditional Roman law, but few can have availed themselves of it. It was not so much a practical proposition as a valuable psychological opening that alleviated the trauma of separation. At the same time, it acted as a moral palliative in what was clearly the thorniest aspect of the law on exposure: the fact that, in contrast with one of the basic principles of Roman law, an individual of free birth could be reduced to slavery by the wishes of another person.

The flexibility of this approach, however, was soon superseded by the opposite tendency, and the laws not only withheld the possibility of recovery but even made infant exposure punishable by death if the parents were free citizens. The results of these measures were, we suspect, negligible. A wide parallel documentation attests how deeply rooted and widespread the phenomenon was, for it thrived well into the Middle Ages in the west and into the Byzantine period in the east, even surviving in the recent history of industrial urbanism.[62]

The failure of strict legislation is indirectly confirmed by a subsequent law passed by Justinian: it guaranteed all exposed children the condition of freedom and denied those who received them the power to enslave them or to reduce them to any other form of dependence, or even to place them in a relationship of patronage. Justinian explained that the measure intended to make a clear moral distinction between the desire for illicit profit and a mere act of compassion. At the same time, those abandoning a child were to be denied the right to recover him with the object of enslaving him.[63] If actually enforced, this law would surely have provoked a considerable increase in the death rate of the exposed. But it is fruitless to pose problems of this kind, or even to try to relate the individual laws to specific demographic or economic situations.[64] In such cases the legislation was

[61] Harris (1994).   [62] Boswell (1989).   [63] *CJ* VIII.51.3 (529); see also *Nov.* 153 (541).
[64] For example, Bianchi Fossati Vanzetti (1983) 223.

clearly very low in practical impact and very high in ideological content. From the emotional point of view, exposure was a central issue round which far too many sins and far too much wretchedness gravitated. It turned parents into putative infanticides (often enough the infant's fate was death). It laid bare the macabre power of uncontrolled sexuality, of both free citizens and slaves, within and outside marriage. It disclosed the avidity of those who exploited the theoretically charitable act of taking in a child as a means of gaining ownership over a human being. Finally, it projected on to the whole of society the shame and contamination of incestuous contact, which could occur anywhere: in brothels as in lawful marriages, in the beds of concubines and adulterers alike. All things considered, the actual survival and subsequent fate of the exposed children were just one aspect of the problem, perhaps not even the most important.

In the abstract, exposure was a serious crime with associations closely resembling those of infanticide. But in the vast majority of cases the offence had compelling material causes that constituted objective conditioning. Raising these issues questioned the whole problem of responsibility: is it better to allow a child to die of hunger or to expose him in the hope that others might take him in? To differentiate the law by introducing a typology of motivations – i.e. distinguishing abandonment caused by indigence from that caused by pettier or less constrictive reasons – would have had the dual effect of undermining the moral principle that the law aimed to uphold and of disrupting the very foundations of the juridical system. Once exposure had entered the province of the law, the only option was to repress it without distinction. The material constrictions, however, doomed the laws to failure; and failure, in turn, provoked even stricter prohibitions and severer punishments. In this way, the law ended up by carrying out, almost exclusively, the functions of a moral imperative.

The laws on exposure can be considered together with those on the sale of infants and the *locatio* of children of working age. The latter was strictly speaking *locatio operarum*, though the laws, in view of the overall context of relationships of dependence, sometimes represented it and classified it as a sale.[65] The legislation thus responded to a need constantly referred to in late antique legislation: that of preserving the family nucleus. In other words, in situations of long-term economic difficulty the break-up of the family could be prevented by the temporary cession of a child. The relinquished child, who would then be housed in the *domus* of a proprietor sufficiently rich to be able to rent labour, would surely be no worse off than before. The possibility of a subsequent return to the nuclear family could also have a dissuasive effect on exposure.

[65] Humbert (1983).

The landlords who were forced – by sheer necessity – to expose or sell the children of their slaves would have been farmers with insufficient reserves to face up to famines or similar adversities. We are therefore dealing with small farms where there was close, daily contact with the slaves. In such contexts, the cession of a *sanguinolentus* born of slaves tended to generate an emotional climate similar to that between free citizens. The right of redemption, which admitted the possibility, at least in theory, of future reunion, helped to reduce the trauma of the event, exactly as it did in the case of free citizens. This established the humanitarian principle that recognized the aspiration of slave family nuclei to remain united, without impairing thereby the right of the *domini* to dispose freely of their *res*. Like other arguments calling for a more humane treatment of slaves, this one had also had its advocates in the past. But it was only under Constantine that it was clearly and formally defined. The humanitarian inspiration of the Constantinian legislation is confirmed by a law on the *fundi patrimoniales vel enfyteuticarii*. The dismemberment of the *possessiones*, the emperor stipulated, must be carried out in such a way as to safeguard the integrity of the *servorum agnatio*, for 'who could tolerate that children should be separated from parents, sisters from brothers, wives from their husbands?'[66]

The strengthening and diffusion of such moral scruples, combined with the decline in the slave supply and the impoverishment of the free farmers, had paradoxical consequences on family stability, for it would appear from certain documents that the slave *agnationes* were more stable than the families that were free but poor. The new epistles of Augustine indicate that the phenomenon intensified in the western areas during the early decades of the fifth century. As a judge, Augustine found himself handling a difficult juridical problem, concerning cases of children illegally sold by free parents and of free adults who had fallen into the hands of slave-dealers. On the subject he appends a revealing note: 'the *mangones* deport those they buy, almost all of whom are free citizens ... Very rare, on the other hand, are the cases of real slaves sold by their lords.'[67] In the same years, the *Vita* of Melania the Younger cites another episode that was an eloquent sign of the times: it told of slaves, freed in large numbers by their lords, rejecting their freedom and carrying their opposition to the verge of revolt.[68] Here it was clearly a case of 'cottaged' slaves (*casarii*), divided into 'family' nuclei not substantially unlike those of the *coloni*, as far as economic functions were concerned. For such people, especially when they belonged to a powerful *domus* unit, slavery offered many advantages, principally that of stability. Freedom, on the other

---

[66] *C.Th.* 11.25.1 = *CJ* III.38.1 (325: Seeck (1919) 88). Though this constitution specifically concerns Sardinia, the principle was certainly general; see Giardina (1988) 138. For confirmation of this principle, in connection with the needs of the census, *CJ* XI.48.7 (371: Seeck (1919) 131).

[67] Aug. *Ep.* 10*, *CSEL* LXXXVIII.46ff.

[68] Pall. *Hist. Laus.* 61.5; *Vita Melaniae* 10f. (*SChrét.* 90); Giardina (1982) 128f.

hand, entailed all the uncertainties and risks of being uprooted. Cassiodorus, celebrating the opulence of the great annual fair of Marcelliana in Lucania, was to recollect all those *pueri* and *puellae* exhibited for sale not because they were slaves but because they were free (*quos non fecit captivatas esse sub pretio, sed libertas*).[69]

IV. WEST AND EAST

It is customary to distinguish the western model of the family, based on the nuclear unit and strongly featuring exogamic matrimony, from that of the east, centred on extended households, agnatic lineages and endogamous marriage patterns. A key role in this distinction is played by Egypt, a region thought to exemplify eastern kinship for many reasons, though particularly because of the custom of marriage between siblings-german. As regards late antiquity, the extent of the Egyptian contribution to this interpretative picture needs to be radically reconsidered. The documents clearly show that, following the *Constitutio Antoniniana*[70] and the spread of Christianity, such marriages became increasingly rare and eventually disappeared altogether. And that is not all. A recent, plausible explanation for the custom has traced its origin to the settlements of the Greek colonists, who adopted a policy of strict closure towards the indigenous population.[71] If, therefore, the phenomenon is explained as an ethnic decision determined by specific historical circumstances, we can obviously no longer use it as evidence either for the specific and primordial nature of Egyptian kinship or for the eastern tendency for siblings-german to intermarry.

The generalization linking close-kin marriages with the eastern empire is too imprecise and needs clarifying. For a start, it would not have occurred to the ancients themselves. In the year 535/6 Justinian issued a law to check the spread of *gamoi athemitoi*, 'unlawful marriages', in the provinces of Osrhoene and Mesopotamia. The marriages in question were consanguineous unions punishable by death: principally those between siblings and between uncle and niece (those between cousins were not prohibited by Byzantine law). While confirming the ban for the future, the emperor agreed to be lenient over past transgressions: those at fault (he said) were peasants who had been led astray by the customs of neighbouring populations (the Persians above all) and whose lives had been disrupted by the numerous recent invasions.[72] A similar measure, this time referring to Mesopotamia, Osrhoene and the Euphratensis, was issued in 566 by Justin II, who again referred to ignorance of the law and to corruption from

---

[69] Cass. *Var.* VIII.33.4.   [70] Hopkins (1980b).

[71] Shaw (1992). On the problem of Egyptian specificity, it is also worth noting that in Egypt the marrying age of girls was in line with the average in the rest of the empire: Bagnall, *Egypt* 189.

[72] Just. *Nov.* 154.

contact with peoples such as the Persians and Saracens.[73] Hence, whereas modern historians have tended to attribute close-kin marriage very broadly to the 'Romans' of Constantinople along with many other peoples of the eastern empire, the Byzantine emperor himself regarded such marriages as geographically and socially confined to the rural populations that were alien to Roman laws and customs.

'East' is thus a singularly vague label, one expected to cover areas as dissimilar as Greece, Lycia, Egypt, Palestine, Syria, Armenia and Mesopotamia. No less vague, however, is the term 'close-kin marriage', which is quite inadequate to describe the differences in family structure between east and west. The modern term covers not only marriages between siblings or between uncle and niece or aunt and nephew, but also those between cousins. But the distance between two cultures that held conflicting views on marriage between cousins (e.g. Roman Africa and Greece in the fifth century A.D.) was not necessarily any greater than that separating a culture that practised marriage between cousins (e.g. Greece) and another that practised marriage between even closer relatives (e.g. Byzantine Mesopotamia).

The most significant distinction between east and west, therefore, concerned marriage between cousins. Theodosius I punished such unions with death. In the year 396 Arcadius confirmed the prohibition but considerably mitigated the punishment. But the law must still have met with strong resistance in the east, for eventually Arcadius lifted the ban (in 405). At the time of Justinian, marriage between cousins was still considered legitimate in Byzantium. In the west, on the other hand, the ban remained in force, as is attested by a law of the year 409.[74] That the disparity in the legal situations of the two parts of the empire actually reflected differences in marriage customs is confirmed by Augustine: marriage between cousins, he declared, was rare (in most of the western regions, we infer) even before it was prohibited by law: *propter gradum propinquitatis fraterno gradui proximum quam raro per mores fiebat, quod fieri per leges licebat.*[75]

---

[73] Justin, *Nov.* 3; the expression *gamoi athemitoi* was not so much a 'euphemism' (Lee (1988) 407) as a general indication comprising all consanguineous marriages except those between cousins (which were permitted by Byzantine law). It is questionable whether it refers only to marriages between brothers and sisters and parents and offspring, and not also (or indeed above all) to those between uncles and nieces. In this connection, see Theodoret, *Ep.* 8, *SChrét.* 40.80, where the custom was considered typical of the Persians. On Iranian customs, see the recent Herrenschmidt (1994); on late antique representations of Persian marriage customs, see Chadwick (1979); for Dura, see Cumont (1924).

[74] For Theodosius' law, see p. 396 above, n. 12; *C.Th.* III.12.3 = *CJ* v.5.6 (396); *CJ* v.4.19 (405); *C.Th.* III.10.1 = *CJ* v.8.1 (409); *Just. Inst.* 1.10.4. The opinion expressed in Patlagean, *Pauvreté* 118ff. (i.e. the banning of marriage between cousins in response to a 'resserrement des liens conjugaux et familiaux') is contradicted by the widespread, traditional practice of marriage between cousins in the Greek world: Bresson (1985) 266. On later developments in Byzantium, Laiou (1992) ch. 1. On the continuity, in the Byzantine age, of the traditional position of the grandfather and the maternal uncle in the Greek family, see Bremmer (1983).

[75] Aug. *Civ.* xv.16. Roda (1979) emphasizes imperial derogations. On the avunculate in the Celtic world, with particular reference to the family of Ausonius, see Guastella (1980).

This polarity between east and west is part of the old problem of eastern influence on Roman law. In late antiquity, this can also be seen in the problem of identifying the different trends in each part of the empire and establishing the connection between these trends and remote anthropological constants. Deducing the area of application of the imperial constitutions from their place of emission or publication is a debatable procedure in any case, but it is especially so for much of the fourth century, given the incompleteness of the documentation and the principle of imperial *unanimitas*. But even laying aside such scruples, we are forced to recognize that the source material often contradicts, when it does not actually confute, the theses one might wish to prove. For example, it has been held that the post-Constantinian legislation directed against mixed-status unions was catering to western needs, which were closer to the tradition of Roman law.[76] But it was a western emperor, Valentinian, who legislated that illegitimate children should have the right to at least a share of their father's inheritance. And it was an eastern emperor, Valens, who disapproved of that law, which was promptly repealed (by Valens himself or his successor).[77] In other cases, the existence of customs that are typically, or prevalently, eastern (and consequently the natural subject of the legislators' special interest) is simply assumed and by no means adequately confirmed by the documents. A case in point is the requirement, to ensure the validity of a marriage, of a written contract specifying the dowry and marriage gifts. Interpreted by some historians as a Greek or eastern custom, it has been correctly ascribed to the church's need to exercise control over the institution of marriage.[78] According to the Claudian *senatus consultum*, a free woman who was a slave's concubine could be reduced to slavery provided she had been warned three times. The warning clause was removed by Constantine, and then reinstated by Julian.[79] It has been claimed that Constantine's measure betrays the influence of Greek customs, which were in favour of automatically reducing women to slavery, and that Julian's reaction was influenced by western customs. But this interpretation is simply not borne out by the sources.[80] As for Constantine's law banning the presence of a concubine in the same house as a lawful marriage, there is nothing to attest that in late antiquity this form of polygamy was so widely spread in the eastern provinces of the empire – and so thinly distributed in the

---

[76] Evans Grubbs (1995) 302f.

[77] *C.Th.* IV.6.4; cf. Lib. *Or* I.145; 195–6. It was only in the fifth century that western legislation started to become more restrictive than that of the east: see below.

[78] Mitteis (1891) 226, 290; Volterra (1937) 248; for a different opinion, Wolff (1939) 83ff.; for the classic problem of the *arrhae sponsaliciae* and the alleged eastern influence on Constantine's betrothal legislation, see the balanced assessment in Evans Grubbs (1995) 174ff.

[79] *C.Th.* IV.12.4 (331); IV.12.5 (362); see also above, p. 396.

[80] Mitteis (1891) 364ff.; Gaudemet (1948) 670; for a different view, Beaucamp (1990) 187.

western parts – as to be a typically eastern phenomenon.[81] The same can be said of abduction.[82] Even the tendency to consider betrothal as a definitive choice has been attributed to eastern, particularly Judaic, influence;[83] it is more convincingly explained as the result of a combination of widespread economic, social and moral factors. These examples clearly show the extent to which historical judgement is conditioned by ideology, especially in a subject such as this. That one or other of these customs was more widely spread in one or other part of the empire is undeniable. What is much more difficult, however, is to distinguish an eastern anthropology from a western one on the basis of the imperial constitutions of the fourth and fifth centuries.

From the doctrinal point of view, there are no significant differences in the records between east and west as regards attitudes to fundamental issues such as betrothal and marriage,[84] and for many centuries the function of the religious rites associated with these events remained substantially the same in Rome and Byzantium.[85]

However, from the first decades of the fifth century, in certain respects western legislation began to take a firmer line than that of the east. This tendency – which was not absolute and included important exceptions[86] – is particularly evident not only in the prohibitions of consanguineous marriage but also in the legislation on both divorce[87] and the inheritance of illegitimate children.[88] Instead of resorting to the argument of 'eastern specificity', we prefer to see the matter as dependent on the different relationships existing between the secular and the religious powers in the two parts. In the east, where the state was stronger, imperial law was able to withstand the demands of the ecclesiastical authorities and to represent the sensibilities of the majority of its subjects more effectively. In the west, exposed as it was to internal and external threats, the state was more amenable to the pressures of the bishops.

With the fall of Rome and the establishment of the Romano-Germanic kingdoms, the history of the Roman family was separated into two parallel, yet interlinked, processes, each of which was further divided into a myriad

---

[81] For a different view, Wolff (1945) 40f.; Evans Grubbs (1995) 299; see in particular Vatin (1970) 204.

[82] Evans Grubbs (1989) 67ff. greatly underestimates the importance of the data from the Latin rhetorical works. On other aspects of this problem, see Volterra (1937).   [83] Cohen (1949).

[84] See, respectively, Anné (1941) 31 and Gaudemet (1978b) 27.

[85] The most significant changes occurred in Byzantium in the ninth century when decisive importance was attributed to betrothal and the marriage blessing: L'Huillier (1987).

[86] See, for example, the provision introduced by the western emperor Majorian in 458: an attempt to promote marriages between the nobility, to encourage the remarriage of widows and to stop parents from consigning virgins to convents for patrimonial reasons (Nov. 6).

[87] The greater leniency of eastern legislation on divorce can be observed by comparing C.Th. III.16.2 (421; modified in CJ IX.9.34) with Theod. Nov. 12 (439), CJ V.17.8 (449), Val. Nov. 35.11 (452) and CJ V.17.9 (497). In general, see Volterra (1975).   [88] C.Th. IV.6.6 (405); IV.6.7 (426/427); IV.6.8 (428).

individual situations both in the Mediterranean world and in continental Europe. Anyone wishing to devote a single book to the subsequent chapters of the history of the ideal-types that we call the 'eastern family' and the 'western family' faces a truly demanding task. For apart from negotiating the labyrinthine links between individual instance and general rule, he would also be expected to classify modes of acculturation, identify sociological constants, propose historical comparisons and reconstruct actual relationships. It is perhaps not difficult to see why these parallel lives still await their Plutarch.

CHAPTER 15

FAMILY AND FRIENDSHIP IN THE WEST

IAN N. WOOD

At the beginning of the fifth century the senatorial aristocracy of the late empire seemed well assured of its future. Its great dynasties, the Anicii and Symmachi among them, appear full of confidence in the letter collections of the period – those of Symmachus himself, but also of Jerome, Augustine and Paulinus of Nola.[1] Nor were they much shaken by the initial break-up of the western empire, despite panic-stricken reactions to the arrival of the barbarians and to the invasions of the Huns. At the end of the fifth century the Italian aristocracy appears as confident as ever in the inscriptions of the Colosseum[2] and in the letters of Ennodius of Pavia. Its Gallic counterpart, a little less grand in status, but of nearly comparable wealth, dominates the letter collections of Sidonius Apollinaris, Ruricius of Limoges and Avitus of Vienne, as well as having a significant profile in that of Ennodius (Provençal by birth, albeit Italian in his career).[3] By the mid sixth century, however, the greatest of these dynasties were no longer a power in the west: Justinian's Ostrogothic wars had destroyed their Italian base, although the Anicii themselves were still of some importance in Constantinople. However, while the front rank of the aristocracy had collapsed in Italy, in the successor states of Gaul its provincial counterpart survived,[4] as is again evidenced by a letter collection, this time the poetic epistles of Venantius Fortunatus.[5] In all probability it had also managed to hang on to much of its wealth. Moreover, these families had not held themselves aloof from the political changes which followed the failure of the western empire; instead they, or at least individual members of the Gallo-Roman aristocracy, were involved in the new kingdoms of the Visigoths, Burgundians and Franks, whether at a local level as bishops, or at the level of the state, as counsellors.[6] As such they appear in the *Ten Books of Histories* of Gregory of Tours, who was himself a

[1] See above all, on the aristocrats, Matthews (1975); Arnheim (1972) 103–42; on friendship, Brown (1992) 45–6; White (1992); Clark (1990) 11–42; on Paulinus of Nola, Fabre (1949); on the letter collections, Matthews (1974) 58–99.   [2] Chastagnol (1966).   [3] Wood (1993a); Mathisen (1981).
[4] Stroheker (1948) remains the classic work.   [5] Brown (1996) 103.
[6] For a study of one individual and his family in the first half of this transitional period, see Harries (1994); more generally, Mathisen (1993).

member of the traditional senatorial class.[7] This combined evidence provides an opportunity for considering the history of the family, in its aristocratic guise, during the transition from the Roman empire to the successor states.

At a lower social level, if one confines one's enquiries to the Roman and sub-Roman population in the west, the history of the family is much less informative. In north-east Italy and in Istria mosaic panels on the floors of fifth- and sixth-century churches, recording donations, show apparently ordinary families acting together to make gifts.[8] Some saints came from among the non-aristocratic property-holders. Just occasionally, evidence like that provided by St Patrick on his father and grandfather in Britain throws light on a lesser family group – though here the problem of dating makes it difficult to determine whether the information relates largely to the fourth century or to the fifth.[9]

The evidence for the new Germanic population entering the empire is at first sight similar in distribution. Certainly at the very highest level – that is, at the level of royalty – the evidence is relatively good. The two greatest Gothic families, the Amals and the Balts, the ruling dynasties of the Ostrogoths and the Visigoths respectively, are well attested for the late fifth and early sixth century, even though much of the evidence relating to those dynasties was clearly elaborated at the hands of Theoderic the Great and Cassiodorus.[10] From the 480s, at least, the Merovingians provide a wealth of salacious stories which give an entrée into the family life of Frankish royalty. Among the Franks the next level of society – the non-royal aristocracy – is invisible in the fifth- and sixth-century legal evidence, so much so as to have prompted the question as to whether it existed at all. For all the silence of the legal sources, the regular discovery of Frankish high-status graves from this period suggests that this is an evidential lacuna rather than proof of any real absence of an aristocratic class.[11]

While the Frankish aristocracy presents a problem of interpretation, the law codes of the successor states shed light on the family structure of the rank and file, among the Franks as among other barbarian peoples.[12] This makes it possible occasionally to look beyond the highest classes of society, the kings, their immediate family and the traditional senatorial aristocracy. For the most part, however, the ensuing discussion will concentrate on the most powerful families in the fifth- and sixth-century west. It will look first at the senatorial aristocracy, essentially that of Gaul, where the evidence is most extensive, at the senatorial *familia*, and at its possessions. Thereafter, the criteria used by the senatorial aristocracy in defining itself will be considered:

---

[7] Mathisen (1984).   [8] Caillet (1993), esp. 447–8.
[9] Patrick, *Confessio* 1, ed. R. P. C. Hanson, *SChrét.* 249 (Paris 1978); see also the discussion, *ibid.* pp. 24–8, although the argument in favour of an early date is not persuasive.
[10] Wolfram (1988); Heather (1989).   [11] James (1988) 219–24.   [12] Murray (1983).

types of descent groups, together with broader approaches to the definition of the family, as suggested by literature and religion. Comparison will then be made with the Frankish and Burgundian evidence for family structures and attitudes. Before concluding, a sideways glance will be cast in the direction of the other great bond in late antique and early medieval society – the bond of friendship, which worked in parallel to the bonds of family, and which is likewise documented in the letter collections.

The Roman or sub-Roman household or *familia* of the fifth and sixth century was a large group. Where it is possible to reconstruct a family tree[13] it is clear that a high birth rate was common and that families could be size-able – something perhaps exacerbated by the absence of child exposure in a Christian world.[14] Apart from parents and children, the *familia*, at least of the greater families, included officials and servants of various sorts, among them household slaves.[15] One such slave, whose history is related by Gregory of Tours, was Andarchius, a member of the household of the Auvergnat aristocrat, Felix. Having impressed his master by his intelligence and learning, he dispossessed him and married his daughter, only to be killed by other slaves in the household, who objected to his usurpation of status and his arrogant behaviour.[16] The story provides a vignette of life in a great household, from Felix and his daughter to the learned, clever and ambitious Andarchius and down to his fellow slaves, who preferred the *status quo* to the more open social world implied by the upward mobility of their former companion.

Andarchius had his eyes on the property of Felix, as well his daughter. In all likelihood this property would have been scattered in numerous estates across a large geographical area. Before the fall of the western empire the geographical distribution of land held by members of the late Roman sena-torial aristocracy was extraordinary, as can be seen from comments on the estates of Melania the Younger, the distribution of which stretched from Spain to Italy and Britain to Africa[17] – or even the estates of Paulinus of Pella, who held lands in both halves of the empire until he lost control of them as a result of the migration and settlement of the barbarians.[18] Although such holdings were no longer possible in the late fifth century, Gallo-Roman aristocrats still held properties which were widely scattered within the provinces of Gaul: the lands of their successors were similarly dis-persed across the kingdom of the Franks throughout the following centu-ries.[19] In the fifth century most will have possessed urban villas, as, to judge

[13] See, for instance, the genealogies in Stroheker (1948).

[14] For child exposure in the Roman empire, Garnsey and Saller (1987) 138.

[15] Compare Garnsey and Saller (1987) 126–47.

[16] Greg. Tur. *Hist.* IV.46. Compare the reaction of the slaves in *Vitas Patrum Emeritensium* 3, ed. J. N. Garvin (Washington 1946).   [17] *Vita Melaniae* 11, 19, ed. D. Gorce, *SChrét.* 90 (Paris 1962).

[18] Paulinus of Pella, *Eucharisticos* lines 408–19, ed. C. Moussy, *Paulin de Pella, Poème d'Action de Grâces et de Prière, SChrét.* 209 (Paris, 1974).   [19] Wood, *Merovingian Kingdoms* (1994) 206–11.

by his references to Lyons, did Sidonius Apollinaris,[20] though it is possible that a city residence became less desirable as the amenities of urban life declined. More important were the rural estates, some of them of considerable pretension, like the lakeside villa of Avitus, Gallo-Roman senator and subsequently emperor, at Aydat,[21] or the hilltop fortress of Pontius Leontius.[22] From Sidonius' descriptions, even allowing for the fact that they are literary set-pieces,[23] it is possible to see these houses as working units: in some cases one can even see some of the minutiae of spatial arrangements – for instance, the division of a library, where there was an area for the men, with books of philosophy, and another for the women, with books of devotion.[24] A century later, Venantius Fortunatus described some aspects of the properties of the sixth-century Gallo-Roman aristocracy and indeed of their Germanic counterparts, including their oratories and their gardens. Among the aristocrats so fêted were the descendants of Pontius Leontius.[25] Estates and their transmission from generation to generation were as important to the senatorial aristocracy of the sixth century as they had been over a hundred years earlier, when Salvian saw desire for property and its transmission to the next generation as central to the vices of the rich of his day.[26]

This concern with family and inheritance can also be seen in mirror image in the early history of monasticism, since monasticism challenged the notions both of a family line and of inherited property.[27] The early bewilderment at Paulinus of Nola's decision to opt out of the traditional pattern of senatorial life shows exactly how much the aristocracy valued continuity of blood.[28] The blatant inversion of social norms performed by ascetics at the end of the fifth century continued to meet with opposition. John of Réomé left Burgundy for Lérins.[29] He was subsequently recognized, and brought back on the instructions of the bishop of Langres to his district of origin. There he founded a monastery, but still refused to have any but the most formal contact with his mother.[30] John, moreover, is one of those saints who takes us a degree down the social scale – still within the ranks of property-holders,[31] but no longer within the senatorial aristocracy. As elsewhere, extreme asceticism throve on an exact contradiction of social norms. Its rejection of family and heirs, which can also be seen in the sixth-century history of Patroclus of Bourges,[32] and its attempt

---

[20] Harries (1994) 36–47.   [21] Sid. Ap. *Ep.* 2.2, ed. W. B. Anderson (London 1936–65).
[22] Sid. Ap. *Carm.* XXII.   [23] Harries (1994) 10.
[24] Sid. Ap. *Ep.* 2.9.4–5. For a study of comparable material in Africa, Thébert (1987) 313–409.
[25] Venantius Fortunatus, *Carm.* 1.14–16, ed. F. Leo, *MGH, AA* 4 (1) (Berlin 1881).
[26] Salv. *Timothei ad Ecclesiam Libri IIII* ed. G. Lagarrigue, *SChrét.* 176 (Paris 1971).
[27] Van Uytfanghe (1987) 31, 72–4.   [28] Matthews (1975) 152–3.
[29] Jonas, *Vita Iohannis* 4, ed. B. Krusch, *MGH, SRM* 3 (Hanover 1896).
[30] Jonas, *Vita Iohannis* 6; Van Uytfanghe (1987) 31, 74.
[31] Jonas, *Vita Iohannis* 1; Van Uytfanghe (1987) 169.
[32] Cf. Greg. Tur. *Liber Vitae Patrum* IX.1, ed. B. Krusch, *MGH, SRM* 1 (2) (Hanover 1885). For a discussion of later Merovingian examples, Van Uytfanghe (1987) 186–92.

to divest itself of family possessions may, therefore, be taken as illustrative of the normal endorsement of those aspects of aristocratic or propertied life.

Land could and did pass through both the male and the female line. This is clear enough at the beginning of the fifth century from the case of Melania, and more generally from the evidence of the Theodosian Code.[33] It is also implied by what we know of the estates held by the family of Gregory of Tours in the sixth century. After his father's death Gregory and his mother lived on their estates in the Auvergne and Burgundy.[34] The Auvergnat estates are likely to have come from Gregory's father, but the Burgundian lands must have been in the possession of Gregory's maternal kin. It is not, therefore, surprising that the evidence suggests that kin groups were essentially cognatic – that is, that maternal relatives had considerable significance – even if modern reconstructions of family trees tend to emphasize the paternal line. Indeed, the most famous late Roman family of all, the Anicii, died out in the male line in the course of the fourth century, and the name was passed on through the female line.[35] Moreover, although sixth-century Gallo-Roman families have been accorded such names as Apollinares, Aviti and Ruricii, there is very little evidence that such appellations were commonly used in Gaul after the fifth century. While it is true that patterns of name-giving can be established for various families, most individuals in the sixth century are referred to by a single name only, even when they are known to have had more than one. All in all, while it is often possible to reconstruct a patrilineal *gens*, this was not the only way of categorizing the family in the sub-Roman west.

The clearest assessment of matrilineal and patrilineal kin comes from Sidonius Apollinaris. Writing to his friend Aper he says that 'In any statement of one's genealogy the father's side takes a privileged position; nevertheless, we owe a great deal to our mothers as well; for it is not right that some slighter honour should be given to the truth that we were our mother's burden than to the fact that we are our father's seed.'[36] Sidonius goes on to describe Aper as the scion of the families of both his parents, and celebrated his joint origins in the Auvergne and the Autunois.[37] It was doubtless easier to present both sides of the family as significant because of the social status of Aper's maternal kin. Most aristocrats of the fifth and sixth century, however, appear to have married within their own social group. Again, a glance at the genealogies which have been reconstructed for the period reveals how intertwined were those families about whom

---

[33] *C.Th.* VIII.18 (see also II.24.2; V.1.5; VIII.19.1; IX.14.3; IX.42.1; XVI.5.7), ed. T. Mommsen, 2nd edn (Berlin 1954).   [34] Wood (1994) 8.   [35] Demandt (1989) 82.

[36] Sid. Ap. *Ep.* 4.21.1, trans. Anderson.

[37] Sid. Ap. *Ep.* 4.21.2. For Sidonius' own maternal kin, see Harries (1994) 31; for similar attitudes already in Pliny, see Garnsey and Saller (1987) 128, 141.

anything is known.[38] It is perhaps significant that Ennodius does not name the parents of his nephew Parthenius, since the boy's mother seems to have married below her social station.[39] Marriage within a confined social group seems to have continued to be the norm among the aristocracy for much of the sixth century. It is clear that both sides of Gregory of Tours' family were of the same status, and that he held his maternal and paternal relatives in equal regard. Among the clerics he revered in his family were a paternal uncle, Gallus of Clermont,[40] and a maternal uncle, Nicetius of Lyons,[41] each of whom was partially responsible for his upbringing.[42] Gregory, who was encouraged to write by his mother,[43] offers a very even coverage of both sides of his family in his *Ten Books of Histories*, and in his hagiography.[44]

Gregory provides evidence for numerous generations of his family, theoretically going as far back, in one case, as the second century.[45] The letter collections of the fifth and sixth century are not so wide-ranging in their chronological coverage, although they perhaps give more intimate insights into attitudes towards the family. Sidonius' comment on the paternal and maternal kin of Aper might be seen as something of a rhetorical flourish. Not so his outburst after some peasants had accidentally disturbed his paternal grandfather's grave, which led him to horsewhip them, and then to consider setting up a proper monument.[46] On his own parents he is remarkably silent, more so than on his father-in-law, although this may say more about power and patronage than about family structures, since Avitus was not only Sidonius' father-in-law but also, briefly, emperor, and as such, inevitably, Sidonius' patron.[47] More intimate are Sidonius' letters to and about his son Apollinaris, which describe his attempts to provide him with a literary education, teaching him Terence, and which lament his failure.[48] These are all the more interesting because the letter collections of Ruricius and Avitus of Vienne reveal Apollinaris as an arbiter of taste in the next generation,[49] suggesting that some of Sidonius' lessons ultimately did bear fruit.

For Avitus of Vienne, Sidonius, probably his maternal uncle, was *Sidonius meus*.[50] For Ruricius of Limoges Sidonius was a more distant relative,[51] but

---

[38] Stroheker (1948); Wood (1992) 10–11.

[39] Ennodius xciv, ed. F. Vogel, *MGH, AA* 7 (Berlin 1885).   [40] Greg. Tur. *Liber Vitae Patrum* VI.

[41] Greg. Tur. *Liber Vitae Patrum* VIII.   [42] Van Dam (1993) 52–62.

[43] Greg. Tur. *Liber de Virtutibus sancti Martini* I pref., ed. B. Krusch, *MGH, SRM* I (2); Greg. Tur. *Hist.* pref., ed. B. Krusch and W. Levison, *MGH, SRM* I (Hanover 1951).   [44] Van Dam (1993) 50–81.

[45] On Vettius Epagathus, Greg. Tur. *Hist.* 1.29, 31. On his relationship with Gregory's family, Greg. Tur. *Liber Vitae Patrum* VI.1.   [46] Sid. Ap. *Ep.* 3.12; Wood (1996).   [47] Harries (1994) 31.

[48] Sid. Ap. *Epp.* 4.12.1; 9.1.5. On the significance of literature for the Gallo-Roman aristocracy of the fifth and sixth century, Mathisen (1993) 105–18.

[49] Ruricius, *Epp.* 2.26.41, ed. B. Krusch, *MGH, AA* 8 (Berlin 1887); Avitus, *Ep.* 51, ed. R. Peiper, *MGH, AA* 6 (2) (Berlin 1883).   [50] Avitus, *Ep.* 51. On the relationship, Mathisen (1981) 97–100.

[51] On the relationship, Mathisen (1981) 101–3; Stroheker (1948) 209–10.

the association was treasured: he was *Sollius noster*,[52] suggesting that distant kin could be worth cultivating, if they were of high enough status or repute. This is not to say that Ruricius or Avitus were mercenary in their family affections. Avitus supported Sidonius' son Apollinaris, in so far as support was possible, given that they lived in mutually hostile kingdoms.[53] The dismemberment of the western empire and the division of Gaul into rival states during the late fifth and early sixth century could present very considerable problems for those wishing to maintain family ties and old friendships across new borders: the creation of frontiers within the old empire brought with it a heightening of suspicion and the possibility of treason accusations – as can be seen not just from the problems faced by Avitus and Apollinaris, but also by Caesarius in their own generation[54] and Sidonius Apollinaris a generation earlier.[55]

Ruricius' correspondence does not record such problems. His attachments are at their most apparent in his letters written to Namatius and Ceraunia, the parents of his daughter-in-law, after the girl's death. Here the bishop of Limoges reveals depths of emotion not always apparent in his often over-literary writings.[56] His lament for the deceased shows something of his attitude towards the next generation of the family: she was 'a solace of life, hope for the future, ornament of the family, joy of the heart, light of the eyes'. Nor did the family connection end with the girl's death; Ruricius continued to correspond with both Ceraunia and Namatius, separately as well as together.[57] Ennodius of Pavia showed a similar concern with the next generation. He took a considerable interest in his nephews. He was concerned about his sister Euprepia, and her son Lupicinus, after the death of Euprepia's husband.[58] Following the death of another sister, he took it upon himself to ensure that her child, Parthenius, had a good education, recommending him to the great rhetor Deuterius at Rome.[59] In so doing, Ennodius also provides us with precious information on the survival of schooling in Rome through to the beginning of the sixth century – evidence which is complemented for Gaul by Ruricius' references to the education of the children of his circle at the hands of the rhetor Hesperius,[60] but which contrasts with the home-based education which Sidonius had given to Apollinaris for at least a part of his upbringing.[61] Ennodius unquestionably had his eye on future generations of his family. As a childless cleric he obviously had to look beyond his own immediate descent group; more specifically he was active on behalf of his sisters' children: once again, his actions were those of maternal kin.

---

[52] Ruricius, *Ep.* 2.26.   [53] Avitus, *Epp.* 24, 36, 51, 52.
[54] *Vita Caesarii* 1.21, ed. B. Krusch, *MGH, SRM* 3.   [55] Sid. Ap. *Ep.* 9.3.1; 9.5.1.
[56] Ruricius, *Ep.* 2.4.   [57] Ruricius, *Epp.* 2.5, 15, 50, 62.   [58] Ennodius lxxxiv.
[59] Ennodius xciv, ccxxv, cclviii, ccclxix. On the intellectual world of Ennodius see also Kirkby (1981).   [60] Ruricius, *Epp.* 1.3–5.   [61] Sid. Ap. *Ep.* 4.12.1.

Apart from the letters addressed to Sidonius' son, the now fragmentary letter collection of Avitus also includes letters to his own brother, another Apollinaris.[62] Clearly the two brothers were extremely close. Equally close was the relationship between the two brothers and at least one of their two sisters, even though no correspondence of Avitus to any one of his female kin survives. In a remarkable letter Apollinaris describes to his brother a nightmare, in which a blood-red dove appeared to him, something he experienced after he had forgotten to commemorate the death-date of one of their sisters.[63] It is a letter which is paralleled by an equally arresting letter of Ennodius of Pavia, who saw a ghost of his relative Cynegia, which reprimanded him for not composing an epitaph for her tomb, an omission he instantly remedied.[64] The vision and the ghostly visitation suggest that, among the senatorial aristocracy, the relationship between the family and its members drew on much that lay beyond the terms of reference of the New Testament. Two Christian bishops of the early sixth century were overcome with guilt in the face of manifestations of their dead relatives. Their reactions seem to draw on pagan assumptions about ancestral spirits; Sidonius' anger at the desecration of his grandfather's grave might reasonably be placed in the same context.[65]

The absence or near-absence of letters addressed to women in the letter collections of Sidonius, Avitus and to a lesser extent Ruricius is worth noting – though its significance is by no means apparent: letters, after all, are only likely to cast light on the relationships of those living some distance apart. Clearly, women were not insignificant to Sidonius, Avitus or Ruricius. Ruricius' circle of female correspondents is slightly wider than those of the other two, though not greatly so. Ceraunia he wrote to jointly with her husband Namatius[66] and separately as a would-be ascetic.[67] He wrote to two other husband-and-wife teams, Eudomius and Melanthia,[68] and Parthenius and Papianilla.[69] By contrast, Ennodius corresponded with a number of women, as well as his sisters. This comparative absence of female correspondents in the collections of Sidonius, Avitus and Ruricius is highlighted not only by the greater number of female recipients of the writings of Ennodius, but also by the clear importance of women among the recipients of the poems of Venantius Fortunatus. In Avitus' works the absence is, however, compensated for by one of the great expressions of family piety, the epic poem the *Consolatoria de castitatis laude*, which is nothing more nor less that an exploration of the history of virginity among the bishop's female relatives.[70] Moreover, these virgins were, in the eyes of the bishop, the outstanding saints of the family, easily eclipsing the virtues of their male counterparts.

---

[62] Avitus, *Epp.* 13, 14, 27, 61, 71, 72, 87, 88. [63] Avitus, *Ep.* 13; see also 14; Wood (1996).
[64] Ennodius ccclxi, ccclxii; Wood (1996). [65] Sid. Ap. *Ep.* 3.12. [66] Ruricius, *Epp.* 2.1, 2, 3, 4.
[67] Ruricius, *Epp.* 2.15, 50. [68] Ruricius, *Ep.* 2.39. [69] Ruricius, *Ep.* 2.37.
[70] Avitus, *Carm.* VI.

Through a remarkable religious inversion, virginity, not fecundity, has become the salvation of the family. Indeed, it may be symptomatic of Avitus' perspective that we know nothing of one sister who may have had children.[71]

Avitus' poem is not only remarkable for the light it sheds on the bishop's family, but also for what it implies about the origins of what have been called *Adelsheiliger*, aristocratic saints. The *Adelsheiliger* are often associated with the Germanic aristocracy of the late Merovingian and Carolingian periods.[72] The origins of a concern with saintly relatives must, however, long antedate this. The *Consolatoria de castitatis laude* constitutes the most remarkable hymn to sanctity among the members of a late Roman family. Moreover, in his concern to commemorate the death-date of his sister, Apollinaris was intent on celebrating a date which could easily have developed into a saint's festival.[73] Nor does Avitus provide the earliest example of family interest in holy relatives. Sidonius had already noted the importance of Frontina to Aper's family.[74]

The writings of Gregory of Tours throw complementary light on the phenomenon of family saints among the aristocracy in the mid to late sixth century, illuminating the issue through narrative. Not only could Gregory boast relationship with seventeen previous bishops of Tours,[75] he could also claim descent from one of the Lyons martyrs of 177,[76] and he portrayed as saints his great-grandfather, Gregory of Langres,[77] as well as two uncles, Gallus of Clermont[78] and Nicetius of Lyons.[79] Although he is careful to avoid too bald a statement of his relationship with the saints of his family, it is clear that for Gregory the sanctity of his kin was a matter of considerable pride and importance.[80] Few Germanic families of the eighth or ninth century could boast as many saints as could that of Gregory of Tours. From the seventh century, only the hagiography relating to Gertrude of Nivelles seems concerned with the notion of a family saint.[81] For the seventh-century Pippinids and their descendents, the eighth-century Carolingians, Gertrude had a significance not unlike that of the female relatives of Avitus of Vienne. In short, the *Adelsheiliger*, aristocratic saints, were a development of late Roman family piety – perhaps more specifically of the piety of the Christian aristocracy of sub-Roman Gaul. They were not, in origin, Germanic.

In its development of the notion of *Adelsheiliger*, the Merovingian aristocracy of the seventh and eighth century seems to have drawn on traditions

---

[71] Avitus, *Carm.* VI lines 19–23 refers to the four children of Audentia: three of them, Avitus, Apollinaris and Fuscina, are well evidenced in Avitus' works.   [72] Graus (1965); Prinz (1967).

[73] Fuscina was indeed remembered as a saint: *Vita Fuscinulae*, ed. *Catalogus codicum hagiographicorum latinorum in Bibliotheca Nationali Parisiensi* III (Brussels 1893) 563–5.   [74] Sid. Ap. *Ep.* 4.21.4.

[75] Greg. Tur. *Hist.* V.49; Mathisen (1984).   [76] Greg. Tur. *Hist.* 1.29.31; *Liber Vitae Patrum* VI 1.

[77] Greg. Tur. *Liber Vitae Patrum* VII.   [78] Greg. Tur. *Liber Vitae Patrum* VI.

[79] Greg. Tur. *Liber Vitae Patrum* VIII.   [80] Wood (1994) 36–46.

[81] *Vita Geretrudis*, ed. B. Krusch, *MGH, SRM* 2 (Hanover 1888).

already established by the senatorial aristocracy of fifth- and sixth-century Gaul. In other respects, too, the Germanic family shared much with its Roman counterparts. At the highest of social levels Germanic and Roman families even intermarried, despite imperial legislation to the contrary.[82] The starting-point for an investigation of the Germanic family, however, must be the codes of the early Germanic kingdoms. At least four of these antedate the mid sixth century, among them the Frankish *Pactus Legis Salicae*, whose first recension seems to have originated in the years prior to 507,[83] and the *Liber Constitutionum* of the Burgundians, issued in 517.[84] The codes themselves are deeply influenced by Roman law,[85] but on the other hand there is no reason to believe that the picture given of the Germanic family is anything other than accurate. In general, the laws define a system of kinship dominated by men and by paternal kin, but not exclusively so – to see the system as agnatic does not reflect the full range of the evidence, which implies a cognatic pattern of kinship, and often the dominance of the nuclear family.[86] Certainly, within the Frankish context there was a type of land defined as Salic land, which could only be inherited by males.[87] There were, however, other types of property, including land, which could be inherited by females.[88] Further, the special status of Salic land was removed by Chilperic I in the second half of the sixth century.[89] It is, in fact, likely that this land was not of a type traditional among Germanic peoples, but was rather land which was in origin associated with the military arrangements of the later Roman empire, and thus necessarily confined to males.[90]

Inheritance patterns, even among the Franks, do not, therefore, imply a simple patrilineal society. Early-sixth-century Germanic legislation relating to sexual intercourse, on the other hand, suggests rather more indulgence towards male than towards female sexuality. For a Frankish male to have sex with his own female servant was apparently not frowned upon, although sex with someone else's female servant incurred a hefty fine,[91] and a man who married the female slave of another was supposed to be reduced to servitude.[92] Even the status of the offspring of a king could be questioned if the mother was a slave. When Guntram had a son by the slave girl Marcatrude, Sagittarius, bishop of Gap, perhaps following Roman rather than Frankish law, seems to have claimed that the child was the property of the girl's master.[93] Not that Roman and Germanic law necessarily differed greatly over the issue of intercourse between slaves and free. Constantine ordered a free woman cohabiting with a slave to be executed

[82] Demandt (1989) 76–80 for the contrary legislation of *C.Th.* III.14.1 and its Germanic derivatives.
[83] Wood, *Merovingian Kingdoms* 108–13.
[84] Wood (1986) 10; the two other codes are the Code of Euric and the *Edictum Theodorici*.
[85] Wormald (1977). [86] Murray (1983); see also Ausenda (1995).
[87] *PLS* 59, 6, ed. Eckhardt (1962). [88] *PLS* 59, 1–5. [89] *PLS* 108. [90] Anderson (1995).
[91] *PLS* 35, 1–2. [92] *PLS* 13, 9.
[93] Greg. Tur. *Hist.* V.20; *C.Th.* IV.6.3; IV.6.7; IV.8.7: XII.19.1; see also *PLS* 13, 9.

and her partner burnt.[94] In both the Frankish and the Burgundian kingdoms intercourse between a male slave and a free woman was also regarded
as heinous: among the Burgundians, if the woman had not consented to
having sex, the slave was to be killed; if she did consent, both were to die.[95]

In most instances, but not in all, the woman was less free in sexual
matters than the male. This does not mean, however, that women were less
important to the family line than were males. Indeed, one might argue that
the need for them to confine their sexual activity only emphasizes their centrality to the family and the descent group, which depended upon their
sexual purity. This is clear from the importance accorded to virginity at the
time of marriage, and from the *morgengab* owed by the husband to his wife
on taking that virginity.[96] It is also clear from the value placed on nubile and
pregnant women in the law codes.[97] It is clearest of all in the alarm caused
by the circulation of slurs directed against the virtue of Chilperic I's queen,
Fredegund, slurs which necessarily called into question the legitimacy of
the king's heirs.[98] From a legal point of view, women were thought of primarily as wives and mothers.[99] Among the Burgundians, a woman who left
her husband, apparently as an act of divorce, was smothered in mire.[100] In
the seventh century, however, women of the Merovingian kingdom had a
little more say than is apparent in the early law codes. Legal formulae, many
of which were based on Roman law but which seem to have served generally as models for regional communities within the Romanized areas of the
Frankish kingdom, recognized the possibility of divorce by mutual
consent.[101] Also in the early seventh century, Chlothar II explicitly
acknowledged that a woman might refuse to marry if she desired to follow
the religious life.[102] In certain limited respects Germanic women had
gained some of the rights of their male counterparts.

At the highest level of Germanic society the queen was always a figure
of considerable importance, and not simply as the recipient of the sperm
of the royal male. On a number of occasions in the late sixth and seventh
century the person of the queen seems to have been crucial to the succession: this can be argued for Goiswinth among the Visigoths,[103] Gundiperga
among the Lombards[104] and Bilichildis among the Franks.[105] Nor was it

---

[94] *C.Th.* IX.9.1; see also IV.12.1, 3–7 where the woman is enslaved.
[95] *PLS* 13, 7–8; *Liber Constitutionum* xxxv, 1–2, ed. L. R. de Salis, *Leges Burgundionum, MGH, Leges* 2
(1) (Hanover 1892). It seems that this legislation was expected to apply to the whole population of the
kingdom, both Germanic and Roman: Wood (1986) 11.
[96] *PLS* 13, 14; *Liber Constitutionum* xxiv, 1.   [97] *PLS* 67 e.   [98] Wood (1993b) 257–9.
[99] For a general exploration of these issues see Stafford (1983); Wood, *Merovingian Kingdoms* 120–39.
[100] *Liber Constitutionum* xxxiv, 1.
[101] Marculf, *Formulae* II.30, ed. K. Zeumer, *MGH, Formulae Merowingici et Karolini Aevi* (Hanover 1886);
Formulae Turonenses 19, ed. Zeumer.
[102] Chlothar II, *Edictum* 18, ed. A. Boretius, *MGH, Capitularia Regum Francorum* 1 (Hanover 1883).
[103] Nelson (1991) 469.   [104] Fredegar, IV.50, 51, 70, ed. B. Krusch, *MGH, SRM* 2 (Hanover 1888).
[105] Wood, *Merovingian Kingdoms* 223.

only at the royal level that descent could be seen in female terms. In the early eighth century, bishop Hugo of Rouen, although the son of a Pippinid male, was remembered as the descendant of his maternal grandmother, Anstrude.[106] Nevertheless, a queen's power depended largely on her association with a living king, whether as wife or as mother – it was this association which provided her with her opportunities. When her husband died, or her son ceased to be dependent on her, she was very nearly powerless. The importance of royal or aristocratic women was not, however, simply biological. Much of a queen's influence was related to her control of the royal household, as well as her role in the provision of a king's heirs;[107] in short, she was responsible for the continuity of the royal family and for its possessions. Traditionally, at least, women were also thought of as the guardians of the family's status in another sense: they are often depicted as the forces driving men towards the blood-feud, whether or not this was actually the case.[108] By contrast, they could help to preserve the peace through the role they played in marriage alliances.[109] As we have seen, they would also come to play a substantial role in another aspect of family status, its holiness.

While the significance of women within the family was rather more than might seem implied by certain laws, the position of men was rather more constrained than might be assumed. Essentially what was at issue was the protection of family and household units. These were not challenged when a man had sex with his own slaves, but they were in almost every other sexual act outside the marriage bed. Legislation against adultery was, therefore, ferocious: in the Burgundian kingdom adulterers caught in the act were to be killed;[110] among the Franks rape of a betrothed girl elicited a heavy fine,[111] while the adulterous association of a man and a woman whose husband was still living was treated on a par with murder, and also incurred a heavy financial composition.[112] In other words, the law championed the family rather than any individual – male or female – within it.

This did not, however, limit the sexual unions of the early Merovingians. The main point of doubt is whether the Frankish royal family practised serial monogamy, polygamy or concubinage. This in its turn is linked to the question of whether the Merovingians made a distinction between marriage and informal liaisons. Some kings, like Sigibert I,[113] seem to have taken marriage very seriously. Others went in for a succession of liaisons, and this had an impact on the question of inheritance. Could the offspring

---

[106] *Ibid.* 261.   [107] Stafford (1983) 93–114, 143–65.

[108] E.g. Greg. Tur. *Hist.* III.6; see Wood, *Merovingian Kingdoms* 43.

[109] For Theoderic's marriage alliances, Procop.*Wars* V.12.21–2, ed. and trans. H. B. Dewing (London 1914–28); *Anon. Valesianus* 11.63, 68, 70, ed. J. Moreau, *Excerpta Valesiana* (Leipzig 1961); Jord. *Get.* 58 (297–9), ed. T. Mommsen, *MGH, AA* 5 (Berlin 1882).

[110] *Liber Constitutionum* lxviii, 1; compare *Liber Constitutionum* xliv.   [111] *PLS* 13, 14.

[112] *PLS* 15, 1.   [113] Greg. Tur. *Hist.* IV.27.

of a king and a slave girl be regarded as royal? Gregory of Tours appears to have thought so, but Sagittarius disagreed – and he certainly had the law on his side.[114] Not all kings, however, wanted to acknowledge their offspring: Chlothar I denied, probably falsely, that he was the father of Gundovald.[115]

A mere glance at the royal genealogy reveals that a string of liaisons with women of all classes was the norm for most Merovingian kings. They indulged in nothing like the social snobbery of the Gallo-Roman aristocracy. Among the wives of the sixth-century Merovingians were foreign princesses[116] and the daughters of a wool carder.[117] In the case of Theudebert I, he associated with Deuteria, despite the fact that she was already the wife of a Gallo-Roman aristocrat. Although he was persuaded to set her aside for a while, it was ultimately her decision to arrange the death of her own daughter, who she thought might prove too appealing to the king's eye, that finally ended the relationship.[118]

There is little to suggest that Tacitus' view of the sexual purity of the early Germans held true in the sixth century, despite the savagery of the laws against divorce and against the intercourse of woman and slave. Although the Franks, or more particularly the kings of the Franks, provide the worst examples of excess, there are examples from other classes and other peoples as well. Among the most interesting cases is one recorded in the *Liber Constitutionum* of the Burgundians, concerning Aunegild and Balthamod.[119] Aunegild, a widow, was betrothed with the consent of her parents to the king's sword-bearer, Fredegisil, but, even after receiving her bride-price, she fell for Balthamod and regularly had intercourse with him. The crime was thought worthy of death, but since the case was judged at Easter – the very Easter court of 517 at which the *Liber Constitutionum* of the Burgundians was issued – leniency was granted, and Aunegild had to pay her blood-price to Fredegisil, while Balthamod had equally to pay his *wergild* unless he could prove that he was unaware that the woman was already betrothed. Not that such behaviour should be seen as the preserve of the Germanic peoples. In his *Histories* Gregory of Tours records the long, and not very salubrious, story of a Gallo-Roman pair, Eulalius and Tetradia – a story which involved adultery, elopement and finally murder.[120]

For all this, there are examples of very genuine affection within the families of the Germanic kings of the late fifth and early sixth century. Both Avitus of Vienne and Remigius of Rheims had occasion to write letters of condolence to their respective rulers. Avitus addressed the Burgundian king, Gundobad, in somewhat brutal terms, insisting that his daughter was

---

[114] Greg. Tur. *Hist.* v.20.   [115] Greg. Tur. *Hist.* vi.24; Wood (1993b) 264; Bachrach (1994) 6–8.
[116] For Chlothild, Galswinth, Brunhild, see Greg. Tur. *Hist.* ii.28; iv.27–8.
[117] Greg. Tur. *Hist.* iv.26.   [118] Greg. Tur. *Hist.* iii.26.   [119] *Liber Constitutionum* lii.
[120] Greg. Tur. *Hist.* x.8.

destined for heaven, whilst brusquely telling the king to turn his mind back to the matter of government.[121] So, too, Remigius counselled the Frankish king, Clovis, against excessive grief following the death of a sister, and reminded him of the necessity of ruling.[122] Perhaps unexpectedly, Germanic kings of the migration period were genuinely overcome with grief at the loss of close female relatives. Nor is it only the grief of kings about their womenfolk that is recorded in the sources: Radegund's sorrow at the death of her cousin, Amalfred, in far-away Byzantium is preserved in a poem of Venantius Fortunatus,[123] while Brunhild's concerns for her daughter, Ingund, and her grandson, Athanagild, who also died in Byzantine territory, are the subject of numerous letters.[124]

Clovis' concern for his family involved more than his immediate kin – though it did not extend to distant cousins.[125] His attitude towards his ancestors seems to have been a factor in his initial unwillingness to convert to Catholicism. Avitus of Vienne congratulated him on abandoning their beliefs.[126] The bishop's positive comments suggest that Clovis had reservations about abandoning his predecessors much as Radbod, king of the Frisians, is said to have done in the eighth century: on hearing that they would remain in hell while he would be welcomed to heaven, Radbod opted for their company, according to a somewhat picaresque story, which cannot be historically accurate in its current form, but which may reflect a genuine dilemma for Germanic peoples on the verge of Christianity.[127] Oddly enough, having abandoned the religion of his father, Childeric, Clovis and his successors seem quickly to have forgotten the exact whereabouts of Childeric's grave[128] – which contrasts rather sharply with Sidonius' concern for the burial place of his grandfather. It is all the more remarkable in that feasts at the graves of the dead were a continuing problem for those intent on the Christianization of the Germanic peoples – suggesting that the grave and continuing rituals associated with it were a central focus even for the non-aristocratic family.[129]

Comparison between the Roman and the Germanic family, at least at the highest level of society, does not suggest a simple contrast between complex Roman structures and clear-cut, agnatic, Germanic structures. This is true even if one considers a practice supposedly central to the kin-based structures of Germanic society and, one might assume, absent from a society ordered by the rational processes of Roman law: the feud. The feud could be, as has long been recognized, a force for order rather than

---

[121] Avitus, *Ep.* 5.   [122] *Epist. Austras.* 1, ed. W. Gundlach, *MGH, Epistolae* 3 (Berlin 1892).

[123] Venantius Fortunatus, *Carm.* Ad Artachin (Appendix iii).

[124] *Epist. Austras.* 27, 28, 43, 44, 45.   [125] Greg. Tur. *Hist.* 11.42.   [126] Avitus, *Ep.* 46.

[127] *Vita Vulframni* 9, ed. W. Levison, *MGH, SRM* 5 (Hanover 1910); Lebecq (1994).

[128] Wood, *Merovingian Kingdoms* 44. The fact that a church of St Brice was later built in the neighbourhood may, however, indicate that some tradition of Merovingian association with the cemetery remained.   [129] *Concilium Germanicum* 5, ed. A. Werminghoff, *MGH, Concilia* 2 (Hanover 1906–8).

for chaos. It was in the interests of the kin-group not to lay itself open to the possibility of retaliation for killing, and therefore to encourage and support an offer of financial compensation.[130] Perhaps the relative absence of stories relating to the feud are an indication of the success of the mere threat of retaliation. On the other hand, those examples of feud known from the fifth and sixth century do not suggest that the feud, when it did break out, was prosecuted on a vast scale, involving a widespread kin-group.

The two most eye-catching feuds of the sixth century may not have been feuds at all. The idea that the Frankish destruction of the Burgundian kingdom in the 520s and 530s resulted entirely from a deep-seated grudge held by queen Chlothild against her cousin Sigismund and, more particularly, her uncle Gundobad, whom she blamed for her father's death, is an idea which is scarcely sustained by events, even though the interpretation was first set out in the early Middle Ages.[131] Nor is there any early evidence for thinking that much of the political unrest of the second half of the sixth century resulted from queen Brunhild's desire to avenge herself on Chilperic, who had murdered her sister Galswinth, in order to return to his liaison with Fredegund.[132] Both these interpretations may have more to do with the gradual recasting of history as epic than with the realities of sixth-century politics.

There are, however, two very much more squalid tales which might be seen as illustrative of the reality of the blood-feud. The better-known of them is that of Chramnesind and Sichar. In fact, Chramnesind's family was not involved in the earliest stages of the conflict, which began with the murder by an unnamed man of the servant of a friend of Sichar. When Sichar attempted to take vengeance, he was met by Austregisl, who killed four of his servants. At this point the case went to law and Austregisl had to hand over for safe-keeping the gold and silver taken in the course of the conflict. It was only at this stage that Chramnesind's family became involved, and in the first instance merely as safe-keepers of the gold. Sichar, however, was determined to get the treasure back before the case went to court, and did so, killing the father, uncle and brother of Chramnesind in the process. Gregory of Tours, as the local bishop, then intervened with offers of compensation, which Chramnesind rejected, until a further attempt had been made on Sichar's life and more of his servants had been killed. Thereafter Sichar and Chramnesind became friends. It was not until Sichar, in his cups, insulted Chramnesind, by pointing out how much his friend had gained financially out of his father's murder, that the latter felt obliged to take revenge.[133] This is no clear-cut feud, with well-defined

[130] Wallace-Hadrill (1962) 125–6.   [131] Wood, *Merovingian Kingdoms* 43.   [132] *Ibid.* 127.
[133] Greg. Tur. *Hist.* VII.47; IX.19.

groups of kin lined up on either side. Such feuding as there is is inextricable from the failed attempts to deal with the conflict through the normal process of the courts. Innocent bystanders get dragged into the mayhem, and the most numerous casualties are the servants, whom even Gregory of Tours seems to have seen as expendable. In the final stages it is a tale of compensation, drunkenness and hurt pride.

There is a second story which might equally have been cast as a tale of feud. The archdeacon of Langres, Peter, was thought to have been responsible for the death of the bishop-elect of the diocese, Tetricus. As a result, Tetricus' son, Silvester, murdered the archdeacon.[134] This second story is never described as a story of feud, for it concerns Gallo-Romans: Peter was the brother of Gregory of Tours; moreover, the conflict was confined to a single kin-group, for both Silvester and Peter were relatives of Tetricus. It is, nevertheless, a story of kinship-based vengeance. Indeed, conflicts were as likely to take place within kin-groups as between hostile families, as can be seen easily enough from the history of the Merovingians themselves. By the mid sixth century the family-orientated behaviour of the Gallo-Romans was not necessarily different from that of their Germanic counterparts.[135]

However different Frankish and Gallo-Roman family structures may once have been, they were increasingly bound by the same law. Incest legislation, in particular, affected both groups equally. As defined by secular sources, incest could include marriage to a distant cousin[136] or even to 'consanguineous relatives' *tout court*.[137] By the end of the sixth century the punishment for such a marriage was death. It was not only secular legislation, however, which impinged. The church canons, and more particularly the canons of councils held within the Burgundian and Frankish kingdoms, dealt regularly with incest.[138] In this the Gallic church was strikingly more determined than other churches of the period.

The legislation scarcely had any impact on the Merovingian family itself. In our narrative sources, which cover the highest levels of society, incest is rarely identified as a problem: there is only one case of marriage between cousins in the Merovingian kingdom, and that took place in the mid seventh century for political reasons.[139] The liaisons of Chlothar I first with Ingund and then, concomitantly, with her sister, Aregund, ought to have been branded as incest, but if they were, the condemnation scarcely

---

[134] Greg. Tur. *Hist.* v.5.

[135] For comments on the absence of real distinction between the civilized and the uncivilized, Goffart (1988) 212.   [136] *PLS* 13 6, 11.

[137] *PLS, capitulare* 6, 1, 2; compare *Liber Constitutionum* xxxvi.

[138] Orleans (511) c. 18; Epaon (517) c. 30; Lyons (518–23) c. 1; Orleans (533) c. 10; Clermont (535) c. 12; Orleans (538) c. 11; Paris (556–73) c. 4; Auxerre (561–605) c. 27–32; Tours (567) c. 22; Mâcon (581–3) c. 11; Lyons (583) c. 4; Mâcon (585) c. 18; Paris (614) c. 16; Clichy (626–7) c. 10, ed. C. de Clercq, *Concilia Galliae A.511–A.695, CCSL* 148A (Turnhout 1963).   [139] Wood, *Merovingian Kingdoms* 223.

affected that uxorious monarch.[140] The one case of incest which caused a religious and political crisis was the marriage of Stephanus to Palladia, the sister of his dead wife, shortly after 518. Stephanus, who was presumably a Gallo-Roman, was the treasurer of the Burgundian king Sigismund, whose decision to support his treasurer led to a withdrawal of co-operation from his bishops.[141] It may be significant that the case followed shortly after the council of Epaon, the council which saw the first detailed legislation against incest.[142]

Although it was a Gallo-Roman official who fell foul of this legislation at the council of Lyons, it is likely to have been at the lowest end of the social scale that the canons caused most difficulties. The upper classes of late and sub-Roman Gaul had contacts over a wide region, and marriage outside their immediate kin can have presented few problems. Among the lower orders of society, marriage outside a confined geographical area or social group would have been almost impossible – it may well not have been desirable, if families wanted to keep the few possessions they had within a closed circle. As a result, they are likely to have been affected by incest legislation more consistently than their masters.[143] In the course of the early Middle Ages, the church defined and redefined what constituted the prohibited degrees of marriage. Whether one accepts that this was part of a deliberate policy developed by the church[144] or whether one sees it as a rather less calculated attempt to define marital purity, the net result is likely to have made legal marriage in small communities more and more difficult.

The chief division in family practice in the fifth and sixth century is, therefore, less likely to have lain between Roman and Germanic – despite all the individual quirks of the senatorial aristocracy or of the Merovingians – than between the relatively closed worlds of village or peasant life and the very much more open world of royalty and the aristocracy. The peasantry had limited geographical horizons and a very small array of strategies for preserving their land and property. At the upper level of society the horizons were much wider, and the strategies available more numerous.

In considering the family of the monarch and the aristocracy it would be wrong to concentrate solely on the bonds of marriage. The *familia* included the whole household, and it also spilt over into the world of clientship. In the Roman world the *clientela* of an aristocrat was central to his status. Because the carrying of arms was legally restricted before the fifth century, this *clientela* was necessarily civilian. The practice of civilian patronage continued throughout the fifth and sixth century – Ruricius and other members of his circle made great play of addressing those of their fellows

---

[140] Greg. Tur. *Hist.* IV.3.   [141] Council of Lyons (518–23) c. 1.
[142] Epaon (517) c. 30. It should be noted that Agde (506) c. 61 was thought by Munier to be an interpolation, *CCSL* 148.   [143] Rouche (1987) 470–1.   [144] Goody (1983) 134–46.

who had helped them in any way as *patronus*,[145] and it can be seen more seriously in the letters of recommendation written by Sidonius[146] and Avitus.[147] Bishops played an increasingly important role as patrons in the fifth and sixth century.[148] The career of Venantius Fortunatus in the mid sixth century depended on patronage: it was for his patrons that he, as a foreigner without personal status and with no kin to protect him, wrote the majority of his earlier poems.[149] Such support might easily have been exercised by the senatorial aristocracy of the fourth century.

In other respects patterns of patronage changed in the fifth and sixth century, most notably with the militarization of society. It would have been legally impossible for a Roman aristocrat of the fourth century to have gathered the private following which Sidonius' brother-in-law Ecdicius put together to relieve the Visigothic siege of Clermont, even if it numbered only eighteen men.[150] Such a force must have been raised from tenants on Ecdicius' own estates and from others indebted to him in one way or another. The private followings of such Gallo-Romans as Mummolus who feature in the pages of Gregory of Tours[151] must likewise have been composed of clients of one sort or another. Nor is it possible to distinguish between the military following of a Gallo-Roman like Mummolus and that of a Frank like Rauching.[152] In part, this is a question of evidence: no detail survives to help us understand the recruitment of private armies. Precious little, indeed, survives to illuminate the recruitment of the personal following of a king, his *antrustiones*, though the Frankish king Theudebert I is seen offering money to potential followers after the death of his father, Theuderic I, in 533.[153] Despite the lacunae in our evidence it is not difficult to see in these developments parallels between the exclusively civilian bonds of clientship of the Roman period and the military bonds of *fidelitas* of later periods.

Clientship evolved in the face of the military changes which beset the west during the fifth and sixth century. Patronal relations were also affected by religious developments, and not just at the etherial level of the relationship between a patron saint and his congregation.[154] In the course of the sixth century baptismal sponsors appear in our narrative sources. Gregory of Tours forgave Eberulf because he was godfather to the man's son.[155] Guntram Boso sought protection from bishop Ageric of Verdun, thinking that he had special influence as godfather to the king.[156] Queen Brunhild offered clemency to Berthefred on the grounds that she was his daughter's godmother.[157] In 613 Chlothar II spared his godson Merovech, while killing

[145] See for example Ruricius *Epp.* 1.1, 2, 7, 8, 9, etc. See also Faustus, *Epp.* 7, 8, 14, ed. B. Krusch, *MGH, AA* 8. [146] E.g. Sid. Ap. *Ep.* 6.4. [147] Avitus, *Ep.* 11. [148] Mathisen (1993) 93–7. [149] George (1992) 22–34. [150] Sid. Ap. *Ep.* 3.3, 3. [151] Greg. Tur. *Hist.* VII.38. [152] Greg. Tur. *Hist.* VIII.26. [153] Greg. Tur. *Hist.* III.23. [154] E.g. Brown (1996) 64. [155] Greg. Tur. *Hist.* VII.22. [156] Greg. Tur. *Hist.* IX.8. [157] Greg. Tur. *Hist.* IX.9.

the boy's brothers.[158] In seventh-century England baptismal sponsorship came to play a very significant role in power politics.[159] In sixth-century Francia it had not been so fully exploited, but Guntram made a point of standing as baptismal sponsor to his nephew, Chlothar II.[160] Baptismal relationships, however, were not always open to manipulation, for increasingly in the eighth century they were subjected to the laws of incest, alongside relationships determined by blood or marriage.[161]

Parallel to patronage, which was the bond between those of unequal status, there was friendship, essentially the bond between those of equal status. The one could draw on the ideology of the other, as in the description of a long-established friend as *patronus*. The majority of our evidence for late Roman and for early medieval friendship comes, as does our evidence for affection within the family group, from the letter collections of the period. The letters of Symmachus provide one model for the understanding of friendship in the fourth century;[162] those of Sidonius, Ruricius, Avitus and Ennodius are models for the late fifth and early sixth century.[163] As a pagan, Symmachus' approach to friendship was necessarily, if only subtly, different from that of the Christian letter-writers. Central here was the use of the term *caritas*, with its Christian resonance, alongside the traditional *amicitia*. Perhaps especially significant in the evolution of this Christian friendship was Paulinus of Nola.[164]

The Christianization of friendship, however, went deeper than the introduction of a Christian vocabulary. Friendship depended on the meeting, or even joining, of two souls,[165] and the soul was definitely within the field of theological speculation. The most sophisticated theological debate to have taken place in Gaul in the fifth century concerned the nature of the soul. An anonymous letter, actually written by Faustus of Riez, argued for the soul's corporeality.[166] Sidonius Apollinaris, not realizing that the letter was by his old mentor Faustus, asked Claudianus Mamertus, brother of the bishop of Vienne, to consider the argument:[167] Claudianus replied with the *De statu animae*, arguing for the incorporeality of the soul.[168] Although the argument between Faustus and Claudianus is not couched in terms of an exploration of friendship, the question of whether the soul was or was not corporeal necessarily had implications for the contemporary understanding of the working of friendship. In the letters of Avitus and Ruricius, the souls of friends often overcome physical separation in one way or another.[169] It is not,

---

[158] Fredegar IV.42, ed. B. Krusch, *MGH, SRM* 2 (Hanover 1888).
[159] Angenendt (1986); more generally, Angenendt (1984).   [160] Greg. Tur. *Hist.* VIII.9; X.28.
[161] Lynch (1986) 219–57.   [162] Matthews (1974).   [163] Wood (1993a).
[164] Fabre (1949); see also White (1992) 146–63.   [165] See for example Ruricius, *Epp.* 1.1; 2.10, 52.
[166] Faustus, *Ep.* 20.
[167] Sid. Ap. *Ep.* 4.2; Claudianus Mamertus, *De Statu Animae, praef.*, ed. A. Engelbrecht, *CSEL* XI (Vienna 1885).   [168] On the debate, Fortin (1959).
[169] E.g. Ruricius, *Epp.* 1.6, 9, 10, 18; 2.1, 2, 3, 4, 10, 32, 52; Avitus, *Epp.* 50, 52, 77, 78, 79, 93.

therefore, surprising that this, the most original theological debate of fifth-century Gaul, should have emerged from the literary circle of Sidonius – both Faustus and Claudianus were his correspondents – which throve on the exercise of friendship, expressed through the medium of letters.

Nor was the debate over the soul the only point where theology and friendship overlapped. Pope Gelasius also drew on notions of friendship when comparing the bonds that bound the orthodox and those that bound the heretics. Between the orthodox the bond of friendship, *amicitia*, could rightly be described as *caritas*; relations with the heretics ought to be relations of hatred, *odium*, for their friendship was like a disease, *contagium*.[170] Friendship was, therefore, not just a pleasurable adjunct to Christian life, but central to it – just as it had been for the senatorial aristocracy of the Roman empire,[171] only now it regularly had a religious colouring.

As in the case of Symmachus and his friends, the exercise of friendship through correspondence continued to be central to the cohesion of a particular class. The cultivation of bonds of friendship was as important as the exploitation of family ties to the survival of the senatorial class of late antique Gaul. In Sidonius' case this can be seen in his careful lobbying of friends during his exile, making sure that he had allies at the court of Euric.[172] Indeed, friendship may well have played a more vital role in the crises of the fifth century than it had done before, since the very survival of a class and a social structure might have been in question. It is not, therefore, surprising that Gallo-Roman letter-writers of the sixth century came to include Germanic magnates, and even kings, among their correspondents. These new arrivals could not be ignored even by the senatorial aristocracy. Already by the early years of the sixth century Avitus of Vienne was in correspondence with Gundobad, and not merely on purely formal issues.[173] He would subsequently correspond on yet more friendly terms with Gundobad's son Sigismund.[174] Remigius of Rheims corresponded with Clovis.[175] Remigius' letters survive in a collection put together in the east Frankish court, probably at the end of the sixth century, and the collection, the *Epistolae Austrasiacae*, may have been used as a manual of model correspondence, as may have been the case also with the letters of Avitus and Ruricius.[176] Among the *Epistolae Austrasiacae* are letters from members of the Germanic aristocracy as well as from Gallo-Roman bishops.[177] Also writing in the late sixth century, Venantius Fortunatus further elaborated the cult of friendship in his verse-letters to his patrons, to Gallo-Roman and Germanic aristocrats, and to members of the royal family. He needed

---

[170] Gelasius, *Ep.* 7, 4, ed. A. Thiel, *Epistolae Romanorum Pontificum Genuinae* (Brunsberg 1868); see also Wood (1993a) 35–6.   [171] Matthews (1974).   [172] Sid. Ap. *Epp.* 4.22; 8.3; 8.9.

[173] Avitus, *Ep.* 5.   [174] Avitus, *Epp.* 23, 31, 32, 45, 49, 76, 77, 79, 91, 92.

[175] *Epist. Austras.* 1–2.   [176] Wood (1993a) 40.

[177] See the letters of the regent Gogo, *Epist. Austras.* 13, 16, 22, 48.

their patronage, but he also gave the cult of friendship a particular twist, through his use of verse, and through his penchant for the word *dulcedo*, which he sometimes used as an alternative to *amicitia* or *caritas*.[178] Moreover, the tradition of *amicitia* exercised through letters continued into the seventh century, down to the correspondence of Desiderius of Cahors, where friendship still provided the cement holding together a peer group, now scattered throughout the Merovingian kingdom, and away from the royal court.[179]

Friendship worked alongside the family and indeed helped to preserve the social influence of the family at the upper ends of society. Its networks came to include the new Germanic aristocracy of the fifth and sixth century, and even royal families. It was part of the process of social amalgamation which took place in the sub-Roman period. On the other hand, this social amalgamation may not have been as major a shift as one might have expected. There were enough points in common between the leading Germanic families and their Gallo-Roman counterparts to facilitate mutual understanding – and despite the senatorial aristocracy's social pretensions, even marriage and other liaisons between the two groups followed. At a royal, and thus in some respects atypical, level, the marriage of Galla Placidia and Athaulf provided an early model,[180] the association of Theudebert and Deuteria a later, more sexually-charged example. For both groups the realities of survival and accommodation were more important than any abstract structure of kinship which may once have provided a norm. At its most revealing the evidence takes the reader into a world of real emotions, whether grief, friendship or simple lust, showing that they could be as important as many of the social traditions which made up the notion of family during the transitional period from empire to successor states.

---

[178] Not that Fortunatus was the first person to use *dulcedo* in this way: see, for example, Ruricius, *Epp.* 1.18; 2.37. See Curtius (1953) 412–13.   [179] Wood (1993a) 42.
[180] For a fuller study of such marriages, Demandt (1989).

CHAPTER 16

STATE, LORDSHIP AND COMMUNITY IN THE WEST (*c.* A.D. 400–600)

PETER HEATHER

This chapter will examine some of the overlapping groups – communities – in which individuals acted for different purposes, and the transformation of these communities, in the period *c.* 400–600. It is focused on the west, because it was here that the greatest changes in our period took place, and where there was least continuity through imperial institutions such as the army and administration. The chapter draws on, and is intended to reflect, recent work on the social history of the early medieval period, and examines both horizontal ties, bonds between relatively equal peer groups, and vertical ties, such as those of patronage and support between lord and follower.[1] It is divided into two parts. The first section focuses on the different sense of community operating at the level of the political centre: the Roman empire as a whole and the kingdoms which succeeded it. The spotlight is then transferred to more local communities. The two types of community are, of course, closely linked. An overall theme of the whole essay, indeed, is that socio-political transformations at the centre had profound effects upon the construction of local community, and vice versa.

I. THE COMMUNITY OF THE REALM

In *c.* 400, western Europe was dominated by the Roman empire. Britain south of Hadrian's Wall, France, the Iberian peninsula, the Benelux countries, Italy and much of Germany and Austria were under its direct rule. Roman power also loomed over the empire's neighbours. By *c.* 600, this European superstate had given way to a series of far from stable successor states: kingdoms built around Franks and Burgundians in France and Benelux, Visigoths and Sueves south of the Pyrenees, Ostrogoths and Lombards in Italy, Anglo-Saxons in southern and eastern Britain. The first half of this essay is concerned with the transformations in political economy which accompanied this fundamental revolution in European history. How did these new kingdoms compare, as states, to their Roman

---

[1] It is also by way of an essay: a first attempt at descriptive analysis rather than an authoritative treatment, which makes no claim to comprehensive knowledge of the relevant literature.

predecessor, and how had they generated political boundaries in the minds of their subjects, where previously there had been none?

1. *Imperial heritage*

In the late Roman empire, central government was exercised from central imperial courts,[2] local government from *civitas* capitals: urban centres controlling dependent rural hinterlands. Situated between court and *civitas* were regional administrative centres – praetorian prefectures, sometimes in their own capitals – and a non-uniform range of assemblies, from provincial level upwards, in which local élites would periodically gather. From *c.* 400, two regional forums had particular importance in the west: the Gallic council in Arles and the Roman senate in Italy.[3]

The fourth century had seen the ever tighter linking of these levels, both formally and informally. Traditionally, cities had been governed by councils of city landowners: decurions or curials. From the third century onwards, however, curials tended to graduate to imperial bureaucratic service, leaving many fewer decurions available to undertake the numerous tasks which the imperial authorities continued to assign to local councils. The new imperial bureaucracy which thus had emerged by *c.* 400 A.D. made Roman emperors powerful on two levels. It gathered and processed information, and wrote legislation, redistributing large amounts of wealth, and making much of the empire operate as some kind of a unity. It was also a patronage machine. By *c.* 400 A.D., around 3,000 very good bureaucratic jobs (those leading to senatorial status) existed in each half of empire, and the total size of the bureaucracy was around 24,000. The system also encompassed long waiting-lists for established posts and ever decreasing lengths of service; both these features maximized the number of jobs available.

Bureaucratic numbers largely increased through consumer demand. In the fourth century, it was increasingly in central government, rather than cities, that money was to be made, and bureaucratic service also brought in its wake senatorial status and a series of other rights and privileges. By 400, these honours defined a class of retired imperial servants – *honorati* – who constituted a new local élite, whose dominance depended precisely on participation in central structures of the empire.[4] The political communities generated around this changing structure were complex. Local pre-eminence demanded that western landowners made efforts to become *honorati*. Those who failed might fall into a second grade of local landowner. The

---

[2] From the time of Valentinian and Valens (364) two imperial courts became the norm: an eastern one at Constantinople, and a western at Trier or Milan, and later Ravenna.

[3] General survey: Jones, *LRE* chs. 11, 19. For a more political treatment, Heather (1998).

[4] In more detail, Heather (1994).

peers of the *honorati* were to be found to some extent among the other families of their *civitas* who had responded to the new challenges, but for the most part at the regional level. Contact between such men might be established during the phase of life spent in imperial service. Above them, there remained a higher élite who dominated the top offices at court, and the successful *honoratus* would seek their patronage.[5]

Local success thus demanded a considerable investment of time and effort in imperial structures. Indeed, the *sine qua non* for entry into the imperial bureaucracy was a traditional classical literary education, which required ten years or more of private schooling with the *grammaticus*.[6] Thus, much of the childhood, let alone the adult life, of even ordinary members of the late Roman élite was shaped by the need to be successful in a political game whose rules were dictated from the centre. Local and regional political communities all the way from Britain to North Africa continued to have great importance, but this is hardly surprising. Much more noteworthy is the fact that there was a real sense in which all Roman landowners, marked out by their specific literary culture, were made at least potentially part of one community by imperial political structures and their accompanying ideologies.[7]

2. *Transformations in political economy*

By A.D. 600, a series of royal courts had replaced one imperial centre. None of the successor kingdoms occupied an area as big as a late Roman prefecture, let alone the western empire as a whole. In former Roman Britain, the political landscape consisted of a host of small kingdoms, British and Anglo-Saxon, many occupying only part of an old Roman *civitas*.[8] In sheer physical distance, therefore, the new states did not face the communications problems of the old empire. On a whole series of other levels, their difficulties were serious and manifold.

Not least, the new states had to establish political boundaries – on the ground and in people's perceptions – where none had previously existed. The new political boundaries did not coincide with Roman regional boundaries, and, in the first instance, surviving Roman landowners maintained contacts across the new frontiers.[9] Indeed, the political élites of the new kingdoms were made up of disparate groups of at least two kinds. The

---

[5] By the fifth century, senators were graded in three ranks: *clarissimi, spectabiles* and *illustres*, in order of seniority. Increasingly, the first two became honorific, with most privileges and active membership of the senate accruing to *illustres* alone: Jones, *LRE* ch. 15. [6] Kaster (1988) esp. chs. 1–2.

[7] Not, of course, that the empire managed to integrate all the élites within its notional borders to the same degree.

[8] On Anglo-Saxon and Celtic Britain, see respectively Bassett (1988) and Dark (1994).

[9] E.g. ch. 15 (Wood), pp. 434–6 above; cf. the letter collections of Ruricius of Limoges and Sidonius Apollinaris.

successor states were actually created by a mixture of military and diplomatic aggression on the part of armed groups of outsiders, labelled Goths, Franks, Burgundians, etc., in our sources. On the other hand, they all also contained large numbers of indigenous Romans, in many cases even members of the former Roman landowning élite, who – close to the Mediterranean, at least – survived imperial collapse in significant numbers.

In traditional historiography, the outsiders were categorized as 'barbarians' (using the Romans' own terms of reference: see below) and seen as ethnically distinct groups (both from each other, and from Romans) whose mind-sets were totally inimical to the Roman way of life. More recently, it has been stressed that most of them had long been in contact with Roman civilization, even if originating in areas beyond the frontier, and that many had graduated to independent statehood of their own via a period in the military service of the empire. The unchanging nature of their identities – previously largely assumed – has also been questioned.[10] There is much to be said for these revisionist points, and their overall implication. The process of state formation involved transformations as much for the incomers as for the inhabitants of the former Roman empire.

There is a danger, however, of losing sight of the revolution that the appearance of these successor states represents. They were born in violence, and while some Romans were ready to accommodate themselves to the new powers in the land, many others resisted with determination.[11] I would also argue that the group or ethnic identities of some of the intruders, even if subject to on-going transformation, were substantial historical phenomena whose nature shaped that of the states they formed. The kingdom-forming Visigoths and Ostrogoths, for instance, were new political units created in the process of migration, but seem to have consisted largely of groups who were already identified by others and by themselves as 'Goths'. They were dominated, indeed, by a numerous – if still minority – élite caste of freemen, who gave them coherence and became – in the first instance, at least – the major military and political force of the new kingdoms. Some of the law codes promulgated in the new kingdoms likewise assign much higher status, measured in terms of *wergild*, to full (i.e. 'free') members of the intruding force than to surviving Romans.[12] Thus, in many cases old mind-sets had to be changed and new patterns of allegiance and political action built up, particularly among élites, if the new kingdoms were to flourish. The task was made more difficult by a series of

[10] The revisionist impulse started in many ways with Wenskus (1961) and continued on the continent in the work of Herwig Wolfram and the Vienna school around him. A more radical approach from a different direction can be found in e.g. Goffart (1981), (1989) and *Barbarians and Romans* esp. ch. 1 and conclusion.   [11] Heather (1995a).

[12] Goths: Heather (1996) esp. ch. 10; cf. Heather (1995b). *Lex Salica* and Ine's Law both assign surviving natives *wergilds* one-half of those of the now dominant intruders.

transformations which shifted the balance of power between centre and locality substantially in favour of the latter.

(a) The militarization of landowning élites

Defence in the later Roman empire was the province of a professional army of several hundred thousands. It was paid for by large-scale taxation, particularly of agricultural activity (a land-tax). The raising of these revenues required a powerful state machine, voluminous records and a basic willingness to pay. The state endeavoured to foster such a willingness by stressing that tax paid for the army, and hence for security; it is generally considered by modern scholars that most revenue was targeted in that direction.[13] By c. 600, the landowning élites of western Europe were providing military manpower directly, however, instead of paying for professionals to do the job. That new landowners from the immigrant groups (Goths, Franks, etc.) continued to fight, once settled, has never been doubted. Wherever they survived, however, Roman landowning élites, or rather their descendants, also came to be drawn upon for military service.[14]

For Frankish Gaul, the most useful source is the writing of Gregory of Tours. He never specifies the precise military obligation enforced by Merovingian kings, but there certainly was one, since he reports its application to particular individuals.[15] Much of the fighting in the sixth century was done by forces drawn directly from *civitates*, and a particular story about the war of 568 between Sigibert and Guntramn makes it clear that these were not garrison troops but citizen militias. In this case, a military reverse suffered by a contingent from Clermont-Ferrand caused the death of many of the city's leading men. And when the particular militias that Gregory happens to mention are plotted on a map (see Fig. 17), most fall outside the areas of substantial Frankish settlement.[16] Likewise, the main royal officers in the cities – counts (*comites*, singular *comes*) and dukes (*duces*, *dux*) – clearly had military as well as administrative and legal roles. The names and biographies of many of the men holding such positions show that descendants of Roman landowners, as well as Franks, regularly filled them.[17]

In the case of Visigothic Spain, legal materials likewise demonstrate that military obligations were applied to Roman and Goth alike. Gothic kings

[13] Jones, *LRE* ch. 17; Elton (1996).

[14] The current orthodoxy, in so far as one exists, portrays surviving Roman landowners retreating to villas, libraries and episcopal sees: e.g. Van Dam (1985); Mathisen (1993); Heinzelmann (1976).

[15] Punishments for those failing to appear: Greg. Tur. *Hist.* v.26; vi.12; vii.42; cf. *Laws of the Ripuarian Franks* 68.1–2.

[16] War of 568: Greg. Tur. *Hist.* iv.30. Gregory mentions citizen militias from Agen, Angoulême, Clermont, Bayeux, Blois, Bordeaux, Bourges, Chartres, Châteaudun, Le Mans, Nantes, Orleans, Périgueux, Poitiers, Saintes, Toulouse, Tours and Vely; cf. Bachrach (1972) 66–7.

[17] Gallo-Roman dukes and patricians: e.g. Agricola, Amatus, Asclepius, Celsus, Desiderius, Ennodius, Gedinus, Mummolus, Nicetius: on all of whom see relevant entries in *PLRE* iii. The military aspect of the office of count is demonstrated by e.g. Greg. Tur. *Hist.* iv.30; viii.36.

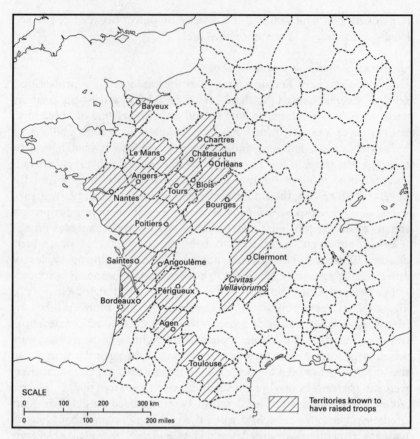

Fig. 17 City territories of Gaul known (from Gregory of Tours' *Histories*) to have raised troops in
the sixth century

were already enforcing this before their loss of southern Gaul, since 'senators' (i.e. Roman landowners) fought for them at Vouillé (or Voulon) in 507.[18] Italy, of course, was eventually divided between Lombards and Byzantines.[19] For the Lombard kingdom we lack early sources. All one can say is that, if any Roman landowners did survive the invasion period, they quickly came to be treated as an integral part of the kingdom and were expected, as in Gaul and Spain, to provide the same services for their kings as descendants of original Lombards. For Byzantine Italy, the situation is harder to read. Justinian's wars had adverse effects upon the senatorial land-

[18] *Visigothic Code* 9.2: detailed laws on levying, esp. 9.2.8–9 which specify the liability falling on Romans as well as Goths. Vouillé/Voulon: Greg. Tur. *Hist.* 11.37.

[19] During the interlude of Ostrogothic rule, many Romans served in garrison forces, but (with certain exceptions) field army service seems to have been reserved for Theoderic's Gothic followers: Heather (1996) ch. 8.

owning class, but some, at least, survived. By 600, however, they cease to figure in the higher social and political echelons around Rome and Ravenna, which were dominated by a new class of militarized landowners. Whether this represents a transformation of the old élite, the rise of a brand new one, or something in between, is unclear. The old senatorial élite proclaimed itself by naming-practices which celebrated familial connections. Around 600, however, a new practice, based on a limited canon of saints' names, came to predominate. It is hard to know, therefore, whether the old class had survived by militarizing itself and adopting new naming-habits, or whether an entirely new élite had replaced it.[20] Either way, Italy essentially repeats the pattern already observed in Gaul and Spain, whereby a militarized landowning élite, whatever its provenance, came to dominance in the social landscape. For Britain, we have still less evidence. Nevertheless, although processes of transformation are again difficult to chart, it seems clear that any members of the Romano-British élite who had managed to survive into the sixth century had undergone a similar transformation into military landowners.[21]

The rise of militarized landowning élites across western Europe obviated the need for professional armies (although the élites of Byzantine Italy remained much more professional than their counterparts in the Germanic kingdoms).[22] This had important political effects upon the nature of the successor states. For, although the main point of the Roman army had been defence against outsiders, it could also be used to maintain internal order, as the massacre in Thessalonica and the fears aroused by the riot of the statues in Antioch, two fourth-century examples, demonstrate.[23] Once military forces ceased to be independent of local élites, the political problems inherent in fighting local dissidents became more acute. There was also the problem that the élites of any dissident area would themselves be armed, and hence more difficult to subdue. This is not to say that post-Roman kings could not use their new-style military forces to counter internal dissent. In the sixth century, for instance, the Frankish king Guntramn overcame the pretender Gundovald, who had the support of certain elements in the Frankish élite, and, in the seventh, the Visigothic king Wamba defeated Paulus, whose power base lay north of the Pyrenees.[24] Indeed, all kings probably still had some essentially professional household troops. Nevertheless, the militarization of landed élites did swing the balance of power away from the centre and towards localities.

---

[20] Brown, *Gentlemen and Officers* esp. ch. 2 and 4.
[21] A subject much explored in the works of Leslie Alcock; see esp. Alcock (1987) and (1989).
[22] Brown, *Gentlemen and Officers* ch. 4, 6, 8.
[23] Thessalonica: Soz. *HE* vii.25; cf. Larson (1970). Antioch: Heather (1994) 30–1. The fourth century also saw the suppression of revolts in Britain: e.g. Amm. Marc. xxvii.8.6–10; xxviii.3.1–8.
[24] Gundovald: *PLRE* iii.566–7; Paulus: Julian, *Hist. Wamb.* in *MGH, SRM* 5.

(b) The decline of taxation

The post-Roman period also saw a decline in the taxation of agricultural production.[25] This had a number of causes. In some areas, the highly trained groups responsible for the sophisticated record-keeping and currency-management necessary for its assessment and collection were, in all probability, simply swept away in the chaos of the invasion period. It is hard to imagine, for instance, their survival in post-Roman Britain. Linked to this, whether as cause or effect is the collapse of some crucial elements of the economy – particularly coinage and exchange – which rendered the extraction of an agricultural surplus in usable form much more difficult.

The decline in taxation was also linked to the disappearance of professional armies. If landowners were now directly responsible for their own defence – the basic justification for taxation under the empire – why should they also pay land-tax? Some successor-state kings did inherit rights to tax, but then gave them away. Judging from Gregory of Tours, for instance, taxation was a major issue in sixth-century Gaul. His narrative includes not only examples of kings extracting revenues but also of kings coming under considerable pressure to remit them. A major element in explaining this, on the face of it, rather odd phenomenon is that kings seem never to have taxed their original Frankish, Gothic or other followers. Thus, as similar military services came to be demanded as well from the descendants of Roman elements of the population, so the political pressure built up for similar tax breaks all round.[26] Administrative difficulties and political pressures may well have combined. As tax became more difficult to collect, both administratively and politically, it became easier for kings to buy support via grants of tax remission, than to raise revenue in the form of coin and produce and then redistribute it.

The erosion of tax structures, like the disappearance of professional armies, significantly altered the balance of political power in the post-Roman world. Drawing on the largest sector of the economy, the land-tax had brought in large sums of annually renewable income. All of one year's income could be spent without reducing revenue for the next. Once taxation ceased to be a major factor in royal finance, however, kings were often forced to rely on grants of land from the royal fisc to reward or buy support. Once a piece of land had been alienated, however, a king could no longer derive any income from it. Thus, when a political economy comes to rely on land itself (economic capital) rather than recycled interest on it in the form of taxation, it becomes much more difficult for kings to reward followers in one year without reducing their own income for the next. The traditional orthodoxy, indeed, is that the operation of such a

---

[25] Durliat's arguments to the contrary (1990b) are not convincing; cf. Wickham (1993b).
[26] Cf. Wickham (1984); Wood (1990).

dynamic led inexorably to shifts of wealth from kings to their noble supporters. This model has been applied particularly to the Merovingian dynasty in Gaul, held to have lost first its land and then its power.

The contrast is, of course, too simple. In the Roman empire, most tax revenue was committed to paying a professional army (although the existence of this force was a significant level of power: see p. 443 above), and the state often had to fall back on unpopular extra taxes (superindictions).[27] Medieval kings, likewise, had some sources of renewable revenue (customs and tolls, for instance) and other types of reward with which to attract support: confirmations of title, grants of office (whether ecclesiastical or secular) and so on. Moreover, royal fiscs could grow as well as diminish. Many gifts had to be made at the beginning of a reign to establish good relationships with the men of power in the localities who would be crucial to its long-term success. But, on the other hand, processes such as confiscations from defeated opponents would bring other land back into the fisc in the course of the reign. The wife of the dead Mummolus, for instance, was left destitute after the Gundovald affair. Hence, a long-lived king might recoup much, if not all, of his initial expenditure. Nevertheless, the tendency, in other than a very successful reign, is likely to have been towards royal impoverishment and the enrichment of noble supporters, and a series of civil wars or early royal deaths might lead to large losses to the fisc.[28]

(c) The limitations of bureaucracy

In the successor states, the militarization of landowning élites also combined with losses of function to reduce the size and importance of bureaucratic structures. The need for bureaucrats to run tax-machinery and monitor spending, for instance, steadily diminished. In most areas, however, kings continued to employ some bureaucrats who maintained some Roman traditions. Parthenius, for instance, related to an emperor of the mid fifth century, was *magister officiorum et patricius* for the Frankish king Theudebert in the mid sixth. The vast network of late Roman bureaucratic openings, however, had ceased to exist. It is impossible to estimate numbers accurately, but each royal court probably maintained a few tens, rather than thousands, of bureaucrats. The number of jobs at the local level was similarly reduced. The workhorse of royal government on the ground was the count of the city (*comes civitatis*), but there was only one such post per *civitas*. In total, there were only 122 *civitates* in Gaul, not all of which survived as units into the post-Roman period, and therefore 122 *comites*, to whom can be added a few, seemingly *ad hominem*, higher commands (*duces*). Central and local bureaucratic structures, which had previously focused the

[27] It was a superindiction which generated the riot of the statues in Antioch: cf. p. 443 above, n. 23.
[28] Model and its critique: Wood, *Merovingian Kingdoms* esp. ch. 4; several of the essays in Davies and Fouracre (1986) (esp. those of Fouracre, Wood and Ganz).

attention of thousands of leading landowners per generation in western Europe on the state, lost much of their political importance.[29]

In sum, the successor states were not copies on a smaller scale of the Roman empire. As states, they operated in different ways, without large-scale taxation, professional armies or extensive bureaucracies. Hence, the post-Roman world generated many autonomous, if not independent, local communities, and a related tendency towards political fragmentation. Indeed, where early medieval kingdoms did successfully retain their coherence over the long run, the influence of outside factors can often be detected. Periods of relative Frankish and Visigothic monarchical power, for instance, coincided with expansionary campaigns, giving kings access to additional sources of wealth. Or, the reverse side of the coin, the Lombards seem to have recreated their monarchy in Italy when the threat of Frankish invasion made an overall ruler useful.[30] In other circumstances, however, the élites of post-Roman Europe had much less reason to take account of the political centre than their Roman predecessors.

3. Court and community in the post-Roman west

None of this means that successor-state kings were powerless, and the history of post-Roman Europe cannot be understood simply as the failure of the state. Manipulating and building upon Roman elements other than taxation, defence and bureaucracy – as well, probably, as non-Roman traditions (although these are harder to penetrate) – the successor states, to greater and lesser extents, bonded their constituent landowners together into political societies based as much on consent as on the calculation of individual ambition.

Not least, of course, the courts of successor kings remained centres of patronage, even if royal income was on a reduced scale. And a king's gifts could have a more than straightforward significance. A striking feature of the period is the garnet-encrusted cloisonné jewellery often found in burials, at least some of it gifts from royal treasuries. The garnet was the precious stone closest in colour to the imperial purple of Roman emperors and was thus used by them in their regalia. Justinian appears with some of this jewellery in the San Vitale mosaic. Apart from being a rich gift, therefore, such jewellery also made a symbolic claim to power and authority: a manipulation of the mental heritage created by nearly half a millennium of domination wielded by purple-clad emperors.[31] To illustrate this further, I will examine,

---

[29] Parthenius: *PLRE* II.833–4. General survey: Barnwell (1992). Ostrogothic Italy was something of an exception, but the *Variae* of Cassiodorus should not be taken as face-value proof of Roman continuity, even if Barnwell (1992) ch. 15 pushes his critique too far.

[30] The arguments of Reuter (1985) and (1991) can certainly be applied to Merovingian contexts; cf. Collins (1983b). On Lombard Italy, see Wickham (1981) 28ff.; Harrison (1993) *passim*.

[31] Arrhenius (1985).

in the sections which follow, how the manipulation of the Roman heritage in religion and law, to take two fundamental aspects of kingship, helped bond together the élites of the successor kingdoms.

(a) Religion

According to the ideology of the late empire, the Divinity (after Constantine, the Christian God) was the chief upholder of the state, and the state existed to further the divine plan for mankind. Emperors were thus much more than secular rulers, and the fully-fledged Byzantine definition of the emperor as God's vicegerent on earth was only the final stage in a long process of development: the combination of New and Old Testament images and Hellenistic concepts of kingship.[32] The end of empire in the west substituted several kings for one emperor, but led to little diminution in the ideological claims being made. Visigothic and Ostrogothic kings, Frankish, Burgundian and others, all, as they converted to Christianity, presented themselves as appointed by God.[33] In the longer term, this ideological stance had some entirely practical effects in heightening a sense of community in the new realms.

Monarchs were responsible, for instance, for calling church councils. Particularly in the Visigothic kingdom of the later sixth and seventh century, and the Merovingian of the sixth century, this resulted in a regular sequence of councils when a large proportion of the religious leadership of the kingdom gathered together to discuss and legislate on the issues of the day. There was an international dimension to such activity, of course, because the church always regarded itself as not confined by political boundaries. A kingdom's extent, however, both decided participation – which bishops should attend – and dictated certain formal elements of behaviour. Surviving proceedings suggest, for instance, that councils opened with prayers for the king, whatever his brand of Christianity. Thus a Catholic Roman synod of 499 began with prayers for the Arian Theoderic. The priests shouted thirty times 'Hear us Christ. Long live Theoderic.'[34] Where a regular pattern of assemblies was established, religious leaders became used to operating as a defined body and to responding to a particular leadership. On these levels, assemblies added a sense of religious community to the political boundaries of the new kingdoms.[35]

---

[32] See, for instance, Dvornik (1966) esp. ch. 8, 10–12; Liebeschuetz (1979) 197ff.

[33] The *Variae* of Cassiodorus and Ennodius' *Panegyric* make this claim about Theoderic; cf. Heather (1993). Julian of Toledo's *Historia Wambae* and the councils of Toledo are some of many texts making the same claim about Visigothic kings: cf. Collins (1977). Merovingians: Wood, *Merovingian Kingdoms* 66ff.   [34] *Acta synh. habit. Romae* 1, in *MGH, AA* 12, p. 405.

[35] On Merovingian and Hispanic councils, see respectively Pontal (1989) and Orlandis and Ramos-Lissen (1981). Anglo-Saxon church councils were less restricted to individual kingdoms, but royal influence, and particularly that of overkings, was still substantial: Cubitt (1995) 39ff. This may well have contributed to the development of a wider Anglo-Saxon (later English) consciousness.

That Catholic kings, at least, also appointed bishops reinforced the links between political and religious community. In practice, any would-be bishop had to make himself known at court, moving outside his own locality. Bishop Gregory's election at Tours, for instance, was opposed by the archdeacon Riculf, who seems to have been a local candidate. But Gregory was physically at court (that of Sigibert), his family had a much higher political profile, and it was Gregory who got the job. This close association of king and bishop also posed potential problems. The root of Gregory's difficulties with king Chilperic was the fact that he was the appointee of Chilperic's brother Sigibert and hence an object of suspicion when Tours passed into Chilperic's hands. Bishops served for life and must often have outlived the kings who appointed them.[36] Even so, the practical power to appoint bishops meant that – at higher levels, at least – the religious life of any kingdom revolved around kings and their courts.[37]

At first sight, these patterns of the later sixth and seventh century do not apply to the preceding century or so. Between c. 450 and 550, the monarchs and a substantial element of the political élite of many of the new and emerging successor states (the Ostrogothic, Burgundian and Vandal kingdoms, and Visigothic Spain before its conversion to Catholicism at the Third Council of Toledo in 587) did not subscribe to Catholic Christianity, but were so-called Arian Christians. Some of these kingdoms, particularly that of the Vandals under Geiseric and Huneric,[38] witnessed periods when Catholics were persecuted, but perhaps more striking is the extent to which the observations already made remain applicable.

The Ostrogothic king Theoderic was concerned in all his propaganda and in every ceremonial act to stress that his rule was divinely ordained, and that he stood in a particular relationship to God. He was involved in the calling of church councils, and maintained, for the most part, good relations with the Catholic church. The papacy called upon him to settle disputed elections, and consulted him on ending the Acacian schism with the Greek east. Caesarius of Arles, likewise, obtained his papal vicariate through Theoderic's intervention, and exploited the political unification of his religious province by the Ostrogoths in the 520s (previously it had been partly under Burgundian rule) to initiate a series of reforming councils. In the Ostrogothic kingdom, even the king's Arianism did not prevent Catholic churchmen from working around and through his power.[39]

---

[36] See generally Wood, *Merovingian Kingdoms* ch. 5.

[37] This tendency was very partially countered by the existence of the papacy and the concept of a universal church. Churchmen were well aware of belonging to a wider Christian community, and considerable prestige attached to the papacy. But, as Peter Brown has recently put it, the western church consisted of 'Micro Christendoms': Brown (1996) esp. ch. 13.

[38] Famously described by Victor of Vita, *CSEL* 7.

[39] Heather (1996) ch. 8; cf. Moorhead (1992) 194ff. on the Acacian schism, and Klingshirn (1994) ch. 5.

Even persecuting non-Catholic kings were, on occasion, motivated by the same ideological heritage; in their view, of course, they were the 'orthodox', and so-called Catholics the heretics. In 484, the Vandal king Huneric unleased a religious offensive which was quite unlike his father Geiseric's preceding moments of persecution. A council of all religious, Catholics and non-Nicenes, was called in Carthage, a definition of faith pushed through, and action taken to enforce adherence to that definition. As the form of his royal edicts underlines, Huneric was acting in all this like those fourth-century emperors who subscribed to and enforced a variety of religious settlements in the aftermath of the Council of Nicaea.[40] The underlying idea was that there should be a single definition of Christian faith for the realm, and that state power should be used to enforce it. The policy of the Visigothic king Leovigild in the 580s was very similar. It was designed not to crack down on Catholics so much as to establish a uniform religious settlement – in this case, based on a doctrinal compromise – for the entire kingdom.[41]

As these examples show, when pushed through against the wishes of a critical mass of the population, or its religious leadership, policies designed to promote religious unity could themselves create division, as they had done in the fourth-century empire as a whole and were doing in the fifth- and sixth-century east. In papyri from Italy, however, the Arian religion is referred to as *lex Gothorum*, and this may provide a key to the religious harmony that largely prevailed outside the Vandal kingdom. Where Arianism was treated by kings as the religion of the intruding conquerors (Goths, Burgundians, etc.), then it was possible to have peace. Churchmen such as Caesarius of Arles could respond by taking the 'render unto Caesar' passage to mean that all earthly rulers were appointed by God for some reason and, wherever possible, should be honoured.[42]

In the longer term, Arianism was destroyed by Byzantine or Frankish conquest (respectively of the Vandals and Ostrogoths, and of the Burgundians) or undermined by the conversions to Catholicism which followed on from prolonged co-existence with Catholic, former Roman, populations.[43] By 600, therefore, Catholicism was almost universally accepted, and the old Roman idea of the kingdom as a religious unit became even less problematic. Kings and churchmen could get on with the business of generating community through the regular religious ceremonial life of the kingdom and the scramble for higher church appointments.

---

[40] Vict. Vit. *Hist. Pers.* bks 2–3.

[41] Thompson (1969) 78ff. argued that Leovigild was being deliberately divisive, but this seems mistaken; cf. Collins (1983a) ch. 2.

[42] *Lex Gothorum*: Tjäder (1982) 268 n. 3; cf. Klingshirn (1994) 88ff. Gregory of Tours, by contrast, often vents his hatred of Arians, but if Gregory had lived under Arian kings, his opinions would probably have been more moderate.　　[43] The case with the Visigoths; cf. Thompson (1960).

(b) Law

That a sense of legal community should play a similarly important role in the new realms was a further adaptation of Roman heritage. Ideologically, the Roman educated classes saw written law as the main factor differentiating their society from that of 'barbarians' beyond the frontier. In the Roman view, only men who had graduated to the higher level of rationality generated by a classical education (whether in Latin or Greek) were able to subordinate their immediate desires to a legal structure which treated all alike and which, by that fact, achieved the best possible outcome for all. Nor was law – in imperial circles, at least – seen as something created by men for human convenience. Rather, it was essential to the divine plan for the cosmos, since it was both cause and effect of realizing that state of higher rationality which was the Divinity's overall aim for humanity. The Christianization of the empire merely heightened the religious significance attached to written law as the generator of 'correct' social order – the powerful example of the Old Testament reinforcing established Roman views. By contrast, 'barbarian' societies, where divinely-inspired written law failed to prevail, were anarchies, where individuals pursued immediate sensory pleasure, living more like animals than men.[44]

Some vestiges of this ideology influenced most successor states. Most obviously, it stimulated the production of written legal texts for groups who had not previously possessed them. Visigoths, Burgundians, Franks, Anglo-Saxons and Lombards all produced written legal texts through direct or indirect contact with Roman example. In part, written law could be used to emphasize the legal role of monarchs, enhancing kingship, but written texts also demonstrated that the group concerned were not mere 'barbarians'. The Ostrogothic king Theoderic made the same claim by *not* producing a separate Ostrogothic law code, since he could present his regime as preserving Roman law unchanged.

In some successor states, this ideological heritage found more profound expression in an overt public approach taken to law. Since law, after the Roman example, symbolized divinely ordained social order and consensus, both the rhetoric in which texts were couched and the ceremonies surrounding their publication reflected these ideas. Prefaces to the many law codes generated in the new states commonly refer to the deep care for the kingdom on the part of king and great men – religious and other – expressed in the act of producing a text. Examples of such language can be found in Burgundian, Lombard and Visigothic texts amongst others,

---

[44] In more detail, with primary refs.: Heather (1993) 324, 329–30. Hence law figures centrally in late antique comparisons of Roman and barbarian: Orosius' account of Athaulf (*Hist. ad Pag.* VII.42.3–3: he could not replace *Romania* with *Gothia* because the Goths were too uncivilized to obey law), and Priscus' conversation with the Roman merchant turned Hunnic warrior (the latter finally agrees, in tears that written law guarantees the superiority of Roman life: ed. Blockley fr. 11.2, p. 272, lines 508–10).

with the *Lex Salica* of the Franks providing an interesting variant. Its earliest preface mentions no king and credits its production to four wise lawgivers, although later versions and modificatory edicts revert to a more traditional style, and emphasize again the co-operation of king and great men.[45]

In some cases, rhetoric was matched by public ceremonial. Different seventh-century revisions of the Visigothic legal code (the *Forum Iudicum*) were presented by the reigning king to various of the periodic public assemblies of the great religious and secular magnates of the Spanish kingdom which gathered at Toledo.[46] The *Liber Constitutionum* of the Burgundians, similarly, has a Preface sealed by more than thirty *comites* – leading lay magnates – of the kingdom. We must surely imagine a formal signing, or rather sealing, ceremony conducted at the Burgundian court when the text was first promulgated. In the Frankish kingdom, likewise, the three surviving edicts of Childebert (dated 1 March 594, 595 and 596) were all presented at assemblies, and those of Guntramn (585) and Chlothar (614) published in the aftermath of church councils.[47]

Written law was thus an expression of divinely ordained order and consensus, and its rhetoric and ceremonial presentation stressed its role in generating a sense of community within the different kingdoms. The degree to which practical legal structures (courts, judges, etc.) provided a further social cement, making successor states actual legal communities in the everyday practice of dispute settlement, is harder to estimate. In some cases, a unified structure of real importance was created. The Visigothic Code was regularly updated to incorporate new royal rulings. The text itself was required to be used; cases it failed to cover were to be referred to the king; and there existed a network of royally certified courts and royally appointed judges. The Islamic conquest of the kingdom means that no pre-eighth-century charters survive to confirm that the text's demands were being fulfilled, but its prescriptions were followed very closely in the Carolingian period – the first moment we can check.[48] In Italy, likewise, a similar royally authorized network of courts operated in the Ostrogothic kingdom of the sixth century, and the Lombard kingdom developed comparable structures in the later seventh and eighth century.[49]

North of the Alps and Pyrenees, the pattern is not so clear. Frankish and Anglo-Saxon kings issued law codes and modificatory edicts, but it is unclear whether these were part of a coherent, centrally directed legal structure. References in both Frankish law codes – *Lex Salica* and *Lex Ribuaria* – imply that these texts were originally viewed as partial collections, behind

---

[45] On all these texts, see further ch. 10 (Charles-Edwards), pp. 260–87 above.
[46] Cf. Collins (1983a) 24ff.   [47] Cf. Wood, *Merovingian Kingdoms*, ch. 7.
[48] Structure: Wormald (1977); King (1972); Collins (1983a) 24ff. Law in practice: Collins (1985) and (1986).   [49] Ostrogothic Italy: Moorhead (1992) 75ff. Lombards: Wickham (1986).

which stood a much larger body of unwritten customary law. References to law – *lex/leges* – in actual cases from seventh-century Gaul suggest the same. Legal authority was held to reside in local men learned in Frankish law (the so-called *rachinburgii*), rather than in a centrally controlled system of courts and justice.[50] Little is known of early Anglo-Saxon systems, but it seems unlikely that they more resembled the Gothic and Lombard kingdoms than the Frankish. Even so, written law does seem to have been used north of the Channel to push through Christianization.[51]

Indeed, even where central legal structures were much less developed, there could still be one important sense in which the kingdom might function as a legal community. Of this, some late Merovingian *placita* – documents recording the final settlement of particular cases – provide an excellent illustration. On a series of occasions in the later seventh century, substantial numbers of secular and ecclesiastical magnates gathered at the royal court to witness disputes between two or more of their number. The king convened the case, the assembly of magnates helped him judge it, and all put their names to the final settlement. For the case of the orphan Ingramnus against Amalbert in February 692 or 693, for instance, some twelve bishops and another forty secular magnates (together with many unnamed followers) gathered at the court of Clovis III.[52] Many of these magnates may have run their own localities like mafia bosses, but the fact that disputes between their number were fought out before their peer group, in a meeting convened by the king, guaranteed a real sense of legal community within the realm.

4. *Involvement, identity and ethnicity*

The Roman inheritance in law and religion thus provided an ideological justification for some sense of community at the highest level in the new states of western Europe. More important, the pursuit and presentation of these ideologies generated a series of occasions and modes of behaviour which allowed the kingdoms' constituent landowning élites to function in reality as a single body. Would-be bishops and counts had to make themselves known, whatever their familial background, to their kings; kings convened more or less regular assemblies of secular and religious magnates; and the great of the kingdom might gather under the chairmanship of the king to settle their disputes. All of these activities led substantial numbers of the élite of any kingdom to meet and, in certain cases, to act as one body. Such occasions provided a real social cement for the new kingdoms – the moments when ties were forged between members of their landowning élites.

---

[50] Wood, *Merovingian Kingdoms* ch. 7; Wood (1986).
[51] Cf. Wormald (1977); modified now by Wormald (1995).
[52] Wood, *Merovingian Kingdoms* 262–3; cf. Fouracre (1986).

These moments were supplemented by a number of other mechanisms, not least the tendency for successor-state kings to itinerate. Whatever their other functions, such cycles of movement allowed kings to make contact with considerable numbers of the landowners within the kingdom. This imposed royal government in areas which might be beyond its normal reach. Fredegar's description of the crowds in Burgundy, flocking to win legal redress from Dagobert when he arrived in the region, is a classic illustration. Itineration also generated a series of social occasions which reinforced senses of community among the élite: everything from formal displays of royal sovereignty to feasts, to hunting.[53]

In the later Roman empire, landowners came to court (physically or metaphorically) to maintain their élite status. In the post-Roman west, monarchs visited the landowners to assert their royalty; and, as we have seen, there were other ways in which central power was structurally weakened in the transformations associated with the end of the Roman empire. Nevertheless, the mechanisms available to successor-state kings were powerful enough to work one major transformation of their own: the dissolution of any ethnic divide between the Roman and non-Roman elements out of which most of the kingdoms had originally been constructed.

By c. A.D. 650, perhaps earlier in some kingdoms, a fundamental transformation in perceptions of identity had worked itself out. Ethnic terms were still used: 'Burgundian', 'Goth', 'Frank', etc., on the one hand, 'Roman' on the other. The words had lost, however, their old significance. In the Hispanic kingdom, 'Goths' were the élite landowners of the realm, whatever their biological origins. The politically enfranchised class of freemen, the definers and bearers of 'Gothicness' in the migration period, had been broken up, as immigrant Gothic and indigenous Roman landowners made common cause to create a new élite. Visigothic legislation mirrors the process: picking out 'greater' and 'lesser' freemen, who eventually came to be ascribed different *wergilds*.[54] Elsewhere, the evidence for the process is less good, but it does appear to have happened wherever Roman landowners survived the initial chaos of invasion. Thus the seventh-century 'Franci' of Neustria were a nexus of some half-dozen or so leading landowning families of the region who engaged in political competition with one another at the highest level. And already in the early-sixth-century Burgundian kingdom, legislative provisions reflect both the dominance of a relatively small Burgundian élite – rather than an extensive freemen caste – and its intermixing with surviving Roman landowners.[55]

[53] Some different aspects of itineration: Ewig (1963); Leyser (1979); Charles-Edwards (1988).

[54] Heather (1996) 283ff., commenting on the original and revised versions of the *Visigothic Code* at 8.4.16.

[55] Franci: Gerberding (1987) 167–8. Burgundians: Amory (1993) (who to my mind overstates the speed of intermingling and the amount of confusion it generated).

A number of factors had brought about this ethnic redefinition. One mechanism was intermarriage. Only the Visigoths are known to have maintained a formal ban on intermarriage between Roman and Goth, but it was probably never very effective, and was overturned under Leovigild (572–86: Visigothic Code 3.1.1). Marriages across ethnic lines would only have been constructed in the first place, however, because common interests had already formed between Roman and immigrant, so that other factors must first have been at work. Not least important was the actual process of settling outsiders on former Roman territory. In some cases, the Roman tax system, or elements of it, played a role; but the process always, to my mind, primarily involved redistributions of land. We do not know how the land was allocated among the immigrant groups, but differences of status already existed (see pp. 462–3 below), so that, as has long been suspected, it is most unlikely that land was distributed equally to all immigrants.[56] This provides a convincing context for assimilation on two levels. First, particularly at the upper levels of society, Roman and non-Roman landowners of equivalent wealth would have had much in common. Second, as wealth differentials grew, vertical bonds of patronage within the incoming freemen classes would have increased in importance (see p. 463 below). One can well imagine them hardening sufficiently over time to break up the ethnic unity of incoming groups of freemen: the process reflected in Visigothic legislation. To this essentially economic explanation, we can also add a growing similarity of function and culture, as military service was demanded of Roman landowners (or their descendants), and immigrants adopted such aspects of the Roman heritage as Latin Christianity and written law, and themselves sought profitable bishoprics.

Perhaps above all, however, since identity is generally created and hardened in conflict, the disappearance of the Roman state removed the force which had sustained the old separate identities and drawn a firm line between Romans and outsiders. From 476, new and more immediate conflicts, between the inhabitants of different parts of Gaul, Italy and Spain, served to create new identities. And in all this, the new royal courts of the successor states played a fundamental role. Their kings may have had fewer and weaker levers of central power, but it was still at court that office, secular and ecclesiastical, was sought, struggles for power were fought out, élite marriages concocted, and élite children, whatever their background, inculcated with a common martial, but also Latin Christian, culture. Thus, just after Toledo III, Claudius, a royal military officer of Roman background, put down a revolt by Goths against the Gothic king Reccared. By 650, terms such as Goth, Burgundian and Frank designated

---

[56] Goffart, *Barbarians and Romans* produced an argument, which has had considerable influence, that incomers were given not land but a share of tax proceeds. I, among many others, am unconvinced; cf. Wood (1990); Barnish (1986). Processes of distribution were highlighted by Thompson (1963).

the élite landowners of a particular region, rather than a politically distinct caste of militarized immigrants. The royal courts of the post-Roman west were central to this transformation.[57]

II. PEERS AND LORDS: LOCAL COMMUNITIES

The basic local political unit of the Roman empire was the *civitas* (city), encompassing both an urban centre and a dependent rural territory. Within this unit, taxes were allocated and collected, and smaller legal issues settled by the *defensor civitatis* (an innovation of the mid fourth century). The urban centre also acted as a religious, political, economic and, indeed, cultural focus for the population of its dependent territory. Officially at least, the later Roman empire continued to value the classical urbanism it had inherited from the Greeks, and saw the public institutions (*fora*, etc.) and communal amusements (bath, theatres, etc.) of the self-governing town as the ideal type of human community.[58]

The fourth century had seen both the growth of an imperial bureaucracy and wholesale transfers of financial assets away from the cities (see p. 438 above), but the *civitas* continued to shape basic senses of local community. Most of the new imperial bureaucrats retained strong roots in their local communities. Periods of service were short, and the imperial authorities used retired *honorati* for important jobs in their localities, such as supervising tax reassessments. *Honorati* likewise tended to have made good contacts while serving at the centre, and were thus in great demand as patrons. While there was no longer one council of landowners (the *curia*), the administrative functions focused upon the *civitas* (tax, law, etc.) continued to make it the local community *par excellence* for *honorati*, *principales* and all other members of the empire's landowning classes.[59]

1. *The end of the civitas?*

In part of the post-Roman west, local *civitas* communities continued to play roles of fundamental importance. Sixth-century Visigothic Spain, for instance, provides the examples of Cordoba and Seville, which threw off central government and acted entirely independently – the former for twenty-two years.[60] In Italy, taking a longer perspective, the city remained a vital structure in the landscape to the end of the first millennium and

---

[57] Claudius: *Lives of the Fathers of Merida, CCSL* 116, 5.10. Different visions of intermixing: Heather (1996) 284ff. (Visigothic kingdom); Halsall (1995) 26–32 (Frankish); Amory (1997) esp. ch. 3 (Ostrogothic), although I would argue that Theoderic's Goths brought many of their women with them, and were dominated by a political élite of free warriors (Heather (1996) 170–2 and App. 1). Hence they were originally more coherent than Amory would allow.
[58] With strongly Christian overtones, this ideal still suffuses the mid-sixth-century *Buildings* of Procopius. [59] E.g. Liebeschuetz (1972) esp. pt v; Heather (1994) 25ff. [60] Collins (1980).

beyond. Nor were these towns merely collections of buildings; they operated as real centres of community, serving a variety of legal, economic,
political and cultural functions for the surrounding countryside. The
Lombards settled their sub-groups within city units, and hence themselves
subsequently became city-based. Thus, in eighth-century Lucca, over half
the twenty or so largish landowners of the territory seem to have lived
within the city itself. In most of sixth-century Gaul, likewise, curias continued to exist, municipal archives charted patterns of local landholding, and,
on the basis of this information, taxes continued to be raised. Sixth-century
Merovingian saints' lives also identify their heroes by *civitas* of origin.[61]

As we have seen, *civitas* contingents, comprising levies of landowners
and their dependants, became central to the military capability of the new
kingdoms. The leading men of each city territory were thus given a whole
new series of reasons and occasions to work together to their common
interest. Indeed, city contingents sometimes operated on their own
account. Gregory's *Histories*, for instance, record an attack by the men of
Orleans, allied with those of Blois, on Châteaudun and Chartres (*Hist.*
VII.2). It seems likely that the military organization of other successor
states, particularly Visigothic Spain, also encompassed such contingents.
Here, at least, the enforcement of recruiting laws was the task of city
authorities, and, as we have seen, Mérida and Seville were able to field their
own independent military forces.[62]

The city likewise remained a centre of local legal community. Alongside
the *defensor civitatis*, the remit of episcopal courts, in secular as well as religious matters, had been recognized and progressively defined from the time
of Constantine, the bishop being expected to reconcile rather than assign
penalties when settling disputes.[63] Both civil and religious courts continued
to operate in the *civitates* of the post-Roman west. Most successor states
appointed officers to individual cities: *comites civitatis* (counts of the city) in
Merovingian Gaul, Gothic Spain and Italy, and *duces* among the
Lombards.[64] Responsible for financial and military affairs, the count also
presided over a court of first resort. At the same time, bishops' courts continued to function, and even became more prominent, as bishops themselves gradually acquired powers (see pp. 457–9 below). The city remained,
therefore, a centre of local legal community.

Ideally, one would like to cite detailed case histories at this point. Most
accounts of legal practice in the early Middle Ages are provided by charters, however, and little such material is available for the immediate post-
Roman period. The legal role of bishops is well documented, however, in
sixth-century Merovingian Gaul, and *formulae* provide some material for

---

[61] See generally ch. 8 (Liebeschuetz), pp. 229–36 above, with refs.   [62] As above, n. 60.
[63] Jones, *LRE* ch. 14.
[64] *Comites civitatis:* Barnwell (1992) 35–6, 80–1, 88, 108–11, 151–2. *Duces:* Wickham (1981) 80ff.

reconstructing the operations of a comital court. The first formula in a surviving collection from Clermont, for instance, mentions a *vir laudabilis*, presumably the count, who presided over the meeting, the *defensor (civitatis)*, and the presence of numerous local notables (*honorati*). The practice in both late Roman and Carolingian times was for the president of the court to make and enforce critical decisions in consultation with the assembled local landowners. There is every reason to think that this would also have been the procedure in the intervening period.[65] A picture of *civitas*-based episcopal and comital courts dominating local dispute settlement is precisely that suggested by the most famous post-Roman case of them all: the feud which broke out in Tours in the time of bishop Gregory. The men involved were of sufficient standing for the case eventually to make its way to the king, but, in the first instance, a tribunal of Touraine citizens, the count's court and even the bishop attempted to halt the feud's progress. Noteworthy, too, is the way that Gregory acted against the letter of the law, offering church funds to promote reconciliation.[66] Some bishops at least, then, continued the established Roman traditions of their courts.

In his proper sphere, too, the steadily rising profile of the bishop in the post-Roman west reinforced the importance of the city to local senses of community. The establishment of episcopal sees substantially followed the administrative pattern of the Roman empire, each *civitas* having its own bishop. One obvious reflection of the increasing importance of the bishop and of Christianity was the changing architectural face of the late antique city. Post-Roman cities in the west tended to be dominated by episcopal complexes: of cathedral and satellite churches, bishop's palace, and bapistery, and perhaps with attendant urban monasteries and lodgings for pilgrims.[67] Much has rightly been written about the rise within the town of the bishop's secular power, which this physical domination reflects, but the bishop's role within the Christian hierarchy also made the city the religious centre of the local community.

The fourth century had seen the rise of the holy man: self-appointed religious authorities whose lives and posthumous cults potentially challenged the dominance of bishops. In the late and post-Roman west, this and other challenges to the bishop were met head-on. The later fourth century saw a switch of hagiographical emphasis towards the monk-bishop – most famously in Sulpicius Severus' *Life of Martin of Tours*. At the same time, bishops exercised their rights to regulate asceticism. Gregory of Tours preserves a nice example of a would-be stylite tearfully

---

[65] Late Roman procedure: Heather (1994) 25ff. Carolingian procedure emerges clearly from Davies and Fouracre (1986) esp. 214ff. Clermont: *Formulae Avernenses* 1, *MGH, Legum* 5, with Wood (1986) 12ff.; cf. James (1983).

[66] Greg. Tur. *Hist* VII.47; IX.19. For commentary from a different angle, see Wallace-Hadrill (1962).

[67] See e.g. ch. 8 (Liebeschuetz), pp. 209–10, 217–19 and 230 above.

accepting episcopal authority as the bishops lured him down and then smashed his pillar (*Hist.* VIII.15). Bishops also acted to regulate the cults of martyrs and other saints within their dioceses, many such cults coming to centre on dead and often related predecessors in local episcopal office. There was nothing particular about Gaul in this respect. The *Lives of the Fathers of Mérida* reveal a similarly close association between the bishops of that city and the martyr cult of Eulalia. Liturgy too could be used to keep the religious community whole in the face of a proliferation of different saints' cults within individual *civitates*. Processions, for instance, were used as a device to ensure that, on special occasions, every church and cult centre of a city could be incorporated into the one celebration. The congregation would start at the bishop's cathedral and move round the different cult sites, emphasizing that all operated under the one episcopally controlled umbrella.

Aristocrats posed a different challenge. As the political cohesion of curias broke up, the tendency increased for aristocrats to live on country estates. Hence sixth-century Gallic church councils ordained that aristocrats should celebrate the major festivals of the religious year in towns. In similar vein, a major feature of the conversion of northern Europe (north and south of the Channel) was a period of aristocratic monastic foundation in the countryside. These rural religious institutions, at least in part, superseded episcopal structures. Thus, the former *civitas* territory of Trier was broken up into four *pagi* (German *Gaue*), in each of which aristocratic monasteries, such as Echternach and Prum, acted as new religious centres. The extent to which such foundations created alternative religious communities, functioning independently of bishops, is unclear. Did aristocrats' dependants receive their Christianity, such as it was, via their lords' foundations? In seventh-century Anglo-Saxon England, this may have been so, since the foundation of monasteries coincided with a shortage of bishops.[68]

Elsewhere in the post-Roman west, however, bishops again responded very positively to the challenge of spreading Christianity to the countryside. The old episcopal monopoly on preaching was broken by the bishops themselves. A council chaired by bishop Caesarius of Arles in 529 was the first to allow priests to preach in the countryside, and the practice gradually spread through Gaul and Spain as the century progressed. This development was vital if the new religion was to be spread outside of urban centres, allowing preaching to take place simultaneously at many centres within one diocese: necessary, controlled devolution rather than an undermining of episcopal power. At the same time, bishops of Tours, at least,

[68] For a general introduction to these developments, see e.g. James (1982) chs. 2, 4, 9; Hillgarth (1986); Brown (1996) esp. chs. 6–8. More specific contributions: Rousseau, *Ascetics*; Stancliffe (1983); Heinzelmann (1976); Van Dam, *Leadership and Community* pt 4; Van Dam (1993) ch. 2; Collins (1980).

were tackling the problem from another angle, establishing satellite religious centres in the countryside. By Gregory's death, there were over forty such establishments in the Touraine, and there is no reason to think Tours unique. A proto-parish system was already emerging in the countryside of sixth-century Europe, allowing Christianity to spread under the bishop's co-ordinating eye.[69]

The *civitas* thus continued to shape senses of local political, legal and religious community in large parts of Gaul, Spain and Italy in the immediate post-Roman period. There were, of course, also discontinuities. The disappearance of secular public buildings marked the end of a long tradition, the displacement of a whole way of life. Peer landowning groups in local society no longer gathered as a curial body in city council chambers but expressed solidarity and pursued rivalries when gathered to fight together in city levies or as assessors in the courts of the local count. There was, moreover, wide regional variation. In some areas, the old Roman cities failed to survive even the first shock of the end of empire. In Britain and north-eastern Gaul, violence and social revolution combined to remake the political landscape. Neither the boundaries of the host of small Anglo-Saxon kingdoms which had emerged by *c*. 600 nor, perhaps more surprisingly, those of their British counterparts bore much relation to the *civitas* geography of the Roman period. Bishops did survive among the British, though not among the pagan Anglo-Saxons, but their sees were also not based on the old *civitates*.[70]

North-eastern Gaul did not witness political fragmentation on the same scale, but, here too, new patterns were generated. The area throws up not *comites civitatis* but *grafios* in charge of *pagi*, and even where larger solidarities emerged, they did so on new bases. Several former Roman units combined, for example, in the Champagne, creating, amongst other things, a military group who tended to act together like the city-based levies to the south and west. While the settlement of outsiders in Spain, southern Gaul and Italy was dictated by, or at least does not seem to have disrupted, the existing *civitas* structure, further north there was much greater discontinuity.[71]

Moreover, even where *civitas* units did survive the invasion period, there were other forces at work which, in some places at least, eventually dismantled them. The Roman *civitas* had many roles. Of central importance was its position as the local administrative centre for the state: the unit of taxation, the court of first resort, and so on. As we have seen, the post-Roman

[69] Preaching: Klingshirn (1994); cf. Hillgarth (1980). Proto-parish systems: the essays of Stancliffe and Fouracre in Baker (1979) with the studies collected in *Cristianizzazione* (1982). Much recent work on the establishment of parish and proto-parish systems has been done in England, where these processes did not take place within *civitas* structures: see generally Blair and Sharpe (1992).

[70] Political structures: as p. 439 above, n. 8. Ecclesiastical structures: Davies (1982) ch. 6.

[71] See generally James (1982) 58–62; Halsall (1995) esp. ch. 8–9 provides a detailed case study.

world witnessed a considerable simplification in state machinery. In broad terms, the state increasingly imposed less pressure on local societies to act through the unit of the *civitas*, and, with the removal of this outside stimulus, different collectivities could assume greater importance.

This was a far-reaching process, and no comprehensive survey of it can be attempted here. The way it tended to work, however, can be approached through an examination of powers of taxation. One important mechanism leading to a general decline in the importance of taxation was the granting of immunities. The effect of such grants is summarized in the Frankish king Chlothar II's *praeceptio* and edict of 614. This forbade royal agents to demand payment of taxes and other public charges from the lands of immunists. The formulary of Marculf goes into further detail:

no public agent may enter [the land of an immunist] to hear legal proceedings, to take the peace-money [*fredus*], to procure lodgings or victuals, or to take sureties, or, for one reason or another, to use force . . . or to demand payments . . .[72]

Thus a grant of immunity removed a block of land from its existing administrative unit – usually a *civitas* and its count – making the immunist directly answerable to the king for his remaining obligations, such as military service. Where such grants proliferated, *civitas* communities would obviously fragment.

Immunities have long formed part of the 'sacred rhetoric' of early medieval western historiography, and have been seen as central to the erosion of Merovingian state power and the rise of the Carolingians. But immunists, as a group, owed special allegiance to the king, and should perhaps rather be seen as favoured royal supporters. Much more to the point for present purposes is whether immunities were granted to lay as well as ecclesiastical landowners in the Merovingian period. The sources show that in principle they might be, but no specific example survives from the sixth or seventh century. However, documents from this period survive only spasmodically, and essentially via church archives, so the absence of lay immunists from the documentary record is perhaps only to be expected. Certainly, by late Merovingian times, many *civitates* had lost their cohesion. The early-eighth-century correspondence of Boniface, for instance, seems to reflect a world of small, administratively independent lordships. Likewise, seventh-century kings restricted their rights to exercise a free choice in appointing counts and bishops to *civitates*, agreeing to confine their choice to local men. This development seems inconceivable if huge amounts of territory, as in the sixth century, were still controlled from *civitas* centres. Kings were probably willing to exercise less control over cities only

---

[72] *Form. Marc.* 1.4, ed. A. Uddholm, Uppsala 1962, trans. James (1982) 62. The text refers to an ecclesiastical immunist, but Chlothar's edict refers to grants being made to both secular and ecclesiastical *potentes*.

because cities were exercising control over a smaller percentage of the kingdom.[73]

Outside Frankish Gaul, such processes took longer to unfold. In Lombard Italy, the state continued to operate through the *civitates* to a much greater extent. Only with the collapse of Carolingian rule, and the *incastellamento* of the later ninth century and beyond, did the Roman administrative landscape finally fragment.[74] For Spain, there is at present a much less clear picture. There is a little evidence, however, that, although strong in certain areas of the peninsula in the sixth century (see p. 455 above), in others the *civitas* structure had begun to break down. The *Life of St Emilian* (26) refers in passing to a mysterious 'senate of Cantabria' (not a pre-existing Roman unit) whose independence was suppressed by Leovigild. A chance survival from the late sixth century likewise demonstrates that taxation was then being assessed on several cities as a group and levied by royal officials, rather than as the responsibility of individual *civitates* and their curias.[75] The Islamic conquerors of the kingdom also made a treaty in 713 with a Visigothic noble named Theodemir, whose semi-independent lordship was acknowledged over seven towns of south-east Spain.[76] Whether this fief represented another late Visigothic grouping of previously independent *civitates* or an *ad hoc* creation of the Arab invasion period, however, remains unclear.

Across post-Roman Europe, then, there were wide variations in the history of the *civitas*. In some areas, the fifth-century invasions delivered a *coup de grâce*. In others, *civitates* survived to play important roles in the successor states, sometimes for many centuries. Everywhere, however, the role of the city community was, if gradually, undermined by the disappearance of those state institutions which had demanded the creation and maintenance of the *civitas* network. There is reason to think that this process of communal dissolution was paralleled by an increase in the degree of private dominion being exercised by at least the larger landowners. It is to this subject that the final part of this essay will turn.

2. *Local lordship and its limitations*

As we have seen, the erosion of the state in the post-Roman period generated some increase in local autonomy. More than that, it led to adjustments in the social bonds operating at all levels of local society. The evidence strongly suggests that, in the longer term, the post-Roman

---

[73] I generally follow here James (1982) 62–4. For revisionist views, Fouracre (1995); cf. Ganz (1995) 12–16. I am not, however, totally convinced that the lack of documented lay immunists is significant.

[74] See e.g. Wickham (1981) 163ff.

[75] The so-called *De Fisco Barcinonensi*; for discussion, see King (1972) 69–70.

[76] Collins (1983a) 153–4.

west was transformed by the appearance of increasingly rigid social stratifications, themselves based firmly upon further transformations in the rural economy.

(a) Freemen and nobles

Across the different successor states, a free class seems to have been characterized by certain rights and obligations: a particular status defined by relatively high *wergild*, attendance at public assemblies (for legal and other matters), and a personal military obligation.[77] The relevant law codes mention the *franci* of the Merovingian kingdoms or the *arimanni* of the Lombard. Freemen are also prominent in the Visigothic codes, and, among the Ostrogoths of Italy, Procopius distinguishes an obviously large class of notables who should probably also be identified as freemen.[78] Weapon-burials in early Anglo-Saxon England probably also reflect not so much fighters *per se*, as men claiming the same critical free status.[79] This legal categorization was not just confined to immigrant warrior groups, but also extended to resident Roman populations. The *Pactus Legis Salicae*, for instance, assigns to different categories of Romans *wergilds* half the value of the equivalent Frankish group.[80]

Over time, this initially prominent class disappeared as a major political force. It seems probable, indeed, that the decline of centralizing state structures into largely autonomous lordships was accompanied by a breakdown in the legal homogeneity of the free class. The unity of this group was originally upheld by the state (or common public consent, in less sophisticated contexts) for a number of purposes: most obviously defence but also, via assemblies, political unanimity. It was a unity artificially imposed upon men among whom there already existed significant differences in wealth. In Roman society, for instance, inherited differentials of wealth and status had by c. A.D. 400 separated out the landowning class, as we have seen, into a number of layers: *honorati*, *principales* and ordinary curials. Hence Gregory of Tours identifies many Roman families of sixth-century Gaul as 'senatorial', even if the law codes do not assign senators a separate, higher *wergild*. Archaeological investigations of Germanic societies of the Roman Iron Age likewise suggest a picture of considerable and increasing social stratification. This would be entirely in tune with the literary evidence from the migration period. More and less powerful individuals clearly existed among the sixth-century Franks, and something akin to a noble class can be seen within Gothic society from the fourth century onwards.[81]

---

[77] The old view, based on rather partial readings of Tacitus, that the Germanic groups of the migration period were composed almost entirely of such men has been superseded. A good historiographical survey is Wickham (1992).   [78] Heather (1996) App. 2.   [79] Härke (1990) and (1992).

[80] Compare on freemen, for instance, *Lex Salica* 41.1 and 5, with 41.8 and 9; cf. 43.4 equating Romans with freedmen and boys, or *Decretio Childeberti* 3.7.

[81] Roman Iron Age: Hedeager (1987) and (1988). Franks: Irsigler (1979); Grahn-Hoek (1976). Goths: Heather (1996) 57–8, 299ff.

As the public institutions of the successor states became less able to shape local society, it seems likely that these inherent economic inequalities (among both Romans and non-Romans) prevailed. As a result, lesser (i.e. essentially poorer) freemen entered into tighter and more subservient relations with their richer neighbours, prompting a diminution in their status and the rise of entrenched local high-status groups. Once such groups had established their superiority to such an extent that it was heritable, then we can start usefully to consider them as 'nobilities'.

In Frankish Gaul, the new lordships of the seventh century seem to have been associated with precisely this kind of social redefinition. A range of archaeological and literary evidence, for instance, suggests that the Frankish heartland of Austrasia saw noble families entrench their hold on local society to an unprecedented degree around the year 600. We have already come across the *franci* of late-seventh-century Neustria, not as a large group of freemen warriors, but as a small group of noble families.[82] Elsewhere, the pace of change varied. Visigothic laws of the sixth century distinguish lesser and greater freemen, but, at that time, despite vertical ties of patronage, all shared the same *wergild*. Only later in the seventh century were they ascribed different *wergilds* – probably marking the moment at which status became essentially an inherited attribute.[83] In Italy, we have seventh-century references to a few great Lombard families, and the laws clearly expect that lesser Lombard *arimanni* might be bound by grants of land to greater freemen. Only in the eighth and ninth centuries, however, do *arimanni* disappear.[84]

These kinds of processes were not everywhere triumphant. Ninth-century east Breton society was composed of self-governing small-scale communities – *plebes* – where all free landowners, no matter how small their holdings, played a considerable part in the running of local affairs. Processes of dispute settlement are best evidenced in the surviving material, and the likelihood of an individual taking on particular roles (judge, assessor, expert witness, surety, etc.) did vary with wealth, but only slightly. In this society, the key right was to be recognized as a free local landowner, and greater lordship played no dominant role. Even here, however, there is a caveat. This society is made accessible by the survival of the charter collection of the great Benedictine house of Redon, founded in the area in 832. The monastery's archive preserved material about the *plebes* only because they later became part and parcel of its own title deeds. In the later ninth century, Redon became the dominant landowner in the region, acquiring considerable powers of lordship. This material thus illustrates both the long-term

---

[82] Halsall (1995) ch. 9.   [83] Heather (1996) 283ff.

[84] Great families: *Rothari's Edict* pref.; cf. *Laws of Liutprand* 62 on greater and lesser freemen. More generally, Wickham (1981) 134ff. None the less, it is likely that substantial numbers of smaller free landowners survived very generally in Carolingian Europe beneath a politicized aristocratic élite: Wickham (1992) with refs.

survival of a world where it was chiefly important to be a free landowner, but also the kinds of processes which might lead to its destruction.[85]

(b) Freedmen

A second feature of the social structures of the post-Roman west is the prominence and redefinition of a class of freedmen (*liberti*). Such a category had long existed within Roman society, but, in the post-Roman period, it evolved a new form. This was characterized by a permanent inherited dependence of freed persons and their offspring towards the manumitter and his or her descendants. The offspring of Roman freedmen, by contrast, acquired total freedom. In Gaul, the new type of freedmen had become an important social grouping by the end of the seventh century at the latest. In the early-eighth-century will of Abbo of Provence, they form the most numerous category of persons mentioned. In Spain, the church seems to have made considerable use of this new style of manumission in the early seventh century, with lay lords following suit later. From Italy there is less evidence, but the mid-seventh-century edict of Rothari again includes a series of provisions concerning this class.[86]

What prompted the evolution of a class of new, permanently dependent *liberti*? For Visigothic Spain, it has been argued that they were generated in an attempt to square the demands of Christian ethics with an existing pattern of material, especially landed, wealth. Emerging Christian morality declared the freeing of slaves to be a good thing, particularly for saintly bishops. This tended to dissipate church assets, however, since people were as important as land in agricultural production. Permanently dependent *liberti* thus offered Christian gentlemen – ecclesiastical or lay – the opportunity to make their manumissions while, at the same time, preserving the tied labour force which was central to their wealth.[87] There is an obvious plausibility to this picture.

I suspect, however, that the new *liberti* may also have something to do with the militarization of society in the post-Roman world. According to Visigothic law codes, all *liberti* were required to fight with their lords when the army was mobilized. This prescription applied to only a percentage – 5 per cent, raised to 10 per cent by king Wamba – of full slaves. A similar distinction operated in the Merovingian kingdom, where *liberti* seem to have been classed among the arms-bearing groups of society and expected to fight, again under the aegis of their lord.[88] The popularity of freedmen

---

[85] Davies (1988) esp. chs. 3–7. Whether this peasant society represents unbroken continuity from the late Roman world is unclear.

[86] Will of Abbo: Geary (1985) 91–9. Spain: Claude (1980). *Rothari's Edict passim* on *aldii*, esp. 76–102.

[87] Claude (1980).

[88] *Visigothic Code* 9.2.8–9. *Salic Law* 26.1; although *Laws of the Ripuarian Franks* 60–1 distinguishes church freedman from other *liberti*.

for landlords, therefore, may well have had something to do with the necessity – as military obligations became generalized in post-Roman society – of building a body of armed retainers with the requisite military traditions and expertise.

(c) Slaves, serfs and estates

Such upward social movement on the part of some slaves was paralleled by a decline in the status of some formerly free peasants. We have already encountered the long-term decline of poorer freemen in the Lombard, Visigothic and Frankish kingdoms. Not dissimilar processes were already working themselves out in late Roman society, which witnessed a major decline in the status of formerly free tenant farmers (*coloni*), who did not own the lands they worked. This particular group of *coloni* – in technical terms, the *adscripticii* – were tied to their lands by the Roman state in an attempt to turn the countryside into stable units of agricultural production, and hence facilitate the collection of taxes. For the same reason, the imperial authorities also forbade agricultural slaves to be sold separately from the land they worked. And as differences between the rights of some formerly free tenants and some slaves started to disappear, the power of landlords over the *adscripticii* increased. From 365, *adscripticii* were denied the right to alienate any property without the landowner's permission. In 371, landlords were made personally responsible for collecting their taxes, removing any contact *adscripticii* may have had with imperial officials. In 396, they were debarred from suing their landlords (except for extracting more than the customary rent), and, from the early fifth century, they required their landowner's consent to be ordained or to enter a monastery. Hence, in the sixth-century east, Justinian could reasonably claim to see no difference between *adscripticii* and slaves.[89]

There is no way of knowing what percentage of the rural population was composed of *adscripticii*, and hence whether this evolution marks a general strengthening of the social, legal and economic dominance of the landlord classes. In fact, this transformation was only one among several, some very long-term, which, as we have seen, were all leading, if slowly, towards a greater predominance of vertical ties of lordship in the local communities of the post-Roman west. The break-up of the *civitas* unit, the decline in status of lesser freemen, the appearance of *liberti* and a general shift in patterns of slavery – all were probably just as important as the fate of the late Roman *coloni* in generating the rise of a class of dominant landlords.

Lurking not very far in the background here is the thorny problem of manorialization: the spread of what is often considered the characteristic form of medieval estate organization. The classic medieval manor was a

---

[89] Jones, *LRE* 795–803 remains the essential starting-point for any discussion of the late colonate.

landed estate divided into two parts (hence 'bi-partite'). One was worked by the tenants of the estate to provide for their own sustenance. The other part – the demesne – provided for the needs of the lord and was worked by the tenants, who, in addition to various renders of produce, owed substantial labour services to the estate.[90] Did late and post-Roman developments mark an important stage in the formation of this characteristic rural production unit of the medieval period?

There is some reason to think that at least its first foundations may have been laid in the late Roman period and after. Detailed information on estate organization in western Europe in the period 400–600 is rare to the point of non-existence. No estate surveys survive, and very few charters, and there is little to compare to the rich evidence provided by papyri from contemporary Byzantine Egypt. However, an isolated piece of evidence reveals that in the territory of Padua in c. A.D. 550, tenants (coloni) of the church of Ravenna were obliged to undertake heavy labour services on their lord's demesnes, amounting to between one and three days per week (in addition to various renders). As always, it is difficult to know what to make of an isolated example. There is no other Italian evidence for characteristically manorial organization for another two centuries, and the tenants of the papacy's Sicilian estates in c. 600 seem to have owed only renders and no labour service.[91] On the other hand, it is wildly unlikely that chance has preserved evidence from the only manorially organized estate of sixth-century Italy.

More generally, although this is again a much disputed question, it has been argued that some (not necessarily all) villas in the late Roman period were tending to become centres of rural population rather than remaining the dwelling-places of individual landowners. Agache's aerial surveys in the Somme basin in northern France showed that many villages of the region, deserted later in the medieval period, had a Roman villa underneath. Arguments have also been advanced from place-name and other evidence for seeing Roman villas as the generators of medieval villages across much of the rest of the Frankish kingdom. If so, this would suggest that in the late and post-Roman periods, the Roman villa in Gaul at least underwent a transformation highly comparable to the process of nucleation observable later in other areas of Europe, when dispersed rural populations gathered in concentrated settlements.[92] As we have seen, the diminution in status of tenant cultivators – the adscripticii, at least – was also creating, at broadly the same time, a labour force highly subservient to the landowning class. It is at least worth suggesting that a nucleation of settlement around some villas in our period was accompanied by an extension of landlord control over the relevant parts of the rural population.

---

[90] A good historiographical introduction is Rösener (1989) 9–28.   [91] Wickham (1981) 99–100.

[92] Agache (1970); cf., more generally, Percival (1976) esp. chs. 8–9. Some bibliographical orientation on nucleation and manorialization: Cheyette (1977); Blair (1991) ch. 1; Hildebrandt (1988).

The argument cannot be pressed. It is entirely possible to have a marked increase in vertical bonds of lordship within a society, without, in the first instance at least, generating a world of nucleated great estates. In the Metz region of north-eastern Francia, an established nobility, passing on inherited status, seems to have emerged in the eighth century, but bi-partite manors only in the ninth.[93] Nucleation of settlement can also occur without generating any increase in the powers of landlords. Villages existed across much of the Mediterranean region in the Roman period without manors coming into existence, and, acting as human collectivities, they could even frustrate the designs of landowners.[94]

Indeed, across much of northern Europe, it was only long after the fall of Rome that processes of nucleation and manorialization worked themselves out. The subject has been explored to greatest depth for Anglo-Saxon England, where these processes can be dated, in the arable lands of central and southern England, between the seventh and the ninth century; further north it was still under way in the twelfth. In the Frankish kingdom, the Carolingian polyptychs demonstrate the existence of bi-partite estates on monastic holdings in its north-central heartlands by the ninth century, but the system was clearly not new at that point. The seventh and eighth centuries have been suggested as the moment of their evolution. Elsewhere, the position is far from clear, but the eighth and ninth centuries would seem to have been an important period of bi-partite estate formation in Lombard Italy. Outside Roman Europe, the demonstrable date for nucleation is generally even later. Nucleated rural settlements in Saxony, for example, seem to have resulted from the imposition of Carolingian lordship there in the ninth century and beyond.[95] Nevertheless, a local society dominated by an élite of free peasants survived in parts of Brittany well into the ninth century, and such societies had probably prevailed across much of western Europe up to the Carolingian period.[96]

Conclusions can only be tentative, but some broad outlines of development seem clear. In the long term, the rural landscape was remade into a series of estate units, under the domination of a powerful landlord class. These formed the primary local communities for medieval peasants. Some of the necessary transformations underlying this process were already under way in the late imperial period, and some late Roman landlords may have already essentially turned their estates into manors. Where the migration period saw substantial settlements of outsiders, such as around Metz, these processes were probably halted or even reversed as lands were

[93] Halsall (1995) 262ff.
[94] The experience of Libanius in Antioch: Liebeschuetz (1972) 67–71 with refs. On all these issues, see further ch. 12 (Ward-Perkins), pp. 327–33 above.
[95] Anglo-Saxon England: Unwin (1988). Carolingian polyptychs: e.g. Duby (1974). Italy: Wickham (1981) 100ff. Saxony: Nitz (1988).   [96] Brittany: see above, n. 85; cf. Wickham (1992).

divided between members of the intruding freemen classes. As we have seen, however, the importance of the freemen class was eventually eclipsed everywhere by the rise of a stable class of larger landowners, perhaps by as early as *c.* 600 in the Frankish kingdom, although actual manorialization may have followed rather later. It remains an open but interesting question whether surviving manorially organized late Roman estates presented the more powerful freemen among immigrant groups with exciting new ideas about how to extend their social pre-eminence.

CHAPTER 17

ARMIES AND SOCIETY IN THE LATER ROMAN WORLD

MICHAEL WHITBY

The Roman empire was a structure created and sustained by force that had to be available for deployment both against external threats to the state's existence and against any of its inhabitants who attempted to reject or avoid its authority. But for its first 250 years the empire managed to maintain a considerable separation between civilian and military spheres: soldiers were legally and socially distinct from civilians, and to a large extent geographically as well, since most major concentrations of troops were located along the empire's frontiers. As a result, many of the 'inner' provinces could appear demilitarized:[1] soldiers might pass along the arterial roads or be on hand when a new census was held, but they were outsiders, in the main recruited from, stationed in and demobilized into other less civilized (i.e. less urbanized) parts of the empire, either the periphery or the uplands and other marginal areas. There was also, however, a close mutual interdependence: the army consumed much of the surplus product of the prosperous peaceful provinces, so that soldier and civilian were tied economically; the emperor was both commander-in-chief of the armies and the ultimate source of law, political authority and social status; provincial governors and most other commanders of armies were members of the senate, the pinnacle of the civilian social structure.

In the late empire this tidy picture was greatly complicated, primarily as a result of extensive tribal invasions: provinces and cities that had once been unmilitary had to remilitarize themselves; the army became an important potential means of political and social advancement, successful tribes created new centres of power where new rules governed relationships; all the time the military had to extract resources from an economy that was often suffering the effects of war. Over all, the military became increasingly prominent in the different parts of the Roman, or former Roman, world, but at differing speeds. What was happening in much of the west in the fifth century only became noticeable in the east about 150 to 200 years later, after a period when the east appeared to be moving in the opposite direction. This progression parallels that of the Graeco-Roman

---

[1] Cornell (1993) 165–8; cf. Rich in Rich and Shipley (1993) 6.

469

cities[2] – not surprisingly, since the civilian ideals enshrined in urban life were being challenged by the militarization of local élites, while this process of militarization reflected the changing social and economic balances within individual communities.

This chapter investigates the ways in which the army, as well as less official types of military force, influenced political and social change in the fields of imperial or royal authority, the preservation of public order, the relationships of core and periphery, and the links between soldiers and civilians. In most of these aspects it is a case of pointing to and explaining the separate development of eastern and western parts of the empire (though with the Balkan provinces regularly being close to the western model).

I. MILITARY POWER AND AUTHORITY

At the very centre of society the military played a key role in determining who wielded power, by involvement in accession ceremonies or usurpations, and by maintaining law and order; those who commanded and deployed military force on such occasions naturally expected to reap benefits in terms of increased influence and status. Within the Roman empire the army (or groups purporting to represent it) participated in the choice and confirmation of new emperors. For the east, where imperial succession was relatively well-ordered until the bloody usurpation of Phocas, many of the accession ceremonies are recorded in Constantine Porphyrogenitus' *Book of Ceremonies* or in contemporary writers.[3] The succession of Marcian to Theodosius II in 450 was performed at the parade ground at the Hebdomon, and the new emperor was probably elevated ceremonially by soldiers, in spite of the fact that his betrothal to Theodosius' sister Pulcheria provided dynastic legitimacy.[4] The ceremonies for Leo's accession in 457 also demonstrate the centrality of the army: Leo was crowned first by Busalgus, a quartermaster (*campiductor*), at which point the military standards that had been placed on the ground were lifted up; Leo attributed his selection to 'God the almighty and your decision, most brave fellow soldiers'. The responding acclamations from the spectators emphasized the position of the army – 'The army, with you as ruler, victorious; the army, with you as ruler, fortunate' – and Leo's first thoughts were about rewarding the troops.[5]

Subsequent eastern accessions were centred on the Hippodrome and the adjacent palace, and units of the palace guards, the *scholae*, *candidati* and *excubitores*, naturally played a more prominent part, even to the extent of

---

[2] Cf. ch. 8 (Liebeschuetz), pp. 207–10 above. [3] MacCormack (1981) III.9; Olster (1993) 159–63.
[4] *Chron. Pasch.* 590.8–12; cf. Burgess (1993/4). [5] *De Caer.* I. 91, pp. 410–12.

fighting each other during the deliberations that preceded the elevation of Justin I in 518,[6] the only occasion between Leo I and Phocas when there was no clear dynastic successor. The changes in ceremonial location and in the military units involved might indicate that the field army lost influence while the palace guards increased in importance; this, however, should not be inferred solely from accession ceremonies, since in the 450s the ascendancy of the general Aspar in Constantinople may have ensured extra prominence for the mobile army. There had always been tension between the 'inside' power of the imperial guards – originally the praetorians in their camp on the outskirts of Rome – and the provincial armies: greater proximity normally allowed the guards to decide inheritance within a dynasty, as with Claudius in 41 and Nero in 54, whereas the greater muscle of the frontier legions would conclude non-dynastic succession, as in the year of the four emperors in 68–9 or in the civil war which followed Commodus' assassination in 192. Thus, the prominence of the guards at successions in Constantinople after Leo is one token of the east's ability to arrange a more civilian and orderly presentation of the continuity of imperial rule: the accession ceremonies were public demonstrations of the links that held together the overlapping spheres of imperial, religious, civilian and military authority.

In the west, both in the remnant of the Roman empire and in the tribal kingdoms, the military were regularly prominent at the moment of succession. In 425 Valentinian III could only inherit his grandfather's throne with the support of a large eastern army which ousted the usurper John from Ravenna. In 455 Avitus was placed on the throne of Italy through the support first of the Visigoths under Theoderic at Toulouse, which was then backed up by the Gallo-Roman aristocracy at Ugernum. After the deposition of Avitus by the Italian army in 456, all subsequent successions were determined either by the *magister militum* in Italy (first Ricimer, then Odoacer) or by the intervention of the eastern emperor, whose nominee Anthemius and representatives Olybrius and Julius Nepos all briefly held power. Military force determined who occupied the throne, or indeed whether it should be left vacant, until Theoderic the Amal captured Ravenna and created the Ostrogothic kingdom by conquest.

Most of the tribal kingdoms reveal a conflict between the dynastic aspirations of the dominant family and the military claims of their associates and retinues. This is most clear in Merovingian Gaul, where the successive partitions of Clovis' spear-won territory between his sons, and then his grandsons, were determined by military might. A son, such as Theuderic's heir Theudebert I in 533, would need the support of his *leudes*, or military following, to counter the ambitions of uncles or cousins; a royal claimant

[6] *De Caer.* 1.93.

would be eliminated when abandoned by his military backers, as Gundovald discovered at St Bertrand-de-Comminges in 585; an ambitious heir like Chramn might even attempt to pre-empt his father's death by carving out a personal kingdom. Lombard Italy was another society whose political superstructure was dominated by its military nobility: after the deaths of Alboin and Cleph, the nobles decided to do without a king for ten years until military needs led them to proclaim Cleph's son, Authari, in 584.[7]

Ostrogothic Italy during Theoderic's long reign might appear more civilized and civilian than other kingdoms, but this was an impression deliberately fostered by the regime and propagated to its civilian Italian subjects by its spokesman, Cassiodorus. Theoderic seems to have appreciated the benefits of cultivating the non-military ingredients of royal power, perhaps in imitation of contemporary developments at Constantinople, but his daughter Amalasuintha's attempts to give her son Athalaric a Roman education were frustrated, since the majority of Goths were not prepared to move so rapidly from the traditional warlike ethos of their society. Theoderic had never forgotten the military basis of his position, as is indicated by his concern, like a Persian monarch, to ensure that his military subordinates attended court regularly to receive the king's gifts.[8] After his death, Amal authority quickly disintegrated, to reveal the fragility of the dynastic aspects of his power. Theodahad could rely on disgruntled members of the nobility in his manoeuvres against Amalasuintha, and, after his own military ineptitude became clear in the early stages of the Byzantine reconquest, the Goths chose a sequence of warriors as kings: Vitigis, Ildibad, Eraric (who indeed was Rugian rather than Goth), Totila and Teias.

The military units which helped influence the choice of royal or imperial master also enhanced the standing of their commanders, so that warfare was an important determinant of social prominence. The fifth century appears as a period of warlords and kingmakers in both halves of the empire. For two decades the west was dominated by the patrician and *magister militum* Aetius. Although his father Gaudentius held military command, it was Aetius' personal connections with sources of troops that made him important: Huns, recruited perhaps through contacts established while serving as a hostage, permitted him to survive his involvement with the usurper John and various later mishaps; he may also have annexed the followers of his rival Boniface, whose wife and estates he certainly took over. Aetius' career as military protector of Valentinian III appeared to achieve the dream of many late Roman soldiers – namely, marriage into the imperial family – when his son Gaudentius was betrothed to Valentinian's

---

[7] Wood, *Merovingian Kingdoms* 56–60; Bachrach (1972) 31; Wickham (1981) 30–2.
[8] Heather (1995b).

daughter Placidia. But, as so often, success was quickly followed by disaster when Valentinian, perhaps urged on by the aristocratic senator Petronius Maximus, personally murdered Aetius. The eastern equivalent of Aetius was the family of Ardabur, whose son Aspar was the dominant figure at the accessions of Marcian and Leo I, and whose grandson Patricius was married to Leo's daughter Leontia and proclaimed Caesar – at which point the family was eliminated at the emperor Leo's instigation. The western rivalry of Aetius and Boniface was paralleled in the east by that between Aspar the Alan and Zeno the Isaurian. As with Aetius, both rivals had access to sources of power independent of the state: the Ardabur family was linked to the Gothic war-leaders Plintha and Theoderic Strabo, while Zeno's background opened connections to a range of Isaurian supporters of varying reliability.

It is possible to construct a complex family tree that incorporates into a single seemingly unified stream most of the prominent military men and ruling families from the fourth century to the sixth,[9] but this apparent family unity reflects the truism that rulers wanted to annex potential sources of military support, while war-leaders desired the social prestige and economic rewards that the emperor controlled. The family of Anastasius illustrates the mutual interdependence of the different élites.[10] The army was only one of the avenues to social advancement, while the existence of large secular and administrative hierarchies provided alternative routes and ensured that education remained almost as important a vehicle for social mobility as military prowess. This is most clearly the case in the complex society of the eastern empire, but even in the west a stable kingdom used its power of patronage to attract civilian supporters: senators who served the Ostrogothic court were rewarded with land grants in the Po valley, while the Visigothic court at Toulouse might offer employment to an expert in Latin letters.[11] Although many generals did come from professional military backgrounds, the hypothesis of Carrié that there was a definitive separation of civilian and military careers relies too heavily on the anti-military and anti-barbarian rhetoric of Libanius and Synesius. The thesis cannot be substantiated, at least in the east: the families of military men like Areobindus and Armatus attempted to establish themselves in civilian society, while the holders of palatine offices like Celer, Tiberius or Maurice might command armies in the field.[12]

The potential political threat from military commanders could be reduced by the choice as generals of relatives or close associates. In this respect a turning-point was marked by Zeno's success in ousting the usurper Basiliscus and breaking the power of his former supporter, the

---

[9] Demandt (1989). [10] Cameron (1978). [11] Schäfer (1991); Harries (1994) 130–1.
[12] Carrié (1986) 485–7, relying on passages like Lib. *Or.* 11.37–40 and Syn. *De Regno* (on which see Cameron and Long (1993) ch. 4). For details on individuals see *PLRE* II and III.

Isaurian Illus; thereafter, throughout the sixth century, eastern emperors retained control of their military establishment. Emperors did not campaign in person, with the exception of a planned expedition by Zeno and two sorties into the Balkans by Maurice, but most had some experience of active command before reaching the throne. Relatives of Anastasius, Justinian, Justin II, Maurice, Phocas and Heraclius regularly served as generals. Members, particularly officers, of the imperial bodyguard could also be expected to be loyal after promotion to independent command: Belisarius and Sittas under Justinian, Comentiolus under Maurice. Thus, Belisarius declined to exploit his African or Italian successes against Justinian, even when Justinian's unpopularity gave hope of success. A further source of reliable generals were the leaders of relatively small tribal groups, especially those with a short history of contact with the Romans, men such as the Gepid Mundo, the Slav Chilbuldius or the Herul Philemuth. Eunuchs were another type of dependable outsiders: Solomon, a former retainer of Belisarius, was Justinian's most successful commander in Africa after the reconquest, while the Persarmenian Narses, an outsider in two senses, controlled distant Italy from 552 until his death in Justin II's reign.

It is difficult to cite comparable examples from the western empire, where the military tended to dominate civilians, in contrast to the east, where civilians managed the military. The career of Belisarius, the rival of Aetius as the most famous general in this period, illustrates the latter point. Belisarius' origins were sufficiently obscure for his parents' names to be unrecorded, but service in the bodyguard of the future emperor Justinian led to military command in 527. In due course, glamorous victories in the west brought him a devoted army, enormous wealth and the chance of a royal throne at Ravenna, but he could still be humbled by the emperor, symbolically in the triumph that commemorated his Vandal victory when he performed obeisance to Justinian beside the captive Gelimer, and effectively in 542 when he lost control of his personal following. It is possible that personal weakness and indecision, faults noted in Procopius' *Secret History*, played a part in Belisarius' failure to assert himself more fully, but his position was also undermined by the sheer size of the eastern empire and the diversity of its armed forces: these ensured that the dominance of any great figure was always likely to be challenged. Belisarius' problems with uncooperative colleagues or subordinates in Italy in the late 530s and 540s can be paralleled by dissension in the eastern army in 502–3, and again in the 570s and 580s: the issue was not confined to one individual.

The ability of the civilian élite to marginalize the general is relevant to the ultimate failure of conspiracies and usurpations in the east until those of Phocas and Heraclius. Only the attempt of Basiliscus achieved brief success, and this was virtually a dynastic squabble, since he was the brother of Zeno's mother-in-law, Verina; even so, Zeno quickly mobilized sufficient support in the east to regain control. Other substantial revolts, such as those of Illus against Zeno and Vitalian against Anastasius, achieved success in one particular region but could not then extend their success to other areas. Mutinies by particular armies, in Africa in the 530s and the east in 588–9, remained confined to their area of operations. Some of the most serious threats to imperial control were posed by non-military members of the court: the bankers' plot in 562, the suspected actions of Aetherius in 560 and again in 566, or the conspiracy by a group of officials, senators and guardsmen against the outsider Phocas in 605.[13] These reflect the belief of civilians that they could control society and, presumably with the co-operation of some powerful officials or members of the imperial family (as in the planned Persarmenian coup of 548), change their master. Even the success of Phocas' own coup in 602 can lend support to this picture of an essentially civilian society, since the mutinous army seems to have canvassed other candidates as the replacement for Maurice before turning finally to its own leader. Heraclius, too, after the deposition of Phocas, stressed the role of the senate in his coup and in the choice of new emperor.[14]

II. THE MAINTENANCE OF ORDER

Far from undermining imperial power, military force in the east was a crucial element in the maintenance of authority. Law and order in the capital and other major cities had to be upheld by a combination of personal display and the occasional deployment of violence.[15] Imperial processions were accompanied by guards and other soldiers to magnify the impact of the emperor's appearance and to restore order if the spectators turned to violence, as on Maurice's procession to Blachernae at Candlemas 602. The extreme instance is the Nika riot of 532 when Justinian, faced by massive popular upheaval and the desertion of parts of the imperial guard, appealed for help to the troops stationed outside the city; these men, presumably drawn from the units commanded by the *magister militum praesentalis* which were quartered conveniently close to the capital, had to fight their way through the city to the imperial palace, after which Justinian could at last take the initiative and plan the destruction of the rioters. Like Anastasius when confronted by fierce religious rioting in 512, Justinian attempted to calm the mob by appearing in the *kathisma*, but, after this failed, troops were sent to the Hippodrome to massacre those present. The death toll was exceptional, but the mechanics of urban control were not:

[13] Malalas 493.1–495.5 with *Exc. de Insid.* fr. 49 and Theophanes 237.15–238.18; *PLRE* III *s.v.* Aetherius 2; *Chron. Pasch.* 696.6–17 with Theophanes 294.27–295.13, 297.12–298.4.
[14] Theophylact VIII.8.5; Nicephorus ch. 2 with *Chron. Pasch.* 708.4–9.
[15] Lintott (1968) chs. 7–11; Nippel (1984).

personal intervention by a senior official – the *comes excubitorum, curopalatus* or city prefect – would be backed up by action by the *excubitores*, who would be supplemented, if necessary, by regular troops.[16]

Rioting in the capital city had extra significance, since the manifestation of anarchy on the streets had implications for the emperor's reputation, but other major cities in the eastern empire had analogous problems. After the Vandal sack of Rome in 455, however, no city in the west had the critical mass to sustain a comparable urban explosion, though a specific grievance might provoke uproar, as when the inhabitants of Trier killed the unpopular tax-gatherer Parthenius.[17] The riots at Antioch are best attested, though even here the evidence only reveals exceptional cases of violence.[18] The task of maintaining order fell to the *comes Orientis* and the prefect of the watch. Their regular resources were insufficient to impose peace, as the riots of 507 revealed when, in spite of the presence of a Gothic guard and the support of the Blue faction, the prefect of the watch, Menas, was disembowelled by the Greens and the *comes* Procopius fled the city.[19] A new *comes* could restore order, but he presumably arrived with a draft of reinforcements from outside, and there is no evidence that there was a large garrison permanently stationed inside the city: certainly in 540 it was necessary to move troops into Antioch in an attempt to thwart the Persian attack. The troubles a century later at the end of Phocas' reign highlight the same issues. The *comes Orientis* Bonosus and the general Cottanas could not initially quell Jewish disturbances in the city, during which the patriarch Anastasius had been killed, but after withdrawing to gather troops they could impose order with the help of the local Blues.[20]

In Alexandria the standard problems of policing a megalopolis were compounded by religious issues. The patriarch could organize considerable violence through his patronage of monks and other ascetics, violence which could be exported to other cities, as Dioscorus demonstrated at the 'Robber' synod of Ephesus in 449. Further, the doctrinal affiliation of the mass of Egyptians was often at odds with the emperor's preference, and this opposition generated violence. Proterius, successor to the deposed Dioscorus, could only be installed through the support of troops; initially the rioters, led by members of urban guilds, forced the soldiers to retreat into the Serapaeum, which was then set on fire with considerable casualties, and order was only restored by the arrival of 2,000 reinforcements from Constantinople; but Proterius was never accepted, as the emperor Marcian admitted in a letter to the praetorian prefect in 455 when the penalties against Manichees were extended to his opponents, and he was eventually lynched by his flock in 457.[21] As at Antioch, there were limits to what

[16] Malalas 394.11–395.5 (*c.* 500–7); 483.9–13 (547); 490.16–491.17 (561); *Exc. de Insid.* Malalas fr. 51 (565). [17] Greg. Tur. *Hist.* III.36. [18] Isaac, *Limits of Empire* 270–7. [19] Malalas 395.20–398.4. [20] Theophanes 296.17–25; *Doctrina Jacobi* 1.40. [21] Frend, *Monophysite Movement* 148–55.

soldiers could do in the long term to impose order on a reluctant population in a megalopolis, a problem not confined to antiquity.[22]

Maintaining provincial law and order has been seen as a primary function, along with external conquest, of the whole Roman military machine.[23] Any special event might require the despatch of troops to maintain control: when Symeon Stylites died on his column in 459 the people of Antioch demanded his body to act as a talisman against earthquakes, and the *comes Orientis* Ardabur had to send a guard of Gothic soldiers to ensure that the body was not torn apart by relic-hunters between Qalat Seman and the city.[24]

Even in the more urbanized east there were areas that remained on the edges of imperial authority in the fifth century, the most notorious being Isauria, a traditional area where altitude conferred immunity from unwelcome official demands.[25] Here the involvement of the bellicose mountaineers in central imperial politics between the 440s and the 490s – namely, during the career of Tarasicodissa-Zeno – stimulated closer links with empire-wide developments, symbolized by the construction of the lavish churches at Alahan. But when centralist ambitions were thwarted, regional rebellion flared. In 484 Zeno's attempt to dominate Illus led to four years of fighting. Illus attracted the support of Leontius, the Isaurian *magister militum per Thraciam*, whom Zeno had sent against him, and of client satraps of Armenia; he had Leontius proclaimed emperor, but Zeno's generals managed to isolate the rebels in the fort of Papyrius; the transfer of the property of Illus' relatives to the cities of Isauria will have helped to undermine his local support. The failure of the Isaurians to secure the throne in 491 caused renewed fighting: Anastasius had Zeno's brother Longinus relegated to Egypt, but two other unrelated Isaurians, Longinus of Cardala and Longinus of Selinus, sustained a revolt in Isauria until 498, relying on weapons and money stored there by Zeno. Anastasius eventually reasserted imperial control, and the transfer thereafter of Isaurians to Thrace imposed order, or at least ensured that problems remained sufficiently local to escape notice.[26]

The Tzani and the Samaritans were other upland peoples reluctant to accept imperial authority. The Tzani were only fully subjected to Roman control in 528/9, but a brief revolt in 558 required the intervention of troops from the Roman army in Lazica. Order was restored by Theodore, himself a Tzan by birth, whose military career illustrates the overall success of Justinian's policy of incorporating this people.[27] In Samaria the primary function of troops was the suppression of religious strife. The Samaritans,

---

[22] Bagnall, *Egypt* 164.   [23] Isaac, *Limits of Empire* ch. 1–2.   [24] Malalas 369.10–16.
[25] For fourth-century troubles here, see Matthews (1989) 355–67.
[26] *PLRE* II *s.v.* Illus 1, Leontius 17, Zenon 7, Longinus 3 and 4.
[27] Procop. *Buildings* III.6; Agathias, *Hist.* v.1–2; *PLRE* III *s.v.* Theodorus 21.

stirred to revolt in 529 by religious persecution, managed to proclaim a brigand leader, Julian, as emperor and capture Neapolis. It took a little time for Theodore, *dux* of Palestine, to co-ordinate the official reaction with John (probably a fellow *dux*) and the leader of a local Arab tribe, but the Samaritan resistance in the mountains was then suppressed with considerable bloodshed. A Samaritan revolt in 556 appears to have been confined to Caesarea, although the death of the local governor during the troubles again illustrates the fact that authorities rarely had sufficient forces on hand to quell violence immediately.[28]

Many eastern provinces were afflicted by lower levels of disorder, as is indicated by Justinian's overhaul of provincial administration that began in the 530s. The intention was to strengthen administrative control by eliminating conflicts between civilian and military authority: in Pisidia and Lycaonia the governor was upgraded to the rank of *praetor*, an enlarged Paphlagonia also received a *praetor*, while a *moderator* was appointed to an enlarged Helenopontus – salaries were higher, and civil and military power combined. In Thrace the amalgamation of two vicariates into a praetorship was intended to stop quarrelling and improve the defence and administration of the hinterland of Constantinople. Brigandage, however, remained a problem, as malefactors migrated across provincial boundaries to evade justice: in 548 a supra-provincial authority had to be introduced in the Pontic provinces, a vicar who controlled soldiers as well as financial and civil officials, and in central Asia Minor a *biokolutes*, preventer of violence, was to co-ordinate action in Lycaonia, Lycia, Pisidia and the two Phrygias.[29] In some parts of the empire, such as the Sinai peninsula, where wandering Arabs caused problems, troops regularly had to provide protection for travellers.[30]

Brigandage could describe various activities, and the diverse nature of the challenge to authority is indicated by a Justinianic law relating to Honorias and by the problems of Cappadocia. A law concerning the suppression of brigands was addressed to the large and small proprietors of the city of Adrianople: this stipulated that no landowner was to have more than five men in his retinue, whereas ten had been allowed at the time of an earlier investigation. These retinues of lance-bearers or horsemen allowed the individual landowner to take the law into his own hands. In Cappadocia there were large imperial estates managed by the *praepositus sacri cubiculi*, whose influence at court might have guaranteed efficient control, but the province also contained several very wealthy landowners whose armed retainers might annex imperial property and intimidate the local governor and his subordinates.[31]

[28] Just. *Nov.* 103; Malalas 445.19–447.21; 487.10–488.3.
[29] Jones, *LRE* 280–2, 294; in 553 the *biokolutes'* authority was confined to Lycaonia and Lycia.
[30] Isaac, *Limits of Empire* 205.
[31] Feissel and Kaygusuz (1985) 399–401, 410–15 (cf. *Nov.* 30); Just. *Nov.* 30.

The efficient exercise of imperial or royal authority required a substantial community of interest between such local grandees and the monarch. In the east, the emperor preserved the balance in his own favour. Even in the Balkans, when the obscure Scamareis took advantage of the severe disruption caused by Slav invasions to rob an Avar embassy, Tiberius could identify the guilty and restore some of the property; under Maurice a savage brigand chief was persuaded by a personal letter from the emperor to stop his activities and come to court.[32] Brigands might well be people of some local prominence who had become marginalized, perhaps through no particular fault of their own, and whom it was important for emperors to reattach to the proper channels of authority: a good example of the process is the fourth-century Gallic brigand Charietto, a man whose support for an unsuccessful usurper destroyed his connections with the imperial centre, but who was then brought back into the fold by Julian.

In the west, the inability of the emperor to maintain such control led to the emergence of 'warlordism'.[33] Local groups had to undertake their own protection with scant regard to central interests: depending on the point of view of the source, their leaders might be termed 'kings', as were Aegidius and Syagrius in their principality at Soissons, or the groups dismissed as bagaudae, whether it is correct to interpret these contentious people as the Gallic equivalent of the private retinues of magnates in Asia Minor or as peasant communities that had relocated themselves away from areas of regular fighting. The members of such communities may well have acknowledged imperial authority in theory, but have been more reluctant to accept it in practice, especially if their preferred emperor was no longer in control.[34] The establishment both of the Visigoths in Aquitaine and, more certainly, of Alans in northern Gaul has been seen as an imperial response to such loss of civilian authority in parts of Gaul, and Aetius was prepared to use the Alans to regain control of subject Romans; if this hypothesis is correct, the strategy brought no more than short-term relief, since the main beneficiaries were the tribes.[35]

Within the emerging tribal kingdoms, rulers faced similar problems of authority, albeit on a smaller scale. In Visigothic Spain, kings had a fundamental problem in attempting to make royal authority anything more than nominal outside the immediate location of the court: in the mid sixth century the inhabitants of Cordoba could rout the king, appropriate his treasure and, like Mérida, maintain virtual independence for several years. Such determined conduct required joint action by local Romans and Visigoths against their supposed master.[36] The king had no less difficulty than a Roman emperor in retaining full control over his military following

[32] Menander fr. 15.6; Farka (1993–4).   [33] Whittaker (1994) ch. 7.
[34] Van Dam, *Leadership and Community* ch. 1.3; Drinkwater (1992); cf. ch. 18 (Wood), pp. 502–9 below.
[35] Wood, *Merovingian Kingdoms* 8–12; Burns (1992) 56–7.   [36] Collins (1980) 198–201.

once it had been given its own property. In Merovingian Gaul, Theuderic employed his army to discipline the Auvergne, probably in 523, after a false rumour of the king's death had led some Arvernians to switch allegiance to Childebert; even the royal army found it difficult to capture fortresses with their local garrisons. This campaign reveals the complexities of royal authority: the army, disgruntled by Theuderic's refusal to join his half-brothers in an attack on the Burgundians and seeking an alternative source of booty, forced the king to conduct the punitive invasion; thus, Theuderic's regional assertion of authority was combined with a demonstration of the power of the military over the king.[37] The Merovingian kingdom had emerged from the amalgamation, often forcible, of the heterogeneous war-bands that dominated northern France in the late fifth century, and this fact conditioned the subsequent relationship of kings and army.

Theoderic the Amal was well aware of the same problem, since in his early days in the Balkans he had experienced the crisis of a recalcitrant war-band when his followers threatened to switch allegiance to Theoderic Strabo, who at the time appeared to be a better patron; in due course Theoderic could turn to his advantage a war-band's fluidity, when he won over the followers of Strabo's son, Recitach. As an establishment figure at Ravenna, Theoderic had to reward his following with the land grants for which they had struggled so long in the Balkans. This dispersal of the war-band might well have encouraged the emergence of local centres of power, but Theoderic appears to have countered this centrifugal danger by demanding the regular attendance at court of the members of his army.[38]

III. LOCAL AND CENTRAL

The role of armies in maintaining order was crucial for the image of a particular regime. Preservation of internal stability and external security were fundamental elements in the ideology of the Roman emperor, and were largely adopted in the tribal kingdoms, since failure by any ruler to guarantee protection was an invitation to others to intervene, either locals organizing self-help or new protectors arriving from outside. The physical and literary rhetoric of Justinian's building works proclaimed that the emperor was ensuring the defence of frontiers and the protection of the empire's inhabitants: for example, with regard to the Balkans, Procopius asserted that Justinian had re-established the Danube as the boundary, and provided protection throughout the interior of the provinces by constructing towers, while for reconquered Africa Justinian legislated to reintroduce an

---

[37] Wood, *Merovingian Kingdoms* 52–3; Bachrach (1972) 20–2.   [38] Heather (1995b).

efficient garrison of frontier troops with some central reserve.[39] Theoderic the Amal made arrangements for the defence of his kingdom's coasts when a naval attack from the east was rumoured, while Carcassonne was rewarded by the Visigoths with urban status in recognition of its importance as a frontier town and strategic fortress for protecting Spain.[40]

Rulers had to appear to be concerned for their subjects or face the consequences. It is no coincidence that the end of Roman rule in Britain is regarded as the withdrawal of Roman garrisons by Honorius, since an area that had to defend itself could not be expected, or forced, to contribute taxes to the imperial treasury, although it was only in retrospect that any such move could be seen as decisive and final.[41] Tiberius came close to signalling the abandonment of Rome in 578/9 when he instructed the senatorial ambassadors who brought the traditional payment in gold to mark his accession to take the money back and spend it locally on their own defence, but here imperial interest did not disappear completely.[42] The Avar Chagan understood the connection. At Anchialus in 588 he donned the imperial robes dedicated there by the empress Anastasia, and challenged Maurice's authority over the Balkans by offering the cities the chance to pay their taxes to the Avars in return for protection.[43] The only regime that blatantly took little interest in the safety of its civilian inhabitants was the Vandal kingdom. Here, city fortifications were officially slighted, putting locals at the mercy of Moorish raiders, but from the Vandal perspective it was more important to eliminate potential centres of resistance than to court the good will of subject Romans.

Weakness at the centre entailed a remilitarization of local society. In some cases this had imperial sanction, as in 440 when Valentinian III responded to Vandal naval attacks by encouraging local organization of defences, but more often initiatives reflected local despair at imperial inaction. At Clermont-Ferrand, Sidonius' brother-in-law Ecdicius, with eighteen companions and presumably numerous lesser followers, rescued the city from the Visigoths; at the time, Sidonius still believed that the empire was interested in retaining control of the Auvergne, but he was soon to be disabused.[44] In the early empire, the imposition of a garrison on a city can be seen as detrimental, a drain on local resources,[45] but in the late empire any disadvantages were outweighed by the greater military threats and the closer integration of soldier and civilian: the Roman world had reverted to a condition in which warfare was much more familiar to a wider range of its inhabitants than at any time since the late republic. Remilitarization of

---

[39] Procop. *Buildings* IV.1.1–14; *CJ* 1.27.2.8; cf. Bagnall, *Egypt* 161–72, *contra* Isaac, *Limits of Empire* 393–4.   [40] Cass. *Variae* v.17; James (1980a) 226.

[41] Whittaker (1994) 239; cf. ch. 18 (Wood), pp. 504–6 below.   [42] Zos. VI.10; Menander fr. 22.

[43] Michael the Syrian x.21, p. 361.   [44] Val. *Nov.* 9; cf. also *C.Th.* VII.18.14, IX.14.2. Sid. Ap. *Ep.* 3.3.

[45] Poulter (1992) 120.

the countryside affected patterns of settlement, by encouraging people to move from the vulnerable lowland sites and return to more defensible, often pre-Roman, hill-top sites, or to attach themselves to the protection of a local patron, the landowner who would soon become warlord.[46]

Towns and cities showed interest in retaining control of 'their' troops. The classic case here is Asemus, a small town just south of the Danube frontier which had a strong tradition of self-help: in the 440s the locals protected themselves against Attila's Huns, while in 592 under the leadership of their bishop they barricaded the city against Maurice's brother Peter when he attempted to enrol the impressive local garrison in his field army. The consequences of the loss of a garrison are illustrated by the fate of Topirus, where the Slavs killed the professional defenders after luring them outside the walls and then overcame the resistance, however fierce, of the local civilians; at Thessalonica in 586 the gravity of the Avar attack was heightened by the absence of the praetorian prefect with his troops on a mission to southern Greece.[47] The desire to control troops locally lies behind one of pope Gregory's quarrels with Maurice. The emperor had used Gregory as a channel for transferring money for the pay of the soldiers at Rome, but he was then extremely vexed when Gregory personally distributed the cash, since this would imply that the pope was now paymaster and so affect the soldiers' sense of priorities; Gregory's recurrent complaints about the lack of a garrison at Rome and the different interests of the exarch at Ravenna are directly relevant to this dispute.[48]

A similar process had probably been under way in the west during the fifth century. Here there is an apparent discrepancy between the paucity of Roman troops available for combating major threats, such as Attila's invasion in 451, when the bulk of Aetius' army comprised federates and allied Visigoths, and the existence of local Roman units whose continuing efficacy is indicated by accounts of their actions in the sixth century. In the Burgundian kingdom there appears to have been a fusion of Gallo-Roman and German military elements, which permitted this area to support a standing army that was commanded by *patricii*, often Gallo-Romans; this may have originated in an essential similarity between Gallo-Roman and German aristocrats, men who possessed personal military followings, but the structure was sufficiently stable to survive the elimination of Burgundian leadership, since Merovingian rulers continued the pre-existing arrangements for organization and command.[49]

In the main parts of the Merovingian world there is a noticeable military division between the north-east (Austrasia) and the south and west (Neustria and Aquitaine): in the latter, local levies, usually based on towns

---

[46] Wightman (1985) 246–50; Casey (1993) 266–7; cf. ch. 18 (Wood), p. 511 below.
[47] Priscus fr. 9.3.39–80; Theophylact VII.3; Procop. *Wars* VII.38.9–23; *Miracula S. Dem.* 1.128.
[48] Greg. *Reg.* V.30, 34, 36, 38–9.   [49] Bachrach (1972) 23, 41; cf. Bachrach (1993) 58.

or cities but on a provincial footing in the case of Champagne, contributed significantly to military activity, whereas in the former there is no evidence for locally-based forces (Fig. 17, p. 442 above). This distinction is likely to have originated in the different fates of these areas during the invasions and migrations of the late fourth and early fifth century: nearer the Rhine frontier, urban life was overwhelmed whereas, in the hinterland, communities often had the time to organize themselves on a new military footing, which was then preserved under Visigothic and Merovingian control.

The new 'urban' troops will have had diverse origins: in some cases the local élite may have supplied the men, but at Bazas in 414 there is evidence for a small group of Alans attaching itself to the town.[50] These urban levies constituted an important part of royal military resources, and it was essential for Merovingian kings to retain control of them through the local magnates who commanded them. They appear to have operated on a seasonal basis, with campaigns lasting a few weeks or months, and not to have been deployed outside the kingdom – for example, on expeditions to Italy or Spain – but for the defence of their locality and attacks on neighbouring regions they were highly effective. Furthermore, these remilitarized Gallo-Romans were no less enthusiastic than their Germanic contemporaries about fighting when booty was in prospect. Numerous inhabitants of Tours joined their levy's expedition against Gundovald, though the men of Poitiers ambushed them and dashed their hopes.[51]

Toleration or encouragement of local military organization was bound to challenge the operation of central power. If this development is one aspect of imperial disintegration in the west in the fifth century, there are signs that the east could have experienced the same fate. At Thessalonica in 478/9 the inhabitants' distrust of the emperor boiled over into a riot in which they overthrew Zeno's statues and threatened to dismember the praetorian prefect and burn down his palace; the situation was calmed by the local clergy, who helped the citizens to arrange the protection of their own city, with custody of the keys being transferred from the prefect to the archbishop.[52] A century later Thessalonica still had an efficient system for mobilizing the urban population to man the walls.[53] The inhabitants of the Balkans, like those of the west, had to cope with regular insecurity. As a result, local society became more militarized, but if these local military men were not in receipt of imperial salaries – and the interruption of salaries to *limitanei* suggests that they were not – loyalties to the centre would be eroded.

The infrequency of military action on the eastern frontier throughout the fifth century ensured that cities there did not develop local military

[50] Paulinus of Pella, *Euch.* 377–98.   [51] Bachrach (1972) 65–8; Greg. Tur. *Hist.* VII.28.
[52] Malchus fr. 20.5–19.   [53] *Miracula S. Dem.* 1.107.

organization so quickly, and Anastasius' reassertion of a more civilian style of government was also a deterrent. But here too resistance to Persian attacks in the sixth century regularly involved the co-operation of imperial troops and local civilians: eastern landowners had been given permission to build defences, and at Amida in 502/3 part of the wall circuit was guarded by local monks, while at Antioch in 540 and Jerusalem in 614 it was the local circus factions who exhibited the fiercest opposition to the Persians.[54] In these three instances the Persians overcame the Roman defenders, and this may point to another reason why there is less evidence for the damaging centrifugal consequences of local military action on the eastern frontier than in the Balkans and the west. Warfare against the Persians usually entailed the deployment of an imperial army which could repress separatist tendencies, as Edessa experienced in 602/3, and there was little hope that a city or region could sustain an independent existence in the face of Persian might – deportation to southern Iraq was a more plausible fate for the Romans, while massacre and pillage terminated a brief period of autonomy at Persian Nisibis in 602.[55] The direct clash of the two great powers of the ancient world helped to ensure that their common frontier was an area of strong central control, not of disintegration.

Religion and imperial expenditure were the keys to preserving attachments to the centre, sometimes in combination, as at Sergiopolis and the monastery at Mount Sinai, where major religious shrines that served as a focus for a mobile population received substantial imperial benefactions which fulfilled both pious and strategic purposes.[56] At Edessa the story of the *acheiropoietos* image, the miraculous representation of Christ that was believed to guarantee the city's safety, created a local focus for loyalties. But the city had also received lavish gifts from the imperial family after the devastating flood of 525, and it knew Persian strength at first hand. In the religious version of the repulse of the Persian attack in 544, the icon's power was linked to the united efforts of soldiers and citizens in effecting the destruction of the Persian ramp. In the 580s an *acheiropoietos* image accompanied the mobile army at Solachon in 586, where Philippicus first paraded the icon to improve his troops' morale, and then consigned it to a local bishop who led neighbouring civilians in prayers for a Roman victory, another successful tripartite combination.[57] On the Persian side of the frontier, religion was no less important: Persian kings were sensitive to the extension of Christianity, they encouraged the spread of Zoroastrian

---

[54] Procop. *Wars* i.7.22, Zachariah, *HE* vii.4; Procop. *Wars* ii.8.28–9; Antiochus Strategus chs. 2–3, 5. Isaac, *Limits of Empire* 252–6; Segal (1955) 113.

[55] *Anon. Guidi* 6–7; *Chron. Seert* 74–5 (*PO* xiii.507–13).

[56] Procop. *Buildings* ii.9, v.8; Cameron, *Procopius* 96–8.

[57] Evagr. *HE* iv 27; Theophylact ii.3.4–9.

practices in Christian Armenia and Iberia, and monitored the behaviour of bishops at major frontier cities like Nisibis and Chlomaron.[58]

In the east the situation was changed by two factors in the early seventh century: the repeated destruction through civil war and Persian victories of the Roman mobile armies, and the development by Khusro II of a religious formula for weakening allegiance to Constantinople – those who would subscribe to Jacobite or Nestorian doctrines would be left unharmed by the Persians, and only the Chalcedonians with their perceived attachment to the emperor would be victimized.[59] This development is undoubtedly relevant to Heraclius' attempt to reunite the Christian churches after his triumph over the Persians. Heraclius only managed to conquer the Persians through propaganda that transformed the conflict from a secular struggle into a religious crusade.[60] Once imperial authority was reasserted over the east, Heraclius set about reintegrating the divided Christian communities. The discussions with the Monophysites are the better known, since these produced the heretical Monothelete and Monergist formulae which split Roman Christendom, but the overtures to the Nestorian hierarchy that resulted in the *catholicus* Isho-Yahb III participating in a Chalcedonian service in Constantinople were just as significant. Emperors appreciated the importance of reliable and competent bishops in control of key cities, especially in areas of military insecurity, as shown by Maurice's request to pope Gregory for permission to replace a demented bishop at Justiniana Prima.[61] Heraclius, however, lacked the time to recreate a reliable episcopal structure after 628. Crusading zeal saved the empire once, but it was difficult to repeat the feat against the Arabs. The presence or expectation of an imperial army would stimulate resistance, but otherwise the willingness of the Arabs to tolerate Christians and the disruption caused by Heraclius' recent christological initiatives combined to undermine central allegiances.[62]

IV. SOLDIER AND CIVILIAN

Religion could serve to unite soldier and civilian in the defence of their country. There is also, however, plenty of evidence that points to severe tensions: this is not surprising, since a sizeable body of soldiers, young men trained to be combative, will seldom be popular with the members of the civilian society with which it has to interact, whether in Aldershot or Edessa. The military ethos would encourage contempt for the non-fighters, whose main function, from the military perspective, was to feed, water, house and generally support the more important activities of the

---

[58] Procop. *Wars* 1.12.3–4; Whitby, *Maurice* 216–18.   [59] Agapius, *PO* VIII.460.
[60] George of Pisidia, *Heraclias*.   [61] Greg. *Reg.* XI.29; cf. Dagron (1984a) 16–17.
[62] Kaegi (1992) 213–18 (with reference to the subsequent search for scapegoats).

military. Troop movements inevitably generated friction and complaints, which are attested in the surviving evidence, but the problem is to establish what was the normal state of affairs. Narrative histories focus on exceptional cases, while papyri record particular disputes, almost invariably from one prejudiced side, but these may not illustrate the less acrimonious relationship of the longer term: a British colonel who drove a regiment of tanks across a north German field of asparagus generated a storm of local protest that belied the overall nature of links between occupying army and natives. These caveats need to be remembered while reviewing the negative evidence. Soldiers did bring some benefits to the places where they served, and the local civilians may not have been above attempting to exploit the military for their own ends. Soldiers had possessions which might be stolen by the hosts on whom they were billeted, while it was the economic vulnerability of soldiers as a captive market that had underlain the promulgation of Diocletian's Prices Edict.[63]

The Roman world had always been a violent society with a tradition of permitting a considerable element of self-help, sometimes physical, in the resolution of disputes.[64] Roman law had developed around this foundation as a means of curtailing its damaging consequences, and the great legal enterprises of Theodosius II and Justinian represented the culmination of these attempts; they ensured that the rule of law could be presented as characteristic of Romans, a feature of civilization and power which differentiated Rome from the tribal monarchs, who might, though, be stimulated to imitation.[65] But legal pronouncements could not eliminate violence, and the various parts of the Roman and post-Roman world reveal, not surprisingly, its acceptance and exploitation at all levels of society. Custodians of the law were not above resorting to illegal force when necessary. The emperors Leo and Zeno both used assassination to remove the rival families of Aspar and Armatus, Valentinian III was personally involved in the murder of Aetius, and Theoderic the Amal permitted the bludgeoning to death of Boethius. If Justinian was more civilized in treating those accused of plotting against him, his rise to the throne had been accompanied by a deployment of urban violence against potential rivals that was difficult to repress at the start of his reign. Brute force was always an option when dealing with recalcitrant opposition: Belisarius used threats to remove pope Silverius from Rome and subsequently colluded in his elimination; shortly before the Fifth Oecumenical Council pope Vigilius was dragged to a meeting with Justinian from an altar where he had taken refuge, with such violence that the altar collapsed on top of him; Monophysites constructed a catalogue of the oppression to which they had

[63] Bagnall, *Egypt* 172–80, 219–25; Frank (1933–40) v.307–421, with Whitakker (1994) 111.
[64] Lintott (1968) chs. 1–2.
[65] Priscus, fr. 6.2.419–510; cf. ch. 10 (Charles-Edwards), pp. 284–7 above.

been subjected.[66] In the provinces local officials might take the law into their own hands: Dioscorus of Aphrodito complained against the depredations effected by the pagarch Menas' henchmen – though here, as often, it is essential to remember that we only have the 'victim's' side of the dispute.[67]

Churchmen also deployed violence for their own ends. Dioscorus brought soldiers to Ephesus to ensure the ratification of his doctrinal views, while Severus of Antioch obtained support for his Monophysite views from Asiaticus, the *dux* of Phoenicia Libanensis, who expelled the bishops of Epiphania and Arethusa for insulting Severus. Severus was also assisted by Conon the bandit-chaser, *lestodioktes*, who had received instructions from Calliopus, a deputy *magister militum* and correspondent of Severus.[68] Hilary of Arles, when making ordinations in outlying parts of his diocese, was accompanied by an armed escort to see that his nominees were imposed. Such use of force in church affairs was prohibited by pope Leo; Valentinian III backed the pope and required provincial governors to cooperate in disciplining unruly bishops, but at local level, violence appeared normal and effective. If a bishop did not use force to secure his nominations, it was quite possible that a *magister militum* would use troops to install his man: bishops were important leaders of secular society, a dual role symbolized by Germanus of Auxerre's decision to retain his general's cloak as a reminder of his previous career.[69]

Leading clerics used violence, and others used it against them. Bishop Cautinus of Clermont abandoned an annual pilgrimage to Brioude for fear that the prince Chramn's men would not respect the holy occasion; rules of sanctuary were manipulated to the benefit of the powerful, so that Merovech and Guntram Boso camped with their armed followers in Gregory's church at Tours, bringing royal retaliation on the city, while Guntram moved his daughters in and out of sanctuary according to the vagaries of his career;[70] murder might be committed in the forecourt of a church, and the cleric Quintanus was killed at the altar.[71]

Army, church and court were the three great consumers of resources in the late Roman world, with the army as the greatest of these, a highly complex mechanism for the appropriation, consumption and hence redistribution of resources, economic and human; its requirements affected every tax-payer, or even tax-defaulter. In these days of military retrenchment and consequent hopes of extra resources for reallocation, it is worth

[66] Procop. *Secret History* 1.14; *Liber Pontif.* Silverius, Vigilius; John Eph. *Lives* 24 (John of Tela), 25 (John of Hephaestopolis), 47 (refugees in Constantinople).

[67] MacCoull, *Dioscorus* 23–8. [68] *PLRE* II.164 *s.v.* Asiaticus and II.252–3 *s.v.* Calliopus 6.

[69] Heinzelmann (1992) 241–2, 246; Van Dam (1992) 326.

[70] Bachrach (1972) 48–9; Wood, *Merovingian Kingdoms* 83.

[71] Wood, *Merovingian Kingdoms* 75, 82; each story included an element of divine retribution which marked historiographically what was acceptable behaviour.

stressing that military inactivity had costs for the Romans.[72] Along the Danube and Rhine frontiers, any perceived weakness in defences would embolden those outside to attack or demand more peace-money, as for example the Avars did in 578, whereas successful action could allow troops to support themselves from the profits of conquest – or so Maurice believed when ordering the Danube army to winter north of the river in 602. Even on the more stable Persian frontier, where cross-border traffic was regulated by treaties, an impression of power would help to restrain Arabs and other clients and deter opportunist Persian aggression.

Troops required regular supplies, and one of the determinants for the location of major military concentrations, and hence for the siting of frontiers, was the availability of the necessary goods and services – hence a preference for river frontiers, with their greater ease of transport.[73] The frontier armies were a crucial element in the empire's complex circulatory economy, receiving the surplus product of provinces in the hinterland and serving to stimulate agriculture and other forms of production there.[74] Units had always supervised the acquisition of some of their supplies, which might be produced from neighbouring lands under their control – hence the absence of villas in north Britain – or acquired through the kind of long-distance operations attested in the Vindolanda tablets.[75] Greater reliance on payment in kind as a result of disruptions to the economic system in the third century affected the nature of the process, since the military might now be involved in the acquisition of their pay as well as their food. That this caused problems is evident from the numerous laws in the Theodosian and Justinianic Codes about taxes in kind, subsistence allowance, and requisitioned services: use of incorrect measures, fixing of compulsory purchase prices, adjustment of proportions between cash and kind, and excessive exactions of transport all caused problems.[76] An officer might often have the power to flout the law, however strictly it was drafted: when Rome was besieged in 546 the garrison commander, Bessas, speculated in grain at the expense of the civilians.[77]

Whatever the problems, however, the fiscal–military system continued to function in most of the eastern empire – the stomach that fed the arms, to adopt the imagery of Corippus. The ideal was for each military region to be self-supporting as far as possible. Anastasius attempted to ensure that each diocese produced sufficient supplies for its own ordinary requirements through payment of the land-tax in kind. He acknowledged, however, that in Thrace the numerous troops could not be supplied in this way because of the disrupted state of local agriculture, and so permitted the regular continuation of compulsory purchases, *coemptio*. But even here

[72] Cf. Lieu (1986).   [73] Whittaker (1994) ch. 4.   [74] Hopkins (1980a).
[75] Breeze (1984) 264–86; Bowman (1994) 42–9.
[76] *C.Th.* XI.1, VII.4; Isaac, *Limits of Empire* 285–97.   [77] Procop. *Wars.* VII.17; 19.14.

the emperor's ability to produce or deny supplies was a vital element in dealings with Gothic war-bands. One of the advantages of the Justinianic *quaestura exercitus* which connected the administration of Thrace and the more settled areas of Caria and the Aegean islands was that this permitted a greater degree of self-sufficiency within an administrative unit. Problems could still occur, and troops delayed outside Adrianople in 551 experienced hunger.[78] Later in the century Tiberius, granting a 25 per cent reduction of tax payments in gold for the next four years to celebrate his elevation to Caesar, maintained levies in kind and specifically referred to the continuation of such payments from Mesopotamia and Osrhoene for storage and military purposes.[79] The western empire failed to sustain this centralized economic–military system, a cause as well as a symptom of its decline. There the transformation of the military into groups supported by settlement on land represented a major change in the nature of the state, its authority and ability to collect and deploy resources.[80]

People also had to be moved from the civilian to the military sector. In normal circumstances recruitment probably worked fairly smoothly, through a combination of hereditary service, volunteering and conscription from within the empire, coupled with the employment of foreign mercenaries. But even a smooth operation might have significant consequences for individuals: the fact that the father of St Saba was drafted from his native Cappadocia into a unit of Isaurians who came to be stationed in Alexandria meant that the saint's mother accompanied her husband to Egypt and the young Saba was brought up by relatives.[81] At times of pressure, and especially military crisis, harsher methods had to be used, as potential recruits tried to evade enrolment by self-mutilation or attachment to a powerful patron. Under Maurice in the 580s even monasteries did not provide safe refuge, as recruiting officers were sent in to obtain the desperately needed soldiers by force.[82]

If troops in fixed locations created problems for civilians, their movement aroused even more: supplies would have to be found along their route, and accommodation provided. In the east the tax system was efficient enough to see that supplies were available for distribution, either through the storage of regular receipts in kind or through the exaction of supplementary levies. Arrangements for provisioning the public transport system were claimed to be beneficial to remote rural areas, which might lack an alternative market for their produce.[83] The billeting of troops, however, generated a significant body of legislation, and an inscription from the Thebaid in Egypt attests the construction by local inhabitants of a hostel specifically for the needs of soldiers; restoration of the building was supervised by the local bishop.[84] In the

---

[78] Corippus II.249–53; *CJ* X.27.2.10; Procop. *Wars* VII.40.39; Jones, *LRE* 280.   [79] *Nov.* 163.
[80] Cf. Wickham (1981) 40.   [81] Cyr. Scyth. *V. Sabae* I.   [82] Michael the Syrian X.21, vol. II p. 362.
[83] Bagnall, *Egypt* 172–3; Procop. *Secret History* 30.11; Hendy, *Studies* 606–8.   [84] Gascou (1994).

west, where the complex fiscal system could not have survived the tribal migrations of the early fifth century and the allocation to war-bands of substantial territories for settlement, the passage of troops was bound to be more disruptive. A signal distinction of Clovis' attack on the Visigoths in 507 was his order forbidding his followers to plunder church lands along their route: only grass and water could be taken, and a transgressor was personally killed by Clovis (a similar story is told of the Persian king Hormizd IV).[85] On the campaign against Septimania in 585 the Frankish army, which contained various urban contingents, killed, burned and pillaged even before entering enemy territory, and after the expedition's failure the churches around Clermont near the main road were stripped of their plate; the journey from Paris to Spain of the princess Rigunth in 584 was almost as destructive through the combination of casual pillaging and unpaid requisitioning. In the Balkans in the 480s the Goths of Theoderic, allegedly the friend of Zeno, drove off cattle and killed farmers in Thrace.[86]

Armies might pillage their own side, but the depredations of an enemy were far worse: from Antioch in 540, Dara in 573, Singidunum in 595, Jerusalem in 614 or Cyprus in 649/50 thousands of captives were led away, along with transportable booty that might extend to marble columns and mosaic *tesserae*.[87] Decades of fighting in Italy resulted in destruction at almost every important city and fortress, with the exception of Ravenna, and had a long-term impact on settlement patterns.[88] Casualties would have been as great. Outside Naissus the bones of those killed in the city's capture by Attila were still littering the river bank years later, and any successful besieging army was likely to go berserk once inside a place that had resisted their efforts, as at Amida in 502 or Dara in 573. Only speedy surrender could avoid such destruction, though the bargain might not always be kept, as Apamea discovered in 540 after opening its gates to Khusro. Few transported captives would ever return. In Persia they would be settled in special communities, such as Khusro's New Antioch, while north of the Danube they would be incorporated in the subject populations of the Hun or Avar federations, perhaps as the basis for a separate military unit, as with the tribe led by Maurus/Kouber; the Slavs had the reputation of being abnormally kind to their captives, who might choose not to return home if offered the chance.[89] A long-delayed home-coming had its own problems, as revealed by the survivors of the Hunnic sack of Aquileia who discovered that their wives had innocently remarried. Invasions created refugees:

---

[85] Greg. Tur. *Hist.* II.37; Tabari 265–8 (Nöldeke). Cf. Belisarius in Africa: Procop. *Wars* III.16.1–8.
[86] Malchus fr. 18.4.2–7; Greg. Tur. *Hist.* VIII.30; VI.45.
[87] Procop. *Wars* II.9.14–18; John Eph. *HE* VI.6–7; Theophylact VI.10.1; Antiochus Strategus 9–17; Chrysos (1993) 10. [88] Brown, *Gentlemen and Officers* 39–42.
[89] Priscus fr. 11.2.51–5; Joshua 53; John Eph. *HE* VI.5–6; Procop. *Wars* II.14.1–4 with Theophylact v.6.11–7.3; *Miracula S. Dem.* II.286–8; Maurice, *Strat.* XI.4.8–16. Thompson (1982) 84–6, 100–9.

the men of property whose attempted escape from Salona precipitated their city's capture by the Croats, the fugitives from Naissus and Justiniana Prima who spread terrifying stories about the Avars' siege engines, the abbot Eustathius driven by the Persian storm from his monastery near Ankara and deprived of his books, or the starving common people who gathered for help at the monastery where the patriarch Eutychius was in exile in Pontus.[90]

The sudden arrival of troops would disrupt the economic structure of even the best-organized cities. Famine in Antioch in 363 is plausibly connected with the presence of Julian's army *en route* to Persia, and the troubles caused at Edessa when it became the base for the eastern army during the war of 502–5 are detailed in the *Chronicle of Joshua*: each household had to supply ten pounds of iron for last-minute repairs to the defences, wheat was provided for a compulsory baking of bread for the soldiers, while there is a catalogue of abuses committed by the quartered defenders upon their hosts – robbery, violence, rape, drunkenness and murder – until the aggrieved citizens posted complaints against the general.[91] In Egypt the monk Shenoute denounced soldiers for pillaging towns, fields and monasteries, and for despoiling people; this contributes to a centuries-old tradition of complaints about soldiers giving a 'shaking down' to civilians. The official army is only one aspect of military activity,[92] and if the officers of a garrison army were reluctant to punish their soldiers' crimes, it is not surprising that misbehaviour by an individual soldier outside the group would also be condoned. The story of Euphemia and the Goth narrates how a soldier attempted to obtain a slave by promising marriage to a young Edessene, who only discovered that he was already married after she was far from home; naturally this Christian tale has a happy ending, and the proud Goth was punished by the laws of the Romans. But soldiers did not always escape military punishment: at Corinth two imprisoned *bucellarii* of the prefect (presumably of Illyricum) scratched on the wall a plea for divine help in achieving their freedom.[93]

At Edessa, though, it was admitted that not all soldiers were guilty of misbehaviour, and it is worth reviewing the benefits that military activity or presence might bring. Protection is the most obvious, and even billeted troops might provide this, as Paulinus of Pella bemoaned when his house, at whose exemption he had originally rejoiced, was sacked.[94] Travel would be made safer on those roads that were regularly patrolled. Booty enriched the successful soldier: Maurice's Balkan army was affronted when the

[90] Thomas the Archdeacon 26–7; *Miracula S. Dem.* II.200; letter of Antiochus the monk, *PG* LXXXIX.1421–8; Eustratius, *Life of Eutychius, PG* LXXXVI.2, col. 2344B.   [91] Joshua 86, 93–6.

[92] Patlagean, *Pauvreté* 313–15; Bagnall, *Egypt* 180.

[93] Segal (1970) 140–1, quoting Burkitt (1913); Feissel and Philippidis-Braat (1985) p. 361 no. 22.

[94] Paulinus of Pella, *Euch.* 281–90.

emperor tried to annex its personal profits, and it was something which required special protection on campaigns. The lucky officer could become very wealthy, like the Isaurian Arbazacius in 404/5 or the rapacious Bessas at Rome in 546; civilians might also benefit, as when the landowners of Martyropolis stripped Persian corpses outside their city.[95] Captives could be used to resettle underpopulated areas – for example, the Persian Christians from Arzanene who were sent to Cyprus to revitalize that island. Veteran soldiers, or groups of foreign mercenaries between bouts of activity, could perform a similar function while helping to protect their newly acquired lands. These would ideally be settled with wives and families to ensure stability and commitment to the region, as with the 30,000 Armenian families that Maurice was alleged to have planned to move to Thrace. A group of warriors without women remained volatile, as for example the 300 followers of the Lombard Ildigisal who could quickly abandon their settlement on imperial property when their leader was insulted.[96]

Military expenditure was also a benefit. The proximity of major concentrations of troops has been suggested as one of the factors that contributed to the prosperity of the Syrian countryside throughout late antiquity.[97] The creation of Dara introduced a very large sum of imperial money into a frontier region: employment was provided to numerous local civilians during the construction, and a large new market was created that stimulated the agricultural development of the plain below the city, which is crossed by a complex irrigation network. On the Tur Abdin plateau above the new city villages flourished, with substantial new constructions under the impact of imperial salaries and new building skills. Dara is an exceptional case, partly for its size, partly for the survival of the physical evidence, but fortification work at many other sites would have had proportionate effects. It seems, contrary to earlier imperial traditions, that the army might rely on civilian labour for military constructions, since the attempt to fortify Mindon and the clearance of the moat at Carthage both used civilians.[98]

Where troops remained stationed for any length of time, they soon established close links with local society. Quite apart from specific lands which were allocated to certain categories of troops, but which might be appropriated by civilians, soldiers regularly owned property in their own right or married people who did, as the epitaph of Flavia, wife of the tribune who perhaps commanded the garrison at Larissa, records.[99] The economic life of the Theodosian camel corps stationed at Nessana in the

---

[95] Theophylact vi.7.6–8.1; Maurice, *Strat.* v; *PLRE* ii.127–8; Procop. *Wars* vii.17; Malalas 469.1–3.
[96] Theophylact iii.15.13–15; Evagr. *HE* v.19; *De Rebus Bellicis* 5; Sebeos 20; Procop. *Wars* viii.27.1–18.　　[97] Liebeschuetz (1972) 80.
[98] Zachariah, *HE* vi.6; Procop. *Wars* i.13.2–3; iii.23.19.
[99] Avramea and Feissel (1994) 361–2 no. 4.

Negev is revealed by a dossier of documents. Part, at least, of the unit was recruited locally and it formed a stable social group; its members were naturally involved in local transactions of houses and land, which would be registered at the civilian record office in nearby Elusa; this land, owned by the soldiers in a private capacity, was subject to normal taxation.[100] Such landowning soldiers did not necessarily become soldier-farmers, whose military activities might be curtailed by the rhythms of the agricultural year; rather, they were like other men of status, *rentiers* who could cultivate their lands through tenants or other dependants. From Egypt, there is evidence both for the itinerant soldier Flavius Taurinus leasing out his property through middlemen, and for Flavius Donatiolus, a member of the *equites Mauri scutarii* at Hermopolis, leasing arable land from a local landowner.[101]

Static units in Egypt reveal patterns of economic integration comparable to Nessana. The fourth-century Abbinaeus archive provides evidence for a local military commander as the recipient of petitions, in some cases from civilians, who should not have been presenting their complaints to him. The units stationed at Syene, Philae and Elephantine in the late sixth century were the dominant members of local society, who combined non-military activities such as that of boatman with membership of their regiments. These units might appear underemployed, with property and other financial transactions and the supervision of the grain supply as their main concerns,[102] but there were serious frontier threats in the fifth century from the Blemmyes and Nobades, and the rural unrest in the Delta *c*. 600 for which we have evidence is unlikely to have been unique. In Italy the Byzantine army of occupation quickly dug itself into local society, providing evidence for the coalescence of military, property and administrative power.[103] Everywhere soldiers, and especially officers, will have been powerful people whose influence inevitably undercut that of other patrons and generated the disgruntled outburst of Libanius about the improper behaviour of soldiers in the hinterland of Antioch.[104] His strong self-interest needs to be remembered when assessing his complaints, and also the fact that Antioch, an imperial residence for much of the fourth century, may have been exceptionally affected by the spending power of officers' salaries. But soldiers could be victims as well as exploiters. Busas at Appiaria was refused ransom by the town's inhabitants, allegedly because one prominent individual had seduced his wife.[105]

Another positive aspect of the Roman army, at least in the east, where a balance was maintained between internal and external recruits, was its continuing power to civilize outsiders. In the west, where the Germanic noble

[100] Isaac *Limits of Empire* 209; Nessana doc. 24 in Kraemer (1958).
[101] Bagnall, *Egypt* 151 n. 12; Jones, *LRE* 662.   [102] Jones, *LRE* 662; Whittaker (1994) 144–5, 263.
[103] Brown, *Gentlemen and Officers* 101–8.   [104] Cf. Bagnall, *Egypt* 173 and ch. 6; Lib. *Or.* XLVII.
[105] Theophylact II.16.7.

with his war-band was the dominant military figure, it is probable that the remnants of Romano-provincial forces, under the command of their land-lord-warlords, adopted 'barbarian' attitudes and ideals. Peter Brown has pointed to an ill documented change in lifestyle that brought to a provincial nobility, now isolated from the imperial court, more frequent opportunities for fighting.[106] Nevertheless, even in post-reconquest Italy, an extremely debilitated society, there is evidence in property transactions and legal disputes for the continuing fusion of the remnants of Theoderic's Goths with Romans, and it is likely that the Bulgar mercenaries in the Byzantine armies also rapidly assimilated themselves.[107] Elsewhere in the west, the process was not all one way: Arbogast, a descendant of the Frankish *magister militum* Arbogast of the late fourth century, held office as *comes Trevirorum* and received letters from Sidonius which praised his Latin culture; he asked Sidonius to compose a work of scriptural exegesis, without success, and ended up as bishop of Chartres.[108]

The rise to power of local commanders had a much greater impact on local society, and indeed the overall operation of the empire, than the much-discussed issue of the gradual introduction into territories under Byzantine control of the 'theme system', the term used to designate the territorial administrative units that underpinned the main Byzantine armies after the mid seventh century.[109] Themes can be seen as the inescapable administrative corollary of the gradual change in the nature of Roman military organization that had been under way, intermittently, for over two centuries. In the tribal west, armies had been localized at an early stage in the process, when war-bands took control of specific areas. In the eastern half of the empire, the Balkan provinces tended to follow the western model, and territory was allocated, or alienated, to tribal groups during the fifth and sixth century, a process which culminated in the establishment of Slav, Serb, Croat and Bulgar groups within the Danube frontier in the seventh century with only nominal imperial sanction. On the eastern frontier, the greater vitality of urban life dictated a different development. Here the imperial presence was strong and the type of fragmentation and piecemeal allocation of territories to war-bands was impractical: conquest and appropriation of territory would either be on a vast scale, as the Persians achieved in the period 610–28 and the Arabs in the 630s, or at a very local and unsustained level, as with the Persian capture of Amida in 502/3 or Dara in 573. But once the Roman armies had been driven out of this urbanized sector and forced to regroup to the north-west in central Anatolia, the nature of their deployment had to take account of the very different structures of provincial society in these areas: cities were few and far between, and the

---

[106] Brown, *Religion and Society* 233.   [107] Brown, *Gentlemen and Officers* 75–6, 70.
[108] *PLRE* II.128–9, with Heinzelmann (1982) *s.v.*
[109] For this see Haldon, *Byzantium in the Seventh Century* ch. 6; Hendy, *Studies* 619–62.

powerful landowners whose depredations of imperial property Justinian had tried to check were dominant. The eastern and Armenian armies reestablished themselves in areas where they had to create their own infrastructure for provision of supplies, recruits and pay. The result was a territorially based army, which provincial magnates undoubtedly found it opportune to join; the nature of military organization then determined the organization of civilian authority.

CHAPTER 18

THE NORTH-WESTERN PROVINCES

IAN N. WOOD

The period between the accession of the Roman emperor Valentinian III in 425 and the death of the Visigothic king Leovigild in 586 inevitably occupies a central position in the debates relating to the transition from classical to medieval in western Europe, and more specifically to the questions of continuity and discontinuity.[1] There is, however, another way of reading this century and a half, and that is as a period in its own right. Several historians working on fifth- and sixth-century Britain have, for instance, argued that between the history of the late Roman province of Britannia and that of Anglo-Saxon England lies a shorter but none the less distinct period that has been called 'sub-Roman'.[2]

Britain can, of course, be seen as experiencing a history radically different from that even of the other parts of western Europe. Its western half was one of only two areas of the erstwhile Roman empire to witness the re-emergence of Celtic kings, and the other area where a similar development occurred, Brittany, had a history inseparable from that of Britain itself. Meanwhile, or perhaps subsequently, Latin language and culture were more thoroughly destroyed in the Germanic kingdoms of eastern Britain than in any other part of what had been the Roman west. Yet the distinctions between Britain and the rest of western Europe may seem clearer to us now, when examined with the benefit of hindsight, than they were at the time. Other regions in western Europe passed through an intermediate 'sub-Roman' phase between the collapse of imperial Roman government and the establishment of a new barbarian regime: this is clear for Gallaecia in Spain, Aremorica and the area controlled by Aegidius in Gaul, as well as Noricum. Certainly there are chronological differences between the sub-Roman periods in each of these regions. In Britain it started earlier and lasted longer than in most places: in Soissons it began with the murder of Majorian in 461 and ended with the defeat of Aegidius' son Syagrius at the hands of Clovis, in c. 486: in Noricum it was a relatively late development, and its end is unclear, because the history of Noricum Ripense after the departure of the

---

[1] E.g. Drinkwater and Elton (eds.), *Fifth-Century Gaul*.

[2] The notion of a discrete period was central to Morris (1973): see more recently Esmonde Cleary (1989); Higham (1992); Dark (1994).

disciples of Severinus in 488 is totally lost to us. Nevertheless, it is worth comparing the sub- and post-Roman histories of these regions, not because they form a geographical unit, which they do not, but because they constitute a particular development in the history of western Europe.[3]

The sources also make comparison between these regions possible. Although no detailed chronicle source survives for the whole region, Hydatius provides an account primarily of Gallaecia, which shows something of the confused nature of this 'sub-Roman' period in that region. Rather sketchier, but valuable for Aremorica and Britain, is the *Chronicle of 452*. Although the narrative history of Britain composed by Gildas in his *De Excidio Britanniae* leaves much to be desired, it provides points of comparison, on the one hand with Patrick's works, and on the other with those of the moralizing theologians writing in Gaul in the first half of the fifth century. Also crossing this geographical divide is the *Vita Germani*, the *Life* of a bishop of Auxerre written by a priest of Lyons, Constantius, in *c.* 480. As a work of hagiography this last text stands comparison with various other stants' *Lives*, notably those of Severinus of Noricum, the Fathers of Jura, Genovefa of Paris and Vedast of Arras. With these last two texts we come to the mainstream of Frankish history, and to a comparative plethora of sources. At the same time the *Vita Germani* itself offers connections with an earlier, more southerly and more Roman world, since Constantius was a close friend of the Gallo-Roman aristocrat and later bishop of Clermont, Sidonius Apollinaris, who dedicated his letter collection to him.[4]

It would be misleading to suggest that these written sources for the north-western fringes of the Roman world in the mid and late fifth century are plentiful. It would be equally misguided to assume that they are easy to interpret, not least because their authors all had their own agendas. Even the chroniclers, in their meagre annals, offer an interpretation rather than an account of the events they were living through, and their inspiration is theological rather than historical.[5] Other genres of writing were yet more open to manipulation.[6] It is particularly unfortunate that for many of the developments in northern Gaul and in Noricum we are dependent almost entirely on works of hagiography for our information. It may be symptomatic of the period that hagiography is central to our understanding – but there is always the possibility that a historical interpretation based upon the *Lives* of saints has mistaken theological or pastoral meditation for fact, and that experiences in these frontier areas were rather closer to those described in Sidonius' letters, some of which do indeed relate to northern Gaul.

[3] Some of the similarities were explored by E. A. Thompson in his numerous articles on Britain, as well as in his articles on the Suevic kingdom and Noricum: see, in particular, Thompson (1982). See also Brown (1996) 76–92.

[4] Sid. Ap. *Epp.* 1.1, 7.18, 8.16, ed. W. B. Anderson (London 1936–65): Harries (1994) 7–9.

[5] Muhlberger (1990) 267–71.   [6] For the evidence for southern Gaul, see Wood (1992).

Alongside the literary texts there is the witness of archaeology. On the whole, however, the archaeological material for the period, rich though it is, illuminates general trends, particularly in burial custom and living conditions. Such information is not easily combined with a written record that deals primarily with matters ecclesiastical and political. Despite the vast numbers of cemeterial finds from the fifth and early sixth century, it is rare to find a grave that is so firmly dated that it can be fitted into a precise historical context: the one obvious exception is the grave of the Frankish king Childeric at Tournai, which is especially valuable because it is the grave of a known individual whose career is recorded and whose death can be ascribed with some certainty to the year 481 or thereabouts. Leaving aside the cemetery evidence, that of treasure hoards is also awkward. Of the British hoards, Mildenhall, Water Newton and Hoxne antedate our period, though in the latter case, only just. The hoard from Traprain Law in Scotland may, however, belong to the early fifth century, and show something of the Roman treasure available to a native prince, living in what had been the frontier zone of the Roman province. From the continent, the hoard from Kaiseraugst seems to belong to the mid fourth century, and the treasure named after Sevso, its owner, who lived apparently in Pannonia, may be dated a little later. There is, in any case, always a danger in trying to associate a hoard, or indeed a destruction layer in a villa or town, with an individual crisis, unless the archaeological finds and the literary texts can be shown to dovetail precisely. Even a text as precise about urban destruction as the *Vita Severini* is difficult to correlate with the archaeological evidence currently available for Noricum. In Britain the discoveries of sub-Roman structures built in timber at Wroxeter and Birdoswald are reminders of how much may have been missed by earlier generations of archaeologists.[7] Urban archaeology in France is also shedding increasing light on the history of the late Roman town, and it seems likely that over the period as a whole there was a marked urban decline, although at the same time, in parts of Gaul at least, this went hand in hand with the development of new suburban foci, notably around the increasingly significant shrines of martyrs and saints.[8]

Although it is possible to construct a narrative for the period, it can at best be a sketch of a time of intense military activity and social change. In 406 or 407 the Rhine frontier broke, and hordes of Vandals, Alans and Sueves crossed first into Gaul and then into Spain, where they fought each other as much as they plundered the Roman province, until the Vandals departed for Africa in 429. In 411 the Visigoths left Italy, in the first instance for Aquitaine. They too moved on to Spain, only to be recalled to Aquitaine in 418 or 419.[9] From their base in Toulouse they usually acted as

[7] On Wroxeter, Barker (1990).   [8] See in general the volumes of Gauthier *et al.* (1986–).
[9] On the question of the date Wood (1992) 15.

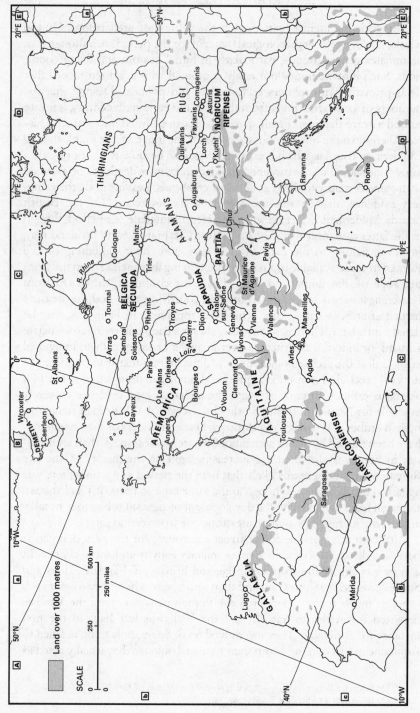

Map 9 The northern and western provinces (places mentioned in chapter 18)

agents for the empire, regularly attacking the Sueves, but also occasionally turning against their Roman masters. Meanwhile, the high seas were also routes for piracy: Britannia, which was under threat from Picts in the north, was plagued by Irish in the west, who took, among other captives, the young Patrick – not that the British themselves were above piracy, as can be seen from Patrick's letter to Coroticus. Nor were the Irish merely plunderers. The ogham stones of south-west Wales reveal the existence of an Irish settlement in Demetia (Dyfed) in the fifth century, a segment of which seems to have split off subsequently to found the kingdom of Brycheiniog (Brecon).[10] To the south of Britain, maritime Franks and Saxons presented a constant threat, as they did to the coasts of Gaul.[11] Heruls are even known to have raided the coast of north-western Spain.[12] Presumably they had set sail from Denmark, where part of the tribe was to be found in the sixth century.[13]

Imperial control of much of northern Gaul and Spain can only have been intermittent after the first two decades of the century,[14] and it seems to have depended increasingly on the use of barbarians federates, not only the Visigoths in Toulouse, but also from the late 430s or early 440s the Alans in Aremorica and the Burgundians in Sapaudia.[15] Britain, which had effectively had to fend for itself since 407, was left to its own fate, and its decision to copy imperial policy in employing Saxons backfired badly with a Saxon revolt.[16] On the continent, however, the policy was successful enough for Aetius, or rather his Gallic henchmen, to be able to put together a sizeable confederacy to oppose Attila at the Catalaunian Plains in 451.[17] In the event, this was to prove the last major intervention of the Huns within the lands of the western empire – and although the west survived, it did so only just, and, to judge by the hagiography of the period, with a considerable scar on its psyche. The murder of Aetius in 454, or, perhaps more important, that of Valentinian III a year later, undermined what fragile unity still remained. Avitus, as a Gallo-Roman, and Majorian had some short-lived successes in Gaul and Spain, but the rapid turn-over of emperors in the ensuing period exacerbated the divisions between the Romans and their federates, and from the 460s onwards individual barbarian groups carved out kingdoms for themselves. The Vandals had already done so in Africa, as had the Sueves in Spain, but now in the 470s the Visigoths under Euric followed suit, to be followed after 476 by the

---

[10] Thomas (1994) 51–87, 113–62.   [11] Wood (1990); Haywood (1991).

[12] Hydat. *Chron.* n. 164, 189, ed. R. W. Burgess, *The Chronicle of Hydatius and the Consularia Constantinopolitana* (Oxford 1993), pp. 106–7, 110–11.

[13] Procop. *Wars* VI.15, ed. H . B. Dewing (London 1914–40).   [14] Wood (1987) 256–60.

[15] *Chronicle of 452*, 124, 127, 128, ed. T. Mommsen, *MGH, AA* 9 (Berlin 1892).

[16] Gildas, *De Excidio Britanniae* 23, ed. and trans. M. Winterbottom, *Gildas: The Ruin of Britain and Other Works* (Chichester 1978).

[17] Jordanes, *Get.* 36.191, ed. T. Mommsen, *MGH, AA* 5 (Berlin 1882).

Burgundians.[18] North of the Loire, independent Roman and Frankish enclaves, notably those of Aegidius and Childeric, were established.[19] On the Danube, Noricum Ripense also passed out of imperial control. This fragmentation was, however, only momentary – at least in Gaul, where the emergence of the Merovingians under Childeric's son, Clovis, reunited the north in a single kingdom. In the course of the first half of the sixth century Aquitaine and, in time, Burgundy and the Rhône valley were attached to this northern core. Squeezed out of most of their Gallic possessions, the Visigoths turned their attention to Spain, and by the end of the sixth century they had control of almost the whole of the peninsula, having destroyed the Suevic kingdom in the process. In Spain and northern Gaul the fifth and early sixth centuries were a time of dissolution and reunification. In Britain the unification was to be a long while in the future.

Although there is a case for seeing this period of dissolution and reunification as something specifically 'sub-Roman', it is useful to begin with what is often taken to be a late Roman problem: the bagaudae. Bagaudae are attested in the third century, but above all in the fifth, coming to the fore around the year 410 and lasting as a significant threat until the 440s. In the problems that they pose, and in their relations both with the imperial government and with the barbarians, they introduce and shed some light on the problems of the sub-Roman world.

According to the *Chronicle of 452*, in around the year 435 a man called Tibatto led a Bagaudic rebellion, apparently in Aremorica – that is, north of the Loire. This rebellion was put down two years later. Germanus of Auxerre's attempt to avert bloodshed at this stage of the proceedings is recorded by his hagiographer, Constantius.[20] Nevertheless, again according to the *Chronicle of 452*, another bagauda flared up some eleven years later. Meanwhile in Spain Hydatius recorded that the *dux utriusque militiae* Asturius killed a large number of bagaudae from Tarraconensis in 442.[21] Bagaudae are also mentioned in Spanish Aracelli in 443,[22] and Basilius is said to have gathered a group of bagaudae, who then killed some federates as well as bishop Leo in the church at Tyriasso.[23] It is possible to add to these fragments evidence relating to Britain, since Zosimus records that the rebellion of the British against the government of Constantine III, which took place sometime after 407, was the model on which the Aremorican rebellion was based.[24]

---

[18] Harries (1994) 222–38.   [19] Harries (1994) 223–4.
[20] Constantius, *Vita Germani* 28, 40, ed. R. Borius, *SChrét*. 112 (Paris 1965). On the implications of this for the death of Germanus, see Wood (1984) 14–16.   [21] Hydat. *Chron*. n. 117.
[22] Hydat. *Chron*. n. 120.   [23] Hydat. *Chron*. n. 133.
[24] Zos. VI.5.2–3, ed. F. Paschoud (Paris 1971–89).

We may also be able to go some way towards understanding the nature of the bagaudae: according to the *Chronicle of 452* they were mainly servile; according to Salvian of Marseilles, writing in the 440s, they were essentially those oppressed by social circumstances, the government and the law.[25] It might be possible to go further still, if we add to this information that of a unique late Roman comedy called the *Querolus*, which describes a lawless, egalitarian society north of the Loire.[26] An all-embracing interpretation of peasant unrest can be squeezed from these diverse clues.[27]

There are, however, grave problems with this reading. First, there is nothing in the evidence for Britain to suggest that the rebellion was class-based. It seems rather to have been a rebellion against Constantine III, intended to facilitate renewed contact with and help from Honorius at Ravenna.[28] If the Aremorican rebellion really was modelled on the British, then it is unlikely to have been a servile movement: if it were a servile movement, which may be implied by the *Querolus*, then Zosimus' linking of the two events is likely to be wrong. As for the rebellion of Tibatto in the 430s, this could be lower-class, but by 437 the rebels were seeking an accord with the emperor, or rather with Aetius. The subsequent rebellion in the late 440s was led by a doctor, Eudoxius, whom the *Chronicle of 452* seems not to have seen as servile. With regard to the Spanish bagaudae, nothing about them, other than their geographical origin, is known, though the fact that Basilius teamed up with the Suevic king Rechiarius may suggest that he was a capable warlord rather than a peasant.

There is a second point: our knowledge of the bagaudae is transmitted through a series of texts, each of which has a very different agenda. The *Querolus* was written to please the circle of Exuperantius, who had subdued a bagaudic revolt in Aremorica in 417:[29] its author could afford to laugh at the libertarians north of the Loire. The concerns of the *De Gubernatione Dei* are entirely different: Salvian's explanation for the disasters of his own time, like that of other Gallic and Italian moralists of the period, involved a radical critique of the social, economic and moral structures of the fifth-century empire, and for Salvian the bagaudae afforded one opportunity to expose Gallic corruption. Hydatius, himself a bishop, knew of bagaudae as the murderers of a bishop – not surprisingly, they receive no sympathy from him. These pieces may all belong to different jig-saws.

We are on safer ground, with regard to the bagaudae, if we place them within a much broader spectrum of reactions to the failure of Roman rule.[30]

[25] Salv. *De Gub. Dei* v.22, 24–6, ed. F. Pauly, *CSEL* 8 (Vienna 1883).
[26] *Querolus sive Aulularia* ed. G. Ranstrand (Göteborg 1951) p. 7: see Thompson (1952) 11–23. Most recently, and critically, see Drinkwater (1992).   [27] E.g. Thompson (1952).   [28] Wood (1984) 5–6.
[29] Rutilius Namatianus, *De reditu suo* I lines 213–16, ed. E. Doblhofer (Heidelberg 1972–7).
[30] Van Dam, *Leadership and Community* 25–56; Drinkwater (1992).

Some aspects of this were long-standing: there is nothing new in the injustice described by Salvian; all that was new was the opportunity to opt out, an opportunity afforded specifically by the crisis in Gaul in the 430s and 440s. Those opting out might on occasion have belonged to the lower orders of society, but others among the disaffected could have been regional *potentes* looking to create a local power structure in a vacuum left by a failing imperial government. These bagaudae may have had something in common with the rebellious Nori and Juthungi mentioned by Hydatius,[31] who were active further east before being put down by Aetius, and with the other bandit groups of the region who appear later in the *Vita Severini*.[32] Yet not everyone wanted to opt out: the Britons, in their rebellion against Constantine, were apparently looking for a *rapprochement* with Honorius.

Further south we also find a debate, albeit of a somewhat different kind, over whether to remain inside the empire or to opt out. As the emperors failed to protect their subjects, the extent to which one should co-operate with the barbarians became an increasingly significant issue. The question appears to have been central to Sidonius at the time of the trial of Arvandus, sometime praetorian prefect of Gaul, who seems not to have regarded as treasonable correspondence with Euric, urging him to attack the British supporters of the emperor Anthemius and to divide Gaul with the Burgundians.[33] In other words, there was a range of possible reactions to the failure of imperial governmental structures, and it is the opening up, and the subsequent closing down, of these possibilities which is the hallmark of this 'sub-Roman' period.

To investigate this further, it is useful to consider reactions to the failure of the military, not least because this failure is one of the central criteria for the end of the Roman world,[34] a point that was already perceived in the early sixth century: Eugippius, for instance, explicitly links the survival of the empire with the payment of Roman troops,[35] And Sidonius may have come to similar conclusions a generation earlier.[36] The run-down of the Roman army was something which affected different provinces at different moments. Britain, having seen the majority of its troops withdrawn to the continent by Constantine III in *c.* 407, was apparently appealing for military aid, without success, around 410; in other regions of the north-west a Roman military presence was spasmodic until the 450s,[37] and in Noricum it seems to have lasted even longer. The end of the Roman army and the lack of a standing army in the successor states was to have a momentous effect on social and economic structures. The barbarian kingdoms founded

---

[31] Hydat. *Chron.* nn. 83, 85: compare *Chronicle of 452* 106 (431).
[32] Eugippius, *Vita Severini* 10 (*scamarae*) ed. P. Régerat, *SChrét.* 374 (Paris 1991); see also 2.
[33] Sid. Ap. *Ep.* 1.7; Harries (1994) 159–66.   [34] Cf. the seminal article of Wickham (1984).
[35] Eugippius, *Vita Severini* 20, 1, ed. P. Régerat, *SChrét.* 374 (Paris 1991).   [36] Sid. Ap. *Ep.* 2.1, 4.
[37] Wood (1987) 258–60.

in the late fifth and the sixth century depended not on a paid army but on the personal followings of kings and aristocrats, as well as on military obligations. Gone was the need for heavy taxation, and hence much of the rationale of the late Roman state.[38]

The initial responses to the absence of a Roman army differed radically in different regions. After their rebellion against Constantine III, the Britons appear to have asked Honorius to send troops to help defend them against barbarian raids. The emperor, however, who was in no position to spare soldiers in 410 or thereabouts, responded by repealing the *Lex Julia de Vi Publica*: the Britons were now allowed to bear arms and defend themselves. Even if we conclude that Zosimus was wrong to associate this act with Britain rather than Bruttium,[39] Gildas appears to imply a similar set of measures – and he may be thought to confirm Zosimus' narrative.[40] Indeed, Gildas actually goes further, in saying that the Romans instructed the Britons in various military strategies.[41]

Clearly, the Britons did organize their own self-defence. Apparently in 429 they were able to defeat a combined force of Picts and Saxons, even if they required military advice from bishop Germanus of Auxerre, supposedly resorting to the somewhat unusual tactic of shouting 'Hallelujah' at the enemy.[42] The role of Germanus here, as of Lupus and Severinus in the later military histories of Troyes and Noricum, is difficult to assess. It may, but does not necessarily, support the cases that Germanus and Severinus had significant secular, and even military, careers before entering the ecclesiastical life.[43] It may merely reflect an extraordinary extension of ecclesiastical influence in a period when power structures were ill-defined, or it may be no more than a literary or hagiographic *topos*.

Whatever the reason for the success of the Britons against the Picts and the Saxons in 429,[44] a decade or more later a new military crisis occasioned a further appeal to the imperial court.[45] The crisis may have been caused by a revolt of Saxon federates, or alternatively the failure of the appeal may have led to the employment and subsequent revolt of the federates.[46] In either case, Britain was still working along firmly Roman lines as late as the 440s. An appeal to Aetius was certainly an appeal to re-enter the military structures of the Roman empire, while the use of barbarian federates was

---

[38] Wickham (1984) 19–20.

[39] See, however, the dismissal of the possibility by Thompson (1977) 315 n. 43.

[40] Gildas, *De Excidio Britanniae* 17–18; Wood (1984) 5.   [41] Gildas, *De Excidio Britanniae* 18.

[42] Constantius, *Vita Germani* 17–18; on the possibility that much of this story is symbolic, Wood (1984) 11–12.

[43] On Germanus' early career, Constantius, *Vita Germani*, ed. R. Borius, *SChrét.* 112 (Paris 1965) 33–5; on Severinus' early career, Eugippius, *Vita Severini*, ed. P. Régerat, *SChrét.* 374 (Paris 1991) 96–102.

[44] On this issue see Myres (1960); Morris (1965); and especially the critical comments of Liebeschuetz (1963) and (1967).   [45] Gildas, *De Excidio Britanniae* 20.

[46] On the problems of squaring the chronology of Gildas with the *Chronicle of 452*, Wood (1984) 19–20.

a long-standing Roman policy. It was also a policy which in the fifth century brought with it considerable danger, as the Britons found to their cost when the Saxons revolted. The decision of one group of Britons, under the leadership of Ambrosius Aurelianus, to rely on its own military strength, rather than on that of Rome or on federates, marks a move away from the policy of reintegration into the imperial sphere, apparently espoused by Vortigern and the council of the Britains, in their appeal to Aetius.[47]

By contrast with Britain, Spain seems to have seen no such emergence of a native military tradition, outside the bagaudae and various brigand troops,[48] despite the decision of two Spanish aristocrats loyal to the emperor Honorius to arm their slaves in opposition to the forces of the usurper Constantine III.[49] For the most part, military operations in the north-western part of the peninsula, and probably further south, were conducted by Roman generals, their barbarian federates or by independent barbarian groups. Once, we hear of a crowd repelling a Herul raid against the coast of Lugo,[50] but more often the Hispano-Romans appear as unarmed civilians, suffering at the hands of barbarians. The population of Noricum is also, for the most part, merely the butt of barbarian and brigand raids, though we hear something from Eugippius of their use of *Fluchtburgen* (refuge sites).[51] In Comagenis, at least in the earlier part of Severinus' time there, the civilian population were guarded by federates – and the federates were none too popular: their panic, caused by an earthquake, and their ensuing massacre of each other were regarded as a miraculous salvation.[52] Moreover, for as long as they were paid, there were other troops in Noricum, but according to Eugippius they depended on the advice of Severinus.[53] Only on one occasion do we hear of a force of locals attacking an enemy.[54]

For the most part, Gallaecia and Noricum appear to have followed the pattern which can be found in Britain before 410 – they depended on Roman troops or federates, and otherwise sought shelter as best they could. Federates were also much in evidence in Gaul: famously in the settlement of the Visigoths in Aquitaine, and later of the Burgundians in Sapaudia and the Alans in Aremorica and Valence.[55] The most northerly of these settlements, that in Aremorica, is remarkably well evidenced because it is not only recorded in the *Chronicle of 452*, but also in the *Vita Germani*: the region was deliberately handed over by the central government to the Alans

---

[47] Gildas, *De Excidio Britanniae* 25.   [48] Hydat. *Chron.* nn. 117, 120, 133.
[49] Oros. *Hist. Ad. Pag.* VII.40.5–7, ed. C. Zangemeister, *CSEL* 5 (Vienna 1882); compare Zos. VI.4.
[50] Hydat. *Chron.* n. 164.   [51] Eugippius, *Vita Severini* 25.3; 30.1.
[52] Eugippius, *Vita Severini* 1.2; 2.1.   [53] Eugippius, *Vita Severini* 4.2–5; 20.
[54] Eugippus, *Vita Severini* 27.1–2.
[55] *Chronicle of 452* 124, 127, 128, ed. T. Mommsen, *MGH, AA* 9 (Berlin 1892); see Thompson (1956).

because of the bagaudic uprising of Tibatto.[56] The subsequent activities of the Alans seem to have been somewhat high-handed, to say the least – they dispossessed the landowning classes (*domini*), which may or may not have been what Aetius wanted.[57] Perhaps rather closer to the experience of the people of Comagenis was that of Sidonius in Lyons, where he objected to the Burgundians stationed in his house.[58]

In parts of Gaul it is also possible to find parallels to the more aggressive policies of Ambrosius Aurelianus. While Sidonius, by this time bishop in Clermont, raised the morale of his flock – much as numerous other bishops seem to have done – his brother-in-law Ecdicius broke the Visigothic siege of the city, apparently with only eighteen men,[59] a number subsequently reduced yet further by Gregory of Tours to a mere ten.[60] Ecdicius showed what a man with military experience and a private following could manage in central Gaul.[61] For such a man Nepos' cession of Clermont to the Visigoths would have been nothing short of betrayal.[62] Another independent military figure, albeit one whose career as a warlord grew directly out of imperial service, was Aegidius. Effectively left without an emperor to follow after the murder of his patron Majorian, he ploughed his own furrow in northern Gaul with the troops he had with him at the time of his master's death.[63] As a result, he was able to set up something like a kingdom of his own, based on Soissons, though how far beyond that it stretched must be open to doubt.[64] There is certainly nothing to suggest that Aegidius or his son Syagrius ruled over the Aremoricans, whose submission to the Franks is noted, somewhat obscurely, in the pages of Procopius.[65]

The one other late Roman military leader in northern or central Gaul in the second half of the century of whom we know anything more than his name was the Briton Riothamus, who sailed from Britain or Brittany and proceeded to Bourges with substantial forces, even if not with the 12,000 spoken of by Jordanes. He is said to have done so in response to an appeal for help from the emperor Anthemius.[66] Riothamus was defeated by the Visigothic king Euric, and retired to the Lyonnais with his remaining troops, where they were still numerous enough to cause problems for the local inhabitants.[67] Almost everything about Riothamus is a mystery. If he indeed came from Britain, why should a man with so many troops abandon the island at a time when the Saxons were not apparently dominant? Does he represent a legitimist faction, determined to stay within the empire at all

---

[56] Constantius, *Vita Germani* 6.28; 7.40; *Chronicle of 452* 117, 119, 127.   [57] *Chronicle of 452* 127.

[58] Sid. Ap. *Carm.* xii; compare *Ep.* 3.4.1 for a more general assessment of the threat posed by federates.   [59] Sid. Ap. *Ep.* 3.3.3; see the comments of Harries (1994) 228–9.

[60] Greg. Tur. *Hist.* ii.24, ed. B. Krusch and W. Levison, *MGH, SRM* i (Hanover 1951).

[61] On this private army, Harries (1994) 228–9.   [62] Sid. Ap. *Ep.* 7.7.5.

[63] Elton (1992) 172–4.   [64] James (1988) 67–71.   [65] Procop. *Wars*, v.12.12–15.

[66] Jord. *Get.* 237–8; cf. Sid. Ap. *Ep.* 1.7.5.   [67] Sid. Ap. *Ep.* 3.9.

costs? That, at least, seems to be the implication of his fighting for Anthemius.

What Riothamus cannot illustrate is the formation of Brittany. On the continent he is associated with Berry and the Lyonnais. The migration of Britons to western Aremorica is curiously difficult to trace. While it is true that the region came to be called Britannia by the late fifth century, and that there were British ecclesiastics and saints there from that period onwards,[68] there is no clear evidence for a large-scale migration – and there is no good reason to read Gildas as describing one, even though he does state that some people fled overseas during the Saxon uprising of the mid fifth century.[69] It may well be that the migration of a limited number of powerful families, within what had long been a single cultural province, uniting western Britain and Brittany, was enough to provide western Aremorica with its new name and to prompt certain linguistic developments.

While Riothamus and Ecdicius may represent groups intent on remaining within the empire, Aegidius in Gaul and Ambrosius Aurelianus in Britain apparently represent groups willing to opt out. Aegidius seems to have remained loyal to the memory of Majorian, but he was certainly not loyal to succeeding emperors. Gregory of Tours, writing in the 570s, could remember Aegidius' son Syagrius as a king of the Romans, *Romanorum rex*.[70] Ambrosius is often represented as a more Roman figure than Vortigern, because of the latter's involvement in the settlement of Saxons in Britain, yet in employing federates Vortigern was not necessarily breaking from the empire, while Ambrosius was undoubtedly behaving in as independent a fashion as was Aegidius. Moreover, if Gildas is right to say that Ambrosius' parents wore the purple,[71] he came from a family of usurpers.

It is possible to see Aegidius and Ambrosius as transitional figures in a development of 'sub-Roman' kingship, a development which came to fruition in western Britain, but which was stopped short in Gaul with the defeat and execution of Aegidius' son, Syagrius, at the hands of the Frank, Clovis.[72] Clearly there were Celtic elements in the lifestyle and in the somewhat relaxed attitude towards holy orders of the five sixth-century kings – Aurelius Caninus, Constantine, Cuneglasus, Maglocunus and Vortipor – castigated by Gildas,[73] but they were also heirs to a Roman past.[74] Two of them had ostentatiously Roman names and Vortipor may have been the Voteporix commemorated as *Protector* by the Latin memorial stone at Castell Dwyran.[75] Equally Roman is the remarkable group of inscriptions

---

[68] The evidence is collected by Jackson (1953) 12–16, and Chadwick (1969) 193–226. The case for substantial numbers migrating, however, depends on assumptions about the differences between British and Gaulish and on the nature of the linguistic impact of the British.

[69] Gildas, *De Excidio Britanniae* 25.   [70] Greg. Tur. *Hist.* 11.27.

[71] Gildas, *De Excidio Britanniae* 25.   [72] Greg. Tur. *Hist.* 11.27.

[73] Gildas, *De Excidio Britanniae* 28–36; Kerlouegan (1987) 526–45.   [74] Dark (1994) 110.

[75] Thomas (1994) 82.

from Penmachno, in the mountains of north Wales.[76] Already in the mid to late fifth cetury Britain could boast at least one more warlord, Patrick's *bête noire*, Coroticus – probably a pirate rather than a representative of any legitimate institutional power, but nevertheless another example of the military life made possible by the withdrawal of the Roman army, and the exhortation to self-help. The continental counterpart to Coroticus may not have been Aegidius, but rather a bagaudic leader, such as the Spaniard Basilius.[77] Yet British pirates are only one end of a spectrum of military possibilities opened up by the failure of the imperial government to protect its citizens.

In certain areas of northern Gaul, as in Britain, military failure was accompanied by governmental failure. Although the Merovingian kings of the Franks managed to govern with something like a Roman administration, and even to tax their Gallo-Roman subjects in the late sixth century, there is no reason to assume that there was absolute governmental continuity throughout northern Gaul up to that time.[78] In discussing the period of barbarian invasion Salvian records the destruction or devastation of Cologne, Mainz and Trier.[79] His account may be largely hyperbolic, and there was certainly some continuity in all three places: in Cologne it may have been considerable.[80] In Aremorica the normal structures of government and society are likely to have failed during the fifth century, even if the Franks managed to put the clock back to the east of modern Brittany half a century later. Salvian's picture of the free society north of the Loire suggests anything but the normal functioning of administrative institutions, and the narrative of events in the Loire valley in the 460s provided by Gregory of Tours, who was apparently dependent on a chronicle compiled in Angers, suggests something like total military chaos in the region of Angers, Bourges and Déols.[81] By the last quarter of the century there were Frankish enclaves not only in Tournai, where Childeric was buried, but also in Cambrai, and perhaps, although by no means certainly, as far west as Le Mans.[82] Further, gaps in some episcopal lists may suggest that there was some disruption in the ecclesiastical organization of northeastern Gaul at the time, although other interpretations of the lacunae are possible.[83] Certainly it should be noted that such a gap may be no more than an evidential hiccup. Nevertheless, other societies have been temporarily broken apart by war, and patched together again subsequently. It is as well to remember that the continuities apparent from the vantage point

[76] Dark (1994) 110.　　[77] Hydat. *Chron.* 133.
[78] The fullest discussion of Merovingian taxation is Goffart (1989).
[79] Salv. *De Gub. Dei* VI.39, 72–7, 82, 85–9.
[80] Ewig (1954) 56–60; Heinemeyer (1979); Wightman (1985); Schütte (1995).
[81] Greg. Tur. *Hist.* II.18–19; for the Angers origin of the material, note the use of the verb *venire* in ch. 18.　　[82] Greg. Tur. *Hist.* II.42.　　[83] Griffe (1964–6) II.134–6.

of the later sixth century may have been completely invisible a century earlier.

Mixed in with this picture of collapse, however, is a picture of remarkable continuity. Writers in the south of Gaul presented the early fifth century as a period of calamity, but their successors in the second half of the century chose to emphasize the continuance of Roman tradition.[84] Archaeology supports the written word in suggesting continuity in such southern cities as Vienne, Arles and Marseilles. At the same time, despite the crises in the Loire valley in the 460s, Sidonius continued to number northern bishops and aristocrats among his correspondents. Among the bishops were Agroecius of Sens,[85] Euphronius of Autun,[86] Lupus of Troyes,[87] Nunechius of Nantes,[88] Perpetuus of Tours,[89] Principius of Soissons,[90] Prosper of Orleans[91] and Remigius of Rheims.[92] Agroecius and Euphronius he consulted over the election of Simplicius to the see of Bourges, while he informed Perpetuus of the result. Along with Paulinus of Périgueux, he supplied Perpetuus with verses for the newly rebuilt church of St Martin.[93] This church was being built during precisely the years that Aegidius, Childeric, Paul, the Saxon Odoacer and the Visigoths were fighting in the Loire valley – it was truly a capsule of eternity in a very unstable world.[94] Aegidius himself may have been a benefactor of St Martin's, but of him Sidonius says not a word.[95] Sidonius did nevertheless correspond with Principius, the bishop of Soissons, which seems to have been Aegidius' power base. Perhaps even more remarkable, Sidonius' friend Volusianus set off for his estate in the Bayeux region in the late 460s.[96]

Among Sidonius' northern correspondents, Remigius provides a valuable thread through the chaos of the late fifth century. Unfortunately many of the sources for Remigius are late, not least the *Vita* rewritten by Hincmar in the ninth century. Nevertheless, he appears as a correspondent of Sidonius in 471 or thereabouts.[97] In the ensuing years the *civitas* of Rheims must have fallen into the hands of the Frankish king Childeric, since Remigius wrote to the king's son, Clovis, when he took over the province of Belgica Secunda in succession to his father.[98] The letter presupposes a good deal of organizational continuity in the province. Remigius was later to baptize Clovis,[99] and to play some role in church appointments in the last years of his reign.[100] The bishop's will, preserved like that of his

---

[84] Wood (1992) 9–10.   [85] Sid. Ap. *Ep.* 7.5.   [86] Sid. Ap. *Epp.* 7.8; 9.2.
[87] Sid. Ap. *Epp.* 6.1; 6.11.   [88] Sid. Ap. *Ep.* 8.13.   [89] Sid. Ap. *Ep.* 7.9.
[90] Sid. Ap. *Epp.* 8.14; 9.10.   [91] Sid. Ap. *Ep.* 8.15.   [92] Sid. Ap. *Ep.* 9.7.
[93] Sid. Ap. *Ep.* 4.18.4–5; Greg. Tur. *Hist.* 11.14; Harries (1994) 116; Van Dam (1993) 18, 314–16.
[94] Van Dam, *Leadership and Community* 230–55: Brown (1996) 64.   [95] Harries (1994) 98–9, 247–8.
[96] Sid. Ap. *Ep.* 4.18.2.   [97] Sid. Ap. *Ep.* 9.7.
[98] *Epist. Austras.* 2, ed. W. Gundlach, *MGH, Epistolae* 3 (Berlin 1892).   [99] Greg. Tur. *Hist.* 11.31.
[100] *Epist. Austras.* 3.

predecessor Bennadius,[101] is a remarkable document of the continuation of senatorial landholding in the north.[102]

It is, in fact, impossible to generalize over the question of continuity and discontinuity in Gallia and Germania: even within Noricum Ripense the fate of individual towns, as described by Eugippius, varied. At Lauriacum (Lorch) religious life lasted beyond the days of Severinus,[103] and the case for continuity is yet stronger further west in Augsburg,[104] and stronger still at Chur in Rhaetia.[105] Britannia, too, presents a remarkably mixed picture. The sheer variety is perhaps clearest in south and west Wales, where the newly created Irish kingdom of Demetia bordered the more Romanized south, with its renowned monastic centre of Llanilltud Fawr (Llantwit Major), which appears to have been a significant centre of Latin education into the sixth century.[106]

In other places of the north-west for which we have anything like a detailed narrative, the sources highlight the ecclesiastical management of social crisis, rather than any governmental continuity, at least during the period of barbarian migration and of the establishment of the successor states. This is apparent as far south as the Rhône valley, where Patiens, bishop of Lyons – himself the dedicatee of Constantius' *Vita Germani* – supervised the distribution of corn.[107] At Orleans Anianus was supposedly responsible for the ransoming of prisoners,[108] as well as the organization of the city's defences against Attila.[109] He was regarded as a plausible subject for Sidonius' literary skills.[110] Lupus of Troyes was likewise credited with saving his flock from the ravages of Attila's Huns, and he did so, interestingly enough, by instructing them to reoccupy a hill-fort outside the city[111] – a policy which might be compared with the use of *Fluchtburgen* in Noricum[112] and the revival of hill-forts in sub-Roman Britain. In part, the activity of bishops such as Patiens of Lyons, Lupus of Troyes or – slightly later and further south – Caesarius of Arles[113] may reflect the very real powers they had been given since 312.[114] Yet the sources do not confine their comments on such social leadership to bishops. Severinus was apparently offered a bishopric,[115] but his actions were those of a charismatic leader. As such, he organized the management of corn distribution at Favianis until more supplies arrived from Rhaetia,[116] he arranged

[101] Flodoard, *Hist. Eccles. Remensis* 1.9, ed. J. Heller and G. Waitz, *MGH, Scriptores* XIII (Hanover 1881); Harries (1994) 218–19.

[102] *Testamentum Remigii*, ed. B. Krusch, *MGH, SRM* 3, pp. 336–47; Wood, *Merovingian Kingdoms* 211–12.

[103] Wolfram (1987) 57. [104] Wolfram (1987) 115–17. [105] Wolfram (1987) 113–15.

[106] *Vita Samsonis* 7–20, ed. R. Fawtier, *La Vie de saint Samson: Essai de critique hagiographique*, Bibliothèque de l'École des Hautes Études 197 (Paris 1912). [107] Sid. Ap. *Ep.* 6.12.5.

[108] *Vita Aniani* 3, ed. B. Krusch *MGH, SRM* 3 (Hanover 1896); for a possible early date for the life, see Griffe (1964–6) II.54–5. [109] *Vita Aniani* 4. [110] Sid. Ap. *Ep.* 8.15.2.

[111] *Vita Lupi* 6, ed. B. Krusch, *MGH, SRM* 3; for an early date for the *Vita Lupi*, see Ewig (1978).

[112] Eugippius, *Vita Severini* 25.3; 30.1. [113] *Vita Caesarii*, ed. B. Krusch, *MGH, SRM* 3.

[114] Heinzelmann (1976); Scheibelreiter (1983). [115] Eugippius, *Vita Severini* 9.4.

[116] Eugippius, *Vita Severini* 3.

for the collection of clothes,[117] and more generally of a tithe, to support the poor.[118] He was constantly occupied in the ransom of Roman captives.[119] More miraculously, he ended the threat of floods at Quintanis,[120] and he provided the poor of Lauriacum with oil.[121]

It was not, however, only churchmen who emerged as charismatic leaders in this period of crisis. We hear of the virgin Genovefa, who is said to have organized famine relief in Paris,[122] and also to have freed prisoners, much to the aggravation of the Frankish king, Childeric.[123] The *Vita Genovefae* may well cast its heroine rather unrealistically in the mould of a bishop,[124] but it appears to have been written as early as 520,[125] and the actions it attributes to the saint may not be fiction. Stripped of its literary models, what is extraordinary about the career of Genovefa is not her lay status but simply the fact that she was a woman, the only one to achieve such prominence as a saint in the north in this transitional period. Patrick thought the Gallo-Romans notable for the ransoming of captives.[126] In addition to his exploits in raising the siege of Clermont, Ecdicius was remembered for relieving a famine in Burgundy out of his own resources; he was rewarded, according to Gregory of Tours, with the heavenly promise that neither he nor his heirs would ever lack food.[127] Charisma was not confined to churchmen or even, in the case of Ecdicius, to saints.

Where churchmen and saints held an advantage was in their ability to make moral capital out of the situation in which they found themselves. The message of Salvian and the other Gallic moralists sprang very precisely from the crisis of the fifth century – it was a reaction to disaster. Not surprisingly, a model of safety achieved through prayer, fasting and good works was put forward. The Britons defeated the Picts and Saxons after following Germanus' instructions that they should receive baptism.[128] Genovefa was said to have saved Paris from Attila by persuading its female citizens to fast,[129] and Orleans was also supposedly saved from the Huns because Anianus instructed the people to pray and process round the city.[130] A similar tactic would be used against the Franks a century later, when the population of Saragossa went into mourning and carried the relics of St Vincent round the walls to counter Childebert's siege.[131] One of the most influential of all processions, the minor Rogations, was instituted in Vienne about the year 470 by Bishop Mamertus, though to ward off earthquakes rather than barbarians.[132] By 473 Sidonius was following

---

[117] Eugippius, *Vita Severini* 29.   [118] Eugippius, *Vita Severini* 17.   [119] Eugippius, *Vita Severini* 9.1.
[120] Eugippius, *Vita Severini* 15.   [121] Eugippius, *Vita Severini* 28.
[122] *Vita Genovefae* 35, 39, 40, ed. B. Krusch, *MGH, SRM* 3.   [123] *Vita Genovefae* 26.
[124] Wood (1988) 378.   [125] Heinzelmann and Poulin (1986).
[126] Patrick, *Epistola ad Milites Corotici* 14, ed. R. P. C. Hanson, *SChrét.* 249 (Paris 1978).
[127] Greg. Tur. *Hist.* 11.24.   [128] Constantius, *Vita Germani* 17.   [129] *Vita Genovefae* 12.
[130] *Vita Aniani* 8, 9.   [131] Greg. Tur. *Hist.* 111.29.
[132] Sid. Ap. *Ep.* 14.2; Avitus, *hom.* 6, ed. R. Peiper, *MGH, AA* 6 (2) (Berlin 1883).

suit in Clermont, though he seems to have been thinking more about barbarians than natural disasters.[133]

The *Vita Severini* provides yet more examples of religious actions performed to avert crisis. Asturis was destroyed because its people would not fast when the saint told them to; news of its destruction made the people of Comagenis more inclined to obey him: their fasting was also rewarded with the destruction of the federate troops who were bothering rather than defending them.[134] In Favianis, Severinus urged penance to avert a famine.[135] Fasting ended a plague of grasshoppers at Cucullae (Kuchl).[136] Later, prayer protected the *burgi* of Noricum from the Heruls.[137] At Lauriacum, prayer, fasting and alms-giving preceded Severinus' miraculous provision of oil to the poor.[138]

On many of these occasions, Eugippius points the moral by introducing a dissident into the story: the people of Asturis who would not fast and were destroyed; Procula, whose greed kept her from providing corn for the people of Favianis; those inhabitants of Quintanis who were killed when they refused to evacuate their town, despite Severinus' advice – for one of the saint's skills was that he knew when to give up;[139] and the man of Cucullae who went to inspect his fields rather than pray – naturally, it was his crops that were eaten by the grasshoppers. In his case, Severinus seized on the man's misfortunes to point the need for prayer. The anecdote, as recounted by Eugippius, may well reflect a genuine tendency on the part of the charismatics of the period to exploit whatever incidents supported their call to repentance.

In all this we are not far from Salvian, on the one hand, or Gildas, on the other. Even more than Severinus, Salvian and Gildas preached repentance – and although the ultimate fate of Britain, and indeed Gildas' own probable departure for Brittany, may imply that his message fell on deaf ears,[140] the narrative of the *De Excidio Britanniae* does suggest that twice in the fifth century some sort of moral crusade did have an impact on British morale.[141] In the ninth century, if not earlier, Germanus, possibly a British saint Garmon rather than the bishop of Auxerre, was remembered as having reprimanded Vortigern.[142] That the British church was powerful is also apparent from Patrick's *Confessio*,[143] although both Patrick and Gildas suggest that the majority of churchmen were lacking in moral stature.[144] To emphasize the moral crusaders may indeed be to fall for the religious propaganda

---

[133] Sid. Ap. *Ep.* 7.1; Harries (1994) 227–8.   [134] Eugippius, *Vita Severini* 2.
[135] Eugippius, *Vita Severini* 3.   [136] Eugippius, *Vita Severini* 12.   [137] Eugippius, *Vita Severini* 24.
[138] Eugippius, *Vita Severini* 28.   [139] Eugippius, *Vita Severini* 27; compare 22.
[140] Cf. the reading of Bede, *HE* 1.22, ed. B. Colgrave and R. A. B. Mynors, *Bede's Ecclesiastical History of the English* (Oxford 1969).   [141] Gildas, *De Excidio Britanniae* 20, 25.
[142] *Historia Brittonum* 24, ed. D. N. Dumville, *The Historia Brittonum, The Vatican Recension* (Cambridge 1985).   [143] Patrick, *Confessio* 10, 13, 26, 27, 37, ed. Hanson *SChrét.* 249.
[144] Gildas, *De Excidio Britanniae* 66–91.

which lies at the heart of much of the hagiography, as well the moral dia-
tribes, of the fifth and sixth century. Nevertheless, the consonance between
a widely scattered group of sources does suggest that we should recognize
the association of charismatic preaching and survival as a factor in the peculiarly unstable days of the mid and late fifth and early sixth century.
Moreover, even if we deny the actuality of what is described in the *vitae* of
fifth-century saints, many of the texts themselves were written in the fifth
or early sixth century, and the image they present must have had some resonance. In other words, whether as reality or literary construct, the fifth
century had its charismatic leaders.

Living saints seem therefore to have played a significant role in amelio-
rating the experiences of Romans during the crisis period of the barbarian
migration and settlement. Dead saints could also have an influence. That
their lives were recorded is in itself an indication of the importance attached
to their memory. Of wider impact were the cults which grew up around the
tombs of holy men. The development of the cult of St Martin by Perpetuus
is only the most eye-catching example of what was common in much of
fifth-century Gaul and elsewhere: the propagation of saint-cults to provide
foci of consolation in an age of fragmentation and uncertainty. Already at
the turn of the century Victricius of Rouen had made much of the relics in
his care.[145] Elsewhere in the north, Euphronius of Autun developed the cult
of the martyr Symphorian;[146] Gregory of Langres was responsible for the
promotion of the cult of Benignus of Dijon and perhaps also of a host of
associated cults.[147] In so doing he, like other bishops of the time, provided
his diocese, and indeed the surrounding dioceses, with a whole new
Christian past. The hagiographers were not above fabricating information
about the saints they promoted, some of whom may have been invented *ex
nihilo*. Further south, cities like Clermont under Sidonius bristled with saint-
cults.[148] A generation later, Lyons could be described as being defended by
its basilicas, each of which housed the relics of saints, rather than by its
defences.[149] The relics of saints, in Gaul as elsewhere, were a very present
help against external threat. Not surprisingly, Germanus of Auxerre, when
in Britain, interested himself in the cult of Alban, identifying the tomb,
removing some relics from it and installing other relics of continental saints
in their place; in so doing he may not only have been thinking about the
safety of Britain — it is likely that he wished to signify that Alban was a
martyr of the whole church, and not the patron of Pelagian heretics.[150] On
his return to Auxerre he may well have commissioned the first *Passio* of the

---

[145] Victricius, *De laude sanctorum* ed. J.-P. Migne, *PL* xx, cols. 443–58.

[146] Greg. Tur. *Hist.* ii.15; he may also have been responsible for the composition of the *Passio
Symphoriani, Acta Sanctorum*, August iv (Brussels 1867), pp. 491–8.

[147] Greg. Tur. *Liber in Gloria Martyrum* 50, ed. B. Krusch, *MGH, SRM* i (2) (Hanover 1885).

[148] Harries (1994) 197–202.   [149] Avitus, *hom.* 24.   [150] Wood (1984) 12–13.

British martyr.[151] In Britain itself, Alban continued to be revered down to the days of Gildas, who also noted the cult of Julius and Aaron, probably based at Caerleon.[152]

Bishops and charismatics established themselves, or at least were remembered as establishing themselves, not only in the eyes of their own congregations and colleagues, but also in the eyes of the barbarians.[153] Their *vitae* record numerous confrontations between kings and holy men. Germanus seized the bridle of Goar's horse, and his action gained him the admiration of the king.[154] His contemporary, Lupus of Troyes, wrote to the Alaman king Gebavult, rebuking him for his raids and persuading him to release the captives taken.[155] Again, however, the largest number of anecdotes relate to Severinus. The Rugian king Flaccitheus and his son Feletheus turned to the saint for advice.[156] Feletheus' wife, Giso, however, was unimpressed. She urged on her husband the baptism of Catholics as Arians and also the capture of Romans. She ignored Severinus' appeal to stop her wickedness, but was punished when captive goldsmiths held her son to ransom. Nor was Feletheus always easy to deal with. Hearing that many Romans had taken refuge in Lauriacum, he marched against the town, intending to move them closer to his own power centre, in order to impose tribute on them. He saw these Romans as his people, and wanted to ensure that the Thuringians and Alamans did not get their hands on them. Even so, Severinus persuaded the king to let them return to their own homes.[157]

Before he died, the saint admonished Feletheus and Giso once again,[158] and he also attacked the king's brother, Ferderuchus, for taking Romans captive.[159] The prince nevertheless went so far as to plunder Severinus' monastery after the saint's death – but he was soon killed by his nephew, who in turn was defeated by Odoacer and fled to Theoderic the Amal.[160] Nor was it only with the Rugi that Severinus had to deal. He also arranged the return of numerous prisoners taken by the Alaman king Gibuld – perhaps to be identified with Gebavult in the *Vita Lupi*.[161]

In the *Vita Severini* we see a society gradually slipping out of Roman rule, but never quite becoming part of a barbarian state. Feletheus regarded the people of Noricum Ripense as his subjects (*subiectos*) – or, to be more precise, he was determined that no other barbarian ruler should profit from them[162] – but he did not actually annex their territory. Technically speaking, at least, the province was not part of a barbarian kingdom while Severinus was alive. Predatory barbarians are also in evidence in the chronicle of Hydatius, but in Gallaecia there appears to have been no charismatic

[151] Wood (1984) 13.   [152] Gildas, *De Excidio Britanniae* 10.   [153] Brown (1996) 77.
[154] Constantius, *Vita Germani* VI.28.   [155] *Vita Lupi* 10.   [156] Eugippius, *Vita Severini* 5, 8.
[157] Eugippius, *Vita Severini* 31.   [158] Eugippius, *Vita Severini* 40.   [159] Eugippius, *Vita Severini* 42.
[160] Eugippius, *Vita Severini* 44.   [161] Eugippius, *Vita Severini* 19.   [162] Brown (1996) 77.

opponent to the kings of the Sueves. Hydatius, who was more than aware of his own inadequacies,[163] was himself taken prisoner, only to be released after three months through the grace of God.[164] There is no sense here of a dramatic confrontation between cleric and barbarian, just sadness at the destruction of the church of Aquae Flaviae and relief that the traitors who had organized his capture caused no further damage.[165] Hydatius' world is one not of charismatics but of unsuccessful legations, each of which failed to tame the Sueves, and of military operations by Romans and later by Visigothic federates, which usually proved equally unproductive. Even the fact that, for a while, the Sueves were ruled by a Catholic monarch, and not, like the majority of the barbarians, by an Arian, was no comfort. Rechiarius was as bad as the rest of them, invading Gallaecia as soon as he became king,[166] then celebrating his marriage to the daughter of the Visigothic king Theoderic with a raid on Vasconia.[167] The same year, 449, he joined the bagaudic leader Basilius in a raid on Caesaraugusta.[168] After a few years in which he is absent from Hydatius' chronicle, he reappears, plundering Tarraconensis and taking the prisoners back to Gallaecia.[169] He had, however, overreached himself, and the emperor Avitus sent Theoderic against him. The result was defeat for the Sueves, and although Rechiarius escaped, he was captured and murdered.[170] Hydatius comments that the kingdom of the Sueves was 'destroyed and brought to an end'. Interesting here is the chronicler's contemporary recognition of barbarian kingdoms (*regna*) within the Roman empire (itself a *regnum*). He uses the word *regnum* in his description of Athaulf's succession to Alaric in 410, and for all subsequent Visigothic successions.[171] So, too, the Alans are described as having a *regnum* as early as 418,[172] and the Vandals a decade later.[173] Suevic succession is also described in regnal terms,[174] and although their kingdom was supposedly destroyed with the defeat of Rechiarius, it reappears in 457.[175] Hydatius knew that the empire's frontiers were about to fall,[176] but there were already kingdoms within the empire, and he watched helplessly as something which he regarded as very like the Last Days unfolded before his eyes.

Hydatius' bleak picture of wars, embassies and embryonic kingdoms, present even while the emperor was trying to re-establish his power, may have been closer to the experience of most fifth-century Romans in Spain, Gaul, Noricum and Britain than the more colourful worlds described in the *Vita Germani*, the *Vita Severini* or the *Vita Genovefae* – although even those

---

[163] Hydat. *Chron.* praef.   [164] Hydat. *Chron.* 196 (460), 202.
[165] On the tone of the chronicle, see Muhlberger (1990) 212–45.   [166] Hydat. *Chron.* 129 (448).
[167] Hydat. *Chron.* 132 (449).   [168] Hydat. *Chron.* 134 (449).   [169] Hydat. *Chron.* 165 (456).
[170] Hydat. *Chron.* 166, 168 (456–7).
[171] Hydat. *Chron.* 37 (410), 52 (416), 62 (419), 145 (451), 148 (453–4), 234 (466–7).
[172] Hydat. *Chron.* 60 (418).   [173] Hydat. *Chron.* 79 (428).   [174] Hydat. *Chron.* 106 (438), 129 (448).
[175] Hydat. *Chron.* 180 (457).   [176] Hydat. *Chron.* praef. 6.

are somewhat doom-laden landscapes. On the other hand, it may be that Gallaecia suffered precisely because no charismatic religious leader emerged to outface the Suevic kings.

Gallaecia may have been unusual among the peripheral zones of the Roman west in not having a charismatic leader. In the south Spanish city of Mérida a line of bishops established themselves as leaders of their community, although their holiness was perhaps secondary to the economic resources they built up.[177] Nor was the periphery the only area where there were saints capable of taking on, and supposedly outfacing, barbarians. Caesarius of Arles was a match for Theoderic the Amal,[178] and, already in the chronicle of Prosper of Aquitaine, pope Leo is said to have impressed Attila.[179] A century earlier, of course, Ambrose had outfaced Theodosius. In general, however, the role of the charismatics in the transition from Roman empire to barbarian kingdom in southern Gaul and Italy seems to have been less than it was in some of the more peripheral regions. Yet here, too, bishops generally played a very conspicuous role in the many diplomatic negotiations which went on during this period. Epiphanius of Pavia, for instance, negotiated with Euric as well as with Gundobad.[180] Equally significantly, four bishops were entrusted with negotiating the final stages of the cession of Clermont to the Visigoths.[181]

Although our sources suggest that it was charismatic clerics who stepped into the breach caused by the failure of the Roman empire, there were other individuals who attempted to use the remnants of imperial authority. The barbarians themselves often acted as officials of the old empire, both before and after becoming kings – and their kingdoms were built on Roman foundations, which in the south had been less shaken than further north. These southern leaders, the Ostrogoths in Italy, the Visigoths in Aquitaine and the Burgundians in the Rhône valley, were also drawn to some extent into the established social patterns of the upper classes of the late Roman empire. We can see this as early as the mid 450s in Sidonius' picture of the daily routine of the Visigothic king Theoderic: church attendance and official duties, followed by inspection of the stables, hunting, the midday meal, then a short siesta – or, even better, a game of dice – then a resumption of royal duties before dinner. As Sidonius remarked, it was advisable to lose a game against the king to get one's suit preferred.[182] Theoderic's brother, the rather more rebarbative Euric, was in time the focus of an equally Romanized court, centred on the Roman city of Toulouse, where the verses of Sidonius were well received.[183] Meanwhile, at the same court, more northerly barbarians – Saxons, Franks, maritime

---

[177] *Vitas Sanctorum Patrum Emeretensium* ed. J. N. Garvin (Washington 1946).
[178] *Vita Caesarii* 1.36–8.   [179] Prosper, s.a. 452, ed. T. Mommsen, *MGH, AA* 9 (Berlin 1892).
[180] Ennod. *Vita Epiph.* 85–94, 136–77, ed. F. Vogel, *MGH, AA* 7 (Berlin 1885).
[181] Sid. Ap. *Ep.* 7.6.10.   [182] Sid. Ap. *Ep.* 1.2.4–10.   [183] Sid. Ap. *Epp.* 4.8.1; 8.9.

Heruls and Burgundians, as well as Ostrogothic insurgents against the Huns – queued for audience.[184]

The expansion of the Visigoths under Euric, particularly in the early 470s, finally broke imperial power in Gaul. Yet this most disruptive of the barbarian kings to rule in Gaul also played a significant role in the continuance of certain aspects of Roman government, for it is he who is the earliest barbarian king known to have issued a law code.[185] In terms of the preservation of Roman tradition, his son went one degree further, issuing an abridgement of the Theodosian Code, the so-called *Breviary of Alaric*, for his Roman subjects in 506. Despite the Arianism of these two monarchs, and despite the brief period of persecution experienced by the Catholic church in those areas captured by Euric in the 470s,[186] they were largely on good terms with their Gallo-Roman bishops, who met under Alaric II's aegis at Agde in 506 and who opened the council with prayers for the king.[187] This apparently flourishing sub-Roman kingdom, however, was brought to a sudden end in 507 with Alaric's defeat and death at the hands of Clovis at the battle known as Vouillé, although it was probably fought at Voulon.[188]

The equally Romanized kingdom of the Burgundians, based on the Rhône valley and centred on the towns of Chalon-sur-Saône, Geneva and Lyons, survived a little longer. The Burgundians, or what remained of them after their defeat at the hands of Aetius,[189] had been settled in Sapaudia, the territory between Geneva and Neufchâtel.[190] While there, they took advantage of the crisis following the deposition of the emperor Avitus to make a special arrangement with the senators of Gaul.[191] The new emperor, Majorian, however, forced them back, presumably to Sapaudia.[192] We next meet the Burgundians controlling Lyons and Geneva as Roman officials. Chilperic acted as *magister militum* of Gaul under the emperor Glycerius and, as such, appears in the letters of Sidonius Apollinaris. In the changing political circumstances of the 470s the job was not an easy one, not least when Glycerius was superseded by Julius Nepos.[193] In such circumstances Chilperic's government was wide open to criticism: he was as liable to the admonitions of a holy man as were his Rugian contemporaries. Lupicinus, one of the so-called Jura Fathers, rebuked him for his harsh treatment of the poor, calling him an impostor.[194] Chilperic was naturally impressed.

---

[184] Sid. Ap. *Ep.* 8.9.5.   [185] Wolfram (1988) 194–5.
[186] Sid. Ap. *Ep.* 7.6: a letter which should be understood as both rhetorical and belonging to very specific circumstances.
[187] Council of Agde (506), praef., ed. C. Munier, *Concilia Galliae A.314–A.506*, CSEL 148 (Turnhout 1963).   [188] Gerberding (1987) 41.   [189] *Chronicle of 452* 118 (436).
[190] *Chronicle of 452* 128 (443); on the problem of the date, Wood (1992) 14–15.
[191] Marius of Avenches, s.a. 456, ed. J. Favrod, *La Chronique de Marius d'Avenches (455–581)* (Lausanne 1991).   [192] Sid. Ap. *Carm.* v.564–71; Harries (1994) 85–6.   [193] Sid. Ap. *Epp.* 5.6.2; 5.7.1.
[194] *Vita Patrum Iurensium* 92–5 (=II.10), ed. F. Martine, *Vie des Pères du Jura*, SChrét. 142 (Paris 1968); see also Greg. Tur. *Liber Vitae Patrum* 1.5, ed. Krusch, *MGH, SRM* 1 (2).

This may well be more than a hagiographic *topos*: the Burgundian is known from Sidonius' letters to have worked happily with the Catholic bishop of Lyons, Patiens. More specifically, he is said to have praised the bishop's banquets, while his wife admired his fasts.[195]

Nor was Chilperic the last Burgundian ruler to have a Roman title and to act in concert with his Catholic clergy. His own rule came to an end in unclear circumstances in *c*. 474. At about that time Gundobad, son-in-law and successor to the *magister militum* Ricimer, left Italy, and established himself, with his brothers, as ruler of that part of Gaul controlled by the Burgundians.[196] In time, Gundobad was to dispose of his brothers. Even as king, despite the absence of an emperor in the west, Gundobad appears to have kept the title of *magister militum*. On his death, his son Sigismund wrote to the emperor Anastasius, asking to take over his father's office.[197]

Like many of the kings of the period, including his uncle Chilperic, Gundobad had to deal with a charismatic cleric – this time the Italian, Epiphanius of Pavia, who demanded the return of prisoners taken by the Burgundians in a raid on Italy.[198] Also like Chilperic, Gundobad was closely associated with his bishops, notably with Avitus of Vienne, with whom he corresponded regularly. He did so despite the fact that he is the only king of the Burgundians known to have ruled as an Arian. Avitus was also a close confidant of Gundobad's son, Sigismund, who converted to Catholicism before his accession. Interestingly, despite his Catholicism, he fell foul of his bishops, who effectively withdrew their support from him over a case of incest, which he apparently condoned.[199] Not long after, his kingdom was the object of a Frankish invasion, and he was handed over to king Chlodomer, who had him thrown down a well.[200] His body was later transferred to the monastery of St Maurice d'Agaune, where he became the focus of the first royal saint-cult of the Middle Ages.[201]

Although to posterity Sigismund was important as a saint, the most important action of his reign was arguably the compilation of the *Liber Constitutionum* of the Burgundians.[202] This law book, which was issued at the Easter court of 517, includes a number of edicts promulgated by the king's predecessors. Both in the form of its legislation and in its contents, the *Liber Constitutionum* is a very much more Roman document than the *Pactus Legis Salicae* issued by Clovis, probably a decade or more earlier.[203] The laws of the *Liber Constitutionum* were addressed to the leading officials of the kingdom's cities, the *comites* of the *civitates*, both Burgundian and Roman.[204] They were

---

[195] Sid. Ap. *Ep.* 6.12.3.   [196] Greg. Tur. *Hist.* 11.28.   [197] Avitus, *Ep.* 93.
[198] Ennod. *Vita Epiph.* 136–77.   [199] Council of Lyons (519), ed. R. Peiper, *MGH, AA* 6 (2).
[200] Greg. Tur. *Hist.* 111.6.   [201] Paxton (1993).   [202] Wood (1986) 10.
[203] Wood, *Merovingian Kingdoms* 108–13.
[204] *Liber Constitutionum, prima constitutio* ed. L. R. von Salis, *Leges Burgundionum, MGH, Leges* 2 (1) (Hanover 1892).

to be enforced on the whole population of the kingdom, Roman or barbarian, by officials who represented the continuance of fifth-century regional government.

The Burgundian kingdom, like the kingdom of Toulouse, could build directly on the Roman past. What disruption there had been was less severe than the disruption further north, despite a civil war in 500 culminating in the siege of Vienne.[205] Like the kingdom of Toulouse, however, the Burgundian kingdom fell prey to the Franks – momentarily, in 524, when Sigismund was handed over to Chlodomer, and permanently, after 534, when Childebert I and Chlothar I took over the kingdom.[206] Thereafter it was to be one of the major units in the Merovingian kingdom of the Franks.

The Frankish kingdom of the mid sixth century enclosed a sizeable area of land stretching from Germany east of the Rhine to the Pyrenees, and from the Alps to the North Sea. It was a kingdom of infinite variety, and not just because it was divided into a series of separate units centred on Paris, Orleans, Soissons and Rheims. Geographically, it included land which had never been part of the Roman empire, together with regions that had suffered greatly during the migration period, and other regions which had scarcely suffered at all. In Burgundy, in Aquitaine, which had been part of the kingdom of Toulouse, and perhaps above all in Provence, there was considerable continuity from the imperial past. Whatever the variety, the Merovingians came more and more, in the course of the sixth century, to cultivate an image of *romanitas*. Indeed, it is often not possible to say whether we are dealing with Roman continuity or revival.

A use of Roman forms is apparent even at the lowest levels of government. Collections of *formulae*, particularly from Clermont, Angers and Bourges,[207] show that the town archives were still in use for the registration of property. In fact, we know more about the functioning of the town archives of Gaul in the Merovingian period than under the Roman empire. From the will of bishop Bertram, made at the start of the seventh century, we know that the *gesta municipalia* were in operation in the city of Le Mans.[208] Such documentation suggests remarkable continuity, even in the north – though it may not be prudent to extrapolate the evidence for one city and apply it to all. It is, however, clear that Frankish cities were usually managed by *comites*, acting as their predecessors had done in the fifth century, although in a number of places, and increasingly, the power of the *comes* passed to the bishop. The reasons for this transfer of power are by no means clear and were probably varied, depending on the traditions of a see and the relations of an individual bishop with the king. Whether in the

[205] Marius of Avenches, s.a. 500; Greg. Tur. *Hist.* 11.32–3.   [206] Greg. Tur. *Hist.* 111.6, 11.
[207] Ed. K. Zeumer, *MGH, Formulae Merowingici et Karolini Aevi* (Hanover 1886); Wood (1986) 9.
[208] Wood, *Merovingian Kingdoms* 208.

hands of the bishop or the *comes*, however, local administration was largely derived from Roman antecedents.

There are other indications of continuing Roman practice at a higher level of government, not least in tax collection, which continued in attenuated forms, apparently organized by Gallo-Romans. Theudebert, who ruled over the east Frankish kingdom with his capital at Rheims, had as his right-hand man the Roman aristocrat Parthenius. On Theudebert's death, those who had suffered at Parthenius' hands, Franks who thought they should not be subject to taxation, took advantage of the absence of royal protection and lynched him.[209] His case is an interesting one, for it shows a Roman aristocrat involving himself in governmental affairs. Clearly, he was attempting to keep certain types of Roman administration running; but he was also thought to be doing something new in taxing the Franks.[210] This was something more than mere continuity. The same may be true of Chilperic's attempts to collect taxes: not content with old tax registers, he attempted to draw up new registers. In Limoges, at least, the attempt was not appreciated, and the tax-gatherer, Mark, narrowly escaped lynching.[211] Although Chilperic is described as imposing new taxes, Childebert II is said to have revised the tax registers not long afterwards, merely to make them more equitable.[212]

In the course of the sixth century *romanitas* did not merely continue. It was positively cultivated, perhaps even revived, at the Frankish court. On Childeric's death, the Gallo-Roman bishop of Rheims, Remigius, wrote to his son, Clovis, advising him of his duties as governor of Belgica Secunda.[213] Twenty-seven years later, in 508, Clovis was supposedly hailed as *consul aut augustus*.[214] Childeric had belonged to a transitional world: presumably Remigius addressed him much as he was to address his son, but his grave reveals him as being at least as much a pagan warrior as a Roman federate.[215] Clovis, at the end of his reign, appears far more Romanized, as well as Christian. While his father had been in conflict with Genovefa, Clovis is said to have freed prisoners at her request, and ultimately built a church in her honour.[216] Like Feletheus on the Danube, he is said to have sought the advice of holy men, notably of Vedast, later bishop of Arras,[217] but it is clear from the letters of Remigius that Clovis often got his own way with the clergy.[218]

Saints continued to advise and inveigh against Merovingian kings in the sixth century,[219] but the background to their confrontations was by then a well-established state rather than war-torn Paris or the undefended banks

---

[209] Greg. Tur. *Hist.* III.36.   [210] Greg. Tur. *Hist.* III.36.   [211] Greg. Tur. *Hist.* v.28.
[212] Greg. Tur. *Hist.* IX.30.   [213] *Epist. Austras.* 2.   [214] Greg. Tur. *Hist.* II.38.
[215] Wood, *Merovingian Kingdoms* 40.   [216] *Vita Genovefae* 56: Daly (1994) 629–31.
[217] Jonas, *Vita Vedastis* 3, ed. B. Krusch, MGH, SRM 3.   [218] *Epist. Austras.* 3.
[219] Wood, *Merovingian Kingdoms* 73.

of the Danube. Nevertheless, there is nothing to suggest that Clovis'
immediate successors were as concerned with Roman titles as was their
contemporary, Sigismund of the Burgundians. A generation later, however,
things looked very different. Clovis' grandson, Theudebert, deliberately
cultivated an imperial style, not least in the context of his involvement in
the Ostrogothic wars in Italy. To the annoyance of the Byzantines, he
started to issue gold coins with his own portrait.[220] His son, Theudebald,
was concerned to demonstrate the extent of his hegemony to the
Byzantine ruler Justinian.[221] So too were other Merovingian rulers.[222] At the
same time, they started to hold horse races in true imperial style.[223] Clovis'
grandson, Chilperic I, restored circuses in Paris and Soissons for that
specific reason.[224] The *romanitas* of the Merovingians of the second half of
the sixth century is even more apparent in the poetry of Venantius
Fortunatus, not least in his epithalamium for the marriage of Chilperic's
half-brother, Sigibert I, and the Visigothic princess, Brunhild. Under one
of the descendants of Sigibert, a collection of letters was made, providing
evidence of and models for the cultivation of letter-writing at court.[225]

After the catastrophe of the fifth century, the sixth century – in Gaul, at
least – was a time of revival. So much so that it is by no means clear where
there is total continuity and where restoration. In most places continuity is
likely at the most basic of administrative levels. Higher levels of government are more likely to have been subject to a process of re-creation. The
same is likely to be true for Spain as well. Here the evidence is markedly less
good than for Gaul. Our best source is Hydatius, and he is concerned primarily with the north-west, and his chronicle comes to an end in 469.
Thereafter the evidence is distinctly fragmentary. The precise chronology,
and even the geography, of the Visigothic settlement of Spain is a matter
for speculation. Nor does the collapse of the kingdom of Toulouse, and
the subsequent transfer of the Visigothic centre of power to Spain, immediately lead to an increase in our documentation. One or two cities are well-
evidenced – above all, Mérida, which in the pages of the *Vitas Patrum
Emeretensium*, at least, does not seem to have been affected much by the
initial settlement of the Goths.[226] The complex theological changes
espoused by Leovigild in the 570s apparently had more impact on the city,
or rather on its bishops.

Leovigild's religious policies were only one aspect of a highly energetic
reign which also saw the final crushing of the Suevic kingdom of
Gallaecia,[227] which had survived, despite the defeat of Rechiarius, and

[220] Procop. *Wars*. VII.33.5–6.   [221] *Epist. Austras.* 20.   [222] Procop. *Wars*. VIII.20.9.
[223] Procop. *Wars*. VII.33.5.   [224] Greg. Tur. *Hist.* V.17.   [225] Wood (1993) 40.
[226] *Vitas Sanctorum Patrum Emeretensium*, ed. J. N. Garvin (Washington 1946).
[227] Isidore, *Historia Gothorum, Wandalorum, Sueborum* 49, ed. T. Mommsen, *MGH, AA* 11 (Berlin 1894).

which, in the course of the sixth century, under the episcopal leadership of Martin of Braga, had become rather more civilized than Hydatius could have hoped. More significant for Visigothic kingship was Leovigild's development of a royal style, modelled much more closely on imperial style than that of his predecessors. Like Theudebert, half a century before him, Leovigild paid attention to the iconography of his coinage.[228] He also adopted a new *regalia* and took to sitting on a throne.[229] He even founded a city, Reccopolis, named after his son Reccared.[230] More so, apparently, even than the Merovingians of the second half of the sixth century, Leovigild recreated Roman style. His successors were able to go further. In abandoning Arianism they were able to harness to their cause a number of highly talented Hispano-Romans, not least Isidore of Seville.

In the course of the sixth century the Visigothic kings of Spain, like the Merovingian kings of the Franks, came to present themselves in a guise that looked back to the Roman empire. After the disruptions of the fifth, the sixth century turned out to be a period of rebuilding. It could not be a perfect re-creation, for too much had changed in the course of the migration period; nevertheless, the style of these kings and their kingdoms was largely Roman. In the far west, however, Brittany continued its own rather eccentric pattern of development, as did Britain itself across the Channel. Whereas Merovingian Gaul fell back into the social and governmental traditions of the later Roman empire, in Britain and Brittany the more open structures of the mid fifth century continued. In western Britain there emerged a curious fusion of Celtic and Roman, in which the Celtic predominated but without entirely obliterating a sense of *romanitas*.[231] In eastern Britain, the developments of the late fifth and early sixth century are unfortunately almost invisible. Given the varieties of experience on the continent, it would be unwise to assume that a single cultural, political or social model held good for the whole of what would become England. Places where federates were stationed may have experienced little more than a sharp military coup, perhaps disguised, as related by the ninth-century *Historia Brittonum*, by a marriage alliance.[232] Some British enclaves may even have survived for some while in the new Saxon-dominated world.[233] Elsewhere there will have been conquest and, probably further west, assimilation and acculturation. It is, however, only with the establishment of new Germanic kingdoms in the later sixth and seventh centuries, and with their conversion to Christianity, that eastern Britain re-enters the historical stage – as the land of the English. The creation of the English kingdoms effectively brought an end to the 'sub-Roman' period, which continued in the west of the island for longer still. Whatever continuities

---

[228] Hillgarth (1966). [229] Isidore, *Historia Gothorum, Wandalorum, Sueborum* 51.
[230] Isidore, *Historia Gothorum, Wandalorum, Sueborum* 51. [231] Dark (1994); Dumville (1995).
[232] *Historia Brittonum* 24. [233] Bassett (1989) 21–2.

there were between Roman Britain and Saxon England were transmitted through a 'sub-Roman' world rather different from what had come before or what came after.

Even more than that of sixth-century Britain, the history of post-Roman Noricum is a blank. After the departure of the followers of Severinus, with the body of their master, to Italy in 488, there is only the occasional reference in Procopius and Paul the Deacon to barbarians settled in or passing through the region. Unlike Visigothic Spain or Merovingian Gaul, Noricum did not weather the crisis of the fifth century in such a way as to be able to reconstruct something of the Roman world. Yet in many respects its experiences during the migration period were not so different from those of Britain, north-eastern Gaul or Gallaecia. It was the subsequent absence of a power capable of re-creating something of the earlier systems of government and organization that proved crucial to its distinctive development. Whereas the Franks in Gaul and the Visigoths in Spain look like the heirs of the Roman empire, their contemporaries in Britain and Noricum do not. The extent to which a region saw reconstruction in the sixth century was as important in the development of what had been the north-western provinces of the Roman empire as were the dislocations of the fifth.

CHAPTER 19

ITALY, A.D. 425–605

MARK HUMPHRIES

In 425, in the circus at Aquileia, the emperor Valentinian III watched the ritual humiliation and execution of the defeated usurper John. This bloody spectacle celebrated the restoration of Italy to its rightful place as the centre of Roman imperial rule after two years of secessionist government.[1] Less than two centuries later, in 605, the Constantinopolitan emperor Phocas ratified a series of treaties with the Lombards which acknowledged, implicitly if not explicitly, that large areas of Italy had been lost to imperial rule.[2] Between these events occurred the dismemberment of Roman Italy, together with its increasing marginalization in the empire. At the outset of this period, Italy was still the centre of the empire; by its end, however, it had become a frontier province, fought over by Lombard potentates and Byzantine military governors.

This chapter will trace this political fragmentation and show how it was reflected in the transformation of local society throughout Italy. The political disintegration has long been known. Certain stretches of Italian history in the fifth and sixth century are narrated in detail by contemporary historians and chroniclers, although overall the coverage is rather patchy, while the epistolary, exegetical and hagiographical works of Gregory the Great present a haunting vision of Italy after decades of debilitating wars. At an institutional level, the letters of Cassiodorus give valuable insights into the administration of Ostrogothic Italy, while inscriptions, though not so numerous as for earlier periods, add further detail to the picture, announcing the ambitions of rulers or recording the achievements of local aristocrats. Such sources, of course, present their own interpretative problems, as factors like ideology impinge on their credibility.[3] We must look elsewhere for insights into the more mundane realities of life in Italy in the fifth and sixth century. From Ravenna, a remarkable dossier of papyrus documents illuminates the daily concerns of Italian landowners.[4] For the metamorphosis of local society throughout the peninsula, however, much new detail has been provided by the greatly increased scope and sophistication

---

[1] McCormick, *Eternal Victory* 59–60.   [2] Paul. Diac. *Hist. Lang.* iv.35.
[3] See e.g. Rouche (1986) on Gregory's letters; cf. Petersen (1984) on the *Dialogus*.
[4] Tjäder (1954–82).

of Italian archaeology over the last three decades. Both excavation and regional survey have helped qualify the picture presented by the literary sources, although archaeological survey, because it is most useful in detecting processes over the *longue durée*, is less demonstrative in showing short-term change than historians might wish.[5] By reading archaeological, documentary and literary evidence side by side, it is possible to achieve a wide-ranging picture of Italy's fate in late antiquity, fitting political developments – which often seemed cataclysmic to the participants – into a broader context of Italian social evolution. It will emerge that the process is one of gradual metamorphosis, which saw the growing entrenchment of local society, punctuated by moments of sudden rupture, such as the Justinianic wars or the Lombard invasions.

It cannot be doubted that the fifth and sixth century witnessed a substantial transformation of Italian society. Under Valentinian III, Italy was still united by social, economic and communications networks much as it had been since the days of the late republic. During the middle empire, to be sure, this unity had come under pressure, but it was only in our period that Italy split asunder.[6] Italy's political unity had outlived the ostensible end of Roman rule and survived intact under Ostrogothic government. In this sense, the initial serenity of Italy's post-imperial experience stands in marked contrast to the instability which engulfed the rest of western Europe in the fifth century.[7] Only in the decades after Justinian's decision to bring Italy back into the empire was the peninsula torn apart by war and invasion. The social, economic and cultural horizons of local communities contracted, and although the old Roman roads, which had helped unite the peninsula, were still used, much of their traffic now consisted of Lombard and Byzantine armies competing for Italian territory.

I. ITALIAN INTERESTS AND THE END OF THE WESTERN EMPIRE
(425–76)

Valentinian III's restoration seemed to guarantee the re-establishment of the old political order in Italy. But the system was in reality falling apart, with the relationship between Italy and the rest of western Europe becoming strained. This facet of imperial collapse was reflected in the tension between Italian interests and non-Italian, especially Gallic, incumbents of the throne. Just as Italy was becoming politically isolated from the rest of the west, so too it had to rely increasingly on its own economic and military resources. The Vandal conquest of Africa was a crucial catalyst. First, while trade between Africa and Italy certainly continued, Rome could no longer depend on the region as the major source of its corn dole. Hence, the city was forced to rely more on Italian resources, transforming the eco-

---

[5] Barker (1991) 53–4.   [6] Dyson (1990) 215–44.   [7] Cf. ch. 18 (Wood), pp. 499–517 above.

nomic relationship between the city and the rest of the peninsula and Sicily.[8] Secondly, Geiseric's success in organizing a fleet opened Italy to barbarian attack from the south as well as along its traditional frontier in the north. Vulnerability from north and south was frighteningly realized with the invasion of Italy by Attila and the Huns in 452, soon followed by the Vandal sack of Rome in 455.

It is no accident that these events precipitated a series of political crises in Italy, with emperors and leading generals being chosen and disposed of according to how their actions pleased Italian opinion, an issue complicated by the complex and sometimes divergent interests of groups within the ruling élite. Under Valentinian, the new Vandal threat to Italy prompted the fortification of Naples and Terracina on the Tyrrhenian coastline.[9] In 454, the *magister militum* Aetius was executed, probably a victim of Valentinian's need to placate Italian interests. During the Hunnic crisis, Aetius had failed to defend Italy from Attila, in stark contrast to the energy he displayed in protecting Gaul; furthermore, he had even suggested that the emperor should abandon Italy. The next year, Valentinian was himself murdered by two of Aetius' former associates. His replacement, Petronius Maximus, did not last long, and by the time of Geiseric's attack on Rome, Italian fortunes were once more in non-Italian hands. With the throne now occupied by a Gallic aristocrat, Avitus, who failed to defend Rome and Italy against the Vandal onslaught, the situation was ripe for a violent confrontation between the two interest groups. At Placentia (Piacenza) in 456, Avitus was defeated and deposed by the generals Majorian, who subsequently became emperor, and Ricimer.[10] As emperor, Majorian strove to unite the disparate interests of Gaul, the Visigoths and Italy against the Vandal threat. Whatever the initial successes of his enterprise, it ended in the capture of his fleet by Geiseric, followed by his deposition and execution at Ricimer's hands at Dertona (Tortona) in 461.[11]

Ricimer's new choice of emperor, the Lucanian aristocrat Libius Severus, reveals the extent to which he depended on Italian support to maintain his supremacy. To be sure, Majorian had also courted the favour of Italy, but Ricimer – who first came to prominence as a commander defending Italy against the Vandals – made it the foundation of his regime and the focus of his policies. For much of the 460s, he devoted his energies to neutralizing the Vandal threat by diplomacy and military action.[12]

When Severus died in 465, Ricimer made no move to replace him, and for almost two years he dominated Italian affairs without any rival. In the

---

[8] Trade between Africa and Italy after 439 is a vexed problem: Wickham (1988) 190–3 on continuity (cf. ch. 20 (Cameron), pp. 556–7 below). For other areas: Wilson (1990) 330–1; Arthur (1989) 133–4; Barnish (1987); Small and Buck (1993) 28–9.   [9] Christie and Rushworth (1988) 81–7.
[10] Harries (1994) 76–80.
[11] For very different appraisals of Majorian, cf. Harries (1994) ch. 4 and O'Flynn (1983) 104–11.
[12] O'Flynn (1983) 104–28.

end it was the eastern emperor, Leo I, who precipitated change, despatching a naval expedition against the Vandals and sending the eastern general and patrician Anthemius to Italy as its new Augustus. Anthemius seemingly attracted considerable support in Rome itself: the city held out for five months on his behalf when it was besieged by Ricimer's forces in 472.[13] But the hostility between him and Ricimer was never more than thinly disguised, and it seems – if Ennodius' reference to Ricimer as *princeps* can be taken seriously – that by the end Ricimer ruled what was in essence an independent northern Italy.[14] Again it seems that Ricimer relied on an Italian power base. When his hostility to Anthemius became open with the condemnation and accusation of his associate Romanus, Ricimer seems to have pursued his own independent Vandal policy, a move which surely would have cultivated favour in Italy.[15]

Ultimately Anthemius was ousted, and his replacement provides a final indication of Ricimer's dependence on Italian loyalties. The new emperor, Olybrius, was a pleasing candidate to the Italians. He came from the Anicii, a prominent senatorial clan, and was therefore a more attractive personality to the Italians than the Greek Anthemius. Moreover, Olybrius had strong family connections with Geiseric, so his elevation promised the cessation of Vandal hostilities.[16] Such hopes were short-lived: Ricimer died soon after making his new appointment, and Olybrius followed him to the grave after a reign of only seven months.[17] But the later stages of Ricimer's ascendancy did more than fail to resolve the Vandal problem: they also highlighted the increasing strain between Italian interests and those of the eastern emperors. Neither Olybrius' appointment, nor that of his successor Glycerius, was accepted by Constantinople.

Similarly, eastern candidates proved to be unacceptable emperors in Italy. The last to be sent, Nepos was expelled by his *magister militum* Orestes, who set up his own son, Romulus, on the throne. But Orestes failed to appreciate the power of the army in Italy, and when he rejected its demand for land, the soldiery looked to another of its commanders, Odoacer, as champion. Orestes was slain at Ticinum (Pavia), while Romulus was deposed and sent into retirement in Campania. Odoacer was proclaimed king by the troops, and the decision was accepted by the senate, which sent a delegation to persuade the eastern emperor Zeno to ratify the arrangement. Unsurprisingly, Zeno refused, but with Odoacar's elevation as king, Italy had taken a fateful step: it was now effectively independent of Constantinople, and all peaceful efforts to restore it to the empire would end in failure.[18]

[13] Joh. Ant. fr. 209.1.   [14] Ennod. *Vita Epiph.* 53; cf. O'Flynn (1983) 119–21.
[15] Joh. Ant. fr. 207.   [16] Clover (1978).   [17] Marc. Com. *Chron.* s.a. 472.2.
[18] Procop. *Wars* v.1.2–8; Malchus fr. 14 Blockley.

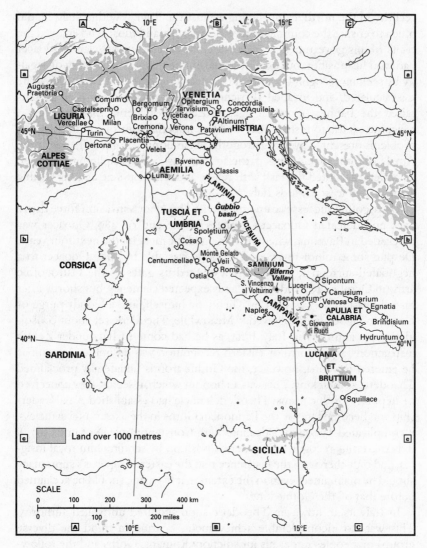

Map 10 Late Roman and Ostrogothic Italy 425–535

II. ODOACER AND THEODERIC (476–526)

Odoacer was to enjoy his new kingdom for thirteen years before Zeno could interfere again in Italian affairs. His policies, like those of Ricimer before him, were geared to consolidating the defence of Italy. He achieved an early diplomatic success with the Vandals, securing the return of Sicily – apart from the area of Lilybaeum – from Geiseric. He also sought greater security in the north, campaigning against the Rugi.[19] Within Italy, he did much to ensure the continuation of normal life, and those who enjoyed the fruits of his government were aristocratic and senatorial clans. Odoacer had won his position by force of arms, but he maintained a show of legality by seeking recognition from the eastern emperor.[20] Then, in 486/7, he miscalculated, and invaded Illyricum at precisely the same time as Illus raised the banner of revolt against Zeno. For Zeno, this provided a welcome excuse to restore Italy to direct imperial control and to solve the problems presented by the Ostrogoths in Pannonia. He gave Theoderic the Amal, *magister militum* and patrician, the task of disciplining Odoacer. Theoderic accepted the task with relish, and late in 488 he and his Gothic army turned west towards Italy.[21]

Ostrogothic successes came swiftly, as Theoderic's invasion force drove back and defeated Odoacer's armies. By the end of 489, Odoacer was blockaded in Ravenna, where he remained for most of the next four years. Despite some minor reverses, Theoderic was able to bring Odoacer to a negotiated surrender, and Ravenna opened its gates to the Ostrogothic army in October 493. Odoacer plainly expected clemency, but shortly after his submission he was slain by Theoderic himself, and a bloody purge of his surviving relatives followed.[22] Meanwhile, Theoderic set about consolidating his authority in Italy. First, as he had come to Italy under Zeno's instructions, some form of eastern recognition was desirable. As soon as he entered Ravenna, however, the Gothic troops unilaterally proclaimed Theoderic as their king. This was an honour which, it seems, they conceived of in purely Gothic terms: Theoderic's uncle had established Amal leadership and become king of the Pannonian Goths in the 450s.[23] Nevertheless, it complicated Theoderic's dealings with Constantinople. Not until 497/8 did Anastasius recognize Theoderic's position by sending him royal insignia, and only then with the insistence that the eastern emperor's supremacy should be maintained, even to the extent that his name should be acclaimed before that of the Gothic king.[24]

In Italy itself, however, Theoderic soon acquired unrivalled authority. This was no inconsiderable achievement, bearing in mind the diverse groups of peoples under his jurisdiction: Romans, Goths and the followers of Odoacer. He also managed, as an Arian himself, to secure the allegiance of a largely Catholic Italy, while also defending minority groups such as the Jews.[25] From the time he had forged the various Pannonian Goths and assorted Danubian tribes into the people customarily designated as the Ostrogoths, Theoderic had shown a genius for uniting seem-

---

[19] *Anon. Val.* 10.48.   [20] Chastagnol (1966); Barnwell (1992) 134–5, 155–6.
[21] Heather, *Goths and Romans* 295–308.   [22] *Anon. Val.* 11.55–6; John. Ant. fr. 214a.
[23] *Anon. Val.* 12.57–8; Jord. *Get.* 52.268–71; cf. Heather, *Goths and Romans* 240–2, 311–12.
[24] Wolfram (1988) 284–8.   [25] Moorhead (1992) 97–100.

ingly disparate groups.[26] In Italy, he displayed this flair to its greatest extent, creating what, for at least one chronicler, could be seen as a golden age of peace and prosperity.[27]

First, the Goths. Much modern study of Theoderic's authority over his Gothic followers has been misled by the elaborate Amal genealogy worked out by Cassiodorus and reflected in Jordanes' *Getica*. While the construction of such a lineage gave Theoderic's rule a firm ideological underpinning, the maintenance of his leadership mainly depended, as it always had done, on his accomplishments as a warrior. In this respect, Theoderic had shown his skill by the series of campaigns culminating in the conquest of Italy. Thereafter, successful campaigns in Dalmatia, the Rhaetian Alps and southern Gaul, which led to the enlargement of the Ostrogothic kingdom, helped preserve the image of Theoderic as a successful military leader.[28]

As well as seeing Theoderic as a triumphant warrior, the Goths looked to their king for other benefits. The army which had invaded Italy was perhaps as large as 25,000; together with its dependants, this means a very large Gothic population demanding sustenance. While some have argued that Theoderic sought to maintain this contingent purely through the mechanism of tax allocations, it is hard to image such a large Gothic population entering Italy without receiving land to settle.[29] There would certainly have been garrisons in major cities such as Rome and in frontier zones such as the Julian Alps. Gothic settlement was more extensive than this: archaeological, literary and toponomastic evidence points to the presence of Goths scattered throughout Italy, with notable concentrations around Ravenna, in the upper Po valley and above all in Picenum.[30] As well as being their source of land, Theoderic was the fount of justice and patronage. That legal redress and political and social advancement depended on Theoderic helped to cement his authority throughout his long reign.[31]

The majority of Theoderic's subjects were the Roman inhabitants of Italy, and his ultimate success in consolidating his kingdom would depend on his ability to integrate them. Like Odoacer, he relied heavily on local élites as the backbone of his administration. When his kingdom expanded into southern Gaul and Dalmatia, he exploited the existing links that the north Italian aristocracy had with those regions.[32] He was conscious, too, of his image as ruler. He could be clement: coming as an Arian Goth to a largely Catholic Italy, he never gained a reputation as a persecutor, in marked contrast to his Vandal co-religionists in Africa.[33] Moreover, he

---

[26] Heather, *Goths and Romans* 320–3.   [27] *Anon. Val.* 12.59–62; cf. Jahn (1989).
[28] Heather (1995) 145–52; Heather (1996) 230–5.
[29] Barnish (1986) *contra* Goffart, *Barbarians and Romans* 58–102.
[30] Esp. Bierbrauer (1975); cf. Battisti (1956).   [31] Heather (1995) 158–65.
[32] Barnwell (1992) 155–65; Barnish (1988) 134–5.   [33] Moorhead (1992) 89–97.

could wear an appealingly Roman mask. While, like Odoacer, he most usually called himself *rex*, he seems not to have objected when, on an inscription recording the restoration of the Via Appia at Terracina, a hyperbolic official called him 'king Theoderic, forever Augustus' (*rex Theodericus semper Augustus*). In a similar vein, the Romans supposedly thought of Theoderic as a new Trajan or Valentinian. Theoderic fostered such images by basing life at his court on models drawn from imperial ceremonial.[34]

It would be misleading, however, to claim that Theoderic's attempts at integrating the disparate elements under his rule resulted in unqualified success. Among the peoples that accompanied him from the Balkans, for example, the Rugi refused to intermarry with the king's Gothic subjects, preserving an independence which lasted until the dying days of the kingdom. Even among his Gothic subjects, Theoderic's authority could amount to little more than ratifying decisions they made independently of him.[35] The greatest area of tension was the king's relationship with the Roman population. Despite the images of harmony preserved by Cassiodorus, Ennodius and the *Anonymus Valesianus*, it is clear that there had been the potential for confrontation from very early in Theoderic's Italian career. At the time of his arrival, he had threatened to confiscate senatorial properties if the owners did not abandon allegiance to Odoacer. Moreover, Theoderic's own expressions of *romanitas* had been tempered by the uneasiness of his relationship with Constantinople.[36] In the end, the result proved catastrophic for members of the Roman élite whose cultural activities had led them into close contact with Constantinople. In the last two years of his reign, when various aspects of his government seemed to have fallen into disarray, Theoderic turned on sections of the Roman aristocracy, suspecting them of treasonable contact with Constantinople.[37]

Despite these problems, the kingdom left by Theoderic at his death in 526 was a remarkable achievement. Whereas barbarian take-over in Spain, Gaul and Britain had resulted in considerable social dislocation, Italy had slipped almost imperceptibly from empire to kingdom. Even so, the situation at his death was ominous. The man who had rewarded Cassiodorus' elaborate reconstruction of the Amal genealogy had failed signally to produce an heir of his own. Ultimately his choice devolved on his grandson, Athalaric.[38] But when Theoderic died, the new king was still a child. This provoked a power struggle among the Gothic élite which led to the eclipse of the Amal line, starkly revealing how fragile was the unity to which Theoderic had devoted so much of his energy.

---

[34] *CIL* 10.6850–1; cf. *Anon. Val.* 12.60; Heather (1996) 221–35.
[35] Procop. *Wars* VII.2; Cass. *Var.* VIII.26.   [36] Heather (1996) 227–30.
[37] Moorhead (1992) 212–45.   [38] Heather (1995) 165–72.

III. THE END OF THE OSTROGOTHIC KINGDOM (526–68)

Foremost among those contending for influence was Theoderic's daughter and Athalaric's mother, Amalasuintha. Although her position was precarious, she showed herself to be a shrewd manipulator, and for eight years the machinery of government acted smoothly under her guidance in Athalaric's name. She pursued further the pro-Roman policies of Theoderic's earlier years, ensuring that Athalaric received a full Roman education and seeking to make reparations for the deterioration in Gotho–Roman relations in the mid 520s. Yet behind this serene façade there lurked a deep unease. At the time of a conspiracy hatched against her by members of the Gothic élite, she loaded a ship with supplies and treasures in readiness for sudden flight to the east.[39] Her relationship with the new Byzantine emperor Justinian went further. During Belisarius' campaigns against the Vandals in 533–4, Byzantine forces were able to use Ostrogothic Sicily as an important staging-point on the way to Africa.[40] Already during these campaigns, however, there were indications of the traumatic period that was about to engulf Italy. Gothic forces took advantage of Vandal disarray to seize Lilybaeum, which had been held by the Vandals since 476 and possession of which had been confirmed by Theoderic as part of his diplomatic initiatives in 500. Belisarius protested at the illegality of the move, threatening hostilities if the Goths did not give up their new conquest.[41]

The tenuousness of Amalasuintha's domination was exposed by Athalaric's death in October 534. She elevated her cousin Theodahad in an effort to maintain control, but within two months, she had been incarcerated; by the next spring, she had been murdered. Theodahad's reign proved disastrous. Frankish power increased north of the Alps as Ostrogothic influence there faded. More seriously, a breach with Constantinople seemed likely. In the course of 535, Sicily succumbed to Byzantine forces, allowing Belisarius to enter Syracuse in triumph on 31 December; meanwhile, Justinian's armies eroded Ostrogothic possessions in Dalmatia. But if it seemed that such reverses might provoke Theodahad to negotiate surrender, a major Gothic victory at Salona in 536 gave the king the bravado to repudiate Justinian's diplomatic overtures. The result was a more vigorous Byzantine counter-offensive. Dalmatia was swiftly cleared of its Ostrogothic garrisons, while a large army under Belisarius crossed the straits of Messina from Sicily. The war for the conquest of Italy had begun.

Theodahad's reaction was to wait in Ravenna. By the time he chose to take the field, in response to Belisarius' capture of Naples, the Gothic élite

---

[39] Procop. *Wars* v.2.22–9.   [40] Procop. *Wars* III.14.5–6.
[41] Procop. *Wars* IV.5.11–25; cf. Wilson (1990) 336–7.

was thoroughly disillusioned with him. Encamped near Terracina, they reverted to the old principle of choosing a leader of established military skill as their king: their choice fell on Vitigis, a proven warrior. Theodahad fled for Ravenna, but Vitigis' agents overtook and murdered him. For the next four years, Vitigis sought to check Belisarius' advance through central Italy. By 540, however, he found himself blockaded in Ravenna, with little option but to surrender to the Byzantine army.

With the capture of Ravenna, it might well have seemed that the war was over. Just as well: in the east, a revival of Persian fortunes was posing severe problems for Justinian.[42] Any confidence about the Italian situation proved ill-founded. Shortly after Vitigis' surrender, two Gothic leaders in northern Italy, Uraias and Ildibad, raised a revolt. While this posed a new threat to Byzantine ambitions, it also demonstrated the inherent disunity of the Gothic forces by this stage of the war: Ildibad had Uraias assassinated, but not long afterwards was himself murdered by the Rugian leader Eraric. In turn, Ildibad's nephew, Totila, engineered Eraric's death, and afterwards found himself proclaimed king.

In Totila, the Goths found a leader who was able to stand up to Byzantine aggression. The war for Italy entered a new phase. For much of the 540s, Totila was successful in dismembering Belisarius' conquests, although it seems that he never lost sight of obtaining a negotiated settlement to the war.[43] But in 551 the Persian war ended with a peace treaty, and Justinian was able to devote most of his attention to Italy. The new Byzantine commander there, the Armenian eunuch Narses, proved a match for the daring Totila, and his army was far larger than any that the Goths could put into the field. In mid 552, Totila's army was defeated in the Apennines, the king himself dying of a wound sustained in battle. Once again, however, the Goths proved tenacious in their resistance: the full submission of Italy was not achieved until Narses took Verona and Brescia in 562.

Justinian celebrated the conquest of Italy with grandiose propaganda. An inscription on the Ponte Salario just outside Rome proclaimed 'the restoration of the liberty of the city of Rome and the whole of Italy', while an anonymous chronicler asserted that, through Narses' victories, Italy had been restored to its 'former happiness'.[44] The memory of the Ostrogothic kingdom was obliterated. Depictions of the king and his courtiers were removed from the mosaics in Theoderic's great church of S. Apollinaire Nuovo at Ravenna. Some even went so far as to claim that the Goths were expelled from Italy, though this is plainly untrue.[45] But the euphoria which engendered such claims and actions was misplaced. Italy had not emerged

---

[42] Moorhead (1994) 86–98.   [43] Heather (1996) 267–9.
[44] *CIL* 6.1199; *Auctarii Havniensis Extrema* 3 (ed. Th. Mommsen, *MGH, AA* 9.337).
[45] Procop. *Wars* VIII.35.36–7; but cf. Agathias 1.1.1. Cf. p. 548 below, n. 118.

from Justinian's wars in a condition of restored happiness: there had been considerable destruction in major cities such as Naples and Rome, and members of local aristocracies had been compelled to flee their homes. In the countryside slaves had abandoned rural estates to join one or other of the opposing armies, and many places – even the rich Po valley – had been afflicted by famine.[46] Surveying the devastation, pope Pelagius I lamented the ransacking of papal estates.[47]

IV. FORGING THE LOMBARD KINGDOM (568–605)

Justinian's dream of restoring the western empire had brought Italy little more than misery. How bitter, then, that the achievement should prove so ephemeral. In 568 the Julian Alps were breached once more, as a Lombard army led by Alboin – whether at the invitation of the Byzantines or out of fear of increasing Avar power in Pannonia – descended on Venetia and the Po valley.[48] The reaction in Italy to this incursion typified the exhausted condition of the peninsula after thirty years of war. Byzantine resistance was the strongest, as imperial armies fought to retain the territory reconquered less than a decade before. Soon it became clear, however, that Byzantine resources were insufficient to halt the Lombard advance. Alliances were forged with other barbarians, as when Tiberius II induced the Franks to invade Italy in 577.[49] Ticinum (Pavia) put up a dogged resistance until 572, but elsewhere Italian communities capitulated without any notable struggle. The only alternative to surrender was flight. As Alboin's army entered his city, archbishop Honoratus of Milan fled across the Apennines to Byzantine Genoa. Venetia, in particular, experienced considerable displacement of its population. While many undoubtedly continued to occupy old settlements such as Altinum (Altino) and Opitergium (Oderzo), others, often under the leadership of their bishops, sought safety in the islands of the lagoons, leading to the foundation of new centres, such as Torcello and Heraclia. Even Aquileia, once the greatest city of the region, shared this fate, as archbishop Paulinus moved the apparatus of his see to Grado.[50]

The Lombard advance was rapid, and by the end of 569 most of the Po valley had fallen under their control. Only the Byzantine territories around Genoa, Ravenna and along the coast of Venetia, as well as some isolated inland areas, offered any significant resistance.[51] As compared with the

---

[46] Cities: Procop. *Wars* v.10.28–9 (Naples), VIII.33.14 (Rome). Runaway slaves: *P. Ital.* 13. Famine: Procop. *Wars* VI.20.18–21.   [47] Pelagius I, *Ep.* 49 (in *MGH Epistolae* 3.73).
[48] Christie (1995) 60–3, in favour of a Byzantine initiative; cf., however, ch. 5 (Collins), p. 130 above.
[49] Men. Prot. 25, 29; cf. Paul. Diac. *Hist. Lang.* III.13.
[50] Leciejewicz, Tabaczynska and Tabaczynski (1977), esp. 1–7, 287–94; Rando (1994) 13–34.
[51] Wickham (1981) 31; Christie (1990).

Ostrogothic achievement a century earlier, however, the Lombard conquests lacked coherence. Theoderic, while he relied in large measure on the acquiescence of his Ostrogothic followers, had been a strong ruler capable of welding the disparate elements in his kingdom into a united whole. Alboin, it seems, never enjoyed such unchallenged leadership. Just as the Lombard conquests divided Italy into Byzantine and non-Byzantine regions, so the lack of Lombard unity contributed to the territorial dismemberment of the peninsula.

The inherent disunity of the Lombards was apparent already, according to Paul the Deacon, in the army that Alboin led into Italy.[52] In order to consolidate his conquests, therefore, Alboin set up his nephew Gisulf as duke (*dux*) of Friuli at Cividale in 569. Gisulf was charged with the defence of the Julian Alps, in which task he was to use various leading Lombard kinship groups (*farae*), presumably in an effort to forge some sort of unity out of the diverse Lombard group by establishing ties of dependence with Alboin's family.[53] Any such unity, however, was an illusion, and in 572, internal Lombard dissension – encouraged, it seems, by the Byzantines – led to Alboin's assassination at Verona. His successor, Cleph, lasted only two years, after which there was an interregnum of ten years, during which Lombard power in northern Italy was split between dukes in the major cities.[54]

The emergence of Lombard duchies in central and southern Italy may also point to disunity among Alboin's followers. By 570 a certain Zotto had established himself as duke of Benevento: little is known about him, and it is not clear whether his Lombard war-band campaigned in the south with or without Alboin's blessing.[55] Another Lombard duchy developed at Spoleto during the interregnum. It first appears in our sources when the duke, Faroald, led his army against Ravenna's harbour suburb, Classe, prompting the suspicion that Faroald originally may have commanded Lombard federates serving with the Byzantines.[56] Certainly, Gregory I mentions several Lombards serving in the Byzantine army, highlighting their lack of ethnic solidarity.[57]

United or not, the Lombards proved a fatal blow to Byzantine dreams of a united Italy under imperial rule. Time after time, Byzantine armies failed to contain the Lombard advance, and by the end of the century, the territorial encroachment of Lombard power was seriously threatening the integrity of those remaining Byzantine possessions in Italy. The new duchy at Spoleto controlled the ancient Via Flaminia, the easiest crossing-point of

---

[52] Paul. Diac. *Hist. Lang.* II.26: 'In fact it is certain that Alboin led with him to Italy a multitude made up of different peoples led either by their own or other kings.'   [53] Paul. Diac. *Hist. Lang.* II.9.

[54] Paul. Diac. *Hist. Lang.* II.27–32. Cf. Gasparri (1978) 12–17, 48 (for a duke Alboin at Milan during the interregnum).   [55] Gasparri (1978) 86.   [56] Paul. Diac. *Hist. Lang.* III.13; cf. Gasparri (1978) 73.

[57] Brown, *Gentlemen and Officers* 70–5.

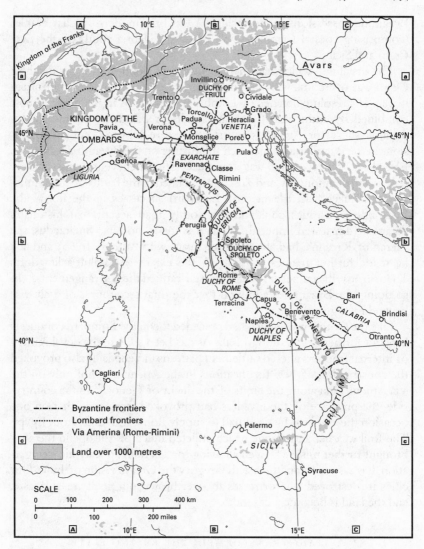

Map 11 Lombard and Byzantine Italy *c.* A.D. 600

the Apennines, jeopardizing communications between Rome and the Byzantine enclaves in the Pentapolis and the exarchate of Ravenna. In response, the Byzantines consolidated a more northerly route through Perugia, the Via Amerina, fortifying the mountain passes along its length.[58] South of Rome, the rising Lombard power at Benevento confined

[58] Cf. Schmiedt (1974) 591–604.

Byzantine possessions to the duchies of Calabria (modern Apulia), Naples (comprising coastal Campania and modern Calabria south of the river Crati) and Sicily.[59]

The instability which had marked Lombard politics after the death of Cleph was overcome with the reinstatement of the monarchy by Authari in 584. His resolute defence of Lombard possessions in the north against combined Byzantine and Frankish assaults prepared the ground for his dynamic successor, Agilulf (590–616), to restore unity to Lombard possessions in the Po valley and encroach still further on the Byzantine territories. Elsewhere, however, he was less successful. Benevento and Spoleto retained their autonomy, and Tuscany remained in the hands of quasi-independent dukes.[60] In the face of Lombard successes in the north, the Byzantine authorities could do little other than accept that Justinian's dream of a restored imperial Italy had come to nothing. Smaragdus, the exarch of Ravenna, had already made peace with Authari. In 603 and 604 he made further treaties recognizing the extent of Agilulf's kingdom. Then, in 605, the emperor Phocas himself ratified these arrangements.[61] In so doing, the Byzantines admitted that the total reconquest of Italy was beyond their grasp.

Like the Gothic wars which had preceded them, the Lombard conquests brought further devastation to Italy. As has been shown, the development of internal frontiers altered settlement patterns in Venetia. It also provoked the construction of new fortifications in the Apennines, not only on the Via Amerina but along the limits of the duchy of Genoa.[62] In the countryside, the presence of the invaders had provoked famine, so that on one occasion the emperor Justin II had to supply Rome with corn from Egypt. The foul weather and plague which afflicted much of Europe in the 580s brought further misery.[63] Even allowing for a certain apocalyptic exaggeration, it is easy to sympathize with Gregory the Great's vision of Italy: 'Our cities are destroyed; our fortresses are overthrown; our fields are laid waste; and the land is become a desert.'[64]

V. ITALY TRANSFORMED: THE RULING ÉLITE

The fifth and sixth centuries saw the utter transformation of Italian political fortunes. At the outset, Italy had been the centre of an empire, albeit a crumbling one. With its metamorphosis into a conglomeration of Byzantine marches and Lombard principalities came a radical realignment of its ruling élite. Under Valentinian III, Odoacer and Theoderic, the

---

[59] Diehl (1888) 6–78.   [60] Wickham (1981) 32–4.   [61] Paul. Diac. *Hist. Lang.* III.18; IV.28, 32, 35.
[62] Christie (1990).
[63] Egyptian corn: *Lib. Pont.* 1.308. Natural disasters: Coronatus, *Vita Zenonis* 9; Greg. Mag. *Dial.* 3.19.2; Paul. Diac. *Hist. Lang.* III.23.   [64] Greg. Mag. *Hom. in Ezech.* 2.6.22.

senate was still fêted by the court.[65] It was not, however, quite so powerful as it had been in the fourth century. The shrinkage of the empire meant that there were fewer offices open to senators. Moreover, officials were increasingly selected from outside its ranks, among local Italian élites or educated professionals. As a result, the senate's influence outside Rome contracted, forcing its members to look increasingly inward. Some turned to cultural pursuits, preserving the literary heritage of Rome. Others turned to the church, but not to the same extent as their fellow aristocrats in Gaul. In Rome, the alliance suffered periodic breakdowns; one such, the Laurentian schism (499–507), led to lasting recrimination. The Gothic wars, with their several sieges of Rome, had a devastating effect on the city and its institutions, and the increasing Lombard threat reduced the importance of civilian administrators. By the late sixth century, the senate itself had ceased to function as an institution, and in the early seventh, the curia was converted into a church. Members of the senatorial order lived on, but they did so now on their rural estates, particularly in southern Italy and Sicily. For some, the trauma of post-imperial experience was too much, and they left Italy for the surviving empire at Constantinople.[66]

The retrenchment of some members of the senatorial aristocracy points to one of the major transformations of the ruling élite in this period. Local aristocrats became increasingly important, not just in their own regions but as agents of the ruling power. Some, such as the Cassiodori of Squillace or the Opiliones of Patavium (Padua), sought to infiltrate the senatorial aristocracy, either by marriage or by holding office at Rome. They also maintained a strong interest in the affairs of their home provinces, where they were particularly prominent as patrons of the church. Ultimately, most saw their destinies on their estates rather than at Rome: when Cassiodorus retired to his monastic foundation at Squillace, he was acting in a fashion typical of his class. Others, however, never even saw Rome as a political goal, and, like Parecorius Apollinaris, governor of Venetia and Histria and sponsor of the *basilica apostolorum* at Aquileia, they limited their ambitions to their native regions.[67]

By the early seventh century, however, power was moving away from such traditional élites to a new military aristocracy. To an extent, this had been prefigured by the dominance of important military figures in the last days of the western empire, such as Ricimer, Orestes, Odoacer and Theoderic. But, by *c.* 600, even the most mundane business of administration was being invested in military officials, who acted as judges in a variety of civilian and ecclesiastical matters. This ascendancy in military and civil affairs was enhanced as leading members of the army came to possess considerable

---

[65] Chastagnol (1966).
[66] Barnish (1988) 120–30; Brown, *Gentlemen and Officers* 21–38; Matthews (1967) 502–5.
[67] Barnish (1988) 130–66; Pietri (1982); Schäfer (1991).

tracts of land. As this circumstance grew more entrenched, and as patterns of settlement in Byzantine territories increasingly focused on fortified *castra*, the distinction between the new military aristocracy and local élites became blurred. The system was reflected in the upper echelons of government too, with the duties of governor entrusted to the exarch, an office which, if its remit was unclear at first, was unequivocally military by *c.* 600.[68] A similar development occurred under the Lombards, particularly in the frontier duchies like Friuli: well into the seventh century, weapons are a major feature of Lombard burials in such areas.[69] Although they had started out from very different positions, Lombard and Byzantine societies in Italy had come to look essentially similar by the seventh century, with both dominated by a militarized landed aristocracy.

VI. THE CHURCH AND THE PAPACY

Just as the traditional aristocracy of Italy was transformed in this period, so too was the position of the church, especially at Rome. Some elements in the transition were evident already by the 420s. During the Gothic invasions of Italy in the early fifth century, bishops such as Chromatius of Aquileia and Maximus of Turin had shown considerable skill as civic leaders, rallying their congregations at times of crisis.[70] The uncertain times of the later fifth and sixth century accelerated this process, and in many places by the time of the Lombard invasions the bishop had become the most prominent citizen. Hence, it was bishop Felix of Tarvisium (Treviso) who negotiated his city's surrender to Alboin in 568, while Gregory the Great exhorted the bishops of Terracina, Misenum and Cagliari to maintain their towns' defences.[71] There can be no more graphic demonstration of the rising social prominence of the church than the topographical changes which occurred in many Italian cities, whereby the civic centre came to be focused on the main church building. Aquileia provides a stark example of the phenomenon: in 452 the city was sacked by Attila, and when it rose again it was enclosed by a smaller circuit of walls which left the old Roman civic centre, the forum, outside, but which contained the cathedral church at its heart.[72] Beyond the confines of individual centres, the church inherited the old Roman administrative and social networks which underlay the development of episcopal dioceses.[73] In response to its increased prominence in society, the church developed an elaborate bureaucracy. Although this evolution is best attested at Rome, the existence of local networks is demonstrated by the dedications of *defensores ecclesiae* in a sixth-century basilica excavated at Trieste.[74] For all his dreams of a restored

---

[68] Brown, *Gentlemen and Officers* 46–60, 101–25.   [69] Christie (1995) 126–39.
[70] Lizzi (1989) chs. 4 and 5.   [71] Paul. Diac. *Hist. Lang.* ii.12; Greg. Mag. *Epp.* 8.19; 9.21, 195.
[72] Jäggi (1990).   [73] Otranto (1990) 16–21, 79–93; Rando (1994) 21–34.   [74] Zovatto (1966).

empire, Justinian had little choice but to accept the new role of the church. In the Pragmatic Sanction of 554, which outlined the provisions for the government of Italy, much of the minutiae of administration was devolved upon its bishops.[75]

The change was most spectacular at Rome. Since the episcopate of Damasus I (366–84), the Roman church had sought to extend its influence over much of Italy and beyond. In the mid fifth century, the process was given a boost by the activities of Leo the Great, whose term as pontiff (440–61) included the Hunnic invasions and the Vandal sack. Both provided him with an opportunity to behave as a statesman, acting as protector of his community. As Attila advanced on Rome, Leo met him and secured the deliverance of the Eternal City, and after Geiseric's Vandals had ransacked it, he did much to restore confidence. At the same time, Leo's pontificate saw a more elaborate formulation of Petrine supremacy, granting his relationships with bishops in Italy – and beyond – a firmer ideological basis. None was more unremitting in his defence of this supremacy than Gelasius I (492–6), even to the extent of berating the emperor on issues of authority and power; he was no less doctrinaire in his dealings with the Italian episcopate.[76]

As defender of Rome against its enemies and guarantor of its ideological supremacy, the papacy was coming to fill the role once performed by the emperors. Another expression of this was the way in which the Roman church came to administer corn distributions in the city, and, as a necessary buttress to this activity, administer sizeable estates throughout Italy. Excavations at Monte Gelato revealed a site dating to the fourth, fifth and sixth centuries which comprised a church and associated agricultural buildings.[77] The widespread existence of papal estates is confirmed by references to donations, by the emperor and aristocratic notables, in the *Liber Pontificalis*, and by constant reference to them in papal correspondence. This points to another area of administration where the papacy was replacing the secular government: whereas previously the corn dole had been organized by imperial and then Ostrogothic officials, increasingly it was coming under the control of the church. To be sure, this would have been a natural development of Christian charity, but by the early seventh century it was clearly an important element in the administrative machinery of the Roman church. Indeed, it did not always go smoothly: pope Sabinian (604–6) made himself unpopular when he chose to alleviate famine by selling corn from papal granaries, rather than distributing it free.[78] This transformation of papal power can be observed in unique detail in the pontificate of Gregory the Great (590–604), whose surviving letters

[75] Moorhead (1994) 111, 118.   [76] Richards (1979) 20–5, 62–7; Otranto (1990) 95–107.
[77] King and Potter (1992) 168–9.
[78] Paul. Diac. *Vita S. Gregorii* 29 (*PL* LXXV.58); cf. *Lib. Pont.* 1.315.

provide a rare insight into the administration of the Roman church and its estates. Gregory's pontificate coincided with the final phase of the territorial dismemberment of Italy, and the interests displayed in his writings reflect the process clearly: on him devolved the task of organizing military defence, diplomatic missions to the Lombards, and the supply of water and grain to the people of Rome.[79]

The popes were not the only bishops to consolidate their position in the uneasy days of the sixth century. Throughout Italy, bishops sought to promote the prestige and influence of their sees. In Apulia, the development of the cult of the Archangel Michael on Monte Gargano gave the bishops of nearby Sipontum considerable clout in local ecclesiastical politics. Moreover, the development of the Archangel's sanctuary as a major pilgrimage centre gave Sipontum sufficient prestige to grant it a relatively untraumatic transition from Byzantine to Lombard political control.[80] The growth of Sipontum is but one example of an explosion in episcopal patronage of the cult of saints in Italy. It had occurred with papal blessing: none other than Gelasius I had supported Laurentius of Sipontum's development of the sanctuary. Elsewhere, however, the cult of saints could provoke certain tensions between local churches and papal claims of supremacy. In northern Italy, both Aquileia and Ravenna developed traditions of apostolic foundation which threatened the ecclesiastical supremacy of Rome. Indeed, the cult of St Apollinaris gave Ravenna's church enough prestige for Constans II to grant the see autocephalous status in 666.[81] The fragmentation of Italy in late antiquity was manifesting itself, then, in how the church was developing as a political and administrative institution.

Ecclesiastical developments also mirrored Italy's transformation from notional centre of empire to Byzantine frontier province, particularly in the relationship between the papacy and Constantinople. This reflected Constantinople's claim, as the New Rome on the Bosphorus, to equal prestige with the Old Rome in the west. Already in 381, the bishop of the eastern capital was accorded 'an honorary seniority after the bishop of Rome' because of Constantinople's status as the New Rome, a decision amplified at the Council of Chalcedon in 451.[82] Constantinople even sought to rival Rome's apostolic primacy. As popes from Damasus I onwards invoked the Petrine succession as a major buttress of Roman supremacy, so the church of Constantinople sought to increase its own prestige by association with the apostle Andrew.[83] So far as the bishops of Rome were concerned, however, such claims were vitiated by Constantinople's absence from the list

---

[79] For what follows, see esp. Richards (1980).   [80] Otranto (1983).

[81] Picard (1988); Markus (1981).

[82] Council of Constantinople (381), canon 3; Council of Chalcedon, canon 28.

[83] Dvornik (1958).

of primatial sees established at the Council of Nicaea in 325, however much the eastern episcopate might acclaim Constantinople's 'honorary seniority' at later councils.[84]

The division of the empire in 395 exacerbated these tensions between Rome and Constantinole. To a pope like Leo I, the removal of the imperial presence from Rome only served to highlight God's plan for the Christian greatness of the city, and efforts to give Constantinople a status similar to that of Rome met with strong opposition.[85] In this climate, conflict, when it came, was severe. In 484, pope Felix III excommunicated bishop Acacius of Constantinople because of his communion with anti-Chalcedonian, Monophysite clergy such as Peter Mongus, patriarch of Alexandria. This hard-line attitude towards Constantinople was maintained by Felix's successor, Gelasius I, but with the accession of the Chalcedonian Justin I in 518 conditions were right for a settlement between the churches.[86] Nevertheless, as the presence at Rome from the mid 490s of the Scythian monk Dionysius Exiguus shows, the Acacian schism had not led to a complete severing of links between eastern and western churches.

Links between Rome and Constantinople persisted under the Ostrogoths, but it was not until the last years of Theoderic's reign that the relationship – like that between Roman senators and the eastern capital – was perceived to have had any political character.[87] With the accession of Justinian, however, political co-operation between the papacy and the empire grew stronger, as the emperor sought the advice of pope Agapitus (535–6) on matters of orthodoxy. Yet the honeymoon did not last: following the Fifth Oecumenical Council in 553, Agapitus' successor, Vigilius, found himself coerced into accepting the condemnation of the writing known as the Three Chapters. Many western bishops – chief among them the north Italians and Istrians led by Paulinus of Aquileia – now repudiated the leadership of the papacy, initiating a schism that afflicted the Italian churches until 607 and forcing the church of Rome into a deeper political alliance with Constantinople.[88]

After Vigilius' death, the relationship between the papacy and the empire was guided as much by secular as by ecclesiastical concerns. Under Justinian, the weight of the Byzantine army in Italy was manoeuvred in support of the papacy's condemnation of the Three Chapters, as when Narses acted as protector of Pelagius I's investiture as pope in 556. With the arrival of the Lombards, however, the relationship began to change. As Byzantine concerns focused primarily on the defence of imperial territories against Lombard encroachment, the papacy found that it was increasingly thrown back on its own resources – and, for a time, those of the

---

[84] Meyendorff (1989) 156–8, 179–84.   [85] Leo I, *Sermo* 82. 1; Meyendorff (1989) 59–66, 148–58.
[86] Dvornik (1966) 59–67; Richards (1979) 100–13.   [87] Moorhead (1992) 235–42.
[88] Herrin, *Formation of Christendom* 119–27; Meyendorff (1989) 235–45.

church of Ravenna – in its defence of the condemnation of the Three Chapters.[89] By the pontificates of Pelagius II (579–90) and Gregory the Great, the position of the papacy was becoming increasingly beleaguered. In Italy, the church of Ravenna was no longer a malleable ally, while in the east the bishop of Constantinople, using the title 'oecumenical patriarch', was once more challenging the Roman church's apostolic primacy. Co-operation between Rome and Constantinople was always seen as desirable, and throughout his pontificate, Gregory the Great sought to achieve peaceful coexistence while at no time compromising his conviction of Roman pre-eminence. Gregory was a realist, and his dealings with the eastern court reveal a pragmatic politician seeking to secure imperial support for papal supremacy. It was this pragmatism that led him to write with enthusiasm to the new emperor Phocas, shortly after he had deposed and executed his predecessor Maurice, a man whom Gregory had befriended in his years as pope Pelagius II's legate in Constantinople.[90]

By the age of Gregory and Phocas, the relationship between Rome and Constantinople epitomized the post-Justinianic status of Italy in the empire. While the papacy existed in that part of Italy under Byzantine control, the Roman church was by no means submissive to Constantinopolitan dictates, whether imperial or ecclesiastical. In part, this reflected the administrative importance of the pope, which at times was recognized by the emperor, as when Phocas yielded to Boniface III's request that Rome be recognized as apostolic and the 'head of all churches' (*caput omnium ecclesiarum*) and gave the Pantheon to Boniface IV for use as a church.[91] During the seventh and eighth centuries, links between Byzantium and the papacy remained strong: many popes were themselves easterners, and they maintained close links with the opponents of Monotheletism and iconoclasm. Yet there can be no denying the uneasiness in relations between pope and emperor in the seventh century. Popes could be uncompromising in the defence of their apostolic prestige, while emperors were as ruthless in their treatment of obdurate popes as they were with inefficient provincial governors, periodically deporting to Constantinople those who caused the imperial authorities trouble.[92]

VII. SETTLEMENT AND SOCIETY

The transformation of the ruling élite and the transformation of the church were significant aspects of social change in fifth- and sixth-century Italy, and, as has been seen, the process had ramifications for patterns of

---

[89] Markus (1981) 567–73.
[90] Greg. Mag. *Epp.* 13.34, 42; for commentary, see Herrin, *Formation of Christendom* 179–181 *contra* Richards (1980) 226–7.   [91] *Lib. Pont.* 1.317; Paul. Diac. *Hist. Lang.* IV.36.
[92] Herrin, *Formation of Christendom* 250–90.

landholding. Indeed, changes in settlement throughout Italy reflect social evolution at its most basic level. Between the mid fifth and the early seventh century, the cities of Italy underwent a profound transformation. As noted above, ecclesiastical building had substantially altered the sacred topography of Italian cities, reflecting the enhanced social profile of the church. Patronage of such ventures varies from centre to centre. In the municipalities, church construction was largely an expression of patronage by local secular and ecclesiastical élites.[93] In administrative centres like Rome, Ravenna or, later, Pavia, much building was undertaken at the expense of the ruling power, whether Roman, Ostrogothic, Byzantine or Lombard.[94] Imperial and royal patronage also made its mark on cities in terms of secular architecture. Ravenna, for example, was the seat of late Roman, Ostrogothic and Byzantine government, so that in addition to fine churches, it also boasted mausolea and palaces for its rulers, venues for public entertainment, and buildings such as warehouses necessary for the upkeep of a major court centre. Palaces were found elsewhere: Theoderic had residences at Verona and Ticinum (Pavia), while the Lombards favoured Pavia, Milan and Monza.[95]

Cities were susceptible to rather more ominous changes. After 535, war became a basic fact of life for many communities. The narratives of Procopius and Paul the Deacon and the correspondence of Gregory the Great are littered with references to sieges and the renovation or construction of fortifications. Sometimes the consolidation of existing defences was not enough. As has been seen, the citizens of many cities in Venetia chose to abandon the old sites of their towns and move to safer locations in the lagoons. Elsewhere, the response was to move to higher ground, sometimes occupying old fortresses first used in the late Roman period. Excavations of such sites at Invillino in Friuli and Castelseprio near Milan have yielded very few Germanic artefacts, suggesting that they were occupied mainly by Roman populations.[96] Meanwhile, in the Byzantine territories of central and southern Italy, the sixth century saw the development of well-defended military *castra*, some of which attracted substantial civilian populations seeking refuge in uncertain times.[97] Northern parts of Apulia seem to have suffered considerable urban decline in the wars, with major centres like Canusium (Canosa) becoming dependent on their neighbours in the secular and ecclesiastical administration of the region.[98]

Change in terms of religious ethos, which had prompted extensive church building, also brought different social habits which could impinge

---

[93] Ward-Perkins, *Public Building* 51–84; Caillet (1993).
[94] Ward-Perkins, *Public Building*, esp. 236–45; Wharton (1995) 105–47.
[95] Ravenna: Deichmann (1969); Johnson (1988). Other centres: *Anon. Val.* 14.82, 87; Ward-Perkins, *Public Building* 157–70.   [96] Christie (1991).   [97] Brown (1978).
[98] Martin (1993) 146–60; Otranto (1990) 251–8.

on the fabric of cities. In many places, for example, the practice of intra-mural burial became common, and not just for the relics of saints; as a consequence, one of the traditional divisions between city and surburb came to be eroded.[99] Yet none of this means that the fifth and sixth century saw a total break with the Roman past, and while there was a certain amount of contraction in terms of city populations, there was also a great deal of continuity throughout late antiquity and into the Middle Ages. In many centres, particularly in the Po valley, the urban fabric proved remarkably resilient to change well into the Middle Ages. Indeed, even today, Roman street grids are well preserved at Cremona, Pavia, Verona and Padua, to name only a few, reflecting the control exercised by civic authorities over urban construction.[100] Such urban continuity is not altogether surprising: even after the Lombard invasions, towns and cities remained the centres of commerce and administration.[101]

There was change in the countryside, too. Some form of prosperity in the south might be expected as a result of the increased economic reliance of Rome on the region after the loss of Africa. There is abundant evidence in Cassiodorus' *Variae* that southern Italy did indeed flourish.[102] This was not empty rhetoric, for it is reflected in the archaeological record. Evidence of increased rural settlement in the survey area around S. Giovanni di Ruoti, the discovery of pig bones in many late antique sites, and the identification of amphorae types specifically identified with the region's wine industry confirm Cassiodorus' testimony that the south prospered under the Ostrogoths.[103] It was not the only region to do so; in the far north-east, Histria – rich in oil, vines and corn – came to be known as Ravenna's Campania.[104] Following the Byzantine invasion of 535, however, this prosperity was severely compromised. Belisarius' forces, on crossing from Sicily, ravaged first the rich lands of Bruttium and Lucania. As the war dragged on, agricultural life throughout Italy was disrupted, leading in some years to famine. Again, the archaeological record confirms the picture: in Lucania there is an appreciable decline in rural settlement from the middle of the sixth century.[105]

In some places, such apparent rural decline must be set against the persistence of activities which stretch back into prehistoric times. This is particularly so in the mountainous regions of central and southern Italy, where ancient drove-roads connecting winter and summer pastures continued to be used throughout late antiquity.[106] Other continuities can be observed. In

[99] For Rome: Meneghini and Santangeli Valenzani (1993); cf. Sicilian examples in Wilson (1990) 331–2.   [100] Ward-Perkins, *Public Building* 179–86.   [101] Harrison (1993); Ward-Perkins (1988).

[102] Notably his eulogy at *Var.* VIII.33.3 of 'industrious Campania, or wealthy Bruttium, or Calabria rich in cattle, or prosperous Apulia'.

[103] Small and Buck (1993) 22, 28; Barnish (1987); Arthur (1989) 134–9.

[104] Cass. *Var.* XII.22.3; cf. XII.24; XII.26.2–3.

[105] Cass. *Var.* XII.5.3; Procop. *Wars* VI.20.21; Christie (1996); Small and Buck (1993) 22, 28–9.

[106] Gabba (1985) 381–7; but cf. Staffa (1995) 328.

various parts of the Po valley, for instance, extensive tracts of Roman centuriation have survived into modern times. As this entails the maintenance of both drainage ditches and land divisions, its persistence probably indicates the continued vitality of agricultural life in these zones. Many of these rural survivals occur close to towns and cities where Roman street grids were conserved into the Middle Ages and beyond, suggesting that urban and rural continuity were interdependent.[107] As in so much else, the picture varies from region to region. Moreover, such changes cannot always be blamed on social decline: natural phenomena also played a role. At Aquileia, the silting up of the river Natiso rendered the city's harbour more and more unusable after the fourth century.[108] Likewise, stagnation set in much earlier than the sixth century at some places: the Gubbio basin in the central Apennines, for example, began its decline in the third century.[109] At Luna (Luni) on the Tyrrhenian coast, a flourishing early imperial agricultural system had been abandoned long before the start of our period.[110] Recent archaeological survey in the Biferno valley in southern Samnium shows a similar pattern of decline, retrenchment and disappearance of settlements.[111] Often it is difficult to attribute these changes to specific events, emphasizing the extent to which such results derived from survey represent a picture of the historical *longue durée*. Indeed, some places may have experienced little change at all: Sicily, spared most of the fighting which disrupted the rest of Italy, seems to have remained prosperous into the early Middle Ages.[112]

The pattern of entrenchment throughout Italy extends to what can be elucidated about inter-regional trade in the fifth and sixth century. Cassiodorus once boasted that Rome 'was fed by supplies furnished even from far off regions, and that this imported abundance was reserved for it'.[113] Despite the disruption caused by the Vandal conquest, long-distance trade seems to have been maintained in the coastal cities of Italy in the later fifth century: deposits of African red-slip ware are found at Rome, Naples and Luna, as well as in their immediate vicinities.[114] Inland, however, the situation shows a marked change, particularly in the sixth century. Excavations in central Italy have shown a marked increase of coarse ware fragments in pottery assemblages, while African red-slip ware is found less frequently and in smaller quantities. This does not represent a drop in demand for non-local goods, however, since at precisely the same time local potters in southern Italy started producing vessels which imitated African designs. Rather, it seems that the supply was no longer penetrating

---

[107] Ward-Perkins (1988) 23. [108] Schmiedt (1978) 236–42.
[109] Malone, Stoddart *et al.* (1994) 181. [110] Ward-Perkins *et al.* (1986).
[111] Barker *et al.* (1995) 236–40; cf. Staffa (1995) 317–18, 322.
[112] Brown, *Gentlemen and Officers* 27–8. [113] Cass. *Var.* XI.39.1.
[114] Hodges and Whitehouse (1983) 36–42; Moreland (1993) 95–6, 99–101; Staffa (1995) 326.

inland areas by the later sixth century, suggesting a contraction of long-distance trade within Italy.[115] Once again, the political fragmentation of Italy was being felt in other areas of life.

VIII. ITALIAN IDENTITIES IN LATE ANTIQUITY

Under Valentinian III, Italy was still, fundamentally, a Roman territory. To be sure, there were plenty of non-Romans about, particularly in the army,[116] but the identity of the region as Roman had remained essentially unchanged since the early empire. By the time of Phocas and Agilulf that situation had changed entirely: large swathes of Italian territory were under the control of Lombard or Byzantine Greek overlords; the old aristocracy had contracted; the unity of Italy had been shattered. This process was accompanied over two centuries by a constant renegotation of Italian identity, as the peninsula's population came to terms with the radical transformation of politics, society and the economy.

Of course, it would be erroneous to suggest that there was such a thing as a single Italian identity, even under Valentinian III. The distinction between the aristocracies of northern Italy, who had strong connections with Gaul and Dalmatia, and those in Rome and the south are reasonably clear.[117] In Rome itself, the religious identity of the senatorial order developed from the heady paganism of the late fourth century to the entrenched Christianity of the sixth. But Roman aristocrats never lost sight of their cultural heritage, pagan though it was, and many of them devoted their energies to preparing editions of the Latin classics. To an extent, this was a consolation: from the mid fifth century, the influence of the senate was in decline, and though Odoacer and Theoderic might court its allegiance, their gestures were primarily cultural, not political. Of course, cultural identities could become fused with notions of political resistance – the dark days at the end of Theoderic's reign were enough to show that – but effective power now lay elsewhere, in the hands of Germanic warlords, local aristocrats or Byzantine administrators.

This is not to say that Roman identity was unimportant. Theoderic and his successors were concerned to depict themselves as inheritors of the empire just as much as the Roman population of Italy. The mosaics of S. Apollinare Nuovo in Ravenna showed Theoderic in a very Roman palace, surrounded by the paraphernalia of Roman court ritual.[118] Even the Lombards, less Romanized than Theoderic's Goths, learned the value of certain aspects of Roman culture, particularly court ceremonial.[119] Roman identity was central, too, in the propaganda of the Byzantine reconquest,

---

[115] Moreland (1993) 96–8.   [116] E.g. Mazzoleni (1976).   [117] Barnish (1988) 134–8.
[118] Heather (1996) 222–7.   [119] McCormick, *Eternal Victory* 284–96.

as emperors from Justinian to Phocas claimed to be restoring Italy's ancient *libertas*. Such declarations found only partial sympathy in Italy. In 591, to be sure, some bishops from the diocese of Aquileia wrote to the emperor Maurice begging for the restoration of imperial rule. But their conception of Roman rule was a religious one, contrasting the Byzantine *sancta res publica* with the Lombard yoke.[120] The letter originated in the context of north Italian resistance to Justinian's condemnation of the Three Chapters, and the ultimate fate of the Aquileian church reveals how fragile Roman identity was by the early seventh century. In 610, the episcopal election was split. One group elected Candidianus, residing at Grado and loyal to Rome and Constantinople. An opposing group, still refusing to accept the condemnation of the Three Chapters, elected their own candidate, John, and left Grado for old Aquileia, where they placed themselves under the political protection of duke Gisulf of Friuli.[121]

Nor did all Goths or Lombards share their rulers' enthusiasm for things Roman. When Amalasuintha chose to give Athalaric a Roman education, she provoked disapproval among the Goths of Italy.[122] Even after the collapse of their kingdom some Goths retained a discrete identity as late as the eighth century.[123] And of course, the Ostrogoths – in stark contrast to the later behaviour of the Visigoths or the Lombards – never became Catholic Christians, but held fast to their Arianism down to the demise of their kingdom. Under the Lombards, the vestiges of Roman culture were fewer still. While the figure of Agilulf on the crown from the Val di Nievole in Tuscany depicts him as *dominus noster* and flanks him with Victories, such echoes of Roman ceremonial are tempered by the king's beard, droopy moustache and the sword on his lap, all very Germanic.[124] The Lombards, too, retained elements of their Germanic culture. While some aspects of their administration, such as the office of duke, had Roman antecedents, other elements were wholly alien to Italian soil, such as the use of *farae* to govern subdivisions of the duchies. Moreover, while the kings and dukes quickly adopted Latin as their language of government, other Lombards, such as those who scratched the runic graffiti at the Archangel's sanctuary on Monte Gargano, retained their own tongue.[125] Such resistance to the Latin culture of Italy was to have far-reaching consequences. The overlay of Germanic elements in Lombard territories, and, indeed, Greek ones in the Byzantine provinces, assisted the linguistic transformation of Italy, creating the wide diversity of regional dialects which were a characteristic of the country until comparatively recently.[126]

---

[120] Greg. Mag. *Reg.* 1.16a.   [121] Paul. Diac. *Hist. Lang.* IV.33.   [122] Procop. *Wars* V.2.6–17.
[123] Schiaparelli (1929–33) II.279 (no. 228) records a certain Staviles 'living according to the law of the Goths' (*legem uiuens Gothorum*) near Brescia in 769.   [124] McCormick, *Eternal Victory* 289–91.
[125] Titles: Wickham (1981) 39; Christie (1995) 110–26. Graffiti: Otranto (1990) 200–2.
[126] Devoto (1978) 137–47, 177–89.

IX. CONCLUSION

Under Lombards and Byzantines, then, Italy was very different from the territory restored to Valentinian in 425. The pace of change had varied from region to region, but, overall, Italy underwent a process markedly different from the rest of western Europe. Whereas Gaul, Spain and Britain had experienced considerable disruption in the fifth century, with the restoration of some form of equilibrium in the sixth, the situation in Italy was almost completely the reverse. The deposition of the last emperor passed almost without notice. Under Ostrogothic government the peninsula saw considerable continuity with the Roman past, even if not all members of the Roman élite acquiesced in Theoderic's regime. The forcible reintegration of Italy into the empire by Justinian, however, belatedly brought to Italy its share of cultural, economic, social and political dislocation.

To a major extent, of course, Roman Italy had always been a conglomeration of regions united by the veneer of Roman civilization and government. Under Theoderic that veneer had held firm, but Justinian's reconquest set in motion a sequence of events that caused the structures of the Roman state to collapse and the peninsula to disintegrate into separate regions.[127] The tumultuous events of the later sixth century saw Italy torn apart between the new reality of Lombard power and the outmoded aspirations of the imperial government in Constantinople. Such contradictions were echoed at the beginning of the seventh century by the complex reactions of Phocas to the new state of Italian affairs. In one sense, Phocas tacitly recognized that Italy was largely lost to the empire when he ratified Smaragdus' treaties with Agilulf. Yet if by such actions Phocas seemed to acknowledge the changed nature of Italian political realities, he was prone to ideological conservatism. In 608, Smaragdus erected a column and gilded statue in Phocas' honour by the Rostra in the Roman forum. On its base an inscription claimed that Phocas was 'triumphator, forever Augustus' who had achieved peace and *libertas* for Italy:[128] the rhetoric is substantially the same as that of Justinian.

By the early seventh century, the very act of setting up the column, statue and inscription represented an anachronistic view of Rome and Italy and their place in the empire. While the shift in power from Ravenna to Constantinople meant that Italy was now a mere frontier province of the Byzantine empire, the idea that it was an imperial possession continued to beguile the emperors of Constantinople, and sixty years after Phocas one last attempt was made to restore Italy to the empire. In 662, Constans II came to Italy in person, aiming to wrest Italy from Lombard hands. Despite some early successes in southern Italy, Constans failed to achieve his ambi-

---

[127] Wickham (1981) 1–5, 9–14.   [128] *CIL* 6.1200.

tion. The fiscal cupidity of his regime – which included the despatch of Roman treasures to Constantinople – aroused contempt in Italy and Sicily, and few will have mourned his death, by an assassin's hand, in his bath at Syracuse in 668.[129] With Constans' death imperial ambitions in Italy came to an ignominious end. Byzantine territories were eroded further by the Lombards in the seventh century. Romuald of Benevento (671–87) conquered most of the duchy of Calabria, apart from the area around Otranto.[130] In the north, king Rothari (636–52) had already obliterated the duchy of Genoa and extended Lombard possessions in Venetia before Constans' western campaigns.[131] Although Byzantine interest in Italian and papal affairs continued in the succeeding centuries, and a rump province existed – and even expanded – in Apulia until the beginning of the second millennium, it was clear that much of Italy's destiny lay outside the empire.[132] Constans' failure was followed by a more lasting peace treaty in c. 680 which made clear what Phocas had acknowledged in his ratifications of 605: the wars fought between Lombards and Byzantines had brought ancient Italy to an end.[133]

---

[129] Paul. Diac. *Hist. Lang.* v.11; *Lib. Pont.* 1.343. Haldon, *Byzantium in the Seventh Century* 59–61.
[130] Paul. Diac. *Hist. Lang.* vi.1.   [131] Fredegar, *Chron.* iv.71; Paul. Diac. *Hist. Lang.* iv.45.
[132] Kreutz (1991) 62–6; Brown (1995) 320–48.   [133] Dölger (1924) no. 240.

CHAPTER 20

VANDAL AND BYZANTINE AFRICA

AVERIL CAMERON

The period from A.D. 425 to the eve of Islam was a momentous one for North Africa. At its start, what is now seen to have been one of the most prosperous and urbanized of Roman provinces, even if that development came somewhat later than elsewhere, passed without real struggle into Vandal control. The monarchy then established lasted until A.D. 533/4, when a Byzantine force under Belisarius re-established Roman rule, again with surprising speed. The new province established by Justinian's Pragmatic Sanction of 534 endured in theory, if not fully in reality, until the fall of Carthage itself to the Arabs in A.D. 698; even though Arab armies had defeated and killed a Byzantine exarch in 646–7[1] and founded an Islamic city at Kairouan in 662, ties between the province and Constantinople were not entirely broken.

These changes of fortune also implied political, religious and economic changes which have been the subject of much recent discussion. The main stimulus for this re-examination has come from archaeology – first and foremost the important series of excavations conducted by a number of national teams at Carthage during the 1970s under the general auspices of UNESCO; these have provided, in many cases for the first time, reliable information at least about parts of the city and its development during this and other periods, and have stimulated and made possible further important developments in such disciplines as the study of ceramics. In turn, the results of these excavations, even though not all are yet fully published, have contributed to the re-examination of issues such as long-distance trade and its place in the Mediterranean economy in the sixth and seventh century. One result has been that the period of Vandal rule in North Africa is no longer seen as one of severe economic decline; rather, overseas trade continued as before. In assessing the level of this exchange, historians have depended heavily on the recently developed study of late Roman pottery, and in particular of late Roman African slipwares. But recent work on Justinian's fortifications in North Africa, survey evidence and work on some major sites, if as yet only incomplete, is also enabling historians to

---

[1] Gregory: *PLRE* III.554, *s.v.* Fl. Gregorius 19.

revise old views of the impact of Byzantine reconquest. A further important change has been the discarding of the colonial model of interpretation, which had long dominated the study of Roman Africa. Often regarded as 'western', and therefore neglected by Byzantinists, North Africa is at last beginning to be recognized as an area of major importance for the general history of the late sixth and seventh century.[2]

I. THE VANDAL CONQUEST AND VANDAL RULE (429–534)

Led by their king, Geiseric, the Vandals crossed the Straits of Gibraltar and entered Roman Africa in A.D. 429. Hippo Regius, on the coast near the border between modern Algeria and Tunisia, the site of Augustine's bishopric, was burnt in 431, only months after Augustine's death in late August 429. In 435 parts of Numidia were conceded to the Vandals by treaty, and in 439 they occupied Carthage; a second treaty in 442, hastily agreed after a Vandal fleet had reached Sicily and threatened Italy, gave them Proconsular Africa, Byzacena, Tripolitania and part of Numidia, while plans were set in hand for a marriage between Geiseric's son Huneric and Eudocia, the daughter of Valentinian III.[3] A band probably totalling in 429 no more than 80,000, including non-combatants,[4] thus went almost unchecked by the provincial armies. External attempts to check or overthrow them – in particular, naval expeditions planned by Majorian in 460 and Leo I in 468 – also failed disastrously. Meanwhile, the Vandals had gained control of Corsica, Sardinia and the Balearics, and in 455 even sacked Rome and took the empress Eudoxia and her daughters Eudocia and Galla Placidia prisoners (Vict. Vit. *Hist. Pers.* 1.24; Procop. *Wars* III.5.1–6); Mauretania and Sicily also came under Vandal sway. After 468 there was little chance of further action against them from the west, and they were raiding the coast of Illyricum when the eastern government under Zeno concluded a peace with them in 475;[5] this peace lasted until Belisarius' expedition. Geiseric was succeeded in 477 by his son Huneric (477–84); after him came Gunthamund (484–96), Thrasamund (496–523), Hilderic (523–30), the son of Huneric and Eudocia, and Gelimer, the last

---

[2] See Mattingly and Hitchner (1995) 209–13 for an excellent survey, with rich bibliography; also Duval (1990), (1993). The standard works on Vandal and Byzantine Africa are still Courtois (1955) and Diehl (1896) (on Courtois, see Mattingly and Hitchner (1995) 210; Lepelley (1989) 30). For the literary sources for the Byzantine period see Cameron (1982), an early attempt at a synthesis; Pringle (1981) is a valuable and detailed study of military aspects. Fundamental on the prosperity of late Roman Africa are Lepelley, *Cités* and Lepelley (1989). For methodology, and for the limitations of archaeological evidence, see Roskams (1996).

[3] Main sources for the period: Victor of Vita, *History of the Vandal Persecution* trans. Moorhead (1992); Procopius, *Wars* III.1–9 (on which see Goffart, *Barbarians and Romans* 62–9)); Prosper, *Chron.*; Hydatius, *Cont. Chron.*; see also Ferrandus, *Vita Fulgentii* and Victor of Tonnena, *Chron.* In general see Courtois (1955); Diesner (1966); narrative in Bury, *LRE* I.

[4] For the number see Goffart, *Barbarians and Romans* 231–4.   [5] Malchus fr. 5 Blockley.

Vandal king (530–4), who walked as a captive in Belisarius' triumphal procession in Constantinople.[6]

Like barbarian settlers elsewhere in the western empire, the Vandals were greatly outnumbered by the existing population. As the self-appointed chronicler of Catholic persecution by the Arian Vandals, Victor of Vita, who seems himself to have accompanied the Catholic clergy exiled by Huneric, emphasizes the damage done by the invaders and the prosperity that had gone before.[7] The unpopularity of the landowning class may have meant that the arrival of the Vandals was not unwelcome to some sections of the population,[8] and the invaders were able to rely on Roman Africans such as Fulgentius, who was later to become bishop of Ruspe and a leader of the Catholic opposition, to maintain their administration. However, much of our literary evidence for the period comes from hostile Catholic churchmen, and the picture is necessarily mixed: moreover, direct Vandal influence was concentrated in the Proconsular province. As a consequence, the so-called *sortes Vandalorum*, the lands which they allocated to themselves and which represented a division between Vandals and Romans, by no means affected all Roman landowners.[9]

According to his biographer, although Fulgentius' grandfather had fled to Italy when the Vandals took Carthage, his father and uncle had succeeded in recovering the family estates near Thelepte in Byzacena, and Fulgentius spent his early life managing the estates and holding the position of *procurator*.[10] The *Tablettes Albertini*, wooden tablets on which are recorded in ink acts of sale from A.D. 493–6, demonstrate the continuance of late Roman landowning practice and indicate that new trees are being planted.[11] While it is hard to find evidence of continuing curial patronage after the Vandal conquest, signs of continuity include attestations of a number of *flamines perpetui* and *sacerdotales*; even though Christian, the Roman élite continued to hold the traditional titles, whether the imperial cult had been appropriated by the Vandal kings, who called themselves *reges*, or whether the titles still carried an imperial connotation.[12] A law of Huneric (484) lists the Roman hierarchy in traditional terminology,[13] while the Vandal kings used the mint of Carthage to issue coins with titulature and iconography derived from imperial usage.[14] By the end of the Vandal period, poets such as Luxorius and Florentinus, whose poems survive in

---

[6] Gelimer and his life in exile: Cameron (1989).

[7] Vict. Vit. *Hist. persec.* 1.3–12, with 11.28, 32; cf. also Possidius, *Vita Augustini* 28. Despite 1.1, which seems to refer to A.D. 488–9, most indications in Victor's work point to 484 as the date of composition: Moorhead (1992) xvi–xvii.   [8] E.g. Diesner (1966) 51ff.; Frend (1978) 480–2.

[9] For the *sortes*, see Procop. *Wars* III.5.11–15; Vict. Vit. *Hist. persec.* 1.12–14, both highly coloured (see Goffart, *Barbarians and Romans* 68); Clover (1982a) 667–8.   [10] Ferrandus, *Vita Fulgentii* 1.13, 8–10.

[11] Courtois *et al.* (1952); cf. Bonnal and Février (1966–7).

[12] Chastagnol and Duval (1974); Clover (1982a), (1989).   [13] Vict. Vit. *Hist. persec.* III.3–14.

[14] Clover (1986).

the *Latin Anthology*, were praising Vandal rule in a style reminiscent of imperial panegyric; there was clearly also some cultural and linguistic intermingling, even if on a limited scale.[15] But life under such a regime was not easy: even if there was a semblance of continuity, the curial patronage so amply documented for the period before the Vandal conquest seems to have come to an abrupt end, and there are no public inscriptions from the Vandal period. When the Vandals employed Catholics in the royal palace, the Catholics found it politic to dress like Vandals,[16] and the Roman poet Dracontius fell foul of Gunthamund and was imprisoned for it.[17]

The Catholic hierarchy, fresh from its recent harsh measures against the Donatists, soon itself experienced periods of persecution from the Arian Vandals. As a result, it developed a strong sense of identity, defined by opposition, which was to continue into the Byzantine period.[18] Geiseric had made the church a target at first with an eye to its wealth, but his successor Huneric went further and tried to enforce Arianism, calling a council reminiscent of the anti-Donatist Council of 411, and following it with a general edict against Catholics in 483 and 484;[19] Geiseric had left the see of Carthage vacant from 440 to 454, and again from 457 to 481, and forbade ordinations in Zeugitana and Proconsular Africa. The extent to which Victor's evidence can be trusted in detail is uncertain, but the policy of persecution and exile continued under Gunthamund and Thrasamund, in whose reign Fulgentius of Ruspe became a leader of the bishops exiled to Sardinia and elsewhere. On their side, the Catholic hierarchy used pamphlets and propaganda to enhance their sense of living under a tyranny. A bishops' list with additional notations, known as the *Notitia provinciarum et civitatum Africae*, whose reliability has been doubted, gives the number of 466 for the bishops attending the conference in 483, with their subsequent fates; most were allegedly exiled, either within Africa itself or in Corsica.[20] Fulgentius, who had been exiled himself, later engaged in formal debate with Thrasamund on points of doctrine.[21] The experience of harassment and exile served to strengthen the resolve of the bishops; at the end of the Vandal period a council held at Carthage in 525 under the more tolerant Hilderic was able to deal with issues internal to the Catholic church in Africa, and prepared some of the ground for the stand it was later to take against Justinian.[22] More immediately, however, the Byzantine victory in 534 was accompanied by the public overthrow of Arianism and the reinstatement of the orthodox.

[15] Luxorius: Rosenblum (1962); Florentinus (*Anth. Lat.* 371): Clover (1982b); Clover (1986) 9–10; Cameron (1982) 30.   [16] Vict. Vit. *Hist. persec.* 11.8.   [17] Clover (1989) 62–6.   [18] Parsons (1994).
[19] Vict. Vit. *Hist. persec.* 1.29–51; 11.23, 39; Huneric as persecutor: Procop. *Wars* 111.8.3–5.
[20] Parsons (1994) ch. 6.
[21] Ferrandus, *Vita Fulgentii* 19–21; cf. his *Tres libri ad Thrasamundum* and *Responsiones contra Arianos*, *CCSL* 91, 91A. Thrasamund: Procop. *Wars* 111.8.8–10.   [22] Courtois (1955) 304–10.

The attempt to trace the impact of Vandal rule from the material remains yields ambiguous results, and certain developments perceptible in the fifth and sixth century, such as increased ecclesiastical building and signs of encroachment on traditional public spaces, are common to other areas in late antiquity.[23] The evidence of the archaeological record is inevitably incomplete and often hard to interpret. At Carthage itself, some monuments may have been falling into disrepair or partly destroyed; Victor of Vita claims that the Vandals completely destroyed the odeon, the theatre, the temple of Memoria and the Via Caelestis, and some archaeological confirmation has been found in the case of the circular monument, the odeon, the theatre, the Byrsa and to some extent also for the Theodosian wall, the circular harbour and the circus.[24] The fifth and early sixth century have not yielded mosaic floors comparable with those of the fourth-century villas.[25] But city life continued, the Vandal kings themselves engaging in building enterprises, and Vandal nobles possessed fine houses and suburban villas with gardens.[26] Against Victor of Vita we may cite the fulsome eulogy of Carthage and its buildings by Florentinus in the *Latin Anthology*.[27] Church building also continued; the large basilica at Bir el Knissia, Carthage, for example, which underwent substantial alterations in the later sixth century and was still flourishing in the seventh century, was built in the late Vandal period.[28] Outside the cities, important recent evidence comes from archaeological surveys, notably (for the central areas) at Segermes and Kasserine, with important results also from Caesarea in Mauretania and the Libyan valleys; not all the final results are as yet published.[29] These allow a far broader approach than before to North African agricultural systems – in particular, the effects of water installations; they do not suggest a sharp change in the Vandal period, which continued to benefit from the enormous growth in sedentarization in earlier periods, which brought with it economic growth on a major scale, and from the wealth of Roman Africa in the fourth century. Fortified farms or other small rural buildings, probably private in origin, are a feature which was to develop further in the Byzantine period.

The understanding of the role played by Vandal Africa in general patterns of long-distance Mediterranean trade has been revolutionized in the last generation by the scientific study of African pottery (ARS, African red-slip ware) from this period, beginning with the fundamental work of John Hayes; similar results have been obtained using other evidence

---

[23] Humphrey (1980); Mattingly and Hitchner (1995) 210. Cities: Brett and Fentress (1996) 79–80.
[24] Vict. Vit. *Hist. persec.* 1.8; see Mattingly and Hitchner (1995) 210.   [25] Lepelley (1992).
[26] Clover (1982b) 13–15; the epigrams of Luxorius make it clear that games and entertainments were still popular: Rosenblum (1962).   [27] *Anth. Lat.* 376.   [28] Stevens *et al.* (1993).
[29] References and general discussion in Mattingly and Hitchner (1995) 189–96; an important kiln survey is also under way.

Map 12 The central provinces of Vandal and Byzantine Africa

– for instance, lamps.[30] Far from being cut off from the rest of the
Mediterranean, African exports continued throughout the period, and
indeed up to the seventh century; interpretation of the evidence remains
controversial, but while there is evidence of decline from the mid fifth
century, combined with a significant increase in imports of eastern
amphorae to the west, the argument is one of scale. Geiseric's aggressive
policy against Italy cannot have helped the cause of African exports; yet
kiln evidence shows that at Lepti Minus, for example, production was
continuous. Indeed, the ending of the *annona* at Rome, which had acted
as a stimulus to African production but also deprived the province itself
of much of the grain which it produced, may have increased local
resources during the Vandal period. It is not clear to what extent the level
of long-distance exchange was affected by the substitution for Roman
currency exports to North Africa of a local Vandal coinage and the continued use of fourth-century bronze.[31]

[30] See *ibid.* 200–5, with Panella (1989), (1993); in general, Giardina (ed.), *Società romana* III; Fulford, in
Fulford and Peacock (eds.) (1984). Discussion in Wickham (1988), especially at 190–3; Mattingly (1988).
[31] References in Mattingly and Hitchner (1995) nn. 386–7.

The study of Vandal and Byzantine Africa, as of Roman Africa, has been dominated in the past by attitudes derived from the modern experience of colonialism, which has indeed provided the researchers and their milieux, as well as their subject matter. Notions of a thin veneer of civilization established by some process of 'Romanization' over a large native population, or ideas of frontiers as protective barriers instead of zones of contact, have been central to this approach. The processes first of recognizing the models applied in older scholarship and then of deciding in what direction to replace them are still in their early stages.[32] As yet, neither Vandal nor Byzantine Africa has featured as prominently in this debate as has the Roman period; nor has either been the subject of the same level of discussion about ethnic and cultural definition as have other geographical areas in late antiquity, notably Egypt and the near east. For a variety of reasons, the level of scholarship with regard to North Africa on such questions remains undeveloped, even in relation to topics like Donatism that are comparatively well-studied. But with the impact first of the Arian Vandals and then, with the Byzantine conquest, of the eastern armies and administration, new levels of complexity were added to an already complex situation. In their important survey, Mattingly and Hitchner argue for a move away from the existing models of two cultures, or of resistance and reaction, towards a more integrated and 'African' approach, replacing that of much of the earlier modern literature, which, as they point out, has tended to adopt the bias inherent in the contemporary Roman and Byzantine sources.[33]

Outside Vandal territory the picture is varied. Attempts were made to compensate Roman landowners for their losses at the hands of the Vandals,[34] and there is evidence for fine houses and mosaics at Cuicul/Djemila and Cherchel, but elsewhere, as at Lepcis and Sabratha to the east, things were less secure. A central phenomenon of the Vandal and Byzantine periods is the increasingly important role played by the Mauri or Berber 'kingdoms' in the mountains of the Aurès and to the south and south-east of the Vandal areas; one of these groups, the Leuathae, still pagan, came from the east, from the area of Cyrenaica, but others – for instance, in Mauretania – were already Christianized, and used Latin. Though the Byzantines were able to win a spectacular success over the Vandals, they found some of these groups more formidable opponents; they feature far more prominently in Arab accounts of the Islamic conquest of Africa in the seventh century than do the Byzantines, and were destined to have a far longer history in the province. Corippus' *Iohannis*, a Latin hexameter poem in eight books praising the campaigns of the Byzantine general John Troglita in the 540s, is a major source of informa-

[32] *Ibid.* 169–70, 209; Roskams (1996) 175–80.
[33] See e.g. their comments on the historiography of Donatism, Mattingly and Hitchner (1995) n. 439.
[34] *Nov. Val.* 34 (A.D. 451).

tion about the Berbers, who are as yet imperfectly understood;[35] during John's campaigns the heavily-armed Byzantine cavalry met an enemy who were camel-riders and for whom they were unprepared. Pastoralists, and comprising both transhumants and sedentaries, these tribal groups had benefited from the loosening of control during the period of Vandal rule, and the advent of the Byzantines presented a direct challenge to them. Already, before the end of the Vandal period, the Leuathae were established in Byzacena, but it seems unlikely that their importance was appreciated by Justinian and his advisers when they decided to send an army to Africa in 533.[36] But by the mid century, and with John Troglita's campaigns, the Byzantines had achieved some success, pushing back the Leuathae and destroying the main cult centre at Ghirza, south of Lepcis.

II. THE BYZANTINE CONQUEST AND BYZANTINE RULE

Whether late Vandal Africa already represented a run-down and struggling province when Justinian decided to invade depends, therefore, on what evidence one chooses to use; it was certainly ripe for the picking. The Byzantine expedition, consisting of some 15,000 infantry and cavalry, set sail from Constantinople in the summer of 533 under the command of Belisarius; after putting in at Sicily and receiving the news that Gelimer was himself away from Carthage, and that most of his army had been sent to Sardinia, the Byzantines landed at Caput Vada (Ras Kapoudia), on the east coast of Tunisia.[37] The campaign was a useful distraction after the Nika revolt of the previous year, and hostilities with Persia had recently ended. Besides, Justinian had a pretext: Hilderic, who had been well-disposed towards Byzantium, had been deposed and imprisoned in 530 by Gelimer, who had responded haughtily to Justinian's protest.[38] The first encounter took place at Ad Decimum outside Carthage, and on the day after the feast of St Cyprian (14 September) Belisarius led his troops into Carthage, sat on Gelimer's throne and feasted on food prepared for the Vandal king in his palace; among those who were present was the historian Procopius, who is our main source.[39] Meanwhile, Gelimer had had Hilderic killed and had fled himself.

The two armies met at Tricamarum in December, and again the Byzantines prevailed. Gelimer fled to the mountains and soon gave himself up: the Vandals were defeated.[40] A praetorian prefect of Africa was established, to

---

[35] See Frend (1978) 484–5; Pringle (1981) 1.13–16; cf. the series of articles by G. Camps, e.g. Camps (1984), with Modéran (1991). Brett and Fentress (1996) puts the subject on a new footing; see especially 70–80.   [36] The wisdom of the decision was questioned, according to Procop. *Wars* III.10.2–6.

[37] For the campaigns that followed, see Pringle (1981) 1.16–22.   [38] Procop. *Wars* III.9.5–26.

[39] Procop. *Wars* 20–1.

[40] Justinian assumed the titles of Vandalicus and Africanus as early as 21 November 533, before the battle of Tricamarum: Const. *Imp. maiestatem*, *CIC* I, *Inst.*, xxi, and cf. *CJ* 1.27.1 (A.D. 534).

oversee in addition Sardinia, Corsica, the Balearics and Septem, at the tip of Mauretania Tingitana; the eunuch Solomon was appointed to this position, and was given military powers as well when Belisarius returned to Constantinople with the captive Gelimer to celebrate a great triumph and to answer in person insinuations made against him.[41] In a ruthless and efficient move, the Vandal males were settled in the east and exploited as military manpower, thus effectively destroying the former governing élite.

But almost at once Solomon had to face Berber attacks in Byzacena and Numidia, while the uncertainties surrounding property rights and imperial action on religious matters in the newly restored province led in 536 to serious rebellion within Solomon's army; many soldiers had married Vandal captives, and had an interest in the family property of their wives, while others were Arians, whose religion had been forbidden by a law of 535.[42] Such was the danger that Solomon and Procopius fled to Sicily, while Carthage was sacked by its own garrison. The situation was only relieved by incisive action by Justinian's cousin Germanus, sent to Africa in 536, and Solomon was reappointed in 539; he was killed at Kasserine in 544.[43] The Berbers in Numidia had played an equivocal role as they watched the warring parties; Solomon therefore lost no time in driving them back towards Mauretania and, in doing so, gained control of the old Mauretania Sitifensis, although Byzantine Africa remained smaller in extent than Roman North Africa. Meanwhile, already in 535 a church council had been held in Carthage on the question of whether the former clergy who had converted could be received into the Catholic church, and whether their baptism was valid.

Except on certain ecclesiastical matters, we are poorly informed about internal affairs in North Africa in the sixth and still more in the seventh century. The account in Procopius' *Wars* focuses firmly on the Byzantine army rather than the local population (though he gives a different, if highly coloured, account in the *Secret History* (18.1–21)). At *Wars* VIII.17.20–1 (A.D. 553–4) Procopius sums up the story of Byzantine rule to date, admitting the high cost to the country of years of war and mutiny; for most of the period the Byzantines faced rebels within their own army as well as having to fight off Berber attacks. Solomon's nephew Sergius, appointed in 544, utterly mishandled the military situation and was recalled to Constantinople in 545; a new commander, Areobindus, fought unsuccessfully against Guntharis, a further rebel, who thus gained possession of Carthage in the winter of 545–6; Areobindus was treacherously murdered by him, only for Guntharis to be assassinated in turn.[44] The campaigns of

---

[41] Events: Stein, *Bas-Empire* II.318–28.
[42] Just. *Nov.* 37, 6–8; the mutiny of Stotzas: Pringle (1981) I.22–7.
[43] For Procopius' narrative and allusions to internal affairs, see Cameron, *Procopius* 176–8.
[44] *PLRE* III.107–9, *s.v.* Areobindus 2; III.574–6, *s.v.* Guntharis 2.

John Troglita in 546–8, praised in Corippus' *Iohannis*, restored quiet for a time,[45] but the same poet writing in 566–7 refers to the *miseri Afri*.[46] In the *Iohannis*, he tells little beyond the sphere of military campaigns, though we learn that he was directing his poem at the *proceres* of Carthage (*praef.*, 1), perhaps as an apologia for the Byzantines and their previous military failures.[47] Both Procopius and Corippus operate within crude categories which permit little understanding of the real ethnic and cultural circumstances, and both relegate the Berber tribes simply to the realm of barbarians;[48] neither shows any awareness of the indignant response of the African church to Justinian's religious policy in the 540s (see below).

During the 570s and 580s fighting with the Mauri continued, claiming the lives of several Byzantine generals; however, Gennadius, appointed *magister militum Africae* by Tiberius II in 578, killed their leader, Garmul, and strengthened Byzantine fortifications.[49] By the end of the century, after the reforms of Maurice (582–602), the province was relatively prosperous and peaceful. A detailed list of towns, bishoprics and metropolitan sees is given in what remains of the *Descriptio urbis Romani* by an early-seventh-century writer, George of Cyprus.[50] The Armenian-born patrician Heraclius, who became exarch before the deposition of the emperor Maurice in November 602, was able to mint coins, engage mercenaries and despatch a naval force to Constantinople against the tyrant Phocas in 609–10 under his son, also called Heraclius, and an army under his nephew Nicetas. The two-pronged attack was successful, and Phocas was overthrown, whereupon Heraclius the younger became emperor.[51] Little more is known, however, of internal affairs in Africa until the time of Maximus Confessor, who spent two periods in Carthage, culminating in his successful debate there in 646 with the Monothelite Pyrrhus, the former patriarch of Constantinople, after which he left Africa for Rome, where he was the leading mover at the Lateran Synod of 649. Shortly after the debate between Maximus and Pyrrhus, the exarch Gregory seems to have declared himself emperor in a bid against Constans II, only to be defeated and killed by the Arabs near Sbeitla in A.D. 647.[52] The Byzantine sources tell us little or nothing about Africa in the later seventh century, though this is partly or wholly attributable to their general inadequacy. Although coin hoards from the late seventh century suggest that the government in Constantinople was still interested in North Africa, Byzantine historical sources are reduced to a few laconic notices in the ninth-century chronicles of Theophanes and Nicephorus.

---

[45] *PLRE* III.644–9, *s.v.* Ioannes 36, *qui et* Troglita.   [46] *In laudem Iustini, Pan. Anast.* 37.
[47] So Cameron (1982) 37–9.
[48] Cameron (1982) 39–40 (Corippus); Cameron, *Procopius* 184–7 (Procopius).
[49] Pringle (1981) I.40–1; see Durliat (1981) no. 28 (Khenchela).
[50] Ed. H. Gelzer (Leipzig 1890); see Pringle (1981) I.42–3. The lists are found today as part of a later compilation.   [51] Sources: *PLRE* III.584–7, *s.v.* Heraclius 3 and 4; see Pringle (1981) I.43–5.
[52] Pringle (1981) I.46–7.

The end came in A.D. 698 after an unsuccessful attempt by the Byzantines to save Carthage from capture by the Arabs.[53]

Within a decade of Belisarius' triumph, Justinian's religious policy provoked indignation among the African bishops. Traditionally looking towards Rome, they reacted with shock and concern when they found that, in his anxiety to placate the Monophysites, the emperor was prepared to condemn writings they themselves held in respect. North African bishops including Reparatus of Carthage, Facundus of Hermiane and Primasius of Hadrumetum were among the leaders of the opposition to Justinian's condemnation of the Three Chapters; these and others were summoned to Constantinople after they had formally condemned pope Vigilius in 550 at a council in Carthage, and were given summary treatment in the years that followed.[54] Those who had not succumbed, meanwhile, were equally staunch in their opposition to Justinian's final theological initiatives in the last year of his life, in the course of which he deposed the patriarch of Constantinople. This protracted struggle between African bishops and Constantinople led to many of the African clergy, including the bishop of Carthage, being deposed and replaced by others who would be more amenable.[55] As in the case of the Catholics under Vandal persecution, surviving accounts are written to a large degree in order to heroicize the objectors; yet enough of their own theological treatises are preserved and enough is known about the Three Chapters affair and the Fifth Oecumenical Council in 553–4 to show that the general outline is reliable.

Late in the sixth century, fitful light is shed on North African Christianity by some letters of pope Gregory I (590–604) which may indicate the continuing influence of Donatism, unless indeed they tell us more about Gregory's own assumptions and worries.[56] But the next substantial amount of documentary evidence comes from the seventh century, and tells again of the African church, or parts of it, taking up a stance of opposition towards Constantinople. By then, Greek was the language used by the eastern monk, theologian and religious leader, Maximus Confessor, in his letters to clerics and members of the administration, and in his public debate with Pyrrhus of Constantinople. Maximus spent two periods in North Africa, first in the 620s and 630s and again in the 640s. He influenced a strong North African contingent to follow him to Rome, where the Lateran Synod was held in 649, and he was prominent in its deliberations

---

[53] Coins of Constans II: Guéry, Morrisson and Slim (1982); events of A.D. 698: Theoph. *Chron*, p. 370 de Boor.

[54] Cameron (1982) 46–8. A main source is the *Chronicle* of Victor of Tonnena, who was among those imprisoned.   [55] Vict. Tunn. *Chron*. s.aa. 553–5; for the African bishops see Maier (1973).

[56] Cameron (1982) 49–51, with Markus (1964), (1979). Against the view of Donatism as identifiable with rural resistance (Frend (1952)) see Mattingly and Hitchner (1995), works cited in n. 439.

and in the composition of its *acta*.[57] Maximus' older friend Sophronius, himself the pupil of John Moschus and another link with the Greek monasteries of Palestine (he was to become patriarch of Jerusalem, 634–8), had been in Egypt before it was overrun by the Persians in 617. From there, a stream of refugees fled towards Carthage, which with the rest of North Africa escaped Persian conquest. Eastern monasteries were by now established in the city, and it was from one of them that Maximus wrote during his first stay in Carthage of his disapproval of the emperor Heraclius' order for forced baptism of Jews in 632 and of the new danger from the Arabs. A Christian dialogue, the so-called *Doctrina Jacobi nuper baptizati*, probably of the late 630s, claims to tell the story of a converted Jew who had been engaged in trade in Carthage.[58] During the 640s Maximus emerged as the champion of religious opposition to the Monothelete policies of Heraclius (610–41) and his successor, Constans II (641–8), and for a brief period there was intense communication between Rome, Constantinople and Carthage. After the Lateran Synod and the exile and death of pope Martin I (653), Maximus was himself exiled to Thrace (655) and then to Lazica, where he died (662). Although the emperor Constans II spent the last part of his reign in the west, in Italy and Sicily, where he was murdered in 668, little more is heard now of Byzantine North Africa. Maximus' departure for Rome in the late 640s coincided with the defeat and death of the exarch Gregory in battle against an Arab army; the Islamic *miṣr* or garrison-city of Kairouan had been founded by 670, and accounts of the final conquest in Arabic sources are more interested in the mysterious Berber queen, the Kāhina, than they are in the Rūm, as the Byzantines are termed.[59]

Unlike the beginning of Vandal settlement, which had been the result of the arrival of a new population group from outside the province, the Byzantine conquest, it seems, brought soldiers and officials into the province, rather than family groups. To what extent the overall level of population may have changed is unclear; in the early seventh century, while some refugees arrived from the east, there may have been some degree of depopulation.[60] The departure of Maximus and his supporters for Italy before 649 may itself have been a sign for further emigration in the direction of Sicily and south Italy, where Greek-speaking monks and clergy from the east became an increasingly significant element during the seventh and eighth century.[61]

The available evidence does not permit us to trace the full impact of the Byzantine or 'Roman' reconquest as fully as one would like, but some light

[57] Chadwick (1974); further, Cameron (1993).
[58] Ed. Déroche in Dagron and Déroche (1991); see also Dagron in *ibid.*   [59] See Brett (1978).
[60] Settlement: Sjörström (1993).
[61] Cameron (1993); Cuoq (1984) 122–72. For evidence of possible depopulation in Byzantine Africa see also Pringle (1981) 1.114.

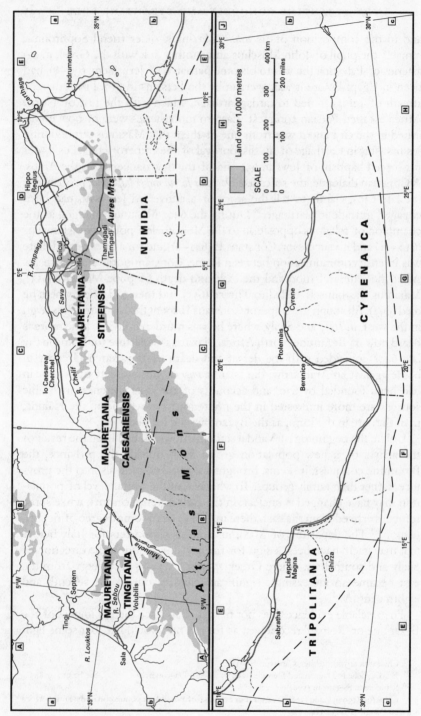

Map 13 North Africa in Vandal and Byzantine times

can be shed on particular aspects.[62] The use of Greek and the presence of eastern officials, for example, are attested by their official seals, which survive even though the documents themselves have perished.[63] Some Greek names appear among the funerary epitaphs, and eastern saints, who have already begun to feature in the North African evidence, become more numerous; there is evidence of the deposition of their relics at North African sites on a number of occasions in the sixth and seventh century,[64] though we lack evidence of the cult of images which was now of growing importance in the east. The letters of Maximus Confessor indicate the existence of a number of monasteries, apparently with monks and nuns of eastern origin.[65] Other scraps of evidence from the late sixth century point to the continuing existence of Latin in monastic life, even if only to attest the carriage of manuscripts and the transplantation of monks from North Africa to Visigothic Spain.[66] Justinian established a praetorian prefect for North Africa, with responsibility for seven governors in charge of Proconsularis, Byzacena, Tripolitania, Numidia, Mauretania Sitifensis, Mauretania Caesariensis and Sardinia. Solomon, the first prefect, also held the military command, with five military *duces* under him. Some of the territory assigned to the *duces* was more theoretical than real, but they were instructed to attempt to recover as much as possible of the former Roman areas that had been lost under the Vandals.[67] The restoration of property taken by the Vandals was also decreed, including churches taken over by Arians; this led initially to discontent and even rebellion in the army, as we have seen. By the end of the century an exarch had replaced the *magister militum*, but there was still a praetorian prefect in addition in pope Gregory's day.[68] A major role of the new imperial administration was naturally to exact taxes from the provincials; this proved highly unpopular at first,[69] but there is little evidence as to its later impact, and appeals made by African landowners in the later sixth century against Justinian's relaxation of the law pertaining to *adscripticii* show an equal concern with the continued availability of labour.[70] There is equally little evidence for the survival or renewal of municipal and provincial organization; a *defensor urbis* is attested at Ammaedara, but references to local notables in general, as to the involvement of bishops with urban organization, suggest that towns were increasingly run by the combined influence of the bishop

---

[62] See the discussion in Pringle (1981) 1.109–20.   [63] Morrisson and Seibt (1982).

[64] See Duval (1982) 1, nos. 106, 112, 126; 11.561ff., 657–70. Funerary epitaphs, largely still Latin: Ennabli (1975), (1982) (Carthage); Prévot (1984) (Maktar); Duval and Prévot (1975) (Haidra); Pringle (1981) 1.116–17, with Cameron (1982) 50–1 and Cameron (1993).

[65] Maximus' letters are to be found mostly in Migne, *PG* xci.   [66] See Cameron (1982) 52–3.

[67] Jones, *LRE* 1.273–4; according to Durliat (1979) the office of *magister militum Africae* came into being only in the late 570s. For detailed discussion of the military and provincial organization as a whole see Pringle (1981) 1.55–89.

[68] Jones, *LRE* 1.313; the administrative reforms of Maurice: Pringle (1981) 1.41–3.

[69] See Procop. *Wars* III.19.3–4.   [70] Justin II, *Nov.* 6 (A.D. 570); Tiberius II, *Nov.* 13 (A.D. 582).

and the local *possessores*.[71] A degree of local euergetism evidently continued, both in relation to church building and decoration and to secular monuments, including fortifications.[72]

The latter constitute one class of material evidence which has been relatively well studied of late, a full survey and gazetteer by Denys Pringle and a corpus of dedicatory inscriptions from works of defence by J. Durliat having appeared in the same year; in addition, Saharan and coastal frontier fortifications have been studied by P. Trousset.[73] Procopius' *Buildings* gives a detailed but incomplete description of Justinian's works of defence in North Africa up to the date of its completion in A.D. 553–4;[74] however, the work is an imperial panegyric, and therefore tends both to exaggerate the degree of imperial achievement and to ascribe everything possible directly to the emperor. Justinian's programme in North Africa had two main aims, the defensive and the religious, the latter including a church of the Virgin at Carthage and another (one of five churches) at Lepcis; in addition, imperial initiatives were directed towards certain prestige urban sites, including Carthage, where building included *stoai*, a bath and a fortified monastery,[75] and Lepcis, where the old imperial palace was restored.[76] City walls whose construction or repair is attributed to Justinian include those of Carthage and Hadrumetum; Procopius names no less than twenty-eight cities which he says the emperor fortified, as well as seven forts,[77] while J. Durliat's catalogue of inscriptional evidence from works of defence amounts to some thirty-eight items.[78] However, only two fortresses have been fully excavated (Ksar Lemsa and Timgad).[79] The size of the army stationed in Africa is difficult to compute from the size and layout of these installations, which vary greatly; Timgad provides the best-investigated example and one of the largest so far (0.75 ha).[80] The initiative and the responsibility for defensive works were shared: the imperial authorities sought to control and monopolize major defensive building, to the extent that twenty-four inscriptions attest the activity in this regard of Solomon as praetorian prefect, acting on behalf of the emperor.[81] Later, the responsibility lay ultimately with the *magister militum Africae*, although local initia-

---

[71] See Pringle (1981) 1.117–18; *tribuni*, attested as the commanders of town garrisons, may also have acquired some civil roles.

[72] Examples are cited by Pringle (1981) 1.118. Individuals named in inscriptions on defensive works include imperial officials, civilians and bishops; however, the last two groups may also have been acting as agents for funds that came from elsewhere (Pringle (1981) 1.90–3).

[73] Pringle (1981); Durliat (1981); Trousset (1985), (1991).

[74] Procop. *Buildings* VI.2–7, with commentaries by Rubin (1954), Pülhorn (1977); discussion in Cameron, *Procopius* 180–7.   [75] Procop. *Buildings* VI.5.8–11.   [76] Procop. *Buildings* VI.4.5.

[77] Pringle (1981) 1.80, in the context of a discussion of the garrisoning of the province; for detailed discussion see Pringle's valuable gazetteer of fortified sites (1981) 1.171–313, with corpus of inscriptions at 315–39, and Appendixes 2 and 5, pp. 123, 126–7.   [78] Durliat (1981).

[79] See Mattingly and Hitchner (1995) 212–12; Pringle (1981) 1.85.

[80] Discussion: Pringle (1981) 1.83–9.   [81] Durliat (1981) 93–8.

tives were not ruled out.[82] Similarly, the cost might be found either from central funds or by the local communities or *possessores* or *priores* themselves; a *castrum* at Aïn Ksar was erected by local *cives*, at their own expense, in the reign of Tiberius II, with a list of their names inscribed on the stone.[83]

The actual extent of building attested, whether by Procopius or by the existence of inscriptions, may have been less than it seems: walls represented an important element of what defined a city in ideological terms, and despite Procopius' claim that the Vandals dismantled all existing Roman defensive installations in Africa, they allowed local communities to construct defences against the Mauri;[84] it is also Procopius' habit to claim building operations as novel rather than as restorations, in order to shed more glory on Justinian. Fortified villas and villages, moreover, owe more to local initiative than to central impetus, and perhaps also to a move towards rural settlement.[85] Nor is it plausible, even though the literary sources may suggest it, to think of Byzantine fortifications in North Africa in terms of lines of defence designed to keep invaders out;[86] the Mauri who now posed the principal threat were in fact established well within the restored province, as well as outside its borders.

Justinian's emphasis on churches as well as works of defence[87] is in a sense indicative of the changing urban topography, here as elsewhere, though generalization is made more hazardous than usual by the fact that it is normally only ecclesiastical and defensive structures that are datable.[88] Eastern influences have been detected in capitals and mosaics, and church building and restoration continued in several places, as at Sbeitla, and sometimes on a large scale, as in the case of the basilicas at Kelibia and Belalis Maior.[89] At Sbeitla, however, the churches coexisted with fortified dwellings, and by the seventh century an oil press sat squarely over what had been the main Roman thoroughfare. Procopius claims that the city of Lepcis, deserted and buried in sand, was restored by Justinian, even if not to its former size; Sabratha, too, was fortified and benefited from church building, though its public spaces, like others elsewhere, were overlaid with houses and shops.[90] 'Encroachment' on to the open spaces and late antique civic areas was a feature of Byzantine Africa, as in other parts of the Mediterranean, and has been detected in a number of the areas excavated

---

[82] Durliat (1981) 98–100.   [83] Durliat (1981) no. 29.

[84] See Durliat (1981) 109–11. For the size of the areas enclosed by walls see Pringle (1981) 1.119–20.

[85] See Mattingly and Hitchner (1995) n. 490.

[86] So Diehl (1896); see, however, Pringle (1981) 1.94–9. Pringle points out that Diehl's model in fact depended partly on the supposed example provided by the Euphrates frontier; however, the nature of late Roman defences in this area has recently been reassessed itself (see Isaac, *Limits of Empire*).

[87] See the statement of policy at Procop. *Buildings* VI.2.18–19.

[88] As remarked by Pringle (1981) 1.118.

[89] Sbeitla: Duval (1964); for the basilica and the striking inscribed font at Kelibia, see Cintas and Duval (1958); Mahjoubi (1978).

[90] Procop. *Buildings* VI.4.1–5, 11–13; cf. Mattingly and Hitchner (1995) 212.

at Carthage where, as at other sites, it is accompanied by increasing numbers of burials within the city itself;[91] similar changes can be observed, for example, at Sétif.[92]

Carthage itself provides an instructive example, even though the archaeological evidence is concentrated in certain areas of the city, thus making a general view difficult. The new administration naturally undertook certain projects in the city, especially in the early years; thus, the Theodosian wall was repaired and a ditch dug there, and building work undertaken at the circular harbour, as well as the north side of the harbour and the island, although there is room for disagreement as to the fit between Procopius' account at *Buildings* VI.5.8–11 and the new archaeological evidence; as yet, the identification of his 'maritime agora', church of the Virgin and 'Mandrakion', described as a fortified monastery near the harbour, remains unclear, and the persuasiveness of his account partly depends on his claims as to the level of destruction or neglect in the Vandal period.[93] Nevertheless, the Byzantines were clearly ready to invest, at least in Carthage, in urban construction that was not solely defensive or religious.[94] Large urban dwellings were still in use during the sixth century, but several of those working in the UNESCO project, especially the University of Michigan and Canadian teams, have reported later subdivision and inhumation within the city.[95] While some of these developments have been ascribed to an influx of refugees from Egypt in the early seventh century, it is also clear that, irrespective of its particular circumstances as the political and administrative centre, the city of Carthage was experiencing the same changes that were happening on other urban sites.[96]

When the Arabs arrived in North Africa in the middle of the seventh century, they found a province still rich in oil and corn production. Corn was still going from Africa to Constantinople in the reign of Heraclius, although the state bread distribution there was formally ended in A.D. 618; the Persians took Egypt, the main source of grain for this purpose, in the following year.[97] Goods were still being exported from North Africa to the eastern Mediterranean in the middle of the seventh century, but to a lesser extent than before;[98] by the second half of the seventh century, imports to the province from the east, which had grown steadily by the end of the sixth

[91] See Humphrey (1980) 113–16.

[92] Mattingly and Hitchner (1995) 213; further remarks by Pringle (1981) 1.118–20; Cameron (1989) 180–1.

[93] Procop. *Buildings* VI.5.1–7; summary and references at Mattingly and Hitchner (1995) 212; on the limitations of 'Justinianic Carthage' see Gros (1985) 124–6; on Procopius, see Cameron, *Procopius* 181–2.   [94] Roskams (1996) 162–3.

[95] See Humphrey (1980); reports and other information from the various excavations have been published regularly since 1987 by the Institut National d'Archéologie et d'Art de Tunisie in its CEDAC Carthage Bulletin.

[96] Humphrey (1980) 117; cf. Roskams (1996) 163–4 ('settlement shift'), 166–7 ('seventh-century demise').   [97] *Chron. Pasch.* p. 711 Bonn, s.a. 618.   [98] Fulford (1984).

century, now fall off dramatically.[99] The explanations both for the growth of this extensive long-distance exchange involving North Africa and for its eventual decline, as for the role played by trade and the activities of large landowners, are as yet still unclear; within the space of two centuries African landowners had had to adjust, first, to Vandal occupation and with it the cessation of the grain *annona* and all that it meant in terms of production and costs, and then to a reconquest or 'restoration' of Roman government, with its centre at Constantinople rather than Rome – a restoration, moreover, which reimposed the land-tax and encouraged the development of an axis between North Africa and the eastern Mediterranean. After apparent success in the late sixth century, the province experienced a progressive reduction in the degree of Byzantine involvement, a process hastened by the Persian and Arab invasions of the eastern Mediterranean.[100]

[99] Anselmino *et al.* (1986) 191–5; cf. Panella (1986) 454–9; Panella (1989) 138–41. North African pottery in the Aegean, sixth to seventh century: Abadie-Reynal (1989) 156–8.

[100] See Wickham (1988) 190–3.

CHAPTER 21*a*

ASIA MINOR AND CYPRUS

CHARLOTTE ROUECHÉ

I. SOURCES

The literary evidence for the history of Asia Minor and Cyprus is abundant for every period, but it suffers to some extent from too much familiarity: Asia Minor and Cyprus were the homeland of so many writers and readers. There was nothing exotic about this area, the heartland of the eastern empire, and so authors felt little need to describe it; much has to be deduced from what they assume. Furthermore, the chief characteristic of Asia Minor and Cyprus in the fifth and sixth century was that they were at peace, so that there was little to recount in historical narratives. The exception, here as in other things, is Isauria, whose turbulent history in the fifth century brought it into the history of the empire.

The lack of 'historical' events can therefore convey a spurious air of immobility. In such a situation, the contribution of archaeological evidence is particularly important; and as the archaeology of this region in this period has developed, it has revealed more and more evidence of marked change. The majority of early excavations concentrated on city sites, and it was common for the late Roman material to be dealt with cursorily during the search for 'more interesting' periods. More recently, excavators have come to treat such material more attentively; moreover, since the 1950s, archaeologists have been surveying the countryside, and their work is starting to provide a more balanced picture of this very large area. Recent work on Roman defences and fortifications has also produced a great deal of evidence for the period. Because of the changes in approach and emphasis, and also because so much archaeological work is going on at present, it is necessary to look at the most recent work possible, while remembering that one year's observations are sometimes reversed by those made a year later.[1]

[1] For Asia Minor, regular reports in English are to be found in 'Archaeology in Anatolia', edited by Professor M. Mellink, in the *American Journal of Archaeology*, and normally in *Anatolian Studies*; regular summary articles, 'Archaeology in Asia Minor', appear every five years in *Archaeological Reports*, published with the *Journal of Hellenic Studies*. An important source of information is the reports on current work – in various languages, but usually in Turkish – which are given by excavators at the annual symposia organized by the Turkish Department of Antiquities. For Cyprus, the principal source is the annual *Report of the Department of Antiquities in Cyprus*; summary reports also appear every five years or so in *Archaeological Reports*.

Inscriptions continued to be set up in many cities of the region, but there is an enormous decrease in quantity between the Roman and the late Roman period. As a result, at very many sites there are only a few late Roman inscriptions, which are sometimes hard to find and even harder to evaluate in the epigraphic corpora.[2]

In assessing both inscriptions and archaeological material there is a recurrent problem of terminology: one author will describe as 'Byzantine' what another will call 'late Roman', and it is necessary to be extremely careful in reading such descriptions. It is also true that, because the archaeology of this period has developed relatively recently, the criteria for dating material within the late Roman period are still rather hazy; but each season's work is increasing archaeological accuracy in such matters. This is a field where our understanding may be radically different in another ten years.

Archaeological discoveries have therefore broken the silence of the historical sources. The picture which they provide complements that provided in the saints' *Lives*; these texts, which emerge as a literary genre in late antiquity, provide a new kind of information by focusing on individuals who lived outside the world of the urban élite. While they are written with no intention of informing us about social and political issues, much can be learned from their assumptions and from the incidental events which are mentioned in them. Lycia in the mid sixth century is brought alive by the *Life of Nicholas of Sion*, just as Galatia at the end of the same century is evoked in the *Life of Theodore of Sykeon*, and in both cases archaeological work in the area concerned confirms the witness of the text.[3] What becomes clear is that, while few events worthy of 'official' history were taking place, the way of life for individuals and communities in the area was changing significantly.[4]

II. THE POLITICAL GEOGRAPHY

Asia Minor is a term of convenience. The large land mass which corresponds roughly to the Asian territory of modern-day Turkey was never in antiquity a historical and cultural unity; it was inhabited by various peoples, speaking a number of different languages, who were from time to time controlled by a single political authority. Over the millennia, this authority had

---

[2] The only collection of such material, Grégoire (1922), was intended to be the first volume of a series, which never materialized. It is still worth consulting; but the best current source of information on such material is the section on Christian epigraphy in the 'Bulletin épigraphique', a survey of Greek inscriptions published annually in the *Revue des Études Grecques*. The easiest source of information in English is the 'Review of Roman Inscriptions' which normally appears every five years in the *Journal of Roman Studies*.

[3] *The Life of St Nicholas of Sion* ed. Ševčenko and Ševčenko (1984); *The Life of Theodore of Sykeon* trans. Dawes and Baynes (1948).

[4] For central Asia Minor this is brought out, with an exemplary use of both archaeological and textual evidence, by Mitchell, *Anatolia* II. For the best account of Cyprus in this period see Chrysos (1993), and, for the end of the period, Cameron (1992).

most often been located outside Asia Minor. The Hellenization which followed the conquests of Alexander provided the first unifying cultural force; all over the region, cities developed on the Greek model, where Greek was spoken, and local cults were interpreted through Greek religion. From the first century A.D. the whole area came under the single political control of the Romans, and experienced several centuries of remarkable security and prosperity.

But the apparent uniformity of public institutions did not eliminate ancient distinctions. When the large Roman units of government were broken down into smaller provinces under the tetrarchy, the new provinces were based on ancient tribal units and kingdoms – Phrygia, Lydia, Caria, etc. – because these still represented real entities; Phrygian, for example, was still being spoken in the fifth century A.D.[5] Local myths and foundation stories were still being recorded in local histories at the end of the fifth century, and many are reflected in Nonnus' fifth-century poem, the *Dionysiaca*. For all the importance of the cities, therefore, there was also an underlying tradition of older and larger political units. Indeed, the replacement of the huge administrative units of the Roman empire by smaller provinces, especially in Asia Minor, seems to have meant that those provinces came to be increasingly important to their inhabitants. It is striking that by the sixth century many people chose to describe themselves as inhabitants of their province – as 'the Lydian' or 'the Cappadocian' – rather than as citizens of particular towns. In so doing, they were using elegant archaism, since the smaller provinces were largely based on older historical units; but the usage may also reveal something as to where their loyalties now lay.

During the second and third century, the demands, above all, of defence had drawn emperors to set up headquarters in the east – for example, at Antioch; but it was only under the tetrarchy that this process started to be formalized, with the development of several 'capitals', including one in Asia Minor, at Nicomedia. The political ecology of the whole region was transformed when this process culminated in the establishment of a permanent imperial capital at Constantinople in 324, which had particularly profound implications for Asia Minor: for the first time for many centuries, the ruling power of the entire area was located on the borders of Asia Minor itself. From 395 the eastern part of the empire was governed from Constantinople; in 476, the deposition of the last western emperor left Constantinople as the only capital of the Roman empire.

This transformation had a major impact on the ruling classes of the cities of Asia Minor. Membership of the imperial senate now no longer involved long and complicated journeys. Moreover, over the same period, the nature of imperial administration in the region had been transformed.

[5] Socr. *HE* v.23.

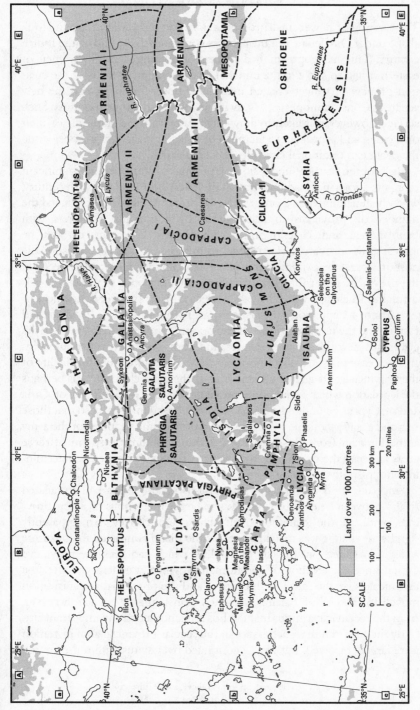

Map 14 Asia Minor and Cyprus

The creation of newer small provinces started in the third century and took shape under Diocletian, but the process continued to the end of the fourth century. This development had met an increasing demand by men of eastern origin to serve in the imperial administration in the east; the creation of new provinces created many new posts for them, and the new senate at Constantinople grew very rapidly during the fourth century. Such service, however, was likely to draw them away from the public life of their own cities, and is probably a factor to be taken into account in considering the decline in traditional civic life discussed earlier.[6]

Beyond the further subdivision of provinces, there were no significant reorganizations in the administration of Asia Minor until the sixth century, when Justinian initiated a programme of reforms. He slightly reduced the number of provinces in Asia Minor by combining Honorias with Paphlagonia, and Helenopontus with Pontus Polemoniacus, but he increased the provinces of Armenia from three to four. He abolished the post of vicar – the administrative office between the praetorian prefect and the provincial governors. Recently discovered evidence suggests that this formalized a change which had already taken place. In several provinces of Asia Minor – Cappadocia I, Galatia Prima, Lycaonia, Phrygia Pacatiana and Pisidia, and the newly expanded Helenopontus and Honorias – he gave the governors new titles, higher salaries, and both civil and military authority. It is not easy to assess how important these alterations were for the life of the provincials. Of all his reforms, one of the most elaborate was perhaps the legislation which brought the provinces of the Greek islands, of Caria and of Cyprus all under the *quaestor exercitus*, based in Thrace, so that those rich and easily accessible provinces could provide the supplies for the army at the Thracian front; this suggests both the continuing prosperity of these areas and also the overriding importance of military finance in determining administrative decisions.[7]

Since the third century, the subdivisions of provinces had stimulated rivalry between cities as to which was to be the metropolis of a new province, with all the benefits which that could convey. An apparently significant change was made in Cyprus; the island continued to constitute a single province, but the city of Paphos, which had been the provincial capital since the creation of the Roman province, was demoted after the earthquakes of the mid fourth century, and the provincial administration moved to the city of Salamis, renamed Constantia. It is clear, however, from the recent excavations that Paphos remained a rich and important city.

By the fifth century, such issues in the secular provincial administration were largely resolved, but rivalry continued over status within the church

---

[6] See ch. 16 (Heather), pp. 437–68 above, and Heather (1994).
[7] Just. *Nov.* 8, 24, 25, 28, 29 (all of 535), 30, 31 (536).

hierarchy. Thus, the ancient and traditional conflict between Nicaea and Nicomedia, which had continued throughout the Roman imperial period, survived at an ecclesiastical level and had to be resolved at the Council of Chalcedon (451). The Council of Nicaea had formalized an arrangement by which the metropolis of a secular province was also the metropolitan archbishopric of a coterminous diocese, and this continued to be the general rule. By the sixth century, the system seems to have stabilized, so that when Justinian combined several provinces he specified that this should not affect the church administration.[8]

It is arguable that the coincidence of diocese and province further enhanced the sense, mentioned above, of 'belonging' to a province. The council of bishops of a province could meet regularly and form an effective pressure group. The most striking example of this is provided by the bishops of Cyprus, who petitioned the Council of Ephesus (431) to confirm their right to select and consecrate their own metropolitan bishop, giving their island a unique status within the church. When this status was called in question again, in 488, the metropolitan Anthemius was guided by a dream to discover the body of St Barnabas, buried with his own copy of the gospel according to St Matthew; this evidence of apostolic foundation was sufficient to ensure the continued independence of the archbishopric, together with particular privileges from the emperor Zeno, including the right to sign documents, as the emperor did, in red ink. Such developments may have been far more significant to the inhabitants of a province than modifications in the imperial administration, and they must have reinforced the local authority of bishops.[9]

III. THE HISTORICAL FRAMEWORK

Asia Minor differs most strikingly from other parts of the empire at this period in one crucial respect: it was virtually unaffected by war. During the anarchic years of the third century, Goths had harried coastal cities, and the forces of Palmyra had at one stage invaded the peninsula. But by the end of the third century Roman control was secure, and would continue to be until the Persian attacks of the early seventh century. During the fifth century, as huge areas of Roman territory came under foreign control, Asia Minor was untouched by external threats; not only was it buffered by Armenia and Syria to the east, and Greece and Thrace to the west, but the strategic position of Constantinople, powerfully fortified by land and in control of crucial sea-routes, offered vital protection. The security of this area must have reduced the contemporary sense of

---

[8] For secular rivalry see Roueché, *Aphrodisias*; for rivalries within the church hierarchy, Jones, *LRE* 873–94; for Cyprus, Jones, *LRE* 873 and Hill (1949) 276–8.

[9] *ACO* i.ii.vii, 118–22, with Jones, *LRE* 873.

catastrophe, and contributed to a sense that the other losses were ones that could be made up.

That is not to say that Asia Minor was entirely at peace. There had always been tensions between the comfortable city-dwellers and the inhabitants of the countryside; and from the third century onwards, there are indications that the less urbanized tribes in parts of the peninsula were giving increasing trouble. Chief among these were the Isaurians, of south-eastern Asia Minor, who had been pacified with some difficulty in the first century B.C.; they revolted again in the 270s, and developed their activities further during the fourth and more particularly the fifth century, when they are reported as attacking settlements as far away as Cappadocia and Pamphylia. By the fifth century, this situation was reflected in the administrative organization of the area: the *Notitia Dignitatum* shows a *comes* and troops stationed in Isauria at the end of the fourth century, and by the later fifth century there were also military commands in the three adjacent provinces of Pamphylia, Pisidia and Lycaonia, in response to the increasing threat from this source.[10] Despite these arrangements, here as in other parts of the empire local magnates tended increasingly to ensure their own security and control by maintaining bodies of armed retainers; during the sixth century there was more than one attempt by the imperial government to restrain this development in Asia Minor (see further below).

Like other warlike enemies of Rome, the Isaurians also produced substantial numbers of troops for the Roman armies. In 474 this tradition acquired political significance when Tarasicodissa, an Isaurian who had risen to power by his military career, became emperor and took the name Zeno. The difficulties which he then faced were characteristic of such a situation; once Zeno had been elevated, other Isaurian chieftains felt themselves to be no less qualified to run the empire than he was. Throughout his reign, Zeno had to deal with revolts in which power was brokered between himself and other Isaurian and barbarian chieftains. He defeated the first attempts with the support of the Isaurian general Illus; but a few years later, in 483, Illus himself revolted, relying on power and connections in Isauria and Cilicia, and perhaps inspired by the success of Odoacer in taking power in Italy in 476. But the Isaurians, for all their strength, and the impregnability of their local terrain, were essentially less of a threat than the other barbarian forces whom the empire deployed, in that they had no kinship with powers beyond the Roman borders and no access to foreign frontiers; Illus negotiated ineffectively with the Persians and the Armenians, but he was defeated by Zeno in 488, and Isauria was finally reduced and pacified under Anastasius in 498.[11]

---

[10] *CJ* XII.59.10.5 of 471–2.   [11] See further ch. 2 (Lee), pp. 50–3 above.

However, although Asia Minor and Cyprus do not appear in the historical records as involved in any other major military undertakings, they were
perhaps more vulnerable than we might assume to the effects of war beyond
their borders. The former patriarch of Constantinople, Eutychius, in exile
at Amasea in the early 570s, had to cope with a famine created by a sudden
influx of refugees fleeing the Persians.[12] In 578 the emperor Tiberius settled
Armenian prisoners of war in Cyprus;[13] and throughout the sixth century
there are hints that people displaced by war were moving westwards. The
Life of Theodore of Sykeon is chiefly taken up with local events in the villages of his area; but Theodore had been conceived in an inn on the main
military road which led from Constantinople to Ancyra and the eastern
frontier, and the later chapters of his life are full of intimations of disaster,
as the reign of Phocas began and the Persian raids on the east intensified.
When the Persians finally broke into Asia Minor, their attacks were the culmination of several decades of progressive destabilization.

IV. THE CITIES

Despite this, it is clear that Asia Minor and Cyprus were essentially at peace
in the fifth and sixth century. This is of particular importance, since it is
clear that many aspects of life in the area did change; these changes cannot
therefore be explained as principally the result of pressure from external
forces, as in other provinces. One development that does suggest an
increased sense of insecurity is the building or rebuilding of fortifications
which took place in a considerable number of cities during the late Roman
period. Such structures are extremely difficult to date, and in earlier years
there was a tendency to date them all in the third century, which was seen
as a 'difficult' time, when it seemed reasonable for cities to adopt
fortifications; this is apparently what did happen at, for example, Ancyra
and Miletus.

But at many sites closer study has made it clear that the situation is much
more complex, although many fortifications remain undatable. In some
peaceful areas, such as Galatia and Lycaonia, Hellenistic fortifications were
rebuilt, but not very carefully. At Aphrodisias, city walls were built for the
first time in the fourth century, and repaired in the fifth; they seem to have
followed the outline of the Roman city, as did the late walls, of indetermi-
nate date, at Nysa on the Maeander. At Smyrna, the walls were built or
repaired under Arcadius. At Sagalassos, the late Roman walls appear to
have been built in the early fifth century, probably as a defence against the
inroads of the Isaurians; they enclosed most, but not all, of the Roman city,
as did the late Roman walls at Oenoanda. Amorium was substantially

---

[12] Eustratius, *Vita Eutychii* 61 (*PG* LXXXVI.2, 2344B).   [13] See Chrysos (1993) 9.

fortified under Zeno – again, probably in response to the Isaurian threat. It was apparently only at the end of the period, in the early seventh century, that fortifications were limited to the most defensible part of the city – as in the case of the Acropolis at Aphrodisias and Phaselis, or the later walls at Side, and the small circuit at Magnesia. Work on this subject is continuing, and the identification of phases of construction is likely to become more precise.[14] It may be that at some places – for example, Aphrodisias – where we do not know of any substantial threat, the new fortifications were intended as much to add to the prestige of the city as to provide for its defence; but it is also worth considering that such fortifications might be intended to meet not a serious 'political' threat, worthy of record in the historical narrative, but an overall increase in small-scale brigandage and robbery. The new walls may reflect a gradual shift in the relationship between the 'city' and the 'country' (see further below).[15]

The fortification or refortification of many of the cities of Asia Minor, and also the extensive re-use of materials in late Roman building, tended to lead earlier scholars to see an overall decline of the cities from the end of the third century. Recently, however, the subject has received closer attention as a result of the work of Clive Foss. As well as publishing studies of the later Roman period at three important cities – Ancyra, Ephesus and Sardis – he drew attention to the flourishing condition of many other cities during the fifth and sixth century. In his view, this period of prosperity came to a sudden end with the Persian invasions of Asia Minor and Cyprus in the second and third decades of the seventh century, leading to the virtual extinction of the cities, or their reduction to fortified *castra*. While this explanation has been disputed (see further below), a result of his work has been to draw the attention of historians and archaeologists to the late antique period at a wide range of sites.[16]

Some sites clearly fell out of use in late antiquity – most obviously, those such as the oracle at Claros, or the shrine of Leto at Xanthos, where the whole focus of the place was on pagan religious activity. These developments were, however, paralleled by the growth of new Christian pilgrimage sites, which became the recipients of substantial patronage. Thus the emperor Zeno provided a substantial new church for his local cult of St Thecla near Seleuceia on the Calycadnus; the life and miracles of Thecla were presented in a new Greek text of the same period. Justinian visited the shrine of St Michael at Germia, whose church also probably dated

[14] Important progress in the understanding and dating of such structures is being made by David Winfield and Clive Foss; see Winfield and Foss (1987).

[15] On the problems of peacekeeping in the Roman and later Roman period in Asia Minor see Hopwood (1983) and (1989), with bibliography.

[16] Foss's general arguments were set out in two overview articles, Foss (1975) and (1977a), as well as in studies of Ankara, Ephesus and Sardis. These and other articles are usefully reprinted in Foss (1990). For an update on the debate see Russell (1986), Whittow (1990) and Foss (1994).

from the late fifth century, as does the great pilgrimage complex at Alahan. These major centres received imperial patronage, and drew large numbers of visitors.[17]

The majority of cities continued to exist, but also changed internally. Certain structures fell out of use, and spolia from such buildings were used for new constructions. Most noticeably, of course, temples were abandoned; thus at Sagalassos one temple was used to make a tower in the fortifications, and the temple of Antoninus Pius, the most impressive building at Sagalassos, had its gables and cornices carefully removed and stored in rows, in order to re-use the frieze blocks in other buildings. Some temples were used as quarries for building materials over a considerable period, as at Ephesus and Sardis; but from the early fifth century onwards some abandoned temples were converted into Christian basilicas, as at Aphrodisias, Pergamum and Sagalassos. These were not just lazy adaptations of existing structures, but careful feats of engineering; at Sagalassos, the blocks of the temple of Dionysus, re-used in a fifth-century basilica, were apparently numbered during dismantling for easy reassembly. At other sites churches were built over temples, as at Side. Elsewhere, churches were established in imposing positions which did not necessarily have significant associations, but were carefully chosen and prepared: thus the basilica at Soloi was placed in a dominating position, requiring substantial terracing.[18] Such imposing building programmes were matched by the accumulation of treasures by churches, exemplified by the rich sixth-century silver treasure found at Kumluca in Lycia.[19]

Even more striking than the location of churches is the sheer quantity of church buildings which can be dated to the fifth or sixth century: thus at Anemurium four churches were built within the city, and at least five more in the immediate vicinity; at Cremna a considerable number of basilicas were inserted into the residential area of the city. Churches appear in unexpected places, such as the small church constructed in part of the theatre at Side, presumably to commemorate martyrs who had died there; this may be paralleled by the painting of Christian frescoes, perhaps in the first half of the sixth century, in the corridor behind the stage of the theatre at Aphrodisias. All these developments, of course, reflect the growing presence of Christianity, and are paralleled by the increasing status of the bishops in civic society. The basilica at Curium, constructed in the first half of the fifth century, was built with generous provision for catechumens and a large baptistery, suggesting that mass conversions were under way at this time. But building activity was not restricted to the Christian community; the synagogue at Sardis was repaired and improved throughout the period,

---

[17] For the fullest account of such a centre in Asia Minor see Gough (1985); on its function see Mango (1986) and (1991). [18] On the impact of such changes see Cormack (1990a).
[19] See Boyd and Mango (1992), especially 1–88 and plates.

although less lavishly during the sixth century, and the synagogue at Side was being repaired in the late fourth and early fifth century.

Although the great civic temples were disintegrating during the fifth century, it is clear that pagan worship did continue in Asia Minor and Cyprus throughout the period. The mentions of Christ and of Apollo on the fifth-century mosaics of the house of Eustolius at Curium are paralleled by invocations of Aphrodite in inscriptions from Aphrodisias in the late fifth century. It is rash to place too much weight on the use of pagan imagery and language, when this was the normal means of expression for all educated people. But at Aphrodisias we know of an avowedly pagan circle, at least among the élite, who welcomed the pagan philosopher Asclepiodotus of Alexandria when he came to settle there. Such people might have been the owners of small pagan statuettes and two figures of Egyptian divinities found in the excavation of a lavish house, probably of the fifth century.

These discoveries might only suggest a taste for the old-fashioned at Aphrodisias, but recent excavation has uncovered a striking series of sculpted portraits of philosophers from the late fourth or fifth century in a substantial and centrally-located building. This seems to confirm the evidence that Aphrodisias was a centre for Neoplatonist teaching at this period, where Asclepiodotus would have had a valuable contribution to make. He and other philosophers travelled throughout the eastern Mediterranean, and were concerned to keep alive the traditions of pagan worship – thus Proclus, who originally came from Lycia but made his career in Athens, visited Lydia, both to study and to encourage proper pagan religious practice there. Paganism could even have political significance: pagans at Aphrodisias made sacrifices for the success of the revolt of Illus in Isauria. But perhaps more significant than this activity in the upper levels of society is the fact that when John of Ephesus was working as a missionary in the 540s, he could claim to have baptized 80,000 pagans in Asia, Caria, Lydia and Phrygia; this suggests that in some cases cities with an apparently 'Christianized' civic centre might be surrounded by a relatively unaltered pagan countryside.[20]

Even if a cultivated élite retained an interest in philosophy, however, the old idea of a civic education for all the young men of a city seems to have evaporated in the third century, and there seems to have been no further use for the great gymnasia of antiquity, which were expensive to run. In at least two abandoned gymnasia at Ephesus, churches were built. But the bath complexes which were often associated with gymnasia stayed in use; thus at Salamis-Constantia in the fifth century, while the ruins of the gymnasium

---

[20] Lydia: Marinus, *Life of Proclus* 15, with Fowden (1990); Illus: Zacharias of Mitylene, *Life of Severus* 40; John of Ephesus, *Lives of the Eastern Saints* (*PO* XVIII.681). For a discussion of paganism in Asia Minor at this period see Trombley, *Hellenic Religion* II.52–133.

were redeveloped, the baths were cleared of debris and put back into use, and a similar redevelopment took place at Sardis. At Anemurium, the palaestra was abandoned and built over by houses and shops; but two bath complexes were maintained, and a third, smaller, one was built. It was apparently in the early fifth century that Scholasticia restored the bath complex beside the street of the Kuretes in the centre of Ephesus. Baths continued to be repaired and maintained at many other sites, such as Aphrodisias, Didyma and Oenoanda, where, as at Side, the aqueduct was also repaired in this period. Theatres largely remained in use, although stadia tended to be altered; recent excavations have revealed a church built into the substructure of the stadium at Ephesus.

Along with these developments came the construction of new kinds of buildings for new purposes. One new category was that of the residential and administrative complexes required for the new church hierarchy; such buildings are coming to be recognized at various sites, although they may sometimes be hard to distinguish from the similar buildings which were also constructed at about the same time for governors at provincial capitals. These buildings themselves are also closely related to the large and lavish private houses which were built or restored in many cities of Asia Minor and Cyprus in this period, as for example Sardis, Aphrodisias or Salamis; particularly striking are the houses at Paphos, which were richly decorated with mosaics in the fifth century.

Parallel with the development of large private houses in this period was the extensive building of shops and other small-scale (presumably private) structures. A typical complex is that of the Byzantine shops at Sardis, constructed in the fifth century and destroyed in the seventh; even if they were less formally organized than shops of the Roman period, they represented new investment. There is considerable evidence for continuing and lively trade in this period. This is brought most vividly alive by the inscriptions from the cemetery at Korykos, in southern Asia Minor, where members of a very large number of different trades recorded their professional status on their tombstones; the interest of these texts – which appear to be largely of the fifth century – is not just as evidence of economic activity, but also as showing the importance of such activity to a man's status in society. The recent excavations at Sagalassos have uncovered an important centre for the manufacture of pottery: 'The position of at least ten kilns has been identified. They range in date from the Late Hellenistic period to the early sixth century A.D. The extent of the quarter makes it clear that Sagalassos must have been a major production centre in Southern Turkey working for an export market.'[21] At several coastal settlements in Lycia granaries and other storage facilities were being built in late antiquity.[22]

---

[21] Mitchell, Owens and Waelkens (1989) 74; cf. Waelkens (1993) 48. [22] Foss (1994).

Shifts in priorities produced another fundamental change in the appearance of the cities during this period – the abandonment of a number of public spaces. At Phaselis, probably in the fifth century, a large basilica – almost certainly a church, but just possibly a secular building – was built in the agora, in the middle of an open space; similarly, a large Christian basilica was built in the centre of the agora at Iasos, perhaps in the sixth century. It is easy to see that many of the functions of an agora – in civic self-government and pagan religion – may have been less relevant to this period, while energetic commercial life still used the pattern of streets lined with shops. This is exemplified at Ephesus, where the great open *Staatsmarkt* area at the upper part of the site, which had been the centre of religious and political life, was abandoned and occupied by small dwellings; spolia from the public buildings there were used elsewhere on the site. But, during the late fourth and early fifth century, the main streets in the lower, western, part of the site were retained and even remodelled – most strikingly, the great Arcadiane, leading from the theatre to the harbour, which was equipped with street-lighting. Moreover, the agora in the lower town was restored in the late fourth century, and remained in use – even if perhaps only for commercial purposes.

In general, after a slack period in the early fourth century, the fifth and the sixth century saw energetic building activity at many cities, such as Side, Aphrodisias, Anemurium and the cities of Pamphylia and Pisidia. Recent excavations at Amorium are uncovering a city which received new city walls, and a new lease of life, principally under the emperor Zeno. At Miletus, this surge of activity seems to have come even later: 'Work has demonstrated that, after a period of stagnation in the 4th and 5th centuries A.D., Miletus once again enjoyed a period of lively building activity in the 6th and 7th centuries.'[23]

One of the biggest changes in the late Roman period is the enormous reduction in the number of inscriptions. As a result, we know less than we would like about the government of these cities. But, after the end of the fourth century, the traditional formulae naming the Council and People as the governing entity disappear. Instead, works are undertaken by the council, by local benefactors, or by the bishop of a city – reflecting developments in the legislation, where civic matters come increasingly to be entrusted to bishops and local landowners. It is worth noting that this change may be reflected in the archaeological record described above, where church buildings, commercial activities and private houses invade some of the previously civic spaces.

At many sites, as has been shown, new buildings used spolia from previous structures, now redundant; but this should not overshadow the

[23] W. Müller-Wiener in Mitchell (1985) 85.

achievement of the civic governments in maintaining their splendour well into the sixth century. At Aphrodisias, for example, when parts of the colonnade of the so-called portico of Tiberius collapsed, apparently in the sixth century, the western side was reconstructed by a single generous donor, while several others contributed to the restoration of the south side. Some of the architrave blocks had been damaged; they were carefully replaced with blocks, several cut from spolia, which attempted to copy the sculpture of the original monument.

V. CITY AND COUNTRYSIDE

Different, but undoubtedly related, changes can be detected in the archaeology of the countryside. As travel in the area has become easier, especially since the Second World War, archaeologists have found more village sites of the late Roman period. Many of these apparently started to develop in the third century A.D., and flourished until the end of the sixth, some even growing into cities.

This has provoked a debate which is far from being resolved: did such settlements grow at the expense of the cities or in response to the prosperity of the cities themselves? The evidence is still being uncovered, and is not simple to evaluate; it also varies between regions. One of the first of such surveys to be published was of the Troad, where a large number of new village sites – some of which may have developed from villas – seem to have been established in the late second or third century, and grew steadily in size. 'Roughly speaking, the fifth–sixth century would seem to be the critical time in which the balance was being tipped from the cities to the rural settlements ... We have the impression that churches must have been built in many places around the sixth century. On the archaeological evidence we should consider that period to be one of the most flourishing in the history of the Troad.' Meanwhile, the ancient city of Ilion appears to have been inhabited until the sixth century, when it was abandoned.[24] A similar pattern is emerging from recent survey work in western Cyprus. But the extent of rural survey in Asia Minor is still very limited, and our understanding is dangerously dependent on small amounts of undatable material, and anecdotal evidence.

In Lycia, several village sites in the hills immediately behind the coast showed important growth, and the first stone buildings at these sites – some of them very impressive – were built in the fifth and sixth century. But further inland, small towns were dwindling into rough settlements, probably under pressure from brigandage. There is considerable debate as to how this evidence should be interpreted; Martin Harrison detected a

---

[24] Cook (1973) 369–73 (villages), 102 (Ilion).

retreat from the coastal cities to settlements in the immediate interior, while Clive Foss sees the prosperity of these settlements as created by movement towards the coast as the interior became less secure. One enigmatic site is that of Arycanda, an ancient settlement in one of the Lycian valleys; there the city remained in good repair into the sixth century, but during the fifth century a fortified town was established on the adjoining hill (at Arif), which coexisted for some time with the earlier city before the latter was abandoned at the end of the sixth century.[25]

Moreover, the countryside was being fundamentally altered by the spread of monasticism; monastic communities were spreading into rural and perhaps into undercultivated land. Many of the impressive monasteries which developed all over Asia Minor at this period will have been built on the property of rich landowners, as in the case of the communities founded by the family of Basil of Caesarea. The monastery of Holy Sion in Lycia seems to have been set up by a rich local benefactor, apparently on family land, in the first half of the sixth century, and the *Life of Nicholas of Sion* records the saintly life of its first *hegumen*, the nephew of the founder. But monastic foundations were also established by humbler patrons, and yet other communities evolved around the activities of a holy man, such as that which developed around Theodore of Sykeon.

The development of a monastic centre would seem to have provided a new focus for the local rural communities; during the plague and famine of the 540s Nicholas went round the villages in the area, providing food. In the account of his life, the nearest city, Myra, which was also the provincial capital, appears as relatively unimportant; the mission of the saint takes place in a well-populated countryside, confirming in the descriptions the archaeological evidence, mentioned above, for rural buildings in fifth- and sixth-century Lycia. Similarly, in the world of Theodore of Sykeon cities play no important role, but, like Nicholas, he has extensive dealings with village communities. In both *Lives* it is made clear that there is tension between the city-dwellers and the country communities: in the *Life of Nicholas* the inhabitants of Myra accused Nicholas of encouraging country farmers to cut off supplies during the Justinianic plague. Later in the sixth century, Theodore of Sykeon was forced to resign the position of bishop of Anastasiopolis, apparently because he was accused of encouraging peasants on church property to resist unfair demands for rent.

All this evidence waits to be explained; it may be that the country settlements grew to the detriment of the cities, but this may be too simple an explanation, since there was not necessarily a clear divide between town

---

[25] Arycanda/Arif: Harrison and Lawson (1979). For a very lucid summary of work on Lycia, with a useful bibliography, see Foss (1994).

and country in antiquity: one way of understanding the *raison d'être* of many of the cities which acquired substantial public buildings in the second and third century is to see them as the monumental civic centres for groups of villages. Equally, the owners of the country estates are likely to be the same people as the rich residents of the city houses – and also, perhaps, the senators of the Constantinople senate.

Such landowners had always been concerned to defend their property, and it has been mentioned above that local security seems to have been an increasing problem; an inscription recently found in Paphlagonia, together with laws in the imperial codes, shows that the imperial government was very concerned to control the development of private militias by landowners.[26] In such circumstances, imperial office could be used to provide legitimacy for the *status quo*. The new power structure may be illustrated by the career of Marthanes, a Cilician landowner who was appointed by Justinian with imperial authority to keep the peace in his own province of Cilicia – an appointment which broke all the earlier regulations preventing the appointment of local citizens to such office, and enabled Marthanes to exercise tyrannical power. Similarly, but less dramatically, a governor of the late fifth or early sixth century at Aphrodisias, Vitianus, was honoured there as being a local citizen. It seems likely that the ruling class of the provinces were now in a position to use imperial office to reinforce their control, and had less and less need of the old civic political system.

VI. THE END OF THE CIVIC ERA

Recent research has shown, at site after site, that buildings fell out of use, and settlements contracted, in the late sixth or early seventh century. Considerable energy and acrimony have gone into discussions of the exact date and the causes of this change. It may be that this question, like others discussed here, cannot yet admit of solution – or of the same solution for every site. The most striking phenomenon is the building of new fortification walls at many sites, protecting a far smaller part of the town than before (see above); unfortunately, such fortifications are often peculiarly hard to date closely. At Sagalassos, the centre for the manufacture of pottery which had flourished for several centuries came to an end in the early sixth century, and no material later than the early sixth century has been found on the site. For whatever reason, it was apparently at about this time that the inhabitants moved to the neighbouring site of Aglasun, where a small settlement developed, preserving the name of the older city. At Paphos, the 'House of Theseus' was probably abandoned in

---

[26] Feissel (1985); Just. *Ed.* 8, *Nov.* 29, 30.

the late sixth century; similarly, a substantial town house at Sardis, which appears to have been developed and extended until the end of the fifth century, seems gradually to have fallen out of use during the sixth. At Anemurium, buildings apparently fell into disuse – even churches, built in the preceding centuries, and baths, which had been maintained since Roman times – at a date around 580. While not all such changes can be closely dated, several can be shown to have occurred before the upheavals of the early seventh century.

From 603, for twenty years, the Persians dominated the east and made several raids into Asia Minor; from 610 onwards, Asia Minor was also the base of operations for Heraclius and his army. Those areas, such as Cyprus, which were not the centres of military activity were affected by a steady flow of displaced persons – such as John the Almsgiver, patriarch of Alexandria, who fled home to his native Cyprus in 619. There can be no doubt as to the debilitating effect of this long campaign. The advance of the Arabs in the 630s brought new pressures. We have a particularly dramatic account of what was to follow in an inscription found in the basilica at Soloi, recording the Arab invasions of 649 and 650, when it is claimed that 120,000 and 50,000 prisoners were carried off; but it must also be pointed out that the inscription was set up, in a newly restored basilica, by 655. Such explicit evidence is, however, exceptional, and much is left for us to deduce.

For a thousand years in Asia Minor, Graeco-Roman life was concentrated on cities; even for the many who lived in the country, almost all lived within the orbit of a city, and probably went there at least once a year, to participate in the religious festivals which were part of the self-definition of such communities. During the third century A.D., civic life altered – as is most drastically illustrated by the diminution in inscriptions – and it appears that the relative importance of rural communities began to grow; the spread of the new, universal religion of Christianity offered such communities an opportunity to establish religious centres equivalent to those found in the cities. Cities continued to provide an important economic and social function, not least as the seat of the bishops; but it is clear that, at some sites, such activity was dwindling even during the sixth century.[27] The cataclysms, firstly, of the plague in the mid sixth century, and of the wars of the early seventh, seems to have speeded up this process. But in some senses, perhaps, it did not matter as much as may appear. Asia Minor was to continue to be the power-house of the empire based in Constantinople for another five hundred years. The institutions which withered in the late sixth century or the early seventh were no longer important. The rural

[27] See Brandes (1988). On this process throughout the empire see ch. 8 (Liebeschuetz), pp. 209–10 above.

society which had always been essential to the cities now made a different use of them; some were abandoned, but many survived as places of refuge and small-scale trade centres, although no longer as the focus for public display or political interaction. What had ended was the 'civic' period of the polis as a political and social entity; the details of that transformation will continue to be illuminated by further archaeological discoveries in Asia Minor and Cyprus.

CHAPTER 21b

SYRIA, PALESTINE AND MESOPOTAMIA

HUGH KENNEDY

The eastern seaboard of the Mediterranean and its hinterland comprised some of the richest areas of the eastern Roman empire in late antiquity. Geographically, the area is most easily understood as a series of different climatic zones running north–south. Along the Mediterranean seaboard there is a well-watered strip which provides rich agricultural lands. In the north, this belt is comparatively narrow where the mountains of Syria and Phoenica Maritima come down almost to the sea. Only in a few places, like the vicinity of Antioch and inland from Tripolis, are there extensive fertile plains. In Palestine the fertile area becomes more extensive, though increasingly arid in the south. The mountains themselves vary greatly in character. In Syria II the mountains along the coast are poor and sparsely inhabited, and further south the high summits of Phoenicia Maritima form an effective barrier between coastal cities like Berytus and inland Damascus. In Palestine, on the other hand, the hills are gentler and more densely settled with villages and towns, including Jerusalem.

Inland, the rift valley runs all the way north–south from Syria I to Palestine III. In the north, where the Orontes flows through it, the rift valley is bordered on the east by the limestone massifs – rounded, rocky hills which supported intensive settlement in late antiquity. Further south, both the Biqa valley around Heliopolis (Baalbek) and the Jordan valley were well populated and included such important cities as Tiberias and Scythopolis (Baysān, Bet She'an). Even in the arid lands of the Wādī 'Araba south of the Dead Sea, the Byzantine period saw important settlements.

East of the rift valley, there is a belt of watered fertile land which includes such populated areas as the Auranitis (Ḥawrān) around Bostra and the hills of Moab. The eastern frontier of this land is represented by the 200 mm isohyet (the limits of the area with an annual rainfall of 200 mm) which marks the furthest boundary of settled agriculture. This line bulges eastward to include the Ḥaurān in the south, and in the north extends as far as the Euphrates. Here the grain-growing plains of Euphratensis, Osrhoene and Mesopotamia, between the anti-Taurus to the north and the Syrian desert to the south, supported numerous towns and villages. This area was, however, sadly exposed to attacks from the east; no natural barriers separated it from the lands of the Persian empire, and its exposure always meant that the towns and villages of this area suffered badly in any hostilities between the two empires.

The people of these areas were separated into distinct but mingling groups, divided by language into Greek, Syriac (a north Syrian and Mesopotamian version of the Aramaic lingua franca of the ancient near east which also developed as a literary language) and Arabic speakers. The division was partly a geographical one: on the whole, Greek was spoken in the settlements along the Mediterranean coast, whereas Syriac was widespread in the hinterland, especially in Syria and the north-eastern provinces. The division was partly social as well, the inhabitants of large towns tending to speak Greek while Syriac was the language of the villages. Having said that, it is clear that Syriac was also spoken in towns, and we find examples of people with clearly Semitic names erecting inscriptions in Greek.[1] Arabic remained essentially the language of the nomads and those along the fringes of the desert, though it seems to have been expanding by the end of the sixth century.[2]

There were also important Jewish communities in many of the main cities like Antioch and Edessa in antiquity, but little is known of their history in the later fifth and sixth century.[3] They were also to be found in the small villages and towns of Galilee, the Golan (Gaulanitis) and parts of southern Palestine. Historical narratives and religious polemic tell of persecution and rebellion, but the archaeological record gives a more positive picture. True, 'the numbers of churches in the Land of Israel constructed during this period is close to three hundred whereas only a few score synagogues were built at that time',[4] but good-quality buildings continued to be constructed throughout, with activity peaking in the late third and early fourth century, and again during the sixth. Many of these were in small country towns and villages, suggesting the survival of numerous Jewish communities in quiet rural prosperity.[5]

---

[1] See Sartre (1985) 142–9 and the 'index onomastique', 165–276 for numerous examples; also MacAdam (1986) 101–46.

[2] For the settlement of Arabs in the villages of Syria along the fringes of the desert and the Damascus area after the break-up of the Ghassānid federation in 581, see Sartre (1982) 191–2; for a more general account of the Arab presence in Syria in the early seventh century, Donner (1981) 101–11; for Arab expansion in Iraq in the sixth century, Morony (1984) 214–23. Further, ch. 22c (Conrad), p. 691 below, and in general Shahīd (1995).

[3] For the meagre evidence for Jewish life in Antioch, Downey (1961) 571; in Edessa, Segal (1970) 103–4. Sartre (1985) 158–9 found no evidence of Jews in Bostra after the early fifth century, and the same seems to be true of Scythopolis: see Binns (1994) 135–7; for Caesarea, Levine (1985) 135–9. Further, Cameron (1996).

[4] Hachlili (1988) 370, 399–400. For a general survey of the synagogues in Palestine, Levine (1981), which concentrates on archaeological and artistic aspects; the most recent discussion is Urman and Flesher (1995).   [5] See, for example, the communities of the Golan described in Urman (1985).

The Samaritans[6] comprised a much smaller minority, concentrated in the area around Neopolis (Nablus) and the site of their ancient temple at Mt Gerazim. In the third century, under the leadership of Baba Rabba, they had experienced a period of prosperity and religious revival but, like the Jews, they found the Christian empire of the late fifth and sixth century increasingly oppressive.

Syria in late antiquity, or at least until the mid sixth century, enjoyed something of a golden age. True, there were famines and riots, and the lot of the peasantry was frequently one of toil and indebtedness, but it was also a period of comparative peace and prosperity and considerable achievement in intellectual and architectural matters. And if you were to be asked which part of the ancient world you would like to live in as a peasant, you could do worse than opt for one of the villages by the great monastery of St Symeon Stylites, in the northern Syrian hills between Antioch and Aleppo, in the reign of Anastasius (491–518).

The administrative geography of the area was essentially that of Diocletian's reforms, with some later alterations. The whole area was included within the diocese of Oriens, and the *comes Orientis*, based at Antioch, was in theory the leading figure in the civil administration, but by the sixth century his office was often united with that of the governor of Syria I, and the provinces were more or less autonomous. The area under discussion was divided into a number of provinces. From north to south along the eastern shore of the Mediterranean was Syria I, with its metropolis at Antioch. In about 425, in the reign of Theodosius II, Syria had been divided and Syria II established with its capital at Apamea, though this was sometimes subordinate to Syria I. In about 529, for reasons which are not clear, Justinian arranged a further division when he created a new small province of Theodorias with its capital at Laodicea (Lattakia) which incorporated the small coastal towns of Paltos Gabala (Jeble) and Balaneai (Banyas) in Syria I and Syrian II.[7]

Further south were the two Phoenicias, Phoenicia Maritima (metropolis Tyre) and, inland from that, Phoenica Libanensis, the capital of which was Damascus and which stretched far to the east to include Palmyra (Tadmur) in the heart of the Syrian desert.

From about 425 onwards, Palestine was divided into three provinces, Palestine I, the metropolis of which was Caesarea and which included most of the coastal lands as well as Jerusalem and Judaea, and Palestine II, which was ruled from Scythopolis in the Jordan valley and which covered Galilee and the Golan. In the south, Palestine III stretched from the Mediterranean around Gaza eastwards to include the Negev, the southern rift valley and the hills of Edom. In theory, the capital was at remote Petra but, in prac-

---

[6] There is little recent discussion of the Samaritans in late antiquity but see Crown, Pummer and Tal (1993); for Samaritan revolts see pp. 593 and 598 below.   [7] Malalas p. 448 Bonn.

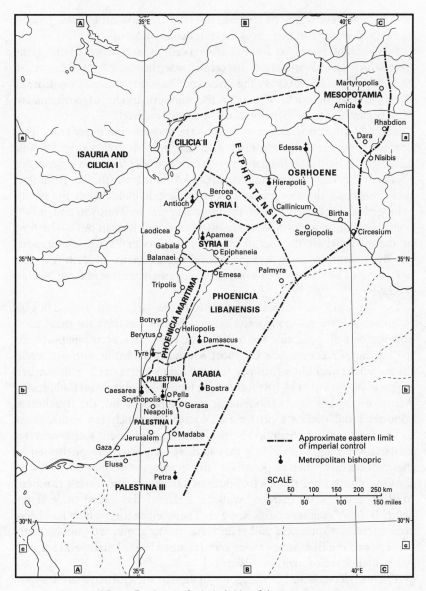

Map 15 Provinces and principal cities of the east A.D. 500

tice, Elusa in the Negev seems to have been the most important centre in the fifth and sixth century.[8] The province of Arabia, originally established by Trajan in 106, had been truncated in the south by the creation of Palestine III.[9] Bostra remained the capital in late antiquity, but the province

[8] See Gutwein (1981).
[9] The borders of the province in late antiquity are discussed in Sartre (1982) 64–75.

only included the southern Ḥaurān, the hilly area around Gerasa (Jerash) and Philadelphia (Amman), and the mountains of Moab.

Inland from Syria I lay Euphratensis along the west bank of the great river which gave it its name. Its capital was the ancient cult centre of Hierapolis (Manbij). Across the river lay Osrhoene, centred on Edessa (Urfa), and to the north of that on the southern fringes of Armenia lay Mesopotamia with its metropolis of Amida (Diyarbakir).

The eastern frontiers of the empire were undefined in many years. The northernmost section of frontier, as it had been determined by Jovian's treaty of 363 with the Persians, ran from the upper Tigris in a generally south-easterly direction along the flanks of Mount Izala (the Tur Abdin) in such a way that the mountains were in Byzantine hands while the plains belonged to the Persians. Here the boundary was well known, and at two points Byzantine fortifications directly confronted Persian ones. The first of these was where the fort of Rhabdion overlooks Persian Sisauranon, just five kilometres away, and the second some seventy kilometres to the west, where Dara was placed to observe movement westward from Nisibis (Nusaybin).[10]

Further south, where lack of water meant that large armies could not be maintained, there was no frontier as such, but we can trace the most easterly outposts of Byzantine control. On the Euphrates, at its junction with the Khabur, Circesium was the most advanced Byzantine outpost, while the Sasanians held Dura Europas, which Shapur had taken in 256. Further defence was provided by fortifications at Birtha (Halebiye) and Callinicum. Across the Syrian desert the frontier was unmarked, but the Byzantines controlled the outposts on Strata Diocletiana, which ran south from Callinicum through Sergiopolis to Palmyra, and then south-west to Damascus, though it is unlikely that all these outposts were garrisoned in the sixth century, when responsibility for security passed into the hands of the Ghassānids after about 530. South of Damascus, the eastern frontiers of Byzantine control marched with the limits of the settled lands as far south as Aila (ʿAqaba) on the Red Sea. The frontier forts which had been constructed on such sites as Lejjūn were mostly abandoned by the sixth century, and the Byzantine empire was defended by diplomacy and subsidy rather than force of arms in this area.[11]

The overall command of the armies in the east was entrusted to the *magister militum per Orientem*, who was based in Antioch, where he had his *praetorium*. There were *duces* to command the local forces, although it is not clear

[10] For the frontier in this area see Whitby (1986) and Whitby *Maurice* 197–213; also Palmer (1990) 4–6.

[11] For the Ghassānids see Sartre (1982) 177–88 and Shahīd (1995). The disbanding of the *limitanei* is claimed by Procopius (*Anecdota* XXIV.12–14) and some would see the archaeological evidence as confirming this; see Parker (1986); for evidence of the decay of the fortress at Lejjūn in the mid sixth century, Parker *et al.* (1987). Sartre (1982) 195–6 notes the almost total absence of fortifications in the Negev in the early seventh century.

that every province had one, and in 528 additional *duces* were established at Circesium in Mesopotamia and Palmyra in Phoenicia Libanensis to defend obvious invasion routes. As in other areas of late Roman administration, the hierarchies and responsibilities were not rigidly adhered to. The emperor communicated directly with provincial governors and *duces*, and on occasion the *magister militum* constructed buildings in Antioch, while the *comes Orientis* was put in charge of the development and garrisoning of Palmyra. One *comes Orientis*, Ephraemius, even became patriarch in 527. Justinian seems to have been concerned to maintain the status of the civilian governors *vis-à-vis* the *duces*, and in 535–6 the governor of Palestine I became a proconsul and those of Arabia and Phoenicia Libanensis were honoured with the new title of *moderator*. It is likely that the regular succession of officials continued at least until the Persian invasions of the early seventh century, but the evidence for this is very scanty and, for example, we do not know the name of any of the *duces* of the province of Arabia after Flavius Paulus in 580.[12]

The degree of military preparedness seems to have varied from time to time and place to place. Those provinces which directly bordered on the Persian empire – Mesopotamia, Osrhoene and Euphratensis – must have had permanent garrisons of *numeri* of the imperial army, at such strong points as Amida, Edessa and Circesium. Palmyra was garrisoned by *numeri* early in Justinian's reign. In the sixth century, major fortifications were built at strategic places on the Persian frontier and the remains of these can still be seen at Dara, Birtha on the Euphrates and Sergiopolis.[13]

Other areas seem to have had few regular troops: in the major Persian invasion of 540, Hierapolis, Beroea (Aleppo) and Apamea all paid ransoms to the invaders, having, it would appear, insufficient garrisons to defend them. Antioch, faced by the same invasion, was poorly defended and was dependent on 6,000 troops hurriedly summoned from Lebanon and on volunteers from within the city. Their combined efforts could not save it from the horrors of pillage and mass deportations.[14] The governors and *duces* of Scythopolis and Caesarea seem to have been equally ill-prepared to face the Samaritan revolts of 529 and 556, and it is said that, after the rebellion of 529, the governor of Scythopolis, Bassus, was executed and the *dux* Theodoros removed from office and put under arrest.[15]

The ecclesiastical administration echoed the civilian one. At the start of the period, all the churches in the area were subordinate to the patriarch of Antioch, just as the secular administration was presided over by the *comes Orientis*. In each province, the church was governed by a metropolitan based in the capital and bishops in all the main towns.[16] At the Council of

---

[12] Sartre (1982) 108–12 discusses the evidence for the sixth-century governors of Arabia.
[13] On Dara: Whitby (1986b) and the comments in Cameron, *Procopius* 107–8; on Zenobia: Lauffray (1983); on Rusafa: Karnapp (1976).
[14] See Procop. *Wars* II and Downey (1961) 533–46; Liebeschuetz (1977) and Cameron, *Procopius* 152–70.   [15] Malalas pp. 445–7 Bonn.   [16] These structures are detailed in Devreesse (1945).

Chalcedon in 451, however, this tidy system was disrupted when Jerusalem became an independent patriarchate presiding over the bishops of the three Palestinian provinces, including the metropolitan of Caesarea, who had previously been his superior.[17] When Theodorias was made into a separate province by Justinian, it did not acquire a separate ecclesiastical identity, and the bishop of Laodicea remained subordinate to Antioch.

A further and more serious confusion in the ecclesiastical organization was the establishment of an alternative and parallel hierarchy in the patriarchate of Antioch in the wake of the Monophysite schism. This rival hierarchy was largely a result of the missionary efforts of the Monophysite Jacob Baradaeus – hence the designation of the Syrian Monophysite church as Jacobite. Originally under the patronage of the empress Theodora, Jacob travelled extensively in the provinces of Syria and Asia Minor between 542 and 578 consecrating metropolitans, bishops and priests. This rival hierarchy took the established ecclesiastical titles, including that of patriarch of Antioch, but they were seldom able to reside in the cities from which they took their titles. Many of them were monks from rural monasteries in Syria and Mesopotamia and lived either in their monasteries or as wandering preachers.[18] The Monophysite hierarchy was also supported by the Ghassānids, and in the province of Arabia there were two bishops of Bostra, a Chalcedonian one in the city and a Monophysite one in the Ghassānid encampments.[19] Despite intermittent attempts at compromise, the divisions hardened in the late sixth and early seventh century, and the great majority of Syriac-speaking monasteries and villages remained loyal to the Jacobite patriarch, based on the monastery of Gubba Barraya, east of Aleppo. Although there is no evidence that the Monophysite populations aided or encouraged the Persian invasion of 611 which swept away the Byzantine political structures, the Jacobite patriarch of Antioch wrote to his colleague in Alexandria: 'The world rejoiced in peace and love, because the Chalcedonian night has been chased away.'[20]

Only once did these provinces and their armies play a major role in the making and unmaking of emperors. Zeno came from neighbouring Isauria and served as *magister militum per Orientem* before ascending the imperial throne in 474. In 482–4 the rival Isaurian leader Illus made Antioch his base in an attempt to put Leontius on the imperial throne. Although his claims were accepted in the city, his troops were easily defeated, and he fled to his native Isauria, where he was eventually killed in 488. Apart from this

---

[17] On the status of Jerusalem in this period see Honigmann (1950); before Chalcedon: *ibid.* 238, 245–6.   [18] See Honigmann (1954), a study of one important monastery.

[19] Honigmann (1951); see also Meyendorff (1989) 229–30 and 266–71; ch. 27 (Allen), pp. 824–33 below. For Bostra: Sartre (1985) 110–12.

[20] Severus b. al-Muqaffaʾ, *History of the Patriarchs* ed. and trans. Evett (*PO* 1 (1907) 481), quoted by Meyendorff in his discussion of this period (1989) 270–1.

episode, which may suggest that Syria was not a viable power base, the political history of this area is restricted to the comings and goings of the *comites Orientis* in Antioch, occasional urban riots and the sporadic rebellions of the Jews and Samaritans in Palestine.

The main threat to the peace and stability of this area between 425 and 600 was from Persian invasions. Persian armies never used the direct desert crossing to Palestine or Arabia but always attacked through the settled areas of Euphratensis, Osrhoene and Mesopotamia, and it was these areas, along with Syria I and II, which bore the brunt of the invasions. After a long period of peace, hostilities broke out in 502–3 when Kavadh attacked and captured Amida, slaughtering a large number of its citizens, and went on to besiege Edessa and ravage the surrounding country. The *casus belli* in this instance was that the emperor Anastasius had, from 483, refused to continue the subsidy previously paid to the Persians for the defence of the Caucasus passes on the grounds that the Persians had refused to return Nisibis, which they claimed had been ceded to them by Jovian in 363 for 120 years. In 503 and 504 large Roman armies counter-attacked, and Amida was restored to imperial control.[21] In 505 a seven-year truce was signed, and Anastasius began the building of the great fortress at Dara, later improved by Justinian, immediately across the frontier from Nisibis.

Hostilities broke out again in the Caucasus in 527 at the end of the reign of Justin I and spread to Mesopotamia, where the then *magister militum per Orientem*, Belisarius was defeated at Callinicum in 531. The fighting was ended by the death of Kavadh and the accession of Khusro I Anushirvan in 532, and a peace agreement by which the Romans paid a lump sum in commutation of the subsidy. This peace lasted until 540, when Khusro, attracted by the weakened defences of the eastern frontier while Justinian's efforts were directed to the west, invaded again, apparently more interested in money than in conquest. Most of the cities, including the provincial capitals of Edessa, Hierapolis and Apamea, duly paid, but as a result of imperial promises of military support and divided counsels within the city (it seems that the patriarch Ephraemius wanted to agree to peace but was prevented by commissioners sent by Justinian) Antioch attempted to resist. The result was the most serious military disaster to afflict Syria in this period. Antioch fell, the city was burned and large numbers of its inhabitants forcibly resettled in Iraq.

After this catastrophe, hostilities soon petered out, and there is no sign that Khusro sought to make permanent conquests. The outbreak of plague in the Roman east in 542 and the successful defence of Edessa by Roman forces in 544 resulted in a truce in 545 in which Justinian again agreed to a

---

[21] Malalas pp. 398–9 Bonn; for a full and vivid narrative of these campaigns W. Wright, *The Chronicle of Joshua the Stylite* (London 1882) caps. xlviii–lxxxi.

substantial cash payment. This peace lasted until 572, when the Romans attempted to take advantage of perceived Persian weakness in Armenia and Nisibis, and open warfare again broke out. Unfortunately, the Romans underestimated their opponents' strength, and Khusro retaliated in 573 by raiding and sacking Apamea, the capital of Syria II.[22] In the same year, the Persians also took the key frontier fortress of Dara. Hostilities dragged on for some twenty years after this, even during the years of truce from 574 to 578. In 591, however, Khusro II was obliged to ask Maurice for help in recovering his throne and was happy to return Dara and Martyropolis, which had been handed over to the Persians by treachery.[23]

The close of the sixth century saw the frontier very much as it had been in 425. The Romans were in control of Dara but never regained Nisibis. The Persian wars had been a burden on the central treasury but, apart from a few major disasters – Amida in 503, Antioch in 540, and Dara and Apamea in 573 – and intermittent ravaging of the countryside of Osrhoene and Mesopotamia, they do not seem to have caused major damage to the provinces and there were many years of uninterrupted peace.

The only other external threat came from the desert. The desert frontiers of Syria and Palestine were very difficult to defend: frontier forts were easily bypassed by swiftly moving bands of bedouin raiders. From the fifth century onwards, the imperial authorities had realized that it was important to secure bedouin allies and increasingly turned to diplomacy and subsidy as a cheaper and more effective way of defending the settled areas than military force. From the end of the fourth century, the leaders of the tribe of Salīḥ seem to have been recognized as phylarchs or managers of the Arab tribes allied to the empire.[24] At the end of the fifth century, the Salīḥid phylarchy, about which we have very little information, was challenged by the arrival of two new tribes in the area, Kinda and Ghassān. In 491 Emesa (Homs) was sacked by the Arabs and in 498 Ghassān raided Palestine and, although they were defeated by the *dux* Romanos, they continued to pose a threat. Probably in 503, Salīḥ were replaced as phylarchs by the chiefs of Ghassān and Kinda. From 503 to 528 it seems as if each province had its phylarch working alongside the *dux*, and in 529 the *dux* of Palestine was assisted by the phylarch of the province in the suppression of the Samaritan revolt.

In 531 Justinian recognized al-Ḥārith b. Jabala the Ghassānid as chief phylarch, in overall charge of the defence of the frontier between the Euphrates and the Red Sea, probably to give him power and status equal to

---

[22] The sack is described by John of Ephesus, *HE* (ed. with Latin trans. E. W. Brooks, *CSCO, Scriptores Syri* 54 (Louvain 1952)), VI.6. The wealth and importance of Apamea in this period have been confirmed by recent excavations, on which see Balty (1981).

[23] See Whitby, *Maurice* 276–304 for a full account of the Persian wars of this period.

[24] On Salih: Sartre (1982) 146–9, 153–62, and Kawar (1958); Shahīd (1989).

the Lakhmid kings of al-Ḥīra, who performed a similar role on the desert frontiers of the Persian empire. For fifty years the Ghassānids more or less kept the peace on the desert frontier, defeated the Lakhmids of al-Ḥīra (notably at Halima near Chalcis in 551), and formed an important contingent in Byzantine armies fighting the Persians, as at Callinicum in 531. When al-Ḥārith died in 569, he was succeeded by his son al-Mundhir. In 581 the emperor Tiberius ordered the arrest of the phylarch al-Mundhir b. al-Ḥārith because he feared the Monophysite sympathies of the Ghassānids and their general unreliability. The Ghassānid system collapsed, and in 583 their supporters attacked Bostra, the capital of Arabia, and ravaged the surrounding area.[25] The defences of the desert frontier were left in disarray, and tribes which had followed them dispersed. The Byzantines still retained allies among the bedouin, some of whom, like the Judhām of southern Jordan, fought vigorously against the first Muslim incursions. Members of the Ghassānid ruling house fought in the armies of the empire at the battle of the Yarmuk in 636, but there can be no doubt that the disappearance of the Ghassānid system was one reason why Muslim forces were able to penetrate Byzantine Syria so effectively from 632 on.[26]

While the politics of the area were comparatively placid, the same cannot be said of the religious history. The area was the birthplace of Christianity, its bishoprics were amongst the oldest Chritian institutions in the empire, and its monasteries and ascetics were rivalled only by those in Egypt. By 425 the majority of the towns were at least nominally Christian, the public performance of pagan rites had been outlawed and some of the major temples destroyed.[27] Pagan cults persisted with considerable vigour in some places, notably at Carrhae (Harran), right through the period.[28] In Edessa, in many ways the spiritual centre of Syriac Christianity, sacrifices were still being made to Zeus at the end of the sixth century. The *magister militum per Orientem* Illus promised to restore pagan cults during his rebellion against the emperor Zeno (481–8), and this attracted some support, though it is not clear how widespread this was.[29] John of Ephesus says that the Christians of Heliopolis were a small and oppressed minority and that when an imperial agent came to put an end to the persecution they were suffering, he uncovered a pagan network in which the *vicarius* of Edessa and the patriarch of Antioch, no less, were alleged to have been implicated.[30] In the countryside,

---

[25] John Eph. *HE* III.40–5, 56; Sartre (1982) 189–94; Shahīd (1995) (a different view).
[26] For the situation at the time of the Muslim conquests, Kaegi (1992) 52–5; in general, Shahīd (1995), with ch. 22c (Conrad), pp. 695–700 below.
[27] For the destruction of the temple of Zeus at Apamea (c. 390) and the Marneion at Gaza in 402 see Trombley, *Hellenic Religion* I.123–9 and 1.187–245.
[28] For Harran, where the pagan cult is well attested from Islamic times, see Green (1992). For the cults of Syria in general: Drijvers (1982).   [29] Trombley, *Hellenic Religion* 81–4, 93–4.
[30] John Eph. *HE* III.27–34; see Bowersock, *Hellenism* 35–40.

too, paganism persisted, especially in remote areas: the Christianization of the limestone massif east of Antioch was largely complete by 420, whereas pagan cults survived in the rural Ḥaurān until the late sixth century.[31]

In the late fifth and sixth century, tensions between the Jewish and Samaritan communities in Palestine and the Christian authorities seem to have been increasing. The Samaritans had not traditionally been militant but, apparently because of Christian attempts to remove sacred relics from Joseph's tomb, they raised a revolt in 484. Churches which had been built on their sacred Mt Gerazim and in Neapolis were destroyed, and they crowned one Justus or Justasas as their king. Caesarea was taken, many Christians were killed and Justasas celebrated victory games, but their success was short-lived. Troops sent by the emperor Zeno put down the rebellion, and Justasas was executed. In 529 there was another revolt. In June communal riots between Samaritans, Christians and Jews broke out in Scythopolis, and many parts of the city were burned by the Samaritans (at least, according to the account of the Christian chronicler Malalas).[32] Fearing the emperor's wrath, the Samaritans broke into open rebellion. Again they crowned a king/messiah called Julian, churches were burned and the provincial capital of Scythopolis taken and held. When Justinian reasserted Byzantine control, large numbers of Samaritans were killed, and the Ghassānid phylarch is said to have taken 20,000 boys and girls and sold them in Persia and India (probably, in fact, south Arabia or Ethiopia) as slaves. Malalas alleges that there were 50,000 Samaritan exiles at the Persian court who encouraged Kavadh to invade Byzantine territory, promising to hand over their own land, all Palestine and the holy places. There may well be no truth in these accusations, but they illustrate the kinds of inter-communal tensions which could arise in the sixth century.

On the whole, the Jews were more passive, even in the face of the increasingly hostile legislation of Justinian, but there are signs of growing militancy in the late sixth century. In 556 Samaritans and Jews allegedly took advantage of trouble between the Greens and the Blues in Caesarea to attack the Christians, and succeeded in killing the governor and storming his palace.[33] There are a number of reports which claim that the Jews joined the Persians in attacking the Christians in the invasion of 614. However, recent scholarship has shown that the evidence for this is based almost entirely on Christian polemical writing of the early Islamic period and has more to do with explaining Christian defeat than with historical accuracy.[34]

In contrast to the comparative tranquillity of political life, church life in this area was always vigorous and was marked by passionate disputes.[35] The

---

[31] Trombley, *Hellenic Religion* 34–5.   [32] Malalas pp. 445–7 Bonn; cf. Binns (1994) 138–9.
[33] Malalas pp. 487–8 Bonn.   [34] See Cameron (1994) and (1996); Schick (1995).
[35] For full accounts, Frend, *Monophysite Movement*; Meyendorff, *Imperial Unity* 165–292; and ch. 27 (Allen), pp. 824–8 below.

theological issues raised by the Monophysite controversy are discussed elsewhere in this volume (see pp. 818–33 below), and it is the political and social dimensions which are to be addressed here. The Monophysite controversy affected all the churches of the empire in one way or another, but nowhere else did it cause such violent dispute as in the patriarchate of Antioch, because here it became associated with other social and cultural divisions which aroused popular passions.

The dispute over the definition of orthodoxy accepted by the Council of Chalcedon in 451 expressed deep divisions over the understanding of the central Christian mystery of the incarnation. The contrast between the full humanity of Christ stressed by the Dyophysites (who of course accepted his divine nature as well) contrasted with the emphasis on the single, divine nature of Christ upheld by the Monophysites.

There was also something of a linguistic divide. Monophysite doctrines were espoused and expounded in the main by Syriac speakers and writers. Even in the case of Monophysite thinkers fully educated in the Greek tradition, like Severus of Antioch (d. 538), their writings have survived in Syriac versions. Others, like Severus' radical ally, Philoxenus of Hierapolis (d. 523), and the historian John of Ephesus, wrote only in Syriac. In general, Chalcedonian Christianity found its popular support in the cities and among the Greek-speaking élite, especially within the ambit of the patriarchate of Jerusalem, while the Syriac-speaking small towns and villages, away from the coast and towards the Persian frontier, were more solidly Monophysite.

The Monophysite movement in Syria found its staunchest adherents among the monks. Even before Chalcedon, monks like Mar Barsawma (d. 459), who spoke no Greek, were openly hostile to episcopal authority. Syrian monasticism tended to be anarchic and individualist,[36] and many monks objected to being subordinate to a hierarchy, especially if the hierarchs spoke a different language and held questionable theological views. The monastic nature of the Monophysite community became even more pronounced after 518, when imperial pressure ensured that all the established bishops were firmly Chalcedonian. It was Monophysite monks, especially those of the frontier monastery at Qartmin, near Dara, who ensured that the council called by the *patricius* John, on the orders of Justin II, to try to resolve the issue at Callinicum in 567, ended in failure.[37]

There were also notable regional differences. By the mid sixth century, when the alternative Monophysite hierarchy was being established, we can see that Syria I, Euphratensis, Osrhoene and Mesopotamia had large, probably majority, Monophysite communities. In contrast, Syria II and the Phoenicias were mostly Chalcedonian. However, the Ghassānids were firm

---

[36] See Vööbus (1958–9) for the full richness of the Syrian ascetic tradition.   [37] Palmer (1990) 150.

supporters of the Monophysites. Adherents to the Monophysite creed were subject to bouts of persecution but, despite rumours that Monophysite monks had betrayed Amida to the Persians in 503, it would be wrong to see the movement as anti-imperial or in any way 'nationalist' or separatist: the Monophysites simply wanted to be part of a Christian empire which was, in their sense, orthodox.[38]

The balance of power between the communities in the patriarchate of Antioch reflected political changes in Constantinople as well as local opinion. From 451 to 518 the key issue was the control of the office of patriarch itself, for the patriarch alone had power to consecrate new bishops and so change the complexion of the hierarchy. Until his death in 488, the key figure among the Monophysites of Antioch was Peter the Fuller, who was patriarch no less than three times, interrupted by two periods of exile. At this stage, much of the population of the city itself seems to have had Monophysite sympathies, and the unfortunate Chalcedonian patriarch Stephen was stabbed to death by his own clergy, using sharpened reed pens, in 479.[39]

In 482 the *Henotikon* of Zeno provided a framework within which the two parties could agree to differ, and some of the violence went out of the dispute. This tolerant policy was continued by Anastasius. In 512, however, Severus became patriarch of Antioch and succeeded in winning over the emperor Anastasius to a more militantly Monophysite position, while Philoxenus of Hierapolis won Euphratensis for the cause. From 512 to 518 the Monophysites were supreme in Antioch, though opponents remained in Syria II and among the monks of Phoenicia II, who went so far as to write to Rome seeking support. The accession in 518 of Justin I, a westerner seeking reconciliation with Rome, led to a violent reversal of policy. The hierarchy was swiftly changed: Severus was obliged to retire to Monophysite Alexandria and the new patriarch Paul, called 'the Jew', began active persecution of the Monophysites, until removed by the emperor for his excesses. Monophysite bishops were replaced and Monophysite monks expelled from their monasteries to find even more austere retreats in the mountains and deserts.

The years 531 to 536 saw a relaxation of persecution because of the pro-Monophysite actions of the empress Theodora but, as Justinian sought to win over the implacably Chalcedonian church of Rome, after 536 the persecution was started up with renewed intensity. This seems finally to have convinced Severus, still the spiritual leader of the Monophysites, to accede to the demands of militants like John of Tella

---

[38] On which see Meyendorff, *Imperial Unity* 251–4; the loyalty of Monophysite communities to the empire in the late sixth century is noted by Whitby (*Maurice* 213–15). Ghassānids: Shahīd (1995).
[39] Malalas p. 381 Bonn.

(martyred in 536) and Jacob Bar'Addai to begin the consecration of an alternative Monophysite hierarchy, which set the seal on the schism. For the rest of the century, the northern provinces of the patriarchate of Antioch saw continuous strife between an officially supported urban hierarchy and a rural populace which largely rejected it and sought their spiritual leadership elsewhere.

The dispute took a very different turn in the patriarchate of Jerusalem. The bishop at the time of Chalcedon, Juvenal, had gone to the council with Monophysite convictions but seems to have been persuaded to change his mind by the erection of his see into an independent patriarchate, something previous bishops had tried but failed to achieve. On his return, he was execrated as a traitor by the Monophysite populace and had to be guarded by imperial troops, while the bishop of Scythopolis was murdered for his Chalcedonian views; however, opinion gradually shifted in favour of Chalcedon. This was partly a question of local ecclesiastical pride: to anathematize Chalcedon, as the Monophysites demanded, would be to undermine the patriarchal status of Jerusalem which had been agreed there. The church in Palestine was also much more influenced by Constantinople and the west because of the constant arrival of overseas pilgrims, some of whom stayed and became monks. The monasteries of the Judaean desert, the spiritual power-houses of the patriarchate of Jerusalem, were very different from those in Syria. While Syrian monasteries recruited men of local experience from the local areas, the Judaean monasteries attracted recruits from all over the empire. The greatest of these, Euthymius (d. 473) and Mar Saba (d. 532), founder of the famous, still surviving, monastery in the Judaean desert which bears his name, were firm supporters of Chalcedon. In this way, despite setbacks like the deposition of the Chalcedonian patriarch Elias during the high noon of Monophysite power in 516, Jerusalem remained as firmly and completely committed to Chalcedon as the Egyptian church did to the Monophysite cause.[40]

The disputes of Chalcedon gathered pace against a background of expanding settlement and over-all economic (and probably demographic) growth. The evidence for this can be found in the unique archaeological record of the region, which is unrivalled in this period for its extent and scope but is not always easy to interpret. There are a number of problems in the use of archaeological evidence for the assessment of economic prosperity. The most obvious of these is the chronology. Much of the dating of sites rests on ceramic evidence which is not clear enough to make distinctions between fifth, sixth and seventh century or even between Byzantine

---

[40] See Patrich (1995); Binns (1994); and Honigmann (1950) 247–61. For the archaeology of the Palestinian monasteries, Hirschfeld (1992).

and early Islamic.[41] There is also a tendency among historians to see the Byzantine period as a sort of plateau and the Persian and Arab invasions of the early seventh century as marking a dramatic break in the social and economic life of the area:[42] in reality, economic and social change probably occurred over a much longer time-span. While it is sometimes possible to be certain when buildings were constructed, it is much more difficult to know when they fell into ruin or disuse. Furthermore, it is not always clear what archaeological evidence tells us about economic prosperity: the building of monasteries, for example, could be an indicator of economic expansion as people endowed the church with their surplus wealth, or it could be a sign that monasteries were expanding their lands at the expense of impoverished or depopulated villages. Equally, the intrusion of poorly built structures on to public open spaces like streets and squares, which seems to happen in the sixth century in Antioch, Apamea, Scythopolis, Gerasa and Madaba, among other sites, could show the general decay of urban life or, conversely, that increased commercial pressures meant that every part of the urban area had to be exploited to the full.[43] All generalizations about the economic history of this period have to be treated with some caution.

The fifth and early sixth centuries were characterized by continued building activities in major cities and the expansion of settlement into marginal lands in mountainous and semi-arid zones. The planned city with its broad, paved, usually colonnaded streets remained the ideal of urban builders. When Justinian rebuilt Antioch after 540, Procopius describes how 'he laid it out with stoas and agoras, dividing all the blocks of houses by means of streets and making water-channels, fountains and sewers, all of which the city now boasts. He built theatres and baths for it, ornamenting it with all the other buildings by which the prosperity of a city is wont to be shown.'[44] When Anastasius constructed the fortress of Dara, he equipped it with 'two public baths, churches, colonnades, warehouses for storing grain and two cisterns for water'. In the archaeological record, the clearest evidence for large-scale street layout in the period is emerging at Scythopolis, capital of Palestine II, where the city-centre streets were rebuilt and extended in the early decades of the sixth century.[45] There is

---

[41] For example, both Orssaud using ceramic material from the limestone massif of northern Syria and Watson using the material from Pella have recently emphasized that the pattern is one of continuity and slow evolution and that there are no clear breaks between the early sixth and the mid eighth century; see Orssaud (1992) and Watson (1992) and the *table ronde* 'De la céramique Byzantine à la céramique Omeyyade' in Canivet and Rey-Coquais (1992) 195–212.

[42] Tchalenko's discussion in *Villages* of the economic life of the villages of the limestone massif is based on the assumption that this society collapsed with the Muslim conquests. For a recent example of the same attitudes, see Shereshevski (1991) 222–3; cf. the critique in Cameron (1994) 91–3; for a helpful overview of the debate see Foss (1995).

[43] Kennedy (1985); also Kennedy (1986a) and the recent discussion in Di Segni (1995). For building and architecture see ch. 31 (Mango), pp. 918–71 below.   [44] Procop. *Buildings* II.10.2–25.

[45] Tsafrir and Foerster (1994).

further evidence from Jerusalem, where Justinian laid out or extended a broad, new colonnaded *cardo* or main paved thoroughfare to lead to the portico of his Nea church.[46] Chroniclers of the period also record numerous instances where the emperors sent money or remitted taxes to aid rebuilding after earthquakes or other disasters.

A particular problem is posed by the buildings at Androna (al-Andarin) and Qasr Ibn Wardan (ancient name unknown), on the fringes of the desert north-east of Hama. At Androna there is a series of churches, two of which are dated to the sixth century, and a square barracks built by 'the most estimable Thomas' in 558. At Qasr Ibn Wardan there is a church, palace and barracks complex of great elegance and sophistication with an inscription of 564. Unfortunately, nothing more is known of Thomas, and we have no idea of the name of the builder of Qasr Ibn Wardan.[47] Given the complete absence of literary or epigraphic evidence, there is no reason to assume that these buildings were imperial fortifications, especially as there is little evidence for imperial building of any kind in the near east in the last decade of Justinian's reign. We should probably ascribe these large-scale projects to local initiative – the governor, a local magnate or the Ghassānids.

Government patronage extended to individual buildings, although after the mid fifth century these are mostly churches. Among the most impressive projects were Zeno's patronage of the building of the great church of St Symeon Stylites in the limestone hills between Antioch and Aleppo (*c.* 476–91) and Justinian's vast Nea (dedicated 543) in Jerusalem,[48] both of them new foundations, but humbler establishments also benefited, as can be seen from the example of the monastery of Qartmin, on the remote Tigris frontier, where the main church, which still survives, was constructed by the emperor Anastasius.[49]

Imperial building activity can also be seen in fortifications. The threat of Persian attacks meant that Justinian's government reconstructed the walls of Antioch and Apamea. In Edessa the damage done by the disastrous flood of 525 was repaired by Justin I and Justinian, who restored the walls and the cathedral and built a dam to divert the flood-water of the river Scirtos which still exists today.[50] Imposing fortifications were constructed at Sergiopolis in the Syrian desert and Birtha on the Euphrates. At Sergiopolis, these consisted of a vast rectangle of walls 500 × 400 metres which contained the city with its churches, including the great basilica of the Holy Cross, dedicated in 559. At Birtha, a triangle of impressive walls

---

[46] Avigad (1984) 213–29.
[47] The best discussion of these buildings is still in Butler (1907–20) Section B, pp. 47–63.
[48] On the building history of the shrine of St Symeon: Tchalenko, *Villages* 1.223–76; for the Nea: Avigad (1984) 229–46; on Syrian stylites and their architectural remains: Peña, Castellana and Fernandez (1987).   [49] Palmer (1990) 113–48.   [50] Segal (1970) 187–9.

about 400 × 300 metres, with a citadel at the apex and the shorter side along the river, enclosed a small garrison town with a forum, baths and at least two churches.[51]

Imperial patronage was largely confined to provincial capitals and frontier fortifications. Cathedrals and churches were often built at the instigation of bishops.[52] The great cathedral at Bostra, one of the most important buildings in the entire area, was dedicated in 512/13 by bishop Julianus and there is no mention of imperial patronage.[53] As far as we can tell, the fine series of churches at Gerasa, which continue through to the early-seventh-century church of bishop Genesius (611), were all constructed by local patrons.[54] At Gerasa it was the bishop Placcus who built new, smaller, public baths in 454–5 to replace the vast classical *thermae* which had fallen out of use.[55] Major church-building schemes from the sixth century have also been revealed at Apamea, where the cathedral was reconstructed in the 530s by bishop Paul, and a round church and an atrium church were built at about the same time. In Edessa in the fifth century a whole series of churches were built by bishops. Bishop Hiba (436–57) was especially renowned for his lavish patronage: in 437–8 he gave a great silver altar to the cathedral and built a magnificent new church of the Twelve Apostles and an extramural church of St Sergius. His successor, bishop Nona, built extensively, including a church of St John the Baptist, with thirty-two columns of red marble, and an infirmary for the poor outside the south gate. As late as the time of the emperor Maurice, bishop Severus built himself a palace and a street called the New Portico.[56]

It was not, however, in the greater cities that the true vitality and prosperity of the late antique near east can be seen, but in the villages and small country towns of the area. Our knowledge of these is derived almost entirely from archaeological sources. The most important evidence is to be found in marginal areas, including the uplands of the limestone massifs of northern Syria (the so-called 'Dead Cities'), the basalt areas of the Ḥaurān and the Negev areas of Palestine III.[57] In all these areas, settlement was more extensive in the fifth and early sixth century than it had been under the principate. In all these areas, too, the communities have common features. The largest settlements can be called towns, but they are very different in character from the *poleis* of the classical period or, indeed, from a contemporary provincial capital like Scythopolis. Typical examples like Kapropera (al-Bara) in northern Syria, Umm al-Jimal (ancient name

---

[51] See p. 592 above, n. 11.

[52] For church architecture in Palestine see Crowfoot (1941) and Tsafrir (1993); for Syria: Lassus (1947).   [53] Sartre (1985) 124–5.

[54] For the superb series of churches at Gerasa see Kraeling (1938) 171–262.

[55] Kraeling (1938) 265–9.   [56] For building in Edessa: Segal (1970) 183–91.

[57] For the villages of the limestone massifs see Tchalenko, *Villages*, and Tate (1992); for the Ḥaurān: Villeneuve (1985); for the Negev: Shereshevski (1991). In general: Cameron and King (1994).

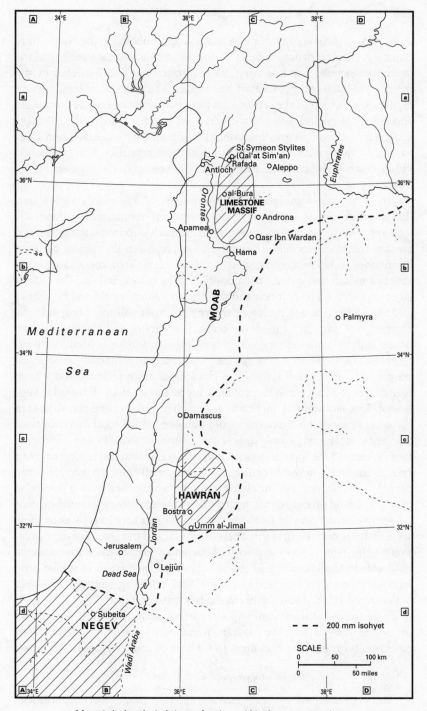

Map 16 Archaeological sites and regions within the eastern provinces

unknown) in the southern Ḥaurān and Soboda (Subeita) in the Negev have common characteristics: there is no formal urban planning at all, and the streets are narrow winding lanes, without porticoes and bordered by the mostly windowless outer walls of the houses. The only public buildings are churches, of which all the settlements have two or more, but the houses are sometimes large and well-built, centred on internal courtyards. All these settlements expanded greatly during the fifth and sixth century, and most of the surviving building can be dated to these centuries. The unplanned village-town is the characteristic feature of late antique settlement in the near east.

The economic foundation of this prosperity was clearly agriculture, though some towns, notably Tyre, were probably in some sense industrial.[58] The apparent prosperity of communities in such unpromising agricultural areas as the limestone hills of northern Syria has been the subject of some discussion. In his pioneering work on these areas, Tchalenko[59] suggested that this wealth was based on a monoculture of olives, and that the hill villages exported oil to Antioch and the Mediterranean world and bought in grain and other necessities from the rest of Syria. All this prosperity, he claimed, was brought to an abrupt end by the Persian and Muslim invasion of the early seventh century, which cut off the area from its Mediterranean markets. This vision of a specialized, market-orientated agricultural economy is attractive but has been challenged more recently, and it now seems that agriculture was probably more mixed than Tchalenko suggested. Tate has pointed out that very few olive presses have been found in the area, certainly no more than would be needed for local consumption; that finds of animal bones suggest that animal husbandry was an important element in the local economy; and that settlement did not come to an end in the early seventh century but continued into the early Islamic period.[60] He argues for mixed peasant farming rather than a specialist economy based on cash crops, but this does not entirely explain the evident prosperity of the area in late antiquity in contrast to a lack of detectable settlement during the first three centuries A.D. and the apparent depopulation of the eighth, ninth and tenth. Villeneuve[61] notes the importance of vineyards in the Ḥaurān, and this is supported by references in the early Islamic sources to the trade in wine and other agricultural products between the Ḥaurān and Arabia in the late sixth century.[62]

There were also significant regional variations. In the limestone massifs of northern Syria and the Ḥaurān, most of the evidence comes from inscriptions on standing buildings. In the area of modern Jordan, however,

---

[58] See Rey-Coquais (1977) 152–61; for prosperity see also Walmsley (1996).
[59] Tchalenko, *Villages*: his general theories are discussed in 1.377–438.
[60] See Tate (1992). See also the extended excavation report from Déhès, a small village in the limestone massif, Sodini *et al.* (1980).   [61] Villeneuve (1985) 121–5.   [62] See Paret (1960).

the most important sources of information are the mosaic floors of churches whose built structures have almost entirely disappeared. These have revealed an astonishing upsurge of building activity lasting until after the Islamic conquests. The most famous of these are probably the mosaics of Madaba (including the famous map of the Holy Land) and Mount Nebo.[63] An illustration of the importance of archaeological evidence in this enquiry can be seen at Petra. Until recently it was thought that Petra in late antiquity was something of a ghost town,[64] but the discovery in 1990 of a major church with high-quality mosaics and marble furnishings must lead to a reassessment of this verdict.[65] At present the church is dated to the late fifth and early sixth century and may have been abandoned after the earthquake of 551. The silence of the literary sources should not lead us to assume that there was no cultural or economic activity in an area.

In Palestine, pilgrims and imperial subsidies for church building must have brought money into the area. Wealthy refugees from the west, like Melania the Younger (d. 439), settled in the area and distributed their vast assets in pious benefactions. The most famous of these patrons was the empress Eudocia (d. 460), who settled in Jerusalem from 441 onward. Though estranged from her husband and the imperial court, she still enjoyed huge wealth, with which she endowed the churches and monasteries of the region.[66] Melania and Eudocia seem to have no parallels in the sixth century, but pilgrims continued to arrive from the west, like the Piacenza pilgrim whose account of his journey (c. 570) still survives,[67] and they must have contributed to the local economy in a more modest way. Justinian's building projects in Jerusalem, the extended *cardo* and the great Nea church, must have brought in revenue as well.

Using this material to examine the general economic history of the area is fraught with problems, and the results of new excavations, like the church at Petra, can suddenly upset accepted hypotheses. At present it looks as if the period from the early fifth century to about 540 was one of gradually expanding settlement and extensive new building of both domestic houses and churches, though there may have been exceptions to this in areas like the countryside around Edessa which were subject to destructive Persian attacks. After the mid sixth century, this expansion of settlement ceased in many areas and regional variations become much more noticeable.

There is some evidence for the decline of the coastal cities, though because of repeated rebuilding, the evidence here is very difficult to assess.

---

[63] See Piccirillo (1989) and Donner (1992).   [64] Gutwein (1981) 13.
[65] For a preliminary publication see Fiema (1993) 1–3; an important find of sixth-century papyri provides new evidence of local economic life.   [66] See Holum, *Empresses*; Hunt, *Holy Land Pilgrimage*.
[67] Antonini Placentini, *Itinerarium* ed. P. Geyer (*CCSL* 175, pp. 127–74); English trans. Wilkinson (1977) 79–89.

There is an almost total absence of literary, archaeological or epigraphic evidence from this area in the second half of the sixth century. Berytus, which had grown in importance in late antiquity, was severely damaged by an earthquake followed by a fire in 550–1, and when the Piacenza pilgrim passed through in about 570 the bishop told him that the famous law school had ceased to function as a result of the earthquake.[68] Smaller towns like Tripolis, Botrys and Byblos are also said to have suffered badly.[69] It may well be the case that the shift of population and economic activity away from the coast to inland towns, like Damascus, Homs and Aleppo, so noticeable in the first century of Muslim rule, may have begun earlier. Further south, Tyre, capital of Phoenicia Libanensis, seems to have preserved some urban life, and the Piacenza pilgrim noted textile manufacture and brothels in the city;[70] its inhabitants put up a vigorous resistance to the attacks of the Persians in the early seventh century. Caesarea,[71] too, seems to have maintained some sort of urban life down to the Muslim conquests, and Arab sources[72] mention a garrison and markets there, though whether this included all the vast area of the antique city or only the restricted fortified perimeter around the theatre is unclear.

The evidence from inland cities is problematic. We can say with some certainty that there is no evidence, literary or epigraphic, of significant construction in the provincial capitals of Apamea, Bostra or Scythopolis after 540, and we know that Apamea was sacked by the Persians in 573 and Bostra by the Arabs in 583. Antioch was rebuilt on Justinian's orders after the Persian conquest of 540 and the earthquake of 542, though the archaeological and literary evidence for this rebuilding is limited. It is also important to stress that we have virtually no information on cities like Beroea and Damascus which may well have been late antique 'success stories'.

Demographically and economically, the rural areas may have been more resilient. The evidence from the limestone massifs of northern Syria seems to show that domestic building virtually ceased after the mid sixth century: in the small but prosperous village of Refada by the monastery of St Symeon Stylites, for example, there is a series of elegant houses, some with columned porticoes, dated from 341 to 516, but nothing from the second half of the sixth century.[73] It seems, however, that the building of churches and monasteries still continued: for example, the monastery of Braij, in the country surrounded by its own fields, seems to have been built in the late sixth century.[74]

---

[68] Antonini Placentini, *Itinerarium* cap. 1, p. 129; cf. Agathias, *Hist.* 11.15.

[69] See Malalas p. 485 Bonn.   [70] *Itinerarium* cap. 2, pp. 129–30.

[71] For a pessimistic assessment of Caesarea in late antiquity see Levine (1985) 135–9.

[72] al-Balādurī, *Futuḥ al-Buldān* ed. M. J. de Goeje (Leiden 1866), pp. 141–2. al-Balādurī also notes (pp. 117–18) that Umayyad rulers made efforts to rebuild and repopulate the coastal cities of Tyre and Acre, which are described as being in ruins, but whether this was the result of the invasions of the early seventh century or a more gradual decline is not clear.   [73] Tchalenko, *Villages* 1.194–7.

[74] Tchalenko, *Villages* 124–5, 158–9, 173.

It may be that church building demonstrates continuing prosperity but there are other possible explanations. One is that the division of the church into separate Monophysite and Dyophysite communities meant that more churches were required to accommodate divided congregations. It is also possible that demographic decline, possibly caused by plague, allowed churches and monasteries to build up large landholdings.

The position in Jordan seems to have been very different, with evidence of large numbers of new, or at least newly decorated, churches from the sixth and seventh century. This prosperity was maintained here in a way in which it was not in the north, especially in the villages and rural monasteries which provide us with the evidence.[75] It may well be that increasing trade with Arabia, notably in wine, oil and grain, was responsible for this, and that the archaeological record confirms the importance of this trade reflected in the early Islamic literary tradition.[76] The evidence from the Negev gives us much less in the way of chronological information, and the Jordanian tradition of mosaic floors seems to have been entirely absent. It is by no means clear whether the depopulation of these settlements was a product or a prelude to the Islamic conquests. The remains of a small mosque beside the entrance to the south church in Subeita[77] suggests that the town was still inhabited in the mid seventh century and that the Muslim settlers were, initially at least, small in number and accepted peacefully.

The causes of change were a combination of natural disasters and foreign invasion. Of the natural disasters, the plague was the most widespread, appearing in the area in 542 and reappearing with grim regularity throughout the late sixth century and, indeed, later.[78] There has been some tendency in the recent literature to play down the effects of plague on society, but there seems no reason to doubt that the loss of life was enormous and that the recurrent outbreaks make it difficult to envisage a sustained demographic recovery. It is also probable that densely populated cities and villages would have suffered worse than nomad areas.

The demographic effects of plague were compounded by a period of violent seismic activity. The most famous earthquakes were those which destroyed Antioch in 526 (in which Malalas estimated that 250,000 people died)[79] and Berytus and other cities of the Lebanese littoral in 551. It seems

---

[75] See the fine series of mosaic floors published in Piccirillo (1994); Whittow (1990).

[76] See p. 604 above, n. 55. The existence of this or any other trade in late pre-Islamic Arabia has recently been questioned by Crone (1987), but, while most scholars would accept that the overland incense trade with South Arabia had long since disappeared, it seems clear that there was still a more localized trade between the pastoralists of the desert and the agriculturalists of the settled areas in such mundane goods as wine, wheat and hides; see ch. 22c (Conrad), pp. 686–8 below.

[77] Shereshevski (1991) 74.

[78] The best account of the plague remains Conrad (1981). See also Conrad (1986). For a sceptical view of the importance of the plague, Durliat (1989) in *Hommes et richesses* and the response by J.-N. Biraben in the same volume, pp. 121–5. The importance of the plague has been reaffirmed in Conrad (1994). [79] Malalas pp. 419–20 Bonn.

that, despite imperial aid, neither Antioch nor Berytus fully recovered from these disasters. These were only the most destructive (and best recorded) of many tremors at this period. The Persian conquests of Antioch in 540 and Apamea in 573 both resulted in widespread destruction and large-scale deportations.

The end of expansion did not mean that the survivors were necessarily impoverished, and it is possible that some individuals may have become more prosperous as they took over vacant land, but it did mean, as in Europe after the Black Death, that many marginal lands were lost to settled agriculture.

The early seventh century saw dramatic changes in the political status of the Byzantine Near East. From 603 Khusro II began his great offensive, ostensibly to avenge the deposition of the emperor Maurice the previous year. This invasion was much more far-reaching than any of its predecessors.[80] Edessa was taken in 609, Antioch in 611 and Jerusalem and Tyre in 614, a campaign in which the Persians were allegedly helped by an uprising of the Jewish population. Persian rule lasted until 628, when Heraclius defeated the Persian armies in Iraq and caused them to withdraw from the Roman near east. The historical sources for the Persian conquest are very poor and the archaeological evidence is not much more helpful: apart from a set of polo goal-posts in the hippodrome at Gerasa, there are no monuments which can be ascribed to the period of Persian rule with any certainty. The extent of the destruction they caused is also problematic, and the nature of the evidence makes it impossible to distinguish damage done by the Persians from that which resulted from the Muslim conquests from 632 onwards.[81]

The Muslim conquest is often seen as a major rupture in the historical continuity of the area, but there is in fact little evidence of widespread destruction. The Arabic sources for the conquests, though full, are often confused about chronology and contain numerous *topoi*, so the detail on specific conquests needs to be treated with some caution,[82] but the general outlines are clear. The earliest Muslim raids seem to have begun in 633, the year after Muḥammad's death. The invaders avoided confrontation with large Byzantine forces but took over much of the land on the fringes of the desert. Probably in 634 Khālid b. al-Walīd arrived with reinforcements from Iraq, and the Muslims began to besiege and take urban centres including Bostra, Scythopolis and Damascus. This provoked a response from the Byzantine authorities, and Heraclius despatched units of the imperial army. However, these were defeated at the battles of Ajnadayn, near Pella, and the Yarmuk between 634 and 636. After this, the way lay

[80] A somewhat lurid narrative account of the Persian conquest is given in Stratos (1968) 107–11.
[81] For the problems of assessing the impact of the Persian invasions, Schick (1992) 107–19; Schick (1995).   [82] See North (1994).

open for the occupation of the rest of the country, including the coastal cities and Antioch itself. By around 647–8 the whole of Syria was in Muslim hands.[83] After the defeat of the Byzantine field armies, most cities surrendered peacefully on easy terms. Only at Damascus and Caesarea does there seem to have been any prolonged and organized resistance.

Our understanding of the Muslim conquests is determined by the view we take of the Near East at the time of their arrival. In the present state of historical research, it is possible to suggest that a major military victory, at the battle of the Yarmuk in 636, was followed by the largely peaceful penetration of a sparsely populated land by nomad or semi-nomad tribesmen, and many of the changes often ascribed to the Muslim conquests, like the decline of the coastal cities and the evolution of new patterns of urban planning, were continuations of trends already established in late antiquity. The Muslims certainly brought a new ruling class, and a new dominant religion and language eventually replaced the Christian Greek and Syriac world of antiquity, but even so, the conquests were only one factor among many in the long evolution of the economic and social life of town and country.

[83] See Donner (1981) 91–155 and Kaegi (1992); ch. 22c (Conrad), pp. 695–9 below.

CHAPTER 21c

EGYPT

JAMES G. KEENAN

By the year 425, Egypt had achieved a provincial arrangement that would last for well over a century.[1] A single province under the principate, it had come under Diocletian to be divided into three smaller provinces. It all began in the last decade of the third century when a new province of Thebaid, coterminous with the old Theban *epistrategia*, was created out of the southern part of the original province of Egypt (Aegyptus); subse-

---

[1] Literary and legal notices for the history of Egypt after 425 are scattered; some will be found in the text and notes below. A text of Justinian's Edict XIII is included in *Corpus Iuris Civilis*, vol. III (*Novellae*), 6th edn, by R. Schoell and W. Kroll (Berlin 1954), 780–95. The fourth-century record of monastic traditions, preserved in Greek, Latin and Coptic texts, yields in the fifth century to the Coptic writings of Shenoute and Besa. What is unique about Egypt, in this as in other periods, is its wealth of documentary evidence preserved on papyrus. Any account of Egypt must rely heavily on this. The years 425–600 are represented by a few papyri in Latin and Coptic, by a great number in Greek, some from the fifth century, but most from the sixth. Important editions include: *P.Monac.* (revised as *P.Münch.*), *P.Lond.* v.1722–37 (for Syene's Patermuthis archive); *P.Cair.Masp.* I–III, *P.Lond.* v, *P.Flor.* III 279–342, *P.Mich.* XIII, *P.Michael.* 40–60 (for Aphrodito); *BGU* XII, *P.Herm.* (for Hermopolis); *P.Oxy.* I and XVI, and *PSI* VIII (for Oxyrhynchus); *Stud.Pal.* III, VIII, XX, *SB*, especially vol. I, *BGU* (*passim*), and some volumes in the *CPR* series, most recently X and XIV (for the Fayum). Papyri from these and other editions are cited according to the conventions set out in J. F. Oates, R. S. Bagnall, W. H. Willis and K. A. Worp, *Checklist of Editions of Greek and Latin Papyri, Ostraca and Tablets* 4th edn (*Bulletin of the American Society of Papyrologists* Suppl. 7: Atlanta, GA, 1992).

The papyrus evidence, despite its richness, has its limitations. One is that it derives from a limited number of sites, none of which can be taken as typical of Egypt as a whole. The most important of these are (from south to north): Syene, Aphrodito, Hermopolis, Oxyrhynchus and the Fayum (Arsinoite nome). Of these, Oxyrhynchus has drawn the most scholarly attention, the Fayum (the state of whose documentation is improving, but still in great disarray) the least.

Besides its geographical spottiness, the papyrus evidence is limited in other, equally important ways. The papyri mostly concern local and regional, rarely imperial events. The plague of 542, for example, extensively described in Procopius (*Wars* II.22–3), finds but one obscure and probably figurative allusion in the papyri (*P.Cair.Masp.* III 67283 with ed. intro.). When papyri do refer to seemingly important events, it is necessary to resort to speculation in seeking their 'fit' into the larger imperial scheme. See, for example, Maehler (1976). Similar, though probably more successful, have been efforts to find the 'fit' between the documentary papyri and the late imperial law codes (esp. *C.Th.*, *CJ*, Just. *Nov.*), though see the remarks of A. H. M. Jones, *JHS* 71 (1951) 271, on how hard it is 'to weave together the bits and patches of the papyri with the tangled skein of the Codes and Novels'.

For bibliographical guidance beyond what is provided here, see A. Bataille, *Les papyrus* (Paris 1955: Traité d'études byzantines II); O. Montevecchi, *La papirologia*, 2nd edn (Milan 1988), pt 4, esp. 259–61, 578 (for papyrus archives); H.-A. Rupprecht, *Kleine Einführung in die Papyruskunde* (Darmstadt 1994), *passim*. My thanks to Terry G. Wilfong for the map that locates places mentioned in this discussion and for advice on Coptic and other late sources.

quently, Libya was separated off to become its own province. Each new province had its own governor, but all three – Aegyptus, Thebaid, Libya – were subject to the plenipotentiary authority of the Augustal prefect, resident in Alexandria.

By the latter part of the fourth century, when Ammianus Marcellinus was penning his well-known digression on Egypt (22.15–16), the threefold division into Aegyptus, Libya and the Thebaid seemed to the historian to have dated 'to ancient times' (*priscis temporibus*); other subdivisions were the creations of more recent times (*posteritas*). A province of Augustamnica, a revival of the short-lived Aegyptus Herculia, consisting of the eastern Delta and the old Heptanomia, had been created out of the territory of Aegyptus, which retained the western Delta, including the city of Alexandria; and the province of Libya had come to be divided into Pentapolis (Libya Superior) and 'Drier' Libya (Libya Inferior).

At some time verging on 381, Egypt's cluster of five provinces became a self-standing diocese, and shortly after, probably between 386 and the century's end, yet another province was created: Arcadia, named for the emperor Arcadius (d. 408), was deducted (mostly) from Augustamnica. First mentioned in the papyri towards the very end of the fourth century, the new province found inclusion in the lists of Egyptian provinces in the *Notitia Dignitatum*, in parts that were probably revised in 395 or shortly after.[2] It was roughly equivalent to the old 'Seven-Nome Region', Heptanomia, but lacked the important middle Egyptian city of Hermopolis, which belonged to the Thebaid.[3]

The six-province nomenclature (Libya Superior, Libya Inferior, Thebaid, Aegyptus, Arcadia, Augustamnica) is, then, the one that is found in the *Notitia Dignitatum*.[4] A half-century later, the same provinces, in a different order, in terms closer to Ammianus' but less correctly spelt, are represented in the *Laterculus* of Polemius Silvius, A.D. 448.[5] All six provinces were directly subject to the Augustal prefect as head of the Egyptian diocese and, through him, subject to the praetorian prefect of the East. It was not until 539 that new, major changes were effected, this time by Justinian. The details were recorded in the emperor's Thirteenth Edict,[6] and from what survives of the edict's damaged text, it is clear that already

---

[2] Kramer (1992); *Notitia Dignitatum* ed. Seeck, *Or.* 1.85, 11.29, XXIII.6 = 13; Jones, *LRE* Appendix 11. Cf. Keenan (1977). See now *P.Oxy.* LXIII 4371, 4385, with introductions; 4386, 10 n.

[3] *SB* 1 5337 mentions five Arcadian cities and one district: Herakleopolis, Cynopolis, Memphis, Letopolis, Nilopolis and 'the Arsinoite'.

[4] *Or.* XXIII.1–14; Augustamnica was mistakenly excluded from *Or.* 1.80–5 and 11.24–9, cf. Jones, *LRE* 1417.

[5] *Not. Dig.* ed. Seeck, pp. 259–60 (*Aegyptus, Augustamnis, Thebaida, Libia sicca, Libia pentapolis, Archadia*), cf. Jones, *LRE* 1451, 1461.

[6] For the vexed question of the edict's date, see Rémondon (1955). For papyrus fragments of the edict, see now *P.Oxy.* LXIII 4400.

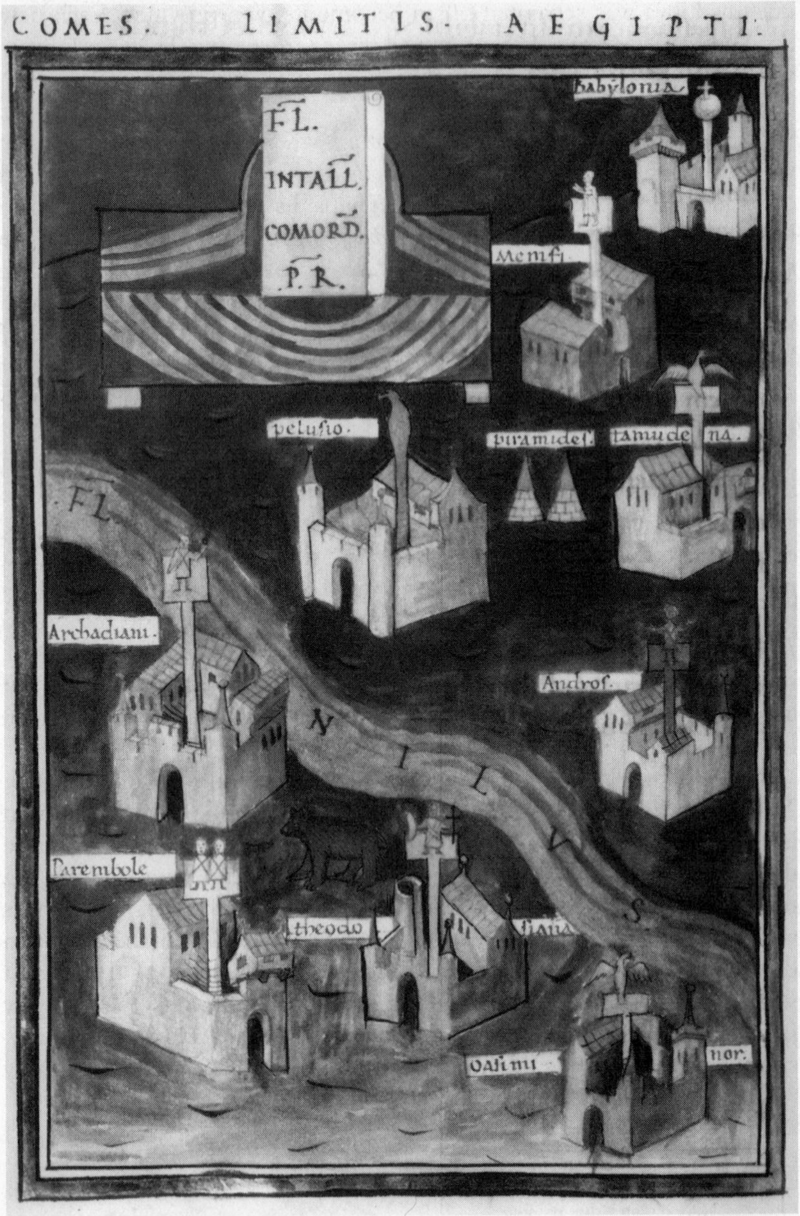

Fig. 18 Leaf from the *Notitia Dignitatum*. Fifteenth-century copy of a Carolingian original. Insignia of the *comes limitis Aegypti* (Count of the Egyptian Frontier) with a schematic map of the Egyptian delta region. The Bodleian Library, Oxford. MS Canon. Misc. 378, fol. 113r. (Photo: courtesy of the Bodleian Library)

some of the Egyptian provinces – Aegyptus, Augustamnica, Thebaid – had been divided in two. By Justinian's reforms, the Augustal prefect was deprived of control over the Egyptian diocese. His exercise of military and civil authority was restricted to Aegyptus I and II, and he had a subordinate civil governor for Aegyptus II. An Augustal duke of the Thebaid had military and civil authority over that province, but with subordinate civil governors for both its upper (southern) and lower (northern) halves. Libya had a duke with a subordinate civil governor.

For the remaining three provinces – Augustamnica, Pentapolis, Arcadia – speculation is needed, because the parts of Edict XIII that concern Augustamnica are damaged, while those that concerned Pentapolis and Arcadia are lost. It has been assumed that Augustamnica, subdivided into I and II, was treated like the Thebaid, Pentapolis – if it was included in the reform – like Libya.[7] The papyri are not as helpful as one might have expected in filling the gaps, if not for Pentapolis,[8] at least for Augustamnica and Arcadia. It is clear none the less from papyri of (mainly) Oxyrhynchite provenance that Arcadia was not subdivided. It had a civil governor, a *praeses*; papyri available to date do not mention a military governor, a *dux Arcadiae*, until A.D. 636.[9] It is therefore possible that Arcadia's treatment in Edict XIII was unlike that of any other province. It may simply have had a civil governor with some coercive police authority; its duke may have been a later creation, perhaps in response to crisis.[10]

In theory, the Egyptian provinces were independent of one another and individually subject, again as for most of the fourth century, to the praetorian prefect of the East. In practice, however, it is difficult to assess the extent to which the subdivided provinces – Aegyptus, Augustamnica, Thebaid – were effectively distinct; and without question, the collection of grain for Constantinople, eight million *artabs* a year according to Edict XIII (chapter 8), required co-operation among all the Egyptian provinces, under the general supervision of the Augustal prefect in Alexandria. Alexandria, strictly speaking, was limited to being the senior capital of the two provinces of Aegyptus; but regardless of its restricted provincial embrace, it remained Egypt's chief city and one of the great metropolises of the eastern empire, an often turbulent centre of education and religion, a thriving centre for manufacture, banking, commerce, shipping and law.[11]

Each Egyptian governor, whether Augustal prefect, duke or *praeses*, had of course his own staff (*officium*, τάξις). A typical civil staff like that of the

---

[7] Jones, *LRE* 281.   [8] Pentapolis in the papyri: *P.Cair.Masp.* II 67168 – a rare glimpse.
[9] *P.Prag.* I 64.   [10] Keenan (1977).
[11] Bowman (1986) ch. 7; Chuvin, *Chronicle* esp. 105–11; *The Coptic Encyclopedia* (New York 1991) 1.95–103, *s.v.* Alexandria in late antiquity (H. Heinen); *P.Oxy.* I 144 (= *FIRA* III.156) and 151; *P.Cair.Masp.* II 67126, with Keenan (1992); *PSI* I 76, with Keenan (1978).

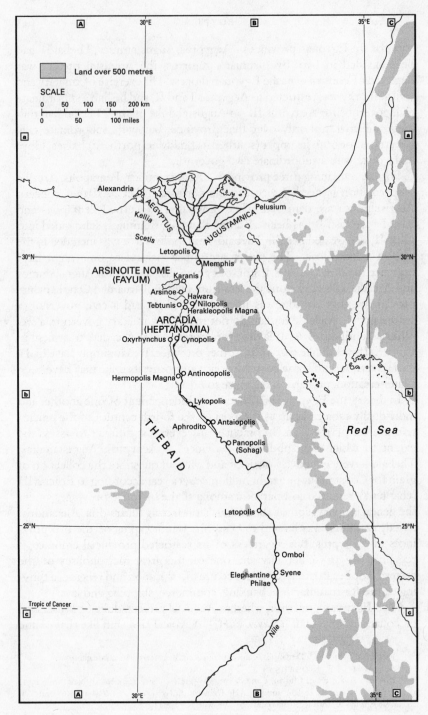

A   30°E   **B**   35°E   **C**

Land over 500 metres

SCALE

| 0 | 50 | 100 | 150 | 200 km |

| 0 | 50 | | 100 miles |

a

Alexandria

Kellia

AEGYPTUS

Scetis

AUGUSTAMNICA

Pelusium

30°N   Letopolis

Memphis

ARSINOITE NOME
(FAYUM)

Karanis

Arsinoe

Hawara

Tebtunis   Nilopolis

Herakleopolis Magna

ARCADIA
(HEPTANOMIA)

Oxyrhynchus   Cynopolis

Hermopolis Magna   Antinoopolis

b

Lykopolis

Aphrodito   Antaiopolis

T H E B A I D

Panopolis
(Sohag)

Red Sea

b

Latopolis

25°N

Omboi

Elephantine   Syene
Philae

Tropic of Cancer

c

Nile

c

A   30°E   **B**   35°E   **C**

Map 17 Egypt

praeses of Thebaid had, according to the *Notitia Dignitatum*,[12] a chief (*princeps*), adjutants (*cornicularius, adiutor*), an accountant (*numerarius*), several types of clerks (*commentariensis, ab actis, a libellis, exceptores*) and other officials (*cohortalini*). The papyri serve to confirm and extend, and to some extent clarify, the often confusing vocabulary of late imperial bureaucracy, but their evidence almost exclusively derives from the provinces of Arcadia and Thebaid. This is due to the often-remarked accidental nature of the finds. Arcadia is familiar because Oxyrhynchus, its capital,[13] is a rich source of late papyri. The Thebaid is well-known because of papyri from its capital, Antinoopolis, but more so because of papyri from other Thebaid provenances, especially Hermopolis and Aphrodito.

This papyrus evidence tends to be casual and scattered and private in nature. A herald (*praeco*) on the staff of the *praeses* in Antinoopolis, for example, borrows money from an Antinoopolite widow; a clerk (*scriniarius*) on the staff of the duke of the Thebaid, originating from Hermopolis, buys part of a house in Antinoopolis; a 'stenographer' (ταχυγράφος) on the staff of the *praeses* of Arcadia, whose home is in the Arsinoite, rents a flat in Oxyrhynchus, no doubt to secure a residence near his workplace.[14] But there are occasions when the evidence on staff officers is more focused. In one private letter, for example, a stenographer (*exceptor*) is seen travelling in the company of his superior, the provincial governor (ἄρχων), probably the *praeses* of Arcadia; the stenographer writes to his mother in Oxyrhynchus. The letter indicates that communication, official and private, was being conducted through aides called *symmachoi* (armed messengers) and *singulares* (despatch riders). Another letter, addressed to an *exceptor*, mentions a *praeses* (ἄρχων), probably (again) the governor of Arcadia, and various members of his *officium*: an *ab actis*, a *numerarius* and *officiales*.[15] Still more important is a late-fifth-century list of officials belonging to the staff of the *praeses* of the Thebaid: two lawyers (*scholastici*) and an assistant lawyer, three chief clerks (*proximi*), an 'assistant in the secretariat', an 'under-assistant' (*subadiuva*), two stenographers (*exceptores*), five despatch riders (*singulares*) and one or more 'couriers' (*cursores*).[16]

Given the variety of titles, it will not be surprising to learn that there were distinctions in grade and rewards among these civil servants, partly depending on the importance of the staff to which they were assigned, partly on whether their work was clerical or not.[17] This is well illustrated in two wills. In one, from sixth-century Oxyrhynchus, Flavius Pousi, a courier (*cursor*) attached to the praesidial (i.e. civil) *officium* of Arcadia, leaves shares of his

---

[12] *Or.* XLIV 6–15, cf. Jones, *LRE* 593–6.

[13] *P.Oxy.* LVIII 3932.6 n., citing Georgius Cyprius, *Descriptio orbis romani* ed. H. Gelzer (Bibl. Teubner), 745.   [14] *P.Mich.* XI 607 (569), *P.Berl.Zill.* 6 (527/65), *P.Oxy.* XVI 1965 (553).

[15] *P.Oxy.* LVIII 3932, *P.Mich.* XI 624 (both sixth century).

[16] *CPR* XIV 39 (late fifth century); cf. *P.Cair.Masp.* I 67054, *P.Oxy.* VIII 1108.   [17] Jones (1949).

house to a religious institution (one half), his wife (one quarter) and another woman (one quarter). His wife receives, in addition to her own clothing and personal ornaments, all the household furniture. The mystery woman receives specified articles, including a platter, three spoons and a third share of the testator's winter and summer clothing; two of Pousi's fellow couriers are assigned the rest of his wardobe. One half of his pension is set aside for burial expenses and, by a common practice, for endowment offerings (προσφοραί) for requiem masses and eucharists (ἀγάπαι) for his soul's repose.[18] The other half goes to his wife. Pousi's elaborate autograph signature to his will, recapitulating its essential terms, is full of mistakes, suggestive of serviceable but unrefined training in letters. Among the witnesses is Pousi's 'boss', the chief (*primicerius*) of the provincial office's school (*schola*) of heralds.[19]

The second will, from several indications a draft, not a final copy, was drawn up in Antinoopolis on 31 March 567.[20] The testator is Flavius Theodore, stenographer (*exceptor*) on the ducal *officium* of the Thebaid, son of a deceased lawyer (*scholasticus*) of the Forum of the Thebaid.[21] The will, in prolix style, names as heirs (1) the monastery of Apa Shenoute in the Panopolite nome, (2) a subsidiary monastery named for Apa Mousaios and (3) Theodore's maternal grandmother, Heraïs. By its provisions, the Shenoute monastery is to receive the bulk of Theodore's landed property, in the Hermopolite, Antinoopolite and Panopolite nomes (and elsewhere), and urban properties in Antinoopolis and Hermopolis, the yearly income and rents from all these to be expended on 'pious distributions'. A house in Antinoopolis, with its stable, inherited from Theodore's father, is to be sold by the monastery, the proceeds to go for the ransoming of prisoners and other 'pious distributions'. Property that had come to Theodore by inheritance from his deceased wife is to be sold off to finance good works in her name. Theodore's movable property is assigned to the Apa Mousaios monastery and is at least partly to be devoted to the remission of his sins. Grandmother Heraïs is to receive a farm (κτῆμα) whose name and location are left blank in the text. Theodore frees all his slaves; they get to keep their 'nest eggs' (*peculia*) and are assigned cash legacies of six *solidi* apiece. Finally, by another legacy, Theodore's nurse and her daughter are to receive by way of trust a yearly pension of twelve *solidi* from his monastic heirs.

The contrast between the estate of Pousi, a non-clerical official on a civil staff, and the estate of Theodore, a stenographer on a ducal staff, can hardly

---

[18] For the practice and for the link between offerings and masses: Wipszycka (1972) ch. III, esp. 65–70. Cf. *P.Cair.Masp.* I 67003.   [19] *P.Oxy.* XVI 1901.

[20] *P.Cair.Masp.* III 67312; *PLRE* IIIB.1253 (Fl. Theodorus 27).

[21] Theodore's name and his position in the ducal *officium* are badly damaged in the papyrus. The editor considered the one 'probable enough', the other 'doubtful'; there is no doubt that, whatever his position, the man was a civilian official on the duke's staff. For convenience' sake the name and title are retained in the discussion that follows.

be more striking. In Pousi's, three spoons merit mention; in Theodore's, the properties are apparently so extensive that no effort is made to describe them in detail. It is no wonder, then, that Pousi has been judged 'a poor man', 'a humble civil servant', Theodore 'a man of rank and substance'.[22] There is no way, however, to determine whether either estate is in any way typical of what a praesidial courier or a ducal stenographer might be expected to have inherited or acquired and bequeathed; but there is a sense that Theodore's substance outstripped his office and that the reverse was true for Pousi. Nevertheless, both wills, but especially Theodore's, raise for any description of late antique Egypt issues of broad concern, to which attention may now be drawn.

First, both wills give evidence of thorough Christianization in sentiment and in fact. Although Christianity by tradition made an early appearance in Egypt, its progress in the countryside is virtually imperceptible in its first three centuries. The most striking documents, so-called *libelli* of the Decian persecution, A.D. 250, are in effect negative evidence (though implying a corresponding positive). These certificates of pagan sacrifice attest that the individuals concerned sacrificed, poured libations and tasted the sacrificial meats – that, accordingly, they were *not* Christian.[23] It is only in the fourth century that Christianization, following the great persecution of 303–4, experienced a 'take-off' of such magnitude as to leave a noticeable imprint in the documentary papyri. As the fourth century progresses, the papyri present increasingly numerous references to churches and clergy, while implying for the latter a hierarchical structure of bishops, priests and deacons.[24] There were later pagan survivals. A festival of the Nile, though perhaps conducted without blood sacrifice, is evidenced as late as 424.[25] Pagans continued to teach philosophy at Alexandria through the fifth and into the sixth century. These included, before his conversion, Flavius Horapollon, native to the village of Phenebythis of Egypt's Panopolite nome, whose metropolis was a hotbed of late antique paganism.[26] The temples on the island of Philai, including the famous Isis temple, remained open and active till their destruction by Justinian's general Narses in the mid sixth century. Nevertheless, Christianity had become virtually universal in Egypt in the fifth century, thoroughly universal in the sixth, penetrating, as a variety of evidence attests, as far south as the First Cataract frontier.[27] Elsewhere, but only by way of example, twelve priests and five deacons, implying the existence of from twelve to seventeen churches in the supposedly declining village of Karanis in the Fayum, are evidenced in a

---

[22] Jones, *LRE* 595–6, 895, 599 (in that order).   [23] *P.Oxy.* LVIII 3929, with intro.
[24] Bagnall, *Egypt* ch. 8, for this and for much that follows.   [25] *P.Oxy.* XLIII 3148.
[26] *P.Cair.Masp.* III 67295, *PLRE* II.569–70 (Fl. Horapollon 2). Cf. Rémondon (1952).
[27] MacCoull (1990).

papyrus of A.D. 439. A century later, ten churches (at least), named for Mother Mary, for the Holy Apostles and for various saints (mainly martyrs), were to be found in the middle Egyptian village of Aphrodito.[28] Churches like these need not have been large either in their physical structures or in their congregations, but they were apparently everywhere.

So also were monasteries – of various kinds and in assorted environments: hermitages in natural caves or in rock-cut Pharaonic tombs on the line of desert hills above the Nile valley; underground dwellings in the desert plains near Esna (ancient Latopolis) in Upper Egypt and at Kellia ('Cells') off the western Delta north of Wadi Natrun (ancient Scetis; Fig. 49, p. 944 below); Pachomian foundations for communal (cenobitic) living on the sites of deserted villages in the Thebaid; Melitian and orthodox monasteries on the Fayum's desert edge near Hawara; but it just so happens that in Theodore's will an especially renowned Coptic monastery comes into play. For the monastery of Apa Shenoute, heir to most of Theodore's estate, was none other than the famous White Monastery (Deir el-Abyad), built around 440 on the 'mountain of Athribis' on the edge of the western desert hills near present-day Sohâg.[29]

Like other monasteries, the White Monastery early on counted on bequests of necessities to help feed and clothe its monks and nuns in a cenobitic community reported to number some 4,000 souls; but as time passed it became an economic force in its own right, able to support by charity thousands of refugees in times of famine and turmoil.[30] By the sixth century, the properties of the White Monastery and other religious institutions in Egypt had become substantial. Besides what it acquired by Theodore's will, the White Monastery under its abbot ('archimandrite') owned land in the arable area of the village of Phthla ('the Cultivation') near Aphrodito in the Antaiopolite nome.[31] Through a lay steward ($\pi\rho o\nu o\eta\tau\dot\eta s$), it leased this land out to a local entrepreneur named Aurelius Phoibammon. He in turn, as middleman, guaranteed the land's farming through a series of sub-leases and work contracts. Similar arrangements must have been in place for the lands the monastery inherited from Theodore. The monastery as landlord would have been, like Theodore himself when alive, an absentee.[32]

Possibly ironical in all of this is that Theodore's will is a most decidedly representative Byzantine Greek document, dictated in Greek for writing in Greek.[33] It favours a community whose early heads – Pgol, Shenoute, Besa

---

[28] *P.Haun.* III 58 (re-edited by J. R. Rea, *ZPE* 99 (1993) 89–95); *P.Cair.Masp.* III 67283.

[29] In addition to Bagnall, *Egypt* ch. 8: Jones (1991); *Vita prima sancti Pachomii* 12, 54; *SB* I 5174–5, with McGing (1990); Gascou (1990). White Monastery: *The Coptic Encyclopedia* III.761–70. Monastery locations: Timm (1983).   [30] Shenoute, *Opera* ed. J. Leipoldt, III.67–71; Leipoldt (1902–3); Kuhn (1954).

[31] *P.Ross.Georg.* III 48 (sixth century).   [32] Keenan (1980) and (1985a).

[33] Like *P.Cair.Masp.* II 67151 (570), the will of Flavius Phoibammon, chief doctor of Antinoopolis. Contrast *MChr.* 319 (sixth century), the will of bishop Abraham of Hermouthis, dictated in Egyptian for transcription in Greek.

Fig. 19 Relief from the upper half of a limestone grave-marker showing a bearded monk with hands raised in prayer. Saqqara, sixth or seventh century A.D. Dumbarton Oaks BL-270. (Photo: courtesy of Dumbarton Oaks, Washington, DC)

– were Sahidic-speaking Copts. The second of these, Shenoute, exhibited in his day a virulent antipathy toward 'Hellenes', that is, Hellenized Egyptians of the upper classes, who would have included in their numbers imperial bureaucrats like Theodore.[34] Moreover, Theodore's will was not only in Greek, but in a very florid Greek. This floridity, construed by earlier scholars as a mark of pomposity and extravagance, servility and degeneracy, is nowadays more likely to be seen as an artful and purposeful extension of the classical rhetorical tradition.[35] Part of the training behind such exercises in the writing of Greek, especially when connected with the study of law, entailed the study of Latin even when it was no longer strictly required.

A natural result was the proliferation of Latin loanwords in late Greek documents from Egypt.[36] One interesting example in Theodore's will is στάβλον, Latin *stabulum*. It will be recalled that Theodore's house in

---

[34] Cf. Trimbie (1986) 268.   [35] MacCoull, *Dioscorus*, esp. ch. 2; Kovelman (1991).
[36] Maas, *John Lydus* 13, 25, 27, 29–30 and *passim*. Loanwords: Daris (1991).

Antinoopolis had a stable, a word that suggests, at the very least, that Theodore owned and kept horses; at most, that, like other landlords of dispersed properties, he had his own 'postal service' (*cursus velox*).[37] He may even have kept racehorses for the circus, a wildly popular entertainment, not only in a megalopolis like Constantinople or Alexandria, but also in Egyptian provincial capitals like Oxyrhynchus and, Theodore's own hometown, Antinoopolis. A unique codex leaf excavated there in 1914 contains a fragmentary painting of five charioteers in Roman dress, wearing the colours of three of the four circus factions (red, blue, green). The physical remains of Antinoopolis' circus suggest it was second in Egypt only to Alexandria's in size and magnificence.[38]

More to the point in Theodore's will, however, is its technical legal vocabulary, which included loanwords like *codicilli* ('codicils'), *epistula fideicommissaria* ('fideicommissary letter') and *peculium* ('nest egg'); but most extraordinary among these words is the reference to a *ius Falcidium* ('Falcidian right') based on a Roman law over six hundred years old, the Lex Falcidia of 40 B.C., whose purpose was to limit legacies to three-quarters the value of an inheritance. In his own will, Theodore seemingly envisages his grandmother complaining that the will's legacies were too great; but he must also have sensed that in any litigation his will should have withstood challenge because so much had been set aside for the kinds of 'charitable purposes' (*piae causae*) favoured in Justinian's legislation.[39]

Much time has so far been spent on Theodore's will, but its value as a mechanism for identifying phenomena typical of late antique Egypt has not quite been exhausted. Three more items are worth remark.

First, in the will's final clauses, Theodore manumits his slaves and establishes trust funds for his nurse and her daughter. Apparent in these measures is a fundamental characteristic of Egyptian slavery in this as in earlier periods of history – that is, slavery was an urban rather than a rural phenomenon. Egypt was a land whose agriculture, even as conducted on great estates, depended on the toil of a large class of peasants, not the efforts of gangs of agricultural slaves. What slaves there were – and these were seemingly much fewer in late than in early imperial times – tended rather to be domestic slaves owned by those in society's higher reaches.[40]

Second, some of the proceeds of Theodore's estate were to be devoted to the pious cause of ransoming prisoners.[41] The will does not specify, but

---

[37] Esp. *P.Oxy.* 1 138 (610/11), Apiones of Oxyrhynchus.

[38] In general: Cameron, *Circus Factions*; Antinoopolis: Turner (1973) (the codex leaf); Humphrey (1986) 513–16.

[39] Berger (1953) 552 *s.v.* Lex Falcidia (citing *Inst.* 11.22, *D.* 35.2; 3; *CJ* VI.50) and 629–30 *s.v.* piae causae (citing *CJ* 1.3). In general: Hagemann (1953). [40] Bagnall, *Egypt* ch. 6. Cf. Fichman [Fikhman] (1973).

[41] Cf. Just. *Nov.* 65 (538), 120.9 (544); Shenoute, *Opera* ed. Leipoldt, III.69–77. In general: Amirante (1957).

Fig. 20 Fragment of a papyrus codex with illustration of five charioteers
(and part of a sixth) wearing jackets in the colours of three of the four circus
factions. Antinoopolis, c. 500. (Photo: courtesy of the Egypt Exploration Society)

the original editor and those who have followed him assume that the prisoners in question were persons kidnapped by desert nomads, especially the
Blemmyes, in raids on the Nile valley. Toward the close of the third century
Diocletian had secured Egypt's southern frontier,[42] but there were later
break-throughs, and the full length of the Nile valley could not, in any
event, always be safeguarded. The Thebaid was especially vulnerable to
attack, and there are indications that the second quarter of the fifth century

[42] Procop. *Wars* 1.19.27–37.

was a time of special tribulation. One Blemmyan captive in this period was the exiled ex-patriarch Nestorius.[43] There followed a revolt by the Blemmyes and Nobades, suppressed by the Romans in 451 and concluded by a treaty whose terms included the ransom-free return of Roman captives.[44] The treaty was soon violated. Sixth-century papyri point to more trouble with the desert tribes, establishing that 'in the olden times of our parents', probably around 500, 'the vile Blemmyes' had ransacked Antaiopolis in middle Egypt, destroying its basilica and its public baths; that the Blemmyes had likewise, later in the sixth century, pillaged the city of Omboi in upper Egypt. By mid century a unit of 'Justinian's Numidians' (*Numidae Iustiniani*), 508 men strong, had been stationed by the emperor's orders at Hermopolis for the purpose of protecting the Thebaid and for the 'repulse of every barbarian attack'.[45] But events and measures like these and like the third Blemmyan war (563–8) must in the end be set against the backdrop of generally peaceful relations between Romans and Blemmyes, the peace achieved by Athanasius, duke of the Thebaid, in the early 570s not long after the drafting of Theodore's will, the tranquil conduct of business between Romans and Blemmyes in Latopolis, and the apparent calm in the First Cataract frontier zone with its garrisons of local militia at Syene, Elephantine and Philai.[46]

Third, Theodore's position shows him to have been a bureaucrat who served in the same provincial government as his father, that of the Thebaid, under its duke. His father, dead by 567, had been a lawyer (*scholasticus*) of the 'Thebaid's Forum', *forum Thebaidos*. Another document may establish that Theodore had a brother serving the same provincial court that his father had served.[47] This tendency of sons to follow their fathers into government service is evidenced elsewhere in the papyri.[48] It was a natural and easy course, but it was also one that came to the attention of late imperial social legislation, especially in the fourth century.[49] By one view, the laws, and particularly *C.Th.* VII.22.2 (331), aimed to enforce hereditary service among staff officials; but by another, the aims were more limited. They were to keep officials from jumping from one *officium* to another, to ensure that sons enrolled in the same *officium* in which their fathers had served, and to see to it that wealthy staff officials on retirement did not escape certain financial obligations to the crown.[50]

---

[43] *W.Chr.* 6, in the new edition by Feissel and Worp (1988) (p. 104 for Nestorius' captivity); Shenoute, *Opera* ed. Leipoldt, III.67–77, with Leipoldt (1902–3).   [44] Priscus fr. 21 (Dindorf).

[45] Antaiopolis: *P.Cair.Masp.* I 67009 v 16–20; Omboi: *P.Cair.Masp.* I 67004; Hermopolis: *P.Cair.Masp.* III 67321, *P.Lond.* v 1663, *SB* v 8028.

[46] Gascou (1975) esp. 206; *P.Cair.Masp.* I 67097 v BC, with MacCoull, *Dioscorus* 113–15 (Athanasius); *BGU* III 972 (Latopolis contract); Keenan (1990) esp. 144–5.

[47] *P.Cair.Masp.* II 67169 + III 67169 *bis*.   [48] *P.Lond.* v 1714; *BGU* I 306 + *SB* VI 9592.

[49] Generally, Keenan (1975).

[50] Jones, *Roman Economy* ch. 21, 396–418, at 403–4; Jones, *LRE* 594–5.

Theodore's following his father in service in the same *officium* thus fits both an expected familial pattern and a pattern sanctioned by late imperial law. But where did provincial staff officials like Theodore ultimately come from? The answer, reasonable but more assumed than proven, is that they belonged to the provincial élite, and in many cases were men of the curial class who in earlier times would have sought recognition through service as members of municipal councils. Although the councils apparently continued to function down into the reign of Anastasius (491–518), the papyrus evidence disappears shortly after 370 when the records for the Oxyrhynchus council (βουλή) come to a close.[51] The curial class, from which members of the municipal councils had been and perhaps continued to be drawn, persevered and sometimes prospered in Egypt to the end of Byzantine rule. Some of its members became counts, others reached high office, many were substantial landowners.[52] Still others must have sought political advancement through government service at the provincial, or even higher, level in a world where despite, or rather because of, the fragmentation of provinces, 'power was more tightly channeled toward the imperial center at Constantinople'.[53]

In this gesture of following his father into bureaucratic service, Theodore, whether of the curial class or not,[54] typified the provincial élite of his age; but he is – finally – representative in yet one last and perhaps most important respect – namely, in representing the common link between private wealth and public service. The wealth, as typical of antiquity as a whole, took the form of landed estates run by agents and stewards for their absentee owners. In fact, the very existence of the provincial political and cultural élites of late antiquity, and of the bureaucracies they served, depended on the possibility and fruits of absentee landlordism. Late antique Egypt presents many examples of this on various levels,[55] but far and away best known is that presented by the Apion family of Oxyrhynchus.

Although the history of the family can be notionally traced back to the mid fifth century, the first known household head with the name Apion only comes into evidence toward the close of the century, and then he appears

[51] Bagnall, *Egypt* ch. 2; Maas, *John Lydus* 19. Later evidence is scrappy and sometimes indirect: Geremek (1990).

[52] Counts: *P.Oxy.* xvi 2002, *Stud.Pal.* xx 218. High office: Bernand (1969) ii.216 (decurion who is *dux et Augustalis* of the Thebaid). *Curiales* as landlords: e.g. *P.Cair.Masp.* i 67113, *SB* vi 9587, *Stud.Pal.* ii 218 (sixth- and seventh-century land leases), *P.Cair.Masp.* ii 67134, 67135, iii 67327, *PSI* viii 935 (sixth-century rent receipts); further (assorted fifth-century evidence): *P.Michael.* 33, *P.Oxy.* vi 902, 913.

[53] Maas, *John Lydus* chs. 1–2. (The quotation is from p. 20.)

[54] If *P.Cair.Masp.* ii 67169 + iii 67169 *bis* concerns his brother, then Theodore's grandfather would have been a count (*comes*). [55] Discussion and examples: Keenan (1974) 284–6 and notes.

as a landlord, not at Oxyrhynchus, but at Herakleopolis Magna.[56] It is this Apion's son, Flavius Strategius, who first appears as a great landlord (γεουχῶν, *magnus possessor*) at Oxyrhynchus in a document dating to 497.[57] The father, still alive, had been honoured with consular rank; the son had attained high, though perhaps purely honorary, military rank as a 'count of the most devoted domestics' (*comes devotissimorum domesticorum*). Apion the father has been identified with 'Apion the Egyptian', the leading patrician who served as 'quartermaster-general' for the army Anastasius despatched to relieve the town of Amida from Persian siege in 503.[58] The expedition failed. Apion, when at Edessa, was relieved of his duties. In May 504 he was, by one account,[59] summoned from Alexandria to Constantinople and charged with having conspired against the expedition's leading general, Areobindus. He apparently spent the next several years in the imperial capital, until the exile that led to his compulsory ordination at Nicaea in 511.

In 518, the accession of Justin I returned Apion to favour and raised him promptly to the praetorian prefecture of the East, perhaps following upon a conversion from Monophysitism to Chalcedonian orthodoxy. The office was not long held. Apion is last mentioned as prefect on 1 December 518; his successor was in place by 19 November 519.[60] He apparently survived into the early years of Justinian's reign, dying by 532 or at some early date in 533. If this is the Apion who is to be credited with having founded his family's fortunes, that effort must have been made in the fifth century, before his sixth-century service and detention abroad, and by means that are lost in the documentary record. It is likelier, though sheerly speculative, that he was not the founder but the inheritor of the family fortune, and that the work of accumulation had been that of his father or grandfather, unknown to us but active in the middle third of the fifth century or even earlier.

Strategius, the son of this Apion, is named in Edict XIII (chapters 15, 16) as having been prefect of Egypt around 523. He reappears in a text of uncertain date as a *magister militum* (στρατηλάτης) with consular rank, both seemingly honorary titles, to which another, the patriciate, was added by 530. At the same time, he was a 'leading citizen' (πρωτεύων) of both Herakleopolis and Oxyrhynchus.[61] In 532 he presided over a synod of

---

[56] *SB* vi 9152 (492), *Stud.Pal.* xx 129 (497); cf. (perhaps) *P.Oxy.* xvi 1877 (*c.* 488). Discussions on the family and its members: *P.Oxy.* xvi 1829.24 n.; Hardy (1931) and (1968); *PLRE* ii.110–12 (Apion 1, Apion 2, Fl. Apion 3), 1034–6 (Fl. Strategius 8 and 9) and Stemma 27 on p. 1325; Gascou (1985) esp. App. 1 (pp. 61–75), with full presentation of the evidence. An earlier generation of the family has been recently identified. See *P.Oxy.* lxiii 4389 (439) and references in the note to line 1.

[57] *P.Oxy.* xvi 1982. A possible earlier (489) appearance is in *P.Flor.* iii 325 (cf. Gascou (1985) 63 n. 356) where Strategius (restored) appears as a *politeuomenos*, i.e. *curialis*, of Oxyrhynchus and *magnus possessor* (γεουχῶν).

[58] Hardy (1931) 25–6, Gascou (1985) 62, *PLRE* ii.111–12 (Apion 2); *contra P.Oxy.* 1829.24 n.

[59] Josh. Styl. *Chron.* (Wright) 58.   [60] *CJ* vii.63.3; v.27.7.

[61] *P.Oxy.* xvi 1984; xxvii 2779, similarly in xvi 1983 of A.D. 535. The significance of the term πρωτεύων is unclear: Hardy (1931) 32 n. 4; Gascou (1985) 64; *PLRE* ii.1036.

Monophysite and Chalcedonian bishops at Constantinople. Shortly after, he began service as the empire's chief financial officer, count of the sacred largesses. Besides duties that must have included overseeing the financing of the construction of St Sophia, Strategius served on several occasions as Justinian's roving ambassador. It is assignments like these that suggest that the ordinary consulship bestowed in 539 upon his son, Flavius Apion (II), was a reward or memorial for the father's distinguished career, an honour to the family more than to Apion the man, who – to judge from the portrait medallion on his consular diptych, discovered in 1860 in the cathedral at Oviedo (Spain) – was still quite young, destined to survive his own consular year by nearly forty more.[62]

With this appointment, the Apion family reached its political zenith. Flavius Apion II first appears in the papyri in 543 as *consul ordinarius* and great landlord at Oxyrhynchus. As late as 577 he appears as former ordinary consul, patrician and great landlord. His death fell between 577 and 579.[63] It is to be presumed that Apion spent the earlier part of his public career in the imperial capital, but returned to Egypt toward mid century, 548/50, to take up his post as duke of the Thebaid.[64] After that, he served for a long time as pagarch in the pagarchy of the Arsinoites and Theodosiopolites (the old Arsinoite nome) where some of his ancestral property lay. In this office, his primary responsibility was the collection of taxes for those parts of the district that were not specifically excluded from his authority by imperial grants of 'autopragia'.[65] Apion appears first in this office, and also as *magister militum*, in 556; subsequently as pagarch and ex-consul.[66] The extent to which he exercised his duties as pagarch by proxy, rather than in person, is an insoluble problem. He was still pagarch at the time of his death, by which time (unless it was a posthumous honour) he had also been named 'first patrician' (*protopatricius*), perhaps implying his presidency of the senate in Constantinople.[67] Following his death, his estate went undivided to his heirs, the most important of whom was his son, another Strategius, Strategius II, about whom little is known.[68]

It is the usually unnamed heirs of Apion II who prevail in the family's documentary record from 579 till 586/7, when they at last escape from anonymity.[69] When they do, the heirs turn out to be Flavia Praeiecta, a woman

[62] Hardy (1931) 32; Gascou (1985) 65; *PLRE* IIIB.1200–1 (Strategius). Apion diptych: *CIL* II.2699 = Dessau, *ILS* I.1310; medallion: Schefold (1945) with plates 3 and 4; career: *PLRE* IIIA.96–8 (Fl. Strategius Apion Strategius Apion 3). [63] *P.Oxy.* XVI 1985; 1896; I 135.

[64] *P.Oxy.* I 130, with *P.Lond.* V 1708.79 and the long discussion in the relevant note, together with Gascou's equally long discussion of the attendant dating (and other) problems: (1985) 66 n. 370.

[65] Liebeschuetz (1974). Synoptic discussion and full bibliography: *The Coptic Encyclopedia* VI.1871–2, s.v. Pagarch (B. Verbeeck). [66] *BGU* I 305, *CPR* XIV 10.

[67] *P.Oxy.* XVI 1976 (582) and other documents; Gascou (1985) 66 and references in n. 374.

[68] *P.Oxy.* XVI 1829 is the key proof, though far from problem-free, of Strategius II's position as principal heir to Apion II. [69] *P.Oxy.* I 135, many other refs. in Gascou (1985) 68 n. 382.

of consular rank (ὑπάτισσα, *femina consularis*), either the wife or the sister of Strategius II (who had apparently died), and her two sons – another Apion (Apion III) and George, both with honorary consular rank.[70] George appears so far only once in the papyri; Praeiecta and Apion appear in tandem in papyri of 590 and 591, the mother acting with and possibly on behalf of her son, still a minor.[71] By 593, Apion is acting on his own and Praeiecta has disappeared.[72] His marriage to Eusebia, daughter of a Roman aristocratic family with friendly ties to the future pope Gregory the Great, must already have taken place.[73]

Apion III appears in documents of 593 and later as sole owner of the family's estates in Oxyrhynchus and as honorary consul. By 604/5 he had attained the patriciate and continued to hold that dignity till (at least) mid year 619. He was dead by the very beginning of 620, but his 'glorious household' continued as an economic unit for another year or so, fading from history early in the decade of the Persian conquest and occupation (619–29).[74] Apion III had, among other children, a son, Strategius (III), still a youth at the turn of the century, and no longer confused (as he once was) with another Flavius Strategius, a contemporary of Apion III, who was apparently from a collateral line of the family that was more active in the Arsinoite and Herakleopolite nomes than in the Oxyrhynchite. This older Strategius, first mentioned in a papyrus of 591,[75] and now commonly referred to as 'pseudo-Strategius III', was himself an honorary consul, and eventually a patrician. He is perhaps best known from documents of the first decade of the seventh century that show him as pagarch of the Arsinoite and Theodosiopolite pagarchy, as Apion II had been before him.[76] A person of eminence, he is credited with having prevented a schism between the Egyptian Monophysite and Syrian churches at an Alexandrian synod in 616;[77] but like Apion III, pseudo-Strategius III and his household disappear from history in the early years of the Persian occupation.

It is clear from this summary that the Apion family had a long and distinguished history, traceable for some six generations from the late fifth into the early seventh century. If there are any trends to be perceived in all this,

---

[70] *P.Oxy.* xviii 2196; *PLRE* iiib.1049 (Fl. Praeiecta 2). Praeiecta appears in most discussions (and stemmata) as Strategius II's wife; for arguments that she was his sister: *CPR* xiv, p. 43 n. 1.

[71] *PLRE* iiia.515 (Fl. Georgius 10); *P.Oxy.* xix 2243, xvi 1989–90, *P.Erl.* 67.

[72] *P.Oxy.* xviii 2202, additional refs. in Gascou (1985) 70 n. 387, to which may be added numerous new references in *P.Oxy.* lviii.

[73] Cameron (1979) 225–7; Gascou (1985) 70; *PLRE* iiia.98–9 (Fl. Apion 4). Eusebia and her mother figure often in Gregory's epistles, but leave no imprint in the documentary papyri.

[74] Details in *P.Oxy.* lviii 3939.4–5 n., 3959 intro.   [75] *P.Oxy.* lviii 3935.

[76] Gascou (1985) 70–1 and n. 392; *CPR* xiv, pp. 41–8; *PLRE* iiib.1203–4 (Fl. Strategius 10).

[77] Hardy (1931) 35–6, Gascou (1985) 70–1.

one is that earlier household heads were more prominent than later ones on the imperial political scene; Apion I and Strategius I must often have been away from home on foreign assignment. It was once thought that the later Apiones had retrenched, content with honorary dignities and provincial or local offices, possibly becoming more Egyptian than their predecessors, possibly reconverting to Monophysitism, choosing to live in Egypt instead of the imperial capital. It is now thought that the family's glory remained undimmed and that its members continued to move in Constantinople's social circles, spending more time away from than in Egypt.[78]

What the papyri contribute to the corporate history of the Apion family is a rough but, as new papyri come to be published, increasingly refined chronological outline of births and deaths, of offices held and honours bestowed. This in itself is an important contribution, but it is rather to an understanding of the economic foundation for the Apion social and political success, the family's landed wealth and its management, that the papyri contribute most. A full treatment cannot be given here, but a sketch of the Apion holdings at Oxyrhynchus (the best-known) and the principal features in their management cannot be avoided.[79]

Although hard statistical evidence is lacking, one estimate, with an indirect basis on payments in kind for the ἐμβολή (grain shipments for Constantinople), puts the extent of Apion holdings in the Oxyrhynchite nome and the neighbouring Cynopolite at 112,000 arouras (75,000 acres) out of a total available 280,000 arouras, roughly two-fifths the arable land in those districts.[80] The presence of twenty stewards, προνοηταί, in an account for Apion holdings just in the Oxyrhynchite is another telling if imprecise indication, as is the fact that each pronoêtês normally had charge of several 'estates' (κτήματα).[81] Apion holdings in the Arsinoite and Herakleopolite nomes are assumed also to have been large, but the documents give no inkling whatsoever of their measure. Whatever their size, the usual view is that the Apion estates did not conform to modern notions of what estates are. That is, they did not form in any given area a coherent territorial block. Instead they were scattered through various rural hamlets (ἐποίκια) in the orbits of nome villages. The spread of the Apion properties, not only in the Oxyrhynchite and neighbouring Cynopolite districts, but also in the Herakleopolite and Arsinoite, together with the frequent absenteeism of the family heads, necessitated for their operation an extensive private bureaucracy of agents (διοικηταί), clerks (chartularii), stewards (pronoêtai), and bankers. It also required a communications network that included both an 'express post' (cursus velox) and a slow post by land, with

[78] Gascou (1985) 74–5; Cameron (1979) 225–7, esp. 225 n. 22, 227 n. 34.
[79] I rely heavily on Hardy (1931) for what follows. [80] Jones, LRE 780, 784.
[81] P.Oxy. xvi 2032, 1 136 (= WChr. 383).

their stables and riders (*symmachoi*, messengers), and estate boats with their sailors (ναῦται) for river travel and transport.[82]

The earliest document from the Oxyrhynchite part of the archive, A.D. 497, includes features that show that the Apion estate system was already fully developed and brings the realization that, despite efforts to the contrary,[83] barring new discoveries, there will never be any way for the historian to trace its origins or early development. The document in question[84] is of a type common in the archive, a so-called receipt for agricultural machinery. In its formulaic structure there lies an embedded narrative, a little drama:[85] an Apion tenant acknowledges that he has found need of a piece of agricultural machinery, in this case (as in many others: presumably axles were most liable to wear or breaking) a new axle for a water wheel (μηχανή). He has 'gone up' from his rural hamlet (ἐποίκιον), part of an Apion estate (κτῆμα), to the city, Oxyrhynchus, and received the needed part. He promises to irrigate faultlessly a plot of land called Thryeis. He will in due time pay his rents to the estate account.

Typical features include the Apion ownership of the 'means of production' – not just the land, but the estate's more expensive equipment: the irrigation machines and their spare parts, in addition to the oil presses, mills and bakeries evidenced in other documents. The Oxyrhynchus estate's 'company store' lies in the city, but the farmlands are outside. Typical is the formulary on which this specific document is based: the resulting document turns out to be more like a formal contract between two parties, landlord and tenant, than would seemingly be required in the normal course of operating an agricultural enterprise, where a verbal agreement or a short written receipt should have sufficed. The formula is not only elaborate, but long-lasting; it is found as late as 616.[86] Most significant is that the tenant farmer is styled an ἐναπόγραφος γεωργός in the Greek text, a term which is a linguistic equivalent to a Latin term found in the late imperial law codes: *colonus adscripticius*. The laws proclaim that the status of such individuals was barely distinguishable from that of slaves.[87] They were, it seems, 'tied to the soil'; but this, according to a recent argument,[88] was accomplished, not by public intervention, but by a process of private registration or listing (ἀπογραφή). The tenant first entered upon a contractual arrangement with his landlord (a work contract, a lease). The landlord then agreed to pay his tenant's taxes for him and the tenant came to be registered in his landlord's census.

Curiously, nearly all *enapographoi* in the papyri are to be found in documents from Oxyrhynchus,[89] and most of these Oxyrhynchite documents

---

[82] See esp. *P.Oxy.* I 136 (= *WChr.* 383), contract for hire of a *pronoētēs*, A.D. 583.

[83] Fikhman (1975).   [84] *P.Oxy.* XVI 1982.   [85] Hardy (1931) 127–8.   [86] *P.Oxy.* XVI 1991.

[87] E.g. *CJ* XI.48.21 (530), Jones, *LRE* 801; but for the realities, see Fikhman (1991) and Sirks (1993).

[88] Sirks (1993).

[89] Exceptions: *SB* XVIII 13949 (541): Oxyrhynchite landlords, two *enapographoi* from a Herakleopolite hamlet.

concern the Apions and their tenants. Besides showing Apion *coloni* going up to the city for machinery parts, they frequently show them being sworn for in documents that have come to be called sureties or guarantees (*cautionnements*, *Bürgschaft-urkunden*).[90] In some of these the formulary is, like that for agricultural machinery receipts, surprisingly elaborate and equally long-lived.[91] In a leading example of the genre,[92] an Oxyrhynchus lead-worker named Aurelius Pamouthius goes bail for a *colonus* named Aurelius Abraham from the Apion estate (*ktêma*) of Great Tarouthinas in the Oxyrhynchite nome. Pamouthius guarantees that Abraham will remain on his assigned estate together with his 'family and wife and animals and furniture'. If Abraham's presence is required by his landlords (the heirs of Apion II), Pamouthius will ensure Abraham's production in the same public place where he received him, 'the jail of the said glorious house'.

The mention of the jail of the glorious house suggests that the Apiones exercised a coercive authority that impinged on the official coercive authority of the government. This, in fact, was reinforced by their employment of soldiers known as 'doughboys' or 'biscuit eaters', *bucellarii*.[93] These in Apion estate accounts appear often to be of foreign, sometimes Gothic, origin; they were paid in kind (in grain, meat, wine and oil) and in cash, and served the glorious house as a mercenary police force.

The presence of an estate jail and the employment of *bucellarii* are at first glance shocking because these were two practices, following upon that of patronage, that late imperial legislation tried vainly to check – yet the Apiones were closely connected to the imperial court.[94] And these two practices, added to the existence of great estates farmed by *coloni adscripticii* ('serfs'), are most responsible for the impression that the Apion household, that Oxyrhynchus with its other great landlords, that late antique Egypt as a whole was 'feudal' in the medieval sense of the term, and that the great houses of Egypt were resistant to and in conflict with the imperial government.[95] Nowadays, it is argued that the Apion and other great houses of Egypt were not working in conflict with the imperial government, but rather with its (eventual) approval and sanction. It is not only that *bucellarii* may have been at least semi-official in character,[96] privately mustered with government approval, but that if private interests in Egypt had not (for example) assumed the upkeep and repair of the irrigation works, the economy would have collapsed and the imperial capital itself would have

[90] Summary discussion with a list of parallel documents in Fikhman (1981).

[91] Latest example, *P.Oxy.* LVIII 3959 (Persian period, 620).

[92] *P.Oxy.* I 135 (579), with several reprintings: *WChr.* 384, Meyer, *JJP* 51, *Sel.Pap.* I 26, *FIRA* III 13.

[93] Hardy (1931) esp. 60–71, cf. Robinson (1968); Liebeschuetz, *Barbarians and Bishops* 43–7; Schmitt (1994).   [94] Keenan (1975) esp. 243–4 and n. 14.

[95] Early and most influential presentation of the 'feudal model': Bell (1917). See Keenan (1993).

[96] Gascou (1985). Cf. on the *bucellarii* Liebeschuetz, *Barbarians and Bishops* 43–7.

Fig. 21 Deed of surety sworn by a lead-worker, Aurelius Pamouthius, on behalf of Aurelius
Abraham, *colonus adscripticius* to the heirs of the Oxyrhynchus landlord, Flavius Apion, 579. *P.Oxy.*
135. (Photo: courtesy of the Egypt Exploration Society. Copyright: The Egyptian Museum, Cairo)

become vulnerable to famine.[97] The new view may in effect be more a refinement than a rejection of the feudal model. Whether the new view is right or not (it does seem to fly in the face of some of the legal evidence), the old one was wrong in laying too much stress on, and generalizing too much from, the evidence from Oxyrhynchus, to the neglect of other sites: Hermopolis, for example, one of whose estates was judged on the basis of a long agricultural ledger to have been 'managed with great wisdom and great humanity',[98] and even more so the middle Egyptian village of Aphrodito.

The sixth-century history of that village and its regional and imperial connections can be partially reconstructed thanks to the survival of an archive preserved by one Flavius Dioscorus.[99] Although Dioscorus himself was probably not born until around 520, the archive includes a few papers of earlier date. The family's Egyptian roots are intimated by the name of its earliest known member, 'old man Psimanobet',[100] who presumably reached his prime in the mid fifth century. Psimanobet, whose Egyptian name signified 'son of the gooseherd', had a son, Dioscorus, who in turn had children, including a son named Apollos. It is this Apollos, father of Flavius Dioscorus, whose activities come to light initially in the Dioscorus papyri. He first appears in 514 as a village headman (πρωτοκωμήτης) of Aphrodito, appearing later, in the 530s, as a member of the village's board of 'contributaries' (συντελεσταί), jointly responsible for the village's tax collection.[101] He may also have served the local great landlord, count Ammonius, as 'collector' (ὑποδέκτης);[102] but all the while he was operating as an entrepreneur in his own right, taking land in lease concurrently from many absentee landlords – from curiales of Antaiopolis, from bureaucrats and lawyers from Panopolis and (probably) Antinoopolis, and from one of the village churches. He sublet these parcels or saw by other means to their being worked by a local force of free tenant farmers.[103] In the last decade of his life, by 538, Apollos became a monk,[104] without fully retiring from worldly business. The year 541 found him in the imperial capital in the company of his fraternal nephew, a priest named Victor. There the two villagers took out a loan of twenty solidi from a banker named Flavius Anastasius, a 'waiter of the sacred table', due for repayment four months

[97] See on the irrigation works, their operation and maintenance, Bonneau (1970), with special attention to the Apiones.   [98] Schnebel (1928).

[99] Discussions of the village and its chief family: Bell (1944); Keenan (1984a); MacCoull, Dioscorus esp. 1–15; Gagos and van Minnen (1994). Dioscorus' career: PLRE IIIA.404–6 (Fl. Dioscorus 5), differing in some details from what is presented here.   [100] P.Lond. v 1691.15–16.

[101] First appearance: P.Flor. III 280; Apollos' career: Keenan (1984b).

[102] Hardy (1931) 144; Thomas (1987) 61, 72, approved by MacCoull (1993a) 21 n. 2. Count Ammonius: PLRE IIIA.56–7 (Fl. Ammonius I).

[103] A critical document is P.Cair.Masp. III 67327; discussion: Keenan (1985a), cf. Thomas (1987) 72–3.   [104] PSI VIII 933.

later in Alexandria.[105] Before his death in 547 Apollos founded a monastery named for the 'Holy Christ-Bearing Apostles', appointing his own son,
the family's second Dioscorus, as the foundation's lay 'curator' (φρον-
τιστής).[106]

This Dioscorus, so it seems, received a fine literary, rhetorical and legal
education, paid for by his entrepreneurial and upwardly mobile father. It is
usually assumed that this educational polish was applied in Alexandria, a
flourishing, cosmopolitan 'university town', where, in Dioscorus' day, a
major intellectual figure would have been John Philoponus,[107] the prolific
grammarian, philosopher and theologian. So it is perhaps a bit ironic that
in Dioscorus' first dated occurrence in the papyri, in A.D. 543, he appears
as victim of a typically rustic trespass: the standing crops in a field he was
holding, apparently under lease from a local monastery, had been trampled,
uprooted and mired, thanks to an unruly drover who had run his sheep
through them.[108] Like his father before him, Dioscorus travelled to
Constantinople. He was there in 551 to defend the right of Aphrodito to
collect its own taxes (the privilege called 'autopragia', 'self-collection')
without interference from the district's pagarch. It was on that visit that he
and some fellow villagers secured a rescript from Justinian and hired two
exsecutores negotii ('executors of the business'), one of them a count of the
sacred consistory, both of them citizens of Leontopolis in Cappadocia, to
assist in enforcing the village's claimed rights against the pagarch's alleged
violations back home.[109] That in Constantinople he met Romanos the
Melodist, and in later retrospect commemorated the occasion with an
acrostic poem in his honour, is an attractive but problematic bit of speculation.[110]

Back in Egypt, Dioscorus had by A.D. 566 taken up residence in the provincial capital, Antinoopolis. There he put his legal training to use, settling
disputes and drawing up contracts and other documents in Greek and in
Coptic,[111] including the will of Flavius Theodore discussed above. This was
one of many papers Dioscorus brought back to Aphrodito on his return
in 573. The remarkable thing about the documents written in Antinoopolis
is that they were often on very large sheets of papyrus which Dioscorus
saved for scrap. On their versos he composed, in autograph drafts showing

[105] *P.Cair.Masp.* II 67126; discussion: Keenan (1992).
[106] See esp. *P.Cair.Masp.* I 67096, cf. Thomas (1987) 64, 73.
[107] *RE* IX.2 (1916) 1764–95 (Kroll).   [108] *P.Cair.Masp.* I 67087, with Keenan (1985b).
[109] Critical documents include *P.Cair.Masp.* I 67024 (rescript), 67032 (contract with *exsecutores negotii*,
also accessible as Meyer, *JJP* 52 and *FIRA* III 179), *SB* IV 7438 (letter of recommendation for
Dioscorus); synoptic discussion with pertinent references: Keenan (1975) 244–6. Further, esp. on
P.Cair.Masp. 67024: Geraci (1979) with extensive bibliography.
[110] Kuehn (1990) (for the connection); van Minnen (1992) esp. 97–8 (opposed).
[111] MacCoull, *Dioscorus* esp. ch. 2 (pp. 16–56); cf. MacCoull (1981) and (1986b) (= MacCoull (1993b)
chs. XII and X).

corrections, what were once judged the last and worst Greek poems – birthday and wedding poems, panegyrics, encomiums and 'salutations' (χαιρετισμοί) – antiquity had produced; but these are now being re-evaluated with a new sense of their artistry that largely stems from a new appreciation for the *Weltanschauung* they reveal.[112] They are the bookish poems of a scholar whose library included codices and rolls of Homer, Aristophanes, Menander (including a likely lawyer's favourite, the arbitration scene from the *Epitrepontes*)[113] and Eupolis, the poetry of Anacreon, a life of the orator Isocrates and a Greek–Coptic glossary.[114]

This archive, then, was the collection of an educated, bilingual, perhaps even trilingual, lawyer; it is full of information on Dioscorus' general milieu, but also on more mundane matters like his village's society and economy. In this evidence we find that, in contrast to the great landlords of Oxyrhynchus and their *coloni*, Aphrodito's core was its small landholders.[115] 'For the village consists of smallholders (λεπτοκτήτορες)', according to a long petition to the duke of the Thebaid,[116] and wretched though they at times claim to have been (when it suited their purposes),[117] they seem on the whole to have been prosperous and well-organized: prosperous enough to send delegations to Constantinople to plead their case before the crown, and organized into a '*collegium* of village headmen (πρωτοκωμῆται), contributaries (συντελεσταί) and landowners (κτήτορες)' to represent the village in its formal business.[118] The village claimed, besides, the special protection of the 'divine house' (*divina domus*) of the empress Theodora and could gather as signatories in a report to her: eleven priests, a reader, a deacon and a monk; twenty-two landholders and a village headman; two notaries; the heads of the guilds of smiths, fullers, carpenters, weavers, boatwrights, wine merchants – and more.[119]

The village itself,[120] a former nome metropolis since demoted, dominated a number of surrounding satellite villages. Located on a tell in the Nile flood-plain, it was surrounded by land in quarters (πεδιάδες) named for the four main compass points. The land was sometimes classed as estates (κτήματα), farms (γεώργια) and pastures (βοσκήματα), in an apparently descending order of value. Estates, sometimes amply described, included such things as cisterns, wine vats, towers, vegetable gardens, vineyards and

---

[112] Early (negative) appraisal: Maspero (1911). Current standard edition for most of the poems: Heitsch (1963) 127–52; a new edition by J.-L. Fournet is in preparation. See further Viljamaa (1968). Re-evaluation: Baldwin (1984) II.327–31; MacCoull, *Dioscorus* esp. ch. 3 (pp. 57–146); Kuehn (1995).

[113] This point is made in Gagos and van Minnen (1994) 33–4.

[114] List of works: Bell (1944) 27; Homer: *P.Cair.Masp.* II 67172–4; life of Isocrates: *P.Cair.Masp.* II 67175; Anacreon: *P.Cair.Masp.* I 67097 v F, with MacCoull, *Dioscorus* esp. 119–21; glossary: Bell and Crum (1925). [115] For much of what follows: Keenan (1984a). [116] *P.Lond.* v 1674.95–6.

[117] E.g. *P.Cair.Masp.* I 67002.2. [118] *P.Cair.Masp.* I 67001.

[119] *Divina domus*: Zingale (1984–5); signatories: *P.Cair.Masp.* III 67283 with intro. and Jones, *LRE* 847–8. [120] Topographical and other data in Calderini (1966) 303–414.

orchards with trees of various kinds – date palms, olives, mulberries, citrons, acacias.[121] There were monasteries outside the village and numerous churches within. Also within were private houses, some of reputed grandeur, and in one part of town, houses owned or formerly owned by a shepherd, a vetch-seller, a cook, a smith, a headman and a priest.[122] There must also have been houses or shops in which artisans plied their crafts – smiths, fullers, carpenters, weavers, the boatwrights who made wickerwork skiffs for canal and river travel – and where wine merchants sold their wares.[123] There were walled-in gardens in the residential areas; a record office, storehouse, threshing-floor, guardhouse; an olive works on Isis street; potteries and a monastic hostel.[124]

The sense conveyed by all of this – when added to the agrarian dealings of Apollos, the literary efforts of his son, and the villagers' journeys to Constantinople – is one of vitality, activity and variety, not, as was once maintained, 'appalling dullness'; and the sense of variety might be further developed by appealing to other archives: the Taurinus archive from Hermopolis, for example, with its landowning soldiers and bureaucrats, or the Patermuthis archive from Syene (modern Aswan), with its border guards and boatmen, house sales and inheritance disputes.[125] The Dioscorus archive ends with unfortunate abruptness with a document of no great significance, a pasture lease dated to 5 April 585;[126] but Dioscorus' village reappears in the early eighth century with another important (and final) Greek-Egyptian archive, embodied in the correspondence between the district pagarch, Flavius Basilius, and the Arab governor of Egypt, Kurrah ibn Sharik. There the linguistic shift from administrative Greek to Arabic is clearly seen to be under way.[127]

The intervening years, in particular those down to 642, were marked by a turbulent and confusing rush of events, of great significance for Egypt and for the Byzantine empire at large. The record, especially for events set forth in the damaged, biased but invaluable *Chronicle* of John, bishop of Nikiu,[128] gives an unremitting series of examples of courage and cowardice, carnage and cruelty on all sides. There was, of course, the familiar street violence in Alexandria, ignited by politics and religion, tempered at

---

[121] See esp. *P.Mich.* xiii 666, cf. *P.Cair.Masp.* 1 67097 r, iii 67300.8–9, *P.Lond.* v 1695.4–9, *P.Michael.* 48.16–17.   [122] *P.Cair.Masp.* 1 67002 ii 24 (grand old houses); *P.Mich.* xiii 665.

[123] Evidence in MacCoull (1984) (= MacCoull (1993b) ch. xx). Comparable variety in other Egyptian locales: Fikhman (1965) (in Russian).

[124] Calderini (1966) 303–414: *P.Lond.* v 1691, *P.Cair.Masp.* 1 67109 (gardens); *P.Flor.* iii 285 (olive works).

[125] Taurinus archive: *BGU* xii, with extensive introduction by H. Maehler, cf. now also Palme (1994). Patermuthis archive: *P.Münch., P.Lond.* v 1722–37, with Farber (1986) and the series of articles in *BASP* 27 (1990) 111–62.   [126] *P.Cair.Masp.* iii 67325 iv r.   [127] See e.g. *P.Lond.* iv, cf. Abbott (1938).

[128] Charles (1916).

times by the charities of John III, 'the Almsgiver', the revered Chalcedonian patriarch, 610–19.[129] Just before his patriarchate, Alexandria was thrown into turmoil by the revolt of Heraclius against the unpopular emperor Phocas. The very end of his patriarchate was attended and followed by the Persian invasion and occupation of 619–29.[130] This in turn was prelude to the Arab invasion and the final occupation of Egypt, 639–42, under ʿAmr ibn al-ʿAsi. In these last-mentioned years began the process whereby Egypt and its people adopted the Arabic language and became overwhelmingly Islamic in faith. So also began the process whereby Greek culture in Egypt disappeared and the indigenous Coptic culture was much eclipsed.[131] As a result of the Arab conquest, in addition to the magnificent city of Alexandria, the Byzantine empire forever lost Constantinople's principal source of food and a substantial portion of the annual imperial revenues.[132] The human toll, especially at the beginning of this transformation, was, by all accounts, enormous. The story of what happened in that period was, at the beginning of the twentieth century, brilliantly reconstructed and retold, but in an old-fashioned, largely pre-papyrological way.[133] That story, which continues the one sketched above, now begs retelling with a full accounting for the papyrological evidence.[134]

[129] Monks (1953).
[130] *The Coptic Encyclopedia* VI.1938–41, *s.v.* Persians in Egypt (R. Altheim-Stiehl).
[131] MacCoull (1989) (= MacCoull (1993b) ch. XXVI); and see also Samir (1986).
[132] Haldon, *Byzantium in the Seventh Century* esp. 10–11; Haas (1997) 337–51; Fraser (1993) [1995].
[133] Butler (1978), cf. *The Coptic Encyclopedia* I.183–9, *s.v.* Arab conquest of Egypt (P. M. Fraser).
[134] For the evidence see Fraser's extensive 'Additional Bibliography' in Butler (1978), with Bagnall's review, *Classical Journal* 75 (1979–80) 347–8; also: MacCoull (1986a) (= MacCoull (1993b) ch. XII). An important, recently published seventh-century document: Gascou (1994).

CHAPTER 22a

THE SASANID MONARCHY

ZE'EV RUBIN

I. ROMANS AND SASANIDS

A chapter dealing with Iranian feudalism in a distinguished series dedicated to *The Rise and Fall of the Roman World* bears the title *Iran, Rome's Greatest Enemy*. This title is more than merely a justification for the inclusion of a chapter on Iran in a series whose subject is Roman history. It also reflects a host of fears and prejudices fostered for long centuries in the Roman world, since the trauma of Crassus' defeat by the Parthians at Carrhae. Not even extended periods of decline and internal disarray within the Parthian monarchy, in the course of which it was repeatedly invaded by the Roman army, could dispel the myth of the uncompromising threat posed by Iran to the Roman order. The replacement of the Parthian Arsacid dynasty by a new vigorous one, based in Fars, namely the Sasanid dynasty, at a time when the Roman empire itself was facing one of its severest crises, only aggravated its inhabitants' deeply rooted fear of Iran. Ancient writers in the Roman *oikoumene* passed on this attitude to modern western scholars.[1]

It is the Sasanid bogeyman which has left a deep imprint in modern historiography. The Sasanid state is widely regarded as a much more centralized and effective political entity than its Parthian counterpart, with a far better army. The great pretensions and aspirations of its monarchs are believed to have been fed by the fervour of religious fanaticism, inspired by the Zoroastrian priesthood, which is commonly depicted as a well organized state church. No wonder that such a state posed the gravest threat to its greatest rival – the other great power of late antiquity.[2] Each of these accepted beliefs raises a multitude of problems, and a fundamental revision is called for. Only a few of the more salient points can be dealt with in the present brief survey.

The Sasanid empire embraced two distinct geographical areas, the very fertile lowlands of Mesopotamia and the Iranian uplands, which were separated from each other by the mighty Zagros chain that stretched from the

---

[1] Widengren (1976). In general, see the contributions in Yar-Shater (1983); also Schippmann (1990), Herrmann (1977), Christensen (1944). There are detailed bibliographic essays in Wiesehöfer (1996) 282–300. [2] Howard-Johnston (1995); Lee (1993) 15–25.

Kurdistan highlands to the fringes of the Persian Gulf in the south.[3] Mesopotamia, where a complex irrigation system permitted dense settlement, was the economic heart of the Persian realm, whose rich agriculture generated the largest part of the Sasanid state's tax revenues and supported a network of major cities: Ctesiphon, the capital; Veh Ardashir, on the west bank of the Tigris opposite Ctesiphon, which was founded by the first Sasanid monarch; Perozshapur on the Euphrates, which commemorated the site of Shapur I's victory over Gordian and exploited the large number of Roman captives secured then; and Veh Antiok Khusrau, which was a similar foundation by Khusro I to celebrate his capture of Antioch on the Orontes and provide a home for the captives and booty from his successful 540 campaign. By contrast, the Iranian plateau was sparsely settled, with the main centres of habitation clustered around and along the sources of water emerging from the Zagros: rainfall is low, and beyond the reach of rivers and *qanats* (underground water channels) lay the expanse of the Gedrosian Desert in the south-east, where much of Alexander's army had perished in 324 B.C., and the salt desert of the Great Kavir to the north. On the fringes of the Sasanid world were further distinct areas of considerable military importance: the sub-Caucasian zone in the north-west, where Iran competed for influence with Rome among the nobilities of Armenia, Lazica, Iberia and Albania and attempted to control movements across the Caucasus passes, and the wide expanses of Transoxiana, where Iran had to confront its traditional enemies, the succession of nomadic federations of the Central Asian steppes, the Hephthalites or White Huns who dominated the frontier in the fourth and fifth century and the Turks who co-operated with Khusro I in the elimination of their mutual enemy, the Hephthalites, in the 550s and then rapidly emerged as a much more powerful threat during the rest of the sixth century. The vast barrier of the Zagros restricted communications to a limited number of major passes, so that the structural backbone of the empire was simple: from the economic and political heartland of lower Mesopotamia, routes up the Tigris led to the area of conflict with Rome in the north and north-west, while the road to the east crossed the Zagros into Media and then continued along the southern flanks of the Elburz range, another major defining mountain range, towards Khorasan and the frontier.

The Sasanid heartland was located in Fars, the relatively fertile region at the south-western end of the Iranian plateau, where the family combined positions of religious authority (the chief priesthood of the temple of Anahita at Istakhr) and secular power (governorship of Darabjird). After two decades in which a strong local power base was transformed into authority over the Iranian plateau, Ardashir descended to the Mesopotamian lowlands, overthrew the Arsacid monarch and was crowned King of Kings at

[3] Comprehensive discussion of all aspects of Iranian geography in Fisher (1968).

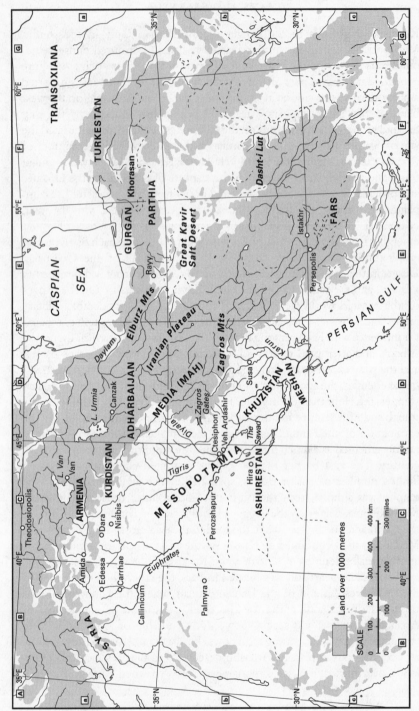

Map 18 Sasanid Iran

Ctesiphon in 226. Military success, and in particular conflict with Rome, was an important mechanism for demonstrating the legitimacy of the new regime. The initial thrusts of the two first Sasanid monarchs, Ardashir I (224–40) and Shapur I (240–70), against the Roman east turned out, in the long run, to be little more than a series of wars of plunder: the Romans were defeated three times in the field, with the emperor Valerian being captured at Edessa in 260; the great cities of Nisibis, Carrhae and Antioch were sacked; and ravaging extended into Cappadocia and Cilicia as well as Syria – but there were no permanent gains.[4] Under their immediate successors, aggressive initiative seems to have passed momentarily to the Romans. The conflicts between the two empires at that time brought to the foreground the problem of Armenia, which was to be a major bone of contention for most of the following century. The attempt of king Narseh (293–302) to regain the upper hand ended in humiliating defeat by the Romans in 297, followed by a no less humiliating treaty. The tide was partly reversed during the long reign of Shapur II (309–79). The wars fought between the two powers at the time were largely over contested frontier lands – first and foremost Armenia and northern Mesopotamia. Stability began to emerge after Julian's invasion in 363 permitted the Persians to regain Nisibis and other territories in upper Mesopotamia, and this was reinforced by the treaty between Shapur III (383–8) and Theodosius I in 384, which arranged the division of Armenia.[5]

This ushered in a long period of relative quiet in the relations between the eastern Roman empire and Persia, apart from two brief conflicts, in 421–2 and 440–1. On the first occasion, the dispute was caused by the Roman reception of Christian fugitives, especially from the Arab tribes allied to Persia: Yazdgard I (399–421) had been favourably disposed towards Christians and other minority religious groups within his kingdom, but energetic Christian missionary activity seems eventually to have forced him to permit persecution; an Arab chief, Aspabad, was instructed to prevent the flight of Christian converts to the Romans, but he in fact joined the exodus, converted and, now renamed Peter, became bishop for the wandering tribal groups in the desert.[6] Persian demands for subsidies towards the cost of defending the Caspian passes (the so-called Gates) caused the second conflict, when Yazdgard II (438–57) attempted to exploit Theodosius' concern over the Vandal capture of Carthage. On each occasion Roman armies checked Persian attacks and peace was rapidly restored, with renewed treaties that contained clauses to regulate the alleged origins of the war.[7]

A plausible explanation for the change from persistent warfare in the third and fourth century to peaceful relations in the fifth is provided by the

---

[4] Sources in Dodgeon and Lieu (1991) 9–67.
[5] Rubin (1986); Frye in Yar-Shater (1983) 153–70; Blockley (1992) 39–45; Whitby, *Maurice* 197–218.
[6] Cyril of Scythopolis, *Life of Euthymius* 10, on which see Rubin (1986) 679–81 and Blockley (1992) 199 n. 28.   [7] Blockley (1992) 56–61; Frye (1984) 320–1.

other external problems which faced successive rulers: developments in the west and the Balkans, as well as internal problems in Isauria, commanded the attention of the emperor at Constantinople, while Sasanid kings had to contend with the equally serious threat posed by the Hephthalites on their north-east frontier. This Sasanid problem is not regularly reported in our sources. The succession of Greek classicizing historians from Priscus of Panium through to Theophylact Simocatta narrate diplomacy and warfare that involved Romans and Sasanids, but only rarely extend their horizons further east.[8] Sasanid sources are mostly preserved for us through compilations from the Islamic period, of which the most important are the *Annals* of al-Tabari in Arabic and the *Shahnama* or *Book of Kings* of Firdawsi in new Persian. Both date from the tenth century and depend on lost Iranian sources in which anecdotal material had substantially ousted reliable information, so that the resulting narratives are dominated by charming and exotic stories. Though al-Tabari attempted to cut his way through the more sensational of his source material and produce a sober historical narrative, he still incorporated two parallel versions of Sasanid history; it is not safe to trust his information uncritically.[9] Furthermore, these Iranian sources are more informative for the royal court and internal affairs and, like their Roman counterparts, are silent about a difficult frontier relationship in which the Persians were often at a disadvantage. Only for the reign of Peroz (459–84) is there substantial information about Persian–Hephthalite relations, partly because Peroz was defeated in 464/5 when the Roman ambassador Eusebius was accompanying the royal army, partly because two decades later Peroz perished with much of his army in a catastrophic attempt to reverse the previous humiliation.[10]

The death of Peroz was followed by a period of dynastic weakness in Iran: Peroz' brother Valash ruled for four years (484–8) before being overthrown by Peroz' son Kavadh (488–96), who relied on Hephthalite support. Kavadh, however, was in turn ousted by the nobility and replaced by his brother Zamaspes (496–8), but he was returned to power (498–531) with Hephthalite assistance, after marrying the king's daughter. His reign witnessed the rise of the Mazdakite 'movement' (see p. 655 below), which advocated communal rights over property, and perhaps also women; it appears to have received some support from the king, and can be interpreted as an attempt to undermine the entrenched power of the hereditary aristocracy. An indirect consequence of Kavadh's dynastic problems was the resurgence of warfare with Rome: Kavadh undoubtedly needed money to repay the Hephthalites and to enhance his position as supreme patron within Persia, and this led to a request to the Romans for contributions towards the costs

---

[8] Discussions in Blockley (1981); Cameron (1969/70); Cameron, *Procopius*; Blockley (1985); Whitby, *Maurice*.   [9] Howard-Johnston (1995) 169–72.   [10] Procop. *Wars* 1.3–4.

of defending the Caspian Gates. Anastasius' refusal provided a pretext for war (502–5), in which Kavadh secured considerable prestige and booty through the capture of Theodosiopolis and Amida during his first campaign, whereafter Roman generals gradually stabilized the position.[11]

In the sixth century, Roman–Persian relations are characterized by two opposite tendencies: the recollection of the relatively harmonious fifth century, during which elaborate diplomatic practices for managing relations had emerged, and international rivalry caused both by weaknesses in the position of the Persian king and by mutual suspicions of each other's intentions. Towards the end of Kavadh's reign, in 527, war again broke out: tension was already increasing because of competition for the allegiance of the sub-Caucasian principalities, where acceptance of Christianity by local rulers threatened to weaken loyalties to Persia, but the flashpoint came when Justin I refused to co-operate with Kavadh's plans to ensure the succession of his third son, Khusro. Overall, the Persians were on the offensive, but a sequence of invasions failed to result in the capture of any major Roman city, and two pitched battles, at Dara in 530 and Callinicum in 531, resulted in one victory for either side. Hostilities were concluded in the Endless Peace of 532, when the new Persian king, Khusro I (531–79), accepted a lump sum of 11,000 pounds of gold in lieu of regular contributions for the defence of the Caucasus.[12]

Peace did not last. Justinian exploited the quiet on his eastern frontier to launch the reconquest of Africa and Italy, but his startling victories were brought to Khusro's attention; jealousy fuelled suspicions about Justinian's long-term intentions, and Khusro exploited a dispute between client Arab tribes to attack in 540. After spectacular Persian successes in this first campaign, the Romans organized their defences, and after 545 a truce confined fighting to Lazica. The respective Arab allies continued their own conflict until in 554 the Ghassanid allies of Rome secured a decisive victory near Chalcis, in which the Lakhmid king al-Mundhir, the scourge of Roman provinces for the previous half-century, was killed. Peace finally came in 562 with an agreement that was intended to endure for fifty years; the detailed terms, which illustrate the range of disputed issues that might provoke conflict, are preserved in an important fragment of Menander Protector.[13] Peace lasted for a decade, but on this occasion the Romans were the agressors: Justin II objected to paying for peace (at the rate of 30,000 *solidi* per year) and believed that he could count on the support of the Turkish federation in Central Asia, which had replaced the Hephthalites as Persia's north-eastern neighbours, to crush their common enemy. Two decades of fighting were concluded when Khusro I's son and successor, Hormizd (579–90), was overthrown in a palace

[11] Joshua the Stylite 43–66; Procop. *Wars* 1.7–10; Theophanes 144–9; Zachariah 151–64. Blockley (1992) 89–96. [12] Procop. *Wars* 1.11–22; Malalas 427–73.
[13] Procop. *Wars* 11; Menander fr. 6.1 (Blockley).

coup; Hormizd's son, Khusro II (590–628), was almost immediately challenged by Vahram, who had gained great glory from defeating the Turks and
was the first non-Sasanid to secure the throne. Khusro sought assistance
from the emperor Maurice, was reinstated by a Roman army in 591, and
peace was again arranged.[14]

The final conflict of the two great rivals of the ancient world broke out
in 602, when Khusro took advantage of the murder of his benefactor
Maurice and the arrival in Persia of Maurice's eldest son Theodosius (or at
least a plausible imitator); Khusro could shed the image of Roman client,
present himself as the supporter of international ties of gratitude and
friendship, and obtain significant booty and military glory into the bargain.
For twenty-five years the conflict ranged across the whole of the near east,
from Chalcedon on the Bosphorus to Canzak on the Iranian plateau, until
a daring counter-offensive by the emperor Heraclius prompted the Persian
nobility to overthrow Khusro in 628.[15] Once more peace was restored, but
the defeated Sasanid dynasty lapsed into a bout of rapid turnover of rulers
(eight rulers within five years, including, for forty days, the Christian and
non-Sasanid Shahvaraz). The last Sasanid ruler, Yazdgard III (633–51), had
only just ascended the throne when he had to confront Islamic attacks; the
diminution of royal prestige and the weakness of his armies after a quarter
of a century of unsuccessful warfare against the Romans made Persia particularly vulnerable, and Yazdgard was forced to flee to the north-east,
where he was eventually killed.

Wars and animosity loom large in the record of the relations between
Rome and Persia, both of which presented a claim to universal ascendancy.
The imprint they have left on the Roman sources tends to obscure the fact
that both sides could also exploit a rhetoric of peace and co-operative relations. The Sasanids, who had to contend with a succession of nomadic and
semi-nomadic powers along their long continental frontiers, tried to
impress on the Romans in their diplomatic dealings that they were defending these frontiers for their mutual benefit. This claim justified repeated
demands for diplomatic subsidies, but Sasanid internal propaganda
depicted these as tribute, which aggravated Roman resistance to the payments:[16] international prestige was one of the factors that individual
Sasanid monarchs used in order to balance the divergent constituencies
within their realm and preserve their own supreme position.

II. ROYAL LEGITIMATION

The best evidence for examining Sasanid royal ideology comes from the
first century or so of the dynasty, and, although it is possible to detect

---

[14] Theophylact i–v; Whitby, *Maurice* 250–304.   [15] Howard-Johnston (1994); Stratos (1968).
[16] Rubin (1986); also Braund (1994) 270–1.

developments thereafter, the basic principles apply throughout the regime's history. Shapur I was the first to claim the title King of Kings of Iran and non-Iran, whereas his father, Ardashir, had contented himself with the title King of Kings of Iran only. The legitimation of the new royal dynasty in its own realm was the immediate task that the early Sasanids had to face, and it is to this subject that we ought to turn first. The great official state inscriptions from the early Sasanid period do not conceal the newness of the dynasty. The *Res Gestae Divi Saporis* – a list of the exploits of king Shapur I (240–70), on the so-called Ka'ba of Zardusht (Cube of Zoroaster), an Achaemenid tower at Naqsh-i Rustam, a royal Achaemenid burial area near the ancient capital of Persepolis – traces the royal geneaology back three generations, through his father Ardashir to his grandfather Papak. On the Paikuli inscription, set up by king Narseh (293–302) in commemoration of his successful bid for supreme power and his victory over his nephew Bahram III, there is only one significant addition. The dynasty is described 'the seed of the Sasanids', elucidating to some extent the role of 'the lord Sasan', mentioned in the *Res Gestae Divi Saporis* as a recipient of an honorary cult, but not explicitly as a forebear of the dynasty. None of the other remaining six inscriptions that allude to the genealogy of the Sasanid kings adds anything of significance.[17]

The great pictures that accompany many of these inscriptions present the key elements of legitimate royal authority: the king and his entourage unseat their rivals in a dramatic joust; foreign enemies demonstrate their submission, including in some scenes the Roman emperor, who arrives at speed to acknowledge Sasanid mastery, kneels before his conqueror or lies prostrate at his feet; and the proper transfer of power at each accession is symbolized by grand ceremonies involving king and court; in some pictures, divine investiture is symbolized by the figure of Ahura Mazda or Anahita handing over a diadem to the king.[18] The monuments present a self-fulfilling legitimation. Supernatural sanction for the Sasanid house is demonstrated by the sequence of royal victories through which the Sasanids have achieved power; royal gratitude for this divine support is displayed by the establishment of a series of ritual fires. It is noticeable that no attempt is made to conceal the totally aggressive character of the king's bellicose activity. This self-glorification in divinely sponsored aggression is repeated three times in the *Res Gestae Divi Saporis*. According to the ideology enunciated in this document, wars of conquest are the duty of a good king and military success proves legitimacy.[19]

Externally, or at least with regard to the Roman empire, which is the only area for which we have evidence, Sasanid strategies for legitimation were slightly more complex. Victory was still crucial, but warfare ought to have

[17] Back (1978) 284–371 (*Res Gestae*); Huyse (1999); Humbach and Skjaervø (1983) (Paikuli).
[18] Pictures in Ghirshman (1962) 135–201.   [19] Whitby (1994).

some justifiction. In his *Res Gestae*, two of Shapur's three expeditions against the Romans are presented as responses to Roman aggression; one of the three versions of the inscription is in Greek, and its contents were probably proclaimed to the inhabitants of the Roman empire, or to its former inhabitants resettled in Iran.[20] More significantly, three historians writing in the Roman empire – Cassius Dio (LXXX.3.3) and Herodian (VI.2.1–5) from the third century, Ammianus Marcellinus from the fourth (XVII.5.3–8) – record how Sasanid envoys presented territorial demands on the Romans in terms of the revival of the old Achaemenid empire.[21] The repeated Roman refusal to return what rightly belonged to the new dynasty was sufficient justification for war.

If the Achaemenid heritage was important in their western diplomatic dealings, there is no evidence that it was significant for internal legitimation. Although Ardashir and Shapur I chose to glorify themselves at Naqsh-i Rustam, near Persepolis, a site rich in Achaemenid association,[22] the possible connection is not voiced in their public inscriptions. The site was chosen for its monumental and awe-inspiring nature, and there is no evidence that those who beheld these monuments were aware of their specific Achaemenid associations, or indeed of the pristine greatness of the Achaemenids themselves. The modern name of the site, Naqsh-i Rustam (with its reference to the hero of Iranian epic tradition), indicates the extent to which folk memory can msirepresent the true nature of such sites. When Shapur I refers to his ancestors' domain in his *Res Gestae*, this is merely to state that exiles from the Roman empire were settled in Iran on crown lands – specifically in Fars, Khuzistan and Ashurestan. Again, this is not a reminiscence of the Achaemenid empire or a claim to legitimation as their heirs.[23]

It has been alternatively suggested that the Sasanids' claims to legitimation harked back not to the Achaemenids but to the Kayanids, the heroic mythical rulers of Iran long before the historical Achaemenids.[24] However, this hypothesis is not supported in the inscriptions: Shapur I only traced his genealogy back to his grandfather Papak, and did not claim universal kingship before his own reign (he is the first 'King of Kings of Iranians and non-Iranians'). More striking is the absence of any allusion to the dynasty's Kayanid origin in Narseh's Paikuli inscription, precisely in the context where its description as the 'the seed of the Sasanids' invited a link

---

[20] English translation, based mainly on the Parthian and Middle Persian versions, in Frye (1984) 371–3.

[21] Whitby, *Maurice*; Potter (1990) 373 argues that Persian demands were reshaped to fit the presuppositions of Roman historiographical traditions.

[22] Wiesehöfer (1994) 207–8 and (1996) 27–8, 154–5; Lee (1993) 21–2.

[23] As suggested by Wiesehöfer (1994) 208, cf. 220–1; (1996) 155, 165–6; cf. also Lukonin (1961) 23 for a less extravagant interpretation of this passage.

[24] For a full development of this hypothesis, see Yar-Shater (1971).

with a more glorious house. Kayanid names (e.g. Kavadh, Khusro) only enter royal nomenclature in the late fifth century and probably reflect a change at that time in strategies for dynastic legitimation. Furthermore, it is the mythological Kayanid link which eventually introduces into royal genealogies an Achaemenid element that had not been present in previous centuries. This Achaemenid link was clearly derived from the *Alexander Romance*, which had become popular at the Sasanid court in the first half of the sixth century. The Sasanid genealogies preserved in Arabic and New Persian sources that derive from lost Pahlavi historiography reflect, as often, the conditions and traditions of the last century of Sasanid rule; little genuine knowledge was preserved.[25]

III. SASANID KINGS AND THE ZOROASTRIAN PRIESTS

Divine sanction was an important part of royal legitimation, and it is there-fore necessary to investigate the relations between monarchs and the Zoroastrian priesthood, the repository of pristine mythological traditions. The orthodox view that Sasanid kings relied on the support of the Zoroastrian priesthood, whose beliefs they in turn actively encouraged and whose power within their realm they enhanced, has been largely modified in recent decades.[26] True, the term *mazdesn*, 'Mazda-worshipping', recurs frequently on the Sasanid monuments as a royal epithet, but this need not imply automatic recognition of one organized priesthood as sole exponent of this deity's cult. Kings could perhaps best consolidate royal power by fostering variety, both inside the 'Zoroastrian church' and between different religions.

For the orthodox view, difficulties arise already with the personality of the founder of the dynasty, Ardashir I. According to the Zoroastrian tradi-tion enshrined in the *Denkard*, a post-Sasanid Zoroastrian encyclopedia, this monarch ought to be considered as the great restorer of the Zoroastrian faith, under whose aegis the priest Tansar collected the scat-tered remnants of the Avestan books that had survived though the period after Alexander's conquests.[27] The picture that emerges from the *Res Gestae Divi Saporis* is rather different: it makes no mention either of Tansar or of any other member of the Zoroastrian priesthood except Kirder, whose appearance is rather inconspicuous. Ardashir himself can reliably be described as a worshipper of Anahita of Stakhr, whereas evidence of his attachment to Ahura Mazda is more equivocal. As worshipped by the early Sasanids, Anahita was the goddess of victory at whose shrine the severed heads of vanquished enemies were habitually dedicated. If the devotion of

[25] Cf. Nöldeke (1887) 87–8; (1920) 13.   [26] For a survey of views, see Schippmann (1990) 92–102.
[27] Shaki (1981).

Ardashir and of his immediate successors to this goddess can be considered as part and parcel of a Zoroastrian orthodoxy, then this orthdoxy must have been entirely different from the kind of orthodoxy assumed in his glorification in the *Denkard*.[28]

The absence of any clear reference to an organized clergy in the *Res Gestae Divi Saporis* is at odds with the role ascribed by modern scholars to a 'Zoroastrian church', at least under the early Sasanid kings. This gap is not filled by the far-reaching claims made in four inscriptions celebrating the career of Kirder, the one priestly character who does figure on Shapur's monument. Kirder was promoted within the Zoroastrian priesthood from a mere *herbed* under Shapur I to the rank of a *mobed* (*mgwpt*, i.e. chief *magus*) under his immediate successors, Hormizd I, Bahram I and Bahram II. Bahram II bestowed additional honours and supposedly authorized Kirder to enforce Zoroastrianism and persecute heresies and other religions. This only indicates that this king was attached to the kind of Zoroastrianism preached by Kirder, which is more than can be said of Shapur I.[29]

The extent of Shapur I's Zoroastrian piety as it emerges from his own *Res Gestae* is not entirely clear. He was indeed the founder of many fire-temples throughout his realm, according to his own testimony as well as to Kirder. Yet fire-temples were sacred not only to Ahura Mazda but also to Anahita, and Shapur's favourable attitude to Zoroastrianism should be conceived in the framework of a religious eclecticism that could also accommodate Manichaeism.[30] Furthermore, the fact that he granted Kirder sweeping powers to conduct the affairs of his religion, without matching these powers with the appropriate titulature (*herbed*, whatever its meaning, appears to be a rather modest title), suggests that Kirder was a court-priest, not the designated head of a powerful church. Some tension between Kirder in this function and some of his brethren cannot be ruled out. Kirder's statement, reiterated on his inscriptions as a refrain, that under his leadership *many* of the *magi* (not all of them) were happy and prosperous, implies an attempt to mute the voices of an opposition. The early Sasanid monarchs, far from depending on an already powerful organization for vital support, may rather have helped Zoroastrian clergy to improve their position in a fluid and competitive religious milieu.

It is usually assumed that under Narseh (293–302) the influence of the Zoroastrian priesthood declined, but that it regained much of the lost ground under Shapur II (309–79). The figure of Aturpat, son of Mahrspand, looms large in the post-Sasanid Zoroastrian literature, where he is depicted as a model of Zoroastrian orthodoxy who submitted himself

---

[28] Chaumont (1958); Duchesne-Guillemin in Yar-Shater (1983) 874–97.

[29] Back (1978) 384–488; Duchesne-Guillemin in Yar-Shater (1983) 878–84.

[30] Wikander (1946) 52–124; Chaumont (1958) 162–3; Lieu (1994) 24–5, 35–6 for Manichaeism in the Sasanid empire.

to the ordeal of molten metal to refute heretics whose precise doctrine is disputed. It would have been quite natural to visualize Aturpat as standing at the head of a mighty Zoroastrian hierarchic organization, authorized by the king himself to administer the institutions of the only fully recognized official state religion. On the other hand, the hierarchy within what we habitually conceive of as 'the Zoroastrian church' probably did not become fully established until much later. It is only under Yazdgard II (439–57) that the high priest Mihr-Shapur, who had already distinguished himself under previous reigns as a persecutor of Christians, is called *modaban mobad (magupatan magupat)*, the earliest reliable attestation of this title. But even then the relative positions of *mobeds* and *herbeds* in the organization of Zoroastrian clergy are not entirely clear. The title *herbedan herbed*, conferred upon Zurvandad, the son of Yazdgard's powerful prime minister, Mihr-Narseh, has been interpreted as evidence for a hierarchy distinct from that of the *mobeds* within the Zoroastrian church.

The Zoroastrian priesthood appears to have gained a truly undisputed position as the sole representative of the one and only state religion in the course of the fifth century. It is precisely at this time that a sudden proliferation of Avestan names borne by members of the royal house, and the appearance of the title *kavi (kay)* on the coins of its kings, mark a crucial stage in the fabrication of the Kayanid genealogy as a source of legitimation of the Sasanid dynasty. Yet the Zoroastrian priesthood was soon to suffer a severe blow under Kavadh I (488–96; 499–531), during the Mazdakite revolt (on which, see p. 655 below). The reign of Khusro I appears to have been a period of harmony between the monarchy and the Zoroastrian priesthood, but it was a priesthood restored by the king following the Mazdakite débâcle, and consequently more dependent on the king than before. Under Khusro's successors, Zoroastrian influence seems to have declined: Khusro II (590–628), rather than follow his predecessors in the grand-scale establishment of fire-temples staffed with a vast multitude of *herbedan*, relied heavily on Christians, who included his favourite wife, his finance officer and his chief general; Zoroastrian tradition, as reflected in the apocalyptic composition *Jamasp Namagh*, branded him as an unjust and tyrannical king.[31]

The personality of Mihr-Narseh, Yazdgard II's prime minister, highlights the problem of orthodoxy and heterodoxy in the Zoroastrian religion of the Sasanid period. From Armenian sources dealing with the persecution he launched against the Christians in Armenia, it is plain that he was an adherent of Zurvan i Akanarag – that is, Infinite Time:[32] his son's name, Zurvandad, is certainly a theophoric name, celebrating this rather shadowy

---

[31] Duchesne-Guillemin, in Yar-Shater (1983) 896; cf. Boyce in Yar-Shater (1983) 1160.
[32] Elishe Vardapet in Langlois (1869) 190–1; cf. Eznik of Kolb in Boyce (1984) 97–8.

divine personification (such names seem to have been common among the Iranian nobles under the Sasanids). The role of this divinity in the Zoroastrian pantheon is much disputed, but represents a trend in Zoroastrian religion which attempted to provide a unifying monistic framework for its fundamentally dualistic theology: Ohurmazd, the good principle, and Ahriman, the evil principle, were depicted as the twin sons of Infinite Time. There is, however, little reliable information: the Pahlavi Zoroastrian literature of the post-Sasanid period is virtually silent, whereas contemporary non-Sasanid and non-Zoroastrian sources suggest that this doctrine was the orthodoxy endorsed by the Sasanid kings.[33]

Various attempts have been made to overcome the discrepancy. It has been postulated that the orthdoxy reflected in the extant Zoroastrian literature triumphed only after the collapse of the Sasanid monarchy, in the context of rivalry between supporters of the old national religion and the new Islamic monotheism, so that the former monistic orthodoxy was deliberately suppressed.[34] According to another view, the story of Zurvanism is one of intermittent success: whereas under some kings it was indeed the accepted orthodoxy, under others the pendulum swung in the opposite direction and the dualistic trend became dominant. Dualism was finally triumphant under Khusro I (531–79), whose reign also constitutes a decisive stage in the canonization of the surviving Avestan Nasks and in the development of Zoroastrian theological literature. Attempts have also been made to play down the significance of Zurvanism, either as a fad entertained by the upper classes or as a popular version of Zoroastrianism, and, at any rate, as nothing tantamount to a heresy in its familiar Christian sense.[35]

Perhaps the best way of approaching a solution is to get rid of the notion of a Sasanid Zoroastrian church analogous in its position to that of the Christian church in the late Roman empire, intent upon using secular support to impose a uniform doctrine within its ranks. The truth may well have been that although the early Sasanid kings had found Zoroastrianism, as represented and propounded by the estate of the *magi*, the most potent religious factor in many of their domains, they were not always prepared to allow it to become the sole officially dominant state religion. Thus, for example, Anahita, who seemingly fades out after the reign of Narseh, springs again into prominence under the last Sasanids, from Khusro II to Yazdgard III (633–51).[36]

Furthermore, the fact that some Sasanid kings, like Shapur I, were prepared to unleash the Zoroastrian priesthood against the Christians in the

[33] Christensen (1944) 149–54; Boyce (1979) 112–13, 160–1.

[34] Boyce (1979) 160–1; cf. Boyce (1984) 96–9.

[35] Zaehner (1955); reaction in Boyce (1957), (1990); Frye (1959), (1984) 321 with n. 27; Shaked (1979) xxxiv.6.   [36] Wikander (1946) 55–6; Duchesne-Guillemin in Yar-Shater (1983) 897.

service of their own policies does not mean that they themselves subscribed to any version of Zoroastrianism as the binding orthodoxy. Attitudes towards this religion appear to have varied according to circumstances and the tempers of individual kings. A sober monarch like Shapur I was quite capable of striking an alliance of convenience with the Zoroastrian clergy while keeping his options open by toying with Manichaeism. Shapur II, a notorious persecutor of the Christians, may well have played off dualism against Zurvanism precisely in order to check the growth of an excessively strong, unified priestly caste. Yazdgard I (399–421) was favourably inclined towards Christianity and Judaism for most of his reign.[37] On the other hand, such kings as Bahram I and Bahram II may be described as truly pious Zoroastrians in the version adhered to by Kirder – probably but not certainly that of dualism.

The attitude of the Sasanid monarchs towards Nestorian Christianity is another consideration against the interpretation of their religious policy exclusively in terms of their Zoroastrian piety. After it had been condemned as a heresy at the Council of Ephesus in 431, believers in this creed found a relatively safe haven in the Sasanid empire. A Nestorian school was founded in Nisibis by fugitive Nestorian teachers from Edessa, Bar Sauma and Narsai, in 457, and flourished in that city, particularly under the king Peroz (459–84), when the Zoroastrian priesthood appears to have been at the peak of its power. There was no danger in a policy of toleration towards a religious sect which was banned within the eastern Roman empire while its emperors were either Chalcedonian or inclined to Monophysitism. On the other hand, even a king like Khusro I, who could afford to be tolerant without marring his relations with a Zoroastrian priesthood which was firmly in his control, could not or would not prevent persecution, even of Nestorians, after war against Rome flared up in 540. Khusro II is habitually described as philo-Christian, but the picture is more complex: he astutely played off Monophysites, whose cause was advocated at court by his favourite wife, Shirin, and her influential physician, Gabriel, against Nestorians, who found a faithful champion in his powerful finance minister, Yazdin. Towards the end of his reign, when his empire succumbed to a Byzantine invasion, he reversed his policy of general toleration, and threatened a wave of persecutions.[38]

IV. KINGS AND NOBLES

The Sasanid monarchy has a reputation for better organization and greater centralization than its Arsacid predecessor. But the notion that the Arsacid

[37] Widengren (1961) 139–42; Rubin (1986) 679–81.
[38] Duchesne-Guillemin in Yar-Shater (1983) 889–90; Khuzistan Chronicle chs. 8, 11, 18, 26.

kingdom was in essence a cluster of largely independent political entities, held together in little more than a semblance of formal allegiance to a shadowy central royal authority, may have its roots in tendentious Sasanid traditions. These treat the whole of the Seleucid and Arsacid periods as that of the 'petty kings' or 'tribal kings' (*muluk al-tawa'if*) and, in clear contrast, depict the Sasanid monarchy established by Ardashir as a coherent and effective political and military power. In the Sasanid sixth-century historical romance, the *Karnamag Ardasher i Papakan*, the fragmentation of Alexander's empire into 240 small states is the foil to Ardashir's expoits; the impression produced by the *Khwaday-namag* tradition, as reflected principally by al-Tabari, is that Ardashir's rise to power was in effect a long succession of wars for the unification of Iran.[39]

Greek and Latin sources give the point of view of contemporary outside observers, which helps to modify this distorted picture, especially with regard to the Parthian empire. These sources, though, also suggest that the establishment of the Sasanid monarchy was a dramatic development: the new energetic drive displayed by an incipient power is all too easy to contrast with the patchy picture of a lethargic Parthian kingdom. The result is a widespread consensus among modern scholars that the statehood of the Sasanid monarchy was more advanced than that of the Arsacid one. A more balanced picture emerges when Sasanid institutions are examined without being distorted by the propagandistic vein that prevails in many of the extant sources: the dynasty was new, but many of its structures were inherited.

The territorial extent of the Sasanid empire was vast but the control exercised by central government was not uniformly effective.[40] Evidence for the foundation of cities by the Sasanid monarchs after Ardashir, chiefly on the detailed data preserved by Tabari, indicates that their activity was confined to a rather limited area. It basically comprised territories conquered by Ardashir I during his wars against the Arsacids and their vassal kinglets – i.e. the provinces of Fars, Meshan, the Sawad and Mah (Media): Sasanid kings did not encroach upon territories held by the great lords of the realm, some of whom belonged to houses whose roots reached far back to the Parthian era (see further below). To this rule, only one exception can be shown. Occasionally, cities were established in newly acquired border zones where the king's lordship by right of conquest could not be contested, or in remote provinces where royal authority was being re-established. A notable example

---

[39] *Karnamak Artakhshir-i Papakan* ed. Edalji Kersaspji Antia (Bombay 1900) ch. 1, 1–5 (English trans.) and Nöldeke (1878) 35–8 for annotated German trans.; Tabari 813–20 (Leiden edition) = Nöldeke (1879) 1–22 (German trans.); also Bosworth (1999) 1–18 for an annotated English translation.

[40] The efficacy of royal control is stressed by Howard-Johnston (1995), but his model is based on a hypothetical interpretation of archaeological finds rather than the more explicit literary evidence. Limitations on ability to tax: Altheim and Stiehl (1954) 47–8.

is the foundation of Ram Peroz in the region of Rayy, Roshan Peroz on the border of Gurgan and the Gates of Sul, and Shahram Peroz in Adharbaijan: all these were clearly foundations of Peroz (459–84) and were located in areas affected by his wars against the Hephthalites.[41] Foundation of a city represented a substantial investment of manpower and resources, and kings only undertook these in locations where they would benefit themselves, not one of their overmighty nobles.

The picture of a well-ordered hierarchic society, controlled and regulated by a strong monarchy, has to be reassessed. This picture emerges from later literary sources from the Islamic period, such as al-Tabari, al-Mas'udi, Ps. al-Jahiz[42] and The Letter of Tansar, a letter attributed to the powerful third-century herbed but probably composed three centuries later, which is preserved in Ibn Isfandyar's Ta'rikh-i Tabaristan, the use of which involves serious problems of Quellenforschung.[43] But these complex issues can be avoided, since the epigraphic sources from the earlier Sasanid period, notably the third century and the first half of the fourth, anticipate and corroborate this later testimony. The inscriptions suggest that already under Shapur I the framework of a social hierarchy had been formally established. The highest rung, immediately below the King of Kings, was that of the shahrdaran, virtually independent kings, whose number seems to have been much lower under the Sasanids than the Arsacids; they tended to be senior members of the royal dynasty, officially ruling their kingdoms as royal apanages. Below them ranked the vaspuhragan, apparently princes of the royal family who held no official post in the royal court. Third in rank were the vuzurgan. This group comprised the members of the great noble houses Suren, Karin, the Lords of Undigan, and others. As late as the end of the fifth century, the unruly heads of these houses admitted only a nominal allegiance to the central power but were virtually independent in their hereditary territorial domains. The fourth and the lowest rung documented on the inscriptions was the azadan, minor gentry of free status, distinct from the other nobility but probably also dependent on them in many cases; from this lesser nobility were recruited the mounted warriors, asavaran, who were the core of the Sasanid army.[44]

The stratification that emerges from the later, literary sources is more general and reflects the (post-Sasanid) Avestan concept of social stratification. The priests (asronan) appear at the top of the ladder. They are followed by the military estate (artestaran). The third estate is that of

[41] Altheim and Stiehl (1954) 12–18; cf. Lukonin (1961) 12–19, specifically on the foundations of Ardashir I and Shapur I.
[42] Tabari 821 (Leiden) = Nöldeke (1979) 21. al-Masudi, Muruj al-Dhahab (ed. De Maynard and De Courteille) 2, 156–63; al-Jahiz, Kitab al-Taj 21–8 (ed. Ahmed Zeki Pacha) = Pellat (1954) 51–6 (French trans.). [43] Boyce (1968).
[44] For these categories, see Schippmann (1990) 82; cf. Wiesehöfer (1994) 228–43; (1996) 171–6.

the royal bureaucracy (*dibiran*, i.e. scribes). Finally, the commoners are enumerated, subdivided into peasants (*vastaryoshan*) and artisans (*hutuxshan*). If the two hierarchies, inscriptional and literary, are to be amalgamated, the inscriptional hierarchy of nobility should be seen as an expansion of the second estate in the literary sources; on the other hand, the literary hierarchy may not be contemporaneous, since there is no evidence for a separate priestly caste in the early period.

Royal power and influence depended to a large degree on effective control of the *shahrdaran* as well as on the active support of the majority of the *vuzurgan*, or equivalent groups, whatever their names in later periods. Their co-operation would be needed for the recruitment of the *asavaran* who owed allegiance to them, and their consent would be required for the imposition of royal taxation within their domains. Sasanid military organization has been described as 'feudal', basically similar to its Arsacid predecessor, and this definition may help us to understand how the Sasanid system functioned. From our meagre information about remuneration for the professional core of soldiery, we may conclude that it was supported through land grants rather than paid in money or kind. Thus it is tempting to accept the notion of enfeoffment, which by its very nature entails bonds of trust and dependence that may be described as ties of vassalage. Yet, if this picture provides a fairly accurate idea of the relationship between the king and warriors conscripted in his own domain, as well as of that between the grandees and their own warriors, it does not reveal the realities of the links between king and grandees. The latter's domains might have been considered as fiefs from the former, but in most cases this status would only have been theoretical, since forfeiture of such 'fiefs' to the crown could hardly be enforced by means of a simple legal procedure, without the need to resort to arms: as in any feudal monarchy, there was no guarantee that every Sasanid king could control all the grandees all the time.

V. TAXATION AND MILITARY ORGANIZATION

In an empire which minted a stable silver coinage, the *drahm*, throughout most of its history, this continuing resort to grants of land in return for military service calls for an explanation. The *drahm* was the only denomination in constant circulation, which raises the question whether such a simple economic system can be described as a truly advanced monetary economy. Gold *dinars* were issued occasionally – not, so it seems, for purposes of monetary circulation, but rather in commemoration of solemn events. Bronze change seems to have been issued only very intermittently, perhaps in response to specific demands, as at Merv; the volume progressively decreased, which poses problems for the mechanics of everyday economic exchanges.[45] The assumption that Arsacid copper coinage was still used in many parts of the Sasanid kingdom is unconvincing,[46] and the conclusion must be that much economic activity was based on barter.

This situation explains a good deal about the Sasanid system of taxation before the beginning of the sixth century. It was based on crop-sharing, the exaction of agricultural produce proportionate to annual yield, as assessed by royal tax-collectors on the spot, and levied in kind. In addition, a poll tax was imposed on most subjects, which may largely have been paid in money, though part was perhaps commuted to goods. The system was inefficient and wasteful, especially with regard to the land-tax; it was subject to frequent fluctuations, and allowed little scope for advance financial planning. The necessity of waiting for the tax-collector with the crops untouched in the field or on the tree involved the risk that some would be damaged or destroyed before being enjoyed by farmers or the king. Only lands held directly by the king could be effectively taxed in this manner, but even on royal domains the avarice of corrupt tax-assessors will have hampered collection.[47]

Towards the end of the fifth century, the burden of taxation on the peasantry seems to have become increasingly oppressive: the complex relations with the Hephthalite khanate, the threat of which loomed in the east, resulted in heavy demands when recurrent famines were compelling kings to grant occasional, and not entirely adequate, tax remissions. This oppression contributed significantly to the popularity of Mazdak, a heretic Zoroastrian priest, who advocated the economic equality of all human beings and regarded the higher classes of the Sasanid kingdom as the worst enemies of his doctrines. For some time he managed to enlist the support of king Kavadh himself, who appears to have used this movement precisely to humble his recalcitrant nobility.[48] When he ultimately turned his back upon the movement and allowed his son to put it down, the battered nobles needed royal support to recuperate and regain a fraction of their former grandeur. They were obviously in no position to form a viable opposition to the one serious attempt to introduce a tax reform in the Sasanid realm, begun apparently towards the end of Kavadh I's reign (531) and continued by his son Khusro I Anushirwan.[49]

On the basis of a general land survey, a new system for exacting the land-tax was devised. Fixed rates of tax were imposed on agricultural land

---

[45] See Göbl in Altheim and Stiehl (1954) 96–9; cf. Göbl (1971) 25–30; Göbl in Yar-Shater (1983) 328–9. On Merv, see Loginov and Nikitin 1993.

[46] Göbl in Altheim and Stiehl (1954) 98; also Göbl (1971), where continued circulation is only suggested for the earlier period, and no explanation is offered for the subsequent mechanics of exchange.

[47] For a very different picture, see Howard-Johnston (1995), who postulates the existence of an efficient tax-raising system not dissimilar to that in the Roman empire.

[48] For summary and bibliography on Mazdak, see Guidi (1992); Crone (1991).

[49] For more detailed discussion of sources, see Rubin (1995).

according to its size and according to the kind of crops raised; the tax was calculated in the *drahm* currency, but some at least probably continued to be levied in kind, calculated according to the current value of the produce in *drahms*. This new system, if efficiently applied, would enable a monarch to anticipate incomes and budget expenses. It might be seen as oppressive on the peasantry, primarily because the fixed *drahm* rates apparently disregarded fluctuations in agricultural yield caused by drought, other natural calamities or war, but this is to ignore the best testimony about the reform: if a distinction is drawn between the reform's institution and operation in Khusro's reign, and what it subsequently became, the system appears reasonably efficient and fair. It considerably augmented crown revenues, but also included a mechanism that enabled constant revision and made tax rebates and remissions possible where and when necessary.

The fiscal reform was accompanied by an agricultural reform. Dispossessed farmers were restored to their lands, financial help was available to enable them to restart cultivation, and a mechanism was instituted to assist farms affected by natural disasters. The overall result should have been to maintain a system of small farms that might be easily taxed, and to prevent the growth of huge estates whose powerful owners might accumulate privileges and immunities, and obstruct effective taxation.

Khusro's reform was meant to have a lasting impact on Sasanid military organization by providing the king with a standing army of crack units of horsemen (*asavaran*), under his direct command and permanently at his disposal, who received a salary, at least when on foreign campaign. This body of *palatini* was recruited among young nobles as well as the country gentry, the *dehkanan*, who wished to start a military career. On the frontiers, troops recruited from the nomadic periphery of the Sasanid empire (e.g. Turks), as well as from semi-independent enclaves within it (e.g. Daylam in the mountainous region of Gilan), might be employed to repel invasions or check them until the arrival of the mobile crack units.

Khusro's system appears to have enjoyed moderate success for a few decades, until the difficulties that beset the Sasanid monarchy exposed its weaknesses. In the fiscal area, its proper functioning depended on internal stability, external security and continuing financial prosperity, backed up by revenues other than the land and poll taxes (e.g. taxes on international trade, especially the silk trade, booty from foreign wars, tributes and diplomatic subsidies, etc.). These supplementary sources of income were necessary to ensure the smooth running of the control mechanism that was integral to Khusro's system. However, its stability as a whole depended too much on a delicate balance which only a very powerful monarch could maintain at the best of times, and in the vast Sasanid monarchy, with its long continental frontiers, it was exposed to the dangers that threatened the empire itself. Growing military commitments increased financial demands and pressure on the tax-payers, thereby threatening the system; if central government lost effective control, abuse and corruption might swamp arrangements.

A neglected source which appears reliable on this issue, the *Sirat Anushirwan* embedded in Ibn Misqawayh's *Tajarib al-Umam*, indicates that Khusro, towards the end of his reign, was hard put to keep his system functioning.[50] The control mechanism proved to be as susceptible to corruption as the taxation machinery that had to be controlled. Furthermore, the strained relations between soldier and civilian, especially in the remoter zones, exacted their toll. In effect, the king could restrain only the soldiers under his direct command from despoiling the rural tax-payers, as is shown by the restrictions imposed by Hormizd IV (579–90) on a journey to Mah. It is probable, however, that already during the last days of his father many of the cavalrymen no longer owed direct allegiance to the king, but had become again retainers of greater and virtually independent landlords. A brief glance at the aftermath of Khusro's military reforms may provide the clue to understanding what happened.

The fragility of the financial arrangements that underpinned the standing army militated against enduring success for Khusro's reforms. If, as suggested above, the Sasanid economy was never fully monetized, the need to provide for the soldiers' everyday needs, at times mostly in goods, will have encouraged the reinstitution of enfeoffment as the standard military contract, even among the lower ranks. Thus, following a limited period when Khusro seriously attempted to sustain his new standing army, already in his own lifetime the *asavaran* were increasingly reverting to an enfeoffed estate, even though the tendency of such allotments to become hereditary, with the consequent problems caused by alienation, had to be faced.[51] Khusro's reforms were, at best, of such limited duration and impact that their scope and intent might be questioned.

From the royal perspective, the high nobility was a more serious problem even than the cavalrymen. The Mazdakite revolt and its aftermath made possible a feudal system more directly dependent on the king than ever before: the nobility restored by Khusro himself was firmly beholden to the king, so there could be no doubts about the origin of its estates and the nature of the services owed to the crown. But the nobility soon returned to its pristine positions of power. The notion that the supreme military commanders and ministers of state were now salaried civil servants is contradicted by the limited available evidence. Thus, for example, Khusro's nominees as *spahbads* – the four supreme military commands he created to supersede the old office of the *artestaransalar* – must have been mighty territorial lords right from the

[50] Discussion in Rubin (1995) 237–9, 279–84.

[51] Theophylact III.15.4 states that Persian troops did not receive a proper salary during service within the kingdom's borders, but had to rely on 'customary distributions' from the king. This contradicts the hypothesis of a salaried standing army in Howard-Johnston (1995).

start, as the very territorial nature of their command suggests. The same is true about the *marzbans*, the commanders of the frontier provinces.

The delusion that the direct dependence of Khusro's nobility on the king as its restorer and benefactor would make it enduringly more tractable and obedient shatters in view of the role played by people of this class under subsequent reigns, quite apart from the revolts in Khusro's first decade. Vahram Chobin of the noble house of Mihran, the first serious pretender outside the royal house since the establishment of the Sasanid dynasty, was supported by many disgruntled nobles. Khusro II overcame him with great difficulty in 591, but only with the expensive support of the Byzantine emperor Maurice.[52] Later, the Sasanid monarchy was rocked by other major revolts, such as those of Bistam and Bindoe, Khusro's relatives and allies turned his foes, and of his powerful general, Shahrvaraz, who was to depose his grandson Ardashir III and claim the throne.[53] By the time of the Arab conquest, local rulers, especially in the east and in the Caspian provinces, had become virtually independent. The same is indicated by the confused Arabic traditions concerning Yemen after its conquest by the Persians in the last decade of Khusro Anushirwan's reign. The growing independence of the great landlords meant that sooner or later they would inevitably control not only their own retinues of fighting men but also independent taxation in their own domains. Thus, for example, according to Dinawari, the rebel Bistam instituted taxation in the territories under his rule (Khorasan Qumis, Gurgan and Tabaristan) and in the process remitted half the land-tax.[54] Other potentates, not in direct revolt against the king, may have acted less openly but may not have been impelled by the requirements of war propaganda to be as generous.

Under Khusro II, oriental sources record impressive data about royal revenues, which might suggest that the machinery devised by Khusro I was still operating smoothly, and that Khusro II made even better use of it than his grandfather.[55] But the full narrative of Tabari conveys a different impression: the revenues were not the product of regular taxation but are to be explained, in part, by the influx of booty from Byzantine territories (the rich spoils of Alexandria and Jerusalem), and in part by extreme measures of extortion. It was primarily as an efficient operator of the taxation machinery that Khusro's Nestorian finance minister (*vastaryoshansalar*), Yazdin, endeared himself to his lord; the favourable *Khuzistan Chronicle* insists on the vast amounts of money that he sent to the treasury from the sunrise of one day to the sunrise of the next.[56] Such extortions seem to have involved not only the imposition of an unbearable burden on tax-

---

[52] Theophylact iv–v; Whitby, *Maurice* 276–308.   [53] Whitby (1994) 252–3.
[54] Dinawari p. 102 (ed. Guirgass).
[55] Altheim and Stiehl (1954) 41–2; Altheim and Stiehl (1957) 52–3.
[56] *Khuz. Chron.* 23; Tabari 1041–3; cf. Nöldeke (1879) 351–6.

payers in the royal domain but also an attempt to reintroduce direct royal taxation in the domains of grandees, who had by now come to regard this as a blatant encroachment upon their privileges: the nobles proved to be the ultimate cause of his downfall. Thus Khusro II's riches cannot be attributed to the tax reforms of Khusro I.

VI. SASANID COLLAPSE

The last decades of the Sasanid dynasty are the story of a chain of violent upheavals, which expose all the inherent weaknesses of the huge empire. The reforms of Khusro I did constitute a serious attempt to cope with these weaknesses and to re-establish the king's position on a firmer basis. They failed in the long run because they strove to superimpose the framework of a fully centralized state, with a salaried civil bureaucracy and army, financed by an efficient and easily manageable taxation apparatus, on a realm which proved too weak to carry these heavy burdens. The political and military organization of its vast territories was too flimsy, the economic infrastructure was too primitive, and the social structure was fixed by traditions that could not be easily transformed. Khusro's own conservatism was a characteristic reflection of these traditions, for it was Khusro who did a lot to restore the battered nobility to its traditional powers after the Mazdakite interlude.

Warfare had always been the primary activity of the Sasanid state, but even by its own standards the last century of its existence witnessed a sustained intensity of campaigning that may have weakened the structures of society. After the outbreak of war against Justin I in 527, there were only twenty-eight years of formal peace with Rome until the conclusive victory of Heraclius in 628 – and this is to ignore the recurrent tensions which embroiled the Arab satellites of the rival empires, Sasanid involvement in the affairs of the Arabian peninsula and the struggle to maintain control in sub-Caucasian principalities such as Suania and Albania. We know much less about the sequence of campaigns on the north-eastern frontier, but these were probably more debilitating. Khusro's apparent triumph over the Hephthalites in the 550s was only achieved through alliance with the rising Turkish federation, which now replaced the Hephthalites as Persia's neighbours and soon constituted a far more powerful threat during the 570s and 580s.[57] No less than Justinian, Khusro was repeatedly involved in wars on more than one front, and the expenses of eastern campaigning probably proved much heavier than the gains from spoils, ransoms and payments stipulated in his treaties with Rome.

The success of the state depended ultimately on the character and reputation of the king, and there was a recurrent danger that such a personal

---

[57] Menander fr. 10.3; 13.5 (Blockley); Theophylact III.6.9–14.

monarchy would experience bouts of severe dynastic competition: thus, the long reigns of both Shapur I and Shapur II were both followed by shorter periods of instability. This danger may have been increased in the sixth century by the withdrawal of Persian kings from regular active participation in warfare, a move which fundamentally changed the nature of royal legitimation. Early rulers from the house of Sasan had demonstrated divine favour for their rule through personal victories, but the successors of Khusro I relied on others to win their wars.[58] From the royal perspective, legitimacy ran in the family, but the nobility and armies might prefer to give their loyalty to a successful commander such as the non-Sasanid Vahram Chobin or Shahvaraz. The existence of substantial minority religious groups, Jews as well as Christians, allowed an established ruler to secure his position by balancing their different claims against the majority Zoroastrians, but it also meant that a rival could promote himself by seeking the support of one particular group: Vahram Chobin is known for his links with the Jews.

In spite of the attempted reforms of Khusro, the Sasanid state remained a fairly simple structure in which much economic and military power rested with the feudal nobility. Royal authority was bolstered by a supremacy of patronage, but this required a regular inflow of wealth for redistribution. Wars against the Romans provided considerable short-term gains, and Roman peace payments under the Endless Peace (532) and the Fifty Years Peace (562) were also important, but it is impossible to calculate how much of this wealth drained eastwards, almost immediately, to the Hephthalites or the Turks. The monetarized heartland of the Sasanid state (as of its Achaemenid antecedent) lay in the rich agricultural lands of Mesopotamia and lower Iraq, areas susceptible to attack from the west, and it seems to have been impossible to increase their tax revenues in the long term.

It is ironic that the most successful Sasanid conqueror, Khusro II, must also bear responsibility for the monarchy's subsequent rapid collapse. In the first decade of his reign, his status as a virtual puppet of the Romans must have contributed to support for the long-running rebellion of Bistam in the east.[59] The overthrow of his patron Maurice in 602 gave Khusro an opportunity to assert his independence, and the disorganization of Roman defences, particularly during the civil war between supporters of Phocas and Heraclius in 609–11, permitted Khusro to transform the sequence of traditional lucrative frontier campaigns into a massive expansionist thrust towards the west. But, whereas a war of pillage replenished royal coffers, the annexation of territories reduced the inflow of funds and meant that the newly acquired resources had to be devoted to the maintenance of

---

[58] Whitby (1994).
[59] *Niyayat al Irab*, Ms. Qq.225, fol. 185a; summarized in Browne (1900) 240; Firdausi, *Shanamah* 2791–6 (ed. S. Nafisy); trans. Jules Mohl, vol. VII (1878) 143–50.

troops in remote regions. Furthermore, Khusro's successful armies had little direct contact with their distant monarch, but were tied more closely to their victorious commanders: as a result, the soldiers of Shahvaraz supported their general when he was threatened by the king. In the 620s, Heraclius' campaigns into the heart of Persia exposed the fragility of Khusro's achievements, and prompted a palace coup that introduced the most severe bout of dynastic instability that the Sasanid state had ever experienced. The return of booty to the Romans combined with the destruction caused by campaigns in Mesopotamia to leave the monarchy short of wealth and prestige at the very moment when the Arabs started to raid across the Euphrates. Yazdgard III (633–51) was forced to abandon Iraq in 638/9 and thereafter lacked the resources and reputation to challenge the new Islamic superpower: the Iranian nobility abandoned the Sasanids and transferred their allegiance to the Muslim rulers, who offered stability, while the rural majority continued to pay their taxes to support a new élite.

CHAPTER 22b

ARMENIA IN THE FIFTH AND SIXTH CENTURY

R. W. THOMSON

'Armenia' has always had an ambiguous place between the major powers, be they the east Roman empire and Sasanian Iran, the Byzantine empire and the caliphate, or the Ottoman empire and the Safavids. Armenian loyalties have not been consistent, either in support of a coherent internal policy or with regard to external diplomacy. The very definition of 'Armenia' highlights the problem. Does the term refer to a geographical entity – and if so, what are its borders? Or does it refer to a people with common bonds – and if so, are those bonds linguistic, religious, cultural or political?[1]

[1] The emphasis in this chapter will be on Armenian reactions to events as expressed by the native historians. The principal Armenian sources for the period are:

Agathangelos: an anonymous history, written at the end of the fifth century, which gives the traditional account of the conversion of king Trdat and the missionary activity of St Gregory the Illuminator at the beginning of the previous century. Although replete with legendary tales and hagiographical commonplaces, it is important for the Armenian Arsacid reaction to the overthrow of the Parthian Arsacid dynasty by the Sasanians.

The *Buzandaran*: this traces the history of Armenia from the death of king Trdat *c.* 330 to the division of the country into Roman and Iranian spheres *c.* 387. The author is unknown. The work is a compilation of epic tales describing the *gestes* of the Arsacid dynasty, the noble house of the Mamikonean family (which played the leading role in the fourth and fifth century), and the descendants of Gregory in the patriarchate. It is the last witness to the disappearing Iranian traditions of Armenia, although the Christian author did not himself comprehend the original significance of all the aspects of social and political life which he described.

Koriwn: a disciple of the inventor of the Armenian script, Mashtots. His biography of the master is probably the earliest original composition in Armenian.

Moses of Khoren: author of a history of Armenia from the days of Noah to the death of Mashtots, whose pupil he claims to be. Very important as the first account of Armenian origins, in which oral traditions are integrated into the schema of Eusebius' *Chronicle*, it is the most learned of early Armenian histories. Moses used many Greek, Jewish and Syriac sources (via Armenian translations). But his strong pro-Bagratid bias and his clear distortions of previous writers suggest a later authorship than that claimed. The date and authenticity are hotly contested. But it is significant that the Bagratids did not gain their ultimate prominence until the eighth century, and Moses' history is not quoted until the tenth.

Elishe: unknown author of a history describing the revolt against Yazdgard II in 450–1, the defeat of the Armenian army led by Vardan Mamikonean at Avarayr, and the ensuing imprisonment of surviving Armenian nobles. This is probably not an eye-witness account as claimed, but a rewriting of the shorter version of these events in Lazar. Its great importance is the adaptation of the story of the Maccabees to the Armenian situation, and the identification of Christian with patriotic virtues. A sophisticated literary work, it shaped Armenian attitudes to the interaction of religion and politics down to the present time.

Despite the conversion of king Tiridates to Christianity, probably in 314,[2] and the establishment of an organized church, the continuing strength of Iranian traditions and the cultural and kinship ties of the Armenian nobility to Iran made Armenia an uncertain ally for the Romans. Yet since the Armenian monarchy was a branch of the Arsacid dynasty which had been overthrown by the Sasanians in 224, relations between Armenia and Iran were already strained. Tiridates' conversion compounded an already difficult situation, for the shahs naturally became suspicious of the future loyalty of Armenians to their Iranian heritage.[3] In the fifth century, attempts by the shahs to impose Zoroastrianism led to armed conflict – while to the west, the Armenians found their relationship with fellow Christians increasingly marred by their involvement in the struggles over orthodoxy. The division of Armenia c. 387 into two monarchies and two spheres of influence – a large Iranian sector east of the forty-first parallel of longitude, and a much smaller Roman sector west of that line up to the Euphrates – did not solve 'the Armenian question'.[4] Both powers were to find Armenia a difficult neighbour.

In the Roman sector (Inner Armenia) king Arshak soon died. His subjects were straightway placed under direct imperial rule through a *comes Armeniae*; on the other hand, the traditional rights of the Armenian princes in that area were not abrogated.[5] They enjoyed immunity from taxation, and no military garrisons were imposed. Procopius claims that it was this military weakness that later led Justinian to tighten his control. He observed that 'Armenia was always in a state of disorder, and for this reason an easy prey for the barbarians.'[6] He might have added that social, religious and cultural ties with their kinsmen across the border could not enhance security.

Laxar of P'arp: author of a history of Armenia from 387, picking up where the *Buxandaran* ends, to the appointment of Vahan Mamikonean as governor of Persian Armenia in 484. His history is an encomium of the Mamikonean family. But despite its bias, it is valuable as an account by someone who knew the major participants. (Most other early Armenian histories are by unknown authors and of uncertain date.)

Sebeos: a 'History of Heraclius' by a bishop Sebeos is mentioned by Armenian authors of the tenth and later centuries, but their quotations do not match the untitled text discovered in the early nineteenth century and published as the work of Sebeos. This anonymous work is important, none the less, as a product of the seventh century by an author familiar with events in the Armenian patriarchate. The emphasis is on Armenia in the context of Byzantine–Iranian rivalry from the time of Maurice (582–602) to the accession of Muawiya as caliph in 661.

Book of Letters: a compilation of documents dealing with ecclesiastical matters from the fifth to the thirteenth century. Of particular importance are the letters exchanged between official representatives of the Armenian church and foreign dignitaries of the Greek-speaking imperial church in the Byzantine empire, of the Syriac-speaking church in Iran, and of the church in Georgia.

[2] This is the usually accepted date for the consecration of Gregory at Caesarea, which marks the beginning of the formal organization of the church in Armenia. For the origins of Christianity in Armenia see Thomson (1988/9).

[3] For the Iranian heritage in Armenia see Garsoïan (1976), and for the religious background Russell (1987). [4] For this division and the geographical setting see Adontz (1970) ch. 1.

[5] Toumanoff (1963) 133–4. [6] Procop. *Buildings* iii.1.16. Loeb translation.

Not until the sixth century did Justinian do away with the traditional rights of the Armenian princes in a series of moves between 528 and 535. Armenian lands west of the border with Iran were then fully integrated into the empire as the four provinces of Armenia I–IV.[7]

It was in eastern Armenia – the sector under Persian suzerainty, which composed about four-fifths of the earlier kingdom – that the major cultural and religious developments of this period had their origin. Yet the border between the two sectors was no solid wall. Although Armenian writers rarely refer explicitly to the border, through the communities in the west contacts between the imperial capital and Persian Armenia were promoted and sustained.

In eastern Armenia the centrifugal tendencies of the leading princely families rapidly overcame the weakened monarchy. The rights and privileges of the noble families, jealously guarded over generations and considered more fundamental than royal authority, had been recognized by the Arsacids and legitimized. The office of *sparapet*, or chief military officer, for example, was the perquisite of the Mamikonean family, which played the leading role in politics during the fifth and sixth century. The role of coronant belonged by hereditary right to their principal rivals, the Bagratunis, who did not attain the leading role until the eighth century.

In Arsacid Armenia there were some fifty noble families of varied size and power, each with its own military forces.[8] Cities played little political or cultural role, despite their economic significance.[9] The focus of noble life was the family holdings. The territories of the Mamikoneans were in Tayk', Bagrevand and Taron – i.e. much of north central Armenia. The homeland of the Bagratunis was in Sper, but they gradually acquired territories to the south-west. A branch of this family was established in eastern Georgia (Iberia to the Greeks, K'art'li to the Georgians). To the south-east of Lake Van another family, the Artsrunis, were settled. They acquired land between Lake Van and the Araxes, and were later to become the principal rivals of the Bagratunis. After the demise of the royal line, these families pursued their own interests with regard to Rome or Persia, conducting, as it were, an individual foreign policy. Eastern Armenia was thus not a stable unity.

This traditional pattern of society was reinforced by the growth of an organized Armenian church. Armenian historians of the fifth and sixth century often stress the 'national' role of the church and the leadership of the patriarchs. But they do not explain that the bishoprics were established in the princely families, reinforcing the authority of the princes. This

---

[7] See further p. 672 below.
[8] Toumanoff (1963) 147–259 is devoted to 'The states and dynasties of Caucasia in the formative centuries', with detailed information on the different noble families.
[9] Garsoïan (1984/5). For the economic situation see Manandian (1965) ch. 4.

Armenian pattern, reflecting Armenian society of the time, was very different from that in the empire, which was based on the relative importance of the cities where the bishops were resident. Furthermore, the Armenian patriarchate until the death of Sahak in 439 was itself regarded as a hereditary perquisite of the Pahlavuni family, just as were other offices of state in other families.[10]

Unhappy with any diminution of their privileges, the magnates of eastern Armenia quarrelled with king Khusro (who had been installed in 387 when Arshak moved to western Armenia) and succeeded in having him deposed in favour of his son Vramshapur. The weaker the monarchy – from their point of view – the better, and soon the princes came to regard the shah himself as their immediate sovereign. On Vramshapur's death his father was briefly reinstated; then Yazdgerd I appointed his own son, Shapur. On Yazdgard's death in 420 Shapur failed to win the succession to the Sasanian throne. Vram V permitted Vramshapur's son Ardeshir to reign, but he too was unpopular. In 428 Vram agreed to accept the direct submission of the Armenian princes. The monarchy was abolished, and a Persian governor, the *marzpan*, installed at Dvin.[11] The *marzpan* was responsible for collecting taxes; the princes provided military service to the shah in person with their private armies. In their own lands they were autonomous.

In this way, the shah took advantage of age-long Armenian practices to increase Persian control of Armenia. Recognizing the importance of the church in that valuable province, he attempted to strengthen his hand even more by deposing the patriarch Sahak, who represented continuity with the past through his descent from St Gregory the Illuminator and whose outlook allied him to Greek cultural interests. Sahak was replaced by an insignificant appointee, to be succeeded by two Syrians.[12] Vram's policy with regard to the political administration of Armenia was moderate and successful. But his interference in ecclesiastical affairs was less well received. And his successor's harsher measures, aimed at integrating Armenia more closely into the Sasanian empire, eventually sparked outright rebellion. The passion of those who resisted – resistance was by no means unanimous – reflects the increased Armenian allegiance to the church and to Christianity as their birthright. The terms 'patrimonial' or 'ancestral way of life' originally used for the secular realm – where they applied to personal estates or the monarchy – were adapted by early Armenian historians to the religious sphere, where they now defined Christianity and the church within an Armenian context.

Yet Christianity was hardly 'an ancestral way of life' in fifth-century Armenia. The anonymous historian known as Agathangelos, who gives the

---

[10] Garsoïan (1984) esp. 233–5.   [11] For this office see Christensen (1944) 131–9.
[12] For these three – Surmak, Brkisho and Shmuel – see Garitte (1952) 99–102.

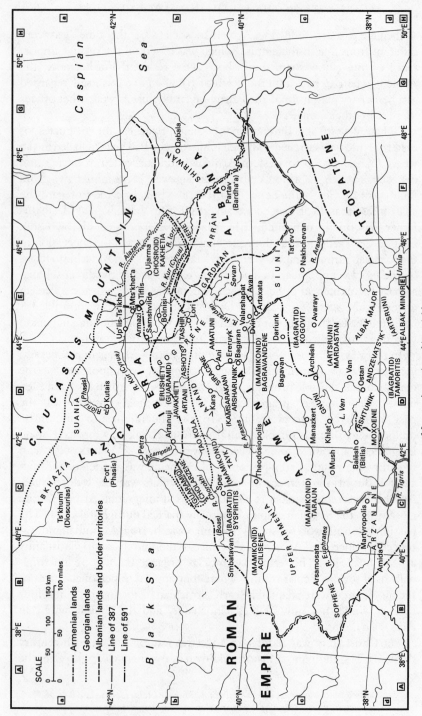

Map 19 Armenia and its neighbours

standard account of the conversion of the country, claims that Gregory visited the whole Caucasus, baptized millions of Armenians and established hundreds of bishoprics.[13] But he was too optimistic. The process of conversion took many generations, and the church met with opposition on many fronts. The *Buzandaran* paints a vivid picture of the pro-Iranian tendencies of many noble families, whose allegiance to the shah was strengthened by the acceptance of magism. For many the Christian message, which reached Armenia from Syria in the south and from Asia Minor to the west, was a foreign faith.[14] The fact that no written medium for the Armenian language existed in the fourth century added to the difficulty of strengthening the church's position and overcoming resistance to this alien innovation. So the invention of a script for the native tongue *c.* A.D. 400 by Mashtots marked a very significant stage in the conversion of Armenia, though it was not in itself the last step in that process.

Mashtots had received a Greek education and rose to a prominent position in the royal chancellery, but withdrew in order to lead a hermit's life. In due course he attracted disciples and, with support from the patriarch Sahak and king Vramshapur, formed a script based on the Greek model – i.e. a fully alphabetical script with separate characters for each consonant and vowel. With only minor modifications, it has remained in continuous use down to the present day. His disciples were sent to Syria and Asia Minor to learn Syriac and Greek and to make translations of books needed for the church. Rapidly a corpus of biblical, liturgical, theological and historical texts was made available. The circle around Mashtots began to create original works as well, and their interests soon extended to secular studies as pursued in the contemporary schools and universities of the eastern Mediterranean – they produced works of philosophy, grammar and rhetoric, and of scientific enquiry.[15]

The development of a specifically Armenian literature – in the broadest sense of the term – brought several consequences: an increasing sense of solidarity among Armenians on either side of the Roman–Iranian border, a stronger voice in national affairs for church authorities as a body that spoke for interests broader than those of individual families, and a greater involvement in the ecclesiastical questions that were shaking the eastern Roman empire. Armenia's liturgical practice was greatly influenced by Jerusalem. Many from Armenia and Georgia made pilgrimages to the Holy Land, and some stayed on as monks. The theological exegesis of Syria

[13] For a comparison of the various recensions and versions of this history see the introduction to Thomson (1976).

[14] There is no general study in a western language of the impact of the Syrian strain in Armenian Christianity more recent than that of Ter-Minassiantz (1904). Aspects of Syrian liturgical influence are brought out by Winkler (1982), which has a good bibliography.

[15] For a survey of the early period see Thomson (1980) and in general Renoux (1993).

made a great impact, and the Greek fathers of the fourth century were well-known. As the Armenians forged their own traditions in matters of practice, their attitudes with regard to matters of faith were sharpened by involvement in the burning issues of the day. This heightened sense of commitment to a faith associated with the Roman empire could only be regarded with concern by the rulers of the Sasanian world in which most of Armenia lay.

Yazdgard II's attempt to impose magism by force in 450 prompted immediate resistance by the church authorities; popular resentment coalesced around the prince of the Mamikonean family, Vardan. He was related by marriage to the patriarch Sahak, whose daughter his father had married, and his family played the leading role in contemporary Armenian politics. Like many other Armenian princes, Vardan had earlier temporized by submitting to magism when summoned to court. But he agreed to lead the revolt, and one of his brothers went with a delegation to seek aid from Theodosius II. The latter died in July, and Marcian refused to become involved in Armenia, having many distractions closer to home in the Balkans.[16]

For that first year the Armenians held off the Persian forces. But faced with dissension in their own ranks, they could not resist a large Persian army sent to Armenia in 451. In June, Vardan and many nobles met their deaths on the field of Avarayr in eastern central Armenia; other leaders, both clerical and lay, were taken in captivity to the region of Nishapur. Resistance in a military sense was thus ended. But Armenia was a valuable asset to the Sasanian empire, and calmer views prevailed. Forced conversion to magism was dropped, and an uneasy peace marked the next generation. During the reign of Peroz (459–84) the imprisoned leaders of the rebellion were released.

The close ties between Armenia and Georgia were the indirect cause of the next attempt to loosen Iranian control. A daughter of Vardan Mamikonean, Shushanik, had married the governor of the neighbouring province of Gugark', Vazgen. But he accepted magism, in return for which he was given a royal princess to wife. His first wife, Shushanik, died of subsequent ill-treatment, and was to become a martyred saint revered on both sides of the Armenian–Georgian border.[17] Her *Life* is the first original composition in Georgian, a script for that language having been formed in the early fifth century (by Mashtots, according to Armenian writers). The Georgian king, Vakhtang-Gorgasal, eventually put Vazgen to death in 482, thereby incurring the immediate wrath of his lord, shah Peroz. In this emergency Vakhtang sought aid from Huns beyond the Caucasus and from his

---

[16] This revolt is not mentioned in contemporary Greek sources. For the date of Elishe's classic description and its relation to the version of Lazar see the introduction to Thomson (1982).

[17] Peeters (1935) discusses the original text by Jacob of Tsurtav and later versions in their historical setting.

Christian neighbours to the south. Vardan's nephew, Vahan Mamikonean, now the leading prince of that family, thus found himself at the head of the Armenian forces engaged in another rebellion, thirty-one years after his uncle's death.

Military success was no more possible now than it was earlier. Armenian–Georgian co-operation was marred by mutual antagonisms, brought out clearly by the historian Lazar, who describes this period in detail – Vahan being the patron and hero of his *History*. The Armenian troops were forced to withdraw to the mountains of north-western Armenia. They were rent by internal dissensions, the Persians always finding supporters among the Armenian nobility. On the other hand, the Persian forces were not at full strength, since Peroz had taken a large army to attack the Hephthalites. His unexpected defeat and death on the battlefield in 484 entirely changed the situation. Anxious to placate their fractious subjects, whose Christian ties to the Roman empire were a potential source of danger, the Persians removed their governor. In his place, the prince of the most prominent local noble family was appointed *marzpan*. Thus Vahan Mamikonean gained the measure of internal autonomy for which his uncle Vardan had died in 451.

The attention of Armenian historians moves rapidly from Vahan's success to the involvement of Armenia in the Byzantine–Persian wars of the late sixth and early seventh century. In doing so, they ignore the growing estrangement of the Armenian from the imperial church – a rift with cultural and political consequences of the first magnitude.

The increasing importance of the church as a cultural institution following the abolition of the monarchy in 428 is not of itself surprising. It was the only institution that cut across factional lines, and it was the only medium through which literary and artistic endeavours could be realized on any meaningful scale. Individuals with financial backing would still attend the universities of the eastern Mediterranean; Greek and Syriac as well as Armenian sources attest to the presence of Armenian students in Antioch, Beirut, Alexandria, Athens and elsewhere. But government service as a career for the educated was no longer an option after 428; the only major patron of education and learning was the church, and only the church could offer advancement for the ambitious and a haven for the studious. The complaints of Anania of Shirak in the seventh century that his fellow countrymen did not admire learning suggest that without patronage a teaching career was difficult.[18] There were cities in Armenia, but they did not play the cultural role of an Antioch or an Athens, with organized schools and subsidized professorial chairs.

The relationship of the Armenian church to the larger Greek world was thus of importance. Armenians were always admirers of Greek learning,

---

[18] His short 'Autobiography' is a unique document in early Armenian literature.

but their attitude to Constantinople was ambivalent. In part, such an attitude reflected the political situation; a pro-Greek attitude could arouse suspicions of disloyalty to the shah. Some part was played by the very different
backgrounds of Armenians and Greeks – and, not least, the strong Syrian
strain in Armenian ecclesiastical life, church ritual and theological exegesis
prevented any automatic acceptance of things Greek. An official break
between the churches was long in coming. But the steps which led to that
eventually irrevocable rupture deserve a brief review.

Luckily, the Armenian reaction to the theological questions that divided
the Greek *oikumene* – debates which gave the Armenians an opportunity to
define more carefully their own position – is well documented in the *Book
of Letters*. The first three sections of this unique collection of official documents comprise exchanges of letters between Armenian ecclesiastical
authorities and members of the imperial church of the eastern
Roman/Byzantine empire, representatives of the Syriac-speaking church
in Iran, and ecclesiastics in Georgia, covering the fifth, sixth and seventh
century. The earliest is a letter by Acacius, bishop of Melitene, written soon
after the Council of Ephesus, held in 431.[19]

Melitene had been one of the cities where the pupils of Mashtots had
pursued their study of Greek. Acacius had met Mashtots on the latter's
travels in Roman territory, and was well informed of events in Armenia.
He had recently played a significant role in the Council of Ephesus, where
Nestorius and other Antiochene theologians had been condemned. So he
took alarm when he heard that works by Theodore of Mopsuestia were
being read in Armenia. For Theodore was a prominent biblical exegete of
the Antiochene school, whose interpretation of the Incarnation had been
rejected at Ephesus. But Armenian interest in Theodore was not surprising, since the tradition he represented had been strong in Edessa, the centre
of Syriac-speaking Christian culture. It was to Edessa that Mashtots had
gone in his search for an Armenian script, and it was in Edessa that many
of his pupils studied. The reply to Acacius' letter, signed by Sahak as prelate
of the Armenian church, was polite but guarded, denying any Armenian
involvement in heresy yet not specifying any heresy by name. A second
letter was sent by Acacius to the secular authorities of Armenia. It had been
prompted by Syrian priests who reported that the influence of 'Nestorian'
ideas in Armenia was continuing. But it passed without response.

Of greater impact was a letter from the patriarch of Constantinople,
Proclus. This time it was not foreign Syrians, but two pupils of Mashtots
who had taken the initiative. While in the capital to translate Greek texts,
they approached the patriarch for an authoritative interpretation of the

---

[19] For the Armenian correspondence with Acacius and the patriarch Proclus see Tallon (1955). The
Armenian reaction to the theological disputes is discussed in Sarkissian (1975). For the debates within
the eastern Roman empire see in general Grillmeier, *Christ in Christian Tradition*.

doctrine of the Incarnation. That this was not an official solicitation by the Armenian authorities is clear from an apology by a third Armenian disciple, Eznik, who had studied in Edessa before going to Constantinople. Proclus responded by addressing a detailed exposition of the matter to the bishops of Armenia. The Armenian reply was signed by both Sahak and Mashtots. After defining their own faith, they assured the patriarch that no heretical ideas attributable to Theodore were circulating in Armenia. The letter of Proclus, however, was to remain a keystone of Armenian orthodoxy, and this early emphasis on the Council of Ephesus had a profound impact. Ephesus, rather than the Council of Chalcedon, held twenty years later, would be the rallying-cry of Armenian theologians.

The Fourth Oecumenical Council – held across the Bosphorus in Chalcedon in 451 – did not bring peace to the warring parties or solve the theological question of defining the Incarnation in a manner satisfactory to all. The patriarch of Armenia was not represented at Chalcedon, though bishops from Armenian provinces on the Roman side of the frontier were in attendance.[20] Somewhat surprisingly, the early Armenian historians pass over both the Second Council of Ephesus in 449 and that of Chalcedon in 451. It was the emperor Zeno's *Henotikon*, promulgated in 482, that Armenians emphasized as orthodox. (As noted above, in that year Vahan Mamikonean was engaged in open rebellion against the shah, a situation resolved by his eventual appointment as *marzpan*.) Bypassing the recent divisive Council of Chalcedon, in their official pronouncements the Armenians were happy to pledge their allegiance to Nicaea and Ephesus. As they developed their own traditions in ecclesiastical architecture and moulded an individual Armenian literature, they were not at the turn of the century acting in deliberate opposition to what was then the orthodoxy of the empire.

At a council held in 505/6 in Dvin, the residence of the *marzpan* and the main city of Persian Armenia, a group of Syrians from the Persian empire appeared, requesting episcopal consecration for one of their monks, Simeon. These Syrians were not members of the church in Persia which enjoyed the shah's official recognition, but were Monophysites. The Armenian bishops consecrated Simeon and recognized the orthodoxy of these Syrians as being in conformity with their own faith and that of the Greeks. But the zealous Simeon, an opponent of the official church in Persia, persuaded the Armenians to anathematize the Council of Chalcedon as expressing the views of Nestorius.[21] The Armenians did not anathematize the Greek church as such; the *Henotikon* of Zeno was still in force, and he was regarded by the Armenians as 'the blessed emperor'.[22]

---

[20] Garsoïan (1989).   [21] For the career of Simeon see Shahid (1971) 159–79.

[22] In the *Book of Letters*, Zeno is called 'blessed' (49, 140, 268); 'pious' (141, 142, 328); 'orthodox' (126, 262, 277); 'benevolent' (266, 267, 269). For this council in Dvin see Sarkissian (1975) ch. 7: 'The rejection of the council of Chalcedon'.

But this apparent unanimity of the Greek and Armenian churches was misleading. Zeno's policy of compromise with the opponents of Chalcedon was reversed on the accession of Justin. After 518 the imperial church of Constantinople made peace with Rome and stood firmly behind the definitions of Chalcedon. As the sixth century progressed, the Monophysites in Syria and Egypt became more coherently organized, thanks mainly to the labours of Jacob Baradaeus, while their theology found definite expression in the works of Severus of Antioch. The differences apparent at the time of Chalcedon had now become quite clear-cut, and compromise was increasingly difficult.[23]

The Armenians do not seem to have taken any definite steps to repudiate the Greek return to Chalcedonian orthodoxy until they were prompted to do so by another Syrian delegation from Persia, which appeared at another council held in Dvin in 555, again requesting consecration for one of their company. These Syrians were members of a splinter group within the Monophysite church, the Julianists, who held that Christ's body had remained 'incorruptible'.[24] The Armenian patriarch, Nerses II, and his bishops found the Syrians' profession of faith orthodox and consecrated Abdisho. The impact of Julianist ideas was not the most important result of this encounter in 555; in later years there was no unanimity among Armenian theologians on that issue. The significant fact was that the Armenians not only rejected Chalcedon again; they also, for the first time, specifically anathematized the Greek church for upholding that council – which to Armenian eyes had approved the ideas of Nestorius.[25]

Despite these important developments, whose significance was perhaps not obvious at the time, Armenian historians have remarkably little to say about Armenian affairs during the reigns of Justin and Justinian. The first Persian war, which ended in 532, brought no change to the frontiers or the status of the divided country. Even the reorganization of the Armenian territories in the eastern Roman empire by Justinian is passed over by Armenian sources. In 528 the right of Armenian princes to maintain their private military forces was abrogated when the office of *magister militum per Armeniam* was created. The civil standing of the princes was diminished when their traditional rights of inheritance were brought into line with imperial practice. In 536 Armenian territory was reorganized into Armenia I, II, III and IV at the expense of neighbouring land in Cappadocia. The use of the name 'Armenia' is an indication of the strongly Armenian presence west of the Euphrates, which had been increasing rather than diminishing. Now, not only were the Armenians inside the imperial borders

---

[23] For Severus see Frend, *Monophysite Movement* 201–20, and for Jacob Baradaeus *ibid.* 284–7, with ch. 21*b* (Kennedy), p. 594 above.   [24] For this controversy see Draguet (1924).
[25] For this second council of Dvin and the correspondence preserved in the *Book of Letters* see Garitte (1952) 130–75.

deprived of their long-standing rights and governance by traditional princely families (which had been guaranteed in the original treaty), but this significant portion of the total Armenian population was lost to Armenia proper. Imperial authorities did not speak Armenian or encourage allegiance to the Armenian church, as Justinian attempted to impose imperial orthodoxy on his realms. Armenians were useful to the empire in many ways, especially in the army. But an individual Armenian culture flourished henceforth only on the Persian side of the frontier.

Justinian's treatment of his Armenian nobles led to complaints to the shah[26] and Armenian involvement in a conspiracy against the emperor.[27] In 540 hostilities between Byzantium and Persia reopened. Antioch was captured, but Dara resisted the invading Persians. Military operations were confined to Mesopotamia and Lazica during the war, save for an encounter at Dvin in 543. The peace of 545 was one of many made during the long confrontation, which continued into the following century.

There was no overt sign of unrest in Persian Armenia until the latter part of the sixth century. When trouble did break out, it seems to have been caused by the attitude of the Persian *marzpan* of the time, Suren, not by the official policy of the shah. In 571 Suren set up a fire-temple in Dvin and attempted to impose Zoroastrianism on the country. The reaction was parallel to that of 450. Led by Vardan, prince of the Mamikoneans (not to be confused with the leader of the fifth-century revolt), the Armenians rebelled. When Suren returned the following year with reinforcements, he perished in the encounter. However, the Persians retook Dvin, and Vardan fled to Constantinople. Now, for the first time, the consequences of the religious differences became clear. Vardan had to accept communion with the imperial church, while the patriarch, who had fled with him, remained at Constantinople under the cloud of submission to Chalcedon until his death in 574.[28]

Justin II gave Vardan military forces, and Dvin was retaken. But Roman success was not lasting. In 576 Persian forces under Khusro crossed Armenia but failed to capture Karin (Theodosiopolis). After advancing as far as Sebaste, Khusro withdrew and sacked Melitene, but after a confrontation there, he fled back to Persia in confusion. During negotiations the following year, the Roman general Justinian was defeated by Tam Khusro in Basean and Bagrevand,[29] and the Persians retained the frontier fortress of Dara, which they had captured in 573.[30]

But Roman fortunes revived in 590 when the general Vahram Chobin seized the Sasanian throne on the murder of shah Hormizd. The legitimate heir, Khusro II, son of Hormizd, appealed to the emperor Maurice for

---

[26] Toumanoff (1963) 175; Procop. *Wars* 11.3.56.   [27] Adontz (1970) 160–1; Procop. *Wars* 11.3.31.
[28] This rebellion and the 'union' of 572 is discussed in Garitte (1952) 183–275.
[29] Sebeos 71.   [30] Whitby, *Maurice* 264–7.

help, promising in return to cede to the empire all of Armenia as far as Lake Van and Dvin, plus part of Georgia. The offer was accepted, and the Armenians under Mushegh, prince of the Mamikoneans, sided with Khusro and the Byzantines. Their combined forces defeated Vahram the following year at Gandzak in eastern Armenia. Installed as ruler of Persia, Khusro fulfilled his promise: Armenia west of the Hrazdan and Azat rivers passed to Byzantium.

This success for the eastern Roman empire was fraught with a number of consequences for the Armenians. Maurice attempted to integrate Armenia more securely into the empire. He deported significant numbers of Armenians to the Balkans to strengthen his borders there and weaken resistance to imperial rule among Armenians now incorporated into the empire. The Armenian general Mushegh Mamikonean was killed in Thrace.[31] But Maurice sometimes encountered resistance by Armenian soldiers. The Bagratid prince Smbat rebelled and was condemned to the arena. Saved by his strength, according to the Armenian historian (by the clemency of the empress, according to a Greek source), he was exiled to Africa.[32] But it was not long before he was in the east, serving the shah.

The plight of the Armenians between shah and emperor is well expressed in an apocryphal letter which the Armenian historian known as Sebeos claims was sent by Maurice to Khusro: 'They are a perverse and disobedient nation, who stand between us and disturb us. I shall gather mine and send them off to Thrace. You gather yours and order them to be sent to the east. If they die, it is our enemies who die. If they kill, they kill our enemies. Then we shall live in peace. For if they remain in their own land, there will be no repose for us.'[33]

But the most significant aspect of his policy was the attempt to enforce imperial orthodoxy in the newly acquired territories. The Armenian patriarch was summoned to a synod where the union of the churches might be effected – that is, where the Armenians would accept Chalcedon and communicate with the Byzantines. Moses II refused to go and remained in Dvin, just across the border. On this occasion he is credited with a riposte that clearly expressed Armenian resistance to assimilation. It is preserved in a rare pro-Chalcedonian document of Armenian origin: 'I shall not cross the Azat; I shall not eat bread baked [in the oven]; I shall not drink warm water.' The Azat was the river marking the border and is a pun, the word meaning 'free'. The other two comments refer to the differing practices of the liturgy, since Armenians used unleavened bread and did not mix warm water with the wine.[34] Matters of doctrine may figure more prominently in the written records of historians and theologians, but the development of different rituals was no less potent a factor in the estrangement of the churches.

---

[31] Sebeos 90–1. Whitby, *Maurice* 127–8, notes that Sebeos' account seems to be a conflation of several campaigns.   [32] Sebeos 93; cf. Whitby, *Maurice* 127.   [33] Sebeos 86.

[34] For the 'union' of 591 and the comments of Moses II see Garitte (1952) 225–54.

Nevertheless, the Armenian bishops in Byzantine territory did go to Constantinople and accept communion, thus causing a schism in the Armenian church. An anti-patriarch, John, was established by Maurice on his side of the Azat, at Avan. Until the death of Maurice, the dissension continued. But once Byzantine forces withdrew, then Armenian unity was restored. This pattern recurred in the time of Heraclius and again under Justinian II, but proved no more lasting than under Maurice. Despite the fact that many sympathized with the position of the Greek imperial church – and significant groups of Chalcedonian Armenians existed in the succeeding centuries[35] – reunion between the Byzantine and Armenian churches was never effected.

Yet the time of Maurice was remembered as a time of peace. The curious text known as 'Pseudo-Shapuh' – a medley of tales dating from the ninth to the twelfth century, and not the lost work of the ninth-century historian – refers to the proverb: 'As in the time of Maurice, when one lived untroubled.' It also reports that when Maurice summoned his father David, who lived in Armenia, the latter said: 'I cannot come. I prefer my small garden to the Roman empire.' But by cutting off the heads of the largest cabbages in his garden, he indicated to his son's messengers how Maurice should treat his magnates.[36]

Just as Maurice used Armenian arms in the Balkans, so did those Armenian princes on the Persian side of the border continue to provide military service to the shah. The most notable example is the career of Smbat, prince of the Bagratunis, who served at different times both emperor and shah – Armenian loyalties being rarely unequivocal and permanent. Just as Maurice settled colonies of Armenians in the west, so did Smbat find Armenians, Greeks and Syrians deported to Hyrcania when he was serving as governor there for Khusro II. Sebeos notes that the Armenians had even forgotten their own language, and that Smbat remedied this by arranging for the ministry of a priest.[37] The role of language and religion as a means of preserving Armenian identity in colonies outside the homeland was already clear.

At the same time, the Armenians were estranged from their northern neighbours. The Georgians under the Catholicos Kyrion disavowed the Armenian rejection of Chalcedon and henceforth remained firmly committed to the orthodoxy of Constantinople. The final rupture occurred after a series of bitter exchanges. At another council held in Dvin in 608, the Armenians excommunicated the Georgians.[38] But contacts between the two peoples could not be stopped by fiat, not least because of the extensive

---

[35] For Chalcedonian Armenians in later centuries see Arutyunova-Fidanyan (1980).

[36] Ps. Shapuh 49, 51. Cf. Adontz (1934).   [37] Sebeos 96–7.

[38] The Armenian–Georgian correspondence in the *Book of Letters* has not been translated, but many of the documents were quoted by Ukhtanes and may be read in the English rendering of that later historian. But see now Garsoïan (1999).

bonds of consanguinity linking noble families on both sides of the frontier. Pro-Chalcedonian Armenians were particularly numerous in Tayk' and Gugark', where the two peoples mingled.

The downfall of Maurice in 602 gave Khusro an opportunity to recover the Armenian lands ceded to his earlier supporter. The reign of Heraclius, however, was to see the final defeat of Sasanian Persia and the rise of a new power in the near east. These truly epoch-making events lie beyond our present scope. Here it may suffice to note that by the turn of the sixth century the basic structures of an independent Armenian culture had already been created.

Many years earlier Tacitus had referred to the ambivalent role of Armenia and the Armenians between Rome and Parthia: 'A people from the earliest times of equal ambiguity in character and geography ... placed between two great empires, with which they differ frequently.' He described their dealings with both sides, and he knew that fundamentally the Armenians were closer to Iran than to Rome.[39] In Sasanian times as well, the value of Armenia as a vassal state was recognized by the two sides: the eastern Roman empire and Sasanian Iran both sought to control Armenia, to engage its troops and to profit from the gold mines and other natural resources. After the division of the country and the abolition of the monarchy, attempted control became attempted integration – more successful in Roman Armenia than in the much larger eastern sector.

The conversion of the Armenians to Christianity gradually changed their relationship with Iran, but slowly and painfully. The various strands of Christian practice from Jerusalem, Syria and Asia Minor were moulded into a national tradition. But their faith and practice kept the Armenians apart from the imperial church of Constantinople. Armenian scholars created a national literature that was overtly patterned on the Christian literatures in Syriac and Greek, reflecting also the influence of late antique culture which Armenians of the fourth and later centuries absorbed in the schools of the eastern Mediterranean. But the Iranian background was not easily shaken off, and Persian motifs reappeared throughout the centuries. Many Armenians found fame and fortune in the Byzantine empire,[40] but Armenia as a whole was never integrated into the Greek-speaking empire.

When Armenians later reflected on their individuality and the formation of their unique culture, they concentrated on a few specific episodes: the conversion of king Trdat (Tiridates), the invention of the Armenian script and beginnings of a literature in the vernacular, and the heroic resistance to Sasanian attempts to impose magism. The interpreters of those events, no matter how far removed or tendentious, became the classic authors *par*

---

[39] Tacitus, *Annals* II.56; XIII.34. My translation.
[40] Cf. Charanis (1963) and for a later period Kazhdan (1975).

excellence. And the images of those events as expressed in the classic histories gave meaning to succeeding generations who sought to understand the role and fate of Armenia in an unfriendly world.

Armenia may have played a larger role in the politics of the near east in the time of Tigran the Great, as Moses Khorenatsi rightly stated: 'He extended the borders of our territory, and established them at their extreme limits in antiquity. He was envied by all who lived in his time, while he and his epoch were admired by posterity.'[41] Yet Tigran and military success were not the typical models in terms of which Armenians thought of their present and their future. Imagery of a 'golden age' described the harmony of king Tiridates and St Gregory the Illuminator, while wishful prophecies foresaw the eradication of present woes by the restoration of the descendants of the one to the Arsacid throne and of the descendants of the other to the patriarchate. More powerful than the memory of the heroic Tigran was the model of the Maccabees, whose defence of ancestral customs and an individual religious culture evoked a strong response in Armenian minds.[42] So in the fifth and sixth centuries the image of an Armenian 'classical' age was created. Perhaps exaggerated in retrospect, it none the less depicted a people who could not be assimilated into either of the imperial powers.

[41] Moses 1.24 – though he has dated this Tigran far too early.
[42] See the introduction to Thomson (1982) for the details. Such imagery was applied by the tenth-century Thomas Artsruni to the Muslim rulers, and is frequently found in later Armenian writers.

CHAPTER 22c

THE ARABS*

LAWRENCE I. CONRAD

I. INTRODUCTION: THE QUESTION OF SOURCES

In the present state of our knowledge it is not difficult to describe the physical setting for pre-Islamic Arabian history, and new archaeological discoveries in Saudi Arabia, Yemen, Jordan and the Gulf are producing much valuable and unique evidence. Over the past century a vast body of epigraphical material – some 50,000 north and south Arabian inscriptions and the inscribed sticks now emerging by the hundreds in northern Yemen – has provided a wealth of information on the societies of the peninsula, especially the bedouins.[1] But all this seldom provides a coherent picture of the course of events, as opposed to vignettes and bare details, and thus does not replace a literary historical tradition. There are external epigraphic records of the Arabs and Arabia, and historical sources – especially in Greek and Syriac – are often helpful.[2] But this information too is profoundly discontinuous, and in any case represents the perspective of outsiders who regarded the Arabs as barbarian marauders and most of Arabia as a menacing wasteland.[3]

There is voluminous material on the subject in the Arabic sources, but herein lies the problem.[4] The relevant accounts, including a vast bulk of poetry, are frequently attributed to the pre-Islamic period or otherwise presented as describing events and conditions of that time, but apart from the Qur'ān the sources containing these accounts are at least two centuries later. In times past it seemed reasonable simply to compare the various accounts to determine which seemed most likely to be true. More recently, however, it has become clear that the Arabic sources on the Arabs in pre-Islamic Arabia – and indeed, on the first century of Islamic history as a whole – represent a fluid corpus that adopted a range of argumentative views on issues important at the time the accounts were being transmitted and the sources compiled; the result was the colouring and reshaping of

---

* I would like to thank Fidelity and William Lancaster and Michael Macdonald for their valuable comments and suggestions.

[1] See, e.g., Robin (1991); Macdonald (1995a).
[2] See Papathomopoulos (1984); Segal (1984); MacAdam (1989).
[3] On the distorted image of bedouins among settled folk, see Shaw 1982–3.
[4] Two still-valuable overviews are Olinder (1927) 11–19; Caskel (1927–30).

much early and possibly genuine material and the creation of many new accounts.[5] Most importantly, pre-Islamic Arabia played an important role in early Islamic kerygma. In explanation of the success of Islam and the Arab conquerors, Muslim scholars and transmitters interpreted Islam's emergence from Arabia as part of God's divine plan.[6] Part of this conception involved presentation of the pre-Islamic Arabs as naïve coarse barbarians – ragged ignorant nomads and eaters of snakes and lizards, for example – and Arabia as a quintessential wasteland. This contrasted sharply with the powerful and sophisticated peoples of the empires to the north and the richness and fertility of their lands; obviously, the Arab victories against such formidable foes could only have been won by God's permission and as part of his plan for mankind.[7] This paradigm is manifestly kerygmatic, and while it may at various points correspond to historical reality it does not spring from that reality. In each case, then, the historian must judge – often on insecure grounds – the extent to which the motifs and stereotypes of this kerygma have affected his sources.[8]

II. THE ARABS IN LATE ANTIQUITY

Extant references to 'Arabs' begin in the ninth century B.C.,[9] and in ensuing centuries attest to their presence in Arabia, Syria and Iraq and their interaction with the peoples of adjacent lands, encouraged in part by the Roman and Persian policy of using Arab groups to protect their desert flanks and perform military functions as confederates and auxiliaries. In Syria, Arab presence was prominent all along the fringe between the desert and the sown,[10] and inscriptions and literary sources confirm that many Arabs took up settled life in rural villages.[11] The hinterlands of inland Syrian cities were partly populated by Arabs, and major cities such as Damascus and Beroea (Aleppo) had significant Arab populations. In such situations Arabs certainly knew Greek and/or Syriac, and perhaps as their first languages.[12] Arabs were also to be found through the pastoral steppe lands of northern Mesopotamia, where monks in the Jacobite and Nestorian monasteries occasionally comment on them.[13] In Iraq there were large groupings of

---

[5] Ahlwardt (1872); Ḥusayn (1927) 171–86; Caskel (1930); Blachère (1952–66) 1.85–127, 166–86; Birkeland (1956); Arafat (1958); Caskel (1966) 1.1–71 (with the review in Henninger (1966)); Crone (1987) 203–30.   [6] See the discussion in Conrad (forthcoming).

[7] Conrad (1987b) 39–40 and n. 46; (1998a) 238.

[8] The gravity of the source-critical problems is stressed in Whittow (1999), a detailed critique of the volumes on 'Byzantium and the Arabs' by Irfan Shahīd (specifically, Shahīd (1995)), which, though full of valuable information, pose serious problems and need always to be used with caution.

[9] Eph'al (1984) 75–7; Macdonald (1995a).

[10] Dussaud (1955) 51–161; Mayerson (1963); Sartre (1982).

[11] MacAdam (1983); Millar (1993b) 428–36.

[12] Nau (1933) 19–24; Trimingham (1979) 116–24; Shahīd (1989) 134–45.

[13] Nau (1933) 15–18, 24–6; Charles (1936) 64–70; Trimingham (1979) 145–58.

Arabs; settled Arabs lived as both peasants and townsmen along the western fringes of Iraq, and al-Ḥīra, the focus of Arab sedentary life in the area, was deemed an Arab town. Most were converts to Christianity, many spoke Aramaic and Persian, and they were largely assimilated to Sasanian culture.[14]

The sources referring to the Arabs describe them in various ways. In Greek and Syriac they were most usually called *sarakenoi* and *ṭayyāyē*, terms which refer to their tribal origin or to their character as travellers to the inner desert.[15] In Arabic, interestingly enough, the terms *ʿarab* and its plural *aʿrāb* are generally used to refer to tribal nomads. Though the settled folk of Arabia shared much in common with the nomads, they nevertheless drew a sharp distinction between themselves and the bedouins (and rightly – a tribesman is not necessarily a nomad). It is true that by the sixth century A.D. the Arabic language had spread through most of Arabia (if not so much in the south) and engendered a common oral culture based largely on poetry of often exceptional quality.[16] But in none of this should one see evidence of a supposed archetype for Arab unity in any ethnic, geographical or political sense.

The basis for Arab social organization was the tribe.[17] Genealogical studies in early Islamic times were already elaborating the lineages and interrelationships of the tribes in great detail. The Arabs comprised two great groupings, northern and southern; the former were traced to an eponymous founder named ʿAdnān and the latter to a similar figure called Qaḥṭān, and both were further divided into smaller sections and subgroupings. Ancient Arab history is routinely presented in the sources as determined by these tribal considerations,[18] but modern anthropology has cast doubt on this and has raised the question of whether such a thing as a 'tribe' even exists. While the term is problematic, it seems excessive to resolve a conceptual difficulty by denying the existence of its object.[19] The notion of the tribe, however ambiguous, has always been important in traditional Arab society; in pre-Islamic Arabia there can be no doubt that kinship determined social organization.[20] The problem can perhaps best be formulated as revolving around the questions of how far back this was meaningfully traced, and how stable perceptions of kinship were.

---

[14] Charles (1936) 55–61; Morony (1984) 214–23.
[15] Macdonald (1995b) 95–6. Other views: Christides (1972); Graf and O'Connor (1977); O'Connor (1986).   [16] Fück (1950) 1–28; Blachère (1952–66) 1.66–82; Gabrieli (1959b); von Grunebaum (1963).
[17] See Caskel (1962); and for modern parallels, Musil (1928) 44–60; Jabbur (1995) 261–8, 286–306.
[18] Caskel (1966) 1.1–71.
[19] *Inter alia*, Schneider (1984). Cf. the discussion in Crone (1986) 48–55; (1993) 354–63; Tapper (1990) 60–4.
[20] Even with respect to Arabs from south Arabia, where Dostal's hypotheses (1984) would lead us to expect social organization along other lines. Note that in all three of the early Arab urban foundations in Egypt and Iraq, the Arab conquerors – even Yemeni contingents – organized themselves according to tribe. See Pellat (1953) 22–34; Djaït (1986) 73–135; Kubiak (1987) 58–75.

Individuals were very often aware of their primordial tribal affiliations, and took pride in the achievements, glories and victories of their ancestors. Similarly, personal enemies often vilified the individual by calling into question his tribe as a whole. In practice, however, the vast tribal coalitions rarely acted as a unified whole, and the socially meaningful unit was the small tenting or village group tracing its origins back four or five generations at most. The perception of common descent was not unimportant to the cohesion of such groups, but even more vital were considerations of common interest. In order to maintain itself, the group had to be able to defend its pasturing grounds, water supplies and other resources from intruders, and its members from injury or harm from outsiders. Dramatic changes in kinship affiliations could occur when, for example, the requirements of contemporary alliances or client relationships dictated a reformulation of historical genealogical affinities.[21] Such shifts could even occur at the level of the great tribal confederations,[22] and were facilitated by the fact that no loss of personal or legal autonomy was involved – a 'client' tribe was not in the state of subservience implied by the western sense of the term.[23]

Through most of Arabia, the welfare of the individual was secured by customary law and the ability of his kin or patron to protect him. If a member of a group were molested or killed, this dishonoured the group as a whole and required either retaliation or compensation. Individuals thus adhered to at least the minimum standards required to remain a member of their group, since an outcast could be killed with impunity.[24] This system provided security and guaranteed the status of tradition and custom.[25] Violence in the form of warfare, feuding and raiding did occur, but the last of these has given rise to much confusion, and its scope and scale have often been exaggerated:[26] there was no glory in raiding a weak tribe or ravaging a defenceless village, and fatalities on either side posed the immediate risk of a blood feud. Prowess in battle was without doubt a highly esteemed virtue, and Arabian society was imbued with a martial spirit that elevated the raid, or *ghazw*, to the level of an institution.[27] Still, this usually involved one powerful tribe raiding another for their animals,[28] and the violence involved was limited by considerations of honour, by the ordinarily small size of raiding parties, and – where weaker groups were concerned – by networks of formal arrangements for protection.

[21] Ibn Khaldūn, *Muqaddima* 1.238.
[22] Goldziher (1967–71) 1.92, 96; Caskel (1953) 8, 15; (1966) 1.31–2, 43–4; 11.22–3, 72, 448; Lancaster (1997) 16–23, 32–4, 151–7. Cf. Gellner (1973). [23] Lancaster (1997) ix, 73, 128–9.
[24] Musil (1928) 426–70, 489–503; Farès (1932) esp. 44–101; Chelhod (1971) esp. 231–341; Stewart (1994) esp. 130–44. [25] Cf. Stewart (1994) 139–43.
[26] Most notoriously in Lammens (1928) 181–236; cf. also Meeker (1979) 111–50.
[27] Musil (1928) 504–661; Jabbur (1995) 348–55; Lancaster (1997) 140–5.
[28] Sweet (1965) 1138–41.

Headship of a tribal unit was vested in a shaykh ('chief', 'elder'; other terms were also used), but the powers of this office were seriously limited, and the shaykh remained in power as long as the tribe felt this was to their benefit. He was expected to lead the tribe, protect its prerogatives and interests, mediate among its members and with other tribes, and serve as an exponent of *muruwwa*, an ethic of masculine virtue bound up in such traits as courage, strength, wisdom, generosity and leadership.[29] While the chief had no power to enforce his decisions, it was of course not in the interest of the group to maintain a leader in power and yet regularly defy his decisions. The shaykh led by example and by exercise of a quality of shrewd opportunistic forbearance called *ḥilm*: he was a mouthpiece of group consensus whose reputation required assent to his judgement.[30]

The exception to all this was the south, where plentiful rainfall, carried by monsoon winds, allowed for levels of agriculture, population and sedentary development not possible elsewhere. The numerous small towns of the region thrived on the spice trade and enjoyed the stability of a highly developed agrarian economy with extensive terrace farming and irrigation. The towns were closely spaced settlements of tall tower-dwellings, often with a distinct 'centre', and their organization tended to promote commercial and professional bonds at the expense of large-scale kinship ties. Out of this stability there arose a number of coherent regimes with indentifiable political centres: Maʿīn, Sabaʾ, Qatabān and Ḥaḍramawt, based respectively at Qarnaw, Maʾrib, Tamnaʿ and Shabwa. The most dynamic of them was Sabaʾ, which by the third and fourth century A.D. had managed to annex the territories of all the others.

The south Arabian entities were ruled by figures early on called *mukarribs*, or 'federators'. It has long been held that this office was hereditary and had a distinctly religious function, but this now seems unlikely.[31] Not unexpectedly, social differentiation reached levels unknown in lands to the north. The sedentary tribes were led by powerful chieftains known as *qayls*, and at the other end of the spectrum both serfdom and slavery were well-established institutions. Nomads were held in check by granting them lands in exchange for military services, thus rendering them dependent upon the regime.

III. ARABIAN RELIGIOUS TRADITIONS

The social organization of pre-Islamic Arabia was closely bound up with considerations of religion, and it is in this area that problems of methodology and source criticism are most acute. Issues such as borrowing from

---

[29] Goldziher (1967–71) I.11–44.   [30] See Pellat (1962–3), (1973). Cf. also Lancaster 1997, 87–9.
[31] Robin (1991) 52, 55.

more advanced civilizations, the starting-points and relative antiquity of religious forms, the roles of animism and totemism, and differences between sedentary and nomadic peoples have been and remain highly controversial, and in many cases important arguments involve value judgements about nomads and, similarly, supposed distinctions between 'high' and 'low' forms of religious expression. There is also the problem that the Arabic sources, where the vast bulk of our source material is to be found, can hardly be said to offer an objective view of pre-Islamic religion. The folly of idol-worship and the credulity of its adherents are routinely stressed in stereotyped ways. One tale describes how a tribe fashioned an idol out of *ḥays* (dried curd mixed with dates and clarified butter) and worshipped it for a time, but eventually devoured it during a famine, leading to a poet's wry comment:

> The tribe of Ḥanīfa ate their lord
> When dearth and hunger swept the land,
> Fearing naught for consequences
> From their lord's avenging hand.[32]

Inspired by Qur'ānic criticisms,[33] Arabic sources also present 'bedouins' as indifferent to matters of faith.[34]

Arabian polytheism took several forms,[35] one of which was stone-worship. Greek and Syriac sources presented this as adoration of lifeless rocks, but such objects were not deities in themselves, but their dwelling-places or the focus of the rituals of the cult. Offerings were made at the site, and ritual observances included circumambulation of the stone. The best-known example is of course the Ka'ba in Mecca, but we are told that other places had such cultic foci.[36] These foci were often surrounded by a sacred territory, usually called a *ḥaram* in the north and a *ḥawta* in the south. These were precincts associated with the sanctity of worship and sacrifice, and violence and killing, including hunting, were forbidden there. Holy men were in charge of these precincts, and their descendants enjoyed a special religious esteem.[37] Also prominent was religious observance revolving around idols – again, with the idol probably representing the deity being worshipped. The names of many idols are known from ancient poetry and from later prose works drawing on this verse, and important new details pertaining to Yathrib (Medina) may be indicative of a more general pattern. Here clans each had an idol in a room belonging to all of the clan. The idol was venerated there and sacrifices were made to it. People also had wooden

---

[32] Ibn Qutayba, *Ma'ārif* 621.
[33] Sūrat al-Tawba (9), v. 90 (= Arberry, 189–90): procrastinators, liars, malingerers; vv. 97–8, 101 (= Arberry, 190–1): hypocrites, stubborn in unbelief, opportunists; Sūrat al-Fatḥ (48), v. 11 (= Arberry, 532): dissemblers, malicious, corrupt; Sūrat al-Ḥujurāt (49), v. 14 (= Arberry, 538): superficial in belief.
[34] Cf. Bashear (1997) 7–14.   [35] Arafat (1968).
[36] This is made especially clear in Lughda al-Iṣfahānī, *Bilād al-'arab* 32.   [37] Sergeant (1962).

idols in their homes, and made similar observances at that level. To offend the idol was an offence against the honour of the head of the house and a matter for retaliation, and there is some evidence that these idols were intended to be figures of ancestors. There was thus a hierarchy of idols, corresponding to the social status of their owners.[38]

There is good evidence of star-worship and astral divinities as well. The widely venerated al-Lāt (a sky goddess) and al-ʿUzza (possibly the morning star) may have been representations of Venus, and Byzantine polemics against Islam claim that the Islamic slogan *Allāhu akbar*, 'God is great', has as its origin a cry of devotion in astral religion.[39] The worship of astral divinities has also been connected with the veneration of idols.

The attitude of the ancient Arabs toward their gods was entirely empirical and pragmatic. Though they did consider problems of human existence and the meaning of life,[40] they did not look to their deities for the answers. They regarded their gods as the ultimate sources of worldly phenomena beyond human control, such as disease, rain, fertility, and personal and communal adversities of various kinds; they worshipped the gods in expectation of their assistance, but they did not revere them or consider that they owed unwavering commitment to them.[41]

Monotheistic religion was also known in Arabia from an early date. The influx of Jews into Arabia is difficult to trace, but probably had much to do with the failure of the Jewish revolt and the destruction of the Temple in A.D. 70, and the gradual spread of Christianity over the next three centuries. In south Arabia, Judaism enjoyed considerable success in the fifth and early sixth century, and to the north there were important Jewish communities at various places, primarily Yathrib. There Judaism seems to have had deep and powerful roots, if one may judge from reports that in pre-Islamic times the Jews there had three times as many fortified compounds (*quṣūr*) as all the other non-Jewish clans combined,[42] and that in the latter half of the sixth century the Jewish clans of Qurayẓa and al-Naḍīr collected taxes from the other tribes.[43] The question of Jewish influences in Arabia and on Islam has become highly sensitive in modern scholarship, but there can be no doubt that such influences were profoundly important; the Qurʾān itself contains many tales and accounts of Jewish origin, as also do early Islamic religious lore and scholarship.[44]

---

[38] Lecker (1993).   [39] On this see Rotter (1993); Hoyland (1997) 105–7.

[40] E.g. the ephemeral joys of youth and the ultimate fate of either death or senility: Zuhayr, *Dīwān* 29; al-ʿAskarī, *Awāʾil* 1.57.

[41] Wellhausen (1897) 213–14; Crone (1987) 237–41.

[42] Ibn al-Najjār, *Al-Durra al-thamīna* 325. Cf. Conrad (1981) 22.

[43] Ibn Khurradādhbih, *Al-Masālik wa-l-mamālik* 128; Yāqūt, *Muʿjam al-buldān*, IV.460. Cf. Kister (1968) 145–7.

[44] On the Jews of pre-Islamic Arabia, see Newby (1988) 14–77; and on influences, Geiger (1833); Rosenthal (1961) 3–46; Nagel (1967); Rubin (1995) esp. 32, 217–25.

The Christianization of the Roman empire in the fourth century opened the way for the large-scale spread of the faith along and beyond the empire's frontiers, including Arabia.[45] Along the Syrian desert fringe from the Red Sea to the Euphrates, it spread to the Arab tribes via monasteries and wandering missionaries, primarily Monophysite. In some cases, as with the Taghlib and Ghassān, entire tribes converted; tribal settlements such as al-Jābiya and Jāsim, south of Damascus, became ecclesiastical centres too. These tribes were familiar with at least basic observances, yet remained completely within Arab tribal culture as well.[46] Along the Iraqi frontier the spread of Christianity was somewhat slower, perhaps because a network of Nestorian monasteries in the area took longer to appear than had been the case among the Monophysites.[47] Still, al-Ḥīra, the Lakhmid base, was the seat of a bishopric by A.D. 410.[48] Further south, there were major Christian communities at such centres as Najrān and Ṣanʿāʾ, and small ecclesiastical outposts along the Arabian coast of the Persian Gulf. In such centres, specifically Monophysite or Nestorian forms of Christianity were practised, but elsewhere the Arab tribesman's main contact with the faith was via individual monks and hermits, and there confessional boundaries may have been less sharply drawn.[49]

Other currents influenced by Judaism and Christianity remained distinct from both. These trends revolved around two notions: that of a 'high god', and a belief in what was called *ḥanīfiya*. Little can be said about belief in a 'high god' in ancient Arabia, apart from the fact that, as elsewhere in the Near East,[50] some held that a god called Allāh held a certain dignity and status above the other deities of the Arabian pantheon and was extolled as a deity to whom one could turn in case of particular need.[51] On *ḥanīfiya* there is more information.[52] The Qurʾān makes it the religion of Abraham and associates it, on the one hand, with belief in a single God and, on the other, with rejection of idolatry and repudiation of worship of the sun, moon and stars. In particular, and most importantly, it reflects not the pragmatic attitude toward religion described above, in which the individual worships his god(s) in expectation of services with respect to worldly needs beyond his control, but rather a submissive devotion to and faith in God for his own sake. *Ḥanīfiya* is also distinct from Christianity and Judaism; in several passages its adherent (a *ḥanīf*) is equated with a Muslim, and in one variant to the Qurʾānic text *ḥanīfiya* replaces Islam as the 'true religion'.[53]

---

[45] For an overview, see Charles (1936); Trimingham (1979).
[46] For a valuable anthology of the verse of early Arab Christian poets, see Cheikho (1890). Cf. also Conrad (1994) 30, 31, 51. [47] Cf. Brock (1982). [48] *Synodicon orientale* 36.
[49] On the Qurʾānic evidence, see Ahrens (1930); Michaud (1960); Parrinder (1965); Bowman (1967); Robinson (1991). The relevant Qurʾānic verses, with the commentaries from many *tafsīr*s, are assembled in Abū Wandī *et al.* (1996). [50] Teixidor (1977) 17, 161–2.
[51] Watt (1979); Welch (1979); Rubin (1981).
[52] For differing interpretations, see Gibb (1962); Rubin (1990); Rippin (1991).
[53] Jeffery (1937) 32, *ad* Sūrat Āl ʿImrān (3), v. 19; = Arberry, 47.

Other sources suggest that there were *ḥanīf*s in various parts of Arabia, that the movement was one of individuals rather than religious communities, and that Mecca was important to its adherents. Other details are less reliable, and there is no evidence to link *ḥanīfiya* with south Arabian inscriptions attesting to worship of a god called al-Raḥmān, 'the Merciful', one of the Islamic names for God. But the fact that the tradition on the *ḥanīf*s makes some of them doubters or enemies of Muḥammad suggests that it should not be dismissed entirely as later prophetic annunciation or the tidying up of a pagan past.

Of interest in this respect is the testimony of Sozomen (d. before 448), who from the vantage point of Gaza in southern Palestine offered the following comments on Arab religion:

It seems that the Saracens were descended from Ishmael, son of Abraham, and hence were originally called Ishmaelites. Their mother Hagar was a slave, so in order to hide the shame of their origin they took the name of Saracens, pretending to be descended from Sarah, the wife of Abraham. As such is their descent, they practise circumcision like the Jews, abstain from eating pork, and adhere to numerous other Jewish observances and practices. In so far as they in any sense diverge from the observances of that people, this arises from the passage of time and their contacts with other neighbouring peoples . . . It seems likely that with the passage of time their ancient customs fell into disuse as they gradually took to observing the customs of other peoples. Eventually, when some of their tribe came into contact with the Jews, they learned from them the facts of their true origin and returned to observance of Hebrew custom and law. In fact, even at the present time there are some of them who live their lives in accordance with the Jewish law.[54]

The connection with Judaism may reflect an inclination to associate false belief with the machinations of Jews.[55] As to the Abrahamic religion attested in the text, while the connection is circumstantial and Sozomen wrote long before the testimony of the Qur'ān, the Islamic scripture may refer to continuing monotheistic trends in Arabia that it wishes to distance from earlier monotheistic faiths now viewed as rivals.

IV. ECONOMIC LIFE IN ARABIA

It is difficult to generalize on the notion of an Arabian 'economy', since the internal economic situation in the peninsula varied from place to place and depended on whether a community was settled or nomadic. As noted above, the south had a lively village economy based on terrace farming and irrigation; but even here, production was primarily limited to foodstuffs and

---

[54] Soz. *HE* VI.38.10–14. Cf. Cook (1983) 81; Millar (1993a) 42–4.
[55] On the topos of the scheming Jews, see Schafer (1997).

use-value goods. South Arabian spices and incense were much sought-after items for centuries, and undoubtedly fortunes were made from trade in them,[56] but overland trade in such goods appears to have collapsed by the first or second century A.D.[57]

In the rest of the peninsula the economy was far more rudimentary. The interior of the peninsula consists of various types of steppe land where, in most years, no major cultivation can be sustained because of lack of water. Reliable water supplies come from wells and oasis springs, and it was around these that Arabia's towns developed. The date palm dominated agriculture in many places, and this and other crops were often cultivated in large walled gardens (*ḥawā'iṭ*) scattered over whatever patches of arable land there were in or around a settlement. Goats and sheep were kept, and items produced for sale included hides and leather, wool, cloth, dairy products, raisins, dates, wine, and utensils and weapons of various kinds. Gold and silver were mined, but often figured as a replacement for currency rather than as an export item; perfume was produced, especially in Aden and Najrān, but beyond the Arabian and Syrian markets it could not compete with the cheaper products of such Byzantine centres as Alexandria.[58] Arabian traders in late antiquity were thus known to their neighbours – in Palestine, for example – as bearers not of costly luxury items, but rather of animals, wool, hides, oil and grains.[59]

Bedouins, on the other hand, were largely herders and pastoralists, though members of many tribes settled for varying periods of time and others engaged in opportunistic agriculture – for example by sowing on a fertile watered plot on their way somewhere else, and then reaping when they returned. Tenting groups travelled in recognized tribal territories, their schedules and movements (and willingness to encroach on the lands of other tribes) largely dictated by the needs of their animals. Those who lived along the desert fringes tended sheep and goats, as well as the single-humped dromedary camel; groups venturing into the depths of the Arabian steppe lands did best with camels, but on occasion are known to have taken goats and sheep as well. For barter or sale, nomads could offer such animal products as hides, leather, wool and dairy products.

The symbiosis between village-dwellers and nomads was important to the whole economic structure of Arabia. Leather, for example, was an extremely important product and was the plastic of its day; everything from buckets to items of clothing was made from it, and agriculture could not have been maintained without huge supplies of leather for ropes, irrigation

---

[56] Groom (1981).   [57] The last reference to it is in the *Periplus maris erythraei* xxvii.

[58] Dunlop (1957) 37–40; Crone (1987) 87–97.

[59] Krauss (1916) 335–6; Kraemer (ed.), *Excavatons at Nessana* III: *Non-Literary Papyri* 251–60 no. 89. The Palestinian church at Dayr al-'Adasa, dedicated in 621, has a mosaic floor bearing various rural scenes, including one of a caravan of camels carrying oil or wine jars; see Balty (1989) 149–51.

equipment, harness and so forth. Apart from exchanges (often quite complex) of goods and services, bedouins played a major role in economic development. There is evidence, for example, that parts of different tribes concluded sharecropping agreements and worked together to promote and protect agriculture.[60] Certain villages also specialized in serving the needs of nomads, and oases and springs where herds could be watered attracted settlements that thrived on trade with the nomads. Relations were further dictated by the need of settled merchants to move their goods through lands controlled by nomads, and hence to remain on good terms with the tribes.[61]

Arabian domestic trade thus consisted of caravans of camels organized by settled merchants and protected and guided by bedouins who controlled the lands through which the caravans passed. Seasonal fairs were often held, especially around religious shrines, and security at such important times was guaranteed by the declaration of sacred periods during which no raiding or fighting was to occur.[62] The goods being traded were for the most part not costly items, but rather the basic goods and commodities that people needed to live. This in turn limited the distance and duration that the caravans could travel, since the longer the journey was, the more expensive the goods would be at their destination;[63] that is, the longer the contemplated journey was in both distance and time, the more precious the goods being carried would have to be in order to generate sufficient income to make the journey feasible economically. The internal trade of Arabia thus seems to have involved the transport of goods on short or medium-length journeys, and it is probably this factor that accounts for the proliferation of market centres. The sources present a picture of lively markets dotting the steppe landscape of the peninsula; wells, springs and small villages were all attractive sites for established market activities, though the scale of such operations was probably small.[64] In some cases, commerce was encouraged by banning private land ownership within the market precinct (thus preventing dominance by a few successful merchants) and suspending taxes and fees on traders and visitors.[65]

---

[60] Al-Bakrī, Mu'jam mā sta'jam 1.77–8. Cf. Kister (1979) 70 on similar arrangements at the time of the Prophet. The same system is still widespread today.

[61] See Simon (1989) 78–86; Morony (1984) 218–19; Donner (1989) 77–8; and for modern examples, Jabbur (1995) 1–2, 5–8, 32–8, 250. Cf. also Nelson (1970).

[62] Wellhausen (1897) 84–94; Brunschvig (1976) 1.113–18; Crone (1987) 87–108.

[63] Jones (1955) 164; Hendy (1986) 556–7. Cf. also Crone (1987) 7. Not all trade was profit-driven, however; see Villiers (1940).

[64] Lughda al-Iṣfahānī, Bilād al-'arab e.g. 224, 227, 243, 333–4, 335, 345, 358, 361, 397; Muḥammad ibn Ḥabīb, Muḥabbar 263–8; al-Marzūqī, Kitāb al-azmina wa-l-amkina 161–70. Cf. also al-Afghānī (1960); Ḥammūr (1979).   [65] Kister (1965); Dostal (1979); Lecker (1986).

V. IMPERIUM AND IMPERIAL POLITICS

It will be seen from the above that there was little in Arabia to attract the attention of the great powers of late antiquity, and at first it was only Arabia's role athwart the route to the east that lent it any importance to them. This factor alone was sufficient to make Arabia a focus of imperial manoeuvring and power politics, but trade operated in conjunction with other factors as well. The spread of Christianity and to a lesser extent Judaism in Arabia reflects the interest of external powers from an early date. In fact, it was the great triad of politics, trade and religion that determined the course of events there from late antiquity onward, with trade providing an imperial momentum later transferred to the other two.

All around the peripheries of Arabia the impact of imperium was being felt. Behind the Roman presence advancing in the north came Roman roads, way stations and forts, reflecting an increasing interest in control of what lay beyond. Far more vigorous, however, were the inroads by the Sasanians, who, with their capital at Ctesiphon, the rich agricultural alluvium of Iraq, and the Persian Gulf trade to consider, had a more immediate stake in Arabia. Settlements were founded up and down the Gulf, and Oman was annexed by Shāpūr I (reigned 241–72). In the fourth century, Arab raids provoked a punitive expedition that reached as far as the Ḥijāz. Discovery of silver and copper in the Najd led to the foundation of a Sasanian outpost at Shamām.[66]

The rivalry between the two powers was exacerbated by several factors. The establishment under Constantine of a Christian empire based at Constantinople made competition with Persia more immediate and provided yet another arena for intrigue and dispute. But more important by far was the evolution of the rival polities themselves. From largely decentralized and culturally diverse empires tolerant of a broad range of contradictory ideologies and traditions, both developed into world powers using political, economic and military strength, justified by élitist ideologies and spurred by aspirations to universal dominion, to pursue imperial aims increasingly dictated from the capital. These states, the empires of Byzantium and the Sasanians, competed for control of the west Asian heartland and adopted more global strategies in efforts to promote their own interests and undermine those of their rival.[67] Thus, while the rise of Christianity led to the collapse of the market for the incense consumed so massively and ostentatiously by pagan Rome,[68] the demise of this formerly

---

[66] Nöldeke (1879) 56; Dunlop (1957) 40; Crone (1987) 46.
[67] Fowden (1993) esp. 24–36, 80–137, though the focus on monotheism and the stress on premeditated planning from the centre seem overstated. Cf. Crone (1987) 47.
[68] Müller (1978) 733–64; Groom (1981) 162; Crone (1987) 27.

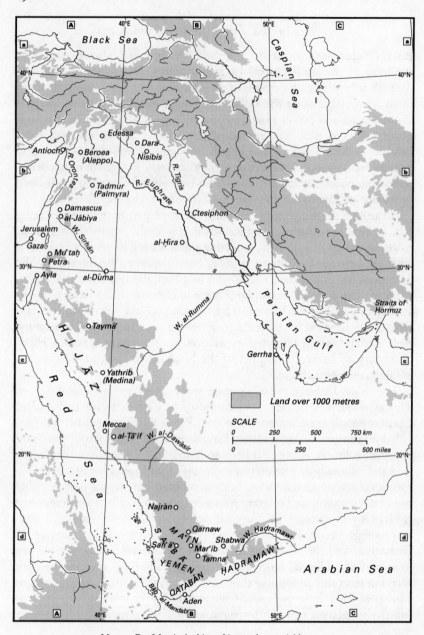

Map 20 Pre-Islamic Arabia and its northern neighbours

crucial aspect of the eastern trade was more than replaced by new rivalries of an unprecedented intensity.

The new level of conflict ushered in by the escalating competition between the two great powers manifested itself in several ways where Arabia and the Arabs were concerned. First, a pronounced religious element was introduced into the struggle, primarily in the southern part of the peninsula and surrounding lands. Monophysite missionary activity[69] led to the conversion of Ethiopia to Christianity in the fourth century and the spread of the faith in Yemen and elsewhere in south Arabia. The Christian presence noted frequently in the Qur'ān was probably the result of commercial contacts with Syria. The Sasanians, on the other hand, supported the spread of the rival confession of the Nestorians and also encouraged the Ḥimyarites, a predominantly Jewish regime which ruled most of south Arabia and had influence elsewhere. Religious rivalries played instrumental roles in an Ethiopian invasion of Yemen in about 518 and shortly thereafter a civil war among the Ḥimyarites between Christian and Jewish factions. This struggle led to a persecution of Christians in south Arabia under the Ḥimyarite Dhū Nuwās, and in the 520s culminated in the massacre of the Christians of Najrān. Ethiopia responded with a second invasion, killed Dhū Nuwās, and once again installed a puppet regime in Yemen. The power of the Ethiopian governor, however, was soon usurped by a certain Abraha, who established himself as the paramount authority in the south; among the Meccans he was remembered as the leader of an expedition that they viewed as a campaign against themselves, but that in fact was a move (in 552) against tribal forces to the east.

Second, the peninsula was gradually encircled and penetrated by external forces. The Sasanians established trading posts beyond the Straits of Hormuz as far as Aden and in the sixth century occupied Yemen. Persian authority extended as far as Yathrib, where taxes were collected by the Jewish tribes of Qurayẓa and al-Naḍīr and in part sent on to a Persian 'governor of the desert' (marzubān al-bādiya).[70] Byzantium, on the other hand, still had trade through Clysma and Ayla to protect,[71] and sought a sea route to the east that would not be subject to Persian taxes and interference. It thus tried to extend its influence down the Red Sea and battled against pirates and adventurers to maintain control of ports and customs stations; epigraphical evidence places Byzantine forces nearly 1,000 km south of Damascus in the mid sixth century.[72] It also used its new Christian ally, Ethiopia, to pursue its economic interests and intervene militarily in the affairs of the south, and encouraged the Ḥimyarites to attack Persian interests.[73]

---

[69] Altheim and Stiehl (1971–3) 1.393–431; Shahīd (1971) 252–60.

[70] Christensen (1944) 373–4; Altheim and Stiehl (1957) 149–50; Whitehouse and Williamson (1973); Frye (1983). [71] E.g. Wilkinson (1977) 88.

[72] Cf. for example, Abel (1938); Seyrig (1941); Simon (1989) 34. [73] Smith (1954) 427.

Third, both powers used tribal allies in Arabia to further their own interests, protect their Arabian frontier zones, and confront the tribal forces of
the other side. Such a tactic was not new. Rome and Persia had routinely
used tribal auxiliaries in various capacities,[74] and in the late fifth and early
sixth century the Ḥimyarites in Yemen co-opted the great north Arabian
tribal confederation of Kinda into acting in their interest and controlling
caravan traffic along the routes from Yemen to Syria and Iraq. Kinda eventually extended its control over all of central Arabia, as well as part of the
Ḥijāz and areas along the Persian Gulf coast, and in the early sixth century
it was attacking both Byzantine and Sasanian targets along the desert
fringes of Syria and Iraq. Seeking to avoid further incursions and gain a
strong tribal ally against forces acting for the Sasanians, the Byzantines
reached an understanding with the confederation and on several occasions
sent embassies to promote good relations. Kinda thus became an ally of
Byzantium; turning against the Sasanians, it gained considerable authority
in the hinterlands of south-western Iraq and even occupied al-Ḥīra for a
time.[75] Its primary sponsors remained the Ḥimyarites in Yemen, however,
and as this regime declined, so also did the fortunes of Kinda.

The Sasanians' main tribal ally was the Lakhmids, a tribe that had established itself in north-eastern Arabia by the fourth century A.D. and founded
a stable base at al-Ḥīra. There had been contacts and relations between the
two sides in the past, but the combination of deteriorating relations with
Byzantium and the spectre of powerful Kinda forces allied to Byzantium and
positioned within easy striking distance of Ctesphon and the agricultural
plains of Iraq led the Sasanians to support and encourage the Lakhmids with
renewed vigour. The latter had long been subordinate to Kinda, and double
marriages between them had been arranged at least twice in the past.
Nevertheless, by about 504 the new Lakhmid chieftain al-Mundhir III ibn al-
Nuʿmān (reigned 504–54) was able to rid himself of Kinda suzerainty and
launch operations against the confederation with a well-organized army.[76]
Fighting over the next two decades ended with the utter disintegration of
Kinda and the extension of Lakhmid authority over their rival's former
clients among the Arab tribes. By the 540s the Lakhmids held sway over
many of the tribes of central Arabia and over towns as far west as Mecca.[77]

Byzantium was thus forced to turn to other Arab clients for the protection of its position and interests. Its choice fell on the Ghassānids, a
south Arabian tribe, closely related to the Kinda, that had migrated to
northern Arabia and Syria in the fifth century and established itself as

---

[74] On Rome, see Shahīd (1984) 52–63; and on the fifth-century Ṣālihids in particular, see Shahīd
(1958), (1989) (to be used with caution).

[75] Olinder (1927) 32–93; Simon (1989) 42–6; Lecker (1994); Shahīd (1995) 1.148–60.

[76] Rothstein (1899) 134–8; Altheim and Stiehl (1957) 117–23; Kister (1968) 165–7.

[77] Rothstein (1899); Simon (1967), (1989) 27–30, 42–6, 55–8, 149–52; ʿAbd al-Ghanī (1993) 11–23.

the pre-eminent power on the desert fringe there. Compared to the Lakhmids, the Ghassānids were a more nomadic group; though they were often associated with the camping-ground called al-Jābiya sixty-five km southwest of Damascus, they had no real fixed centre comparable to that of the Lakhmids at al-Ḥīra. Their influence was not as broad-ranging as that of the Lakhmids, and though they had trading connections with Iraq through Nisibis and Dara, their control over the relevant routes was tenuous. Nevertheless, Byzantium granted the Ghassānid shaykh the title of phylarch and showered him with honours, privileges and money. In return, it was expected that the chieftain would keep his own tribe under control and protect imperial interests from other tribes as well.[78]

The Ghassānids and Lakhmids, confronting one another across the Syrian desert, were thus drawn into the series of great Byzantine–Persian wars that began in 502 and ended with a decisive Byzantine victory in 628. Significant fighting between them began in the 520s and continued sporadically for sixty years, with dire consequences for the agricultural infrastructure of both Syria and Iraq. Several observers describe the destruction in Syria,[79] and whatever survived the passage of raiding parties and military expeditions was exposed to the brigands and outlaws hovering around such forces.[80]

The military strife tends to overshadow other developments in which the two sides were variously involved. The Ghassānids were responsible for the establishment of several small towns in the hinterlands south of Damascus and perhaps also for some of the so-called 'desert palaces' of the Syrian steppe.[81] Sponsors of Monophysite Christianity, they also erected numerous churches and monasteries. In Iraq, al-Ḥīra grew from a camp (which is what the name means in Arabic) into a lively Arab town noted for its churches and monasteries, impressive residential compounds and taverns. Persian Gulf shipping could sail up the Euphrates as far as al-Ḥīra, and Lakhmid income included proceeds not only from raids but also from agricultural rents and produce, trade, and taxes from tribes they controlled. There also seems to have been a nascent literary tradition emerging there.[82] Both sides, especially the Lakhmids, were also major patrons of Arab oral culture, and some of the most important poets of pre-Islamic times gained generous support from Ghassānid or Lakhmid shaykhs.[83]

---

[78] Nöldeke (1887); Simon (1989) 27–32, 55–8; Sartre (1982); Peters (1984). On the term phylarch, which originated as a post in the provincial administration, not necessarily relating to nomads, see Macdonald (1993) 368–77.

[79] John Moschus, *Pratum spirituale* 2957–8, 2995–8, 3023–4 nos. 99, 133, 155; Delehaye (1927) 23–4; al-Ṭabarī, *Ta'rīkh* I.1007 (cf. also Nöldeke (1879) 299 n. 4); al-Washshā', *Kitāb al-fāḍil* fol. 105r. Cf. also Foss (1975); (1977) 68–71; Schick (1995) 25, 31–3.

[80] Abū l-Baqā', *Al-Manāqib al-mazyadīya* I.105–6. Early Islamic works on *jihād* also mention the problems posed by these elements.   [81] Gaube (1984).

[82] Much valuable material is collected in 'Abd al-Ghanī (1993) 25–138.

[83] Nicholson (1907) 38–54; Blachère (1952–66) II.293–356; 'Abd al-Ghanī (1993) 365–469.

The history of the Arab client regimes is important, but they were not central in the imperial planning of either Byzantium or Persia, in which they figured mainly as threats that had to be countered.[84] Little is known from the Lakhmid and Persian side, but Byzantine emperors, political strategists and historians like Procopius certainly held the Ghassānids in low esteem. The Byzantines had little faith in the abilities, motives or intentions of their Arab allies. The treaty of 561, for example, expresses dissatisfaction with Saracen adherence to treaty terms in the past, comes close to calling them smugglers and traitors, and warns of harsh punishment for lawbreakers.[85] When Ghassānid phylarchs refused to adhere to Chalcedonian orthodoxy, they were exiled. Byzantium made overtures to the Lakhmids when it suited them to do so, and the lack of trust and commitment worked both ways: the capture of Dara by Khusro Anushirvan (reigned 531–79) probably involved some negotiations with the Ghassānid phylarch al-Mundhir ibn al-Ḥārith (reigned 569–82).[86]

Neither side survived the manoeuvrings of their patrons or the broader conflict engulfing the Near East in the sixth century. In 581 al-Mundhir was arrested by the emperor Tiberius (reigned 578–82) and exiled to Sicily in a religious dispute, and in 584 his son and successor al-Nuʿmān joined him. Fragmented by the emperor Maurice (reigned 582–602) into a host of smaller entities and riven with dissension and conflict over the deposition of two leaders within four years, the Ghassānid phylarchate rapidly fell apart. Forces from the tribe are mentioned in accounts of the Arab conquest of Syria, but not in a leading role.[87] The Lakhmids survived a while longer, but during the reign of Khusro II Parviz (reigned 590–628) they were displaced in favour of a similarly decentralized system. The Sasanians also promoted the position of the Banū Ḥanīfa, which roamed in the desert on their southern flank.[88] Later, when a force of Persian troops and Arab auxiliaries sought to quell a desert revolt in about 610, the imperial army was beaten at Dhū Qār, thus marking the first time that the tribes had been able to defeat the Sasanians in battle.[89] It also illustrates how the demise of the Arab client regimes marked not the shift from one system of frontier defence to another, but rather the opening of a great power vacuum extending from the desert fringes of Syria and Iraq all the way to central Arabia. Inhabitants of the peninsula remembered that they had once been 'trapped on top of a rock between the two lions, Persia and Byzantium'.[90] But as the next decade was to reveal, these

[84] Important discussion in Whitby (1992).   [85] Menander fr. vi.i.320–2, 332–40.
[86] Whitby, *Maurice* 257–8. Cf. also the Nemara Inscription of A.D. 328, which has Arabs in the eastern Ḥawrān in contact with both the Romans and the Persians; Bowersock (1983) 138–47; Bellamy (1985).
[87] Nöldeke (1887) 33–45; Shahīd (1995) 1.455–71, 634–41, 648–51.
[88] Al-Aʿshā, *Dīwān* 72–87 no. 13, esp. 86 vv. 47–9; Abū l-Faraj al-Iṣfahānī, *Aghānī* xvii.318–22.
[89] Nöldeke (1879) 332–5; Rothstein (1899) 120–3.
[90] Qatāda (d. 735) in al-Ṭabarī, *Tafsīr* ix.145, *ad* Sūrat al-Anfāl (8), v. 26. Cf. Kister (1968) 143–4.

days were gone forever and the Persian setback at Dhū Qār was but a hint of things to come.

VI. MECCA, MUḤAMMAD AND THE RISE OF ISLAM

In about 552[91] a boy named Muḥammad ibn ʿAbd Allāh was born into a minor clan of the tribe of Quraysh, which was settled in and around the shrine centre of Mecca in the Ḥijāz, about 900 km south of Syria. A trader by profession, he participated in the caravan trade of Arabia and visited Syria on several occasions. In about 610 he began to preach a monotheistic faith called 'submission to God', or Islam, and summoned his fellow Meccans to prepare for the Last Judgement. Difficulties in Mecca and the erosion of vital support had by 622 reached the point where he was obliged to move to Yathrib, 300 km to the north. This shift, the *hijra*,[92] proved to be of crucial importance, for in Yathrib, henceforth called Medina (al-Madīna, probably referring not to 'the city', but to the Prophet's house), the ranks of his followers increased dramatically. Raids on the caravans, camps and villages of his enemies met with success and further expanded his support. He returned to Mecca in triumph in 630, and by the time of his death in 632 his authority extended over much of Arabia. The rest was brought under control by the first caliph, Abū Bakr (reigned 632–4), and Muslim forces went on to campaigns of conquest that in less than a century created an empire extending from Spain to central Asia.

How all this occurred and why it focused on Muḥammad, Mecca and the late sixth century are questions that early Muslims took up themselves,[93] and that have comprised a major concern of modern historical research. In the 1950s Watt proposed a socio-economic solution. Mecca was a major centre for overland caravan trade, and its merchants and others grew wealthy on the profits from commerce in such precious items as incense, spices, gemstones, gold and so forth. This widened the gap between the rich and the poor and led to social malaise as crass materialism eroded traditional values. Muḥammad's message was essentially a response to this crisis.[94] More recently, however, serious challenges have been made to the notions of a lucrative Arabian trade in luxury items, of Mecca as an important entrepôt, and hence of some serious crisis provoking a religious response.[95] It may thus be useful to indicate the ways in which points made above contribute to the discussion.

---

[91] For the date, see Conrad (1987a).   [92] Crone (1994).

[93] But not immediately; see Donner (1998) 75–85.

[94] Watt (1953) 1–29 and in numerous publications of his thereafter. Cf. the review by Bousquet (1954).

[95] Simon (1975), trans. Simon (1989); Peters (1988); Crone (1987). Cf. the highly polemical review of Crone in Serjeant (1990) and the reply in Crone (1992).

Mecca, a place completely unknown to any non-Arabic source of the pre-Islamic period, lies off the main routes of communications in western Arabia. The site itself is barren, inhospitable and incapable of sustaining agriculture for more than a minuscule population. Even had there been a lucrative international trade passing through the Ḥijāz in the sixth century, it would not have found an attractive or logical stopping-point at Mecca, which owed its success to its status as a shrine and pilgrimage centre. As at certain other shrines in Arabia, pilgrims came to circumambulate a rock, in this case associated with an unroofed building called the Kaʿba, and perform religious rituals with strong affinities to those of Judaism: offerings and animal sacrifice, washing and concern for ritual purity, prayer, recitation of fixed liturgies and so forth.[96] There are indications that, early on, there was little resident population at the site: 'People would perform the pilgrimage and then disperse, leaving Mecca empty with no one living in it.'[97]

The success and expansion of Mecca were due to the administrative and political skills of its keepers, the tribe of Quraysh. The Kaʿba seems to have been a shrine of the god Hubal,[98] but in the religiously pluralistic milieu of pagan Arabia it must not have been difficult to promote it as a place where other deities could be worshipped as well. A greater achievement was convincing other tribes to honour the sanctity of the *ḥaram* of Mecca and to suspend raiding during the sacred months when pilgrims came. As agriculture was not possible at Mecca, it had to bring in food from elsewhere and so was at the mercy of nearby tribes in any case. The very fact that Mecca survived, much less prospered, thus reflects the diplomatic skills of Quraysh. The Islamic tradition, of course, makes much of the *a priori* importance of Quraysh, but this is surely something that emerged within the paradigm of a sedentary tribe seeking to protect and promote its interests through skilful manipulation of relations with the nomadic tribes around it. There was mutual advantage in the prosperity of Mecca: trade with pilgrims, import and marketing of foodstuffs and other necessities, and collection and distribution of taxes levied in kind for feeding and watering pilgrims.[99]

It may even be that Quraysh was able to organize a profitable trade with Syria, perhaps as a result of disruption to the agricultural productivity of the Levant caused by the destruction of the Persian wars, numerous droughts in Syria,[100] and the repeated visitations of bubonic plague after 541.[101]

The message that Muḥammad preached in the milieu of a prosperous Mecca was in many ways a familiar one, and in others quite a novelty.[102] His summons to the worship of one God recalled the notion of a 'high god',

[96] Hawting (1982); Rubin (1986).   [97] Al-Bakrī, *Muʿjam mā staʿjam* 1.89, citing al-Kalbī (d. 763).
[98] Cf. Wellhausen (1897) 75–6; Crone (1987) 187–95.   [99] E.g. Ibn Hishām 1.1, 83.
[100] Butzer (1957) 362.   [101] Conrad (1994), (1996b).   [102] Cook (1983) 25–60.

and his identification of Islam as the religion of Abraham had important associations with the doctrines of *ḥanīfīya*. As can be seen from the testimony of Sozomen, his call for the restoration of a pristine faith, free from the corruptions that had crept into it, was already a time-honoured tradition in Arabia. The observances he advocated were also well known from either pagan Arabian or Jewish practice: prayer and Friday worship, fasting, pilgrimage, ritual purity, almsgiving, circumcision and dietary laws.[103]

Where Muḥammad broke with tradition was in his insistence on absolute monotheism and his advocacy of a relationship with God that abandoned traditional pragmatic views of religion and summoned man to unconditional commitment and faith in response to God's creative munificence and continuing solicitude. The rejection of pagan eclecticism, however, threatened the entire social and economic position of Quraysh and thus earned him the enmity of their leaders, and among the public at large his message, with its corollaries of reward and punishment in the hereafter, seemed extreme and delusory and evoked little positive response.[104] In order to gain support he had to prove that his God was a winner, and this he achieved by moving to Yathrib (Medina), where he used his expanding following to disrupt Meccan commerce and food supplies.[105] His military success made him a force to be reckoned with: the tribal arrangements so carefully nurtured by Mecca over the years soon fell apart in the face of this challenge, while the victories of the new religion provided the worldly success which Arabs demanded of their gods and also appealed to the Arabs' warrior ethic. Islam also had a broad appeal on other grounds. The Qur'ān presented itself as a universal scripture 'in clear Arabic speech',[106] and thus took advantage of the position of the Arabic language as the common cultural tongue of Arabia and a basis for common action.[107] Arabs could also identify with one another, despite their tribal distinctions, on the basis of a shared participation in Arabian tribal organization and custom, a heritage of similar cultural and religious experience in pagan systems and folklore, and a long history of trade and commerce, revolving around fairs and religious shrines, that engendered a certain feeling of familiarity around the peninsula.

It has often been asserted that the Arab conquests were of essentially Islamic inspiration. The kerygmatic tradition of Islam of course sees things this way, and the Armenian chronicle (written in the 660s), attributed to the bishop Sebeos, also has Muḥammad urging his followers to advance and claim the land promised to them by God as the descendants

---

[103] Goitein (1968) 73–125; Bashear (1984) 441–514; Rippin (1990–3) 1.86–99.
[104] Cf. Izutsu (1966) 45–54.   [105] Discussion in Donner (1977).
[106] Sūrat al-Naḥl (16), v. 103; Sūrat al-Shuʿarāʾ (26), v. 195 (=Arberry, 100, 379). Cf. also Sūrat Ibrāhīm (14), v. 4 (=Arberry, 246).
[107] Blachère (1952–66) ii.230–41, (1956); von Grunebaum (1963); Bashear (1997) 54–5.

of Abraham.[108] It therefore seems probable that there was a religious agenda to the conquests from the start, and it is certainly true that without the unifying factor of Islam there would probably have been no conquest at all.

But the arguments of leaders and advocates are one thing, and the response of the fighters themselves is another. Even in Mecca and Medina the teachings of Muḥammad and the text of the Qur'ān were still known in only fragmentary fashion, and it is difficult to see how most tribesmen elsewhere could have had more than a vague and trivial knowledge of either so soon after the Prophet's death. Many warriors who joined the conquest forces had only recently fought against the Prophet himself, or resisted the effort of the first two caliphs to bring Arabia under their control. It is also implausible that tribal warriors all over Arabia could so quickly have abandoned the pragmatic and worldly attitude toward religion that had prevailed for centuries, in favour of one that expected genuine commitment to the one God. There is, in fact, good evidence on the conquests showing that this was not the case at all.[109]

This is not to detract from the centrality of the message of Islam to Muḥammad's own sense of mission and purpose, and probably to that of others around him. One may also concede that Islam enabled the Muslim leadership to mobilize warriors in a way that transcended important differences, and it is likely that Islamic slogans and admonitions of various kinds were frequently inspiring to fighters on the ground. But if the faith played an important role in uniting and mobilizing the tribes, it was nevertheless waves of tribal forces, motivated primarily by traditional tribal ambitions and goals, that broke over Syria, Iraq and Egypt, beginning in the 630s.

It is unlikely that either Syria or Iraq could have withstood the advance of forces of this kind, given the constitution of their defences after the end of the last Persian war in 628, only six years before the first Arab advance. The Arab armies were not simply marshalled in Medina and then sent forth with the caliph's instructions; providing food, fodder and water for an army of thousands of men and animals would have been extremely difficult. The norm was rather for small contingents gradually to expand as other groups joined them on the march; the sources make it clear that commanders were expected to engage in such recruiting along the way, to ensure that the newcomers were armed and equipped, and to 'keep each tribe distinct from the

---

[108] Sebeos, *Histoire d'Héraclius* 95–6. Cf. also the quotations from Dionysius of Tell Maḥrē (d. 845) in Michael I Qīndāsī, *Chronique de Michel le Syrien* II.403–5 (trans.); IV.404–8 (text); *Chronicon ad annum Christi 1234 pertinens* I.227–30 (text); I.178–80 (trans.). Discussion in Crone and Cook (1977) 8–10; Hoyland (1997) 124–30.

[109] E.g. al-Walīd ibn Muslim (d. 810) in Ibn ʿAsākir I.461–2; al-Ṭabarī, *Taʾrīkh* I.2922; al-Maqrīzī, *Khiṭaṭ* I.75.

others and in its proper place'.[110] In this way a small force could soon swell to thousands as warriors joined its ranks in expectation of adventure, fighting and plunder.

The situation was made more difficult by the fact that confronting the Arabs on this scale posed entirely new military problems. Both powers were accustomed to dealing with Arabs as bands of raiders and had planned their frontier defences accordingly. Watchtowers and forts, many of them abandoned for centuries in any case, were inadequate to deter the forces that now swept past them, and whereas the old Roman system had anticipated incursions by single uncoordinated bands, it was now confronted by penetration at many points simultaneously. It was probably also difficult to determine exactly where the enemy was at any given time, for when battle was not imminent an Arab army tended to fragment into bands of warriors roaming the countryside.

Finally, and as the above example shows, Arab strategy was often highly reactive and thus difficult to counter or predict. Incursions into Iraq, for example, seem to have begun when the tribe of Rabīʿa, of the Banū Shaybān, was obliged by drought in Arabia to migrate to Iraqi territory, where the Sasanian authorities permitted them to graze their herds on promise of good behaviour. But the presence of these tribal elements eventually led to friction, which the Rabīʿa quite naturally interpreted as unwarranted reneging on an agreed arrangement. When they called on their kinsmen elsewhere for support, the crisis quickly escalated into full-scale conflict between Arab and Persian forces.[111]

It is difficult to guess whether either of the great powers would have been able to stem the military momentum that was building in Arabia, even had they correctly gauged the threat it posed. With Kinda, the Ghassānids and the Lakhmids all in a state of either collapse or disarray, the growing strategic power of Islam was able to develop in what otherwise amounted to a political void; the real source of the danger confronting the empires was effectively beyond their reach from the beginning. Byzantium and Persia could fight armies that violated their frontiers, but could not stop the process that was generating these armies in the first place. Initial victories over the Arabs at Muʾta in Syria in 632 and the battle of the Bridge in Iraq in 634 thus proved no deterrent, as in earlier times would have been the case.[112]

What overwhelmed the Byzantines and Sasanians was thus the ability of the message and charismatic personality of Muḥammad to mobilize the tribal might of Arabia at a level of unity never experienced among the Arabs either before or since. Unprepared for defence on the scale required

[110] Ibn ʿAsākir 1.446.   [111] Ibn Aʿtham al-Kūfī, Kitāb al-futūḥ 1.88–9.
[112] Donner (1981) 105–11, 190–202; Kaegi (1992) 71–4, 79–83.

to counter this new threat and unable to marshal tribal allies of their own
to strike at their foe in his own heartlands, both were forced to fight deep
within their own territories and suffered defeats that simply encouraged
further incursions on a larger scale. Greek and Persian field armies were
crushed in one disastrous battle after another, leaving cities to endure sieges
without hope of relief and encouraging resistance everywhere else to evap-
orate in short order.[113]

[113] Donner (1981) 119–220; Kaegi (1992) 88–180.

CHAPTER 23

THE BALKANS AND GREECE 420–602

MICHAEL WHITBY

I. INTRODUCTION

The 420s mark a turning-point in the history of the Balkan provinces of the Roman empire. Since the 370s the region had been under pressure from various tribes who were themselves being stimulated to challenge the strength of imperial defences by the threat posed to them by the westward movement of the awesome Huns across the south Russian steppe. By 420, but not much before, the Huns had reached the Danube, establishing themselves on the Hungarian plain, asserting their authority over other tribal groups along the Danube, and beginning to challenge Roman imperial authority in both west and east.[1] South of the river, the prosperity of urban and rural life varied. Most cities survived the period of Gothic ravaging and settlement, partly because Goths were not skilled besiegers, but rural hinterlands upon which the vitality of cities depended had been seriously affected. This stimulated a significant change in the pattern of settlement, with the abandonment of isolated rural villages that previously had served as nuclei for exploiting the countryside and a migration of population to the safety of urban defences or upland refuges.[2] Some cities might benefit from an influx of wealthy rural inhabitants who now relocated their grand villas inside the walls, while others in more exposed places received impoverished country people but lost their élites. Walls were strengthened or rebuilt, perhaps to enclose a restricted, more defensible, circuit, though habitation might still extend beyond the central defended area, as at Athens. Urban and rural prosperity basically increased with distance from the Danube, in areas which had been less intensively ravaged in the fourth century and where, as for example in the Thracian plains, the expansion of Constantinople stimulated interest in the countryside and made agricultural land a desirable commodity.

North of the Stara Planina, however, and particularly in Pannonia, conditions were very different. Although some areas seem to have remained prosperous until the Hun raids of the mid fifth century – for example, Upper

[1] Heather, *Goths and Romans* 227–30; Heather (1995); Whitby, *Maurice* 66–7.
[2] Amm. Marc. xxxi.6.4; 15.15; Poulter (1983b) 90.

Moesia[3] – others were already suffering depopulation in the fourth century, and hence were available for settlement by numerous tribesmen who had to be accommodated under the agreements reached by Theodosius I. Contrary to previous practice, these incomers remained under the control of their own leaders and retained their individual identities, so that they were less susceptible to Roman authority. The creation *c.* 420 of the new post of *comes foederatorum*, whose first known holder was Areobindus,[4] may have been intended to remedy this, but in the north civilian life remained insecure, even within walled cities: the start of the transfer of Nicopolis ad Istrum from an open site in the Yantra valley to Tsarevets hill at Veliko Trnovo, a secluded site protected by river and ravines, is dated to this period. The dangers are revealed by the fate of Noviodunum in Scythia which was seized in the 430s by Roman allies, the Rubi (probably Rugi) under Valips, who deterred a Roman counterattack by placing the children of his captives on the ramparts.[5] The efficacy of Danubian defences was undermined both by the presence of these potentially unruly elements to the south of the river and by the loss of Pannonia, where Roman authority had been shaky since the late fourth century. Pannonia controlled the main military route between the eastern and western parts of the empire that ran from Singidunum (Belgrade) up the Sava valley towards Aquileia at the head of the Adriatic, and occupation of this area by Goths or Huns gave them easy access in both directions; it took time for the Romans to readjust to this fact, but the route of Olympiodorus' embassy to the Huns, which seems to have proceeded from Constantinople by sea to Aquileia and then on by land to the middle Danube, may reflect the threat to road travel. The fate of Pannonia is illustrated by the decline of Sirmium from a major provincial capital and occasional imperial residence to an impoverished refuge where the local population sought shelter in decaying buildings.[6] Claudian's panegyric of Stilicho optimistically describes Pannonian life, but also hints at the urban blockade experienced by the Pannonians rather than any restoration of imperial control. After 420 Pannonia was only attached to the empire briefly and intermittently.

An anecdote in Olympiodorus is suggestive of the fate awaiting the Balkans: Valerius, governor of Thrace under Constantius (421–3), dug up three silver statues of captive barbarians that had been buried facing north; shortly afterwards, Goths poured over Thrace and Huns and Sarmatians over Illyricum and Thrace. Stories of the damaging removal of prophylactic emblems are common, and the chronology of Valerius' supposed action can be disputed,[7] but it reflects a belief that Balkan life had dramatically changed.

---

[3] Mócsy (1974) 351.   [4] Jones, *LRE* 665; *PLRE* II.145–6.
[5] Poulter (1983b) 96–7; Priscus fr. 5.
[6] Mócsy (1974); Eadie (1982); Bavant (1984); Claudian, *II Cons.* II.191ff.
[7] Olympiod. fr. 27; for date, see *PLRE* II.1144 *s.v.* Valerius 4.

It also illustrates a problem in the evidence available for understanding developments. For the fifth century there is no complete historical narrative, although the fragments of Priscus and Malchus, primarily devoted to diplomacy, contain important information about relations with Huns and Goths and some incidental, but revealing, comments about the situation within the Balkans. For the sixth century, the literary evidence is rather better: although Procopius did not consider Balkan warfare worthy of separate treatment, he did record significant events and there are signs in *Wars* VIII that he had realized the importance of the Balkans; his narrative was continued by Agathias, who narrated the Kotrigur invasion of 558/9, Menander, whose fragments record Roman diplomacy with the expanding Avar federation, and Theophylact, whose account, often obscure, covers the last major Roman campaigns on the Danube frontier. Their information can be supplemented by Procopius, *Buildings* IV, a panegyrical description of works in the Balkans attributed to Justinian; a few laws that proclaim changes in administration; and the *Strategikon* attributed to Maurice, which describes tactics for use against the two main Balkan enemies in the late sixth century, the Slavs and the Avars. These sources share a Constantinopolitan perspective, but some breadth is provided by the *Miracula* of St Demetrius and the *Chronicle of Monemvasia*, which describe actions from the viewpoint respectively of Thessalonica and the Peloponnese, and the letters of pope Gregory, which shed some light on ecclesiastical administration in Illyricum.

Archaeology is a vital, but often frustrating, addition. Decline in urban fabric can be illustrated by destruction of and repairs to buildings; changes to the organization of urban space reflect living conditions; and the discovery of hill-top settlements reveals new patterns of habitation; but few sites have been thoroughly excavated, publication of results lags far behind, and the fragmentary remains of late antiquity have not always attracted the attention of investigators. A particular problem lies in the classification of material as Roman or non-Roman: poor-quality 'squatter' dwellings may represent a movement either of non-Roman tribesmen on to a site or of rural refugees whose living standards might not resemble those traditionally associated with Romanized urban dwellers; they may also have housed the impoverished remnants of the urban population. Similarly, pottery identified as 'Slavic' may not be such an accurate diagnostic tool, and brooches and buckles could belong just as well to German recruits in Roman service as to tribal war-bands. Archaeological discoveries will continue to improve our understanding of the development of the Balkans in this period, but it would be unrealistic to expect dramatic or rapid progress: there is a long-term need to build up a series of local pictures from which eventually a new synthesis can be attempted.[8]

---

[8] Baratte (1984); Popović (1975), (1978); also other contributions to *Villes*.

II. THE HUNS

The Huns, by origin nomads from central Asia, were the warrior élite of a federation whose strength rose and fell with the assimilation and subsequent revolt of a variety of tribal groups, Huns, Sarmatians, Goths and other Germans. Their period of supremacy on the Danube lasted no longer than a generation, from the 420s to the 450s, but this was sufficient for them to have a profound effect on both halves of the empire. Before the 420s Huns had been strong and ambitious but the Romans had been able to cope, as is shown by the fate of Uldin: a leader of the Hun tribes near the Danube, after fighting for the Romans in Thrace and Italy he invaded the empire on his own account, and rejected peace terms on the grounds that he could subjugate every region of the earth that was illumined by the sun; however, his subordinate commanders were seduced by Roman diplomacy, and he fled in defeat as his followers deserted.[9] The significant development in the 420s was the consolidation of authority within a single ruling family, that of Rua, who was succeeded by his nephews Attila and Bleda, the sons of Mundiuch; after Bleda's death in 445, probably in a power struggle within the ruling family, Attila wielded sole authority until his death in 453, after which dissension between his sons quickly caused his federation to disintegrate as important constituents asserted their independence. Within this generation, the dramatic rise of Hunnic power is reflected in the annual payments from the eastern empire: in the 430s Rua obtained an increase from 350 to 700 pounds of gold, there may have been a further rise in 442, and in 447 the annual payment was set at 2,100 pounds of gold, just over 150,000 *solidi*, and the Romans were required to pay outstanding instalments assessed at 6,000 pounds of gold. These payments were represented as the provision of supplies for a Roman general, a rank that was accorded Attila to save face,[10] but they were not the only peaceful gains for the Huns, since their envoys regularly received gifts. With the involvement of Attila in the west and his subsequent death, the eastern emperor Marcian terminated payments, and Attila's sons could not again enforce them.

Hunnic success depended upon the personal authority of their leader, which was founded on success in battle, as is suggested in the stories about the discovery and presentation to Attila of the sword of Mars, or the allegorical substitution of Attila's bow for the man.[11] It was consolidated by control of patronage – for example, the distribution of Roman gifts which Attila ensured were widely spread through deliberate variation in the composition of embassies – and by honorific treatment at the royal court. The

[9] Soz. *HE* ix.5.
[10] Priscus frr. 2.35-8; 9.3.1-10; 11.2.627-31; Zuckerman (1994) 166 doubts the increase in 442.
[11] Jord. *Get.* 35.183; Priscus fr. 12; Jord. *Get.* 49.254-5.

latter is well illustrated by Priscus' own experiences as envoy to Attila in 448: at a ceremonial banquet Onegesius sat to the right of Attila, the position of honour, and his status was also reflected in the size of his compound, which contained a Roman bathing suite with skilled attendant, by Attila's courteous treatment of his wife and by his employment on an important mission to the Akatziri.[12] But the key to the long-term preservation of authority was a controlled terror that made it impractical to plot against Attila and impossible to escape his revenge: the lesson of Uldin's fate had been learnt. As a result, Romans could not employ traditional tactics of diplomatic subversion. A Hun envoy, Edeco, was prepared to accept bribes from the *cubicularius* Chrysaphius to assassinate Attila, but on returning to court revealed the plot: loyalty was strengthened by awareness that his fellow ambassador, Orestes, might report him to Attila. Onegesius, a man through whom the Romans hoped to influence Attila, preferred loyal servitude among the Huns to Roman wealth.[13] The Romans were consistently denied the chance to acquire friendly Huns who might be used to subvert Attila's position, and this was the principal reason why the return of fugitives was a regular demand in negotiations.[14] Attila was not concerned about a leakage of precious manpower, since his military resources were ample as long as his authority was unchallenged, and the numbers of fugitives seem to have been comparatively small, capable of being recorded on lists and once being specified as seventeen;[15] rather, it was a demonstration to all followers that no one could escape his clutches. On one occasion when the Romans were obliged to return fugitives of royal descent, Mama and Atakam, they were at once impaled, even before they had been escorted back to Hunnic territory. It is likely that most fugitives were from the class of leading men, identifiable individuals from tribes under Hunnic control who might hope that association with the Romans would lead to their reinstatement as tribal leaders. In these ways Attila dominated the social pyramid of the Hun federation: the leaders at court, Attila's advisers, diplomats and military commanders, were loyal and they preserved the allegiance of the units under their control. Disobedience was punished swiftly and publicly, with the guilty being impaled or gibbeted and left as warnings to others.[16]

Military success, patronage of leading men, and terror ensured that Hunnic control extended over all the tribes along the Danube and the northern shore of the Black Sea. In part, this has to be inferred from the process of the disintegration of the Hun federation, when Gepids, various groups of Goths, and Bulgar tribes emerged to trouble the Romans, but it

---

[12] Priscus frr. 10; 13.1.33–7; 11.2.361–72, 378–85, 241–3.   [13] Priscus fr. 11.2.126–31, 536–41.
[14] E.g. Priscus frr. 2.6–7, 29–31; 6.1.8–9; 9.1.3; 9.3.1–10, 35–8; 10.2; 11.1.6–7; 11.2.181–3, 195–201; 15.4.10.   [15] *Contra* Thompson (1948) 177–8; Priscus fr. 11.2.12–13.
[16] Priscus frr. 2.40–3; 11.2.343; 14.58–65; cf. Zuckerman (1994) 163.

is also apparent from the composition of Attila's army at the battle of the Catalaunian Plains, where a large contingent of Goths fought for him. There are hints about how this control was imposed. Rua's first attested diplomatic contact with the eastern empire came when he learnt that certain Danubian tribes – the Amilzuri, Itimari, Tunsures, Boisci and others – were planning to enter Roman service at a time when he was determined to dominate them himself.[17] The process of asserting Hunnic control is revealed in the description of the submission of the Akatziri: an error in Roman diplomacy had insulted the leading king of this people, Kuridach, who summoned Attila to help against his fellow kings; his colleagues submitted, but Kuridach himself then refused an invitation to meet Attila and so preserved his own power; the remainder of the Akatziri were placed under the control of Attila's eldest son, Ellac, whose installation was entrusted to Onegesius.[18] Thereafter, the manpower of the Akatziri would be available for use on Hunnic campaigns.

Key elements in Hunnic success against the Romans were their diplomatic perceptiveness and a proficiency at siege warfare that distinguished them from most of Rome's other tribal enemies. Some aspects of Attila's diplomacy have already been mentioned: his control over ambassadors' actions even at a distance and his careful distribution of rewards and opportunities. The dénouement of the Roman attempt to subvert Edeco reveals his tactical skill: after learning of the plot, Attila bided his time, laying a trap for the interpreter Vigilas, the Roman go-between in the affair, so that he was caught in possession of money whose purpose he could not explain. This ensured maximum embarrassment for Theodosius and Chrysaphius: Attila's envoy, Eslas, could berate the emperor in public with little prospect of contradiction, and hostility towards the powerful eunuch *cubicularius* would be reinforced among those who now saw that his unsuccessful plotting had endangered their lives.[19] Attila's personal behaviour kept Roman envoys at a psychological disadvantage: his rapid changes of mood might, superficially, seem the irrational behaviour of a barbarian, but Priscus' description of their impact on his fellow ambassadors suggests that Attila knew what he was doing. The chief ambassador Maximinus, downcast at the apparent futility of his whole journey, lay on the grass in despair while Priscus attempted to rescue the mission by flattering Scottas, a leading Hun; the ambassadors were then subjected to contrasting outbursts of rage and displays of hospitality as they attempted to win favour with people of influence at Attila's court. Attila had established himself as diplomatic patron, with the Roman envoys as suppliants grateful for modest tokens of favour, for which they waited outside the royal compound like a traditional Roman client. Ambassadors from the western empire were simultaneously

---

[17] Priscus fr. 2.1–4.   [18] Priscus fr. 11.2.241–59.   [19] Priscus fr. 15.

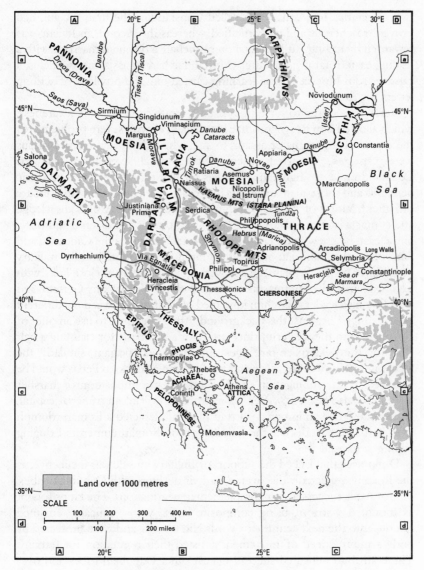

Map 21 The Balkans and Greece

subjected to the same treatment.[20] But Attila knew that diplomacy with the
sophisticated Romans could not rely just on personal passion, and ensured
that he was supplied with people of suitable education to present his
written messages to emperors in appropriate form. Aetius had furnished

[20] Priscus fr. 11.2.

two secretaries for Attila, both called Constantius; the first, a Gaul, had
proved treacherous and was crucified, whereas the second, an Italian, was
rewarded by having Attila pursue on his behalf a disputed marriage with a
leading eastern family; the latter Constantius had an assistant, Rusticius, a
captive from Moesia, whose learning earned him the privilege of writing
letters for Attila.[21]

Attila also seems to have possessed a strategic diplomatic awareness,
which allowed him to synchronize his challenges with severe problems for
the empire: his first major assault in 441, when Viminacium and Naissus
were captured, occurred when a large naval expedition had left
Constantinople to fight the Vandals in Africa, while his diplomatic
demands and subsequent invasions in the late 440s coincided with pressure
on other frontiers of the eastern empire.[22] The range of Attila's knowledge
and contacts is impressive, as befitted his ambitions to universal authority:
in the east, he knew that Persia could be attacked across the Caucasus, and
had some information about the geography of the route and the military
capabilities of the Persians; in the west, quite apart from close links with
leading Romans like Aetius, his contacts with the Vandal king Geiseric and
with Frankish leaders kept him informed of relations between the different
tribal groups.[23] Against this background, Attila's decision to use an offer of
marriage from the western princess Honoria as a basis for claiming a half
share of the western empire does not appear extravagant; similarly, the
assessment of informed associates that a Hunnic attack on Persia would be
followed by the subjugation of the Romans and imposition of harsher
terms was also realistic. After his capture of Milan, an imperial capital,
Attila redesigned an imperial portrait that had depicted a Roman triumph
over barbarians to display the humiliation of Roman emperors bringing
tribute to himself.[24]

Diplomacy that lacked the support of military muscle was ineffective, as
the Romans repeatedly discovered in their dealings with Danubian tribes,
but for Attila success in war complemented negotiations. The Huns fought
as mounted warriors, using composite bows, whose efficacy remained
famous into the next century,[25] swords and lassoes, and were protected by
body armour; speed of movement assisted their reputation for ferocity.
These attributes ensured success against other Danubian tribes and over
Roman field armies, which had a substantial component of Germanic
tribesmen whose fighting capabilities and equipment were likely to be
similar to those of tribesmen north of the river. But what distinguished the
Huns and rendered their impact on the empire much more serious than
that of ordinary invaders was their ability to capture strongly fortified and

---

[21] Priscus frr. 11.2.329–43; 14.1–51.   [22] Priscus fr. 10; chronology: Croke (1983).
[23] Priscus fr. 11.2.596–619; Jord. *Get.* 36.184; Priscus fr. 20.3. Discussion in Clover (1973).
[24] Priscus frr. 20; 11.2.620–35; *Suda* M.405.   [25] Procop. *Wars* v.27.27; VI.1.9.

stoutly defended Roman cities, the centres of Roman power, wealth and administration that had been able to withstand the earlier Gothic incursions. Some places fell through treachery, as when Margus was handed over by its bishop, but accounts of attacks on Naissus and Aquileia indicate that the Huns had access to quite sophisticated siege technology, probably supplied by military captives or the remnants of the Roman population of Pannonia, whose best chance of lucrative employment was now in Hunnic service.[26] At Naissus, Priscus describes towers that could be wheeled up to the ramparts and provide protection for attacking archers, substantial battering rams and assault ladders; although there are signs that his account has been affected by historiographical traditions of siege narrative, there is no justification for dismissing the narrative as invention: Naissus was captured and thoroughly sacked. At Aquileia there is less detail about the technical equipment, and the siege may have lasted longer,[27] but Attila was still able to collapse a section of the defences and storm the city. Apart from mechanical devices, it is clear that Attila, controlling large reserves of subject manpower, was content to sacrifice lives in frontal assaults. The results are recorded in the sources: in the northern Balkans most of the major cities succumbed, Naissus being joined by Viminacium, Ratiaria, Philippopolis, Arcadiopolis and Constantia; the destruction was so extensive that it could be claimed that only Adrianople and Heracleia on the Sea of Marmara survived. In the sixth century Procopius could comment on the Huns' inexperience at siege warfare, but there is no justification for reading this assessment back into the fifth century.[28]

The consequences for the Romans were serious: Hun ravaging, which extended as far south as Thermopylae, depopulated parts of Illyricum and Thrace; urban defences no longer offered a secure refuge for inhabitants and their wealth. In spite of being strengthened in 443, the Roman frontier on the Danube ceased to exist from Pannonia as far east as Novae in Thrace. Attila demanded that along the whole of this distance a stretch of land five days' journey wide must be left uncultivated; the place for commercial exchange in Illyria should no longer be on the Danube but at ravaged Naissus, itself adjudged to be five days from the river. Thus Roman territory was to be clearly separated from Attila's, which would reduce the chances for Roman interference in Hunnic affairs; on the other hand, Attila might choose to use this region for hunting, an activity that provided a convenient disguise for military preparations.[29] To counter this threat, new fortifications were built: Constantinople had already been provided with a massive set of new land walls earlier in Theodosius' reign (413), and these

[26] Mócsy (1974) 357.
[27] Priscus fr. 6.2; Blockley (1981) 54; Jord. *Get.* 42.220; Procop. *Wars* III.4.30–5.
[28] Theophanes 102–3; Procop. *Buildings* IV.3.21–2; *contra* Croke (1978) 257.
[29] Theod. *Nov.* 24; Priscus frr. 11.1.9–14; 11.2.74–8.

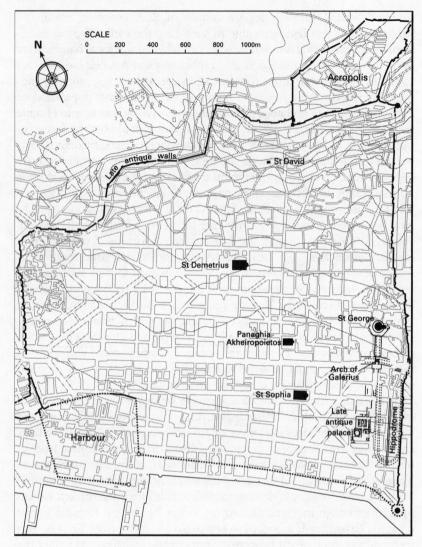

Fig. 22 The walls of Thessalonica. (After Spieser (1984a))

were reinforced in the late 440s by the construction of Long Walls, which ran from the Black Sea to Selymbria on the Sea of Marmara; another long wall was built at the Isthmus of Corinth, to deny access to the Peloponnese, and the defences at Thermopylae were probably also strengthened at this time. The administration of the Illyrian prefecture was moved from Sirmium to Thessalonica, which was provided in the early 440s with a massive set of walls that are largely extant (see Fig. 22); in due course these were complemented by the construction of major administrative buildings and grand churches.[30] The economic consequences of the transfer to the Huns of thousands of pounds of gold were serious, and, although Priscus' sorrow for the plight of senators selling their furniture and wives' jewellery may not be deserved by these traditional exploiters of privilege, all tax-payers will have had to contribute at a time when revenues from the Balkan provinces were curtailed by extensive ravaging. The wealth that was distrib-uted to notables like Onegesius or wives like Hereka, or that was evident on the banquet tables at Attila's court, was in large part lost to the Roman empire; only a portion will have filtered back south, through the markets established during various negotiations, whereas much remained outside and contributed to the impressive Hunnic-period treasures discovered beyond the Danube.[31] Imperial authority was severely damaged, and in those cities which survived there are signs that local interests would be placed above those of the empire: at Asemus, the garrison ambushed a Hunnic convoy of booty and prisoners, and the inhabitants then resisted demands that liberated captives should be restored or at least ransomed, even though this complicated negotiations at a higher level. Local initiative protected this fortified settlement, though even here the general level of insecurity is revealed by the fate of certain children who had been captured while pasturing flocks outside the walls.[32]

Hun invasions were a disaster both for the Roman state and for individ-ual Romans, and there is no justification for the theory that lower-class Romans gave the Huns an enthusiastic welcome or that traders in the eastern empire regarded the mercantile opportunities of Hunnic power as sufficient to offset their destructiveness.[33] It is true that the survivors of the Romanized population of Pannonia will have passed into Hunnic control in the 430s, so that wealth and power had now to be achieved through pat-ronage from the Huns: this explains the prominence at the Hun court of upper-class Romans like Orestes, the father of the future western emperor Romulus. Also some ordinary Romans served the Huns after being cap-tured, and benefited as a result, but it is dangerous to generalize from the few examples that Priscus encountered during the embassy to Attila. Rusticius the secretary had expert knowledge which made him a valuable asset, while the anonymous trader from Viminacium whose knowledge of Greek attracted Priscus' attention was scarcely an ordinary individual, since it was military prowess in Hunnic service that secured him liberty and a respectable place in the retinue of Onegesius.[34] Thus the trader's com-plaints about Roman failings, to which in any case Priscus provided a long and moving response that prompted the trader to admit tearfully the

---

[30] Croke (1981); Spieser (1984a); Whitby (1985); Gregory (1992).
[31] For illustrations, see *Germanen* parts 3–5 and Wolfram (1985).   [32] Priscus fr. 9.3.
[33] Thompson (1948) 54–6; 184–203.   [34] Priscus fr. 11.2.422–35.

benefits of Roman law and life, have to be interpreted carefully: they do not prove that life was better for everyone under the Huns, and it must be remembered that far more Romans ended up as bleached skeletons, such as those that made it difficult for Priscus and his fellow envoys to find a clean camp site outside Naissus even seven years after the city's sack,[35] than as privileged Hun servants.

III. FROM THE HUNS TO THE AVARS

The fragmentation of the Hun federation following Attila's unexpected death changed but did not remove the threat to the Balkan provinces, since in place of a unified group whose leader was usually amenable to negotiations, there emerged a complicated array of competing tribal groups. This state of affairs persisted from the mid fifth century until the Avars began to reimpose unity under the authority of their Chagan in the 560s. On occasions the Romans could turn disunity to their advantage: for example, in the 460s Roman generals blockaded a heterogeneous tribal group; an officer of Hunnic descent in the Roman army, Celchal, persuaded the Goths among the starving enemy to attack their Hunnic comrades by reminding them of the exploitation to which Huns normally subjected Goths, and the Romans took advantage of the consequent massacre. But on other occasions Romans suffered from the fragmentation, since instability north of the Danube prompted tribesmen to regard Roman territory to the south as an escape route or a resource to be exploited: the movement of the Amal-led Goths into the empire in the 460s has plausibly been attributed to their inability to achieve conclusive domination in power struggles north of the river, while in 551 the Gepids summoned help from the Kotrigurs, but when 12,000 troops arrived too early for action against their intended foes, the Lombards, the Gepids ferried them across the Danube to gain satisfaction in Roman territory. A separate problem in these years was the emergence of the Vandal navy as a threat to southern Greece in the 460s and 470s, when the Ionian islands, the western Peloponnese and, probably, Athens all suffered.[36]

It was the Gepids who effected the collapse of Hunnic power when they led a coalition of Germanic tribes which defeated their former masters at the river Nedao in Pannonia in 454; thereafter, they established themselves as masters of Pannonia, and achieved the status of Roman allies, although their loyalty was not exceptional. Attila's sons failed to co-ordinate their actions, and no son emerged as sole leader, so that the mighty Huns rapidly descended to the level of other tribal groups. Two Gothic groups, each of

---

[35] Priscus fr. 11.2.52-5.
[36] Priscus fr. 49; Heather, *Goths and Romans* 247-50; Procop. *Wars* VIII.18; Frantz (1988) 78.

about 10,000–15,000 fighting men, emerged as the main tormentors of the Balkans from the 460s to 489. The two leaders, Theoderic Strabo and Theoderic the Amal, were rivals for the allegiance of their followers and the grant of territory and imperial titles, with their associated salaries; their competition was exploited by the emperor Zeno, but in return the Goths could take advantage of Zeno's insecurity and win concessions by participating in the civil strife of his reign.[37]

The accounts of Gothic movement provide some information about conditions within the Balkans. Places in which Gothic contingents were settled for any length of time were likely to be suffering from depopulation, since Goths were regularly interested in land which they could work – demands for food were only a short-term remedy.[38] This might have been inferred about the land north of the Stara Planina, which had suffered most from earlier invasions, where the Amali based themselves from 474 to 478 in the vicinity of Novae and Marcianopolis, but the presence of Strabo's troops on the Thracian plain south of the mountains suggests that there were empty lands there as well; Strabo had probably contributed to this, since Zeno later complained about how he had 'damaged the inhabitants of Thrace, cutting off their hands . . . and displacing all farmers'.[39] Depopulation is explicitly mentioned in Dardania, which Zeno offered to Theoderic the Amal in 479 as having 'much beautiful and fertile land, lacking inhabitants, farming which he could support his army in abundance of everything'. Elsewhere, ravaging ensured the destruction of agriculture: in 478, as they were being pushed out of the Thracian plain, the Amali devastated the area near Rhodope, 'all the best of the land in Thrace', where they drove off herds, killed what they could not take and obliterated all agriculture – it is not recorded whether the suffering farmers were Romans or followers of Theoderic Strabo.[40] Prosperity, however, was possible in areas that escaped ravaging for any significant length of time: in 479 Lychnidus could be described as 'a prosperous city full of old wealth', and towards the Adriatic in Epirus and near the Dalmatian coastline there are signs of continuing wealth.[41]

In their search for food and land the Goths inevitably came into conflict with the cities and other fortifications, since these offered security and were storehouses for local agricultural surpluses. The latter point is illustrated by the Amali's experience outside Heracleia in Macedonia, probably Heracleia Lyncestis: the Amali were utterly destitute, but during negotiations with Zeno they were provided with supplies by the local bishop; at their departure they demanded grain and wine for their journey towards Dyrrachium, but the local population had taken refuge in a strong fortress, from where

[37] Malchus frr. 15.31–6; 18.3.15–16; 22.16–17.
[38] Malchus fr. 18.3.5–7; cf. fr. 20.54–5, 204; Heather, *Goths and Romans* 258–9.
[39] Malchus frr. 18.2.13; 15.18–20.   [40] Malchus frr. 20.202–4; 18.4.4–7.
[41] Malchus fr. 20.141–2; Popović (1984); Wilkes (1969) 419–20.

they rejected the Goths' request, and the Goths' only response was to burn the deserted city before departing.[42] Theoderic Strabo had a comparable experience in 473 when, although he managed to capture Arcadiopolis by starvation, his own army was also afflicted by famine: it was no easier to find food outside a beleaguered city than inside. The emperor's command of food reserves was an important factor in negotiations with the Goths.

The bishop of Heracleia's behaviour is an example of a local leader taking the initiative in securing the well-being of his own people, and there are other signs of the defence of local self-interest being combined with a lack of confidence in the emperor. In 478 the inhabitants of Thessalonica, suspecting that Zeno wanted to give their city to the Amali, overthrew imperial statues and attacked the prefect and his office; they were calmed by the clergy, but insisted on removing the keys of the city gates from the prefect and entrusting them to the archbishop, and they organized themselves into a guard. Shortly afterwards, at Dyrrachium, Theoderic was able to exploit similar apprehensions when he sent Sidimund with a fake message to warn the inhabitants that the Amali were about to move into their territory with Zeno's approval and that they should contemplate gathering their possessions and seeking refuge on islands or in other cities; the trick worked, and Theoderic occupied the city.[43]

The opportune death of Theoderic Strabo and his son Recitach's inability to hold the loyalty of his followers permitted the consolidation of the Gothic groups under Amal control, and the new dynasty set about inventing a long history to justify its current pre-eminence.[44] Theoderic the Amal's Goths were encouraged to depart to Italy, which gave limited respite to the Balkan provinces. New tribal groups emerged on the Danube, but it took time for these to consolidate their positions and in the meantime the new emperor Anastasius, a native of Dyrrachium, was gradually able to reassert Roman authority along and within the Danube frontier. This was a slow business, and most progress seems to have been made along the lower Danube, especially in Scythia Minor, where there is evidence for reconstruction at several sites; the Roman navy's ability to control the Black Sea and the Danube was probably an important element in this process.

Beyond the Danube there was no single dominant tribal group. In Pannonia the Gepids acted as federate allies, and were probably used to observe and pressurize the Ostrogoths, who controlled Dalmatia. But when in 537 Justinian recovered Dalmatia, relations with the Gepids deteriorated, and Justinian made an alliance with the Lombards, neighbours and rivals of the Gepids. One other important group was active in this region, the Heruls,

---

[42] Malchus fr. 20.35–42, 94–100; cf. *Vita S. Hypatii* (pp. 61.11–63.8) for a *castellum* acting as a food distribution-point to country dwellers impoverished by Hun attacks.   [43] Malchus fr. 20.5–19; 20.63–98.

[44] Heather (1989); Heather, *Goths and Romans* 322–30; Burns (1984) chs. 2–3 is far too credulous, Wolfram (1988) 248–58 more sceptical.

who achieved the distinction of being called 'the most evil of all mankind'. Part of this tribe, perhaps as many as 4,500 fighting men, had been settled in Illyricum by Anastasius, and then in the vicinity of Singidunum by Justinian, who secured the conversion and baptism of the leading men; their brutality made them useful recruits for imperial armies.[45] Further east on the lower Danube, the main hostile groups were now Bulgars and Slavs. The Bulgars were Hunnic and comprised a number of groups, those nearer the Danube being remnants of Attila's followers, while others known as Kotrigurs and Utigurs dwelt farther east, north of the Black Sea; these were being disturbed by tribal reshuffling caused ultimately by the Avars, who had begun to re-enact the westward movement of the Huns. Under Zeno and Anastasius, Bulgars served in Roman armies, but in the 540s and 550s the Kotrigurs ravaged widely, reaching the land walls of Constantinople and the Isthmus of Corinth. Justinian's main response was to manipulate the rivalry between Utigurs and Kotrigurs, and in due course to accept the Avars as a new diplomatic pawn in the trans-Danubian game; the Kotrigurs are later found as a sub-group within the Avar federation.[46]

In the long term, the Slavs, were the most significant of the new groups on the Danube, which they had reached by the start of the sixth century, though the exact course of their migrations cannot be specified since it is notoriously difficult to identify Slavs archaeologically.[47] They lived in simple agricultural communities in forest clearings – small villages of huts which might have subterranean entrances, often located close to rivers; under threat, they might take refuge in woods or lakes and marshes. Their social structure was rudimentary, and the normal unit of organization was probably the family group or a few such groups combined into a clan, who might share a common hill-fort.[48] They were adept fighters on their chosen ground, and some Slavs – for example, Chilbuldius – achieved prominence in Roman service. For military purposes they might combine into larger bodies, but as with many of Rome's tribal neighbours, leaders of such units possessed relatively little personal authority and were dependent upon the co-operation of their leading men, the heads of family groups. Roman writers could identify two distinct groups, Slavs and Antes, the latter living further from the Danube frontier and perhaps being more socially advanced than other Slavs, in that they had a money- and slave-owning society and a recognized leadership with whom the Romans could nego-tiate, a type of diplomacy that was rendered impractical by the anarchy of other Slav groups.[49] It is likely that, as with other tribal groups, proximity to the Roman empire and regular warfare, against Bulgars and Avars as well

[45] Procop. *Wars* VI.14.36; VII.34.43; Croke (1982) 132.
[46] Procop. *Wars* VIII.18–19, 25; Agathias, *Hist.* V.11–25; Menander fr. 12.5.90–3.
[47] Baratte (1984); Gimbutas (1971) ch. 1–4 for their previous history.   [48] Gimbutas (1971) ch. 7.
[49] Maurice, *Strat.* XI.4; Procop. *Wars* VII.14; Jord. *Get.* 23.119.

as Romans, stimulated considerable social and political change among the
Slavs during the sixth century. The chronology of their invasions is difficult
to establish, since their attacks may have coincided with those of other,
more prominent, tribes such as the Bulgars, and hence may be concealed.[50]
The earliest attested incursions were in 517; there was extensive raiding in
530 at a time of Bulgar attacks; and in 545 a Slav group was defeated in
Thrace by Herul federates. In 549 3,000 Slavs ravaged Thrace and
Illyricum, defeating imperial cavalry and capturing the city of Topirus; in
551 a Slav band was intending to assail Thessalonica but was diverted
towards Dalmatia by the fortuitous presence of an army under Germanus,
who was recruiting troops for service in Italy; in the same year other Slavs
reached the Long Walls of Constantinople and devastated the Thracian
plains, and in 552 Slavs plundered Illyricum and then escaped with the assistance of the Gepids, who saved them from Roman pursuit by ferrying
them across the Danube for a *solidus* per person.[51]

In spite of the best efforts of emperors, especially Anastasius and
Justinian, the Balkan provinces remained an unsettled area. Anastasius'
actions in the eastern Balkans were undermined by the troubles associated
with Vitalian's revolt, which was centred on the lower Danube and the
Black Sea coast, while under Justinian the Balkans had to cede precedence
to military activity elsewhere in the empire: after the start of the western
reconquest this became a serious problem – Balkan military commanders
are found in action in Italy and large numbers of troops were recruited in
the Balkans for service in the west. Germanus in 549/50 and Narses in 551,
both *en route* for Italy, encountered invaders in the Balkans but concentrated
on their western missions rather than attend to the immediate threat.[52]
Agathias, in a highly critical assessment of Justinian's policies in the context
of Zabergan's invasion, complains of demoralized soldiers cheated of their
pay, drastically reduced troop numbers, and remaining forces transferred
elsewhere;[53] accounts of Slav and Bulgar raids give an impression of an
empty land across which invaders could move with impunity. An illustration is provided by the exploits of Ildigisal, a Lombard who had been
settled with 300 followers in Thrace: in 552, discontented by his treatment
in Constantinople, Ildigisal fled with a few companions to Apri, where they
joined other Lombards, raided the imperial horse pastures, defeated the
Kotrigurs settled in Thrace who attempted to oppose them, fled across
Thrace without further opposition, and escaped to the Gepids after killing
the commanders of a Roman force in Illyricum.[54] There was clearly empty
land available for the settlement of contingents like these Lombards and
Kotrigurs, as well as the Heruls mentioned above.

[50] Lemerle (1954) 284; Ferjančič (1984) 88–9.   [51] Procop. *Wars* VII.38; 40; VIII.25.
[52] Procop. *Wars* VII.39–40; Agathias, *Hist.* I.19.1; Procop. *Wars* VII.40; VIII.21.
[53] Agathias, *Hist.* V.13.7–14.4.   [54] Procop. *Wars* VIII.27.

The grimness of the situation should not, however, be exaggerated. The ability to find troops to recruit is an indication of some sort of successful habitation, even if some recruits were tribesmen newly introduced for that purpose. Viewed from the outside, the Balkans were still a land of milk and honey, as is revealed in the Utigurs' complaints about Justinian's reception of their Kotrigur enemies. Justinianic legislation suggests that land in the Balkans was a desirable commodity, an asset that unscrupulous lenders might attempt to obtain from their debtors in Haemimontus and Illyricum; legislation against this applied to both soldiers and civilians, and a law about redeeming captives from barbarians reveals that there was an active market for land.[55] Decades of impoverishment had undermined administration, especially in Thrace, but attempts to remedy this were initiated by Anastasius and taken further by Justinian: Thrace was joined with more prosperous regions – Cyprus, Caria and the Aegean islands – in a unit known as the *quaestura exercitus*, and was provided with a new rank of governor, a Justinianic *praetor*, with enhanced powers and a specific duty to attend to local defences.[56] In Illyricum, where the greater security and prosperity of the southern areas would have helped the prefect in Thessalonica to control the more threatened northern parts of his prefecture, Justinian attempted at a moment of confidence to move some aspects of administration further north: a separate metropolitan see was created at his new city of Justiniana Prima, supposedly for the convenience of the inhabitants. Bishops provided secular as well as spiritual leadership, as can be seen from the complaints of the citizens of Thessalonica about the absence of their archbishop during a crisis in 535.[57]

Diplomacy and fortifications were emperors' twin strategies for defending the Balkans. Lombards were incited to act against Gepids, Antes against Slavs, Utigurs against Kotrigurs. Tribal groups or smaller war-bands could be solicited into imperial service, to be rewarded with lands and military titles that brought salaries or provisions. Critics of Justinian complained that such policies merely encouraged tribes to cause more trouble in the expectation of greater rewards from the supine empire, but Menander offered a positive assessment of his preference for avoiding war. The frequent failure of large armies during Anastasius' reign, and again in 529–30, to crush opponents in the Balkans tends to support Menander's judgement.[58] Pressure along the frontier was eased sufficiently for Justinian to reinforce Roman control of the Danube as far upstream as Singidunum, and the operations of the Roman fleet and the ability of Roman commanders to watch known crossing-points could restrict, if not ultimately prevent, fresh invasions.

---

[55] Procop. *Wars* VIII.19; *Nov.* 32, 33; 65.   [56] *Nov.* 41; 26; Hendy, *Studies* 397–404.
[57] *Nov.* 11; *Life* of David, cited by Hoddinott (1963) 89ff.
[58] Menander fr. 5.1–2; Cameron (1970) 125–7.

The defences of Balkan cities and towns were strengthened both by Anastasius and Justinian. The latter's contribution is more prominent, thanks to the panegyrical account in Procopius, *Buildings* IV. This offers the names of about 600 places in the Balkans at which Justinian is said to have organized building work; two long lists of constructions in Illyricum and Thrace can plausibly be traced to official lists,[59] so that Procopius may have had reasonable information about imperial intentions, though the extent to which these were realized remains in dispute. It is impossible to corroborate Procopius' evidence, and probably always will be, both because many of the places mentioned have not been identified and because in the absence of inscriptions it is difficult to date construction work precisely or show that an emperor financed work executed during his reign. Critics of Procopius tend to seize on rhetorical pronouncements about the extent and efficacy of Justinian's achievements, the type of propaganda that is also evident in *Novel* 11, or assume that there was a strategic programme underlying the information that Procopius organizes into administrative areas.[60] A more balanced approach is possible. Justinian was interested in the Balkans: it was his birthplace, the central area where many of the fortifications were located possessed substantial mineral wealth, and the whole region's security affected the safety of Constantinople and its suburbs. As a result, Justinian instructed his new *praetor* to attend to construction works and report any that required substantial expenditure. Frontier defence was accepted as an imperial duty, but did not entail the existence of a grand strategic plan:[61] rather, existing sites would be fortified, strengthened or repaired, depending upon what appeared best at a local level or was requested by local inhabitants. As a result, various types of site are probably recorded in Procopius: frontier fortresses in the vicinity of the Danube which constituted the empire's front line; settlements along the main roads that ensured the maintenance of imperial communications but also offered invaders avenues for penetrating the interior; major cities; and upland refuge sites to which the harassed population of the Balkans had been moving since the Gothic incursions of the fourth century. Few new settlements were created by Justinian, but his actions were perhaps important for reintegrating within the empire the scattered communities that had been created as populations shifted from the low-level cities and roadside sites to safer upland locations. The new city and ecclesiastical capital at Justiniana Prima, plausibly identified with the remains at Tsaricin Grad (see Fig. 23), represents an exception in the broader context of Justinian's activity in the Balkans. These fortifications, with a few exceptions such as the walls at Thermopylae, Corinth or the

[59] Beševliev (1970) 74–7.
[60] For a hostile assessment see, for example, Wozniak (1982); for discussion, Whitby, *Maurice* 71–8.
[61] *Nov.* 26.4; for criticism of modernizing notions, see Isaac, *Limits of Empire* ch. 9.

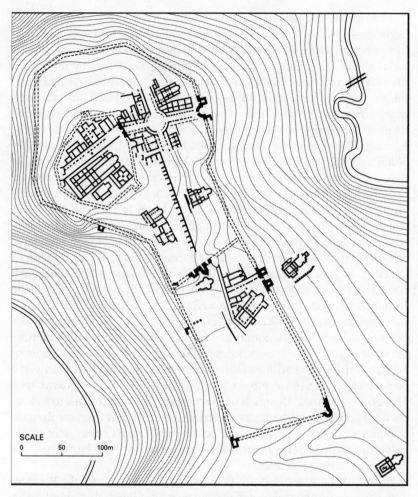

Fig. 23 Tsaricin Grad (Justiniana Prima). (After Bavant in *Villes et peuplement.*) For a different
reconstruction of the walled circuit, see Fig. 41, p. 922 below

Chersonese, were not intended by themselves to prevent the movement of
invaders but to shelter the local population and ensure that when danger
passed there were people who could return to the cultivation of the surrounding country. Only significant garrison troops, or a mobile army,
could oppose roving war-bands directly, whereas for a city to commit its
limited local resources outside its defences might court disaster, as at
Topirus, which was captured by Slavs after its armed men had been lured
from the walls and killed.[62]

[62] Procop. *Wars* VII.38.

Towards the end of Justinian's reign, a new tribal group entered Roman horizons – the Avars, who were introduced to the Roman commander in Lazica by the Alans, an approach which indicates that they were currently located near the Caucasus; although displaced westwards by the rise of Turkish power in the central Asian steppes, they appear to have had a formidable military reputation, analogous to that of the Huns. Justinian welcomed them as recruits to the trans-Danubian diplomatic game, rewarded them with presents, and encouraged them to attack tribes hostile to the Romans; Bulgar and other Hunnic tribes were crushed, and the Antes were plundered.[63] These successes increased Avar strength and confidence, so that they extended their control west from the Caucasus towards the Danube, but their power was still modest, since Justinian was able to keep the Danube defended against them, and at Justin II's accession the new emperor rebuked Avar envoys in public without provoking immediate retaliation. Avar involvement in a new round of strife between Lombards and Gepids led to the departure of the former to Italy, the subjugation of the latter, and the acquisition of the whole of Pannonia, which henceforth constituted the Avar homeland. New recruits and military successes, on the Danube and against the Franks, allowed the Avars to create a federation, a successor to that of Attila and with comparable strengths and weaknesses. Baian, the Avar Chagan, dominated through terror an increasing number of subject groups such as Kotrigurs, Gepids, Slavs and even a unit of Romano-natives; archaeological investigations in Hungary have discovered cemeteries of Avars or subject groups, the Avars being equated with Mongol-type burials.[64] Symbols of power and gifts for patronage to followers were important to the Avars, and these were extorted from the Romans as diplomatic gifts or payments for peace; the Chagan's pretensions might be enhanced by imperial robes, whose export to northern barbarians was prohibited in later centuries.[65]

From 568 the Avars disputed possession of Sirmium with the Romans, who had only recently recovered the city from the Gepids. In the early 570s, before the outbreak of war in the east, the Romans could force the Chagan to retire from the city walls without reward, even if they were defeated in battle. But the transfer of resources away from the Balkans, especially after Tiberius recruited a large army there in 574/5, weakened defences along the Danube. The first to take advantage were Slavs near the lower Danube who were probably prompted by a desire to escape from the encroaching power

---

[63] Menander fr. 5.1–3; Kollautz and Miyakawa (1970) 1.134–47.

[64] *Mirac. S. Dem.* 11.284–6; László (1955); Lengyel and Radan (1980) 408–16; Kollautz and Miyakawa (1970) 1.184–99.

[65] Theophylact 1.3.8–13; Menander 12.5.56–68; Michael the Syrian XI.21; Constantine Porphyrogenitus, *De Administrando Imperio* 13. *Germanen* part 6 for illustrations of the wealth of burial treasures.

of the Avars. Widespread Slav raiding began in 577, and Tiberius' only response was to employ the Avars, who had their own quarrel with the Slavs, to attack Slav territory. This revealed the extent of Roman weakness, and the Avars renewed their attempts on Sirmium, eventually capturing the city in 581/2 after a three-year blockade.[66] In the first decade of Maurice's reign the Avars re-enacted the attacks of Attila's Huns: like them, they were capable of capturing fortified cities, at least north of the Stara Planina, and as long as the Persian war continued, there was little that the Romans could do but purchase a peace, at a price that rose from 80,000 to 100,000 *solidi* in 584. At the same time Slav raiding continued, partly encouraged by the Avars but also partly stimulated by fear of them. Slav bands reached the Long Walls of Constantinople in 584, Thessalonica was briefly attacked in 586, and their raiding extended as far south as Athens, Corinth and into the Peloponnese.[67] In the 590s the termination of the Persian war allowed a greater concentration on Balkan affairs, and the narrative of Roman campaigns suggests a gradual reassertion of control across the countryside to the south of the Danube, the reopening of communications with isolated cities that had survived the years of ravaging, and the extension of the war to the north of the Danube to instil in Slavs and Avars a fear of Roman power; attention was paid to their enemies' military capabilities, aspects of Avar organization and equipment were copied, suitable tactics and strategies were devised, and by 602 it appeared that the Romans had begun to dominate the Slavs on the lower Danube and to create dissension within the Avar federation based in Pannonia.[68]

IV. FROM ROMAN TO POST-ROMAN

So far, the progress of this chapter has been dictated by the sequence of invaders whose activities determined the pace and direction of developments. On the other hand, although lack of evidence makes it difficult to analyse the region's history from the perspective of its Roman inhabitants, some attempt must be made if the fundamental changes in population and organization that occurred at the end of the Roman period are to be understood. If in the early fifth century the northern Balkans were already a war zone trampled by tribal bands and Roman armies, the southern Balkans and in particular peninsular Greece had as yet escaped severe damage. A survey of the history of Athens from the Gothic attack in 396 to the Slav arrival in the 580s is divided into three phases – 'prosperity, decline and disaster' – and, although Athens had certain unique features, this paradigm is clearly of much wider application in the southern province of Achaea.[69]

---

[66] Menander frr. 21, 25, 27.   [67] Theophylact 1.3.1–7.6; Whitby, *Maurice* 140–51.
[68] Whitby, *Maurice* 156–65, 176–81.   [69] Frantz (1988) ch. IV.

Archaeological field surveys in Greece are increasingly building up a picture of considerable intensification of settlement and land use in the fourth and fifth century after more than half a millennium of abatement: in Boeotia the density of rural settlement was striking, and, though this may be explained to an extent by a decline of smaller townships and the transfer of population to rural estates, the results belie Zosimus' complaint (v.5.7) about the area's continuing impoverishment. Surveys in other areas – for example, the Argolid – have confirmed this resurgence of the Greek countryside; marginal land was being reoccupied, and it is even possible to talk of a return to the population density of classical times. Attica shared this trend.[70]

In Athens itself, the long-running investigations of the Agora have revealed rapid rebuilding after the destruction associated with Alaric's Goths in 396 (see Fig. 24); indeed, the recovery appears more substantial than in the aftermath of the Herul attack in the third century. Two factors made Athens special – the prosperity of its Neoplatonic philosophy school and an imperial marriage. The reputation of Athens as a centre for philosophical education was re-established by Plutarch, who died in the early 430s, and continued by its most famous representative, Proclus, who led the school for almost half a century until his death in 485. Although Synesius, writing to his brother, probably in 410, had poked fun at the Plutarchean sophists who attracted students with Attic honey rather than the fame of their eloquence (*Ep.* 136), the Athenian intellectuals made a significant contribution to the local economy – like a modern university in a small town such as Lampeter or St Andrews. The teachers themselves may not have been sufficiently wealthy to own the large houses excavated on the north slope of the Areopagus, but they were closely connected with the members of the local élite who lived there, and with the provincial officials who could finance major building works: thus the restoration of the Library of Hadrian was organized by the praetorian prefect of Illyricum, Herculius, whose statue was placed on the façade by the sophist Plutarch.[71] The educational establishment was relevant to the imperial marriage: Athenaïs, selected as Theodosius II's bride in 421 and renamed Eudocia, was daughter of Leontius, a teacher at Athens. A plausible suggestion is that the grand Palace of the Giants, which occupied most of the central portion of the old agora (see Fig. 25), was built to mark the promotion of this local family to imperial dignity; at any rate, Eudocia's brother Gessius was praetorian prefect of Illyricum in the 420s, and a statue of Eudocia stood in front of the palace.[72] It is possible that the one-third

[70] Bintliff and Snodgrass (1985) 147–8; Runnels and van Audel (1987) 319–20; Alcock (1989) 13; Fowden (1988) 54–5.

[71] Frantz (1988) 57–8, 37–49 (modifications in Fowden (1990) 495–6); Cameron and Long (1993) 56–7.   [72] Frantz (1988) ch. 5 (by Homer Thompson), with Fowden (1990) 497–9.

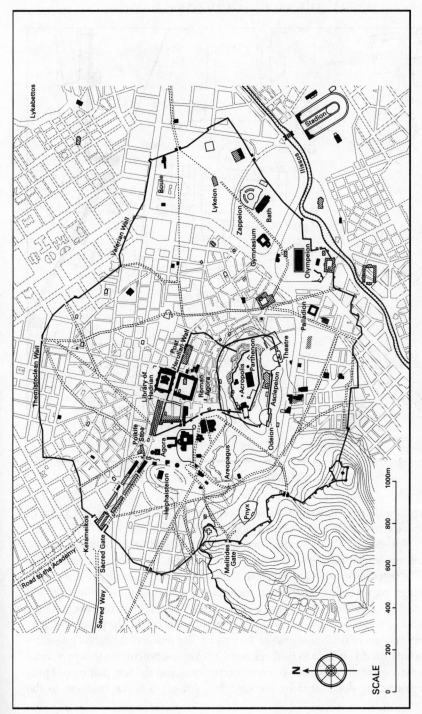

Fig 24 Athens in the fifth century A.D. (After Frantz (1988))

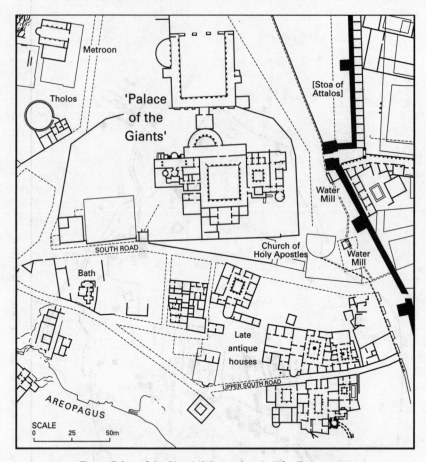

Fig. 25 'Palace of the Giants' (Athenian Agora). (After Frantz (1988))

reduction in taxation in Achaea, authorized in October 424 (*C.Th.* XI.1.33), was a consequence of the province's imperial contacts.

Possession of philosophers and an empress made Athens a little different, but its development was not out of line with that of other provincial cities. The inscriptions of Corinth from the fifth and sixth century reveal a wide range of activities: agriculture, including goatherds, pheasant-rearing and market gardening, trade, including tailors, cobblers and furriers, and the retinue and support services required by the presence of the provincial governor – there is even a graffito by two of the praetorian prefect's *bucellarii* asking for divine help in their release form imprisonment. Smaller provincial towns naturally produce very few inscriptions, and the few that record professions are dominated by the church.[73] Athens was not immune to the

---

[73] Feissel and Philippidis-Braat (1985) part I.

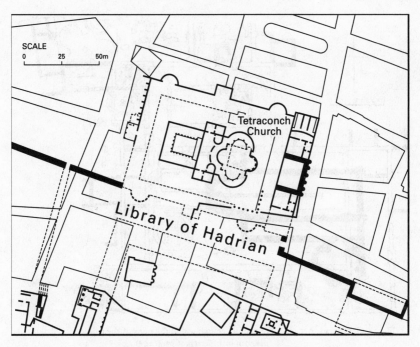

Fig. 26 Library of Hadrian. (After Frantz (1988))

growth in power and visibility of Christianity, and it is possible to infer from inscriptions that there was a gradual but significant conversion in the century 350–450. The philosophers remained solidly pagan, but they may not have determined the religious affiliations of their fellow citizens: Proclus had briefly to retire from Athens to Lydia in the late 440s, and a plausible specu-lation is that he was evading Christian pressure; there is no firm evidence for the religious views of ordinary Athenians, but Proclus' devotion in attend-ing the rural shrines of Attica on their feast days was probably abnormal. A church of a striking tetraconch design was built in the courtyard of the Library of Hadrian in the early fifth century (see Fig. 26), and it may be right to connect this with Eudocia, who was an intellectual in her own right but also a convert to Christianity with a record of church building and other ben-efactions; two basilicas were constructed in the south-eastern part of the city by the Ilissos stream. A significant blow to pagan morale would have been struck when the cult statues were removed from the Parthenon and Asclepieion and access to the temples prohibited, a development which probably occurred towards the end of Proclus' life.[74]

At Athens, continuity of occupation makes it impossible to identify all the new Christian buildings that were erected, but from elsewhere in

[74] Frantz (1988) 72–3; Fowden 499–501; Trombley, *Hellenic Religion* ch. IV.

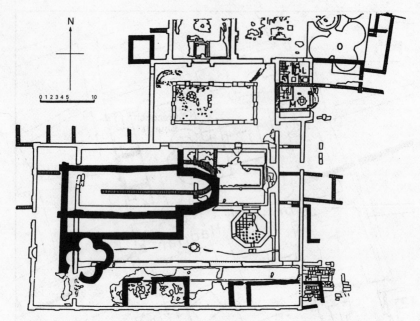

Fig. 27 Gamzigrad (Acquis), sixth-century church within the ruins of the palace of Galerius.
(After Bavant in *Villes et peuplement* 268)

Greece there is plenty of evidence for the erection and decoration of substantial churches and other ecclesiastical structures – for example, at
Distomo and Kirra in Phocis, or Nea Anchialos in southern Thessaly,
where there was clearly a flourishing Christian community; in Macedonia,
at Kitros and Makryialos, late Roman basilicas have been discovered within
the past decade, while at Philippi the decoration of the episcopal palace has
revealed that the bishop lived in conditions to match the impressive group
of basilicas in the centre of his town.[75] At Thessalonica, as at Athens, the
late fifth century seems to have been the crucial period for the monumental establishment of Christianity at the centre of the city: the city's patron
saint and protector, Demetrius, received a grand church, the unused mausoleum of Galerius was converted into a church to St George with lavish
mosaic decorations, and there were also churches for St David and the
Panaghia Akheiropoietos; these are just the structures that survive.[76] As
Christian buildings were becoming more prominent in the provincial cities
and towns, so the bishops were emerging as the dominant local figures: the
role of the bishops at Thessalonica and Heracleia during the passage of
Theoderic's Goths in 478 has already been noted; this is matched at a lesser
level by bishop Epiphanius who was responsible for a construction at

[75] All information reported in *Archaeological Reports for 1990–1991*.   [76] Spieser (1984a).

Thebes, or the learned bishop Peter commemorated in verse on a mosaic inscription.[77]

Those areas of the Balkans less accessible to northern invaders preserved their prosperity, or at least avoided serious decline, until the sixth century, but thereafter there is a rapid and catastrophic collapse: field surveys note the almost complete abandonment of the countryside, while in towns and other significant sites the level of material culture dropped dramatically and the fabric of society appears to have unravelled. In peninsular Greece, Athens may have led the decline, depending on what impact Justinian's prohibition on pagan participation in teaching in 529 had on the local economy: the careful concealment of pagan statues at one of the large houses on the Areopagus at about that date is suggestive, but should not be pushed too far.[78] In the mid sixth century Bulgars ravaged northern and central Greece, and by the 580s central Greece and the Peloponnese had also become the targets for Slav attacks and the location, perhaps, of some Slav settlement. By the late sixth century it is no longer possible to identify a north/south divide in the Balkans, since the whole region was suffering from extreme disruption as raiders caused considerable depopulation and destruction, with no respite for recovery.

In some cities the population departed *en masse*: thus at Lissus in Dalmatia and Euria in Epirus, local clergy seem to have led their flocks to safety, in Italy and Corfu respectively, in the 590s.[79] For the Peloponnese, the *Chronicle of Monemvasia* records migrations to Italy, Sicily, offshore islands or isolated refuges such as Monemvasia, at which a bishopric was now established; the *Chronicle* also asserts that the Peloponnese passed out of imperial control in 587/8, only to be recovered in the early eighth century. Although the status of this text is much discussed and its information may well be exaggerated in certain respects, the general impression of developments is at least credible; this literary evidence coincides with the picture of utter desolation recorded in the Argolid field survey.[80] On the other hand, all was not lost until after 600 and the termination of energetic campaigning along the Danube under Phocas and the transfer of troops to Asia Minor by Heraclius: in 592 pope Gregory could refer to a general recovery in Illyricum from the effects of invasions, which encouraged him to reorganize the church's possessions there, and his letters suggest the survival of ecclesiastical order in Macedonia, peninsular Greece and along the Adriatic coast.[81]

Those who managed to flee into exile were the lucky ones, since both Slavs and Avars are known to have removed large numbers of captives for

---

[77] Avramea and Feissel (1987) nos. 6 and 7.
[78] Frantz (1988) 84–92; caution in Fowden (1990) 496.   [79] Greg. *Reg.* II.37; VIII.32; XIV.7–8.
[80] Charanis (1950); Whitby, *Maurice* 125–6.
[81] *Reg.* II.23; III.6, 38; VI.7; IX.156; Whitby, *Maurice* 112–15.

exploitation in their homelands; though these might be liberated through military action, their allegiance to the empire was thereafter considered suspect, so that even release was a mixed blessing.[82] The Slavs' reputation for kind treatment of captives, and opportunities for lucrative service with the successful Avars, will have weakened the attractions of loyalty to Rome. More importantly, perhaps, the region was experiencing a steady process of demographic and cultural change as the settlement of Germanic and Hunnic tribesmen within the Balkans since the fourth century blurred distinctions between inhabitants north and south of the Danube. The invasions must have caused heavy casualties, particularly as the Avars, like the Huns, were capable of undertaking sieges and organizing effective blockades: an inscription from Sirmium, in poor Greek, attests the agony of this city in 580: 'Lord Christ, help the city and smite the Avars, and watch over Romania and the writer; Amen'; the prayer went unanswered, and the Avar Chagan had no compunction about taking false oaths on the Bible.[83] Even Slavs could overrun the walls of Topirus in 552, and defences of the lower cities at Athens and Corinth c. 582. The absence of Thessalonican coins in northern Illyricum has been suggested as an indication of lack of economic activity in the sixth century, possibly of major depopulation; granted the link between coinage production and army pay, this absence probably reflects a lack of soldiers, or at least of soldiers whose units were still closely attached to the imperial system, unlike the unpaid garrison at Pessau in Noricum or the soldiers at Asemus.[84] Maurice believed that there was sufficient room in Thrace for the settlement of 30,000 Armenian families, which would each provide a new soldier.[85]

In this period of uncertainty, urban settlements were in fundamental conflict with the invaders,[86] partly because city walls protected the surpluses of food and reserves of wealth that interested tribesmen, partly because the movement of tribes into an area destroyed agricultural prosperity, constricted a city's vitality, and prompted the flight of leading inhabitants to places of greater safety: at Salona, attempted flight by the upper classes prompted the city's fall in 638/9, while the refugees from Serdica and Naissus at Thessalonica c. 620 were probably similar people.[87] Cities might be choked to death as the more Romanized elements of their population departed, and it is significant that at many Balkan sites the last phases of 'Roman' occupation are difficult to distinguish from 'barbarian' control, with so-called squatter inhabitation of ruined buildings. Part of the problem is the lack of publications of seventh-century structures, which are usually unprepossessing and appear uninteresting, and the tendency of archaeologists to date material to the fifth/sixth century on the

[82] Maurice, *Strat.* XI.4.131–6.   [83] Menander fr. 25.1.76–87.
[84] Metcalf (1984); cf. Lemerle (1984) 520. *Life* of Severinus 20.1; Theophylact VII.3.
[85] Sebeos 8.   [86] Lemerle (1984) 516; *contra* Howard-Johnston (1983).
[87] Thomas the Archdeacon 26–7; *Mirac. S. Dem.* II.200.

basis that civilized life had collapsed by the seventh century, so that there could be no significant archaeological evidence thereafter. In addition, at Isthmia, one of the best-published sites in southern Greece, which has produced the first quantity of Slavic pottery outside a cemetery context, it has proved impossible to establish the identity of the inhabitants: they may have been Greeks who chose to use 'Slavic' pottery, or settled Slavs who maintained close contacts with the Byzantine authorities at nearby Corinth.[88]

Travel and communications were now endangered throughout the Balkans, which will have enhanced the separatist tendencies already evident in the north in the fifth century. Pope Gregory wrote to the bishop of Corinth in 591 with a specific request that he assist with a papal messenger's journey to Constantinople (*Register* 1.26). Avar envoys returning from Constantinople were ambushed by Scamareis, who stole horses, silver and other equipment; the identity of these Scamareis is unknown, though the fact that Tiberius could track down the culprits and recover some of the goods suggests they were an identifiable community, perhaps analogous to the western bagaudae. An Avar ambassador was murdered by Slavs within the empire, and in Justinian's reign the Slavs are reported to have isolated the Roman city of Adina in Scythia Minor.[89] Outside cities there was considerable insecurity. At Appiaria a local leader was captured and held to ransom after a hunting expedition took him away from the walls, a repetition of the fate of Asemus' shepherds in the 440s. Asemus itself survived beyond the end of the sixth century and provides the best example of local separatism: in 594, with their bishop as leader, the inhabitants barricaded their city against an imperial army and mocked the general Peter, the emperor Maurice's brother, because he had attempted to enlist their garrison – local safety came first, and Asemus had learnt to fend for itself during a decade without imperial contact. At nearby Novae, Peter was received more favourably, though the insistence with which he was pressed to remain to celebrate the festival of the local martyr Lupus may also reveal consequences of isolation: his presence could allow the citizens to commemorate their saint without fear of surprise attack. The importance of bishops in maintaining morale is demonstrated at Justiniana Prima, where Maurice intervened in an attempt to have a demented bishop replaced quickly, lest the city fall to the enemy through lack of ecclesiastical guidance. The first book of the *Miracles* of St Demetrius was composed by bishop John of Thessalonica in the early seventh century, when his city was coming under such severe pressure that it was dangerous to venture beyond the walls and the inhabitants desperately needed reassurance that their man at the heavenly court would continue to protect them.[90]

[88] Gregory (1993) 156–9.   [89] Men. frr. 15.6; 25.2.32–6; Procop. *Buildings* IV.7.13; Farkas (1993–4).
[90] Theophylact VII.3.1–10, 2.17–18; Greg. *Reg.* XI.29; Whitby, *Maurice* 115–17.

The *Life of Gregentius*, although a fictitious text, presents a convincing picture of living conditions: Gregentius, a native of the Balkans, avoided capture during a tribal raid by taking refuge in a fort, but those inhabitants who did not reach a nearby town were captured or slaughtered. Only after a tribe was firmly established in an area were more stable relations possible with Roman communities which survived: at Singidunum the Avars appear to have been happy to permit survivors to remain in their captured city until the reappearance of a Roman army disturbed the arrangement, and at the height of their power in 589 the Chagan offered security to city-dwellers if they paid taxes to the Avars instead of the Romans.[91] Near Thessalonica in the seventh century good relations were gradually built up between the citizens and local Slavs, particularly between leaders on each side, as some Slavs came to appreciate the benefits of Roman civilization. Thessalonica, however, was a rarity in surviving as a Roman city beyond the mid seventh century, as the restoration of Roman authority in Maurice's second decade was undermined by the resumption of eastern war and imperial dissension; apart from the immediate hinterland of Constantinople, Roman control was soon restricted to coastal areas where small communities could support and defend themselves. An expedition led by Justinian II suffered heavily in an ambush while returning from Thessalonica to the capital in 688 (Theophanes 364.11–18).

In much of the Balkans there was a complete break between the Roman and post-Roman worlds. In Bulgaria there was some continuity of language and administrative skills in the short term, probably transmitted by the inhabitants of cities along the Black Sea, but the majority of the territory north of the Stara Planina was already occupied by Slav tribes when Asparuch led in the new Bulgar ruling élite in 680. In peninsular Greece enough of the native population survived for the reconnection of this area with the Byzantine world to be an unremarkable process, but many had probably had to take refuge in the mountains and other safe areas; there may already be signs of the process of incorporation into the Byzantine cultural world in the seventh-century settlement at Isthmia, where the inhabitants were sedentary agriculturalists inhabiting buildings partly built of stone. Throughout most of the Balkans, however, the future lay with the non-Roman elements: Croats and Serbs were settled in the north-west during Heraclius' reign, the Bulgars controlled the north-east, while the Slavs spread into whatever land was available. Centuries of Graeco-Roman influence and control disappeared, and the new groups with their own languages and identities were only brought slowly into a Christian commonwealth through considerable missionary activity.[92]

---

[91] Theophylact VII.10–11; Michael the Syrian XI.21.
[92] Howard-Johnston (1983); Obolensky (1971) chs. 2–3.

CHAPTER 24

THE ORGANIZATION OF THE CHURCH

STUART GEORGE HALL

I. BISHOPS AND PATRIARCHS

The fifth-century church inherited an organization matching that of the empire.[1] Each community usually had its bishop, though increasingly presbyters or sometimes deacons deputized for the bishop in governing congregations. Above the local bishop stood the bishop of the metropolis, the metropolian (μητροπολίτης), whose position had been codified at Nicaea in 325. Superior to the metropolitan, the city which was the centre of an imperial diocese (ἐπαρχία) attained comparable status in the church, and its bishop was called 'archbishop' (ἀρχιεπίσκοπος). This term was frequently used of the bishops of Rome, Alexandria and Antioch at the Council of Ephesus in 431, the same sees which had been named as exercising territorial superiority in the canons of Nicaea in 325. The term 'archbishop' was limited to those of such standing till about 500. After that it is more widely used, first of metropolitans, then of others whose independence was being asserted. The term 'patriarch' (πατριάρχης) then began to be applied to the bishops of the greater sees. 'Patriarch' was first used of the ancient biblical figures, and had been adopted for leading officers by the Jewish communities before Constantine's time. Its rare use for Christian figures began to be extended to the superior bishops in documents associated with the Council of Chalcedon in 451.[2] That council also specified that the metropolitan bishops of the imperial dioceses of Pontus, Asia and Thrace should be ordained by the bishop of Constantinople; thus the metropolitans of Cappadocian Caesarea, Ephesus and Philippopolis, who were to ordain bishops in their respective imperial provinces and any pendent sees among the barbarians, were declared subordinate to the capital.[3] Chalcedon also rewarded the conversion of Juvenal of Jerusalem (422–58) to the imperial theology by upgrading his see to rank among the patriarchates: he was confirmed in control of the metropolitans of the

---

[1] Jones, *LRE* 873–937, and the related notes, can only be admired and palely imitated in the space available here. Baus, Beck, Ewig and Vogt (1980) is also useful, especially chs. 13–21, 27 and 28–31. See also Ducellier, *L'Église byzantine*, especially for the relations of church and emperor.

[2] See *PGL s.v.* ἀρχιεπίσκοπος, πατριάρχης.   [3] Canon 28.

three Palestines, Caesarea, Scythopolis and Petra; 'Arabia' (Bostra) would be added in 553. Thus five ancient patriarchates enjoy super-metropolitan powers: Rome, Constantinople, Alexandria, Antioch and Jerusalem. These are consistently referred to in the documents of the sixth century, and constitute the 'pentarchy'.[4]

There were, however, different perceptions of this patriarchal system. Rome remained pre-eminent in the west, being the only western apostolic see – that is, founded (as was believed) by the apostles themselves. Its bishops, however, regarded their primacy as extending to the east, and steadily enlarged both its theory and practice. Celestine of Rome in 430 commissioned Cyril of Alexandria to depose Nestorius if he would not repent, 'appropriating to yourself the authority of our see, and using our position'.[5] So Cyril acted as and for the bishop of Rome. Sixtus III (432–40) of Rome in 433 ratified the Formula of Union by which the disorders of the Council of Ephesus were resolved, acting in concert with Alexandria, Antioch and Constantinople, but emphasizing the importance of agreeing with the tradition of Peter.[6] His successor Leo I (440–61) condemned Eutyches in 448–9. Eutyches was not only christologically unsound, but rejected the Formula of 433 as an improper addition to the Nicene Creed.

Leo intensified the idea of Petrine tradition by using the principle of inheritance, claiming that the bishops of Rome inherited the bishopric and primacy of Peter: Peter was not only the source of Roman tradition, but was present in his heir and successor. The primacy of Peter among the apostles was the same as the primacy of his successors among the bishops. Leo not only preached this view, but advanced it in practice. His greatest success was in bringing to heel bishop Hilary of Arles, an ascetic trained in Lérins, who expected the highest standards of his fellow bishops. Hilary held councils and deposed and ordained bishops without reference to Rome. He went beyond his immediate jurisdiction in the province of Viennensis. Leo not only argued his case to the bishops, emphasizing his authority as successor of Peter, but achieved an imperial *Constitutio* from Valentinian III in 445, ratifying his own sentence. Hilary was allowed to remain a bishop in Arles, but deprived even of his normal metropolitan powers. The *Constitutio* forbade the bishops of the Gallic or other provinces to do anything without the authority of 'the venerable Pope of the Eternal City', and the enactments of the apostolic see were to be law for all.[7]

With the collapse of imperial order in the west, Constantinople became for most purposes the centre of Christendom, as well as of the empire.

---

[4] See Gahbauer (1993), (1996).
[5] Celestine, *Ep.* 11.3–4 (*ACO* I.I.I. p. 76); for a fuller account see ch. 27 (Allen), pp. 811–34 below.
[6] Sixtus III, *Ep.* 6.   [7] See generally Studer (1991).

Constantinople lacked the territorial superiority affirmed in the canons of Nicaea in 325 for Rome, Alexandria and Antioch, as well as the apostolic name claimed by them. Among its bishops, John Chrysostom had been deposed because he interfered to suppress simony in churches in Asia, where his writ did not run, and heard appeals against the condemnation by Theophilus of Alexandria of Origenist monks. Nestorius similarly incurred the hostility of senior colleagues by seeming to hear appeals against the judgements of Alexandria and Rome,[8] and by intervening in parts of Asia Minor and also in Macedonia, where the bishop of Thessalonica's special relation to Rome made it particularly sensitive.[9] Constantinople's standing was clarified at the Council of Chalcedon, as already stated. Along with territorial jurisdiction went a primacy of honour as second to 'great and elder Rome', asserted in 381 at the Council of Constantinople and strengthened in 451 at Chalcedon. It was then claimed that the Fathers in 381 'gave equal privileges to the most holy throne of New Rome, judging with reason that the city which was honoured with the sovereignty and senate, and which enjoyed equal privileges with the elder royal Rome, should also be magnified like her in ecclesiastical matters, being the second after her'.[10] Leo rejected this formula, which expresses the civic grounds of ecclesiastical primacy at the expense of its theological ground. He based his rejection on the canon of Nicaea which gave such honour only to the apostolic sees; Nicaea could not be challenged merely on civil grounds.[11] Emperors and bishops in Constantinople would alike ignore Leo's repudiation.

The affirmation of Constantinople in 451 was not unopposed in the east. Alexandrian bishops had complicated local constituencies to manage, with ecclesiastical rivalries, competing doctrines, communal tensions, non-Christian religion and culture, and large and quarrelsome monastic communities throughout their diocesan territory. With this they must reconcile the need to assure themselves that they would not be isolated in the empire. Cyril's quarrel with Nestorius was essentially over jurisdiction: Nestorius gave ear to the appeals of persons condemned by Cyril in disciplinary hearings, thus implying appellate power.[12] Cyril's successor Dioscorus tried to reaffirm Alexandria's hegemony, succumbing to Constantinople and Rome in 451. In Egypt itself after Chalcedon only imperial force could impose Proterius as bishop until his assassination in 457. Timothy Aelurus (457–77) thereafter enjoyed wide local support, while his Chalcedonian rival Timothy Salophakialos (460–82) had only a few families hostile to the Dioscuran party and one powerful monastery

---

[8] The non-doctrinal aspects of this dispute are emphasized in McGuckin (1994) ch. 1.

[9] Leo, *Ep.* 98.4; 105.2; 106.5.   [10] Canon 28; cf. Leo, *Ep.* 98.4.   [11] Leo, *Ep.* 98.4; 105.2.

[12] The story is often told: recently by McGuckin (1994) ch. 1; also the introduction to Wickham (1983) and Wickham's article in *TRE* 24. For developing conciliar theory, see Sieben (1986) 231–69.

at Canopus. Peter Mongus (477–90), succeeding Timothy Aelurus, by judicious patronage and pressure balanced reconciliation with the empire by subscribing to the *Henotikon*, won over rival 'Monophysite' factions, and destroyed the remaining strongholds both of non-Christian cult and of Chalcedonian theology at Canopus.[13] The defection of Juvenal of Jerusalem to supporting the empire at Chalcedon confirmed patriarchal standing for his see, but split his local churches between Chalcedonians and Monophysites. Syria also, and the great prize of Antioch, suffered continual changes in response to shifts of imperial policy and local rivalries. But in neither of these areas was the superiority of Constantinople challenged constitutionally.

Another issue for Constantinople was the quarrel about the title 'oecumenical patriarch' (πατριάρχης οἰκουμενικός). 'Oecumenical' means 'worldwide', but it is used technically to refer to the imperial (i.e. worldwide) authority of a body or person: so there are imperially ratified 'oecumenical councils', and after Justinian abolished the philosophical schools in 529 there are 'oecumenical teachers' at Constantinople. Dioscorus was addressed as 'oecumenical patriarch' in 449, being seen as restorer of the true conciliar theology; so was Leo I when appealed to by Dioscorus' enemies, and later Roman popes by eastern appellants. When first taken by a patriarch of Constantinople, John the Faster in 595, it was seen at Rome as usurping a Roman title, and furious opposition resulted.[14]

The bishop of Constantinople was near the seat of power. The promotion of his see was of interest to the emperor, and communication was easy. Communication and influence from further afield were possible but could be very expensive, or liable to interception and suppression. But the patriarch was also subject to imperial pressure, much more than his Roman colleague. 536 was a critical year. Constantinople had been divided from Rome in the Acacian schism (484–519). Its healing had been accompanied by the condemnation and exile of leading figures, who nevertheless continued promoting their cause, as Severus of Antioch did in Egypt. By 531 the emperor was attempting a reconciliation with the Monophysites, using the new patriarch, Anthimus, but his eirenic scheme foundered through the arrival of the pope Agapitus I in the spring of 536 as ambassador from Theodahad. Agapitus refused communion with Anthimus, ostensibly because he had previously been bishop of Trebizond: translations were frequent enough, but since 325 could always be denounced.[15] In 536 Anthimus was dropped by Justinian, and Agapitus' policy was implemented by the new patriarch Menas (536–52), who anathematized leading Monophysites like Theodosius of

---

[13] See Haas (1993).
[14] *PGL s.v.* οἰκουμενικός, πατριάρχης; thorough analysis in Tuilier (1966).
[15] Council of Nicaea, canon 15; cf. the first part of Scholz (1992).

Alexandria and even Severus. These events precipitated the setting up of independent Monophysite churches in Egypt and Syria: Theodosius from the capital supervised by letter his Egyptian congregations, and in 542 ordained missionary bishops for the Arabian and Syrian provinces. These were Theodore of Arabia and Jacob Baradaeus (Bar'Addai). The latter, though chiefly responding to pastoral need in ordaining many hundreds of priests before his death in 578, also consolidated the divisions by ordaining Sergius of Pella as patriarch of Antioch in 557/8. The Monophysite churches (always fissiparous) were now separate from the imperial.

The imperial and patriarchal system was again tested by the controversy over the Three Chapters.[16] The initial document of 543/5 and the anathemas pressed upon the bishops in 551 had only Justinian's authority. The west was hostile, and the papal *apocrisarii* withdrew from communion with Menas. Vigilius of Rome (537–55) was required to attend in Constantinople in 547. His repeated shifts and contradictions are notorious. Justinian exposed Vigilius' prevarications to the council, which expunged his name from their prayer-diptychs without excommunicating him. Vigilius at the end of 553 gave full assent to the condemnation of the Three Chapters, and was finally allowed to travel home. He died in 555 before reaching Rome. His successor Pelagius, who gave Justinian what he wanted in order to gain the appointment, was to change sides again when he returned to the west.[17]

All of this shows how hard it was to unify the Christian body of the empire. Justinian expected to govern the church in his domain; but he was frustrated by the religious passions of the easterns and by the inflexibility of Rome. That see was acknowledged to hold a necessary or primary place in settling worldwide affairs; but it was tied by its own traditions, theologically grounded in Peter, and by its western constituency, unable to take the steps which would enable the emperor to come to terms with the eastern dissidents. The expedient of a council also failed: it could not satisfy both pope and emperor, whose assent and enforcement are understood parts of the process, or engage the theological dissidents of the east. To achieve church unity more flexible views of tradition and dogma were needed. The bishops of Rome increasingly became a point of stability, as was recognized even by unsympathetic overlords. Theoderic II at Ravenna, acting as a Christian monarch, took pains to settle the Laurentian schism in 498, hearing the parties and arranging a compromise. Appeal was repeatedly made to him by Laurence's supporters, and it was not until 506 that Symmachus was finally confirmed as bishop and got possession of all the church buildings in the city.[18]

---

[16] See ch. 27 below.   [17] Beck in Baus, Beck, Ewig and Vogt (1980) 452–5.
[18] Baus in Baus, Beck, Ewig and Vogt (1980) 620–1.

II. COUNCILS AND CLERGY

Each bishop ruled his own church as final judge, and his judgement could not be undone by another. His sanction against offenders was excommunication, a grave matter affecting the whole life and career of the person concerned. Appeal could be made higher in the church, and the fifth canon of Nicaea established a system for this: the metropolitan must assemble his bishops twice a year, before Lent and in the autumn, to review and normally to ratify all decisions. The system was not scrupulously applied, and the rule had often to be repeated. Of the bishop's council or the metropolitan's we get only occasional reports, and few full records. They were of local and temporary interest. Only when wider national or imperial concerns led to special assemblies from more than one province do the records sometimes survive.

This state of affairs is well illustrated from Merovingian Gaul. Most councils engaged more than one metropolitan province; only two are provincial and one diocesan. Surviving records reflect the fact that major councils were often called by royal power. The model is provided by Constantine and Nicaea; so Clovis, who from his conversion in 496 becomes a 'new Constantine', constitutes his state church with the Council of Orleans (511). The council acknowledges that it meets at his command, and seeks his approval of its decrees. Its first three canons deal with a matter of civil concern: the right of criminals to asylum. Only then does it turn to the more usual occupations of councils – largely rules for the clergy and monks, and some liturgical items. The relation to royal authority had already figured large in the holding of councils. The total of fourteen provinces never met together until the Fifth Council of Paris in 614; but thirteen were represented by the sixty-five bishops at Orleans V in 549. We have records of only one diocesan synod, the undatable Auxerre, and of a number limited to the province of Arles, which was lively and large, with twenty-three dioceses.[19]

The bishops often repeat decrees of earlier councils. Already in the Council of Agde in 506 the compilation called *Statuta Ecclesiae Antiqua* plays an important role.[20] The modern editions trace the parallels from council to council.[21] These same documents illustrate the concerns of the bishops. One is always the purity of the clergy. Minimum ages (twenty-five for a deacon, thirty for a presbyter) are stipulated. Slaves may not be ordained without enfranchisement. From 524 (Arles IV can. 2) laymen could not be ordained direct to the diaconate or presbyterate. Acceptability to the civil authority is required, but only rarely is there any concern for educational

[19] Gaudemet and Basdevant (1989) 33–4 differs slightly from the count in Wallace-Hadrill (1983) 94–5.   [20] Ed. Munier (1963a).
[21] For the concerns of the councils, Gaudemet and Basdevant (1989) 44–59.

qualifications. If married, clergy must abstain from sexual intercourse, and may not retain a female other than a close relative in their house. Clergy may not be twice married, and their widows must stay single. Clergy may not attend the circus or hunt. Liturgical occasions must be properly observed, and these are imposed especially on bishops, along with their pastoral, homiletic and charitable duties, the giving of absolution to the penitent and the writing of recommendations. Jurisdictional questions figure largely. Property might be held in one diocese by persons resident in another, and if churches are built and staffed there, ecclesiastical allegiance must be sorted out. This is especially tricky where the property is owned by another bishop. The disposal of church property is frequently an issue, and there are stringent canons about what happens on the death of a cleric. The duty of metropolitans to call provincial synods annually, or more frequently, is prescribed. Potential bishops must have their discipline and their faith tested before election. They must not (like Caesarius of Arles) be chosen by their predecessors. New ecclesial offices arise to deal with the problems of organization: archpresbyters, archdeacons, and even archsubdeacons appear. Relations with the kings sometimes figure, and the royal prerogative in appointing bishops can sometimes be asserted (Orleans V, 549, can. 10) and sometimes repudiated (Paris III, 546/573, can. 8); the part in elections of the people, the clergy, the bishops and the metropolitan are repeatedly affirmed. Where the laity are concerned, marriage rules loom large: the fear of incest is obsessive.[22] Marriage or other contact with heretics and Jews is banned or restricted. Only rarely are doctrinal matters tackled; the classic exception is Caesarius' Council of Orange in 529, when the Augustinian position was comprehensively asserted against the semi-Pelagians. Such matters do not come to the fore, even when regimes are changing from 'Arian' to Catholic overlords.[23] Much of this may be interpreted inversely: where a practice is repeatedly banned, it is presumably common. The influence of the civil power led to many worldly men being appointed to the clericate, and the constant concern of councils with clergy discipline, as well as with the doctrinal competence of bishops, reflects this fact.

A remarkable absentee in the Merovingian canons is the pope. The only reference appears to be the right to consult the apostolic see through the metropolitan about the date of Easter.[24] This reflects political conditions, and perhaps the absence of any primacy among the metropolitans further

---

[22] Gaudemet and Basdevant (1989) 57.

[23] The Council of Épaone in 517, presided over by Avitus of Vienne after Sigismund's rise to power, had only two references to heretics and their buildings. The same applies to the momentous Council of Toledo III in 589, after Reccared's conversion (see Orlandi in Orlandi and Ramos-Lisson (1981) 95–117, esp. 110–11).

[24] Orleans IV, 541, can. 1 (not can. 2 as in Gaudemet and Basdevant (1989) 48 n. 4).

north. Caesarius at Arles (bishop 500–43) exercised the papal vicariate, and exchanged letters with the bishops of Rome about conciliar decisions in his area. When in 533 his council at Marseilles condemned and deposed Contumeliosus of Riez, this drew a rebuke from Agapitus of Rome.[25]

The patriarchal system provided a further point of consultation, appeal and decision. Disputes between metropolitans or charges against them came to the patriarchal bishop. When support was needed, he could assemble metropolitans and bishops to meet. Each case was unique: there were no metropolitans in Egypt, and the heads of churches were summoned to Alexandria from time to time. Two particular arrangements deserve mention. Rome had its own metropolitan authority in central Italy, *Roma suburbicaria*, whose leaders formed the Roman Synod. But this advised the pope on matters affecting the wider church: for example, Celestine I in 430 and Leo I in 449 in relation to the christological crises in the east. At Constantinople, which had no such traditional province, the unique phenomenon of the *synodos endemousa* or 'Resident Synod' arose: the archbishop would assemble to advise him the bishops (and sometimes others) who were at that time in the capital. These might be quite numerous. The Resident Synod would meet regularly, but could take major decisions, such as condemning Eutyches in 448.[26]

Much more is known about the councils intended to be 'oecumenical', especially those of Ephesus in 431 and Chalcedon in 451, of which full records survive. From these we know that they were called by imperial mandate. In spite of his commission from Rome, Cyril in 430 could not begin his council at Ephesus until he had induced the emperor's representative, Candidianus, to read out the imperial *sacra* authorizing the meeting.[27] The same document stipulated the various roles of the participants: good order and the exclusion of strangers were an imperial responsibility, doctrine was ecclesiastical. The history of this and the other great councils shows that the two could not be so readily separated. Once an agreement had been reached, however, the assembly would announce its decisions to the emperor, and he would enforce what was decided. Procedure was modelled on that of the senate.[28]

From the perspective of our documentation one might assume that councils and controversies occupied much of the time of ancient churchmen. This is not the case. Some of their work and preoccupations can be deduced from material like the Merovingian councils.

Occasionally we get closer insights about the clergy. An investigation of the church at Mopsuestia in preparation for the Oecumenical Council of

[25] But see Langgärtner (1964).

[26] Jones, *LRE* 890 translates ἐνδημοῦσα as 'visiting', but the word indicates its permanent (or domestic) character: Baus in Baus, Beck, Ewig and Vogt (1980) 245: Hajjar (1962).

[27] McGuckin (1994) 74–9.   [28] Dvornik (1934) and (1966).

553 showed that there were seventeen presbyters and deacons above fifty years old. This might suggest a total of fifty. Besides them, there were sub-deacons, acolytes and readers, all counted as *in clero*. These minor offices were sometimes filled by young men: six of the older clergy had been *in clero* at less than eleven years old and one as young as five, though readers of under eighteen were now forbidden. This is a large number for a modest town. Justinian limited the clerical staff of four churches in Constantinople itself to sixty priests, a hundred deacons, ninety subdeacons, a hundred and ten readers, twenty-five singers, a hundred doorkeepers and forty deacon-esses.[29] Age restrictions were not rigorously applied. At the age of eighteen the charismatic and ascetic monk Theodore of Sykeon was tonsured and ordained reader, subdeacon, deacon and presbyter on successive days. His bishop recognized that this act was uncanonical, but justified it from scrip-ture, and expressed the confidence that he would rise to become a bishop.[30] There is no evidence that most clergy were trained except by experience in the work. They were normally expected to rise through the minor orders to the presbyterate. They would therefore be hearing and reading the scrip-tures and liturgical texts, and hearing the preaching of the bishop and pres-byters quite regularly. The need for regular direction in their functions is reflected in the growth of new offices, such as archpriest, archdeacon and archsubdeacon.

The bishop might, especially in Gaul, be drawn from secular life because of his gifts or his family connections. Sidonius Apollinaris (431–*c.* 486), son and grandson of prefects of Gaul, married the daughter of Avitus and went with him to Rome in 456. After Avitus' fall and Maiorinus' death, he retired to his estates in the Auvergne and cultivated literature and friend-ships, writing classically correct verse and ornate prose. Called to be city prefect at Rome in 468, he retired again, and was probably a priest before his ordination as bishop of Clermont-Ferrand (Arvernum) in 471. As bishop, he encouraged resistance to the Visigoths but, after an exile, sub-mitted.[31] Venantius Fortunatus (*c.* 535–*c.* 610), a north Italian poet and orator educated at Ravenna, went to Gaul on pilgrimage and was ordained at Poitiers, where he was asociated with queen Radegund's convent and suc-ceeded as bishop in 597.[32] The historian Gregory of Tours (*c.* 538–94) was of a senatorial Gallo-Roman family, with twelve bishops in his family's past. In 573 he became bishop of Tours, which St Martin's relics made a great spiritual centre. He moves fluently and lives dangerously amid warring Merovingian kings and queens.[33] The bishop at this period is more likely to

---

[29] Jones, *LRE* 910–14 and Wickham (1995) 4–6; I have used Wickham's reading of the Mopsuestia evidence, against Jones.   [30] *Vie de Théodore de Sykéon* ed. Festugière (1970) 28.
[31] Pricoco (1990), (1967); Harries (1994).
[32] Navarra (1990); Brennan (1985); George (1992).
[33] Pietri (1985) has full documentation; see also Van Dam (1993).

have risen among the monks, and then been promoted among the clergy. This meant that he had usually opportunity for biblical and patristic learning, and would be a spiritual man of whom miraculous powers might be expected. Such, for example, was the patriarch Eutychius (c. 513–82).[34] At the age of twelve he was sent from Augustopolis in Phrygia to Constantinople for his secular education. Becoming a monk, he was pressed to become bishop of Zaliches, but gave himself to the bishop of Amasea, who was at Constantinople. He was made a reader and tonsured, then deacon, and at the minimum age of thirty was ordained presbyter. He lived in the monastery at Amasea, and was responsible for its administration, with the title Catholicus. After ruling his monks for eighteen years he was sent to Constantinople for the council on the Three Chapters. His biblical skill commended him to the authorities, especially when he found a biblical precedent for condemning heretics who had died in full communion with the church. He was appointed patriarch in place of Menas in 552. We need not follow the later vicissitudes of his career, but only note that at varous stages, but especially in exile in Amasea, his miraculous gifts are displayed, at least according to his biographer. Promoting a holy monk, even with stupendous miraculous gifts, could be a disaster if he lacked administrative skills, as occurred with Theodore of Sykeon. Having allegedly acquired miraculous gifts and holy orders as the result of terrible penances in his youth, Theodore was demanded as bishop by the 'clergy and landowners' of Anastasiopolis. But he soon had to be allowed by patriarch and emperor to demit office, despite his continuing miracles and the reluctance of his metropolitan.[35]

In the west, aristocratic background and monastic training often combine. Eucherius of Lyons (died c. 449) was probably of a senatorial family. In middle life he retired to Lérins, the new centre of ascetic learning, with his wife, and became a noted writer on the ascetic life before becoming bishop of Lyons before 441; his two sons shared his retreat and both became bishops (Veranus at Vence and Salonius at Geneva).[36] Caesarius of Arles is more than an ordinary bishop, but rises in typical fashion. Born in 470 of a noble family of Chalon-sur-Saône, he joined the minor clergy at eighteen, and in 490 fled to Lérins. Moving to Arles, he joined a community of monks in a noble household. Eonius the metropolitan, a relative, had him trained in rhetoric, then about 499 ordained him deacon and priest, and sent him to reorganize a community of monks. In 502 Eonius before his death got the agreement of clergy and of the Visigothic king Alaric II (484–507) to Caesarius' succession. As bishop, Caesarius dealt successfully with rulers like Theoderic. He visited Rome

[34] Eustratius, *Vita S. Eutychii*, ed. Laga, *CCSG* 25; Cameron (1990).
[35] *Vie de Théodore de Sykéon* ed. Festugière (1970) 58, 73–8.
[36] Documents and life in Wickham (1982a).

and received the pallium, the scarf signifying metropolitan power, from pope Symmachus (496–514), and superiority not only over the Gallic churches but over Spain as well. The combination of asceticism and nepotism apparent in his own rise appears also in his famous convent. The first abbesses were his sister and his niece. He rebuilt it after the siege of 508 and transferred church property to endow his foundation, in defiance of existing canons, though with authorization from Rome. He lived there, and endowed it in his will.[37]

III. FINANCE

The wealth of the church affected the economy of the whole empire.[38] The clergy in the cities enjoyed regular pay. In country areas the presbyters and deacons might have to work at farming or other gainful craft. A church's income derived from two chief sources: the offerings of the faithful, and endowments in the form of rents. There were also government grants, but these seem to have been mainly charitable funds administered by the church.[39] The biblical tenth or tithe was not imposed, but was seen as a model of voluntary generosity.[40] Endowments began seriously with Constantine I, but were soon huge, especially in Rome and Constantinople. A constant stream of gifts, including the estates of deceased clergy, swelled the property. In the sixth century, popes, Gallic councils and the emperor Justinian all forbade the setting up of new churches without sufficient endowment to pay the clergy.[41] The Register of Gregory I shows that the pope gave much attention to the management of his estates, 'the Patrimony of Peter', through agents in Sicily, Italy and Gaul. His administrative efficiency enabled him to deal effectively with the immense social and humanitarian problems which afflicted Rome as a result of war and plague. Bishops were supposed not to alienate lands or goods, but often did. Various forms of simony, such as a candidate for the episcopate promising to give church lands to those who support him, were rife and often banned, notably at Rome under Odoacer and Theoderic. The emperor Leo in 470 decreed against it at Constantinople, and this rule was variously repeated by Anastasius and Justinian.[42] Protection of the church's property was an important reason for the attempts to impose celibacy on the clergy. Reluctantly approving the appointment of a married bishop in Syracuse, pope Pelagius I (556–61) insisted on a complete listing

[37] *Caesarii Arelatensis Opera Omnia* (*CCSL* 103–4: 2.292–343 for the ancient *Vita Caesarii*). For literature see Collins (1981); Klingshirn (1990). See also Beck (1950).

[38] The chapters by Jones in *LRE* and *The Roman Economy* are indispensable and rarely superseded, though occasionally his interpretation is challenged, as by Greenslade (1965) 222.

[39] Jones, *LRE* 898–9.

[40] A special penance at the second council of Tours; recommended as a neglected practice at the second council of Matisco in 585.   [41] Jones, *LRE* 900.   [42] Jones, *LRE* 896–8.

of his private property, so that on his death he did not bequeath ecclesiastical goods to his children.[43] City churches were often under the direct control of the bishop, and were called in the west *tituli*. Independently endowed churches (*parochiae* or *dioceses*) existed in some, usually more rural, areas. The bishop might control the central funds himself, or (as the twenty-sixth canon of Chalcedon required) appoint a manager (οἰκονόμος). Funds were shared between the staff, the buildings and charity in varying proportions. In earlier times the bishop's control was absolute. In their Suburbicarian province the popes now had the bishops divide all income into four parts, for the bishop, the clergy, the maintenance of the cathedral and its *tituli*, and the poor. Other places had a threefold division, without the poor, or gave endowment income to the bishop, while he shared other offerings with the clergy. Similarly, practice varied as between fixed stipends and equal shares: multiplying clergy on stipends could impoverish a church.[44] The biggest differences in clergy pay were caused by differences in church wealth. Justinian's grading of sees below the patriarchates ranged from those worth (probably to the bishop personally) over thirty pounds gold per annum to those with less than two pounds. Cyril could find 2,500 pounds to spend on his campaign against Nestorius, plus gifts in kind. Theodore of Sykeon got a *solidus* a day, about five pounds per annum, at Anastasiopolis. The episcopally paid clergy of cathedral and *tituli* were usually better off than their colleagues in the independent *parochiae*, benefiting from better endowments and congregations.[45]

IV. TEACHING

Christianity is a doctrine, historical, philosophical and practical. Dedicated bishops always set store by teaching. Caesarius illustrates this in the late empire. He delegated financial duties to free him for preaching. The doors of Arles cathedral were shut to make people stay for the preaching, and when absent he had the clergy read his sermons in his place. He urged the duty of preaching on fellow bishops, and had copies of his sermons distributed in Gaul, Spain and Italy. Collections of sermons were therefore made in his lifetime, many of which survive. They have strong moral emphasis: common sins like lying and adultery are rebuked, and simple religion encouraged, notably repentance, tithing, almsgiving, and Bible-reading. Homiliaries thereafter became familiar books in churches, the Gallican, Roman and Toledan being influential examples.[46] Caesarius' rule for the nuns was imitated all over Gaul.[47] This story of the high-born

---

[43] Pelagius, *Ep.* 33 to Cethegus; cf. Vogt in Baus, Beck, Ewig and Vogt (1980) 653.
[44] Jones, *LRE* 900–4.   [45] Jones, *LRE* 905–7.
[46] Sermons in *CCSL* 103–4 and *SChrét.* 175, 243, 330; also Grégoire (1966).
[47] Caesarius of Arles, *Œuvres monastiques* I (*SChrét.* 345); McCarthy (1960).

Christian who learns the ascetic life, is promoted in the church, deals with governments and writes improving literature has many lesser parallels in his own area, such as Eucherius of Lyons and Gennadius of Marseilles. The influence of the literary activity involved should not be underestimated. There flows out from centres like Lérins and Arles a steady stream of books. All of these provide bases for Christian living, and are used at all levels to promote morality and holiness. They include copies of the scriptures, martyrologies and saints' lives (increasingly concerned with the achievements of ascetics), works of notable Fathers on exegesis, morality and doctrine, and, increasingly, liturgical texts and collections of canons. Comparable things may be said of other centres, old and new: in the west, Cassiodorus' foundation at Vivarium deserves notice, and in the east Constantinople and Jerusalem rise steadily, alongside Alexandria and Antioch (notably under Severus).

The rise of Gregory I as bishop of Rome (590–604) brought various developments in the west. He was well qualified.[48] He numbered two bishops of Rome among his ancestors. His father was a senator, and he himself became prefect of Rome. He founded the monastery of St Andrew in Rome, and dedicated all the family estates at his disposal to endowing monasteries; his sisters had all become nuns. In 579 Pelagius II (579–90) sent him to Constantinople as papal *apocrisarius*, and he stayed on bad terms with the patriarchs till 586. He returned to his monastery, and was forced out by popular demand to become bishop in 590. In war-torn Italy he served the city well by negotiating peace with the Lombards. He tried to re-establish a semblance of unity in the Italian churches, where competing imperial and Lombard ('Arian') policies aggravated church tensions, as in the Three Chapters controversy. His Register reveals worldwide interests and activities. He clearly had a good administrative mind and made good appointments. The management of the Patrimony of Peter through his agents in Sicily, Italy and Gaul helped to strengthen the resources of the papacy. He used this and other methods to deal with the immense social and humanitarian problems which afflicted Rome as a result of war and plague.

His persistent influence lies, however, elsewhere. The *Regula pastoralis*, which he composed early in his episcopate, sets out the goals and methods of a bishop.[49] The spiritual qualifications, and the continuing spiritual training, of the bishop himself are considered. The third and longest of the four parts is particularly important, emphasizing the pastor's educational duty in training believers of all varieties and levels for their life in the church, and the temptations they must overcome. This work was transmitted all over

---

[48] Articles with bibliographies: Recchia (1990); Markus (1985); see also Richards (1980).
[49] See Rommel and Morel (1992).

Europe, and has shaped the attitudes and practices of countless clergy. Gregory's numerous exegetical works often draw on earlier writers, but are also original. His *Dialogues*, which include the biography of Benedict, constitute a justification for the life of ascetic holiness in the face of the impending end of the world, as well as exhibiting the ascetical prowess of the western church (notably Benedict) against the eastern.[50] Gregory's convictions flowed from the established law and custom of the church as he understood it. The Roman church was fortified with a massive set of records. These had been ably sifted and made accessible by such scholars as Dionysius Exiguus, who had not only calculated the fundamentals of the Christian calendar as it exists to the present, but early in the sixth century had translated and systematized the findings of past councils and the decrees of past popes.[51]

[50] *Dialogues* ed. de Vogüé (1978–80).
[51] Bibliography in Richter (1982); see also Dekkers (1995), nos. 652–4; 1284–6.

CHAPTER 25

MONASTICISM

PHILIP ROUSSEAU

Devotion to asceticism was a highly visible and in some ways alarming feature of the late Roman world. That thousands of men and women were ready to adopt a life of radical simplicity, sexual abstinence and apparent indifference to wealth, status and power, and that even larger numbers were willing to admire if not imitate their choice, tells us something remarkable about the society in which they lived. Restrictions in diet and sexual behaviour had been accepted for centuries; and abnegation was frequently accompanied by a rejection of influence in public affairs and of privilege and property. Christians, however, from the third century onwards, were responsible for an unprecedented upsurge in ascetic devotion. The movement transformed town as well as countryside: famous exemplars may have congregated at first in remoter districts; but a new class of citizen became more widely evident at an early stage. Distinguished at times by an appalling emaciation of the body, by filth and infestation, by ragged, colourless and skimpy clothes, large numbers of these ascetics converged, at moments of crisis, on the cities themselves, forming virtual mobs that were capable not only of menace but of real power. Within a relatively short time, they occupied special and prominent buildings, administered successful rural estates, broadcast their views in public fora, and gained the ear of those in power – invading, in other words, the chief components of the late Roman polity.

This outburst of negation – against the body, the family, the accepted canons of economic and political success – demands historical explanation. There was a view of the self and of the world that gave the ascetic movement its cohesion, its capacity for organic development and its broadening appeal. Conversely, the structure and growth of its institutions at once encouraged and protected the ascetic urge. To that extent, the phenomenon had a life and significance of its own. Yet ascetics developed also a subtle relationship with society at large. They regarded their interpretation of human nature, of psychology and anthropology, as defining both the power and the destiny of any human person. So the stable society they created for themselves – its routine, its economy, its sense of order and authority – stood also as an invitation, a call to 'conversion'. Ascetics could appear eccentric, 'alternative', even anarchic. Yet they did not merely abandon, let alone undermine or destroy, traditional society. They were participants in a wide public debate – about the nature of authority and leadership, about the appropriate mechanisms of social formation, about the very tradition to which Christianity was entitled to appeal. Although their own system was never likely to usurp or absorb all others, the tolerance and admiration they inspired was proof of the central role they had to play in the definition of a Christian society.

In describing and explaining, therefore, the structures of the ascetic life, we have to recognize the influence of ideology – both the theories proper to the ascetic communities themselves, and the principles that affected their relations with the outside world. By the early fifth century, of course, precedents had been established; in particular, a widespread preference for community life. The earliest archaeological evidence in Egypt, from the 'Cells' just south of the Delta, shows how quickly the little brick shelters of the solitaries made famous in the *Sayings of the Desert Fathers* were gathered around common courtyards and buildings within a low perimeter wall, providing company while preserving independence.[1] It is no surprise to find that, while more isolated heroes like Antony remained prominent in ascetic literature, the formal prescriptions of Pachomius and Basil gained increasing allegiance, in both east and west, and for theoretical reasons. If those ascetics who could read were still content with anecdote and individual portrait – and the Greek *Sayings* themselves, the *Pratum Spirituale* or *Spiritual Meadow* of John Moschus, and a long series of Latin *Vitae* suggest that that was the case – they did so amidst a growing crowd of coenobitic colleagues. It was within that community structure that monks now conducted their debates as to how they should organize their lives. Should they pursue a 'contemplative' or an 'active' life? The choice they faced, in the language of the time, was between 'theory' and 'practice' (θεωρία and πρακτική), between vision and love, between prayer and reflection on the one hand and a concern for the ignorant and needy on the other; but, whatever the option, it was to be embraced in the company of fellow devotees.

If ideology governed structure, we need to arm ourselves from the outset with a clear understanding of ascetic literature – an understanding of the varied circumstances, forms and motives that colour the material upon which we depend. Broadly speaking, we catch in the sources, at various moments of frozen textuality, what was in fact a developing tradition, in which 'rules' and biographies (not always easily distinguished) attracted additions, made often undeclared adjustments and abandoned embarrassing antecedents. Now and again, a writer might look back in a more ordered and reflective way, and make a calculated statement about

[1] Walters (1974) 9f., 102f.

spiritual values, effective practices and hallowed or authentic genealogies. Biographies could serve that reflective purpose also, as well as treatises on virtue or prayer. Finally, any extended text could then be broken up again, and pasted piecemeal within the rolling narratives of the ascetic world.

The classic example of such development we have mentioned already – the *Sayings of the Desert Fathers* or *Apophthegmata Patrum*. As they stand in our printed editions, the *Sayings* date from a period at least a little later than that studied here. In addition to preserved elements of an originally oral tradition, gathered from a range of places, but in the first instance, perhaps, from Egyptian exiles in Palestine, they included brief extracts from longer *Lives*, some of which we possess, and collections of embryonic 'rules'. It is possible to observe, also, not least by reference to independently preserved though shorter collections, some of the staggered phases through which the literary accumulation of the *Sayings* themselves progressed.[2] In the matter of 'rules' more generally, the work of Jerome on Pachomius and of Rufinus on Basil, when compared with later compilations, demonstrate the piecemeal way in which at first such guidance was formulated and dispersed: an impression corroborated in biographical accounts.[3]

A readiness to add moss to such rolling stones did not die out in later periods. John Moschus is the best example (died 619). He travelled widely, collecting stories about ascetics here and there; but he did not attempt to build, on the strength of that, an integrated picture of the religious life. To some extent he reflected thereby the conditions of his age. By then, monastic communities were less bound together under the banners of theological party than they had been earlier in the sixth century, and more threatened by the newer and rather different pressure of Persian aggression.[4] The central motive in Moschus' work (as, perhaps, in the *Apophthegmata* before him) was to record, as quickly as possible and as confusedly as might be necessary, a way of life that seemed at any moment likely to disappear. It is ironic that such improvisation in the face of apparent decline should contribute, within the framework of monastic literature as a whole, to a reversal of the process, whereby values challenged in the sixth-century setting could be recollected and admired with almost canonic tranquillity in the more assured circumstances of later Byzantine monasticism. Turning back to what Moschus might have regarded as the secure heyday of the ascetic movement, as recorded earlier in the sixth century by Cyril of Scythopolis and John of Ephesus, we sense at once that we are dealing with texts more consciously governed by a thesis (largely doctrinal), even if anecdote and hitherto scattered literary sources can be detected in

---

[2] The best existing introduction is Guy (1962); but the forthcoming edition of the *Sayings* by Chiara Faraggiana will carry interpretation much further forward.

[3] The development of the Basilian 'rules' is the best documented, by Gribomont (1953).

[4] Binns (1994) 49.

their compositions. These authors were more settled, wedded to the interests of particular institutions, with access to libraries, albeit modest. They worked in an atmosphere of enquiry, even scholarship; and their books were preserved precisely by the survival of the physical resources upon which they depended.[5]

We have to be on our guard, therefore, not to confuse the development of the literature itself with the development of forms of the ascetic life. A suspicion, for example, that disjointed anecdotes, passed orally from hermit to hermit, found their way eventually into the libraries of complex communities is in any case a simplistic assessment of the surviving texts and dangerously wedded to the notion that those texts reflect directly the changing social patterns of the world that produced them. So, for example, when Cyril describes a 'return to the cities' on the part of Palestinian monks – a development described below – we should not imagine that all monks in Palestine viewed their world in that way or shared in his delight.[6]

When we do try to explain either the pace or the direction of development in ascetic society, the lasting and, at times, paradoxical popularity of Egyptian-based literature can tempt us to adopt a diffusionist view, taking Egypt as the fount and all other places as dependent. Certainly, Egypt came to occupy a special place in the Christian understanding of asceticism; and its practices were adopted more and more elsewhere, supplanting local and in some cases ancient traditions. That did not happen, however, simply by transporting the 'rules' of Pachomius or any other prescriptive text to different parts of the empire. By the early years of the fifth century, the legacy of Pachomius, originating in the Thebaid, had in any case been modified by his disciples and by transmission northwards within Egypt itself. Besa's *Life of Shenoute*, for example, whatever the attachment of its hero to rigorous order, shows him operating happily within an ascetic society quite loose in structure and tolerant of mobility, at one moment loving solitude, at another in contact with the secular world: more akin to what we find in Rufinus, Palladius and the *Sayings of the Fathers*, and sympathetic to the traditions of the north. There is revealing irony in the fact that a man of Shenoute's character, recommending the practices he did, could claim the heritage of Pachomius, from whom, in fact, he differed enormously both in spirit and in monastic discipline.[7]

Similar caution will temper our view of early Palestinian asceticism. Hilarion – supposedly a Palestinian pioneer, made famous by Jerome in a

---

[5] Binns (1994) 57f.

[6] For the phrase and its significance, together with appeal to the idiosyncratic character of church life in Scythopolis, see Binns (1994) 121f.

[7] Besa, *Vita Shenoudi* (*CSCO Script. Copt.* 16) 119, 123, 144, 173. Shenoute died at an extremely advanced age, probably in A.D. 466. A useful and fully documented account is provided by Elm (1994) 296–310.

brief and partly fictional *Life*, and founder of an ascetic settlement near Gaza – was a declared admirer of the Egyptian Antony. Epiphanius, later bishop of Salamis in Cyprus, had also been to Egypt, was inspired by Hilarion, and sowed the seeds of another community in the Gaza region. He continued (uncanonically) to maintain a close interest in Palestinian affairs. As the fourth century came to a close, an increasing number of ascetics had begun to leave Egypt, sometimes because of persecution but also sensing decline, abandoning in particular the more loosely structured settlements in Nitria and Scetis. Notable among them were Porphyry, the later bishop of Gaza (leaving in 377), Silvanus, originally from Palestine (leaving in 380), and Esaias (who left soon after 440 and did not die – again, near Gaza – until 489).

Such men may have preserved at least some Egyptian values in their new home, passing on stories and traditions to new companions and disciples.[8] Yet even older, according to tradition, was the career of Chariton, originally from Iconium in Asia Minor. As a 'foreigner', he is a fitting archetype of the enthusiastic pilgrims attracted in ever greater numbers by Palestine's growing status as the 'holy land', beautified and enriched by imperial generosity and aristocratic patronage.[9] He eventually settled further north than Gaza, first in country to the west of Jericho and then south of Jerusalem beyond Bethlehem, founding what came to be known as the Old Laura (Greek *laura*) or Souka (Syriac *shouqa*). These words have come to be associated with markets or bazaars, with their long, narrow streets of shops and stalls: thus, in the desert, a precipitous path wound past caves in the *wadi* walls, each housing its ascetic. They were not hermits in a strict sense, for the *laura* possessed also a communal church and a bakehouse, to which all repaired on Saturday, sharing in vigils and a meal of bread, vegetables and dates, and in the Sunday eucharist. Then, having collected fresh material for basket work and other crafts, and a further supply of food, they returned to their caves to work and pray alone during the other days of the week. In that early generation, therefore, most of the characteristics of Palestinian asceticism were set in place – economic as well as social: for its future prosperity depended for the most part on donations from novices, admirers and high-ranking patrons (chiefly in cash and food, more rarely in parcels of land), simple horticulture and handicraft contributing no more than a supplement.

Chariton is presented in hagiography as a rival, indeed a predecessor, of the Egyptian Antony; but his association with Asia Minor – reared as he

---

[8] Still the fundamental survey is that offered by Chitty (1966), which may now be supplemented by Gould (1993) and Binns (1994), although the latter may exaggerate Egyptian influence (157f.).

[9] Hirschfeld (1992) 2, 11, 71. For pilgrimage and Christian developments in fourth-century and fifth-century Palestine, see Hunt, *Holy Land Prilgrimage* and Walker, *Holy City, Holy Places?* The surviving biography of Chariton is late and has to be used with caution, since it may justify custom he never foresaw: see Garitte (1941) and the English translation by Di Segni in Wimbush (1990) 393–421.

was not far to the west of Basil's Cappadocia – brought Palestine into touch
with quite another centre of fourth-century ascetic experiment. The great
hero of Palestinian monasticism in the next century, Euthymius, came
from the same part of the world – from Melitene, on the eastern fringe of
Cappadocia: even more within the orbit of Basil and his associates. Before
travelling south, he had served in the household of his local bishop, and
had exercised some authority over nearby monasteries.[10] Several of his first
disciples in Palestine had similar origins. That is not to suggest that he
introduced Basilian monachism into Palestine – far from it: for he long subscribed to the *laura* pattern, developed an admiration for what he discovered of Egyptian asceticism, and was himself disposed to even greater
withdrawal. (No more did the refugees from Egypt bring with them an
unadulterated admiration for Pachomius, of whom, perhaps, many knew
little.) Nevertheless, ascetic practice in Palestine from the beginning of the
fifth century was open to influence from the north as well as the south, its
original enthusiasms thus overlaid by patterns developed elsewhere.

That makes it a good place to observe the internal debates that came to
enliven ascetic communities. In 411, Euthymius, who had been in Palestine
since 405, established with his friend Theoctistus a *laura* in the Wadi el-
Mukallik, which flows down to the Dead Sea from the Jerusalem–Jericho
road.[11] He himself eventually settled in greater seclusion some 5 km distant.
A contrast was thus established, and acquired the status of an ancient rule:
Euthymius sent new recruits to Theoctistus, who introduced them to the
principles of asceticism – 'humility and obedience' – in a tightly controlled
and communal environment; only then were they allowed to graduate to a
more isolated life. The experience of living in a community, numbering
perhaps thirty or forty men, thus became an accepted part of the ascetic
regime, even if regarded as preliminary to higher practice.[12] Conflict between
the two disciplines was in that way avoided: both were to play their part
within one system of personal development. Also involved was a distinctive
relationship between master and disciple: Theoctistus dealt with admirers
and dependants, while Euthymius enjoyed the luxury of secluded prayer.

In spite of Euthymius' enduring (though often frustrated) attachment to
solitude, one should not underestimate the importance of the community

---

[10] Cyr. Scyth. *Vita Euthymii* 3f. The world of Euthymius and his successors, and of his biographer
Cyril of Scythopolis, is vividly described by Hirschfeld (1992), with copious bibliography; see also Price
(1991). (Cyril enjoyed a link of his own with Cappadocia and with Euthymius, through the latter's disciple Cosmas, who was consecrated bishop of Scythopolis in the late 460s.) Hirschfeld's account of
diet, dress and furniture (82–101) is particularly relevant to later *cænobia*; but his economic descriptions
(102–11) make wide reference and point to a marked contrast with Egyptian monasticism in its
Byzantine heyday.

[11] For what follows, see *V. Euthym.* 8f. For his Palestinian experience hitherto, conscious of Chariton
but geared to productive labour and generosity, see 6f.

[12] Cyr. Scyth. *Vita Sabae* 7. One might compare the attitude of Shenoute, for whom solitude was a
test of virtue and reunion with the *cænobium* its reward: *V. Shen.* 38f.

within his system. Weekends were always shared with others; and a *laura* developed its own economy, requiring the supervision of a steward and his subordinates (bakers, cooks and storekeepers), who lived out their period of office within the communal buildings. The steward would oversee the collection and distribution of raw materials among the ascetics, and the marketing of their produce. In the more northern region, topography could also contribute to integration: for some of the *laurai* here (although not that of Theoctistus itself) were established on flatter ground and acquired more cohesion. Common prayer on Saturdays and Sundays encouraged complex rituals in well-furnished churches; a feature reinforced in monasteries built close to centres of pilgrimage (increasingly common in the Jericho region, close to the Jordan river). Euthymius wished his own retreat to become a *cœnobium* at his death – a wish fulfilled in 482.[13] Most striking of all, the regular movement from community to solitude was seen as compatible with a principle of stability: monks should avoid 'a feeling of resentment or loathing towards the place where we are and towards our companions'; and Euthymius retained a 'fear that our rule be subverted by change of place'. Nor did he lose entirely a readiness to share in the pastoral activities of the church, preaching to outsiders, baptizing, and collaborating with the local bishop – in every respect a precedent for later developments.[14]

Further south, near Gaza, Esaias exemplified the same pattern. He had lived in a *cœnobium* before moving to Scetis. After leaving Egypt, he shut himself up in a cell, while Peter, his disciple, dealt with visitors. Yet he was ready to legislate for more organized followers, and was not untouched by the controversies of the church in his day.[15] The pattern persisted. Severus, the later patriarch of Antioch, adopted a solitary life near Gaza but built also a monastery for his gathering admirers. A more formal stage, perhaps, is illustrated by the monastery of Gerasimus – another Asian arrival in Palestine, from Lycia. His *cœnobium*, built in the Jericho plain probably between A.D. 440 and 460, was actually sited in the midst of the cells of the *laura* itself, still with the function of training the less experienced.

Sabas, Euthymius' successor as the dominant monastic figure in Palestine, was originally from Argaeus, close to Basil's Caesarea. He first

---

[13] Chitty (1966) 102f.

[14] Community arrangements: *V. Euthym.* 17f. Liturgy: *V. Euthym.* 28f. (Note also the implications of 48; and compare *V. Sab.* 32, 36.) Own cell a *cœnobium*: *V. Euthym.* 39 (an ordered liturgy and hospitality to strangers were to be central). Stability: *V. Euthym.* 19, tr. Price (1991) 26. Pastoral responsibility: *V. Euthym.* 10, 12, 14f. Euthymius' habitual Lenten retreat finds an interesting and contemporary parallel in Eparchius of Clermont-Ferrand (Greg. Tur. *Hist.* 11.21). The earliest monastic churches for which we have archaeological evidence were built no differently from those in settled centres, and seem designed to fulfil the same liturgical and pastoral needs: see Walters (1974) 34f.

[15] For convenience of reference, see Chitty (1966) 73f. and Chitty (1971); also Zacharias of Mitylene, *HE (CSCO Script. Syr.* 3, 5–6) v.9, vi.3.

practised asceticism, like Euthymius, in his native district, in a large and
well-developed monastery. Again it was Jerusalem – just as in the case of
Euthymius – that first attracted him to Palestine, rather than the Judaean
desert. Like many before him, Euthymius sent him to be schooled by
Theoctistus; and then he practised asceticism in a remoter cave. The
description of his regime sums up the pattern of Palestinian practice:
'spending the day in physical labour and passing the night without sleep in
giving praise to God, making humility and obedience the root and foundation of his life, and showing aptitude and great zeal in the office of the holy
liturgy'.[16] Once he had attracted disciples of his own, he exercised over
them an authority based predominantly on his own experience – the hallmark of the charismatic master in the north Egyptian tradition. He also
acquired in time, however, a Theoctistus of his own – another
Cappadocian, named Theodosius, with whom he divided authority.
Theodosius, near Jerusalem, governed coenobites in the spirit of Basil, his
fellow countryman. By this time, in the 470s, *cænobia* were becoming established features of the desert fringe: extensive walled communities with
refectories and dormitories for more than a hundred monks, together with
accommodation for visitors and for the sick, the buildings added to decade
by decade. A large church provided the setting not only for the eucharist
but for regular hymns and psalms. Sabas, meanwhile, in his 'Great Laura',
closer to the Dead Sea, commanded more scattered ascetics; but he also
developed something akin to 'rules', which were general enough to be
imposed upon later foundations as they were established. Here too, prayer
as well as discipline was catered for, the monks in their weekday cells
responding to the same signal that summoned their coenobitic colleagues.[17]
So, while leading a life of some freedom and eccentricity, Sabas busied
himself with the material details of an increasingly complex and prosperous empire. Patrons in Jerusalem were a source of regular funds; but he also
travelled on two occasions to Constantinople, in A.D. 511–12 and 531,
where he gained apparently easy access to the court, and returned with considerable wealth for his communities. His own Great Laura thus acquired
a coenobitic offshoot, a hospital and a new church.[18]

When it came to relations with bishops, Palestinian monasticism had by
this time adopted a style of administration peculiar to itself, reflecting in
part the small scale of the desert region and its easy access to Jerusalem.[19]
The patriarch of the city appointed one ascetic – Sabas being only the most

[16] *V. Sab.* 8, tr. Price (1991) 100. Earlier asceticism: *V. Sab.* 1f. First endeavours in Palestine: *V. Euthym.* 31; *V. Sab.* 7f.

[17] Authority: *V. Sab.* 16. Relations with Theodosius: *V. Sab.* 30, 65; *V. Jo. Hesych.* 6 (see Hirschfeld (1992) 15, and Binns (1994) 45). 'Rules': *V. Sab.* 42, 74, 76.

[18] *V. Sab.* 18, 25, 32; 27, 31, 35; 51f., 71f.; Patrich (1995).

[19] Emphasis on a close link between monks and church in Palestine is the chief mark of Binns (1994). On Jerusalem, see especially 80f., 178f.

famous – to be archimandrite (that is, overall superior) for all the monks of the diocese. The communities were thus bound to the patriarch in a single system. That was why Sabas was in such frequent contact with episcopal affairs: he was always willing to travel up to Jerusalem, not only to consult with the bishop but to lodge and dine with him and his associates, enjoying at least occasionally a comfort that may surprise us.

There had been, for a long time, ascetics in Jerusalem itself. That was inevitable, given the city's increasing importance as a centre of pilgrimage. The most famous were on the Mount of Olives, associated with the name of the elder Melania, and increasingly disdained by the less clerically orientated Jerome in Bethlehem. Melania encouraged hard work and reflective reading, in a style of which even Pachomius would have approved. The Jerusalem communities were marked also by a certain Basilian character (significantly attractive to ascetics for a time in this very city); a character associated not only with the proximity of the bishop but also with the numerous hostels built in Jerusalem, and with a related care for the poor. The *Life* of the younger Melania, who reached Jerusalem some forty years later, provides evidence that such traditions persisted over more than one generation. Gerontius, her biographer, may disappoint us by dwelling more on Melania's personal asceticism than on the details of her monastic ordinance. Yet she had obviously come to value the mutual respect and moderated self-denial encouraged by the common life, and set in place a detailed routine of liturgical prayer in her communities, which were built within the city. She also mixed easily with bishops and other churchmen.[20]

It was with that tradition of urban monasticism and episcopal patronage that Sabas was now associated (together with his colleague Theodosius), putting in place an even wider network of authority and dependence that drew city and desert together. The process was undoubtedly encouraged by the shifting allegiance of Jerusalem to the Council of Chalcedon (A.D. 451). The patriarch Juvenal lost, for a time, his authority, following ambiguous resistance to the decisions of the council; and he was replaced briefly by a monk. Returning with force in 453, Juvenal presided over a period of some antagonism between himself and ascetics. Euthymius quietly supported his authority, but was relatively isolated in doing so.[21] Elpidius and Gerontius, general archimandrites, took the opposing side. The situation was resolved only with the accession of Martyrius as patriarch in 478, which represented a victory for the clergy – a victory that Sabas was willing to accept. Esaias

---

[20] *Vita Melaniae* 36, 40f. Melania had already set up monastic houses for both men and women during a stay in Africa, under the shadow of another bishop and ascetic legislator, Augustine. In that instance, Gerontius is frustratingly vague (perhaps he knew less) (22f.) but mentions (among the women) reading, fasting, prayer and spiritual direction. Augustine's own enterprises will be discussed below. Gerontius himself was later to achieve prominence in the very same *milieu*.

[21] *V. Euthym.* 27. For events in Jerusalem meanwhile, see 28f.

of Scetis and others, correspondingly, withdrew to Gaza.[22] By that time, no doubt, the growing willingness of desert ascetics to give the *cænobium* permanent status, the fact that many more of them remained within community walls than graduated to the more independent life of a personal cell, and the associated emphasis on carefully preserved property and growing liturgical sophistication, all gave the episcopate an increasing foothold in monastic circles. Perhaps nothing symbolized the growing liaison more than the feeling among Sabas' followers that he could not exercise effective leadership unless he were ordained a priest.[23] That ordination was achieved by subterfuge in 490; and Sabas succeeded as general archimandrite in 492.

Three features of ascetic experience, therefore, became obvious in Palestine: submission to the episcopate, a carefully controlled hierarchy of masters and disciples, and a calculated encouragement of the community life. While remaining capable of sustaining a variety of styles, the Palestinian regime betrayed an openness to church life, not only in its subjection to episcopal authority, but also in the associated complexity of its liturgical celebrations, and in its willingness to undertake the conversion and pastoral care of people beyond its immediate boundaries.

When we move further north, to Syria proper, and in particular to the country around Antioch, the scene appears to change. Our chief source of information for the first part of our period (and, indeed, reaching back beyond it) is Theodoret, bishop of Cyrrhus and author of an *Historia religiosa*, which describes the lives of prominent Syrian ascetics. His most famous subject is undoubtedly Symeon Stylites; and Symeon and his imitators, bizarre and extreme in their ascetic discipline, have tended to dominate the imagination of later readers.[24] Yet very few of Theodoret's vignettes depict such lives; and the careful reader soon discerns both the anxieties of a bishop and the persistent influence of the coenobitic life. The Syrian church had long been rigorist and demanding in its view of Christian commitment, probably owing little in the process to anything but it own reflection upon the gospel. It was at the same time intensely devoted to the notion of community and to the authority of the bishop; and it would be surprising to find any contrary emphasis from the pen of one of its leading churchmen. In story after story, Theodoret refers to the coenobitic background of his heroes. He gives full details of a coenobitic regime, with reference to the liturgy of monks, their reception of guests ('the divine work of hospitality'), their general order and hard work.[25] He

---

[22] Zach. *HE* III.4, VI.1; John Eph. *Lives* 25. See Binns (1994) 189f.

[23] *V. Sab.* 19. Hirschfeld sees Sabas' promotion as a victory for the desert ascetics ((1992) 14f.); but it was achieved at a price.

[24] Theodoret of Cyrrhus, *Historia religiosa* XXVI. For Symeon, see the texts translated and introduced by Robert Doran (1992). The *Life* of Daniel the Stylite is also of interest (trans. in Dawes and Baynes, (1977)).

[25] Theod. *HR* (*SChrét.* 234) II.5, III.2, 12, V.2, X.3 (liturgy); III.14, 20 (quoted), VIII.2, X.4f (guests); III.22, X.2 (general).

reveals, in a pattern now familiar, the development from a holy man's solitary cell, through the attraction of disciples, to the establishment of a clear coenobitic regime.[26] Yet – and here is a Syrian feature that will recur – small groups that were gathered around a master continued to subdivide the larger communities.[27]

Ascetics also maintained a close relationship with society at large. Theodoret was anxious to emphasize that proximity to village life was no impediment to ascetic virtue.[28] Archaeological and epigraphic evidence corroborates the impression that monastic communities, like ecclesiastical sites in general, gradually acquired in Syria a central place in the rural economy, in both alluvial and mountainous country, either by association with a village or villages or by inclusion within an extensive estate. In the sixth century, under the influence of growing Monophysite confidence, churches and hostels of increasing size and grandeur catered for popular devotion, while extensive farm buildings, often some distance from the monastery itself, reached out into cultivated land. Cereal crops provided for monastic and local needs; but the extensive cultivation of olives points to sale and trade on a considerable scale.[29] There is no reason to suppose that the process was not under way in Theodoret's time, although many of the earliest monastic communities in Syria failed to maintain themselves in the century that followed – reflecting in part the contemporary shifts in theological loyalty but also, perhaps, the growing need to develop sites more conducive to agricultural exploitation and pastoral accessibility. Theodoret himself welcomed, certainly, a degree of social and even pastoral concern among monks,[30] and reported without surprise that it was from ascetic society that bishops were often drawn.[31]

He was ready on several occasions to interfere directly in the lives of monks, precisely in order to preserve communal discipline and to criticize idiosyncrasy or self-will. His approach was not always welcomed, and he could find himself puzzled by some of the practices he discovered.[32] His treatment of Symeon was particularly charged with hesitation, tempered only partly by the popularity of the man, which he clearly found hard to explain or accept. Symeon, after all, had first practised asceticism in a coenobitic setting, had proved constantly disobedient and disruptive, and

---

[26] Theod. *HR* II.3, III.4, V.3, VI.13, X.3. A static distinction between two states is very rare: XXVII.1. Compare *V. Sab.* 35.   [27] Theod. *HR* II.6, IV.5.   [28] Theod. *HR* IV.1, XIV.2, 5, XXV.1.

[29] See expecially Tchalenko, *Villages* I (in which specifically monastic references are interwoven with other material), and the Appendix by André Caquot, an invaluable gazetteer with bibliography (*Villages* III.63–106).

[30] Theod. *HR* I.7, XXII.7; and IV.4, 8f. XVII.3 is rare in its 'mediating' or 'patronal' authority. This is the context of Peter Brown's famous analysis, 'The rise and function of the Holy Man' (1971), which is taken by Palmer ((1990) 107f.) to apply also in the Tur 'Abdin. Clearly, there are anecdotes which support the view; but a coenobitic and, indeed, pastoral context is almost always implied: see Rousseau (1995).   [31] Theod. *HR* II.9, III.5, V.8, X.9, XVII.1, 8.   [32] Theod. *HR* XXI.10f., 33, XXII.6.

remained, even after his departure, surprisingly restless.[33] Theodoret came to regard him as an unwelcome competitor in the exercise of public and spiritual authority. He unhesitatingly used his subordinates to counter that influence, and was grudging in his regard for the stylite, quick to hint that many others might share his disapproval. If we take Theodoret as a guide, therefore, we have to believe that in Syria, too, the communal life was gaining some ascendancy, under the increasing watchfulness of episcopal authority, even while the old loyalties of master and disciple, as in Palestine, were far from fading.

Taking Palestine and Syria together, therefore, it becomes clear that, by the middle of the fifth century, a principle espoused by the Council of Chalcedon was already on its way to acceptance over a wide area of the eastern empire (and, as we shall see, much the same could be said of the west). Monasteries – whatever the word might imply in this or that situation – were to be subject to bishops, at least at their foundation and in their external relations. Ascetics were not to wander from place to place, at the risk of their reputation, but to stay in one community, devoting themselves to fasting and prayer.[34] That monastic preoccupation had gradually eclipsed (largely because it had absorbed) an older world of virgins and widows, independent enthusiasts, and the urban households of a pious élite. The prescriptions of Chalcedon were also drawn up in the context of religious controversy; and we have to note the extent to which, by that time, ascetics of various sorts had been drawn into the conflicts surrounding Nestorius and Dioscorus. Such involvement contributed in no small degree to making the monasteries an integral part of the episcopal world. In Palestine, the conduct of Euthymius, Saba and their associates had been closely controlled by their attitude to Chalcedon and to the religious policies of the emperors Zeno and Anastasius. In addition, however, to disturbances in Jerusalem, there was widespread monastic unrest in Antioch (particularly during the time of Severus, appointed patriarch in 512), and even more in Alexandria, where alliance between desert and city dated back to the days of Theophilus and Cyril.

All that helps to explain how we pass from the world of Pachomius and Basil to that of Theodoret and Sabas. The great fourth-century pioneers of ascetic discipline might maintain their influence as writers of 'rules', not least as translated into Latin by Jerome and Rufinus; but territorially the centre of ascetic gravity had shifted away from the Nile and from Pontus and Cappadocia. The rise of Jerusalem was one factor, already noted; the other was the corresponding importance of Constantinople – not only a

---

[33] For this and what follows, see Theod. *HR* xxvi, esp. 12, 14f., 23.

[34] Council of Chalcedon, canon 4, Hefele and Leclercq (1907–) II.2: 779. The council's stipulations marked a climax in a longer process: bishops were held responsible for ascetics, in the Theodosian Code, as early as A.D. 398: *C.Th.* IX.40.16.

new capital for the empire but a capital almost built around the piety, even the ascetic piety, of its imperial family.[35] Indeed, the irregularities that Chalcedon was intent upon controlling were most obviously prevalent in the capital itself.

It was in some ways exceptional. As the city had gained prominence during the fourth century, so its religious life became at once more significant and more idiosyncratic. The monks of the city were as much newcomers as any other citizen, unabashed fortune-seekers from elsewhere in the empire, cut loose from the controlling bonds of their own communities, and vigorously opposed to the influence and privilege of clergy in the city. Both John Chrysostom and Nestorius were famously disadvantaged by that conflict.[36] From the beginning, in the 380s, ascetics in Constantinople acquired political supporters among the secular élite. Palladius' *Lausiac History*, written around A.D. 420, both reflected and supported that bid, illustrating what had been, since the time of Evagrius, a long-running infiltration of the educated and governing classes in the east by ascetic devotees.[37] The career of Eutyches in the 440s, protected not least by his association with the powerful eunuch Chrysaphius, followed a pattern to be repeated through many reigns to follow, most famously that of Justinian. It was a far cry from the remote rigour of Pontus or the Thebaid. Ascetics in the capital also took unscrupulous advantage of the notorious piety of the empress and her sister-in-law, just as Palestinians did later, when Eudocia was in self-imposed exile after 443. The result was undoubtedly a loss of discipline, quite belied by the seemingly ordered and uninterrupted liturgy of the *Acoemitae*, the 'Sleepless Ones', probably the most famous but least typical of Constantinople's ascetic communities. It was the ambitious, more numerous and less predictable groups that Chalcedon wished to bring under control: the bishops knew h ow disproportionate and unhealthy their influence had been in the years during and since the Council of Ephesus (A.D. 431). Once, of course, prohibitions and regulations had been set in place, the control and even theological condemnation of 'wandering' ascetics became firmly embedded in the legislative agenda of the church.[38]

One of our richest sources of information about eastern developments in the following century remains the *Lives of the Eastern Saints* by John of Ephesus, written probably between A.D. 566 and 568. One may find this surprising, given John's dedication to the Monophysite cause, which might

---

[35] For the broader background, see Dagron, *Naissance*; Krautheimer (1983); Holum, *Empresses*; and McCormick, *Eternal Victory*. Useful light is shed on the temper of the court by Cameron (1982).

[36] For a succinct account of the earliest monks in Constantinople see Dagron (1970). A great range of detail is provided by Janin (1969): essentially a religious gazetteer of the city, covering the whole Byzantine period, it offers a considerable bibliography and many allusions to development and practice. [37] Context and bibliography are provided by Clark (1992).

[38] See, for example, texts cited in Jones, *LRE* II (1973) 1389 n. 160, to which add Justinian, *Nov.* 79 of A.D. 539, and, in the west, the Council of Orleans (A.D. 511), canon 22.

prompt one to expect a regime at once tainted by heretical association and cut off from the mainstream of Christian development. There is no doubt that the history of monasticism in the sixth-century east was wholly interwoven with the progress of the Monophysite controversy. Monks were at once the most influential leaders of the heretical cause and the most revered victims of orthodox persecution. Shifts of government policy under Zeno and Anastasius, and indeed during the reign of Justinian himself, had a constantly disruptive effect on the practice of the ascetic life – exile, polemic and pastoral concern being the order of the day. Nothing can blind us to the fact, however, that significant numbers (perhaps the majority) of Chrisitans in the eastern empire were willing to accommodate themselves in some degree to the Monophysite party; and only orthodox prejudice can lead one to believe that the Palestinian *laura* had become a dominant model. The majority of the ascetics described by John were certainly from Syria and certainly Monophysite in their loyalty; but his account ranges fully over a great crescent from Thrace to the Nile, and presents us with an image of monastic practice adopted throughout the eastern provinces of the empire.

A recurrent pattern is easy to discern. Each monastery had its archimandrite, and its 'rule' in the sense of customary order: there can be no doubt that, in John's day, that had become the norm, with complex buildings, regular hours and a highly developed liturgy. More than once, he admires explicitly fine craftsmanship in monastic buildings, and the sumptuousness of their church furniture.[39] A monastery, however, would still bear the stamp and often the name of the holy man who had found it. The process of coenobitic development was still based on an original master and the gradual accretion of disciples.[40] Other patterns occurred: the Palestinian rhythm, by which one graduated from community to solitary life; and the development of increasingly ordered forms of devotion among pious families. Within each community – a custom hinted at by Theodoret – masters could still preside over groups of disciples, and even transfer with them to other places. More experienced ascetics practised isolated programmes of self-denial, not always approved of by their peers, but initiated by their own enthusiasm, and carried out in corners and at odd hours of the day or night. Such anecdotes add a voice to the jumbled ground-plan of cells and courtyards revealed by monastic archaeology.[41] John's chief point was to stress

---

[39] John Eph. *Lives* 4, 7, 12, 14, 17f., 20, 31, 33, 35, 42, 47. 9, 12 and 58 give particularly full accounts of buildings and their appointments. For a general survey, see Harvey, *Asceticism and Society in Crisis*. An excellent summary of John's descriptions of the monastic regime is given by Palmer (1990) 81–8; and his book as a whole provides a superb example (the monastery of Qartmin in south-east Turkey) that illustrates, in archaeology and in associated documents, many aspects of Syrian asceticism in this period. Janin's provincial survey (1975), covering large areas of Greece and Asia, offers again a richly documented gazetteer.   [40] John Eph. *Lives* 5f., 22, 27, 34, 54.

[41] The narrative is vividly corroborated by the remains at Qartmin: see Palmer (1990) 97–107.

the way in which the community enfolded those endeavours (even that of stylites), and enjoyed priority of merit. Communities remained open, also, valuing both hospitality and the care of the poor.[42] On the fringes of that ordered world, John described wandering ascetics and radically pious lay persons (in this context women come to greater prominence),[43] who also devoted much of their practical energy to the care of the sick and the poor, and to the entertainment of travellers and strangers.[44] Over all presided the bishop – one of John's chief motives was to show that bishops, also, could be holy! So they exercised their authority over monasteries, characterized as they were by attachment to a sacramental life.[45]

Two things strike one about these vivid accounts. First, monastic order was not an end in itself. One did not base one's life on loyalty to a specific written rule or even to a permanent community. The fundamental social component of the ascetic life was still the relationship between master and disciple. The reputation of the master was the stimulus for the formation and organization of the community in the first place; and the master's own practice and advice was the factor that did most to control the ambition and behaviour of his associates. The monastery and its habitual order were the extended instrument, or at least the protective setting, of a master's formative power. That was why a life governed by 'rules' could still acknowledge some dependence on the biographical tradition enshrined in the *Sayings of the Fathers* and its later supplements and imitations. Second, the *cœnobium*/*laura* relationship observed in Palestine had now entered a new phase, in that the *laura* had come to live in the *cœnobium*. Within a domestic setting that catered for a communal life, men who were psychologically, as it were, hermits pursued in private a programme of prayer and self-discipline within the communal buildings themselves. At the root of the whole enterprise one discovers two fundamental motives: a fear of judgement and a compassion for the unfortunate. The first engendered an urgent sense of responsibility for the direction of one's own life; the second encouraged mercy for others, equally subject not so much to economic or physical misfortune as to a disappointment or weakness entirely like one's own.

Such were the perceptions that did most to shape the structure of eastern monastic life in the fifth and sixth century. Such, also, were the adaptations visited upon the heritage of Pachomius and Basil. The monastic life continued in Asia Minor – the youthful experience of Euthymius and Sabas bears witness to that – even though Constantinople and

---

[42] From community to solitude: John Eph. *Lives* 6 (though in conjunction with other processes), 16, 29 (in which solitaries seek winter refuge in communities). Pious families: 21, 56. (A splendid history of more general character is provided in 58.) Masters and disciples: 2, 3, 15, 29, 32f., 35. Eccentricity within the community: 11, 17, 36, 54. Stylites: 2, 4 (and see the example provided by Palmer (1990) 105f.). Community more meritorious: 3 (very forceful), 4, 13, 15, 19. External relations: 2, 5, 13, 17, 29, 31, 33, 44.   [43] John Eph. *Lives* 12, 27f., 54.   [44] John Eph. *Lives* 31, 39, 45f., 52f., 57.
[45] John Eph. *Lives* 2, 4, 12, 16, 25.

Jerusalem had begun to exert their disturbing pull.[46] In Egypt, where the outlook of Shenoute had modified Pachomian tradition, and where Monophysite self-confidence was less severely disturbed and capable of more organic development, the physical aspects of monastic life in the Delta and along the Nile were quite startlingly changed, precisely in ways that Pachomius had foreseen and feared.[47] Rambling walled *cœnobia* (like Shenoute's 'White Monastery' near Atripe), more populous and more prosperous than before, lay now at the centre of great estates, absorbing the energies of the monks themselves, and providing employment for local peasants. They offered material support in time of famine and unrest, and taxable wealth for the imperial government (which was often returned to them by donation or remission).[48] They were drawn, as a result, into the economy of the church as a whole, sharing under episcopal supervision in the increasing prosperity of the Christian community generally.

In the matter of legislative development, a distinction seems evident between east and west. At the opening of the fifth century, the eastern provinces had already begun to acquire the detailed traditions of order that were to dominate monasticism in the Greek church and its satellites for long afterwards. In the west, on the other hand, the rule that seems most to have influenced later centuries, that of Benedict, would not take shape for a century or more. The distinction, however, is unreal. 'The Rule of Pachomius' or 'the Rule of Basil' did not exist in a hard-and-fast form. The Pachomian material translated into Latin by Jerome did not form a single, coherent corpus; and it is unlikely that such regulations were at any time honoured throughout the coenobitic communities of the Nile valley. Some even of Pachomius' own foundations seceded from his federation soon after his death. The ease with which Shenoute usurped the Pachomian mantle was itself a sign of how diffuse and even insecure his legacy had become. Other collections of rules gained competing influence. Several items in the *Sayings of the Fathers* fall into sequences that are virtually rules in embryo.[49] The *Sayings* focus also on figures like Longinus, superior of the

---

[46] The flourishing establishments in Basil's Caesarea were sadly depleted by the time of his successor Firmus, a century later. See Firmus, *Letters* (*SChrét.* 250) esp. *Epp.* 12 and 43. John Eph. *Lives* 31 describes another species of Basilian *Nachleben* in sixth-century Melitene, on the eastern borders of Cappadocia.

[47] For the tenuous survival of old north-Egyptian traditions, see Chitty (1966) 144f., and Gould (1993) 9f., 185f.

[48] The generosity of patrons, in a society where wealth meant either land and its produce or gold, was thus locked firmly into the local beneficence of hospitality and welfare. The work of Jones and, more recently, Hendy provides a general context and access to a wide international bibliography. Much recent work of an economic nature has focused more on the third and fourth centuries. Useful detail can still be found in Johnson and West (1949) especially 66f. Walters (1974) discusses surviving material evidence of refectories, bakeries and water installations, 99f, 206f., 209f. and 219f., with additional reference at this last point to handicraft and to labour outside the monastery.

[49] For example Moses, 14–18. Such prescriptive dialogues could find their way into narrative sources: see John Eph. *Lives* 3.

Ennaton, a large Delta monastery with Pachomian roots. Esaias of Scetis, another generator and hero of such anecdotes, was not averse to drawing up rules. He clearly worked in the Pachomian tradition, even though he sprang from the exiled northern communities of Egypt that probably created the *Sayings* themselves. As for Basil, his *Regulae* circulated at first in at least two collections, each subject to editing and accretion. They are notable for saying less about monastic institutions than about the development of the ascetic's spiritual life, or else were designed to meet particular needs and to answer particular questions as they arose.[50] The memory of such pioneers survived among the communities they inspired largely because of their personal reputation, enhanced in Pachomius' case by a rich biographical tradition. It may be that the greater influence of Basil was due precisely to his lesser specificity, the detailed prescriptions of Pachomius' actual rules being more difficult to transfer unchanged to other settings. So, even on paper, individual character continued to count for most: one was loyal to reputations as much as to regimes. Wherever a 'rule' does seem discernible, we find constantly an eclectic tendency: ascetics did not adopt the practice of one particular place, whether Caesarea or the Thebaid, but reinforced the customs and recollections of more immediate instructors, or, at the very most, responded admiringly to the wisdom of some figure in the more distant past. Sabas was to prove, in a way that applied to a multitude of monasteries, a typical example: he bequeathed, in A.D. 532, written instructions to his successor; but they represented not one authority but 'the traditions handed down in his monasteries' – only at that late stage, perhaps, committed to writing.[51]

Yet there were developments proper to the west, governed to some extent by precedents in its own provinces. Before the translated *Life of Antony* could gain widespread effect, and certainly before Jerome and Rufinus began to offer the west their own ascetic works and translations, bishops in particular were beginning to make formal prescriptions for ascetic disciples. Eusebius of Vercelli (died 371) and Ambrose of Milan (died 397) are famous examples. Episcopal initiative and control were important features of the development: in some cases, indeed, the bishop's household became the centre of the ascetic endeavour, with the inevitable involvement of members of his clergy. Jerome and Rufinus were, indeed, products of that world; and Augustine (A.D. 354–430) continued the tradition.

His towering stature within the western Christian tradition can often encourage us to forget how local Augustine could be in his initial influence; and that is particularly true of his monastic experiments. Suspicions

---

[50] See Rousseau, *Basil of Caesarea* 354f. and Gribomont (1953).
[51] Cyr. Scyth. *V. Sab.* 76, tr. Price (1991) 191.

aroused in Gaul by his doctrine of grace, at least in the 420s and 430s, and the alternative prestige of Lérins and its satellites no doubt help to explain why his ascetic writings and regulations were slow to make their mark outside North Africa. It is in later ascetic writers – Caesarius, Benedict and Gregory the Great – that his ideas can be more readily detected.[52] Nevertheless, while the earliest relevant texts do suggest a narrow audience and confused compilation, Augustine could justly claim to have been the first monastic legislator of the west. His 'rule' in its primitive form, the so-called *Ordo monasterii*, was probably written, perhaps in collaboration with others in his circle, at the beginning of the 390s, when Jerome and Rufinus had yet to make known to the west the works of Pachomius and Basil. Augustine was living at the time in a community at Thagaste, which he had founded when he returned to Africa from Italy after 388. He undoubtedly set the tone of the 'rule' in the opening section of what was otherwise a laconic document, emphasizing love of God and neighbour. A cycle of prayer and work was broken by a period of reading and a late afternoon meal. Goods were to be held in common, but there was commerce with the outside world. Obedience was demanded within a hierarchy of *pater* and *praepositus*.[53] Augustine's models had been inspired by the east, but were Italian in origin: he imbibed the tradition at second hand. He also placed the ascetic endeavour firmly within the context of the church as a whole. Finally, he developed his devotion to the monastic life alongside his famous sensibility to what he regarded as the weakness and complexity of the human psyche: destined for eternal fulfilment, but needing guidance and authority.

Once established in Hippo in 391, Augustine developed his ideas for a monastery entirely his own, producing his *Praeceptum*. He attached charac-teristic importance to the pattern of life followed by the first Christians in Jerusalem, as portrayed in Acts. The original church was the perfect mon-astery, with property held in common, and intense affection among its members. Given the variety of ability characteristic of human experience, the only way to maintain that 'unity of heart and soul' was to develop a sense of responsibility for other people, acknowledging dependence upon the virtuous, and rallying to the aid of the weak. A system of superiors still monitored behaviour, but in collaboration with the community and for the community's sake, conscious always of their own vulnerability in the sight of God. At the same time, the 'rule' had an authority of its own, being read aloud each week. Prayer was clearly ordered, although the opportunity for private reflection was still safeguarded, according to the Egyptian tradition.

---

[52] All three will be dealt with below. Caesarius' *Statuta* 21 (*Quæ aliquid*) is a striking example: compare Aug. *Praec.* 1.5f., III.3f. The relevant Augustinian texts are edited by Verheijen (1967).
[53] Love: Aug. *Ordo* 1. Routine: 2f; see also 9. Common property: 4. External relations: 8. Obedience: 6.

As we would expect of Augustine, obedience in such a world was at once the exercise and the guarantee of true freedom, not mere submission to a law.[54] The contrast with developments in Gaul will be striking. Instead of a monk who later became a bishop, we have a bishop who was learning more and more what it meant to be a monk. The redeeming security and necessary order of the church provided the model for the monastic life; and its function as the household of God was as important as the structures of authority within it. That social emphasis and reflective skill meant that Augustine's influence would transform any preoccupation with daily order and obedience; and it was to be in the *Rule* of Benedict that the coalition was finally most perfectly achieved.

Perhaps the most famous 'monk-bishop' of an earlier generation was Martin of Tours (died A.D. 397).[55] In Gaul itself (he was actually born on the Danube frontier), he appears to have been something of a monastic pioneer, although he had depended as a young man on encouragement by Hilary of Poitiers (died A.D. 367). The *Life* of Martin by Sulpicius Severus, written around the time of its hero's death, and the same author's *Dialogues*, written a few years later, present us with a vivid though highly tendentious account. Drawing upon eastern sources, both literary and anecdotal, Sulpicius' descriptions of Martin's ascetic regime may depend as much on the models he admired as on the reports he received. Nevertheless, he provides us with good reason to believe that some form of organized, communal asceticism was in place in the region of Poitiers and Tours by the 360s. After his consecration, Martin continued to live a visibly ascetic life (to the horror of some churchmen), to retreat at times to his own foundations, and to maintain supervision of their progress. Structures appear to have been loose, each ascetic living in a simple cabin or cave. There is allusion to literary interests, supporting, perhaps, a pastoral and anti-heretical impulse; but details are sketchy.[56] Martin's subsequent influence was largely restricted to the western parts of Gaul. He may have awakened interest in Britain and Ireland; but there is little evidence that his cult, for all its popularity and prestige both north and south, was accompanied, at least in the Gallic cities where it took root, by a specific and corresponding enthusiasm for anything that could be described as Martinian monasticism.

Of greater importance were developments in south-eastern Gaul, in the Rhône valley and around Marseilles. Here the pioneer was Honoratus, who, with the encouragement of Leontius, bishop of Fréjus, founded a

---

[54] Influence of Acts: Aug. *Praec.* 1.2f., III.3f., IV.8. Superiors: VII.1f. 'Rule': VIII.2. Prayer: II.1f; the continuum of each ascetic's inner life was never ignored, III.2. Obedience: VIII.1 (the point had already been made briefly in the *Ordo* 1of.).

[55] Still the most authoritative account of asceticism in Gaul is that of Prinz (1965).

[56] Most of the information is in Sulpicius Severus, *V. Mart.* x. Maintaining earlier asceticism: 1f. Regular retreats to Marmoutier: 3f. Cabins or caves: 5. Literary pursuits: 6, and note reference to monks as future bishops: 8f. For Hilary, v.1f., and churchmen's horror, IX.3.

monastery on the island of Lérins (between Cannes and Antibes), and later became bishop of Arles (in A.D. 426). Honoratus had previously travelled in the east, perhaps even in Egypt and Syria; and he brought to his Gallic foundation the practices he observed or learnt of on his journey. This transference of eastern ideas was more direct than in the case of Martin. Although we have little certain textual evidence of the earliest regime at Lérins itself – it is likely that the canons of monastic practice were committed to writing only gradually – it is clear that a regular round of work and prayer, a system that included both coenobites and solitaries, and a detailed pattern of government under a designated superior were quickly established according to eastern models.[57] As the century progressed, a whole series of regulae began to appear, some in the Rhône valley, some across the Alps, almost all linked with Lérins to some degree, and all indebted to the heritage of Pachomius and Basil. Thus there sprang into being on western soil a stream of ideas and practices that would flow eventually into the prescriptions of Caesarius in Arles and of Benedict and his predecessors in Italy.[58]

From that same south-eastern Gallic milieu come the writings of John Cassian, an easterner by origin, who, after extensive travels in Palestine and Egypt, had settled in Gaul and had, by c. 415, founded two monasteries near Marseilles. For his own monks and for other communities already beginning to grow nearby (including that of Honoratus at Lérins), he wrote his Institutes and Conferences, which were greatly honoured and not infrequently imitated in the centuries to follow. In practical matters, the Institutes concentrated on the admission of novices and on the round of daily prayer. The singing of psalms at evening and in the night hours now became more ordered, with a split between 'nocturns' proper and a dawn service of disputed character, reflecting an amalgamation of Egyptian and Palestinian practice, but carried to a new level of formality. And instead of leaving the daylight hours to personal reflection (meditatio), brief 'offices' that we now know as 'terce', 'sext' and 'none' provided a more rigid and spaced-out framework. Enduring vagueness and obscurity, however, remind us that traditions had yet to congeal into patterns familiar to Benedict a century later.[59]

Cassian prescribed otherwise very little. It seems that he felt his duty was more to describe and gently recommend eastern practices, leaving his readers (at first envisaged as potential superiors themselves) to decide how

[57] Hilary's Life of Honoratus (something of a misnomer) provides a little institutional information. Adalbert de Vogüé (1982) argued with vigour that the so-called 'Rule of the Four Fathers' was the rule operating at Lérins from the earliest days. Its connection with the monastery appears to be beyond doubt; but its date is much less easily discovered.

[58] There can be no doubt that, in spite of difficulties in matters of dating and dependence, the account of this tradition given by De Vogüé (1982) is the most cohesive and appealing currently available.

[59] Concerning novices, De institutis (CSEL 17) I discusses the symbolism of a monk's clothing and IV.1–7 the experience of renouncing the world. The round of prayer: II and III.

those might best be imitated. They were to govern, in any case, more by example than by rule.[60] The bulk of the *Inistitutes* (Books v–xii) was devoted to spiritual guidance, under the headings of eight vices and how they might best be countered. The *Conferences* were similar in effect, reporting conversations with well-known ascetics of northern Egypt: offering, in other words, instruction from the lips of ascetic masters. Where Cassian did discuss relations between superiors and subjects, his emphasis was on formation – on the desire of the disciple and the wisdom of the teacher. The setting evoked, moreover, was predominantly eremitical: the solitary life was still acknowledged as the ascetic's characteristic ideal. There can be no doubt, nevertheless, that Cassian's intentions, like his audience, were coenobitic, and that the virtues and practices he encouraged were those proper to community life.[61] It is one of his claims to genius that he was able to respect an ancient Egyptian tradition, while nevertheless adapting it thoroughly to the new monasteries of Gaul. Thus the apparent conversations of old masters were transformed into an independently available text with an authority of its own.[62]

Once in place, those southern experiments and precedents set the tone for monasticism in Gaul until the end of the sixth century. (They also provided a context for interaction between Gaul, Britain and Ireland: Patrick was to some degree a disciple of Honoratus.)[63] Yet the close relationship between ascetics and the episcopate in Gaul, already evident in Cassian's career,[64] makes it difficult to assess the significance of specifically monastic developments in the province. Lérins quickly became a virtual school for bishops – not only of Arles, as in the case of Honoratus and his successor Hilary (died 449), but of several other dioceses: Eucherius' Lyons, for example, and the Riez of Faustus.[65] Such promotions did not represent merely enthusiasm for ascetic candidates, 'common assumption' though their suitability might have been.[66] The acquisition of a see depended as much on the patronage of the powerful, and reflected new aristocratic ambitions within an increasingly isolated province.[67] The men concerned

[60] Cassian, *Inst.* preface 4f., confirmed in *Conlationes* (*CSEL* 13) preface to 1. *Inst.* iv.17–18 discusses food.
[61] That emphasis becomes more and more evident as the *Conferences* proceed, but is heavily accentuated in xix. [62] Cassian, *Con.* prefaces to xi and xviii. Adaptation to the west: *Inst.* 1.10.
[63] Although it was not as a monk that he journeyed to Ireland and worked there.
[64] His prefaces in the *Institutes* and *Conferences* bear witness to a complex web of relationships; and he had come to Gaul in the first place under the patronage of Proculus of Arles. See Rousseau, *Ascetics* 174f., 217f.
[65] Sid. Ap. *Ep.* 6.1.3; 9.3.4. Lérins was not the only source of such recruits. Rusticius of Narbonne, whose episcopate spanned more than thirty years (from A.D. 427), was a monk from St Victor, one of Cassian's foundations in Marseilles. It was to him that Jerome wrote, recommending an ascetic career as the visible guarantee of worthiness for the priesthood: *Ep.* 125.17.
[66] *Familiaris . . . præsumptio*. Boniface of Rome, *Ep.* 'Exigit dilectio', PL xx.669f.
[67] See Mathisen (1989), (1993), and Drinkwater and Elton, *Fifth-Century Gaul*.

were members of the social and political élite; and that counted for as much
as their ascetic experience. The notorious conflict between Ravennius of
Arles, for example, and Theodore of Fréjus, fostered by the recalcitrant
independence of Faustus, abbot of Lérins before he became bishop of
Riez, hints at more than a debate between priests and monks. Their testy
relations with Leo, the bishop of Rome, add to the implications.[68]

We are dealing here with attitudes and events that lie outside the narrow
sphere of ascetic history and acquire their clearest significance in relation to
post-imperial politics. Yet those developments had a direct and perhaps
damaging effect on monastic practice: for the ambitious bishops who thus
retained some trace of monastic formation played out the rest of their
careers, and exercised their enduring patronage of monastic foundations,
within the cities over which they came virtually to rule. Caesarius, in the next
century, belonged very much, as we shall see, in that world (the monastery
governed by his sister Caesaria was built, eventually, in the heart of Arles);[69]
and what we read later in the pages of Gregory of Tours bears witness to
the survival not only of Caesarius' own prescriptions but of a bond between
bishop and monk that far outweighed in Gregory's mind any independence
among ascetic institutions. Aurelianus of Arles and Ferreolus of Uzès are
perfect examples of the trend.[70] The urban monasteries patronized by
Frankish royalty were built on the same species of opportunism: their
founders, whether religious or lay, indulged their piety as one means among
others of reinforcing their hold over cities and their *territoria*. Partly in the
service of that development, heroic solitaries in the old style, still gathering
about themselves loyal disciples, were sucked into an ecclesiastical system
with more on its agenda than abstemious self-discipline.

The period between Caesarius and Cassian, punctuated as it is by the
regulæ already referred to, can be brought to life in even greater detail by a
collection of lives devoted to the 'Fathers of the Jura', Romanus, Lupicinus
and Eugendus, successive abbots of Condat and its associated houses in
the upper reaches of the Rhône valley system.[71] These three lives present
us with a transition from the virtual isolation of Romanus in his early years
to the highly ordered community of Eugendus, recognizably similar to the
monastery of his contemporary Caesarius (and, indeed, of Benedict and

[68] *Concilia Galliae A. 314–A. 506* ed. C. Munier (*CCSL* 149) 132f. Faustus became bishop of Riez some
ten years later, after more than twenty-five years as abbot, and died c. A.D. 490. The details of this controversy are treated fully by Mathisen (1989) 173–205; see especially 195f. In this particular instance (A.D.
451), the bishop of Fréjus was specifically warned to keep his nose out of the monastery's internal
affairs: a stipulation that modified significantly the exactly contemporary strictures of Chalcedon.
[69] *Vita sancti Cæsarii* (trans. W. Klingshirn, Liverpool, 1994) 1.28 and 35. Aurelianus, his later successor (A.D. 546–51), followed his example: see following note.
[70] For texts and references, see Desprez (1980).
[71] The biographies cover the period from c. 435 to the death of Eugendus in 510, and were probably written shortly after that date. Romanus died c. 460, Lupicinus in 490.

his Italian predecessors). Yet Romanus was fully aware of the rich tradition within which he had begun to work. Although there is little sign that he wrote or had access to a rule,[72] details of organization familiar in the east were taken for granted: individual cells, a place of prayer, a hostel for visitors; attention to fasting and watching; a distinction between the regular prayer and reading of the solitary and the manual labour of the coenobite; but, under Romanus, a combination of the two.[73] He, like Cassian, was chary of subservience to clerics, and was anxious to adapt the practices of the east to the needs and abilities of his associates.[74] There are hints that his regime was deliberately more lenient than that of Lupicinus, who had already begun to make an independent mark in a satellite community.[75]

With Lupicinus, we enter a more ordered world. There is specific reference to a monastic liturgy – the *vespertina synaxis* of the east. The monastery possessed an *œconomus*: its relations with visitors and dependants were becoming more controlled. Lupicinus enjoyed a growing reputation among secular associates, and could be seen as a threatening critic of civil authority, undermined as it was by sin. Most important, growing attention was paid to the place of obedience in the community. Custom, the example of others, and the advice of the abbot were combined to call into question personal judgement, even when it aimed at more rigorous observance. The governing principles, however, were the need for balance and the schooling of inner motive, not the regimentation of behaviour.[76]

Eugendus, finally, offered a contrast, not only in his more detailed government but also in his settled life: he exemplified a *stabilitas loci* absent in the careers of his predecessors – the assumption (reinforced by Chalcedon) that ascetics would remain in one institution for the whole of their lives. That sprang in his case, perhaps, from a personal inclination to study; and, in spite of his reputation as a legislator, Eugendus displayed other signs of eccentricity. After fire had destroyed the old buildings at Condat, dating back perhaps even to Romanus' day, he set the monastery on a new path, insisting on a single dormitory for all ('setting aside the custom of eastern archimandrites'), and on rigorous adherence to a common life. The author comments on his attachment to Cassian, in preference to Basil, Pachomius and even Lérins itself, because of that master's ability to adapt his recommendations to the conditions of the west. The actual 'rule' of Eugendus is not described: reference is made instead to

---

[72] Note the vagueness of *V. Rom.* 4, 11, 36; see Martine (1968). Precision was to come with Eugendus, 59; and Romanus was chary of setting too precise a standard, 32f. But custom was distinct from the authority of the master himself. 36.   [73] *V. Rom.* 28, 15 and 10 respectively.

[74] *V. Rom.* 18f., 28, 33. Hilary of Arles is specifically criticized.   [75] *V. Rom.* 17, 24.

[76] Eastern observances: *V. Lup.* 64f. Organization: 68. External relations: 92f. (Compare the judicial influence of the Gallic recluse Eparchius: Greg. Tur. *Hist.* vi.8.) Obedience: 75f. Gregory's rather different account of Lupicinus and Romanus, *V. pat* 1, reveals not only his different interests but the shifting values of monastic Gaul in the sixth century.

customs enforced elsewhere.[77] Certainly, there are accounts of an ordered liturgy, common and regular meals (for some monks at least, two a day), and abbatial authority. Eugendus tried to control the gifts that the community received and the troubled visitors that flocked to its gates. Yet his dying requests referred in only a general way to the 'institutes of the fathers'. He prayed alone in the cemetery or under a favourite tree. His monks travelled, even to Rome, in search of relics. He allotted tasks in the community according to the talents of individual monks, exercising that insight into the character of each subject that was typical of the old charismatic masters of the Egyptian desert. In some ways, therefore, this coenobitic hero was not so very different from Leunianus of Vienne, living in the solitude of a cell, yet 'ruling monks' and supervising a nearby convent.[78]

The prestige of Lérins and its satellites reached a peak in the career and writings of Caesarius of Arles (died 543). His monastic formation included a period at Lérins; and, after becoming bishop in A.D. 503, he wrote a *Regula monachorum* and longer and more informative *Statuta sanctarum virginum*.[79] One has to be cautious about the meaning he attached to *regula*. Its constant conjunction with other words – *institutio regulæ, discretio et regula* – reminds us that the *regula* itself was still regarded as part of a wider tradition – 'canonical scripture and the books of the ancient fathers'.[80] His written prescriptions are larded like sermons with exhortations to virtue, and reflect upon attitude as much as behaviour.[81] The authority of the abbot or abbess was by now well-established, but balanced by the delegated duties of a *præpositus* and subject to the influence of *seniores*. Caesarius envisaged a fully coenobitic regime, with none of the privacy associated with the cells of the *laura*; and again there is an emphasis on *stabilitas loci*. Women are specifically catered for. Extra care is taken to protect their seclusion. In contrast to their male counterparts, they will pray more than they work (although they also copied books). The bulk of Caesarius' *Rules* is devoted to fasting and liturgy. The latter, by his day, had reached a high degree of detailed sophistication, with variations from season to season and a complex succession of antiphonal and unison psalmody, interspersed with readings. Overshadowing this regime was the bishop himself (a significant resolution of debates in the previous century); but his authority

---

[77] De Vogüé (1982) II.452 discusses possible connections between the so-called *Regula orientalis* and Condat under Lupicinus and Eugendus.

[78] Stability: *V. Eug.* 126. Rebuilding and its results: 162, 170 (*refutato archmandritarum orientalium instari*, ed. Martine (1968), 422), 173. Monastic regime: 129f., 131, 151, 171. External relations: 147, 172. Death: 177. His prayer: 129, 153f. Travelling monks: 153f. Charismatic insight: 149. Leunianus: 128.

[79] Note that the numeration and nomenclature of *PL* LXVII.1099–104, 1107–20 are not always used by more recent and more reliable editors.

[80] *Statuta* 26 (*Et quamvis*), 30 (*Ad cellarium*), 35 (at *Matri quæ*), 47 (*Te vero*); *Recapitulatio*, 62 (*Et licet*), 72 (*Vos tamen, PL tandem*). Compare *regulari sceptro* in Greg. Tur. *V. pat.* XVI.1, ed. 275.

[81] *Reg. mon.* ed. G. Morin (Maredsous 1942) 151:8f.; 152:8f. (*PL* 13, 19). See especially *Sermons* 233–6.

was carefully defined, and the domestic liberty of the nuns was fully respected.[82] Caesarius also made detailed provision for the endowment of his communities: the preservation of his will allows us a rare glimpse into such arrangements, as it carefully identifies the blocks of land upon which future prosperity would depend.[83]

In spite of selection, the main development is clear. The east provided the first models, and preserved the reputation of the ascetic master and of the *laura* system. Custom and anecdote provided the authority for order, and a move away from that tradition was slow and never total.[84] Yet the common dormitory, the common refectory, the importance of shared labour and the prominence of the abbot became increasingly the norm. The bishop and the secular patron retained some ultimate influence, not least because both shared in the ambition and privilege of the aristocratic élite.

About the following century in Gaul, we gain most from a reading of Gregory of Tours (died 594). His *Histories* are less useful than his more deliberately religious works – the *Liber vitae patrum* and the *De gloria confessorum* – which have the added advantage of placing clearly coenobitic enterprises in a rich context of eccentric variety; but there is one interesting oddity in his more secular record – Radegund. Royal status made her circumstance exceptional; but the fortunes of her community show the pressures that could be brought to bear upon Caesarius' legacy.[85] In the hagiographical works, however, predictable patterns emerge. Travellers from the east continued to reinforce Palestinian and Syrian customs.[86] Men solitary in spirit and practice lived within communities or in close dependence upon them. They might even be their founders.[87] Such communities

---

[82] Superiors: *Reg. mon.* ed. Morin, 151:3f. (*PL* 11); see also 152:1f. (*PL* 16), and *Statuta* 35 (at *Matri quae*). Common life: *Reg. mon.* ed. Morin, 150:13 (*PL* 3); *Statuta* 9 (*Nulli liceat*). Stability: *Statuta* 2 (at *Si qua*). Women: *Statuta* 39 (*Convivium*), 42f. (from *Illud ante*). Bishops: *Statuta* 36 (*Ante omnia propter*), 43 (*Ante omnia observandum*); *Recapitulatio* 64 (*Illud etiam*), 72 (*Vos tamen, PL tandem*); and compare Greg. Tur. *Gloria* 79. Books: *Vita sancti Caesarii* 1.58.   [83] Ed. Morin, 283–9. See also *Vita* II.8f., 47.

[84] Witness the splendid portrait in Greg. Tur. *Hist.* VI.6 – an eastern ascetic in Gaul who even imported his own food! One may note how the *Apophthegmata*, when translated into Latin, were rearranged according to theme – though still in no way constituting a rule.

[85] For other instances of royal involvement, see Greg. Tur. *V. pat.* VI and XII; and compare 1.5 with *V. Lup.* 92–5. Gregory's personal interest in the famous 'rebellion' that occurred after Radegund's death prompts him to describe the practices of the convent and its endowment with land, which led to the development of widespread estates with officials and tied labourers, supporting an army of domestic servants responsible for the upkeep of urban buildings: *Hist.* VI.29, IX.39f., X.15f. For a brief but authoritative account, see Wood, *Merovingian Kingdoms* 136–9.

[86] Greg. Tur. *V. pat.* III (urban and generous), XIII and XV (characteristically penitential). See also *Hist.* IV.32 (an ascetic who 'stands' – very Syrian), VI.6 (a hermit's imported herbs, and much else), VII.31 (a merchant with St Sergius' finger), X.26 (a Syrian bishop), and X.31 with II.39 (a travelled abbot).

[87] *V. pat.* IV.3, IX; *Gloria* 37 (*iuxta regulas monasteriorum . . . secretius tamen atque peculiarius*, ed. Krusch, 321), 85. Having accustomed ourselves to the often extensive communities of the east, it is worth attending to hints at scale: three monks, for example, in *V. pat.* XV; *collectis secum paucis monachis* in *Gloria* 79, ed. Krusch, 347. Yet Gregory the Great would attribute Rome's safety from the Lombards to the prayers of 3,000 nuns within its walls, *Ep.* 7.23. A founder: *V. pat.* IX.

were soon endowed with fields and woodland, came under the influence of royal patronage, and spawned their own dependent foundations.[88] Cassian and Martin are mentioned still.[89] In Gregory's anecdotes we see at one and the same time the development of a rich monastic culture along the reaches of the Loire and the lasting influence of the Rhône communities, reaching into areas further north. Economic conditions are faithfully recorded. Gardens provided for immediate needs; but cereal crops were also grown, and ascetics worked on the land of others.[90] In a couple of instances, a more rural monastery and the nearby village appear to have been almost intertwined, both in close association with the local church.[91] Such vignettes provide us with a more secure image of varied monastic practice in the sixth-century west (for we shall discover parallels in Benedict's Italy), and modify the rigid impression we might gain from the hopeful prescriptions of church councils (presided over, of course, by bishops eager to maintain a disciplined conformity and to assert their pastoral rights).[92]

Both the tone and the motive of those conciliar decrees remind us that the Gallic church in the sixth century, in ascetic matters as in others, was in need of reform. A weary sense of decline, characteristic of the period generally in both east and west, is evident in many of the specifically ascetic sources we have examined; and we need not attribute it always to outraged conservatism or tremulous eschatology. Gregory himself, albeit a bishop with little experience of monasticism in his own life, and not unsusceptible to the advantages of local eminence or royal patronage, had an honest enough sense of the room for improvement. Yet the crucial pressure, in the case of specifically monastic reform, came from outside the Frankish kingdoms, and is exemplified most obviously in the career of the Irishman Columbanus. Born in the 540s, he arrived in Gaul just as Gregory was completing his *Histories*. After travelling in the Loire region (providing further

[88] *V. pat.* XII. See also the account of Martius, XIV, with subordinate *præpositus*.

[89] *V. pat.* XX.3, following the suggestion of James (1985) 157. Compare possible dependence on Martin – *post magistri dogmata*, ed. B. Krusch; 330 – *Gloria* 56.

[90] *V. pat.* X.1 (garden and hired labour), XVIII.2 (corn and a mill); *Gloria* 23 (where the attractiveness of the garden is also stressed), 81 (bees), 96.   [91] *Gloria* 22f., 56.

[92] The council of Orleans (A.D. 511) set the tone for the coming century: 'Abbots should think of themselves, in the interests of religious humility, as subject to the authority of bishops; and, if in any matter they act in breach of the rule, the bishops should correct them' (canon 19, ed. C. de Clerq *Concilia Galliae, A.511–A. 695 (CCSL* 148A) 1963, 10). See also Épaone (A.D. 517), canon 19 (episcopal control over succession); Orleans (A.D. 533), canon 21 (vague subjection to episcopal *præcepta*); Arles (A.D. 554), canons 2 and 3 (fairly broad); Tours (A.D. 567), canon 17 (excommunication; but note that canon 7 required the bishop to act in co-operation with other abbots); Narbonne (A.D. 589), canon 6 (against harbouring criminals); and Auxerre (late sixth century), canons 23–6 (various specific controls). Few councils in sixth-century Gaul concerned themselves with the internal discipline of monastic communities. The council of Tours (A.D. 567) was unusual in insisting on a common dormitory (rather than individual or shared cells), and drew up rules for fasting (canons 15 and 18). If, on the other hand, a monk withdrew from a community – 'to build himself a cell', for example: a practice viewed with caution, but allowed for – then he exposed himself to direct episcopal control: Orleans (A.D. 511), canon 22.

evidence of its contacts across the Channel), he established a monastery at Luxeuil in Burgundy, some 150 km north of Condat. It developed eventually into an important centre of medieval monasticism, together with Bobbio, which Columbanus founded later in northern Italy. He died in A.D. 615.

There is a certain irony in this startling and far from welcome intrusion. Fifth-century monks had made a contribution to developments in Ireland, often via Britain and its more immediate Celtic neighbours: not only Patrick, but also shadowy figures like Riochatus (a friend of Faustus of Riez),[93] the disciples and successors of Ninian at Whithorn (the famous *Candida Casa*, dedicated to Martin of Tours),[94] and of Illtud and David in Wales.[95] Now the influence began to flow strongly in the other direction. Columbanus' original rules – the *Regula monachorum* and the *Regula cœnobialis* – were written during his earliest years in south-eastern Gaul, before A.D. 610. They owed something to Benedict (proving his growing influence) but more to the older traditions of Basil and Cassian. Like Cassian, Columbanus issued more theoretical advice than positive prescriptions. The harsh and repetitive punishments of the *Regula cœnobialis* – five blows for this offence, fifteen for that – are disappointing in their allusions, betraying only in the baldest terms the silence, order and deference expected of each monk.[96] But more than a century of Irish independence had carried the monastic society of the island away from the stifling control of the secular nobility, harnessed it to a more pastoral concern for rural converts, and charged it with a Celtic vigour and that righteous attachment to high standards in dedication and observance so obvious in the writings of the Welshman Gildas (died *c*. 570).[97] Not surprisingly, the emphasis estranged Columbanus from royalty in Gaul, especially Theuderic II of Burgundy and his notorious grandmother Brunhild. Thanks to his admiration for Gregory the Great and his loyalty to Roman authority generally, he acquired an increasingly detailed knowledge of Benedict's achievements in Italy, continued to introduce his principles into his own regime, and eventually crossed the Alps in search of more sympathetic surroundings.

Two issues have, for more than a generation, dominated the study of Benedict: the relationship between his own *Rule* and the *Regula magistri*, and

---

[93] Sid. Ap. *Ep.* 9.9.   [94] Bede, *HE* III.4.

[95] Illtud may have come from northern Gaul. Much of our information comes from later hagiography, which is unreliable; but dedications and archaeology provide useful hints. Ireland is well placed in the wider European context by Mayr-Harting (1991) esp. (for our purposes) 33–9, 78–85.

[96] Columbanus' works are edited by G. S. M. Walker (Dublin 1957). Wood, *Merovingian Kingdoms*, provides extensive, documented, convenient reference. See also Clarke and Brennan (1981) and the commentaries provided by Adalbert de Vogüé (1989) in collaboration with Pierre Sangiani and Sister Jean-Baptiste Juglar.

[97] His preoccupations were not predominantly monastic; but he may have been a pupil of Illtud, and he travelled abroad as far as Rome in the Ostrogothic period. For some background, see Higham (1994).

the role of Gregory the Great in making Benedict more widely known, especially in the second book of his *Dialogues*. Both investigations have questioned, in a sense, the originality of Benedict; but the answers given have shown at once the traditional nature of his contribution and the particular qualities that mark his genius and lasting significance.

There is now widespread agreement that Benedict drew heavily upon the *Regula magistri*, which was probably written in the vicinity of Rome during the first quarter of the sixth century. By that time, ascetic developments in southern Gaul were well-known in Italy, and political and ecclesiastical events – the Ostrogothic settlement and the attempts to solve the Acacian schism – were encouraging new relationships between the eastern and western sectors of the empire, represented at the ascetic level, for example, by the Latin *Life* of Pachomius written by Dionysius Exiguus, himself an easterner. So, when Sigismund of Burgundy presided over the foundation of the monastery of St Maurice at Agaune in 515, eastern relics were installed and elements adopted from the liturgical practice of the *Acœmitœ* in Constantinople, while prescriptions were borrowed from the heirs of the Lérins tradition. The monastery was destined to exert considerable influence during the century and more to follow.[98]

The unknown 'Master' of the *Regula magistri* was intent upon preserving a detailed system, thoroughly protected against the world around it, in which the common dormitory, refectory and oratory, together with a garden and outhouses, were surrounded by a wall. Other types of ascetic community, more open, more loosely structured and more mobile (and presumably still common), were severely criticized.[99] An abbot, two subordinate and equal superiors, a cellarer, a porter and weekly teams with domestic duties were described in terms not unlike those of Pachomius; but hierarchy was valued for its own sake, based on secular models.[100] An immensely detailed liturgy departed quite significantly from the customs of Lérins, with great stress on reading and *meditatio* – ancient qualities reflected also in the single daily meal. The 'Master' appeared to accept clear divisions in the community, based on literary and technical skill, although he seems to have been aware that the monastery might thereby encourage within its own walls the social divisions of the secular world.[101] The features that distinguish this rule most famously are its careful submission to the authority of the bishop,[102] and its emphasis within the monastery on the submission of pupil to teacher. The very title of 'master' displays that preference. The

[98] The *Acœmitœ* had long had a reputation for attachment to western views of orthodoxy. Among other later impressions, see Greg. Tur. *Hist.* III.5f. For links with Lérins and the Jura, see De Vogüé (1982) 439f., 447; Theurillat (1954) and Masai (1971).

[99] *Regula magistri* (ed. A. de Vogüé, 3 vols.) (*SChrét.*) 105–7)) I.13, LXI and LXXVIII express typical and detailed caution.   [100] See, for example, *Regula magistri* XI.5f.   [101] *Regula magistri* L.72, 76f.

[102] Most clearly formulated in relation to the abbot, *Regula magistri* XCIII.

rule is preoccupied with vertical communication between superior and subject rather than with relationships among the subjects themselves. The document is presented as a series of questions and answers, the disciple seeking guidance, evoking the style of Cassian or Basil, but to different effect.

Here, then, was one of Benedict's sources; but one only. He was in many ways a syncretist, working in a world where Caesarius and his associates could influence developments in Ravenna as easily as in Poitiers.[103] For some considerable time, his own *Rule* was to be popularized most effectively in conjunction with Caesarius and with the later Columbanus. Even more important, his use of the *Regula magistri* was tempered in a fundamental way by his dependence on the more social emphases of Augustine. Reading his *Rule*, one is reminded constantly of the 'Master', and yet astonished no less frequently by the skilfully interwoven attention to community life. In the combination that did most to characterize his achievement, the community now balanced, within a trinity of influences, the impact of both the abbot and the rule. Obviously by the time his own *Rule* had developed, circumstances in Italy had changed once again, with the Gothic kingdom in disarray, the armies and administrators of Justinian increasingly in command, and the loyalties of Italians at once weakened and divided. It was a world in which the very definition of community was open to reassessment, and where the ability to maintain an effective economy was subject not only to the stress of war but also to the loss of political focus and identity. No wonder Benedict was more hesitant than his most famous Italian model, offering in his own *Rule* no more than 'the rudiments of monastic observance', a 'little rule for beginners'. Cassian, the *Vitæ patrum* and the rules of Basil were deemed more exhaustive guides.[104]

We owe our biographical knowledge of Benedict to Gregory the Great. The critical problem is whether the portrait provided in the latter's *Dialogues* (completed in A.D. 594) has accurately recorded the milieu of the *Regula magistri* and of Benedict's own *Rule*. Did Gregory, one might almost say, invent the Benedict who has become so familiar to history? In fact, the correspondences are numerous and convincing. As Gregory wrote himself, 'his life could not have differed from his teaching'.[105] In so far as doubts remain, we have no reason to expect that a biographical account, with its attention to change and incident, should reproduce exactly the impressions we may gain from a series of static prescriptions. Rules are not biographies

---

[103] See Gregory the Great, *Ep.* 12.6; Venantius Fortunatus, *Carm.* VIII.1, and Greg. Tur. *Hist.* III.7, VI.29f.

[104] *Regula Benedicti* (ed. A. de Vogüé, 6 vols. (*SChrét.* 181–6)) LXXIII: *initium conversationis . . . hanc minimam inchoationis regulam*, ed. McCann, 160/162.

[105] Gregory the Great, *Dialogues* (ed. A. de Vogüé, 3 vols. (*SChrét.* 257, 260, 265)) II.36: *nullo modo potuit aliter docere quam vixit*, ed. De Vogüé, 2.242. Gregory's own point was that the *Rule* itself was almost a biography, a portrait of the man.

– a point to bear in mind when we consider the Pachomian corpus or the *vitae* of Gallic wonder-workers.

Nevertheless, Gregory did have points to make that were peculiar to himself. One should not underestimate the complexity of his motives. Like his *Pastoral Care*, the *Dialogues* bear the stamp of the former prefect; of a man used to the exercise of authority and skilful in political as well as moral rhetoric. The audience of the work was not merely ascetic, or even clerical: Gregory wished to present images of practical sanctity to Lombards as well as Romans, to the powerful of the visible world, with whom he felt he had now to collaborate. So his portrait of Benedict is somewhat marked by that context. The irony was that, whether in religious or political terms, neither Benedict nor Gregory could foresee with accuracy, let alone control, the Lombard future.

Central to the *Dialogues*, nevertheless, as to much else from Gregory's pen, was a more intimate concern for the relation between contemplation and action. That could be taken partly, although only partly, as a distinction between monastery and world. He wrestled with the problem of how one might make spiritual insight available to a busier society, without losing the tranquillity and perception of the contemplative state. (As for Benedict – by no means averse, as we shall see, to concern for the outside world – he believed that sustained attention to the realm of the spirit would automatically school a monk to usefulness in the service of others.)

The bishop of Rome was also preoccupied with the issue of authority and leadership. Who was fit to take the helm in yet another set of circumstances? – for the Lombards, occupying the vacuum left by Gothic collapse, had done so amidst widespread destruction, which heralded, in Gregory's view, the imminent end of the world.[106] Perhaps it was that sense of urgency that explained his determination to extend the boundaries of Christendom as far as he could, encouraging at least the beginnings of a missionary fervour among western churchmen. Monks had been no more enthusiastic for such an enterprise previously than any other leaders in the church. Their pastoral endeavours among desert tribesmen or mountain villagers had represented only tiny movements on the Mediterranean map. In the seventh century, by contrast, Columbanus and other exiles – *peregrini pro Christo* – were to develop a quite new enthusiasm for distant travel, even beyond the current boundaries of the empire, dragging disciples of Benedict and other pioneers in their wake. To that extent, at least, they provided circumstances in which a more deliberately pastoral policy, such as that of Gregory himself, could find support and promise growth.[107]

Finally, we would not expect a pope to be indifferent to the economic fortunes of the west, who administered estates under his own jurisdiction

---

[106] *Dial.* III.38.3 especially; see also III.37.21; IV.43.2. That sense of doom is widespread in Gregory's writings, especially in the *Moralia* and his commentary on *Kings*.

[107] Note the judicious caution of Wood, *Merovingian Kingdoms* 311–15.

with laborious scruple, and congratulated in his *Dialogues* a miraculous power among holy men that habitually averted flood and disease, enhanced fertility, and provided abundance in time of famine.

So the *Dialogues* placed Benedict in a broad ascetic context, much of it now familiar.[108] Alongside the many monasteries, described in the first book most of all, Gregory mentioned hermits and near-hermits,[109] and even ascetics who had come from the east, bringing with them customs that would not have seemed out of place in the writings of John of Ephesus or Cyril of Scythopolis.[110] Benedict's contemporaries and immediate disciples would have jostled with such assorted company. Among them we may even include the erudite Cassiodorus (about whom Gregory was silent), an exile in the east after his distinguished but finally embittered career in Ostrogothic government, and now returned to found something approaching a monastery at Vivarium.[111] In the matter of authority, bishops had some pre-eminence, as envisaged by Justinian's Pragmatic Sanction of A.D. 554; but Gregory could be surprisingly cautious about the extent of their control in monastic matters, and recommended in practise a very literal adherence to the precedents established at Chalcedon, keeping bishops well away from the internal affairs of communities, in Gaul as well as Italy. While the third book of the *Dialogues* was devoted to the thesis that bishops could be (or should be) as holy as anyone, and showed them at work among monks, Gregory did not disguise the fact that they could often be at odds with superiors, in spite of being sometimes monks themselves or presiding over ascetic households.[112] Holy men took their own initiatives, founding communities;[113] and, like the clergy, they claimed a right to judge and advise.[114] Not least because of that association, they were portrayed as natural evangelists, as well as supporters of the poor.[115] Laymen exercised a further patronage meanwhile, setting up buildings and even appointing superiors, although their generosity was occasionally rejected.[116] Within that framework of establishment, control and social concern, ascetics of all types worked the land, miraculously and otherwise. While

---

[108] Gregory included his own monastic experience, which may well have become disillusioned, wedged as it was between the careers of a prefect and a pope. His famous letter to Leander, *Ep.* 5.53ᵃ, admitted, in relation to the *quies monasterii, quia habendo non fortiter tenui, quam stricte tenenda fuerit, perdendo cognovi.* See also *Dial.* I, preface.   [109] *Dial.* III.14.2f., 16.1f., 17.1f., 18.1f.; IV.31.2f.

[110] Certainly Isaac the Syrian, living in a church and gathering disciples around himself, *Dial.* III.14.2–5. Possibly the cave-dwelling Martin criticized by Benedict for wearing chains, III.16.9. Probably the Menas of III.26.1f. See also IV.37.3f., 40.10f.

[111] Whatever justice allows us to think of him as a 'monk' has to be based on a reading of his *Institutions* (ed. Mynors (1937)), hardly the work of one *scienter nescius!*

[112] For examples of close bonds between ascetic and clerical careers, see *Dial.* I.4.3f., 9 *passim;* III.13.1, 22.1, 36.1; IV.33 *passim.* Much is implied less directly elsewhere. Gregory's caution was expressed mostly in his letters: see *Ep.* 3.58, 7.12, 13.12.   [113] *Dial.* I.1.3, IV.11.1f.

[114] *Dial.* II.23 and 25 make the connection with Benedict, basing authority on experience and insight.

[115] *Dial.* I.1.5f., 4.8; III.15.2, 34.2f.

[116] *Dial.* II.35.1 provides a detailed instance. See also II.22.1, III.15.2. Contrasting caution is betrayed in III.14.4f., IV.9.1. A peasant surrendered his goods to Benedict for safe keeping, II.31.1f.

some groups were reluctant to accept outside employment (Benedict could be particularly strict in that regard),[117] others hired themselves to neighbouring farmers in a fashion long traditional in the east.[118] 'I can lay claim to no particular profession', said one, 'but I do know how to keep a good garden.'[119] Gardens figure frequently in Gregory's account, hinting perhaps at the commonest form of material support for ascetics, the small-scale cultivation of vegetables.[120] Reference to endowment, therefore, need not suggest large properties;[121] but olives are mentioned, and some ascetics at least had land enough on which to grow grain for their annual needs.[122] Gregory's own correspondence provides useful details of endowments, especially where urban communities depended on revenue from rural properties.[123]

Benedict was presented also as a contemplative, in Gregory's special sense; *scienter nescius et sapienter indoctus*, to use the famous phrase: 'ignorant but informed, untutored but wise'.[124] Hidden in the 'desert' of Subiaco, he attracted disciples, while worrying about the threat to his *contemplatio*; a whole community of ascetics invited him to be their abbot.[125] His eventual influence was the inevitable outcome of his early discipline and understanding. He represented the era (documented no less by Gregory of Tours) when miracles were performed once more by the living and not simply at the tombs of the dead.[126] He founded monasteries of his own in conjunction with lay patrons, exercising that concern for other ascetics that was natural in a monk.[127] Nor did he forget to engage in preaching the Christian faith and alleviating need.[128]

Gregory wished to make one basic point. The *Rule* of Benedict, which he referred to and had undoubtedly consulted, was designed in his eyes to make a particular brand of sanctity available to society as a whole – society being here defined as the Christian church. That sanctity was at once perceptive, powerful and generous, schooled by reflection and service. The discipline of the *Rule* itself conformed entirely to that ideal. When it comes to the order of the monastic day, Cassian, Lérins, Caesarius and the 'Master' will have fortified us against surprises: the variations are in most respects minor and do not touch the essence of the 'Benedictine spirit'. Gregory's occasional references to buildings give solid shape to the way of life

---

[117] *Dial.* 1.7.5, II.12.   [118] *Dial.* 1.4.12, II.32.1f.
[119] *Dial.* III.1.3: *artem quidem aliquam nescio, sed hortum bene excolere scio*, ed. De Vogüé, 2.260.
[120] *Dial.* 1.3.2, 4.7; II.6.1; III.14.6f.; IV.23.1 (produce given to refugees).
[121] *Dial.* 1.7.2. Benedict's straitened circumstances in II.21.1f. hint at limited agricultural opportunities.   [122] *Dial.* 1.7.5; II.33.2; IV.20.2.
[123] *Ep.* 9.137 especially – a Roman example – and see also 2.10, 9.197, 13.12.
[124] *Dial.* II, preface. The paradox is repeated in III.37.20.   [125] *Dial.* II.1f.
[126] *Dial.* II.16.1. For the insight of the living preferred to the power of the dead, see IV.9.
[127] *Dial.* II.22 provides a vivid example. For the principle, see IV.11.3.
[128] Preaching, *Dial.* II.8.2, 19.1; generosity, II.28.1, in the context of 1.3.4 and IV.23.1f.

demanded in the *Rule* – the oratory for prayers, the refectory for common meals, a kitchen, and a hospice for strangers.[129] More important, however, is Benedict's constant attention to the foundations of community life. The abbot was master, but one above all who cared for the weak and was answerable to authorities beyond himself. He presided over a distinct and protected society, whose members varied in their strengths and abilities, although they were not thereby divided according to secular categories and expectations. This community prayed briefly and intensely, and dedicated itself otherwise to work and to service, remaining open always to requests and visitations. It saw itself as making no more than a start in religious devotion, and acknowledged the rich tradition from which it sprang.[130]

The simplicity and earnestness of the Benedictine *Rule* demands of us, as it demanded of the monk himself, an answer to the question: what was the purpose of those institutional experiments? The hesitancy of Benedict himself, the wealth of Gregory's *Dialogues*, the evident variety of ascetic practice, even at the end of the sixth century, all point to an enduring polarity, a cautious attempt to balance contrasting but compatible ambitions. On the one hand, one sought guidance in the development of insight and self-mastery, and preserved a sense of loyalty to ascetic masters and to fellow devotees. On the other hand, one sympathized with the weak and the needy, gave them what help one could, and worked to give more. Obscured at times by demonic fears and eccentric exaggerations, those motives remain evident in the anecdotal sources that provide so much of our information about the east. An attachment to discipleship, mutual encouragement and service was no less evident in western practice. The proliferation of *regulæ* and the textual problems that beset our understanding of their development, coupled with our knowledge that the *Rule* of Benedict did eventually gain paramount authority over an extensive and highly organized system of communities, can blind us to the similarity of practice and attitude that bound all ascetics together. And that consistency of motive and principle does most to remind us how asceticism was linked with and contributed to wider late Roman debates about authority, education and tradition.

There was, indeed, a theory of the ascetic life, widely known and constantly appealed to. Its embodiment in practical discipline was developed in the writings of Evagrius of Pontus (died 399), but the tradition was rooted in the works of Origen, and was extended in other ways by the contemporaries of Evagrius, Basil of Caesarea and the two Gregorys of

---

[129] *Dial.* ii.22.1; to which add ii.8.5, 9 and 10; iii.15.2.

[130] Abbot: *Regula Benedicti* iii.1f.; xxvii.6; lxiv.3f.; lxv. Seclusion: i and lxi. Categories of person: ii.12; but compare xlviii.23 with *Regula magistri* l, and see *Regula Benedicti* ii.18; xxi.4; lix.3. See Gregory's account in *Dial.* ii.20. Prayer: xx.3f. Work: preface, 14, 45. External relations: iv; liii.16; but lxvi.6f. is more aligned to the *Regula magistri*.

Nazianzus and Nyssa. The names of all those men recur constantly in the
ascetic literature of our later period. Cassian was a faithful disciple of
Evagrius; Dorotheus of Gaza, at the other end of the empire and period,
was steeped in the thought of Origen and the Cappadocians. (The date of
Dorotheus' death is unknown. After apprenticeship under the guidance of
Barsanuphius and John at Thavath – Hilarion's native village, close to the
settlement in exile of Esaias of Scetis – he established a monastery of his
own *c.* 540.)

Cassian's writings were charged with an Alexandrian optimism. The
ascetic was made in the image of God; and the perfection of that image,
the re-establishment of union with the creator, was in some sense a natural
expectation, based on the development of innate qualities. The path to
fulfilment lay in self-knowledge and self-mastery. Knowledge became
accurate and effective when λογισμοί, *cogitationes*, the constant movements
of thought and imagination, were identified, ordered and focused in tranquillity. Mastery, a parallel enterprise, consisted in control of πάθοι, *pas-
siones*, the clouded and disturbing movements of the heart. Every external
prescription was seen by Cassian as underpinning that interior task.[131]
'Thought' and 'passion' replaced the demon. The corresponding virtues
were seen as forming a unity. No success against anger, for example, would
weaken the struggle against greed: any step forward would bring its reward
in an integrated drama of self-possession. The result, albeit based on vigi-
lance and effort, was a genuine freedom: freedom from fear of one's own
inadequacy, of temptation, of judgement; freedom that accepted submission to others, because it guaranteed trust and affection. The gradual
achievement of that balance represented in part a movement from πρακτική to θεωρητική, from the 'active' to the 'contemplative' life. It gave
asceticism an historical dimension both personal and social. In the latter
case, the monk acquired a place in the general unfolding of salvation: the
purity of intention that had characterized the early Christians in Jerusalem,
compromised with time, was restored within the monasteries, set, therefore, at the heart of the church. (To that extent, Cassian shared the view of
Augustine.) In the individual's life, one might pass from coenobitic practice
to the more contemplative life of the hermit. In the event, as we know,
Cassian catered most for community life; and in the very passages where
he creates his more general history, he emphasizes the usefulness of asceticism in the company of others.[132]

Moving at once from Cassian to Dorotheus, from Latin back to Greek
and across more than a century, the tenacity of the spiritual tradition is
made obvious by the similarity of their approach. Dorotheus' allusions to
his Palestinian milieu combine the impression gained from Cyril of

---

[131] *Inst.* IV.32f.　　[132] *Con.* XVIII above all; but see also XVI.

Scythopolis with the traditions proper to Esaias and the Egyptian exiles around Gaza. The letters and responses of Barsanuphius continue to reflect the practices of the fifth and early sixth century: the *laura* system of solitaries surrounded by coenobites, served by their close disciples and badgered by the curiosity of laymen and clerics. It seems, however, that against both the rigour and the disorder of that world Dorotheus eventually revolted, feeling obliged to set up a community of his own, for which he wrote the Διδασκαλίαι Ψυχωφελεῖς, his *Instructions for the Help of Souls*. There was still plenty of reference to the practicalities of the monastic regime; to hard work and continuous reflection, with a characteristically eastern emphasis on exile, the life of the 'stranger'; and to respect for the traditions of the elders.[133] The more inward attainments, such as that of humility, Dorotheus' favourite virtue, were seen as part of a history of salvation, reversing Adam's pride; and the Evagrian focus on passion and corresponding virtue was faithfully maintained.[134] Dorotheus recommended constant consultation, the disclosure and assessment of λογισμοί. The relation of master and disciple was essentially one of trust, which was the only acceptable justification for obedience in the Pachomian tradition.[135] Dorotheus was also attentive, like Cassian and Benedict, to relations within the community: relations at once tactful, instructive and warm.[136] In a sense, he had reversed the direction of ascetic theory in a way that both Cassian and Euthymius had recognized: surrendering a passionate desire for ἡσυχία, the silence of the solitary life, in exchange for νῆψις, a tranquil self-possession induced in oneself by the company of others, and then offered to others as the best encouragement in a common task.

It is refreshing to find so sober and considerate a view of self-improvement surviving amidst the turmoil and untidiness of eastern ascetic practice. Successfully transplanted to the west in Cassian's works, it had also inspired both Benedict and Gregory the Great. Ascetics could be cruel both to themselves and to others, with little apparent benefit and a considerable degree of injustice. Yet enough of them paid heed to theoretical principle and held fast to the challenge of combining self-mastery and usefulness. The skill lay in pursuing a vision of God that avoided blindness to the needs and aspirations of others. Basil had known as much, and Pachomius. Nearly two centuries later, the ταπείνωσις, the humility of Dorotheus was echoed in Benedict's *dominici schola servitii*, the 'school of the Lord's service'.[137]

And for all his concern with theory, for all his emphasis on the inner life, there is enough anecdote in Dorotheus' text and enough humanity in the

---

[133] *Didasc.* XI provides many details of the regime; for other points, I.11, II.37, VI.69, XIV.153.
[134] *Didasc.* I.7, XII.134.
[135] See *Didasc.* v.61f., and *Ep.* 2. The attitude of VII.85 was essential to the ἀδιάκριτος ὑπακοή – so often translated 'blind obedience' – of I.25. [136] *Didasc.* IV *passim*, VI.77f., and *Ep.* I.180f.
[137] *Didasc.* I.7; *Regula Benedicti* preface, 45.

man himself to make his work a fitting conclusion to our whole investigation. For the chief impression given by ascetics in that age is of vigorous
independence. In the end, it is not the eccentricities of the hermit or the
discipline of the coenobite that captures chief attention. In particular, the
history of asceticism in the fifth and sixth century does not revolve around
the relative merits and victories of the eremitic and the coenobitic life.
True, much of ascetic literature adopts a position on one side or the other
in that debate; but that may have been a feature more of texts and their
authors than of less self-conscious devotees. Deeper than those social
configurations, there lay a firm belief in discipleship.

The practical implications of such belief were varied. Most obviously,
imitation and respect, perhaps even obedience, and certainly trust were
central to a disciple's life. The ascetic was also, along with the master, heir
to a tradition, partly oral, partly written, perceived in either case as orthodox, guaranteed to reflect and fulfil the will of God, encouraging 'a virtue
and morality that was worthy of the faith'.[138] Discipleship involved also
continuous application, a life of concentrated labour. Regardless of social
complexities, that labour was universally perceived as a mixture of prayer,
fasting and manual work. The quality above all that set that heritage in
motion was authority: an authority recognized in the master, and acquired
in turn by the disciple.

All else we have observed remained subordinate to those concerns. Even
in the most ordered and crowded community, the individual ascetic had
models to admire and personal goals to achieve; and both admiration and
achievement were often dependent on quite intimate relations. There was,
in the end, a hidden stillness to asceticism that community life, paradoxically, could only make more intense. Any doubts we may retain about the
reasonableness or honesty of late Roman asceticism rests precisely on the
ultimate inaccessibility of the individual spirit.

What we can discern, however, is the immense variety of behaviour that
resulted. Wherever we capture a close picture of the formed ascetic in
action, we observe an individual, a man or woman recognizably inspired by
widely accepted practices, but bringing to the tasks of self-improvement an
attitude and a taste entirely their own. 'Holiness', as understood at the time,
was not a matter of conformity to anything so transient as a regular regime,
but was based on the closest possible engagement with the invisible God.
Among those who might claim to have come nearest success, that inner
victory displayed itself upon the surface of each one's personality in ways
that no one else could lay claim to. If there was anything, nevertheless, that
they truly shared, it sprang only, in their eyes, from their being disciples of
a common Lord.

[138] Zach. *HE* 11.5.

CHAPTER 26

HOLY MEN

PETER BROWN

Some time in the 520s, the Great Old Man Barsanuphius, an Egyptian recluse, wrote from his cell in the vicinity of Gaza, in order to comfort a sick and dispirited monk:

> I speak in the presence of Christ, and I do not lie, that I know a servant of God, in our generation, in the present time and in this blessed place, who can also raise the dead in the name of Jesus our Lord, who can drive out demons, cure the incurable sick, and perform other miracles no less than did the apostles . . . for the Lord has in all places his true servants, whom he calls no more *slaves* but *sons* (Galatians 4.7) . . . If someone wishes to say that I am talking nonsense, as I said, let him say so. But if someone should wish to strive to arrive at that high state, let him not hesitate.
>
> (Barsanuphius, *Correspondance* 91, trans. Regnault (1971) 84)

Throughout the Christian world of the fifth and sixth century, the average Christian believer (like the sick monk, Andrew) was encouraged to draw comfort from the expectation that, somewhere, in his own times, even, maybe, in his own region, and so directly accessible to his own distress, a chosen few of his fellows had achieved, usually through prolonged ascetic labour, an exceptional degree of closeness to God. God loved them as his favoured children. He would answer their prayers on behalf of the majority of believers, whose own sins kept them at a distance from him. Thus, when the bubonic plague struck the eastern Mediterranean in 542/3, the Great Old Man wrote at once to reassure his monks on the state of the world:

> There are many who are imploring the mercy of God, and certainly no one is more a lover of mankind than he, but he does not wish to show mercy, for the mass of sins committed in the world stands in his way. There are, however, three men who are perfect before God, who have transcended the measure of human beings and who have received the power to bind and to loose, to remit our faults or to retain them. They *stand upright in the breach* (Psalms 105.23) to ensure that the world is not wiped out at one blow, and, thanks to their prayers, God will chastise with mercy . . . They are John, at Rome, Elias, at Corinth, and another in the province of Jerusalem. And I am confident that they shall obtain that mercy.
>
> (Barsanuphius, *Correspondance* 569, Regnault (1971) 369)

Himself a total recluse, Barsanuphius was unusual in the emphasis that he placed on the power of prayer alone, when offered by such saints. Of the three that he mentioned, one was studiously anonymous, and the other two are not known as 'holy men' from any other sources.

The modern historian of late antiquity, however, tends to approach the issue of sanctity from another direction. He is interested in the well-known phenomenon of the role allotted to living holy persons within the Christian communities, and, more generally, within the religious imagination of the period. What he wishes to find – and finds in impressive abundance – are the writings of those who believed in no uncertain terms that certain figures, 'servants of God', 'friends of God', 'men of God' (persons whom for want of a better term we tend to call 'holy men'), both existed and should be seen to exist. The historian, in fact, concentrates on sources that privilege the fully public deeds of holy men at the expense of the equally intense and effective power of prayer frequently ascribed to more reclusive persons, to holy women quite as much as holy men. This chapter will follow the grain of a modern historiographical interest, in that it isolates for examination one category only of holy persons: it will be about 'holy men', about those 'servants of God', that is, whom contemporaries believed to have been specially chosen by God, in their own time, as in past ages, to show forth the power of his arm, through the *coruscatio*, the forceful lightning-flash, of visible miracles.

Holy men of this kind played a crucial role in the religious imagination of many late antique persons. They made the Christian God present in their own age and locality; and they did so to such an extent that disbelief came to focus less on the existence of the Christian God so much as on his willingness to provide a distant human race – and especially the unkempt inhabitants of a given region – with the crowning mercy of palpable human agents of his will. At the same time as Barsanuphius, near Gaza, was writing his letters, a farmer on the high plateau behind the coastline of Lycia was unimpressed when told by his neighbour of visits to the holy man, Nicholas of Sion:

What is this 'servant of God'? As the Lord God lives, I would not put my trust in any man on earth.   (*Life*, 22, ed. Ševčenko and Ševčenko (1984) 43)

Lapidary though such statements of belief and disbelief might be, their very trenchancy served to veil – from contemporaries quite as much as from modern historians – a whole range of conflicting assumptions that surrounded the figure of the holy man in late antiquity. The very possibility that such persons might exist raised basic questions on the relations between God and human beings that received sharply different answers in different Christian regions.

That sanctity, when achieved, should show itself at all to the world in the form of popular and much sought-after physical 'signs' – such as healing, exorcism, successful intercessory prayer for safety from natural disasters, prophecy, blessing and cursing – was an issue that caused the finest representatives of the selfsame ascetic tradition that produced the overwhelming majority of holy persons to think carefully about what such a gift might mean to those who had received it, and how it should be best deployed. Thus Gregory the Great, in Rome, would 'draw ever new refreshment' from tales told by old men of the deeds of the holy men and women of his native Italy, in his *Dialogues* (Gregory, *Dialogi* 1.10.20). Yet, in the same years, he could write to warn the monk Augustine in A.D. 601 of the very real spiritual perils involved in living up to current expectations as a wonder-working missionary among the barbarians of Kent:

for the weak mind may be raised up by self-esteem, and so the very cause for which it is raised on high, through honour from outsiders, may lead, through vainglory, to an inner fall.   (Gregory, *Registrum* xi.36; also in Bede, *HE* 1.31)

No agreement was reached on such matters by Christian writers of the period. From the Iona of Columba (who died in the same year, 597, as Augustine reached Kent from Rome) to the Nestorian communities of Mesopotamia, Iran and central Asia (whose representatives reached China in the same generation) an unmistakably late antique Christian language of the holy, that expected 'servants of God' to make themselves known to the world at large by 'signs', was spoken in a number of quite distinctive local dialects. Given this situation, the purpose of this chapter is twofold. First, to use the abundant evidence for attitudes towards the activities of living holy persons in various Christian regions to bring into clearer focus, through significant contrasts, the principal outlines of a human geography of the holy within widely differing Christian communities. The second follows from this: it is to seize the characteristics of the period as a whole, from A.D. 425 to around 630, as one stage among many in the long process of Christianization. For the activities of the Christian holy man provide precious evidence for the slow building up, in different ways and in different regions, of what Norman Baynes once called a 'thought-world',[1] a thought-world that came to form the basis of the religious culture of Byzantium, of the medieval west and of the Christian communities of the middle east. It is easy to forget how slowly this thought-world took on unambiguously Christian features in the late antique period. Yet part of the fascination of the Christian hagiography of these centuries is that it enables us to glimpse Christianity itself against its wider background. Christianity

[1] Baynes (1960) 24–46.

appears more clearly in such texts than in any others as a relative newcomer, perched against a very ancient spiritual landscape, whose principal contours, in the form of notions of the nature and function of the holy, had existed long before the rise of the Christian church to public favour. Immovably, if indistinctly, visible out of the corner of the eye in even the most unambiguously Christian texts, these permanent features were renamed or subjected to selective inattention through the very act of recording the hagiographic evidence that has come down to us. As a result, the writing of the lives of active Christian saints became, for contemporaries, a way of learning how to view the supernatural world in Christian terms. The very repetitiveness and stereotyped form of the great majority of our hagiographic sources, qualities which prove tiresome to historians who have tended to use such sources as precious evidence for the day-to-day realities of late Roman society, underline their role as part of a far larger process. Piled one on top of the other over the generations, such stories insensibly steered purveyor and audience alike towards particular views of the working of the holy in the world, and tacitly excluded others.

It is not surprising, therefore, that the period should begin with what would soon become 'classic' works of hagiography, designed to capture the dazzling quality of the heroes of a 'second Apostolic age'.[2] Sulpicius Severus' *Life of Martin* (of 396) and the further defence of his hero's reputation in the *Dialogues* (of 404–6), the *Historia Monachorum* and *Ecclesiastical History* of Rufinus (of 402), the *Lausiac History* of Palladius (of 420) and Theodoret of Cyrrhus' *History of the Friends of God* (of 440) have a stark, black-and-white quality about them: we see the late Roman world lit up in great lightning-flashes coming from the direction of the desert. At the end of our period, by contrast, we are dealing with a 'late classical' flowering of a hagiography marked, rather, by a sense of the holy that is as infinitely differentiated as the tints of an autumn landscape. Cyril of Scythopolis, in his lives of the monks of Palestine (of 558),[3] Gregory, bishop of Tours (573–94), in his *History* and *Eight Books of Miracles* (of the early 590s),[4] the Monophysite John of Ephesus' *Lives of the Eastern Saints* (of the late 560s),[5] the *Spiritual Meadow* of the Chalcedonian, John Moschus (of around 614),[6] the *Dialogues* of Gregory the Great (of 593–4)[7] and the slightly later *Lives* of Symeon the Holy Fool of Emesa and of John the Almsgiver by Leontius of Neapolis (of 641–2)[8] show us a world where the full range of the holy has come to be caught in a fine web of Christian words. A recent study of the workings of social memory has made plain that stories exist to

[2] Ruggini (1981) and Thélamon (1981).   [3] Tr. Price (1991); Flusin (1983).
[4] Esp. *Vita Patrum* tr. James; Van Dam (1988).
[5] Tr. E. W. Brooks, *Lives of the Eastern Saints*, in PO XVII–XIX (1923–5); Harvey, *Asceticism and Society in Crisis*.   [6] Trans. Wortley (1992). Chadwick (1974).   [7] Ed. De Vogüé, *Dialogues*.
[8] Mango (1984a) and Déroche (1995).

provide us with a set of stock explanations which underlie our predisposition to interpret reality in the ways that we do.[9]

In the hagiography of the late sixth century, we are dealing with just this. There is hardly an incident connected with the holy, from Tours to Amida (modern Diyarbekir, eastern Turkey), which is not placed within a narrative framework whose very banality and strong sense of *déjà vu* serves to make it seem utterly matter-of-fact – that this is how the holy works, and in no other way.

It is important to have lingered over the nature of the sources that the historian uses in approaching the holy man. They give the impression that the 'holy man' existed largely in the eye of the believer. This, of course, was not the whole story. Contemporaries believed that sanctity was achieved through ascetic labour, through humility and through the grace of God, according to long traditions of spiritual guidance, of which we have more abundant evidence for this period, the golden age of Christian ascetic wisdom, than that provided by the vivid *Lives* of the saints, which form the basis of modern studies of late antique hagiography. Yet, reassuring – even infectious – though the undemonstrative sanctity of many Christian men and women might be to their fellow believers, contemporaries wanted something more from a holy man. Even though he might be careful always to present himself as no more than one humble 'servant of God' among many, in the quiet manner of a mature monastic tradition, the holy man was frequently approached, in his own lifetime, as

a brilliant star, spreading its rays . . . an unshakeable column . . . who puts demons to flight, who gives healing to the sick, a father to orphans, a food-supply to the poor, a covering to the homeless . . . a source of repentance to all sinners and a staff to the indigent. (*Life of Theodore of Sykeon* 2, ed. Festugière (1970) 2)

To find anything else was disappointing. A peasant who had walked in to Ancona to visit the holy man Constantius was very surprised to be shown a little man perched half-way up a ladder, busily lighting the lamps of the shrine. He had, of course, expected to find a *grandis homo*, a Big Man (Greg. *Dial.* 1.5.5).

Certainly, the holy man came to be seen as such in retrospect. He was almost invariably presented in this manner by those who had developed a strong interest in his reputation – most often by disciples connected with a monastic establishment that had grown perilously large in the lifetime of the saint, and that faced a recession of gifts and visitors once the glory of his living presence had departed. The Syriac *Panegyric* on Symeon Stylites (396–459) was an oratorical performance, designed for the annual gathering

---

[9] Fentress and Wickham (1992) 51.

that commemorated the greatest rain miracle of his career. It was a verbal accompaniment to the spectacular new architecture of the pilgrimage shrine set up around the base of what was now an empty column – a shrine complete with baptistery, monastery, guest-hostel and triumphal way leading up from the plain, that had come to weigh heavily on a once open site occupied by the living Symeon on the limestone ridge at Telnesin.[10] Besa's *Life* of Shenoute of Atripe (385–466) was written for a similar occasion – the annual festival of the great abbot, celebrated beneath the lowering walls of the White Monastery.[11] From Iona to Telnesin and upper Egypt, the *Life* of a saint was less a biography than a recital of *virtutes*, of deeds of power. It was narrated in such a way as to keep alive the expectation that such power would remain available to the pious for as long as the respect once shown to its dead wielder continued to be shown by the outside world to the monastery that guarded the holy man's memory.[12]

Apart from the precious letters of Barsanuphius and fragments of sources, such as the *ostraka* of Epiphanius, a late-sixth-century hermit of Thebes, we seldom catch a holy man in action through documents that stem from himself – still less do we hear him talk about himself. As 'servants of God', many holy men simply placed a high value on self-effacement. But there is more to it than that: a public man in an ancient, epic tradition, the holy man as we usually meet him in his *vita*, was condemned, by the writers of hagiography, to 'utter externality'.[13] It is only where we would least expect it, from the Atlantic coast of fifth-century Ireland, that we learn from the *Confessio* of Patricius the Briton (now known to us as St Patrick) of what it was like to respond, as a slave in Mayo, to the call of holiness in its late antique Christian form:

But after I reached Ireland, well, I pastured the flocks every day and I used to pray many times a day: more and more did my love of God and my fear of Him increase, and my faith grew and my spirit stirred, and as a result I would say up to a hundred prayers in one day, and almost as many at night; I would even stay in the forests and on the mountain and would wake to pray before dawn in all weathers, snow, frost, rain: and I felt no harm and there was no listlessness in me – as I now realise, it was because the Spirit was fervent within me.

(Patricius, *Confessio* 16, trans. A. B. E. Hood, *St Patrick*.
London and Chichester (1978) 44)

What matters for our account, however, as it did for many contemporaries, was how a closeness to God, gained preferably in the wild, was seen to act in the settled world. On this subject each late antique writer of hagiography had his own firm notions of what constituted an appropriate narrative

---

[10] Doran (1992).   [11] Besa, *Vita Sinuthii* 1, tr. Bell (1983) 41.
[12] A fact seen most clearly in the reception of late antique hagiography in Ireland: Picard (1982) and Herbert (1988).   [13] Bakhtin (1981) 133.

of the emergence and function of a holy person. Let us pass from west to east, looking largely at the hagiography of the late sixth century, in order to establish the distinctive features of what folklorists have called the 'oiko-type', the 'home type', the 'locally standardized species' of accounts that both justified and delimited the activities of holy persons in differing Christian environments.[14]

The hagiography of Gaul – not only the works of Gregory of Tours but also earlier sources such as the *Lives of the Fathers of the Jura*[15] – suggest a reticence in the face of living holy men which is, at first sight, surprising in a world that consciously looked back to the classic study of a holy man in action, written by an exact contemporary – the *Life of Martin* by Sulpicius Severus. But it is easy to forget that, with Sulpicius, the memory of Martin lingered for more than a generation as the special preserve of a profoundly alienated segment of the Christian aristocracy of Gaul.[16] Martin's miracles were presented by Sulpicius himself as the desperate last gestures of a prophet in a darkening world. They were performed, in part, to counter the appeal of Antichrist, who, so Martin informed his disciples, had been born in the east and was already a boy of eight (Sulp. Sev. *Dial.* 11.14).

A mood of ambivalence about the claims of living holy persons settled heavily on the Christianity of Gaul. It went back to the *cause célèbre* of Priscillian, who had, after all, been known to have prayed successfully for rain, and yet had ended his life executed as a common sorcerer.[17] The uncertain light of the imagined approach of Antichrist heightened the need for caution. All too many wonder-working 'prophets' came to enjoy a Christ-like veneration in Gaul and Spain in the course of the fifth and sixth century. They turned out to be 'pseudo-prophets', troubling heralds of Antichrist's presence in the world (Sulp. Sev., *V. Mart.* 24; Greg. Tur. *Hist.* x.25). In the panic that accompanied the Hunnish invasion of 451, St Genovefa narrowly escaped being stoned by the citizens of Paris as one such 'pseudo-prophet' (*V. Genovefae* 12, ed. Krusch, *MGH, Script. rer. Mer.* 3 (1896) 219).

At the same time, devout aristocrats who admired those monks who followed in the footsteps of Martin, such as were the late-fifth-century hermits of the Jura, tended to keep memories of the holy 'in the family', as it were, through intense but inward-looking networks of spiritual friendship. The senatorial lady Syagria, for instance, kept the letters of St Eugendus locked away in a cupboard 'to kiss *in lieu* of the right hand of the blessed man', biting on them with her teeth in urgent search for healing (*V. Eugendi, V. Patr. Jur.* iii.12, ed. Martine (1968) 145–6).

One suspects that in Gaul exacting social codes of diffidence among pious aristocrats – oligarchic codes, partly moulded by envy and by a dislike

---

[14] Fentress and Wickham (1992) 74.   [15] Ed. Martine (1968).   [16] Stancliffe (1983) 265–312.
[17] Chadwick (1976).

of *parvenus* of any kind, spiritual or social – combined with a sincere monastic fear of vainglory. *Elatio* might ensue from any display of miraculous
powers, thereby turning the quiet 'temple of the heart' into a 'place of merchandise'. Self-interested drives might creep into the heart of a monk, once
he had the reputation of a wonder-worker to maintain in the face of a notoriously exacting audience of clients (*V. Lupicini, V. Patr. Jur.* 11.15, 114).
Only when dead and in the peace of God's paradise could those dramatic
manifestations of spiritual power and effective patronage, that had been
latent in the soul of the living holy man, blaze forth for the good of all,
because freed by death from the all-too-human stain of vanity (*V. Lupicini,
V. Patr. Jur.* 11.16, 117).

When, in the 580s, Gregory of Tours began to look back to find memories of the holy men of his region, his failure to record more than a few
such persons reflected a complicated situation. On the one hand, as a
Gallo-Roman bishop, he had a strong interest in asserting the pre-eminent
importance of the shrine of his own city, that of St Martin of Tours. But,
loyal though he was to the cults of his adopted city and of his family,
Gregory had no insuperable aversion to other forms of Christian sanctity.
Local memory may have let him down. Though holy men and women had
doubtless played decisive roles, in their own lifetime, in extending the reach
of Christianity far beyond the cities into the countryside of Gaul, Spain
and the Rhine estuary,[18] they did not attract memories that were as enduring as those associated, in Gregory's mind and, one suspects, in the circles
within which he moved, with the urban tombs of the few great, long-dead
bishops. It was around these tombs that the faithful tended to swarm, 'like
happy bees around their hive', leaving on them a patina of expectations of
posthumous acts of power, as they begged the custodian priest for

pieces of wax . . . a little dust . . . a few threads of the tomb-covering, all carrying
off for some specific purpose the same grace of health.

(Greg. Tur. *Vita Patrum* VIII.6)

One need only compare the *Lives of the Fathers* of Gregory of Tours with
the *Life of Euthymius* of Cyril of Scythopolis, written in 556, to realize the
extent of the lacuna brought about by the absence, in Gaul, of enduring
'fixatives' for the memory of holy living persons. In the monastic communities of the Judaean desert, memory itself could stand still for over a
century. The miracles that Cyril witnessed in 544 at the tomb of Euthymius,
who had been buried in 473, in the underground cave that had served him
as a cell, took place as long after Euthymius' death as did any which
Gregory witnessed among the tombs of Gaul. But the links between the
generations were stronger in a world of great monasteries than they were

---

[18] See esp. Hillgarth (1987), which corrects Brown (1981) 18–127, and Delaplace (1992).

among the more hesitant Christian communities of Gaul. Memory was supported by the intense and stable relationship of spiritual fathers to their disciples: John the Hesychast, the spiritual father of Cyril, had himself been the spiritual son of Sabas, who had, in turn, been directed, in his choice of monastery, by none other than Euthymius. In the monastic foundations of the area, every rock, cave and wadi told its own, unmoving story of former ascetic occupants. As a result, Cyril, writing at the end of the reign of Justinian, was able to reach back into the very first decades of the fifth century (Cyr. Scyth. *V. Euthymii* 60).

When Gregory the Great wrote his *Dialogues* in Rome in 593/4 (a decade later, that is, than Gregory of Tours' *Libri Miraculorum*), he also found himself confronted with mere shards of local memory. Lombard invasions in the past twenty years had destroyed many of the sites that had once been associated with holy men. Benedict's Monte Cassino had been sacked; the sieve that hung in the church at Nursia as testimony to his first miracle had disappeared; Lombard raids had effectively wiped out the ecclesiastical organization of many of the cities of Campania and the Apennines that had boasted holy ascetics in more sheltered times. Though he claimed to write about the 'modern fathers' of Italy, Gregory looked back, in much of his *Dialogues*, across the chasm of the Lombard invasion to the stormy days of Totila's last stand against the Byzantine armies in 546–51 and even, further still, into the peaceful last decades of unchallenged Ostrogothic rule.[19] The days were long past when good bishop Boniface of Ferentis had provided a pair of Goths travelling to the court at Ravenna with a miraculously inexhaustible bottle of wine, and when the holy man Florentius sat quietly in the hills above Nursia, with a pet bear who knew the time of day (Greg. *Dial.* 1.9.4; III.15.4). All this must have seemed poignantly distant to the beleaguered pope of the 590s.

Effectively wrenched, by warfare and emigration, from their local context, the memories that came to Gregory could be organized, by him, according to an 'oikotype' that existed, largely, in his own, resolutely Augustinian mind. The *Dialogues* took the form of a spiritual conversation between Gregory and his loyal friend, the Roman deacon Peter. No other writer of the age was in such a position, or had such a firm intention, to pass local narratives through a theological filter of so fine a mesh.[20]

With Gregory, miracles were far more than an occasion for vainglory – as they were also for Gregory of Tours – sensitive though he was to that aspect of the problem. They were *signa*, signals sent from a distant God through human agents on whom he had conferred the strictly temporary grace of the ability to work wonders and to see, with his own eyes, the hidden things of his providence. For Gregory, to be holy was to cling to

[19] A fact well seen by Cracco (1992).   [20] McCready (1989).

God, to make his will one's own (Greg. *Dial.* 11.23.1). Hence the deep religious dread that might fall on even the most supercilious observer of a holy
man. Abbot Equitius, unselfconsciously tossing hay in his hobnailed boots,
was a man who carried with him nothing less than the awesome weight of
the presence of God (Greg. *Dial.* 1.4.13–14). Yet Gregory was too loyal a
follower of Augustine to believe that an alignment of the human will with
that of God might never waver (Greg. *Dial.* 11.16.7). No permanent and
ever-increasing effervescence of the Holy Spirit could overcome the daily
ruin of the ascetic's fallen human nature. Far from it: nothing was more calculated to upset the fragile equilibrium of the soul's commune with God
than were those outward signs which, from time to time, God willed that a
person of tested sanctity might perform for the good of others. Like the
abrupt flashes of a signalling light, miracles could dazzle those who performed them, even while they arrested the attention of those stubborn
minds who needed the physical challenge of a miracle.

In this attitude, Gregory reached back, through Augustine, to one of the
most austerely intellectualist and anti-materialist traditions of late
Platonism. To perform a miracle was to turn away from the inner, spiritual
fire of contemplation, to view the fainter radiance of God's workings in
the mere world of matter (Greg. *Moralia* 11.91 and xxx.8). Prolonged
engagement in the *publica operatio* of miracles was calculated to place the
unreflective wonder-worker on the edge of a slippery slope. Miracles could
be as certain a cause of the fall of the soul into the world of material cares
as was the burden of public involvement in the fate of the church, under
which, as bishop of Rome, Gregory himself had come to groan, like a giant
straining beneath the oceanic weight of episcopal office. Yet, like bishops,
miracles had their place in God's scheme for the human race, even in
modern times. Gregory's unflinching sense of public mission was bolstered by a robust faith that, in a harmonious *cosmos*, material sign and spiritual reality were never utterly incommensurable: a miracle might point
without ambiguity to the higher, more enduring, spiritual realities that it
made visible, in a single, stunning moment of time.[21] Lingering with frank
patriotism on the narratives of his native land, Gregory, for all his warnings to the less guarded Peter, allowed himself to take comfort in *tam
iucunda miracula*, in so many, sweetly-tempered miracles that showed that
God, at least, had not deserted Italy (Greg. *Dial.* 111.22.4). Only in the chill
shadow of the reign of Antichrist, by contrast with which even Gregory's
own troubled times might seem, on looking back, times of deep peace,
would the church have to face the world with mere words, stripped of its
present dignity – the gift of miracles (Greg. *Moralia* xv.69; xix.16; xxxii.24
and xxxiv.7).

---

[21] Straw (1988) 47–89.

A loyal, if careworn, subject of the east Roman emperors, Gregory had resided for some time in Constantinople. He knew that he did not write in a vacuum. He was careful to enunciate his own, distinctively Latin, 'dialect' of the holy with all the more clarity because he knew that other, subtly different variants of a Christian language of the holy existed in the east. What we find, above all in Syria, but also in Palestine, Egypt and a little later in Constantinople and Asia Minor, are dialects of the holy which, though they differed greatly among themselves, tended to differ even more from those current in the west. They invested living persons with a degree and, above all, with a stability of sanctity that men such as Gregory of Tours and even Gregory the Great preferred to ascribe only to the holy dead. Even when we make due allowance for the fact that much of our evidence reflects the state of mind of great pilgrimage sites, which needed to foster stable and generous expectations of the powers of their wonder-working heroes, we are confronted, in the hagiography of the eastern empire, with a significantly different view of the human person.

The great holy men of the eastern empire were, indeed, 'mourners'. They were penitents, publicly crushed beneath the weight of their own sins. Their fully visible self-mortifications played out, on a heroic scale, the contrition and profound sense of human frailty which every believer was expected to feel, but which few were called upon to experience with such exquisite sensibility. But repentance of epic dimensions was widely deemed to have brought holy persons to a state of loving familiarity with God. The veil which, since Adam's fall, had descended between mankind and the angelic hosts around the throne of God had been worn thin by their prayers. It had become transparent to their tear-worn eyes. Indeed, when Symeon Stylites first mounted his column at Telnesin and, a little later, began to sway backwards and forwards, bowing with a dizzying frequency that riveted the attention of all onlookers – a servant of Theodoret of Cyrrhus counted up to 1,244 such prostrations before giving up – it was because, clearly visible to Symeon, an angel was perpetually bowing in just the same manner before the eucharistic bread that was stored in a little stone niche on one side of his column (Theodoret, *HR* xxvi.22; *V. Sym. Syr.* 98, Doran (1992) 171–2).

For Symeon, perhaps, and certainly for those reared in a mature Syrian tradition who came to watch him, the holy man was, in himself, a 'living sign'. His dramatic way of life was more than the distant blink of a signal from God. It made present with almost perfect congruence in the visible world realities that usually lay beyond human sight. It is as if the angelic world itself had pushed through the veil, to become fully palpable in the figure perched on his column above the plain at Telnesin.[22]

---

[22] Harvey (1988), (1998).

For a human being to stand, in such an unambiguous manner, as an 'angel' among men required a gift of the Holy Spirit more all-consuming and definitive than that bestowed upon each Christian by the grace of baptism (or, to put it differently, a more robust emergence of that grace than was the case with the average believer). Belief in the fervour of the Spirit, that had stirred in Patricius on the coast of Mayo, was taken for granted in Syria. It rested on the firm foundations of a prestigious and long-established theological tradition. It was as bearers of the Holy Spirit, their whole nature 'mixed' with its inspiring energy as inseparably as the fragrance of myrrh penetrated the heavy oil base of a perfume, that Syrian Christians had been accustomed, for centuries, to make Christ present and palpable in this world.

As a result, claims to which Greek bishops had reacted with instant suspicion in the early fifth century, when made on behalf of nameless groups of believers – who earned from their enemies the heresiological label of 'Messalians' (persons who were held to believe that the deep-seated force of evil might be irrevocably driven from the human soul by unremitting, fervent prayer) – were taken for granted as underlying the spiritual achievements of the *nouvelle vague* of stylite hermits and, a little later, despite initial resistance, of the analogous Syrian phenomenon of the 'Sleepless' monks (monks, that is, devoted to unceasing prayer). The holy man settled down, throughout the eastern Mediterranean, as a 'licensed Messalian'.[23]

In both cases, practices that originated in Syria broke through previous cultural frontiers, creating an 'international style' of demonstrative Christian sanctity. 'Stylite', 'hermit' and 'recluse' tended to merge in the terminology of the times. They could be found everywhere. A female stylite is recorded outside Amasea (Amasya) in Pontus. In Egypt, a male stylite is found, according to one papyrus, arranging for a donkey driver to bring water in daily instalments to the monastery that had grown up, apparently at the foot of his column, at Antinoe. Far to the east, in the foothills of the Zagros mountains, Monophysite stylites perched ominously, 'like carrion vultures', on the edge of hostile Nestorian villages.[24] They had come to stay. Consulted by a Muslim leader in the course of the civil wars which accompanied the end of the Umayyad dynasty in the mid eighth century, a stylite attached to a Palestinian monastery answered:

If I tell thee the truth, thou wilt slay me; yet I will declare what God has revealed to me. With the measure with which thou hast measured it shall be measured to thee.

He was proved right on both counts.

[23] Stewart (1991) and Escolan (1999).
[24] Anderson and Cumont (1910) no. 134, 146; *Papyri Greek and Egyptian: In Honour of Eric Gardiner Turner* (1981) no. 54, 198–203; Thomas of Marga, *Book of Governors* III.8, tr. E. A. W. Budge (London 1893) 330–3 and 363.

When Marwan heard this, he commanded that the pillar should be overthrown; and he brought down the old man, and burnt him alive in the fire.

(*History of the Patriarchs of Alexandria* 1.18, ed. B. Evetts, *PO* v.156)

It is some indication of the shifting frontiers of many such Christian dialects of the holy that the *laus perennis*, the 'sleepless' chant of the monks, was soon established in Burgundy and in the Franche-Comté (then, as in the sixteenth century, a frontier zone of piety between the Mediterranean and the north).[25] By contrast, Wulfilaic, a Lombard holy man who had grown up in northern Italy, close to the Byzantine exarchate of Ravenna, received a cool reception in northern Gaul. The bishop of Trier told him to get off his column. There was no place for a *homo ignobilis* such as himself to become the Symeon Stylites of northern Gaul (Greg. Tur. *Hist.* viii.15).

Given the nature of our sources, it is relatively easy to evoke the various, agreed local versions of the place that holy persons might occupy in the memory and expectations of distinct Christian regions. It is less easy to explain the rise and function of the holy man in terms of the wider social and religious world in which he was expected to be active. Here we are faced by a problem of perspective. The foreground of the life and activities of the holy man is supremely well known to us. Vivid and deliberately circumstantial evidence presents the holy man interacting with all manner of persons. The emphasis is placed on specific incidents of healing, good advice, cursing and successful intercession, both with God in heaven and with the powerful on earth. Yet, seen in terms of these sharply delineated actions, the holy man stands out, like a figure in a Chinese landscape, against an indistinct and seemingly measureless background. How to relate foreground and background, the known activities of the holy man with their wider social and religious implications; and hence how to explain their overall significance for contemporaries and their relative importance in relation to other forms of religious activity has remained a tantalizing problem. It is a problem that admits no single, unambiguous solution. Let us, therefore, begin with what is easiest to know, with the foreground.

It must never be forgotten that the holy man's activities, though usually presented in the sources as dramatic and exceptional, were no more than a highly visible peak in a spiritual landscape that rose gently upwards from the expectations and activities of ordinary Christians in towns and villages. A community of believers, endowed by baptism with the gift of the Holy Spirit, all Christians were potentially 'holy'. In late antique conditions, this fact was expected to be shown by the possession of spiritual powers. To take one well-known example: Augustine's mother, Monica, took for granted that she would receive God-given, premonitory dreams; and

[25] Wood (1981) 16.

Augustine himself believed that he had been cured of toothache by the
prayers of his friends at Cassiciacum, not all of whom were even baptized
(Aug. *Conf.* VI.xiii.23 and IX.iv.12). What Christian writers felt that they
needed to explain was not so much the miraculous gifts of the holy man
but, rather, why such gifts appeared to contemporaries to have drained
away from the average members of the community of believers on to the
persons of a few recipients of divine *charismata* (*Apostolic Constitutions* VIII.1:
PG 1.1061).

Low profile and intermittent expectations of help and comfort from
religious persons (pious men and women and members of the local clergy)
remained usual in any Christian community. The 'religious person', the *vir
religiosus*, the *femina religiosa*, was watched carefully by his or her neighbours
for evidence of virtue and, hence, of spiritual powers that might prove
useful to others. A layman complained to Barsanuphius about himself that
his retiring disposition, his unwillingness to get involved in local politics
and his unusual sexual modesty when visiting the public baths had already
given him an embarrassing reputation for being a holy person
(Barsanuphius, *Correspondance* 771, Regnault (1971) 472). The further step,
to a demand for a show of spiritual power, was a short one. Faced by a nest
of angry wasps, the harvesters of Besne, near Nantes, turned to Friardus,
half in jest and half in earnest:

Let the religious fellow come, the one who is always praying, who makes the sign
of the cross on his eyes and ears, who crosses himself whenever he goes out of
the house.   (Greg. Tur. *Vita Patrum* X.1)

Only Friardus had the power to halt wasps.

Healing substances circulated freely. 'Oil of prayer' could be obtained
from the lamps around the altar of any number of churches, and might be
applied with the prayers of any person with even a moderate reputation for
holiness.[26] In his exile in Amasea (Amasya, Turkey) the patriarch Eutychius
of Constantinople settled down in his monastery to function, in a small
way, as a wonder-worker. A man blinded for perjury was healed by the
prayers of Eutychius after three days of anointing with oil. A woman who
had difficulties with breast-feeding ended up being able to act as wet-nurse
to all the children of her neighbourhood (Eustratius, *V. Eutychii* 58 and 60:
PG LXXXVI.2.2340A and 2341C).

In this world of unspectacular but constant resort to persons with a reputation for sanctity, women, in certain regions, could be quite as important
as men, if not more so. Living at home or in convents close to the city or
village, safely protected from the very real dangers of the wild in which holy
men were supposed to gain their sanctity, holy women were as central to

[26] Till (1960) no. 261, 64.

the supernatural economy of any settled community as was the local well. It was increasingly difficult to believe that men who had not, at some time, vanished into the antithesis of settled life could be fully holy. But women could not vanish from society in this way. Hence the peculiar charge of the holy woman. Profound sanctity and efficacy in prayer was, as it were, trapped by the constraints of society, in an almost uncanny manner, just around the corner. It was enough to look down 'with worldly thoughts' from one's rooftop on to Modegundis at prayer, in her back garden in Tours, to be struck blind (Greg. Tur. *Vita Patrum* xix.1).

Female sanctity was an essential feature of urban life. It was good to come with other married women on Fridays and Saturdays to listen to Febronia read the scriptures in the chapel attached to the local convent (*V. Febroniae* 1.6: *Acta Sanctorum, Jun. V.* 19B, tr. Brock and Harvey (1987) 155). It was reassuring for the *matronae* of Paris to join Genovefa in the baptistery of the cathedral, to hold vigil as the Hunnish armies swept across the plains of Champagne (*V. Genovefae* 12, ed. Krusch 219). Pious women, quite as much as men, were indispensable nodal points, who transmitted the energy of their prayers to a continuous circuit of well-known healing substances, words and gestures which ran through every Christian neighbourhood. A vine leaf moistened with her spittle and the sign of the cross made by her fingers were enough to cure a little boy brought to Modegundis of an agonizing stomach ache (Greg. Tur. *Vita Patrum* xix.3).

Thus, when believers went out to a holy man, they often travelled considerable distances and arrived at a site associated, whenever possible, with the wild antithesis to the settled land. They came as pilgrims, to find

in a 'far' milieu, the basic elements and structures of [their] faith in their unshielded, virgin radiance.[27]

What they usually got, in fact, was 'home cooking'. The supplicants of holy men received exactly the same banal remedies for their ills as circulated at home. But these were now applied by hands known without doubt to be holy, at a place shorn of the disillusionments of everyday life. Precisely because he was thought to be a 'living sign', the holy man could make present to the believer the fiery angels who were forever transparent to his own eyes. Solemn angelic figures, that now stood largely unheeded on the walls of the local churches, became, for an instant, present and active in the sufferer's cure (*V. Sym. Jun.* 39, ed. Van den Ven (1962) 39).

It was the same with the words of the holy man. Any student of the spirituality of the Christian east, as it achieved classical form in this period, knows the primary importance of the link between spiritual father and disciple in the monastic tradition. Centuries of late classical and Christian

---

[27] Turner and Turner (1978) 15.

thought on self-formation had produced the conclusion that full knowledge of the self was possible only for those who were prepared, as spiritual sons, to see their own souls through the quiet eyes of an Old Man.[28]
The Old Man alone, wrote John of Gaza to a monk in an adjoining monastery, 'is absolutely not the plaything of demons' (Barsanuphius,
Correspondance 373, Regnault (1971) 263). Such guidance usually took place
within the narrow confines of a given monastery or monastic region. But
what holy men such as Barsanuphius and John could do at Gaza, and what
Epiphanius did at Thebes in upper Egypt, was to place their authoritative
words at the disposition of a far wider variety of questioners. In a world
where the primary division was not that between the monastery and the
world, or between the clergy and the laity, but the existential chasm between
religious persons and the vast majority who had neither the leisure nor the
inclination for such matters, it was usual for any outstanding person or
monastic establishment to function as a 'monastery without walls' for a
wide network of religiously-minded clients 'in the world'.

Holy men might receive desperate requests for help of every kind, from
words of comfort and prayer to God to direct intervention with the
authorities. This is shown by the *ostraka* found in the monastery of
Epiphanius at Thebes. A woman whose husband had been carried off by
the barbarians wrote:

Be so good, let thy compassion reach me ... for my heart is flown forth from me.
(Crum and Evelyn-White (1926) no. 170, p. 199)

An elderly priest also approached the hermit:

broken, lying abed, being carried in and out ... A great grief is in my heart, night
and day ... be so kind as to appoint for me prayers and a [regime of fasting] convenient to my sickness and old age, and even be it lying down, I will fulfil them.
(Crum and Evelyn-White (1926) no. 11, p. 195)

It was from the Old Men, Barsanuphius and John, that the Christian notables of the Gaza region received advice on all manner of topics. The
codes of Christian deportment proposed in these letters represent the late
flowering of a very ancient *délicatesse*, issuing now with supernatural authority from behind the permanently closed doors of the cell of an Egyptian
recluse. Not least of the good advice provided by the Old Men concerned
dealings with non-Christians. Should a landowner place his wine press at
the disposal of a Jewish neighbour?

If, when it rains, God causes the rain to fall on your fields and not on those of the
Jew, then you also can refuse to press his wine. But as he is full of love for all
mankind ... why should you wish to be inhumane rather than merciful?
(Barsanuphius, *Correspondance* 686, Regnault (1971) 441)

[28] Brown, 'Asceticism pagan and Christian', in *CAH* xiii, 601–31.

The Great Old Man even provided a specimen letter, declining with civility an invitation from a notable to a festival in which acts of non-Christian worship might take place:

Say to him: 'Your Charity knows that those who fear God hold to his commands; and your own habits are to hand to convince you of that, because your own affection for me would never cause you to transgress the precepts of your own ancestral tradition.'   (Barsanuphius, *Correspondance* 776, Regnault (1971) 475)

One should have no illusions on one point. As in all other periods of the ancient world, to cultivate mentors of this kind required wealth and leisure. Holy men were often appropriated by well-to-do persons. The peasants of Lipidiacum wanted to keep the body of Lupicinus, a 'living martyr' whose bloody spittle, the result of his austerities, they would scrape from the walls of his cell as a healing substance. But the body of the dead saint was impounded by a 'respectable woman' from neighbouring Trézelle (Allier): for she claimed it on the strength of having fed the saint from the produce of her villa when he was alive (Greg. Tur. *Vita Patrum* XIII.3).

All over the Christian world, notables collected holy men, drawing constantly on their services and, in turn, contributing to their upkeep and their reputation. Archesilaus of Caesarea Maritima remembered how Zosimas, a hermit from outside Tyre, was staying with him when the saint burst into tears, flooding the pavement of Archesilaus' town house. For Zosimas had heard the roar of the collapse of Antioch in the earthquake of 526. The holy man instantly called for a censer and filled the building with perfume, so as to render it immune from a similar fate. When Archesilaus' wife injured her eye with an embroidery needle, Zosimas stood by, praying and advising the surgeons who handled the injury. But Zosimas declared that it was another friend of the family, John of Choziba, four hundred *stadia* away in the desert of Judaea, to whom God had finally 'given the grace' of healing the injury: it was to John's prayers that he had listened (Evagr. *HE* IV.7).

As a result of patronage by the great, holy men and their disciples found themselves in a situation that generated permanent anxiety. They were frequently settled on marginal lands. They usually drew to themselves, in the heyday of their reputation, large bands of disciples and crowds of pilgrims, many of whom stayed for long periods in their presence. If successful, they required permanent facilities – such as buildings, a water supply and large surpluses of food and money for the poor, the sick and the many strangers. Altogether, the holy man came to weigh heavily on the most vulnerable tracts of the ecology of his region. There was never much wealth or land to go round, even in the most prosperous regions of the late Roman world. There is hardly a single account of the successful establishment of a holy man, from the autobiography of Valerius of Bierzo in seventh-century

Galicia,[29] through Benedict and his enemy, the priest Florentius, at Subiaco
(Greg. *Dial.* II.8.1–4), to the three thousand monks settled in the Judaean
desert,[30] the huge convents outside Amida (all too easily devastated when
the Chalcedonian authorities cut off the food supplies usually offered to
them by a devout laity),[31] to Nestorian convents in northern Iraq, regularly
pillaged by the Kurds (Thomas of Marga, *The Book of Governors* v.17, tr. E.
A. W. Budge (London 1893) 563), where we do not meet examples of
savage competition for scarce resources, waged between the new ascetic
settlements and local leaders, clergy and villagers. When it came to the issue
of oblations – the gifts of agrarian produce and of other forms of wealth
(including, of course, small children) offered to the holy man in exchange
for his blessing – the assertion of holiness almost invariably locked the
saint and his disciples (usually more zealous in this matter than their
master) into a zero-sum game.[32]

Holy men were frequently dependent on patronage – and often on the
crushing patronage of emperors, kings and great landowners. They had to
justify their position by standing, in the eyes of the world, as the quintes-
sence of good patronage. Hence the vividness and circumstantiality of
those accounts which show holy men rebuking the rich, protecting peasants from extortion, arbitrating in local disputes, and facing down high-
ranking officials, even the emperor himself, in the name of the poor, the
oppressed and the condemned. As a result, it has proved tempting to
explain the rise and function of the holy man in many regions of the
Christian world in terms of the manner in which holy men were believed
by their admirers to have played the role of 'the "good patron" writ large'.[33]

To arrive at a more balanced view of the matter, it is worth while stressing the overall tendency of the sources in which these incidents occur. It was
a tendency to render innocent the undoubted wealth and influence of the
holy man's 'establishment'. Put briefly: hagiography achieved its effect by
censoring one side of the gift exchange that took place around the holy man
– the steady, even disquieting, flow of gifts and favours from the outside
world that gave the holy man's activities their appropriate degree of splendour and public recognition. It presented the holy man's activities in terms
of the other side of that exchange – the seemingly effortless, 'gravity-free'

---

[29] Valerius of Bierzo, *Ordo Quaeremoniae* and *Replicatio*, ed. Aherne (1949).
[30] A world now brought alive by Hirschfeld (1992).
[31] John Eph. *Lives of the Eastern Saints* 35, *PO* xviii.607–20; *Chronicon pseudo-Dionysianum* iii.8, tr. R.
Hespel, *CSCO* 507, *Script. Syri* 213 (Louvain 1989) 27–8; see also Palmer (1990).
[32] *V. Sym. Jun.* 130, Van den Ven (1962) 122: a Georgian priest who had set up a healing shrine with
a *hnana* of Symeon was accused of working miracles through sorcery by the priests whose *karpophoriai*
had been intercepted by his shrine.
[33] Brown, 'Holy man' 91 (now in Brown, *Society and the Holy* 129) succumbed with gusto to that temptation. What follows should be read as a corrective to the views advanced in that article: see also Brown
(1983) 10–13, (1998), with Howard-Johnston and Hayward (1999) and Lane Fox (1997).

flow of divine favours, of acts of successful arbitration, plain speaking and intercession on behalf of the community as a whole (as in times of drought) that came from God through the holy man. To be content with one small, but revealing example. By the 580s, visitors to Symeon the Younger on the *Mons Admirabilis*, the Wonder-filled Mountain, outside Antioch (present-day Samandağı, Symeon's mountain), could not but have been impressed by a complex of buildings at the foot of the column of the saint, the splendour of whose surviving capitals alone reflected a *koine* of near eastern princely art that stretched from Constantinople to Kermanshah. Such building, however, so the biographers of Symeon insisted, was the product of Isaurian workers who had worked solely out of gratitude to the saint for the healings that he had bestowed on them.[34] In the same way, the wealth associated with the growing establishment of the holy man (especially as this was continued, after his death, by a monastic community) and the support offered to him in his lifetime by leading persons were frequently explained, in hagiographic sources, by reference to some incident in which an important person, standing for the wealth and power of 'the world' in its most obtrusive and darkened form, was humbled by the holy man through some miracle. Frequently this miracle was performed on behalf of the poor who had sought the saint's protection against the powerful person in question. Wealth that came to the holy man's establishment was made 'clean' in this way, by a dramatic story in which the giver of the wealth was first 'taught a lesson' by the saint.[35] Given this situation, it has been rightly observed that, by the sixth century, the miracle had become 'the specific, quasi-institutional mode of action' through which the holy man impinged on the world.[36]

Altogether, holy men tended to be remembered as having been effectively active in society in a manner that fulfilled, with satisfying congruence, the expectations of any other great patron. They frequently did so in areas which the historian now knows to have been characterized by a vigorous rural population which had taken ever more marginal land into cultivation. This is the case with the astonishing late Roman villages of northern Syria and with the large churches perched on what is now the boar-infested plateau of Karabel above Myra (Demre, Turkey) in Lycia.[37] But we must always remember that the very success of the holy man left his disciples with much to explain. The fact that they did so, and with gusto, in terms of a carefully censored language of 'clean' patronage does not mean that patronage in itself explains the holy man. It is, rather, to the wider features of the religious world in which the holy man moved that we

---

[34] *V. Sym. Jun.* 96, Van den Ven (1962) 74–5; see Van den Ven (1962) II.92–3, who shares my scepticism. On the buildings, see Djobadze, (1986) 57–114.

[35] Similar narratives concerning the wealth of modern Islamic holy men have been acutely observed by Gilsenan (1982) 102–3.   [36] Flusin (1983) 208.

[37] Tate (1992); Harrison (1963); Fowden (1990b).

must turn. Let us conclude, therefore, by sketching, inevitably very briefly, the role of the holy man as 'arbiter of the holy' – that is, as one significant actor among many in the slow and hesitant process of the creation of a Christian 'thought world'.

The Christian holy man emerged at a crucial moment in the overall relig-ious history of post-imperial western Europe and the Byzantine middle east. He was a figure of genuine spiritual power at a time when the holy stretched far beyond the somewhat narrow confines of the triumphant Christian church. It is no coincidence that a figure of the stature of Symeon Stylites should have appeared in northern Syria at just the time when the ecclesiastical structures of the region had been in place for some genera-tions, when the pagan temples had been officially closed for a quarter of a century, but where a strong form of local religious leadership had not yet arisen to negotiate an honourable surrender for the gods. Firmly placed on a column which in itself may have linked his person to ancient memories of holy stones,[38] administering banal and widely-recognized forms of blessing (the *hnana* of the dust from the sacred enclosure beneath his column), summoning local church congregations through their priests to what amounted to gigantic revivalist meetings associated with Christian penitential supplication, Symeon stood on the low slopes of the limestone ridge as a highly personalized challenge to the ancient pilgrimage site on top of Sheikh Barakat. Despite the splendid buildings that were lavished on it after his death, it is not the relatively low-lying area of Telnesin, but the conical shape of Sheikh Barakat that still catches the eye of the travel-ler in the Jebel Sem'an as it towers with an immemorial sacrality above the plain of Dana. In a similar manner, the column of Symeon's later imitator, Symeon the Younger, holds in view – but now at eye-level – the opposing peak of the oracle of Zeus on Mount Kasios.

Symeon negotiated many surrenders of the gods. Bedouin tribesmen burned their idols in his presence (Theodoret, *HR* XXVI.13). Whole villages entered into a 'covenant' with him. A polytheist village in the mountains of Lebanon was told that, if they followed his commands by placing stones carved with the sign of the cross or blessed by portions of his holy dust on the four corners of their fields, and if they destroyed their shrines and household idols, they would enjoy protection from creatures of the wild – from werewolves and ravenous field mice (*V. Sym. Syr.* 61 and 63, Doran (1992) 141 and 143, with comments on 22–3). A century later, villages touched by the ministrations of Symeon the Younger did not abruptly convert from 'paganism' to 'Christianity'. Rather, in a Christian empire that had used many forms of cultural and physical violence against polytheists,

[38] Frankfurter (1990).

the villagers were edged, a little more gently, through a language of sacred violence associated with the blessing and cursing of the wonder-working child-saint in the mountain above them, towards 'behaving a little more like Christians', χριστιανοπρεπῶς πολιτεύεσθαι (*V. Sym. Jun.* 221 and 223, Van den Ven (1962) 191 and 194; cf. 188–20, Van den Ven (1962) 166–9). When the formidable Shenoute of Atripe prophesied to the villagers of Sment in upper Egypt that they would lose their gods, they assumed the worst: 'A governor will surely come and will oppress us' (Till (1936) 65). Instead they got Apa Moyses, whose violence, though spectacular and disastrous for their temples, partook in an ancient language of the sacred, which rendered defeat, if not palatable, at least meaningful.

It is for this reason that, all over the Christian world, the countryside in particular became 'the locus for the elaboration of cultic choices'.[39] For, unlike the European missionaries of a later age, the Christian holy men and women of late antiquity and the early Middle Ages

appeared as representatives of a power superior to that of traditional faiths, but not as purveyors of a dramatically different world view or type of religion.[40]

Filled with the Holy Spirit and more certain than were most Christians of their position in a hierarchy of heavenly powers, in alliance with which they upheld the claims of Christ, their God, holy men (unlike those of us who usually study them) knew spiritual power when they saw it. They frequently engaged it at dangerously close quarters. Not only were long and intimate duels with the local sorcerer almost *de rigueur* in the life of a successful saint; sometimes one senses that the one is a doublet, rather than an enemy, of the other (e.g. *V. Theod. Syk.* 37–8, ed. Festugière (1970) 32–4). At Néris, in the Berry, Patroclus found himself faced at the time of the bubonic plague of 571 by a woman, Leubella, who had received from 'the devil, falsely appearing as saint Martin . . . offerings which would, he said, save the people'. But Patroclus himself had almost succumbed to the temptation to come down from the hills to save the people as a wonder-worker. Only after he received a vision of the 'abominations' of the world to which he had been tempted to return did he go back to his cell, to find genuine 'offerings' – 'a tile on which was the sign of the Lord's cross' (Greg. Tur. *Vita Patrum* IX.2).

What is often ascribed, in the more pensive and monastically orientated sources of the time, to the unhinging effects of *elatio*, of spiritual vainglory, that led to madness in many failed wonder-workers, refers to a far more gripping and specifically late antique phenomenon than mere conceit. We are dealing with figures for whom the boundaries between exorcism and possession, between power over spirits and a quasi-shamanistic power

[39] Boesch-Gajano (1991) 115. [40] Kaplan (1984) 115.

through possession by spirits, were far more fluid than our texts would lead us to suppose.[41] Driven by the torrent of cultic experimentation that raced through many Christian regions, it is not surprising that the mills of hagiographical literature should have come to turn so briskly towards the end of this period, in an effort to reduce the raw grain of so many, frequently ambiguous, experiences of the holy to the fine flour of a few, dominant Christian 'oikotypes'. Such experimentation would not have aroused so much interest if it had occurred only among the peasantry. What was at stake was the putting in order of a Christian 'thought-world' that was, if anything, a more urgent matter for the well-to-do than for the peasantry. The wealthy and the educated were the patrons of holy men and the readers of accounts of their lives. Seen in this light, the activities of the holy man, and especially the manner in which these were recounted in retrospect, represent one stage in the long schooling of the imagination of all classes in late antiquity.

The average well-to-do and thoughtful person lived in many 'thought-worlds'.[42] Potentially exclusive explanatory systems coexisted in his or her mind. The host of the monk Peter the Iberian, an eminent Egyptian, was a good Christian; but he was also 'caught in the error of pagan philosophers, whose ideas he loved greatly' (*V. Petri Iberi*, ed. R. Raabe, Leipzig 1895 72). He employed a magician to cure his daughter. Nor were these systems parallel. They often interlocked as separate parts of a single process of cure. A notable of Alexandria could go to the healing shrine of Sts Cyrus and John to receive a cure from their hands. But he claimed to have done so 'in order that his horoscope should be fulfilled' (*Miracula SS. Cyri et Johannis* 28. 8, *PG* LXXXVII.3504B; and ed. N. Fernandez Marcos (Madrid 1975) 296).

Holy men themselves did not see the matter in terms of a sharp antithesis of Christian and non-Christian. They belonged to a category of persons who were assumed by their supplicants to have access to knowledge of the holy in all its manifestations. The expectations of the neighbourhood committed them to far more than an exclusively Christian art of prayer. A respected saint was a person who was allowed to have the last word in what was usually a long and well-informed discussion of supernatural causality, in which everyone had a say. When Theodore of Sykeon was conceived, his mother, Maria, dreamed that a brilliant star had descended into her womb. Her lover (an acrobatic camel-rider on an imperial mission) was delighted. She would have a baby boy, he said, who would become a bishop. Next, Maria went to a holy man with second sight in a neighbouring village. He concurred.

---

[41] A gripping incident in John Eph. *Lives of the Eastern Saints* 15, *PO* XVII.223–7; John Moschus in *BZ* XXXVIII (1938) 360; Barsanuphius, *Correspondance* 843, Regnault (1971) 501.

[42] This is made particularly clear by Dagron (1981).

A star [he told her] is held to signify the glory of an emperor by those who are expert in interpreting visions; but with you it must not mean this.

Also consulted by Maria, the bishop of Anastasiopolis, 'by God's inspiration, gave her the same interpretation' (*V. Theod. Syk.* 4, ed. Festugière (1970) 4, tr. Dawes and Baynes (1997) 88–9). When Theodore, sure enough, grew up to be both a bishop and a holy man, he functioned in a similar manner:

if any required medical treatment for certain illnesses or surgery or a purging draught or hot springs, this God-inspired man would prescribe the best thing for each, for even in technical matters he had become an experienced doctor . . . and he would always state clearly which doctor they should employ.

(*V. Theod. Syk.* 145, ed. Festugière (1970) 114, Dawes and Baynes (1977) 182; cf. Harvey (1984) 87–93)

Nor did the information flow only in one direction. Viewing the crowds of sufferers around the shrine of St Epiphanius at Salamis in the early seventh century, a 'philosopher' informed the bishop that the majority of those present would be cured by a simple change in diet. Responsible for a crowded healing establishment, the bishop agreed. The philosopher's remedy worked wonders (Anastasius Sinaita, *Quaestiones* 94, *PG* LXXXIX.733A). We know of this from the *Quaestiones* of Anastasius of Sinai, a monastic writer whose highly nuanced discussion of divine providence, health and miracles contains, also, the first disturbing hint of yet another rival explanatory system – that of Islam. Anastasius knew how Arabs could tell from physiognomic traits which of their warriors would die – presumably as a 'martyr' – in battle; and he had heard of the great she-demon who rose from the earth to devour the camel-sacrifices heaped up around the Ka'ba of Mecca (Anastasius Sinaita, *Quaestiones* 20, *PG* LXXXIX.521A; Flusin (1991) 404–5).

In normal conditions, the varying layers of explanation tended to group themselves around the holy man, much as the manifold invisible powers of the universe, even the demons, fell into ranks beneath the one God whom he served. But the possibility of conflict was always present, in which these many layers would fall apart into sharply polarized antithesis. The most banal of these moments of conflict concerned the use of sorcery. This is hardly surprising. Within the Christian community itself, members of the clergy, like the holy man, were frequently deemed to be bearers of comprehensive knowledge of the sacred. Many had knowledge of sorcery. Clergy and lay persons alike were urged to use accustomed Christian healing substances and, above all, to employ names and formulae that were to be found only in the canonical Christian scriptures (Greg. Tur. *De Gloria Confessorum* 1 and 39). But it was far from certain that such a seemingly innocent substance as the 'oil of prayer' would be energized by Christian prayers or by invocations considered to be tainted by sorcery

(Shenoute, *Contra Origenistas* 259, ed. T. Orlandi (Rome 1985) 19; cf. Kropp
(1930) 120).

Though presented as a defence of the faith against 'heathen' customs,
and couched in terms of exhortations directed principally at a Christian
laity deemed to be more mired in non-Christian habits than were their
leaders, the long war on sorcery within the Christian community often took
the form of an internecine feud between rival experts on the sacred among
the monks and clergy themselves. It was a Great Old Man, and not a pagan
sorcerer, not even a Christian layman, who shocked Shenoute of Atripe by
recommending a jackal's claw tied to his right toe as the correct remedy for
his client, a Christian governor (Shenoute, *Contra Origenistas* 821, Orlandi
62). The middle age of Theodore of Sykeon was troubled by an influential
priest, a great sorcerer and philanderer, known as 'the Billy Goat of
Bithynia' (*V. Theod. Syk.* 159, Festugière (1970) 134).

Deadly conflict between members of the clerical élites on theological
issues caused the overlapping systems of explanation to explode. Sorcery
alone could explain the miracles of theological opponents. In the stormy
ecclesiastical history of the fifth and sixth century, we rarely find a holy
man of an opposing party who is not dismissed at one time or another by
his rivals as a mere sorcerer.[43] Occasionally we come upon a precious
moment when a community, as a whole, was forced to make up its mind
as to the meaning of an untoward event. Only then do we realize the
freedom of manoeuvre enjoyed by late Roman persons within the inter-
stices of the explanatory systems that jostled at the back of their minds.
When, in 420, the monk Fronto challenged local noble families and clergy
at Tarragona on an inconclusive charge of sorcery, a servant of count
Asterius burst into the crowded basilica with an armed retinue. Pointing at
Fronto, he roared:

Give me that dog. I will stop his barking . . .

That evening, the servant died of a stroke.

When this happened, all the faithful, frightened by the obvious power of this sign,
ceased to attack me for a little while. But my enemies and the count's whole household . . . demanded that I be punished as a murderer, since I had killed a man with
death-dealing spells. There were even a few of those, totally lacking in faith, who
said that it had all happened by coincidence.   (Aug. *Ep.* 11*.13)

Such uncertainty was not surprising. For many late antique Christians,
the sacred was profoundly faceless and ill-defined. Illusion was always possible. The Great Old Men of the desert had fostered a view of the untrans-

---

[43] Barsauma denounced by the emperor Marcian: Nau (1913) 130; Zu'ura denounced by pope
Agapetus: John Eph. *Lives of the Eastern Saints* 2, *PO* XVII.27. The Nestorians were convinced that the
Monophysites had replaced the relics of Mar Mattai by a sorcery-idol: *The History of Rabban Hormizd*
XVI, tr. E. A. W. Budge (London 1902) 120.

formed human consciousness as a fragile thing, perpetually ringed by demonic mirages. In dreams the demons could take the form of holy figures, Barsanuphius told a worried layman: only the sign of the cross they could not bring themselves to imitate (Barsanuphius, *Correspondance* 416, Regnault (1971) 290). Not every miracle that happened was a true miracle. The power of the demons, and the imminent presence of Antichrist, had deprived mankind of the binocular vision needed to discriminate between holiness and illusion. In the 430s, a monk appeared in Carthage. He applied to the sick oil poured over the bone of a martyr.

He brought hallucinations to play on the blind and the sick ... so that they thought that they had recovered their sight and ability to walk. But in departing from him, the illnesses in whose grip they were held remained.

(Quodvultdeus, *Liber promissionum* VI.6.11)

He left the city in a hurry. Yet just such cures, also performed with the 'oil of saints', only a generation later made the reputation of Daniel, a Syrian recluse and later a famous stylite, established beside the busy ferry across the Bosphorus (near Arnavutköy and Rumeli Hısar) a little to the north of Constantinople (*V. Danielis* 29, with Festugière (1961) II.111 n. 41). Epidemics of healing could be demonically inspired. They might be provoked by false relics – that is, by relics associated with rival Christian factions – such as was the 'polluted' oil left by mistake by a Monophysite monk in the chapel of a great Nestorian monastery (Thomas of Marga, *Book of Governors* VI.6; Budge 612–14). A stampede of sick persons to a holy man might be no more than a plot on the part of the demons to disturb the peace of his monastery (John Eph. *Lives of the Eastern Saints* 4, PO XVII.65).

Belief was never an easy matter, and in times of acute crisis the explanatory system which usually rested on the figure of the Christian holy man might collapse like a pack of cards. A massive public catastrophe, such as the onslaught of the plague, swamped the ministrations of the holy man. It was reassuring to believe that the cloth from the tomb of St Remigius, carried in a litter around Rheims, had created a sacred circuit that held the bubonic plague away from the city (Greg. Tur. *De Gloria Confessorum* 77). But Rheims was fortunate. When the plague first struck the eastern Mediterranean in 542, resort to the prayers of the saints was not the only – indeed, not the first – reflex of the afflicted populations. Demons in the form of angels appeared in Palestine, urging the inhabitants of one city to resume the worship they had once paid to a prominent bronze statue. Elsewhere, the word got round that

If one throws pots out of the house the plague will go from the city,

so that it became unsafe to walk in the streets by reason of the crockery raining down from every window (*Chronicum Anonymum pseudo-Dionysianum*, tr. R. Hespel, *CSCO* 507, *Script. Syri* 213 (Louvain 1989) 64–5 and 81, trans. Witakowski (1996) 79 and 97).

Such incidents were not simply moments of regression in the face of overwhelming, but mercifully infrequent, catastrophe. It is important to realize how little of the public space of late Roman society was occupied by Christian holy persons. The solid gold of demonstrative sanctity was spectacular; but it circulated in strictly delimited channels in what had remained, to an overwhelming extent, a supernatural 'subsistence economy', accustomed to handling life's doubts and cares according to more old-fashioned and low-key methods. To take one example: the high drama associated with the healing of the mentally disturbed through exorcism brought into peculiarly sharp focus the particular 'style' of supernatural power associated with effective Christian sanctity. For that reason, it bulks large in all hagiographic literature. But exorcism never achieved exclusive dominance in the thought-world of contemporaries, nor, when it happened, was it always perceived in the highly dramatic terms favoured by Christian narratives of the display of spiritual power. Many of the exorcistic gestures associated with holy men such as St Martin grew naturally out of recognizable medical practices. Those in a position to visit a shrine or a holy person associated with exorcism would, in any case, have been a small proportion of the population.[44]

As for the theological controversies that rocked the eastern empire in the fifth and sixth century, Christian holy men played an important role in the mobilization of local opinion on either side – all the more so as many influential lay persons made the habit of taking the eucharist only from the 'blessed' hands of known holy men (John Rufus, *Plerophoriae* 22 and 33, *PO* VIII.40 and 75; John Moschus, *Pratum Spirituale* 188, *PG* LXXXVII.3065D). But their opinions on theology carried little weight with the experts on such matters. Considering a theological dictum ascribed to St Spyridon of Cyprus, the great Monophysite theologian Severus of Antioch observed drily that, while Spyridon might have received the 'gift of healing', the holy old man had evidently not received the 'gift of wisdom' (Severus Antioch. *Liber contra impium grammaticum* III.39, tr. J. Lebon, *CSCO* 102, *Script. Syri* 51 (Louvain 1952) 181).

Deeply conscious of the ambiguity of the sacred and fully aware of the limits of its field of action in a complex world, the society that turned to Christian holy persons was more niggardly than our hagiographic sources might lead us, at first sight, to suppose in lavishing credulity upon them. But when they did, they were encouraged to 'stylize' their imagination of the workings of the supernatural in a highly specific way. The holy man was a 'servant' of his God. He was also a 'patron' in that he offered petitions to God on behalf of others. His actions assumed, at a profound level, that the events of this world were the product of conflicting wills (in which

---

[44] Rousselle (1990) 109–86 and Horden (1993) are decisive on this issue.

conflict, the supremely wilful envy of the demons played a crucial role) and that true order meant the ultimate submission of all wills to God, the supreme emperor of the universe. The intimacy of holy persons with their Lord could be as tender as that of a son, a familiar friend, even of a lover. But the overwhelming weight of language, in our texts, presented the holy man in his public *persona* as a courtier. For many regions, this attitude involved far more than an unthinking projection on to the invisible world of the observed working of patronage within the centralized structures of the later Roman empire. To see the invisible world in these clear-cut terms involved making conscious choices between available religious traditions. In 370 Athanasius wrote that, of course, dreams of the future can be vouchsafed to Christian devotees at the shrines of the martyrs. What mattered was how this happened. Many Egyptian Christians seem to have assumed that the martyrs, as 'unconquered' heroes who had overcome the demons of the lower air by their heroic deaths, could now be prevailed upon, by the prayers of believers, to torture the demons yet further (in a long Egyptian tradition, by which higher gods bullied and threatened their subordinates) to reveal their own unearthly knowledge of the future. It was not like that, Athanasius insisted. God sent the dreams because the martyrs acted as ambassadors – *etreupresbeue* – who bore the prayers of the faithful to his court (Athanasius, *Festal Letters*, ed. T. Lefort, *CSCO* 150/151, *Script. Coptici* 19/20 (Louvain 1955) 65/46–7).

The language of patronage at a distant court, of course, had its limits. Only simple folk in Egypt believed, on the strength of an imperial model of the supernatural world, that the Archangel Michael, rather than having been forever present in his mighty role from the first dawn of the creation, had ousted Satan in a *coup d'état* in the palace of heaven; and consequently that, like any other Roman consul, Michael was obliged to scatter the benefits of healing upon his people on the day of his festival, which was, of course, the day when he had received from God the formal scroll of his appointment.[45] But the emphasis on the clash of free wills implied in this model brought a quality of mercy into an otherwise inflexible and potentially profoundly impersonal *cosmos*.

With the notion of freedom came also the notion of sin. The holy man was not only a favoured courtier of the distant emperor of heaven, he was a preacher of repentance. Dramatic changes in health; dramatic changes in the weather; dramatic shifts in the locus of wealth, as gold, precious objects, robes, land, even small children passed from the world to the monastic establishments associated with holy persons: all these highly visible changes were held to have registered the most amazing of all discontinuities – the stirring to contrition of the sinful human heart.

[45] Van Lantschoot (1946).

The great *Lives* of the holy men leave us in no doubt as to that basic Christian oikotype. It did not coincide with other notions of the sacred that were widespread at the time. Some time after the middle of the fifth century, Athens was afflicted by a drought. Rising to the occasion, the great non-Christian philosopher Proclus brought down the rain. The mysterious drone of the sacred bull-roarer, swung above the city by the wise man, restored the burning elements to their harmonious pitch. Himself already something of a lesser god, Proclus' soul was co-opted, through these rites, into the quiet and immemorial routine of government, by which the presiding spirits of a small part of the *cosmos* nurtured the sweet air of his beloved Attica (Marinus, *Vita Procli* 28). For a moment, Proclus joined himself to the loving care of the gods; he did not bow, as a courtier and a sinner, before the sole emperor of heaven.

A few decades earlier, drought had fallen also on the region of Jerusalem. The processions of Christian villagers, bearing crosses and chanting *Kyrie eleison*, that converged on the monastery of the great Euthymius were treated to a very different view of the universe.

'God, Who fashioned us, is good and benevolent, and *His pity extends over all His works*. But [Euthymius added] *our sins stand between us and Him* . . . This is why in His anger He has brought this correction upon us, so that, disciplined by it, and bettered by repentance, we may approach Him in fear and He accordingly may hear us.' On hearing this, they all cried out in unison. 'You yourself, venerable father, must entreat God for us.' [Euthymius then] went into his oratory without making any promises. Casting himself on his face, he begged God with tears to have mercy on His creation . . . As he was praying, there suddenly blew up a south wind, the sky was filled with clouds, heavy rain descended and there was a great storm.

(Cyr. Scyth. *V. Euthymii* 25, tr. Price (1991) 34–5)

Dramatic though such scenes of intercession might be, they did not exhaust expectations of the Christian holy man. Behind the standard, workaday Christian version of a universe made intelligible in terms of sin, affliction and repentance, there always shimmered the majesty of paradise regained – that is, an image not only of a God placated by bursts of human prayer and contrition, offered to him on behalf of others by his favoured servants, but of an entire world rejoicing in the recovery of its lost order. In large areas of eastern Christianity (and, if in a more diffident and spasmodic manner, also in the west) the holy man brought back to the settled world, from his long sojourn in the wilderness, a touch of the haunting completeness of Adam.[46] Nature, characterized by great antithetical categories, fell into place around him. On his pillar at Telnesin, Symeon radiated an order that seeped from his person, standing in prayer before the court of God, into the column itself and the sacred space around it.

---

[46] Flusin (1983) 126–8.

Symeon maintained, as if in microcosm, the fundamental boundaries on which all civilized life was held to depend throughout the near east.[47] The clutter of stuffed deer, lions and snakes at the foot of the column spoke of notable breaches in the boundary between the animal and the human world healed in the name of the saint (*V. Sym. Anton.* 15 and *Appendix* 21, Doran (1992) 93 and 225). Further from Telnesin, the blessing of Symeon on the crosses set up in his name around villages in the mountains of Lebanon maintained the boundaries of the settled land against the encroaching disorder of the wild woods. The sexes, also, were held apart. In the women's enclosure at the foot of the terrain that rose towards the column, a female dragon would take her place, along with the five wives of a visiting Yemeni sheikh, demurely receiving her *hnana*, not from the hands of Symeon, but from the mouth of her male companion (*V. Sym. Syr.* 79 and *V. Sym. Anton. Appendix* 25, Doran (1992) 161 and 227).

Symeon was very much a 'revivalist' of a Syrian Christianity that had always been marked by a strong sense of cosmic order and with a consequent concern for the proper separation of the sexes. But an Adam might also pass beyond, as well as reinforce, boundaries that bulked so large in the minds of contemporaries. An 'angelic' man, the holy man trembled on the borderline of those divisions that usually pitted one segment of late Roman society against the other. Not invariably ordained, he was a layman to whom bishops bowed in reverence, as one above whom the hand of God had appeared. Priest or not, his blessing echoed faithfully the domestic practices of any Christian household. He was studiously accessible to both rich and poor, listening attentively to the humble and surprising the cultivated with his untutored spiritual insight. Even the charged barriers between the sexes opened at his touch. When Sabas passed through Scythopolis in 531–2, his attention was drawn to a woman who lay in the colonnade of the main street, isolated even from her fellow beggars by the stench of an uncontrolled menstrual haemorrhage.

He came over to her in the colonnade and said . . . 'This my hand I lend to you, and I trust in the God that I worship that you will be cured.' Taking the saint's hand, she applied it to the hidden part, and immediately the flux of blood ceased.

(Cyr. Scyth. *V. Sabae* 62, Price (1991) 173)

By such persons, the 'world' itself – that dark place of 'abominations' so often decried in the monastic literature of the time – was healed. In this sense, the holy man was a truly 'angelic' figure. Like the towering angels, he raised his eyes from his clamorous human clientele to contemplate the rich earth, teeming with the possibilities of life. He was responsible to God for all created things. Shenoute was able to stir the tardy Nile to give life once

[47] Well characterized by Doran (1992) 43–5.

again to the land of Egypt; and he did so, not simply as a favoured courtier
of God, but, with an ancient congruence, by first making the life-giving
liquid of his tears fall on the dead sand of his desert retreat beyond the
White Monastery (Besa, *V. Shen.* 102–5, Bell 72–3; see Thélamon (1981)
383).

Christian holy persons had been shot into prominence at this time by an
exceptionally stern and world-denying streak in late antique Christianity.
Those who approached them, and those who remembered their activities,
habitually assumed that they would act upon the spiritual world in terms of
expectations that echoed all that was most abrasively up-to-date in the hierarchical and patronage-ridden social structure of the later Roman empire.
Yet by sharing through their prayers in the concerns of the mighty angels,
holy persons had come to embrace the world. They cradled it, in the
Christian imagination, in terms that did better justice to the notion of a
God who loved his own creation, and so to the tenacious hopes of an overwhelmingly agrarian society locked in the tyrannical, warm embrace of the
earth. By their intercessions, the Christian holy men joined with St Michael
the Archangel to look with mercy on humanity in all its joys and cares:

[on] the strenuous work of our hands . . . the quietness of the oxen and the growth
of the lambs . . . the wool of the sheep and the milk of the goats . . . the growth
of all the fruits of the field . . . the body of the vine and the fullness [which is] in
the wine . . . the fatness and the savour of the olives . . . the slumber of a man and
his rest by night . . . the union of holy matrimony, wherein men beget their children for a blessing . . . in war that destroyeth the ungodly, and establisheth peace,
and delivereth the righteous . . . in the midst of the brethren [who live together]
. . . and towards those who are weary, and when he giveth them strength.

(*Discourse on the Compassion of God and of the Archangel Michael*
tr. E. A. W. Budge, *Miscellaneous Coptic Texts* (London 1915) 757–8)

By playing a role in the slow emergence of an imaginative model of the
world that had a place for such wide-arching prayers, the Christian saints
of late antiquity helped to make Christianity at last, and for a short
moment, before the rise of Islam, the one truly universal religion of much
of Europe and the middle east.

CHAPTER 27

THE DEFINITION AND ENFORCEMENT OF ORTHODOXY

PAULINE ALLEN

The definition of orthodoxy between 425 and 600 finds expression primarily in the decrees or statements of the Oecumenical Councils of Ephesus I (431), Chalcedon (451) and Constantinople II (553), which to a large extent were held at imperial instigation. The difficulties of enforcing such definitions, which often had to be upheld by the legislative, military, and even theological and liturgical interventions of emperors, prove that orthodoxy so defined was by no means acceptable to all Christians in the empire. This was particularly the case with the Council of Chalcedon, for its reception and promulgation, or its rejection and condemnation, were played out not only in imperial and patriarchal circles, but also among great numbers of monks and faithful. What, in fact, constituted right belief? Both proponents and opponents of Chalcedon laid claim to orthdoxy, tracing their pedigree in right belief back to the Council of Nicaea (325). An additional complication in assessing the definitions of orthodoxy in this period and the manner in which they were enforced is caused by the development and differentiation in the expression of doctrine. The interpretation of Chalcedon by its sixth-century adherents, for instance, was to differ from the perception of orthodoxy among their fifth-century counterparts. Furthermore, imperial policies adopted for the enforcement of orthodoxy were often dictated by a desire for ecclesiastical unity rather than for the preservation of right belief, which in such cases was used as an administrative tool. Increasingly, different perceptions of orthodoxy, and contrary opinions regarding its enforcement, caused ruptures not only among Christians of the eastern empire, but between east and west as well.

I. THE COUNCILS OF EPHESUS I AND II

Prior to the First Council of Ephesus two figures dominate the theological debate concerning orthodoxy – Cyril, patriarch of Alexandria (412–44), and the Antiochene Nestorius, who in 428 was appointed by the emperor Theodosius II as patriarch of Constantinople. While this was indeed a conflict of personalities, it was also a confrontation between the Alexandrian school, with its allegorical interpretation of scripture and its emphasis on the one nature of the divine Logos made flesh, and the Antiochene school, which favoured a more literal reading of scripture and stressed the two natures in Christ after the union. It was Nestorius' rejection of the title *Theotokos* (God-bearer) as applied to Mary and his substitution of the word *Christotokos* (Christ-bearer) which particularly drew the ire of Cyril and the Alexandrians. Celestine, bishop of Rome, was also disquieted by the contents of Nestorius' sermons. When a complete dossier of the correspondence which had passed between the two eastern patriarchs reached him, including Cyril's first and second letters to Nestorius, he and his synod condemned Nestorius and charged Cyril with overseeing the doctrinal capitulation of Nestorius or else putting into effect his condemnation (August 430). On 19 November 430, however, the emperor Theodosius intervened – on behalf, as he thought, of his protégé – and convoked a council which was to meet at Ephesus on 7 June the following year. Meanwhile Cyril delivered his ultimatum to Nestorius in the form of a third letter, in which he accused the patriarch of Constantinople of having 'injected the ferment of bizarre and outlandish heresy into congregations not only at Constantinople but all over the world'.[1] To this document were attached twelve anathemata (Twelve Chapters) for his enemy to subscribe. Together with his first two letters to Nestorius, they came to be regarded as a touchstone of orthodoxy in subsequent theological debate.[2]

Nestorius' refusal to accept the Twelve Chapters meant that at Ephesus he would be on trial. As it was, he was condemned and deposed by Cyril and the Alexandrians in the absence both of John of Antioch and his party, and of the Roman delegation. Furthermore, Cyril's third letter and the Twelve Chapters were inserted into the official proceedings of the council, and Mary was proclaimed *Theotokos*. The faith of Nicaea was upheld. The fact that Cyril and his colleague Memnon of Ephesus were in their turn anathematized by the Antiochene party when the latter finally arrived did not help the cause of Nestorius, who was forced to return to Antioch.

Ephesus I was not only a triumph for Cyril and implicitly for orthodoxy as defined in Cyril's third letter to Nestorius, but also a defeat for Nestorius and his christology in Syria. By imperial legislation in 435 Nestorius was banished from the patriarchate of Antioch;[3] in 448 another imperial edict ordered all his works to be burnt.[4] While Nestorian Christianity was to take root beyond the Roman empire in Persia, Nestorius himself was added to the list of names regarded by orthodox Christians as heresiarchs.

After the demise of Nestorius, the Antiochenes and Alexandrians re-established unity between their two patriarchates based on a compromise christological document which became known as the Formula of Reunion.

---

[1] Greek text in Wickham (1983) 12, lines 13–14. The translation is Wickham's (13).
[2] For the text of these anathemata see Wickham (1983) 28–33; on their significance see *ibid.* xxxv–xliii.   [3] *C.Th.* xvi.5.66.   [4] *CJ* i.1.3.

This document is also significant as the first in a series of theological compromises in the debates of the next two centuries. While the agreement was a more successful compromise than most of its kind, the peace effected after the union was none the less uneasy, not least because of the efforts of Cyril and his followers to secure additionally the condemnation of the (deceased) Antiochene theologians, Diodore of Tarsus and Theodore of Mopsuestia. Although Proclus, patriarch of Constantinople (434–46), was unwilling to condone this course of action in his christological work, the *Tome to the Armenians*, Cyril's cause was taken up by Dioscorus, his successor as patriarch of Alexandria in 444, who was both an ardent Cyrillian and a declared opponent of the Antiochene school. On the other side, Theodoret of Cyrrhus and Ibas of Edessa defended the Antiochene teachers strenuously. In the attempts of the Cyrillians here to widen Nestorius' condemnation to include other Antiochenes, we can see the beginnings of the so-called Three Chapters controversy, which was to be fully articulated in the reign of Justinian.

Among the influential monastic body in Constantinople, the archimandrite Eutyches had acquired considerable support for his christological views. While these are not known to us with certainty,[5] as represented by his opponents, such as Theodoret of Cyrrhus, Eutyches implied that Christ was not consubstantial with human beings. Like the emperor, Dioscorus also took the part of the archimandrite, who shared his negative views of the protagonists of the Antiochene school. Eutyches nevertheless met with stiff opposition from Flavian, who had become patriarch of Constantinople in 446, and the home synod of the capital city, who condemned him for his views. The archimandrite's appeal to Leo, bishop of Rome, was backed up by the emperor, who determined to hold another council at Ephesus on 1 August 449 to restore ecclesiastical order. Indeed, the emperor played a significant role in the preparations for this council, since he deputed not Flavian but Dioscorus to convene it, and stipulated the number and nature of its participants. Furthermore, he banned Theodoret from the proceedings. The papal legates who travelled to Ephesus carried a letter from Leo to Flavian, the Tome of Leo, in which the bishop of Rome declared his christological position, affirming Christ to be one single person, but with two natures, divine and human, each of which interacts with the other. The Tome was to become both one of the canons of two-nature christology and an object of hatred by adherents of the one-nature christology. The document was not read, however, during the aggressive and riotous proceedings of the council, presided over by the patriarch of Alexandria, at which Eutyches was rehabilitated, Flavian, Theodoret and Ibas deposed, and Cyril's Twelve Chapters accepted. Amid the triumph for Dioscorus personally and for

[5] See Wickham (1982b) 562.

Alexandrian christology in general, Leo was in a difficult position in that his Tome had not been reconciled with Cyril's Twelve Chapters. The scandalized bishop of Rome called Ephesus II a *latrocinium* or robber council, and, indeed, because it was not accepted in the west as orthodox, the council never achieved oecumenical status.

II. THE COUNCIL OF CHALCEDON

After the death of Theodosius on 28 July 450, his sister Pulcheria and her consort, the emperor Marcian, gave new direction to ecclesiastical matters. Pulcheria had already taken the side of Rome against Ephesus II. Now the new emperor summoned another council, which met at Chalcedon, across the Bosphorus from Constantinople, on 8 October 451. The role of Marcian and Pulcheria in securing new terms for orthodoxy at Chalcedon was significant: not only were they present at the important sixth session, but they entrusted the organization of the proceedings to imperial rather than ecclesiastical officials, thus ensuring orderly procedures.[6] Here the Tome of Leo was declared to be orthodox – that is, in harmony with the Fathers and with Cyril; Dioscorus was deposed, and Theodoret and Ibas restored. The participants also promulgated a definition of faith, which, while it outlawed the extremes of both schools, namely Eutychianism and Nestorianism, and attempted a balance between the christological terminology of each, proclaimed Christ 'in two natures' as opposed to the expression 'from two natures' favoured by the Alexandrians. This definition was problematical from the start because in the east it was seen only as an interpretation of the symbol or creed of Nicaea, whereas for Leo it was an absolute definition which allowed no addition or subtraction.[7] Also critical was the resolution of the council, which later became known as canon 28, whereby

the one hundred and fifty bishops gave the same privileges to the most holy patriarchal throne of New Rome, judging with good reason that the city which was honoured by the presence of the imperial office and the Senate and enjoyed equal privileges with the older imperial Rome, should also be made powerful, like Rome, in ecclesiastical matters, and should hold second place after her.[8]

As a result of this canon, the influence of Alexandria was short-circuited. To the bishop of Rome the canon was also unfavourable, and he was reluctant to accept it explicitly. The issues of the formula 'in two natures' and canon 28 were to cause unrest and resentment among Christians in both east and west in the century that followed, and a lasting division in the churches of the eastern Roman empire.

[6] Meyendorff, *Imperial Unity* 168.   [7] *Ep.* 145 in *ACO* 11.4, no. 87, p. 96, 4–6.
[8] *ACO* 1.1.3, 89, lines 4–9.

III. AFTERMATH OF CHALCEDON

The edict of 7 February 452, by which the emperors Marcian and Valentinian III enjoined their subjects to obey decisions of the council,[9] was promulgated amid turbulence in Palestine, Egypt and Antioch in the aftermath of the council. That monks and people also defined and enforced orthodoxy at this time is clear from such cases as that of Juvenal of Jerusalem, who lost the support of the influential monks in his see, and on his return to Jerusalem after the council was forced to flee in the face of their determined opposition. The amount of popular literature written in the century after Chalcedon both for and against the council demonstrated that reaction to the perceived issues was not confined to the imperial or patriarchal level.

While Marcian had Juvenal restored by force, similar trouble was brewing in Alexandria, where Dioscorus, condemned and excommunicated at Chalcedon, was replaced by his trusted priest Proterius who, however, accepted the council. Since the people and monks remained loyal to Dioscorus and refused to recognize his successor, Proterius could not consolidate his position, despite banishing his chief opponents, the deacon Peter Mongus and the priest Timothy, nicknamed by his opponents Aelurus, 'the Cat' or 'the Weasel', because he was so emaciated from ascetic practices.[10] In 455 Marcian was forced to intervene by issuing another edict, prescribing penalties for those who adhered to the docetic heresies of Apollinaris of Laodicea and Eutyches,[11] i.e. those who refused to accept the Chalcedonian definition of Christ's true humanity and true divinity. Subsequently Proterius was kept in power by a military presence. When, on the emperor's death on 26 January 457, feeling against Proterius heightened, Timothy Aelurus was brought back secretly to Alexandria and consecrated patriarch. Two months later the people lynched Proterius. It was the energetic leadership of Timothy Aelurus, who suppressed or removed bishops who adhered to Chalcedon,[12] which ostensibly prompted Marcian's successor Leo and the ambitious patriarch of Constantinople, Anatolius, to despatch in 457 to Leo of Rome, metropolitans and eminent ascetics in the east a *codex encyclius*, canvassing their opinion on the consecration of Timothy Aelurus and on the status of Chalcedon. The replies which have come down to us reject Timothy, and only one bishop, Amphilochius of Side, seems to have declined to accept the council, possibly because at the gathering itself he had been hit on the head to encourage him to subscribe the conciliar statement.[13] In reaction to these positive replies, Leo of Rome wrote his letter 165, the so-called Second Tome,

---

[9] *ACO* II.2.2, no. 8 (Latin) and II.1.3, no. 23 (Greek).　　[10] Zach. Rh. *HE* IV.1.　　[11] *CJ* I.5.8.
[12] Zach. Rh. *HE* III.10–IV.2; Evagr. *HE* II.8.
[13] *ACO* II.5.9–98. For the alleged coercion of Amphilochius see Zach. Rh. *HE* III.1.

spelling out the defence of Chalcedon. Timothy's position had become untenable, and partly through the efforts of the convinced Chalcedonian Gennadius, the successor of patriarch Anatolius in Constantinople, he was removed from Alexandria at the end of 459 or the beginning of 460. In his exile, however, Timothy wrote influential works condemning Chalcedon.

Meanwhile Antioch was becoming increasingly anti-Chalcedonian,[14] particularly under the leadership of Peter the Fuller, a presbyter whose theology was Cyrillian. Seemingly with help from the Isaurian general Zeno, Peter was consecrated patriarch of Antioch in the absence of the Chalcedonian patriarch, Martyrius. In particular Peter strove to make an anti-Chalcedonian addition to the liturgical hymn known as the *Trishagion* (Thrice-holy), which properly speaking ran: 'Holy God, Holy Strong One, Holy Immortal One, have mercy on us.' The proposed addition of the words 'who was crucified for us' before 'have mercy on us' would have involved a phrase which was used as an anti-Chalcedonian slogan and was seen by Chalcedonians as theopaschite i.e. as proposing that God, although impassible and eternal, had died on the cross. Because of the unrest which this phrase occasioned in Antioch, the emperor Leo intervened, and in 471 Peter was removed.[15]

IV. ZENO AND BASILISCUS

The Isaurian Zeno became emperor on 17 November 474, but the following year was compelled to flee Constantinople because of a palace intrigue, and to see Leo's brother-in-law Basiliscus take his place. The usurper cast his lot with the anti-Chalcedonians:[16] Timothy Aelurus and Peter the Fuller were recalled to their sees, and Basiliscus composed an encyclical, addressed primarily to Timothy, in which the Tome of Leo and the 'innovation' of Chalcedon were anathematized, and the creeds and Councils of Nicaea, Constantinople (381) and Ephesus I and II were upheld.[17] In the conflict concerning Chalcedon this is the first of a series of imperial interventions imposing by force a doctrinal interpretation on the subjects of the empire.[18] Although during Basiliscus' regency the sees of Ephesus, Antioch and Jerusalem were anti-Chalcedonian, there was opposition to the encyclical in Constantinople itself, where patriarch Acacius considered that the rights conferred on his patriarchate by Chalcedon had been rendered ambiguous. Basiliscus was forced to retract his edict in favour of an

---

[14] Where possible, the term 'anti-Chalcedonian' is to be preferred to the pejorative and incorrect word 'Monophysite' in referring to the opponents of the council of 451. See Allen (1993).

[15] Theod. Lect. *HE* ed. Hansen 110.14–15.

[16] For speculations on Basiliscus' motives in this move see Frend, *Monophysite Movement* 169–70.

[17] Zach. Rh. *HE* v.1–2; Evagr. *HE* iii.4; Schwartz (1927) 49–51.

[18] See Meyendorff, *Imperial Unity* 195–6, and 196 n. 46 for a list of these imperial statements down to the seventh century.

antencyclical condemning Nestorius and Eutyches and reaffirming the rights of the patriarchate of Constantinople, and eventually had to leave the capital on the return of Zeno in 476.

On Zeno's return Basiliscus' edicts were promptly rescinded, the ecclesiastical *status quo* was restored, and Acacius' position reinforced. The prominent anti-Chalcedonians Peter the Fuller and Paul of Ephesus were exiled, but Timothy Aelurus died on 31 July 477 before he could be banished. There were obstacles to this restoration, however, and, indeed, to the unity of church and of empire. To begin with, although consecrated irregularly in Timothy Aelurus' stead, Peter Mongus was regarded in Alexandria as the true patriarch. Furthermore the people of Antioch were anti-Chalcedonian, even if Chalcedonian bishops were appointed there and Peter the Fuller was still in exile. It was, in fact, because of the murder of a new Chalcedonian bishop in Antioch that Acacius of Constantinople wrote to pope Simplicius roundly condemning Peter Mongus. In Jerusalem, meanwhile, an uneasy *modus vivendi* existed between the overwhelmingly anti-Chalcedonian monks and the patriarch. It was precisely the compromise in Jerusalem which seems to have inspired the edict promulgated by Zeno in 482 in an attempt to effect religious unity. The *Henotikon* (document of union), as it came to be called, was addressed to the church of Alexandria, Egypt and Cyrenaica; only later when it was enforced generally throughout the empire did it acquire universal relevance. While the edict did not anathematize the Tome, Chalcedon or the formula 'in two natures', stress was placed on the need for unity of belief according to the one and only definition of faith, i.e. that of Nicaea.[19] Apart from Nicaea, the Councils of Constantinople and Ephesus I were acknowledged, and Cyril's Twelve Chapters accepted. Chalcedon was mentioned only in the following crucial sentence: 'Everyone who has held or holds any other opinion, either at present or at another time, whether at Chalcedon or in any synod whatever, we anathematize.' The *Henotikon* was a masterpiece of imperial diplomacy, in which the patriarch Acacius had had a considerable hand, and nominally at least it united Constantinople and Alexandria, while bringing the major eastern sees into communion. In the long run, however, it was to be unsuccessful. For extreme anti-Chalcedonians, especially the monks in Egypt, euphemistically called *Diakrinomenoi* or Hesitants, only an outright condemnation of the Tome and Chalcedon would suffice. In fact the rigorists in Alexandria later separated, being known first as *Aposchistai* (Separatists), and subsequently as *Akephaloi* or Headless Ones, a reference to their seemingly anonymous leadership. But some Chalcedonians too, like Calandion of Antioch, found the edict unacceptable. Rome was also unhappy at the recognition of Peter Mongus inherent in the reconciliation

---

[19] Zach. Rh. *HE* v.8; Evagr. *HE* iii.14; Schwartz (1927) 133.

of Alexandria and Constantinople, at the perceived perfidy of Acacius, and at the jurisdiction which the patriarch of the capital had arrogated to himself in other matters. Alerted by the strict Chalcedonian Sleepless Monks in Constantinople, in 484 pope Felix III excommunicated Acacius, and demanded that the emperor Zeno choose between the apostle Peter and Peter Mongus.[20] This was the beginning of the Acacian schism between east and west, which was to last until the reign of Justin I.

V. ANASTASIUS I

On his accession to the throne after the death of Zeno in April 491, Anastasius I (491–518) determined to use the *Henotikon* as an oecumenical tool, interpreting the document as being in no way an annulment of Chalcedon. In working towards restoring relations with Rome as well, Anastasius tried to make the *Henotikon* the basis of negotiation. However, since he aimed primarily at ecclesiastical peace rather than at a uniform belief, the new emperor was usually willing to allow cities that were pre-dominantly of one persuasion or another to be governed by bishops sym-pathetic to their cause. This policy caused confusion and polarization, according to the sixth-century church historian Evagrius, who identifies three groupings: (1) rigorous anti-Chalcedonians who were satisfied only with a condemnation of Chalcedon and Leo's Tome; (2) rigorous, uncom-promising defenders of Chalcedon; (3) Chalcedonians and anti-Chalcedonians who abided by the *Henotikon*.[21] The emperor's enforcement of the *Henotikon* as the basis for negotiation is demonstrated clearly also by the deposition and exile of the Chalcedonian patriarch of Constantinople, Euphemius (490–6), who did not support the *Henotikon*. On the other hand, adherence to the document availed a patriarch nothing if, like Flavian of Antioch (498–512), he was unable to deal with unrest within his juris-diction.

The reign of Anastasius is decisive for the history of opposition to Chalcedonian orthodoxy in that, as well as proving the failure of compro-mise documents like the *Henotikon*, this period produced two of the great-est theologians of the anti-Chalcedonian 'one nature' (Monophysite) christology – Philoxenus of Mabbug and Severus of Antioch, both of whom tried to enforce an anti-Chalcedonian interpretation of the *Henotikon*. Philoxenus not only induced the monastic body at Antioch to oppose the Chalcedonian patriarch Flavian, but also persuaded Anastasius to have Euphemius' successor Macedonius summon the home synod, where a confession of faith was composed (507?) in which the Antiochene and Leonine tradition as evident in Chalcedon was condemned. In 509, at

---

[20] Felix, *Ep.* 8, in Schwartz (1934) 81, lines 24ff.   [21] Evagr. *HE* III.30.

a synod in Antioch where Philoxenus was present, the *Henotikon* was given a more rigorous interpretation along Monophysite, and especially Alexandrian, lines, but the two-nature christology (Dyophysitism) was not condemned expressly. Meanwhile Severus had gone to the capital with a large group of Palestinian monks to protest against the persecutions of anti-Chalcedonians by patriarch Elias of Jerusalem. The latitude which Anastasius had allowed bishops and patriarchs in their individual sees had not produced the ecclesiastical unity which the emperor desired. This explains the composition of the Typos of the emperor, a document drawn up by Severus (perhaps between 512 and 518), in which Chalcedon and the Tome of Leo were explicitly anathematized. It is doubtful, however, whether the Typos was ever promulgated as official policy.[22] Although the patriarch of Alexandria, John of Nikiu (505–16), was in favour of interpreting the *Henotikon* in an anti-Chalcedonian sense, the synod of Sidon in October 511, at which all the patriarchs of the east were present, retained the *Henotikon* as the basis of negotiations and added to it no anathemata on Chalcedon or the Tome. However, the anti-Chalcedonians were able to secure the deposition of Flavian of Antioch a year later and to see Severus consecrated in his stead on 16 November 512.[23]

During this time, Anastasius' attempts to produce unity had been threatened on the one hand by those who rallied around the Monophysite catch-cry 'who was crucified for us', which was used by Severus' monks, and on the other hand by the Chalcedonian party, of which the Sleepless Monks were some of the most influential and vociferous members. In giving asylum to pro-Chalcedonian refugees from Egypt and acting as informants to the popes in Rome, as well as through instigating a collection of documents which was used as Chalcedonian propaganda, the Sleepless Monks were to be centre-stage in the enforcement of the council of 451 from the time of pope Felix (483–92) until the reign of Justinian. There were two uprisings associated with the contentious formula, the first in 510/11, for which Severus claimed Macedonius, patriarch of Constantinople, was responsible, and the second in 512. In August 511 Macedonius, who was no match for Severus and could not carry out the emperor's eirenic policies, was deposed.[24] Apart from Palestine, the east was now administered by anti-Chalcedonian bishops, and thanks to the efforts of Philoxenus and Severus Monophysitism was in the ascendancy. The *Henotikon*, on the other hand, had once again proved unsuccessful as a tool for enforcing unity, as the depositions of Macedonius and Flavian showed.

Once patriarch, Severus lost no time in anathematizing Chalcedon and the Tome, but he left the *Henotikon* in abeyance. A number of clergy in the

---

[22] See Grillmeier, *Christ in Christian Tradition* II.1 273–9 for an assessment of the contents of the Typos. [23] De Halleux (1963) 70–4. [24] Theod. Lect. *HE* ed. Hansen 139.25–7.

east, however, in particular the bishops of Illyricium under Alcison of Nicopolis, were in favour of Chalcedon and of Rome, and looked to Vitalian, the Thracian count, as their champion. In 512 Vitalian led a revolt against Anastasius, demanding the restoration of Macedonius and Flavian and no addition to the *Trishagion*. On Vitalian's victory in 514 Anastasius agreed to eliminate the addition to the *Trishagion* and to end the breach with Rome, and invited the bishop of Rome to a council to be held at Heracleia. However, his attempts to reach a compromise with pope Hormisdas (514–23) on these issues was unsuccessful,[25] and by the time the emperor died in 518 the breach with Rome was complete. In the wake of Vitalian's success the Scythian monks in Constantinople were advocating the use of a potentially theopaschite formula ('one of the Trinity suffered') in a Chalcedonian but anti-Nestorian sense. At the end of Anastasius' reign the anti-Chalcedonian position had crystallized and been made explicit, in such a way that the major issues in ecclesiastical unity were clear: all hinged on the acceptance or rejection of Chalcedon and the Tome.

VI. JUSTIN I AND JUSTINIAN

There could be no doubt about the agenda awaiting the new emperor Justin I (518–27) on his accession: the populace in Constantinople demanded that he should make his position clear by proclaiming Chalcedon and banishing Severus. This Justin did. The four oecumenical councils were proclaimed, the names of Macedonius and Leo of Rome were restored to the diptychs in Constantinople, and the feast of the Council of Chalcedon was inaugurated (16 July 518). Justin began initiatives to end the schism with Rome, with the support of his nephew, Justinian, and Vitalian. The importance which the emperor attached to the restoration of unity between east and west can be seen from the invidious terms of the *libellus* put forward by pope Hormisdas and signed by John, patriarch of Constantinople, on 28 March 519. Not only did John anathematize the most important opponents of Ephesus and Chalcedon, but he acquiesced in removing from the diptychs the names of all patriarchs of Constantinople, including Acacius, as well as those of the emperors Zeno and Anastasius.[26] After thirty-five years, and seemingly at a great price to the eastern empire, unity was restored between east and west, and Chalcedonian orthodoxy triumphed. But in the east itself the polarization between Chalcedonian and anti-Chalcedonian parties was ever more apparent. Severus had been forced to flee his see a few months after the death of Anastasius. Like Julian of Halicarnassus and others before him, he sought refuge in Alexandria, which was uncompromisingly anti-Chalcedonian. In 519 Philoxenus, too,

[25] Frend, *Monophysite Movement* 231–2.   [26] Guenther (1895) 167.

was forced into exile. Chalcedonian bishops were put in the place of the deposed except in Cilicia I, Phoenicia Maritima and Arabia,[27] and anti-Chalcedonian monks were badly treated. Persecution followed. But even within its own ranks the anti-Chalcedonian movement was experiencing the problems which were to dog its history for the rest of the sixth century, and to impede imperial attempts to enforce Chalcedonian orthodoxy on opponents of the council of 451. These problems arose from theological disputes among Monophysites, such as we see in Egypt between Severus and Julian of Halicarnassus, who disagreed on the manner in which human passions or emotions were attributed to Christ. For Julian the emphasis on the unity of Christ was of primary importance, and the difference between the two natures was secondary. Thus he asserted that to describe the body of Christ as 'corruptible' (*phthartos*), i.e. subject to human suffering, was to call into question the unity of the body with the divinity.[28] Julian's doctrine, which was not always understood properly by his adversaries, attracted opposition not only from anti-Chalcedonians like Severus, who himself wrote several works against it, but also from Chalcedonians. However, Julian's 'aphthartodocetism', as it was dubbed by its enemies, continued to exercise considerable influence, especially in the Alexandrian and Armenian churches.

Justin's nephew, the count Justinian, had been assuming increasing importance in ecclesiastical politics, taking up the cause of the Scythian monks, and advising pope Hormisdas that the Scythian theopaschite formula could be interpreted as anti-Nestorian and orthodox, and so unite Chalcedonians and anti-Chalcedonians. The count also attempted to have Hormisdas review his demands concerning the removal of bishops' names from the diptychs. Hormisdas, however, conceived of using, not being used by, imperial power to enforce orthodoxy as he saw it.

From April to August 527, when Justinian acted as co-regent with his uncle, he passed legislation against heretics, Manichees and Samaritans.[29] This was a foretaste of the policies he was to pursue after becoming sole regent on the death of Justin. Not only was he determined to end the split between Chalcedonians and anti-Chalcedonians, but in edicts early in his reign he enacted penalties against Nestorians, Eutychians, Apollinarians, Montanists and others.[30] Pagans ('Hellenes') were the subject of a particularly energetic and programmatic attack. In a law passed in the year 529[31] pagans are ordered to be baptized with their entire households, or run the risk of being excluded from the state and stripped of all goods and possessions. Pagan teachers are singled out and forbidden to teach, under threat of dire penalty. The promulgation of this stringent legislation, which

---

[27] Honigmann (1951) 25ff.
[28] Draguet (1924); Grillmeier, *Christ in Christian Tradition* II.2 79–110. [29] *CJ* I.I.5.
[30] *CJ* I.5.18. [31] *CJ* I.11.10.

affected chiefly the aristocratic class,[32] resulted in a spate of trials and executions. It was an act which, like the closing of the Neoplatonist academy of Athens and the confiscation of its endowment in 529–32, demonstrated that for Justinian the enforcement of orthodoxy entailed the eradication of paganism. Yet, as the missionary efforts of John of Ephesus were to show a decade later, paganism did survive this onslaught. It has been argued that Justinian's anti-pagan measures, which had a deleterious effect on secular higher education, were responsible for the decay of ancient literature and culture, the renaissance of which had begun under Constantius two centuries earlier.[33]

In the administration of churches and clergy Justinian brought all under his control.[34] His was a total religious policy in which pagans, heretics, Samaritans and Jews were also to accept Chalcedonian orthodoxy, as is evidenced *inter alia* by the concerted mission effort in his reign. On the liturgical front as well, Justinian consequently left little to chance. The liturgical chant, the *Trishagion*, including the formula 'One of the Holy Trinity suffered in the flesh', which the emperor had championed as a tool for ecclesiastical unity even before becoming sole regent, was subsumed into a profession of faith and enshrined in the introduction to his legal code in 528.[35] According to Theophanes,[36] in 535 Justinian ordered that the hymn *Ho monogenes* (which began with the words 'Onlybegotten Son and Word of God') was to be sung in the liturgy at Constantinople. In its terminology the hymn was acceptable to both sides – the anti-Chalcedonian tradition even attributed its introduction to Severus of Antioch. A further step was taken by the emperor at the Council of Constantinople in 553, when an anathema was placed on anyone who did not confess that Christ, 'who was crucified in the flesh, is true God and Lord of glory, and one of the Holy Trinity'.[37] Like the Cherubic hymn introduced into the liturgy in 573–4 by Justin II,[38] the *Ho monogenes* and its manipulation by Justinian show that theology in the sixth century had turned its back on the Antiochene tradition and was tending in an Alexandrian direction.[39] It is also no accident that the great melodist Romanos, who composed his *kontakia* or liturgical hymns during Justinian's reign, is decidedly anti-Nestorian, while reticent about christological heresies in the period before or after Chalcedon.[40]

The nature of Justinian's collaboration with the empress Theodora in ecclesiastical politics is difficult to determine; it has been seen variously as clever or despicable. This is in large part caused by the extreme bias with which she is portrayed in contemporary sources, particularly Procopius of

---

[32] Chuvin, *Chronicle* 135.   [33] Lemerle, *Byzantine Humanism* 77.   [34] *Nov.* 6; *CJ* 1.3.41; 1.3.47.
[35] *CJ* 1.1.5.   [36] *Chron.* A.M. 6028, p. 216 de Boor.   [37] *ACO* IV.1.242.
[38] Cedrenus, *Historiarum compendium*, ed. Niebuhr, vol. 35, 685 lines 3–4.
[39] See further Schulz (1986) 21–2.   [40] Grillmeier, *Christ in Christian Tradition* II.2.513–23.

Caesarea and John of Ephesus.[41] Theodora had Monophysite sympathies and became the patron of Monophysites in exile, sheltering them in one of her palaces. According to the partisan John of Ephesus, these bishops, clergy and ascetics numbered more than five hundred, and one could

go into the palace itself called that of Hormisdas, as into a great and marvellous desert of solitaries, and marvel at their numbers . . . and the same men's spiritual songs which were heard from all sides, and their marvellous canticles and their melancholy voices.[42]

The polarization of the two sides in the debate over Chalcedon, which is particularly evident in the bias of the two most important church histories of the sixth century, those of John of Ephesus and the Chalcedonian Evagrius, went a step further in c. 530, when John of Tella began to ordain Monophysite clergy: this was eventually to lead to the separation of the Monophysite churches. Around 530 Justinian relaxed the persecution of Monophysites, probably in order to be able to organize meetings in Constantinople between Chalcedonian and anti-Chalcedonian bishops and monastic representatives. But the Nika revolt of 532, which threatened the power of the Byzantine monarch, also demonstrated the extent of anti-Chalcedonian feeling in the capital, as well as the necessity of removing all suspicion of Nestorianism from the Chalcedonian position. The meetings of 532/3 between Chalcedonians and anti-Chalcedonians were attended by the patrician Strategius, whose reponsibility it was to report the progress of the discussions to the emperor. The aim of this exercise was to conduct the debate on a purely theological plane, and, by allowing the anti-Chalcedonians to air their grievances against Chalcedon, to remove their doubts and restore an ecclesiastical unity based on acceptance of the council of 451.[43] This can be seen from the fact that Justinian himself presided over the last session of the talks, and that on their conclusion imperial decrees were promulgated, aimed at unifying the empire, accepting four councils, condemning Eutyches, Apollinaris and Nestorius, proposing the anti-Nestorian theopaschite formula of the Scythian monks ('the one who suffered in the flesh is God and one of the Trinity'), but passing over the Tome of Leo.[44] The decrees were accepted in both east and west, and the Sleepless Monks were even condemned by Rome as 'Nestorian'. Further accommodation of the anti-Chalcedonian position can be seen in the ordination of the Monophysite Theodosius to the patriarchate of Alexandria on 10 February 535, a move seemingly engineered by Theodora. The empress also arranged for the Chalcedonian bishop of Trebizond,

[41] Cameron, *Procopius* (1985) 49–83.
[42] John Eph. *Lives of the Eastern Saints* 47, ed. E. W. Brooks, *PO* XVIII.677.
[43] Brock (1981); Speigl (1984); Grillmeier, *Christ in Christian Tradition* II.2 232–48.
[44] *CJ* I.1.6; I.1.7.

Anthimus, to become patriarch of Constantinople. In Alexandria vociferous opposition to Theodosius' accession was roused by the Gaianites, an
offshoot of the Julianists, and the patriarch had to be kept in power by the
intervention of imperial troops. When Theodosius was summoned to
Constantinople, an imperial invitation was extended to Severus to come to
the capital to discuss christological matters with Anthimus. The upshot was
that Severus, Anthimus and Theodosius communicated with each other,[45]
thereby bringing unity and strength to the anti-Chalcedonians and threatening the Chalcedonian position in the east. Strict Chalcedonians in
Palestine and Syria expressed their concern to Rome. At the demand of
pope Agapitus, Anthimus was deposed, and an imperial edict was promulgated (536) anathematizing Severus, Anthimus and their followers, and
ordering that Severus' works be burnt.[46] Severus himself retreated again to
Egypt, where he died on 2 August 538.

Under the protection of Theodora, Theodosius took over Severus' role
as leader of the anti-Chalcedonian party and began ordaining Monophysite
bishops. Between 536 and 538 the empress had attempted to have the anathemata against the Monophysite leaders revoked by using her influence on
Vigilius, the papal legate in Constantinople, and even by contriving his
appointment as pope (29 March 537). This ploy, however, was unsuccessful, and in 540 Vigilius was forced by Justinian to ratify the anathemata of
536.

The reign of Justinian witnessed the rise of yet another christological
controversy, which apparently posed a threat both to Chalcedonian and
anti-Chalcedonian perceptions of orthodoxy, when in the 530s the
Monophysite deacon Themistius, who came from the anti-Julianist party in
Alexandria, promulgated in Constantinople his doctrine concerning the
ignorance of Christ. Just as Christ's body was subject to death and corruption, so too, argued Themistius, was his human mind finite and subject to
ignorance. While this was a logical progression in the opposition to the supposed ideas of Julian of Halicarnassus, the doctrine caused a furore within
anti-Chalcedonian circles, and Themistius and his followers were soon
awarded the sobriquet *Agnoetai* (those who do not know). The debate certainly lasted to the end of the sixth century. It seems as if Chalcedonians
too were attracted to Themistius' ideas, and that Justinian was led to pass
an edict against Agnoetic teaching.[47] Like Julianism before it, this debate
both shows the shortcomings of Monophysite christology, the expression
of which produced an increasing number of splinter groups, and points to
a certain common ground between pro- and anti-Chalcedonians.

While on the Chalcedonian side a concerted defence of Chalcedonian
orthodoxy was being made by such writers as Leontius of Byzantium and

[45] Zach. Rh. *HE* IX.19.   [46] *Nov.* 42.   [47] Brock (1985) 38–9; Van Roey and Allen (1994) 8–9.

Cyril of Scythopolis, among the moderate Chalcedonians we find a tendency to combine acceptance of the Council of Chalcedon and the Tome with a Cyrillian interpretation of Chalcedon. The more radical position within this development (often called neo-Chalcedonianism) was the following. The expression 'in two natures' used of Christ is necessary in order to combat Eutychianism; the term 'from two natures' or the one-nature formula of Cyril has to be used to preclude Nestorianism. Both expressions need to be used together, lest the terminological impasse arising from the Chalcedonian definition continue. Representatives of this school of thought were Nephalius of Alexandria, John of Scythopolis, John the Grammarian and Ephraim of Amida. A more moderate approach, found in Leontius of Jerusalem and in Justinian's edict *On the Right Faith* (551), was to supplement the Chalcedonian definition of faith with Cyrillian terms, particularly those of the Twelve Chapters against Nestorius. Yet in his theological tract the emperor remained firmly on Chalcedonian ground.[48]

Meanwhile, in 542/3, as a consequence of a request for Monophysite bishops by the Arab king al-Harith to Theodora, Theodosius consecrated Jacob Baradaeus (Bar'Addai) metropolitan of Edessa and Theodore of Arabia metropolitan of Bostra. This was a decisive step for the expansion of Monophysitism and for the eventual separation of the anti-Chalcedonian churches. Through the missionary efforts of Jacob and other bishops consecrated by Theodosius, the anti-Chalcedonian cause was strengthened in Asia Minor, Armenia, Syria, Arabia, the Aegean, Egypt and Nubia.[49] The part played by Jacob in particular is reflected in the fact that the Monophysite church in the Syrian region eventually came to be known by the name Jacobite. According to the partisan John of Ephesus, Jacob was so successful 'that all the synodite [i.e. Chalcedonian] bishops from all sides were exasperated, and made threats against him to arrest him and tear him in pieces'.[50] On another missionary front, we find John of Ephesus himself sent in 542 to evangelize pagans in Asia, Caria, Lydia and Phrygia.[51] In 545–6 he cut a swathe through the area around Tralles in Asia Minor.[52] His own claim that 'eighty thousand were converted and rescued from paganism, and ninety-eight churches and twelve monasteries and seven other churches transformed from Jewish synagogues were founded in these four provinces' during his campaign sounds scarcely credible.[53] It may also be doubted whether John converted these pagans to Chalcedonian orthodoxy, but, on the other hand, his missionary expeditions were funded by Justinian, and churches and convents were built after the destruction of pagan temples.[54] Many of

[48] Grillmeier, *Christ in Christian Tradition* 11.2 437–9.   [49] Van Roey (1979).
[50] John Eph. *Lives of the Eastern Saints* 49, ed. Brooks, *PO* 18.693.   [51] John Eph. *HE* 11.44.
[52] John Eph. *HE* 111.3; cf. Chuvin, *Chronicle* 143–4.
[53] John Eph. *Lives of the Eastern Saints* 47, ed. Brooks, *PO* 18.681.   [54] Engelhardt (1974) 16–17.

these churches were in fact dedicated to the Theotokos, whose title had been ratified by the definition of Chalcedon.

Justinian's designs for religious conformity throughout the empire also encompassed the Jews and Samaritans, who became the subject of regulation and legislation to an extent not seen previously during the reign of Christian emperors. Although the Jews fared better than the Samaritans, they too were subject to legal and financial limitations, enumerated in *Novel* 45 from the year 531. Just as he regulated the internal affairs of the churches, so too the emperor intervened in Jewish matters, in *Novel* 146 (A.D. 532) going so far as to legislate for the Bible to be read in synagogues not in Hebrew, but in Latin or Greek, the two official languages of the empire. A body of Jewish dogma was also condemned in the same *Novel*. The Samaritans, for their part, having revolted frequently against the empire in the past, were brought to heel early in Justinian's reign after a revolt in 529, during which they appointed their own emperor.[55] In the legislation of 530[56] they are grouped with Manichaeans and the worst kinds of heretics, and subjected to similar penalties; their synagogues were ordered to be burnt. The relaxation of these stringent measures in *Novel* 120 of 551, as a result of the intercession of bishop Sergius of Caesarea with the emperor, was followed by another bloody revolt four years later, which Justinian sent no less a dignitary than the *magister militum per Orientem* to quell. For their continued resistance to Christianity the Samaritans later had punitive legislation imposed on them by Justinian's successor, Justin II.[57]

In his enforcement of Chalcedonian orthodoxy Justinian had also to deal with the disruption caused by Origenist monks in Palestinian monasteries. In 543 the emperor himself wrote a tract against the controversial third-century theologian Origen and against Origenists, including ten anathemata on Origenistic doctrine.[58] This writing was ratified by a synod in the same year, but in 553 at the Second Council of Constantinople Origen and his works were condemned, together with those of his followers, Evagrius of Pontus and Didymus the Blind. Nevertheless, the emperor's abiding effort was directed towards making Chalcedon acceptable to its opponents. A possibility presented itself, suggested by one of the leaders of the condemned Origenists, Theodore Askidas, whereby suspicion from the Monophysite side concerning the Nestorianism of Chalcedon could be allayed.[59] The plan, which had first emerged among Cyrillians after 431, was a condemnation, on three counts or heads, of the Antiochene Theodore of Mopsuestia and his works, the works of Theodoret against Cyril's Twelve

---

[55] John Malalas, *Chron.* 18; Procop. *Buildings* v.7.   [56] *CJ* 1.5.18–19.
[57] Mich. Syr. *Chron.* ed. Chabot 11.262.   [58] *ACO* 111.189–214.
[59] Unlike e.g. Frend, *Monophysite Movement* 279–80 and Grillmeier, *Christ in Christian Tradition* 11.2 419–23, Meyendorff, *Imperial Unity* 236–7 argues against the involvement of Theodore Askidas in this episode.

Chapters, and the so-called letter of Ibas of Edessa to Maris the Persian, in which the incarnation of the Word was denied and Cyril was accused of being a follower of the heretical Apollinaris of Laodicea. In 544 Justinian issued an edict, no longer extant, condemning these Three Chapters. There were, however, problems associated with these condemnations, and negative outcomes which the emperor could not envisage. In the first place, the Monophysites found the edict unacceptable because it had not rejected the authority of Chalcedon. In the west Justinian's legislation found even stronger opposition, because it was argued that Theodore had died in the peace of the church and Theodoret and Ibas had been vindicated at Chalcedon. Surely the edict represented a betrayal of an inspired council? Vigilius of Rome, who was deeply in Theodora's debt, was not so much invited as brought to Constantinople, the expectation being that he would put the weight of papal authority behind Justinian and subscribe the edict. Afraid of abrogating Chalcedon, the pope initially refused to sign, but then produced the required anathemata in 548, to great opposition in the west. In his tract *On the Right Faith*, published in 551, Justinian reiterated the anathemata of 544. Although this tract also proclaimed four councils and reaffirmed the Council of Chalcedon, the emperor's policy of showing that the council of 451 was anti-Nestorian, true to Cyril and therefore acceptable to its opponents had ended up alienating some Chalcedonians.

Justinian now wished to press on and summon a council to ratify the condemnation of the Three Chapters, but Vigilius would not agree, rightly fearing that the west would not be properly represented at such a gathering. When a council none the less coverned on 5 May 553, the pope refused to participate. Not surprisingly, the Second Council of Constantinople ratified all Justinian's religious policies, professing four councils, the correctness of Cyrillian christological tradition and the Cyrillian or neo-Chalcedonian interpretation of Chalcedon.[60] Despite the fact that Vigilius finally acceped Constantinople II in 554 and was restored to communion with Eutychius, the patriarch of the capital, Justinian had to resort to eliminating opposition to the council's decrees by exiling bishops. The bishops of Africa, in particular, suffered for their resistance to the council, and some of them, like Facundus of Hermiane, who were not exiled, were incarcerated in Constantinople, where Justinian and Eutychius attempted forcefully to show them the error of their ways.[61] Because its oecumenical nature was suspect, the reception of Constantinople II remained ambiguous for more than half a century, not only, but particularly, in the west.[62]

On succeeding Vigilius as bishop of Rome in 555, Pelagius I attempted to win over western opponents of Constantinople II by his profession of

---

[60] Grillmeier, *Christ in Christian Tradition* II.1 459–84; Frank (1991).
[61] On the role of Eutychius in this episode and its hagiographical presentation by his biographer Eustratius see Cameron (1988) 230–1.   [62] Murphy and Sherwood (1974) 127–8.

faith in which only four councils were mentioned. This met with little success, and in fact the provinces of Milan and Aquileia openly rejected the fifth council, thereby inaugurating the Aquileian or Istrian schism, which was to last for over a century. This situation was exploited by the Arian Lombards who invaded Italy in 568, since the church in Lombard territory was in communion neither with Rome nor with Constantinople.[63]

Justinian's strenuous efforts in the direction of appeasing anti-Chalcedonians and thereby restoring ecclesiastical unity continued to be beset both by the separation of the Monophysites from Chalcedonian orthodoxy and by splits within Monophysite ranks, which did not stop with the Julianists and the Agnoetai. In about 577 John Ascotzangès, 'Bottle Shoes', so called because he apparently wore shoes made from the same leather as drinking-bottles, began to teach that in the Godhead there are three substances or natures, just as there are three hypostases.[64] His disciple John Philoponus, an Alexandrian intellectual, became the most able exponent of this doctrine, although the bishops Conon of Tarsus and Eugenius of Seleucia also played a prominent role. The doctrine, which involved an attempt to bring Monophysite christological and trinitarian terminology into alignment by using Aristotelian terms, became known as tritheism, despite the fact that it was merely a verbal tritheism. Theodosius refuted tritheism in 560 in a tractate that was accepted by the majority of Monophysites, although one group, the Condobaudites, refused it recognition and withdrew.[65] Then the controversy seemingly went into abeyance until after the death of Theodosius (566), when certain signatories retracted their consent. Subsequently its history goes hand-in-hand with the activities of Paul of Beit Ūkkāmē ('Paul the Black'). At the request of Theodosius, Paul the Black was ordained patriarch of Antioch in c. 557. This was an unpopular move among Monophysites for reasons which we cannot entirely explain, and led quickly to schism between Jacob Baradaeus and his followers (Jacobites) and the Paulites.

Such was the disarray on the anti-Chalcedonian side when towards the end of his reign Justinian himself, like not a few of his contemporaries both Chalcedonian and Monophysite, espoused some of the tenets of Julianism. This was opposed by senior clergy, notably the patriarchs Eutychius of Constantinople and Anastasius of Antioch, who were consequently deposed and exiled. The emperor was on the point of legislating for a general acceptance of this doctrine when he died in 565.[66]

IV. JUSTINIAN'S SUCCESSORS

Justinian's successor Justin II (565–78) initially had a conciliatory policy in ecclesiastical matters. His first official command was to allow bishops in

---

[63] Goubert (1965) 83; Meyendorff, *Imperial Unity* 311–12.
[64] Mich. Syr. *Chron.* ed. Chabot ii.251–61.
[65] Van Roey and Allen (1994) 129–43, esp. 137, with n. 60.   [66] Evagr. *HE* iv.41.

exile or in hiding to return to their sees, on condition that they maintained the *status quo* and abstained from innovation in matters of the faith.[67] Theodosius died on 22 June 566 before he was able to take advantage of this amnesty, but was given a public funeral in Constantinople, at which, according to one of the sources, Theodora's nephew, the monk Athanasius, publicly anathematized Chalcedon.[68] Like his aunt, Athanasius played a prominent part in Monophysite affairs. In his bid for unity, rather than Chalcedonian orthodoxy, the emperor Justin had the symbol or creed of Constantinople I read aloud at liturgies, thereby leaving Ephesus and Chalcedon in abeyance.[69] In an attempt to smooth the way to unity he convoked a synod of archimandrites, prominent Chalcedonians and anti-Chalcedonians in the capital. When this resulted in a stalemate, the emperor had a statement of faith, which went a long way towards accommodating anti-Chalcedonian demands, proposed at a meeting of anti-Chalcedonians at Callinicum on the Euphrates in 567.[70] The emperor was prepared to declare Christ to be 'from two natures', to proclaim the faith of Nicaea as ratified by Constantinople I and Ephesus I, to condemn the Three Chapters and rehabilitate Severus. The fact that Callinicum was in the heart of Monophysite territory also shows how earnest Justin was in his desire for unity at the expense of Chalcedonian orthodoxy. The Monophysite monks present, however, who regarded themselves as the guardians of christological orthodoxy, would only be satisfied by an explicit denial of two natures in Christ, and the meeting ended in a riot, during which the draft document was torn to pieces by extremist monks. Although he imprisoned uncooperative Monophysite bishops, Justin was still prepared to draft another edict. This too was unacceptable to the Monophysite bishops because it contained no explicit condemnation of Chalcedon.

Rivalry had meanwhile developed between the anti-tritheite Paul of Antioch and Athanasius, who was supported by Conon of Tarsus and Eugenius of Seleucia. Paul had in fact attempted to have himself consecrated as Theodosius' successor, using the wealth he had gained as the beneficiary of Theodosius' will to further his designs on the patriarchate of Alexandria. But the large number of tritheists in Alexandria thwarted Paul's plans by their disingenuous request to Justin to send back to the city the Chalcedonian patriarch, who had been chased from his see.[71] In defeat Paul retired to Syria, to the camp of his friend and supporter, the Arab leader al-Mundhir, and never returned to Antioch. Going to Constantinople, he consented twice to communion with the Chalcedonians there, thus incurring the wrath of his fellow Monophysites. For their part, in 569 Conon and Eugenius were excommunicated from within Monophysite ranks, but they remained active.[72] The fact that they were still supported by Athanasius

---

[67] Evagr. *HE* v.1.   [68] Mich. Syr. *Chron.* ed. Chabot 11.283.   [69] John Biclar. *Chron.* ad a. 567 (?).
[70] Mich. Syr. *Chron.* ed. Chabot 11.285–90. On this meeting at Callinicum see Allen, *Evagrius* 23–5.
[71] Mich. Syr. *Chron.* ed. Chabot 11.253.   [72] Van Roey (1982) and (1985).

enabled them to arrange for discussions in Constantinople with other anti-Chalcedonians – remarkably, under the presidency of the Chalcedonian patriarch John (569–70). The president stipulated that the sole basis of negotiation between the two dissenting parties should be the works of Severus of Antioch. The failure of these discussions was the immediate cause of the publication of an imperial edict in 571, sometimes called the second *Henotikon*.[73] The terms of the edict were moderate, and its inspiration neo-Chalcedonian, but it was much less accommodating to Monophysite demands than the draft edict presented at Callinicum. Although the document is couched in Chalcedonian terms, there is no mention of that council. Justin's aim in this legislation was to unite both Monophysites and Chalcedonians, and Monophysites among themselves, and several Monophysite bishops, including Paul of Antioch and John of Ephesus, were in fact beguiled into communion with the Dyophysites on the understanding that Chalcedon would be anathematized. On withdrawing from communion they were imprisoned, and, with Justin's patience at an end, persecution began in earnest, lasting until the emperor's death in 578. In the west, too, Justin's edict met with little success. However, the prefect of Rome, Gregory, the future pope, was able to persuade the new bishop of Milan, Laurentius, to join communion with Rome, thereby weakening the Aquileian schism.

Between 569 and 571 John Philoponus had written a tract *On the Resurrection*, which was strongly objected to by Conon but approved by Athanasius. Subsequently the tritheists split into two groups, the Cononites and the Athanasians, and the fortunes of tritheism after this point are inglorious. Eugenius fled, Conon was exiled, and Athanasius died in 571.[74] While this split meant the end of tritheist strength, the views of Philoponus and Conon were attacked by both Chalcedonians and Monophysites in various efforts to save orthodox christology.

According to the anti-Chalcedonian bishop and historian John of Ephesus, Justin's successor Tiberius (578–82) continued the persecution instigated by Justin, but in a desultory manner.[75] On his accession there was a demonstration in Constantinople against the Arian Goths, who, in return for their service in the Byzantine army, had been permitted by Tiberius to construct their own church in the capital. This religious tolerance aroused suspicions about the emperor himself, and to clear his orthodoxy he was constrained to take action against the Arians, Montanists and Sabbatians, who were imprisoned but later dismissed on bail.[76] It was during Tiberius' reign, too, that a persecution was waged against pagans, in retaliation for the persecution which the inhabitants of Heliopolis

---

[73] E.g. by Frend, *Monophysite Movement* 322, 366. For the text of the edict see Evagr. *HE* v.4.
[74] Allen, *Evagrius* 38.   [75] John Eph. *HE* iii.15–16; *pace* Frend, *Monophysite Movement* 328.
[76] John Eph. *HE* iii.13.

(Baalbek) had launched against Christians. During this episode alleged evidence emerged of many other instances of pagan cults in the east, particularly in Syria, and the ringleader was identified as Rufinus, a pagan high priest in Antioch, who committed suicide before he could be brought to trial.[77] Finally, in an imperial enquiry, Anatolius, the vicar of the praetorian prefect of Edessa, named the patriarch of Antioch as a collaborator in the sacrifice of a boy at Daphne, outside Antioch. Both vicar and patriarch were taken to Constantinople to be tried, and Anatolius was lynched by the mob in the capital. While the polarity between the accounts of the anti-Chalcedonian John of Ephesus and the Chalcedonian Evagrius, who was in the employ of the patriarch of Antioch at the time, makes a reliable reconstruction of the episode difficult, it is clear that, despite the rigorous legislation of Justinian, paganism did in fact survive in the east until the end of the sixth century, and apparently counted eminent administrators among its adherents.[78]

Increasingly the wars in the Balkans and against Persia were claiming the attention of Tiberius, who is reported as saying that it was enough to contend with the wars against the barbarians, without having to take up arms against his own people as well.[79] Furthermore, because of their fragmentation, the Monophysites posed little threat, especially after the death of the charismatic Jacob Baradaeus on 3 July 578.

The anti-Chalcedonian church, in fact, was in turmoil, and the divisions among monks were so acrimonious that aged and venerable ascetics took to murdering their opponents and had to be imprisoned. At the invitation of Tiberius, al-Mundhir went to Constantinople with his two sons (February 580) in order to convene a Monophysite assembly and to put an end to the incessant quarrels and anathemata.[80] The assembly was a four-way conference between the adherents of Jacob, those of Paul, and the Alexandrians under their patriarch Damian (578–604) on the one hand, and John of Ephesus as representative of mainstream Monophysitism on the other.[81] An eirenic document, which probably hinged on the recognition of Paul, was drawn up and signed by all. On the basis of this success, Tiberius passed an edict of tolerance which was to be proclaimed throughout the patriarchate of Antioch. The Arab prince had given the emperor his word that if troops were not used against Christians (i.e. Monophysites), he, for his part, would make peace. The persecution ceased for a short time, just long enough for Damian to return to Alexandria and start anathematizing Paul. The Jacobites took matters into their own hands and in 581 consecrated Peter of Callinicum patriarch of Antioch.[82] Deceived by Damian, al-Mundhir had been unsuccessful in fulfilling his ambitious promise to restore unity, and,

---

[77] John Eph. *HE* iii.3; contrast Evagr. *HE* iv.18.   [78] Bowersock, *Hellenism* 38–40.
[79] John Eph. *HE* iii.12.   [80] John Eph. *HE* iv. 41; Mich. Syr. *Chron.* ed. Chabot ii.366.
[81] John Eph. *HE* iv.46.   [82] John Eph. *HE* iv.42.

together with his influence over the Monophysite groups, his prestige in the eyes of imperial authority sharply declined.

The hopelessness of attemping to enforce unity, let alone Chalcedonian orthodoxy, on anarchic Monophysite groups had become plain. Although there is little reliable and comprehensive information about ecclesiastical events in the reign of Tiberius' successor Maurice (582–602) because of the polarity between the pro- and anti-Chalcedonian sources, it seems that Maurice too abandoned formal negotiations with Monophysites. Outside the empire he was able to secure Georgia for the Chalcedonian cause, but he was unsuccessful in substituting Chalcedonianism for Monophysitism in Armenia. Notwithstanding the fact that the wars with Persia will have pre-occupied the emperor until the Byzantine victory in 591, there is more than a suggestion that Monophysites were persecuted during his reign. According to John of Ephesus, John the Faster, patriarch of Constantinople at the time (582–95), asked why pagans were given amnesty while Monophysite Christians were persecuted.[83] At the instigation of his nephew Domitian, the metropolitan of Melitene, the emperor apparently gave permission for a per-secution of Monophysites near Melitene, but the persecution cannot have achieved significant proportions, for Maurice became a saint in the Monophysite tradition.[84] In the Nestorian tradition, too, he appears in a hag-iographical light.[85]

Soon after the accession of Peter of Callinicum, another dispute arose in Monophysite circles as a result of the sophist Proba and the archiman-drite Juhannan Barbur, who appear to have applied the philosophical ter-minology of the Alexandrian sophist Stephen to Christ.[86] Their teaching that it was impossible to maintain the difference in natural quality in Christ's natures without confessing at the same time a division and plu-rality of natures brought them close to the Dyophysite position. Their evangelization among Monophysites was so successful that in c. 585 Peter of Callinicum convoked a synod at Goubbā Barrāyā, the headquarters of the Monophysite patriarchate between Aleppo and Mabbug, in order to excommunicate them and check the progress of their doctrine. Together with their followers in many monasteries, Proba and Juhannan Barbur subsequently went over to the Chalcedonian side, where they were accepted by the Chalcedonian patriarch of Antioch, Anastasius (559–70; 593–8).[87]

Stability among Monophysite groups was also threatened by the disso-lution of the Ghassanid federation in 584 after al-Mundhir had fallen under suspicion of treachery to the Byzantine state. Many members of the Arab

[83] John Eph. HE v.15.   [84] Mich. Syr. Chron. ed. Chabot 11.381. See Allen, Evagrius 27.
[85] See Nau (1910) 773–8.   [86] Uthemann (1985) 398–9.
[87] Mich. Syr. Chron. ed. Chabot 11.361–3; Van Roey (1961).

tribes joined the Persians, seriously affecting both the Monophysites, whose political arm was now cut off, and the strategic safety of the empire.

Under Maurice, the perpetual wrangling among Monophysites produced yet another schism in the east. The death of Paul the Black in 581 did not end the bad feeling between the patriarchates of Antioch and Alexandria. In 587 Peter of Antioch, formerly of Callinicum, and Damian of Alexandria came to blows when the Antiochene patriarch criticized Damian's treatise against tritheism. This episode, which was characterized by futile and tempestuous meetings between the patriarchs in Arabia and Alexandria, led to a complete rupture, which was to last until their successors were able to restore unity of a sort in 616.[88]

Although cordial relations existed between east and west at this time, the concerns in the west were different. The Aquileian schism continued there, and on his succession in 590 as bishop of Rome, Gregory was careful to proclaim the four oecumenical councils, likening them to the four gospels, while reserving an ambiguous place for the Second Council of Constantinople.[89] His mission of 596, bringing Christianity to the Anglo-Saxons under the leadership of the monk Augustine, involved none of the doctrinal complications associated with the two main differing interpretations of orthodoxy found in the east.

Although by the end of the sixth century the Council of Chalcedon was generally accepted in the west, in the east the separation between the Monophysite and Chalcedonian churches continued. Among anti-Chalcedonians in Syria and Egypt, in particular, an increasing part was being played by nationalism, fuelled by the long-standing rivalry between Antioch and Alexandria. Whether or not orthodoxy was successfully defined at Chalcedon, its enforcement by emperors and ecclesiastical hierarchy had failed, as had attempts to restore enduring unity between Christians in the empire. Neither imperial legislation, which especially under Justinian became an autocratic tool for enforcing orthodoxy, nor compromise theological statements nor the deposition or exile of their bishops had persuaded convinced anti-Chalcedonians to accept the council of 451 and the Tome of Leo. The Second Council of Constantinople and its attempt to remove all suspicion of Nestorianism from Chalcedon had succeeded only in driving another wedge between east and west. But it was not simply that orthodoxy as defined by Chalcedon had resisted enforcement. Monophysite orthodoxy and cohesion were threatened by the rise of splinter groups and by growing anarchy among the adherents of the one-nature christology.

---

[88] For Peter's side of the dispute see Ebied, Van Roey and Wickham (1981).
[89] Greg. Ep. 3, 10; Murphy and Sherwood (1974) 127–8.

The ironical task of Chalcedonian bishops and highly placed secular officials, to which they were sometimes directed by the imperial government, became to resolve doctrinal squabbles among Monophysite groups in the hope of effecting a unified block with whom Chalcedonians might enter dialogue. Not even the energetic efforts of the emperor Heraclius in the seventh century with his monoenergist and monothelite formulae would succeed in achieving either undisputed orthodoxy or ecclesiastical unity in the empire.

CHAPTER 28

PHILOSOPHY AND PHILOSOPHICAL SCHOOLS[1]

ANNE SHEPPARD

I. INTRODUCTION

The dominant pagan philosophy of the fifth and sixth century A.D. was Neoplatonism. By this period Platonism had absorbed the other philosophical traditions of antiquity. Aristotle was extensively studied but in a Platonist context, and usually as a preparation for the study of Plato himself. Epicureanism and Scepticism had faded away. Many elements of Stoicism do reappear in Neoplatonist logic and metaphysics but altered and transposed so as to fit into a very different philosophical system: the Stoics were materialists, whereas for the Neoplatonists the intelligible world is not only distinct from the material one but superior to it in reality and power. Neoplatonism was initiated by Plotinus in the third century and continued into the fourth by Porphyry, Iamblichus and their followers; by 425 it had spread all over the Mediterranean world. There were several different schools, in the physical sense, and this chapter will consider those in order. I shall begin with the school of Athens, proceed to Alexandria and then conclude with a brief account of philosophy elsewhere in the empire. The two principal schools were in Athens and Alexandria. These schools have often been seen as differing in doctrines and attitudes as well as in their geographical location. However, recent research has undermined this conventional picture.[2] I shall argue later in the chapter that there were some genuine differences in emphasis and attitude between the two schools. However, they both derived from the Iamblichean tradition of Neoplatonism, and I shall begin by summarizing the main features of that tradition.

The contrast between an intelligible world, accessible only to the mind,

---

[1] Several biographical works are important sources for the history of philosophy in this period: Marinus, *Life of Proclus* (English translation in Rosán (1949); discussion in Blumenthal (1984)); Damascius, *Life of Isidorus* (discussion of the period heavily based on Damascius in Athanassiadi (1993), and see now P. Athanassiadi, *Damascius, The Philosophical History* (Athens, 1999)); Zacharias, *Life of Severus*. For bibliography on individual philosophers see Sorabji (1990) 485ff., with the addition of Hoffmann (1994) on Damascius. For the archaeological evidence see Frantz (1988), Roueché, *Aphrodisias* 85–6, Fowden (1990a), Smith (1990).

[2] The Athenian and Alexandrian schools were sharply distinguished in Praechter (1910). For the case against Praechter see, in the first instance, Hadot (1978). For a recent, balanced discussion see Blumenthal (1993).

and the material world perceived by the senses goes back to Plato. In the philosophy of Plotinus this contrast was developed into an elaborate metaphysics in which, above and beyond the material world, there are three further levels or 'hypostases': the One, the source of all other things, Mind or Intellect and finally Soul. Iamblichus and his successors developed this Plotinian metaphysics further, offering more detailed accounts of the three hypostases and their relation to one another, as well as introducing some intermediate levels.

In later Neoplatonism philosophy and religion go hand-in-hand. Iamblichus himself was both a sophisticated philosopher and a pagan 'holy man', credited by Eunapius with performing all kinds of wonders. The same combination reappears in the philosophers of the fifth and sixth century. Proclus, for example, is reported as celebrating the main feasts of all (pagan) religions,[3] while at the same time he integrated the traditional Greek gods into his philosophical system, identifying them with the divine 'henads' which he posited between the One and Mind in order to mediate the transition from the One to the rest of reality. In philosophical terms the supreme entity remains the transcendent One. Here too philosophy and religion come together. The One is beyond Mind and so ultimately inaccessible even to the intellect. It can be reached only by mystical experience. Plotinus writes as one who has had such experience but he always regards it as something which comes only after rigorous intellectual effort.[4] Later Neoplatonists continued to talk in a Plotinian way about mystical experience, but from the time of Iamblichus onwards they also practised the rites of theurgy, a type of religious magic associated with the *Chaldaean Oracles*. The belief that theurgy could assist the soul in its return to the gods and the One opened the way to a less severely intellectual approach to mysticism.

In the third and fourth century Porphyry, Iamblichus and their pupils were firmly opposed to Christianity, although at the same time many Christian thinkers were heavily influenced by Platonism. In the fifth and sixth century attitudes became more diverse. At Athens the philosophers continued to be strongly pagan; Proclus and his successors remained consistently hostile to Christianity. At Alexandria, as we shall see in more detail later, the school gradually moved from paganism through accommodation with Christianity to the situation at the end of the sixth century, in which the last known teachers of Neoplatonism were themselves Christians.

The term 'Neoplatonism' is a modern invention. All the Platonists of late antiquity saw themselves as interpreters of Plato, and from the time of Porphyry onwards commentaries were the main vehicle for the exposition of Neoplatonist ideas. The Neoplatonists commented not only on Plato

---

[3] Marinus ch. 19.   [4] See e.g. Plotinus 6.7.36.6–21.

but also on Aristotle, and tried to harmonize the two, explaining away contradictions wherever that was possible. The desire to synthesize previous thought extended beyond the philosophical authorities. Just as they integrated the pagan gods into their metaphysical system, so they brought together Homer, the Orphic poems and the *Chaldaean Oracles* and found in them the same fundamental ideas as they found in Plato and Aristotle.

II. PHILOSOPHY IN ATHENS

Proclus, the central figure in fifth-century Neoplatonism, was born in 410 or 412. A native of Xanthos in Lycia, he studied rhetoric, Latin and law in Alexandria but then turned to philosophy. It was in pursuit of philosophy that he arrived in Athens in 430/1. He found there a Platonic school directed by Plutarch of Athens and Syrianus. Plutarch, already an old man, died about two years later and Proclus continued his studies with Syrianus. Syrianus died in 437 and Proclus in turn became head of the school. Proclus continued to teach until his death in 485, although Marinus records that his vigour diminished in the last few years of his life. His voluminous output included commentaries on Plato, monographs on providence and evil, systematic works of philosophy such as the *Elements of Theology* and the *Platonic Theology*, works on mathematics and astronomy, works on theurgy and a number of hymns. Much of our knowledge of later Neoplatonism comes from these works of Proclus. He was also a very influential teacher: pupils of his taught philosophy at Alexandria and Aphrodisias, as well as carrying on the tradition in Athens; others moved on from philosophy to political careers.[5]

The Athenian Neoplatonists saw themselves as the spiritual heirs of Plato's Academy. However, the original institution of the Academy no longer existed; the late antique school seems to have been a private foundation, conducted in the house which Proclus inherited from Plutarch and Syrianus. A large house of the period, excavated on the south side of the Acropolis, has plausibly been identified as that of Proclus.[6] Marinus backs up his praise of Proclus' capacity for hard work with an impressive account of how he spent his time. In one day Proclus would give five lectures, or sometimes more, write about seven hundred lines, talk philosophy with his colleagues and give further, oral instruction in the evening. This intense scholarly activity was accompanied by religious devotion: as well as worshipping at night, he prostrated himself before the sun three times a day, at sunrise, midday and sunset.[7] Marinus may be exaggerating the details, but Proclus' own works confirm the general picture of a man who combined energetic teaching, scholarly productivity and deep religious feeling.

---

[5] Saffrey and Westerink (1968) i.ix–lx.
[6] Glucker (1978) 153–8, 248–55, 306–15, 322–9. Frantz (1988) 42–4.   [7] Marinus ch. 22.

What was Proclus teaching? Both at Athens and Alexandria there was by this time a traditional curriculum. Students would start by studying Aristotle, as Proclus himself did. Marinus tells us that Proclus studied Aristotle both in Alexandria and at Athens with Plutarch and Syrianus. Ammonius refers to lectures on Aristotle by Proclus. Aristotle, however, was only a beginning. Students would then move on to study selected dialogues of Plato: the *First Alcibiades*, the *Gorgias*, the *Phaedo*, the *Cratylus*, the *Theaetetus*, the *Sophist*, the *Politicus*, the *Phaedrus*, the *Symposium*, the *Philebus* and finally the *Timaeus* and the *Parmenides*.[8] This list of dialogues, read in this order, would lead the students from ethics to metaphysics; Proclus would presumably guide them through the interpretations of previous commentators, as he does in his written commentaries on Plato, offering in the end either his choice among earlier interpretations or his own, independent view. In his written commentaries he often opts for the interpretation given by Syrianus.

Dialogues outside this canon were not neglected. Proclus wrote a series of essays on the *Republic*, one of which is written up from a special lecture delivered at the annual celebration of Plato's birthday. The Orphic poems and the *Chaldaean Oracles* were also studied.[9]

Marinus depicts Proclus as a model of pagan piety. He describes how Proclus went in for sea-bathing as a form of purification, performed Orphic and Chaldaean purification rites and the rites of the Great Mother, observed the Egyptian holy days and in general kept the religious holidays of all peoples and all nations, celebrating them by vigils and hymns rather than idleness and feasting. Proclus' surviving *Hymns*, modelled on the Homeric Hymns, fit this picture, as does the shrine of Cybele found in the 'House of Proclus'. Marinus also tells stories of Proclus' theurgic ability to work wonders: these included saving Athens from a drought by his rain-making and curing the child Asclepigeneia by praying to Asclepius.[10]

It is clear from Proclus' works that his school was conducted in an atmosphere of enthusiastic paganism. The traditional Greek gods were revered and knowledge of classical Greek literature was assumed. It might seem surprising that this was still possible in the fifth century, but archaeology suggests that Christianity was slower to permeate all sectors of society in Athens than elsewhere. The removal of cult statues from temples and the conversion of those temples into churches were slow processes. Proclus could not just ignore Christianity, however. He does not attack it explicitly but refers in his works to 'impiety', 'ignorance' and 'confusion', using 'code-phrases' which would be readily understood by a sympathetic

---

[8] Marinus chs. 9, 12, 13. Westerink (1962) xxxvii–xl. (Cf. Westerink and Trouillard (1990) lxvii–lxxiv.) Festugière (1969). Lamberz (1987) 5 n. 17.

[9] Proclus, *In Rem Publicam* 1.69.20–71.17. Marinus chs. 26, 27.

[10] Marinus chs. 18, 19, 28, 29, 33. Frantz (1988) 44.

contemporary audience. Marinus reports that Proclus had to leave Athens for a year because of 'a storm'. It seems pretty clear that this storm was a disagreement with the Christian authorities.[11] Yet the school was not a totally pagan enclave. The poet Christodorus of Coptos, whose name indicates his Christianity, wrote a poem on the pupils of Proclus. The poem does not survive and we do not know whether Christodorus himself was among those pupils, but he must have had some connection with the school, however indirect. Marinus mentions that when Proclus first arrived in Athens he was welcomed by his fellow Lycian, Nicolaus of Myra, who was studying in Athens. Nicolaus was a rhetor, whose *Progymnasmata* show some knowledge of Platonism; his name suggests he was a Christian. Most importantly, a significant body of research has drawn attention to the connections between the work of the Christian author known to us as Pseudo-Dionysius the Areopagite and the work of Proclus. In particular, H. D. Saffrey has pointed out a number of close verbal echoes. Saffrey steers clear of trying to identify Pseudo-Dionysius, but whoever he is, he appears remarkably familiar with Proclus' thought and Proclus' phraseology. Relations between pagans and Christians in Athens deteriorated during Proclus' lifetime. Marinus recounts that when the Christians removed the statue of Athene from the Parthenon, probably around 470, a beautiful woman appeared to Proclus in a dream and announced, 'The Lady of Athens wishes to come to live with you.' Pagan worship, it seems, was becoming a private and domestic affair.[12]

Proclus' philosophical views, like his religion, draw on a long tradition. His reputation in modern times is as a great systematizer. His surviving commentaries on Plato survey previous interpretations at length, while the *Elements of Theology* is remarkable for its presentation of Neoplatonic metaphysics as a series of axioms which follow deductively from one another. The range and variety of his work have not always been fully appreciated. He wrote short treatises as well as lengthy commentaries and, like many philosophers of the period, his interests extended into mathematics on the one hand and literature on the other. On the mathematical side, he wrote a commentary on the first book of Euclid's *Elements*. His literary interests are evident not only in his comments on literary aspects of Plato's work but also in his writing of *Hymns* and his attempt, in his essays on the *Republic*, to defend Homeric poetry against Plato's attack.

Proclus taught and wrote in a tradition which placed no value on innovation and originality. Philosophers of this period use appeals to earlier authority as a way of arguing for their views. It is therefore difficult to pick out Proclus' own contributions to philosophy. The doctrine of the divine henads which bridge the gap between the One and the rest of the

---

[11] Marinus ch. 15. Saffrey (1975).   [12] Marinus chs. 10, 30. Felten (1913) xxiff. Saffrey (1982).

Neoplatonic universe, traditionally ascribed to Proclus, goes back to Syrianus.[13] In general the metaphysical system found in Proclus is more elaborately structured than in earlier Neoplatonism; at the same time, Proclus stresses the cohesiveness of the structure and its ultimate dependence on the One. Much of this may go back to Iamblichus, although sometimes we can see Proclus applying the principles of Neoplatonism to produce new solutions to traditional problems. For example, his discussions of how evil can exist in a world ordered by divine providence develop the idea that evil has only a dependent, parasitic existence which he calls *parhypostasis*; this suggestion may go back to Syrianus but is not found earlier.[14]

When Proclus died, his pupil Marinus succeeded him as head of the school. After a few years, Marinus was succeeded first by Isidorus, then by Zenodotus, and finally, probably some time before 515, by Damascius. Between the death of Proclus and the headship of Damascius, the Athenian school suffered a temporary decline. Alexandria, where Ammonius was teaching, was for the moment the dominant philosophical centre. However, under Damascius the Athenian school revived again until its closure in 529. Damascius, probably born around 462, studied both in Alexandria and in Athens. He started his career as a teacher of rhetoric, although he was already acquainted with the Neoplatonic philosophers. He was converted to philosophy by Isidorus and then studied philosophy further, both in Athens and at Alexandria under Ammonius. We do not know just when he returned to Athens to become head of the school there. His surviving philosophical works, commentaries on Plato's *Phaedo*, *Philebus* and *Parmenides* and a treatise *On the First Principles* all, like the works of Proclus before him, derive from his teaching. His *Life of Isidorus*, which survives only in fragments, described the history and personalities of the Neoplatonic school from the end of the fourth century. It, too, was written while Damascius was head of the school, some time between 517 and 526.[15]

Damascius taught the same range of material as Proclus, in a similar way. There is evidence for his teaching of Aristotle, although no certain evidence for written commentaries on Aristotle. There are also references to either lectures or written commentaries on Plato's *First Alcibiades*, *Republic*, *Phaedrus*, *Sophist*, *Timaeus* and *Laws*, and on the *Chaldaean Oracles*. In his surviving works Damascius draws on earlier commentators, particularly Proclus, but shows a good deal of independence and readiness to criticize Proclus. In the treatise *On the First Principles* Damascius argues that above the One there is a further Ineffable principle, completely inaccessible to conceptual thought. This view is not found in Proclus, but Damascius, with a typical Neoplatonic appeal to authority, ascribes it to Iamblichus.[16]

---

[13] Saffrey and Westerink (1978) III.ix–lxxvii.   [14] Sheppard (1982) 9–10. Lloyd (1987).
[15] Westerink and Combès (1986) i.ix–xxvi, xxxiii–lxxii. Tardieu (1990) ch. 1; Hoffmann (1994).
[16] Damascius, *De Principiis* II.1–3.

Damascius was as strongly pagan as Proclus. The references to Christians in the *Life of Isidorus* are veiled but scornful. According to Agathias, Damascius and six other philosophers, including Simplicius and Priscianus Lydus, left Athens for Persia and the court of Khusro I when Justinian in 529 forbade pagans to teach philosophy or law. Traditionally, Justinian's action has been described as 'closing the schools' and it has been assumed that the Neoplatonist philosophers never returned to Athens. Since 1969 there has been considerable discussion by philosophers, historians and archaeologists over what did happen to Damascius and his colleagues. Malalas reports that Justinian sent an edict to Athens prohibiting the teaching there of philosophy and law. This report has regularly been interpreted as referring to the laws prohibiting pagans from teaching found in the *Codex Iustinianus* 1.11.10.2 and 1.5.18.4, although those laws do not refer specifically to Athens. Archaeology suggests that several groups of pagan teachers in Athens were affected by these laws. A group of houses on the Areopagus, plausibly identified as educational establishments, was suddenly abandoned about 530. In one, sculpture was deposited in a well which was then sealed. The 'House of Proclus' too was abandoned some time in the sixth century, although there are no finds which date its abandonment precisely. The combination of literary and archaeological evidence does support the traditional view that the Neoplatonists left Athens in 529 or soon afterwards.

By Agathias' account, the philosophers' stay in Persia was short-lived. The peace treaty signed between Justinian and Khusro in 532 included a provision that they might return to their own ways and live privately, without fear. Where did they go? Damascius, an old man by this time, may have retired to his native Syria. A funerary epigram in the museum at Emesa, dated to 538, is almost identical with an epigram in the *Palatine Anthology* ascribed to Damascius. We do not know when or where Damascius died. In 1969 Alan Cameron suggested that Simplicius, Priscianus Lydus and the others returned to Athens. The only strong evidence for this is a passage from Olympiodorus' *Commentary on the First Alcibiades*, probably written about 560, which says that the *diadochika*, the endowments of the Athenian school, have lasted until the present time in spite of the many confiscations which are taking place. Recently Michel Tardieu has argued that none of the philosophers ever returned to Athens. Instead, Simplicius and others settled in Harran in northern Mesopotamia. Tardieu's case rests on two distinct bodies of evidence. On the one hand there is an allusion in the Arabic writer Mas'udi to a Platonist school in the tenth century at Harran, which was still a pagan city at that time. On the other hand, Tardieu argues that a number of references in Simplicius' works indicate that they were written in that area. Tardieu has even suggested that it was only Damascius who visited Khusro's court; the others never got further than Harran. The references in

Simplicius' works do suggest that he spent some time in Mesopotamia, although they do not prove that he settled there nor that there was a tenth-century Platonist school in Harran which descended directly from the Athenian school of the sixth century. Olympiodorus' remark about the *diadochika* remains puzzling and inadequately explained.[17]

The last known Athenian philosophers, Simplicius and Priscianus Lydus, probably left Athens while they were still in mid career. However, it will be convenient to discuss them here before turning to the school at Alexandria. Little is known of Priscianus. The only two works ascribed to him with certainty are the *Solutiones eorum de quibus dubitavit Chosroes Persarum rex* and the *Metaphrasis in Theophrastum*. The former was presumably a product of the time in Persia, written either during the visit to Khusro or not long afterwards. The latter is a discussion and paraphrase of Theophrastus' views on psychology. It has also been claimed that the commentary on Aristotle's *De anima* ascribed to Simplicius is in fact by Priscianus.[18]

Simplicius' output was far more significant, although many details of his career are uncertain. Simplicius refers to his own studies under Ammonius; he must therefore have been in Alexandria before Ammonius' death, which took place at the latest in 526. He also refers to studying under Damascius, and it is probable that these studies took place in Athens in the period immediately before 529. Simplicius is best known for his voluminous commentaries on Aristotle; he also wrote a commentary on Epictetus' *Encheiridion*. The latter offers a simpler metaphysics than the Aristotle commentaries, and Karl Praechter supposed that it belonged to an early, Alexandrian phase of Simplicius' career, while his Aristotle commentaries were written after he had come under the influence of Damascius and the Athenian school. However, Ilsetraut Hadot has shown that the *Encheiridion* commentary does display acquaintance with Damascius' thought. It simplifies some of the complexities of the Neoplatonic system because it is addressed to beginners in philosophy, not because it was composed in Alexandria. Like earlier Neoplatonic commentaries, it belongs to a context of teaching. Wherever Simplicius was when he wrote it, he appears to have had pupils. Simplicius' commentaries on Aristotle may all be dated after 532 on internal evidence but they seem less closely related to teaching. Like his predecessors, Simplicius offers very full accounts of earlier philosophers' views. Wherever he was, he must have had access to a good library. If some kind of school continued somewhere in the 530s, the pupils may have been fewer and at a

[17] Agathias, *Hist.* II.28–30. Malalas, *Chron.* p. 451.16–21 Bonn. Jalabert and Mouterde (1959) 155, no. 2336. *Anth. Pal.* VII.553. Olympiodorus, *In Alcibiadem* 141.1–3. Cameron (1969). Frantz (1988) 84–92. Tardieu (1986), (1987) (but see the criticisms in Foulkes (1992)); Tardieu (1990) chs. 2–4. Athanassiadi (1993) 24–9; Hoffmann (1994) 556–63.

[18] Bossier and Steel (1972). Steel (1978). Hadot (1978) 193–202.

lower level than in the Athens of Proclus and Damascius; if so, Simplicius will have had more time purely for research.[19]

III. PHILOSOPHY IN ALEXANDRIA

Alexandria was a centre of scholarship from the Hellenistic period onwards. It was there that Plotinus studied under Ammonius Saccas, but there is no evidence of a continuous tradition of Neoplatonic teaching. At the end of the fourth and the beginning of the fifth century, Neoplatonism was being taught by Theon and his daughter Hypatia. Hypatia, as is well known, was lynched by a Christian mob in 415. The Neoplatonic school of the fifth and sixth century represents a fresh start, stimulated perhaps by developments in Athens. There was much coming and going between the two centres. Hierocles, who taught in Alexandria early in the fifth century, was a pupil of Plutarch of Athens. Hermias, a contemporary of Proclus, was, like Proclus, a pupil of Syrianus; his one surviving work, a commentary on Plato's *Phaedrus*, is largely a report of Syrianus' lectures. Hermias' wife, Aedesia, was a relative of Syrianus, who had originally intended that she should marry Proclus. His son, Ammonius, born between 435 and 445, studied at Athens with Proclus before returning to Alexandria to teach. Ammonius in turn taught both Damascius and Simplicius, as well as the Alexandrian philosophers of the next generation, Philoponus and Olympiodorus.

The Alexandrian school, unlike the Athenian, received some form of public funding. Hermias was paid a salary by the city[20] and Ammonius' agreement with the patriarch, to be discussed shortly, had something to do with money. The patriarch may have agreed to support the school, or at least not to cut off municipal funds, in return for concessions by Ammonius.

The close personal links between the Athenian and Alexandrian schools might suggest that there was little difference between them. This is not, however, the traditional view. Since the work of Karl Praechter, it has been conventional to distinguish quite sharply between the two schools. Praechter argued that the Alexandrian school differed from the Athenian in three ways: the Alexandrians had a simpler metaphysics in which the Demiurge, identified with Mind, replaced the One as the supreme principle; they concentrated on the interpretation of Aristotle rather than Plato and interpreted Aristotle in a more sober and level-headed manner than the Athenians did; and they came increasingly under the influence of Christianity. We have already seen that Praechter was wrong to regard Simplicius' commentary on Epictetus' *Encheiridion* as evidence for a simpler, Alexandrian metaphysics. He argued that a similar metaphysics, influenced by Christianity, could be

---

[19] Praechter (1927) 206ff. Hadot (1978) chs. 3, 7, 8. Hadot (1990a).
[20] Damascius, *Life of Isidorus* fr. 124 Zintzen.

found in Hierocles' commentary on the *Golden Verses* of Pythagoras. Ilsetraut Hadot has shown that Hierocles' metaphysics is not significantly different from that of the Athenian Neoplatonists; like Simplicius' *Encheiridion* commentary, it simplifies the system only because it is addressed to beginners.[21]

Hadot has also turned her attention to examining Athenian and Alexandrian styles of commentary. She has compared the introduction to Simplicius' commentary on the *Categories*, commonly regarded as 'Athenian', with the similar introductions to the Alexandrian *Categories* commentaries of Ammonius, Philoponus, Olympiodorus and David (or Elias – the attribution is disputed). All discuss ten questions such as 'What is the classification of Aristotle's writings?', 'What is the end of Aristotle's philosophy?', 'What are the qualities required of the exegete?' according to a standard scheme; they all then proceed to a second set of points relating to the *Categories* in particular and consider the aim of the work, its usefulness, its authenticity, its place in the order of reading Aristotle, the reason for its title and its division into chapters. Hadot argues that both schemes go back in the first instance to a lost work of Proclus, the *Synanagnosis* or *Commentary on a Text under the Direction of a Teacher*, although the second scheme can be traced further back. Wider examination of the Alexandrian commentaries leads her to the more general conclusion that the Alexandrian commentators, like their Athenian contemporaries, seek to harmonize Plato and Aristotle but hold that Plato is superior. This conclusion accords with the conclusions reached by Henry Blumenthal in his study of the Neoplatonic commentaries on the *De anima*. Blumenthal has shown that all the Neoplatonic commentators read the *De anima* through Platonizing spectacles and all sought to harmonize Plato and Aristotle. Individual commentators differ over details but share a common approach.[22]

What then remains of Praechter's picture? Athenian and Alexandrian metaphysics do not differ as radically as he thought; nor do Athenian and Alexandrian styles of commentary. When we also take account of the personal connections between the two groups of philosophers, the division into two schools might seem to lack real significance. Recent work has stressed how much the two schools have in common. Nevertheless, there are still some differences of emphasis and attitude which distinguish the philosophers based in Athens from the philosophers based in Alexandria. There are some differences in their interests as commentators, although the differences are not as great as has been traditionally supposed; there are also differences in the third area to which Praechter drew attention, in their attitudes to Christianity.

---

[21] Praechter (1913). Hadot (1978) chs. 4–6.
[22] Hadot (1987b) (=Hadot (1990b) 21–47); Hadot (1991). Blumenthal (1976), (1977–8), (1981); Mansfeld (1994).

First, the differences in Athenian and Alexandrian interests as commentators. The first Alexandrian commentators, Hierocles and Hermias, studied in Athens under Plutarch and Syrianus respectively, and their scanty surviving work suggests no significant difference between their interests and those of their Athenian teachers. Hierocles' concern with Pythagoras' *Golden Verses* is typical of the period; Hermias' commentary on the *Phaedrus* is, as I have said, largely a report of the lectures of Syrianus. With Ammonius, however, divergence does appear, although Ammonius too studied in Athens, under Proclus. Koenraad Verrycken has examined Ammonius' metaphysics, asking specifically whether, as Praechter thought, Ammonius considered the Demiurge the highest principle.[23] Verrycken argues convincingly that such a view is no more to be found in Ammonius than it is in Hierocles. He considers particularly Asclepius' commentary on Aristotle's *Metaphysics*, which is a faithful report of Ammonius' lectures, and concludes that Ammonius regarded the One as the supreme principle followed, as in Syrianus and Proclus, by the monad and the dyad. However, in those lectures Ammonius has simplified Proclus' metaphysical system in other ways: to quote Verrycken, 'the henads disappear; the Demiurge seems to be simply identified with the divine intellect; there is not much left of Proclus' construction of innumerable triads; the articulation of the intelligible world at levels between the divine Intellect and the sensible world has been blurred. Moreover Ammonius is inclined to remodel the hierarchy of ontological levels into a dichotomy between the creative and the created.'[24] It could be argued that this simplification of metaphysics, like the simplifications found in Hierocles and in Simplicius' *Encheiridion* commentary, is due to the nature of the work being commented on. Aristotle's *Metaphysics* is hardly an elementary work, but in the standard Neoplatonic curriculum Aristotle was covered first, before the student went on to the deeper thought of Plato. Verrycken is well aware of this possibility but argues against it. He points out that the only works of Plato on which Ammonius certainly commented were the *Gorgias* and the *Theaetetus*, both regarded as elementary by the Neoplatonists. There is no record of Ammonius commenting on the *Timaeus* or the *Parmenides*. Ammonius regards Aristotle's *Metaphysics* as the final stage in the study of *Aristotelian* philosophy and he tries to make Aristotle's theology converge with Plato's. Ammonius appears less interested than Proclus in the details of the intelligible world, more concerned with the cosmos. Verrycken finds a similar approach in certain commentaries of Philoponus which derive from Ammonius' lectures. (Philoponus, born around 490, studied under Ammonius and edited some of his lectures. He produced a number of philosophical works but gradually moved away from the teachings of his

---

[23] Verrycken (1990). [24] Verrycken (1990) 226.

master to explicit attacks on both Proclus (in 529) and Aristotle (after 529). He ended his career as a Christian controversialist.)

Verrycken's arguments that Ammonius' metaphysics really differed from those of Proclus are not entirely convincing. Proclus himself readily offers simplified versions of his system when context and occasion demand it. If the henads do disappear from Ammonius' system, they are back again by the time of Olympiodorus.[25] However, it does seem to be true that Ammonius was more interested in Aristotle and less in Plato than Proclus. We have already seen that Ammonius did not comment on the *Timaeus* or the *Parmenides*. Proclus had written lengthy commentaries on both these dialogues, and that in itself might have inhibited Ammonius from writing about them; but it need not have inhibited him from teaching them, making use of Proclus' work. Conversely, Proclus appears less interested in Aristotle, and more prepared to attack him, than Ammonius.

Interesting traces of Proclus' treatment of Aristotle's *De interpretatione* can be found in his commentary on Plato's *Cratylus*, while in a number of other places Proclus discusses Aristotle's view of the divine Intellect. In both cases there are revealing parallels with Ammonius. The more hostile and defensive attitude to Aristotle in the *Cratylus* commentary could be due precisely to the fact that there Proclus is commenting on Plato; the more sympathetic tone of Ammonius might reflect a more sympathetic tone adopted by Proclus when Aristotle himself was under discussion. However, the same difference in tone also appears on a more contentious subject, the treatment of Aristotle's theology. Proclus criticizes Aristotle for failing to draw the conclusion that the divine Intellect must be not only the ultimate object of desire but also the efficient cause which produces the world. In Ammonius, as reported by Asclepius, this criticism becomes a favourable interpretation of Aristotle: according to Ammonius, Aristotle did in fact regard the divine Intellect as an efficient cause.[26]

Support for the claim that these differences of tone are not just produced by the differences of context comes from the work of Proclus' teacher, Syrianus. Syrianus' commentary on Aristotle, *Metaphysics B, Γ, M* and *N* survives. *M* and *N* in particular make difficult reading for a Platonist since they attack the Platonist theory of ideal numbers. Syrianus is quite prepared to go on the attack and to accuse Aristotle of talking nonsense. It is true that in the preface to his commentary on *M* Syrianus speaks with respect and admiration of Aristotle's work in logic, ethics and physics and describes himself as both a fighter on behalf of Platonism and an impartial arbitrator between Aristotle and the disciples of Pythagoras (who, for Syrianus, include Plato). In the subsequent commentary, however, the fighter is more in evidence than the arbitrator. It is Ammonius, in his commentary on the *De interpretatione*,

---

[25] Olympiodorus, *In Alcibiadem* 44.9, 51.16.   [26] Sheppard (1987). Steel (1987).

who picks up the image of Syrianus as an arbitrator, while an anonymous commentary on the *De interpretatione* reports Syrianus as contradicting Aristotle and showing a view of his to be false.[27]

It is true that both Proclus and Syrianus studied and taught Aristotle and, like the other Neoplatonists, regarded his views as fundamentally in harmony with Plato's. However, they are more prepared than Ammonius to criticize Aristotle explicitly, and Proclus evidently preferred to concentrate on Plato when it came to producing written commentary. Ammonius' greater interest in Aristotle has sometimes been connected with his attitude to Christianity: I shall say more about this in a moment. It could also be due to personal preference. Whatever the reason, Philoponus too concentrated on Aristotle, while at Athens Damascius continued Proclus' emphasis on Plato. With the latest Neoplatonists, interests shift again: Olympiodorus, born some time between 495 and 505 and still teaching at Alexandria in 565, produced commentaries on Plato's *Alcibiades, Gorgias* and *Phaedo* as well as on Aristotle's *Categories* and *Meteorologica*, while Simplicius concerned himself primarily with Aristotle. Olympiodorus' *Gorgias* commentary draws on his notes from Ammonius' lectures, while his commentaries on the *Alcibiades* and the *Phaedo* take account of Damascius; one of Simplicius' concerns is to attack the views of Philoponus. By the mid sixth century, interaction between the schools has already dissolved a short-lived distinction between Athenian concentration on Plato and Alexandrian emphasis on Aristotle.

There are no surviving commentaries on Plato by the last Neoplatonic teachers in Alexandria, Elias, David and Stephanus. Commentary on Aristotle's logical works does survive, however; it has also been argued that the third book of the *De anima* commentary attributed to Philoponus is in fact by Stephanus. Elias was probably a pupil of Olympiodorus and describes himself as teaching Aristotelian philosophy as a preliminary to Plato. David too was probably a pupil of Olympiodorus. Stephanus must have been younger, since he was summoned by the emperor Heraclius to teach at Constantinople in 610. There is no clear evidence for Neoplatonic teaching at Alexandria after Stephanus, although it is usually assumed that teaching continued until the Arabs captured the city in 642.[28]

So much for differences between Athenian and Alexandrian interests as commentators. There remains the difficult but important question of attitudes to Christianity. For Praechter, different attitudes to Christianity at

---

[27] Saffrey (1990). Ammonius, *In De interpretatione* 253.12–17. Tarán (1978) 120.13–14.
[28] On Elias see Westerink (1990) 336–9 (cf. Westerink and Trouillard (1990) xxxi–xxxvi). On David, Mahé (1990). On Stephanus, Wolska-Conus (1989). For a different view of the relationships between Elias, David and Stephanus and some arguments for philosophical teaching at Alexandria continuing into the seventh century, see Roueché (1990). An anonymous chronicle of the last Persian kings records that Alexandria was betrayed to the Persians in 617 by one Peter who had gone to Alexandria as a youth to study philosophy (Guidi (1903) 22).

Athens and Alexandria were linked to differences in metaphysics and in types of commentary. He thought that the influence of Christianity could already be discerned in the metaphysics of Hierocles and persisted throughout the life of the Alexandrian school; the concentration on Aristotle and, as he thought, the more sober approach to his work confirmed that the Alexandrians were turning away from the dangerous pagan theology which the Athenian philosophers found in Plato. We have seen that, even if Alexandrian, or at least Ammonian, metaphysics does differ from Athenian in the way suggested by Verrycken, the One is the supreme principle for both groups. The work of Hadot and Verrycken has demolished any suggestion that there is Christian influence here. We have also seen that it was Ammonius who turned the Alexandrian school more strongly towards Aristotle, at least for a time. What was Ammonius' attitude to Christianity? Study of Ammonius' writings reveals no influence of Christianity on his thought: like any good pagan Platonist, he believed in the eternity of the world, in the world soul and in the pre-existence and reincarnation of the human soul.

There is, however, a celebrated report by Damascius that Ammonius 'being greedy and prepared to do anything for money, made agreements' with the patriarch of Alexandria.[29] What did Ammonius agree to? The standard interpretation is that he agreed not to teach Plato; hence, it is supposed, his concentration on Aristotle. If this was the substance of the agreement, it was not faithfully adhered to. Damascius heard Ammonius lecture on Plato some time between 475 and 485, and Olympiodorus listened to a course on the *Gorgias*. The agreement was made either with Peter Mongus, patriarch in 482–9, or with Athanasius II, patriarch *c.* 489–96. It is thus quite possible that Damascius heard Ammonius before the agreement on which he pours scorn was made and that Ammonius did give up teaching Plato for a time but resumed it later when both Peter and Athanasius were dead. There have been other suggestions: that Ammonius pledged himself to silence on pagan doctrines such as the eternity and divinity of the world – if so, the silence did not endure, any more than a silence about Plato; or that Ammonius agreed to teach elementary philosophy courses to ecclesiastics.[30] Neither of these is particularly convincing. A Christian patriarch might conceivably be worried about Ammonius teaching Plato and doctrines associated with Platonism such as the eternity of the world; it seems unlikely that he would want Ammonius to teach his own flock. But something else associated with Neoplatonism would worry a patriarch much more, and that is the practice of theurgy.

As we have already seen, the Athenian Neoplatonists followed in the Iamblichan tradition of practising the magic rites associated with the

[29] Damascius, *Life of Isidorus* fr. 316 Zintzen.   [30] Westerink (1990) 327. Blumenthal (1986) 321–3.

Chaldaean Oracles; they incorporated the theory of cosmic sympathy on which theurgy is based into their philosophical system and regarded the theurgy as a possible route to union with the divine. Hierocles and Hermias are no different from the Athenians in this respect. True, there are no anecdotes about their theurgic activities comparable to the stories Marinus reports about Proclus, but both are familiar with the theoretical basis of theurgy. In Hierocles we find, as in Proclus, a theory of language based on theurgic ideas: both Proclus and Hierocles describe words as *agalmata*, theurgic images, and see the relationship of language to the world as parallel to the relationship between such images and the divine realities they symbolize.[31] Hermias' commentary on the *Phaedrus* includes material on theurgy. Ammonius, however, is silent about both theurgy and the *Chaldaean Oracles*. This may of course reflect his own personal attitudes, but I think it likely that his agreement with the patriarch was an agreement to keep quiet about what Christians would see as pernicious magic. Damascius would have regarded this quite as scornfully as an agreement not to teach Plato. If this is right, Ammonius did make concessions to Christianity in one important area.

The tendency to accommodation with Christianity can also be seen in subsequent Alexandrian philosophers. Philoponus was a Monophysite Christian, and recent scholarship has tended to the view that he was born a Christian. On the other hand, Philoponus stands a little to one side of the Alexandrian school since he never officially taught philosophy. Olympiodorus was a pagan. He maintains the eternity of the world and believes in reincarnation. He also mentions the cult of images, theurgy and the *Chaldaean Oracles*. Like Proclus and Damascius, he sometimes alludes to the prevailing religion of Christianity in terms which are both veiled and contemptuous. Yet in other ways his attitude to Christianity is more conciliatory and more discreet than the attitudes of Proclus and Damascius. Passages in his commentary on the *Gorgias* imply that he was addressing a largely Christian audience, while in the commentary on the *First Alcibiades* he suggests that the *eilēchōs daimōn*, the guardian spirit, is to be understood as conscience. Where Proclus had illustrated the point that agreement is not necessarily evidence of truth by citing the Christians' denial of the existence of the gods, Olympiodorus instead cites the Democriteans and their doctrine of the vacuum.[32] Elias, David and Stephanus were Christians. Elias is perhaps to be identified with the prefect of Illyricum to whom Justinian addressed his *Novel* 153 in December 541. If so, he will have been an orthodox Christian. He still maintains a belief in the eternity of the world but also admits the possibility of miracles understood as direct acts

---

[31] Hirschle (1979).
[32] Olympiodorus, *In Gorgiam* 32–3, 243.16–244.17; *In Alcibiadem* 22.14–23.4, 92.6–7.

of Providence.[33] David has a Christian name. Stephanus is perhaps to be identified both with the Stephanus who around 581 was expelled from the Monophysite church and with the Stephanus who was giving lectures in an orthodox church annexe between 581 and 584.[34] In sixth-century Alexandria, paganism and Christianity seem to be comfortably coexisting: Christianity dominates, but Olympiodorus could openly express pagan views, while Elias could assimilate them to a Christian viewpoint. Doctrinal quarrels within Christianity had become more important than disputes over pagan philosophical ideas.

Neoplatonic attitudes to Christianity may be better understood if they are compared with the attitudes to Christianity found in other intellectuals of the period. Combinations of paganism and Christianity appear in several poets of the time. Nonnus' voluminous *Dionysiaca* is an epic on the legend of Dionysus, but a verse paraphrase of St John's gospel also survives under his name. The attractive poem on the legend of Hero and Leander written by Musaeus uses motifs from Homer and Plato but at the same time appears to be the work of a Christian. Cyrus of Panopolis, the fifth-century politician and Christian bishop, wrote poetry which uses motifs drawn from Homer and Virgil.[35] For Nonnus, Musaeus and Cyrus, pagan tradition provides a literary and mythological frame of reference not incompatible with Christianity. More significant perhaps is Procopius' refusal to go into detail when he mentions a Christian dispute over the nature of God. 'As for me', he declares, '. . . I shall maintain a discreet silence concerning these matters, with the sole object that old and venerable beliefs may not be discredited. For I, for my part, will say nothing whatever about God save that he is altogether good and has all things in his power.'[36]

There is a fair amount of evidence for contacts between the Neoplatonist philosophers and other intellectuals, both pagan and Christian. Hierocles dedicated his work *On Providence* to the pagan historian, poet and diplomat Olympiodorus of Thebes. Pamprepius, another pagan poet from Egypt, was a pupil of Proclus between 473 and 476 before he went to Constantinople and became mixed up in the conspiracy of Illus against the emperor Zeno in 484. I have already mentioned Christodorus of Coptos, the Christian poet whose works included a poem on the pupils of Proclus. Musaeus too may have had some kind of acquaintance with Proclus' work and ideas.[37] We have seen that Proclus and Damascius were well educated in rhetoric. Philoponus is sometimes given the title *grammatikos*, which suggests that he taught what

---

[33] Elias, *In Categorias* 120.16–17, 242.11.   [34] Wolska-Conus (1989) 47–68; Uthemann (1985).
[35] Cameron (1965), (1982).   [36] Procop. *Wars* v.3.7–9, quoted in H. B. Dewing's Loeb translation.
[37] Gelzer (1975) 297ff., esp. 316–22. Although Gelzer's claim that the poem is a deliberate Neoplatonic allegory is not convincing, he does demonstrate some looser connections between Musaeus and Neoplatonism.

we would call language and literature. He is said to have studied with the 'grammarian' Romanus and he wrote two works dealing with accentuation. It has also been suggested that he taught the poet Dioscorus of Aphrodito.[38]

Combining pagan culture with Christianity would be harder for a Neoplatonist philosopher than for a poet or a historian. A Christian poet can comfortably use Homeric motifs or even write a learned poem on Dionysus (if Nonnus was a Christian when he wrote the *Dionysiaca*); a historian like Procopius can avoid committing himself on matters of theology; but a philosopher discussing Aristotle's *Metaphysics* or Plato's *Timaeus* has to decide where he stands on the relationship between the creator God, divine Intellect and the One or on the eternity of the world. But if, in a city like Alexandria, pagans and Christians mixed freely and shared a common culture, then we should not be surprised by Ammonius' agreement with the patriarch, the editing of Ammonius' lectures by the Christian Philoponus and Olympiodorus' instruction of Christian pupils. It is the Athenian Neoplatonists, clinging firmly and almost exclusively to pagan tradition, who are the odd ones out.

Proclus was interested not only in literature but also in astronomy and mathematics. The Alexandrian philosophers had similar interests. Ammonius gave lectures on the work of the second-century Pythagorean, Nicomachus of Gerasa, a mathematician popular among Neoplatonists from Iamblichus onwards; these lectures are incorporated in the commentaries on Nicomachus by Asclepius and Philoponus. Ammonius' immediate successor in his teaching post was a mathematician, Eutocius. Olympiodorus gave lectures on astrology. Philoponus shows considerable knowledge of medicine. Stephanus too had interests in astronomy and astrology, but it remains uncertain whether the Stephanus who taught in Alexandria is the same as the Stephanus of Athens who wrote commentaries on Hippocrates and Galen.

So far, the Alexandrian Neoplatonists have been discussed as teachers, commentators and scholars with wide intellectual interests. Did they make any significant contributions to the development of philosophy? They were the heirs of a long tradition and, like the Athenians, they saw themselves as perpetuators of that tradition, not as innovators. Philoponus is something of an exception. He turned against the tradition to criticize the Aristotelian account of the physical world which was normally accepted by the Neoplatonists. In so doing, he introduced a number of new ideas, notably 'impetus theory'. Aristotle had been puzzled as to what makes a projectile, such as a javelin, continue to move once it has left the thrower's hand. His solution was to say that successive pockets of air behind the javelin received the power to push it onwards. Philoponus suggested

---

[38] MacCoull (1987).

instead that a force, or impetus, could be implanted by the thrower directly into the javelin. This theory was still standard in the time of Galileo. Philoponus also made novel contributions to the discussion of concepts such as velocity, space and light.[39]

Study of Philoponus and the other Alexandrian philosophers requires the ability to penetrate the long-winded form of commentary in which their work is presented. Recent work has highlighted the interesting discussions buried within the commentaries of Philoponus. It may well be that equally interesting material lies concealed in the works of Ammonius or even in those of Olympiodorus, who is commonly dismissed as totally unoriginal. No final conclusions can be drawn about the philosophical importance of the Alexandrian Neoplatonists until individual thinkers have received more detailed and expert study.

IV. PHILOSOPHY ELSEWHERE IN THE EMPIRE

Students came to both Alexandria and Athens from a wide area. In due course some of these students became teachers and spread Neoplatonism to other cities. Aeneas of Gaza, a Christian, appears to have studied at Alexandria under Hierocles before returning to his native city to teach a Christian Neoplatonism.[40] Asclepiodotus, a native of Alexandria who had studied in Athens with Proclus, settled as a teacher at Aphrodisias. He married Damiane, the daughter of another Asclepiodotus, a prominent local citizen who himself had philosophical interests. In fifth-century Aphrodisias, both pagans and Christians occupied important positions. Asclepiodotus of Aphrodisias was a pagan, and the two Asclepiodoti maintained a philosophical school where pagan worship and theurgy flourished. It is not clear whether this school built on any local philosophical tradition. There is some evidence for philosophical activity at Aphrodisias in the second and third century, including the Aristotelian commentaries of Alexander, but little to establish a continuing tradition. However, as at Athens, archaeology confirms the literary evidence for philosophy in the fifth century. Excavations at Aphrodisias have produced not only inscriptions honouring Asclepiodotus of Aphrodisias and Pytheas, a member of the same circle, but also a number of shield portraits and two busts found in a building complex which appears to be a philosophical school. The shield portraits depict both philosophers and pagan cultural heroes (Pindar, Alexander and Alcibiades); the busts appear to represent a philosopher and a sophist. These sculptures may be earlier than the second half

---

[39] Sorabji (1987).
[40] Sheldon-Williams (1967) 483–8. On the problems of dating Aeneas' dialogue *Theophrastus*, see Hadot (1978) 203–4. Glucker (1987) 51–7 argues convincingly that the school of Gaza was primarily a centre for literary and rhetorical studies.

of the fifth century. If Asclepiodotus of Alexandria arrived in Aphrodisias in the late 470s, as Charlotte Roueché supposes, he may well have found a Neoplatonic school already flourishing under the direction of his future father-in-law. No writings survive by any representative of this school, and it may not have lasted very long. Asclepiodotus of Alexandria probably left Aphrodisias in the mid 480s. He and his wife visited the shrine of Isis at Menouthis in Egypt in an attempt to cure Damiane's childlessness. A baby was produced, but the Christians of Alexandria alleged that it had been bought from a priestess and used the affair as a pretext for attacking and destroying the shrine. Asclepiodotus apparently did not return to Aphrodisias. At some point, probably in the sixth century, the shield portraits were removed, broken up and dumped. It seems plausible that Justinian's legislation of 529 affected Aphrodisias as well as Athens.[41]

Another pupil of Proclus, Agapios, taught philosophy to John Lydus in Constantinople. An anonymous dialogue, *On Political Science*, written by a Christian in Constantinople some time before 532, bears witness to the wide diffusion of Neoplatonic teaching among contemporary intellectuals.[42]

This diffusion was not confined to the Greek-speaking world. Neoplatonism spread both westwards, into medieval Europe, and eastwards, into Syria and Armenia. Neoplatonic thought had already influenced writers in Latin in the third and fourth century. Macrobius, Marius Victorinus and Augustine all drew on Plotinus and Porphyry. In the fifth century one Latin writer, Boethius, stands out as strongly influenced by contemporary Greek philosophy. Boethius, born around 480 and executed in prison in 524, drew both on his Latin predecessors and on the Greek thought of his own time. His Christian theology is strongly influenced by Augustine but his works on logic, which include commentaries on Aristotle's *De interpretatione* and *Categories* and on Porphyry's *Isagoge* (an introduction to the *Categories*), show knowledge of fifth-century Greek Neoplatonism, particularly the work of Proclus. Like his Greek contemporaries, and like Iamblichus, he was interested in the works on arithmetic and music by Nicomachus of Gerasa and used them in his own writings on these subjects. It remains, however, uncertain just how much of contemporary Greek thought was known to Boethius and whether he had any direct personal contact with the Greek Neoplatonists. Pierre Courcelle argued that much of Boethius' work was closely parallel to that of Ammonius and suggested that Boethius had actually studied at Alexandria. At the other extreme, James Shiel has argued that Boethius worked from a manuscript of Aristotle's *Organon* with marginal glosses and had no other access to the work of the Greek commentators. Boethius' knowledge of

---

[41] Roueché, *Aphrodisias* 85–96. Smith (1990).
[42] Lydus, *De Magistratibus* III.26. Maas, *John Lydus* ch. 7. Fotiou (1985).

Greek Neoplatonism does appear wider and deeper than Shiel's hypothesis suggests. He was not working in isolation from his Greek contemporaries; yet there is no evidence that he ever set foot in either Athens or Alexandria. It may well be that his knowledge of Greek thought came from reading works of Porphyry, Proclus and others which were available in Italy.[43]

Like Elias, Boethius maintains some Neoplatonic doctrines which one might have supposed incompatible with Christianity, the soul's existence prior to life in the body and the everlastingness of the world. His *Consolation of Philosophy*, written in prison, combines classical literary and philosophical tradition with a Christian outlook and beliefs. Boethius played a major role in the transmission of Greek philosophy in the western European tradition. Latin commentaries on the *Consolation of Philosophy* were written from the ninth century onwards, and the work was translated into medieval English, French and German. His works on logic, arithmetic and music were used in the medieval schools.[44]

By around 600 Greek philosophy was also passing into other linguistic and cultural traditions. Neoplatonic works, particularly from the Alexandrian school, were translated into Syriac and later into Arabic. The works of David were translated into Armenian at the end of the sixth century or the beginning of the seventh. In the seventh century, the Armenian writer Anania of Shirak records in his autobiography that his own, Greek, teacher of philosophy, Tychikos of Trebizond, studied in Constantinople with a teacher from Athens, 'city of philosophers'. This may have been Stephanus, if Stephanus of Alexandria and Stephanus of Athens are indeed the same person.[45] In any case it is striking that in seventh-century Armenia Athens still had the reputation of being the city of philosophers. This was of course its reputation in the classical period, but the persistence of that reputation in late antiquity is due to the Neoplatonists.

---

[43] Courcelle (1948) 257–312. Shiel (1990). Chadwick, *Boethius.*   [44] Gibson (ed.), *Boethius.*
[45] Mahé (1990). Wolska-Conus (1989) 20–4.

CHAPTER 29

EDUCATION IN THE ROMAN EMPIRE

ROBERT BROWNING†

Throughout the fifth and sixth centuries A.D., and to some extent later also, the education of the young followed patterns established in outline almost a thousand years earlier. Changes in content and in institutional arrangements had certainly taken place during the long period. The gradual disappearance in the Greek world of the element of physical training and of the institution which provided for it, the gymnasium, is an example. But change on the whole had been slow and almost imperceptible. Traditional attitudes, methods and values had sunk deep roots in ancient society, roots which remained relatively undisturbed by the social, political and religious changes of the period. Education of all kinds was marked by rigid conservatism. There was no resistance to innovation because there was no innovation to resist. In the words of a recent study, 'Late antique schools of grammar and rhetoric were sound-proof against the outside world, their methods and their status largely untouched by the profound political and religious changes taking place around them.'[1] Such general statements call for some qualification when one looks more closely at particular regions, periods or ethnic groups, but on the whole they provide a valid and important characterization of late antique education and of the culture which it reflected and perpetuated.

The ancient world was and remained largely illiterate. The vast majority of the peasants whose labour sustained its wealth could neither read nor write, and the few who could had had little opportunity to pursue their education any further. However, there clearly were exceptions. Vegetius mentions literate recruits to the Roman army, who were presumably peasants.[2] Education was a function of urban society, serving not only to distinguish the citizen from the countryman, but also to mark an élite within each city. It was, with only a few exceptions, in cities that instruction in 'grammar' – the art of reading, understanding and, on occasion, imitating the works of classical writers in Greek or Latin – and rhetoric – the art of structured and persuasive oral and written communication – was available. The grammarian and the teacher of rhetoric were conspicuous figures in late antique

---

[1] Kaster, *Guardians of Language* ix. [2] Vegetius, *De Re Militari* II.19.

society, about whom a great deal is known. The elementary schoolmaster (*grammatistēs, litterator, ludi magister*) was a more humble individual, whose activities and whose very existence have left few traces in the record of history. He, too, seems to have been largely an urban figure. But there were some elementary schoolmasters in the countryside, especially in the Greek east. They turn up in some of the large villages of Egypt, and towards the end of the sixth century we encounter a *paidodidaskalos* in a remote village of Galatia, and in another village of the same province – which, however, lay on a main strategic road – a future saint is sent at the age of eight to a *didaskalos* to learn *grammata*.[3] How widespread socially and geographically the ability to read was cannot be determined with any pretension to precision. The father of St Symeon the Younger, a maker and seller of perfumes in the fifth century, spent his evenings reading religious books. However, he lived in a small town in northern Syria rather than in a village.[4]

The principles which guided late antique education have been explained and illustrated in the preceding volume of this *History* (see vol. xiii, pp. 665–80). The traditional three-stage system – elementary literacy, grammar and rhetoric – was maintained throughout the fifth and sixth century and later, though the distinctions between the various stages tended to become more blurred than in earlier periods.

Such information as we possess on the content and methods of elementary education in late antiquity is derived mainly from school exercises and similar texts on papyrus, wooden tablets, ostraka (fragments of pottery) and other materials preserved in the rubbish heaps of Egyptian villages and towns. There is no reason to suppose that these are not representative of what took place in schools elsewhere in the Graeco-Roman world, and in the teaching of Latin as well as of Greek. About a hundred such texts survive from the fifth to the eighth century. They do not differ significantly from those of earlier periods, except for the very occasional replacement of pagan by Christian examples.[5] Learning by rote from dictation and copying short texts written by the teacher played a central role in teaching, and there was little attempt to engage the interest of the pupil or to adapt teaching to the psychological development of the juvenile mind. For most schoolchildren the school day must have contained large stretches of numbing boredom.

The traditional methods of learning to read and write developed over the centuries in the Greek and Latin worlds were taken over with little or no modification by other linguistic communities as they became literate. This is illustrated by the corpus of 332 Coptic school texts recently published.[6] Beginning with single letters, the pupils go on to copy the alphabet,

---

[3] Festugière (1970) 5.18, 26.12.   [4] *PG* LXXXVI.2993.
[5] Zalateo (1961); Wouters (1979); Harrauer and Sijpesteijn (1985).   [6] Hasitzka (1990) *passim*.

then syllables, then lists of words – often of names – then formulae for letters, etc., and finally short edifying texts. They also copied lists of numbers, multiplication and other tables, arithmetical rules, exercises and problems. Coptic-speaking students were often expected to learn a little Greek. So we find them copying lists of Greek words with their Coptic equivalents, *sententiae* of Menander with interlinear Coptic translations, and short scriptural texts in both languages. It is interesting and touching to find a seventh-century schoolboy in upper Egypt copying a long list of characters from the *Iliad* in alphabetical order.

Elementary schoolteachers were not in general paid by the state or by municipalities, as were grammarians and rhetoricians, but depended on fees payable by the parents of their pupils. Many children were taught to read and write at home, either by their parents or by private tutors.

Grammarians occupied a more conspicuous social position than elementary schoolmasters, and are consequently far more frequently mentioned by contemporary sources. A recent study identifies 178 Greek or Latin teachers of 'grammar' between the fourth and the sixth century, and lists a further hundred individuals who may have exercised the profession.[7] We possess quite detailed information on the careers of some of these. Unfortunately, we learn little about their day-to-day work.

The aims and methods of the teacher of grammar had changed little over the centuries. The *Grammatikē technē* of Dionysios Thrax and the commentaries which had grown up around it provided the theoretical foundation. Reading and explication of a limited number of classical Greek or Latin poetic texts provided the practical element in the teaching of the grammarian. Damascius, the last head of the Academy in Athens, in the early sixth century, defines grammar as 'the art based on the explication of poets and correct use of the Greek language'.[8] This is almost a direct translation of the definition given by Quintilian five centuries earlier: *recte loquendi scientia et poetarum enarratio*.[9] For both Greek and Latin speakers, grammar was both explanatory and prescriptive. As both languages developed and changed over the centuries, the prescriptive function came more and more to the fore. Preservation of the purity of language as enshrined in a limited number of ancient literary texts became the grammarian's primary aim. As correct speech became the badge of the educated urban upper classes, the grammarian came to play a role in the process of social differentiation. It is probably no accident that many more handbooks of grammar composed in the fourth to sixth century survive in Latin than in Greek. The bearers of culture were fewer in number in the Latin west and felt their position more threatened than in the Greek east. It is perhaps

[7] Kaster, *Guardians of Language*.   [8] *Vita Isidori* fr. 111 Zintzen.
[9] Quintilian, *Institutio Oratoria* 1.4.2.

equally no accident that it is in the late antique west that we find such statements as *Tanto maxime rudibus praestare cognoscimur, qui rusticitatis enormitate
incultique sermonis ordine sauciant, immo deformant examussim normatam orationis
integritatem, politumque lumen eius obfuscant, quanto ipsi a pecudibis videantur*[10] (We
are recognized to be as much superior to the uneducated, who by the form-
lessness of their rusticity and the disorder of their untrained speech wound
and even maim the purity of language guided by strict rule, and obscure the
brilliance of its elegance, which is the fruit of art, as they themselves seem
superior to beasts) and *Experiere per dies quanto excellunt beluis homines, tanto
anteferri rusticis institutos*[11] (You will find out as you go on that just as men
surpass beasts, so the educated surpass the rustic). It is worth remarking
that the first work is addressed to a certain Athanasius, evidently a
Christian, and that Sidonius Apollinaris when he wrote the letter cited was
already a bishop.

Surviving Greek handbooks from the fifth and sixth century are more
original in their approach than their Latin counterparts. They include an
Introductory Rules for the Inflection of Greek Nouns and Verbs[12] (*Eisagogikoi
kanones peri kliseōs onomatōn kai rhēmatōn*) of Theodosios of Alexandria (late
fifth/early sixth century), the *General Rules on Composition*[13] (*kanones katholi-
koi peri syntaxeōs*) of Timotheos of Gaza (late fifth/early sixth century), the
Spelling Book[14] (*Peri orthographias*) of John Charax (sixth century), and several
lexica of uncommon words, including one by a certain Cyril, sometimes
identified with Cyril, patriarch of Alexandria 412–44, a lexicon of rare
words used in literature by Hesychius of Alexandria (fifth/sixth century)
and the *Ethnica* of Stephanus of Byzantium, a vast geographical and eth-
nographical dictionary, which survives only in a later epitome.

In the Latin west the fourth century saw *Artes grammaticae* by
Victorinus,[15] Charisius[16] and Aelius Donatus,[17] all of which are derivative
from earlier manuals. In the fifth century Servius and Pompeius wrote long
commentaries on Donatus,[18] whose longer and shorter *Artes* had become
standard handbooks, while others compiled *Artes grammaticae* which drew
almost exclusively on Donatus. The most original work on Latin grammar,
the *Institutiones* of Priscian,[19] written about 500 in Constantinople, was
influenced by contemporary Greek grammatical doctrine, as was the
shorter *Ars* of his pupil Eutychius,[20] written in the mid sixth century.

These works were intended as handbooks for teachers, not as textbooks
for pupils, and they reveal little about oral teaching, which no doubt varied

---

[10] Diomedes, *Ars Grammatica* (*Grammatici Latini* ed. H. Keil (Leipzig 1857–80) 1) 299.19–23.
[11] Sid. Ap. *Ep.* 4.17.2.   [12] Hilgard (1889–94).   [13] Cramer (1839–41) IV.239–44.
[14] Cramer (1835–7) IV.331–9 (partial edition; the bulk of the work remains unpublished).
[15] *Grammatici Latini* 6.3–184.   [16] *Grammatici Latini* 1.1–269, 524–65.
[17] *Grammatici Latini* 4.355–402.   [18] *Grammatici Latini* 4.405–48; 5.95–312.
[19] *Grammatici Latini* 2–3.   [20] *Grammatici Latini* 5.447–89.

in style and quality from teacher to teacher. However, some of the Latin manuals permit a glimpse of what went on in the classroom. Donatus' *Ars minor* consists of a series of questions and answers designed to help teachers formulate their teaching and test how much of it the students had memorized and understood. Thus the section on the verb begins: *Verbum quid est? Pars orationis cum tempore et persona sine casu aut agere aliquid aut pati aut neutrum significans. Verbis quot accidunt? Septem. Quae? Qualitas, coniugatio, genus, numerus, figura, tempus, persona.* Each of these features of the verb is then defined and its subdivisions set out.[21]

The other principal activity of the grammarian was the explication of poetic texts. This has a long history, in Greek going back beyond the Alexandrian grammarians to the schoolmaster in a fragment of Aristophanes who quizzes his pupils on the meaning of Homeric words, and in Latin to Probus (late first century A.D.) and ultimately to Varro. No continuous commentary on a Greek poetic text survives from late antiquity. But we do possess the commentary on Virgil by Servius, written in the first half of the fifth century, and embodying much earlier material.[22] Servius follows ancient practice in commenting on Virgil's text line by line rather than discussing the structure of the poem as a whole or the place in it of particular episodes or particular characters. His commentary is mainly linguistic, and he only occasionally touches upon mythological, historical or literary questions at any length. His main principles of explanation are *natura, auctoritas* and *usus*, and he easily slides from linguistic description to linguistic prescription. He is alert to ambiguities and to semantic change, and often elucidates a Virgilian passage by quoting Lucretius or Horace or Lucan. But he scarcely ever refers to the spoken language of his own day, as Eustathios was to do in the twelfth century in commenting on Homer. Though he was aware of the existence of variant readings, he never tries to solve a problem of interpretation by emending the text of his manuscript as a modern scholar might do. Fortified by the accumulated learning of his predecessors, he interprets Virgil, not without complacency, in a hermetically sealed world.

His commentary clearly reflects his teaching. But how? Few pupils would have a text of Virgil. The grammarian presumably began his lesson by dictating a passage of the *Aeneid*, which his pupils would copy. Then he would go on to explain the passage, comment on its language and discuss its interpretation. It must have been a slow procedure, not likely to give the pupil a grasp of the larger structure of the poem or a sense of its grandeur. A twelfth-century Greek commentator on Aristotle remarks that schoolboys normally read about thirty lines of Homer a day, while only the brightest

---

[21] On the relation between the teacher's written text and his oral exposition cf. Holtz (1981) 75–100.
[22] Thilo and Hagen (1881–7).

read as many as fifty.[23] These figures are likely to be as true of late antiquity as they were of the Middle Ages.

The teaching of rhetoric in antiquity comprised three distinct stages, which might of course overlap in practice. The pupil began by studying and probably learning by heart a series of short model texts, each illustrating a particular rhetorical genre. These would be explained and commented on by the teacher. Several collections of such preliminary exercises or *progymnasmata* were made in the Greek world, of which the earliest still surviving is that of Aelius Theon of Alexandria (first/second century A.D.). No such collection survives in Latin, but the resemblances in content and arrangement between Quintilian's precepts and Theon's practice bear witness to a common pedagogical tradition, doubtless of Greek origin. The next stage was the study of a theoretical handbook of rhetoric, often structured on the model of a Hellenistic *technē*. Finally the student was required to compose and deliver speeches, both on general moral or political topics and in imaginary legal disputes. Side by side with these three stages went the reading of a selection of speeches by classical writers – Demosthenes, above all, in Greek, Cicero in Latin.

Unlike the grammarian, however, the rhetorician had another role besides teaching. He was expected to give displays of his art in theatres and other public places. These might be merely exhibitions of a virtuosity which was much appreciated by those who had enjoyed a rhetorical education and often admired by those who had not. But he might also be called upon to be the spokesman of his city, delivering epithalamia or funeral orations for local notables, addresses of welcome to high officials, panegyrics on emperors, requests for subventions or privileges, or pleas for clemency. As Choricius observed in his funeral oration for Procopius of Gaza, delivered some time between 530 and 540: 'There are two tests of the excellence of a rhetorician, astounding his audience in the theatre by the wisdom and beauty of his words, and initiating the young in the mysteries of the ancients . . . In his lectures to the young he never let pass a word that was not Attic, nor a thought that was not relevant to his purpose, nor a syllable which spoilt the rhythm of his speech, nor a sentence whose construction failed to please the ear . . . When he came to deliver his own compositions in the theatre – something which he often did in order to kindle in the young a love of eloquence – he astonished every learned ear and charmed all the bystanders.'[24] This public role explains both the close relations which often prevailed between the rhetorician and the governing élite of his city, and the self-complacent aggrandizement of themselves and their craft so characteristic of rhetoricians. A good example of this is to be found in the opening paragraph of John Doxapatres' introductory lecture on the

[23] Michael of Ephesus, *CAG* 20.613 lines 4–7.   [24] Choricius, *Oratio Funebris in Procopium* 7–9.

Progymnasmata of Aphthonius, a text written in the eleventh century, but largely a compilation of tralatician clichés. 'To those who have just come from the study of poetry and its tales of marvels to the great mystery of rhetoric, and who are eager to take their fill of its inspiration and grandeur of thought, it is natural to feel no small sense of astonishment and not ignoble confusion. The greatness of the reputation of the art and its extraordinary renown make it reasonable to feel so much disquiet, and of necessity engender in those of more noble spirit an eagerness commensurate with their amazement. For the more difficult they hear this art to be, and the harder to practise successfully, the greater the enthusiasm with which they prepare themselves to succeed in an enterprise which for the many is hard to comprehend and to grasp with the intellect, and so to become distinguished in eloquence and enjoy widespread fame.'[25]

In late antiquity the general pattern of rhetorical teaching remained the same in east and west, but many innovations made in the Greek world remained virtually unknown in the Latin west. In the east a standard group of textbooks was adopted, probably in the fifth century. The student began by studying the *Progymnasmata* of Libanius' student Aphthonius of Antioch, which replaced earlier collections, but was itself not replaced in general use by the less differentiated *Progymnasmata* of Nikolaos of Myra, professor of rhetoric in Constantinople in the fifth century and friend of the philosopher Proclus. All earlier theoretical handbooks had been superseded by the four treatises of Hermogenes of Tarsus (*c.* 160–*c.* 225) – *Peri staseōn, Peri ideōn, Peri heureseōs* and *Peri methodou deinotētos* – who had introduced a much subtler analysis of style than the earlier doctrine of the three stylistic levels. Both Aphthonius' *Progymnasmata* and Hermogenes' treatises accumulated around themselves numerous commentaries. The earliest, those of Syrianus and Sopatros on Hermogenes, were composed in the fifth or sixth century. Aphthonios and Hermogenes' works regularly occur together in medieval manuscripts, which are probably descended from teachers' manuals of late antiquity. The two treatises on epideictic oratory attributed to Menander were also in use as teaching manuals in late antiquity.

Western rhetorical teaching seems to have remained much as it was in the days of Quintilian. There is no regular corpus of preliminary exercises. Latin handbooks of rhetoric compiled in late antiquity by Julius Victor, Fortunatianus, Julius Severianus, Augustine and Martianus Capella show no trace of knowledge of Hermogenes or Menander. The only exceptions are the fourth-century grammarian Grillius' commentary on Cicero's *De inventione*, which appears to know some Hermogenian definitions, and the sixth-century grammarian Priscian, who introduced Hermogenian matter in his

[25] Rabe (1931) 80–1.

De figuris numerorum. It is probably no accident that Grillius probably and Priscian certainly worked and taught in Constantinople. For late Latin rhetoricians Cicero provided both models of style and theoretical treatises. His *De inventione* was endlessly commented on, as were to a lesser extent his *Partitiones oratoriae* and his *Topica*. Quintilian is the latest authority quoted by most late antique Latin treatises on rhetoric. The causes of this impermeability of late Latin rhetorical teaching are not easy to discern.

Many model declamations used in the later stages of rhetorical education survive from late antiquity both in Greek and in Latin. They allow us a glimpse into the rhetorician's classroom. In Greek there are collections by Libanius (only partly authentic), Himerius, Sopatros, Procopius of Gaza and Choricius. In Latin some of the texts in the two collections of declamations traditionally attributed to Quintilian may have been composed in late antiquity, but they are impossible to date with precision. The eighty-one texts in Sopatros' *Diaireseis zetematōn*[26] are not complete declamations, but analyses of the appropriate arguments and the manner of their presentation. The same is true of some of the shorter Pseudo-Quintilianic declamations. Such texts throw an interesting light on how the late antique teacher of rhetoric set about his business. Two striking features are common to both Greek and Latin rhetorical texts of the period. The first is the predominance of forensic and, to a lesser extent, of political themes. Yet the surviving 'real-life' speeches of Libanius and Themistius, Procopius of Gaza and Choricius, Dioscorus of Aphrodito and the Latin panegyrists, belong with few exceptions to the epideictic genre – encomia, funeral orations, addresses to rulers and the like. There is a curious discrepancy between precept and practice, between the school and the life for which it was intended to prepare. Even more remarkable are the themes of these model declamations. Those dealing with political or moral themes, if in Greek, are set either in fifth-century Athens or in the world of Demosthenes and Alexander the Great, if in Latin, in the last century of the Roman republic. The much more numerous forensic speeches display no knowledge of or interest in Roman law or even the law of contemporary Greek cities. Almost without exception they are set in a timeless world with arbitrary and often fantastic laws. None of these model speeches, political, moral or forensic, betrays any awareness of the Roman empire. When one reflects that a training in rhetoric was regarded as essential both for members of city councils and for those who aspired to play a part in the public life of their province or of the empire as a whole, one cannot but be surprised at this hermetic exclusion of the world in which such men were to pass their lives.

The study of philosophy was never a regular stage in the education of the urban élite, as were grammar and rhetoric. Late antiquity, however, saw

---

[26] Walz (1832–6) VIII.1–385.

a certain revival of philosophical teaching as part of the growth and spread of Neoplatonism as a common world view. Athens and Alexandria were the principal centres of philosophical teaching, with professors who were paid either by the imperial government or by the city authorities or by private endowments. The Alexandrian school was derivative from that of Athens, where the Academy had existed as a teaching institution, if not with unbroken continuity since the death of Plato, at least since the second century B.C. Hermeias, the earliest in a continuous succession of heads of the Alexandrian school, was a pupil of Syrianus (*flor. c.* 430) in Athens, and his son and successor Ammonius had studied in Athens under Proclus (*c.* 411–95). There is no doubt, however, that there were teachers of philosophy in other cities too. John the Lydian in the sixth century tells us incidentally that he studied Plato and Aristotle in Constantinople under Agapius, a pupil of Proclus.[27] It is evident that he did not pursue his philosophical studies in any depth. Later in the sixth century Maximus Confessor is said by some accounts to have studied grammar, rhetoric and philosophy in Constantinople. This may well be a cliché; but Maximus was certainly acquainted with Aristotelian logic.

Philosophical teaching was much more open to attack by the Christian establishment, especially after the end of the fourth century, than was the teaching of grammar and rhetoric, in spite of the pagan tone of much of the teaching material used in connection with these subjects. The reasons are threefold. First, philosophy often concerned itself with such questions as whether the universe was created or uncreated, the relation between the human and the divine, and the foundations of moral conduct, on all of which Christian doctrine had much to say. The second reason was the association, real or supposed, between Neoplatonic philosophy and theurgy or magic. Not all Neoplatonists engaged in these practices, and many distanced themselves sharply from them. But to the prejudiced or uncritical observer, all philosophers were tarred with the same brush. The third reason is the importance which many Neoplatonists attached to the observance of pagan cult ceremonies. A case in point is the great Proclus. Actual persecution of philosophers was rare, until in 529 the Athenian school was caught up in Justinian's campaign against pagans in influential positions. But biographies of Neoplatonist teachers, such as Marinus' *Life of Proclus* and Damascius' *Life of Isidore*, reveal the uneasy and uncertain situation in which the Athenian teachers felt themselves to be. We have less biographical information from Alexandria. But philosophers there must from time to time have recalled the murder of Hypatia by fanatical Christians in 415. Some of the Alexandrian teachers either took care not to give offence to Christian feelings, like Ammonius, son of Hermeias, or were themselves

[27] John Lydus, *De Mag.* III.26.

Christians, like John Philoponus, Elias and David. At any rate, relations appear to have been less tense in Alexandria than in Athens, and the philosophical school there was unaffected by Justinian's purges in 529 and later.

A very large body of writings in Greek connected with philosophical teaching survives from late antiquity, not all of which have been published. They are mainly text-orientated rather than problem-orientated. Much teaching took the form of commentaries on works of Plato or Aristotle, in which the teacher discussed and explained the meaning of the text section by section. These commentaries are partly addressed to beginners (e.g. the Fifth Essay in Proclus' commentary on Plato's *Republic*), and partly to advanced students, who have already some acquaintance with philosophical discourse, perhaps to students who hoped themselves to become professional philosophers; an example is the Sixth Essay in the same commentary of Proclus. As well as commentaries on earlier texts, Neoplatonist teachers also wrote introductory works, prolegomena to philosophy, and elementary treatises on logic, based on Aristotle's logical works and Porphyry's *Commentary on the Categories*. These were addressed to a more general body of students, most of whom may not have made any further study of philosophy. All these works, advanced and elementary, are substantially the texts of lectures given by teachers. Some are still divided into *praxeis* in surviving manuscripts. The average length of a *praxis* is about 800–900 words. If each *praxis* represents a lecture, then the lecture must have been delivered at dictation speed. It is likely, though it can hardly be proved, that most of the commentaries and similar works were delivered in this way, and that the texts which we possess represent what some student had taken down from dictation, rather than the master copy of the teacher's lecture notes. At any rate, their origin is to be sought in a teaching situation. The principal exceptions are the commentaries on Aristotle by Simplicius. They were all composed after he had ceased to teach in 529, and were intended from the first for reading. This may explain their high philosophical quality and the richness of their quotations from earlier philosophers, including the Presocratics. Were it not for Simplicius and his enforced leisure, Empedocles and Parmenides might be mere names for us.[28]

For the late antique Neoplatonists, Plato was the philosopher *par excellence*, and the study of a small selection of his works the culmination of philosophical education. The study of Aristotle was seen as a kind of propaedeutic to 'the greater mysteries of Plato'. But as time went on, Aristotle came to play a predominant role in their teaching, perhaps more in Alexandria than in Athens. Syrianus and Proclus composed commentaries on dialogues of Plato, and Damascius, the last head of the Academy in Athens, commented on the *Parmenides*, the *Philebus* and the *Timaeus*. Simplicius, who had studied

---

[28] On Simplicius' life and works see Hadot (1990a).

in Alexandria before coming to Athens, concerned himself exclusively with Aristotle. In Alexandria Olympiodorus still composed commentaries on Plato of little philosophical significance, but John Philoponus, David and Elias seem to have confined their teaching to Aristotle.

The succession of the heads of the schools of Athens and Alexandria in the fifth and sixth century can be plausibly reconstructed. In Athens Plutarch, a member of a family connected with the Academy for several generations, became head *c.* 410. He was succeeded *c.* 431 by Syrianus, who at an unknown date was succeeded by his pupil Proclus. On Proclus' death in 485 the headship passed successively to Marinus, Isidorus and Damascius, who was dismissed or resigned when the school was closed in 529. In Alexandria Ammonius, son of Hermeias (so called to distinguish him from an earlier homonym) and a pupil of Proclus, died *c.* 520 after heading the school for many years. He was succeeded, perhaps after a short interregnum, by Olympiodorus, who remained head until 565 or later. He in turn was followed by Elias, the first Christian holder of the chair.[29] He was succeeded by David, who in turn was succeeded by Stephanus. The transference of Stephanus to Constantinople some time between 610 and 618, no doubt on account of the Persian occupation of Egypt, probably implied the transference of the whole school.[30] But it is likely that some teachers returned to Alexandria after the end of the occupation, and that some philosophical education went on until the Arab conquest or later.

John Philoponus, a pupil of Ammonius and a Monophysite Christian, whose ideas have interested modern philosophers and historians of science, never became head of the school and may indeed have left it before his death soon after 565. He is sometimes referred to as a grammarian, and may, at least at first, have taught grammar rather than philosophy. In his *De aeternitate mundi contra Proclum* he rejects the traditional view that the superlunary is different in its nature and superior to the sublunar world, and in his *De opificio mundi*, dedicated to Sergius, patriarch of Antioch 546–9, he attempts to reconcile Aristotle's *Physics* with Christian doctrine. The commentaries in his name on several works of Aristotle are actually the notes which he made at Ammonius' lectures with his own additions and comments.[31] Writings of most of these teachers, and sometimes very extensive bodies of writings, survive. We therefore have more detailed information on philosophical teaching than on any other branch of late antique education.

Many students of philosophy, who will already have studied rhetoric, went on to study law in Berytus in the fifth century and probably also in the sixth. An example is Severus, the future Monophysite patriarch of Antioch. Born in Pisidia *c.* 465, he studied rhetoric and philosophy in Alexandria,

[29] *PLRE* III.438. Elias has sometimes been supposed to have been praetorian prefect of Illyricum on the basis of Justinian's *Novels* 130 and 135. But his title *apo eparchōn* is almost certainly honorary.
[30] Wolska-Conus (1989). [31] Sorabji (1987); Wildberg (1988); Verrycken (1990).

then went to Berytus to study law, and on completion of his studies returned to his native city and established himself as rhetor and scholasticus (teacher of rhetoric and law).

From the *Life of Severus*, written by Zacharius Scholasticus, we learn something of the lively student life in Alexandria and Berytus.[32] There was still tension between Christian and pagan students, and many conversions to Christianity.[33] In Berytus a kind of witch-hunt was organized by Christian students, directed against possessors of books on magic – the possession of which by this time was illegal – and denunciations and house searches were frequent.[34] There were booksellers' stalls in the Royal Stoa in Alexandria which were frequented by students, and books seem to have been readily available. When Zacharias Scholasticus moved from Alexandria to Berytus he took with him many books by the fourth-century Fathers.[35] In the law school at Berytus, and possibly also in Athens and Alexandria, teaching went on every day except on Saturday afternoon and Sunday.[36] Some Christian students met in reading circles at weekends to read and discuss patristic texts, including St Basil's *Address to Young Men on the Value of Greek Literature*.[37]

Little useful can be said about philosophical teaching in the Latin west after 425. Augustine, Boethius and Cassiodorus were not primarily teachers. The gradual disappearance of knowledge of Greek in the west from the early fourth century, in spite of a brief and probably somewhat superficial revival in the reign of Theoderic, meant that contact was inexorably lost with the development of Neoplatonist thought in Athens and Alexandria. Such scholars as there were in the west pondered on commentaries rather than on original texts. We hear of teachers of philosophy in various regions of the Latin west, even as far afield as Gaul. Sidonius Apollinaris recalls the philosophers who taught in Arles, but it is not clear whether he is referring to formal teaching or to discussion in a circle of intellectually inclined friends. If there were real teachers, their teaching did not go beyond an elementary school tradition. Justinian's arrangements after the reconquest of Africa and Italy made provision for publicly funded teachers of grammar and rhetoric, but not of philosophy. The broad stream of classical philosophy had been reduced to a meagre trickle. As for the Ostrogothic king Theodahad, who claimed to be a Platonic philosopher, the less said the better.

The early Christian church had often shown some hostility to traditional classical culture as preserved and transmitted by grammarians, rhetoricians and philosophers. Not only was it founded on the study of overtly pagan texts, but it was closely associated with the predominantly pagan establishment. But the spread of Christianity in the fourth century among the urban

---

[32] Kugener (1907) 46, 91–2.   [33] Kugener (1907) 43.   [34] Kugener (1907) 64–70.
[35] Kugener (1907) 48.   [36] Kugener (1907) 52.   [37] Kugener (1907) 53–4.

upper classes who were the bearers of that culture, and the leading role which members of this class began to play in the church hierarchy, led, particularly in the Greek east, to a kind of fusion of Hellenic and Christian culture. John Chrysostom, himself a pupil of Libanius, urged the citizens of Antioch to send their sons to be educated by hermits in the wilderness. It was a utopian project, and he did not press the point for long. What he expected from the monks was religious education, not literary and rhetorical training. Neither in the Greek east nor in the Latin west did the church attempt to set up its own schools in opposition to existing traditional schools. Specifically Christian education was to be given in the family or in the church, while teaching pupils to read with understanding the scriptures and other Christian texts was left to the grammarian. It would have called for an extraordinary effort to do otherwise. How could the church in a brief space of time replace the system of select texts, commentaries, paraphrases, lexica, technical manuals, model speeches, etc., elaborated over the course of centuries, together with the concepts and values which they embodied and perpetuated? And where were the teachers to be found? The church never followed the example of the Jewish communities, who set up their own schools, because, unlike the Jews, it did not see itself as a perpetually marginalized minority. Of course, pagan literature had to be read with discretion. A distinction had sometimes to be made between form and content. Awkward passages had sometimes to be dealt with by allegorical interpretation. St Basil's *Address to Young Men on the Value of Greek Literature*, twice translated into Syriac in the fifth and the seventh century, and into Latin by Leonardo Bruni in Florence in 1403, provided a balanced statement of the attitude of the church in the east: 'We must seek from poets and prose writers and rhetoricians and all men whatever will be advantageous for the care of the soul.'[38] His friend and fellow bishop Gregory of Nazianzus repeatedly emphasized the importance and value of *logoi*, both literature and the culture which it reflected. Choricius in the sixth century puts the matter thus: 'We need a Christian and a pagan schooling; from the one we gain profit for the soul, from the other we learn the witchery of words.'[39] Classical education was even accorded the approval of saints. Among the *Miracles* of St Thecla was the healing of Alypios, a *grammatikos*. The account relates that the saint was *philologos* and *philomousos*, and always took pleasure in those who praised her *logikōteron*.[40] In the sixth century St Cyril of Scythopolis in Palestine emphasizes the utility of classical education, which he himself lacked, in his *Life of Euthymius*.[41] St Gregory of Nyssa sent a copy of his polemic against the heretic Eunomius to Libanius for a verdict on its stylistic merits.

[38] Wilson (1975) 2, 37–9.   [39] Choricius, *Laudatio Marciani Secunda* 9.
[40] Dagron (1978) Miracle 38.2.   [41] *PG* CXIV.596.

In the west the situation was a little less clear. Augustine envisaged a Christian education which could replace the traditional classical education, but never worked out his idea in detail. Both in east and west the grammarian and the rhetorician were left to teach Christian and pagan children alike, using traditional methods and materials.

Monasteries faced peculiar problems of their own. They often admitted novices who were juveniles or adult illiterates. They may have had no need of the culture of the secular world which they had abandoned. But they had to be taught to read the Bible and the essential liturgical texts. Pachomius in Egypt had laid down rules for dealing with illiterate monks, who were almost exclusively Coptic speakers. They were to be given twenty Psalms to learn by heart and tested thrice daily by an older monk. Later they were to be taught letters, syllables, verbs and nouns, i.e. the subjects taught by the elementary schoolmaster.[42] 'Even the unwilling must be taught to read.' The *Regula Magistri* and the *Rule* of St Benedict both insist on monks becoming literate. St Basil desired illiterate oblates, who would be mostly children, to learn to read biblical names and then, surprisingly, to go on to short stories based on Greek mythology. This is one of the few indications in antiquity of the adaptation of educational methods to the interests and abilities of children. However, monastic education in general eschewed all use of profane literature. Occasionally and sparingly, children who were not committed to the religious life were admitted to monastery schools. But in 451 the Council of Chalcedon banned the admission of secular children – *paides kosmikoi* – to any monastery, a ban which has never been formally relaxed.

In those regions of the Roman empire where the population largely spoke neither Greek nor Latin, the situation differed both from that in the Greek east and that of the Latin west. In these communities, members of the local élites had for centuries sought a Greek or Latin education, and by doing so had distanced themselves from their fellow citizens, who spoke their own tongues, were more often than not illiterate, and neither understood nor esteemed classical culture. It was largely thanks to the missionary and pastoral work of the church, especially since the fourth century, that the vernacular tongues of these peoples became literary languages and the people themselves potentially literate. The Syriac, Coptic, Armenian, Georgian and Gothic languages first emerged as vehicles of culture when the Bible, the liturgy and some patristic texts were translated into them, sometimes in an alphabet specially devised for the purpose. Speakers of these languages, who could now become literate without having to learn a foreign language, learnt to read, write and express themselves by the study of Christian texts rather than of profane literature. What they took over

---

[42] Pachomius, *Praecepta* 139–40.

from the Greeks in this process of acculturation was the Christian element in late antique culture. The pagan element was largely filtered out; the few non-Christian texts translated into one or other of these languages in late antiquity, such as Aristotle's logical works, were perceived as playing a propaedeutic role to the study of Christian literature and thought, or as technical manuals. The same process was to repeat itself three centuries later with the creation by Cyril and Methodius and their pupils of a purely Christian literature in Slavonic, and a system of education based upon it. This general characterization is true, with very few exceptions, of translations made in late antiquity. Syriac translators of the ninth century, however, working in a very different milieu and for Muslim patrons, not infrequently translated non-Christian works from Greek into Syriac, and often thence into Arabic.

However, although the structure and methods of schools were scarcely affected by the Christianization of society, the spread of Christianity and its increasingly dominant role in the culture of the age was reflected in other ways. A new reading public was created, side by side with and overlapping with the traditional users of books. The scriptures, liturgical texts, devotional works, and writings of the Fathers of the church were in demand not only by the very large body of clergymen and monks, but by some laymen as well, though we must resist the temptation to exaggerate the dissemination of Christian literature among laymen, as some scholars have done. The church of late antiquity did not encourage the reading by laymen of its basic documents, as many Protestant groups did in the sixteenth and seventeenth century. Entirely new kinds of literature were produced and widely read, of which the most notable were the *Lives* of holy men. Athanasius wrote his *Life of Antony c.* 360. In turn it stimulated a vast production of hagiographical texts in Latin, Syriac and Coptic, as well as in Greek. These texts, particularly those in Greek, varied very much in their literary and linguistic level. Some were clearly written for, if not necessarily by, persons who had not had a traditional literary education, and cared nothing for its values. Santo Mazzarino wrote thirty years ago of 'the democratization of culture in the late empire'.[43] It is probable that there were far more persons who read and sometimes discussed books in the sixth century than in the third. Whether 'democratization' is the best term to describe this phenomenon is another matter. I should prefer to speak of the growth of a new group of culture-bearers and the gradual disintegration of an old one. In the east the new group largely overlapped and fused with the traditional *Kulturträger*. In the west the two groups remained much more distinct.

The demands of this new class of readers strained the resources of traditional book production – which was either commercial or dependent on

[43] Mazzarino (1960) 35ff.

the patronage of magnates. The church had long maintained libraries, to which were attached scriptoria to provide for its own internal needs. These ecclesiastical libraries and scriptoria expanded greatly to meet the increasing demand for Christian texts. When Constantine wanted fifty Bibles for the churches of Constantinople, the book trade of the newly founded capital could not meet this sudden demand, and the emperor had to write to Caesarea in Palestine, where since the days of Origen there had been an active Christian scriptorium.[44] In the Greek east the two systems of book production, secular and Christian, coexisted peacefully. Both Christian and secular texts were copied in similar hands and with similar layout. In the west commercial book production continued in Rome and Ravenna, though probably on a much reduced scale. We hear of a bookseller or copyist Gaudiosus, active in the late fifth and early sixth century in or near the church of St Peter in Vinculis in Rome, and of a sixth-century scriptorium in Ravenna directed by Viliaric – evidently a man of Gothic or other Germanic origin.[45] The surviving commercial copyists, the ecclesiastical scriptoria, and the copyists maintained by the great senatorial magnates of Italy seem in the course of the fifth century to have produced both secular and Christian books. The consul Turcius Rufius Apronianus Asterius 'edited' the Medicean Virgil and the *Paschale Carmen* of Sedulius towards the end of the fifth century,[46] and in the sixth century another consul, Agorius Basilius Mavortius, 'revised' both Horace's *Epodes* and Prudentius.[47] Hagiographic texts, since they sometimes found liturgical use, were presumably included in the books produced by the church for internal use. But one suspects that some of them at least circulated as separate books for the edification of clerics and laymen alike.

Since education in grammar and rhetoric was essential for the urban upper classes, it was natural that from Hellenistic times onwards some teachers should be paid out of municipal funds, just as doctors, athletic coaches and others were so supported. A city which depended exclusively on private teachers who lived on their fees might have found itself with no teacher at all, which would have been a social disaster. In the same way, the Roman state depended on a supply of educated men to run its administration, especially as centralization and bureaucratization increased in the later empire. Considerations of class solidarity would also incline the rulers to subsidize a service essential to the local aristocracy. But neither state nor municipality appears ever to have provided subventions for elementary teachers. There was never a programme of mass literacy in the ancient world; and many of the upper class in the cities probably had their children taught elementary literacy by private tutors.

[44] Eus. *Vita Constantini* IV.36–7.   [45] Cavallo (1975) 117 and nn. 161, 162.   [46] *PLRE* II.173–4.
[47] *PLRE* II.736–7.

Municipal funding of teachers of grammar and rhetoric and sometimes philosophy continued throughout late antiquity, though it was often hindered or interrupted by the impoverishment of the curial class and the accidents of warfare. Such municipally paid teachers were to be found everywhere in the empire. In cities which became imperial residences, as well as in some others, the central government also took a hand in the appointment and payment of teachers.

In Constantinople there had probably been officially appointed teachers since the foundation of the city by Constantine in 330. His son, Constantius II, made provision for a public library in the city,[48] probably to supplement the provision of state support for teachers. In 425 Theodosius II issued several edicts of great interest for the history of education in the capital. The first (*C.Th.* xiv.9.3) makes provision for the appointment of ten Latin and ten Greek grammarians, three Latin and five Greek rhetoricians, one philosopher and two teachers of law. All are to have classrooms allocated to them in the Capitol (*C.Th.* xv.1.3 and 14.9.3). No other person is to teach in any public building, but private teachers may give instruction in the houses of their patrons (*C.Th.* xiv.9.3). Elsewhere in the empire, it seems, anyone could teach grammar or rhetoric in a public place. Another edict deals in detail with the disposition of the rooms for teachers (*C.Th.* xv.1.53). Yet another confers on two Greek grammarians, one Latin grammarian, two rhetoricians and a teacher of law the dignity of *comes primi ordinis* and a rank equivalent to that of ex-*vicarii* (governors of groups of provinces), and goes on to ordain that all official teachers in the capital, provided they are of good character and professional standing, should after twenty years of service be rewarded with the same dignity and rank (*C.Th.* vi.21.1). It is a reasonable inference that the six teachers named in the edict had all been in post for at least twenty years in 425. Imperial recognition of the social role played by teachers of grammar and rhetoric, like that of doctors and others, had long included exemption from taxation and service in municipal councils, and other immunities.[49] The practice goes back at least to the reign of Vespasian. It may well have lapsed to some extent in the third century, but was restored by Constantine by a series of edicts (*C.Th.* xiii.3). Similar immunities were extended to certain teachers of philosophy by Theodosius II in 414 (*C.Th.* xiii.3.16). They are not mentioned in later legislation.

It is not always easy to determine whether a teacher's salary is paid by the central government or by a city council or by both. Libanius, teacher of rhetoric in Antioch in the fourth century, seems to have been indebted for his salary to both emperor and council. But when he argues in a speech for higher salaries for teachers of rhetoric in Antioch, he appears to assume

---

[48] Them. *Or.* iv.59b–61a.   [49] Lemerle (1971) 63–5.

that a decision by council is involved (*Or.* xxxi.16–18). The salaries of some teachers in Gaul in the fourth century seem to have been paid from the *fiscus* (*C.Th.* xiii.3.11), but there is some ambiguity in the language used. For the fifth and sixth centuries there is scarcely any firm evidence for the source or amount of teachers' salaries, other than the edicts of Theodosius II already quoted.

In the high empire the culture of the urban élites was largely shared between the eastern and western halves of the empire. This shared culture is still visible in the temples, theatres, baths and other public buildings from the Yorkshire Ouse to the Euphrates, as well as in the almost identical mosaics sometimes found a thousand miles apart. Greeks, on the whole, did not find it worth while to learn Latin, although some, like Plutarch, Appian, Herodian and Cassius Dio, were at home in the language of their rulers. Educated Romans, on the other hand, were more often than not bilingual, or at any rate had a reasonably good knowledge of Greek. A break begins to appear in the common culture by the late third century. It is significant that the rhetorical concepts of Hermogenes failed to be adopted by Latin teachers of rhetoric, and that the analysis of Greek syntax by Apollonius Dyscolus was not imitated by Latin grammarians until Priscian, who lived and worked in Constantinople. The quasi-bilingual culture of the western-ers gradually gave way to a monoglot Latin culture. Jerome knew Greek very well indeed. But in his famous dream it was Cicero, and not Demosthenes, who held him in thrall. His almost equally learned contemporary Augustine was bored by Greek at school, and never learned enough to understand the Greek church Fathers of the fourth century.[50] The gulf between eastern and western culture was widening. At the same time, however, the transfer of the imperial capital to Constantinople and the increasing bureaucratization of the Roman government meant that more easterners learned Latin in order to further their careers. Libanius laments the abandonment of the study of rhetoric for that of Latin by some of his most promising pupils. Most of these young Greeks probably aimed at no more than a functional knowledge of the language. But in order to learn it they were obliged by the age-old pedagogical tradition to make some study, however superficial, of a few works of Latin literature. The papyri from late antique Egypt contain-ing passages from Virgil with a parallel 'crib' in Greek illustrate vividly how a Hellenophone learned Latin.

In the fifth century large tracts of Roman territory in the west passed into barbarian control, and by the end of the century Italy itself was an Ostrogothic kingdom. In general, the new Germanic rulers were not much interested at first in classical culture, which they saw as a threat to their sense of ethnic identity. But attitudes varied from region to region. In Italy

[50] Aug. *Conf.* 1.13.

schools continued to flourish. The rich and influential senatorial aristocracy and the still numerous upper class of the cities provided a milieu in which they had an important role to play. And the favourable policy of Theoderic, who had spent his youth in Constantinople, helped to preserve the traditional educational structures. Ennodius (473/4–521), bishop of Pavia, paints a picture of flourishing schools in northern Italy.[51] Boethius planned to translate into Latin all of Plato and Aristotle, but was prevented from realizing his project by his early death. The project bears witness both to a lively interest in philosophy and to a declining knowledge of Greek in Italy. He is today remembered for his five theological treatises and above all for his *Consolation of Philosophy*, written while he was in prison awaiting execution.[52]

Cassiodorus (*c.* 487–*c.* 580) proposed to establish a kind of university in Rome, in which classical literature and philosophy would be studied as a preparation for the study of theology. His *Institutiones* provide an idea of the curriculum which he envisaged. However, twenty years of war destroyed not only much of the material fabric of Italy, but also the social fabric of Italian society, and Cassiodorus had to content himself with establishing a monastery at Vivarium in Calabria, where he strove to salvage what he could of classical and Christian culture. Justinian by his Pragmatic Sanction of 554 made some attempt to restore higher education in Rome. Teachers of grammar and rhetoric were to be found in Rome and Ravenna in the second half of the sixth century, under whom the future pope Gregory the Great and the poet Venantius Fortunatus studied, but the Lombard invasion in 568 struck the final blow to traditional education in Italy, leaving monasteries as virtually the sole institutions providing basic literacy.[53]

In North Africa the Vandals at first gave no encouragement to traditional education, and the flight of many of the wealthier citizens must have reduced the support for classical culture. But the new rulers gradually came to appreciate Latin learning, and to acquire a taste for panegyrics of themselves in the classical manner. In the reigns of king Gunthamund (484–96) and king Thrasamund (493–523) schools were established in Carthage. The vast encyclopaedia of Martianus Capella, *De nuptiis Philologiae et Mercurii*,[54] written in the fifth century, testifies to a revived, if somewhat superficial, interest in classical culture. Poetry flourished, as exemplified by the technically correct but shallow poems collected in the *Latin Anthology* and the *De laudibus Dei* of Dracontius.[55] Corippus, the last notable Latin poet in the classical tradition, was educated in Vandal Carthage and composed there in 549 his panegyrical account of the exploits of the Byzantine general John

---

[51] *DBI* 42 (1993) 681–95; Fontaine (1962).   [52] Gibson (ed.), *Boethius*; Chadwick, *Boethius*.
[53] Mommsen (1874); Mynors (1937); cf. O'Donnell (1979); Momigliano (1955).
[54] Cf. Le Moine (1972).   [55] Vollmer (1914).

Troglita before migrating to Constantinople, where he celebrated the accession of Justin II in 565.[56]

Prose writing, mainly of Christian content, flourished in late antique Africa. Typical works are the *Chronicle* of Victor of Tunnuna and the numerous Christian polemical treatises and other works of Fulgentius of Ruspe. Both writers were active in the sixth century. Schools continued to function, albeit on a dwindling scale, until the capture of Carthage by the Arabs in 698.

In Spain the establishment of a Visigothic kingdom marked less of a break than elsewhere in the barbarian west and did not change the dominant role of classical Latin culture. Cities survived unscathed, and new ones were founded by the Visigothic rulers. The Byzantine reconquest of southern Spain, short-lived as it was, encouraged the maintenance of Roman institutions and way of life. The conversion to the Catholic faith of king Reccared in 589 brought Visigoths and Hispano-Romans closer together, and leading Visigothic families intermarried with the surviving senatorial aristocracy. There is little direct evidence for schools, but the general level of culture, and the recently discovered documents written on slate in a late Roman cursive hand, suggest that they had not disappeared. Medicine and law continued to be studied. The Visigothic kings patronized literature, and king Sisebut (612) even dabbled in Latin verse; an astronomical poem in sixty-one hexameters survives from his pen. Eugenius, bishop of Toledo (died 657), revised Dracontius' poem *De laudibus Dei*. Isidore of Seville (*c.* 570–636) must have had a fairly rich library at his disposal when he composed his encyclopaedic *Etymologiae*.[57] John of Toledo (*c.* 642–90) composed minor works on theology and grammar. In 710 Toledo was captured by the Arabs. The Romano-Visigothic culture did not very long survive its fall.

In Gaul the situation was more complex. In the fifth and sixth century the region south of the Loire and the Langres plateau, though ruled by Visigothic, Burgundian and Frankish kings, still belonged culturally and socially to the Mediterranean world, whereas in the north, which was subject to invasions and where Latin culture was more thinly implanted, Roman institutions and social relations largely vanished. In Provence, Burgundy and Aquitaine the old senatorial families survived and flourished in uneasy symbiosis with barbarian rulers. But city life gradually dwindled, and with it public schools, and, indeed, schools of any kind, became few and scattered. The aristocrats had their libraries and included in their entourage men of learning, sometimes slaves. Sidonius Apollinaris (431–90) corresponds with his friends in elegant Latin, peppered with classical allusions and involved figures of speech. His friend, the senator Felix,

---

[56] Diggle and Goodyear (1970); Cameron, *Corippus*.   [57] Fontaine (1959) 846–61, 1174–80.

studies Virgil and Roman law with the help of a slave tutor. Poets and orators follow classical models.[58] Inscriptions are set up in public places, and city officials draw up documents in traditional form. But this elegant society, so conscious of being Roman, was living on an inherited stock of cultural capital which it could not replace. In the late sixth century Gregory of Tours (539–95), though belonging to an ancient Gallo-Roman family, was unable because of the early death of his parents to learn grammar, something which he deeply regretted. Later in life he read Virgil. But his *History of the Franks* and his *Lives* of saints are written in unpolished and sometimes awkward Latin, and his perception of the world about him is almost exclusively a religious one.[59] Desiderius, bishop of Vienne (died 607), scion of an aristocratic family, learnt grammar in Vienne, where there were still teachers in the early sixth century.[60] But when he became bishop towards the end of the century there was no longer any teacher in the city. So the bishop himself set about teaching grammar to a circle of young men, for which he was sternly rebuked by pope Gregory the Great.[61] Yet he was only trying to deal with the problem of educating possible future clergy, a problem which became progressively more urgent during the sixth century throughout the barbarian world. In south-east Gaul there were still men who had not entirely forgotten the literary culture of their forefathers. The biographer(s) of Caesarius of Arles, writing about 550, feared the criticism of their Latinity by the *scholastici* of Provence.[62] Caprasius, a seventh-century monk from Lérins, was horrified to find that Provençal clergy 'studied books of the pagans, fables of poets, comedies and songs'.[63] The Provençal priest Florentius, composed a *Life* of St Rusticula in elegant and correct Latin in the mid seventh century.[64] But by his time the traditional literary culture had become difficult to adapt to the new world of the early Middle Ages.

Though, as we have seen, events took a slightly different course in each of the Germanic kingdoms which were established in former Roman territory, in the end three features appeared in all of them, which sharply distinguished education and culture in the west from that in the east. The first is the loss of the knowledge of Greek. Boethius in Rome could contemplate translating Plato and Aristotle into Latin. Sidonius Apollinaris in Auvergne could still read Menander with his son – presumably because he could not find a teacher of Greek grammar. Isidore of Seville, polymath though he was, in all probability knew no Greek. This loss of contact with Greek language, literature and culture was part of a larger change, the break-up of the unity of the Mediterranean Graeco-Roman world, which affected trade, ecclesiastical relations and much else besides. We must

---

[58] Chadwick (1955).   [59] Convegno Todi (1977); Goffart (1988).   [60] Riché (1972) 233–6.
[61] Greg. Mag. *Ep.* 11.34.   [62] Morin (1942) 297.   [63] *Vita Caprasii, AASS* 1 June, 78.
[64] Riché (1954) 369–77.

remember, however, that here and there pockets of Greek culture survived, particularly in southern Italy and in some church circles in Rome.

The second feature is the separation between classical culture and Christian culture. In the Greek-speaking world much of the classical literary heritage was quietly taken over and adapted by the fourth-century Church Fathers, and absorbed into the Christian Greek culture of Byzantium. In the west much of the Latin cultural heritage was marginalized, or survived in selections as a propaedeutic to the study of Christian literature and thought. Virgil, Horace, Terence, Lucan, Sallust and other classical authors were read, but by fewer and fewer people, and even then in the safety of the schoolroom.[65]

The third common feature was that, as secular schools became fewer, it became more difficult to find literate candidates for training as clergy. Consequently bishops and sometimes priests were obliged to take over what had previously been the work of the *ludi magister* and the grammarian, and teach boys and young men themselves. This led to the first beginnings of what were to become the cathedral schools and parish schools of the Middle Ages. This movement was perhaps most marked in Gaul, but the same need led to the same solution in all other regions of the barbarian west. From the end of the sixth century this rather jejune culture was gradually enriched by the influence of monks from Ireland and England, where some features of classical culture had been better preserved than in continental Europe. But the old educational system was never revived.

In the Greek east, contact with Latin culture was not so immediately lost. There were many Latin-speaking communities in the territories ruled from Constantinople – Africa after 533, Sicily, much of Italy, much of the northern and western Balkans. And there were many Latin speakers in Constantinople itself, beginning with the emperors Justin I and Justinian, and including influential refugees from Africa and Italy and their entourages and descendants. Latin remained the language of the law, the army, the central administration and the imperial court, either exclusively or along with Greek, until the end of the sixth century. So it is scarcely surprising that public and private teachers of Latin were to be found in the capital throughout the fifth and most of the sixth century. Priscian was the greatest of these, but at least twenty-one others are known to us by name. It may, however, be no accident that we have no certain attestation of the presence of a Latin grammarian in Constantinople in the second half of the sixth century. Fewer Latin rhetoricians are known. What emerges from this is that it was possible to obtain a literary education in Latin in Constantinople up to the death of Justinian in 565, and probably later. There must therefore still have been a demand for such an education. Nevertheless, it is clear

---

[65] Kaster, *Guardians of Language* 72ff.

from the use of Greek in most of Justinian's *Novels* and from other indications that effective communication throughout the eastern empire required the use of Greek. The Latin-speaking community in the capital may have become progressively marginalized and isolated, as were the speakers of Syriac and Coptic. The future pope Gregory the Great spent seven years, from 579 to 586, as papal *apocrisiarius* in Constantinople without learning a word of Greek, or so he claims.

NON-LITERARY EDUCATION

Doctors in late antiquity learnt their craft either by a kind of apprenticeship under a senior doctor, or by a formal course of study, or perhaps in both ways. Most large cities had one or more public doctors, who received both a salary from the state or from the city authorities, as well as fees from their wealthier patients. These public doctors appear to have been under an obligation, perhaps customary rather than legal, to teach pupils. This was probably the way in which the majority of doctors learnt medicine. When they had completed their training to the satisfaction of their teacher, they received a letter of attestation or testimonial. The formal study of medicine was pursued above all in Alexandria, where a school of medicine existed until after the Arab conquest in the mid seventh century. The subject was regarded as a branch of philosophy, and several of the teachers of medicine there are described as philosophers. The link between medicine and philosophy was an old one; Galen had already observed that no one could be a good doctor unless he had studied philosophy. David, head of the Alexandrian school of philosophy in the early sixth century, wrote a commentary on Hippocrates' *Prognostica*.[66] Asclepiodotus (late fifth century), a polymath with a touch of charlatanism, studied medicine in Alexandria and taught both medicine and philosophy in Aphrodisias and later in Alexandria. There was also formal teaching of medicine in Constantinople, probably in the fifth century. Agapius, a native of Alexandria, where he studied and probably taught medicine, went to Constantinople in the mid fifth century as a teacher of medicine, perhaps in the framework of the revived 'university' of Theodosius II.[67] Hesychius of Damascus practised and taught medicine in the capital about the same period.[68] His son and pupil Iacobus was *comes et archiatrus* there in the reign of Leo I. He is said to have lived on his official salary and to have charged no fees. He was an advocate of therapy by cold baths, whence his nickname *Psychristos* ('Cooled').[69] He numbered among his patients both Leo I and the philosopher Proclus, and statues of him were set up in Constantinople and Athens.

[66] Westerink (1964). [67] *PLRE* II.32. [68] *PLRE* II.554. [69] *PLRE* II.582–3.

It is likely that the teaching of public doctors had a strong practical emphasis, though one must not underestimate the role that could be played by systematic handbooks. In the Alexandrian medical school, treatises of Galen and Hippocrates – in that order – provided the basis of teaching. They seem to have been commented on in the same way as the works of Aristotle. Several such commentaries survive – e.g. Palladios' on Galen's *De sectis*, and on Book VI of Hippocrates' *Epidemics* and *De fracturis*, as well as a synoptic handbook on fevers variously attributed to Palladius, Theophilus Protospatharius and Stephanus of Alexandria, and a treatise by Paul of Nicaea (or of Nike in Thrace?) on diagnosis and therapy. Doctors who studied in Alexandria often obtained posts as public doctors or *archiatri*, though no doubt many others entered private practice.

The doctor's *Doppelgänger*, the veterinarian (*veterinarius*, *hippiatros*), must have been an important figure in a predominantly agrarian society such as that of the late Roman empire. He certainly had a role to play in the Roman army. We know disappointingly little of how he was trained. There was no institutional arrangement for veterinary education. But there was a body of technical literature, both in Greek and in Latin, which budding veterinarians must have studied, and which, in its turn, reflected the content and arrangement of teaching. In Greek there survive handbooks attributed to Chrion – no doubt a pseudonym – and Apsyrtus of Prusa (late sixth century), and a medieval compilation of excerpts from earlier works entitled *Hippiatrica*. In Latin there are a collection of letters on veterinary practice by Pelagonius (probably fourth century), a *Mulomedicina sive ars veterinaria* attributed to P. Vegetius, probably to be identified with Flavius Vegetius Renatus, author of an *Epitome rei militaris*, and a Latin adaptation of the Greek text of 'Chrion'. To judge by these specimens, the veterinary art lacked the philosophical basis of medicine. Empiricism tempered by superstition is characteristic of veterinary literature. Vegetius attempts a somewhat more elevated style than the authors of the other surviving treatises.

Pleading in courts of law was often, as in earlier times, done by persons trained in rhetoric, who depended on experts for advice on legal matters. Genuine legal education was, however, available, and a far-reaching reform of it was carried out by Justinian in the first decade of his reign. Many students seem to have studied law after completing a course in rhetoric. Until Justinian's reform of Roman law, a knowledge of Latin was essential for the serious study of the subject. The publication of the *Institutes* (533), the *Digest* (533) and the Code (second edition 534) made reference to the original texts of the Roman jurisconsults unnecessary, and since Greek translations of Justinian's *Corpus Iuris* were soon made, professional legal studies became accessible to those who knew little Latin.

The primary source on legal education in late antiquity is Justinian's *Constitutio omnem* (533) which prescribes a programme of instruction based on the new *Corpus Iuris*. It also describes briefly the arrangements previously in force. This Constitution, though no doubt clear to contemporaries, is not entirely free from ambiguity for us. Legal education, it declares, had previously been available in a number of cities, including Alexandria and Caesarea in Palestine. These schools were henceforth to be closed, and the teaching of law confined to Berytus and Constantinople. No mention is made of Rome, which when the Constitution was promulgated was under Ostrogothic rule. But Law had been, and no doubt still was, taught there, and provision was made for the payment of public teachers of law in the Pragmatic Sanction of 554, after the reconquest of Italy.

Before Justinian's reforms, law was studied for four years, with an optional fifth year. The first year was devoted to reading the *Institutes* of Gaius and to the law on dowry, *tutela*, wills and legacies. In their second year, students studied the *prima pars legum* together with portions of the *partes de rebus* and *de iudiciis* (these expressions probably refer to portions of the commentaries of the classical jurists on the Praetorian Edict, particularly those of Ulpian; but their precise meaning is not clear to us). The subject matter of the third year was the remainder of the *partes de rebus* and *de iudiciis*, together with selections from the *responsa* of Papinian. In their fourth year, students studied the *responsa* of Paulus on their own and were not expected to attend lectures. The optional fifth year may have been occupied by the study of imperial constitutions.

The new programme of study instituted by Justinian lasted five years. In their first year, students attended lectures on the *Institutes* and the first part of the *Digest* – probably Books 1–4. The second year was devoted to the study of either Books 5–11 of the *Digest* (*De iudiciis*) or Books 12–19 (*De rebus*), in both cases plus Books 23, 26, 28 and 30, dealing respectively with dowry, *tutela*, wills and legacies. In their third year, students attended lectures on whichever of the sections of the *Digest* they had not covered in their second year, as well as Books 20–2. The fourth year was for private study of the books of the *Digest* up to Book 36, which had not been expounded in the second and third years. The fifth year was for private study of Justinian's Code. The detailed arrangements for this programme escape us, but it seems likely that the same professor taught a group of students through the whole of their five-year course. Students of each year had long had names, no doubt originally unofficial. Freshmen had been known as *dupondii*, the meaning of which is not clear, but it was probably pejorative. Second- and third-year students were known as *Edictales* and *Papinianistae*, and fourth-year students were *lytai*. Justinian, who was fussy about such matters, prescribed the following names: *Iustiniani novi, Edictales, Papinianistae, lytai* and *prolytai*. He also prohibited all traditional student ragging – with what effect we do not know. These matters have been set out in some detail, not only for their intrinsic interest, but also as some indication of the precision with which teaching programmes in other fields may have been organized. No other programme of instruction, however, is likely to have been the subject of imperial legislation. But law had always been a close concern of the Roman state.

Architects and engineers were normally trained by a kind of apprenticeship system. Diocletian's Edict on Maximum Prices establishes a monthly fee payable by or for the pupils of an *architectus magister*. Constantine in an Edict of 334 orders a provincial governor to urge (*impellere*) youths aged eighteen *qui liberales litteras degustaverint* to study architecture, and grants to them and their parents immunity from personal taxes as well as a *salarium competens* (*C.Th.* XIII.4.1). These young men will have completed their studies with the *grammaticus* before going on to study architecture. The profession was not merely literate but cultured. Anthemius of Tralles, the architect of Hagia Sophia in Constantinople, was not only a man of remarkable imagination and technical skill, but was also an applied mathematician and engineer of distinction and author of a surviving treatise *On Unusual Devices* (*Peri paradoxōn mēchanēmatōn*) as well as a lost treatise on *Burning-Mirrors*. He was a member of an unusually talented family, and may well have studied mathematics in Alexandria.[70]

Surveyors probably learnt their craft by a similar system of apprenticeship. Their role in the assessment of taxes gave them unusual importance in the eyes of the state in late antiquity, which probably explains why Diocletian's Edict on Maximum Prices allows them to charge twice as much as architects for teaching pupils. They enjoyed the relatively high social status accorded to practitioners of a profession based on a body of theory enshrined in written texts.

At a much lower social level, and hence much less frequently mentioned in our sources, came the practitioners of fine and applied arts – painters, sculptors, potters, jewellers, mosaicists, etc. They too were taught by an apprenticeship system. But concerning these professions there was no body of theory and no authoritative texts. Diocletian's Edict accords to a portrait-painter 150 *denarii* a day, to a mural painter 75 *denarii*, to a mosaicist 60 *denarii*, and to a mason or carpenter 50 *denarii*. These were not contemptible wages, but they were far below those of the grammarian, the rhetorician, the doctor or the engineer. An enactment of Valentinian I of 374 granting certain tax exemptions to painters shows that they were regarded as *humiliores*, whereas members of the 'literary' professions were *honestiores* (*C.Th.* XIII.4.4).

Somewhere between these two categories came astrologers, apothecaries and the like, as well as shorthand writers. The latter readily found employment in the imperial service and in that of the church, and some

---

[70] Huxley (1959).

rose to the highest positions. Libanius laments the favour shown to short-hand writers and castigates fathers who have their sons taught shorthand rather than rhetoric. Shorthand seems to have been taught not only by specialist teachers but also by some elementary schoolmasters. What information we possess on the teaching of shorthand comes mainly from contracts between fathers – or owners of slaves – and teachers recorded in Egyptian papyri, which tell us nothing about teaching methods or assessment of qualifications. Most of what we do know about teachers of these 'subliterary' subjects comes from sources much earlier than the period under review. But there is no reason to suppose that teaching institutions and methods, or the social status of practitioners of these crafts, were any different in the fifth and sixth century except that the preference given to shorthand writers in the imperial service began to be reduced after the death of Constantius II in 362.

Finally, in a society more and more permeated by Christian ideology, one asks how theology was taught. The short answer is that it was not taught at all, or at least not in any systematic way. Children of Christian families and converts to Christianity might receive elementary instruction in doctrine and behaviour from the local bishop or one of his priests. This could be well done, badly done, or not done at all. We are curiously ignorant of the content and methods of such catechetical teaching in the fifth and sixth century. But it seems very rarely to have risen to the level of systematic instruction in theology. One systematic treatment of Christian theology in Greek is that embodied in the four books of Pseudo-Dionysius the Areopagite, probably written about 500. But this attempt to formulate Christian doctrine in Neoplatonic terms, though it enjoyed immense influence in later centuries, was ill-adapted to serve as a textbook for budding clerics. Bishops were responsible for training clergy in their dioceses. Their teaching, which no doubt varied greatly in thoroughness and clarity, seems to have been based on reading of the scriptures and their exegesis by the church Fathers. John Chrysostom, Severianus of Gabala and Theodore of Mopsuestia all commented at length on books of the Bible in homilies or treatises in the fourth and early fifth century. In the period at present under review, the principal exegetes were Theodoret of Cyrrhus (died 457/8), Hesychius of Jerusalem (died after 451), patriarch Gennadius I of Constantinople (458–71), Cyril of Alexandria (412–44), Olympiodorus (sixth century), Oecumenius (sixth century) and Andrew of Caesarea (563–614) – both of the latter wrote commentaries on the Apocalypse. These often extremely lengthy commentaries were in many cases not intended as textbooks. But soon collections of excerpts from them were compiled and systematically arranged as variorum commentaries or *catenae* on the various books of the Bible, intended both for teaching purposes and for private study. An early compiler of *catenae* was Procopius of Gaza (*c.* 475–528), a teacher of rhetoric by profession. His

Eklogai exēgētikai, which covered the Octateuch and the other historical books of the Old Testament, was read by Photius in the ninth century (*Bibliotheca*, cod. 206). It no longer survives in its original form, but much of it was absorbed into later *catenae*. An epitome of this great *catena* survives both in Greek and in a Latin translation, while abbreviated and/or interpolated versions of Procopius' commentaries on Isaiah, on the Song of Songs, on Proverbs and on Ecclesiastes also survive. A *catena* on the Psalms may be the work of Procopius or of one of his pupils. Several other *catenae* by anonymous compilers can plausibly be dated in the sixth century and linked with teaching activity.[71] Many exegetical works were written in the fifth and sixth century, including Prosper of Aquitaine's commentary on the Psalms, which consists largely of excerpts from Augustine's *Enarrationes in Psalmos*, Maximus of Turin on the Gospels, the younger Arnobius on the Psalms and the Gospels, entirely derivative commentaries on the Apocalypse by Primasius of Hadrumetum and Apringius of Pace, an allegorical exposition of the Song of Songs by Justus of Urgel, and a set of exegetical homilies on the New Testament by one Luculentius. Most of these unoriginal works arose out of the need to train the local clergy. Cassiodorus' *Expositio Psalmorum*, probably written when he was in Constantinople in 540–54, aims a little higher. But only with Gregory the Great's commentaries on Job, Ezekiel and the Psalms do we find exegesis comparable in its learning and penetration with that of Jerome or Augustine.

As has already been observed, the relations between church and school in the Syriac-speaking world were different from those in the Greek-speaking and Latin-speaking regions of the empire. Syriac literature was a Christian creation, with no long tradition. Syriac schools were often attached to churches or monasteries, and the texts which were read and studied in them were religious. There was no sharp separation between the teaching of literacy and the teaching of Christian doctrine. Three schools of higher learning, which included theology as well as grammar, rhetoric and philosophy, all taught in Syriac, were established in Edessa in the late fourth century. In 489 the emperor Zeno closed the so-called Persian school, which was suspected of Nestorian heresy and of pro-Persian leanings, and expelled its teachers. Most of them made their way across the frontier to Nisibis (Nusaybin in south-east Turkey), which had been in Persian hands since 363, and established or perhaps reinforced a similar school there. The statutes of the School of Nisibis, promulgated in 496 after the arrival of the refugee teachers from Edessa, describe the teaching regime in some detail.[72] There were at one time as many as 800 students. The course of study in theology lasted three years. Students were required

---

[71] For a *catalogue raisonné* of Greek catenae cf. Geerard (1974–87) IV.185–259.
[72] Vööbus (1965), especially 110–15, 147–8, 177–87, 203–9, 269–75, 282–9.

to pass a preliminary entrance examination, and to live in a hostel attached to the school, unless it was full, in which case they might seek lodgings in the town. Attendance at classes, which lasted all day, was obligatory, except during the summer vacation. Students must be unmarried, and were forbidden to visit taverns or attend parties in the town. Neither students nor teachers could engage in a trade or handicraft or take any paid employment during the teaching season. The school possessed a library, from which books might be borrowed under strict conditions. Crossing the frontier into Roman territory was strongly discouraged.

The School of Nisibis evidently preserved many of the features of a late antique school of higher education, like that of Alexandria. Junillus, probably to be identified with the official who succeeded Tribonian as *quaestor sacri palatii* in Constantinople in 542, and author of a brief introduction to the Bible, describes a meeting with Paul the Persian, who had taught at 'the school of the Syrians', where 'divine law is taught systematically by rule by public professors, as we teach grammar and rhetoric in secular schools'.[73] But the Nisibis school probably also owed something to Jewish educational tradition and practice, and there was an influential rabbinical school in the town. The School of Nisibis served in its turn as a model for the school of theology which Cassiodorus hoped to establish, first in Rome and later at Vivarium, but which did not outlast its founder.[74]

---

[73] *PL* LXVIII.13b–c; cf. *PLRE* III.742.   [74] Cassiodorus, *Institutiones* praef. 1.

CHAPTER 30

THE VISUAL ARTS

ROBIN CORMACK

Under detailed scrutiny, the period from 425 to 600 is seen to represent a time of significant and conspicuous artistic production and stylistic change and complexity. If the fourth century appears a time of transition, yet dominated by traditional forms and techniques, then in contrast it is easy to see that the fifth century witnesses considerable change, and that by 600 the forms of Christian art have become distinctive, and many of the aspects of later medieval art have been determined. This is the period which produced the present church of St Sophia at Constantinople (532–7), one of the most dramatic and influential buildings in world architecture. This achievement alone gives the period an identity in its own right. Yet in the broad view, it is clear that Christianity adapted rather than rejected the values of classical 'pagan' art. Hence the predominant discussions of the art of this period in terms of continuity and change, or – put more precisely – in terms of classical and non-classical elements, and either their interplay or their independence.

This priority for the art-historical analysis of these centuries is superficially justifiable, but one soon suspects that it may mask a whole set of more serious problems. It may, however, still offer a way of identifying the strengths and weaknesses of the current state of research; the question of the stage of 'classicism' embodied in the art of this period should not necessarily be evaded, so long as one remains aware that it encourages the framing of questions in terms of style, and identifies the issues from the surface appearance. It helps to assess how far the identification of stylistic change is limited in its conceptual value. If it is the case that both pagans and Christians as viewers confronted the artistic representation of their various religious beliefs and values in very similar visual manners, then their cognitive responses to these similar forms must have differed, and we need to find ways of discovering these responses. This must involve setting the evidence of texts against the evidence of art in order to relate visual expression to spiritual and ideological change in this period, and it may ultimately need the framing of pictorial material within parameters set by texts rather than simply by the images themselves.[1] This chapter, however, will track

[1] For a coverage of these issues see Barasch (1992).

questions of pictorial continuity and change, and illuminate the problems of isolating what is classical and non-classical in the material evidence. At the same time, it is accepted that if 'classicism' is taken to be an attitude of mind rather than an essentialist component, the pursuit of the classical may only be a way of seeking to deduce the intentions of the planners and producers of this art. It may turn out to be more constructive for future research to ask how the art functioned among its viewing audience rather than to emphasize the conditions of production.[2]

The art-historical viewing of the period from 425 to 600 has, then, traditionally developed largely along 'formalist' lines. From this perspective, the central questions which emerged were (predictably, perhaps) how to define the essence of the period and how to describe its stylistic character. The formalist emphasis also encouraged a critical assessment of the art of the period, frequently couched in terms of 'decline'; more recently, this negative reaction has been increasingly replaced by more constructive attempts to find the positive 'transformations' of 'early Christian art' into a new art form with its own visual expressiveness; in this respect, art history has conformed with other historical and literary approaches.

Parallel with this critical and general overview of these centuries has been the debate on whether the term 'early Christian art' (or alternatively late antique art) is the appropriate label for the production of all or part of this period – for not all of it was produced in the service of the religion, and even some art produced in the service of the religion does not appear to modern hindsight to be sufficiently 'Christian'.[3] Some have wished to subdivide the period, resisting the idea that 'early Christian art' could label the artistic situation right up to the period of Byzantine iconoclasm in the eighth century. The debate is really about whether it is useful to use a coverall term encompassing all the complex and changing historical circumstances within which a 'European' art was developed. There is also the long-running issue of how far a distinction should be made between the artistic spheres of the 'western' and 'eastern' parts of the Roman empire. But since the production of the sixth century has generally been seen in terms of an attempt by Justinian to produce an international art, there is a case for treating the production of the period as a unity, with certain regional factors operating on occasion, rather than setting up a division in this period between east and west (or between supposed regional or provincial identities). On this model, the best label for the period might be 'early Byzantine', although without the implication that Constantinople was the only centre of production. Nevertheless, there is as yet no agreed

---

[2] Such as Elsner (1995).

[3] For 'discourses' or overlapping 'discourses' see Cameron, *Rhetoric of Empire*, mostly in relation to the verbal: developed in Cameron (1992). Definitions of the period are discussed in Clover and Humphreys (1989) and Shelton (1989).

term which characterizes the production of these centuries, and any term proposed is likely to have conceptual undertones. So to speak of an 'age of Justinian', for example, may seem to express historical reductionism, however much the texts of the court writers such as Procopius, Paul the Silentiary and Corippus may be adduced as contemporary witnesses of the cult of the individual emperor.

The yardstick against which the changes of this period are most often defined is 'antiquity'. The analysis, therefore, has differed according to the definitions of antiquity adopted by the art historian, and how far antiquity was seen as a monolithic concept or itself a complex and changing construct. For some viewers, then, the change from antiquity over this period involved an over-all and radical transition from 'naturalism' to 'abstraction'. For others, the phases through which early Byzantine art went can be related to separate episodes in the history of the art of antiquity, and might represent phases of 'renaissance' or episodes of the more prominent emergence or development of other classical styles and devices (such as frontality in portraiture). All these analyses are open to the criticism that the art historian has exaggerated the history of style over the recognition that Christian art was responding to a whole matrix of demands from religious beliefs and practices.

The formalist treatment of the surviving material has at least enabled a particular set of stylistic stages and issues to be defined, and these have had their various explanations.[4] The most influential commentator has undoubtedly been Ernst Kitzinger: he initially set out his formalist approach in a book constructed within the framework of the British Museum materials (*Early Medieval Art in the British Museum*, 1940), and then subsequently in a series of articles (the majority brought together in a collected edition in 1976) and most systematically in his book *Byzantine Art in the Making* (1977) where he refined his conceptual framework and conclusions.[5] Interestingly, the British Museum has kept his first book in print, in an updated edition, and so one might almost speak of 'British Museum' scholarship to refer to the empirical approach.[6]

I. ARTISTIC EVIDENCE AND ITS INTERPRETATION

The traditional approach has always involved the collation of as many surviving materials as possible in order to build up a deductive picture of the period, while allowing for the 'distortions' due to the disappearance of so much of the original production. Within this frame of reference, the period

---

[4] A key formalist textbook is Morey (1942 and 1953). For a review of the field, see Kessler (1988).

[5] For sweeping criticisms of Kitzinger see C. Mango in the *TLS*, 25 March 1977: 381, followed by a reply on 6 May and subsequent rebuttal.

[6] The empirical approach is maintained in the British Museum exhibition catalogue, Buckton (1994).

can only be viewed as one of random and serious losses, with almost endless scope for speculation about the 'realities' of production. The literature has been particularly engaged with one particular problem (both in our period and in the preceding one): how to solve the question of the *location* of artistic innovation and development. Was Christian art developed in the manuscript (and particularly in the *codex* which Christians were seen to favour as their book form)? Or was the place where the 'new' art was established rather the walls of churches or cemeteries? Or were the minor arts, such as signs on personal gemstones, the carriers of the first Christian art?[7]

None of these alternative scenarios can be adequately reconstructed and assessed, because of the lacunae in the evidence. They all assume the doubtful proposition that a particular artistic medium or genre could be produced and developed in isolation within the culture. Nevertheless, the idea that Christianity as the religion of the book might have developed its pictorial traditions within the medium of biblical manuscripts was once very influential and still underlies much discussion of early Christian art and its diffusion; it cannot be dismissed without mention. Any reappraisal of this debate has repercussions on the high status frequently attributed to manuscript illumination within the artistic production of the period. If the idea that the manuscript was the innovating medium is dropped, much of the conjecture about the quantity and importance of manuscript illumination may appear exaggerated. Pictures in books can instead be treated analytically in new ways – for example, how do they function pictorially and how far can their evidence be integrated with other art of the period?

There are very few surviving luxuriously illuminated Christian manuscripts from the period. The key biblical books are the sixth-century Vienna Genesis, the burnt remnants of the fifth- or sixth-century Cotton Genesis in the British Library, the sixth-century Rossano Gospels, the sixth-century Sinope Gospel fragments, the Rabula Gospels of the year 586, the sixth-century St Augustine Gospels, and the sixth-century Ashburnham Pentateuch. These manuscripts have often been the basis for the reconstruction of lost models and lost affiliations.[8] Recently they have been alternatively treated, not as evidence for the existence of the mass production of illuminated manuscripts in the period, but as unique objects, individually produced for a limited, probably élite, clientele.[9] Similarly, the two Virgil manuscripts (Vatican lat 3225 from Rome in the early fifth century and Vatican lat 3867 of the late fifth or sixth century) and the Milan *Iliad* may be seen as special enterprises, no doubt owing some part of their illumination to earlier models in illustrated manuscripts of a famous text, but nevertheless unique productions rather than representative examples of

---

[7] Murray (1977) and Finney (1994).   [8] Weitzmann (1977).   [9] Lowden (1990) and (1993).

CONVERTANTFRIAMIAMCEALOPHRYGIISQUIFUTURUM
SINMANIBUSVESTRISVESTRAMASCINDISSETINURBEM
VLTROASIAMMAGNODELOCEAADMOENIABELLO
VENTURAMITNOSTROSEAINTAMANERENTCOLIS
TALIBUSIINSIDIISPERIURIIQ·ARTESINONIS
CREDITARESCAPTIQ·DOLISLACRIMISQUECONCTIS·
QUOSNEQUETTDIDESNECCLARISEUSACHILLIS·
NONANNIDOMUEREDECLAINONMILLEEARINAE

Fig. 28 Laocoön. Miniature from the Vatican Virgil, early fifth century. Vatican Library (Cod. Vat.
Lat, 3225, fol. 18v). (Photo: Biblioteca Vaticana)

mass-produced editions.[10] The same may be said of the *De Materia Medica*
of Dioscorides (Vienna ÖNB med.gr.1), produced around 512 in
Constantinople for Anicia Juliana, daughter of the empress Galla
Placidia.[11] It is a special edition with 498 miniatures, mostly of plants, but
with additional texts and pictures from other tracts.

Manuscript illumination remains an important source of information
about artistic craftsmanship and methods during the period. The damaged
physical condition of the Vatican Virgil lat 3225 and the Itala Quedlinburg

[10] Wright (1993) and Bianchi Bandinelli (1955).   [11] Gerstinger (1970).

fragment of the Bible paradoxically offers valuable information about working practices in the first half of the fifth century: flaked miniatures in the former reveal that the artists worked with an underdrawing before applying the pigments, and, in the case of the latter, the scribe wrote down instructions indicating which figures to include in the pictures.[12] The miniatures were made up to some extent from stock types and stock motives (sometimes incongruously linked – as in the Laocoön scene in the Vatican Virgil). Some commentators on this period assume that in all cases artists, whether floor mosaicists, miniature painters or monumental artists, worked from 'pattern books', and that ideas and styles were transmitted mechanically.[13] However, the range of artistic expertise and the actual complexities of production can hardly be reduced to a mentality of copying. A test case is given by the mosaics of the church of Santa Maria Maggiore in Rome (432–40), a major papal commission. These mosaics incorporate some of the same figure motives and compositional schemes as these two manuscripts. But this does not prove that all are linked by the use of common model books; the same congruence of vocabulary might be interpreted as due to the work of the same artists or by the conformity of different artists to the same fashions. The significant visual issue here is the divergence in style between the two parts of the decoration, despite the similarity of the figural and architectural motives: the nave mosaics (which represent stories of Old Testament history and accordingly offered Christians in Rome a new 'past') are illusionistic in a colourful and impressionist manner, whereas the style of the triumphal arch mosaics (representing the New Testament story of the Infancy of Christ) is linear and flat. The pictorial distinction between the 'narrative' emphasis of the nave images and the 'theological' imagery of the triumphal arch around the apse cannot be explained solely by the use of stylistically different 'models' – whether pattern books, illustrated Bible manuscripts, or some other source. Furthermore, the suggestion that some of the details of the scenes of the nave might derive from traditions of the 'Jewish' community rather than from Gentile Christian thinking and that their source might be Jewish pictorial iconography which had entered Christian art through the illustration of manuscripts of the Septuagint cannot be demonstrated. And in any case the planners and artists of these mosaics (and the other art of this period) were influenced by a complex visual experience and a knowledge of ideas from many texts, theological, spiritual (including hymns) and others; to derive precise elements directly from (lost) manuscript illuminations must be excessively speculative.[14]

The cycles in both parts of Santa Maria Maggiore show parallel thinking, and, whatever their sources, are examples of highly developed pictorial

---

[12] Degering and Boekler (1932).
[13] For the materials see Scheller (1963 and 1996); and Conkey and Hastorf (1990).
[14] See Brenk (1975) and (1977).

Fig. 29 Mosaic panel of the Hospitality of Abraham from the nave of S. Maria Maggiore, Rome, 432–40. (Photo: Alinari/Art Resource, NY)

decoration. The nave imagery is more than mere narrative, and involves just as complex symbolic and liturgical references as the triumphal arch. For example, the panel on the left wall nearest to the sanctuary shows a narrative sequence of Abraham meeting the three angels at the oak of Mamre, his hospitality, and their prediction of Sarah's pregnancy, but the evocations are rich and deeply theological: among these are the reference to the typological connection between Sarah and Mary, and the implication that the three angels represent the Trinity and the symbolic meal of bread and wine foretelling the eucharist (which was celebrated in the church itself on the altar in the sanctuary area below the mosaic). Neither of the cycles is a simple narrative.

The decorators of the mosaics have also developed their means of expression far beyond the conventions of the manuscripts of the period, and they have reacted to the problems of a monumental environment. They had to make the scenes somehow visible to the audience despite their height above the colonnade and despite the difficulties of viewing which result from daylight shining through windows. The use of gold around the figures was one response to such problems; it was a device which succeeded in marking and highlighting the principal figures, while at the same time giving them increased symbolic status by their penumbra of gold. Making the imagery visible had its spin-offs, too. This treatment of the scene of Abraham and the three angels can be compared with another rendering in the mosaics in San Vitale in Ravenna over a century later. Here the artists have again explored and refined visual strategies to make the scene readable from the floor of the church (perhaps after study of the S. Maria Maggiore panel itself). In Ravenna a more linear style and an increase in the size and scale of the figures as they are placed higher on the wall have solved the viewing problems. In these churches, the mosaics were set tessera by tessera directly and pragmatically on the walls – not in the studio or in front of manuscripts – and the skills of presentation derive from experience gained in the monuments.

In the face of an art-historical literature which has in general emphasized broad-scale change but failed to offer any consensus on what that change was or how it can be described or explained, it is likely that style history must in future be more closely aligned with the indications of history and literature. If decline is to be replaced by a meaningful notion of transformation, we shall need to be aware of the formalistic contribution but also to go beyond its limitations and accept that we are seeing a religious art under development.[15] Although there are collections of texts about art in this period (notably by C. Mango and C. Davis-Weyer),[16] the implications for the history of art of such evocative authors at Paulinus of Nola, Corippus, Procopius, Choricius of Gaza and Gregory of Tours (among others) have been more signalled than explored by art historians.

The aim of this chapter is to cover the special and distinctive art-historical features of the period from 425 to 600, which does offer an identifiable phase in the history of art, even if it lacks an agreed label. It is a time replete with major works and innovations, which established the

---

[15] Elsner (1995) exploits the primary literature more than Mathews (1993); for a critical review of Mathews, see P. Brown in the *Art Bulletin* 77 (1995) 499–502.

[16] Davis-Weyer (1971) and Mango (1972).

Fig. 30 Mosaic panel of the Hospitality of Abraham and Sacrifice of Isaac in the sanctuary of S. Vitale, Ravenna, 548. (Photo: Alinari/Art Resource, NY)

character of the imagery not only of the Byzantine Middle Ages but of the west as well. The period determined the nature of Christian visual expression and the main art forms of the Middle Ages. It is, however, also characterized (more debatably) as a period which so far diverged from the perceptual art of antiquity into the conceptual art of the Middle Ages that it was the turning-point in Europe from western to non-western art. Despite an 'orientalizing' bias in the art-historical literature, this chapter regards the period as a phase in the history of classicism. The fact that later medieval periods of 'renaissance' (both in the Carolingian west and Byzantine east) seem as likely to draw on models of this period rather than to return to the art of classical antiquity itself points to the need to uncover its precise character in relation to classical art.

There are many signs of change in the early fifth century in comparison with the previous century. Some of these are empirical: in Rome (and Milan), for example, after decades of lively sculptural production, the series of sarcophagi comes to an end, and although Ravenna becomes a minor centre of the production during the fifth and sixth century and Constantinople produces limestone and imperial porphyry sarcophagi, monumental sculpture was clearly not to be a major form of Christian art in this period.[17] The most impressive sculpture of the period was either the portrait sculpture of provincial magnates, such as the magistrates of Aphrodisias and Ephesus, or imperial statues.[18] But even for imperial display, this production was not sustained, and it is debatable whether the famous equestrian statue of Justinian set up in 543–4 in the Augustaion in front of S. Sophia was any more than an adaptation of the old (the horse was probably made in the reign of Theodosius I).[19] It is clear that this period saw the essential demise of the production of traditional sculpture in the round; in this medium we can recognize overall a break with the past. But in particular cases where sculptural commissions were achieved, the relation with the past is not simple. It is true that the base of the obelisk of Theodosius I has reliefs which have encouraged the notion of a period of 'renaissance' of classicism, but the set of statue bases of the monuments of the popular Constantinopolitan charioteer Porphyrios, set up on the spina of the Hippodrome (the latest dating from around 545), are evidence of different aesthetic aims.[20]

Such empirical evidence of shifts in patronage or in taste points to new developments and enterprises. There is the development of sponsorship resulting in complex church architecture and the expansion of the medium of mosaic for monumental decoration and of gold and silver furnishings and fittings for churches.[21] Equally, one of the most significant forms of

---

[17] Lawrence (1945); for further bibliography on sculpture see Effenberger (1986). For an overview see Smith (1985).   [18] Inan and Alföldi-Rosenbaum (1979).   [19] Sodini (1994).
[20] Cameron (1973).   [21] Mango, M. M. (1986) and Boyd and Mango (1992).

art to develop in this period was the icon – the portable painted panel for home and monastery and church use or the larger image for grand church display.[22] But more elusive and more significant is the change in the spiritual character of the art which was produced after 425. A number of works help us to recognize what may perhaps best be described as public art for the institutionalized church; it is in the development of church decoration that we may want to recognize how ecclesiastical thinking and control dominated the development of art over this period. In other words, we need to recognize the importance of a functional Christian art (which cannot be seen superficially as the advertising and presentation of a new religion). Beneath the changing forms we can try to detect a new climate within which art operated – and of course supported and expanded Christian modes of thought. If there was a new culture in which the notion of sin began to dominate and in which new ethical and family values emerged and were promoted, clearly the visual art was fully implicated in the definition and presentation of this Christian identity. While it was in this period that Paulinus of Nola (died 431) and pope Gregory I (590–604) claimed art as 'writing for the illiterate', yet it is clear that the diverse functions which we can detect in the art of this time are more than merely didactic. Indeed, others who wrote about the art reveal a broader understanding of the power of art, and so does the text of Gregory to bishop Serenus of Marseilles: 'To adore images is one thing; to teach with their help what should be ignored is another. What scripture is to the educated, images are to the ignorant, who see through them what they must accept; they read in them what they cannot read in books.'[23]

II. CHURCH AND ART IN THE FIFTH CENTURY

The definitive monument in this period is the church building. The role of the pope, Sixtus III (432–40), in the decoration of Santa Maria Maggiore was prominently signalled at the apex of the triumphal arch with his name as 'seal'.[24] The church was a major dedication to Mary around the time of the Council of Ephesus (431), and whatever the precise connection was between council and church, it is clear that the planners of the decoration belong to a period of concentrated debate on the nature and status of the Virgin and Incarnate Christ. The decoration participates in that debate, and shows how statements can be made visually, which might have been more difficult to articulate so clearly in words. The church itself was a vast

---

[22] The key source of information about the character and types of the painted icon in this period comes from the holdings of the monastery of St Catherine on Sinai: see Weitzmann (1976).

[23] Davis-Weyer (1971) esp. 46 and Duggan (1989).

[24] For the architecture and dating see Krautheimer and others (1937–); for the mosaics, Cecchelli (1967).

wooden-roofed basilica, which has over the succeeding centuries been considerably altered and enhanced. The insertion of transepts in the Baroque period and alterations to the entrance end of the nave mean that only twenty-seven out of the original forty-two panels over the entablature of the colonnade survive; and at the apse end, the extension of the sanctuary in the Middle Ages means that the fifth-century apse decoration is lost; only the (partially restored) mosaics of the triumphal arch have survived here. Nevertheless, the decoration is enormously informative. High on the walls the viewer saw Old Testament scenes, which offered a narrative of the past which, as already suggested, was full of typological hints and evocations. Indeed, the incipient fourth-century interest in typological connections between the Old and New Testaments has clearly become a dominant interest of fifth-century programme planners.[25] Because of the height of the mosaics above the spectator, the scenes (sometimes one, sometimes two in the panel) were hard to read from the floor and this is only partially solved by the use of the gold around key figures. As suggested already, the latter is a technical device to highlight them; but it is also a symbolic enhancement – the figures are framed with divine light. Unlike the art of the catacombs and other examples of earlier Christian art, the scenes offer a denser and fuller narrative, and aim to convey far more than repetitive cases of God's power of salvation. The left wall portrays events from the story of Abraham and Jacob, and the right wall, events from the life of Moses and Joshua. The complexity of the symbolism is best seen by looking further at the panel which completes the sequence on the left wall and abuts the triumphal arch. It shows in sequence the meeting of Abraham with the three angels, his hospitality, and their prophecy that Sarah (despite her age) would bear a son (Genesis 22.1–19). However much narrative may seem a key element of the panel – the figures are dramatically portrayed in an atmospheric landscape, the dwelling-place of Abraham is fully delineated, as is the table at which the angels sit, and the oak tree at Mamre where the event took place is prominently included – yet through the narrative imagery the fifth-century viewer, particularly if educated by sermons, would hardly fail to detect several levels of symbolic associations. The three angels would suggest the Trinity; their announcement of the future pregnancy of Sarah would be recognized as a prefiguration of the birth of Jesus to Mary; and the offering of bread and wine would instantly evoke the eucharist.

Similarly, the registers on the triumphal arch show something more than a narrative of the infancy of Christ. It has been often noted that the stylistic treatment of the triumphal arch is far less atmospheric than the nave cycles, and is conventionally described as more abstract (and so more obviously

---

[25] Malbon (1990).

symbolic). The modern interpretation of this section of the church has led, however, to considerable controversy, and the various viewpoints are irreconcilable.[26] One issue is how closely to relate the imagery to biblical (or even to apocryphal) sources or how far to see it as a tentative visual exploration of the current interpretations of the status of Mary. The latter approach is helped by the fact that technical examination of the mosaics shows that some of the preliminary drawings on the plaster layers on the wall diverge from the final composition. This might be taken to suggest a pictorial development during the course of finalizing the imagery. The issues of interpretation are illustrated immediately if one considers the opening scenes of the set at the top left of the triumphal arch. The first scene might be identified as the Annunciation (Luke 1.26–38), but the composition does not conform to later medieval 'norms'. Mary is seen seated in a throne, in imperial dress and wearing a diadem; and she has a retinue of angels. All this imperial emphasis is unexpected, and certainly far from the gospel account. Equally absent from the gospels is her work of spinning a veil of purple wool for the temple; this is a detail about the early life of Mary taken from the Apocrypha. The angel Gabriel is shown in the sky, flying towards her. To the right is another scene, the Annunciation to Joseph. Although the motif of Mary as queen became a feature of art in Rome from the sixth century, it would seem highly innovative to show the theme at this date; it also seems that the use of the Apocrypha was discouraged at this period. For these reasons, alternative interpretations of the scene have been pursued. The Annunciation, however, remains the most likely reading.

But another scene of the cycle (in the register immediately below) is considerably more arcane within the vocabulary of the art of this period. Where we might have expected the Nativity, we appear to have a unique version of the Adoration of the Magi; the three Magi approach the newly born child (one to the left and two to the right) from each side of a massive jewelled throne. Christ sits upright and has a halo with a small cross above his head. On each side of Christ is a seated woman. The woman to the left resembles the figure of Mary as queen in the Annunciation scene above; the woman to the right, dressed in purple, is a figure one would expect to identify as Mary, since she wears the conventional dress of the mother of Christ. These two figures have caused particular difficulty, some identifying the figures as symbolic figures (one symbolizing the church), some suggesting that one may be Sarah, the wife of Abraham, some seeing the images as two facets of Mary (Mary in glory, Mary in sadness for the fate of Christ). As for the figure of baby Jesus sitting upright on the throne, the identification is hardly controversial (although the surface is much

---

[26] The fundamental exposition is that of Grabar (1936), and many of the controversial interpretations are in reaction to his identifications of the scenes: Brodsky (1966) and Spain (1979) are the most antipathetic to his viewing.

Fig. 31 Mosaics of the Annunciation to Mary and Joseph and of the Adoration of the Magi on the left side of the Triumphal Arch around the apse of S. Maria Maggiore, Rome, 432–40. (Photo: Alinari/Art Resource, NY)

restored), but the imagery is unique and the interpretation therefore elusive. The omission of a separate Nativity scene and the emphasis on the enthroned Christ's audience of the Magi point to a theological controversy about the nature of Christ at the time of the Incarnation.[27]

The nave mosaics and the apse mosaics both exhibit, therefore, a high degree of theological input, and, as visual art, their message is insistently didactic and instructive. It is this aspect which defines their moment in the history of art, so different from some of the more 'frivolous' mid-fourth-century mosaics of Santa Costanza in Rome, which include among the biblical scenes all sorts of traditional 'pagan' decorative imagery, including scenes of the wine harvest. The cycles in Santa Maria Maggiore match well the prescriptions of Paulinus of Nola in Italy and St Nilus of Ancyra in the east, who appealed for the choice of *serious* subjects in church decoration and for intense concentration in front of them on the part of viewer and educators.[28] 'It would be the mark of a firm and manly mind to represent a single cross in the sanctuary, for it is by virtue of the one salutary cross that mankind is being saved and hope is being preached everywhere to those without hope; and to fill the holy church on both sides with pictures from the Old and New Testaments so that the illiterate who are unable to read the Holy Scriptures may, by gazing at the pictures, become mindful of the manly deeds of those who have genuinely served the true God and may be aroused to emulate those glorious and celebrated feats.'

This text of Nilus (if genuine) offers a direct and simple witness of changes in thinking and expression at all levels of the church in the period of the sophisticated papal-sponsored decoration of Santa Maria Maggiore, but it is also a helpful text with a prescriptive message on the nature of proper church decoration. Another church in the Byzantine east extends this evidence of self-conscious didactic and ecclesiastical planning; this is the mosaic decoration of the church now known as the Rotunda in Thessalonica.[29] The exact date of the conversion of the early-fourth-century building (perhaps intended as the mausoleum of Galerius) is still disputed, most opting for a time either in the middle of the fifth century or around 500.[30] The significance of this decoration is its confirmation of the spreading influence of the established church over the choice of imagery. The mosaic decoration of the cupola was in three registers: the apex held a medallion of a large figure of Christ, the second register was of angels and perhaps other heavenly figures, and the best-preserved and lowest register was a set of exquisite architectural façades inhabited by

[27] Hellemo (1989); not discussed in Mathews (1993).

[28] Mango (1972) 32–3 quotes Nilus' *Letter to Prefect Olympiodorus* (*PG* LXXIX.577–80).

[29] Kleinbauer (1972) set out the problems involved in the study of the monument. Recent restoration and investigation do not seem to have resolved the dating.

[30] Spieser (1984) is the fullest archaeological survey.

Fig. 32 Fifth-century mosaics of saints in the cupola of the Rotunda (Church of St George), Thessalonica. (Photo: Conway Library, Courtauld Institute of Art, London)

named Christian figures. The buildings are no doubt meant to evoke the church in heaven, and the figures are saints engaged in the heavenly liturgy. The name of each saint and his festival day is written in the mosaic. What we have in this register is, in other words, a visual church liturgical calendar encircling the dome. There has been considerable discussion about the possible source of the calendar (a factor being that the inclusion of Cosmas and Damian might help in the location and date of the source). But it can at least be said that the choice of saints must represent current commemorations in the city of Thessaloniki and that the conception indicates the attention directed by the church authorities towards the content, value and functions of public church art.

These two sophisticated examples of church decoration are significant indicators of the nature of monumental art in the fifth century. One can of course emphasize the classical past from which this art has emerged. The architectural façades shown in the mosaics of the Rotunda can easily be compared with the wall paintings of Pompeian and Campanian houses; and the stock figures and architectural motives which appear both in the mosaics of Santa Maria Maggiore and in the Virgil manuscripts no doubt have models in Roman art. But since the stylistic appearance of both monuments is so different from those of antiquity and from each other, the identification of classical sources and stylistic traditions may be of only minor value. With such grand interiors it is obvious that the services and the accessories needed for them would need to match the splendour of the walls, and that most attention was directed towards supplying the 'proper' beauty and holiness for the setting in which the clergy operated and society participated.[31]

It was not just the walls of churches that were lavishly decorated in expensive materials; considerable attention was also given to the provision of rich church plate in the fifth and sixth century. Archaeological evidence of vessels in precious metals comes from the east and Asia Minor, and descriptions in the *Liber Pontificalis* show the wealth that accumulated in churches through the gifts of successive donors.[32] These gifts included textiles, and the impressiveness in church decoration of woven textiles is conveyed by the tapestry of the Virgin and Child with apostles, now in the Cleveland Museum.[33] Some liturgical silver might be purchased by churches and monasteries from their own resources, and much was given as votive gifts 'for the remission of sins'. By the middle of the sixth century, the production of these pieces was highly sophisticated and no doubt phenomenally expensive: the Sion Treasure from Asia Minor (now in Dumbarton Oaks and the Antalya Museum) includes large heavy pieces as

[31] MacCormack (1981); Van Dam, *Leadership and Community*; Cameron (1987); McCormick, *Eternal Victory*.   [32] Davis (1989).   [33] Pelikan (1990) is constructed around this tapestry.

Fig. 33 Silver paten (from the Riha Treasure) with partially gilded repoussé relief and niello inscription showing the Communion of the Apostles, probably 577. Byzantine Collection, Dumbarton Oaks, Washington, DC

well as a censer; the Stuma and Riha patens are highly refined productions; and the Cross of Justin II and Sophia, now in the Vatican collections, was an imperial gift with a value far beyond the metal itself.[34] In form and style, much metalwork did tend to be traditional, and it is in this medium that the vocabulary of classicism was most obviously continued and recreated in this period.[35] Another medium which shows the mark of tradition is that of floor mosaic: the vast areas of floor mosaic found in the Great Palace in Constantinople continue to defy a precise dating, actually because of their 'classicism', and are variously attributed to the fifth century, the period

[34] Cruikshank Dodd (1961) and (1973); Mango, M. M. (1986) and Boyd and Mango (1992).
[35] Kitzinger (1976).

of Justinian, or even to more than a century later. The sixth century remains the most likely. On the whole, the production of mosaic pavements was given up in the sixth century, and marble or tiled floors succeeded them.[36]

Similarly, the ivory production of this period has encouraged more debate about chronologies than interpretations.[37] The series of consular diptychs (up to 540), those of the fifth century mostly from Rome and of the sixth century mostly from Constantinople, were produced within a political framework but influenced the production of Christian imagery, and were objects which soon passed into the hands of the church, recycled in several ways.

III. 'THE AGE OF JUSTINIAN'

The fifth century established the nature of early Christian church art. Although historians of iconoclasm have sought to find traces of opposition to the proliferation of images in this period, and no doubt there were critical eyes and attitudes, yet it is best seen as a period of amazing artistic enterprise, particularly in the developing east.[38] Constantinople was no doubt jerry-built in its original growing stage, but the gradual acceptance of the permanence of the city as a capital meant the expansion and elaboration of the arts. Architectural sculpture flourished with the continued exploitation of the Proconnesian quarries, and it has even been suggested that the effects of polished marble revetments in the churches, with the hint of natural pictorial images trapped inside the stone, influenced the aesthetic of this period and encouraged imaginative abstraction.[39]

The key church type during the fifth century was the wooden-roofed basilica, but by a century later the domed church was emerging as the prestige form of ecclesiastical architecture, and this development must have caused churchmen to think even more about the appropriate kind of imagery for interior spaces of this kind. The development of a new architecture, often sponsored by the emperor, resulted in such striking buildings as Sts Sergius and Bacchus (around 530) and St Sophia (532–7), and these influenced other buildings, such as the throne room of the Chrysotriklinos in the Great Palace or, further afield, San Vitale at Ravenna. Equally grand was the church of S. Polyeuktos at Constantinople, built in the 520s (but by the twelfth century in ruins). Its patron, Anicia Juliana (who earlier had commissioned the grand Dioscorides manuscript), proclaimed her imperial descent in a poem sculpted on the walls of the church. The ostentatious sculpture and (probable) domed plan might again be seen as an

---

[36] Maguire (1990).   [37] Volbach (1976) and Cutler (1985).   [38] Murray (1977).
[39] The extreme statement is by Onians (1980).

imperial rather than aristocratic statement.[40] A feature of the architectural ornament of these churches was its distinctly non-classical appearance both in style and in the choice of motives; some of the inspiration for palmettes and other such ornaments has been traced to eastern, particularly Persian, models.

The widespread popularity of the centrally-planned church was a feature of the Byzantine world rather than the west, and, by the later periods, it had become the standard plan for the majority of buildings. The solution followed for the decoration of this type of architecture has in the case of St Sophia generally mystified modern commentators. While Justinian and his planners might have been expected in this commissioned masterpiece to have set out to match the luxuriance of the architecture and its sculptural ornamentation with spectacular figurative mosaics, the actual mosaic programme has been in these terms a surprise. The circumstantial evidence of archaeology (and probably the texts) is that the Justinianic phase was entirely devoid of monumental figurative mosaics.[41] The surprise is that the emperor who was connected with complex iconography on the façade of the Bronze Gate of the Great Palace or in Ravenna or Sinai was satisfied in St Sophia with a mosaic vault decoration which was limited to the sign of the cross, endlessly repeated, or to more neutral patterns and designs. The church which from the moment of its construction symbolized Byzantium was originally devoid of figurative mosaics – all the present panels represent piecemeal additions from the periods after iconoclasm. Whether apse, dome, vaults or narthex, it is safe to conclude that the main decoration was the cross. While this scheme is strangely evocative of the Islamic mosque's equal rejection in later centuries of portraits and narrative, yet the decision is a powerful one visually. Just as the building is permeated with light – and this is the point that Procopius was the first to emphasize – so the decoration of crosses fills the building with the aura of Christianity, the endlessly repeated sign of the life-giving cross. In this respect, the vast spaces and architectural complexities of the church are unified by the one repeated motive. Although conceptual and other explanations are offered in the literature for the lack of figures on the walls – it has been described as 'an architect's church' or it is suggested that time was too short too allow for a full decoration or it is postulated that it represented an incipient iconoclasm on the part of the emperor or his Monophysite wife, and so on – yet perhaps all this speculation is uncalled for. For the viewer in the church, these mosaics offered a highly successful visual, mesmeric effect. This is a case where we can hardly know the intentions of the period, but where we can at least be sensitive to the visual effects of the decision. We can also see by hindsight that St Sophia excelled

[40] Harrison (1989). [41] Mango (1962); and Cameron, *Corippus*.

Fig. 34 The nave of St Sophia, Constantinople (532–7), looking east, when in use as a mosque,
recorded by Gaspare Fossati between 1847 and 1849 (lithograph after a watercolour).
(Photo: Foto Marburg/Art Resource, NY)

as the site for the state ceremonial of Byzantium.[42] Not only was it the largest building of its time, but its interior could be guaranteed to impress, not only the Byzantines – from the first writer on the building, Procopius, and the other court encomiasts like Paul the Silentiary – but visitors from any country.[43] In this respect, the building offered, with its unrepentantly repeated sign of the cross, a statement of the triumph of the Christian religion in front of which all the faithful, whether orthodox or heterodox, must assent to bow and worship. It may have been an inspired decision after all.

In contrast with St Sophia, the redecoration of the churches of Ravenna after the reconquest of 540 is of great visual complexity.[44] The city and harbour of Ravenna had been developed from the mid fifth century, and there were soon resplendent churches in the new city in the marshes. The artists and architects seem to have come from Rome – at least, the stylistic connections with Rome are often close. The so-called Mausoleum of Galla Placidia owes nothing particular to Byzantine art in the east, either in its domical vault or carpet covering of mosaic.

The inclusion of dynastic portraits was a recurrent feature of the churches of the city (the local context is well documented in the later medieval history of Agnellus), and when Theoderic took over the city and made it the centre of a Gothic kingdom, he too employed artists with a knowledge of the art of Rome to decorate his new Arian churches.[45] By the end of the fifth century, Ravenna had two baptisteries and a rival ecclesiastical situation.[46] Theoderic also began the construction of a new basilica dedicated to Christ (c. 500–26). Its walls were decorated with mosaic – in the highest register with New Testament scenes; in the lowest register below the windows were the figures of Christ on one side and the Virgin on the other. At the west end of this long register were topographical representations of the port (Classis) and the palace. Within the palace façade were the dynastic portraits of (probably) Theoderic and court. The style of the upper biblical portraits was simple and direct, reminiscent of Roman mosaics, even perhaps consciously going back, it has been suggested, to the simplicity of the catacombs. The choice of imagery, since it omits the Nativity and the Crucifixion and shows Christ in two forms (beardless in the Miracles scenes and bearded in the Passion scenes), may reflect Arian theology and thinking about the nature and sacrifice of Christ.[47] The decoration of this church, which now carries its later medieval dedication,

---

[42] Mainstone (1988).
[43] Macrides and Magdalino (1988); and Majeska (1984) for the Russian perception. For local myths of the church see the *Narratio* on the building of St Sophia, discussed by Dagron (1984) 191–314.
[44] The fundamental studies are Deichmann (1958) and (1969, 1974, 1976, 1989).
[45] Pizzaro (1995).   [46] Wharton (1987).
[47] Von Simson (1948); Nordström (1953); also Gregg and Groh (1981).

S. Apollinare Nuovo, demonstrates how the forms and content of early Christianity were so well established that even a new group entering the ruling classes was able to manipulate church decorative schemes to declare and proclaim their own particular aims, ambitions and sectarian beliefs. Nothing more obviously shows the rapidly achieved maturity of Christian art than the ability to operate subversively within the norms.

It became a matter of orthodox honour after the reconquest of Ravenna in 540 to obliterate the Arian atmosphere of this church of Christ – operating, of course, within the now established visual discourses. The church was accordingly rededicated, and the patron chosen was St Martin, the famous bishop of Tours and so-called 'hammer of the heretics'; at the same time, various sections of the early-sixth-century mosaics were selectively picked out and replaced. This work was probably carried out under bishop Agnellus (557–70). The mosaic images of Theoderic and his court were removed from their spaces between the columns of the palace façade – carelessly, though, to the modern eye, since the tesserae of their hands were left intact on the columns. Another alteration was that a new cycle of saints was inserted in the central section of the lower register: these were twenty-six named male Catholic martyrs headed by St Martin on the south side; on the north side was a procession of twenty-two female martyrs and virgins. Instead of inserting new representations of the current rulers of Ravenna in the spaces from which Theoderic was removed, these areas were left blank. In fact, portraits of Justinian and Theodora had been set up elsewhere in Ravenna in the newly built orthodox church of San Vitale (which had originally been sponsored by Julius Argentarius).[48]

San Vitale can help to exemplify the stage reached in church decoration by around 548, when it was dedicated; the architecture was planned and building may have begun in the 530s, judging from the similarity of the sculptural style of the capitals with Justinian's Constantinopolitan showpiece churches. The mosaic decoration of San Vitale is now (and perhaps always was) limited to the sanctuary. We retain a very clear view of its general sixth-century appearance, although a considerable amount of restoration has been carried out over the surface, and this robs us of certainty about the precise original treatment of some details. A similar multimedia use of architectural decoration, using stucco, marble and mosaic (which may include precious materials like mother-of-pearl), is found in a church of similar mid-sixth-century date at the head of the Adriatic at Poreč (Parenzo). As a piece of visual organization, the point has already been made that the mosaic has advanced far beyond Santa Maria Maggiore; the figures are now designed to be more easily read from the floor of the

[48] The information about Julius Argentarius (and his sponsorship of 26,000 *solidi*) is from Agnellus XXIV.57, 59: see Mango (1972) 104–5.

Fig 35 Sanctuary and apse with mosaics of Christ between angels and St Vitalis and Bishop Ecclesius, c. 548, S. Vitale, Ravenna. (Photo: Alinari/Art Resource, NY)

church because of the attention to scale and the relative size of the figures as the mosaic stretches higher into the vaults.

The semicircular panel of Abraham is in the prominent tympanum of the left wall, facing the representation of Abel and Melchizedek opposite; both panels are very clearly a reference to the theme of sacrifice and through it to the eucharist which is celebrated in the sanctuary.[49] As in S. Maria Maggiore, the Abraham scene has clear symbolic references – the bread, for example, is marked like the bread of the eucharist; reference to sacrifice is intensified by the inclusion of the Isaac scene. But the flatness and linearity of the Abraham panel style is in contrast to the more impressionist S. Maria Maggiore mosaics. This change of style from the earlier mosaics – for some commentators, this greater distance from antique illusionist style – does have the expressive value that it conveys more starkly the dogmatic significance of the scene.[50] The purpose of the oak tree may be to define the authenticity of the location of the event, but perspectivally the artist ignores its presence – one is not supposed to imagine that Abraham walked literally around the tree as he went from house to table.

The side walls of the sanctuary of San Vitale were, therefore, conspicuously decorated with Old Testament scenes with typological significance, and around them with Old Testament prophets; but these images are symbolically and hierarchically lower on the walls than the evangelist portraits of the New Testament writers (with their emblems) above them. A reading of the mosaics of San Vitale must allow for intersecting currents and levels of symbolic meaning; the selection of subjects is both sophisticated and designed technically to be highly visible. These church walls show the typological, narrative and liturgical evocations which likewise are apparent in the fifth century in Rome; but several additional strands are also to be detected. There are overt references to salvation and paradise in the apse composition (and to the earthly paradise, perhaps, in the luxurious animal and vegetal imagery of the central vault mosaic). Christ is seated on a globe in the apse above the four rivers of paradise and between a 'court' retinue of two archangels; St Vitalis is given his martyr's crown, and the founder of the church, Ecclesius, holds a model of the octagonal church. One also detects that the three figures in the central axis of the sanctuary composition – the young Christ, the lamb in the vault and God the Father at the apex of the opening arch – are a reference to the orthodox concept of the Trinity, and overtly counter to Arian and Monophysite theology.

There are yet other components in the sanctuary decoration, most notably the famous panels, low down and near the altar, which represent (to the left) Justinian (holding a paten for the bread of the eucharist), the current archbishop, Maximian, and his clergy, and the imperial court and army; and opposite them (on the right) the representation of Theodora and

---

[49] Another level of interpretation is proposed by Leach (1983).   [50] Walter (1984).

her retinue, also in full imperial regalia. Theodora holds a chalice for the communion wine; her dress is ornamented with images of the Adoration of the Magi, making their offerings to Christ.[51] It is well known (to us) that Justinian and Theodora never themselves went to Ravenna (the extent of Justinian's travels seems surprisingly limited); and it is probable that Theodora was still alive when the mosaic was dedicated in 547/8 (if so, she died soon after). The meanings of these panels are therefore clearly symbolic, not a commemoration of any actual event: the rulers of Ravenna are present through their icons, just as the emperor was present in all civil and judicial proceedings where his image was displayed.[52] But it has been convincingly argued that their presence in the sanctuary mosaics also illustrates a symbolic presence in the church liturgy: they are participating in the ritual of the procession of the First Entrance of the liturgy.[53] Maximian leads the emperor into the church, and it is clear that, in spatial narrative terms, Theodora is processing from the atrium into the church interior. The settings no doubt suggest more than simple progress across the threshold of the church, since the niche which frames Theodora also conveys her royalty and power. The languages and messages communicated by clothes are incorporated within the languages of art. The extraordinary visibility of Theodora within the sacred area of the church must have been startling: the basis for the (sexist) complaints of Procopius in the *Secret History* about the aggressive power of Theodora is eloquently made visible in this conspicuous positioning of the imperial couple.

It may be that the large ivory chair dated to this period through the inclusion among the carvings of the monogram of Maximian was intended to stand in the sanctuary of San Vitale.[54] Whether it was designed as a 'chair' or as a stand for the display of a book of scripture, it was an extraordinary *tour de force* as a display of ivory. Its panels, which include a cycle of Joseph scenes and gospel images, are, like the mosaics of S. Maria Maggiore, conceived in a range of different styles, some more, some less 'classical'. It is again easier to recognize that through the narratives a number of symbolic references are intended – such as the representation of Joseph and the events of his life as the antetype of a bishop – than to explain their greater or lesser use of classical modes and forms. Another ivory of this period can likewise be understood to include all sorts of classical elements – this is the Barberini diptych in the Louvre.[55] But the essential question for analysis is whether the emperor portrayed should be identified specifically as Justinian, or whether the imagery of triumph has to be handled in a more general way. Is this topicality or the universality of the triumph of the Christian emperor?

The breadth of expression exhibited in the sixth century and noticeably in commissions connected with Justinian is further shown in the decorations

---

[51] Barber (1990) and Clark (1993) esp. 106–10.   [52] Von Simson (1948).   [53] Matthews (1971).
[54] Cecchelli (1936–44).   [55] Durand (1992) cat. no. 20.

of the church of the monastery of St Catherine on Sinai (the dedication to St Catherine is post-Justinianic). Here the names of Justinian and Theodora (now deceased) are carved in the wooden beams of the roof of the basilica, as is the name of the architect (or builder?) Stephanus of Aila, now Eilat. The church (constructed in local stone) thus dates between 548 and 565; and a second inscription in the apse mosaics of the Sinai church mentions the monks involved (the abbot Longinus and the deacon John) and indiction 14; if the mosaic was carried out under the same programme of work, as seems almost certain, it was done in either 550 or 565. The mosaic does not, however, mention or represent the emperor.[56]

The Sinai church was a *martyrium* built on the site of the burning bush, and the mosaic programme of the apse commemorates events in the life of Moses on the triumphal arch (Moses at the Burning Bush, and Moses receiving the Law); the Transfiguration is in the conch, and figures of Old Testament prophets and New Testament apostles are in medallions around the apse (together with an early 'Deesis' composition and the two icons of the monks). Compared with San Vitale (which also includes Moses scenes), the stylistic treatment of the figures is even more 'abstract' and boldly non-illusionistic. The viewers of this mosaic would be the monks of this remote community, together with the intrepid pilgrims who managed to reach such an awesome holy site. All equally would feel insignificant in front of the vast and mystic imagery of the holy light of the Transfiguration. All commentators on this mosaic have emphasized the levels of meaning which they detect in the mosaic: 'eschatological, dogmatic, liturgical, topographic, typological, imperial' (Weitzmann); 'visual exegesis' (Elsner). While it may seem feasible to argue that we can see a chronological development from San Vitale to Sinai 'away' from classicism, the analysis of the functions and evocations of the mosaic programmes suggests that the formal choices were made for more complicated reasons than the weakening of illusionism.

The development of the pilgrimage monastery of Sinai was mentioned by Procopius (and the tenth-century writer Eutychius) as a work of Justinian, but the details of the financial and practical organization of the work are not known. Since sponsorship of other works in the Holy Land which are mentioned in contemporary texts (such as the New Church in Jerusalem) might be delegated through the tax system, it is likely that the monks who are commemorated in the mosaic organized the work. This situation may account for the debate about the origin of the artists. While the architect (and probably the masons of the variety of capitals along the columns of the nave) was local, the panache with which the mosaics are carried out has led to the assumption that the artists were sent out from

---

[56] Forsyth and Weitzmann (1973); Manafis (1990); Elsner (1995) 99–124. Doubts have been expressed whether the inscription in the mosaic is original or added later. Ernest Hawkins pointed out to me that since the sizes of the medallions below the lettering are adjusted to make room for the inscription, all this section of the mosaic is homogeneous.

Constantinople by Justinian (or his court officials). There is clearly insufficient evidence to decide on the provenance of the artists. The only material factor is that the marble revetment around the base of the apse (and other fittings in the sanctuary) is of Proconnesian marble. If this marble was freshly quarried and transported out from the Sea of Marmara, then it might seem reasonable to argue that the mosaicist accompanied the cargo and came from Constantinople. But this was the period when, it has been argued, the use of the quarries was virtually at an end, and the marble may come from a stockpile anywhere – even perhaps in Jerusalem, since churches of the fifth and sixth century in the Negev (and elsewhere) like-wise had access to this marble for their church fittings.[57] Similar discussions about the existence of local mosaicists recur in all parts of the regions involved – from France to Syria. For example, there are three mosaic apses on Cyprus, all representing in diverse imagery the Virgin Mary, from the period before iconoclasm (and very likely all from the sixth century): Kanakaria (recently looted from the site and fragmented), Livadia (recently destroyed) and Kiti.[58] The case proposed – that these mosaics were achieved by imported mosaicists from Syria or Constantinople – is perhaps undermined by the fact that archaeology reveals that an enormous amount of mosaic work was done on the island in this period, sufficient, one might argue, to support a local industry. The same issue emerges in the analysis of the mosaic at Qartmin in Syria from the early sixth century.[59]

The quantity of work and the links between Constantinople and so much enterprise undertaken outside the capital does support the notion that the period of Justinian adds up to an 'age of Justinian'; despite the loose connections between the emperor and the production of the art. All over the Mediterranean one detects artistic contacts and intersections, and the signs of an 'international art'. The writings of the court encomiasts equally support the interpretation that the built environment and the culture of viewing were selfconsciously promoted under the name of the emperor.[60] But clearly art was not all centred on Constantinople, and there is no evidence that the Byzantine capital was the source of all artistic enter-prise: the character of the art of Ravenna is far too complex to support this view.[61] In the same way, the architecture of the period shows many local features.[62]

---

[57] Asgari (1995); a problem here is whether the quarries went entirely out of use in the sixth century or whether the procedures for working in the quarries changed.

[58] Megaw and Hawkins (1977); Megaw and Hawkins have dated the apse of Kiti to the late sixth century; Barber (1991) argues for the late seventh century for Kiti.   [59] Hawkins and Mundell (1973).

[60] Cameron, *Procopius*.   [61] Kostof (1965).

[62] For the evolution of architecture over this period see fundamentally Grabar (1946) and Lassus (1947); also Tchalenko, *Villages*. A more pragmatic coverage is offered by Krautheimer, *Early Christian and Byzantine Architecture* and Mango, *Byzantine Architecture*. The range of possibilities is obvious from a comparison of the Church of the Hundred Gates at Paros; Basilica B at Philippi (unfinished); the church of St John at Ephesus; and Kasr Ibn Wardan in modern Jordan.

IV. CHURCH, MONKS AND ART AT THE END OF THE SIXTH
CENTURY

When the new emperor Justin II succeeded Justinian, the recommended
rhetoric for imperial succession was to claim continuity.[63] But in fact the
overstretching of resources which marks the artistic patronage of the age
of Justinian did not continue, and marked changes in art have been
detected in the late sixth century. Perhaps these were to some extent a
response to crisis, and so fit with the view that artistic change is to be linked
with spiritual and social anxieties. Outbreaks of plague and the fear of premature death may encourage increased artistic patronage (through church
endowments, for example) and may even initiate changes in visual expression. However, studies of the better-documented circumstances around
the time of the Black Death have shown only the complications of the
analysis rather than offering firm guidelines for other periods. The late sixth
century is also a period of foreign invasion and disruption; it might be said
that the dominance of Constantinople in the east was a negative consequence of the decline of other cities, like Antioch, Alexandria and
Jerusalem, rather than a positive imperial policy.[64]

The temptation for the art historian is to relate changing historical
circumstances and the emergence of new types of writing to new forms of
art. A period which produced the Akathistos hymn and numerous *Lives* of
holy men might be supposed also to initiate some kind of matching artistic expression. The most tempting theory is to date the emergence of the
icon to the second half of the sixth century and relate the popularity of the
icon to new forms of spirituality. Weitzmann's catalogue of early icons
from Sinai sees a set of portable icons in the monastery as the gift of
Justinian (in particular, Christ, St Peter and the Virgin with saints).[65] Others
have dated these pieces later, perhaps within the seventh century. In fact,
despite the imprecision about the stylistic dating of these panels, there is
no reason to doubt the existence of painted panels in encaustic or tempera
throughout this period. However, there *may* have been an upsurge in production, as Kitzinger proposed, in the second half of the sixth century.[66]
Likewise the production of portable pilgrim souvenirs from the Holy
Land, such as the base metal ampullae which are now best-known from collections at Bobbio and Monza, *may* have been a development of this
period.[67]

Similarly, there may be a case for linking this supposed increase in devotional materials with the growing influence of monasticism, especially in the
Holy Land and Asia Minor. It would not be true, however, in the present

[63] Cameron, *Corippus*.
[64] Haldon, *Byzantium in the Seventh Century*; Cormack (1990); Wickham (1994).
[65] Weitzmann (1976).   [66] Kitzinger (1976) 91–156.   [67] Grabar (1958).

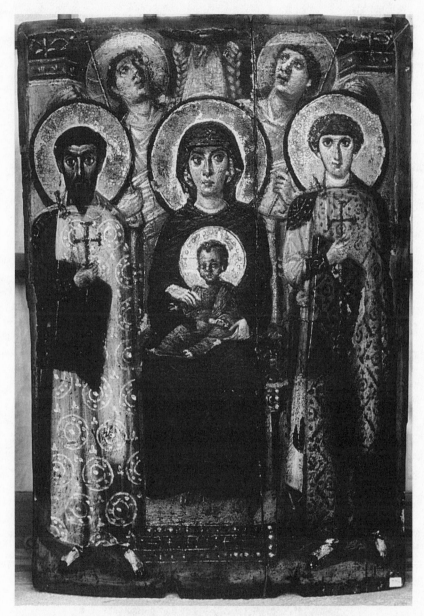

Fig. 36 Encaustic icon of the Virgin and Child with angels and saints, sixth century, in the monastery of St Catherine, Sinai, Egypt. (Photo: Erich Lessing/Art Resource, NY)

Fig. 37 Sixth-century lead ampulla from the Holy Land with the Ascension of Christ. Cathedral Treasury at Monza. (Photo: Foto Marburg/Art Resource, NY)

state of the evidence to say that we can yet date the precise stages of sixth-century developments. The important evidence from Thessalonica and Rome suggests the need for caution over the detail. In the expansion of Thessalonica after the mid-fifth-century development of the city after the prefect of Illyricum moved there, we cannot be sure of the chronology of the various churches and their decoration. In particular, the mosaics of the first decoration of St Demetrius may be as early as the first quarter of the sixth century.[68] Yet they incorporate many expressive and stylistic features which Kitzinger saw as belonging to the early seventh century. The representation of the Virgin Mary in the north inner aisle mosaics has much in common with the icon of the Virgin and saint at Sinai. Kitzinger argued that the icon included significant classical and non-classical elements and that in this period style was being exploited for devotional purposes: that the classicism of the angels and Mary indicated through style their metaphysical status, and that similarly the abstract style of the two saints (Theodore and George or Demetrius) indicated their humanity and function as mediators and receptors of prayers. But the same contrasts of form are found in the church of St Demetrius – and substantially again in the fifth-century consular diptychs. Another church with sets of panels acting as icons is Santa Maria Antiqua in Rome, where again there is a debate about its precise relative chronology, although the case for saying that its first phase of decoration (including the panel of Maria Regina) belongs to the reign of Justin II is strong. These materials from Thessalonica and Rome also introduce questions about the nature of power and patronage in the period; it is clear that the bishop in Thessalonica and the pope in Rome had the advantage of long-term power and prestige, unlike the civil leaders.

The scholarly focus on an 'age of Justinian' may have unduly compartmentalized the developments of the sixth century. The materials from Thessalonica and Rome in particular demonstrate the range of patronage – popes, bishops, monks, governors and leading citizens all feature in the patronage of art in these cities. The church leaders were often long established in city life, while secular officials were in power for relatively short times.[69] These add further complexities of power and status to our understanding of how patronage worked in this period. But it is clear that it was a period of great enterprises successfully carried out; the result was that the Roman empire by the end of the period was visibly and deeply Christianized.

In viewing this visible Christianity, it has become clearer that we have little access to the thought-processes of the planners and artists, who continued to work within a broadly classical vocabulary but were capable of considerable variation in their choices of manner and content (pagan motives continued to be included in art, particularly in floor mosaics and

---

[68] Spieser (1984); Cormack (1989).   [69] Ward-Perkins, *Public Building*.

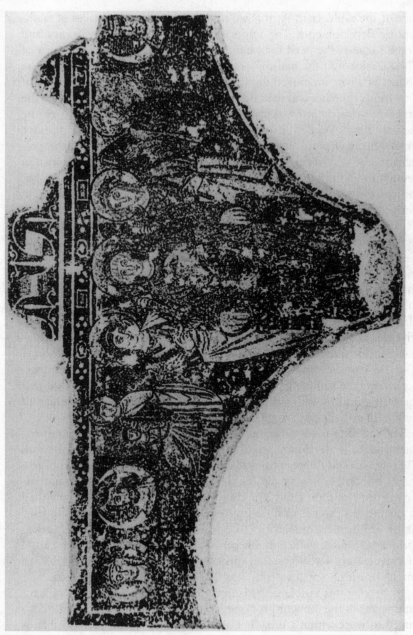

Fig. 38 Sixth-century mosaic panel from the north aisle of the church of St Demetrius, Thessalonica, with the Virgin and Child enthroned between angels and with St Demetrius and a donor, St Theodore and other saints (destroyed 1917). (Photo: Conway Library, Courtauld Institute of Art, London)

metalwork). It seems not until the seventh and eighth century that more introspection was put into the 'proper' nature and uses of Christian art. In our period, whatever the theologians did or did not say, and despite the Second Commandment, Christian art is distinguished by its conspicuous and aggressive use of imagery – with the glaring exception of the walls and vaults of St Sophia. The distinctive aspect of the period is the grand scale of church building and patronage. In this respect, one sees why Procopius was able to construct a long list of monuments, even if we cannot agree that they represent the personal achievement of one individual, Justinian, alone. What is missing from the rhetoric of such a text is the more significant development in the presentation of Christian patronage in the period. We find in church inscriptions a new kind of statement. Images, not only in the churches of Thessalonica like Hosios David and S. Demetrios, but all around the Mediterranean, were increasingly accompanied by the following text: 'For the remission of sins of the person whose name God knows'.[70] Such a discourse in the patronage of art must have profoundly affected also the viewing of art. It eloquently marks the end of classical patterns of euergetism and shows the arrival of the Christian Middle Ages.

[70] Cormack (1989) 1.25.

CHAPTER 31

BUILDING AND ARCHITECTURE

MARLIA MUNDELL MANGO

I. INTRODUCTION

Buildings are the most tangible witnesses of the character of a civilization. Their scale, their function, their elaboration and their novelty as compared to earlier types are all significant pointers. A survey of architecture in the fifth and sixth century leads to one inescapable conclusion: *mutatis mutandis*, life in both city and countryside went on as before in areas under the effective control of the empire. If a citizen of Ephesus of A.D. 300 had been reborn in A.D. 600, he would not have found himself in an alien environment. The forum or agora remained a focus of city life (Fig. 43), as did the bath (Fig. 47) and circus. Of course, most of these traditional buildings were not newly built structures in late antiquity, since most cities had received lavish public buildings in the imperial period. Made to last, they needed upkeep but not replacement, unless they burnt or fell in an earthquake. Unless, therefore, a city was expanding (e.g. Constantinople (Fig. 40), Caesarea, Jerusalem, etc.), was a new foundation (Dara, Justiniana Prima (Fig. 41)) or had been raised in status (Dyrrhachium), there was little call for new public buildings. One novelty was the invasion of the city centres by large churches, but even in this domain, the essential structures had been architecturally developed in the century prior to A.D. 425, although there was still room for expansion. Other new architectural elements were monasteries (Figs. 49–50), *martyria* (Figs. 56–7) and welfare establishments. Village architecture of this period is also abundantly represented by buildings, many still standing to roof height, in the limestone massif of northern Syria: churches, baptisteries, baths, shops, and *andron*, inns, monasteries, houses and tombs (Figs. 42, 54, 60–2).

In addition to standing structures and the archaeological record, knowledge of the architecture in the period is available in a wide variety of narrative and other sources: the *Liber Pontificalis*, Sidonius Apollinaris, Venantius Fortunatus, Gregory of Tours, Malalas, Agnellus and, in particular, Procopius, who describes in detail building carried out over much of the empire during forty years (from the 510s to the 550s).[1] This information is

[1] Mango (1972) 19–145 for a selection of texts in English.

918

supplemented by inscriptions and by laws regulating construction (the height of dwellings, the spaces between them, their access to a water supply, etc.).[2]

Two building trends are apparent in the empire of the fifth and sixth century – a decrease in the west and an increase in the east. At Rome (Fig. 39), a building 'boom' occurs between 380 and 480, precipitated in part by the Gothic and Vandal sackings in 410 and 455, and including the large new churches of Sta Sabina (422/32), Sta Maria Maggiore (432/40) and S. Stefano Rotundo (468/83). At Milan, unsurprisingly, most of the large churches had been built in the fourth century while the city served as a major imperial capital (S. Ambrogio, S. Lorenzo) and, although two bishops continued this work in the fifth and sixth, the two churches known to be erected after 550 are comparatively small in scale. At Ravenna, after a major period of building while the city served as an imperial capital (402–76) and the Ostrogothic capital (until 540), no churches or other public buildings are known to have been erected after S. Severo in 570–95. Although many other churches were built in Italy (e.g. at Vicenza, Verona, Brescia) and Gaul (e.g. at Narbonne, Clermont, Lyons) during the fifth and sixth century – some described by Gregory of Tours – their numbers probably did not reach the number put up in the east.[3]

Constantinople, walled by Constantine in the early fourth century, had continued to expand throughout the fourth century and reached its maximum extent in the fifth (Fig. 40). After its enlargement under Theodosius II (413), the fortified space was not further extended. Yet building within the walls continued and the city benefited from the large construction programme of Justinian, who rebuilt or set up a senate house, a forum, a seaside promenade, a baths complex, a vast cistern, six hospices and four palaces, in addition to thirty-three churches, including St Sophia, the largest building in Christendom until six centuries later. Other eastern cities, such as Antioch, Caesarea Maritima, the capital of Palaestina Prima, and Jerusalem, expanded in size in the fifth or sixth century, adding new buildings both secular and cultic, and new 'symbolic' cities, such as Justiniana Prima in the Balkans (Fig. 41), were founded. At least in the diocese of Oriens, construction in the countryside matched that in the city. In the village of Rihab in the province of Arabia, five churches were built between 594 and 623.[4]

In the late antique city, defensive walls, the water supply, honorific monuments, places of entertainment and cult buildings were all maintained by

[2] Inscriptions: Ward-Perkins, *Public Building*; Mango, M. M. (1984). Laws: Janvier (1969); Saliou (1994).

[3] Rome: Krautheimer (1980) 33–58; Milan: Krautheimer (1983) 68–92; Ravenna: Ward-Perkins, *Public Building* 241–4; other Italian cities: Krautheimer, *Early Christian and Byzantine Architecture* 125–47; Gaul: Greg. Tur. *Hist.* II.14–17, 20, 21, 43; V.45; VII.10; X.31; Venantius Fortunatus, *Carm. passim*.

[4] Constantinople: Mango, *Studies on Constantinople* I.118, 124–8; other eastern cities and Rihab: Mango, M. M. (1984) Gazetteer, I.A.1 430/1–592; VI.B.51; VII.A.1 450–598; VII.A.10 432–630.

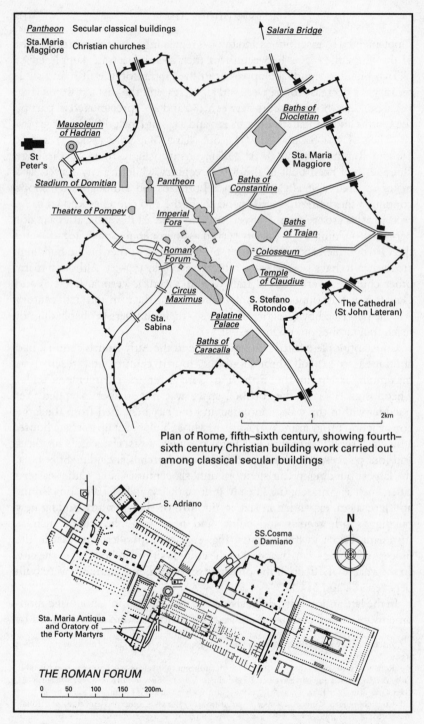

Plan of Rome, fifth–sixth century, showing fourth–
sixth century Christian building work carried out
among classical secular buildings

THE ROMAN FORUM

Fig. 39 Plan of Rome, fifth–sixth century, indicating monuments mentioned in the text

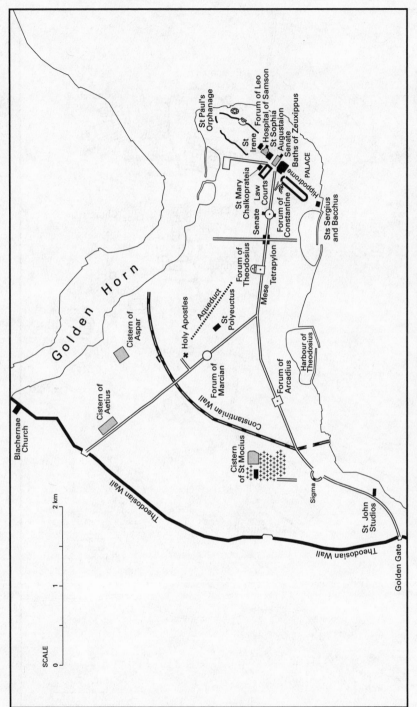

Fig 40 Plan of Constantinople, fifth–sixth century, indicating monuments mentioned in the text

Golden Horn

St Paul's Orphanage

St Irene

Forum of Leo

Hospital of Samson

St Sophia

Augustaion

Senate

Baths of Zeuxippus

PALACE

St Mary Chalkoprateia

Senate

Law Courts

Forum of Constantine

Hippodrome

Sts Sergius and Bacchus

Forum of Theodosius

Mese

Tetrapylon

Cistern of Aspar

Aqueduct

Holy Apostles

St Polyeuctus

Cistern of Aetius

Forum of Marcian

Forum of Arcadius

Harbour of Theodosius

Constantinian Wall

Blachernae Church

Theodosian Wall

Cistern of St Mocius

Sigma

St John Studios

Theodosian Wall

Golden Gate

SCALE
0   1   2 km

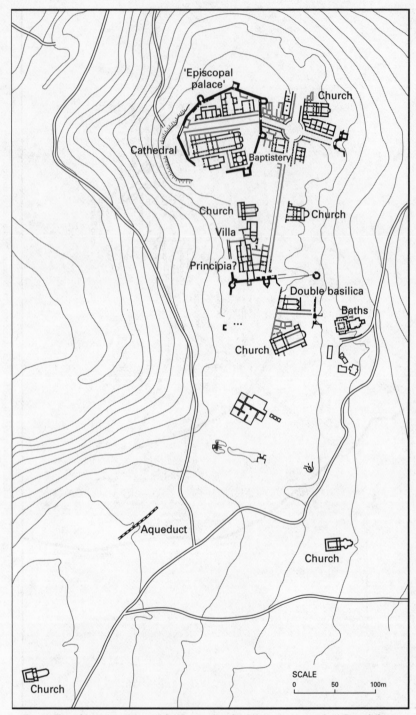

Fig. 41 Plan of Justiniana Prima. (After Bavant, Kondic, Spieser (1990) site plan.) For a different reconstruction of the walled circuit, see Fig. 23, p. 719 above

a combination of state and local money. By law, various public amenities such as harbours, bridges, roads and circuit walls were the responsibility of either the provincial governor or the city; forts were, by contrast, that of military commanders. In the west, Justinian's Pragmatic Sanction of 554 provided for repair to Rome's public buildings, including the Forum, the city's port and aqueducts. The tradition had earlier been maintained by the Romanized Ostrogoths, who prevented spoliation of buildings in Rome (and elsewhere) and provided a fund to maintain the buildings of the city.[5] The last known imperially funded repairs in Rome were those carried out on the Salaria bridge by Narses in 565; in Italy overall, it was the repair of Ravenna's aqueduct by Maurice in c. 600.[6] The ancient tradition of private individuals spending on public buildings was not as marked a feature of our period as it had been earlier, with the important exception of spending on churches. In Italy the last known private funding of a secular public building was the restoration of Rome's theatre of Pompey by Symmachus in 507–12, though private patronage of churches flourished – the most famous instance being the largess of the banker Julianus Argentarius, who financed several churches in sixth-century Ravenna, including San Vitale, S. Apollinare in Classe and S. Michele in Africisco.

In the east, most public building at Constantinople was undertaken by the state, private funding of secular public buildings being less established than at Rome. Building in the diocesan capital Antioch was sponsored in part by members of the imperial family: Eudocia, Theodosius II, Leo, Anastasius, Justin I, Justinian and Maurice, as well as the rebel Illus, and overseen by local state officials; private patronage is, however, also recorded. Privately financed public buildings in the city of Gerasa include at least six out of the ten churches built between 464 and 540.[7]

In late antiquity two types of specialists were responsible for construction; they were known in the Greek-speaking world as the *mechanikos* and the *architekton*. The first, of higher standing, was not just an engineer but an architect with a grounding in mathematics; the *architekton* was a master builder, responsible for the majority of buildings, while an ordinary builder was an *oikodomos* or a *technites*. The architects of Justinian's St Sophia (Fig. 59), Anthemius of Tralles, a prominent mathematician, and Isidore of Miletus, were *mechanikoi*. Texts give the names of other architects: Rufinus of Antioch, who built the cathedral of Gaza under Arcadius, Isidore the Younger, who rebuilt the dome of St Sophia, Stephen of Aila, who was responsible for the monastery church at Mt Sinai, and Asaph and Addai, who built St Sophia at Edessa, are all known from the reign of Justinian.

---

[5] Jones, *LRE* 448–9, 461–2, 734–7; Ward-Perkins, *Public Building* 28–32, 38–48.

[6] Ward-Perkins, *Public Building* 42–5, 70–84, 243–4.

[7] Mango, M. M. (1984) Gazetteer, I.A.I 430/1, 438, 458, 483, 507, 526–7, C540, C588; VII.A.7 464, 526, 529, 531, 533, 540.

The numerous inscriptions of the small area of the limestone massif in northern Syria have yielded a series of named builders (*oikodomoi* and *technitai*) working there between the third and the sixth century (Figs. 42, 62).[8]

Leaving aside works of engineering (defensive walls, aqueducts, harbours),[9] several types of architecture, both secular and religious, will be discussed below under the headings of 'civic and administrative architecture', 'amenities', 'communal accommodation', 'palaces, houses and tombs', and 'churches and synagogues'. Works of building maintenance will also be mentioned to provide a fuller historical picture of the period. Of the three principal areas of elaborate or large-scale architecture in late antiquity – baths, palaces and churches – only the last has been systematically and comprehensively studied by modern scholars.[10]

II. SECULAR ARCHITECTURE

Until recently, excavation, survey, study and publication of late antique architecture has concentrated on religious buildings, thus exaggerating a perceived break in other construction. Yet both archaeology and texts attest to a continuation of urban life in several cities, particularly in the east, which would have demanded, at the least, administrative and commercial architecture. *The Miracles of St Artemius* are set in a seventh-century Constantinople little changed since the fourth. *The Life of Theodore of Sykeon* written in *c.* 612 conveys an impression of urban vitality at Nicomedia. Other texts praise in particular the monumental aspect of a city. Sidonius Apollinaris (*c.* 430–79) does so of Narbonne, listing its 'walls, circuit, shops, gates, porticoes, fora, theatre, shrines, capitol, mints, baths, arches, granaries, markets, fountains, merchandise'. In *c.* 592 Evagrius describes as still standing buildings set up centuries earlier at Antioch: public baths, the law courts, the stoa of Callistus and four civil basilicas, as well as the 'beautiful' palace of the *magister militum*. In 739 a poem in praise of Milan mentions its secular (Roman) monuments with pride – the forum, the paved streets and the aqueduct and bath – all apparently still functioning. Such accounts prove beyond doubt that the ideal of the ordered monumental city remained very close to that of classical times, although excavations, particularly in the west, have revealed the reality of monumental decay – for example, at Luna (the forum) and Verona in *c.* 600.[11]

---

[8] Mango, *Byzantine Architecture* 24–5; Downey (1948).

[9] Defensive walls: Foss and Winfield (1986) 3–13, 25–34, 41–52, 125–31; Lawrence (1983) 171–220. Aqueducts and harbours in Italy: Ward-Perkins, *Public Building* 119–54, 250–5; at Constantinople: Mango, *Studies on Constantinople* I.120–3.

[10] E.g. Krautheimer, *Early Christian and Byzantine Architecture*.

[11] Constantinople: Mango (1980) 78–9; Nicomedia: Foss (1995) 186–7; Narbonne: Sid. Ap. *Carm.* XIII.39–44; Antioch: Mango, M. M. (1984) Gazetteer, I.A.I 592; Milan: Ward-Perkins, *Public Building* 224; Luna: Ward-Perkins (1978); Verona: Hudson (1989).

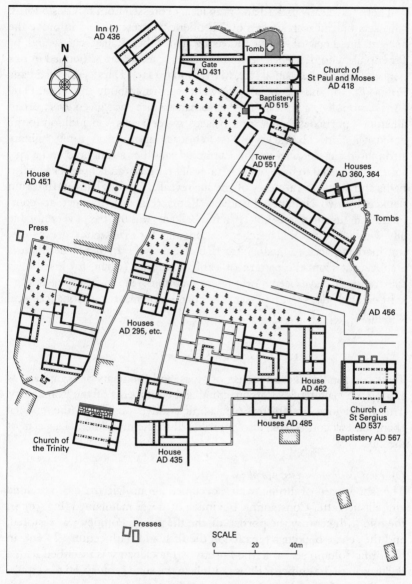

Fig. 42 Plan of Dar Qita, a village in the Jabal Barisha, Syria. Three churches, baptistery and several houses (I–XIX) were built in the fifth and sixth century. Kyros, Symeon and Eusebius, three *technitai*, built one church and two houses, respectively. (After Butler (1920))

There still clearly existed an urban ideal expressed both by Cassiodorus, who sets out measures taken by Theoderic to preserve and improve the ancient buildings of Rome, Ravenna and other Italian cities, and by Procopius, who describes new cities (*poleis*) founded or refounded in this period. Despite their small size, Martyropolis (420), Dara (508), Justiniana Prima (*c.* 530) and Zenobia (550) were seen to embody this ideal. Dara (Anastasiopolis), 'a bulwark of the Roman empire', was given every urban amenity – porticoes, baths, inns, palaces, water works – in addition to the defensive works, barracks and storehouses appropriate for a military stronghold. At Zenobia on the Euphrates, another stronghold and a city, Justinian was said to have built circuit walls, barracks and churches but also baths and porticoes; a survey of the site revealed a public bath and a forum flanked by two churches. Justiniana Prima (Fig. 41), founded to commemorate Justinian's birthplace in the Balkans, was built as 'a very notable city with aqueduct . . . churches . . . lodgings for magistrates, great stoas, fine market-places, fountains, streets, baths, shops'.[12] In these cities there is a shift away from the pattern of earlier centuries (when, for instance, a theatre would have been a prominent feature of the townscape), but the shift certainly does not represent the abandonment of traditional classical urbanism.

1. *Civic and administrative architecture*

Texts cite fora, porticoed streets or stoas, and fountains or nymphaea as among the main types of architectural embellishments of the Roman city. The prestigious architecture of administrative buildings (the council chamber, law courts, etc.) also contributed to the monumental aspects of the city.

(a) *Fora, porticoed streets, nymphaea*

The 'show area' of Rome, which occupied about half the city, was little embellished after Constantine, but much of it was maintained (Fig. 39). In the mid fifth century the portico of the theatre of Pompey was restored, and the senate buildings repaired in the fifth and sixth century. In 608 an honorific column set up in the Forum by Diocletian was inscribed with a dedication to the emperor Phocas. Only in the sixth century did the republican Roman Forum begin to undergo a Christian conversion, starting with two public rooms turned into the church of SS. Cosmas and Damian and a vestibule of the imperial palace converted into Sta Maria Antiqua. Elsewhere in the city, two fora were restored in the mid fifth century.[13] Only

---

[12] Cass. *Variae* I.25; III.30–1, 44; IV.51; XI.39.2; Procop. *Buildings* II.1.4–3.26; 8.11–25; IV.1.19.

[13] Ward Perkins, *Public Building* 45 n. 33, 46–8; Krautheimer (1980) 75–6.

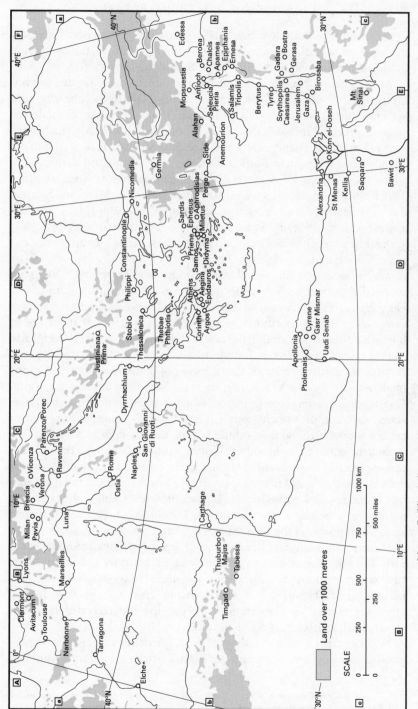

Map 22 Building in late antiquity (places mentioned in chapter 31; see also Map 23, p. 943 below)

in the seventh century does there seem to have been a decisive shift away from the traditional urbanism in Rome, with, for example, the conversion of the senate house into the church of S. Adriano in Foro (625/38).

At Constantinople (Fig. 40), prestige monuments were needed to symbolize the pretensions of the empire. Being New Rome, the city consciously reproduced some of Old Rome's features: a palace/hippodrome complex, fora, a *capitolium*, *thermae*, all set out on 'seven hills'. The historiated columns of Theodosius I and Arcadius imitated that of their supposed ancestor Trajan at Rome. Emperors of the fifth and sixth century added to the series of fora created by earlier emperors – Constantine, Theodosius I and Arcadius – along the main street (the Mese) and beyond, thereby enlarging the city's ceremonial setting. Theodosius II (405–50) built a semicircular portico, the Sigma, west of the Forum of Arcadius (of *c.* 403) in the direction of the city's Golden Gate, where he also set up bronze elephants brought from Athens. The Forum of Marcian (450–7), whose central monolithic column still stands on its base carved with Victories, spanned the street leading north-west to the imperial mausoleum of the Holy Apostles. The Forum of Leo I (457–74) was erected on the ancient acropolis of the city, north-east of the church of St Irene. At 26 metres, its honorific column was among the tallest in the city; the colossal Corinthian capital, recently rediscovered, supported a bronze statue of the emperor, perhaps to be identified with the Colossus of Barletta removed from the medieval city by the Venetians (Fig. 44). The Tetrastoon, a large pre-Constantinian agora (190×95 metres) bounded by four porticoes which lay at the east end of the city, was Constantinople's equivalent of Rome's central forum. Around it stood the Milion, the law courts, St Sophia, the senate, the entrance to the imperial palace, and the Zeuxippus Baths. From this ancient forum a somewhat smaller agora, renamed the Augustaion, was carved, possibly in 459 (Figs. 40, 43). In 532 Justinian rebuilt the surrounding structures and enclosed the Augustaion with a wall and paved it in marble; he replaced a silver statue of Theodosius I with an equestrian statue of himself on top of a masonry column plated in bronze.[14]

Honorific monuments were still being erected in Constantinople in the early seventh century. In 609 Phocas set up a masonry column near the bronze tetrapylon on the Mese (Fig. 40), intended to support a statue of himself; in 612 Heraclius put a monumental cross on top of it. In 614, Heraclius erected in Constantine's Forum the last recorded honorific statue, an equestrian portrait of the patrician Nicetas.[15]

In other cities similar building of fora, porticoes and civil basilicas is known, mostly from texts, and occasionally from excavation. Although

[14] Mango, *Studies on Constantinople* I.123–6; x.1–4; Addenda, 3; Mango (1959) 36–60; Krautheimer, *Early Christian and Byzantine Architecture* 174.　[15] Mango, *Studies on Constantinople* IX.30–1; x.14–17.

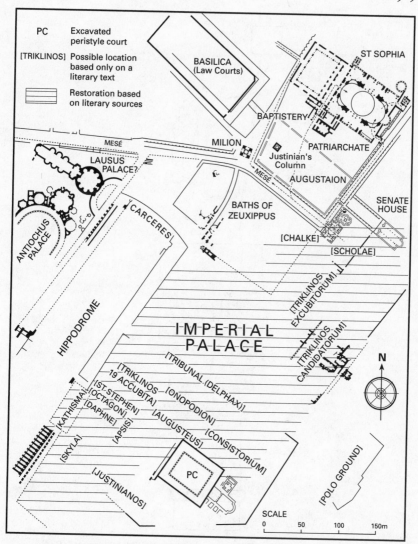

PC — Excavated peristyle court

[TRIKLINOS] — Possible location based only on a literary text

▤ — Restoration based on literary sources

BASILICA (Law Courts)

ST SOPHIA

MESÉ

MILION

BAPTISTERY

PATRIARCHATE

LAUSUS PALACE?

Justinian's Column

MESÉ

AUGUSTAION

ANTIOCHUS PALACE

CARCERES

BATHS OF ZEUXIPPUS

SENATE HOUSE

[CHALKE]

[SCHOLAE]

HIPPODROME

[TRIKLINOS EXCUBITORUM]

IMPERIAL PALACE

[TRIBUNAL (DELPHAX)]

[TRIKLINOS CANDIDATORUM]

N

[TRIKLINOS (ONOPODION)]

19 ACCUBITA

[TRIKLINOS 19 ACCUBITA]

[ST STEPHEN]

[OCTAGON]

[DAPHNE]

[APSIS]

[AUGUSTEUS]

[CONSISTORIUM]

KATHISMA

[SKYLA]

[JUSTINIANOS]

PC

[POLO GROUND]

SCALE
0   50   100   150m

Fig. 43 Plan of Augustaion and surrounding area, Constantinople. (Based on Mango (1959) fig. 1 and Müller-Wiener (1977) fig. 263)

Theoderic provided public buildings in his capitals at Ravenna, Verona and Pavia, most documented cases come from the eastern empire. At Gaza in *c.* 536 rhetorical literature alludes to the construction of a civil basilica and colonnaded street, in addition to baths, a summer theatre and other amenities. Comparable construction occurred at Antioch until the very end of the sixth century, though sadly, aside from the main street, none of these documented buildings was identified in the excavations of the city. What

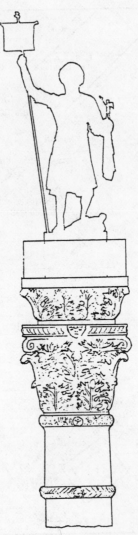

Fig. 44 Column in the Forum of Leo, Constantinople. (From Peschlow (1986) fig. 6)

may have been law courts, a stoa and a basilica were erected there by 433. In the following years, Theodosius II built another basilica known as that of Anatolius, described as 'large and well illuminated'. In *c.* 480 a senator constructed a tetrapylon adorned with bronze as well as two basilicas having 'brilliant stonework' and paved in Proconnesian marble. Following riots in 507, two basilicas, two tetrapyla and the governor's *praetorium* were rebuilt. Porticoes, baths and other public buildings were restored in 526 and

Fig. 45 Ephesus, Arcadiane built *c.* 400 with four honorific columns added during the reign of Justinian. The columns supported statues of the Four Evangelists, a fascinating example of the Christianization of a monument which in its setting and style appears traditional and secular.
(From *Forschungen in Ephesos* (1906) fig. 59)

540 following various disasters, as were, apparently, the law courts after an earthquake in 588.[16]

Comparable late monumental building has been excavated in other cities, where pre-existing monuments were often rebuilt or remodelled during this period, employing re-used materials. At Ephesus, the main porticoed thoroughfares often bear the marks of late antiquity. The long colonnaded Arcadiane, presumably built by Arcadius in *c.* 400 to link the harbour and theatre, incorporated on its south side, opposite the baths rebuilt by Constantius II, an exedra with decorative architecture and a water basin. During the reign of Justinian four large columns, each supporting a statue of an evangelist, were inserted into a central crossing of the street (Fig. 45). In the fifth century, the square in front of Ephesus' theatre and the main porticoed street leading south from it were renovated and repaved in marble. About this time the agora behind it was rebuilt and the nearby Library of Celsus (of the second century) was transformed into a monumental fountain, so that its two-storey façade ornamented with statues was reflected in a pool added below. Two other public fountains of more

[16] Western cities: Ward-Perkins, *Public Building* 30–1, 179–86; Gaza and Antioch: Mango, M. M. (1984) Gazetteer, I.A.1 433, 438, 480, 507, 526, 540, 588; VII.A.21 536–48.

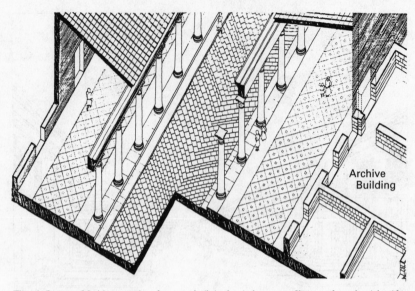

Fig. 46 Caesarea Maritima, porticoed street rebuilt in the sixth century. Shops and, on the right side, the offices of the Archive Building open behind the portico. The central street is paved with slabs and the covered passages have mosaic pavements. (After Holum (1988) fig. 128)

modest dimensions were set up on main streets in Ephesus – one in front of the stadium, the other on the Embolos, at the top of which was also set up in the fifth or sixth century a marble arch decorated in relief with Victories.[17]

At Gerasa, inscriptions attest to the construction of a stoa in 447 and a rebuilding of at least parts of the porticoed cardo to the north and south of the south tetrapylon in 513–30. Antioch's porticoed cardo was rebuilt on a large scale in 540, and at Caesarea in Palestine a secondary porticoed cardo was rebuilt in the sixth century (Fig. 46). To the north-east of this area, near the former temple of Hadrian, another public complex with stairs, an arch and a new pavement was rebuilt in the later sixth century, and two large statues set up, one a second-century portrait of Hadrian. Similar contemporary urban renewal occurred at Scythopolis in Palaestina Secunda, where in 507 a porticoed exedra ringed with shops and embellished with marble was built on Palladius Street (Fig. 47c). Excavations at Tsaricin Grad, identified as Justiniana Prima, have revealed a porticoed main street and a circular piazza with remains of a bronze statue of Justinian(?), as well as baths and churches, all built in the sixth century (Fig. 41).[18]

---

[17] Foss (1979) 46–80.
[18] Gerasa, Caesarea, Antioch: Mango, M. M. (1984) Gazetteer, I.A.1 430; VII.A.1 562, 568; VII.A.7 447; Holum (1988) 174–6, 179–80, 186–7; Scythopolis: Tsafrir and Foerster (1997) 113–14, 121–2, 130; Cariçin Grad: Bavant, Kondic, Spieser (1990) 303–15.

Incorporated into the porticoes of city streets were offices or shops (Figs. 46–7), workshops and housing for artisans, all combined under one roof. These parallel oblong units occupied the space behind the back walls of the porticoes on to which they opened. Facing one side of the Embolos at Ephesus were twelve rectangular vaulted shops and workshops with rooms above, serving as living-quarters for the artisans. At Sardis, similar two-storeyed *ergasteria* (for glassmakers, dyers, ironmongers) formed one side of the porticoed street running beside the Roman bath–gymnasium. Some units at Sardis served as restaurants and a wine shop; others may have been used as residences only.[19]

(b) Administrative buildings

In the fifth and sixth century, imperial administration was sited in the palaces of Ravenna and Constantinople (see below). Next to nothing is known of the architecture of the offices of the prefects. At Rome, that of the *praefectus urbi* was restored in 408/23. At Constantinople (Fig. 40) the residence (see below) and offices of the praetorian prefect (who had a staff of 2,000) were situated by the Forum of Leo; one of its five *scrinia* (departments dealing with Constantinople, Europe, Asia, Pontus and Oriens) was located by the 'middle entrance', while its judicial archives were housed behind the *kathisma* of the Hippodrome, inside the imperial palace. The offices and, presumably, *praetoria* of the urban prefect and master of offices were on the Mese and inside the imperial palace, respectively.[20]

At Caesarea in Palestine a government complex built 560–614 included an archive building and, apparently, a governor's palace and bath (*c.* 550–640). The archive building, identified by inscription as an imperial office (*skrinion*), held accounts for the tax payments from the province; the simple square structure is divided into a large entrance hall and seven rooms (Fig. 46). Justinianic military headquarter buildings (*principia*) have been tentatively identified at Justiniana Prima (Fig. 41) and Zenobia. What is considered the fortified headquarters of the *dux* of Cyrenaica stood on the cardo at Ptolemais, and another building nearby, restored possibly by a governor, has a suite of offices in addition to living-quarters. Two offices (*secreta*) decorated in mosaic survive from the Patriarchal Palace at Constantinople, constructed on the south side of St Sophia by Justin II (565–78) (Fig. 43). A two-storeyed episcopal audience hall survives on the north side of the cathedral atrium at Porec/Parenzo. Like the imperial palace, the residences of governors, *duces* and bishops (see below) may have contained administrative offices.[21]

---

[19] Ephesus: Foss (1979) 73–4; Sardis: Stephens-Crawford (1990).

[20] Rome: Ward-Perkins, *Public Building* 42–3; Constantinople: Mango, *Studies on Constantinople* I.124, Addenda, 1–3.

[21] Caesarea: Holum (1988) 68–71; Ptolemais: Kraeling (1962) 140–60; Constantinople: Mango (1959) 52–6; Porec/Parenzo: Krautheimer, *Early Christian and Byzantine Architecture* 196–7.

At Rome, the *secretarium senatus* was rebuilt in 412/14 following a fire, and the senate house (curia) was restored under the Ostrogoths, though, as we have seen earlier, it was abandoned and turned into a church in the early seventh century. At Constantinople, however, the senate endured until the twelfth century. One of the two senate houses there, that which stood on the Augustaion, was rebuilt after 404, burned during the Nika riot in 532 and subsequently reconstructed by Justinian as a basilica with apse (Fig. 43). Its porch was composed of six enormous white marble columns, four to the front and two behind. As described by Procopius, 'The stoa [thus formed] carries a vaulted roof, and the whole upper portion of the colonnade is adorned with [beautiful] marbles ... and the roof is wonderfully set off by a great number of statues which stand upon it.'[22]

The law courts of Constantinople were situated in the Basilica, a legal and cultural centre near the Augustaion (Fig. 43). Architecturally this was a large court (*c.* 150 metres long) enclosed by four porticoes erected in *c.* 410. The buildings attached to the Basilica included the Public Library (of unknown plan) which in the fifth century was said to contain 120,000 books, and the Octagon, the seat of a university where law courses were given and cases tried; book vendors occupied parts of the porticoes. The Basilica burned down in 476, was rebuilt in 478 and burned again in 532. In the subsequent reconstruction, a vast underground cistern (the Cisterna Basilica) was built beneath the court, and in 542 the prefect Longinus rebuilt the Basilica's porticoes and repaved its court. Justin II set up there a *horologion* (perhaps a sundial).[23]

2. *Amenities: baths and places of entertainment*

(a) Baths

Baths were in the forefront of the development of Roman architecture. Concentric architecture conserved heat, and glass mosaics rendered walls and vaults impermeable. Innovations in the use of concrete facilitated the construction of vaults and domes. Thus the Roman bath chamber, domed or vaulted and decorated in mosaic, is the architectural predecessor, not just of the late antique bath chamber, but of the Byzantine church as well.[24]

In late antiquity, baths were the most popular area of what remained of secular public buildings, except for defensive walls and palaces. By the end of the fourth century, there were eleven *thermae* (each a vast complex laid out symmetrically on an axis leading to the *caldarium*) in Rome and eight in Constantinople. And the *balneum* or *balaneion*, a smaller, asymmetrical bath, usually privately owned, proliferated: there were 856 at Rome and 153 at

---

[22] Rome: Ward-Perkins, *Public Building* 220–1; Krautheimer (1980) 72; Constantinople: Mango (1959) 56–60; Procop. *Buildings* 1.10.6–9.　　[23] Mango (1959) 48–51.

[24] Ward-Perkins (1981) 105–7, 210, 418–21, 430; Sear (1977) 29–30.

Constantinople by A.D. 400. Ostia, Athens and Timgad each had more than a dozen. Whether state owned or privately owned, both *thermae* and *balnea* were open to all for a small entrance fee.[25] By the fifth century, the church started to provide baths exclusively for the poor and for the clergy. At Rome, pope Hilarus (461–8) built two such baths at a monastery and pope Symmachus (498–514) built others. At Ravenna, clerical baths were available to both orthodox and Arians; those of the former were rebuilt by the bishop Victor (537–45).[26] The bishop of Gerasa built a bath in 454 which was restored in 584. Justinian restored the bath 'for soldiers' enjoyment' in the garrisoned city of Circesium. Texts mention the existence of distinct summer baths and winter baths at Antioch, Tripolis, Edessa, Gaza, Epiphania (Hama) and Thuburbo Majus. Although the architectural differences between the two are unclear, some distinctive features set seasonal baths apart: in sixth-century Epiphania a normal bath was converted into a winter bath. A summer bath built at Edessa in 497–504/5 had two basilicas and a *tepidarium*; the local winter bath also had at least two basilicas. The winter bath at Gaza had a dome decorated with a *tabula mundi*.[27]

At Rome, the *thermae* of Agrippa still functioned in the fifth century, the baths on the Aventine were restored in 414 and those of Constantine in 443, while Theoderic restored the Baths of Caracalla (Fig. 39). Of the eight *thermae* at Constantinople listed in the *Notitia urbis Constantinopolitanae* of *c.* 425, four were built, completed or rebuilt in the fifth and sixth century: the *Thermae Constantianae*, built 345–427; the *Honorianae*, finished in 412; the Baths of Achilles, rebuilt in the fifth century; and the Baths of Zeuxippus, rebuilt after 532 (Figs. 40, 43). The bath of Dagistheos north-west of the Hippodrome was started by Anastasius and completed in 528 by Justinian, who also built a marble colonnaded seaside promenade, decorated with statues, at the Arcadianae Baths. Unfortunately, these baths are known only from written sources, aside from parts of the sixth-century Zeuxippus baths, which have been excavated (Fig. 43). Constructed of *opus mixtum*, these included a domed structure and another with a large apse (12 metres wide) facing an extensive court which was possibly a *palaestra*. Two vaulted chambers were excavated separately, as were two granite columns set 27 metres apart and two spiral staircases, of a type often found in imperial *thermae* connecting the *caldarium* with the hypocaust below and the upper storey above. The original Zeuxippus baths had contained eighty classical statues, which were celebrated by a series of epigrams composed by Christodoros of Coptus shortly before the fire of the Nika riot, which destroyed the building in 532. Two inscribed statue bases and a marble slab

---

[25] Yegül (1992) 1–5, 314–23.   [26] Ward-Perkins, *Public Buildings* 135–46.

[27] Mango, M. M. (1984) Gazetteer, VII.A.7 454, 584 (Gerasa); XV.A.17 527–60 (Circesium); I.A.1 360 (Antioch); IV.A.7 450 (Tripolis); XV.A.1 497, 500 (Edessa); VII.A.21 500, 536 (Gaza); II.A.2 6th c. (Epiphania); Yegül (1992) 43, 222, 226–30, 238.

with a relief of a nereid – all of the sixth century – were recovered in the excavations.[28]

In contrast to the imperial *thermae* of the west, which assimilated the Greek *palaestra* to the Roman bath to create a new comprehensive form, the bath in Asia Minor simply grafted the one on to the other to create the bath-gymnasium. Archaeologists have dated most of these to before the fifth century. That at Ephesus, built in the second and third century, was restored in the fifth and redecorated again after that. The bath-gymnasium at Salamis on Cyprus, built in the second century, was repeatedly rebuilt and restored in the fourth, fifth and sixth century, and Heraclius helped to build an aqueduct, which led in its direction, in the seventh. Baths excavated elsewhere in the east may be *thermae* with or without a *palaestra*.[29]

At Antioch, Malalas named nine large baths of the imperial period. The Baths of Valens were restored by Eudocia in 438, and Leo repaired those of Trajan, Hadrian and Severus in 458. Justinian and Theodora built baths there in 527, and Maurice apparently rebuilt a winter and a summer bath in 588. Excavations at Antioch uncovered several large-scale baths, and while none is easily identified with those cited in texts, Bath F (rebuilt in 537, according to an inscription) was apparently laid out symmetrically and on a large scale. At Alexandria, what may also have been a *thermae* building is a large-scale symmetrical bath, restored in the fifth and sixth century. One *thermae* complex at Scythopolis (95 × 60 metres), built in the fifth century and remodelled in the sixth, has a *palaestra* and large propylaeum façade (four columns supporting a pediment) made of reused carved marble (Fig. 47A–B).[30]

The plans of smaller baths with or without *palaestra* vary widely. At Ephesus, a bath rebuilt *c.* 400 had an irregular plan adjusted to the nearly trapezoidal lot available on the congested Embolos. Lacking both *palaestra* and axiality, the bath had two large adjoining halls (an apsed room and a long gallery) to serve as vestibule and *apodyterium*. The bath was paved with marble and mosaic, its walls revetted with marble, and its rooms decorated with statues of the owner Scholasticia herself, Socrates, Menander and a dignitary of the sixth century.[31] Asymmetrical baths built or rebuilt in the fifth and sixth century, with chambers arranged in a row (axial or angular) or in a ring, have been identified in Constantinople, Greece (Philippi, Thebae Phthiotis), Asia Minor (Didyma, Priene, Samos, Perge, Side, Anemorium), Egypt (Kom el-Dosheh), Cyrenaica (Apollonia, Cyrene, Ptolemais, Gasar

---

[28] Rome: Ward-Perkins, *Public Building* 34–5; Yegül (1992) 135, 152; Constantinople: Mango (1984b) IV.388–41; Janin (1964) 216–24; Zeuxippus excavations: Mango (1959) 37–9.

[29] Yegül (1992) 250–313; Mango, M. M. (1984) Gazetteer, XIX.A.1 342, 5th, 528, 618–33.

[30] Antioch: Mango, M. M. (1984) Gazetteer, I.A.1 438, 458, 527, 526/8–537/8, 588; Alexandria: Nielsen (1990) catalogue no. 280, fig. 217; Scythopolis: Tsafrir and Foerster (1997) 131–2 and n. 207.

[31] Foss (1979) 70; Yegül (1992) 288, 290–1.

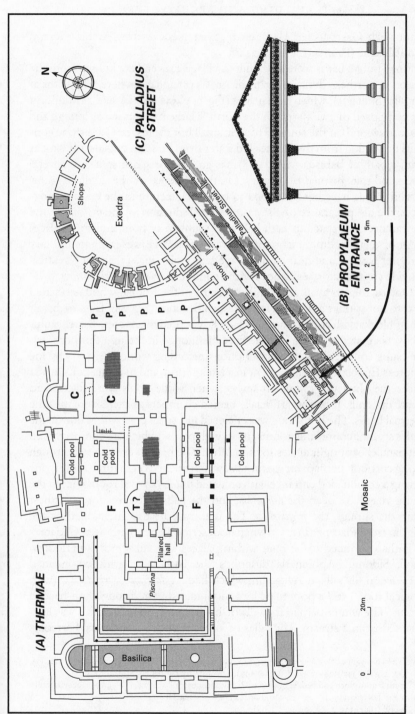

Fig 47 Scythopolis: (a) plan of *thermae* built in the fifth century and remodelled in the sixth, when the 'basilica' and the pools were added in the palaestra on the west side; (b) the propylaeum entrance composed of reused carvings is situated on the south side; (c) porticoed Palladius Street, with shop-lined exedra added, probably in the sixth century. (P = praefurnium; C = caldarium; T = tepidarium; F = frigidarium.) (After Yeivin *et al.* (1987–8) fig. 11 and Tsafrir *et al.* (1993) figs. 56, 60)

Khuraybah, Gasr Mismar, Uadi Senab), Syria (Neocaesarea), Arabia (Gerasa) and Palestine (Emmaus, Philoteria).[32]

Small public baths were also built in villages; several are known from the period in northern Syria, at Androna (in *c.* 558) and elsewhere. The baths at Sergilla (built 473), which has latrines (Fig. 9, p. 331 above), and at Midjleyya are composed of two parts: on the north, a large hall serving as lounge and *apodyterium*, and on the south, a row of small hot rooms; elevated stone conduits projecting from the façades fed water from a cistern outside. Of similar plan, a bath at Babisqa (dated 488) has an interior space split into several levels and transformed by arcades. On the evidence of these village baths, certain trends have been ascribed to bath architecture in the eastern provinces: the disappearance of the *palaestra*, the reduction of the *frigidarium*, the appearance of a spacious bath hall with fountain or pool, and the replacement of a large communal pool by small pools.[33] However, contemporary and later baths at and near Antioch, at Scythopolis (Fig. 47) and at Caesarea, provide contradictory evidence for the continuation of the *frigidarium*.[34]

One of the largest thermo-mineral baths in the Roman world is situated next to hot springs at Gadara in Palaestina Secunda (Fig. 48). Built of basalt ashlar blocks with rubble core and probably roofed in concrete barrel vaults, it covers an area *c.* 50×70 metres. First mentioned in the mid third century, the baths complex has three inscriptions recording work in 443–60 by the empress Eudocia, an enlargement in a later period, and modifications in 664 under the Umayyad caliph Mu'awiya, when some pools were filled in to create dry halls. It has no artificially heated chambers as there were in some thermal baths. The hot spring was enclosed in a small pool within one of the bath's six interconnecting rooms (most with pools), which are compactly laid out parallel or at right angles to each other. The baths were entered through a long corridor, perhaps an *apodyterium*, which opened on to three rooms, one having a colonnaded entrance with arcuated lintel. An oval room next to the spring may have been the *caldarium*, and the hall (55 metres long) furthest from the springs, the *frigidarium*. The bath may be that mentioned by the pilgrim from Piacenza in *c.* 570 when he described lepers bathing at Gadara.[35]

Baths continued to be built within palaces and villas in this period. In Gaul, Sidonius Apollinaris describes the bath suite with colonnaded entrance in his villa at Avitacum, which had a *caldarium*, a *frigidarium* (with 'conical roof') and a pool filled by a mountain stream through lion-headed spouts. The winter bath in the villa of his friend Pontius Leontius was likewise fed from a stream. The villas of other friends (Consentius, Ferreolus

---

[32] Nielsen (1990) catalogue nos. 284, 294, 312, 314, 319, 326–31, 338, 341, 347, 356–9, 370, 372, 373, 379, 387; Yegül (1992) 324–5.   [33] Yegül (1992) 329–39; Charpentier (1994) 113–42.

[34] Bath F at Antioch and bath at Toprak en-Narlica nearby: Stillwell (1941) 8–9, 19–23; Scythopolis: Tsafrir and Foerster (1997) 113, 131–2 and nn. 123–4; Caesarea: Holum (1988) 182–4.

[35] Yegül (1992) 121–4.

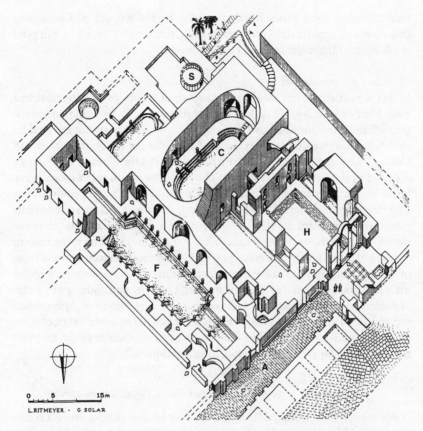

Fig. 48 Gadara, thermal springs, isometric drawing of baths. Improved by the empress Eudocia (443–60) later enlarged, and finally modified by the caliph Muʿawiya in 664. (S = hot spring; C = caldarium; F = frigidarium; A = apodyterium; H = entrance hall with pool). (After Yegül (1992) fig. 136)

and Apollinaris) also had baths.[36] The sixth-century governor's palace at Ephesus contains a bath with *frigidarium*, *tepidarium* and *caldarium*, arranged in two parallel rows, and a villa outside Antioch, possibly built by Ardabur when he was *magister militum per Orientem* at Antioch (453–66), had a bath suite. Another private bath of the mid fifth century, attached to a group of farm buildings at Toprak en Narlica, just east of Antioch, is of the angular row type, reminiscent of the Syrian village baths. An oblong vestibule opens into an octagonal *frigidarium* which recalls a room in *thermae* (Bath C) at Antioch. Decorated with floor mosaics of *Soteria* ('Well-being') and *Apolausis* ('Enjoyment'), the chamber has four corner pools and a larger pool in an alcove. From the octagon a small chamber leads into the *sudatorium* and

[36] Sid. Ap. *Carm.* XVIII–XIX, XXII.179–86; XXIII.495–9; *Epp.* 2.2.4–9; 9.8; 8.4.1.

then the *caldarium*. A latrine lies on the other side of a court. At Caesarea in Palestine a compactly designed private bath, dated 550–640, had a fish pool in addition to the usual hot and cold chambers.[37]

(b) Places of entertainment

In this period, few if any theatres, circuses or other places of entertainment were built or rebuilt – Theoderic's amphitheatre at Pavia being an exception – but their continued use and architectural alterations are attested by excavation and written sources. In the Colosseum at Rome the 'arena and balcony' were repaired in the late fifth century, and the Theatre of Pompey restored in the early sixth (Fig. 39). The emperor Maurice (582–602) gave funds to reconstruct the Hippodrome at Antioch. The Hippodrome at Constantinople, designed for horse-racing, remained the most important public meeting-place in the city, where the populace saw the emperor sitting in the *kathisma* by the palace (Figs. 40, 43). In other cities, the theatre continued to be a major meeting-place for the people, as well as the setting of mimes, pantomimes and games. Inscriptions record restorations in the fifth and sixth century of the theatres at Ephesus and Side, and of the Maiouma *naumachia* theatre at Gerasa (in 533). The theatre at Aphrodisias was modified in the mid fourth century, and imperial and other statues were set up there into the sixth, while the stage area of the theatre of Scythopolis experienced four rebuilding phases in late antiquity.[38]

3. Communal accommodation: barracks, inns, hospitals, monasteries

Some types of communal accommodation in this period share certain architectural features, such as a series of rooms grouped around a court.

(a) Barracks

Barracks are mentioned several times by Procopius in listing Justinian's building accomplishments throughout the empire. Actual remains are available in Syria, where the barracks are square enclosures with accommodation built around the inside of the wall, and incorporate a church or chapel. In barracks (called *kastellos* and dated to 412 in an inscription) at Umm idj-Djemal a chapel is attached to one of the enclosure walls. In the barracks (558/9) at Androna and possibly in those (c. 561) at Qasr Ibn Wardan, a church stands in the centre.[39]

---

[37] Ephesus: Foss (1979) 48–51; Antioch: Stillwell (1938) 95–147; Toprak en-Narlica: Stillwell (1941) 19–23; Caesarea: Holum (1988) 182–4.

[38] Pavia and Rome: Ward-Perkins, *Public Building* 44, 99, 107; Constantinople: Mango (1984b) IV.344–50; Ephesus: Foss (1979) 61; Antioch and Gerasa: Mango, M. M. (1984) Gazetteer, I.A.1 c588; VI.A.7 533; Aphrodisias: Roueché (1991); Scythopolis: Tsafrir *et al.* (1992) 19–22.

[39] Mango, M. M. (1984) Gazetteer, II.B.8 558; II.B.65 c561; VI.B.64 412.

(b) Inns

Several inns (*xenon, xenodochion*) have been identified by inscription in northern Syria. An inn built, possibly in the mid fifth century, outside the north gate of Antioch had a large entrance court and a mosaic pavement, as did an inn (510) in the village of Frikya. Below Qal'at Sim'an (ancient Telanissos) three inns, called *pandocheia*, were constructed in 471 and 479, for the use of pilgrims visiting the column of St Symeon the Elder. Elsewhere in the area, inns having stables on the lower level and accommodation for travellers above were built in 436 at Dar Qita (Fig. 42) and 504. The inn situated inside a fort at Umm al-Halahil may have served as a *metaton* or staging-post between the cities of Chalcis and Epiphania (Hama). Inns were excavated in the monasteries of Mt Nebo and Martyrius (Fig. 50) in Palestine (see below).[40]

(c) Hospitals and orphanotrophia

In this period the Greek word *xenon* or *xenodochion* could apply either to an inn or to a hospital/hospice, the latter also being called a *nosokomeion*. Hospitals are recorded being built in several major cities during this period – at Rome, Alexandria, Antioch and at Constantinople, where several hospitals were established in the fifth and sixth century. These included the hospice for both the destitute and the seriously ill built between St Irene and St Sophia by one Samson before 450 (Fig. 40). Destroyed during the Nika riot in 532, it was rebuilt by Justinian, who made it 'nobler . . . in the beauty of its structure and much larger in the number of its rooms'. The seventh-century *Miracles of St Artemius* relate that a deacon of St Sophia underwent surgery there. The plan of ruins excavated on the site of this hospice reveals a cistern to the east and a large hall with colonnaded entrance to the west.[41]

Not far from the Samson hospice was the orphanage of St Paul, founded by Justin II (Fig. 40). What have been identified as its remains include a row of late antique chambers with colonnaded façade, behind which lie others of medieval date; so large was the orphanage that in the twelfth century Anna Comnena described it as being 'a city within a city'. It had a two-storey residential wing for the poor and sick, an international school and a Georgian nunnery.[42]

(d) Monasteries

The monastic rule of Basil the Great, which represents the norm of Byzantine monasticism, advocated a self-sufficient community. Hence many monasteries were land-based and engaged in agriculture, so that early monasticism is more associated with the countryside than the city. However,

---

[40] Mango, M. M. (1984) Gazetteer, I.A.1 458; I.B.23 436; I.B.45 504/5; I.B.81 471, 479; II.B.27 510; II.B.98.   [41] Miller (1990).   [42] Anna Comnena, *Alexiad* xv.7.3–9; Mango, *Développement* 34.

some monasteries existed within city walls from an early date. The first monastery at Constantinople, that of Dalmatios, was founded in the late fourth century, and by 536 there were nearly eighty monasteries in and around the capital. In the Holy Land, many monasteries were founded at pilgrimage sites to care for the shrine and its visitors; others were foundations of élite individuals, like the empress Eudocia, who wished to be buried in their own establishments with their own clergy praying for their souls. In Palaestina Secunda, a monastery at Scythopolis, founded in c. 560 by a family (titled members of which were buried there), had rooms decorated with floor mosaics and sculpture and was laid out around a hall with a chapel at one corner (Fig. 11, p. 339 above).[43]

Aside from churches, little monastic architecture has survived or been excavated in cities. More is known of the architecture of rural monasteries, from both texts and excavations, which reveal that they contained dormitories, a refectory, stables, workshops, storage buildings, communal tombs and a church or chapel – also, possibly, a bath, an infirmary and an inn. Peter the Iberian's monastery, built near Gaza in c. 488, was described as having two-storey cells, porticoes, courtyards, gardens, cisterns, a tower and a walled church. In many ways, rural monasteries resembled the self-sufficient Roman villa as described by Palladius in the fourth century and by earlier writers. Rural monasteries took two main social and architectural forms – the *laura*, where monks lived separately in cells scattered around the church and service buildings, and the *coenobium*, where monks had communal quarters and refectory and a variety of buildings usually arranged around a courtyard and enclosed by a quadrangular wall.[44]

In Egypt, where monasticism originated, the huge *laura* settlement of Kellia, built in the sixth to the eighth century in the Nile delta, had c. 1,600 walled units, now partially excavated, each containing separate rooms for two monks, a reception room, a kitchen and an oratory, all grouped around a courtyard and often with a well, garden and watch tower, and, sometimes, a small church (Fig. 49). The larger complexes at Kellia serving as community centres also have towers, refectories and several churches. At Bawit in upper Egypt the monastery of Apa Apollo is composed of two churches and several complexes, some with chapels, transverse halls with painted niches interpreted as prayer halls, and tombs. At Saqqara, the necropolis of Memphis, the monks of Apa Jeremias first settled in abandoned mausolea and had a mud-brick chapel and single-aisled refectory; better premises were built only after the Arab conquest.[45]

[43] Mango, *Studies on Constantinople* 1.125; Hirschfeld (1992) 18–58; Scythopolis: Fitzgerald (1939).
[44] Mango, M. M. (1984) Gazetteer, VII.B.44.
[45] Kellia: Bridel (1986); Bawit: Maspero (1931–43); Saqqara: Quibell (1909–12).

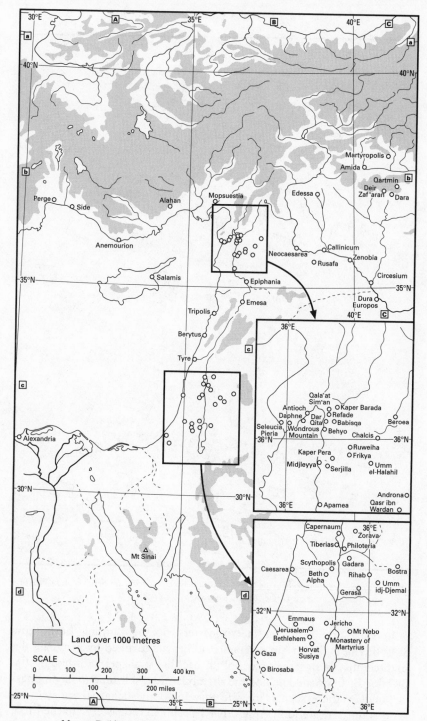

Map 23 Building in the eastern provinces (places mentioned in chapter 31)

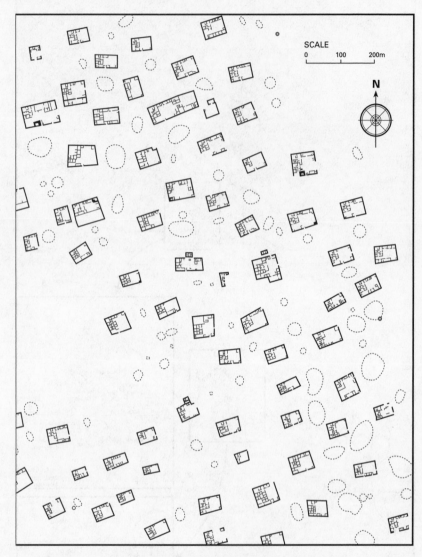

Fig. 49 Kellia, *laura* monastery in the Nile delta built between the sixth and eighth century. Plan of some of the 1600 walled units. (After Bridel (1986))

In Palaestina Tertia, at the monastery of the Burning Bush (now St Catherine's) on Mt Sinai, rebuilt and heavily fortified by Justinian, the sixth-century basilical church, still in use, has a chapel surrounding the Burning Bush situated behind the altar; but other, still-functioning monastic buildings there, such as the refectory and domestic quarters, date from various different periods. At another Palestinian monastery attached to a pilgrimage site, on Mt Nebo in Jordan, where Moses is believed to have viewed the Promised Land before his death, the installations surrounding the church have been excavated and dated – for the most part, to the fifth and sixth century. In addition to the refectory, other areas identified were occupied by the cells of the monks and their superior, a kitchen, bakeries and, possibly, a library (all of which were laid out around courtyards and the atrium of the church, under which lie two cisterns). A long narrow lodging for guests stands on the floor above its own refectory. Similar to the Mt Nebo monastery – but without the pilgrimage church – was that founded before 474 just east of Jerusalem by Martyrius, where the walled quadrilateral complex enclosed refectory, kitchen, cells, church, tombs and service areas, as well as a bath and lavatory, all arranged around a central courtyard, at one corner of which stood stables serving an external inn (Fig. 50). Hundreds of ceramic table and kitchen vessels were excavated there, in addition to a *sigma*-shaped marble dining-table top like those found in a town house at Apamea (see below). Elsewhere in the Judaean desert, sixty monastic sites have been identified, about a quarter of which have been surveyed or excavated. Of these, some, like the monastery of Martyrius, are coenobitic, while nineteen others are *laura* installations with scattered cells.[46]

In Syria, monasteries near Antioch had a separate, sometimes large church, either a basilica or single-nave hall church. By contrast, in the area of Apamea, the monastery church was replaced by an oratory added to one side of a large communal building; this plan is thought to have been introduced from Mesopotamia, where a related form of monastic architecture is known at Qartmin and other sites. Monasteries were built adjacent to the shrines of Symeon Stylites the Elder and the Younger, north-east and south-west of Antioch, at Qal'at Sim'an and Wondrous Mountain, respectively; both had inns for pilgrims and a baptistery (Fig. 62), and the latter was said to contain a kitchen, bakery and granary.[47]

Like the fortified monastery on Mt Sinai, two walled monasteries founded in Mesopotamia in late antiquity continue to function today – those of Qartmin (Mar Gabriel) and Deir Zaf'aran in the Tur 'Abdin. Both complexes also retain sixth-century churches. The first (with a transverse nave and tripartite sanctuary) was possibly built in 512 and is still decorated with wall mosaics and an *opus sectile* pavement, and the second (a compact triconch with tripartite sanctuary) is attributed to *c.* 536 and decorated with elaborate sculpture. Early buildings in these two monasteries include collective tombs, baptisteries and cisterns, built of massive ashlar masonry and some brick.[48]

---

[46] Mt Sinai: Forsyth and Weitzmann (1973); Grossmann (1990); Mt Nebo: Saller (1941); Martyrius: Hirschfeld (1992) 42–5, 99, 197–8; other Judaean monasteries: Hirschfeld (1992) 18–68, 112–212.

[47] Tchalenko, *Villages* I.19–20, 145–73, 178–82, 211–18; Mango, M. M. (1984) Gazetteer, I.B.81–2.

[48] Bell (1982) 132–5, 137–9.

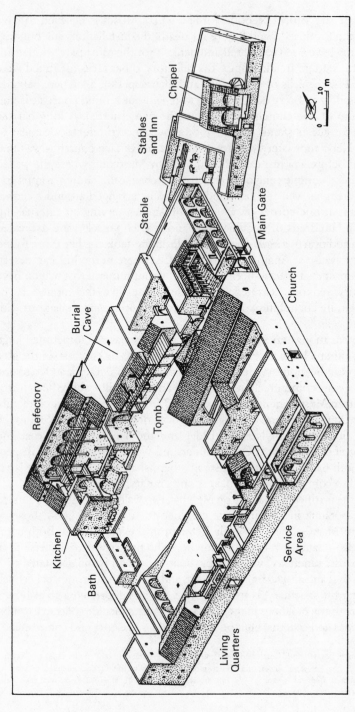

Fig. 50 Near Jerusalem, reconstruction drawing of coenobitic monastery founded in 473 by Martyrius from Cappadocia, later patriarch of Jerusalem. Outside the walled complex containing accommodation and a church for monks is an inn with its own chapel. (From Hirschfeld (1992))

Living Quarters

Bath

Kitchen

Refectory

Burial Cave

Tomb

Stable

Stables and Inn

Chapel

Church

Main Gate

Service Area

0   10 m

4. *Palaces, houses and tombs*

(a) *Palaces and houses*

Palaces

Although no longer a regular imperial residence after 312, the Palatine palace in Rome continued to be maintained, though not enlarged. Texts refer to several palaces at Ravenna, imperial capital from 402: those of Honorius, Galla Placidia, Valentinian III (called 'Ad Laureta', recalling the Daphne section of the Constantinople palace), Odoacer and Theoderic. Theoderic's palace is known to have had an entrance called 'Chalke', a name based on that of the imperial palace at Constantinople, and, apparently, a basilica of Hercules. F. W. Deichmann concluded that most of these various palaces were located in the same urban area – namely, to the east of the Platea Major – and that they were probably situated within the walls of a large military building, possibly a *praetorium*, which had been in use between the first and the fourth century. They probably all formed part of a single sprawling complex, similar to those of Rome and Constantinople. The porticoed façade of Theoderic's 'palatium' is illustrated in a mosaic in the church of S. Apollinare Nuovo, and remains of what may be his palace have been uncovered near the church. The excavated building had a central court with porticoes on two sides, one of which opened into an apsed *triclinium* and a trefoil dining-chamber. Theoderic also built or improved palaces at Pavia and Verona. The latter, situated inside the Castrum, was linked by a portico to the city gate.[49]

The origin and extent of the imperial palace adjacent to the Hippodrome at Constantinople is a matter of great speculation, and several restorations have been attempted, based largely on the descriptions given in the *Book of Ceremonies* (Fig. 43). The entrance to the palace was a monumental vestibule called the Chalke on account of its gilded bronze roof tiles or its great bronze portals. An epigram ascribing a rebuilding of Constantine's Chalke to Anastasius describes the new structure as large and splendid, rectangular or square in plan and with gilded roof tiles. When this was burned during the Nika riot of 532, it was rebuilt by Justinian on a magnificent scale, as described by Procopius. Its rectangular plan was on an east–west axis. Inside, four square piers engaged in the walls carried eight arches, four of which upheld the central dome, while the other four supported vaults. The floor and walls were covered with marble – white set off by green and orange-red. The lateral vaults were decorated in mosaic with scenes of Belisarius' successful campaigns against the Vandals and the Goths. The imperial couple and senators were portrayed in the dome.[50]

---

[49] Ravenna: Deichmann (1989) 49–75; Pavia and Verona: Ward-Perkins, *Public Building* 159–60.
[50] Ebersolt (1910); Mango (1959) 21–35.

Another part of the palace known from the early period, and loosely ascribed to Constantine, is the Hall of the Nineteen Couches, used for state banquets, when 228 persons reclined at table in the antique manner. Justin II (565–78) built the Chrysotriklinos, the main throne room of the palace, known only from written sources. It was octagonal in plan and had a dome supported by eight arches and pierced by sixteen windows. On the east side, an apse held the emperor's throne. The other seven arches opened into semicircular niches. From the written account, it appears that its architecture may have distantly recalled that of Domitian's audience hall in Rome's Palatine and may have reflected Justinian's church of Sts Sergius and Bacchius (Fig. 58). In 578 the emperor Tiberius is recorded to have pulled down a number of buildings to enlarge the palace on one side and to have put up what John of Ephesus describes as 'larger and more magnificent buildings, including a splendid bath' and stables.[51]

An unidentified part of the imperial palace, excavated and dated after 540 on the basis of underlying material, probably formed part of the private quarters (Fig. 43). This discovery consisted of a large peristyle court paved in high-quality mosaics, on to which opened an apsed reception room or *triclinium* paved in marble. Nothing remains of another sixth-century imperial palace, that of the Deuteron, built by Justin II on the main street leading to the Adrianople Gate; this is recorded to have had a private hippodrome, gardens and two columns with statues.[52]

Certain large and luxuriously decorated town houses known from texts and excavations can be identified as *praetoria* or official residences of provincial governors, bishops or other officials, although in the case of many of the excavated buildings it is impossible to be certain if the building concerned is a large privately owned dwelling or a publicly financed palace. The residence of the praetorian prefect at Constantinople was established in the 470s in an existing house with bath suite on the Forum of Leo; this was enlarged in 517 by the addition of an upper storey into which a new bath was built before 551. A text indicates that the governor's *praetorium* at Antioch must have been large: in 526 the Baths of Commodus on the Forum of Valens were converted to this use. At Apamea, a building that has been identified as the palace of the governor of Syria Secunda (a province created *c.* 415) had its entrance from the street in the west wing of the peristyle, while two large *triclinia* project from the east and north wings. The building's decoration included mosaics and stone and stucco sculpture. The massive 'Palace of the Giants' (84×129 metres) built in *c.* 410 at Athens, possibly for official use, had two peristyle complexes linked by a

---

[51] Ebersolt (1910) 58–67, 77–92; Mango (1972) 128.
[52] Brett, Macaulay and Stevenson (1947); Talbot Rice (1958); Mango (1972) 124–5.

(a)

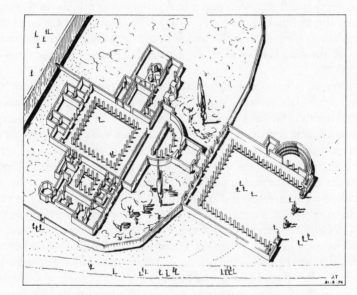

(b)

Fig. 51 Athens, 'Palace of the Giants' of *c.* 410: (a) restoration of the entrance façade and (b) isometric reconstruction of complex. (From Frantz (1988) plate 55)

semicircular portico (Fig. 51). The principal façade was modelled on a triumphal arch, and incorporated colossal figures reused from the Antonine period. What is considered the sixth-century *praetorium* of the proconsul of Asia based at Ephesus has a transverse double-apsed entrance hall (50 metres long) followed by a large reception room somewhat reminiscent of the imperial Chrysotriklinos at Constantinople. Decorated with stucco, painting and floor mosaics, the room, 19 metres square, has four large corner niches and a projecting apse where the seated governor could receive visitors. A bath was attached to one side, and a chapel was added to another. Other possible *praetoria* of the fifth to the sixth century have been found at Ptolemais and Apollonia in Cyrenaica, and at Caesarea in Palestine.[53]

Relatively little is known of episcopal palaces. At Bostra, capital of Arabia, two standing buildings have been identified as episcopal palaces. At least one of the two is a square two-storey building with a central court surrounded by vaulted rooms; the other may also have followed this design. The main reception room, situated on the upper floor, is a tetra-conch. A cruciform building near the cathedral of Justiniana Prima has been identified as its episcopal palace (Fig. 41). At Ravenna, the orthodox episcopal palace, first built in *c.* 450, had a banqueting hall, a mosaiced chapel (which still survives) and a bath, which was rebuilt on a grander scale by the archbishop Victor (537–44). The bishop of Naples added a dining-hall to his palace in the mid fifth century. Only offices decorated with wall mosaics survive from the patriarchal palace in Constantinople (Fig. 43).[54]

Houses at Athens and Aphrodisias – cities noted for philosophical schools during late antiquity – may have provided both living accommodation and teaching facilities for sophists, the latter in the form of a large apse surrounded by colonnades. Apses in these houses had a series of niches to hold sculpture; in those at Aphrodisias were excavated a series of tondo portraits, ascribed to the fifth century, which commemorate Pindar, Alexander and various philosophers. The most elaborate town houses of this period were probably in Constantinople: the remains of two of these have been excavated, situated side by side, to the north of the Hippodrome (Fig. 52). One, if correctly identified as the palace of Lausus, *praepositus sacri cubiculi* in 420, housed a famous collection of statues; the other was identified by inscription as the palace of Antiochus, another *praepositus sacri cubiculi* in *c.* 421. Both buildings had a monumental semi-circular entrance portico. In the Lausus house, this led into a large circular hall, over 20 metres wide, with eight niches in its walls. Beyond this and a double-apsed bay lay an apsed hall 52.5 metres long, covered by a series of cross-vaults; in the sixth century six projecting niches were added to the lateral walls. The sculpture may have been displayed in this long hall.[55]

Less elaborate rich private houses are known from excavation in many cities of the empire, such as the peristyle houses with *triclinia* uncovered at Argos in Greece, at Carthage, at Apollonia in Cyrenaica, at Salamis in

[53] Official residences including Apamea (house 'au triclinos'): Duval (1984) and fig. 2b on p. 475; Constantinople: Mango, *Studies on Constantinople*. Appendix, 1–2; Antioch: Mango, M. M. (1984) Gazetteer, I.A.1 526; Athens: Frantz (1988) 95–116; Ephesus: Foss (1979) 50–1; Ptolemais: Kraeling (1962) 140–60; Apollonia: Goodchild (1976); Caesarea: Holum (1988) 169–71.

[54] Bostra: Butler (1919) 255–60, 286–8; Ravenna and Naples: Ward-Perkins, *Public Building* 177; Constantinople: Mango (1959) 52–6.

[55] Athens: Frantz (1988) 37–48; Aphrodisias: Smith (1991); Constantinople: Müller-Wiener (1977) 125, 238; Mango, Vickers and Francis (1992); Bardill (1997).

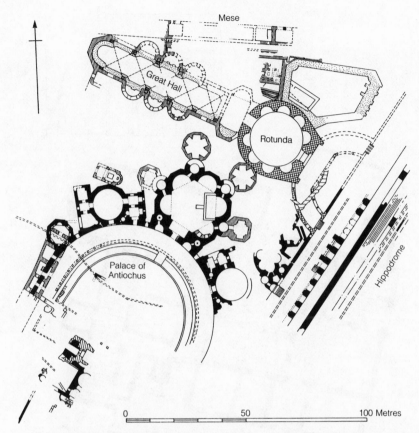

Fig. 52 Constantinople, partial plan of the private palaces of possibly two *praepositi sacri cubiculi*, Antiochus and Lausus, built in the early fifth century. Both houses had semicircular porticoes. (From Bardill (1997) fig. 1)

Cyprus (with elaborate stucco decoration) (Fig. 53) and at Apamea in Syria, the latter being occupied into the seventh century. Many of these late antique houses were elaborately decorated and provided with sophisticated amenities, such as those of the partially excavated house at Aphrodisias, which had an intricate system of water channels and pipes and which was ornamented with statues, two of which, attributed to the fifth century, were recovered.[56]

Multi-storeyed houses and apartment buildings, well known at Rome, were apparently commonplace at Constantinople, judging from the legislation made to limit the number of storeys permissible. No such buildings

[56] Argos: Akerström-Hougen (1974); Carthage: Gazda (1981) 125–78 and Dunbabin (1982) 179–92, p. 188 = reconstruction of the house after A.D. 400; Apollonia: Goodchild (1976); Salamis: Argoud, Callot and Helly (1980); Apamea: Balty (1984) 19–20, 471–501; Aphrodisias: Erim (1990) 27, figs. 29–30.

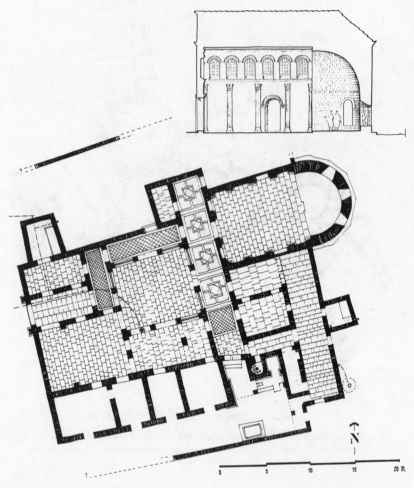

Fig. 53 Salamis, two-storey porticoed house decorated with elaborate stucco work; built in the fifth century and subsequently remodelled. (From Argoud, Callot, Helly (1980) plates XXIII.8 and XLVI)

have been recovered there archaeologically, but two complex blocks of housing (*insulae*) have been excavated at Ephesus. Both were originally built in the first century A.D., but underwent numerous rebuildings into the seventh century. Terraced against the hillside, the five levels of housing extend between the diagonal Embolos and an upper straight street. A vaulted drainage tunnel, six feet high, serviced the buildings, and clay pipes conducted water into them at every level. An elaborate house was rebuilt in the centre of one *insula* and the remainder of the space was given over to smaller middle-class units. The other *insula* also contained two double-storey luxurious peristyle units. Throughout the *insulae*, fountains were common, and frescoes, marble revetment and mosaic decorations are all preserved.[57]

Villas

Sidonius Apollinaris describes several villas of the fifth century in Gaul. His own at Avitacum near Clermont faced north and south to attractive vistas; in addition to its bath suite, it had a portico on the east overlooking a lake, a living-room (*diaeta*), a summer drawing-room (*deversorium*) open to the north, a winter dining-room (*triclinium*) with fireplace, a small dining-room (*cenatiuncula*) with *stibadium* (a semicircular couch) and sideboard, a ladies' dining-room near a storeroom and a weaving-room. The villa of his friend Consentius near Narbonne had colonnades, a bath, a chapel, an entrance court, gardens, olive groves and vineyards. The villa of another friend, Pontius Leontius, had a crescent-shaped atrium, a double portico and marble facing on the façade, as well as a winter house (*hiberna domus*), a dining-room with curved portico and fish tanks, a weaving-room, winter baths, a summer portico and granaries. In the second half of the sixth century, Venantius Fortunatus describes other villas in Gaul which also seem to have been very much in the classical tradition. A singular example of the type from this period in Italy is the villa at S. Giovanni di Ruoti, which was rebuilt in *c.* 460 over an earlier villa (Fig. 10, p. 334 above). The complex includes a reception hall with polygonal apse, a room with a mosaic floor, and another room, of uncertain function, which was roofed with a dome, as well as a tower and stables.[58]

The Roman *villa rustica* is less associated with the eastern empire, although *proasteia* – that is, suburban estates near a city – are well known from written sources. Remains of such villas have been found outside the walls of Caesarea in Palestine. They were also built in the fifth and sixth century between the Constantinian and Theodosian walls of Constantinople (Fig. 40), an area where tessellated pavements of a secular nature have been unearthed. At Daphne, outside Antioch, houses paved in mosaics, some built close together on irregular plans, had two main periods of construction – in the second to the third century and in the fifth to the sixth, when the size of rooms increased; the largest rooms (up to 13 metres wide) may have been courtyards. One large complex, possibly built by Ardabur when he was *magister militum per Orientem* at Antioch (453–66), included a bath. What may be described as a forerunner in eastern Syria of the Arab desert palace is the walled complex built in 561–4 at Qasr ibn Wardan, which includes a palace, a church and barracks. The square symmetrical palace, in *opus mixtum*, centres on an unporticoed court; on the side

---

[57] Foss (1979) 73–7.

[58] Sid. Ap. *Carm.* XXII.4.101–235; *Epp.* 2.2.3–19; 8.iv.1; Venantius Fortunatus, *Carm.* I.18–20; VI.7; VIII.19–21. On the villas' baths see n. 36 above; S. Giovanni di Ruoti: Small and Buck (1994) 75–121.

Fig. 54 Refade in the Jabal Sem'an in Syria, house built in 510. The heavy carved mouldings terminating in large volutes which frame the upper colonnade are characteristic of the region.
(From de Vogüé (1865–77))

opposite the entrance is a suite of apsed rooms on the upper storey which recalls that in the episcopal palace at Bostra (see p. 950 above).[59]

Village houses
In northern Syria some villages, such as Dar Qita (Fig. 42) and Behyo, were composed of small, simple houses, while others, like Refade, contained larger, well-decorated houses (Fig. 54) with certain amenities, such as an upper-storey lavatory. These houses were so well built that some are re-inhabited today. On those with imposing façades, the decoration of niches and mouldings became more elaborate by the sixth century. The plans of houses are marked by consistency: all are organized around a court and on two levels having different functions. The ground floor was used as stables for animals, and the upper floor, which alone had windows, for living-quarters (Fig. 13, p. 353 above). Each room is a separate unit entered from the front. The houses vary from 100 to 2,000 metres square, and are composed of from one to three – rarely four – units, to which are added an entrance porch, a subterranean room, a portico and an olive or wine press. The manner of construction (of the beams, floors, etc.) has been compared with that of houses in Cyrenaica, while other features (a blind ground floor, stone stairs, the placing of cisterns) have been compared to houses in Lycia in Asia Minor.[60]

(b) Tombs
Imperial mausoleums in the fourth century, such as those built for Helena at Rome and for Constantine at Constantinople, were large rotundas. In the fifth and sixth century, imperial and royal tombs in both east and west

[59] Caesarea: Holum (1988) 181–4; Constantinople: Mango, Développement 47; Daphne: Stillwell (1961); Qasr ibn Wardan: Mango, Byzantine Architecture 146–51.   [60] Tate (1992) 15–64.

continued to be structures with a centralized plan. In fifth-century Ravenna, the chapel formerly attached to Sta Croce, which is considered the mausoleum of Galla Placidia of *c.* 450, is cruciform. The second of the two imperial mausoleums adjoining Holy Apostles in Constantinople, added to the north side by Justinian, was likewise cruciform. Theoderic's mausoleum at Ravenna is a two-storeyed rotunda, constructed of Istrian limestone with a monolithic roof, 11 metres in diameter and weighing 300 tons. The decagonal building at Toulouse, known as La Daurade, may have been built as a Visigothic royal mausoleum. Now destroyed, the three-storey blind arcading which covered its walls had colonnettes carved with vine scrolls and niches filled with figural mosaics on a gold ground.[61]

Tombs of a more modest type have been excavated at Istanbul. A tomb standing to its full height just outside the Theodosian land walls in 413–15 has a vestibule and a main chamber which contained five tombs fronted by closure slabs decorated in relief with biblical scenes and portraits of the deceased. Earlier tombs with similar closure slabs, rather than sarcophagi, have been excavated elsewhere in the city. Imposing ashlar stone tombs of the fifth to the sixth century still stand in Syria: a classical tomb with raking stone roof fronted by a pediment, with prominent dentil courses, stands at Ruweyha, while indigenous tower-like tombs with stone pyramidal roof and ornately carved string courses are at Kaper Pera (al-Bara). Elsewhere, such as at Jerusalem and Scythopolis, built tombs with tessellated pavements have been excavated. That at Jerusalem, with an Armenian inscription, has been identified as the burial place of the mother of the mid-sixth-century general Artabanes who served in North Africa.[62] Monastic tombs have been noted above.

III. RELIGIOUS ARCHITECTURE

1. *Churches*

In function, churches were either congregational, or pilgrimage shrines, or monastic. They were built in cities and villages, in forts and monasteries. Chapels were added to churches, dwellings and barracks. In addition to churches built with imperial or other official support, many were financed privately, a form of public benefaction which came to supplant the more traditional forms of civic responsibility borne by the curial class. At the village of Kaper Barada, in northern Syria, various parts of a church are inscribed with separate dedications, indicating piecemeal subscription

[61] Ravenna: Krautheimer, *Early Christian and Byzantine Architecture* 137–8; Constantinople: Mango, *Studies on Constantinople* v.53; Toulouse: Mackie (1994).

[62] Constantinople: Deckers and Sergadoğlu (1995); Mango (1977) 307–15; Syria: Tate (1992) 67–9; Jerusalem and Scythopolis: Mango, M. M. (1984) VII.A.10 6th; VIII.A.1 567.

payment. Consequently, cities had dozens of churches – Justinian built or rebuilt thirty-three at Constantinople alone – and large villages had several: in the provinces of Arabia and Syria, by the early seventh century, Umm idj-Djemal had fifteen churches, Androna had ten, and Rihab had eight, five of which were built between 594 and 623. The relatively small village of Dar Qita had three (Fig. 42).[63]

Architecturally, church building is less complicated than building baths, where there are functional constraints imposed by plumbing and heating, combined with considerable choice in the shape and arrangement of the various components that make up the progression from cold to tepid to hot chambers (Figs. 47–8). The requirements of the church, whether congregational or memorial, were simpler. For the congregational type, the faithful's need for simultaneous participation in a service demanded a single space, while subsidiary spaces such as the baptistery were not necessarily used in sequence with the main church, and did not require direct communication with it (Figs. 41–2, 57, 59, 62). For the memorial church, the venerated place or saint's tomb provided an architectural focus, and additional space was required for pilgrims to circulate and pray in, and for services to be performed in (Figs. 56–7).[64]

Architecturally, churches were of two types – longitudinal and centralized – the first remaining the primary form of western church architecture, the second becoming that of the east. In late antiquity, the basilica was the standard form of church. In the western empire Constantine used it at Rome both for his cathedral, the Lateran, and for the memorial church of St Peter. Simultaneously, and independently of Constantine, a basilica was built in the eastern empire, then under the emperor Licinius, at Tyre, as described by Eusebius of Caesarea. Yet centralized structures also appeared at the outset in the eastern empire – Constantine built the cathedral of Antioch as an octagon, and he used centralized forms for the focal part of the pilgrimage shrines of the Nativity Church at Bethlehem and the Holy Sepulchre at Jerusalem.[65]

(a) The longitudinal church: the basilica and the hall church

The Roman civil basilica, which continued to be built in the secular sphere during late antiquity, had been adopted and adapted for church architecture by the time of Constantine, if not before. In its ecclesiastical form it occasionally had a single aisle (in which case it is termed a 'hall church'), but the great majority of church basilicas were divided into three (Fig. 60) or five (Fig. 56) aisles by piers or big monolithic columns. Most also had a timber roof, with or without a coffered ceiling below, although in areas where long

---

[63] Kaper Barada, Rihab: Mango, M. M. (1984) I.B.41 399–402; VI.B.51; Thantia (Umm idj-Djemal): Lassus (1947) 60–2; Androna: Butler (1920) 47, 52–62; Constantinople: Mango, *Studies on Constantinople* 1.126.   [64] On church architecture and liturgy see Mathews (1971).

[65] Krautheimer, *Early Christian and Byzantine Architecture* 17–44; Mango, *Byzantine Architecture* 58–61.

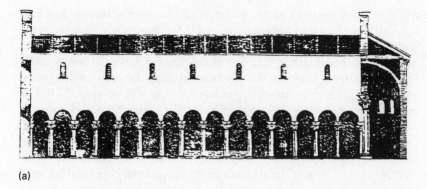

(a)

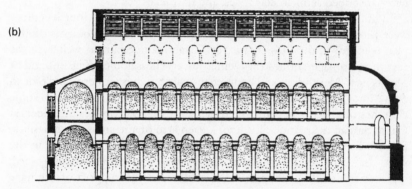

(b)

Fig. 55 Longitudinal sections of (a) Ravenna, cathedral church, showing western features of a long nave and clerestory wall above colonnade (as in the eighteenth century; by Amadesi Buonamici, 1733); (b) Thessalonica, Acheiropoietos church of *c.* 470, showing eastern features of a shorter nave and upper-storey colonnade opening into a gallery above each side aisle. (From Krautheimer, *Early Christian and Byzantine Architecture* fig. 25)

timbers were unobtainable, masonry vaults replaced them. The basilica was equally popular in city and village (Figs. 41–2, 55–6, 60–1). At least six were built in the Syrian village of Androna, and, although Constantinople is better known for its centralized or domed churches (Sts Sergius and Bacchus, St Irene, and St Sophia) (Figs. 58–9), timber-roofed basilicas were built there too in the fifth and sixth century: St John Studios, St Mary Chalkoprateia, the Blachernae church, and those unearthed at Beyazit and in the Saray.[66]

Although all of the same basic type, there were many differences across the empire in the details of the basilica's design. For instance (Fig. 55), western basilicas tend to be longer than eastern ones. In the east there were

[66] Mango, *Byzantine Architecture* 61–79; Krautheimer, *Early Christian and Byzantine Architecture* 74–101. Androna: Butler (1919, 1920) II B, 47, 52–62; Constantinople: Mathews (1971) nos. 5, 15, 34, 39; Procop. *Buildings* 1.3.1–5.

often galleries over the aisles, which made the nave relatively dark and reduced the amount of wall space available for decoration, whereas in the west the absence of galleries allowed a clerestory wall above the nave. There is also considerable variation in the number (basically one or three; Figs. 58, 61) and form of the sanctuary rooms: the end wall might be straight (Fig. 42: two churches), polygonal (Fig. 58) or curved, and, if curved, this apse might be inscribed within the outer end wall (Fig. 61) or project beyond it (Fig. 57). Trefoil sanctuaries are also known. Constantinopolitan churches are noted for polygonal apses and the lack of lateral sanctuary chambers (Figs. 58–9). The congregational church architecture in the villages of the adjacent provinces of Syria Prima and Secunda has been compared. Churches in both groups are primarily basilical and have a tripartite sanctuary (Fig. 42), but those in the second group have galleries, inscribed semicircular apses, and narthexes.[67]

In the west – at Rome and Milan – some basilicas of the fourth century were provided with a transept in front of the sanctuary. Variants of this plan reappear in the fifth century at Tarragona in Spain, as well as in the east in pilgrimage shrines (St Demetrius at Thessalonica (Fig. 56) and St Menas near Alexandria) and congregational churches (at Perge and Side in Asia Minor, at Epidauros, Nea Anchialos and Corinth in Greece). In some churches of cruciform plan – such as that of Symeon Stylites the Elder (at Qalʿat Simʿan near Antioch, c. 470) – each arm of the cross was a basilica. Double basilicas, built side by side, were popular in late antiquity in the west. In some Syrian basilicas strong masonry piers, widely spaced, replaced monolithic columns as the main means of support of the nave walls, thus opening up the space between the central nave and aisles, and affording a more unified area comparable to that of the centralized church (Fig. 61). The basilica could also be combined with a centralized plan, carrying a dome on four massive piers, as in St Irene at Constantinople, or a wooden pyramidal roof, as restored at Germia and Alahan in Asia Minor. In both types, the central bay has lateral arcades between the four piers and the longitudinal axis is extended to the west by two bays. Justinian's St John's at Ephesus (Fig. 57) and Basilica B at Philippi in Thrace combined elements of the transept basilica with the domed centralized building.[68]

(b) The centralized church

In plan, the centralized church is based on a square formed by the internal supports for the roof, which may be a pyramid in wood or a dome in either wood or masonry supported on pendentives (Fig. 59a H) or squinches. In practice, the early Byzantine centralized church is a double shell building

---

[67] Mainstone (1988) 141; Tchalenko, *Villages* II, pls. XI–XII.
[68] Krautheimer, *Early Christian and Byzantine Architecture*, 67–213; Mango, *Byzantine Architecture* 154–60; Mango (1986).

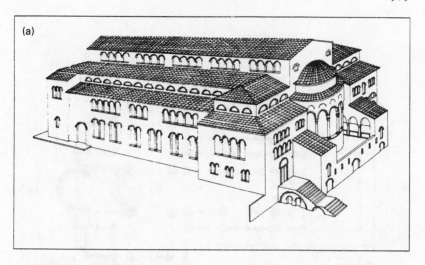

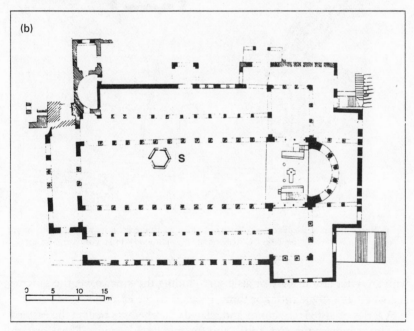

Fig. 56 Thessalonica: (a) reconstruction and (b) plan of the pilgrimage church of the martyr St Demetrius as built in the fifth or sixth century. The transept at the east end was a feature of earlier martyrial churches at Rome; the hexagonal shrine of Demetrius (S) stood in the nave near the north arcade. (From Mango, *Byzantine Architecture* figs. 78–9)

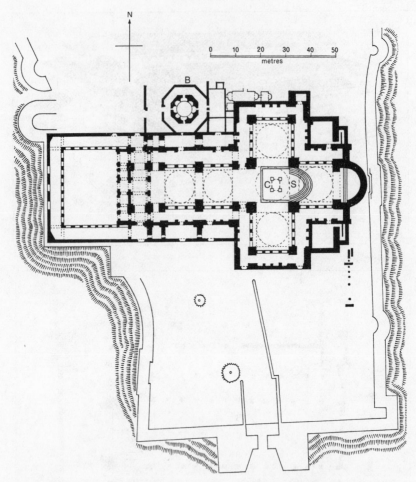

Fig. 57 Ephesus, plan of the pilgrimage church of St John the Evangelist as it was rebuilt with dome by Justinian by 565. (B = baptistery; C = ciborium; S = synthronon.) (From Foss (1979) fig. 34)

with an outer ambulatory or aisle surrounding the inner nave; the sanctuary, whether a single room or three, projects to the east.[69]

A series of aisled tetraconch and related churches was built in the eastern provinces between the later fifth and the mid sixth century. These had an inner chamber defined by colonnades, surrounded by an ambulatory. Churches of this design have been found in the provincial capitals of Apamea, Amida, Rusafa and Bostra, as well as in the cities of Seleucia Pieria,

[69] Krautheimer, *Early Christian and Byzantine Architecture* 153–70; Mango, *Byzantine Architecture* 87–96, 101–23, 132–40.

Beroea and Zorava. Before the recent discovery of a second aisled tetra-conch at Bostra, these churches had all been identified as cathedrals under the patriarchate of Antioch, where the cathedral initiated by Constantine (327–41) was likewise built on a centralized plan – that of an octagon with wooden dome – of which only a general written description survives. Of these churches, only that at Apamea had central supports strong enough to take a masonry dome. The L-shaped piers in the others probably offered sufficient support only for thin upper walls under a light roof in wood.[70]

Two other churches of the sixth century may be compared with the aisled tetraconch churches of the eastern provinces: Sts Sergius and Bacchus, built at Constantinople by Justinian in 524–7, and S. Vitale at Ravenna, built between *c.* 526 and 547. Sts Sergius and Bacchus is a variant of the Bostra group of aisled tetraconches in that its inner chamber and ambulatory are inscribed in a square building with internal diagonal corner niches (Fig. 58). The inner chamber is composed of eight wedge-shaped piers between which four diagonal columnar exedrae alternate with three straight colonnades and the arched opening into the eastern apse. The eight piers support a masonry melon dome divided by ribs into sixteen segments. The dome does not rest on pendentives, but rises from the walls built above the eight supporting arches. The upper arcades of the nave, which open into the galleries, rest on a richly carved flat entablature which incorporates a verse inscription in raised lettering. Originally the church opened on the north side into the palace of Hormisdas and on the south into the basilical church of Sts Peter and Paul (built in 519) with which it shared a narthex, atrium and propylaeum.[71]

Entered across an atrium and through a double-apsed oval narthex, S. Vitale at Ravenna differs from the centralized churches discussed so far in being octagonal both in its inner chamber and outer walls. As in Sts Sergius and Bacchus, the inner octagon is composed of eight wedge-shaped piers, but here seven columnar exedrae and the sanctuary open between them. S. Vitale is eastern in style, rather than Italian, in its inclu-sion of gallery over the cross-vaults of the ambulatory, in its marble deco-ration, and in its walls, built of thin bricks with thick mortar joints rather than the local short, thick bricks. The dome, however, is distinctly Ravennate, made of earthenware tubes laid in horizontal courses, rather than of brick. Unlike the low-slung dome of Sts Sergius and Bacchus, the dome of S. Vitale rests on a drum pierced by eight windows over a zone of squinches between its eight lower arches.[72]

What may have been the largest church built at Constantinople before Justinian's St Sophia was the church of St Polyeuctus erected by Anicia

[70] Kleinbauer (1973).

[71] Mango, *Byzantine Architecture* 101–7; Mango, *Studies on Constaninople* XIII–XIV.

[72] Krautheimer, *Early Christian and Byzantine Architecture* 169–70; Mango, *Byzantine Architecture* 132–4, 138, 140.

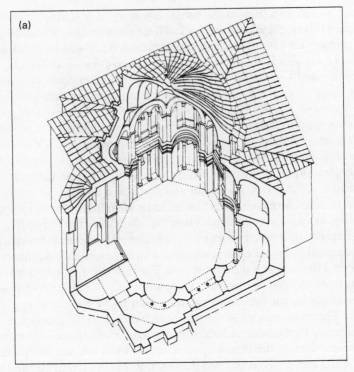

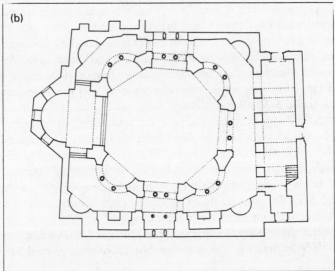

Fig. 58 Constantinople: (a) isometric drawing and (b) plan of Sts Sergius and Bacchus, built by
Justinian in 524–7. In contrast to most aisled tetraconch churches, the increased number and
weight of the internal piers of this church provided an adequate support for a masonry dome.
(From Mango, *Byzantine Architecture* figs. 109–10)

Juliana. Now destroyed, its substructures and debris (including profuse exotic sculptural decoration) have been excavated. Its plan and elevation have been reconstructed as a centralized church with a dome on massive piers surrounded on four sides by aisles, narthex and sanctuary, all of about equal widths. On the north and south sides of the central space stood a pair of two-storey exedrae composed of three niches with a pier in between. The spaces around the domed bay would have been covered with barrel or cross-vaults.[73]

St Sophia, Constantinople, built in 532–7 to replace the cathedral of Theodosius II – a timber-roofed basilica dedicated in 415, which was burned down in the Nika riot – represents a high point in Byzantine technological achievement (Fig. 59, and Fig. 34, p. 904 above). The design of St Sophia has been described as achieved by splitting Sts Sergius and Bacchus (Fig. 58) in half and inserting a central dome.[74] St Sophia's dome on pendentives, 100 Byzantine feet (31 metres) in diameter, stands 56 metres above floor level. The webs between the forty dome ribs are pierced by forty windows. The four main and four secondary piers are of stone up to the springings of the gallery vaults; the four buttress piers are of stone up to the springing of the aisle vaults. The arches, vaults, semi-domes, pendentives and dome are constructed of brick, while the springing course of the dome is a cornice of Proconnesian marble. The monolithic marble columns of the galleries do not stand directly above those at ground level, but redistribute the vertical loads from above. When the church was first built, the nearest comparable domed space was that of the Pantheon in Rome, which was completely centralized, its hemispherical dome set on a cylindrical base of walls. By contrast, St Sophia is a complex domed structure which combines the centrality of an aisled tetraconch with the axiality of a normal basilica. A primary system of masonry (Fig. 59a), located mainly within the nave, carries the principal weight load, and secondary systems, mostly within the enveloping spaces (narthexes, aisles and galleries) support only themselves.

The technological achievement in building St Sophia was, however, flawed: twenty years after completion its dome collapsed and had to be rebuilt. Most scholars attribute the collapse of this original dome to its shallow pitch, which directed its force outwards, creating lateral pressure against the four main piers. According to Agathias, the new dome was built taller, and thus its weight is transmitted downwards in a more vertical path, reducing lateral pressure. However, the dome again collapsed in part in the tenth and in the fourteenth century, so that the present structure incorporates several stages of construction, while retaining the profile of the dome as rebuilt after 557.[75]

---

[73] Harrison (1989).   [74] Mango, *Byzantine Architecture* 106–21, 123.   [75] Mainstone (1988).

(a)

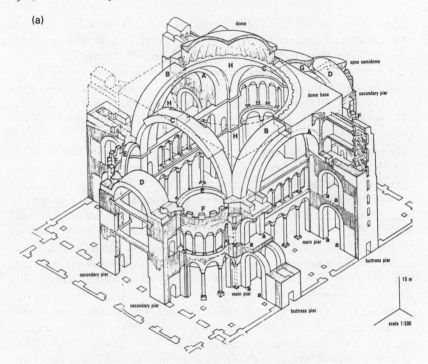

(b)

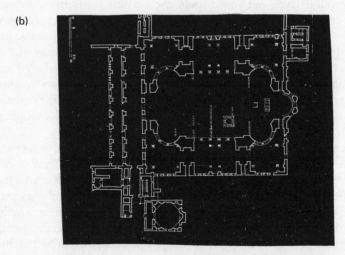

Fig. 59 Constantinople: (a) drawing and (b) plan of St Sophia as rebuilt by Justinian, 532–57. The drawing by R. Mainstone shows the primary structural system with the secondary systems cut away.
(A, C = main arches; B = upper north and south arches; D = east and west barrel vaults;
E = exedrae semidome arches; F = exedrae semidomes (cut away at the top); G = main eastern semidome (western counterpart cut away to show better the structure behind); H = pendentives (western ones cut away to show structure behind); a = pier projections.)
(From Mainstone (1988) ill. 88 and Mango, *Byzantine Architecture* fig. 115)

(c) Bemas and other liturgical furniture

Liturgical furnishings in the church included the chancel screen, altar, ciborium, synthronon and ambo or bema (Figs. 57, 60). Texts attest to their being covered with sheets of silver; some examples have been discovered in Lycia. Unlike the medieval iconostasis, the late antique screen fencing off the chancel was relatively open, being composed of colonnettes supporting an entablature and closed by low parapet panels. The altar was normally a marble slab resting on four colonnettes. The synthronon, which existed only in congregational churches, was a curved, stepped bench for clergy, built against the apse wall and resembling the sophist's bema.[76]

The congregational church nave also had a stone ambo or pulpit which was used for readings during the mass. The ambo was composed of an oval elevated platform reached by two flights of stairs and enclosed by curved parapet slabs. It was connected with the chancel by means of a walled passage, the solea. A different liturgical arrangement prevailed in parts of northern Syria, where congregational churches in thirty-three cities and villages – basilicas, aisled tetraconches and hall churches – had instead a U-shaped bema composed of a large low platform, normally apsed, which was equipped with a synthronon and pulpit (Fig. 60). While it appears to combine both these features as found in other churches, the exact function of this bema, which occupied a large part of the nave, remains unclear, although it was probably used for readings.[77]

(d) Annexes: martyrial chapels and baptisteries

The influence of the cult of saints and relics on the planning of the ordinary congregational church is demonstrated by the addition, often near the sanctuary, of a martyrial chapel to hold reliquaries. In northern Italy and southern Gaul these chapels were often cruciform or trefoil in plan, while in northern Syria an existing south chamber in or adjacent to the tripartite sanctuary was used, and sometimes enlarged, for this purpose (Figs. 60–1). In North Africa, relics were often housed in an apse situated opposite the main apse.[78]

Prominent among the annexes of congregational and pilgrimage churches was the baptistery, which was already part of the third-century house church at Dura Europos. Architecturally, the baptistery was centred on the font or pool which was sunk in the floor; the building itself (externally and/or internally) could be square (Fig. 42), round, cruciform (Fig. 41) or octagonal (Figs. 57, 59, 62) in plan, possibly ringed by an ambulatory (Figs. 57, 62), and was often domed. Octagonal baptisteries

[76] Xydis (1947); Boyd (1992) 31–4, figs. s55.1–s69.1.   [77] Xydis (1947); Tchalenko (1990).

[78] Krautheimer, *Early Christian and Byzantine Architecture* 69, 79, 131–2, 144 and n. 46, 196–8; Lassus (1947) 167–83.

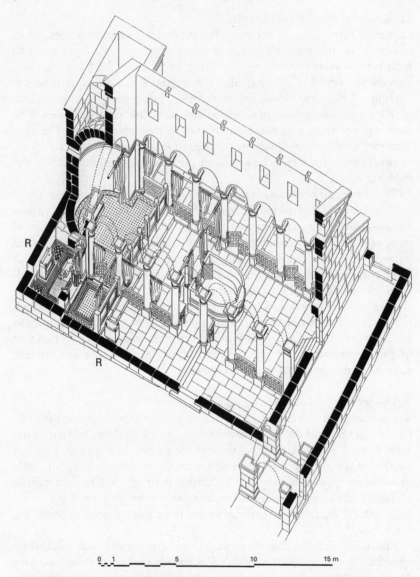

R

R

0 1   5   10   15 m

Fig. 60 Jirade in the Jabal Zawiye in Syria, isometric reconstruction of a village church built in the
fifth century, showing the liturgical furnishings including the altar, the chancel-screen, the
U-shaped bema in the nave and the reliquaries in the north aisle and north-east chamber.
(R = reliquary.) (From Tchalenko (1979) pl. 299)

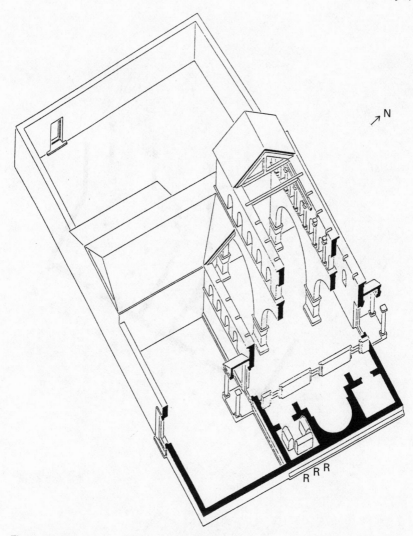

N

Fig. 61 Behyo in the Jabal il Aʻla in Syria, isometric drawing of a village church built probably in the first half of the sixth century. In contrast to the Jirade church (Fig. 60), which has closely spaced columns supporting the lateral arcades, this church has widely spaced piers which open up the space between nave and aisles. (R = reliquary.) (From Tchalenko, *Villages* pl. CXIV)

were built in the fifth century at the Lateran cathedral in Rome, in the sixth century at St Sophia's cathedral in Constantinople (Fig. 59), at Marseilles and at the pilgrimage churches of St John at Ephesus (Fig. 57), St Symeon Stylites (Qalʻat Simʻan) near Antioch (Fig. 62) and St Menas near Alexandria. The two built for the orthodox and Arian cathedrals at Ravenna are still elaborately decorated with mosaic. The two baptisteries

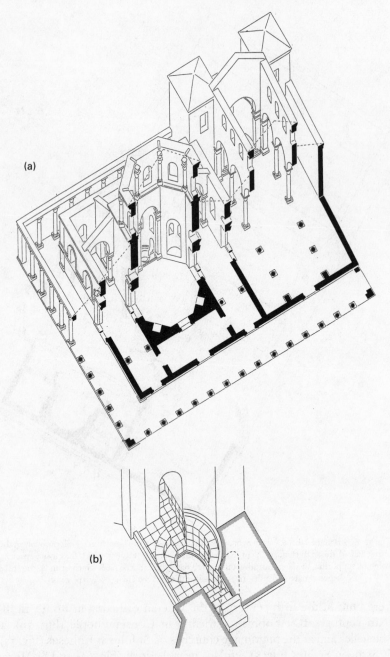

Fig. 62 Telanissos, pilgrimage shrine of St Symeon Stylites the Elder (Qalʿat Simʿan). Isometric drawing of (a) baptistery with adjoining basilical chapel built in *c.* 475–90 by the *technites* Agapius and others and (b) its pool. (From Tchalenko, *Villages* pls. LXXV–LXXVI)

in the village of Dar Qita were built or modified in 515 and 566 respectively (Fig. 42).[79]

2. Synagogues

The synagogue had similar architectural requirements to the church, as it was a place for prayer and reading the Torah, as well as a house of assembly. Attached to its main building could also be a ritual bath, an infirmary and a hostel. Out of some 120 synagogues known, at least 100 are situated in the Holy Land. The largest, however, was excavated at Sardis in Asia Minor. This was probably a secular building which was acquired and converted for use as a synagogue. Like many others, it was basilical in form. Other diaspora synagogues from the Roman period have been excavated at Ostia near Rome, Naro near Carthage and Elche in Spain, and at Stobi, Corinth, Aegina, Delos, Priene, Miletus, Dura Europos, Apamea and perhaps Mopsuestia in Cilicia, Neocaesarea (Dibsi Faraj) on the Euphrates and Emesa (Homs) in Syria. Further diaspora synagogues are known from texts. Those at Antioch, Callinicum, Edessa, Berytus and Gerasa were destroyed or converted to other uses between 350 and 530. In the Holy Land, synagogues are referred to in written sources or have been excavated in both city (including Caesarea, Gaza, Jericho, Scythopolis, Tiberias, Gadara, Birosaba) and village, well-known rural examples being those at Capernaum and Beth Alpha.[80]

What most synagogues shared was prayer directed to Jerusalem (shared also with eastern churches), and the use of Jewish symbols in the decoration. The wall facing Jerusalem had an aedicula or niche on a raised platform for holding the Torah scroll kept in an ark, as at Horvat Susiya in Palaestina Prima (Fig. 63). Recent studies in synagogue architecture have focused on the Torah shrine and on problems of dating. It now seems that, as with other buildings, the sixth century was an important period for synagogue building in the near east. The location of the Torah shrine within the synagogue varied locally. By the fifth century, a church-like apse was sometimes added to an existing synagogue to hold it, replacing the smaller aedicula or niche; by the sixth century, the apse was an integral architectural feature, except in the north of Palestine. Synagogues were often elaborately decorated. The Jerusalem Talmud states that during the late third and fourth century the walls and floors of synagogues started to be decorated and that this was tolerated. Tessellated pavements (illustrating the Temple façade or Torah ark flanked by the menorah, shofar, lulav and ethrog; the zodiac; biblical scenes; animals) were certainly common in synagogues between the fourth and the sixth century.[81]

[79] Khatchatrian (1982).   [80] Levine (1981); Hachlili (1989).
[81] Levine (1981) 15–18; Hachlili (1989) 1–6, 65–100.

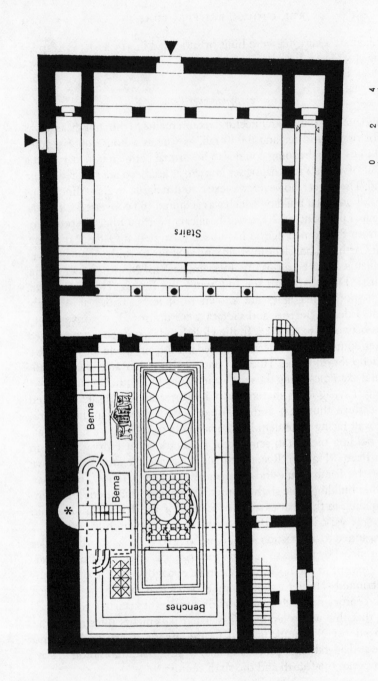

Fig. 63 Horvat Susiya, plan of synagogue. (From Gutman, Yeivin, Netzer (1981) fig. p. 123)

* Assumed niche

IV. CONCLUSION

The period 425 to 600 is traditionally seen as active and innovative only in the building of churches. However, although this was much more marked in the east than in the west (reflecting the greater political stability and prosperity of the former), the fifth and sixth century also saw considerable continuity of the ideal and the reality of the ancient city. Entirely new scaled-down versions were built into the reign of Justinian at Justiniana Prima in the Balkans and Anastasiopolis/Dara in Mesopotamia, while in many other cities porticoed streets, fora, baths, fountains and aqueducts continued to be maintained or even built for public enjoyment, alongside new and elaborately decorated palaces and private houses for the ruling classes.

Continued prosperity and the growth of Christianity did, of course, also foster a boom in church building, and churches did eventually come to replace the public baths as the largest buildings of public congregation. In church architecture our period saw the evolution of what was to prove an enduring split – between the centralized church in the east and the longitudinal basilica in the west. By the mid sixth century, the masonry dome poised on piers had been perfected, exemplified by St Sophia at Constantinople, which was to remain for centuries the largest and most structurally complex church in Christendom. The recent introduction of monasticism occasioned the development of a communal architecture which in a rural setting recalled the Roman villa.

Up until the seventh century, in the east at least, new architectural forms evolved slowly out of old, with no obvious breaks in continuity and development. Continuous traditions of urban life, combined in many regions with favourable economic and political conditions, ensured that this was so. Only in the troubles that beset seventh-century Byzantium did the scale of all building, outside the Moslem east, decline dramatically; and only then were a number of traditional forms of building abandoned for ever.

CONCLUSION

No other volume of *The Cambridge Ancient History* raises such major questions of periodization or historical interpretation as Volume XIV, the last in the series. Indeed, the very decision to extend the original coverage of the series by two extra volumes and to allow an overlap with the new *Cambridge Medieval History* is an indication of the lively state of research on this period and the variety of interpretative schemes currently proposed. We can no longer be content with a simple 'transition from classical antiquity to the Middle Ages', nor can we propose a single point where the line between them may be drawn. The conventional date of the fall of the Roman empire in the west, confidently placed by previous generations in the year A.D. 476, was already found inadequate by Edward Gibbon, while the lack of interest shown in the supposed event by contemporaries has been noted as a problem by many historians.[1] 'Transformation' is now a term more commonly used than 'fall' to describe the process of historical change in the west from the last centuries of classical antiquity to the Middle Ages, and the search for a chronological divide is felt with less urgency than before as concentration focuses instead on a longer time-scale of change. Meanwhile, the historic changes in eastern Europe in the late twentieth century encouraged a re-examination of the processes which led to the formation of Europe, and in particular a reconsideration of what the very concept of Europe might entail.[2]

Despite its similarity of title to the original version of *The Cambridge Ancient History*, a series of fourteen volumes completed at the end of the twentieth century ought indeed to look different from one that appeared over sixty years ago. Volume XIV in particular is different in format. In part, this is a function of the political geography of the period: given the continuity of Roman government in the east and the multiple changes taking place in the west, a unitary narrative is no longer possible, and even the thematic chapters tend to concentrate on either western or eastern material. Moreover, the undoubted vitality of urban life and the richness of the evi-

---

[1] Momigliano (1973); Croke (1983). For the 'Pirenne thesis', see Pirenne (1937); Brown (1974); Hodges and Whitehouse (1983).   [2] Webster and Brown (1997); Davies (1996) introduction.

dence from some of the eastern provinces in the sixth century have given the provincial section a distinct eastern emphasis.

Thus Volume XIV presents problems of organization and definition of subject matter, covering as it does both the collapse of Roman government in the west in the fifth century and the attempt of Justinian to reassert it from Constantinople in the sixth. Justinian's 'reconquest' was not straightforward, spectacular as it seemed in the early stages. The reconquest of Vandal North Africa in A.D. 533–4 was swift and easy, but its consolidation as an imperial province was to prove costly, and in the case of Italy Justinian's great endeavour met with military, logistical and financial difficulties of such magnitude that the war lasted for nearly twenty years. The government of the resulting province was officially organized in a law of A.D. 554; however, partly as a result of the long war and partly because of new movements of peoples unforeseeable by Justinian, Italy remained divided, and the west was fragmented among different kingdoms. There were also consequences for the east from the attempt at reconquest: a heavy pressure on resources and manpower, and resulting political cost. Justinian and his successors continued to try to hold together an empire which stretched from west to east but which was under almost constant pressure from outside, and under centrifugal tension internally, both political and ecclesiastical.[3]

This volume perhaps lays more emphasis on the Roman and imperial perspective than an explicitly medieval European history would do. Yet the vigorous development of newer states and kingdoms in both east and west[4] makes the point of view from the periphery as important as that from the centre, and this is also reflected here – for instance, in the rich material in the provincial section. For this period in particular it is important to recognize that there are legitimately different ways of seeing it. As in the case of the debate between 'continuity' and 'decline', it is largely a matter of where one places the emphasis and why.

For previous generations, and even before Edward Gibbon's *Decline and Fall*, the historiography of the Roman empire was pervaded by the concept of 'decline and fall'. The reasons have been constantly debated, and the rival claims of internal factors and external pressures weighed up against each other; the French historian André Piganiol, for example, famously claimed that Rome did not die but was assassinated, whereas in the Marxist analysis of Geoffrey de Ste Croix the empire was preyed upon from within by its own contradictions and inequalities.[5] There are indeed a number of possible turning-points, such as the Roman defeat at Adrianople in 378. Rome itself was sacked in 410. But the end of an empire is not always signalled by a

---

[3] Cf. Brown (1976).   [4] For the east see Fowden, *Empire to Commonwealth*.
[5] Piganiol (1947); de Ste Croix (1981); see Brown (1967).

dramatic event like the dismantling of the Berlin Wall. Scholars are uncertain whether to lay more stress on the military impact of the barbarians or on the long-term process of acculturation whereby they were gradually brought within the Roman world. In either case, as several contributors to these volumes demonstrate, the barbarians gradually developed their own distinct identities during this process, and their historians used methods such as chronicle, chronography and genealogy to bestow upon them a historical past to rival that of Rome.[6] This creation of new identities is an important feature of the period, not confined to the west or to the new peoples: in the sixth century the Syrian Monophysites in the east redefined themselves as Jacobites, and a hundred years later the Arabs who followed Muhammad acquired a new identity and a new religion capable of lasting until the present day.

A straightforward concept of 'fall' in relation to the Roman empire is in any case difficult, in that the empire based on Constantinople survived. In the sixth century, even though its everyday language was Greek, Justinian's empire was still recognizably Roman, its administrative, fiscal and legal apparatus similar in essentials to the system developed under Diocletian and Constantine. The official titulature of the emperor had not changed, and Justinian saw himself as the restorer of the Roman past, an aspiration warmly endorsed, even if Justinian was criticized in the execution, by the contemporary writer and former bureaucrat, John the Lydian.[7] By the sixth century, Constantinople was a city of perhaps half a million, filled not only with churches and palaces, but also with a panoply of traditional late Roman buildings.[8] Even though the events of the seventh and eighth century, especially the Arab conquests and the consequent loss of most of the eastern provinces, critically undermined this sense of connection with the Roman past, still for centuries to come the Byzantines continued to think of themselves as Romans. It was only in the last period of the empire, under the Palaeologan dynasty, that their intellectual heritage as 'Hellenes', heirs of classical Greece, began to be admitted as worthy of celebration. The challenge for the historian of the period covered in this last volume, therefore, is to avoid subjective or tendentious categorization, even when the terms are used by contemporaries, and to try instead to plot the many shifts and nuances by which continuity of structures and mentality in fact coexisted in dynamic relation with multiple change.

This problem of terminology is especially sharply posed in the case of the eastern empire. From what date is it reasonable to call the emperors in Constantinople and the inhabitants of the eastern empire Byzantines? The question has been much debated among Byzantinists, and two main answers have been given: either the sole reign of Constantine or the founding of

---

[6] Goffart (1988); Heather (1989).   [7] Maas, *John Lydus*.   [8] Mango, *Développement*.

Constantinople (A.D. 324 and 330), or the early seventh century, to coincide with the reign of Heraclius (A.D. 610–41) and the Arab conquests.[9] There are indeed good reasons why those with a focus on the eastern empire, and especially its religious history, might want to start with Constantine, and why the military, economic and administrative changes of the seventh century might also seem to mark a realistic turning-point.[10] However, common usage is in practice inconsistent, and even those who prefer the later date commonly use the term Byzantine to refer, say, to the reign of Justinian, while most Roman historians would find it unnatural to refer to Constantine as Byzantine; in practical terms, the pivotal period is probably the fifth century, when the western empire ceased to exist, leaving only an eastern, 'Byzantine' empire. But there is indeed a danger of seeming to prejudge the relevant issues in imposing a consistent mode of reference, and there has therefore been no aim in this Volume to introduce a rigid periodization. Indeed, that would be contrary to the approach taken by many of the contributors; overlap of terminology is therefore not only to be expected but also in due measure to be welcomed.

Perhaps one of the most striking features of our period is the growing disparity in apparent prosperity, in both town and country, between the east and the west. In contrast to the situation in the west, some of the eastern Mediterranean provinces in the sixth century display signs of a prosperity hardly equalled previously; this is true especially of Palestine and modern Jordan.[11] The basis of this prosperity and the extent to which it was still to be found at the end of the sixth century are the subject of some discussion, as is the scale and significance of the evidence for long-distance trade across the Mediterranean.[12] But it is in general the case that the period saw a shift of wealth and authority to the south and east. In part, this must be due to the disruption caused by barbarian invasion and settlement in the west, but it must also have been brought about by the heavy investment of resources in the east which had been a feature of the Roman empire since the third century. Doctrinal and political differences between east and west – for example, in attitudes towards the Vandal regime in North Africa – were to some degree sharpened by these underlying economic factors, and they must also in part explain the political, military and cultural strength of the east in the sixth century.

Another way of viewing the period covered in Volumes XIII and XIV, or perhaps more accurately from Volume XII onwards, is as 'the age of late antiquity',[13] a period broadly defined as running from the later third century

---

[9] Kazhdan and Constable (1982). Whittow (1996) chooses to begin at A.D. 600.
[10] Haldon, *Byzantium in the Seventh Century*.
[11] Cameron and King (1994); Whittow (1990); Walmsley (1996).   [12] Wickham (1988).
[13] Especially since Brown (1971), on which see the debate 'The world of late antiquity revisited' in *Symbolae Osloenses* 72 (1997): 5–90. See now Bowersock, Brown, Grabar (1999).

A.D. to perhaps the early seventh century, and with a culture or cultures covering, as well as the Mediterranean area, also the bordering regions from Britain and northern Europe all the way to Mesopotamia and the hinterland of Iran. The Christian kingdoms of Georgia, Armenia, Ethiopia and Axum and the civilization of south Yemen have also been seen as falling within this orbit, particularly in view of the influence upon them of Byzantine imperial culture and religion; indeed, one of the more intriguing features of the period is the extent to which Christian influences were felt in pre-Islamic Arabia. The particular advantages of this way of defining and approaching the period lie in the very avoidance of potentially inappropriate categories and subjective and moral terms, and the possibility of an expansive and multiform mode of description equal to the pluriformity of the evidence. It is an approach particularly suited to cultural history, but perhaps less so to structures of government, or economic and military history. Nevertheless, it offers a powerful model within which to encompass historical diversity, and a way of looking at the period which is appealing and recognizable to many modern readers for its multiculturalism and stress on variety.

Questions of interpretation are especially urgent in relation to certain kinds of contemporary evidence, including visual art. In this field, traditional analysis based on the perceived aesthetics of style is particularly apt to lead to subjective judgements about the differences between classical and medieval or Byzantine art, and the reasons for the supposed transition from one to the other. Study of this material needs to be underpinned by a concern for issues of patronage and production and by a greater willingness to take late antique art on its own terms for what it is, rather than for what the modern interpreter thinks it should be. In art history, too, therefore, new models of interpretation are evolving, while historians of late antiquity in turn are today working with a heightened consciousness of the importance of visual and material evidence. It is possible to cite, for example, the lively and varied architectural developments of the period, and the way in which images, especially religious images, were coming to carry an increasing charge of meaning for contemporaries, a precursor to the intense quarrels over their status during the succeeding centuries.[14] If some late antique art looks crude by comparison with the art of classical antiquity,[15] in other cases new artistic forms took shape, indicative of great variety and local skill. Continued contact across the Mediterranean and between Byzantium and the east meant that images in the Byzantine style were to be found in Rome in the sixth and seventh century, that fine exmples of silver dishes and utensils, one of the most impressive legacies of late antiquity, have places of origin as far apart as Britain, Syria and

---

[14] Cormack (1997).   [15] But see ch. 30 (Cormack), pp. 884–917 above.

Sasanian Persia, and that impressive mosaic floors with mythological or classicizing themes were being laid across the empire, from Spain in the west to Cyprus, Antioch and Apamea in Syria, and in many places in Palestine and modern Jordan. We now know that some Christian communities in the eastern provinces were building large new churches and laying elaborate mosaic floors even long after the establishment of Umayyad rule.[16]

It is possible to see in recent scholarship evidence of a breaking down of barriers between traditionally distinct disciplines and their perceived bodies of evidence. Historians of institutions are more ready to admit the relevance of the visual, to realize the power of rhetoric or to draw on literary texts and documents from unexpected sources; religious history is no longer necessarily treated as separate from other sorts of history. This trend indeed seems to reflect the juxtapositions in late antiquity itself, a matter not just of literary or artistic style but of the possibilities offered to and seized by individual people. Thus a rich woman might pretend that she was a beggar and dress in rags; one of the wealthiest couples in the Roman world enrolled on the register of the poor at Jerusalem; a professor from Bordeaux might become praetorian prefect; a former teacher of rhetoric devoted his attention to the art of communicating to the uneducated. Christianization in particular turned things upside down. Surprising juxtapositions give the period life and vigour: a man of senatorial rank hiding away in the desert; an obscure Cretan who became consul; a holy man in a loincloth who thought it clever to humiliate a religious woman by asking her to remove all her clothes in public. Rioting over religious issues coexisted in late-fourth-century Rome with the traditional life of the Roman senate, while in contrast at Constantinople the court in the early fifth century could be described as being like a nunnery. Men and women were segregated, as at the funeral of Macrina, yet could become lifelong friends, like Jerome and the loyal Paula, of whom Palladius quotes Posidonius as remarking that, if she were to die first, at least she would be spared Jerome's bad temper.[17]

It is deceptively easy in the face of such abundant evidence to think of the period as characterized above all by the progress of Christianization. Yet the life and vigour of late antique paganism – or, as some historians prefer, polytheism – is one of the striking discoveries of recent scholarship. The great oracular shrines which Eusebius tried so hard to pretend were dead and silent still attracted visitors in the fourth century. The emperor Julian may have been the only pagan emperor after Constantine (and was vilified by the church for it), but the Neoplatonist Academy at Athens entered one of its most brilliant phases in the fifth and early sixth century,

[16] Piccirillo (1993).   [17] Pall. *Hist. Laus.* 36.

and pagan philosophers travelled in the sixth century on religious pilgrimages to sacred spots in Syria and wrote important and lasting commentaries on Aristotle.[18] How far Christianity had completely won over the population at large by the late sixth century is still an open question: St Nicholas of Sion in Lycia, like pope Gregory in Sardinia, found country people prone to folk practices connected with sacred trees, and it was still more than worth while for Christian literature to insist on the superiority of the faith over 'Hellenism'. Far from indicating an inexorable advance of Christianity towards the position it occupied in the medieval world, this diversity of belief and practice gives late antiquity a vividness and life hardly paralleled in any other period. Another feature of the period is the evident vigour of the well-to-do Jewish communities in Palestine, confident and settled enough to build and decorate substantial synagogues, and numerous enough to attract Christian suspicion and distrust during the Persian invasions of the early seventh century. Christians themselves were divided and sometimes persecuted by fellow Christians in the name of religious unity. There was nothing monolithic about late antique religion.

Late antiquity was a time of change, mental and psychological. It was not a revolution, not an enlightenment, not the discovery of a New World. But the change did involve, as well as the closing in of some of the old, the shifting of mental horizons and the construction of new imagined worlds. The clearest sign of this change is in the breaking down of existing barriers, with a corresponding sense of possibility. Yet a parallel struggle was going on to control the many possibilities that were opening up.[19] It was both a psychological struggle and a struggle of cognition. This was still a world in which Dionysos and Orpheus were very much alive, whether in imaginative recreations in visual art, or in the exotic *mélange* of memory and fancy that is Nonnus' *Dionysiaca*, where the signs of the zodiac exercised a lively fascination, where astrologers at once sprang to mind when someone needed advice, and where a philosopher could still appeal to the example of Heracles and Asclepius, and hold up for imitation the teachings of Pythagoras. It was a world in which synagogues in Galilee or elsewhere were decorated with a rich profusion of plant life, zodiacal signs or even figures such as Orpheus.[20]

It was not surprising that so many people tried so hard to lay down sure guidelines. His disciples reported with admiration the loathing which St Euthymius felt for heresy, spelling out with relish the six types which he most detested. As the possibilities of error proliferated, so did the polemics and the denunciations. Public confrontations took place under the auspices of the emperor, as when a hundred or so eastern monks debated Monophysitism in Constantinople in the early years of Justinian. Justinian and his wife liked nothing better than to debate with the Monophysite

---

[18] Chuvin, *Chronique*; Tardieu (1990).   [19] Lim (1995).   [20] Levine (1981).

monks living in part of the imperial palace, while St Symeon Stylites the Younger would engage astrologers in discussion from the top of his pillar. Endless talking went on. Set answers were produced for the standard questions, but that did not stop it. Letters poured out whenever a dispute arose, and one has the distinct impression that a good deal of enjoyment was to be had from the excitement of the battle. We should not underestimate, either, the sheer joy of problem-solving, the pleasure of interpreting the texts, the fascination of the intellectual puzzle. A pleasure in dialectic or hermeneutics for their own sake is palpable in some of the later theological literature. For some of the intellectual heavyweights, considerable satisfaction must have lain in the activity itself. But no wonder lesser people were confused, and needed whatever help they could get by way of instruction.

The moral and spiritual as well as the social landscape of the period is laid open to view in the copious surviving written material. After centuries of silence or at best of rhetorical displays exploiting misogynistic traditions, the difference between male and female became a topic of attention in learned discourses. Were women to be regarded as having been made in the image of God, or, as the apostle had said, only in that of man? Was the union with God that was seen as the goal of women's asceticism, too, to be defined as a type of *gnosis*, or in a specifically female sense, in terms of mystic marriage? Could real women escape implication in the sin of Eve?[21] Whatever the injunctions in some of the texts, public figures in the world of Christianity did not avoid, but rather sought out, certain – even if self-consciously limited – kinds of association with women. In the early fifth century, Palladius went out of his way to include a section in praise of women in his *Lausiac History*; Evagrius Ponticus and others concerned themselves with women religious,[22] and in the sixth century the empress Theodora transformed herself from a theatre performer of dubious reputation to a virtual saint of the eastern church. In the surviving, and especially in the eastern, literature – monastic tales as well as academic treatises – a central place is taken by issues of the moral and practical relations between the sexes, and the moral tone of family life. The proper exercise of emotion, and of affection, was much discussed, as was the proper behaviour of married people and the remarriage of widows, the best education for little girls and the correct behaviour of those women who elected to look after male religious in supposedly innocent relationships. Peter Brown has pointed to proper deportment as a major concern among contemporaries – how to present oneself in a world of change;[23] such preoccupations ranked only second to worries about the future and the desire to control the environment by resort to soothsayers, astrologers or holy men.[24]

---

[21] Clark (1993); Mattioli (1992).   [22] Elm (1994).
[23] Brown (1992); also Wimbush and Valantasis (1995).   [24] Dagron (1981).

There is, indeed, also new evidence from excavation from which to reconstruct the concerns and life of the time. The epigraphic record of late antique cities like Aphrodisias in Caria and Ephesus in Asia Minor traces their change from Roman imperial centres with confident local élites ready to spend freely on civic adornment to Byzantine bishoprics, much diminished from their former glory; yet seat inscriptions help to reveal the prominence of the Blue and Green factions during the fifth and sixth century, as well as the hierarchical seating arrangement of different groups within the city.[25] Elsewhere, recently discovered charred papyrus scrolls at Petra in southern Jordan show that the city was the home of a substantial Christian population in the sixth century, which engaged in agriculture and bore names which mixed Greek and Arabic. Such evidence is centred on cities, and the study of late antique urbanism is one of the liveliest fields in modern scholarship.[26] There are some common features, to be found in differing combinations across the Mediterranean – the decline of the traditional upper-class house, the reuse of earlier materials (to our eyes often inappropriately), the abandonment of public buildings and spaces associated with the urbanism of an earlier age in favour of impressive defensive and ecclesiastical buildings, and, at the later end of the period, subdivision of houses and the once-forbidden practice of burial within the walls. Yet the occurrences vary in different areas, and the changes happen at differing speeds. Cities in some areas continue to show signs of growth, whereas others manifest decline. Constantly-growing evidence, as more towns are excavated and studied, makes this an often bewildering as well as fascinating area of study, and one in which no general view is as yet possible. Research over recent decades, on individual sites and on big international projects like that at Carthage, has transformed our knowledge of late antique pottery, whether amphorae or fine table-wares, often allowing very precise dating and a clear idea of provenance.[27] It is becoming increasingly possible to map detailed patterns of distribution, although, inevitably, the mechanisms behind it remain the subject of active scholarly debate. At the same time, we also know more about the countryside, including in some cases the continuing prosperity of villages, from the growing number of archaeological surveys, whether in Greece or North Africa, which examine a small area over a long chronological period. And re-examination of known evidence, as in the case of the villages of the limestone massif of northern Syria, is changing older conclusions.[28]

This is a period which has attracted much recent scholarship, and which has seen considerable development in its analysis. From the relevant literature in English one could single out in addition to Jones's *Later Roman*

---

[25] See ch. 21a (Roueché), pp. 570–87 above.
[26] See e.g. Rich (1992); Cameron, *Mediterranean World* ch. 7; Christie and Loseby (1996); Brogiolo (1997).   [27] Hayes (1972); Giardina (1988).   [28] See Tate (1992).

Empire of 1964 and the influential work of Peter Brown, the collection edited by Arnaldo Momigliano in 1963, *The Conflict between Paganism and Christianity in the Fourth Century.*[29] Brown has followed Momigliano in emphasizing the religious and moral changes in late antiquity, and these have captured the imagination of many other scholars. There are also many important and original works on individual topics. But there is no work as yet which reinterprets the political and institutional history of the period by integrating it fully with the large amount of work that has now been done in other fields, whether artistic, literary or cultural. Perhaps it is still too soon for such a large-scale synthesis. But in another sense a multi-authored work, with chapters on the many and varied aspects of the period, for which the evidence itself is so diverse, may be exactly what is needed to convey an impression of the diversity and excitement of the period itself. With Volume XIV we therefore leave the ancient world, not with the sense of some inevitable passage to the Middle Ages, but rather with a sense of open-endedness and possibility. It is doubtful whether, after the spectacular and exhausting success of his campaigns against the Persians, the emperor Heraclius had any idea that they would be followed by equally spectacular Byzantine defeat and the retrenchment of imperial power in the seventh century to a small area surrounding the city of Constantinople. Those events and their interpretation belong more properly in another volume and another series. No doubt part of the explanation for them does lie at an earlier date, and indeed during the period with which we are concerned here. But history does not proceed in accordance with some deterministic scheme, and it is right that our history-books should recognize that fact.

---

[29] On Momigliano (1963) see Consolino (1995).

CHRONOLOGICAL TABLE

A.D.	Emperors	The West	The East
425	Theodosius II (408–50) Valentinian III (425–55)		Reform of teaching in Constantinople
427			First commission to codify laws
428			Nestorius, patriarch of Constantinople
429		Vandals cross to Africa	
431		Aspar and eastern army defeated by Vandals	First Council of Ephesus; deposition of Nestorius
432		Death of Augustine	
435		Revolt of bagaudae in Armorica	Exile of Nestorius
436		Goths besiege Narbonne	
438			Theodosian Code issued
439		Geiseric the Vandal captures Carthage	
440		Vandals ravage Sicily	Yazdgard II attacked eastern provinces Victories for Attila in Balkans
441		Sueves control Baetica and Carthaginiensis	Ascendancy of eunuch Chrysaphius
443			Sweeping successes of Attila in Balkans
447			
449		Embassy to Attila	Second Council of Ephesus (the Robber Synod)
450	Marcian (450–7)	Attila invades Gaul; defeat at Catalaunian Plains	
451			Council of Chalcedon
452		Attila attacks Italy; sack of Aquileia	
453	Death of Pulcheria	Death of Attila	
454		Valentinian III murders Aetius	Huns defeated at River Nedao
455	Avitus (455–7)	Vandals sack Rome	
457	Leo I (457–74) Majorian (457–61)		Aspar controls succession Death of Symeon Stylites

Year	Emperors / Rulers	West	East
460		Expedition of Majorian to Spain v. Vandals	
461	Libius Severus (461–5)	Defeat of Majorian in Spain; Ricimer controls succession	
467	Anthemius (467–72)	Failure of eastern expedition v. Vandals	
468			Overthrow and death of Aspar
471			
472		Death of Ricimer	
473	Glycerius (473–4)		Leo sends Nepos west to depose Glycerius
474	Zeno (474–91) / Nepos (474–5)		Rebellion of Basiliscus; Zeno retires to Isauria
475	Romulus (475–6)	Rebellion of Orestes	
476	Basiliscus (usurper)	Odoacer deposes Romulus Augustulus; Visigoths capture Arles and Marseilles	Return of Zeno; exile and death of Basiliscus
480		Acacian schism divides Rome and Constantinople	Death of Theoderic Strabo
482		Huneric persecutes Catholics	Zeno issues *Henotikon*
484			Rebellion of Illus
489		Theoderic enters Italy	Theoderic the Amal leaves Balkans for Italy
491	Anastasius (491–518)		
492			Rebellion in Isauria
493		Theoderic the Amal captures Ravenna and kills Odoacer	
496			Anastasius deposes Euphemius of Constantinople
497			Suppression of Isaurian revolt
498			Abolition of Chrysargyron tax; coinage reform
502			Kavadh invades eastern provinces; siege of Amida
505			Truce on eastern frontier; construction of Dara
507		Clovis and Franks defeat Visigoths at Vouillé	
511		Clovis' Catholic Council of Orleans; Division of Frankish kingdom on Clovis' death	Anastasius deposes Macedonius of Constantinople
512			Deposition of Flavius of Antioch; Severus succeeds
513			First revolt of Vitalian
515			Defeat of Vitalian
518	Justin I (518–27)	End of Acacian schism	
524		Execution of Boethius	
526	Athalaric (526–34)		
527	Justinian I (527–65)		
528			Commission for codification of Law

A.D.	Emperors	The West	The East
529			First edition of *Codex Iustinianus*
530			Commission to codify Roman jurists
531			Accession of Khusro I, king of Persia
532			Nika riot; 'Endless Peace' with Persia
			Theopaschite Edict
533		Belisarius defeats Vandals	Completion of *Digest* of Roman law, and *Institutes*
534		Pragmatic Sanction to regulate affairs of Africa	Second edition of *Codex Iustinianus*
		Burgundian kingdom taken over by Franks	Triumph of Belisarius at Constantinople
		Regency of Amalasuintha in Italy	
535		Murder of Amalasuintha; Belisarius despatched to Italy	Consulship of Belisarius
536		Belisarius lands in Italy; capture of Naples	
		Belisarius occupies Rome	
537		Siege of Rome	Dedication of rebuilt St Sophia
539		Goths capture Milan and massacre inhabitants	
		Franks invade Italy	
540		Belisarius enters Ravenna	Khusro I attacks Romans; sack of Antioch
			Basilius, the last annual consul
			Jacob Baradaeus appointed bishop of Edessa; creation of separate Monophysite hierarchy
			Bubonic plague strikes Constantinople
542		Belisarius' second expedition to Italy	
544			
546		Totila captures Rome	
547			Pope Vigilius summoned to Constantinople
548	Death of Theodora	Recall of Belisarius	
549		Arrival of Narses in Ravenna	
552		Defeat and death of Totila at Busta Gallorum	
553/4			Fifth Oecumenical Council at Constantinople
554		Pragmatic Sanction to regulate affairs of Italy	
558			First contacts between Avars and Romans
559			Kutrigurs cross Danube; raid breaches Long Walls
561		Division of Frankish kingdom on Chlothar I's death	
562			Plot against Justinian; 50 Years Peace with Persia

Year	Emperor	West / Church	East
563			Rededication of St Sophia after repairs
565	Justin II (565–78)		Justinian adopts Aphthartodocete heresy.
568		Lombards invade Italy	
570			Birth of Muhammad (approx.)
571			Justin's neo-Chalcedonian doctrinal edict.
572			Justin provokes war with Persia
573			Persians capture Dara; insanity of Justin II
574			Truce on eastern frontier
576	Tiberius Caesar		Failure of Khusro's invasion of Armenia
578	Tiberius II (578–82)		Arrest of Ghassanid leader al-Mundhir
581			Avars capture Sirmium
582	Maurice (582–602)		First Avar siege of Thessalonica
586			Slav raids reach Athens and Corinth
587		Reccared the Visigoth converts to Catholicism	
589		Catholic Third Council of Toledo	
590		Pope Gregory the Great (590–604)	Overthrow of Hormizd; flight of Khusro II to Romans
591			Restoration of Khusro II by Romans
594		Death of Gregory of Tours; Mission of Augustine to Britain	
597		Death of Columba	
602	Phocas (602–10)		Revolt of Balkan army; murder of Maurice
609/10		Heraclius in Africa prepares attack on Phocas	Violent opposition to Phocas in Antioch and Egypt
610	Heraclius (610–41)	Nicetas sets out from Africa to attack Egypt	Heraclius captures Constantinople
614			Persians capture Jerusalem and relic of Cross
616			Persian invasion of Egypt
622			Muhammad leaves Medina (Hijra)
627			Victory of Heraclius over Persians at Nineveh
632			Death of Muhammad
636			Battle of River Yarmuk
638			Surrender of Jerusalem to Arabs
640			Arab conquest of Egypt

Visigothic Kings		Vandal Kings		Frankish Kings		Rulers of Italy		Lombard Rulers in Italy		Persian Kings	
Theoderic I	419–51	Geiseric	428–77	Childeric	?–481	Odoacer	476–93			Vahram V	421–38
Theoderic II	453–66	Huneric	477–84	Clovis	c.481–	Theoderic	493–526			Yazdgard II	438–57
					c.511						
Euric	466–84	Gunthamund	484–96	Chlothar I	511–61	Athalaric	526–34			Hormizd III	457–9
Alaric II	484–507	Thrasamund	496–523	Theoderic I	511–33	Theodahad	534–6			Peroz	459–84
Gesalic	507–11	Hilderic	523–30	Childebert I	511–58	Vitigis	536–40			Balash	484–8
Amalric	511–31	Gelimer	530–3	Theodebert I	533–47	Totila	541–52			Kavadh	488–531
Theudis	531–48			Theodebald	547–55			Alboin	568–72	Khusro I	531–79
Theudisclus	548–9			Guntram	561–92			Cleph	572–4	Hormizd IV	579–90
Agila	549–55			Charibert I	561–7			Ducal interregnum	574–84	Vahram Tchobin	590–1
Athanagild	551–68			Sigibert I	561–75			Authari	584–90	Khusro II	590–628
Liuva I	567–71			Chilperic	561–84			Agilulf	590–616		
Leovigild	569–86			Childebert II	575–95/6						
Reccared	586–601			Chlothar II	584–629						
				Theodebert	596–612						
				Theoderic II	596–613						

BIBLIOGRAPHY

ABBREVIATIONS

Full references to editions of primary sources and standard collections can be found in, for example, Lewis and Short, *A Latin Dictionary*, Liddell, Scott and Jones, *Greek Lexicon*, and *Prosopography of the Later Roman Empire*, vols. I–III.

AA	*Auctores Antiquissimi*
AAntHung	*Acta Antiqua Academiae Scientiarium Hungaricae*
AASS	*Acta Sanctorum*, 71 vols. 1863–1940
AB	*Analecta Bollandiana*
ACHCM	*Actes du Congrès d'Histoire et de Civilisation du Maghreb*
ACO	*Acta Conciliorum Oecumenicorum*, ed. E. Schwartz, Berlin, 1914–40; J. Straub, Berlin, 1971–
ACOR	American Centre for Oriental Research, Amman
Actes XI Cong. Int. d.Arch. Chrét.	*Actes du XI Congrès International d'Archéologie Chrétienne*
AHR	*American Historical Review*
AJA	*American Journal of Archaeology*
Anc.H.Bull.	*Ancient History Bulletin*
Annales:ESC	*Annales: Économies, Sociétés, Civilisations*
ANRW	*Aufstieg und Niedergang der römischen Welt*, ed. H. Temporini
Ant. Afr.	*Antiquités Africaines*
AO	*Acta Orientalis*
APF	*Archiv für Papyrusforschung und verwandte Gebiete*
AR	*Archaeological Reports*
ARCA	Classical and Medieval Texts, Papers and Monographs, Liverpool
AS	*Anatolian Studies*
BAR	British Archaeological Reports, Oxford
BASOR	*Bulletin of the American School of Oriental Research*
BASP	*Bulletin of the American Society of Papyrologists*
BF	*Byzantinische Forschungen*
BGU	*Aegyptische Urkunden aus den Königlichen* (later *Staatlichen*) *Museen zu Berlin, Griechische Urkunden*
BIFAO	*Bulletin de l'Institut Français d'Archéologie Orientale*
BMGS	*Byzantine and Modern Greek Studies*

BS	*Byzantine Studies*
BSAA	*Bulletin de la Société archéologique d'Alexandrie*
BSAC	*Bulletin de la Société d'Archéologie Copte*
BSOAS	*Bulletin of the School of Oriental and African Studies*
Byz.	*Byzantion*
Byzslavica	*Byzantinoslavica*
BZ	*Byzantinische Zeitschrift*
CAG	*Commentaria in Aristotelem Graeca*, Berlin, 1891
CCSG	*Corpus Christianorum Series Graeca*
CCSL	*Corpus Christianorum Series Latina*
Cd'É	*Chronique d'Égypte*
CHAAN	*Colloque internationale d'histoire et archéologie de l'Afrique du Nord, Actes*
ChHist	*Church History*
CIC	*Corpus Iuris Civilis*², ed. T. Mommsen, P. Krüger *et al.*, 3 vols., Berlin, 1928–9
CIL	*Corpus Inscriptionum Latinarum*
CJ	*Codex Justinianus*, ed. P. Krüger, Berlin, 1929
CLA	*Codices Latini Antiquiores*, ed. E. A. Lowe, Oxford, 1934–
Class. et Med.	*Classica et Medievalia*
CPh	*Classical Philology*
CPR	*Corpus Papyrorum Raineri*
CQ	*Classical Quarterly*
CRAI	*Comptes rendus de l'Académie des Inscriptions et Belles Lettres*
CSCO	*Corpus Scriptorum Christianorum Orientalium*
CSEL	*Corpus Scriptorum Ecclesiasticorum Latinorum*
C.Th.	*Codex Theodosianus*, ed. T. Mommsen, Berlin, 1905
DOP	*Dumbarton Oaks Papers*
DBI	*Dizionario biografico degli italiani*
EHR	*English Historical Review*
EME	*Early Medieval Europe*
FHG	*Fragmenta Historicorum Graecorum*, ed. C. Müller
FIRA	*Fontes Iuris Romani Anteiustiniani*
GRBS	*Greek, Roman and Byzantine Studies*
Hist. Zeit.	*Historische Zeitschrift*
HSCP	*Harvard Studies in Classical Philology*
HThR	*Harvard Theological Review*
ICS	*Illinois Classical Studies*
IGLS	*Inscriptions grecques et latines de la Syrie*, Paris
ILS	*Inscriptiones Latinae Selectae*
IQ	*Islamic Quarterly*
IVRA	*Ivra. Rivista internazionale di Diritto romano e antico*
JAAR	*Journal of the American Academy of Religion*
JAOS	*Journal of the American Oriental Society*
JbAC	*Jahrbuch für Antike und Christentum*
JEA	*Journal of Egyptian Archaeology*
JEH	*Journal of Ecclesiastical History*

JESHO	*Journal of the Economic and Social History of the Orient*
JFA	*Journal of Field Archaeology*
JHS	*Journal of Hellenic Studies*
JJP	*Journal of Juristic Papyrology*
JÖB	*Jarhbuch der Österreichischen Byzantinistik*
JRA	*Journal of Roman Archaeology*
JRAS	*Journal of the Royal Asiatic Society*
JRS	*Journal of Roman Studies*
JSAI	*Jerusalem Studies in Arabic and Islam*
JSS	*Journal of Semitic Studies*
JThS	*Journal of Theological Studies*
Justinian, *Nov.*	*Corpus Iuris Civilis III, Novellae*, 6th edn, R. Schoell and W. Kroll, Berlin, 1954
MAMA	*Monumenta Asiae Minoris Antiqua*
MChr	*Chrestomathie der Papyruskunde, Juristische Teil*, ed. L. Mitteis
MEFR	*Mélanges de l'École française de Rome (Moyen Âge)*
MGH	*Monumenta Germaniae Historiae*
Mus. Helv.	*Museum Helveticum*
Mus.Phil. Lond.	*Museum Philologicum Londiniense*
NMS	*Nottingham Medieval Studies*
Num.Chron.	*Numismatic Chronicle*
OC	*Oriens Christianum*
OCA	*Orientalia Christiana Analecta*
OCP	*Orientalia Christiana Periodica*
OLA	*Orientalia Lovaniensia Analecta*
OMRO	*Oudheidkundige Mededelingen vit hen Rijksmuseum van Oudheden te Leiden*
OMS	*Opera Minora Selecta*
Oxf. J. Arch.	*Oxford Journal of Archaeology*
PBA	*Proceedings of the British Academy*
PBSR	*Papers of the British School at Rome*
P.Cair.Masp.	*Papyrus grecs d'époque byzantine, Catalogue général des antiquités du Musée du Caire*
PCPS	*Proceedings of the Cambridge Philological Society*
PG	*Patrologia Graeca*
PGL	*A Patristic Greek Lexikon*, ed. G. W. H. Lampe
P.Herm.	*Papyri from Hermopolis and Other Documents of the Byzantine Period*
PL	*Patrologia Latina*
P.Lond.	*Greek Papyri in the British Museum*
PLRE	*Prosopography of the Later Roman Empire* I–III, Cambridge, 1971–92
PLS	*Pactus Legis Salicae*
P.Mich.	*Michigan Papyri*
P.Michael.	*Papyri Michaelidae*
P.Monac.	*Byzantinische Papyri in der Königlichen Hof- und Staatsbibliothek zu München*
PO	*Patrologia Orientalis*

P.Oxy.	*The Oxyrhynchus Papyri*
P&P	*Past and Present*
P.Ross.Georg.	*Papyri russischer und georgischer Sammlungen*
P.Ryl.	*Rylands Papyri*
PSI	*Papyri Greci e Latini, Pubblicazioni della Società Italiana per la Ricerca dei Papiri Greci e Latini in Egitto,* 1912–
P.Warren	*The Warren Papyri* (Papyrologica Lugd.-Bat.) 1, ed. M. David
RAC	*Reallexikon für Antike und Christentum*
RBPH	*Revue belge de philologie et de l'histoire*
RDC	*Revue de droit canonique*
RE	*Pauly–Wissowa–Kroll, Realenzyklopädie der klassischen Altertumswissenschaft.* Stuttgart, 1894–
REA	*Revue des Études Anciennes*
REB	*Revue des Études Byzantines*
REG	*Revue des Études Grecques*
RH	*Revue historique*
RHE	*Revue d'Histoire Ecclésiastique*
RIDA	*Revue Internationale des Droits de l'Antiquité*
SB	*Sammelbuch griechischer Urkunden aus Aegypten*
SCH	*Studies in Church History*
SChrét.	*Sources Chrétiennes*
SCI	*Scripta Classica Israelica*
SCNAC	*Sacrorum Conciliorum Nova et Amplissima Collectio,* ed. J. D. Mansi, Florence, 1759ff.
SDHI	*Studia et Documenta Historiae et Iuris*
SEG	*Supplementum Epigraphicum Graecum*
SI	*Studia Islamica*
SRM	*Scriptores Rerum Merovingicarum*
StPatr.	*Studia Patristica*
StudPal	*Studien zur Paläographie und Papyruskunde*
TAPA	*Transactions of the American Philological Association*
TAVO	*Tübinger Atlas des Vorderen Orients*
T&MByz	*Travaux et Mémoires*
TRE	*Theologische Realenzyklopädie,* ed. G. Krause and G. Müller, Berlin, 1977–
TRHS	*Transactions of the Royal Historical Society*
TU	*Texte und Untersuchungen*
VC	*Vigiliae Christianae*
WChr	U. Wilcken, *Grundzüge und Chrestomathie der Papyruskunde, Historischer Teil,* II. Leipzig–Berlin, 1912
YCS	*Yale Classical Studies*
ZÄS	*Zeitschrift für ägyptische Sprache und Altertumskunde*
ZDMG	*Zeitschrift der deutschen Morgenländischen Gesellschaft*
ZPE	*Zeitschrift für Papyrologie und Epigraphik*
ZRG GA	*Zeitschrift der Savigny-Stiftung für Rechtsgeschichte, Germanistische Abteilung*
ZRG RA	*Zeitschrift der Savigny-Stiftung für Rechtsgeschichte, Romanistische Abteilung*

FREQUENTLY CITED WORKS

Allen, *Evagrius*. Allen, Pauline (1981) *Evagrius Scholasticus the Church Historian.* Louvain

Bagnall, *Egypt*. Bagnall, R. S. (1993) *Egypt in Late Antiquity.* Princeton, NJ

Bagnall *et al.*, *Consuls*. Bagnall, Roger S., Cameron, Alan, Schwartz, Seth, Worp, K. A. (1987) *Consuls of the Later Roman Empire.* Atlanta, GA

Bowersock, *Hellenism*. Bowersock, G. W. (1990) *Hellenism in Late Antiquity.* Ann Arbor, MI, and Cambridge

Brown, 'Holy man'. Brown, Peter (1971) 'The rise and function of the holy man in late antiquity', *JRS* 61: 80–101 (= Brown, *Society and the Holy* 103–52)

Brown, *Religion and Society*. Brown, P. (1972) *Religion and Society in the Age of Saint Augustine.* London

Brown, *Society and the Holy*. Brown, P. (1982) *Society and the Holy in Late Antiquity.* Berkeley and Los Angeles

Brown, *Gentlemen and Officers*. Brown, T. S. (1984) *Gentlemen and Officers: Imperial Administration and Aristocratic Power in Byzantine Italy A.D. 554–800.* London

Bury, *LRE*. Bury, J. B. (1923) *History of the Later Roman Empire from the Death of Theodosius I to the Death of Justinian*, 2 vols. London

Cameron, Alan, *Circus Factions*. Cameron, Alan (1976) *Circus Factions: Blues and Greens at Rome and Byzantium.* Oxford

Cameron, Alan, *Literature and Society*. Alan Cameron (1985) *Literature and Society in the Early Byzantine World.* London

Cameron, Averil, *Changing Cultures*. Averil Cameron (1996) *Changing Cultures in Early Byzantium.* Aldershot

Cameron, Averil, *Corippus*. Corippus, *In laudem Iustini minoris libri quattuor*, ed. with transl. and comm. by Averil Cameron (1976). London

Cameron, Averil, *Mediterranean World*. Cameron, Averil (1993) *The Mediterranean World in Late Antiquity AD 395–600.* London

Cameron, Averil, *Procopius*. Cameron, Averil (1985). *Procopius and the Sixth Century.* London

Cameron, Averil, *Rhetoric of Empire*. Cameron, Averil (1991) *Christianity and the Rhetoric of Empire: The Development of Christian Discourse.* Berkeley and Los Angeles

Capizzi, Carmelo, *Giustiniano*. Capizzi, Carmelo (1994) *Giustiniano I tra politica e religione.* Milan

Carandini *et al.*, *Storia di Roma* III. Carandini, A., Cracco Ruggini, L., Giardina, A. (1993) *Storia di Roma* III. *L'età tardoantica, 1. Crisi e trasformazioni.* Turin

Chadwick, *Boethius*. Chadwick, Henry (1981) *Boethius. The Consolations of Music, Logic, Theology and Philosophy.* Oxford

Chuvin, P., *Chronicle*. Chuvin, P. (1990) *A Chronicle of the Last Pagans*, Eng. transl. by B. A. Archer of part 1 of Chuvin, *Chronique* (Revealing Antiquity 4). Cambridge, MA, and London

Chuvin, *Chronique*. Chuvin, P. (1990) *Chronique des derniers païens: La disparition du paganisme dans l'Empire romain, du règne de Constantin à celui de Justinien.* Paris (2nd edn 1991)

Dagron, *Naissance*. Dagron, G. (1974) *Naissance d'une capitale: Constantinople et ses institutions de 330 à 451* (Bibliothèque byzantine, Études 7). Paris

Downey, *History of Antioch.* Downey, G. (1961) *A History of Antioch in Syria.* Princeton, NJ

Drinkwater and Elton (eds.), *Fifth-Century Gaul.* Drinkwater, J. and Elton, H. (eds.) (1992) *Fifth-century Gaul: A Crisis of Identity?* Cambridge

Ducellier, *L'Église byzantine.* Ducellier, Alain (1990) *L'Église byzantine: Entre Pouvoir et Esprit (313–1204).* Paris

Fowden, *Empire to Commonwealth.* Fowden, Garth (1993) *Empire to Commonwealth: Consequences of Monotheism in Late Antiquity.* Princeton, NJ

Frend, *Monophysite Movement.* Frend, W. H. C. (1972) *The Rise of the Monophysite Movement: Chapters in the History of the Church in the Fifth and Sixth Centuries.* Cambridge

Giardina (ed.), *Società romana.* Giardina, A. (ed.) (1986) *Società romana e impero tardoantico*, 4 vols. (I: *Istituzioni, ceti, economie*; II: *Roma: Politica, economia, paesaggio urbano*; III: *Le merci, gli insediamenti*; IV: *Tradizione dei classici, trasformazioni della cultura*). Rome–Bari

Gibson (ed.), *Boethius.* Gibson, Margaret (ed.) (1981) *Boethius: His Life, Thought and Influence.* Oxford

Goffart, *Barbarians and Romans.* Goffart, W. (1980) *Barbarians and Romans A.D. 418–584: The Techniques of Accommodation.* Princeton, NJ

Gray, *Defence of Chalcedon.* Gray, P. T. R. (1979) *The Defence of Chalcedon in the East (451–553).* Leiden

Grillmeier, *Christ in Christian Tradition.* I^2, II.1–2, II.4 A. Grillmeier, *Christ in Christian Tradition*, Eng. tr., (1975) I^2: *From the Apostolic Age to Chalcedon (451)*, trans. John Bowden; (1995) II: *From the Council of Chalcedon to Gregory the Great (451–604)*, 1. *Reception and Contradiction: The Development of Discussion about Chalcedon from 451 to the Beginning of the Reign of Justinian*, trans. Pauline Allen and John Cawte; 2, in collaboration with Th. Hainthaler, *The Church of Constantinople in the Sixth Century*, trans. John Cawte and Pauline Allen. London

Haldon, *Byzantium in the Seventh Century.* Haldon, J. F. (1990) *Byzantium in the Seventh Century: The Transformation of a Culture.* Cambridge

Harvey, *Asceticism and Society in Crisis.* Harvey, Susan Ashbrook (1990) *Asceticism and Society in Crisis: John of Ephesus and* The Lives of the Eastern Saints. Berkeley and Los Angeles

Heather, *Goths and Romans.* Heather, P. (1991) *Goths and Romans 332–489.* Oxford

Hendy, *Studies.* Hendy, M. F. (1985) *Studies in the Byzantine Monetary Economy c. 300–1450.* Cambridge

Herrin, *Formation of Christendom.* Herrin, Judith (1987) *The Formation of Christendom*, Princeton, NJ, and Oxford

Holum, *Empresses.* Holum, K. (1982) *Theodosian Empresses: Women and Imperial Dominion in Late Antiquity.* Transformation of the Classical Heritage 3. Berkeley and Los Angeles

Hommes et richesses I. J. Lefort and C. Morrisson (eds.) (1989) *Hommes et richesses dans l'empire byzantin* I, IVe–VIe *siècle.* Paris

Hunt, *Holy Land Pilgrimage.* Hunt, E. D. (1982) *Holy Land Pilgrimage in the Later Roman Empire A.D. 312–460.* Oxford (2nd edn 1992)

Isaac, *Limits of Empire.* Isaac, B. (1990) *The Limits of Empire: The Roman Army in the East.* Oxford (2nd edn 1992)

Jeffreys *et al.*, *Chronicle.* Jeffreys, Elizabeth, Jeffreys, Michael, Scott, Roger *et al.* (1986) *The Chronicle of John Malalas: A Translation.* Sydney

Jeffreys *et al.*, *Studies.* Jeffreys, Elizabeth, with Croke, Brian, and Scott, Roger (eds.) (1990) *Studies in John Malalas.* Sydney

Jones, *Cities.* Jones, A. H. M. (1937) *Cities of the Eastern Roman Provinces* (2nd edn 1971). Oxford

Jones, *LRE.* Jones, A. H. M. (1964) *The Later Roman Empire 284–602: A Social, Economic and Administrative Survey*, 3 vols. Oxford; 2 vols. (continuous pagination). Norman, OK

Jones, *Roman Economy.* Jones, A. H. M. (1974) *The Roman Economy: Studies in Ancient Economy and Administrative History*, ed. P. A. Brunt. Oxford

Kaster, *Guardians of Language.* Kaster, R. (1988) *Guardians of Language: The Grammarian and Society in Late Antiquity.* Berkeley, CA

Krautheimer, *Early Christian and Byzantine Architecture.* Krautheimer, R. (1965) *Early Christian and Byzantine Architecture.* Harmondsworth (rev. edns 1975, 1979, 1986)

Lemerle, *Byzantine Humanism.* Lemerle, P. (1986) *Byzantine Humanism*, Engl. transl. by Lindsay, Helen, and Moffatt, Ann (Byzantina Australiensia 3). Canberra

Lepelley, *Cités.* Lepelley, C. (1979–81) *Les cités de l'Afrique romaine au Bas-Empire* (Études Augustiniennes), 2 vols. Paris

Liebeschuetz, *Barbarians and Bishops.* Liebeschuetz, J. H. W. G. (1990) *Barbarians and Bishops: Army, Church and State in the Age of Arcadius and Chrysostom.* Oxford

Maas, *John Lydus.* Maas, Michael (1992) *John Lydus and the Roman Past: Antiquarianism and Politics in the Age of Justinian.* London

McCormick, *Eternal Victory.* McCormick, Michael (1986) *Eternal Victory: Triumphal Rulership in Late Antiquity, Byzantium, and the Early Medieval West.* Cambridge

MacCoull, *Dioscorus.* MacCoull, L. S. B. (1988) *Dioscorus of Aphrodito: His Work and his World.* Berkeley and Los Angeles

Magdalino (ed.), *New Constantines.* Magdalino, Paul (ed.) (1994) *New Constantines: The Rhythm of Imperial Renewal in Byzantium, 4th–13th Centuries.* Aldershot

Mango, *Byzantine Architecture.* Mango, Cyril (1976) *Byzantine Architecture.* New York

Mango, *Développement.* Mango, C. (1985) *Le développement urbain de Constantinople (IVe–VIIe siècles).* Paris

Mango, *Studies on Constantinople.* Mango, Cyril (1993) *Studies on Constantinople.* Aldershot

Meyendorff, *Imperial Unity.* Meyendorff, J. (1989) *Imperial Unity and Christian Divisions: The Church 450–680 A.D.* Crestwood, NY

Mitchell, *Anatolia.* Mitchell, Stephen (1993) *Anatolia: Land, Men and Gods in Asia Minor*, 2 vols. Oxford

Not. Dig. Notitia Dignitatum, ed. O. Seeck, Berlin, 1876

Patlagean, *Pauvreté.* Patlagean, E. (1977) *Pauvreté économique et pauvreté sociale à Byzance (4e–7e siècles).* Paris

Pearson and Goehring (eds.), *Egyptian Christianity.* Pearson, Birger A., and Goehring, James E. (eds.) (1986) *The Roots of Egyptian Christianity: Studies in Antiquity and Christianity.* Philadelphia

Rouché, *Aphrodisias.* Rouché, C. M. (1989) *Aphrodisias in Late Antiquity* (JRS Monographs 5). London

Roueché, *Performers and Partisans.* Roueché, C. M. (1993) *Performers and Partisans at Aphrodisias in the Roman and Late Roman Periods* (JRS Monographs 6). London

Rousseau, *Ascetics.* Rousseau, Philip (1978) *Ascetics, Authority and the Church in the Age of Jerome and Cassian.* Oxford

Rousseau, *Basil of Caesarea.* Rousseau, Philip (1994) *Basil of Caesarea.* Berkeley and Los Angeles

Rousseau, *Pachomius.* Rousseau, Philip (1985) *Pachomius: The Making of a Community in Fourth Century Egypt.* Berkeley and Los Angeles

Stein, *Bas-Empire.* Stein, E. (1968) *Histoire du Bas-Empire* II (transl. by J.-R. Palanque). Amsterdam (repr. of Paris–Bruges edn, 1949)

Tchalenko, *Villages.* Tchalenko, Georges (1953–8) *Villages antiques de la Syrie du nord: Le massif du Bélus à l'époque romaine.* 3 vols. Paris

Trombley, *Hellenic Religion.* Trombley, F. R. (1993–4) *Hellenic Religion and Christianization c. 370–529*, 2 vols. Leiden

Van Dam, *Leadership and Community.* Van Dam, Raymond (1985) *Leadership and Community in Late Antique Gaul.* Berkeley and Los Angeles

Walker, *Holy City, Holy Places?* Walker, Peter (1990) *Holy City, Holy Places? Christian Attitudes to Jerusalem and the Holy Land in the Fourth Century.* Oxford

Ward-Perkins, *Public Building.* Ward-Perkins, B. (1984) *From Classical Antiquity to the Middle Ages: Urban Public Building in Northern and Central Italy, A.D. 300–850.* Oxford

Whitby, *Maurice.* Whitby, L. M. (1988) *The Emperor Maurice and his Historian: Theophylact Simocatta on Persian and Balkan Warfare.* Oxford

Wood, *Merovingian Kingdoms.* Wood, Ian (1994) *The Merovingian Kingdoms 450–751.* Harlow

PART I: CHRONOLOGICAL OVERVIEW (CHS. 1–5)

Alcock, L. (1993) *The Neighbours of the Picts: Angles, Britons & Scots at War and at Home.* Rosemarkie

Alexander, P. J. (1967) *The Oracle of Baalbek.* Washington, DC

Allen, Pauline (1979) 'The "Justinianic" plague', *Byz.* 48: 5–20

Allen, Pauline (1980) 'Neo-Chalcedonianism and the patriarchs of the late sixth century', *Byz.* 50: 5–17

Amelotti, M. (ed.) (1972–94) *Legum Iustiniani Imperatoris Vocabularium* (Subsidia I–IV). Turin

Amelotti, M. (1978) 'Giustiniano tra theologia e diritto', in Archi (ed.) (1978) 133–60

Amelotti, M. and Luzzato, G. L. (1972) *Le costituzioni giustinianee nei papiri e nelle epigrafi.* Milan (= Amelotti (ed.) (1972–94) III)

Amelotti, M. and Zingale, L. M. (1977) *Scritti teologici ed ecclesiastici di Giustiniano.* Milan (= Amelotti (ed.) (1972–94) III)

Amory, P. (1993) 'The meaning and purpose of ethnic terminology in the Burgundian laws', *EME* 2: 1–28

Anderson, P. (1974) *Passages from Antiquity to Feudalism.* London

Archi, G. G. (ed.) (1978) *L'imperatore Giustiniano. Storia e Mito. Giornate di Studio a Ravenna, 14–16 ottobre 1976*. Milan

Baker, D. (ed.) (1976) *The Orthodox Churches and the West* (Studies in Church History 13). Oxford

Barber, C. (1990) 'The imperial panels at San Vitale: a reconsideration', *BMGS* 14: 19–42

Barnish, S. J. B. (1986) 'Taxation, land and barbarian settlement in the western empire', *PBSR* 54: 170–95

Barnish, S. J. B. (1988) 'Transformation and survival in the western senatorial aristocracy, c. A.D. 400–700', *PBSR* 33: 120–55

Barnish, S. J. B. (1989) 'A note on the *collatio glebalis*', *Historia* 38: 254–6

Barnish, S. J. B. (1990) 'Maximian, Cassiodorus, Boethius, Theodehad: literature, philosophy and politics in Ostrogothic Italy', *NMS* 34: 16–32

Barnwell, P. S. (1992) *Emperor, Prefects and Kings: The Roman West, 395–565*. London

Baynes, N. H. (1955) 'Alexandria and Constantinople: a study in ecclesiastical diplomacy', in Baynes, *Byzantine Studies and Other Essays* (London) 97–115

Beaucamp, J. (1990, 1992) *Le statut de la femme à Byzance (4e.–7e. siècle)*, 2 vols. Paris

Biondi, B. (1936) *Giustiniano Primo, principe e legislatore cattolico*. Milan

Biondi, B. (1952) *Il diritto romano cristiano* 1. Milan

Blockley, R. C. (1985) 'Subsidies and diplomacy: Rome and Persia in late antiquity', *Phoenix* 39: 62–74

Blockley, R. C. (1992) *East Roman Foreign Policy: Formation and Conduct from Diocletian to Anastasius*. Liverpool

Bóna, I. (1976) *The Dawn of the Dark Ages: The Gepids and the Lombards in the Carpathian Basin*. Budapest

Brock, S. P. (1995) 'The Syriac background', in M. Lapidge (ed.), *Archbishop Theodore* (Cambridge) 30–52

Brooks, E. W. (1893) 'The emperor Zeno and the Isaurians', *EHR* 8: 209–38

Brown, P. R. L. (1971) *The World of Late Antiquity*. London

Brown, P. R. L. (1982) 'Relics and social status in the age of Gregory of Tours', in Brown, *Society and the Holy* 222–50

Browning, R. (1971, 1987) *Justinian and Theodora*. London

Burgess, R. W. (1993) *The 'Chronicle' of Hydatius and the 'Consularia Constantinopolitana'*. Oxford

Burgess, R. W. (1993–4) 'The accession of Marcian in the light of Chalcedonian apologetic and Monophysite polemic', *BZ* 86/87: 47–68

Burns, T. S. (1980) *The Ostrogoths: Kingship and Society*. Wiesbaden

Burns, T. S. (1984) *A History of the Ostrogoths*. Bloomington

Bury, J. B. (1889) *History of the Later Roman Empire from Arcadius to Irene (395 A.D. to 800 A.D.)*. London

Bury, J. B. (1897) 'The Nika riot', *JHS* 17: 92–119

Bury, J. B. (1928) *The Invasion of Europe by the Barbarians*. London

Cameron, Alan (1965) 'Wandering poets: a literary movement in Byzantine Egypt', *Historia* 14: 470–509

Cameron, Alan (1970) *Claudian*. Oxford

Cameron, Alan (1973) *Porphyrius the Charioteer*. Oxford

Cameron, Alan (1974) 'The date of Priscian's *De laude Anastasiī*, *GRBS* 15: 313–16 (= Alan Cameron, *Literature and Society* V)

Cameron, Alan (1978) 'The house of Anastasius', *GRBS* 19: 259–76 (= Alan Cameron, *Literature and Society* XIV)

Cameron, Alan (1982) 'The empress and the poet: paganism and politics at the court of Theodosius II', *YCS* 27: 217–89 (= Alan Cameron, *Literature and Society* III)

Cameron, Alan, and Long, J. (1993) *Barbarians and Politics at the Court of Arcadius*. Berkeley

Cameron, Alan, and Schauer, D. (1982) 'The last consul: Basilius and his diptych', *JRS* 72: 126–45

Cameron, Averil (1970) *Agathias*. Oxford

Cameron, Averil (1975) 'The empress Sophia', *Byz.* 45: 5–21 (= Averil Cameron (1981) XI)

Cameron, Averil (1976) 'The early religious policies of Justin II', in Baker (ed.) (1976) 51–67 (= Averil Cameron (1981) X)

Cameron, Averil (1977) 'Early Byzantine *Kaiserkritik*: two case histories', *BMGS* 3: 1–17 (= Averil Cameron (1981) IX)

Cameron, Averil (1978) 'The Theotokos in sixth-century Constantinople', *JTS* 29: 79–108 (= Averil Cameron (1981) XVI)

Cameron, Averil (1979) 'Images of authority: élites and icons in late sixth-century Byzantium', *P&P* 84: 3–35 (= Averil Cameron (1981) XVIII)

Cameron, Averil (1980) 'The artistic patronage of Justin II', *Byz.* 50: 62–84 (= Averil Cameron (1981) XII)

Cameron, Averil (1981) *Continuity and Change in Sixth-Century Byzantium*. Aldershot

Cameron, Averil (1982) 'Byzantine Africa: the literary evidence', in J. H. Humphrey (ed.), *Excavations at Carthage 1978* (Ann Arbor) 1–51 (= Averil Cameron, *Changing Cultures* VII)

Cameron, Averil (1987) 'The construction of court ritual: the Byzantine *Book of Ceremonies*', in D. Cannadine and S. Price (eds.), *Rituals of Royalty: Power and Ceremonial in Traditional Societies* (Cambridge) 106–36

Cameron, Averil (1988) 'Eustratius' life of the patriarch Eutychius and the Fifth Ecumenical Council', in Chrysostomides (ed.) (1988) 225–47 (= Averil Cameron, *Changing Cultures* I)

Cameron, Averil (1997) 'Gibbon and Justinian', in R. McKitterick and R. Quinault (eds.), *Edward Gibbon and Empire* (Cambridge) 34–52

Cameron, A. and A. (1966) 'The *Cycle* of Agathias', *JHS* 86: 6–25

Campos, J. (1960) *Juan de Bíclaro*. Madrid

Capizzi, C. (1969) *L'imperatore Anastasio I (491–518)*. Rome

Carile, A. (1978) 'Consenso e dissenso fra propaganda e fronda nelle fonti narrative dell'età Giustinianea', in Archi (ed.) (1978) 37–93

Cavallo, G. (1978) 'La circolazione libraria nell'età di Giustiniano', in Archi (ed.) (1978) 83–132, 149–62

Chadwick, H. (1983) 'The Chalcedonian definition', in *Actes du Concile de Chalcédoine*, sessions III–IV (trans. by A.-J. Festugière) (Geneva) 3–12 (= Chadwick (1991) XVIII)

Chadwick, H. (1991) *Heresy and Orthodoxy in the Early Church*. London

Charlesworth, M. P. (1937) 'The virtues of the Roman emperor', *PBA* 23: 105–33

Charlesworth, M. P. (1943) '*Pietas* and *victoria*: the emperor and the citizen', *JRS* 33: 1–11

Chauvot, A. (1986) *Procope de Gaza, Priscien de Césarée: Panégyriques de l'empereur Anastase Ier.* Bonn

Chauvot, A. (1987) 'Curiales et paysans en Orient à la fin du Ve et au début du VIe siècle: note sur l'institution du *vindex*', in Frézouls (ed.) (1987) 271–81

Christlein, R. (1979) *Die Alamannen: Archäologie eines lebendigen Volkes.* 2nd edn. Stuttgart

Chrysos, E. K. (1966) *Die Bischöfslisten des V. Ökumenischen Konzils (553).* Bonn

Chrysos, E. K. (1971) 'Die angebliche Abschaffung der städtischen Kurien durch Kaiser Anastasios', *Byzantina* 3: 93–102

Chrysos, E. K. and Schwarcz, A. (eds.) (1989) *Das Reich und die Barbaren.* Vienna

Chrysostomides, J. (ed.) (1988) *Kathegetria: Essays Presented to Joan Hussey for her 80th Birthday.* Camberley

Claude, D. (1971) *Adel, Kirche und Königtum im Westgotenreich.* Sigmaringen

Clover, F. M. (1972) 'Geiseric and Attila', *Historia* 22: 104–117 (= Clover (1993) II)

Clover, F. M. (1978) 'The family and early career of Anicius Olybrius', *Historia* 27: 169–96 (= Clover (1993) III)

Clover, F. M. (1982) 'Carthage and the Vandals', in Humphrey (ed.) (1982) 1–22

Clover, F. M. (1989a) 'Felix Karthago', in Clover and Humphreys (eds.) (1989) 129–69

Clover, F. M. (1989b) 'The symbiosis of Romans and Africans in Africa', in Chrysos and Schwarcz (eds.) (1989) 57–73

Clover, F. M. (1993) *The Late Roman West and the Vandals.* Aldershot

Clover, F. M. and Humphreys, R. S. (eds.) (1989) *Tradition and Innovation in Late Antiquity.* Madison, WI

Collins, R. (1983) 'Theodebert I: Rex Magnus Francorum', in Wormald, Bullough and Collins (eds.) (1983) 7–33

Collins, R. (1986) *The Basques.* Oxford

Collins, R. (1991) *Early Medieval Europe, 300–1000.* London

Collins, R. (1992) *Law, Culture and Regionalism in Early Medieval Spain.* Aldershot

Collins, R. (1995) *Early Medieval Spain, 400–1000.* 2nd edn. London

Collins, R. (1996) *Fredegar.* Aldershot

Cormack, R. (1985) *Writing in Gold: Byzantine Society and its Icons.* London

Courtois, C. (1955) *Les Vandales et l'Afrique.* Paris

Croke, B. (1977) 'Evidence for the Hun invasion of Thrace in A.D. 422', *GRBS* 18: 347–67 (= Croke (1992) XII)

Croke, B. (1978) 'The date and circumstances of Marcian's decease, A.D. 457', *Byz.* 58: 5–9 (= Croke (1992) XIII)

Croke, B. (1982) 'The date of the "Anastasian long wall" in Thrace', *GRBS* 23: 59–78 (= Croke (1992) XVII)

Croke, B. (1983a) 'The context and date of Priscus fragment 6', *CP* 78: 296–308 (= Croke (1992) XIV)

Croke, B. (1983b) 'Basiliscus the boy-emperor', *GRBS* 24: 81–91 (= Croke (1992) X)

Croke, B. (1984) 'Dating Theodoret's *Church History* and *Commentary on the Psalms*', *Byz.* 54: 59–74 (= Croke (1992) VII)

Croke, B. (1992) *Christian Chronicles and Byzantine History, 5th–6th Centuries.* Aldershot

Croke, B. (1995) *The Chronicle of Marcellinus* (Byzantina Australiensia 7). Sydney

Crone, P. (1991) 'Kavad's heresy and Mazdak's revolt', *Iran* 29: 21–42

Crow, J. G. (1995) 'The long walls of Thrace', in Mango and Dagron (eds.) (1995) 104–24

Dabrowa, E. (ed.) (1994) *The Roman and Byzantine Army in the East.* Kraków

Dagron, G. (1982) 'Le fils de Léon Ier (463): témoignages concordants de l'hagiographie et de l'astrologie', *AB* 100: 271–5

Dagron, G. (1984) *Constantinople imaginaire, Études sur le recueil des 'Patria'.* Paris

Dagron, G. (1996) *Empereur et prêtre. Étude sur le 'césaropapisme' byzantin.* Paris

Davies, W. (1982) *Wales in the Early Middle Ages.* Leicester

Demicheli, A. M. (ed.) (1994) *Scritti apocrifi di Giustiniano.* Turin (= Amelotti (ed.) (1972–94) IV)

Driscoll, S. T. and Nieke, M. R. (eds.) (1988) *Power and Politics in Early Medieval Britain and Ireland.* Edinburgh

Dumville, D. (1977) 'Sub-Roman Britain: history and legend', *History* 62: 173–92

Dumville, D. (1993) *Saint Patrick, A.D. 493–1993.* Woodbridge

Durliat, J. (1988) 'Le salaire de la paix sociale dans les royaumes barbares (V–VIe siècles), in Wolfram and Schwarcz (eds.) (1988) 21–72

Durliat, J. (1989) 'Le peste du VIe siècle. Pour un nouvel examen des sources byzantines', in *Hommes et richesses* 1.107–20

Ensslin, W. (1947) *Theoderich der Grosse.* Munich

Evans, J. A. S. (1996) *The Age of Justinian. The Circumstances of Imperial Power.* London

Ewig, E. (1952) 'Die fränkischen Teilungen und Teilreiche (511–613)' (*Akademie der Wissenschaften und der Literatur in Mainz, Geistes- und sozialwissenschaftliche Klasse* 9) 651–715

Ewig, E. (1993) *Die Merowinger und das Frankenreich.* 2nd edn. Berlin/Cologne

Farka, C. (1993/4) 'Räuberhorden in Thrakien. Eine unbeachtete Quelle zur Geschichte der Zeit des Kaisers Maurikios', *BZ* 86/87: 462–9

Feissel, D. (1984) 'Deux inscriptions d'Asie Mineure et les consuls de 448 et 452', *BCH* 108: 564–71

Ferreiro, A. (1988) *The Visigoths in Gaul and Spain A.D. 418–711: A Bibliography.* Leiden

Freeman, P. and Kennedy, D. (eds.) (1986) *The Defence of the Roman and Byzantine East* (BAR International Series 297). Oxford

French, D. H. and Lightfoot, C. S. (eds.) (1989) *The Eastern Frontier of the Roman Empire* (BAR International Series 553). Oxford

Frézouls, E. (ed.) (1987) *Sociétés urbaines, sociétés rurales dans l'Asie Mineure et la Syrie hellénistiques et romaines.* Strasbourg

Frye, R. N. (1984) *The History of Ancient Iran.* Munich

Fulford, M. G. (1980) 'Carthage: overseas trade and the political economy, c. AD 400–700', *Reading Medieval Studies* 6: 68–80

García Moreno, L. A. (1974) *Prosopografía del Reino visigodo de Toledo.* Salamanca

García Moreno, L. A. (1989) *Historia de España visigoda.* Madrid

Goffart, W. (1957) 'Byzantine policy in the west under Tiberius II and Maurice: the pretenders Hermengild and Gundovald (579–85)', *Traditio* 13: 73–118

Goffart, W. (1981) 'Rome, Constantinople, and the Barbarians', *AHR* 76: 275–306

Goffart, W. (1989) *Rome's Fall and After*. London and Ronceverte

Goffart, W. (1989) 'The theme of "The Barbarian Invasions" in late antique and modern historiography', in Chrysos and Schwarcz (eds.) (1989) 87–107

González Blanco, A. (ed.) (1986) *Los Visigodos: historia y civilización*. Murcia

González Ruiz, R. (ed.) (1981) *Innovación y continuidad en la España visigótica*. Toledo

Goubert, P. (1951–65) *Byzance avant l'Islam*. vols. i, ii.1–2 Paris

Grahn-Hoek, H. (1976) *Die fränkische Oberschicht im 6. Jahrhundert*. Sigmaringen

Gray, P. (1988) 'Justinian', *TRE* 17.3/4 (Berlin) 478–86

Greatrex, G. (1994) 'The dates of Procopius's works', *BMGS* 18: 101–14

Greatrex, G. (1995) 'The composition of Procopius's *Persian Wars* and John the Cappadocian', *Prudentia* 27.1: 1–13

Greatrex, G. (1998) 'The Nika riot: a reappraisal', *JHS* 118: 60–86

Gregory, T. E. (1979) *Vox Populi: Popular Opinion and Violence in Religious Controversies of the Fifth Century AD*. Columbus, OH

Guillaumont, A. (1969/70) 'Justinien et l'église de Perse', *DOP* 23/24: 39–66

Haldon, J. F. (1979) *Recruitment and Conscription in the Byzantine Army c. 550–950: A Study on the origins of the stratiotika ktemata* (Sitzungsberichte der Österreichischen Akad. der Wissens., phil.-hist. Kl. 357). Vienna

Haldon, J. F. (1984) *Byzantine Praetorians*. Bonn

Harl, K. W. (1990) 'Sacrifice and pagan belief in fifth- and sixth-century Byzantium', *P&P* 128: 7–27

Harmatta, J. (1952) 'The dissolution of the Hun empire', *Acta Archaeologica Hungaricae* 2: 277–304

Harries, J. (1994) '*Pius princeps*: Theodosius II and fifth-century Constantinople', in Magdalino (ed.), *New Constantines* 35–44

Harries, J. (1995) *Sidonius Apollinaris and the Fall of Rome, AD 407–485*. Oxford

Harries, J. and Wood, I. (eds.) (1993) *The Theodosian Code*. London

Harrison, R. M. (1981) 'The emperor Zeno's real name', *BZ* 74: 27–8

Harrison, R. M. (1989) *A Temple for Byzantium*. London and Austin

Harrison, R. M. and Hayes, J. W. (1986) *Excavations at Saraçhane in Istanbul: The Church of St Polyeuktos*. i.1. *The excavations, structures, architectural decoration, small finds, coins, bones and molluscs*. 2. *The pottery* (by J. W. Hayes). Princeton

Heather, P. (1992) 'The emergence of the Visigothic kingdom', in Drinkwater and Elton (eds.), *Fifth-Century Gaul* 88–94

Heather, P. (1994) 'New men for new Constantines: creating an imperial governing class in the eastern Mediterranean', in Magdalino (ed.), *New Constantines* 11–33

Heather, P. (1995) 'The Huns and the end of the Roman empire in western Europe', *EHR* 110: 4–41

Heather, P. (1996) 'Afterword', in Thompson (1996) 238–84

Henry III, P. (1967) 'A mirror for Justinian: the *Ekthesis* of Agapetus Diaconus', *GRBS* 8: 281–308

Herring, E., Whitehouse, R. and Wilkins, J. (eds.) (1991) *Papers of the Fourth Conference of Italian Archaeology*. London

Higgins, M. J. (1939) *The Persian War of the Emperor Maurice (582–602) I The Chronology*. Washington, DC

Hohlfelder, R. L. (1984) 'Marcian's gamble: a reassessment of eastern imperial policy toward Attila A.D. 450–453', *AJAH* 9: 54–69

Holum, K. (1977) 'Pulcheria's crusade A.D. 421–22 and the ideology of imperial victory', *GRBS* 18: 153–72

Honoré, T. (1978) *Tribonian*. London

Hopkins, K. (1978) *Conquerors and Slaves*. Cambridge

Hopwood, K. (1986) 'Towers, territory and terror: how the east was held', in Freeman and Kennedy (eds.) (1986) 343–56

Hopwood, K. (1989) 'Consent and control: how the peace was kept in Rough Cilicia', in French and Lightfoot (eds.) (1989) 191–201

Hughes, K. (1972) *Early Christian Ireland: Introduction to the Sources*. London

Humphrey, J. H. (ed.) (1982) *Excavations at Carthage 1978, conducted by the University of Michigan*. Ann Arbor

James, E. (ed.) (1980) *Visigothic Spain: New Approaches*. Oxford

James, E. (1988a) *The Franks*. Oxford

James, E. (1988b) 'Childéric, Syagrius et la disparition du royaume de Soissons', *Revue Archéologique de Picardie* 3/4: 9–12

Jarman, A. O. H. (ed.) (1988) *Aneirin: Y Gododdin*. Llandysul

Jarnut, J. (1982) *Geschichte der Langobarden*. Stuttgart

Jiménez Garnica, A. (1983) *Orígenes y desarrollo del Reino Visigodo de Tolosa*. Valladolid

Kaegi, W. E. (1968) *Byzantium and the Decline of Rome*. Princeton

Kaegi, W. E. (1981) *Byzantine Military Unrest 471–843*. Amsterdam

Kelly, J. N. D. (1995) *Goldenmouth. The Story of John Chrysostom*. London

Khazanov, A. M. (1984) *Nomads and the Outside World* (trans. J. Crookenden). Cambridge

Kitzinger, E. (1977) *Byzantine Art in the Making*. Cambridge, MA

Lapidge, M. and Dumville, D. (eds.) (1984) *Gildas: New Approaches*. Woodbridge

Lee, A. D. (1993a) 'Evagrius, Paul of Nisibis and the problem of loyalties in the mid-sixth century', *JEH* 44: 569–86

Lee, A. D. (1993b) *Information and Frontiers: Roman Foreign Relations in Late Antiquity*. Cambridge

Lee, A. D. (forthcoming) 'Dirty tricks in late Roman diplomacy'

Lemerle, P. (1971, 1986) *Le premier humanisme byzantin*. Paris (tr. as Lemerle, *Byzantine Humanism*)

Lemerle, P. (ed.) (1981) *Les plus anciens recueils des Miracles de saint Démétrius et la pénétration des Slaves dans les Balkans, 2. Le commentaire*. Paris

Lieu, J., North, J. and Rajak, T. (eds.) (1992) *The Jews among Pagans and Christians in the Roman Empire*. London

Linder, A. (1987) *Jews in Roman Imperial Legislation*. Detroit

Lippold, A. (1973) 'Theodosius II', *RE* Suppl. XIII, 961–1044

MacCormack, S. G. (1981) *Art and Ceremony in Late Antiquity*. Berkeley

Maenchen-Helfen, O. J. (1973) *The World of the Huns*. Berkeley

Magdalino, P. and Macrides, R. (1988) 'The architecture of Ekphrasis: construction and context of Paul the Silentiary's poem on Hagia Sophia', *BMGS* 12: 47–82

Mainstone, R. (1988) *Hagia Sophia*. London

Mango, C. (1959) *The Brazen House. A Study of the Vestibule of the Imperial Palace of Constantinople*. Copenhagen

Mango, C. (1972) 'The church of Saints Sergius and Bacchus at Constantinople and the alleged tradition of octagonal palace churches' (= Mango, *Studies on Constantinople* XIII)

Mango, C. (1975) 'The church of Sts. Sergius and Bacchus once again' (= Mango, *Studies on Constantinople* XIV)

Mango, C. and Dagron, G. (eds.) (1995) *Constantinople and its Hinterland*. Aldershot

Markey, T. S. (1989) 'Germanic in the Mediterranean: Lombards, Vandals, and Visigoths', in Clover and Humphreys (eds.) (1989) 51–71

Mathisen, R. (1979) 'Resistance and reconciliation: Majorian and the Gallic aristocracy after the fall of Avitus', *Francia* 7: 597–627 (= Mathisen (1991) 167–98)

Mathisen, R. (1981) 'Avitus, Italy and the east in A.D. 455–456', *Byz.* 51: 232–47 (= Mathisen (1991) 137–52)

Mathisen, R. (1991) *Studies in the History, Literature and Society of Late Antiquity*. Amsterdam

Matthews, J. F. (1975) *Western Aristocracies and Imperial Court AD 364–425*. Oxford

Matthews, J. F. (1989) *The Roman Empire of Ammianus*. London and Baltimore

Max, G. E. (1979) 'Political intrigue during the reigns of the western Roman emperors Avitus and Majorian', *Historia* 28: 225–37

Mazzucchi, C. M. (1982) *Menae patricii cum Thoma referendario De scientia politica Dialogus*. Milan

Menghin, W. (1985) *Die Langobarden: Archäologie und Geschichte*. Stuttgart

Metcalf, D. M. (1969) *The Origins of the Anastasian Currency Reform*. Amsterdam

Millar, F. (1992) 'The Jews of the Graeco-Roman diaspora between paganism and Christianity, A.D. 312–438', in Lieu, North and Rajak (eds.) (1992) 97–123

Momigliano, A. (1955) 'Cassiodorus and the Italian culture of his time', *PBA* 41: 207–45

Momigliano, A. (1972) 'Popular religious beliefs and the late Roman historians', *SCH* 8: 1–18

Mommaerts, T. S. and Kelly, D. H. (1992) 'The Anicii of Gaul and Rome', in Drinkwater and Elton (eds.), *Fifth-Century Gaul* 111–21

Mommsen, T. (1901) 'Aetius', *Hermes* 76: 516–47

Moorhead, J. (1981) 'The last years of Theoderic', *Historia* 32: 106–20

Moorhead, J. (1983) 'Italian loyalties during Justinian's Gothic war', *Byz.* 53: 575–96

Moorhead, J. (1984) 'Theoderic, Zeno and Odovacer', *BZ* 77: 261–6

Moorhead, J. (1992a) *Theoderic in Italy*. Oxford

Moorhead, J. (1992b) *Victor of Vita: History of the Vandal Persecution*. Liverpool

Muhlberger, S. (1990) *The Fifth-Century Chroniclers*. Liverpool

Nelson, J. L. (1976) 'Symbols in context: rulers' inauguration rituals in Byzantium and the west in the early middle ages', *SCH* 13: 97–119

Obolensky, D. (1971) *The Byzantine Commonwealth*. London

O'Donnell, J. J. (1979) *Cassiodorus*. Berkeley and Los Angeles

O'Flynn, J. M. (1983) *Generalissimos of the Western Roman Empire*. Edmonton

Olajos, T. (1988) *Les sources de Théophylacte Simocatta historien*. Leiden

Olster, D. M. (1993) *The Politics of Usurpation in the Seventh Century: Rhetoric and Revolution in Byzantium*. Amsterdam

Orlandis, J. (1984) *Hispania y Zaragoza en la Antigüedad Tardía*. Saragossa

Orlandis, J. (1988) *Historia del reino visigodo Español*. Madrid

Orlandis, J. (1991) *La vida en España en tiempo de los Godos*. Madrid

Orlandis, J. (1992) *Semblanzas visigodas*. Madrid

Ostrogorsky, G. (1956) *History of the Byzantine State*. Oxford

Painter, K. (1991) 'The silver dish of Ardabur Aspar', in Herring *et al.* (1991) 1.73–80

Patterson, O. (1982) *Slavery and Social Death*. Cambridge, MA

Pérez Sánchez, D. (1989) *El ejército en la sociedad visigoda*. Salamanca

Pertusi, A. (1978) 'Giustiniano e la cultura del suo tempo', in Archi (ed.) (1978) 181–99

Pingree, D. (1976) 'Political horoscopes from the reign of Zeno', *DOP* 30: 133–50

Rabello, A. M. (1987) *Giustiniano, Ebrei e Samaritani, alla luce delle fonti storico-letterarie, ecclesiastiche e giuridiche*. Milan

Richards, J. (1980) *Consul of God*. London

Rodley, L. (1994) *Byzantine Art and Architecture: An Introduction*. Cambridge

Rodríguez Alonso, C. (ed.) (1975) *Las Historias de los Godos, Vándalos y Suevos de Isidoro de Sevilla*. León

Roueché, C. (1986) 'Theodosius II, the cities, and the date of the "Church History" of Sozomen', *JThS* 37: 130–2

Rousseau, P. (1979) 'The death of Boethius: the charge of *maleficium*', *Studi Medievali* 20: 871–89

Rubin, B. (1954) *Prokopios von Kaisareia*. Stuttgart (= art. Prokopios von Kaisareia, *RE* 23.1.273–599, 1959)

Rubin, B. (1960, 1995) *Das Zeitalter Iustinians* I, II (ed. C. Capizzi). Berlin

Saitta, B. (1983) *Studi Visigotici*. Catania

Schwartz, E. (1939) *Drei dogmatische Schriften Iustinians* (Abh. der Bayer. Akad. der Wiss., philosoph.-hist. Abt. 18). Munich

Scott, L. (1976) 'Aspar and the burden of barbarian heritage', *Byzantine Studies/Études byzantines* 3: 59–69

Scott, R. (1985) 'Malalas, the *Secret History* and Justinian's propaganda', *DOP* 39: 99–109

Scott, R. (1987) 'Justinian's coinage and Easter reforms and the date of the *Secret History*', *BMGS* 11: 215–21

Shahīd, I. (1989) *Byzantium and the Arabs in the Fifth Century*. Washington, DC

Shahīd, I. (1995) *Byzantium and the Arabs in the Sixth Century* I, parts 1 and 2. Washington, DC

Shaw, B. D. (1990) 'Bandit highlands and lowland peace: the mountains of Isauria-Cilicia', *JESHO* 33: 199–233, 237–70

Shepard, J. and Franklin, S. (eds.) (1992) *Byzantine Diplomacy*. Aldershot

Small, A. (ed.) (1987) *The Picts: A New Look at Old Problems*. Dundee

Smyth, A. P. (1972) 'The earliest Irish annals', *Proceedings of the Royal Irish Academy* 72C: 1–48

Smyth, A. P. (1984) *Warlords and Holy Men: Scotland AD 800–1000*. London

Stein, E. (1919) *Studien zur Geschichte des byzantinischen Reiches, vornehmlich unter den Kaisern Justinus II. und Tiberius Constantinus*. Stuttgart

Stein, E. (1959) *Histoire du Bas-Empire* I (2nd edn trans. J. R. Palanque from German 1st edn: *Geschichte des spätrömischen Reiches* I, Vienna 1928). Paris

Stein, F. (1991) *Alammanische Siedlung und Kultur: das Reihengräberfeld in Gammertingen*. Sigmaringen

Sundwall, J. (1915) *Weströmische Studien*. Berlin

Tardieu, M. (1990) *Les paysages reliques. Routes et haltes syriennes d'Isidore à Simplicius.* Paris

Thomas, C. (1994) *And Shall these Mute Stones Speak? Post-Roman Inscriptions in Western Britain.* Cardiff

Thompson, E. A. (1948) *A History of Attila and the Huns.* Oxford

Thompson, E. A. (1956) 'The settlement of barbarians in southern Gaul', *JRS* 46: 65–75 (= Thompson (1982) 23–37)

Thompson, E. A. (1969) *The Goths in Spain.* Oxford

Thompson, E. A. (1977) 'The Suevic kingdom of Galicia', *NMS* 21: 3–31 (= Thompson (1982) 161–87)

Thompson, E. A. (1982) *Romans and Barbarians: The Decline of the Western Empire.* Madison, WI

Thompson, E. A. (1985) *Who was Saint Patrick?* Woodbridge

Thompson, E. A. (1996) *The Huns.* Oxford (revised with an afterword by Peter Heather)

Twyman, B. L. (1970) 'Aetius and the aristocracy', *Historia* 19: 480–503

Van Dam, R. (1993) *Saints and their Miracles in Late Antique Gaul.* Princeton

Van de Vyver, M. (1936, 1937, 1938) 'La victoire contre les Alamans et la conversion de Clovis', *RBPh* 15: 859–914, 16: 35–94 and 17: 793–813

Vasiliev, A. A. (1950) *Justin the First.* Cambridge, MA

Wainwright, F. T. (ed.) (1955) *The Problem of the Picts.* London

van der Wal, N. and Stolte, B. H. (eds.) (1994) *Collectio Tripartita: Justinian on Religious and Ecclesiastical Affairs.* Groningen

Wallace-Hadrill, A. (1981) 'The emperor and his virtues', *Historia* 30: 298–323

Weber, R. J. (1989) 'Albinus: the living memory of a 5th-c. personality', *Historia* 38: 472–97

Werner, J. (1962) *Die Langobarden im Pannonien.* Munich

Whitby, Mary (1985) 'The occasion of Paul the Silentiary's *Ekphrasis* of S. Sophia', *CQ* 35: 215–28

Whitby, Michael (1985) 'The long walls of Constantinople', *Byz.* 55: 560–83

Whitby, Michael (1986a) 'Procopius and the development of Roman defences in upper Mesopotamia', in Freeman and Kennedy (eds.) (1986) 717–35

Whitby, Michael (1986b) 'Procopius' description of Dara (*Buildings* 2.1–3)', in Freeman and Kennedy (eds.) (1986) 737–83

Whitby, Michael (1992) 'From frontier to palace: the personal role of the emperor in diplomacy', in Shepard and Franklin (eds.) (1992) 295–303

Whitby, Michael (1994) 'The Persian king at war', in Dabrowa (ed.) (1994) 227–63

Whitby, Michael (1995) 'Recruitment in Roman armies from Justinian to Heraclius (*ca.* 565–615')', in Averil Cameron (ed.), *The Byzantine and Early Islamic Near East* III. *States, Resources and Armies* (Princeton) 61–124

Whitby, Michael and Whitby, Mary (1989) *Chronicon Paschale 284–628 AD* (Translated Texts for Historians 7). Liverpool

Whittaker, C. R. (1994) *Frontiers of the Roman Empire: A Social and Economic Study.* Baltimore

Whittow, M. (1990) 'Ruling the late Roman and early Byzantine city: a continuous history', *P&P* 129: 3–29

Wickham, C. (1981) *Early Medieval Italy, Central Power and Local Society 400–1000*. London

Wickham, C. (1984) 'The other transition. From the ancient world to feudalism', *P&P* 103: 3–36

Wickham, L. R. (1973) review of Frend, *Monophysite Movement, JThS* 24: 591–9

Wolfram, H. (1988) *History of the Goths* (English trans.). Berkeley

Wolfram, H. and Pohl, W. (eds.) (1990) *Typen der Ethnogenese unter besonderer Berücksichtigung der Bayern* (Denkschriften der Österreichischen Akademie der Wissenschaften, phil.-hist. Kl. 201). Vienna

Wolfram, H. and Schwarcz, A. (eds.) (1988) *Anerkennung und Integration: Zu den wirtschaftlichen Grundlagen der Völkerwanderungszeit (400–600)* (Denkschriften der österreichischen Akademie der Wissenschaften, phil.-hist. Kl. 201). Vienna

Wood, I. N. (1984) 'The end of Roman Britain: continental evidence and parallels', in Lapidge and Dumville (eds.) (1984) 1–25

Wood, I. N. (1985) 'Gregory of Tours and Clovis', *RBPh* 63: 249–72

Wood, I. N. (1990) 'Ethnicity and the ethnogenesis of the Burgundians', in Wolfram and Pohl (eds.) (1990) 53–69

Wormald, P., Bullough, D. and Collins, R. (eds.) (1983) *Ideal and Reality in Frankish and Anglo-Saxon Society*. Oxford

Wozniak, F. (1981) 'East Rome, Ravenna and western Illyricum 454–536 AD', *Historia* 30: 351–82

Young, F. (1983) *From Nicaea to Chalcedon*. London

Zecchini, G. (1983) *Aezio: l'ultima difesa dell'Occidente romano*. Rome

Zingale, L. M. (1994) *Nuovi Testi Epigrafi*. Turin (= Amelotti (ed.) (1972–94) IV)

Zöllner, E. (1970) *Geschichte der Franken, bis zur Mitte des 6. Jahrhunderts*. Munich

Zuckerman, C. (1994) 'L'empire d'Orient et les Huns: notes sur Priscus', *T&MByz* 12: 159–82

PART II: GOVERNMENT AND INSTITUTIONS (CHS. 6–11)

Albanese, B. (1991a) 'Sul programma legislativo esposto nel 429 da Theodosio II', in Albanese (1991b) 1669–87

Albanese, B. (1991b) *Scritti giuridici* II. Palermo

Alberti, A. (1933) *La Glossa Torinese e le altre glosse del ms. D III.13 della Biblioteca Nazionale Torino*. Turin

Alfieri, N. (1977) 'L'insediamento urbano sul litorale delle Marche', in Duval and Frézouls (eds.) (1977) 87–98

Alföldy, G. (1974) *Noricum*. London

Alföldy, G. (1987) 'Römisches Städtewesen auf der neukastilianischen Hochebene' (Abhandlungen Heidelberger Akad., phil.-hist. Kl.). Heidelberg

Allen, P. (1979) 'The "Justinianic" Plague', *Byz*. 49: 5–20

Amelotti, M. and Zingale, L. M. (1985) *Le costituzioni giustinianee nei papiri e nelle epigrafi*. 2nd edn. Milan

Anton, H. H. (1986) 'Verfassungsgeschichtliche Kontinuität und Wandlung von der Spätantike zum hohen Mittelalter: das Beispiel Triers', *Francia* 14: 1–25

Arangio-Ruiz, V. (ed.) (1935) '*Frammenti di Gaio*', in *Papiri greci e latini* (Pubblicazioni della Società Italiana per la ricerca dei Papiri greci e latini in Egitto XI 1187) 1–52. Florence

Arangio-Ruiz, V. (ed.) (1953) *'Definizioni e massime giuridiche'*, in *Papiri greci e latini* (Pubblicazioni della Società Italiana per la ricerca dei Papiri greci e latini in Egitto XIII 1348) 196–208. Florence

Archi, G. G. (1937) *L'Epitome Gai.* Milan

Ashburner, W. (1926) 'The Byzantine mutiny act', *JHS* 46: 80–109

Atsma, H. (ed.) (1976) *Spätantikes und fränkisches Gallien.* Munich

Ausbüttel, F. M. (1988) *Die Verwaltung der Städte und Provinzen im spätantiken Italien.* Frankfurt

Aussaresses, F. (1909) *L'Armée byzantine à la fin du VIème siècle d'après le Strategicon de l'empereur Maurice* (Bibliothèque des Universités du Midi 14). Bordeaux

Avramea, A. (1989) 'Les constructions profanes de l'évêque dans l'épigraphie grecque', *Actes XI Congr. Int. d'Arch. Chrét.* 1: 829–35. Rome

Bachrach, B. S. (1971) *Merovingian Military Organisation 481–751.* Minneapolis

Bagnall, R. (1985) 'Agricultural productivity and taxation in later Roman Egypt', *TAPA* 115: 289–308

Bagnall, R. S. and Worp, K. A. (1980) 'Papyrus documentation in Egypt from Constantine to Justinian', in R. Pintaudi (ed.), *Miscellanea Papyrologia* (Florence) 13–23

Bakhit, M. A. and Asfour, M. (eds.) (1986) *Proceedings of the Symposium on Bilad al-Sham During the Byzantine Period.* Amman

Baldovin, J. F. (1987) *The Urban Character of Christian Worship* (Orientalia Christiana Analecta 228). Rome

Balty, J. C. (1980) 'Notes sur l'habitat romain, byzantin et arabe d'Apamée: rapport de synthèse', in *Colloque Apamée de Syrie, Musées Royaux d'Art et Histoire* (Brussels) 471–501

Balty, J. C. (1989) 'Apamée au VIe siècle', in *Hommes et richesses* 1.79–96

Banaji, J. (1992) 'Rural Communities in the Late Empire, A.D. 300–700: Monetary and Economic Aspects' (Oxford D.Phil. thesis)

Barker, G. *et al.* (1985) *Cyrenaica in Antiquity* (BAR International Series 236). Oxford

Barnes, T. D. (1974) 'A law of Julian', *CPh* 69: 288–91

Barnish, S. J. B. (1985) 'The wealth of Iulianus Argentarius', *Byz.* 55: 5–38

Barnish, S. J. B. (1986) 'Taxation, land, and barbarian settlement in the western empire', *PBSR* 54: 170–95

Barnish, S. J. B. (1987) 'Pigs, plebeians and *potentes*', *PBSR* 55: 157–85

Barnish, S. J. B. (1988) 'Transformation and survival in the western senatorial aristocracy, c. A.D. 400–700', *PBSR* 56: 120–55

Barnish, S. J. B. (1989) 'The transformation of classical cities and the Pirenne debate', *JRA* 2: 385–400

Barnish, S. J. B. (1990) 'Maximian, Cassiodorus, Boethius, Theodahad', *NMS* 34: 17–31

Barnish, S. J. B. (1992) *Cassiodorus: Variae.* Liverpool

Barnwell, P. S. (1992) *Emperor, Prefects and Kings: The Roman West, 395–565.* London

Bartlett, R. (1986) *Trial by Fire and Water: The Medieval Judicial Ordeal.* Oxford

Bavand, B. (1989) 'Cadre de vie et habitat urbain en Italie centrale byzantine', *MEFR* 101–2: 465–532

Beck, H. G. (1966) 'Senat und Volk von Konstantinopel' (Sitzungsberichte, Bayerische Akademie der Wissenschaften, phil.-hist. Kl. 6). 10–22

Berger, A. (1958a) 'Leontios 6', *RE* suppl. 7: 373–5

Berger, A. (1958b) 'Leontios 7', *RE* suppl. 7: 375–6

Berger, A. (1988) *Untersuchungen zu den 'Patria Konstantinoupoleos'* (Poikila Byzantina 8). Bonn

von Bethmann-Hollweg, M. A. (1866) *Der Civilprozess des gemeinen Rechts III = Der römische Civilprozess III, Cognitiones*. Bonn

Beyerle, F. (1924) 'Über Normtypen und Erweiterungen der Lex Salica', *ZRG GA* 44: 216–61

Beyerle, F. (1954) 'Zur Textgestalt und Textgeschichte der Lex Burgundionum', *ZRG GA* 71: 23–54

Beyerle, F. (1961) 'Das legislative Werk Chilperichs I', *ZRG GA* 78: 1–38

Beyerle, F. (1962) *Leges Langobardorum 643–866*, 2nd edn. Witzenhausen

Beyerle, F. (1972) 'Die Malberg Glossen der Lex Salica', *ZRG GA* 89: 1–32

Bieler, L. (1963) *The Irish Penitentials*. Dublin

Binchy, D. A. (1956) 'Some Celtic legal terms', *Celtica* 3: 221–31

Binchy, D. A. (ed.) (1979) *Corpus Iuris Hibernici*. Dublin

Biondi, B. (1952–4) *Diritto romano cristiano*. Milan

Biraben, J.-N. (1989) 'Rapport: la peste du VIe siècle dans l'empire byzantin', in *Hommes et richesses* 1.121–5

Birks, P. and McLeod, G. (1987) *Justinian's Institutes*. Ithaca, NY

Blake, H. M., Potter, T. W. and Whitehouse, D. B. (eds.) (1978) *Papers in Italian Archaeology* 1. London

Blockley, R. C. (1969) 'Internal self-policing in the late Roman administration: some evidence from Ammianus Marcellinus', *Class. et Med.* 30: 403–19

Blockley, R. (1985) *The History of Menander the Guardsman*. Liverpool

Blockley, R. C. (1992) *East Roman Foreign Policy, Formation and Conduct from Diocletian to Anastasius*. Leeds

Bognetti, G. P. (1966–8a) *L'età Longobarda*. 4 vols. Milan

Bognetti, G. P. (1966–8b) 'L'editto di Rotari come espediente politico di una monarchia barbarica', in Bognetti (1966–8a) IV.115–35

Bognetti, G. P. (1966–8c) 'S. Maria Foris Portas di Castelseprio e la storia religiosa dei Longobardi', in Bognetti (1966–8a) II.13–683

Bossy, J. (ed.) (1983) *Disputes and Settlements: Law and Human Relations in the West*. Cambridge

Bowman, A. K. (1985) 'Landholding in the Hermopolite nome in the fourth century', *JRS* 75: 137–63

Bowman, A. and Woolf, G. (eds.) (1994) *Literacy and Power in the Roman World*. Cambridge

Brandes, W. (1989) *Die Städte Kleinasiens im 7. und 8. Jahrhundert*. Amsterdam

Brandt, H. (1988) *Zeitkritik in der Spätantike*. Munich

Brooks, A. D. (1986) 'A review of evidence of continuity in British towns in the 5th and 6th centuries', *OJA* 5 (i): 77–102

Brown, P. R. L. (1978) *The Making of Late Antiquity*. Cambridge, MA

Brown, P. R. L. (1992) *Power and Persuasion in Late Antiquity: Towards a Christian Empire*. Madison

Brühl, C.-R. (1975) *Palatium und Civitas. Studien zur Profantopographie spätantiker Civitates. 1. Gallien*. Cologne and Vienna

Brunner, H. (1906, 1928) *Deutsche Rechtsgeschichte*. 2nd edn. Berlin

Bruns, K. G. and Sachau, E. (ed. with German trans.) (1880) *Syrisch-Römisches Rechtsbuch aus dem fünften Jahrhundert.* Leipzig

Buchner, R. (1953) *Die Rechtsquellen,* Beiheft zu Wattenbach-Levison (1952) *Deutschlands Geschichtsquellen im Mittelalter: Vorzeit und Karolinger.* Weimar

Burgmann, L. (1986) 'Neue Zeugnisse der Digestensumme des Anonymos', in Simon (ed.) (1986) 101–16

Burnham, B. C. and Wacher, J. (1990) *The Small Towns of Roman Britain.* London

Bury, J. B. (1910) 'Magistri scriniorum, ἀντιγραφῆς and ῥεφερενδάριοι', *HSCP* 21: 23–9

Bury, J. B. (1911) *The Imperial Administrative System in the Ninth Century, with a revised text of the Kleterologion of Philotheos.* London

Bury, J. B. (1919) 'Justa Grata Honoria', *JRS* 9: 1–13

Butler, R. M. (1959) 'Late Roman town walls in Gaul', *AJ* 116: 25–50

Caimi, J. (1981) 'Iohannis Lydi *de Magistratibus* III.70. Note esegetiche e spunti in tema di fiscalità e legislazione protobizantine', *RSBS* 1: 317–61

Cameron, Alan (1973) *Porphyrius the Charioteer.* Oxford

Cameron, Alan (1978) 'The House of Anastasius', *GRBS* 19: 259–76 (= Alan Cameron, *Literature and Society* XIV)

Cameron, Alan (1981) 'The empress and the poet', *YCS* 27: 217–89 (= Alan Cameron, *Literature and Society* III)

Cameron, Alan, and Cameron, Averil (1966) 'The *Cycle* of Agathias', *JHS* 86: 6–25

Cameron, Alan, and Long, J. (1993) *Barbarians and Politics at the Court of Arcadius.* Berkeley

Cameron, Averil (1967) 'Notes on the Sophiae, the Sophianae and the harbour of Sophia', *Byz.* 37: 11–20 (= Averil Cameron (1981) XIII)

Cameron, Averil (1978) 'The Theotokos in sixth-century Constantinople. A city finds its symbol', *JTS* 29: 79–108 (= Averil Cameron (1981) XVI)

Cameron, Averil (1980) 'The artistic patronage of Justin II', *Byz.* 50: 62–84 (= Averil Cameron (1981) XII)

Cameron, Averil (1981) *Continuity and Change in Sixth-Century Byzantium.* London

Cameron, Averil (1982) 'Byzantine Africa: the literary evidence', in Humphrey (ed.) (1982) 26–92 (= Averil Cameron, *Changing Cultures* VII)

Cameron, Averil (ed.) (1995) *The Byzantine and Early Islamic Near East* III, *States, Resources, Armies.* Princeton

Campbell, J. B. (1984) *The Emperor and the Roman Army 31 BC–AD 235.* Oxford

Canivet, P. and Rey-Coquais, J.-P. (eds.) (1992) *La Syrie de Byzance à l'Islam, VIIe and VIIIe siècles.* Inst. Franç. de Damas. Damascus

Capizzi, C. (1969) *L'Imperatore Anastasio I.* Rome

Carrié, J.-M. (1986) 'L'esercito: trasformazioni funzionali ed economie locali', in Giardina (ed.), *Società romana* 449–88, 760–71

Carrié, J.-M. (1995) 'L'état à la recherche de nouveaux modes de financement des armées (Rome et Byzance, IVe–VIIIe siècles)', in Averil Cameron (ed.) (1995) 27–60

Carver, M. (ed.) (1992) *The Age of Sutton Hoo.* Woodbridge

Cavallo, G. (1984) 'Libri e continuità della cultura antica in età barbarica', in *Magistra barbaritas. I barbari in Italia* (Milan) 603–62

Cesa, M. (1988) *Ennodio: Vita del beatissimo Epifanio vescovo della chiesa pavese* (Bibliotheca di Athenaeum 6). Como

Charanis, P. (1955) 'The significance of coins as evidence for the history of Athens and Corinth in the seventh and eighth centuries', *Historia* 4: 163–7

Charanis, P. (1966) 'Observations on the demography of the Byzantine empire', *Thirteenth International Congress of Byzantine Studies, Main Papers* (Oxford) 1–19 (= Charanis (1972b) 1)

Charanis, P. (1972a) 'The Armenians in the Byzantine empire', *Byzslavica* 22: 196–240 (= Charanis (1972b) v)

Charanis, P. (1972b) *Studies on the Demography of the Byzantine Empire.* London

Charles-Edwards, T. M. (1989) *The Welsh Laws.* Cardiff

Charles-Edwards, T. M. and Kelly, F. (eds.) (1983) *Bechbretha.* Dublin

Chastagnol, A. (1963) 'L'administration du diocèse italien au Bas-Empire', *Historia* 12: 348–79

Chastagnol, A. (1978) *L'album municipal de Timgad.* Bonn

Chastagnol, A. (1979) 'L'empereur Julien et les avocats de Numidie', *Antiquités Africaines* 14: 220–35

Chauvot, A. (1986) *Procope de Gaza, Priscien de Caesarée, panégyriques de l'empereur Anastase I.* Bonn

Chauvot, A. (1987) 'Curiales et paysans en orient à la fin du Ve et au debut du VIe siècle: note sur l'institution du vindex', in Frézouls (ed.) (1987) 271–81

Chrysos, E. (1971) 'Die angebliche Abschaffung der städtischen Kurien durch Kaiser Anastasius', *Byz.* 3: 97–8

Chrysos, E. K. and Schwarcz, A. (eds.) (1989) *Das Reich und die Barbaren* (Veröffentlichungen des Instituts für Österreichische Geschichtsforschung 29). Vienna

Classen, P. (ed.) (1977a) *Recht und Schrift im Mittelalter* (Vorträge und Forschungen 23). Sigmaringen

Classen, P. (1977b) 'Fortleben und Wandel spätrömischen Urkundenwesens im frühen Mittelalter', in Classen (ed.) (1977a) 13–54

Classen, P. (1977c) *Kaiserreskript und Königsurkunde.* 2nd edn. Thessalonica

Classen, P. and Scheibert, P. (eds.) (1964) *Festschrift Percy Ernst Schramm.* Wiesbaden

Claude, D. (1960) *Topographie und Verfassung der Städte Bourges und Poitiers bis in das 11 Jahrhundert* (Historische Studien 380). Lübeck

Claude, D. (1964) 'Untersuchungen zum frühfränkischen Comitat', *ZRG GA* 81: 1–79

Claude, D. (1969) *Die byzantinische Stadt im 6 Jahrhundert.* Munich

Clauss, M. (1980) *Der magister officiorum in der Spätantike (4.–6. Jh.).* Munich

Clauss, M. (1984) 'Urbicius "praepositus imperii"', in *Sodalitas. Scritti in onore di Antonio Guarino III* (Naples) 1245–57

Clover, F. M. (1982) 'Carthage and the Vandals', in Humphrey (ed.) (1982) 1–22

Collinet, P. (1925) *Histoire de l'école de droit de Beyrouth.* Paris

Collins, R. (1983) *Early Medieval Spain 400–1000.* London

Conrad, L. I. (1986) 'The plague in Bilad al-Sham in pre-Islamic times', in Bakhit and Asfour (eds.) (1986) II.143–63

Conrat, M. (1903) *Breviarium Alaricianum.* Leipzig

Coster, C. H. (1935) *The iudicium quinquevirale.* Cambridge, MA

Cotton, H. M., Cockle, W. H. and Millar, F. G. B. (1995) 'The papyrology of the Roman Near East: a survey', *JRS* 85: 214–35

Courtois, C. *et al.* (eds.) (1952) *Tablettes Albertini. Actes privés de l'époque Vandale.* Paris

Cracco Ruggini, L. (1961) *Economia e società nell'Italia annonaria.* Milan

Cracco Ruggini, L. (1971) 'Le associazioni professionali nel mondo romano bizantino', *Settimane di studi* 18: 59–193

Crawford, J. S. (1990) *Byzantine Shops at Sardis.* Cambridge, MA

Crook, J. (1995) *Legal Advocacy in the Roman World.* London

Cüppers, H. (1977) 'Die Stadt Trier und verschiedene Phasen ihres Ausbaues', in Duval and Frézouls (eds.) (1977) 223–8

Dagron, G. (1969) 'Aux origines de la civilisation byzantine: langue de culture et langue d'état', *RH* 241: 23–56

Dagron, G. (1977) 'Le christianisme dans la ville byzantine', *DOP* 31: 3–25 (= Dagron (1984b) IX)

Dagron, G. (1978) *Vie et miracles de Saint Thècle.* Brussels

Dagron, G. (1979) 'Entre village et cité: la bourgade rurale des IVe–VIIe siècles en Orient', *Koinonia* 3: 29–52 (= Dagron (1984b) VIII)

Dagron, G. (1980) 'Two documents concerning mid-sixth century Mopsuestia', in Laiou-Thomadakis (ed.) (1980) 19–30 (= Dagron (1984b) VI)

Dagron, G. (1984a) 'Les villes dans l'Illyricum protobyzantin', in *Villes et peuplement dans l'Illyricum protobyzantin* (1984). (Collection de l'École Française de Rome 77) (Paris) 1–19

Dagron, G. (1984b) *La romanité chrétienne en Orient.* London

Dagron, G. (1989) 'Vie religieuse à Constantinople', *Act. XI Cong. Int. d'Arch. Chrét.* (Rome) II.1069–85

Dagron, G. and Feissel, D. (1987) *Inscriptions de Cilicie.* Paris

Daniel, R. W. (1996) 'The Petra papyri in historical perspective: the dating formulas', ACOR *Newsletter* 8.2 (Winter): 1–4

Daube, D. (1947) *Studies in Biblical Law.* Cambridge

Daube, D. (1956) *Forms of Roman Legislation.* Oxford

Dauphin, C. (1987) 'Les Komai de Palestine', *Proche Orient Chrétien* 3: 251–67

Dauphin, C. M. and Schonfield, J. J. (1983) 'Settlements of the Roman and Byzantine periods on the Golan Heights: preliminary report on the survey 1979–81', *Israel Exploration Journal* 33: 189–206

Davies, W. (1982) 'The Latin charter tradition in western Britain, Brittany and Ireland in the early medieval period', in Whitelock, McKitterick and Dumville (eds.) (1982) 258–80

Davies, W. and Fouracre, P. (eds.) (1986) *The Settlement of Disputes in Early Medieval Europe.* Cambridge

Dazert, H. (1986) *Ergänzungsabgaben und ausserordentliche Lasten im römischen Reich im 4. und frühen 5. Jh. n. Chr.* Freiburg im Breisgau

Declareuil, J. (1910) 'Les comtes de la cité', *Rev. Hist. du Droit Français et Étranger* 34: 794–836

Deichmann, F. W. (1976–89) *Ravenna: Hauptstadt des spätantiken Abendlandes* II.2–3. Wiesbaden and Stuttgart

Delmaire, R. (1989) *Largesses Sacrées et Res Privata: l'aerarium impérial et son administration du IVe au VIe siècle.* Rome

Delmaire, R. (1995) *Les institutions du Bas-Empire romain de Constantin à Justinien. I. Les institutions civiles palatines.* Paris

Demandt, A. (1970) 'Magister militum', *RE* suppl. 12: 553–790

Demandt, A. (1986) 'Der Kelch von Ardabur und Arethusa', *DOP* 40: 113–17

Demandt, A. (1989) *Die spätantike: römische Geschichte von Diocletian bis Justinian, 284–565 n. Chr.* Handbuch der Altertumswissenschaft 3, 6. Munich

Demangel, R. (1949) *Contribution à la topographie de l'Hebdomon.* Paris

Dentzer, J.-M. (1985) *Le Hauran.* I–II. Paris

Dévréesse, R. (1945) *Le patriarcat d'Antioche depuis la paix de l'église jusqu'à la conquête arabe.* Paris

Dhondt, J. (1957) 'L'essor urbain entre Meuse et mer du Nord à l'époque mérovingienne', *Studi in onore di A. Sapori* (Milan) 1.55–78

Dilcher, G. (1964) 'Bischof und Stadtverfassung in Oberitalien', *ZRG GA* 81: 225–66

Dixon, P. (1992) 'The cities are not populated as once they were', in Rich (ed.) (1992) 145–60

Dolezalek, G. (1985) *Repertorium manuscriptorum veterum Codicis Iustiniani.* Frankfurt am Main

Dölger, F. J. (1959) 'Die frühbyzantinisch und byzantinisch beeinflusste Stadt', *Atti del 3 congresso internazionale di studi sull'alto medioevo* (Spoleto) 66–100

Doncel-Voûte, P. (1988) *Les pavements des églises byzantines de Syrie et du Liban.* Louvain

Donner, F. (1981) *The Early Islamic Conquests.* Princeton

d'Ors, A. (1960) *El Código de Eurico: Estudios Visigotices* II, Cuadernos del Instituto Juridico Español 12. Rome and Madrid

Doyle, W. (1996) *Venality: The Sale of Offices in Eighteenth-Century France.* Oxford

Drijvers, H. J. W. (1992) 'The Gospel of the Twelve Apostles: a Syriac apocalypse from the early Islamic period', in Averil Cameron, and L. I. Conrad (eds.), *The Byzantine and Early Islamic Near East* I: *Problems in the Literary Source Material* (Princeton) 189–213

Duchesne, L. (1907) *Fastes épiscopaux de l'ancienne Gaule.* Paris

Dumville, D. N. (1984) 'On the dating of the Breton lawcodes', *Études Celtiques* 21: 207–21

Duncan-Jones, R. P. (1978) 'Pay and numbers in Diocletian's army', *Chiron* 8: 541–60

Dunn, A. (1993) 'The Kommerkiarios, Apotheke, Dromos, Vardarios and the west', *BMGS* 17: 3–24

Durliat, J. (1981) 'Les grands propriétaires africaines et l'état byzantin (533–709)', *Cahiers de Tunisie* 29: 517–31

Durliat, J. (1982) 'Les attributions civiles des évêques byzantines: l'exemple du diocèse d'Afrique 533–709', *JÖB* 32.2: 73–84

Durliat, J. (1984) 'L'administration civile du diocèse byzantin d'Afrique (533–703)', *RSBS* 4: 149–78

Durliat, J. (1989) 'La peste du VIᵉ siècle. Pour un nouvel examen des sources byzantines', in *Hommes et richesses* 1.107–19

Durliat, J. (1990a) *De la ville antique à la ville Byzantine: le problème des subsistances.* Rome

Durliat, J. (1990b) *Les finances publiques de Dioclétien aux Carolingiens (284–889).* Sigmaringen

Duval, N. (1989) 'L'évêque et la cathédrale en Afrique du Nord', *Actes XI Cong. Int. d'Arch. Chrét.* (Rome) 1.354–403

Duval, N. and Caillet, J. P. (1992) *Basiliques chrétiennes de l'Algérie.* Paris

Duval, P.-M. (1959) 'Une enquête sur les enceintes gauloises', *Gallia* 17: 37–62

Duval, P.-M. and Frézouls, E. (eds.) (1977) *Thèmes de recherches sur les villes antiques d'occident*. Paris

Eck, W. (1978) 'Der Einfluss der Konstantinischen Wende auf die Auswahl der Bischöfe im 4 und 5 Jahrhundert', *Chiron* 8: 561–85

Eck, W. (1983) 'Der Episkopat im spätantiken Africa', *HZ* 236: 265–95

Eck, W. (1989) *Religion und Gesellschaft in der römischen Kaiserzeit*. Cologne/Vienna

Eck, W. and Galsterer, H. (1991) *Die Stadt in Oberitalien und in den nordwestlichen Provinzen des römischen Reiches*. Mainz

Eckhardt, K. A. (1954) *Pactus Legis Salicae I, Einführung und 80-Titel Text*. Germanenrechte, NF. Göttingen

Eckhardt, K. A. (1956) *Pactus Legis Salicae II.2, Kapitularien und 70 Titel-Text*. Germanenrechte, NF. Göttingen

Eckhardt, K. A. (1962) *Pactus Legis Salicae. MGH* Legum Sectio 1, iv.1. Hanover

Eckhardt, W. A. (1967) 'Die *Decretio Childeberti* und ihre Überlieferung', *ZRG GA*, 84: 1–71

Elton, H. (1992) 'Defence in fifth-century Gaul', in Drinkwater and Elton (eds.), *Fifth-Century Gaul* 167–76

Ennen, E. (1975) *Die europäische Stadt des Mittelalters*. Göttingen

Ensslin, W. (1942) 'Palatini', *RE* xviii, 1: 2529–60

Ensslin, W. (1961) 'Vindex', *RE* ix, a1: 25–7

Ersch, J. S. and Gruber, J. G. (eds.) (1868) *Allgemeine Encyklopädie der Wissenschaften und der Künste* 1.86

Evenari, M. (1971) *The Negev*. Cambridge, MA

Ewig, E. (1958) 'Volkstum und Volksbewusstsein im Frankenreich des 7. Jahrhunderts', *Settimane di Studi* 5: 609–14 (= Ewig (1976) 1.246–9)

Ewig, E. (1969) 'Die Stellung des Ribuariens in der Verfassungsgeschichte des Merowingerreiches' (Gesellschaft für rheinische Geschichtskunde. Vorträge 18) (= Atsma (ed.) (1976) 450–71)

Ewig, E. (1976) *Spätantikes und fränkisches Gallien*. 2 vols. Munich

Ewig, E. (1988) *Die Merowinger und das Frankenreich*. Stuttgart

Falchi, G. L. (1989) *Sulla codificazione del diritto romano nel V e VI secolo*. Rome

Feissel, D. (1989) 'L'évêque, titres et fonctions d'après les inscriptions jusqu'au VIIe siècle', *Actes XI Cong. Int. d'Arch. Chrét.* (Rome) 1.801–28

Feissel, D. and Kaygusuz, I. (1985) 'Un mandement impérial du VIe siècle dans une inscription d'Hadrianoupolis d'Honoriade', *T&MByz* 9: 397–419

Fentress, E. (1988) 'Sétif, les thermes du Ve siècle', in Mastino (ed.) (1988) 320–37

Ferrill, A. (1986) *The Fall of the Roman Empire: The Military Explanation*. London

Ferrini, C. (ed.) (1884–97) *Institutionum graeca paraphrasis Theophilo antecessori vulgo tributa*. Berlin

Ferrini, C. (1929) 'Gli estratti di Giuliano Ascalonita', in Ferrini, *Opere* 1 (Milan) 443–52

Festugière, A.-J. (1959) *Antioche païenne et chrétienne: Libanius, Chrysostome et les moines de Syrie*. Paris

Février, P. A. (1979) 'Permanence et héritage de l'antiquité dans la topographie des villes de l'occident durant le haut moyen âge', *Settimane di Studi* 21: 41–138

Février, P. A. *et al.* (eds.) (1980) *La ville antique des origines au IXe siècle* (Histoire de la France urbaine (ed. G. Duby) 1). Paris

Fischer, H. T. and Riekhoff-Pauli, S. (1982) *Von den Römern zu den Bajuvaren.* Munich

Fixot, M. (1980) 'Les villes du VIIe au IXe siècle', in Février *et al.* (eds.) (1980) 497–62

Flemming, J. and Hoffmann, G. (1917) *Akten der ephesinischen Synode vom Jahre 449* (Abhandlungen der königlichen Gesellschaft der Wissenschaften Göttingen, phil.-hist. Kl. 15.1)

Fleuriot, L. (1971) 'Un fragment en latin de très anciennes lois bretonnes armoricaines du VIe siècle', *Annales de Bretagne* 78: 601–60

Fontaine, J. (1959) *Isidore de Seville et la culture classique dans l'Espagne wisigothique.* Paris

Forsyth, G. H. and Weitzmann, K. (1966) *The Monastery of Saint Catherine at Mount Sinai.* Ann Arbor

Foss, C. (1975) 'The Persians in Asia Minor and the end of antiquity', *EHR* 90: 721–47 (= Foss (1990) I)

Foss, C. (1976) *Byzantine and Turkish Sardis.* Cambridge, MA

Foss, C. (1977a) 'Archaeology and the "twenty cities of Asia"', *AJA* 81: 469–86 (= Foss (1990) V)

Foss, C. (1977b) 'Late antique and Byzantine Ankara', *DOP* 31: 27–87 (= Foss (1990) VI)

Foss, C. (1977c) 'Attius Philippus and the walls of Side', *ZPE* 26: 172–80 (= Foss (1990) VIII)

Foss, C. (1979) *Ephesus after Antiquity: A Late Antique, Byzantine and Turkish City.* Cambridge

Foss, C. (1990) *History and Archaeology of Byzantine Asia Minor.* Aldershot

Fotiou, A. (1988) 'Recruitment shortages in sixth-century Byzantium', *Byz.* 58: 65–77

Frank, R. I. (1969) *Scholae Palatinae: The Palace Guards of the Later Roman Empire* (Papers and Monographs of the American Academy in Rome 23). Rome

Frank, T. (ed.) (1933–40) *An Economic Survey of Ancient Rome.* 5 vols. Baltimore

Frere, S. S. (1977) 'Verulamium and Canterbury', in Duval and Frézouls (eds.) (1977) 189–95

Frézouls, E. (ed.) (1987) *Sociétés urbaines, sociétés rurales dans l'Asie mineure et la Syrie hellénistique et romaine.* Strasbourg

Frézouls, E. (1988) *Les villes antiques de la France* II. Strasbourg

Gagé, J. (1933) 'Σταυρὸς νικοποιός. La victoire impériale dans l'Empire chrétien', *Revue d'histoire et de philosophie religieuses* 13: 370–400

Ganshof, F. L. (1961) *Was waren die Kapitularien?* Weimar

Garnsey, P., Hopkins, K. and Whittaker, C. R. (eds.) (1983) *Trade in the Ancient Economy.* London

Gascou, J. (1972) 'La détention collégiale de l'autorité pagarchique dans l'Égypte byzantine', *Byz.* 43: 60–72

Gascou, J. (1976a) 'L'institution des Bucellaires', *BIFAO* 72: 143–56

Gascou, J. (1976b) 'Les monastères pachomiens et l'état byzantin', *BIFAO* 76: 157–8

Gascou, J. (1976c) 'Les institutions de l'hippodrome en Égypte byzantine', *BIFAO* 76: 185–212

Gascou, J. (1985) 'Les grands domaines, la cité et l'état en Égypte byzantine', *T&MByz* 9: 1–90

Gascou, J. (1987) 'Le cadastre d'Aphrodito', *T&MByz* 10: 103–48

Gascou, J. (1989) 'Le tableau budgétaire d'Antaeopolis', in *Hommes et richesses* 1.279–313

Gascou, J. (1990) 'Remarques critiques sur la table budgétaire d'Antaeopolis', *ZPE* 82: 97–101

Gaudemet, J. (1958) *L'Église dans l'empire romain, IVe–Ve siècles*. Paris

Gaudemet, J. (1979a) *La formation du droit séculier et du droit de l'église aux IVe et Ve siècles*. 2nd edn. Paris

Gaudemet, J. (1979b) 'Jus et leges', in Gaudemet, *Études de droit romain* I (Camerino) 439–70

Geremek, H. (1981) 'Les *politeuomenoi* égyptiens sont-ils identiques aux *bouleutai?*', *Anagenesis* 1: 231–47

Geremek, H. (1990) 'Sur la question des *boulai* dans les villes égyptiennes au Ve–VIIe siècles', *JJP* 20: 47–54

Giardina, A. (1977) *Aspetti della Burocrazia nel Basso Impero*. Rome

Goffart, W. (1970) 'Did Julian combat venal suffragium? A note on *CTh* 2.29.1', *CPh* 65: 145–51

Goffart, W. (1982) 'Old and new in Merovingian taxation', *P&P* 96: 3–21

Goffart, W. (1989) *Rome's Fall and After*. London

Goodchild, R. (1979) *Libyan Studies* (ed. J. Reynolds). London

Gorges, J.-G. (1979) *Les villas hispano-romaines*. Paris

Greatrex, G. (1996) 'Stephanus, the father of Procopius?', *Medieval Prosopography* 17: 125–45

Gregory, T. E. (1979) *Vox Populi: Popular Opinion and Violence in the Religious Controversies of the 5th Century A.D.* Columbus, OH

Grierson, P. and Blackburn, M. (1986) *Medieval European Coinage* I, *The Early Middle Ages (5th-10th Centuries)*. Cambridge

Grosse, R. (1920) *Römische Militärgeschichte von Gallienus bis zum Beginn der byzantinischen Themenverfassung*. Berlin

Grünewald, M. E. G. (1974) *Spätantike Herrschaftsvillen in den nordwestlichen Provinzen des römischen Reiches*. Vienna

Gui, I., Duval, N. and Caillet, J.-P. (1992) *Basiliques chrétiennes d'Afrique du Nord, pt. I, Inventaire de l'Algérie* (Études Augustiniennes: Antiquités 129). Paris

Guilland, R. (1969) *Études de topographie de Constantinople byzantin* (Berliner byzantinistische Arbeiten 37). Berlin

Guilland, R. (1971) 'Questeur', *Byz.* 41: 78–104

Guillou, A. (1980) 'Transformations des structures socio-économiques dans le monde byzantin du VIe au VIIe siècle', *Zbornik Radova* 19: 72–8

von Halban, A. (1899) *Das römische Recht in den germanischen Volksstaaten* II. Breslau

Haldon, J. F. (1979) *Recruitment and Conscription in the Byzantine Army c. 550–950: A Study on the stratiotika ktemata* (Sitzungsberichte der Österreichischen Akad. der Wissens., phil.-hist. Kl. 357). Vienna

Haldon, J. F. (1984) *Byzantine Praetorians*. Bonn

Haldon, J. F. (1986) 'Ideology and social change in the seventh century: military discontent as a barometer', *Klio* 68: 139–90

Hänel, G. (ed.) (1849) *Lex Romana Visigothorum*. Leipzig

Hänel, G. (1857) *Corpus Legum*. Leipzig

Hänel, G. (ed.) (1873) *Iuliani Epitome Latina Novellarum Iustiniani*. Leipzig

Hannestad, K. (1961) 'Les forces militaires d'après la guerre gothique de Procope', *Class. et Med.* 21: 136–83

Hardy, E. R. (1968) 'The Egyptian policy of Justinian', *DOP* 22: 23–40

Harries, J. (1988) 'The Roman imperial quaestor from Constantine to Theodosius II', *JRS* 78: 148–72

Harries, J. (1992a) 'Christianity and the city in late Roman Gaul', in Rich (ed.) (1992) 77–98

Harries, J. (1992b) 'Sidonius Apollinaris, Rome and the barbarians: a climate of treason?', in Drinkwater and Elton (eds.), *Fifth-Century Gaul* 298–308

Harries, J. (1994a) '*Pius princeps*: Theodosius II and fifth-century Constantinople', in Magdalino (ed.), *New Constantines* 35–44

Harries, J. (1994b) *Sidonius Apollinaris and the Fall of Rome, AD 407–485*. Oxford

Harries, J. and Wood, I. (eds.) (1993) *The Theodosian Code*. London

Harris, W. V. (1989) *Ancient Literacy*. Cambridge, MA

Harrison, R. M. (1979) 'Nouvelles découvertes romaines tardives et paléobyzantines en Lycie', *CRAI* 229–39

Harrison, R. M., *et al.* (1986) *Excavations at Saraçhane in Istanbul* 1. Princeton

Hassall, M. and Ireland, R. (eds.) (1979) *The Anonymus de Rebus Bellicis* (BAR International Series 63). Oxford

Heather, P. (1994) 'New men for new Constantines? Creating an imperial élite in the eastern Mediterranean', in Magdalino (ed.), *New Constantines* 11–33

Heather, P. (1995) 'Theoderic as war-leader', *EME* 4: 145–73

Heidenheimer, A. J., Johnstone, M. and Levine, V. T. (eds.) (1979) *Political Corruption: A Handbook*. New Brunswick

Heimbach, C. W. E. (1868) 'Griechisch-römisches Recht 1 (534–867) 2: Geschichte der Rechtswissenschaft', in Ersch and Gruber (eds.) (1868) 223–98

Heimbach, G. E. (ed.) (1846–51) *Authenticum. Novellarum constitutionum Iustiniani versio vulgata*. Leipzig

Heinzelmann, M. (1976) *Bischofsherrshaft in Gallien*. Munich

Hendy, M. F. (1972) 'Aspects of coin production and fiscal administration in the late Roman and early Byzantine period', *NC* ser. 7, 12: 117–39

Hendy, M. F. (1988) 'From public to private: the western barbarian coinages as a mirror of the disintegration of late Roman state structures', *Viator* 19: 29–78

Hirschfeld, Y. (1992) *The Judaean Desert Monasteries in the Byzantine Period*. New Haven

Hobley, B. (1986) *Roman and Saxon London: A Reappraisal*. London

Hodges, R. and Whitehouse, D. (1983) *Mohammed, Charlemagne and the Origins of Europe*. London

Hoffmann, D. (1969) *Das spätrömische Bewegungsheer und die Notitia Dignitatum*. Düsseldorf

Hohlfelder, R. L. (ed.) (1982) *City, Town and Countryside in the Early Byzantine Era*. New York

Holum, K. (1988) *King Herod's Dream: Caesarea on the Sea*. New York

Holum, K. (1995) 'Inscriptions from the imperial revenue office of Byzantine Caesarea Palestinae', in J. H. Humphrey (ed.) *The Roman and Byzantine Near East: Some Recent Archaeological Research* (*JRA* Supplementary Series 14) (Ann Arbor) 333–45

Holum, K. and Vikan, G. (1979) 'The Trier Ivory, Adventus ceremonial and the relics of St. Stephen', *DOP* 33: 113–33

Honigmann, E. (1951) *Évêques et évêchés monophysites d'Asie antérieure au VIe siècle* (*CSCO* 127 subsid. 17). Louvain

Honoré, T. (1978) *Tribonian.* London

Honoré, T. (1994) *Emperors and Lawyers.* 2nd edn. Oxford

Honoré, T. (1998) *Law in the Crisis of Empire, 379–455 A.D.* Oxford

Hopkins, K. (1978) *Conquerors and Slaves.* Cambridge

Horn, G. (1987) *Die Römer in Nordrheinwestfalen.* Stuttgart

Howard-Johnston, J. D. (1995) 'The two great powers in late antiquity: a comparison', in Averil Cameron (ed.) (1995) 157–226

Humphrey, J. H. (1980) 'Vandal and Byzantine Carthage', in Pedley (ed.) (1980) 85–120

Humphrey, J. H. (ed.) (1982) *Excavations at Carthage 1978 conducted by the University of Michigan.* VII. Ann Arbor

Hunger, H. (1978) *Die hochsprachliche profane Literatur der Byzantiner* II. Munich

Hunt, D. (1993) 'Christianising the Roman empire: the evidence of the Code', in Harries and Wood (eds.) (1993) 143–58

Huschke, P. E., *et al.* (eds.) (1927) *Iurisprudentiae anteiustinianae reliquiae* II. 2. 6th edn. Leipzig

Huxley, G. L. (1977) 'The second dark age of the Peloponnese', *Lakonikai Spoudai* 3: 84–110

Jaeger, H. (1960) 'Justinien et l'episcopalis audientia' *Nouv. Rev. Hist. Droit Franç. et Étr.*, 4 sér. 38: 214–62

James, E. (1982) *The Origins of France: From Clovis to the Capetians 500–1000.* London

James, E. (1983) '*Beati pacifici*: bishops and the law in sixth-century Gaul', in Bossy (ed.) (1983) 25–46

James, E. (1988) *The Franks.* Oxford

Janin, R. (1964) *Constantinople byzantine.* 2nd edn. Paris

Jenkins, D. (1986) *The Law of Hywel Dda: Law Texts from Medieval Wales.* Landysul

Johnson, A. C. and West, L. C. (1949) *Byzantine Egypt: Economic Studies.* Princeton

Johnson, S. (1983) *Late Roman Fortifications.* London

Jolowicz, H. F. and Nicholas, B. (1972) *Historical Introduction to the Study of Roman Law.* 3rd edn. Cambridge

Jones, A. H. M. (1940) *The Greek City from Alexander to Justinian.* Oxford

Jones, A. H. M. (1960) 'Church finance in the fifth and sixth centuries', *JTS* 11: 84–94

Jones, A. H. M., Grierson, P. and Crook, J. A. (1957) 'The authenticity of the "Testamentum S. Remigii"', *RBPh* 35: 356–73

Kaegi, W. (1981) *Byzantine Military Unrest, 471–813.* Amsterdam

Kaegi, W. (1992) *Byzantium and the Early Islamic Conquests.* Cambridge

Kaiser, R. (1979) 'Steuer und Zoll in der Merowingerzeit', *Francia* 7: 1–18

Kaiser, W. (1991) 'Digestenentstehung und Digestenüberlieferung', *ZRG RA* 108: 330–50

Kaplan, M. (1976) *Les propriétés de la Couronne et de l'Église dans l'empire byzantin (V^e–VIe siècles).* Paris

Kaser, M. (1967) 'Vulgarrecht', *RE* vol. IX.A. 2: 1283–1304

Kaser, M. (1975) *Das römische Privatrecht* II. 2nd edn. Munich

Kaser, M. and Hackl, K. (1996) *Das römische Zivilprozessrecht.* 2nd edn. Munich

Kaser, M. and Schwartz, F. (eds.) (1956) *Die Interpretatio zu den Paulussentenzen.* Cologne

Kaufhold, H. (1966) 'Über einige Handschriften der Versionen R I, R II und R III des syrisch-römischen Rechtsbuches', *ZRG RA* 83: 350–57

Kazhdan, H. A. P. (ed.) (1991) *Oxford Dictionary of Byzantium.* Oxford

Keay, S. J. (1988) *Roman Spain.* London

Keay, S. J. (1991) 'New light on Tarraco', *JRA* 4: 383–94

Keenan, J. G. (1990) 'Evidence for the Byzantine army in the Syene papyri', *BASP* 27: 139–50

Kelly, C. (1994) 'Later Roman bureaucracy: going through the files', in Bowman and Woolf (eds.) (1994) 161–76

Kelly, F. (1988) *A Guide to Early Irish Law.* Dublin

Kempf, K. (1964) 'Untersuchungen am Trierer Dom 1961–63', *Germania* 42: 126–41

Kempf, S. J. (1968) 'Grundrissentwicklung und Baugeschichte des Trierer Doms', *Das Münster* 21: 1ff.

Kennedy, H. (1985a) 'From Polis to Madina', *P&P* 106: 3–27

Kennedy, H. (1985b) 'The last century of Byzantine Syria', *BF* 10: 141–83

Kennedy, H. (1992) 'Antioch from Byzantium to Islam and back again', in Rich (ed.) (1992) 181–98

King, C. E. (ed.) (1980) *Imperial Revenue, Expenditure and Monetary Policy in the Fourth Century AD* (BAR International Series 76). Oxford

Kirsten, E. (1954) 'Chorbischof', *RAC* 2: 1105–14

Kirsten, E. (1958) *Die byzantinische Stadt,* Berichte zum XI Internationalen Byzantinisten Kongress. Munich 1: 1–48

Klingshirn, W. (1993) *Caesarius of Arles.* Cambridge

Knütel, R. (1996) 'Christliche Zahlensymbolik im Digestenplan', *ZRG RA* 113: 422–30

Kopecek, T. A. (1974) 'The Cappadocian fathers and civic patriotism', *ChHist* 43: 293–303

Kraeling, C. H. (1938) *Gerasa, City of the Decapolis.* New Haven

Kraemer, C. J. (1958) *Excavations at Nessana, conducted by H. D. Colt, Jr. (vol. III). The Non-Literary Papyri.* Princeton

Krause, J.-V. (1987) *Spätantike Patronatsformen im Westen des römischen Reiches.* Munich

Krautheimer, R. (1966) 'Die Decanneacubita in Konstantinopel', in Schumacher (ed.) (1966) 195–9

Krautschick, S. (1986) 'Zwei Aspekte des Jahres 476', *Historia* 85: 344–71

Kreuter, N. (1993) *Römisches Privatrecht im 5. Jh. n. Chr.* Berlin

Krüger, J. (1990) *Oxyrhynchos in der Kaiserzeit.* Frankfurt am Main

Krüger, P. (1912) *Geschichte der Quellen und Literatur des römischen Rechts.* 2nd edn. Munich

Krüger, P., *et al.* (eds.) (1890) *Collectio librorum iuris anteiustiniani III.* Berlin

Kruse, H. (1934) *Studien zur offiziellen Geltung des Kaiserbildes im römischen Reiche.* Paderborn

Kulakovskij, Y. (1912) *Istoria Vizantii* 2. Kiev

La Rocca, C. (1992) 'Public building and urban change in northern Italy in the early medieval period', in Rich (ed.) (1992) 161–80

Laiou-Thomadakis, A. E. (ed.) (1980) *Charanis Studies*. New Brunswick

Leclercq, H. (1948) 'Chorévêques', in F. Cabrol and H. Leclerq (eds.) (1948) *Dictionnaire d'archéologie chrétienne et de liturgie*. III.1423–52

Lee, A. D. (1993) *Information and Frontiers: Roman Foreign Relations in Late Antiquity*. Cambridge

Leipoldt, J. (1903) *Schenute von Atripe und die Entstehung des nationalen ägyptischen Christentums* (Texte und Untersuchungen 25.1). Leipzig

Lemerle, P. (1971) *Le premier humanisme byzantin*. Paris (trans. as Lemerle, *Byzantine Humanism*)

Lendon, J. E. (1997) *Empire of Honour: The Art of Government in the Roman World*. Oxford

Lestocquoi, J. (1953) 'Le paysage urbain en Gaul', *AESC* 8: 159–72

Levy, E. (1934) 'Neue Bruchstücke aus den Institutionen des Gaius', *ZRG RA* 54: 258–311

Levy, E. (1945) *Pauli Sententiae. A Palingenesia of the Opening Titles as a Specimen of Research in West Roman Vulgar Law*. Ithaca

Levy, E. (1951) *West Roman Vulgar Law. The Law of Property*. Philadelphia

Levy, E. (1956) *Weströmisches Vulgarrecht. Das Obligationenrecht*. Weimar

Levy, E. (1963a) *Gesammelte Schriften* I. Cologne

Levy, E. (1963b) 'Reflections on the first "reception" of Roman law in Germanic states', in Levy (1963a) I.201–9

Lewis, A.R. (1976) 'The dukes of the *regnum Francorum*, AD 550–751', *Speculum* 51: 381–410

Liebeschuetz, W. (1959) 'The finances of Antioch in the fourth century AD', *BZ* 52: 344–56 (= Liebeschuetz (1989) XII)

Liebeschuetz, W. (1972) *Antioch: City and Imperial Administration in the Later Roman Empire*. Oxford

Liebeschuetz, W. (1973) 'The origin of the office of the Pagarch', *BZ* 66: 38–46 (= Liebeschuetz (1989) XVII)

Liebeschuetz, W. (1974) 'The Pagarch: city and imperial administration in Byzantine Egypt', *JJP* 18: 163–8 (= Liebeschuetz (1989) XVIII)

Liebeschuetz, W. (1985) 'Synesius and municipal politics of Cyrenaica in the 5th century AD', *Byz.* 55: 146–64 (= Liebeschuetz (1989) XIV)

Liebeschuetz, W. (1986) 'Why did Synesius become bishop of Ptolemais?', *Byz.* 56: 180–95 (= Liebeschuetz (1989) XV)

Liebeschuetz, W. (1987) 'Government and administration in the late empire', in Wacher (ed.) (1987) 455–69

Liebeschuetz, W. (1989) *From Diocletian to the Arab Conquest: Change in the Late Roman Empire*. Aldershot

Liebeschuetz, W. (1992) 'The end of the ancient city', in Rich (ed.) (1992) 1–49

Liebeschuetz, W. and Kennedy, H. (1988) 'Antioch and the villages of northern Syria in the 4th–6th centuries AD', *NMS* 32: 65–90

Liebs, D. (1971) '*Variae lectiones*. Zwei Juristenschriften', in *Studi in onore di E. Volterra* V (Milan) 51–88

Liebs, D. (1976) 'Römische Provinzialjurisprudenz', in *ANRW* II, 15: 288–362

Liebs, D. (1983) 'Das ius gladii der römischen Provinzgouverneure in der Kaiserzeit', *ZPE* 43: 217–23

Liebs, D. (1985) 'Unverhohlene Brutalität in den Gesetzen der ersten christlichen Kaiser', in Liebs and Luig (eds.) (1985) 89–116

Liebs, D. (1986) Review of H.-J. Horstkotte, *Die Theorie vom spätrömischen 'Zwangsstaat' und das Problem der 'Steuerhaftung'*, *Gnomon* 58: 275–8

Liebs, D. (1987) *Die Jurisprudenz im spätantiken Italien*. Berlin

Liebs, D. (1992) 'Das Gesetz im spätrömischen Recht', in Sellert (ed.) (1992) 11–27

Liebs, D. (1993) *Römische Jurisprudenz in Africa*. Berlin

Liebs, D. and Luig, K. (eds.) (1985) *Römisches Recht in der europäischen Tradition. Symposion aus Anlass des 75. Geburtstages von F. Wieacker*. Ebelsbach

Lieu, S. N. C. (1985) *Manichaeism: in the Later Roman Empire and Medieval China*. Manchester

Loseby, S. (1992) 'Bishops and cathedrals: order and diversity in the fifth century urban landscape of southern Gaul', in Drinkwater and Elton (eds.), *Fifth-Century Gaul* 144–55

Lotter, F. (1971) 'Antonius von Lérins und der Untergang Ufernorikums: ein Beitrag zur Frage der Bevölkerungs Kontinuität im Alpen-Donau-Raum', *HZ* 212: 265–315

Luttwak, E. N. (1976) *The Grand Strategy of the Roman Empire from the First Century A.D. to the Third*. Baltimore

Maas, M. (1986) 'Roman history and Christian ideology in Justinianic reform legislation', *DOP* 40: 17–31

McCail, R. C. (1969) 'The *Cycle* of Agathias: new identifications scrutinised', *JHS* 89: 87–96

MacCormack, S. (1981) *Art and Ceremony in Late Antiquity*. Berkeley

McCormick, M. (1985) 'Analyzing imperial ceremonies', *JÖB* 35: 1–20

McCormick, M. (1989) 'Clovis at Tours, Byzantine public ritual and the origins of medieval ruler symbolism', in Chrysos and Schwarcz (eds.) (1989) 155–80

MacKenzie, M. M. and Roueché, C. (eds.) (1989) *Images of Authority: Papers Presented to Joyce Reynolds on her 70th Birthday*. Cambridge

McKitterick, R. (ed.) (1990) *The Uses of Literacy in Early Medieval Europe*. Cambridge

MacMullen, R. (1980) 'How big was the Roman Imperial Army?', *Klio* 62: 451–60

MacMullen, R. (1987) 'Tax-pressure in the Roman empire', *Latomus* 46: 737–54

MacMullen, R. (1988) *Corruption and the Decline of Rome*. New Haven

Maier, J.-L. (1973) *L'épiscopat de l'Afrique romaine, vandale et byzantine*. Rome

Mamboury, E., Wiegand T., et al. (1934) *Die Kaiserpaläste von Konstantinopel zwischen Hippodrom und Marmara-Meer*. Berlin

Manenti, C. (ed.) (1887–9) *Antiqua summaria codicis Theodosiani* (Studi Senesi nel Circolo Giuridico della R. Università) 3: 257–88; 4: 141–57; 5: 203–311

Mango, C. A. (1959) *The Brazen House: A Study of the Vestibule of the Imperial Palace of Constantinople*. Copenhagen

Mango, C. A. (1975) 'The church of Sts. Sergius and Bacchus once again', *BZ* 68: 385–92 (= Mango, *Studies on Constantinople*, XIV)

Mango, C. A. (1980) *Byzantium: The Empire of New Rome*. London

Mantovani, D. (1987) *Digesto e masse bluhmiane*. Milan

Markus, R. (1990) *The End of Ancient Christianity*. Cambridge

Marrou, H. I. (1956) *A History of Education in Antiquity*. London

Martin, J. and Quint, B. (eds.) (1990) *Christentum und antike Gesellschaft*. Darmstadt

Maspéro, J. (1912) *Organisation militaire de l'Égypte byzantine*. Paris

Mastino, A. (ed.) (1988) *L'Africa Romana*. Sassari

Mathews, T. (1971) *The Early Churches of Constantinople*. University Park, Pennsylvania State University

Mathews, T. (1974) 'Architecture et liturgie dans les premières églises palatiales de Constantinople', *Revue de l'Art* 24: 22–90

Mathisen, R. W. (1984) 'The family of Georgius Florentius Gregorius and the bishops of Tours', *Medievalia et Humanistica* 12: 83–95

Mathisen, R. W. (1992) 'Gallic visitors to Italy, business or pleasure?', in Drinkwater and Elton (eds.), *Fifth-Century Gaul* 228–38

Mathisen, R. W. (1993) *Aristocrats in Barbarian Gaul*. Austin, TX

Matthews, J. F. (1989) *The Roman Empire of Ammianus*. London and Baltimore

Mayerson, P. (1986) 'The Beersheba Edict', *ZPE* 64: 141–8

Mayerson, P. (1988) 'Justinian's *Novel* 103 and the reorganization of Palestine', *BASOR* 269: 65–72

Mazzarino, S. (1951) *Aspetti Sociali del Quarto Secolo*. Rome

Meiggs, R. (1973) *Roman Ostia*. 2nd edn. Oxford

Memmer, M. (1990) 'Der schöne Kauf des guten Sklaven', *ZRG RA* 107: 1–45

Merkel, J. (1888) 'Über römische Gerichtsgebühren', in Merkel, *Abhandlungen aus dem Gebiete des römischen Rechts III* (Halle) 121–74

Millar, F. (1977) *The Emperor and the Roman World*. London

Millet, G. (1925) 'L'origine du logothète général', in *Mélanges d'Histoire du Moyen Âge offerts à M. Ferdinand Lot* (Paris) 563–73

Millett, M. (1990) *The Romanization of Britain*. Cambridge

Mitford, T. B. (1950) 'Some new inscriptions from early Christian Cyprus', *Byz.* 20: 128–32

Modéran, Y. (1993) 'La chronologie de la vie de saint Fulgence de Ruspe et ses incidences sur l'histoire de l'Afrique vandale', *MEFR* 105: 135–88

Mollat, M. (ed.) (1974) *Études sur l'histoire de la pauvreté* 1. Paris

Mommsen, T. (1905) 'Das theodosianische Gesetzbuch', in Mommsen, *Gesammelte Schriften* 11 (Berlin) 371–405

Mommsen, T. (1910) *Gesammelte Schriften* VI. Berlin

Moorhead, J. (1992) *Theoderic in Italy*. Oxford

Morosi, R. (1977) 'L'Officium del prefetto del pretorio nel VI secolo', *Romanobarbarica* 2: 103–48

Morosi, R. (1978) 'Cancellarii in Cassiodoro e in Giovanni Lido', *Romanobarbarica* 3: 127–58

Morosi, R. (1981) 'I Comitiaci, funzionari Romani nell'Italia Ostrogotica', *Quad. Catanesi di Studi Classici e Medievali* 3: 77–111

Morrisson, C. (1970) *Catalogue des monnaies byzantines de la Bibliothèque Nationale* 1. Paris

Moss, J. R. (1973) 'The effects of the policy of Aetius on the history of western Europe', *Historia* 22: 711–31

Mrozek, S. (1978) 'Munificentia privata in den Städten Italiens während der spätrömischen Zeit', *Historia* 27: 355–68

Müller, A. (1912) 'Das Heer Iustinians nach Prokop und Agathias', *Philologus* 71: 101–38

Müller-Wiener, W. (1977) *Bildlexikon zur Topographie Istanbuls*. Tübingen

Murray, A. C. (1986) 'The position of the grafio in the constitutional history of Merovingian Gaul', *Speculum* 64: 787–805

Murray, A. C. (1988) 'From Roman to Frankish Gaul: "Centenarii" and "Centenae" in the administration of the Frankish kingdom', *Traditio* 44: 59–100

Naumann, R. (1965) 'Vorbericht über die Ausgrabungen zwischen Mese und Antiochus-Palast 1964 in Istanbul', *Istanbuler Mitteilungen* 15: 135–48

Naumann, R. and Belting, H. (1966) *Die Euphemiakirche am Hippodrom zu Istanbul und ihre Fresken* (Istanbuler Forschungen 25). Berlin

Nehlsen, H. (1969) Review of Vismara (1967), *ZRG GA* 86: 246–60

Nehlsen, H. (1972) *Sklavenrecht zwischen Antike und Mittelalter: germanisches und römisches Recht in den germanischen Rechtsaufzeichnungen* (Göttinger Studien zur Rechtsgeschichte VII). Göttingen

Nehlsen, H. (1977) 'Aktualität und Effektivität germanischer Rechtsaufzeichnungen', in Classen (ed.) (1977a) 449–502

Nehlsen, H. (1984) 'Codex Euricianus', *Reallexikon der germanischen Altertumskunde* 2nd edn. 5: 42–7

Nelson, H. L. W. (1981) *Überlieferung, Aufbau und Stil von Gai Institutiones*. Leiden

Nelson, H. L. W. (1995) Review of G. Archi, *L'Epitome Gai* (Tijdschrift voor rechtsgeschiedenis 63) 170–7

Nelson, H. L. W. and Manthe, U. (1999) *Gai Institutiones III 88–181. Die Kontraktsobligationen*. Text and commentary. Berlin

Nesbitt, J. W. (1977) 'Double names on early Byzantine seals', *DOP* 31: 111–21

Nicole, J. (1893) *Le livre du préfet*. Geneva

Noailles, P. (1912–14) *Les collections de novelles de l'Empereur Justinien*. Paris

Noble, T. (1990) 'Literacy and the papal government in late antiquity and the early middle ages', in McKitterick (ed.) (1990) 82–108

Noethlichs, K. L. (1981) *Beamtentum und Dienstvergehen. Zur Staatsverwaltung in der Spätantike*. Wiesbaden

Noll, R. (1963) *Das Leben des heiligen Severin*. Berlin

Nörr, D. (1988) 'Zur neuen Faksimile-Ausgabe der *littera Florentina*', *IVRA* 39: 121–36

Oikonomides, N. (1972) *Les listes de préséance byzantines des IXe et Xe siècles*. Paris

Oikonomides, N. (1986) 'Silk trade and production in Byzantium from the sixth to the ninth century: the seals of Kommerkiarioi', *DOP* 40: 33–53

Oikonomides, N. (1987) 'De l'impôt de quantité à l'impôt de distribution à propos du premier cadastre Byzantin (7e–9e siècle)', *Zbornik Radova* 26: 9–19

Oswald, F., Schaefer, L., Sennhauer, H. R. (1966) *Vorromanische Kirchenbauten*. Munich

Palmer, A. (1990) *Monk and Mason on the Tigris Frontier: The Early History of Tur 'Abdin*. Cambridge

Palol, P. de S. (1966) *Demografía y arqueología hispánica de los siglos IV al VIII*. Valladolid

Palol, P. de S. (1967) *Arqueología christiana de la España romana siglos IV–VI*. Madrid

Palol, P. de S. (1968) *Arte hispánico de la época visigoda*. Barcelona

Le pandette di Giustiniano. Storia e fortuna di un codice illustre. Due giornate di studio Firenze, 23–24 giugno 1983. (1983) Florence

Parker, S. T. (ed.) (1987) *The Roman Frontier in Central Jordan. Interim Report on the Limes Arabicus Project, 1980–1985* (BAR International Series 340). Oxford

Patetta, F. (1967) 'Contributi alla storia del diritto romano nel medio evo', in Patetta, *Studi sulle fonti giuridiche medievali*. Turin 121–58

Paverd, F. van de. (1991) *St John Chrysostom: The Homilies on the Statues* (OCA 239). Rome

Pedersen, F. S. (1970) 'On professional qualifications for public posts in late antiquity', *Class. et Med.* 31: 161–213

Pedley, J. G. (ed.) (1980) *New Light on Ancient Carthage*. Ann Arbor

Percival, J. (1992) 'The fifth century villa: new life or death?', in Drinkwater and Elton (eds.), *Fifth-Century Gaul* 156–64

Petrikovits, H. V. (1981) 'Die Spezialisierung des römischen Handwerks: 2, Spätantike', *ZPE* 43: 285–306

Picard, J. C. (1988) *Le souvenir des évêques: sépultures, listes épiscopales et cultes des évêques en Italie du Nord dès l'origine au Xe siècle*. Rome

Pieler, P. E. (1978) 'Byzantinische Rechtsliteratur', in Hunger (1978) II.341–480

Pietri, L. (1983) *La ville de Tours du IVe au VIe siècle: naissance d'une cité chrétienne* (Coll. de l'École Française de Rome 69). Paris

Pirenne, H. (1939) *Mohammed and Charlemagne*. London

Pirling, R. (1986) *Römer und Franken am Niederrhein*. Mainz

Poulter, A. (1990) 'Nicopolis', *Current Archaeology* 121: 37–42

Poulter, A. (1992a) 'The use and abuse of urbanism in the Danubian provinces during the later Roman empire', in Rich (ed.) (1992) 99–135

Poulter, A. (1992b) 'Nicopolis ad Istrum, the anatomy of a Graeco-Roman city', in Schalles, von Hesberg, Zanker (eds.) (1992) 69–86

Pringle, D. (1981) *The Defence of Byzantine Africa from Justinian to the Arab Conquest: An Account of the Military History and Archaeology of the African Provinces in the Sixth and Seventh Centuries* (BAR International Series 99). Oxford

Prinz, F. (1965) *Frühes Mönchtum im Frankenreich*. Munich

Prinz, F. (1971) *Klerus und Krieg im frühen Mittelalter*. Stuttgart

Prinz, F. (1973) 'Die bischofliche Stadtherrschaft im Frankenreich vom 5. bis zum 7. Jahrhundert', *HZ* 217: 1–35

Rackham, O. (1986) *History of the Countryside*. London

Rathbone, D. (1990) 'Villages and population in Graeco-Roman Egypt', *PCPS* 36: 100–42

Reece, R. (1992) 'The end of the city in Roman Britain', in Rich (ed.) (1992) 136–44

Reinink, G. J. (1988) 'Pseudo-Methodius und die Legende vom römischen Endkaiser', in W. Verbeke, D. Verhelst, and A. Welkenhuysen (eds.), *The Use and Abuse of Eschatology in the Middle Ages*. Louvain

Rémondon, R. (1961) 'Soldats de Byzance d'après un papyrus trouvé à Edfou', *Recherches de Papyrologie* 1: 41–93

Rémondon, R. (1965) 'P.Hamb. 56 et P.Lond. 1419 (notes sur les finances d'Aphrodito du VIe siècle au VIIIe', *Égypte Gréco-Romaine* 40: 401–30

Rémondon, R. (1966) 'L'Égypte au Ve siècle de notre ère', *Atti dell'XI Congr. Int. di Papirologia* (Milan) 135–48

Rémondon, R. (1971) 'Le monastère Alexandrin de la Metanoia: était-il bénéficiaire du fisc ou à son service?', *Studi in onore di E. Volterra* v (Milan) 771–81

Rey-Coquais, J. (1977) 'Inscriptions découvertes dans les fouilles de Tyr', *Bull. Mus. Beyrouth* 29

Rich, J. (ed.) (1992) *The City in Late Antiquity*. London

Riché, P. (1957) 'La survivance des écoles publiques en Gaule au Ve siècle', *Le Moyen Age* 63: 421–36

Riché, P. (1965) 'L'enseignement du droit en Gaule du VIe au XIe siècle', *Ius Romanum Medii Aevi* 1.5b: 1–21

Riché, P. (1972) 'L'enseignement et la culture des laïcs dans l'occident pré-carolingien', *Settimane di Studi* 19: 231–51

Riché, P. (1973) *Éducation et culture dans l'occident barbare*. Paris

Robert, L. (1948) 'Épigrammes relatives à des gouverneurs', *Hellenica* 4: 34–114

Robert, L. (1958) 'Inscriptions grecques de Side en Pamphylie, époque impériale et bas empire', *RPh* 32: 15–53

Rochow, I. (1976) 'Die Heidenprozesse unter den Kaisern Tiberius II, Konstantins und Maurikios', in F. Winkelmann and H. Köpstein (eds.) (1976), *Probleme der Herausbildung des Feudalismus* (Berlin) 120–30

Rohr, C. (1997) 'Zum Theoderiche-Panegyricus des Ennodius', *Hermes* 125: 100–17

Roques, D. (1987) *Synésios de Cyrène et la Cyrénaïque du Bas-Empire*. Paris

Rouche, M. (1974) 'La matricule des pauvres: évolution d'une institution de charité du Bas-Empire, jusqu'à la fin du Haut Moyen Âge', in Mollat (ed.) (1974) 83–110

Rouche, M. (1979) *L'Aquitaine dès Wisigoths aux Arabes 418–781*. Paris

Roueché, C. (1979) 'A new inscription from Aphrodisias and the title πατὴρ τῆς πόλεως', *GRBS* 20: 173–85

Roueché, C. (1984) 'Acclamations in the later Roman empire: new evidence from Aphrodisias', *JRS* 74: 181–99

Roueché, C. (1989) 'Floreat Perge', in MacKenzie and Roueché (eds.) (1989) 205–28

Rousseau, P. (1996) 'Inheriting the fifth century: who bequeathed what?', in P. Allen and E. Jeffreys (eds.), *The Sixth Century: End or Beginning?* (1996) (Brisbane) 1–19

Russell, J. (1987) *The Mosaic Inscriptions of Anemurium*. Vienna

Sachau, E. (1907) (ed.) *Syrische Rechtsbücher* 1. Berlin

Saliou, C. (1996) *Le Traité d'urbanisme de Julien d'Ascalon*. Paris

Sanchez-Albornoz y Meduina, C. (1943) *Ruina y extinción del municipio romano en Espana*. Buenos Aires (= Sanchez-Albornoz y Meduina, Y. (1971) 11–147)

Sanchez-Albornoz y Meduina, Y. (1971) *Estudios Visigodos*. Roma

Sartre, M. (1982) *Inscriptions grecques et latines de la Syrie* XIII.1, *Bostra*. Paris

Sartre, M. (1985) *Bostra*. Paris

Sawyer, P. H. and Wood, I. N. (eds.) (1977) *Early Medieval Kingship*. Leeds

Schalles, H.-J., von Hesberg, H., Zanker, P. (eds.) (1992) *Die römische Stadt im 2. Jahrhundert n. Chr.* Cologne

Schellenberg, H. (1965) *Die Interpretationen zu den Paulussentenzen*. Göttingen

Scheltema, H. J. (1962) 'Die Veronensischen Kodexscholien', *Tijdschrift voor Rechtsgeschiedenis* 30: 252f.

Scheltema, H. J. (1966) 'Kobidas', *RIDA* 13: 341–3

Scheltema, H. J. (1970) *L'enseignement de droit des antécesseurs.* Leiden

Scheltema, H. J. (1975) 'Over getallen in het Corpus Iuris Civilis', in *Vrijheid en Recht. Opstellen aangeboden aan Prof. mr. E. H. s'Jacob ter gelegenheid van zijn aftreden als hoogleraar aan de Rijksuniversiteit Groningen* (Zwolle) 227–34

Schindler, K.-H. (1962) 'Consultatio veteris cuiusdam iurisconsulti', *Labeo* 8: 16–61

Schmidt, H. F. (1957) 'Das Weiterleben und die Wiederbelebung antiker Institutionen im mittelalterlichen Städtewesen', *Annali di storia del diritto* 1: 85–135

Schmidt-Wiegand, R. (1959) 'Die kritische Ausgabe der Lex Salica – noch immer ein Problem', *ZRG GA* 76: 301–19

Schmidt-Wiegand, R. (1987) 'Reht und Ewa', in R. Bergmann *et al.* (eds.), *Althochdeutsch* (Germanische Bibliothek, n.s. viii) (Heidelberg) 11.937–58

Schminck, A. (1989) 'Frömmigkeit ziere das Werk. Zur Datierung der 60 Bücher Leons VI' (*Subseciva Groningana* 3) 79–114

Schubert, W. (1969) 'Die rechtliche Sonderstellung der Dekurionen Kurialen in der Kaisergesetzgebung 4.–6. Jhs.', *ZRG RA* 86: 287–331

Schulz, F. (1953) *History of Roman Legal Science.* 2nd edn. Oxford

Schumacher, W. N. (ed.) (1966) *Tortulae. Studien zu altchristlichen und byzantinischen Monumenten.* Rome

Scott, J. A. (1987) 'Sardis. Byzantine and Turkish eras', in E. Guralnick (ed.) *Sardis, 27 years of discovery* (Chicago) 74–87

Scott, R. (1985) 'Malalas, the *Secret History*, and Justinian's propaganda', *DOP* 39: 99–109

Seeck, O. (1919) *Regesten der Kaiser und Päpste für die Jahre 311–476.* Stuttgart

Selb, W. (1964) *Zur Bedeutung des syrisch-römischen Rechtsbuches.* Munich

Selb, W. (1965) 'Zum Plan einer Neuedition des syrisch-römischen Rechtsbuches', *Labeo* 11: 329–40

Selb, W. (ed.) (1990) *Sententiae Syriacae.* Vienna

Sellert, W. (1992) (ed.) *Das Gesetz in Spätantike und frühem Mittelalter.* Göttingen

Ševčenko, I. and N. (1984) *The Life of Nicholas of Sion.* Brookline, MA

Shahīd, I. (= Kawar) (1957) 'The Patriciate of Arethas', *BZ* 52: 321–43 (= Shahīd (1988) III)

Shahīd, I. (1984) *Byzantium and the Arabs in the Fourth Century.* Washington, DC

Shahīd, I. (1988) *Byzantium and the Semitic Orient before the Rise of Islam.* London

Shahīd, I. (1989) *Byzantium and the Arabs in the Fifth Century.* Washington, DC

Shahīd, I. (1995) *Byzantium and the Arabs in the Sixth Century.* Washington, DC

Siems, H. (1984) 'Codex Theodosianus', *Reallexikon der germanischen Altertumskunde* v. 2nd edn. Berlin

Siems, H. (1989) 'Zu Problemen der Bewertung frühmittelalterlicher Rechtstexte', *ZRG GA* 106: 291–305

Sijpesteijn, P. J. (1986) 'Nomination for a liturgy', no. 1 in 'Five Byzantine papyri from the Michigan collection', *ZPE* 62: 133–7

Sijpesteijn, P. J. (1987) 'The title πατὴρ τῆς πόλεως and the papyri', *Tyche* 2: 171–4

Simon, D. (1975) Review of Sitzia (1973), *ZRG RA* 92: 417–24

Simon, D. (1978) 'Marginalien zur Vulgarismusdiskussion', in O. Behrends *et al.* (eds.) *Festschrift für F. Wieacker zum 70. Geburtstag* (Göttingen) 154–74

Simon, D. (ed.) (1986) *Fontes minores* VII. Frankfurt am Main

Simon, D. and Troianos, S. (eds.) (1989) *Das Novellensyntagma des Athanasius von Emesa.* Frankfurt am Main

Simon, D., *et al.* (1977) 'Zum griechischen Novellenindex des Iulian', in Simon (ed.), *Fontes minores* II (Frankfurt am Main) 1–29

Simon, D., *et al.* (1979) 'Eine Fragmentensammlung aus dem Baroccianus 173', in Simon (ed.), *Fontes Minores* III (Frankfurt am Main) 1–23

Sinnigen, W. G. (1964) 'Chiefs of staff and chiefs of the secret service', *BZ* 57: 78–105

Sirks, A. J. B. (1991) *Food for Rome.* Amsterdam

Sirks, A. J. B. (1996a) in R. W. Mathisen and H. Sivan (eds.), *Shifting Frontiers in Late Antiquity* (Aldershot) 147–57

Sirks, A. J. B. (1996b) *Summaria Antiqua Codicis Theodosiani.* Amsterdam

Sirks, A. J. B. (1996c) 'The *summaria antiqua codicis Theodosiani* in the MS. Vat. reg. Lat. 886', *ZRG RA* 113: 243–67

Sitzia, F. (1973) (ed.) *De Actionibus. Edizione e commento.* Milan

Sivan, H. (1992) 'City and countryside in fifth-century Gaul: the example of Bordeaux', in Drinkwater and Elton (eds.), *Fifth-Century Gaul* 132–43

Sjöström, I. (1993) *Tripolitania in Transition: Late Roman and Early Islamic Settlement.* Avebury

Sodini, J.-P. (1989) 'Les groupes épiscopaux de Turquie (à l'exception de la Cilicie)', *Actes XI Cong. Int. d'Arch. Chrét.* (Rome) 1.405–27

Sontis, J. M. (1937) *Die Digestensumme des Anonymus.* Heidelberg

Spagnesi, E. (1986) (ed.) *Le pandette di Giustiniano. Storia e fortuna della littera Florentina. Mostra di codici e documenti 24 giugno – 31 agosto 1983.* Florence

Spieser, J.-M. (1984) 'Les villes en Grèce du IIIe au VIIe s.', in *Villes et peuplement* (1984) 315–38

Sprandel, R. (1957) '*Dux* und *comes* in der Merowingerzeit', *Zeitschrift für Rechtsgeschichte* 74: 41–84

Stein, E. (1919) *Studien zur Geschichte des byzantinischen Reiches, vornehmlich unter den Kaisern Justinus II. und Tiberius Constantinus.* Stuttgart

Stein, P. G. and Lewis, A. D. E. (eds.) (1983) *Studies in Justinian's Institutes in Memory of J. A. C. Thomas.* London

Stern, E. (ed.) (1993) *New Encyclopedia of Archaeological Excavations in the Holy Land.* Jerusalem

Stevens, C. E. (1933) *Sidonius Apollinaris and his Age.* Oxford

Talbot Rice, D. (1958) *The Great Palace of the Byzantine Emperors, Second Report.* Edinburgh

Taradell, M. (1977) 'Les villes romaines dans l'Hispania de l'est', in Duval and Frézouls (eds.) (1977) 97ff.

Tate, G. (1989) 'Les campagnes de Syrie du nord', in *Hommes et richesses* 1.163–86

Tate, G. (1992) *Les campagnes de la Syrie du nord, Ie au VIIe siècles* I (Bibl. archéologique et historique 133). Paris

Tate, G. and Sodini, J.-P. (1980) 'Déhès, recherches sur l'habitat rural', *Syria* 67: 1–303

Teall, J. L. (1985) 'The barbarians in Justinian's armies', *Speculum* 40: 294–322

Teitler, H. C. (1985) *Notarii and Exceptores.* Amsterdam

Teitler, H. C. (1992) 'Un-Roman activities in late antique Gaul: the cases of

Arvandus and Seronatus', in Drinkwater and Elton (eds.), *Fifth-Century Gaul* 309–20

Testini, G., *et al.* (1989) 'La cattedrale in Italia', *Actes XI Cong. Int. d'Arch. Chrét.* (Rome) 1.1–231

Thomas, A. C. (1981) *Christianity in Roman Britain to AD 500.* London

Thompson, E. A. (1969) *The Goths in Spain.* Oxford

Thompson, E. A. (1979) 'Gildas and the history of Britain', *Britannia* 10: 203–26

Thompson, E. A. (1982) *Romans and Barbarians: The Decline of the Western Empire.* Madison, WI

Thompson, E. A. (1984) *St Germanus of Auxerre and the End of Roman Britain.* Wadebridge

Thompson, E. A. (1990) 'Ammianus Marcellinus and Britain', *NMS* 34: 1–15

Tjäder, J.-O. (1954) *Tables.* Lund

Tjäder, J.-O. (1955–82) *Die nichtliterarischen lateinischen Papyri Italiens aus der Zeit 445–700.* Lund and Stockholm

Tomlin, R. S. O. (1976) 'Notitia Dignitatum omnium, tam civilium quam militarium', in R. Goodburn and P. Bartholomew (eds.), *Aspects of the Notitia Dignitatum* (BAR Suppl. Series 15) (Oxford) 189–209

Tomlin, R. S. O. (1987) 'The army of the late empire', in Wacher (ed.) (1987) 1.107–20

Tort-Martorell, C. (1989) *Tradición textual del Codex Iustinianus. Un estudio del Libro 2.* Frankfurt am Main

Traube, L. (1891) 'Untersuchungen zur Überlieferungsgeschichte römischer Schriftsteller', Sitzungsberichte. Bayerische Akademie der Wissenschaften, phil.-hist. Kl.: 387–428

Treitinger, O. (1969) *Die oströmische Kaiser- und Reichsidee nach ihrer Gestaltung im höfischen Zeremoniell.* Darmstadt

Trombley, F. R. (1987) 'Korykos in Cilicia Trachis', *AHB* 1: 16–23

Tsirplanis, C. (1974) 'John Lydus on the imperial administration', *Byz.* 44: 478–502

Vanags, P. (1979) 'Taxation and survival in the late fourth century: the Anonymus' programme of economic reforms', in Hassall and Ireland (eds.) (1979) 47–58

Van Dam, R. (1996) 'Governors of Cappadocia during the fourth century', *Medieval Prosopography* 17: 7–83

Van der Vliet, J. (1993) 'Spätantikes Heidentum in Ägypten im Spiegel der koptischen Literatur', *Riggisberger Berichte I* (Riggisberg) 99–130

Van Ossel, P. (1985) 'Quelques apports récents à l'étude de l'habitat rural galloromain dans la région mosane', *LEC* 53: 7996

Velkov, V. (1962) 'Les campagnes et la population rurale en Thrace aux IVe–VIe siècles', *Byzantinica Bulgarica* 1: 31–66

Vera, D. (1986) 'Forme e funzioni della Rendita Fondiaria nella tarda antichità', in Giardina (ed.), *Società romana* 1.367–447

Veyne, P. (1981) 'Clientèle et corruption au service de l'État: La vénalité des offices dans le Bas-Empire romain', *Annales* 36: 339–60

Viden, G. (1984) *The Roman Chancery Tradition: Studies in the Language of Codex Theodosianus and Cassiodorus' Variae.* Gothenburg

Viereck, H. (1981) '*Imitatio imperii* und *interpretatio Germanica* vor der Wikingerzeit', in R. Zeitler (ed.), *Les pays du Nord et Byzance* (Uppsala) 64–113

Villes et peuplement dans l'Illyricum protobyzantin (1984) (Collection de l'École Française de Rome 77). Rome

Vismara, G. (1967) *Edictum Theodorici*, Ius Romanum Medii Aevi, 1. 2b Milan

Vittinghoff, F. (1958) 'Zur Verfassung der spätantiken Stadt', *Studien zu den Anfängen des europäischen Städtewesens* (Vorträge und Forschungen) 11–39

Vives, J. (1963) *Concilios Visigóticos e Hispano-Romanos*. Barcelona

Vogt, J. (1945) 'Zur Frage des christlichen Einflusses auf die Gesetzgebung Konstantins des Grossen', *Festschrift für L. Wenger* II (Munich) 118–48

Volterra, E. (1983) 'Sulla legge delle citazioni' (Atti dell' Accademia nazionale dei Lincei. Memorie. Classe di scienze morali, storiche e filologiche 8, 27) 185–267

Von Falkenstein, V. (1989) 'Die Städte im byzantinischen Italien', *MEFR* 101–2: 401–64

Vööbus, A. (1958–60) *A History of Ascetism in the Syrian Orient*. Louvain

Vööbus, A. (1972) 'Die Entdeckung neuer wichtiger Quellen für das syrisch-römische Rechtsbuch', *ZRG RA* 89: 348–51

Vööbus, A. (1975) 'A new source for the Syro-Roman Lawbook', *Labeo* 21: 7–9

Voss, W. E. (1982) *Recht und Rhetorik in den Kaisergesetzen der Spätantike*. Frankfurt am Main

Voss, W. E. (1985) 'Der Grundsatz der ärgeren Hand bei Sklaven, Kolonen und Hörigen', in Liebs and Luig (eds.) (1985) 117–84

Wacher, J. (ed.) (1987) *The Roman World*. London

van der Wal, N. (1964) *Manuale Novellarum Justiniani*. Groningen

van der Wal, N. (ed.) (1985) 'Die Paratitla zur Epitome Iuliani', in *Subseciva Groningana* 2: 93–137

van der Wal, N. and Lokin, J. H. A. (1985) *Historiae iuris graeco-romani delineatio*. 2nd edn. Groningen

Waldstein, W. (1980) 'Tribonianus', *ZRG RA* 97: 232–55

Wallace-Hadrill, J. M. (1962) 'The blood-feud of the Franks', in Wallace-Hadrill, *The Long-Haired Kings and Other Studies in Frankish History* (London) 121–47

Wallace-Hadrill, J. M. (1971) *Early Germanic Kingship in England and on the Continent*. Oxford

Walmsley, A. G. (1992) 'The social and economic regime at Fihl (Pella) between the 7th and 9th centuries', in Canivet and Rey-Coqais (eds.) (1992) 249–61

Ward-Perkins, B. (1978) 'Luni, the decline and abandonment of a Roman town', in Blake, Potter and Whitehouse (eds.) (1978) 313–21

Weidemann, K. (1970) 'Zur Topographie von Metz in der Römerzeit und im frühen Mittelalter', *Jahrb. R.-G. Mus. Mainz* 17: 147–171

Wenger, L. (1953) *Die Quellen des römischen Rechts*. Vienna

Wenskus, R. (1964) 'Bemerkungen zum *Thunginus* der Lex Salica', in Classen and Scheibert (eds.) (1964) 217–36

Wessel, H. (2000) *Das Recht der Tablettes Albertini*. Berlin

Wetzler, C. F. (1997) *Rechtsstaat und Absolutismus. Überlegungen zur Verfassung des spätantiken Kaiserreichs anhand von CJ 1.14.8*. Berlin

Whitby, Mary (1987) 'On the omission of a ceremony in mid-sixth century Constantinople: *candidati, curopalatus, silentiarii, excubitores* and others', *Historia* 36: 462–88

Whitby, Michael (1995) 'Recruitment in Roman armies from Justinian to Heraclius (c. 565–615)', in Averil Cameron (ed.) (1995) 61–124

Whitelock, D., McKitterick, R. and Dumville, D. N. (eds.) (1982) *Ireland in Early Mediaeval Europe*. Cambridge

Whittaker, C. R. (1980) 'Inflation and the economy in the fourth century A.D.', in King (ed.) (1980) 1–22

Whittaker, C. R. (1983) 'Late Roman trade and traders', in Garnsey *et al.* (eds.) (1983) 163–80

Whittow, M. (1990) 'Ruling the late Roman and early Byzantine city: a continuous history', *P&P* 129: 3–29

Whittow, M. (1996) *The Making of Orthodox Byzantium, 600–1025*. London

Wickham, C. (1981) *Early Medieval Italy*. London

Wickham, C. (1984) 'The other transition: from the ancient world to feudalism', *P&P* 103: 3–36

Wickham, C. (1988) 'Marx, Sherlock Holmes and late Roman commerce' (review of Giardina, *Società romana* III) *JRS* 78: 183–93

Wickham, L. R. (1995) 'Aspects of clerical life in the early Byzantine church in two scenes: Mopsuestia and Apamea', *JEH* 46: 3–18

Wieacker, F. (1955) *Vulgarismus und Klassizismus im Recht der Spätantike*. Heidelberg

Wieacker, F. (1964) *Recht und Gesellschaft in der Spätantike*. Stuttgart

Wieacker, F. (1983a) *Ausgewählte Schriften* I. Frankfurt am Main

Wieacker, F. (1983b) 'Zur Effektivität des Gesetzes in der späten Antike', in Wieacker (1983a) 222–40

Wieacker, F. (1983c) 'Vulgarrecht und Vulgarismus. Alte und neue Probleme und Diskussionen', in Wieacker (1983a) 241–54

Wightman, E. M. (1978) 'The towns of Gaul with special reference to the north-east', in M. W. Barley (ed.) *European Towns, their Archaeology and Early History*. London

Wightman, E. M. (1985) *Gallia Belgica*. London

Wilkinson, T. J. W. (1990) *Town and Country in S. E. Anatolia: Settlement and Land Use at Kurban Höyük*. Chicago

Willers, D., *et al.* (1993) *Riggisberger Berichte 1, Begegnungen von Heidentum und Christentum in Ägypten*. Riggisberg

Wilson, N. G. (1983) *Scholars of Byzantium*. London

Winkelmann, F. (1978a) 'Zum byzantinischen Staat (Kaiser, Aristokratie, Heer)', in F. Winkelmann, H. Köpstein, H. Ditten and I. Rochow (eds.), *Byzanz im 7. Jahrhundert*. Berlin

Winkelmann, F. (1978b) 'Zur Rolle der Patriarchen von Konstantinopel bei den Kaiserwechseln in frühbyzantinischer Zeit', *Klio* 60: 467–81

Wipszycka, E. (1972) *Les ressources et activités économiques des églises en Égypte du IVe au VIIIe siècle* (Papyrologia Bruxelensia 10)

Wiseman, J. (1984) 'The city in Macedonia Secunda', in *Villes et peuplement dans l'Illyricum protobyzantin* (Paris) 289–313

Wolff, H. (1991) 'Die Kontinuität des städtischen Leben in den nördlichen Grenzprovinzen des römischen Reiches und das Ende der Antike', in Eck and Galsterer (eds.) (1991) 287–318

Wolff, H. J. (1936) 'Römische Grundstückskaufverträge aus dem Vandalenreich', *Tijdschrift voor Rechtsgeschiedenis* 14: 398–420

Wolfram, H. (1988) *History of the Goths,* 2nd edn, trans. T. J. Dunlap. Berkeley

Wood, I. N. (1983) *The Merovingian North Sea* (Occasional Papers on Medieval Topics, no. 1). Alingsås

Wood, I. N. (1986) 'Disputes in late fifth- and sixth-century Gaul: some problems', in Davies and Fouracre (eds.) (1986) 7–22

Wood, I. N. (1990) 'Administration, law and culture in Merovingian Gaul', in McKitterick (ed.) (1990) 63–81

Wood, I. N. (1992) 'Frankish hegemony in England', in Carver (ed.) (1992) 235–77

Wood, I. N. (1993) 'The Code in Merovingian Gaul', in Harries and Wood (eds.) (1993) 159–77

Wormald, P. (1977) '*Lex Scripta* and *Verbum Regis*: legislation and early Germanic kingship from Euric to Cnut', in Sawyer and Wood (eds.) (1977) 105–38

Wormald, P. (1995) '"Inter cetera bona . . . genti suae": lawmaking and peace-keeping in the earliest English kingdoms', *Settimane di Studi* 42: 963–93

Worp, K. A. (1982) 'Byzantine imperial titulature in the Greek documentary papyri: the oath formulas', *ZPE* 45: 199–226

Zachariae von Lingenthal, K. E. (1843a) *Anekdota* III. Leipzig

Zachariae von Lingenthal, K. E. (1843b) 'Edicta praefectorum praetorio ex codicibus mss. Bodleianis, Laurentianis, Marcianis, Vindobonensibus', in Zachariae von Lingenthal (1843a) 227–78

Zachariae von Lingenthal, K. E. (1873a) 'Die griechischen Scholien der rescribierten Handschrift des Codex in der Bibliotek des Domcapitels zu Verona', in Zachariae von Lingenthal (1873b) 313–55

Zachariae von Lingenthal, K. E. (1873b) *Kleine Schriften zür römischen und byzantinischen Rechtsgeschichte* I. Leipzig

Zacos, G., Veglery, A. and Nesbitt, J. W. (1972–84) *Byzantine Lead Seals.* 6 vols. Basel–Bern

Zayadine, F. (ed.) (1986) *Jerash Archaeological Project* I, 1981–1983. Amman

Zayadine, F. (ed.) (1989) *Jerash Archaeological Project* II, 1984–1988. Paris

Zeumer, K. (1886) *Formulae Merowingici et Karolini Aevi* (*MGH* Legum sectio 5). Hanover

Zeumer, K. (1898) 'Geschichte der westgotischen Gesetzgebung, 1' *Neues Archiv* 23: 75–112

Zeumer, K. (1899) 'Zum westgotischen Urkundenwesen', *Neues Archiv* 24: 13–38

Zeumer, K. (1902) *Leges Visigothorum* (*MGH* Leges 1.1). Hanover

Zocco-Rosa, A. (1908–10) *Imperatoris Iustiniani institutionum palingenesia.* Catania

PART III: EAST AND WEST: ECONOMY AND SOCIETY
(CHS. 12–17)

Abadie-Reynal, C. (1989) 'Céramique et commerce dans le bassin égéen du IVe au VIIe siècle', in *Hommes et richesses* I: 143–62

Agache, R. (1970) *Détection aérienne de vestiges proto-historiques, gallo-romains et médiévaux.* Amiens

Alcock, L. (1972) 'By South Cadbury is that Camelot . . .'. The Excavation of Cadbury Castle 1966–1970. London

Alcock, L. (1987) Economy, Society and Warfare among the Britons and Saxons. Cardiff

Alcock, L. (1989) Arthur's Britain. London

Alcock, S. E. (1985) 'Roman imperialism in the Greek landscape', JRA 2: 5–34

Alcock, S. E. (1993) Graecia Capta: The Landscapes of Roman Greece. Cambridge

Alföldy, G. (1974) Noricum. London–Boston

Amory, P. (1993) 'The meaning and purpose of ethnic terminology in the Burgundian laws', EME 2.1: 1–28

Amory, P. (1997) People and Identity in Ostrogothic Italy 489–554. Cambridge

Anderson, T. Jr (1995) 'Roman military colonies in Gaul, Salian ethnogenesis and the forgotten meaning of Pactus Legis Salicae 59.5', EME 4: 129–44

Angenendt, A. (1984) Kaiserherrschaft und Königstaufe: Kaiser, Könige und Päpste als geistliche Patrone in der abendländischen Missionsgeschichte. Berlin

Angenendt, A. (1986) 'The conversion of the Anglo-Saxons considered against the background of early medieval mission', in Angli e Sassoni al di qua e al di là del mare (= XXXII Settimana di studio del Centro Italiano di Studi sull'Alto Medioevo) (Spoleto) II.755–66

Angiolini Martinelli, P. et al. (1968–9) 'Corpus' della scultura paleocristiana, bizantina ed altomedioevale di Ravenna, diretto da Giuseppe Bovini. 3 vols. Rome

Anné, L. (1941) Les rites des fiançailles et la donation pour cause de mariage sous le bas-empire. Louvain

Anselmino, L. et al. (1989) Il castellum del Nador. Storia di una fattoria tra Tipasa e Caesarea (I–VI sec. d. C.) (Monografie di Archeologia Libica XXIII). Rome

Arjava, A. (1988) 'Divorce in later Roman law', Arctos 22: 5–21

Arjava, A. (1996) Women and Law in Late Antiquity. Oxford

Arnheim, M. T. W. (1972) The Senatorial Aristocracy in the Later Roman Empire. Oxford

Arrhenius, B. (1985) Merovingian Garnet Jewellery: Emergence and Social Implications. Stockholm

Arthur, P. and Patterson, H. (1994) 'Ceramics and early medieval central and southern Italy', in Francovich and Noyé (1994) 409–41

Atlante delle forme ceramiche (1981) vol. 1 (Ceramica fine romana nel bacino mediterraneo. Medio e tardo impero) (= supplement to Enciclopedia dell'Arte Antica). Rome

Ausenda, G. (1995) 'The segmentary lineage in contemporary anthropology and among the Lombards', in G. Ausenda (ed.), After Empire: Towards an Ethnology of Europe's Barbarians (Woodbridge) 15–45

Avramea, A. and Feissel, D. (1994) 'Inventaires en vue d'un recueil des incriptions historiques de Byzance IV, inscriptions de Thessalie (à l'exception de Météores)', T&MByz 14: 357–98

Bachrach, B. S. (1972) Merovingian Military Organisation 481–751. Minneapolis

Bachrach, B. S. (1993) 'Grand strategy in the Germanic kingdoms: recruitment of the rank and file', in Vallet and Kazanski (1993) 55–63

Bachrach, B. S. (1994) The Anatomy of a Little War. Boulder

Bagnall, R. (1985) 'Agricultural productivity and taxation in later Roman Egypt', TAPA 115: 289–308

Bagnall, R. (1987) 'Church, state and divorce in late Roman Egypt', in K. L. Selig and R. Somerville (eds.), *Florilegium Clumbianum. Essays in Honour of Paul Oskar Kristeller* (New York) 41–61

Bagnall, R. (1993) 'Slavery and society in late Roman Egypt', in B. Halpern and D. W. Hobson (eds.), *Law, Politics and Society in the Ancient Mediterranean World* (Sheffield) 220–40

Baker, D. (ed.) (1979) *The Church in Town and Countryside* (Studies in Church History 16). Oxford

Barnish, S. J. B. (1986) 'Taxation, land, and barbarian settlement in the western empire', *PBSR* 54: 170–95

Barnwell, P. S. (1992) *Emperor, Prefects and Kings: The Roman West, 395–565*. London

Bassett, S. (1988) *The Origins of Anglo-Saxon Kingdoms*. Leicester

Beaucamp, J. (1990 and 1992a) *Le statut de la femme à Byzance (4e–7e siècle)* 1, *Le droit impérial*; 2, *Les pratiques sociales*. Paris

Beaucamp, J. (1992b) 'L'Égypte byzantine: biens des parents, biens du couple?', in D. Simon (ed.), *Eherecht und Familiengut in Antike und Mittelalter* (Munich) 61–76

Bellinger, A. R. (1938) *Coins from Jerash, 1928–1934* (Numismatic Notes and Monographs no. 81). New York

Bermond Montanari, G. (ed.) (1983) *Ravenna e il porto di Classe. Venti anni di ricerche archeologiche tra Ravenna e Classe*. Bologna

Bettini, M. (1988) 'Il divieto fino al "sesto grado" incluso nel matrimonio romano', *Athenaeum* 66: 69–98

Bettini, M. (1994) 'De la terminologie romaine des cousins', in Bonte (1994) 221–39

Bianchi Fossati Vanzetti, M. (1983) 'Vendita ed esposizione degli infanti da Costantino a Giustiniano', *SDHI* 49: 179–224

Bintliff, J. (1983) 'The development of settlement in south-west Boeotia', in P. Roesch (ed.), *La Béotie antique, Lyon – Saint-Etienne (6–20 mai 1983) Colloques internationaux du Centre National de la Recherche Scientifique* (Paris) 49–70

Bintliff, J. (1985) 'The Boeotia survey', in S. Macready and F. H. Thompson (eds.), *Archaeological Field Survey in Britain and Abroad* (London) 196–216

Biondi, B. (1952–54) *Il diritto romano cristiano*. Milan

Biraben, J.-N. and Le Goff, J. (1969) 'La peste dans le haut Moyen Âge', *Annales* 24: 1484–1510

Bishop, J. (1985) 'Bishops as marital advisors in the ninth century', in J. Kirshner and S. F. Wemple (eds.), *Women of the Medieval World. Essays in Honor of J. H. Mundy* (Oxford) 53–84

Blair, J. (1991) *Early Medieval Surrey: Landholding, Church and Settlement*. Stroud

Blair, J. and Sharpe, R. (eds.) (1992) *Pastoral Care Before the Parish*. Leicester

Bonnassie, R. (1991) *From Slavery to Feudalism in South-Western Europe*. Cambridge

Bonneau, D. (1970) 'L'administration de l'irrigation dans les grands domaines en Égypte au VIe siècle de n.e.', in D. H. Samuel (ed.), *Proceedings of the Twelfth International Congress of Papyrology* (Toronto) 45–62

Bonte, P. (ed.) (1994) *Épouser au plus proche. Inceste, prohibitions et stratégies matrimoniales autour de la Méditerranée*. Paris

Boswell, J. (1989) *The Kindness of Strangers: The Abandonment of Children in Western Europe from Late Antiquity to the Renaissance*. New York

Bowman, A. (1994) *Life and Letters on the Roman Frontier: Vindolanda and its People*. London

Brandes, W. (1989) *Die Städte Kleinasiens im 7. und 8. Jahrhundert*. Berlin

Breeze, D. (1984) 'Demand and supply on the northern frontier', in R. Miket and C. Burgess (eds.), *Between and Beyond the Walls: Essays on the Prehistory and History of North Britain in Honour of George Jobey* (Edinburgh) 32–68

Bremmer, J. (1983) 'The importance of the maternal uncle and grandfather in archaic and classical Greece and early Byzantium', *ZPE* 50: 173–86

Bresson, A. (1985) 'Graphes et réseaux de parenté en Grèce ancienne', in *Informatique et prosopographie, Paris 1984* (Paris) 261–75

Brogiolo, G. P. (1994), 'Castra tardoantichi (IV-metà VI)', in Francovich and Noyé (1994) 151–8

Brogiolo, G. P. and Gelichi, S. (eds.) (1996) *Le ceramiche altomedievali (fine VI–X secolo) in Italia settentrionale: produzione e commerci*, Mantua

Brown, P. R. L. (1988) *The Body and Society: Men, Women and Sexual Renunciation in Early Christianity*. New York

Brown, P. R. L. (1992) *Power and Persuasion in Late Antiquity*. Madison

Brown, P. R. L. (1996) *The Rise of Western Christendom: Triumph and Diversity AD 200–1000*. Oxford

Bruce-Mitford, R. (1975–83) *The Sutton Hoo Ship-Burial*. 3 vols. in 4 parts. London

Burgess, R. W. (1993/4) 'The accession of Marcian in the light of Chalcedonian apologetic and Monophysite polemic', *BZ* 86/87: 47–68

Burkitt, F. C. (1913) *Euphemia and the Goth, with the Acts of the Martyrdom of the Confessors of Edessa*. London

Burns, T. S. (1992) 'The settlement of 418', in Drinkwater and Elton (eds.), *Fifth-Century Gaul* 53–63

Butler, H. C. (1920) *Syria: Publications of the Princeton University Archaeological Expeditions to Syria in 1904-5 and 1909*, II. *Architecture, Section B Northern Syria*. Leiden

Caillet, J.-P. (1993) *L'évergétisme monumental chrétien en Italie et à ses marges* (Collection de l'École Française de Rome, 175). Rome

Cameron, Alan (1978) 'The House of Anastasius', *GRBS* 19: 259–76

Cameron, Alan and Long, J. (1993) *Barbarians and Politics at the Court of Arcadius*. Berkeley

Cameron, Averil (1993) *The Later Roman Empire, A. D. 284–430*. London

Carandini, A. *et al.* (1983) 'Rapporto preliminare delle campagne 1973–77', *Quaderni di Archeologia della Libia* 13: 9–60

Carletti, C. (1977) 'Aspetti biometrici del matrimonio nelle iscrizioni cristiane di Roma', *Augustinianum* 17: 39–51

Carrié, J. M. (1986) 'L'esercito: trasformazioni funzionali ed economie locali', in Giardina (ed.), *Società romana* 449–88, 760–71

Carver, M. O. H. (1993) *Arguments in Stone: Archaeological Research and the European Town in the First Millennium* (Oxbow Monograph 29). Oxford

Casey, P. J. (1993) 'The end of fort garrisons on Hadrian's Wall: a hypothetical model', in Vallet and Kazanski (1993) 259–68

Castagnetti, A. (1979) *L'organizzazione del territorio rurale nel medioevo. Circoscrizioni ecclesiastiche e civili nella 'Langobardia' e nella 'Romania'*. Turin

Castello, C. (1983) 'Assenza d'ispirazione cristiana in C. Th. 3, 16, 1', in *Religion, société et politique. Mélanges en hommage à Jacques Ellul* (Paris) 203–12

Castello, C. (1988) 'Legislazione costantiniana e conciliare in tema di scioglimento degli sponsali e di ratto', in *Atti dell'Accademia Romanistica Costantiniana, VII Convegno Internazionale, 1985* (Perugia) 383–91

Chadwick, H. (1979) 'The relativity of moral codes: Rome and Persia in late antiquity', in W. R. Schoedel and R. M. Wilken (eds.), *Early Christian Literature and the Classical Intellectual Tradition: In Honorem R. M. Grant* (Paris) 135–53

Charles-Edwards, T. (1988) 'Early medieval kingships in the British Isles', in Bassett (1988) 28–39

Charpentier, G. (1994) 'Les bains de Sergilla', *Syria* 71: 113–42

Chastagnol, A. (1966) *Le sénat romain sous le règne d'Odoacre: recherches sur l'épigraphie du Colisée au Ve siècle.* Bonn

Cheyette, F. L. (1977) 'The origins of European villages and the first European expansion', *Journal of Economic History* 37: 182–209

Chrysos, E. K. (1993) 'Cyprus in early Byzantine times', in A. A. M. Bryer and G. S. Georghallides (eds.), *'The Sweet Land of Cyprus', Papers given at the Twenty-Fifth Jubilee Symposium of Byzantine Studies, Birmingham, March 1991* (Nicosia and Birmingham) 3–14

Chrysos, E. K. and Schwarcz, A. (eds.) (1989) *Das Reich und die Barbaren.* Vienna

Clark, E. A. (1990) *The Origenist Controversy: The Cultural Construction of an Early Christian Debate.* Princeton

Claude, D. (1969) *Die byzantinische Stadt im 6. Jahrhundert.* Munich

Claude, D. (1980) 'Freedmen in the Visigothic kingdom', in James (1980a) 159–88

Clover, F. (1989) 'The symbiosis of Romans and Vandals in Africa', in Chrysos and Schwarcz (1989) 57–73

Cohen, B. (1949) 'Betrothal in Jewish and Roman Law', *Proceedings of the American Academy for Jewish Research* 18: 67–135 (= Cohen (1966) *Jewish and Roman Law: A Comparative Study* (New York) 1: 279–349)

Collins, R. (1977) 'Julian of Toledo and the royal succession in late seventh-century Spain', in Sawyer and Wood (1977) 30–49

Collins, R. (1980) 'Mérida and Toledo: 550–585', in James (1980a) 189–219

Collins, R. (1983a) *Early Medieval Spain: Unity in Diversity 400–1000.* London

Collins, R. (1983b) 'Theodebert I: *Res Magnus Francorum*', in P. Wormald (ed.), *Ideal and Reality in Frankish and Anglo-Saxon Society* (Oxford) 7–33

Collins, R. (1985) '*Sicut Lex Gothorum continet*: law and charters in ninth- and tenth-century Leon and Catalonia', *EHR* 100: 489–512

Collins, R. (1986) 'Visigothic law and regional custom in early medieval Spain', in Davies and Fouracre (1986) 85–104

Conrad, L. I. (1986) 'The plague in Bilâd al-Shâm in pre-Islamic times', in M. A. Bakhit and M. Asfour (eds.), *Proceedings of the Symposium on Bilâd al-Shâm during the Byzantine Period (1983)* (Amman) II:143–63

Corbier, M. (1991) 'Constructing kinship in Rome: marriage and divorce, filiation and adoption', in Kertzer and Saller (1991) 127–44

Cornell, T. (1993) 'The end of Roman imperial expansion', in Rich and Shipley (1993) 139–70

Courtois, C., Leschi, L., Perrat, C. and Saumagne, C. (1952) *Tablettes Albertini: actes privés de l'époque vandale.* Paris

Cristianizzazione ed organizzazione ecclesiastica delle campagne nell'alto medioevo: espansione e resistenze (1982) (= XXVIII Settimana di studio del Centro Italiano di Studi sull'Alto Medioevo). Spoleto

Crouzel, H. (1971) *L'Église primitive face au divorce*. Paris

Cubitt, C. (1995) *Anglo-Saxon Church Councils c. 650–c. 850*. Leicester

Cumont, F. (1924) 'Les unions entre proches à Doura et chez les Perses', *Comptes rendus de l'Academie des inscriptions et des belles lettres* 53–62

Cunliffe, B. (1978) *Iron Age Communities in Britain*. 2nd edn. London

Curtius, E. (1953) *European Literature and the Latin Middle Ages*. London (first published as *Europäische Literatur und lateinisches Mittelalter*, Bern 1948)

Dagron, G. (1979) 'Entre village et cité: la bourgade rurale des IVe–VIIe siècles en Orient', *Koinônia* 3: 29–52 (= Dagron (1984b) VIII)

Dagron, G. (1984a) 'Les villes de l'Illyricum protobyzantin', in *Villes et peuplement* (1984) 1–19

Dagron, G. (1984b) *La romanité chrétienne en Orient*. London

Dark, K. R. (1994) *Civitas to Kingdom: British Political Community 300–800*. Leicester

Dauphin, C. (1980) 'Mosaic pavements as an index of prosperity and fashion', *Levant* 12: 112–34

Davies, W. (1982) *Wales in the Early Middle Ages*. Leicester

Davies, W. (1988) *Small Worlds: The Village Community in Early Medieval Brittany*. London

Davies, W. and Fouracre, P. (eds.) (1986) *The Settlement of Disputes in Early Medieval Europe*. Cambridge

Davies, W. and Fouracre, P. (eds.) (1995) *Property and Power in the Early Middle Ages*. Cambridge

Dawes, E. and Baynes, N. H. (1948) *Three Byzantine Saints*. London and Oxford

Demandt, A. (1989) 'The osmosis of late Roman and Germanic aristocracies', in Chrysos and Schwarcz (1989) 75–86

Démians d'Archimbaud, G. (1994) *L'oppidum de Saint-Blaise du Ve au VIIe s.* Paris

Dentzer, J.-M. (ed.) (1985) *Hauran I. Recherches archéologiques sur la Syrie du Sud à l'époque hellénistique et romaine*. Paris

Dodge, H. and Ward-Perkins, B. (eds.) (1992) *Marble in Antiquity. Collected Papers of J. B. Ward-Perkins*. London

Doehaerd, R. (1971) *Le haut moyen âge occidental. Économies et sociétés*. Paris

Drinkwater, J. F. (1992) 'The bacaudae of fifth-century Gaul', in Drinkwater and Elton (eds.) *Fifth-Century Gaul* 208–17

Duby, G. (1974) *The Early Growth of the European Economy*. London

Durliat, J. (1988) 'Le salaire de la paix sociale dans les royaumes barbares (Ve–VIe siècles)', in H. Wolfram and A. Schwarcz (eds.), *Anerkennung und Integration* (Österreichische Akademie der Wissenschaften, phil.-hist. Kl. Denkmalschriften 193) 21–72

Durliat, J. (1989) 'La peste du VIe siècle. Pour un nouvel examen des sources byzantines', in *Hommes et richesses* 1.107–19

Durliat, J. (1990a) *De la ville antique à la ville byzantine. Le problème des subsistances* (Collection de l'École Française de Rome 136). Rome

Durliat, J. (1990b) *Les Finances Publiques de Dioclétien aux Carolingiens (284–888)* (Beihefte der Francia 21). Sigmaringen

Durliat, J. (1993) 'Armée et société vers 600. Le problème des soldes', in Vallet and Kazanski (1993) 31–8

Dvornik, F. (1966) *Early Christian and Byzantine Political Philosophy: Origins and Background*. vol. 2. Washington, DC

Edwards, N. (1990) *The Archaeology of Early Medieval Ireland*. London

Ellis, S. (1985) 'Carthage in the seventh century, an expanding population', *Cahiers des études anciennes* 17: 30–42

Elton, H. (1996) *Warfare in Roman Europe AD 350–420*. Oxford

Empereur, J.-Y. and Picon, M. (1989) 'Les régions de production d'amphores impériales en Méditerranée orientale', in *Amphores romaines et histoire économique: dix ans de recherche* (Collection de l'École Française de Rome 114) (Rome) 223–48

Esmonde Cleary, A. S. (1989) *The Ending of Roman Britain*. London

Evans Grubbs, J. (1989) 'Abduction marriage in antiquity: a law of Constantine (*C. Th.* IX. 24. 1) and its social context', *JRS* 79: 59–83

Evans Grubbs, J. (1995) *Law and Family in Late Antiquity: The Emperor Constantine's Marriage Legislation*. Oxford

Ewig, E. (1963) 'Résidence et capitale pendant le haut Moyen Age', *RH* 230: 25–72

Fabre, P. (1949) *Saint Paulin de Nole et l'amitié chrétienne* (Bibliothèque des Écoles Françaises d'Athènes et de Rome, 161). Paris

Farka, C. (1993–4) 'Räuberhorden in Thrakien. Eine unbeachtete Quelle zur Geschichte der Zeit des Kaisers Maurikios', *BZ* 86/87: 462–9

Feissel, D. and Kaygusuz, I. (1985) 'Un mandement impérial du VIe siècle dans une inscription d'Hadrianoupolis d'Honoriade', *T&MByz* 9: 397–419

Feissel, D. and Philippidis-Braat, A. (1985) 'Inventaires en vue d'un recueil des inscriptions historiques de Byzance III, Inscriptions du Péloponnèse (à l'éxception de Mistra)', *T&MByz* 9: 267–395

Fentress, E. and Perkins, P. (1988) 'Counting African Red Slip Ware', in A. Mastino (ed.), *L'Africa romana. Atti del V convegno di studi, Sassari 11–13 dicembre 1987* 205–14

Festugière, A. J. (ed.) (1970) *Vie de Théodore de Sykéon* (Subsidia Hagiographica 48). Brussels

Finley, M. I. (1973) *The Ancient Economy*. London (2nd edn London 1985)

Fitzgerald, G. M. (1939) *A Sixth-Century Monastery at Beth-Shan (Scythopolis)* (Publications of the Palestine Section of the University Museum, University of Pennsylvania, IV). Philadelphia

Fortin, E. L. (1959) *Christianisme et culture philosophique au cinquième siècle*. Paris

Foss, C. (1975) 'The Persians in Asia Minor and the end of antiquity', *EHR* 90: 721–47

Foss, C. (1979) *Ephesus after Antiquity: A Late Antique, Byzantine and Turkish City*. Cambridge

Foss, C. (1995) 'The near eastern countryside in late antiquity: a review article', *The Roman and Byzantine Near East: Some Recent Archaeological Research* (*JRA* supplementary series 14) 213–34

Fouracre, P. (1986) '*Placita* and the settlement of disputes in later Merovingian Francia', in Davies and Fouracre (1986) 23–44

Fouracre, P. (1995) 'Eternal light and earthly needs: practical aspects of the development of Frankish immunities', in Davies and Fouracre (1995) 53–81

Francovich, R. and Noyé, G. (1994) *La storia dell'Alto Medioevo italiano (VI–X secolo) alla luce dell'archeologia*. Florence

Frank, T. (ed.) (1933–40) *An Economic Survey of Ancient Rome*. 5 vols. Baltimore

Frantz, A. (1988) *Late Antiquity: A. D. 267–700* (= *The Athenian Agora* vol. XXIV). Princeton

Frova, A. (ed.) (1973) *Scavi di Luni. Relazione preliminaire delle campagne di scavo 1970–1971.* Rome

Frova, A. (ed.) (1977) *Scavi di Luni. II. Relazione delle campagne di scavo 1972 – 1973 – 1974.* Rome

Frugoni, C. (1977) 'L'iconografia del matrimonio e della coppia nel Medioevo', in *Il matrimonio nella società altomedievale* II: 901–63

Ganz, D. (1995) 'The ideology of sharing: apostolic community and ecclesiastical property in the early Middle Ages', in Davies and Fouracre (1995) 17–30

Garnsey, P. (1988) *Famine and Food Supply in the Graeco-Roman World.* Cambridge

Garnsey, P. (1996) 'Prolegomenon to a study of the land in the later Roman empire', in J. H. M. Strubbe, R. A. Tybout and H. S. Versnel (eds.), *Energeia: Studies on Ancient History and Epigraphy presented to H. W. Pleket* (Amsterdam) 135–53

Garnsey, P., Hopkins, K. and Whittaker, C. R. (eds.) (1983) *Trade in the Ancient Economy.* London

Garnsey, P. and Saller, R. (1987) *The Roman Empire: Economy, Society and Culture.* London

Gascou, J. (1985) 'Les grands domaines, la cité et l'état en Égypte byzantine. Recherches d'histoire agraire, fiscale et administrative', *T&MByz* 9: 1–90

Gascou, J. (1994) 'Deux inscriptions byzantines de Haute-Égypte', *T&MByz* 12: 323–42

Gaudemet, J. (1948) 'Constantin restaurateur de l'ordre', in *Studi in onore di Siro Solazzi* (Naples) 652–74 (= Gaudemet (1979) II.71–95)

Gaudemet, J. (1950) 'Droit romain et principes canoniques en matière de mariage au bas-empire', in *Studi in memoria di Emilio Albertario* (Milano) II.173–96 (= Gaudemet (1979) III.163–88)

Gaudemet, J. (1970) 'Le lien matrimonial: les incertitudes du Haut Moyen-Age', in *Le lien matrimonial* (Strasbourg) 81–105 (= Gaudemet (1980) 230–89)

Gaudemet, J. (1977) 'Le legs du droit romain en matière matrimoniale', in *Il matrimonio nella società altomedievale* I.139–79 (= Gaudemet (1980) 230–89)

Gaudemet, J. (1978a) 'Tendances nouvelles de la législation familiale au IVe siècle', in *Transformation et conflits au IVe siècle ap. J.-C., Bordeaux 1970* (Bonn) 187–206

Gaudemet, J. (1978b) 'L'intérpretation du principe d'indissolubilité du mariage chrétien au cours du premier millénaire', *Bollettino dell'Istituto di diritto romano* 81: 11–70 (= Gaudemet (1980) 230–89)

Gaudemet, J. (1979) *Études de droit romain.* Camerino

Gaudemet, J. (1980) *Société et mariage.* Strasbourg

Gaudemet, J. (1989) *L'Église dans l'empire romain (IVe–Ve siècles).* Paris

Geary, P. (1985) *Aristocracy in Provence: The Rhone Basin at the Dawn of the Carolingian Age.* Philadelphia

George, J. (1992) *Venantius Fortunatus: A Latin Poet in Merovingian Gaul.* Oxford

Gerberding, R. A. (1987) *The Rise of the Carolingians and the Liber Historiae Francorum.* Oxford

Giannarelli, E. (1980) *La tipologia femminile nella biografia e nell'autobiografia cristiana del IV secolo.* Rome

Giardina, A. (1982) 'Lavoro e storia sociale. Antagonismi e alleanze dall'ellenismo al tardoantico', *Opus* I: 115–46

Giardina, A. (1988) 'Carità eversiva: le donazioni di Melania la Giovane e gli equilibri della società tardoromana', *Studi Storici*: 127–42

Giardina, A. (1994) 'Melania la Santa', in A. Fraschetti (ed.), *Roma al femminile* (Rome–Bari) 259–85

Goffart, W. (1981) 'Rome, Constantinople, and the barbarians', *AHR* 76: 275–306

Goffart, W. (1982) 'Old and new in Merovingian taxation', *P&P* 96: 3–21

Goffart, W. (1988) *The Narrators of Barbarian History*. Princeton

Goffart, W. (1989) 'The theme of "The Barbarian Invasions" in late antique and modern historiography', in Chrysos and Schwarcz (eds.) (1989) 87–107

Goody, J. (1983) *The Development of the Family and Marriage in Europe*. Cambridge

Goody, J. (1990) *The Oriental, the Ancient and the Primitive: Systems of Marriage and the Family in the Pre-industrial Societies of Eurasia*. Cambridge

Goria, F. (1975) *Studi sul matrimonio dell'adultera nel diritto giustinianeo e bizantino*. Turin

Grahn-Hoek, H. (1976) *Die frankische Oberschicht im 6 Jahrhundert. Studien zur ihrer rechtlichen und politischen Stellung*. Sigmaringen

Graus, F. (1965) *Volk, Herrscher und Heiliger im Reich der Merowinger: Studien zur Hagiographie der Merowingerzeit*. Prague

Greene, K. (1986) *The Archaeology of the Roman Economy*. London

Grierson, P. (1982) *Byzantine Coins*. London

Guastella, G. (1980) 'I Parentalia come testo antropologico: l'avunculato nel mondo celtico e nella famiglia di Ausonio', *Materiali e discussioni* 4: 97–124

Halsall, G. (1995) *Settlement and Social Organisation: The Merovingian Region of Metz*. Cambridge

Hardy, E. R. (1931) *The Large Estates of Byzantine Egypt*. New York

Härke, H. (1990) '"Warrior graves?": the background of the Anglo-Saxon burial rite', *P&P* 26: 22–43

Härke, H. (1992) 'Changing symbols in a changing society: the Anglo-Saxon weapon burial rite in the seventh century', in M. O. H. Carver (ed.), *The Age of Sutton Hoo* (London) 149–65

Harper, G. M. (1928) 'Village administration in the Roman province of Syria', *YCS* 1: 105–68

Harries, J. (1994) *Sidonius Apollinaris and the Fall of Rome*. Oxford

Harris, W. V. (1986) 'The Roman father's power of life and death', in R. S. Bagnall and W. V. Harris (eds.), *Studies in Roman Law in Memory of A. A. Schiller* (Leiden) 81–95

Harris, W. V. (1994) 'Child-exposure in the Roman empire', *JRS* 84: 1–22

Harrison, D. (1993) *The Early State and the Towns: Forms of Integration in Lombard Italy, AD 568–774*. Lund

Harrison, R. M. (1986) *Excavations at Saraçhane in Istanbul, Volume I (The Excavations, Structures, Architectural Decoration, Small Finds, Coins, Bones, and Molluscs)*. Princeton

Harrison, R. M. (1989) *A Temple for Byzantium: The Discovery and Excavation of Anicia Juliana's Palace-Church in Istanbul*. London

Hatcher, J. (1977) *Plague, Population and the English Economy 1348–1530*. London

Hayes, J. W. (1972) *Late Roman Pottery: A Catalogue of Roman Fine Wares*. London

Hayes, J. W. (1980) *Supplement to Late Roman Pottery*. London

Hayes, J. W. (1992) *Excavations at Saraçhane in Istanbul, Volume II (The Pottery)*. Princeton

Heather, P. (1989) 'Cassiodorus and the rise of the Amals: genealogy and the Goths under Hun domination', *JRS* 79: 103–28

Heather, P. (1992) 'The emergence of the Visigothic kingdom', in Drinkwater and Elton (eds.), *Fifth-Century Gaul* 84–94

Heather, P. (1993) 'The historical culture of Ostrogothic Italy', *Atti del XIII Congresso internazionale di studi sull'Alto Medioevo* (Spoleto) 317–53

Heather, P. (1994) 'New men for new Constantines. The creation of an imperial elite in the eastern Mediterranean', in Magdalino (ed.), *New Constantines* 11–33

Heather, P. (1995a) 'The Huns and the end of the Roman empire in western Europe', *EHR* 110: 4–41

Heather, P. (1995b) 'Theoderic, king of the Goths', *EME* 4: 145–73

Heather, P. (1996) *The Goths* (Blackwell Peoples of Europe series). Oxford

Heather, P. (1998) 'Senators and senates'. *Cambridge Ancient History* XIII.184–210

Hedeager, L. (1987) 'Empire, frontier and the barbarian hinterland. Rome and northern Europe from AD 1–400', in K. Kristiansen *et al.* (eds.), *Centre and Periphery in the Ancient World* (Cambridge) 125–40

Hedeager, L. (1988) 'The evolution of Germanic Society 1–400 A.D.', in R. F. J. Jones *et al.* (eds.), *First Millennium Papers: Western Europe in the First Millennium* (BAR International Series 401) (Oxford) 129–44

Heinzelmann, M. (1976) *Bischoffsherrschaft in Gallien*. Munich

Heinzelmann, M. (1982) 'Gallische Prosopographie 260–527', *Francia* 10: 531–718

Heinzelmann, M. (1992) 'The "affair" of Hilary of Arles (445) and Gallo-Roman identity in the fifth century', in Drinkwater and Elton (eds.), *Fifth-Century Gaul* 239–51

Heinzelmann, M. (1993) '*Villa* d'après les oeuvres de Grégoire de Tours', in E. Magnou-Nortier (ed.), *Aux sources de la gestion publique. Tome I, Enquête lexicographique sur fundus, villa, domus, mansus* (Lille) 45–70

Herrenschmidt, C. (1994) 'Le *xwêtôdas* ou mariage "incestueux" en Iran ancien', in Bonte (ed.) (1994) 113–25

Hildebrandt, H. (1988) 'Systems of agriculture in central Europe up to the tenth and eleventh centuries', in Hooke (ed.) (1988) 275–90

Hillgarth, J. (1980) 'Popular religion in Visigothic Spain', in James (ed.) (1980a) 3–59

Hillgarth, J. (1986) *Christianity and Paganism, 350–750: The Conversion of Western Europe*. Philadelphia

Hodges, R. (1989) *The Anglo-Saxon Achievement*. London

Hodges, R. and Whitehouse, D. (1983) *Mohammed, Charlemagne and the Origins of Europe*. London

Holum, K. G. *et al.* (1988) *King Herod's Dream. Caesarea on the Sea*. New York and London

Hooke, D. (ed.) (1988) *Anglo-Saxon Settlements*. Oxford

Hope-Taylor, B. (1977) *Yeavering: An Anglo-British Centre of Early Northumbria* (Department of the Environment, Archaeological Reports 7). London

Hopkins, K. (1980a) 'Taxes and trade in the Roman Empire (200 B.C.–A.D. 400)', *JRS* 70: 101–25

Hopkins, K. (1980b) 'Brother–sister marriage in Roman Egypt', *Comparative Studies in Society and History* 22: 303–54

Humbert, M. (1972) *Le remariage à Rome. Étude d'histoire juridique et sociale*. Milan

Humbert, M. (1983) 'Enfants à louer ou à vendre: Augustin et l'autorité parentale (*Ep.* 10* et 24*)', in *Les lettres de Saint Augustin découvertes par Johannes Divjak* (Paris) 189–203

Inscriptions grecques et latines de la Syrie (1929–). Paris

Irsigler, F. (1979) 'On the aristocratic character of early Frankish society', in T. Reuter (ed. and trans.), *The Medieval Nobility* (Amsterdam) 105–36

James, E. (ed.) (1980a) *Visigothic Spain: New Approaches.* Oxford

James, E. (1980b) 'Septimania and its frontier: an archaeological approach', in James (ed.) (1980a) 223–41

James, E. (1982) *The Origins of France: From Clovis to the Capetians 500–1000.* London

James, E. (1983) '*Beati pacifici*: bishops and the law in sixth-century Gaul', in J. Bossy (ed.), *Disputes and Settlements: Law and Human Relations in the West* (Cambridge) 25–46

James, E. (1988) *The Franks.* Oxford

Joxe, F. (1959) 'Le christianisme et l'évolution des sentiments familiaux dans les lettres privées sur papyrus" *AAntHung* 7: 411–20

Kaegi, W. (1992) *Byzantium and the Early Islamic Conquests.* Cambridge

Kantorowicz, E. H. (1960) 'On the golden marriage belt and the marriage rings of the Dumbarton Oaks collection', *DOP* 14: 3–16

Kaplan, M. (1992) *Les hommes et la terre à Byzance du VIe au XIe siècle. Propriété et exploitation du sol* (*Byzantina sorbonica*, 10) Paris

Karlin-Hayter, P. (1992) 'Further notes on Byzantine marriage: raptus-ἁρπαγή or μνηστεῖαι?', *DOP* 46: 135–54

Keenan, J. G. (1980) 'Aurelius Phoibammon, son of Triadelphus: a Byzantine Egyptian land entrepreneur', *BASP* 22: 137–69

Keenan, J. G. (1984) 'The Aphrodite papyri and village life in Byzantine Egypt', *BSAC* 26: 51–63

Keenan, J. G. (1985) 'Notes on absentee landlordism at Aphrodito', *BASP* 22: 137–69

Keenan, J. G. (1993) 'Papyrology and Byzantine historiography', in W. J. Cherf (ed.), *Alpha to Omega: Studies in Honour of George John Szemler on his Sixty-Fifth Birthday* (Chicago) 111–22

Kennedy, H. (1985) 'The last century of Byzantine Syria: a reinterpretation', *BF* 10: 141–83

Kertzer, D. I. and Saller, R. P. (eds.) (1991) *The Family in Italy from Antiquity to the Present.* New Haven and London

King, P. D. (1972) *Law and Society in the Visigothic Kingdom.* Cambridge

Kirkby, H. (1981) 'The scholar and his public', in Gibson (ed.), *Boethius* 44–69

Klingshirn, W. E. (1994) *Caesarius of Arles: The Making of a Christian Community in Gaul.* Cambridge

Kondic, V. (1984) 'Les formes des fortifications protobyzantines dans la région des Portes de Fer', in *Villes et peuplement* (1984) 131–61

Kraemer, C. J. (1958) *Excavations at Nessana, conducted by H. A. Colt, Jr* III, *The Non-Literary Papyri.* Princeton

Krautheimer, R. (1980) *Rome: Profile of a City, 312–1308.* Princeton

Laiou, A. E. (1985) 'Consensus facit nuptias – et non. Pope Nicholas I's *Responsa* to the Bulgarians as a source for Byzantine marriage customs', *RJ* 4: 189–201

(= no. IV of Laiou, *Gender, Society and Economic Life in Byzantium*, London Variorum 1992)

Laiou, A. E. (1992) *Mariage, amour et parenté à Byzance aux XIe–XIIIe siècles*. Paris

Laiou, A. E. (1993) 'Sex, consent, and coercion in Byzantium', in A. E. Laiou (ed.), *Consent and Coercion to Sex and Marriage in Ancient and Medieval Societies* (Washington) 109–221

Lambrechts, P. (1937) 'Le commerce des "Syriens" en Gaule du haut empire à l'époque mérovingienne', *AC* 6: 35–61

Larson, C. W. R. (1970) 'Theodosius and the Thessalonian massacre revisited – yet again', in F. L. Cross (ed.), *Studia Patristica* 10 (Texte und Untersuchungen 107) (Berlin) 297–301

Latouche, R. (1967) *The Birth of the Western Economy*. London (first published, in French, 1956)

Lebecq, S. (1994) 'Le baptême manqué du roi Radbod', in *Les assises du pouvoir: temps mediévaux: territoires africains: Mélanges Jean Devisse* (Valenciennes) 141–50

Lee, A. D. (1988) 'Close-kin marriage in late antique Mesopotamia', *GRBS* 29: 403–13

Lemaire, A. (1929) 'Origine de la règle *"Nullum sine dote fiat conjugium"*', in *Mélanges P. Fournier* (Paris) 415–24

Lepelley, C. (1983) 'Liberté, colonat et esclavage d'après la Lettre 24*: la jurisdiction épiscopale *"de liberali causa"*', in *Les lettres de Saint Augustin découvertes par Johannes Divjak* (Paris) 329–42

Levi, D. (1947) *Antioch Mosaic Pavements*. Princeton

Lewit, T. (1991) *Agricultural Production in the Roman Economy A.D. 200–400* (BAR International Series 568). Oxford

Leyser, K. (1979) *Rule and Conflict in an Early Medieval Society*. London

L'Huillier, P. (1987) 'Novella 89 of Leo the Wise on marriage: an insight into its theoretical and practical impact', *Greek Orthodox Theological Review* 32.2: 153–62

Liebeschuetz, J. H. W. G. (1972) *Antioch, City and Imperial Administration in the Later Roman Empire*. Oxford

Liebeschuetz, J. H. W. G. (1979) *Continuity and Change in Roman Religion*. Oxford

Liebeschuetz, J. H. W. G. (1993) 'The end of the Roman army in the western empire', in Rich and Shipley (1993) 265–76

Lieu, S. (1986) 'Captives, refugees and exiles: a study of cross-frontier civilian movements between Rome and Persia from Valerian to Julian', in P. Freeman and D. Kennedy (eds.), *The Defence of the Roman and Byzantine East* (BAR International Series 297.ii) (Oxford) 475–505

Lintott, A. (1968) *Violence in Republican Rome*. Oxford

Longnon, A. (1878) *Géographie de la Gaule au VIe siècle*. Paris

Loseby, S. T. (1992) 'Marseille: a late antique success story?', *JRS* 82: 165–85

Lot, F. (1921) 'Conjectures démographique sur la France au IXe siècle', *Le Moyen Âge* 32: 1–27 and 109–37

Lot, F. (1928) *L'impôt foncier et la capitation personnelle sous le Bas-Empire et à l'époque franque* (Bibliothèque de l'école des hautes études 253). Paris

Lynch, J. H. (1986) *Godparents and Kinship in Early Medieval Europe*. Princeton

MacCormack, S. (1981) *Art and Ceremony in Late Antiquity*. Berkeley

MacMullen, R. (1963) *Soldier and Civilian in the Later Roman Empire*. Cambridge

MacMullen, R. (1987) 'Late Roman slavery', *Historia* 26: 359–82

MacMullen, R. (1988) *Corruption and the Decline of Rome*. New Haven

Mallory, J. P. and McNeill, T. E. (1991) *The Archaeology of Ulster: From Colonization to Plantation*. Belfast

Mathisen, R. W. (1981) 'Epistolography, literary circles and family ties in late Roman Gaul', *TAPA* 111: 95–109

Mathisen, R. W. (1984) 'The family of Georgius Florentius Gregorius and the bishops of Tours', *Medievalia et Humanistica* 12: 83–95

Mathisen, R. W. (1993) *Roman Aristocrats in Barbarian Gaul: Strategies for Survival in an Age of Transition*. Austin

Il Matrimonio nella società altomedievale (1977). Spoleto (XXIV Settimana di studio del Centro Italiano di Studi sull'Alto Medioevo)

Matthews, J. F. (1974) 'The letters of Symmachus', in J. W. Binns (ed.), *Latin Literature of the Fourth Century* (London) 58–99

Matthews, J. F. (1975) *Western Aristocracies and Imperial Court A.D. 364–425*. Oxford

Matthews, J. F. (1989) *The Roman Empire of Ammianus*. London and Baltimore

Mattingly, D. J. (1995) *Tripolitania*. London

Mattingly, D. J. and Hayes, J. W. (1992) 'Nador and fortified farms in North Africa', *JRA* 5: 408–18

Mattingly, D. J. and Hitchner, R. B. (1995) 'Roman Africa: an archaeological review', *JRS* 85: 165–213

Millar, F. (1981) 'The world of the *Golden Ass*', *JRS* 71: 63–75

Millett, M. (1990) *The Romanization of Britain*. Cambridge

Millett, M. (1991) 'Pottery: population or supply pattern? The *Ager Tarraconensis* approach', in G. Barker and J. Lloyd (eds.), *Roman Landscapes: Archaeological Survey in the Mediterranean Region* (Archaeological Monographs of the British School at Rome 2) (London) 18–28

Mitchell, F. (1976) *The Irish Landscape*. London

Mitteis, L. (1891) *Reichsrecht und Volksrecht in den östlichen Provinzen des römischen Kaiserreichs*. Leipzig

Moorhead, J. (1992) *Theoderic in Italy*. Oxford

Moreau, Ph. (1994) 'Le mariage dans les degrés rapprochés. Le dossier romain (Ier siècle av. J.-C. – IIIe siècle ap. J.-C.)', in Bonte (ed.) (1994) 59–78

Morrison, C. (1986) 'Byzance au VIIe siècle: le témoignage de la numismatique', in *Byzantium: Tribute to Andreas Stratos* (Athens) 1.149–63

Müller-Wiener, W. (1986) 'Von der Polis zum Kastron. Wandlungen der Stadt im ägäischem Raum von der Antike zum Mittelalter', *Gymnasium* 93: 435–75

Murialdo, G., Bertolotti, F., Falcetti, C., Palazzi, P. and Paroli, L. (1997) 'La suppellettile da mensa e da cucina nel VII secolo in Liguria: l'esempio di un sito fortificato', in S. Gelichi (ed.), *I Congresso Nazionale di Archaeologia Medievale, Pisa 29–31 maggio 1997*. Florence

Murray, A. C. (1983) *Germanic Kinship Structure*. Toronto

Nelson, J. (1991) 'A propos des femmes royales dans les rapports entre le monde wisigothique et le monde franc à l'époque de Reccared', in *XIV centenario Concilio III de Toledo 589–1989* (Madrid) 465–76

Nippel, W. (1984) 'Policing Rome', *JRS* 74: 20–9

Nitz, H.-J. (1988) 'Settlement structures and settlement systems of the Frankish central state in Carolingian and Ottonian times', in Hooke (1988) 249–73

Olster, D. M. (1993) *The Politics of Usurpation in the Seventh Century: Rhetoric and Revolution in Byzantium*. Amsterdam

Orestano, R. (1951) *La struttura giuridica del matrimonio romano dal diritto classico al diritto giustinianeo*. Milan

Orlandis, J. and Ramos-Lissen, D. (1981) *Die Synoden auf der iberischen Halbinsel bis zum Einbruch des Islam (711)*. Paderborn

Orrsaud, D. (1992) 'De la céramique byzantine à la céramique islamique. Quelques hypothèses à partir du mobilier trouvé a Déhès', in P. Canivet and J.-P. Rey-Coquais (eds.), *La Syrie de Byzance à l'Islam* (Damascus) 219–28

Ovadiah, A. (1970) *Corpus of the Byzantine Churches in the Holy Land*. Bonn

Paroli, L. and Delogu, P. (eds.) (1993) *La storia economica di Roma nell'alto Medioevo alla luce dei recenti scavi archeologici*. Florence

Patlagean, E. (1973) 'L'enfant et son avenir dans la famille byzantine (IVe–XIIe siècles)', *Annales de démographie historique* 86–93 (= no. x of Patlagean, *Structure sociale, famille, chrétienté à Byzance, IVe–XIe siècle*, London Variorum 1981)

Patlagean, E. (1978) 'Familles chrétiennes d'Asie Mineure et histoire démographique du IVème siècle', in *Transformation et conflits au IVème siècle ap. J.-C.* (Bonn) 169–86 (= no. ix of Patlagean, *Structure sociale, famille, chrétienté à Byzance, IVe–XIe siècle*, London Variorum 1981)

Peacock, D. P. S. (1982) *Pottery in the Roman World: An Ethnoarchaeological Approach*. London and New York

Peacock, D. P. S. and Williams, D. F. (1986) *Amphorae and the Roman Economy: An Introductory Guide*. London and New York

Percival, J. (1976) *The Roman Villa*. London

Percival, J. (1992) 'The fifth-century villa: new life or death postponed?', in Drinkwater and Elton (eds.), *Fifth-Century Gaul*: 156–66

Piccirillo, M. (1985) 'Rural settlement in Byzantine Jordan', in A. Hadidi (ed.), *Studies in the History and Archaeology of Jordan* ii (Amman) 257–61

Piccirillo, M. (1993) *The Mosaics of Jordan*. Amman

La Pietra ollare dalla preistoria all'età moderna (1987). Como

Pietri, Ch. (1979) 'Le mariage chrétien à Rome', in J. Delumeau (ed.), *Histoire vécue du peuple chrétien* (Toulouse) i. 105–31

Pietri, L. (1983) *La ville de Tours du IVe au VIe siècle. Naissance d'une cité chrétienne* (Collection de l'École Française de Rome 69). Rome

Pirenne, H. (1939) *Mohammed and Charlemagne*. London (first published as *Mahomet et Charlemagne* (Paris and Brussels) 1937)

Pontal, O. (1989) *Histoire des conciles mérovingiens*. Paris

Popovic, V. (1984) 'Byzantins, Slaves et autochthones dans les provinces de Prévalitane et Nouvelle Épire', in *Villes et peuplement* (1984) 181–243

Poulter, A. (1992) 'The use and abuse of urbanism in the Danubian provinces during the later Roman empire', in J. Rich (ed.), *The City in Late Antiquity* (London) 99–135

Pringle, D. (1981) *The Defence of Byzantine Africa from Justinian to the Arab Conquest: An Account of the Military History and Archaeology of the African Provinces in the Sixth and Seventh Centuries* (BAR International Series 99). Oxford

Prinz, F. (1967) 'Heiligenkult und Adelsherrschaft im Spiegel merowingischer Hagiographie', *Hist. Zeit.* 204: 529–44

Randsborg, K. (1991) *The First Millennium A.D. in Europe and the Mediterranean: An Archaeological Essay*. Cambridge

Randsborg, K. (1992) 'Barbarians, classical antiquity and the rise of western Europe. An archaeological essay', *P&P* 137: 8–24

Rebuffat, R. (1993) 'Introduction au colloque', in Vallet and Kazanski (1993) 5–9

Rémondon, R. (1965) 'P. Hamb. 56 et P. Lond. 1419 (notes sur les finances d'Aphrodito du VIe siècle au VIIe)', *Chronique d'Égypte* 40: 401–30

Reuter, T. (1985) 'Plunder and tribute in the Carolingian empire,' *TRHS* 35: 75–94

Reuter, T. (1991) 'The end of Carolingian military expansion', in P. Godman and R. Collins (eds.), *Charlemagne's Heir: New Perspectives on the Reign of Louis the Pious* (Oxford) 391–405

Reynolds, P. (1995) *Trade in the Western Mediterranean, A.D. 400–700: The Ceramic Evidence* (BAR International Series 604). Oxford

Reynolds, P. L. (1994) *Marriage in the Western Church: The Christianization of Marriage during the Patristic and Early Medieval Periods*. Leiden, New York and Cologne

Rich, J. and Shipley, G. (1993) *War and Society in the Roman World*. London

Richards, J. (1979) *The Popes and the Papacy in the Early Middle Ages, 476–752*. London

Riley, J. A. (1979) 'The coarse pottery', in *Excavations at Sidi Khrebish Benghazi (Berenice)* II, ed. J. A. Lloyd (*Tripoli*, supplement to *Libya Antiqua* v, vol. II) 91–465

Ritzer, K. (1981) *Formen, Riten und religiöses Brauchtum der Eheschliessung in den christlichen Kirchen des ersten Jahrtausends*. 2nd edn. Münster

Roda, S. (1979) 'Il matrimonio fra cugini germani nella legislazione tardoimperiale', *SDHI* 45: 289–309

Rösener, W. (ed.) (1989) *Strukturen der Grundherrschaft im frühen Mittelalter*. Göttingen

Rossiter, J. J. (1990) 'Villas vandales; le *suburbium* de Carthage au début du VIe siècle de notre ère', in *Actes du IVe Colloque international sur l'histoire de l'Afrique du Nord (Strasbourg 1988)* vol. 1 (*Carthage et son territoire dans l'Antiquité*) (Paris) 221–7

Rouche, M. (1979) *L'Aquitaine des Wisigoths aux Arabes 418–781. Naissance d'une région*. Paris

Rouche, M. (1983) 'La destinée des biens de Saint Remi durant le haut moyen âge', in W. Janssen and D. Lohrmann (eds.) *Villa – Curtis – Grangia* (Munich) 46–61

Rouche, M. (1987) 'The early Middle Ages in the west', in P. Veyne (ed.), *A History of Private Life from Pagan Rome to Byzantium* (Cambridge, MA) 411–549

Rubin, R. (1989) 'The debate over climatic changes in the Negev, fourth–seventh centuries C.E.', *Palestine Exploration Quarterly* 1989: 71–8

Ruggini, L. (1959) 'Ebrei e orientali nell'Italia settentrionale fra il IV e il VI secolo d. Cr.', *Studia et documenta historiae et iuris* 25: 187–308

Saller, R. P. (1991a) 'European family history and Roman law', *Continuity and Change* 6: 335–46

Saller, R. P. (1991b) 'Roman heirship strategies in principle and in practice', in Kertzer and Saller (1991) 26–47

Saller, R. P. (1994) *Property and Death in the Roman Family*. Cambridge

Saller, R. P. and Shaw, B. D. (1984) 'Tombstones and Roman family relations in the Principate: civilians, soldiers and slaves', *JRS* 74: 124–56

Samson, R. (1987) 'The Merovingian nobleman's house: castle or villa?', *JMH* 13: 287–315

Sargenti, M. (1986) 'Matrimonio cristiano e società pagana', *SDHI* 51: 367–91 (= Sargenti, *Studi sul diritto del tardo impero*, Padua 1986: 343–73)

Sartre, M. (1985) *Bostra des origines à l'Islam*. Paris

Sawyer, P. H. and Wood, I. N. (eds.) (1977) *Early Medieval Kingship*. Leeds

Schäfer, C. (1991) *Der weströmische Senat als Träger des antiker Kontinuität unter den Ostgotenkönigen (490–540 n. Chr.)*. St Katharinen

Seeck, O. (1919) *Regesten der Kaiser und Päpste für die Jahre 311 bis 476 n. Chr*. Stuttgart

Segal, J. B. (1955) 'Mesopotamian communities from Julian to the rise of Islam', *PBA* 41: 109–41

Segal, J. B. (1970) *Edessa: 'The Blessed City'*. Oxford

Shaw, B. D. (1984) 'Latin funerary epigraphy and family life in the later Roman empire', *Historia* 33: 457–97

Shaw, B. D. (1987a) 'The family in late antiquity: the experience of Augustine', *P&P* 115: 3–51

Shaw, B. D. (1987b) 'The age of Roman girls at marriage: some reconsiderations', *JRS* 77: 30–46

Shaw, B. D. (1991) 'The cultural meaning of death: age and gender in the Roman family', in Kertzer and Saller (1991) 66–90

Shaw, B. D. (1992) 'Explaining incest: brother–sister marriage in Graeco-Roman Egypt', *Man* n.s. 27: 267–99

Shaw, B. D. and Saller, R. P. (1984) 'Close-kin marriage in Roman society?', *Man* n.s. 19: 432–44

Slack, P. (1990) *The Impact of Plague in Tudor and Stuart England*. Oxford

Small, A. M. and Buck, R. J. (1994) *The Excavations of San Giovanni di Ruoti*, I. *The Villas and their Environment*. Toronto

Sodini, J.-P. (1989) 'Le commerce des marbres à l'époque protobyzantine', in *Hommes et richesses* I.163–86

Sodini, J.-P. *et al.* (1980) 'Déhès (Syrie du Nord): campagnes I–III (1976–1978). Recherches sur l'habitat rural', *Syria* 57: 1–304

Spagnuolo Vigorita, T. (1984) *Exsecranda pernicies. Delatori e fisco nell'età di Costantino*. Naples

Spieser, J.-M. (1984) 'Les villes en Grèce du IIIe au VIIe s.', in *Villes et peuplement* (1984) 315–38

Stafford, P. (1983) *Queens, Concubines and Dowagers*. London

Stancliffe, C. (1983) *St Martin and his Hagiographer*. Oxford

Stroheker, K. F. (1948) *Der senatorische Adel im spätantiken Gallien*. Tübingen

Talbot, A. M. (1990) 'The Byzantine family and monastery', *DOP* 44: 119–29

Tate, G. (1992) *Les campagnes de la Syrie du nord du IIe au VIIe siècle. Un example d'expansion démographique et économique à la fin de l'Antiquité* (Institut Français d'Archéologie du Proche-Orient, Bibliothèque archéologique et historique 133). Paris

Thébert, Y. (1987) 'Private life and domestic architecture in Roman Africa', in P. Veyne (ed.), *A History of Private Life: From Pagan Rome to Byzantium* (Cambridge, MA) 313–409

Thomas, J. P. (1987) *Private Religious Foundations in the Byzantine Empire*. Washington, DC

Thompson, E. A. (1960) 'The conversion of the Visigoths to Catholicism', *NMS* 4: 4–35

Thompson, E. A. (1963) 'The Visigoths from Fritigern to Euric', *Historia* 12: 105–26

Thompson, E. A. (1969) *The Goths in Spain*. Oxford

Thompson, E. A. (1982) *Romans and Barbarians. The Decline of the Western Empire.* Madison, WI

Tjäder, J.-O. (1982) *Die nichtliterarischen lateinischen Papyri Italiens aus der Zeit 445–700,* vol. 2. Stockholm

Toubert, P. (1973) *Les structures du Latium médieval* 2 vols. (Bibliothèque des Écoles Françaises d'Athènes et de Rome 221). Rome

Toubert, P. (1977) 'La théorie du mariage chez les moralistes carolingiens', in *Il matrimonio nella società altomedievale* II.233–82

Treadgold, W. (1995) *Byzantium and its Army 284–1081.* Stanford

Treggiari, S. (1991) *Roman Marriage.* Iusti Coniuges *from the Time of Cicero to the Time of Ulpian.* Oxford

Trier Kaiserresidenz und Bischofssitz. Die Stadt in spätantiker und frühchristlicher Zeit (1984). Mainz

Troplong, R.-Th. (1843) *De l'influence du christianisme sur le droit civil des Romains.* Paris

Unwin, T. (1988) 'Towards a model of Anglo-Scandinavian rural settlement in England', in Hooke (1988) 77–98

Vallet, F. and Kazanski, M. (1993) *L'Armée romaine et les barbares du IIIe au VIIe siècle* (Association française d'archéologie mérovingienne et Musée des antiquités nationales). Rouen

Van Dam, R. (1992) 'The Pirenne thesis and fifth-century Gaul', in Drinkwater and Elton (eds.), *Fifth-Century Gaul* 321–33

Van Dam, R. (1993) *Saints and their Miracles in Late Antique Gaul.* Princeton

Van Ossel, P. (1992) *Établissements ruraux de l'Antiquité tardive dans le nord de la Gaule.* Paris

Van Uytfanghe, M. (1987) *Stylisation et condition humaine dans l'hagiographie mérovingienne (600–750).* Brussels

Vatin, Cl. (1970) *Recherches sur le mariage et la condition de la femme mariée à l'époque hellénistique.* Paris

Vera, D. (1995) 'Dalla "Villa Perfecta" alla villa di Palladio: sulle trasformazioni del sistema agrario in Italia fra Principato e Dominato (2a parte)', *Athenaeum* 83: 331–56

Villeneuve, F. (1985) 'L'économie rurale et la vie des campagnes dans le Hauran antique (Ier siècle ap. J.-C.). Une approche', in Dentzer (1985) 63–138

Villes et peuplement dans l'Illyricum protobyzantin (1984) (Collection de l'École Française de Rome 77). Rome

Vita-Finzi, C. (1969) *The Mediterranean Valleys: Geological Changes in Historical Times.* Cambridge

Vogel, C. (1966) 'L'âge des époux chrétiens au moment de contracter mariage, d'après les inscriptions paléochrétiennes', *RDC* 16: 355–66

Vogel, C. (1977) 'Les rites de la célébration du mariage: leur signification dans la formation du lien durant le haut Moyen Âge', in *Il matrimonio nella società altomedievale* I.397–465

Vogel, C. (1982) 'Application du principe de l'"économie" en matière de divorce dans le droit canonique oriental', *RDC* 32: 81–100

Volterra, E. (1937) *Diritto romano e diritti orientali.* Bologna (reprinted Naples 1983)

Volterra, E. (1967) 'Famiglia (diritto romano)', in *Enciclopedia del diritto* (Milan) XVI.723–44

Volterra, E. (1975) 'Matrimonio (diritto romano)', in *Enciclopedia del diritto* (Milan) xxv.726–807

Wallace-Hadrill, J. M. (1962) 'The blood-feud of the Franks', in *The Long-Haired Kings and Other Studies in Frankish History* (London) 121–47

Walmsley, A. (1988) 'Pella/Fihl after the Islamic conquest (A.D. 635–c. 900): a convergence of literary and archaeological data', *Mediterranean Archaeology* 1.142–59

Ward-Perkins, B., Mills, N., Gadd, D. and Delano Smith, C. (1986) 'Luni and the Ager Lunensis: the rise and fall of a Roman town and its territory', *PBSR* 54: 81–146

Ward-Perkins, J. B. (1968) 'The Ager Veientanus north and east of Veii', PBSR 36: 1–218

Ward-Perkins, J. B. *et al.* (1986) 'Town houses at Ptolemais, Cyrenaica', *Libyan Studies* 17: 109–53

Watson, P. (1992) 'Change in foreign and regional economic links with Pella in the seventh century A.D.: the ceramic evidence', in P. Canivet and J.-P. Rey-Coquais (eds.), *La Syrie de Byzance à l'Islam* (Damascus) 233–48

Weiss, E. (1908) 'Endogamie und Exogamie im römischen Kaiserreich', *ZRG RA* 29: 340–69

Wenskus, R. (1961) *Stammesbildung und Verfassung: Das Werden der frühmittelalterlichen Gentes.* Cologne

Whitby, M. (1996) 'Recruitment in the Roman armies from Justinian to Heraclius (*ca.* 565–615)', in Cameron, Averil (ed.), *The Byzantine and Early Islamic Near East*, III: *States, Resources and Armies* (Princeton) 61–124

White, C. (1992) *Christian Friendship in the Fourth Century.* Cambridge

Whittaker, C. R. (1985) 'Trade and the aristocracy in the Roman empire', *Opus* 4: 49–75

Whittaker, C. R. (1993) 'Landlords and warlords in the later Roman Empire', in Rich and Shipley (1993) 277–302

Whittaker, C. R. (1994) *Frontiers of the Roman Empire: A Social and Economic Study.* Baltimore

Wickham, C. (1981) *Early Medieval Italy: Central Power and Local Society 400–1000.* London

Wickham, C. (1984) 'The other transition: from the ancient world to feudalism', *P&P* 103: 3–36

Wickham, C. (1986) 'Land disputes and their social framework in Lombard–Carolingian Italy, 700–900', in Davies and Fouracre (1986) 105–24

Wickham, C. (1988) 'L'Italia e l'alto medioevo', *AM* 15: 105–24

Wickham, C. (1992) 'Problems of comparing rural societies in early medieval western Europe', *TRHS* 6th series, 2: 221–46

Wickham, C. (1993) 'La chute de Rome n'aura pas lieu. À propos d'un livre récent', *Le Moyen Âge* 99: 107–26

Wightman, E. (1985) *Gallia Belgica.* London

Wipszycka, E. (1972) *Les ressources et les activités économiques des églises en Égypte du IVe au VIIIe siècle* (Papyrologica Bruxellensia 10). Brussels

Wolff, H. J. (1939) *Written and Unwritten Marriages in Hellenistic and Postclassical Roman Law.* Haverford

Wolff, H. J. (1945) 'The background of the post-classical legislation on illegitimacy', *Seminar* 3: 21–45

Wolff, H. J. (1950) 'Doctrinal trends in postclassical Roman marriage law', *ZRG RA* 67: 261–319

Wolfram, H. (1988) *History of the Goths*. Berkeley, Los Angeles and London (first published as *Geschichte der Goten*, Munich 1979)

Wolfram, H. (1993) 'L'armée romaine comme modèle pour l'*Exercitus barbarorum*', in Vallet and Kazanski (1993) 11–15

Wood, I. N. (1986) 'Disputes in late fifth- and sixth-century Gaul: some problems', in Davies and Fouracre (eds.) (1986) 7–22

Wood, I. N. (1990) 'Ethnicity and the ethnogenesis of the Burgundians', in Wolfram, H. and Pohl, W. (eds.), *Typen der Ethnogenese unter besonderer Berücksichtigung der Bayern* (Denkschriften der Österreichischen Akademie der Wissenschaften, phil.-hist. Kl. 201) (Vienna) 53–69

Wood, I. N. (1992) 'Continuity or calamity? The constraints of literary models', in Drinkwater and Elton (eds.), *Fifth-Century Gaul* 9–18

Wood, I. N. (1993a) 'Letters and letter-collections from antiquity to the Middle Ages: the prose works of Avitus of Vienne', in M. A. Meyer (ed.), *The Culture of Christendom* (London) 29–43

Wood, I. N. (1993b) 'The Secret Histories of Gregory of Tours', *RBPH* 71: 253–70

Wood, I. N. (1994) *Gregory of Tours*. Bangor

Wood, I. N. (1996) 'Sépultures ecclésiastiques et sénatoriales dans le bassin du Rhône (400–600)', *Médiévales* 31: 13–27

Woolf, G. (1993) 'Roman peace', in Rich and Shipley (1993) 171–94

Wormald, P. (1977) '*Lex scripta* and *verbum regis*: legislation and Germanic kingship from Euric to Cnut', in P. H. Sawyer and I. N. Wood (eds.), *Early Medieval Kingship* (Leeds) 105–38

Wormald, P. (1995) '*Inter cetera bona . . . genti suae*: law-making and peace-keeping in the earliest English kingdoms', in *La giustizia nell'alto medioevo* (XLII Settimana di studio del Centro Italiano di Studi sull'Alto Medioevo) (Spoleto) 963–996

Zanker, P. (1975) 'Grabreliefs römischer Freigelassener', *Jahrbuch des deutschen archäologischen Instituts* 90: 267–315

Zayadine, F. (ed.) (1986) *Jerash Archaeological Project 1981–1983*. Amman

Zuckerman, C. (1994) 'L'empire d'Orient et les Huns: notes sur Priscus', *T&MByz* 12: 159–82

PART IV: THE PROVINCES AND THE NON-ROMAN WORLD (CHS. 18–23)

CH. 18: THE NORTH-WESTERN PROVINCES

Barker, P. (ed.) (1990) *From Roman Viroconium to Medieval Wroxeter*. Worcester

Bassett, S. (1989) 'In search of the origins of Anglo-Saxon kingdoms', in S. Bassett (ed.), *The Origins of Anglo-Saxon Kingdoms* (London) 3–27

Brown, P. (1996) *The Rise of Western Christendom: Triumph and Diversity AD 200–1000*. Oxford

Chadwick, N. (1969) *Early Brittany*. Cardiff

Daly, W. M. (1994) 'Clovis: how barbaric, how pagan?', *Speculum* 69: 619–64

Dark, K. (1994) *From Civitas to Kingdom: British Political Continuity 300–800*. Leicester

Drinkwater, J. (1992) 'The bacaudae of fifth-century Gaul', in Drinkwater and Elton (eds.), *Fifth-Century Gaul* 208–17

Dumville, D. N. (1995) 'The idea of government in sub-Roman Britain', in G. Ausenda (ed.), *After Empire: Towards an Ethnology of Europe's Barbarians* (Woodbridge) 177–204

Elton, H. (1992) 'Defence in fifth-century Gaul', in Drinkwater and Elton (eds.), *Fifth-Century Gaul* 167–76

Esmonde Cleary, S. (1989) *The Ending of Roman Britain*. London

Ewig. E. (1954) *Trier im Merowingerreich: Civitas, Stadt, Bistum*. Trier

Ewig, E. (1978) 'Bemerkungen zur Vita des Bischofs Lupus von Troyes', in K. Hauck and H. Mordek, *Geschichtsschreibung und geistiges Leben im Mittelalter* (Cologne) 14–26

Gauthier, N. *et al.* (1986–) *La topographie chrétienne de la Gaule*. Paris

Gerberding, R. A. (1987) *The Rise of the Carolingians and the Liber Historiae Francorum*. Oxford

Goffart, W. (1989) 'Old and new in Merovingian taxation', in W. Goffart, *Rome's Fall and After* (London) 213–31

Griffe, E. (1964–6) *La Gaule chrétienne à l'époque romaine*, 3 vols. 2nd edn. Paris

Harries, J. (1994) *Sidonius Apollinaris and the Fall of Rome*. Oxford

Haywood, J. (1991) *Dark Age Naval Power: A Reassessment of Frankish and Anglo-Saxon Seafaring Activity*. London

Heinemeyer, K. (1979) *Das Erzbistum Mainz in römischer und fränkischer Zeit*. Marburg

Heinzelmann, M. (1976) *Bischofsherrschaft in Gallien*. Munich

Heinzelmann, M. and Poulin, J.-C. (1986) *Les Vies anciennes de sainte Geneviève de Paris: Étude critique*. Paris

Higham, N. (1992) *Rome, Britain and the Anglo-Saxons*. London

Hillgarth, J. N. (1966) 'Coins and chronicles: propaganda in sixth-century Spain and the Byzantine background', *Historia* 15: 483–508

Jackson, K. H. (1953) *Language and History in Early Britain*. Edinburgh

James, E. (1988) *The Franks*. Oxford

Kerlouegan, F. (1987) *Le De Excidio Britanniae de Gildas: les destinées de la culture latine dans l'île de Bretagne au VIe siècle*. Paris

Liebeschuetz, W. (1963) 'Did the Pelagian movement have social aims?', *Historia* 12: 227–41

Liebeschuetz, W. (1967) 'Pelagian evidence on the last period of Roman Britain?', *Latomus* 26: 436–47

Morris, J. (1965) 'Pelagian literature', *JThS* n.s. 16: 26–60

Morris, J. (1973) *The Age of Arthur*. Chichester

Muhlberger, S. (1990) *The Fifth-Century Chroniclers*. Leeds

Myres, J. N. L. (1960) 'Pelagius and the end of Roman rule in Britain', *JRS* 50: 21–36

Paxton, F. (1993) 'Power and the power to heal: the cult of St Sigismund of Burgundy', *EME* 2: 95–110

Scheibelreiter, G. (1983) *Der Bischof in merowingischer Zeit*. Vienna

Schütte, S. (1995) 'Continuity problems and authority structures in Cologne', in G. Ausenda (ed.), *After Empire: Towards an Ethnology of Europe's Barbarians* (Woodbridge) 163–9

Thomas, C. (1994) *And Shall These Mute Stones Speak?* Cardiff

Thompson, E. A. (1952) 'Peasant revolts in late Roman Gaul and Spain', *P&P* 2: 11–23

Thompson, E. A. (1956) 'The settlement of the barbarians in southern Gaul', *JRS* 46: 65–75

Thompson, E. A. (1977) 'Britain A.D. 406–410', *Britannia* 8: 303–18

Thompson, E. A. (1982) *Romans and Barbarians: The Decline of the Western Empire.* Madison

Van Dam, R. (1993) *Saints and their Miracles in Late Antique Gaul.* Princeton

Wickham, C. (1984) 'The other transition: from the ancient world to feudalism', *P&P* 103: 3–36

Wightman, E. M. (1985) *Gallia Belgica.* London

Wolfram, H. (1987) *Die Geburt Mitteleuropas.* Vienna

Wolfram, H. (1988) *History of the Goths.* Berkeley

Wood, I. N. (1984) 'The end of Roman Britain: continental evidence and parallels', in M. Lapidge and D. N. Dumville (eds.), *Gildas: New Approaches* (Woodbridge) 1–25

Wood, I. N. (1986) 'Disputes in late fifth- and sixth-century Gaul: some problems', in W. Davies and P. Fouracre (eds.), *The Settlement of Disputes in Early Medieval Europe* (Cambridge) 7–22

Wood, I. N. (1987) 'The fall of the western empire and the end of Roman Britain', *Britannia* 18: 251–60

Wood, I. N. (1988) 'Forgery in Merovingian hagiography', in *MGH Schriften 33, Fälschungen im Mittelalter* 5 (Hanover) 369–84

Wood, I. N. (1990) 'The Channel from the fourth to the seventh centuries', in S. McGrail (ed.), *Maritime Celts, Frisians and Saxons, CBA Research Report* 71: 93–7

Wood, I. N. (1992) 'Continuity or calamity?: the constraints of literary models', in Drinkwater and Elton (eds.), *Fifth-Century Gaul* 9–18

Wood, I. N. (1993) 'Letters and letter-collections from antiquity to the early Middle Ages: the prose works of Avitus of Vienne', in M. A. Meyer (ed.), *The Culture of Christendom* 29–43

CH. 19: ITALY, A.D. 425–605

Amory, P. (1997) *People and Identity in Ostrogothic Italy, 489–554.* Cambridge

Arthur, P. (1989) 'Some observations on the economy of Bruttium under the later Roman empire', *JRA* 2: 133–42

Barker, G. (1991) 'Two Italys, one valley: an *Annaliste* perspective', in J. Bintliff (ed.), *The Annales School and Archaeology* (London) 34–56

Barker, G. *et al.* (1995) *A Mediterranean Valley: Landscape Archaeology and Annales History in the Biferno Valley.* London and New York

Barnish, S. J. B. (1986) 'Taxation, land and barbarian settlement in the western empire', *PBSR* 54: 170–98

Barnish, S. J. B. (1987) 'Pigs, plebeians and *potentes*: Rome's economic hinterland, *c.* 350–600 A.D.', *PBSR* 55: 157–85

Barnish, S. J. B. (1988) 'Transformation and survival in the western senatorial aristocracy, *c.* A.D. 400–700', *PBSR* 56: 120–55

Barnwell, P. S. (1992) *Emperor, Prefects and Kings: The Roman West, 395–565.* London

Battisti, C. (1956) 'L'elemento gotico nella toponomastica e nel lessico italiano', *Sett.* 3: 621–49

Bierbrauer, V. (1975) *Die ostgotischen Grab- und Schatzfunde in Italien.* Spoleto

Blake, H. McK., Potter, T. W. and Whitehouse, D. B. (eds.) (1978) *Papers in Italian Archaeology* 1. Oxford

Brown, T. S. (1978) 'Settlement and military policy in Byzantine Italy', in Blake, Potter and Whitehouse (1978) 323–38

Brown, T. S. (1995) 'Byzantine Italy, *c.* 680–*c.* 876', *The New Cambridge Medieval History* 11 (Cambridge): 320–48

Caillet, J. P. (1993) *L'évergétisme monumental chrétien en Italie et à ses marges.* Rome

Chastagnol, A. (1966) *Le sénat romain sous le règne d'Odoacre. Recherches sur l'épigraphie du Colisée au Ve siècle.* Bonn

Christie, N. (1990) 'Byzantine Liguria: an imperial province against the Longobards, A.D. 568–643', *PBSR* 58: 229–71

Christie, N. (1991) 'The Alps as a frontier, AD 168–774', *JRA* 4: 410–30

Christie, N. (1995) *The Lombards.* Oxford

Christie, N. (1996) 'Barren fields? Landscapes and settlements in late Roman and post-Roman Italy', in G. Shipley and J. Salmon (eds.), *Human Landscapes in Classical Antiquity: Environment and Culture* (London) 254–83

Christie, N. and Rushworth, A. (1988) 'Urban fortification and defensive strategy in fifth and sixth century Italy: the case of Terracina', *JRA* 1: 73–88

Clover, F. M. (1978) 'The family and early career of Anicius Olybrius', *Hist.* 27: 169–96

Davis, R. (1992) *The Lives of the Eighth-Century Popes.* Liverpool

Deichman, F. W. (1969) *Ravenna. Haupstadt des spätantiken Abendlandes* 1. *Geschichte und Monumente.* Wiesbaden

Devoto, G. (1978) *The Languages of Italy.* Chicago

Diehl, C. (1888) *Études sur l'administration byzantine dans l'exarchat de Ravenne (568–751).* Paris

Dölger, F. (1924) *Regesten der Kaiserurkunden des oströmischen Reiches* 1. Berlin

Dvornik, F. (1958) *The Idea of Apostolicity in Byzantium and the Legend of the Apostle Andrew.* Washington, DC

Dvornik, F. (1966) *Byzantium and the Roman Primacy.* New York

Dyson, S. L. (1990) *Community and Society in Roman Italy.* Baltimore

Gabba, E. (1985) 'La transumanza nell'Italia romana. Evidenze e problemi. Qualche prospettiva per l'età altomedievale', *Sett.* 31: 373–89

Gasparri, S. (1978) *I duchi longobardi.* Rome

Harries, J. D. (1994) *Sidonius Apollinaris and the Fall of Rome.* Oxford

Harrison, D. (1993) *The Early State and the Towns: Forms of Integration in Lombard Italy AD 568–774.* Lund

Heather, P. (1995) 'Theoderic, king of Goths', *EME* 4: 145–73

Heather, P. (1996) *The Goths.* Oxford

Hodges, R. and Whitehouse, D. (1983) *Mohammed, Charlemagne and the Origins of Europe.* London

Jäggi, C. (1990) 'Aspekte der städtebaulichen Entwicklung Aquileias in frühchristlicher Zeit', *JbAC* 33: 158–96

Jahn, W. (1989) *Felicitas est secuta Italiam*: Bemerkungen zur Lage der römischen Bevölkerung im 6. Jahrhundert in Italien', *Klio* 71: 410–13

Johnson, M. J. (1988) 'Toward a history of Theoderic's building program', *DOP* 42: 73–96

King, A. and Potter, T. (1992) 'Mola di Monte Gelato in the early Middle Ages: an interim report on the excavations 1986–9', in E. Herring, R. Whitehouse and J. Wilkins (eds.), *Papers of the Fourth Conference of Italian Archaeology. 4. New Developments in Italian Archaeology, Part 2* (London) 165–76

Kreutz, B. M. (1991) *Before the Normans: Southern Italy in the Ninth and Tenth Centuries.* Philadelphia

Leciejewicz, L., Tabaczynska, E. and Tabaczynski, S. (1977) *Torcello. Scavi 1962–63.* Rome

Lizzi, R. (1989) *Vescovi e strutture ecclesiastiche nella città tardoantica.* Como

Malone, C., Stoddart, S. *et al.* (1994) *Territory, Time and State. The Archaeological Development of the Gubbio Basin.* Cambridge

Markus, R. A. (1981) 'Ravenna and Rome, 554–600', *Byz.* 51: 556–78

Martin, J.-M. (1993) *La Pouille du VIe au XIIe siècle.* Rome

Matthews, J. F. (1967) 'Continuity in a Roman family: the Rufii Festi of Volsinii', *Hist.* 16: 484–509

Mazzoleni, D. (1976) 'Nomi di barbari nelle iscrizioni paleocristiane della *Venetia et Histria*', *Romanobarbarica* 1: 159–80

Meneghini, R. and Santangeli Valenzani, R. (1993) 'Sepolture intramuranee e paesaggio urbano a Roma tra V e VII secolo', in L. Paroli and P. Delogu (eds.), *La Storia economica di Roma nell'alto Medioevo alla luce dei recenti scavi archeologici* (Florence) 89–111

Moorhead, J. (1992) *Theoderic in Italy.* Oxford

Moorhead, J. (1994) *Justinian.* London

Moreland, J. (1993) 'Wilderness, wasteland, depopulation and the end of the Roman empire?', *Accordia Research Papers* 4: 89–110

O'Flynn, J. M. (1983) *Generalissimos of the Western Roman Empire.* Edmonton

Otranto, G. (1983) 'Il *Liber de apparitione*, il santuario di S. Michele sul Gargano e i Longobardi del Ducato di Benevento', in M. Sordi (ed.), *Santuari e politica nel mondo antico* (Milan) 210–45

Otranto, G. (1990) *Italia meridionale e Puglia paleocristiane.* Bari

Petersen, J. M. (1984) *The* Dialogues *of Gregory the Great in their Late Antique Cultural Background.* Toronto

Picard, J. C. (1988) *Le souvenir des évêques: sépultures, listes épiscopales et cultes des évêques en Italie du Nord dès l'origine aux Xe siècle.* Rome

Pietri, C. (1982) 'Une aristocratie provinciale et la mission chrétienne: l'exemple de la *Venetia*', *Antichità Altoadriatiche* 22: 89–137

Rando, D. (1994) *Una chiesa di frontiera. Le istituzioni ecclesiastiche veneziane nei secoli VI–XII.* Bologna

Richards, J. (1979) *The Popes and the Papacy in the Early Middle Ages 476–752.* London

Richards, J. (1980) *Consul of God: The Life and Times of Gregory the Great.* London

Rouche, M. (1986) 'Grégoire le Grand face à la situation économique de son temps', in J. Fontaine, R. Gillet and S. Pellistrandi (eds.), *Grégoire le Grand* (Paris) 41–57

Ruggini, L. (1961) *Economia e società nell'* Italia Annonaria. *Rapporti fra agricoltura e commercio dal IV al VI secolo d. C.* Milan

Schäfer, C. (1991) *Der weströmische Senat als Träger antiker Kontinuität unter den Ostgotenkönigen.* St Katharinen

Schiaparelli, L. (ed.) (1929–33) *Codice diplomatico Longobardo.* 2 vols. Rome

Schmiedt, G. (1974) 'Città scomparse e città di nuova formazione in Italia in relazione al sistema di comunicazione', *Sett.* 21: 503–607

Schmiedt, G. (1978) 'I porti italiani nell'alto medioevo', *Sett.* 25: 129–254

Sirago, V. A. (1987) 'Italia e Italianità nelle *Variae* di Cassiodoro', *Studi Tardoantichi* 4 (= *Hestíasis. Studi di tarda antichità offerti a Salvatore Calderone* 4) 129–62

Small, A. M. and Buck, R. J. (1993) *The Excavation of San Giovanni di Ruoti.* 1. *The Villas and their Environment.* Toronto

Staffa, A. R. (1995) 'L'Abruzzo tardoantico ed altomedievale nelle fonti archeologiche: urbanesimo, popolamento rurale, economia e cultura materiale', in N. Christie (ed.), *Settlement and Economy in Italy 1500 BC–AD 1500. Papers of the Fifth Conference of Italian Archaeology* (Oxford) 317–30

Stein, E. (1939) 'La disparition du sénat de Rome à la fin du VIe siècle', *Académie royale de la Belgique. Bulletin de la Classe des Lettres*[5] 25: 308–22

Tabacco, G. (1989) *The Struggle for Power in Medieval Italy: Structures of Political Rule.* Cambridge

Tjäder, J.-O. (1954–82) *Die nichtliterarischen lateinischen Papyri Italiens aus der Zeit 445–700.* Lund and Stockholm

Ward-Perkins, B. (1988) 'The towns of northern Italy: rebirth or renewal?', in R. Hodges and B. Hobley (eds.), *The Rebirth of Towns in the West AD 700–1050* (London) 16–27

Ward-Perkins, B. *et al.* (1986) 'Luni and the *Ager Lunensis.* The rise and fall of a Roman town and its territory', *PBSR* 54: 81–146

Wharton, A. J. (1995) *Refiguring the Post Classical City: Dura Europus, Jerash, Jerusalem and Ravenna.* Cambridge

Wickham, C. (1981) *Early Medieval Italy.* London

Wickham, C. (1988) 'Marx, Sherlock Holmes, and late Roman commerce', *JRS* 78: 183–93

Wilson, R. J. A. (1990) *Sicily under the Roman Empire.* Warminster

Wolfram, H. (1988) *History of the Goths.* Berkeley and Los Angeles

Zovatto, P. L. (1966) 'Il *defensor ecclesiae* e le iscrizioni musive di Trieste', *RSCI* 20: 1–8

Abadie-Reynal, C. (1989) 'Céramique et commerce dans le bassin égéen du IVe au VIe siècle', in *Hommes et richesses* 1.143–59

Anselmino, L., Panella, C., Valenzani, R. S., Tortorella, S. (1986) 'Cartagine', in Giardina, *Società romana* III.163–95

Bonnal, J.-P. and Février, P.-A. (1966–7) 'Ostraka de la région de Bir Trouch', *Bull. d'archéol. algérienne* 2: 239–49

Brett, M. (1978) 'The Arab conquest and the rise of Islam in North Africa', in Fage (ed.) (1978) 490–555, at 505–13 ('The advance into the Maghrib')

Brett, M. and Fentress, E. (1996) *The Berbers*. Oxford

Cameron, Averil (1982) 'Byzantine Africa – the literary evidence', in Humphrey (ed.) (1982) 29–62 (= Cameron, *Changing Cultures* VII)

Cameron, Averil (1989) 'Gelimer's laughter: the case of Byzantine Africa', in Clover and Humphreys (eds.) (1989) 171–90 (= Cameron, *Changing Cultures* VIII)

Cameron, Averil (1993) 'The Byzantine reconquest of Africa and the impact of Greek culture', *Graeco-Arabica* V: 153–65 (= Cameron, *Changing Cultures* x)

Camps, G. (1984) 'Rex gentium et Maurorum et Romanorum. Recherches sur les royaumes de Maurétanie aux VIe et VIIe siècles', *Ant. Afr.* 20: 183–218

Chadwick, H. (1974) 'John Moschus and his friend Sophronius the sophist', *JThS* n.s. 25: 41–74

Chastagnol, A. and Duval, N. (1974) 'Les survivances du culte impérial dans l'Afrique du Nord à l'époque vandale', in *Mélanges d'histoire ancienne offerts à William Seston* (Paris) 87–118

Christie, N. and Loseby, S. T. (eds.) (1996) *Towns in Transition: Urban Evolution in Late Antiquity and the Early Middle Ages*. Aldershot

Chrysos, E. and Schwartz, A. (eds.) (1989) *Das Reich und die Barbaren*. Vienna

Cintas, J. and Duval, N. (1958) 'L'église du prêtre Felix (région de Kélibia)', *Karthago* 9: 155–265

Clover, F. M. (1982a) 'Emperor worship in Vandal Africa', in Wirth (ed.) (1982) 661–74

Clover, F. M. (1982b) 'Carthage and the Vandals', in Humphrey (ed.) (1982) 1–22

Clover, F. M. (1986) 'Felix Karthago', *DOP* 40: 1–16

Clover, F. M. (1989) 'The symbiosis of Romans and Vandals in Africa', in Chrysos and Schwartz (eds.) (1989) 57–73

Clover, F. M. and Humphreys, R. S. (eds.) (1989) *Tradition and Innovation in Late Antiquity*. Madison

Courtois, C. (1954) *Victor de Vita et son oeuvre*. Algiers

Courtois, C. (1955) *Les Vandales et l'Afrique*. Paris

Courtois, C. et al. (1952) *Tablettes Albertini: Actes privés de l'époque vandale (fin du Ve siècle)*. Paris

Cuoq, J. (1984) *L'Église d'Afrique du Nord du IIe du XIIe siècle*. Paris

Dagron, G. and Déroche, V. (eds.) (1991) 'Juifs et chrétiens dans l'Orient au VIIe siècle', *T&MByz* 11: 17–273 (Dagron, 17–46, 'Introduction historique'; Déroche, 47–229, ed. and trans., *Doctrina Jacobi nuper baptizati*)

Diehl, C. (1896) *L'Afrique byzantine* I–II. Paris

Diesner, J. (1966) *Das Vandalenreich*. Stuttgart

Durliat, J. (1979) 'Magister militum-stratelates dans l'empire byzantin (VIe–VIIe siècles)', *BZ* 72: 306–320

Durliat, J. (1981) *Les dédicaces d'ouvrages de défense dans l'Afrique byzantine* (Coll. de l'École Française de Rome 49). Rome

Duval, N. (1964) 'Observations sur l'urbanisme tardif de Sufetula (Tunisie)', *Cahiers de Tunisie* 45–6: 88–103

Duval, N. (1990) 'Quinze ans de recherches archéologiques sur l'antiquité tardive en Afrique du nord 1975–1990. I, généralités et Tunisie (Carthage)', *REA* 92: 349–87

Duval, N. (1993) 'Deuxième chronique et suppléments à généralités et Carthage', *REA* 95: 583–640

Duval, N. and Prévot, F. (1975) *Recherches archéologiques à Haidra I. Les inscriptions chrétiennes.* Rome

Duval, Y. (1982) *Loca Sanctorum Africae*, 2 vols. Paris

Ennabli, L. (1975) *Les inscriptions funéraires chrétiennes de la basilique dite de Sainte-Monique à Carthage.* Rome

Ennabli, L. (1982) *Les inscriptions funéraires chrétiennes de Carthage II. La basilique de Mcidfa.* Rome

Ennabli, L. (1992). *Inscriptions funéraires chrétiennes à Carthage III: Carthage intra muros et extra muros.* Paris and Rome

Fage, J. D. (ed.) (1978) *The Cambridge History of Africa* II. Cambridge

Février, P. A. (1989) *Approches du Maghreb romain*, 2 vols. Aix-en-Provence

Frend, W. H. C. (1952) *The Donatist Church* (2nd edn 1971). Oxford

Frend, W. H. C. (1978) 'The Christian period in Mediterranean Africa, c. 200 to 700', in Fage (ed.) (1978) 410–89

Fulford, M. G. (1984) 'The long-distance trade and communications of Carthage, c. A.D. 400 to c. A.D. 650', in Fulford and Peacock (eds.) (1984) 255–62

Fulford, M. G. and Peacock, D. P. S. (eds.) (1984) *Excavations at Carthage I.2. The Avenue du Président Habib Bourguiba, Salammbo. The Pottery and Other Ceramic Objects from the Site.* Sheffield

Gros, P. (ed.) (1985) *Mission archéologique française à Carthage. Byrsa III. Rapport sur les campagnes de fouilles de 1977 à 1980: la basilique orientale et ses abords* (Coll. de l'École Française de Rome 41). Rome

Guéry, R., Morrisson, C., Slim, H. (1982) *Recherches archéologiques franco-tunisiennes à Rougga III. Le trésor de monnaies d'or byzantines.* Rome

Humphrey, J. H. (1980) 'Vandal and Byzantine Carthage: some new archaeological evidence', in Pedley (ed.) (1980) 85–120

Humphrey, J. H. (ed.) (1982) *Excavations at Carthage 1978 conducted by the University of Michigan* VII. Michigan

Humphrey, J. H. (ed.) (1988) *The Circus and a Byzantine Cemetery at Carthage* I. Ann Arbor

Hurst, H. (1995) *Excavations at Carthage: II.1. The Circular Harbour, North Side.* Oxford

Hurst, H. R. and Roskams, S. P. (eds.) (1984) *Excavations at Carthage I.1. The Avenue du Président Habib Bourguiba, Salammbo I, The Site and Finds other than Pottery.* Sheffield

Kaegi, Jr, W. E. (1965) 'Arianism and the Byzantine army in Africa, 533–546', *Traditio* 21: 23–53

Lepelley, C. (1989) 'Peuplement et richesses de l'Afrique romaine tardive', in *Hommes et richesses* I.17–30

Lepelley, C. (1992) 'The survival and fall of the classical city in late Roman Africa', in Rich (ed.) (1992) 50–76

Mahjoubi, A. (1978) *Recherches d'histoire et d'archéologie à Henchir al-Faouar (Tunisie). La cité de Belalitani Maiores.*

Maier, J. (1973) *L'Épiscopat de l'Afrique romaine, vandale et byzantine.* Rome

Markus, R. A. (1964) 'Donatism – the last phase', *SCH* 1: 118–26

Markus, R. A. (1967) 'The imperial administration and the church in Byzantine Africa', *ChHist* 36: 18–23

Markus, R. A. (1979) 'Country bishops in Byzantine Africa', *ChHist* 16: 1–15

Mattingly, D. (1988) 'Oil for export? A comparison of Libyan, Spanish and Tunisian oil production in the Roman Empire', *JRA* 1: 33–56

Mattingly, D. J. (1995) *Tripolitania*. London

Mattingly, D. and Hitchner, R. B. (1995) 'Roman Africa: an archaeological review', *JRS* 85: 165–213

Modéran, Y. (1986) 'Corippe et l'occupation byzantine de l'Afrique: pour une nouvelle lecture de la Johannide', *Ant. Afr.* 22: 195–212

Modéran, Y. (1991) 'Le découverte des Maures. Réflexions sur la reconquête byzantine de l'Afrique en 533', *ACHCM* 5: 211–33

Moorhead, J. (1992) *Victor of Vita: History of the Vandal Persecution* (Translated Texts for Historians 10). Liverpool

Morrisson, C. and Seibt, W. (1982) 'Sceaux de commerciaires byzantins du VIIe siècle trouvés à Carthage', *Revue numismatique* 24: 222–41

Panella, C. (1986) 'Le merci: produzioni, itinerari e destini', in Giardina (ed.), *Società romana* III.431–59

Panella, C. (1989) 'Gli scambi nel mediterraneo occidentale dal IV al VII secolo', in *Hommes et richesses* I.129–41

Panella, C. (1993) 'Merci e scambi nel mediterraneo tardoantico', in Carandini *et al.* (eds.) (1993) 613–97

Parsons, J. (1994) 'The African Catholic Church under the Vandals 429–533'. Unpublished Ph.D. thesis. London

Pedley, J. G. (ed.) (1980) *New Light on Ancient Carthage*. Ann Arbor

Prévot, F. (1984) *Recherches archéologiques franco-tunisiennes à Maktar V. Les inscriptions chrétiennes*. Rome

Pringle, D. (1981) *The Defence of Byzantine Africa from Justinian to the Arab Conquest*, 2 vols. (BAR International Series 99(i)). Oxford

Pülhorn, W. (1977): see Veh (1977)

Rich, J. (ed.) (1992) *The City in Late Antiquity*. London

Rosenblum, M. (1962) *Luxorius: A Latin Poet among the Vandals*. New York

Roskams, S. (1996) 'Urban transition in North Africa: Roman and medieval towns of the Maghreb', in Christie and Loseby (eds.) (1996) 159–83

Rubin, B. (1954) *Prokopios von Kaisareia. RE* 23.1.273–599

Sjörström, I. (1993) *Tripolitania in Transition: Late Roman to Early Islamic Settlement*. Aldershot

Stevens, S. T. *et al.* (1993) *Bir el Knissia at Carthage: A Rediscovered Cemetery Church, Report no. 1, JRA* Supp. Ser. 7. Ann Arbor

Trousset, P. (1985) 'Les "fines antiquae" et la reconquête byzantine en Afrique', *CHAAN* 2: 361–76

Trousset, P. (1991) 'Les défenses côtières byzantines de Byzacène', *Limes* 15: 347–53

Veh, O. (ed.) (1977) *Procopii Opera. De Aedificiis*, with commentary by W. Pülhorn

Wickham, C. (1988) 'Marx, Sherlock Holmes and late Roman commerce', *JRS* 78: 183–93

Wirth, G. (ed.) (1982) *Romanitas-Christianitas: Untersuchungen zur Geschichte und Literatur der römischen Kaiserzeit.* Berlin

CH. 21*a*: ASIA MINOR AND CYPRUS

Argoud, G. *et al.* (1980) *Salamine de Chypre XI, Une résidence byzantine, 'l'huilerie'.* Paris
Belke, K. (1984) *Galatien und Lykaonien. Tabula Imperii Byzantini* 4. Vienna
Belke, K. (1994) 'Galatien in der Spätantike', in Schwertheim (ed.) (1994) 171–88
Boyd, S. and Mango, M. Mundell (eds.) (1992) *Ecclesiastical Silver Plate in Sixth-Century Byzantium.* Washington, DC
Brandes, W. (1988) *Die Städte Kleinasiens in 7 und 8 Jahrhundert.* Berlin
Brandt, H. (1992) *Gesellschaft und Wirtschaft Pamphyliens und Pisidiens im Altertum.* Bonn
Bryer. A. A. M. and Georghallides, G. S. (eds.) (1993) *The Sweet Land of Cyprus: Papers given at the 25th Jubilee Symposium of Byzantine Studies, Birmingham 1991.* Nicosia
Cameron, Averil (1992) 'Cyprus at the time of the Arab Conquests', Ἐπετερίς της Κυπριακῆς Ἐταιρείας Ἱστορικῶν Σπουδῶν 1: 27–50 (= Cameron, *Changing Cultures* VI)
Chrysos, E. (1993) 'Cyprus in Early Byzantine times', in Bryer and Georghallides (eds.) (1993) 3–14
Cook, J. M. (1973) *The Troad.* Oxford
Cook, J. M. and Blackman, D. J. (1971) 'Archaeology in western Asia Minor, 1965–70', *AR* 17: 33–62
Cormack, R. (1981) 'The classical tradition in the Byzantine provincial city: the evidence of Thessalonike and Aphrodisias', in Mullett and Scott (eds.) (1981) 103–18
Cormack, R. (1990a) 'Byzantine Aphrodisias: changing the symbolic map of a city', *PCPS* 216: 26–41
Cormack, R. (1990b) 'The temple as the cathedral', in Roueché and Erim (eds.) (1990) 75–88
Cormack, R. (1991) 'The wall-painting of St Michael in the Theatre', in Smith and Erim (eds.) (1991) 109–22
Coulton, J. (1983) 'The buildings of Oenoanda', *PCPS* 209: 1–20
Crawford, J. Stephens (1990) *The Byzantine Shops at Sardis.* Cambridge, MA
Dagron, G. and Feissel, D. (1987) *Inscriptions de Cilicie.* Paris
Daszewski, W. A. (1977) *Nea Paphos II, La mosaïque de Thésée.* Warsaw
Daszewski, W. A. (1985) 'Researches at New Paphos 1965–1984', in Karageorghis (ed.) (1985) 277–91
Dawes, E. and Baynes, N. H. (trans.) (1948) *Three Byzantine Saints.* London and Oxford (reissued 1977)
Feissel, D. (1985) 'Un mandement impérial du VIe siècle dans une inscription d'Adrianoupolis d'Honoriade', *T&MByz* 9: 397–419
Fejfer, J. and Mathiesen, H. E. (1991) 'The Danish Akamas project', in *Report of the Department of Antiquities of Cyprus* 211–23
Foss, C. (1975) 'The Persians in Asia Minor and the end of antiquity', *EHR* 90: 721–47 (= Foss (1990) I)

Foss, C. (1976) *Byzantine and Turkish Sardis*. Cambridge, MA

Foss, C. (1977a) 'Archaeology and the "Twenty Cities" of Byzantine Asia', *AJA* 81: 469–86 (= Foss (1990) II)

Foss, C. (1977b) 'Late antique and Byzantine Ankara', *DOP* 31: 29–87 (= Foss (1990) VI)

Foss, C. (1977c) 'Attius Philippus and the walls of Side', *ZPE* 26: 172–80 (= Foss (1990) VIII)

Foss, C. (1979) *Ephesus after Antiquity: A Late Antique, Byzantine and Turkish City*. Cambridge

Foss, C. (1990) *History and Archaeology of Byzantine Asia Minor*. Aldershot

Foss, C. (1991) 'Cities and villages of Lycia in the Life of St Nicholas of Holy Zion', *Greek Orthodox Theological Review* 36: 303–39

Foss, C. (1993) 'Lycia in history', in J. Morganstern (ed.), *The Fort at Dereagzi* (Tübingen) 16–20

Foss, C. (1994) 'The Lycian coast in the Byzantine age', *DOP* 48: 1–52

Fowden, G. (1990) 'Religious developments in late Roman Lycia: topographical preliminaries', *Μελετήματα, Κέντρο Ελληνικής και Ρωμαικής Αρχαιότητος, Εθνικό ίδρυμα Ερευνών* 10:343–72

des Gagniers, J. and Tran Tam Tinh (1985) *Soloi: Dix campagnes de fouilles 1964–1974*. Sainte-Foy

Gough, M. (1985) *Alahan, an Early Christian Monastery in Southern Turkey*. Toronto

Grégoire, H. (1922) *Recueil des inscriptions grecques-chrétiennes d'Asie Mineure* I. Paris

Harrison, R. M. (1963) 'Churches and chapels in central Lycia', *AS* 13: 117–51

Harrison, R. M. (1981) 'Town and country in late Roman Lycia', *IX Türk Tarih Kongresi* I: 383–7. Ankara

Harrison, R. M. (1990) 'Amorium 1989', *AS* 40: 205–18

Harrison, R. M. (1991) 'Amorium excavations 1990', *AS* 41: 215–29

Harrison, R. M. (1992) 'Amorium excavations 1991', *AS* 42: 207–22

Harrison, R. M., Christie, N. *et al.* (1993) 'Excavations at Amorium: 1992 Interim Report', *AS* 43: 147–62

Harrison, R. M. and Lawson, G. R. J. (1979) 'An early Byzantine town at Arif in Lycia', *Yayla* 2: 13–17

Haspels, C. H. (1971) *The Highlands of Phrygia*. Princeton

Heather, P. (1994) 'New men for New Constantines? Creating an imperial élite in the eastern Mediterranean', in Magdalino (ed.), *New Constantines* 11–33

Hild, F. and Hellenkemper, H. (1990) *Kilikien und Isaurien. Tabula Imperii Byzantini* 5. Vienna

Hild, F. and Restle, M. (1981) *Kappadokien. Tabula Imperii Byzantini* 2. Vienna

Hill, G. (1949) *History of Cyprus* I. Cambridge

Hopwood, K. (1983) 'Policing the hinterland: Rough Cilicia and Isauria', in Mitchell (ed.) (1983) 173–87

Hopwood, K. (1989) 'Bandits, élites and rural order', in Wallace-Hadrill (ed.) (1989) 173–87

Karageorghis, V. (1969) *Salamis in Cyprus*. London

Karageorghis, V. (ed.) (1985) *Archaeology in Cyprus 1960–1985*. Nicosia (includes an extensive bibliography)

Mackenzie, M. M. and Roueché, C. (eds.) (1989) *Images of Authority: Papers presented to Joyce Reynolds*. Cambridge

Mango, C. (1986) 'The pilgrimage centre of St Michael at Germia', *JÖB* 36: 117–32

Mango, C. (1991) 'Germia: a postscript', *JÖB* 41: 297–306

Megaw, A. H. S. (1974) 'Byzantine architecture and decoration in Cyprus', *DOP* 28: 59–88

Megaw, A. H. S. (1985) 'Progress in early Christian and medieval archeology', in Karageorghis (ed.) (1985) 292–8

Mitchell, S. (ed.) (1983) *Armies and Frontiers in Roman and Byzantine Anatolia* (BAR International Series 156). Oxford

Mitchell, S. (1985) 'Archaeology in Asia Minor, 1979–84', *AR* 31: 70–105

Mitchell, S. (1990) 'Archaeology in Asia Minor, 1985–89', *AR* 36: 83–131

Mitchell, S. and McNicoll, A. W. (1979) 'Archaeology in western and southern Asia Minor, 1971–78', *AR* 25: 59–90

Mitchell, S., Owens, E. and Waelkens, M. (1989) 'Ariassos and Sagalassos 1988', *AS* 39: 61–77

Mitford, T. B. (1971) *The Inscriptions of Kourion.* Philadelphia

Müller-Wiener, W. (1989) 'Bischofsresidenzen im östlichen Mittelmeer-raum 3. Kleinasien und Armenien', *Actes XI Cong. Int. d'Arch. Chrét.* 1 (Rome) 670–86

Mullett, M. and Scott, R. (eds.) (1981) *Byzantium and the Classical Tradition.* Birmingham

Nikolaou, K. (1966) 'Archaeology in Cyprus, 1961–66', *AR* 12: 27–43

Nikolaou, K. (1969) 'Archaeology in Cyprus, 1966–69', *AR* 15: 40–54

Nikolaou, K. (1976) 'Archaeology in Cyprus, 1969–76', *AR* 22: 34–66

Nikolaou, K. (1981) 'Archaeology in Cyprus, 1976–80', *AR* 27: 49–72

Nollé, J. (1993) *Side im Altertum* 1. Cologne

Papageorghiou, A. (1993) 'Cities and countryside at the end of antiquity and the beginning of the Middle Ages in Cyprus', in Bryer and Georghallides (eds.) (1993) 27–51

Radt, W. (1988) *Pergamon. Geschichte und Bauten, Funde und Erforschung einer antiken Metropole.* Cologne

Rautman, M. L. (1995) 'A late Roman townhouse at Sardis', in Schwertheim (ed.) (1995) 49–66

Roueché, C. (1989) 'Floreat Perge', in Mackenzie and Roueché (eds.) (1989) 206–28

Roueché, C. and Erim, K. T. (eds.) (1990) *Aphrodisias Papers.* Ann Arbor

Roueché, C. and Smith, R. R. R. (eds.) (1996) *Aphrodisias Papers* 3. Ann Arbor

Rougé, J. (1966) 'L'Histoire Auguste et l'Isaurie au IVe siècle', *REA* 68: 28–315

Russell, J. (1986) 'Transformation in early Byzantine life: the contributions and limitations of archaeological evidence', *17th International Byzantine Congress, Major Papers* (New York) 137–54

Russell, J. (1987) *The Mosaic Inscriptions of Anemurium.* Vienna

Schäfer, J. (1981) *Phaselis.* Tübingen

Schwerthelm, E. (ed.) (1992) *Forschungen in Pisidien* (Asia-Minor Studien 8). Bonn

Schwertheim, E. (ed.) (1994) *Forschungen in Galatien* (Asia-Minor Studien 12). Bonn

Schwertheim, E. (ed.) (1995) *Forschungen in Lydien* (Asia Minor Studien 17). Bonn

Ševčenko, I. and Ševčenko, N. P. (trans.) (1984) *The Life of St Nicholas of Sion.* Brookline

Smith, R. R. R. (1990) 'Late Roman philosopher portraits from Aphrodisias', *JRS* 80: 127–55

Smith, R. R. R. and Erim, K. T. (eds.) (1991) *Aphrodisias Papers* 2. Ann Arbor

Sodini, J.-P. (1989) 'Les groupes épiscopaux de Turquie', *Actes X Cong. Int d'Arch. Chrét.* I (Rome) 406–26

Symons, D. J. (1987) 'Archaeology in Cyprus, 1981–85', *AR* 33: 62–77

Waelkens, M. (1991) 'The excavations at Sagalassos 1990', *AS* 41: 197–213

Waelkens, M. (1992a) 'The excavations at Sagalassos 1991', *AS* 42: 79–98

Waelkens, M. (1992b) 'Die neuen Forschungen (1985–1989) und die belgischen Ausgrabungen (1990–1991) in Sagalassos', in Schwertheim (ed.) (1992) 43–60

Waelkens, M. (ed.) (1993) *Sagalassos I.* Leuven

Waelkens, M. and Poblome, J. (1993) *Sagalassos II.* Leuven

Wallace-Hadrill, A. (ed.) (1989) *Patronage in Ancient Society.* London

Whittow, M. (1990) 'Ruling the late Roman and early Byzantine city: a continuous history', *P&P* 129: 3–29

Winfield, D. and Foss, C. (1987) *Byzantine Fortifications.* Pretoria

Yegül, F. K. (1986) *The Bath-Gymnasium Complex at Sardis.* Harvard

CH. 21*b*: SYRIA, PALESTINE AND MESOPOTAMIA

Alon, G. (1980) *The Jews in their Land in the Talmudic Age (70–640 C.E.).* 2 vols. Jerusalem

Avi-Yonah, M. (1976) *The Jews of Palestine: A Political History from the Bar Kokhba War to the Arab Conquest.* Oxford

Avigad, N. (1984) *Discovering Jerusalem.* Oxford

Balty, J. C. (1981) *Guide d'Apamée.* Brussels

Binns, J. (1994) *Ascetics and Ambassadors of Christ: The Monasteries of Palestine 314–631.* Oxford

Bowersock, G. W. (1982) *Roman Arabia.* Cambridge, MA

Burns, R. (1992) *Monuments of Syria: An Historical Guide.* London

Butler, H. C. (1907–20) *Publications of the Princeton University Archaeological Expedition to Syria 1904–5, 1909.* Leiden

Cameron, Averil (1994) 'The Jews in seventh-century Palestine', *SCI* 13: 75–93

Cameron, Averil (1996) 'Byzantines and Jews: some recent work on early Byzantium', *BMGS* 20: 249–74

Cameron, Averil, and King, G. R. D. (1994) *The Byzantine and Islamic Near East II Land Use and Settlement Patterns* (Studies in Late Antiquity and Islam 1). Princeton

Canivet, P. and Rey-Coquais, J.-P. (eds.) (1992) *La Syrie de Byzance à l'Islam.* Damascus

Conrad, L. I. (1981) 'The Plague in the Early Medieval Near East'. Unpublished PhD thesis. Princeton

Conrad, L. I. (1986) 'The plague in Bilad al-Sham in pre-Islamic times', in M. A. al-Bakhit, and A. Asfur (eds.), *Proceedings of the Symposium on Bilad al-Sham during the Byzantine Period* II (Amman) 143–63

Conrad, L. I. (1994) 'Epidemic disease in central Syria in the late sixth century: some new insights from the verse of Hassan b. Thabit', *BMGS* 18: 12–58

Crone, P. (1987) *Meccan Trade and the Rise of Islam.* Princeton

Crowfoot, J. W. (1941) *Early Churches in Palestine.* The Schweich Lectures in Biblical Archaeology, 1937. London

Crown, A. D., Pummer, R. and Tal, A. (eds.) (1993) *A Companion to Samaritan Studies*. Tübingen

Dentzer, J.-M. (ed.) (1985) *Hauran* I: *Recherches archéologiques sur la Syrie du sud à l'époque hellénistique et romaine*. Paris

Devreesse, R. (1945) *Le patriarcat d'Antioche depuis la paix de l'église jusqu'à la conquête Arabe*. Paris

Di Segni, L. (1995) 'The involvement of local, municipal and provincial authorities in urban building in late antique Palestine and Arabia', in *JRA* Supplement 14: 312–32

Donner, F. M. (1981) *The Early Islamic Conquests*. Princeton

Donner, H. (1992) *The Mosaic Map of Madaba*. Kampen

Drijvers, H. J. W. (1982) 'The persistence of pagan cults and practices in Christian Syria', in N. Garsoian (ed.), *East of Byzantium: Syria and Armenia in the Formative Period* (Washington, DC) 35–45

Durliat, J. (1989) 'La peste du VIe siècle: pour un nouvel examen des sources byzantines', in *Hommes et Richesses* 1.107–19

Fiema, Z. T. (1993) 'The Petra project', ACOR *Newsletter* 5.1: 1–3

Foss, C. (1995) 'The near eastern countryside in late antiquity: a review article' in *JRA*, supplementary series 14: 213–34

Freeman, P. and Kennedy, D. (1986) *The Defence of the Roman and Byzantine East* (BAR International Series 297). Oxford

Gil, M. (1992) *A History of Palestine, 634–1099*. Cambridge

Grabar, O. (1978) *City in the Desert*. Cambridge, MA

Green, T. M. (1992) *The City of the Moon God: Religious Traditions of Harran*. Leiden

Gregory, S. and Kennedy, D. (1985) *Sir Aurel Stein's Limes Reports* (BAR International Series 272). Oxford

Gutwein, K. C. (1981) *Third Palestine*. Washington, DC

Hachlili, R. (1988) *Ancient Jewish Art and Archaeology in the Land of Israel*. Leiden

Hirschfeld, Y. (1992) *The Judaean Desert Monasteries in the Byzantine Period*. New Haven and London

Honigmann, E. (1935) *Die Ostgrenze des byzantinischen Reiches von 363 bis 1071*. Brussels

Honigmann, E. (1950) 'Juvenal of Jerusalem', *DOP* 5: 209–79

Honigmann, E. (1951) *Évêques et évêchés monophysites d'Asie antérieures du VIe siècle* (*CSCO Subsidia* 2). Louvain

Honigmann, E. (1954) *Le couvent de Barsauma et le patriarcat jacobite d'Antioche et de la Syrie* (*CSCO Subsidia* 7). Louvain

Kaegi, W. E. (1992) *Byzantium and the Early Islamic Conquests*. Cambridge

Karnapp, W. (1976) *Die Stadtmauer von Resafa in Syrien*. Berlin

Kawar, I. (1958) 'The last days of Salih', *Arabica* 5: 145–58

Kennedy, H. (1985) 'From Polis to Medina: urban change in late antique and early Islamic Syria', *P&P* 106: 3–27

Kennedy, H. (1986a) 'The last century of Byzantine Syria: a reconsideration' *BF* 10: 141–83

Kennedy, H. (1986b) *The Prophet and the Age of the Caliphates*. London

Kennedy, H. and Liebeschuetz, W. (1989) 'Antioch and the villages of northern Syria in the fifth and sixth centuries', *NMS* 32: 65–90

Kraeling, C. H. (1938) *Gerasa: City of the Decapolis*. New Haven

Lassus, J. (1947) *Sanctuaires chrétiens de Syrie*. Paris

Lauffray, J. (1983) *Halabiyya-Zenobia: place forte du limes oriental et la Haute-Mésopotamie au VIe siècle*. Paris

Levine, L. I. (1981) *Ancient Synagogues Revealed*. Jerusalem

Levine, L. I. (1985) *Caesarea under Roman Rule*. Leiden

Liebeschuetz, J. H. W. G. (1977) 'The defences of Syria in the sixth century', *Vorträge des 10 Internationalen Limeskongress* (Cologne) 487–99

MacAdam, H. (1986) *Studies in the History of the Roman Province of Arabia* (BAR International Series 125). Oxford

Morony, M. (1984) *Iraq after the Muslim Conquest*. Princeton

Northedge, A. (1993) *Studies on Roman and Islamic Amman I: Site and Architecture*. Oxford

Noth, A. (1994) *The Early Arabic Historical Tradition: A Source-Critical Study* 2nd edn, with Lawrence I. Conrad (Studies in late Antiquity and early Islam 3). Princeton

Orssaud, D. (1992) 'De la céramique Byzantine à la céramique Islamique', in Canivet and Rey-Coquais (1992) 219–28

Palmer, A. (1990) *Monk and Mason on the Tigris Frontier: The Early History of the Tur 'Abdin*. Cambridge

Paret, R. (1960) 'Les villes de Syrie du sud et les routes commerciales d'Arabie à la fin du VIe siècle', in F. Dölger and H. G. Beck (eds.) (1960) *Akten des XI Internationalen Byzantinisten-Kongress, München, 1958* (Munich) 438–44

Parker, S. T. (1986) 'Retrospective on the Arabian frontier after a decade of research', BAR International Series 297 (Oxford) 633–60

Parker, S. T., *et al.* (1987) 'The legionary fortress of El-Lejjun', BAR International Series 340 (Oxford) 183–428

Patrich, J. (1995) *Sabas, Leader of Palestinian Monasticism. A Comparative Study of Eastern Monasticism, Fourth to Seventh Centuries* (Dumbarton Oaks Studies 32). Washington, DC

Peña, I., Castellana, C. and Fernandez, R. (1987) *Les Stylites Syriens*. Milan

Piccirillo, M. (1989) *Chiese e mosaici di Madaba*. Jerusalem

Piccirillo, M. (1994) *The Mosaics of Jordan*. ACOR Publications 1. Amman and Baltimore

Rey-Coquais, J.-P. (1977) *Inscriptions grecques et latines découvertes dans les fouilles de Tyr. 1. Inscriptions de la nécropole*, Bulletin du Musée de Beyrouth 29. Paris

Rostovtzeff, M. (1932) *Caravan Cities*. Oxford

Sartre, M. (1982) *Trois études sur l'Arabie romaine et byzantine*. Brussels

Sartre, M. (1985) *Bostra: des origines à l'Islam*. Paris

Schick, R. (1992) 'Jordan on the eve of the Muslim Conquest A.D. 602–34', in Canivet and Rey-Coquais (1992) 107–19

Schick, R. (1995) *The Christian Communities of Palestine from Byzantine to Islamic Rule: An Historical and Archaeological Study* (Studies in late Antiquity and early Islam 2). Princeton

Segal, A. (1988) *Town Planning and Architecture in Provincia Arabia* (BAR International Series 419) Oxford

Segal, J. B. (1970) *Edessa 'The Blessed City'*. Oxford

Shahīd, I. (1989) *Byzantium and the Arabs in the Fifth Century*. Washington, DC

Shahīd, I. (1995) *Byzantium and the Arabs in the Sixth Century*. 2 vols. Washington, DC

Shereshevski, J. (1991) *Byzantine Urban Settlements in the Negev Desert*. Jerusalem

Sodini, J.-P., *et al*. (1980) 'Dehès (Syrie du nord), campagnes I–III (1976–78): recherches sur l'habitat rural', *Syria* 57: 1–304

Stratos, A. N. (1968) *Byzantium in the Seventh Century* I. Amsterdam

Tate, G. (1992) *Les Campagnes de la Syrie du Nord du IIe au VIIe siècle*. Paris

Tsafrir, Y. (ed.) (1993) *Ancient Churches Revealed*. Jerusalem

Tsafrir, Y. and Foerster, G. (1994) 'From Scythopolis to Baysān – changing concepts of urbanism', in Cameron and King (eds.) 95–115

Urman, D. (1985) *The Golan: A Profile of a Region During the Roman and Byzantine Period* (BAR International Series 269). Oxford

Urman, D. and Flesher, P. (eds.) (1995) *Ancient Synagogues*. Leiden

Villeneuve, F. (1985) 'L'économie rurale et la vie des campagnes dans le Hauran antique', in Dentzer (1985) 63–129

Vööbus, A. (1958–9) *History of Asceticism in the Syrian Orient*. 2 vols. (*CSCO Subisida* 14, 19). Louvain

de Vries, B. (1981) 'The Umm el-Jimal Project, 1972–7', *BASOR* 244: 52–73

Walmsley, A. (1996) 'Byzantine Palestine and Arabia: urban prosperity in late antiquity', in N. Christie and S. T. Loseby (eds.), *Towns in Transition: Urban Evolution in Late Antiquity and the Early Middle Ages* (Aldershot) 126–58

Watson, P. (1992) 'Change in foreign and regional links with Pella in the seventh century A.D.: the ceramic evidence', in Canivet and Rey-Coquais (1992) 233–48

Whitby, L. M. (1986a) 'Procopius and the development of Roman defences in Upper Mesopotamia', in Freeman and Kennedy (1986) 717–35

Whitby, L. M. (1986b) 'Procopius on Dara', in Freeman and Kennedy (1986) 737–83

Whittow, M. (1990) 'Ruling the late Roman and early Byzantine city: a continuous history', *P&P* 129: 3–29

Wilkinson, J. (1977) *Jerusalem Pilgrims before the Crusades*. Warminster

Woolley, C. L. and Lawrence, T. E. (1914–15) *The Wilderness of Zin*. London

CH. 21*c*: EGYPT

Abbott, N. (1938) *The Kurrah Papyri from Aphrodito in the Oriental Institute* (The Oriental Institute of the University of Chicago Studies in Ancient Oriental Civilization, 15). Chicago

Amirante, L. (1957) 'Appunti per la storia della "Redemptio ab Hostibus"', *Labeo* 3: 171–220

Baldwin, B. (1984) 'Dioscorus of Aphrodito: the worst poet of antiquity?', *Atti del XVII Congresso Internazionale di Papirologia* II (Naples) 327–31

Bell, H. I. (1917) 'The Byzantine servile state in Egypt', *JEA* 4: 86–106

Bell, H. I. (1944) 'An Egyptian village in the age of Justinian', *JHS* 64: 21–36

Bell, H. I. (1948) *Egypt from Alexander the Great to the Arab Conquest: A Study in the Diffusion and Decay of Hellenism*. Oxford

Bell, H. I. and Crum, W. E. (1925) 'A Greek-Coptic glossary', *Aegyptus* 6: 177–226

Berger, A. (1953) *Encyclopedic Dictionary of Roman Law*. Philadelphia

Bernand, E. (1969) *Les inscriptions grecques de Philae*. Paris

Bonneau, D. (1970) 'L'administration de l'irrigation dans les grands domaines en Égypte au VIe siècle de N.E.', *Proceedings of the Twelfth International Congress of Papyrology* (Toronto) 45–62

Bowman, A. K. (1986) *Egypt after the Pharaohs, 332 BC–AD 642*. Berkeley and Los Angeles

Butler, A. J. (1978) *The Arab Conquest of Egypt and the Last Thirty Years of Roman Domination* (2nd edn, ed. P. M. Fraser). Oxford

Calderini, A. (1966) *Dizionario dei nomi geographici e topografici dell'Egitto greco-romano*. 1.2. Madrid

Cameron, Averil (1979) 'A nativity poem of the sixth century A.D.', *CPh* 74: 222–32

Charles, R. H. (trans.) (1916) *The Chronicle of John, Coptic Bishop of Nikiu (c. 690 A.D.)*. London (repr. Amsterdam, n.d.)

The Coptic Encyclopedia (ed. A. S. Atiya) (1991) 8 vols. New York

Daris, S. (1991) *Il lessico latino nel greco d'Egitto* (2nd edn) (Estudis de papirologia i filologia biblica 2). Barcelona

Farber, J. (1986) 'The Patermuthis archive: a third look', *BASP* 23: 81–98

Feissel, D. and Worp, K. A. (1988) 'La requête d'Appion, évêque de Syène, à Théodose II: P. Leid. Z révisé', *OMRO* 68: 97–108

Fikhman, I. F. (1965) *Egypt on the Confines of Two Epochs* (Russian). Moscow

Fichman [Fikhman], I. F. (1973) 'Sklaven und Sklavenarbeit im spätrömischen Oxyrhynchos', *Jahrbuch für Wirtschaftsgeschichte* 2: 149–206

Fikhman, I. F. (1975) 'Quelques données sur la genèse de la grande propriété foncière à Oxyrhynchus', in *Le monde grec: Hommages à Claire Préaux* (Brussels) 784–90

Fikhman, I. F. (1981) 'Les cautionnements pour les *coloni adscripticii*', *Proceedings of the Sixteenth International Congress of Papyrology* (Chico) 469–77

Fikhman, I. F. (1991) 'Esclaves et colons en Égypte byzantine', *Analecta Papyrologica* 3: 7–17

Fraser, P. M. (1993) [1995] 'Byzantine Alexandria: decline and fall', *BSA* 45: 91–106

Gagos, T. and van Minnen, P. (1994) *Settling a Dispute: Towards a Legal Anthropology of Late Antique Egypt* (New Texts from Ancient Cultures 1). Ann Arbor

Gascou, J. (1975) 'Militaires étrangers en Égypte byzantine', *BIFAO* 75: 203–6

Gascou, J. (1985) 'Les grands domaines, la cité et l'état en Égypte byzantine', *T&MByz* 9: 1–90

Gascou, J. (1990) 'Nabla/Labla', *CdÉ* 65: 111–15

Gascou, J. (1994) *Un codex fiscal hermopolite (P. Sorb. II 69)* (Amer. Stud. Pap. 32). Atlanta

Gelzer, M. (1909) *Studien zur byzantinischen Verwaltung Ägyptens* (Leipziger historische Abhandlungen 13). Leipzig

Geraci, G. (1979) 'Per una storia dell'amministrazione fiscale nell'Egitto del VI secolo d.C.: Dioskoros e l'autopragia di Aphrodito', *Actes du XVe Congrès International de Papyrologie* (Brussels) IV.195–205

Geremek, H. (1990) 'Sur la question des *BOULAI* dans les villes égyptiennes aux Ve–VIIe siècles', *JJP* 20: 47–54

Haas, C. (1997) *Alexandria in Late Antiquity: Topography and Social Conflict*. Baltimore

Hagemann, H.-R. (1953) *Die Stellung der Piae Causae nach justinianischem Rechte*. Basel

Hardy, E. R. (1931) *The Large Estates of Byzantine Egypt*. New York

Hardy, E. R. (1968) 'The Egyptian policy of Justinian', *DOP* 22: 23–41

Heitsch, E. (1963) *Die griechischen Dichterfragmente der römischen Kaiserzeit* I (2nd edn rev.) (Abhandlungen der Akademie der Wissenschaften in Göttingen, philologisch-historische Klasse, dritte Folge 49). Göttingen

Humphrey, J. H. (1986) *Roman Circuses: Arenas for Chariot Racing.* London

Johnson, A. C. and West, L. C. (1949) *Byzantine Egypt: Economic Studies* (Princeton University Studies in Papyrology 6). Princeton

Jones, A. H. M. (1949) 'The Roman civil service (clerical and sub-clerical grades)', *JRS* 39: 38–55 (= *Studies in Roman Government and Law* (Oxford, 1960) 151–75)

Jones, M. (1991) 'The early Christian sites at Tell el-Amarna and Sheikh Said', *JEA* 77: 129–44

Keenan, J. G. (1973, 1974) 'The names Flavius and Aurelius as status designations in later Roman Egypt', *ZPE* 11: 33–63; 13: 283–304

Keenan, J. G. (1975) 'On law and society in late Roman Egypt', *ZPE* 17: 237–50

Keenan, J. G. (1977) 'The provincial administration of Egyptian Arcadia', *Mus. Phil. Lond.* 2: 193–202

Keenan, J. G. (1978) 'The case of Flavia Christodote: observations on PSI I 76', *ZPE* 29: 191–209

Keenan, J. G. (1980) 'Aurelius Phoibammon son of Triadelphus: a Byzantine Egyptian land entrepreneur', *BASP* 17: 145–54

Keenan, J. G. (1984a) 'The Aphrodito papyri and village life in Byzantine Egypt', *BSAC* 26: 51–63

Keenan, J. G. (1984b) 'Aurelius Apollos and the Aphrodito village élite', *Atti del XVII Congresso Internazionale di Papirologia* (Naples) III.957–63

Keenan, J. G. (1985a) 'Notes on absentee landlordism at Aphrodito', *BASP* 22: 137–69

Keenan, J. G. (1985b) 'Village shepherds and social tension in Byzantine Egypt', *YCS* 28: 245–59

Keenan, J. G. (1990) 'Evidence for the Byzantine army in the Syene papyri', *BASP* 27: 139–50

Keenan, J. G. (1992) 'A Constantinople loan, A.D. 541', *BASP* 29: 175–82

Keenan, J. G. (1993) 'Papyrology and Byzantine historiography', *BASP* 30: 137–44

Kovelman, A. B. (1991) 'From logos to myth: Egyptian petitions of the 5th–7th centuries', *BASP* 28: 135–52

Kramer, J. (1992) 'Schreiben der Prätorialpräfekten des Jahres 399 an den *praeses provinciae Arcadiae* in lateinischer und griechischer Version', *Tyche* 7: 157–62

Kuehn, C. (1990) 'Dioskoros of Aphrodito and Romanos the Melodist', *BASP* 27: 103–7

Kuehn, C. (1995) *Channels of Imperishable Fire: The Beginnings of Christian Mystical Poetry and Dioscorus of Aphrodito.* New York

Kuhn, K. H. (1954) 'A fifth century Egyptian abbot', *JThS* n.s. 5: 36–48; 174–87

Leipoldt, J. (1902–3) 'Berichte Schenutes über Einfälle der Nubier in Ägypten', *ZÄS* 40: 126–40

Liebeschuetz, W. [=J. H. W. G.] (1974) 'The pagarch, the city and imperial administration in Byzantine Egypt', *JJP* 18: 163–8

MacCoull, L. S. B. (1981) 'The Coptic archive of Dioscorus of Aphrodito', *Cd'É* 56: 185–93 (= MacCoull (1993b) II)

MacCoull, L. S. B. (1984) 'Notes on the social structure of late antique Aphrodito', *BSAC* 26: 65–77 (= MacCoull (1993b) xx)

MacCoull, L. S. B. (1986a) 'Coptic Egypt during the Persian occupation: the papyrological evidence', *Studi classici e orientali* 36: 307–13 (= MacCoull (1993b) XII)

MacCoull, L. S. B. (1986b) 'Dioscorus and the dukes: an aspect of Coptic Hellenism in the sixth century', *BS* 13: 30–40 (= MacCoull (1993b) x)

MacCoull, L. S. B. (1989) 'The strange death of Coptic culture', *Coptic Church Review* 10: 35–45 (= MacCoull (1993b) XXVI)

MacCoull, L. S. B. (1990) 'Christianity at Syene/Elephantine/Philae', *BASP* 27: 151–62

MacCoull, L. S. B. (1993a) 'The Apa Apollos monastery of Pharoou (Aphrodito) and its papyrus archive', *Le Muséon* 106: 21–63

MacCoull, L. S. B. (1993b) *Coptic Perspectives on Late Antiquity*. Aldershot

McGing, B. (1990) 'Melitian monks at Labla', *Tyche* 5: 67–94

Maehler, M. (1976) 'Trouble in Alexandria in a letter of the sixth century', *GRBS* 17: 197–203

Maspéro, J. (1911) 'Un dernier poète grec, Dioscore, fils d'Apollos', *REG* 24: 426–81

Maspéro, J. (1912) *Organisation militaire de l'Égypte byzantine* (Bibliothèque de l'École des Hautes Études, Sciences historiques et philologiques 201). Paris

Minnen, P. van (1992) 'Isocrates and Menander in late antique perspective', *GRBS* 33: 87–98

Monks, G. R. (1953) 'The church of Alexandria and the city's economic life in the sixth century', *Speculum* 28: 349–62

Palme, B. (1994) 'Flavius Sarapodorus, ein *agens in rebus* aus Hermupolis', *APF* 40: 42–68

Rémondon, R. (1952) 'L'Égypte et la suprême résistance au Christianisme (Ve–VIIe siècles)', *BIFAO* 51: 63–78

Rémondon, R. (1955) 'L'édit XIII de Justinien a-t-il été promulgué en 539?', *CdÉ* 30: 112–21

Robinson, O. (1968) 'Private prisons', *RIDA* ser. 3, 15: 389–98

Rouillard, G. (1928) *L'administration civile de l'Égypte byzantine* (2nd edn). Paris

Samir, Khalil, S. J. (1986) 'Arabic sources for early Egyptian Christianity', in Pearson and Goehring (eds.), *Egyptian Christianity* 82–97

Schefold, K. (1945) 'Ein Bildnismedallion der Zeit Justinians', *Mus. Helv.* 2: 48–53

Schmitt, O. (1994) 'Die *Bucellarii*. Eine Studie zum militärischen Gefolgschaftswesen in der Spätantike', *Tyche* 9: 147–74

Schnebel, M. (1928) 'An agricultural ledger in P. Bad. 95', *JEA* 14: 34–45

Sirks, B. (1993) 'Reconsidering the Roman colonate', *ZRGRA* 110: 331–69

Thomas, J. P. (1987) *Private Religious Foundations in the Byzantine Empire*. Washington, DC

Timm, S. (1983) *Tübinger Atlas des Vorderen Orients* (TAVO) B VI 15: *Ägypten. Das Christentum bis zur Araberzeit (bis zum 7 Jahrhundert)*. Wiesbaden

Trimbie, J. (1986) 'The state of research on the career of Shenoute of Atripe', in Pearson and Goehring (eds.), *Egyptian Christianity* 258–70

Turner, E. G. (1973) 'The charioteers from Antinoe', *JHS* 93: 192–5 (with colour plates)

Viljamaa, T. (1968) *Studies in Encomiastic Poetry of the Early Byzantine Period*

(Commentationes Humanarum Litterarum, Societas Scientiarum Fennica 42.2). Helsinki

Wipszycka, E. (1972) *Les ressources et les activités économiques des églises en Égypte du IVe au VIIIe siècle* (Pap. Brux. 10). Brussels

Zingale, L. M. (1984–5) 'Osservazioni sulla *domus divina* di Teodora', *Annali della Facoltà di Giurisprudenza di Genova* 20: 142–9

CH. 22*a*: THE SASANID MONARCHY

Altheim, F. and Stiehl, R. (1954) *Ein Asiatischer Staat, Feudalismus unter den Sasaniden und ihren Nachbaren*. Wiesbaden

Altheim, F. and Stiehl, R. (1957) *Finanzgeschichte der Spätantike*. Frankfurt am Main

Asmussen, J. P. (1975) *Manichaean Literature*. Delmar, NY

Back, M. (1978) 'Die sassanidischen Staatsinschriften', *Acta Iranica* 8

Baynes, N. H. (1960) 'Rome and Armenia in the fourth century', in *Byzantine Studies and Other Essays* (London) 186–208

Blockley, R. C. (1981) *The Fragmentary Classicising Historians of the Later Roman Empire* 1 (ARCA 10). Liverpool

Blockley, R. C. (1985) *Menander the Guardsman* (ARCA 17). Liverpool

Blockley, R. C. (1992) *East Roman Foreign Policy* (ARCA 30). Leeds

Böhlig, A. (1980) *Die Gnosis. Dritter Band, der Manichäismus*, in *Die Bibliothek der alten Welt*. Zurich and Munich

Bosworth, C. E. (1999) *The History of al-Ṭabarī, V: The Sasanids, the Byzantines, the Lakhmids and Yemen* (translated and annotated). New York

Boyce, M. (1957) 'Some Reflections about Zurvanism', *BSOAS* 19–2: 305–16

Boyce, M. (1968) *The Letter of Tansar*. Rome

Boyce, M. (1979) *Zoroastrians, their Religious Beliefs and Practices*. London and New York

Boyce, M. (1984) *Textual Sources for the Study of Zoroastrianism*. Manchester

Boyce, M. (1990) 'Some further reflections on Zurvanism', *Acta Iranica* 16: 20–9

Braund, D. (1994) *Georgia in Antiquity, a History of Colchis and Transcaucasian Iberia, 550 BC–AD 562* (Oxford) 238–314

Browne, E. G. (1900) 'Some account of the Arabic work entitled "Nihāyatu'l-irab fī, akhbari' l-Furs wa'l-'Arab"', *JRAS*: 195–259

Cameron, Averil (1969/70) 'Agathias on the Sassanians', *DOP* 23/24: 67–183

Cameron, Averil (1995) (ed.) *The Byzantine and Early Islamic Near East. III States, Resources and Armies* (Studies in Late Antiquity and Early Islam 1). Princeton

Chaumont, M.-L. (1958) 'Le culte d'Anahita à Staxr et les premiers Sassanides', *RHR* 153: 154–75

Chaumont, M.-L. (1960) 'Recherches sur le clergé Zorastrien: Le herbad', *RHR* 157: 54–80; 158: 161–79

Chaumont, M.-L. (1976) 'L'Arménie entre Rome et l'Iran I. De l'avènement d'Auguste à l'avènement de Dioclétien', *ANRW* II, 9.1: 71–194

Chaumont, M.-L. (1988) *La Christianisation de l'empire iranien des origines aux persecutions du IVe siècle* (*CSCO Subsidia* 80). Louvain

Christensen, A. (1925) *Le règne du roi Kawadh et le communisme Mazdakite*. Copenhagen

Christensen, A. (1944) *L'Iran sous les Sassanides*. Copenhagen

Crone, P. (1991) 'Kavad's heresy and Mazdak's revolt', *Iran* 29: 21–42

Dabrowa, E. (ed.) (1994) *The Roman and Byzantine Army in the East.* Kraków

Dodgeon, M. and Lieu, S. N. C. (1991) *The Roman Eastern Frontier and the Persian Wars, AD 226–363: A Documentary History.* London and New York

Fisher, W. B. (1968) (ed.) *The Cambridge History of Iran* I, *The Land of Iran.* Cambridge

Frye, R. N. (1959) 'Zurvanism again', *HThR* 52: 63–73

Frye, R. N. (1984) *The History of Ancient Iran* (Munich) 287–339

Ghirshman, R. (1962) *Iran, Parthians and Sassanians.* London

Göbl, R. (1971) *Sasanian Numismatics.* Würzburg

Goodblat, D. M. (1979) 'The poll tax in Sassanian Babylonia', *JESHO* 22: 233–95

Grignaschi, M. (1971) 'La riforma tributaria di Hosro I e il feudalismo sassanide', in *La Persia nel medioevo,* Accademia nazionale dei Lincei (Rome) 88–138

Guidi, M. [Morony, M.] (1992) 'Mazdak', *Encyclopaedia of Islam* 2nd edn, VI.949–52

Hahn, I. (1959) 'Sassanidische und spätrömische Besteuerung', *AAntHung* 7: 149–60

Herrmann, G. (1977) *The Iranian Revival.* London

Howard-Johnston, J. D. (1994) 'The official history of Heraclius' Persian campaigns' in Dabrowa (ed.) (1994) 57–87

Howard-Johnston, J. D. (1995) 'The two great powers in late antiquity: a comparison', in Averil Cameron (ed.) (1995) 157–226

Humbach, H. and Skjaervø, P. O. (1983) *The Sassanian Inscription of Paikuli.* Wiesbaden

Huyse, P. (1999) 'Die dreisprächige Inschrift Šaburs I an der Ka'aba-i Zarduŝt', *Corpus Inscriptionum Iranicarum* III, *Pahlavi Inscriptions* I. London

Klíma, O. (1957) *Mazdak. Geschichte einer sozialen Bewegung im Sassanidischen Persien.* Prague

Klíma, O. (1977) *Beiträge zur Geschichte des Mazdakismus.* Prague

Labourt, J. (1904) *Le Christianisme dans l'empire Perse sous la dynastie Sassanide.* Paris

Langlois, V. (1867, 1869) *Collection des historiens anciens et modernes de l'Arménie,* 2 vols. Paris

Lee, A. D. (1993) *Information and Frontiers: Roman Foreign Relations in Late Antiquity.* Cambridge

Lieu, S. N. C. (1994) *Manichaeism in Mesopotamia and the Roman Near East.* Leiden

Loginov, S. D. and Nikitin, A. B. (1993a) 'Sasanian coins of the third century from Merv', *Mesopotamia* 18: 225–46

Loginov, S. D. and Nikitin, A. B. (1993b) 'Coins of Shapur II from Merv', *Mesopotamia* 18: 247–69

Loginov, S. D. and Nikitin, A. B. (1993c) 'Sasanian coins of the late 4th–7th centuries from Merv', *Mesopotamia* 18: 271–316

Lukonin, V. G. (1961) *Iran v epokhu pervykh Sasanidov.* Leningrad

Millar, F. (1993) *The Roman Near East, 31 BC–AD 337.* Cambridge, MA

Nöldeke, T. (1878) *Geschichte des Artachsir i Papakan* (Beiträge zur Kunde der indogermanischen Sprachen 4) (Göttingen) 24–69

Nöldeke, T. (1879) *Geschichte der Perser und Araber zur Zeit der Sasaniden.* Leiden

Nöldeke, T. (1887) *Aufsätze zur persischen Geschichte.* Leipzig

Nöldeke, T. (1920) *Das iranische Nationalepos.* 2nd edn. Leipzig

Pellat, C. (1954) *Le Livre de la couronne.* Paris

Pigulevskaya, N. V. (= Pigulevskaja, N.) (1937) 'K voprosu o podatnoj reforme Khosroya Anushervana', *Vestnik Drevnej Istorii* 1: 143–54

Pigulevskaya, N. V. (1946) *Vizantiya i Iran na rubezhe VI i VII vekov.* Moscow and Leningrad

Pigulevskaja, N. (1963) *Les villes de l'état Iranien aux époques Parthe et Sassanide.* Paris

Potter, D. S. (1990) *Prophecy and History in the Crisis of the Roman Empire, a Historical Commentary on the Thirteenth Sibylline Oracle.* Oxford

Rubin, Z. (1986) 'Diplomacy and war in the relations between Byzantium and the Sassanids in the fifth century AD' (BAR International Series 297) (Oxford) 677–95

Rubin, Z. (1995) 'The reforms of Khusro Anushirwan', in Averil Cameron (ed.) (1995) 227–97

Schippmann, K. (1990) *Grundzüge der Geschichte des Sasanidischen Reiches.* Darmstadt

Shaked, S. (1979) *The Wisdom of the Sasanian Sages (Denkard VI)* (Persian Heritage Series 34). Boulder, CO

Shaked, S. (forthcoming) 'Zoroastrians and others in Sasanian Iran', in L. I. Conrad (ed.), *Late Antiquity and Early Islam IV. Patterns of Communal Identity in the Byzantine and Early Islamic Near East* (Studies in Late Antiquity and Early Islam). Princeton

Shaki, M. (1981) 'The Denkard account of the history of the Zoroastrian Scriptures', *Archív Orientální* 49: 114–25

Solodukho, J. A. (1948) 'Podati i povinosti v Irake v III–V nashej ëry', *Sovetskoe Vostokovedenie* 5: 55–72

Stratos, A. N. (1968) *Byzantium in the Seventh Century I: 602–34.* Amsterdam

Whitby, M. (1994) 'The Persian king at war', in Dabrowa (ed.) (1994) 227–63

Widengren, G. (1956) 'Recherches sur le féodalisme iranien', *Orientalia Suecana* 5: 79–182

Widengren, G. (1961) 'The status of the Jews in the Sassanian Empire', *Iranica Antiqua* 1–2: 117–62

Widengren, G. (1965) *Die Religionen Irans.* Stuttgart

Widengren, G. (1967) *Der Feudalismus im alten Iran.* Cologne and Opladen

Widengren, G. (1976) 'Iran der grosse Gegner Roms: Königsgewalt, Feudalismus, Militärwesen', *ANRW* II, 9.1: 219–306

Wiesehöfer, J. (1996) *Ancient Persia.* London (translation of Wiesehöfer, J. (1998) *Das antike Persien, von 550 v. Chr. bis 650 n. Chr.* Munich and Zurich

Wikander, S. (1946) *Feuerpriester in Kleinasien und Iran.* Lund

Wolski, J. (1976) 'Iran und Rom. Versuch einer historischen Wertung der gegenseitigen Beziehungen', *ANRW* II, 9.1: 195–214

Yar-Shater, E. (1971) 'Were the Sasanians heirs to the Achaemenids?', in *La Persia nel Medioevo* (Accademia nazionale dei Lincei) 517–33

Yar-Shater, E. (1983) (ed.) *The Cambridge History of Iran* III. *The Seleucid, Parthian, and Sasanian Periods.* Cambridge

Zaehner, R. C. (1955) *Zurvan: A Zoroastrian Dilemma.* Oxford

Zaehner, R. C. (1975) *The Dawn and Twilight of Zoroastrianism.* London

CH. 22*b*: ARMENIA IN THE FIFTH AND SIXTH CENTURY

Adontz, N. (1934) 'Les légendes de Maurice et de Constantin V', in *Mélanges Bidez* (Annuaire de l'Institut de Philologie et d'Histoire orientales et slaves 2) 1–9 (= *Études arméno-byzantines* (Lisbon) 125–36)

Adontz, N. (1970) *Armenia in the Period of Justinian: The Political Conditions Based on the Naxarar System* (translated with partial revisions, a bibliographical note, and appendices by N. G. Garsoïan). Lisbon

Agathangelos, *Patmutʿiwn Hayocʿ* (ed. G. Ter-Mkrtčʿean and S. Kanayeancʿ) (1909) Tiflis (repr. Delmar, NY, 1980). English trans.: see Thomson (1976)

Arutyunova-Fidanyan, V. A. (1980) *Armyane-khalkedoniti na vostochnikh granitsakh Vizantijskov imperii*. Erevan

Berbérian, H. (1964) 'Autobiographie d'Anania Sirakecʿi', *Revue des études arméniennes* n.s. 1: 189–94

Book of Letters: Girk Tʿłtʿocʿ ed. Y. Izmiteancʿ (1901). Tiflis

Charanis, P. (1963) *The Armenians in the Byzantine Empire*. Lisbon

Christensen, A. (1944) *L'Iran sous les Sassanides* (2nd edn). Paris

Draguet, R. (1924) *Julien d'Halicarnasse et sa controverse avec Sévère d'Antioche sur l'incorruptibilité du corps du Christ*. Louvain

Elishe, *Ełišei vasn Vardanay ew Hayocʿ Paterazmin* (ed. E. Ter-Minasyan) (1957) Erevan (repr. Delmar, NY, 1993). English transl.: see Thomson (1982)

Garitte, G. (1952) *La Narratio de Rebus Armeniae* (*CSCO Subsidia* 4). Louvain

Garsoïan, N. G. (1976) 'Prolegomena to a study of the Iranian elements in Arsacid Armenia', *Handes Amsorya* 90: 177–234 (= Garsoïan (1985) x)

Garsoïan, N. G. (1984) 'Secular jurisdiction over the Armenian church (fourth–seventh centuries)', in *Okeanos: Essays presened to Ihor Ševčenko* (Harvard Ukrainian Studies 7) 220–50 (= Garsoïan (1985) ix)

Garsoïan, N. G. (1984/5) 'The early-mediaeval Armenian city: an alien element?', in *Ancient Studies in Memory of Elias Bickerman, The Journal of the Ancient Near Eastern Society* 16/17: 67–83

Garsoïan, N. G. (1985) *Armenia between Byzantium and the Sasanians*. Aldershot

Garsoïan, N. G. (1989) 'Some preliminary precisions on the separation of the Armenian and Imperial Churches: 1. The presence of "Armenian" bishops at the first five Oecumenical Councils', in J. Chrysostomides (ed.) *Kathegetria. Essays Presented to Joan Hussey* (Camberley) 249–85

Garsoïan, N. G. (1996) 'Quelques précisions préliminaires sur le schisme entre les églises byzantine et arménienne au sujet du concile de Chalcédoine: 11. La date et les circonstances de la rupture', in *L'Arménie et Byzance. Histoire et Culture* (Byzantina Sorbonensia 12) 99–112

Garsoïan, N. G. (1999) *L'Église arménienne et le grand schisme d'Orient* (*CSCO* 574). Louvain

Goubert, P. (1951) *Byzance avant l'Islam* vol. 1: *Byzance et l'Orient sous les successeurs de Justinien. L'empereur Maurice*. Paris

Kazhdan, A. P. (1975) *Armyane v sostave gospodstvyuschego klassa Vizantijskoj imperii v XXI–XII vv.* Erevan

Koriwn, *Varkʿ Maštocʿi* (ed. M. Abełean) (1941) (repr. Delmar, NY, 1985, with English translation by B. Norehad). German trans.: Winkler, G. (1994) *Koriwns Biographie des Mesrop Maštocʿ* (Orientalia Christiana Analecta 245). Rome

Lazar of Pʿarp, *Patmutʿiwn Hayocʿ* (ed. G. Ter-Mkrtčʿean and S. Malxasean) (1904) Tiflis (repr. Delmar, NY, 1985). English trans.: see Thomson (1991)

Manandian, H. (1965) *The Trade and Cities of Armenia in Relation to Ancient World Trade*. Lisbon

Moses of Khoren, *Patmut'iwn Hayoc'* (ed. M. Abełean and S. Yarut'iwnean) (1913) Tiflis (rep. Delmar, NY, 1984). English trans.: see Thomson (1978)

P'awstos Buzand, *Buzandaran Patmut'iwnk'* (ed. K'. Patkanean) (1883) St Petersburg (repr. Delmar, NY, 1984). English trans.: Garsoïan, N. G. (1989) *The Epic Histories (Buzandaran Patmut'iwnk')*. Cambridge, MA

Peeters, P. (1935) 'Sainte Sousanik, martyre en Arméno-Géorgie', *AB* 53: 5–48, 245–307

Pseudo-Shapuh: Thomson, R. W. (1988/89) 'The anonymous story-teller (also known as "Pseudo-Šapuh")', *Revue des études arméniennes* 21: 171–232

Renoux, Ch. (1993) 'Langue et littérature arméniennes', in M. Albert *et al.* (eds.), *Christianismes orientaux* (Paris) 109–66

Russell, J. R. (1987) *Zoroastrianism in Armenia*. Cambridge, MA

Sarkissian, K. (1975) *The Council of Chalcedon and the Armenian Church* (2nd edn). New York

Sebeos, *Patmut'iwn Sebeosi* (ed. G. Abgaryan) (1979) Erevan. English trans.: see Thomson and Howard-Johnston (1999)

Shahīd, I. (1971) *The Martyrs of Najran. New Documents* (Subsidia Hagiographica 49). Brussels

Tallon, M. (1955) 'Livre des Lettres, 1er Groupe: Documents concernant les relations avec les Grecs', *Mélanges de l'Université Saint Joseph* 32: 1–146 (also printed separately)

Ter-Minassiantz, E. (1904) *Die armenische Kirche in ihren Beziehungen zu den syrischen Kirchen bis zum Ende des 13. Jahrhunderts nach den armenischen und syrischen Quellen* (Texte und Untersuchungen 16). Leipzig

Thomson, R. W. (1976) *Agathangelos: History of the Armenians*, trans. R. W. Thomson. Albany

Thomson, R. W. (1978) *Moses Khorenats'i: History of the Armenians*, trans. R. W. Thomson. Cambridge, MA

Thomson, R. W. (1980) 'The formation of the Armenian literary tradition', in N. G. Garsoïan, T. F. Mathews and R. W. Thomson (eds.), *East of Byzantium: Syria and Armenia in the Formative Period* (Washington, DC) 135–50 (= Thomson (1994) IV)

Thomson, R. W. (1982) *Elishe: History of Vardan and the Armenian War*, trans. R. W. Thomson. Cambridge, MA

Thomson, R. W. (1988/9) 'Mission, conversion, and Christianization: the Armenian example', *Harvard Ukrainian Studies* 12/13: 28–45 (= Thomson (1994) III)

Thomson, R. W. (1991) *The History of Lazar P'arpec'i*, trans. R. W. Thomson. Atlanta

Thomson, R. W. (1994) *Studies in Armenian Literature and Christianity*. Aldershot

Thomson, R. W. and Howard-Johnston, J. (1999) *The Armenian History attributed to Sebeos*, 2 parts (Translated Texts for Historians 31). Liverpool

Toumanoff, C. (1963) *Studies in Christian Caucasian History*. Washington, DC

Ukhtanes (1985) *History of Armenia*, Part II: *History of the Severance of the Georgians from the Armenians* (translated by Z. Arzoumanian) (1985). Fort Lauderdale

Winkler, G. (1982) *Das armenische Initiationsrituale* (*OCA* 217). Rome

Abū l-Baqāʾ Hibat Allāh al-Ḥillī (d. early sixth/twelfth century). *Al-Manāqib al-mazyadīya fī akhbār al-mulūk al-asadīya*. Ed. Ṣāliḥ Mūsā Darādka and Muḥammad ʿAbd al-Qādir Khuraysāt. 2 vols. Amman, 1984

Abū ʿUbayda, Maʿmar ibn Muthannā al-Taymī (d. 204/819). *Naqāʾiḍ Jarīr wa-l-Farazdaq*. Ed. A. A. Bevan. 3 vols. Leiden, 1905–12

al-Aʿshā Maymūn. *Dīwān*. Ed. Rudolf Geyer. London, 1928

al-ʿAskarī, Abū Hilāl al-Ḥasan ibn ʿAbd Allāh ibn Sahl (d. 395/1004). *Kitāb al-awāʾil*. Ed. Walīd Qaṣṣāb and Muḥammad al-Miṣrī. 2 vols. 2nd edn. Riyadh, 1401/1981

al-Azdī, Abū Ismāʿīl Muḥammad ibn ʿAbd Allāh al-Baṣrī (f. *c.* 180/796). *Futūḥ al-Shām*. Ed. W. N. Lees. Calcutta, 1854

Arberry, A. J. (trans.). *The Koran Interpreted*. London, 1955

al-Azraqī, Abū l-Walīd Muḥammad ibn ʿAbd Allāh ibn Aḥmad (d. *c.* 250/865). *Akhbār Makka wa-mā jāʾa fīhā min al-āthār*. Ed. Rushdī al-Ṣāliḥ Malḥas. 2 vols. Beirut, 1403/1983

al-Bakrī, Abū ʿUbayd ʿAbd Allāh ibn ʿAbd al-ʿAzīz (d. 487/1094). *Muʿjam mā staʿjam fī asmāʾ al-bilād wa-l-mawāḍiʿ*. Ed. Muṣṭafā al-Saqqā. 4 vols. Cairo, 1364–71/1945–51

al-Balādhurī, Abū l-Ḥasan Aḥmad ibn Yaḥyā ibn Jābir (d. 279/892). *Ansāb al-ashrāf*, I. Ed. Muḥammad Ḥamīd Allāh. Cairo, 1959
    Futūḥ al-buldān. Ed. M. J. de Goeje. Leiden, 1866

Cheikho, Louis. *Shuʿarāʾ al-naṣrānīya*. 2 vols. Beirut, 1890

Chronicon ad annum Christi 1234 pertinens. Ed. and trans. J. B. Chabot. 4 vols. Paris, 1916–20

Ibn ʿAbd Rabbih, Shihāb al-Dīn Abū ʿUmar Aḥmad ibn Muḥammad (d. 328/940). *Al-ʿIqd al-farīd*. Ed. Aḥmad Amīn, Aḥmad al-Zayn and Ibrāhīm al-Abyārī. 7 vols. Cairo, 1368–84/1949–65

Ibn ʿAsākir, Abū l-Qāsim ʿAlī ibn al-Ḥasan ibn Hibat Allāh (d. 571/1176). *Tārīkh madīnat Dimashq*, I. Ed. Ṣalāḥ al-Dīn al-Munajjid. Damascus, 1951

Ibn Aʿtham al-Kūfī, Abū Muḥammad Aḥmad (wr. 204/819). *Kitāb al-futūḥ*. Ed. Muḥammad ʿAbd al-Muʿīd Khān *et al.* 8 vols. Hyderabad, 1388–95/1968–75

Ibn Ḥabīb, Abū Jaʿfar Muḥammad al-Baghdādī (d. 245/860). *Kitāb al-muḥabbar*. Ed. Ilse Lichtenstädter. Hyderabad, 1361/1942

Ibn Hishām, Abū Muḥammad ʿAbd al-Malik al-Maʿāfirī (d. 218/834). *Sīrat Rasūl Allāh*. Ed. Ferdinand Wüstenfeld. 2 vols. Göttingen, 1858–60

Ibn Khaldūn, ʿImād al-Din Abū Zayd ʿAbd al-Raḥmān ibn Muḥammad (d. 808/1405). *Al-Muqaddima*. Ed. E. M. Quatremère. 3 vols. Paris, 1858

Ibn Khurradādhbih, Abū l-Qāsim ʿUbayd Allāh ibn ʿAbd Allāh (d. *c.* 300/911). *Al-Masālik wa-l-mamālik*. Ed. M. J. de Goeje. Leiden, 1889

Ibn al-Najjār, Abū ʿAbd Allāh Muḥammad ibn Maḥmūd (d. 643/1245). *Al-Durra al-thamīna fī taʾrīkh al-Madīna*, printed as an appendix to al-Fāsī (d. 832/1429), *Shifāʾ al-gharām bi-akhbār al-balad al-ḥarām*, II. Mecca, 1956

Ibn Qutayba, Abū Muḥammad ʿAbd Allāh ibn Muslim (d. 276/889). *Kitāb al-maʿārif*. Ed. Tharwat ʿUkkāsha. 2nd edn. Cairo, 1969

al-Iṣfahānī, Abū l-Faraj ʿAlī ibn al-Ḥusayn (d. 356/967). *Kitāb al-aghānī*. Ed. Aḥmad Zakī al-ʿAdawī *et al.* 24 vols. Cairo, 1345–94/1927–74

Jeffery, Arthur. *Materials for the History of the Text of the Qurʾān*. Leiden, 1937

John Moschus (d. 634). *Pratum Spirituale*. PG LXXXVII.2852–3112

John of Ephesus (d. *c.* 586). *Historia Ecclesiastica*, III. Ed. and trans. E. W. Brooks. 2 vols. Paris, 1935

Kraemer, Casper J. (ed.) *Excavations at Nessana*, III: *Non-Literary Papyri*. Princeton, 1958

Lughda al-Iṣfahānī, Abū ʿAlī al-Ḥasan ibn ʿAbd Allāh (f. *c.* 261/875). *Bilād al-ʿarab*. Ed. Ḥamad al-Jāsir and Ṣāliḥ Aḥmad al-ʿAlī. Riyadh, 1387/1968

al-Maqrīzī, Abū l-ʿAbbās Aḥmad ibn ʿAlī (d. 845/1442). *Al-Mawāʿiz wa-l-iʿtibār bi-dhikr al-khiṭaṭ wa-l-āthār*. 2 vols. Būlāq, AH 1270

al-Marzūqī, Abū ʿAlī Aḥmad ibn Muḥammad (d. 421/1030). *Kitāb al-azmina wa-l-amkina*. 2 vols. Hyderabad, AH 1332

Menander (wr. 580s). *Fragmenta*. Ed. and trans. R. C. Blockley, *The History of Menander the Guardsman*. Liverpool, 1985

Michael I Qīndāsī (d. 1199). *Chronique de Michel le Syrien*. Ed. and trans. J.-B. Chabot. 4 vols. Paris, 1899–1924

Periplus maris erythraei. Ed. and trans. Lionel Casson. Princeton, 1989

Sebeos (wr. 660s). *Histoire d'Héraclius*. Trans. Frédéric Macler. Paris, 1904

Sophronius (d. *c.* 639). *Life of John the Almsgiver*. Ed. Hippolyte Delehaye, 'Une vie inédite de saint Jean l'Aumonier', *AB* 45 (1927) 19–25

Sozomen (d. before 448). *Historia Ecclesiastica* (Kirchengeschichte). Ed. Joseph Bidez and Günther Christian Hansen. Berlin, 1960

Synodicon Orientale. Ed. and trans. J.-B. Chabot. Paris, 1902

al-Ṭabarī, Abū Jaʿfar Muḥammad ibn Jarīr (d. 310/922). *Tafsīr*. 30 vols. Cairo AH 1330 *Taʾrīkh al-rusul wa-l-mulūk*. Ed. M. J. de Goeje *et al.* 15 vols. Leiden, 1879–1901

Theophanes Confessor (d. 818). *Chronographia*. Ed. Carl de Boor. 2 vols. Leipzig, 1883–5

al-Wāqidī, Abū ʿAbd Allāh Muḥammad ibn ʿUmar ibn Wāqid (d. 207/822). *Kitāb al-maghāzī*. Ed. Marsden Jones. 3 vols. London, 1966

al-Washshāʾ, Abū l-Ṭayyib Muḥammad ibn Aḥmad (d. 325/936). *Kitāb al-fāḍil*. British Library MS. Or. 6499

Wilkinson, John. *Jerusalem Pilgrims before the Crusades*. Warminster, 1977

Yāqūt ibn ʿAbd Allāh al-Ḥamawī, Abū ʿAbd Allāh (d. 626/1229). *Muʿjam al-buldān*. Ed. Ferdinand Wüstenfeld. 6 vols. Leipzig, 1866–73

Zuhayr ibn Abī Sulmā (d. *c.* 609). *Dīwān*, with the commentary of Thaʿlab (d. 291/904). Cairo, 1363/1944

Secondary Sources

ʿAbd al-Ghanī, ʿĀ. (1993) *Taʾrīkh al-Ḥīra fī l-jāhilīya wa-l-Islām*. Damascus

Abel, F.-M. (1938) 'l'Ile de Jotabe', *RB* 47: 510–38

Abū Wandī, Riyāḍ, *et al.* (1996) *ʿĪsā wa-Maryam fī l-Qurʾān wa-l-tafāsīr*. Amman

al-Afghānī, S. (1960) *Aswāq al-ʿarab fī l-jāhilīya wa-l-Islām*. Damascus

Ahlwardt, W. (1872) *Bemerkungen über die Ächtheit der alten arabischen Gedichte*. Greifswald

Ahrens, K. (1930) 'Christliches im Qoran', *ZDMG* 84: 15–68, 148–90

Altheim, F. and Stiehl, R. (1957) *Finanzgeschichte der Spätantike.* Frankfurt am Main

Altheim, F. and Stiehl, R. (1971–3) *Christentum am Roten Meer.* 2 vols. Berlin

Arafat, W. (1958) 'Early critics of the authenticity of the poetry of the *Sīra*', *BSOAS* 21: 453–63

Arafat, W. (1965) 'An aspect of the forger's art in early Islamic poetry', *BSOAS* 28: 477–82

Arafat, W. (1968) 'Fact and fiction in the history of pre-Islamic idol-worship', *IQ* 12: 9–21

Balty, J. (1989) 'Mosaïques antiques de Syrie et de Jordanie', in M. Piccirillo, *Mosaïques byzantines de Jordanie* (Lyons) 149–60

Bashear, S. (1984) *Muqaddima ilā l-ta'rīkh al-ākhar.* Jerusalem

Bashear, S. (1997) *Arabs and Others in Early Islam.* Princeton

Bellamy, J. A. (1985) 'A new reading of the Namārah Inscription', *JAOS* 105: 31–51

Birkeland, H. (1956) *The Lord Guideth: Studies on Primitive Islam.* Oslo

Blachère, R. (1952–66) *Histoire de la littérature arabe des origines à la fin du XVe siècle de J.-C.* 3 vols. Paris

Blachère, R. (1956) 'Regards sur l'"acculturation" des arabo-musulmans jusque vers 40/661', *Arabica* 3: 247–65

Bousquet, G. H. (1954) 'Un explication marxiste de l'Islam par un ecclésiastique épiscopalien', *Hesperis* 41: 231–47

Bowersock, G. W. (1983) *Roman Arabia.* Cambridge, MA

Bowman, J. (1967) 'The debt of Islam to Monophysite Christianity', in E. C. B. MacLaurin (ed.), *Essays in Honour of G. W. Thatcher* (Sydney) 201–40

Brock, S. (1982) 'Christians in the Sasanid empire: a case of divided loyalties', in S. Mews (ed.), *Religion and National Identity* (Studies in Church History 18) (Oxford) 1–19

Brunschvig, R. (1976) 'Coup d'oeil sur l'histoire des foires à travers l'Islam', in his *Études d'islamologie* (Paris) 1.113–44

Butzer, K. W. (1957) 'Der Umweltfaktor in der grossen arabischen Expansion', *Saeculum* 8: 359–71

Caskel, W. (1927–30) 'Die einheimischen Quellen zur Geschichte Nord-Arabiens vor dem Islam', *Islamica* 3: 331–41

Caskel, W. (1930) 'Aijâm al-ʿarab. Studien zur altarabischen Epik', *Islamica* 3: fasc. 5 (Ergänzungsheft), 1–99

Caskel, W. (1953) *Die Bedeutung der Beduinen in der Geschichte der Araber.* Cologne and Opladen

Caskel, W. (1962) 'Der arabische Stamm vor dem Islam und seine gesellschaftliche und juridische Organisation', in *Dalla tribù allo stato* (Rome) 139–49

Caskel, W. (1966) *Ğamharat an-Nasab. Das genealogische Werk des Hišām ibn Muḥammad al-Kalbī.* 2 vols. Leiden

Caton, S. C. (1990) 'Anthropological theories of tribe and state formation in the Middle East: ideology and the semiotics of power', in P. S. Khoury and J. Kostiner (eds.), *Tribes and State Formation in the Middle East* (Berkeley) 74–108

Charles, H. (1936) *Le christianisme des arabes nomades sur le limes et dans le désert syro-mésopotamien aux alentours de l'hégire.* Paris

Chelhod, J. (1971) *Le droit dans la société bedouine.* Paris

Christensen, A. (1944) *L'Iran sous les sassanides*. 2nd edn. Copenhagen

Christides, V. (1972) 'The names *Arabes, Sarakenoi*, etc. and their false Byzantine etymologies', *BZ* 65: 329–33

Conrad, L. I. (1981) 'The *Quṣūr* of medieval Islam: some implications for the social history of the Near East', *Al-Abḥāth* 29: 7–23

Conrad, L. I. (1987a) 'Abraha and Muḥammad: some observations apropos of chronology and literary topoi in the early Arabic historical tradition', *BSOAS* 50: 225–40

Conrad, L. I. (1987b) 'Al-Azdī's History of the Arab Conquests in Bilād al-Shām: some historiographical observations', in M. A. Bakhit (ed.), *Proceedings of the Second Symposium on the History of Bilād al-Shām during the Early Islamic Period up to 40 A.H./640 A.D.: The Fourth International Conference on the History of Bilād al-Shām* (Amman) 1.28–62

Conrad, L. I. (1994) 'Epidemic disease in central Syria in the late sixth century: some new insights form the verse of Ḥassān ibn Thābit', *BMGS* 18: 12–58

Conrad, L. I. (1996a) 'The Arabs and the Colossus', *JRAS*, third series, 6: 165–87

Conrad, L. I. (1996b) 'Die Pest und ihr Umfeld im Nahen Osten des frühen Mittelalters', *Der Islam* 73: 81–112

Conrad, L. I. (1998) 'Futūḥ', in J. Meisami and P. Starkey (eds.), *Companion to Arabic Literature* (London) 237–40

Conrad, L. I. (forthcoming) *Muhammadanea Edessensis: Muḥammad and the Faith of Islam in Christian Discussions in Early ʿAbbāsid Edessa*. Princeton

Conrad, L. I. (forthcoming) 'The early Arab urban foundations in Iraq and Egypt: implications for trade and exchange', in L. I. Conrad and G. R. D. King (eds.), *The Byzantine and Early Islamic Near East, v: Trade and Exchange*. Princeton

Cook, M. (1983) *Muhammad*. Oxford

Crone, P. (1986) 'The tribe and the state', in J. A. Hall (ed.), *States in History* (Oxford) 48–77

Crone, P. (1987) *Meccan Trade and the Rise of Islam*. Oxford

Crone, P. (1992) 'Serjeant and Meccan trade', *Arabica* 39: 216–40

Crone, P. (1993) 'Tribes and states in the Middle East', *JRAS*, third series, 3: 353–76

Crone, P. (1994) 'The first-century concept of *Hiǧra*', *Arabica* 41: 352–87

Crone, P. and Cook, M. (1977) *Hagarism*. Cambridge

Delehaye, H. (1927): see Sophronius, under Sources

Djaït, H. (1986) *Al-Kūfa: naissance de la ville islamique*. Paris

Donner, F. M. (1977) 'Mecca's food supplies and Muḥammad's boycott', *JESHO* 20: 249–66

Donner, F. M. (1981) *The Early Islamic Conquests*. Princeton

Donner, F. M. (1989) 'The role of nomads in the Near East in late antiquity (400–800 C.E.)', in F. M. Clover and R. S. Humphreys (eds.), *Tradition and Innovation in Late Antiquity* (Madison) 73–85

Donner, F. M. (1998) *Narratives of Islamic Origins: The Beginnings of Islamic Historical Writing*. Princeton

Dostal, W. (1979) *Der Markt von Ṣanʿāʾ*. Vienna

Dostal, W. (1984) 'Towards a model of cultural evolution in Arabia', in A. T. Ansary (ed.), *Studies in the History of Arabia, II: Pre-Islamic Arabia* (Riyadh) 185–91

Dunlop, D. M. (1957) 'Sources of gold and silver according to al-Hamdānī', *SI* 8: 29–49

Dussaud, R. (1955) *La pénétration des arabes en Syrie avant l'Islam*. Paris

Eph'al, I. (1984) *The Ancient Arabs: Nomads on the Borders of the Fertile Crescent, 9th–5th Centuries B.C.* Jerusalem

Fahd, T. (ed.) (1989) *L'Arabie préislamique et son environnement historique et culturel*. Leiden

Farès, B. (1932) *L'honneur chez les arabes avant l'Islam*. Paris

Foss, C. (1975) 'The Persians in Asia Minor and the end of antiquity', *EHR* 90: 721–47

Foss, C. (1977) 'Late antique and Byzantine Ankara', *DOP* 31: 29–87

Frye, R. N. (1983) 'Bahrain under the Sasanians', in D. T. Potts (ed.), *Dilmun: New Studies in the Archaeology and History of Bahrain* (Berlin) 167–70

Fück, J. (1950) *'Arabīya. Untersuchungen zur arabischen Sprach- und Stilgeschichte*. Berlin

Fück, J. (1981) *Arabische Kultur und Islam im Mittelalter: Ausgewählte Schriften*. Weimar

Gabrieli, F. (ed.) (1959a) *L'antica società beduina*. Rome

Gabrieli, F. (1959b) 'La letteratura beduina preislamica', in Gabrieli (ed.), *L'antica società beduina* (Rome) 95–114

Gaube, H. (1984) 'Arabs in sixth-century Syria: some archaeological observations', in *Proceedings of the First International Conference on Bilād al-Shām* (Amman) 61–6

Geiger, A. (1833) *Was hat Mohammed aus dem Judenthume aufgenommen?* Bonn

Gellner, E. (1973) 'The concept of kinship', in his *Cause and Meaning in the Social Sciences*, ed. I. C. Jarvie and J. Agassi (London) 163–82

Gibb, H. A. R. (1962) 'Pre-Islamic monotheism in Arabia', *HThR* 55: 269–80

Goitein, S. D. (1968) *Studies in Islamic History and Institutions*. Leiden

Goldziher, I. (1967–71) *Muslim Studies*, ed. and trans. S. M. Stern and C. R. Barber. 2 vols. London

Graf, D. and O'Connor, M. (1977) 'The origin of the term Saracen and the Rawaffa inscription', *BS* 4: 52–66

Griffith, S. H. (1985) 'The Gospel in Arabic: an inquiry into its appearance in the first Abbasid century', *OC* 69: 126–67

Groom, N. (1981) *Frankincense and Myrrh: A Study of the Arabian Incense Trade*. London and New York

von Grunebaum, G. E. (1963) 'The nature of Arab unity before Islam', *Arabica* 10: 5–23

Ḥammūr, 'I.M. (1979) *Aswāq al-'arab: 'arḍ adabī ta'rīkhī li-l-aswāq al-mawsimīya al-'āmma 'inda l-'arab*. Beirut

Hawting, G. R. (1982) 'The origins of the Islamic sanctuary at Mecca', in G. H. A. Juynboll (ed.), *Studies on the First Century of Islamic Society* (Carbondale) 25–47

Henninger, J. (1966) 'Altarabische Genealogie (zu einem neuerschienenen Werk)', *Anthropos* 61: 852–70

Hoyland, R. (1997) *Seeing Islam as Others Saw It: A Survey and Evaluation of Christian, Jewish and Zoroastrian Writings on Early Islam*. Princeton

Ḥusayn, Ṭ. (1927) *Fī l-adab al-jāhilī*. Cairo, 1345/1927

Izutsu, T. (1966) *Ethico-Religious Concepts in the Qur'ān*. Montreal

Jabbur, J. S. (1959) ''Abu-al-Duhur: the Ruwalah Uṭfah', in J. Kritzeck and R. B. Winder (eds.), *The World of Islam: Studies in Honour of Philip K. Hitti* (London) 195–8

Jabbur, J. S. (1995) *The Bedouins and the Desert: Aspects of Nomadic Life in the Arab East*, trans. L. I. Conrad, ed. S. J. Jabbur and L. I. Conrad. Albany

Jacob, G. (1897) *Altarabisches Beduineneleben*. Berlin

Jones, A. H. M. (1955) 'The economic life of the towns of the Roman empire', *Recueils de la Société Jean Bodin* 161–92

Kaegi, W. E. (1992) *Byzantium and the Early Islamic Conquests*. Cambridge

Khoury, P. S. and Kostiner, J. (eds.) (1990) *Tribes and State Formation in the Middle East*. Berkeley

Kister, M. J. (1965) 'The market of the Prophet', *JESHO* 8: 272–6

Kister, M. J. (1968) 'Al-Ḥīra: some notes on its relations with Arabia', *Arabica* 15: 143–69

Kister, M. J. (1979) 'Some reports concerning al-Ṭāʾif', *JSAI* 1: 61–91

Krauss, S. (1916) 'Talmudische Nachrichten über Arabien', *ZDMG* 70: 321–53

Kubiak, W. B. (1987) *Al-Fustat: Its Foundation and Early Urban Development*. Cairo

Lammens, H. (1928) *L'Arabie occidentale avant l'hégire*. Beirut

Lancaster, W. (1997) *The Rwala Bedouin Today*. 2nd edn. Prospect Heights, IL

Lecker, M. (1986) 'On the markets of Medina (Yathrib) in pre-Islamic and early Islamic times', *JSAI* 8: 133–47

Lecker, M. (1993) 'Idol worship in pre-Islamic Medina (Yathrib)', *Le Muséon* 106: 331–46

Lecker, M. (1994) 'Kinda on the eve of Islam and during the *Ridda*', *JRAS*, third series, 4: 333–56

MacAdam, H. I. (1983) 'Epigraphy and village life in southern Syria during the Roman and early Byzantine periods', *Berytus* 31: 103–15

MacAdam, H. I. (1989) 'Strabo, Pliny the Elder and Ptolemy of Alexandria: three views of ancient Arabia and its peoples', in T. Fahd (ed.), *L'Arabie préislamique et son environnement historique et culturel* (Leiden) 289–320

Macdonald, M. C. A. (1993) 'Nomads and the Ḥawrān in the late Hellenistic and Roman periods: a reassessment of the epigraphic evidence', *Syria* 70: 303–413

Macdonald, M. C. A. (1995a) 'North Arabia in the first millennium BCE', in J. M. Sasson (ed.), *Civilizations of the Ancient Near East* (New York) II.1355–69

Macdonald, M. C. A. (1995b) 'Quelques réflexions sur les saracènes, l'inscription de Rawwāfa et l'armée romaine', in H. Lozachmead (ed.), *Présence arabe dans le croissant fertile avant l'hégire* (Paris) 93–101

Mayerson, P. (1963) 'The desert of southern Palestine according to Byzantine sources', *Proceedings of the American Philosophical Society* 107: 160–72

Meeker, M. E. (1979) *Literature and Violence in North Arabia*. Cambridge

Michaud, H. (1960) *Jésus selon le Coran*. Neuchâtel

Millar, F. (1993a) 'Hagar, Ishmael, Josephus and the origins of Islam', *JJS* 44: 23–45

Millar, F. (1993b) *The Roman Near East, 31 BC–AD 337*. Cambridge, MA

Morony, M. G. (1984) *Iraq after the Muslim Conquest*. Princeton

Müller, W. W. (1978) *Weihrauch. Ein arabisches Produkt und seine Bedeutung in der Antike*, in Pauly–Wissowa, *RE*, Supp. xv. Munich

Musil, A. (1928) *The Manners and Customs of the Rwala Bedouins*. New York

Nagel, T. (1967) *Die Qiṣaṣ al-anbiyāʾ. Ein Beitrag zur arabischen Literaturgeschichte*. Bonn

Nau, F. (1933) *Les arabes chrétiens de Mésopotamie et de Syrie du VIIe au VIIIe siècle*. Paris

Nelson, C. (ed.) (1970) *The Desert and the Sown: Nomads in the Wider Society*. Berkeley

Newby, G. D. (1988) *A History of the Jews of Arabia*. Columbia, SC

Nicholson, R. A. (1907) *A Literary History of the Arabs*. London

Nöldeke, T. (1879) *Geschichte der Perser und Araber zur Zeit der Sasaniden*. Leiden

Nöldeke, T. (1887) *Die ghassânischen Fürsten aus dem Hause Gafna's*. Berlin

O'Connor, M. P. (1986) 'The etymology of Saracen in Aramaic and pre-Islamic Arabic contexts', in P. Freeman and D. Kennedy (eds.), *The Defence of the Roman and Byzantine East* (Oxford) 11.603–32

Olinder, G. (1927) *The Kings of Kinda of the Family of Ākil al-Murār*. Lund and Leipzig

Papathomopoulos, M. (1984) 'Greek sources for the history of the Arabs in the pre-Islamic period', *Graeco–Arabica* 3: 203–6

Parrinder, G. (1965) *Jesus in the Qur'ān*. London

Pellat, C. (1953) *Le milieu basrien et la formation de Ğāḥiz*. Paris

Pellat, C. (1962–3) 'Concept of *Ḥilm* in Islamic ethics', *Bulletin of the Institute of Islamic Studies* 6–7: 1–12

Pellat, C. (1973) *Risālā fī l-ḥilm*. Beirut

Peters, F. E. (1984) 'The Arabs on the frontier of Syria before Islam', in *Proceedings of the First International Conference on Bilād al-Shām* (Amman) 141–73

Peters, F. E. (1988) 'The commerce of Mecca before Islam', in F. Kazemi and R. D. McChesney (eds.), *A Way Prepared: Essays in Honor of Richard Bayly Winder* (New York) 3–26

Rippin, A. (1990–3) *Muslims: Their Beliefs and Practices*. 2 vols. London

Rippin, A. (1991) 'RHMNN and the *Ḥanīf*s', in W. Hallaq and D. P. Little (eds.), *Islamic Studies Presented to Charles J. Adams* (Leiden) 153–68

Robin, C. (1991) *L'Arabie antique de Karb'îl à Mahomet: nouvelles données sur l'histoire des arabes grâce aux inscriptions*. Aix-en-Provence

Robinson, N. (1991) *Christ in Islam and Christianity: The Representation of Jesus in the Qur'ān and the Classical Muslim Commentaries*. London

Rosenthal, E. I. J. (1961) *Judaism and Islam*. London and New York

Rothstein, G. (1899) *Die Dynastie der Laḥmiden in al-Ḥīra*. Berlin

Rotter, G. (1993) 'Der *veneris dies* im vorislamischen Mekka, eine neue Deutung des namens "Europa" und eine Erklärung für *kobar*= Venus', *Der Islam* 70: 112–32

Rubin, U. (1981) '*Al-Ṣamad* and the High God', *Der Islam* 61: 197–214

Rubin, U. (1986) 'The Ka'ba: aspects of its ritual functions and position in pre-Islamic and early Islamic times', *JSAI* 8: 97–131

Rubin, U. (1990) '*Ḥanīfiyya* and Ka'ba: an inquiry into the Arabian pre-Islamic background of *Dīn Ibrāhīm*', *JSAI* 13: 85–112

Rubin, U. (1995) *The Eye of the Beholder: The Life of Muḥammad as Viewed by the Early Muslims – a Textual Analysis*. Princeton

Sartre, M. (1982) 'Tribus et clans dans le Hawran antique', *Syria* 59: 77–92

Schafer, P. (1997) *Judeophobia: Attitudes towards the Jews in the Ancient World*. Cambridge, MA

Schick, R. (1995) *The Christian Communities of Palestine from Byzantine to Islamic Rule: A Historical and Archaeological Study*. Princeton

Schneider, D. M. (1984) *A Critique of the Study of Kinship*. Ann Arbor

Segal, J. B. (1984) 'Arabs in Syriac literature before the rise of Islam', *JSAI* 4: 89–123

Serjeant, R. B. (1962) '*Ḥaram* and *Ḥawṭah*: the sacred enclave in Arabia', in A. Badawi (ed.), *Mélanges Taha Husain* (Cairo) 41–58

Serjeant, R. B. (1990) 'Meccan trade and the rise of Islam: misconceptions and flawed polemics', *JAOS* 110: 472–86

Seyrig, P. (1941) 'Postes romains sur la route de Médine', *Syria* 22: 218–23

Shahīd, I. (1958) 'The last days of Ṣāliḥ', *Arabica* 5: 145–58

Shahīd, I. (1971) *The Martyrs of Najrân: New Documents.* Brussels

Shahīd, I. (1984) *Rome and the Arabs: A Prolegomenon to the Study of Byzantium and the Arabs.* Washington, DC

Shahīd, I. (1989) *Byzantium and the Arabs in the Fifth Century.* Washington, DC

Shahīd, I. (1995) *Byzantium and the Arabs in the Sixth Century.* 2 vols. Washington, DC

Shaw, B. D. (1982–3) '"Eaters of flesh, drinkers of milk": the ancient Mediterranean ideology of the pastoral nomad', *Ancient Society* 13–14: 5–31

Simon, R. (1967) 'L'inscription Ry 506 et la préhistoire de la Mecque', *AO* 20: 325–37

Simon, R. (1975) *A mekkai kereskedelem kialakulása és jellege.* Budapest

Simon, R. (1989) *Meccan Trade and Islam: Problems of Origin and Structure*, trans. F. Sós. Budapest

Smith, S. (1954) 'Events in Arabia in the sixth entury A.D.', *BSOAS* 16: 425–68

Stewart, F. (1994) *Honor.* Chicago

Sweet, L. E. (1965) 'Camel raiding of north Arabian bedouin: a mechanism of ecological adaptation', *American Anthropologist* 67: 1132–50

Tapper, R. (1990) 'Anthropologists, historians, and tribespeople on tribe and state formation in the Middle East', in P. S. Khoury and J. Kostiner (eds.), *Tribes and State Formation in the Middle East* (Berkeley) 48–73

Teixidor, J. (1977) *The Pagan God: Popular Religion in the Greco-Roman Near East.* Princeton

Trimingham, J. S. (1979) *Christianity among the Arabs in Pre-Islamic Times.* London and New York

Villiers, A. (1940) *Sons of Sindbad.* London

Watt, W. M. (1953) *Muhammad at Mecca.* Oxford

Watt, W. M. (1979) 'The Qur'ān and belief in a "High God"', *Der Islam* 56: 205–11

Welch, A. T. (1979) 'Allāh and other supernatural beings: the emergence of the Qur'ānic doctrine of *Tawḥīd*', *JAAR* 47: 733–58

Wellhausen, J. (1897) *Reste arabischen Heidentums.* 2nd edn. Berlin

Whitby, M. (1992) 'Greek historical writing after Procopius: variety and vitality', in Averil Cameron and L. I. Conrad (eds.), *The Late Antique and Early Islamic Near East*, 1: *Problems in the Literary Source Material* (Princeton) 25–80

Whitehouse, D. and Williamson, A. (1973) 'Sasanian maritime trade', *Iran* 11: 29–48

Whittow, M. (1999) 'Rome and the Jafnids: writing the history of a 6th-c. tribal dynasty', in J. Humphrey (ed.), *The Roman and Byzantine Near East 2. Some Recent Archaeological Research*, *JRA* supp. series 31 (Portsmouth, RI) 207–24

Adshead, K. (1990) 'Procopius' *poliorcetica*: continuities and discontinuities', in G. Clarke (ed.), *Reading the Past in Late Antiquity* (Rushcutters Bay, NSW) 93–119

Alcock, S. E. (1989) 'Roman imperialism in the Greek landscape, 200 B.C.–200 A.D.', *JRA* 2: 5–34

Avraméa, A. and Feissel, D. (1987) 'Inventaires en vue d'un recueil des inscriptions historiques de Byzance. III. Inscriptions de Thessalie (à l'exception des Météores)', *T&MByz* 11: 357–98

Baratte, F. (1984) 'Les témoignages archéologiques de la présence Slave au sud du Danube', in *Villes et peuplement* (1984) 11–61

Bavant, B. (1984) 'La ville dans le nord de l'Illyricum (Pannonie, Mésie I, Dacie et Dardanie)', in *Villes et peuplement* (1984) 245–88

Beševliev, V. (1970) *Zur Deutung der Kastellnamen in Prokops Werk 'De Aedificiis'.* Amsterdam

Bintliff, J. M. and Snodgrass, A. M. (1985) 'The Cambridge/Bradford Boeotian expedition: the first four years', *JFA* 12: 123–61

Blockley, R. C. (1981, 1983) *The Fragmentary Classicising Historians of the Later Roman Empire* I–II (ARCA 10, 6). Liverpool

Blockley, R. C. (1992) *East Roman Foreign Policy, Formation and Conduct from Diocletian to Anastasius* (ARCA 30). Leeds

Browning, R. (1975) *Byzantium and Bulgaria.* London

Burns, T. S. (1980) *The Ostrogoths: Kingship and Society* (Historia Einzelschriften 26). Wiesbaden

Burns, T. S. (1984) *A History of the Ostrogoths.* Bloomington, IN

Cameron, Alan and Long, J. (1993) *Barbarians and Politics at the Court of Arcadius.* Berkeley and Los Angeles

Cameron, Averil (1970) *Agathias.* Oxford

Charanis, P. (1950) 'The Chronicle of Monemvasia and the question of the Slavonic settlements in Greece', *DOP* 5: 139–66

Clover, F. (1973) 'Geiseric and Attila', *Hist.* 23: 104–17

Cormack, R. (1985) *Writing in Gold: Byzantine Society and its Icons.* London

Croke, B. (1978) 'Hormisdas and the late Roman walls of Thessalonika', *GRBS* 19: 251–8

Croke, B. (1980) 'Justinian's Bulgar victory celebration', *Byzslavica* 41: 188–95

Croke, B. (1981) 'Thessalonika's early Byzantine palaces', *Byz.* 51: 475–83

Croke, B. (1982) 'Mundo the Gepid: from freebooter to Roman general', *Chiron* 12: 125–35

Croke, B. (1983) 'The context and date of Priscus fragment 6', *CP* 78: 297–308

Dagron, G. (1984) 'Les villes dans l'Illyricum protobyzantin', in *Villes et peuplement* (1984) 1–20

Dunn, A. (1994) 'The transition from *polis* to *kastron* in the Balkans (III–VIIcc.): general and regional perspectives', *BMGS* 18: 60–80

Duval, N. and Popovič, V. (1984) *Caričin Grad* I (Coll. de l'École Française de Rome 75). Rome

Eadie, J. W. (1982) 'City and countryside in late Roman Pannonia: the *regio Sirmiensis*', in Hohlfelder (ed.) (1982) 25–42

Farkas, C. (1993–4) 'Räuberhorden in Thrakien. Eine unbeachtete Quelle zur Geschichte der Zeit des Kaisers Maurikios', *BZ* 86–7: 462–9

Feissel, D. and Philippidis-Braat, A. (1985) 'Inventaires en vue d'un recueil des inscriptions historiques de Byzance. IV. Inscriptions du Péloponnèse (à l'exception de Mistra)', *T&MByz* 10: 267–395

Ferjančič, B. (1984) 'Invasions et installations des Slaves dans les Balkans', in *Villes et peuplement* (1984) 85–109

Fowden, G. (1988) 'City and mountain in late Roman Attica', *JHS* 108: 48–59

Fowden, G. (1990) 'The Athenian agora and the progress of Christianity', JRA 3: 494–501

Frantz, A. (1988) *The Athenian Agora XXIV. Late Antiquity: A.D. 267–700.* Princeton *Germanen, Hunen und Awaren, Schätze der Völkerwanderungszeit* (1987) (Germanisches Nationalmuseum). Nuremberg

Gimbutas, M. (1971) *The Slavs.* London

Gregory, T. E. (1982) 'Fortification and urban design in early Byzantine Greece', in Hohlfelder (ed.) (1982) 43–64

Gregory, T. E. (1992) 'Kastro and diateichisma as responses to early Byzantine frontier collapse', *Byz.* 62: 235–53

Gregory, T. E. (1993) 'An early Byzantine (Dark Age) settlement at Isthmia', in Gregory (ed.), *The Corinthia in the Roman Period (JRA* suppl. ser. 8) 149–59

Haussig, H. W. (1953) 'Theophylakts Exkurs über die skythischen Völker', *Byz.* 23: 275–462

Heather, P. (1989) 'Cassiodorus and the rise of the Amals: genealogy and the Goths under Hun domination', *JRS* 79: 103–28

Heather, P. (1995) 'The Huns and the end of the Roman empire in western Europe', *EHR* 110: 4–41

Heather, P. and Matthews, J. (1991) *The Goths in the Fourth Century.* Liverpool

Hoddinott, R. F. (1963) *Early Byzantine Churches in Macedonia and Southern Serbia.* London

Hoddinott, R. F. (1975) *Bulgaria in Antiquity.* London

Hohlfelder, R. L. (ed.) (1982) *City, Town and Countryside in the Early Byzantine Era.* New York

Howard-Johnston, J. D. (1983) 'Urban continuity in the Balkans in the Early Middle Ages', in Poulter (ed.) (1983a) 242–54

Kollautz, A. and Miyakawa, H. (1970) *Geschichte und Kultur eines völkerwanderungszeitlichen Nomadenvolkes. Die Jou-Jan der Mongolei und die Awaren in Mitteleuropa.* Klagenfurt

Kovrig, I. (1955) 'Contribution au problème de l'occupation de la Hongroie per les Avares', *Acta Archaeologica* 6: 163–91

László, G. (1955) 'Études archéologiques sur l'histoire de la société des Avares', *Archaeologica Hungarica* 34

Lemerle, P. (1954) 'Invasions et migrations dans les Balkans depuis la fin de l'époque romaine jusqu'au VIIe siècle', *RH* 211: 264–308

Lemerle, P. (ed.) (1981) *Les plus anciens recueils des Miracles de Saint Démétrius et la pénétration des Slaves dans les Balkans 2. Le commentaire.* Paris

Lemerle, P. (1984) 'Conclusion', in *Villes et peuplement* (1984) 501–21

Lengyel, A. and Radan, G. T. B. (1980) *The Archaeology of Roman Pannonia.* Budapest

Maenchen-Helfen, J. O. (1973) *The World of the Huns.* Berkeley and Los Angeles

Metcalf, D. M. (1984) 'The mint of Thessalonica in the early Byzantine period', in *Villes et peuplement* (1984) 111–29

Mócsy, A. (1974) *Pannonia and Upper Moesia.* London

Musset, L. (1975) *The Germanic Invasions: The Making of Europe AD 400–600.* London

Obolensky, D. (1971) *The Byzantine Commonwealth.* London

Pohl. W. (1980) 'Die Gepiden und die *gentes* an der mittleren Donau nach dem Zerfall des Attilareiche', in Wolfram and Dain (eds.) (1980) 239–305

Popovič, Vl. (1975) 'Les témoins archéologiques des invasions avaro-slaves dans l'Illyricum byzantin', *MEFR* 87: 445–504

Popovič, Vl. (1978) 'La descente des Koutrigours, des Slaves et des Avars vers la mer Égée: le témoignage de l'archéologie', *CRAI* 596–648

Popovič, Vl. (ed.) (1981) 'Note sur l'habitat paléoslave', in Lemerle (ed.) (1981) 235–41

Popovič, Vl. (1984) 'Byzantins, Slaves et autochthones dans les provinces de Prévalitane et Nouvelle Épire', in *Villes et peuplement* (1984) 181–243

Poulter, A. G. (ed.) (1983a) *Ancient Bulgaria.* Nottingham

Poulter, A. G. (1983b) 'Town and country in Moesia Inferior', in Poulter (ed.) (1983a) 74–118

Runnels, C. N. and van Audel, T. H. (1987) 'The evolution of settlement in the Southern Argolid, Greece: an economic explanation', *Hesperia* 56: 303–34

Sorlin, I. (1981) 'Slaves et Sklavènes avant et dans les miracles de Saint Démétrius', in Lemerle (ed.) (1981) 219–34

Spieser, J. M. (1973) 'Inventaires en vue d'un recueil des inscriptions historiques de Byzance. 1. Les inscriptions de Thessalonique', *T&MByz* 5: 145–80

Spieser, J. M. (1984a) *Thessalonique et ses monuments du IVe au VIe siècle. Contribution à l'étude d'une ville paléochrétienne.* Paris

Spieser, J. M. (1984b) 'La ville en Grèce du IIIe au VIIe siècle', in *Villes et peuplement* (1984) 315–40

Teodor, D. G. (1984) 'Origines et voies de pénétration des Slaves au sud du Bas-Danube (VIe–VIIe siècles)', in *Villes et peuplement* (1984) 63–84

Thompson, E. A. (1948) *The History of Attila and the Huns.* Oxford

Toynbee, A. (1973) *Constantine Porphyrogenitus and his World.* Oxford

Trombley, F. R. (1989) 'Boeotia in late antiquity: epigraphic evidence on society, economy and Christianization', in Harmut Beister and John Buckler (eds.), *Boiotika. Vorträge vom 5. Int. Böotien-Kolloquium zu Ehren von Siegfried Leuffer, Inst f. alte Geschichte, Ludwig-Maximilians-Universität München, 13–17 Juni, 1986* (Munich) 215–28

Velkov, V. (1977) *Cities in Thrace and Dacia in Late Antiquity.* Amsterdam

Villes et peuplement dans l'Illyricum protobyzantin (1984) (Collection de l'École Française de Rome LXXVII). Rome

Whitby, M. (1985) 'The long walls of Constantinople', *Byz.* 55: 560–83

Wilkes, J. J. (1969) *Dalmatia.* London

Wolfram, H. (1985) *Treasures on the Danube: Barbarian Invaders and the Roman Inheritance.* Vienna

Wolfram, H. (1988) *History of the Goths* (trans. Thomas J. Dunlap). Berkeley and Los Angeles

Wolfram, H. and Dain, F. (eds.) (1980) *Die Völker an der mittleren und unteren Donau im fünften und sechsten Jahrhundert* (Öst. Akad. der Wiss., phil.-hist. Kl., Denkschr. 145) Vienna

Wozniak, F. E. (1982) 'The Justinianic fortification of interior Illyricum', in Hohlfelder (ed.) (1982) 199–209

Zásterová, B. (1971) *Les Avares et les Slaves dans la Tactique de Maurice*. (Rozpravy Ceskoslovenské akadamie ved, r. spol. lxxxi/3)

Zuckerman, C. (1994) 'L'empire d'Orient et les Huns: notes sur Priscus', *T&MByz* 12: 159–82

PART V: RELIGION AND CULTURE (CHS. 24–31)

Aherne, C. M. (1949) *Valerio of Bierzo*. Washington, DC

Akerström-Hougen, G. (1974) *The Calendar and Hunting Mosaics of the Villa of the Falconer in Argos*. Stockholm

Allen, P. (1993) 'Monophysiten', *TRE* 23: 219–33

Anderson, J. G. C. and Cumont, F. (1910) *Studia Pontica*. Brussels

Argoud, G., Callot, O. and Helly, B. (1980) *Une résidence byzantine, l'Huileries* (Salamine de Chypre XI). Paris

Armstrong, A. H. (ed.) (1967) *Cambridge History of Later Greek and Early Medieval Philosophy*. Cambridge

Asgari, N. (1995) 'The Proconnesian production of architectural elements in late antiquity, based on evidence from the marble quarries', in Mango and Dagron (eds.) (1995) 263–88

Athanassiadi, P. (1993) 'Persecution and response in late paganism: the evidence of Damascius', *JHS* 113: 1–29

Athanassiadi, P. (1999) '*Damascius. The Philosophical History*. Athens

Bakhtin, M. M. (1981) *The Dialogic Imagination*. Austin, TX

Balty, J. (ed.) (1984) *Aspects de l'architecture domestique d'Apamée* (Apamée de Syrie. Bilan des recherches archéologiques 1973–1979). Brussels

Barasch, M. (1992) *Icon: Studies in the History of an Idea*. New York

Barber, C. (1990) 'The imperial panels at San Vitale: a reconsideration', *BMGS* 14: 19–42

Barber, C. (1991) 'The Koimesis Church, Nicaea: the limits of representation on the eve of Iconoclasm', *JÖB* 41: 43–60

Bardill, J. (1997) 'The palace of Lausus and nearby monuments in Constantinople: a topographical study', *AJA* 101: 67–95

Baus, K., Beck, H.-G., Ewig, E., Vogt, H. J. (1980) *The Imperial Church from Constantine to the Early Middle Ages* (= Jedin, H. (ed.) (1980) *History of the Church* II, London) (tr. from *Handbuch der Kirchengeschichte* (1973/75) ii/1–2, Freiburg-im-Br.)

Bavant, B., Kondic, V. and Spieser, J.-M. (eds.) (1990) *Caričin Grad* II. Belgrade and Rome

Baynes, N. H. (1960) 'The thought-world of east Rome', in Baynes, *Byzantine Studies and Other Essays*. London

Beck, H. G. (1950) *The Pastoral Care of Souls in South-East France during the Sixth Century* (Analecta Gregoriana 51). Rome

Bell, D. N. (tr.) (1983) *The Life of Shenoute by Besa* (Cistercian Studies 73). Kalamazoo

Bell, G. (1982) *The Churches and Monasteries of the Tur 'Abdin* (ed. and annotated M. Mundell Mango). London

di Berardino, A. (ed.) (1992) *Encyclopedia of the Early Church* (tr. from the Italian by Adrian Walford). 2 vols. Cambridge (= *Dizionario Patristico e di Antichità Cristiana*, Casale Monferrato 1983/88)

Bianchi Bandinelli, R. (1955) *Hellenistic-Byzantine Miniatures of the Iliad (Ilias Ambrosiana)*. Olten

Bieler, L. (1986) *Studies on the Life and Legend of St Patrick* (edited by Richard Sharpe). London

Binns, J. (1994) *Ascetics and Ambassadors of Christ: The Monasteries of Palestine, 314–631*. Oxford

Blumenthal, H. J. (1976) 'Neoplatonic elements in the *De anima* commentaries', *Phronesis* 21: 64–87 (= Sorabji (ed.) (1990) 305–24)

Blumenthal, H. J. (1977–8) 'Neoplatonic interpretations of Aristotle on *phantasia*', *Review of Metaphysics* 31: 242–57

Blumenthal, H. J. (1981) 'Some Platonist readings of Aristotle', *PCPS* n.s. 27: 1–16

Blumenthal, H. J. (1984) 'Marinus' Life of Proclus: Neoplatonist biography', *Byz.* 54: 469–94

Blumenthal, H. J. (1986) 'John Philoponus: Alexandrian Platonist?', *Hermes* 114: 314–35

Blumenthal, H. J. (1993) 'Alexandria as a centre of philosophy in later classical antiquity', *ICS* 18: 307–25

Boesch-Gajano, S. (1991) 'Uso e abuso del miracolo nella cultura altomedioevale', in *Les Fonctions des saints dans le monde occidental (IIIe–XIIIe siècle)* (Collection de l'École Française de Rome 149) (Rome) 109–22

Bossier, F. and Steel, C. (1972) 'Priscianus Lydus en de "de anima" van Pseudo(?)-Simplicius', *Tijdschrift voor filosofie* 34: 761–822

Bowersock, G. W., Brown, P. and Grabar, O. (eds.) (1999) *Late Antiquity: A Guide to the Postclassical World*. Cambridge, MA

Boyd, S. A. (1992) 'A "metropolitan" treasure from a church in the provinces: an introduction to the study of the Sion Treasure', in Boyd and Mango (eds.) (1992) 5–38

Boyd, S. A. and Mango, M. M. (eds.) (1992) *Ecclesiastical Silver Plate in Sixth-Century Byzantium*. Washington, DC

Brenk, B. (1975) *Die frühchristlichen Mosaiken in S. Maria Maggiore zu Rom*. Wiesbaden

Brenk, B. (1977) *Spätantike und frühes Christentum*. Frankfurt

Brennan, B. (1985) 'The career of Venantius Fortunatus', *Traditio* 41: 49–68

Brett, G., Macaulay, W. J. and Stevenson, R. B. K. (1947) *The Great Palace of the Byzantine Emperors*. Oxford

Bridel, P. (1986) *Le site monastique copte des Kellia. Sources historiques et explorations archéologiques*. Geneva

Brock, S. (1973) 'Early Syrian asceticism', *Numen* 20: 1–19 (= Brock (1984) *Syriac Perspectives on Late Antiquity* (London) 1)

Brock, S. (1981) 'The conversations with the Syrian Orthodox under Justinian (532)', *OCP* 47: 87–121

Brock, S. (1985) 'A monothelete florilegium in Syriac', in C. Laga, J. A. Munitiz, L. van Rompay (eds.), *After Chalcedon: Studies in Theology and Church History Offered to Prof. A. Van Roey for his 70th birthday* (Louvain) 35–45

Brock, S. and Harvey, S. A. (1987) *Holy Women of the Syrian Orient*. Berkeley and Los Angeles

Brodsky, N. A. (1966) *L'iconographie oubliée de l'Arc Éphésien de Sainte Marie Majeur à Rome*. Brussels

Brown, P. R. L. (1976) 'Town, village and Holy Man: the case of Syria', in D. M. Pippidi (ed.), *Assimilation et résistance à la culture gréco-romaine dans le monde ancien*. Bucharest 213–20 (= Brown, *Society and the Holy* 153–65)

Brown, P. R. L. (1981) *The Cult of the Saints: Its Rise and Function in Latin Christianity* (Haskell Lectures on History of Religions, n.s. 2). Chicago

Brown, P. R. L. (1983) 'The saint as exemplar', *Representations* 1: 1–25

Brown, P. R. L. (1998) 'The rise and function of the holy man in late antiquity, 1971–1997', *Journal of Early Christian Studies* 6: 353–76

Brundage, J. A. (1987) *Law, Sex, and Christian Society in Medieval Europe*. Chicago and London

Buckton, D. (ed.) (1994) *Byzantium: Treasures of Byzantine Art and Culture from British Collections*. London

Bundy, D. D. (1979) 'Jacob Baradaeus. The state of research, a review of sources and a new approach', *Le Muséon* 91: 45–86

Butler, E. C. (1924) *Benedictine Monachism*. London (repr. Cambridge and New York, 1961)

Butler, H. C. (1919, 1920) *Publications of the Princeton University Archaeological Expedition to Syria in 1904–1905 and 1909*. II *Architecture*. A. *Southern Syria* (1919) B. *Northern Syria* (1920). Leiden

Cameron, Alan (1965) 'Wandering poets: a literary movement in Byzantine Egypt', *Historia* 14: 470–509 (= Cameron, *Literature and Society* I)

Cameron, Alan (1969) 'The last days of the Academy at Athens', *PCPS* n.s. 15: 7–29 (= Cameron, *Literature and Society* XIII)

Cameron, Alan (1973) *Porphyrius the Charioteer*. Oxford

Cameron, Alan (1982) 'The empress and the poet: paganism and politics at the court of Theodosius II', in J. Winkler and G. Williams (eds.), *Later Greek Literature* (Yale Classical Studies 27) 217–89 (= Cameron, *Literature and Society* III)

Cameron, Averil (1987) 'The construction of court ritual: the Byzantine *Book of Ceremonies*', in D. Cannadine and S. Price (eds.), *Rituals of Royalty* (Cambridge) 106–36

Cameron, Averil (1988) 'Eustratius' *Life* of the patriarch Eutychius and the Fifth Ecumenical Council', in J. Chrysostomides (ed.), *Kathegetria. Essays Presented to Joan Hussey on her 80th Birthday* (Camberley) 225–47

Cameron, Averil (1990) 'Models of the past in the late sixth century: the Life of the patriarch Eutychius', in Clarke, Graeme *et al.* (eds.), *Reading the Past in Late Antiquity* (Rushcutters Bay) 205–33

Cameron, Averil (1992) 'The language of images: the rise of icons and Christian representation', in D. Wood (ed.), *The Church and the Arts* (Oxford) 1–42 (Studies in Church History 28) (= Cameron, *Cultural Changes* XII)

Canivet, P. (1977) *Le monachisme syrien selon Théodoret de Cyr* (Théologie historique 42). Paris

Cavallo, G. (ed.) (1975) *Libri, editori e pubblico nel mondo antico*. Rome and Bari

Cecchelli, C. (1936–44) *La cattedra di Massimiano*. Rome

Cecchelli, C. (1967) *I mosaici della basilica di S. Maria Maggiore*. Rome

Chabot, J. B. (ed. and tr.) (1908, 1933) *Documenta ad origines monophysitarum illustran-das (CSCO*, Scr. Syr. 2.37). Paris, Louvain

Chadwick, H. (1974) 'John Moschus and his friend Sophronius the Sophist', *JThS* 25: 41–74

Chadwick, H. E. (1976) *Priscillian of Avila*. Oxford

Chadwick, N. (1955) *Poetry and Letters in Early Christian Gaul*. London

Chadwick, O. (1950) *John Cassian*. 2nd edn, 1986. Cambridge

Charpentier, G. (1994) 'Les bains de Sergilla', *Syria* 71: 113–42

Chesnut, G. F. (1986) *The First Christian Histories: Eusebius, Socrates, Sozomen, Theodoret, and Evagrius* (2nd edn, revised and enlarged). Macon, GA

Chitty, D. (1966) *The Desert a City: An Introduction to the Study of Egyptian and Palestinian Monasticism under the Christian Empire*. Oxford

Chitty, D. (1971) 'Abba Isaiah', *JThS* n.s. 22: 47–72

Clark, E. A. (1984) *The Life of Melania the Younger*. New York and Toronto

Clark, E. A. (1992) *The Origenist Controversy: The Cultural Construction of an Early Christian Debate*. Princeton

Clark, G. (1993) *Women in Late Antiquity: Pagan and Christian Lifestyles*. Oxford

Clarke, H. B. and Brennan, M. (eds.) (1981) *Columbanus and Merovingian Monasticism* (BAR International Series, 113). Oxford

Clover, F. M. and Humphreys, R. S. (eds.) (1989) *Tradition and Innovation in Late Antiquity*. Madison and London

Collins, R. C. (1981) 'Caesarius von Arles', *TRE* 7: 531–6

Conkey, M. and Hastorf, C. (1990) *The Uses of Style in Archaeology*. Cambridge

Convegno Todi (1977) *Gregorio di Tours. Convegno del Centro di Studi sulla spiritualità medievale, 10–13 ottobre 1971 (Convegni 12)*. Todi

Cormack, R. (1985) *Writing in Gold: Byzantine Society and its Icons*. London

Cormack, R. (1989) *The Byzantine Eye: Studies in Art and Patronage*. London Variorum

Cormack, R. (1990) 'Byzantine Aphrodisias. Changing the symbolic map of a city', *PCPS* 216 (n.s. 36): 26–41

Courcelle, P. (1948) *Les lettres grecques en occident de Macrobe à Cassiodore*. Paris

Cracco, G. (1992) 'Il tempo fuori del monastero: tentazione o missione?', *Codex Aquilarensis* 6: 119–34

Cramer, A. (1835–7) *Anecdota graeca e codd. manuscriptis bibliothecarum Oxoniensium*. Oxford

Cramer, A. (1839–41) *Anecdota Parisiensia e codd. manuscriptis bibliothecae regiae Parisiensis*. Oxford

Cruikshank Dodd, E. (1961) *Byzantine Silver Stamps*. Washington, DC

Cruikshank Dodd, E. (1973) *Byzantine Silver Treasures*. Bern

Crum, W. E. and Evelyn-White, H. G. (1926) *The Monastery of Epiphanius of Thebes. Part 2*. New York

Cutler, A. (1985) *The Craft of Ivory: Sources, Techniques and Uses in the Mediterranean World A.D. 200–1400*. Washington, DC

Dagron, G. (1970) 'Les moines et la ville. Le monachisme à Constantinople jusqu'au Concile de Chalcédoine (451)', *T&MByz* 4: 229–76 (= Dagron (1984) *La romanité chrétienne en Orient. Héritages et mutations* (London) VII)

Dagron, G. (1978) *Vie et miracles de Sainte Thècle*. Brussels

Dagron, G. (1981) 'Le saint, le savant, l'astrologue', in *Hagiographie, cultures et sociétés, IVe–XIIe siècles* (Paris) 143–56

Dagron, G. (1984) *Constantinople imaginaire*. Paris

Dagron, G. (1992) 'L'ombre d'un doute: l'hagiographie en question, VIe–XIe siècle', *DOP* 46: 59–68

Davis, R. (tr.) (1989) *The Book of Pontiffs (Liber Pontificalis)* (Translated Texts for Historians, Latin Series 5). Liverpool

Davis-Weyer, C. (1971) *Early Medieval Art, 300–1150*. Englewood Cliffs, NJ

Dawes, E. and Baynes, N. H. (trans.) (1977) *Three Byzantine Saints*. London and Oxford

De Vogüé, A. (1966) 'La Règle du Maître et les Dialogues de S. Grégoire', *RHE* 61: 44–76

De Vogüé, A. (1966a) *Grégoire le Grand. Dialogues (SChrét.* 251, 260, 265). Paris

De Vogüé, A. (1976) 'Benoît, modèle de vie spirituelle d'après le deuxième livre des Dialogues de Saint Grégoire', *Collectanea Cisterciensia* 38: 147–57

De Vogüé, A. (1977) *La Règle de saint Benoît*, VII: *Commentaire doctrinal et spirituel*. Paris

De Vogüé, A. (1982) *Les Règles des saints pères*. Introduction, texte critique, traduction et notes par Adalbert de Vogüé. *SChrét.* 297–8. Paris

De Vogüé, A. (1989) *Saint Columban. Règles et pénitentiels monastiques*. Abbaye de Bellefontaine, Bégrolles-en-Mauges

De Vogüé, M. (1865–77) *Syrie centrale, architecture civile et religieuse, du Ie au VIIe siècle*. Paris

Deckers, J. G. and Sergadoğlu, Ü. (1995) 'Das Hypogäum beim Silivri-Kapi in Istanbul', in *Akten des XII. Internationalen Kongresses für Christliche Archäologie, Bonn, 22.–28. September 1991* ed. J. Engemann, II. Vatican City and Münster (1995) 674–81, pls. 85–6

Degering, H. and Boekler, A. (1932) *Die Quedlingburger Italafragment*. Berlin

Deichmann, F. W. (1958) *Frühchristliche Bauten und Mosaiken von Ravenna*. Baden-Baden

Deichmann, F. W. (1969, 1974, 1976, 1989) *Ravenna. Hauptstadt des spätantiken Abendlandes*, vol. 1. *Geschichte und Monumente*. Wiesbaden; *Kommentar*, vol. 2 part 1. Wiesbaden; *Kommentar*, vol. 2 part 2. Wiesbaden; *Kommentar*, vol. 2 part 3. Stuttgart

Dekkers, E. (1995) *Clavis Patrum Latinorum, editio tertia (CCSL)*. Steenbrugge

Delaplace, C. (1992) 'Ermites et ascètes à fin de l'antiquité et leur fonction dans la société rurale. L'exemple de la Gaule', *MEFR* 104: 981–1024

Déroche, V. (1995) *Études sur Léontios de Néapolis*. Uppsala

Desprez, V. (1980) *Règles monastiques d'Occident: IVe–Ve siècle, d'Augustin à Ferréol*. French trans. with introductions and notes (Vie monastique, 9; Spiritualité orientale, 9). Abbaye de Bellefontaine, Bégrolles-en-Mauges

Diggle, J. and Goodyear, F. (eds.) (1970) *Corippus. Johannidos seu De bellis Libycis libri VIII*. Cambridge

Djobadze, W. (1986) *Archaeological Investigations in the Region West of Antioch-on-the-Orontes*. Wiesbaden

Doran, R. (tr.) (1992) *The Lives of Symeon Stylites* (Cistercian Studies 112). Kalamazoo

Downey, G. (1948) 'Byzantine architects, their training and methods', *Byz.* 18: 99–118

Draguet, R. (1924) *Julien d'Halicarnasse et sa controverse avec Sévère d'Antioche sur l'incorruptibilité du corps du Christ.* Louvain

Duchesne, L. (1925) *L'Église au VI⁰ siècle.* Paris

Duggan, L. G. (1989) 'Was art really the "book of the illiterate"?' *Word and Image* 5: 227–51

Dumville, D. N. (ed.) (1993) *Saint Patrick, A.D. 493–1993.* Woodbridge and Rochester, NY

Dunbabin, K. M. D. (1982) 'The marine mosaic (no. 16) from the House of the Greek Charioteers', in *Excavations at Carthage 1978 conducted by the University of Michigan* 7, ed. J. H. Humphrey. Ann Arbor (1982) 179–92

Durand, J. (ed.) (1992) *Byzance. L'art byzantin dans les collections publiques françaises.* Paris

Duval, N. (1984) 'Les maisons d'Apamée et l'architecture "palatiale" de l'antiquité tardive', in Balty (1984) 447–70

Duval, N. (1994) 'L'architecture chrétienne et les pratiques liturgiques en Jordanie en rapport avec la Palestine: recherches nouvelles', in K. Painter (ed.), *Churches Built in Ancient Times.* London

Dvornik, F. (1934) 'The authority of the state', *The Christian East* 14: 95–108

Dvornik, F. (1966) *Early Christian and Byzantine Political Philosophy,* 2 vols. Washington, DC

Ebersolt, J. (1910) *Le grand palais de Constantinople et le Livre de Ceremonies.* Paris

Ebied, R. Y., Van Roey, A., Wickham, L. R. (eds.) (1981) *Peter of Callinicum. Anti-Tritheist Dossier* (OLA 10). Louvain

Edwards, N. (1990) *The Archaeology of Early Medieval Ireland.* London

Effenberger, A. (1986) *Frühchristliche Kunst und Kultur. Von den Anfängen bis zum 7. Jahrundert.* Leipzig

Elm, S. (1994) *'Virgins of God': The Making of Asceticism in Late Antiquity.* Oxford

Elsner, J. (1995) *Art and the Roman Viewer: The Transformation of Art from the Pagan World to Christianity.* Cambridge

Engelhardt, I. (1974) *Mission und Politik in Byzanz. Ein Beitrag zur Strukturanalyse byzantinischer Mission zur Zeit Justins und Justinians* (Miscellanea Byzantina Monacensia 19). Munich

Erim, K. T. (1990) 'Recent work at Aphrodisias', in C. Roueché and K. T. Erim (eds.), *Aphrodisias Papers: Recent Work on Architecture and Sculpture* (Ann Arbor) 9–36

Escolan, P. (1999) *Monachisme et Église: le monachisme syrien du IV⁰ au VII⁰ siècle: un ministère charismatique.* Paris

Evans, G. R. (1986) *The Thought of Gregory the Great* (Cambridge Studies in Medieval Life and Thought, fourth series, 2). Cambridge

Felten, J. (ed.) (1913) *Nicolaus. Progymnasmata.* Leipzig

Fentress, J. and Wickham, C. (1992) *Social Memory.* Oxford

Ferguson, E. (ed.) (1990) *Encyclopedia of Early Christianity.* Chicago and London

Festugière, A. J. (tr.) (1961) *Les Moines d'Orient II: Les Moines de Constantinople.* Paris

Festugière, A. J. (1969) 'L'ordre de lecture des dialogues de Platon aux Ve/VIe siècles', *MH* 26: 281–96

Festugière, A. J. (ed.) (1970) *Vie de Théodore de Sykéon* (Subsidia Hagiographica 48). Brussels

Finney, P. C. (1994) *The Invisible God: The Earliest Christians on Art.* Oxford

Fitzgerald, G. M. (1939) *A Sixth Century Monastery at Beth Shan (Scythopolis).* Philadelphia

Flusin, B. (1983) *Miracle et histoire dans l'œuvre de Cyrille de Scythopolis.* Paris

Flusin, B. (1991) 'Démons et Sarrasins. L'auteur et le propos des *Diègèmata Stèriktika* d'Anastase le Sinaïte', *T&MByz* XI

Fontaine, J. (1959) *Isidore de Séville et la culture classique dans l'Espagne wisigothique.* Paris

Fontaine, J. (1962) 'Ennodius', *RAC* 5: 398–421

Forschungen in Ephesos (1906). Vienna (Österreichischen archaeologischen Institut)

Forsyth, G. H. and Weitzmann, K. (1973) *The Monastery of Saint Catherine at Mount Sinai: The Church and Fortress of Justinian.* Ann Arbor

Foss, C. (1979) *Ephesus after Antiquity: A Late Antique, Byzantine and Turkish City.* Cambridge

Foss, C. (1994) 'The Lycian coast in the Byzantine age', *DOP* 48: 1–52

Foss, C. (1995) 'Nicomedia and Constantinople', in Mango and Dagron (eds.) (1995) 181–90

Foss, C. and Winfield, D. (1986) *Byzantine Fortification: An Introduction.* Pretoria

Fotiou, A. S. (1985) 'Plato's philosopher king in the political thought of sixth-century Byzantium', *Florilegium* 71: 17–29

Foulkes, P. (1992) 'Where was Simplicius?', *JHS* 112: 143

Fowden, G. (1990a) 'The Athenian agora and the progress of Christianity', *JRA* 3: 494–501

Fowden, G. (1990b) 'Religious developments in late Roman Lycia', *Meletemata tou K.E.R.A.* (Athens) 10: 343–72

Frank, G. L. C. (1991) 'The Council of Constantinople II as a model reconciliation council', *Theological Studies* 52: 636–50

Frankfurter, D. T. M. (1990) 'Stylites and *phallobates*: pillar religions in late antique Syria', *VC* 44: 168–98

Frantz, A. (1988) *The Athenian Agora XXIV: Late Antiquity A.D. 267–700.* Princeton

Frend, W. (1973) 'Severus of Antioch and the rise of the Monophysite hierarchy', *OCA* 195: 261–75

Frend, W. (1984) *The Rise of Christianity.* London

Gahbauer, F. R. (1993) *Die Patriarchietheorie. Ein Modell der Kirchenleitung von den Anfangen bis zur Gegenwart.* Frankfurt

Gahbauer, F. R. (1996) 'Patriarchat I', *TRE* 26: 85–91

Garitte, G. (1941) 'La Vie prémetaphrastique de S. Chariton', *Bulletin de l'Institut Historique Belge de Rome* 21: 16–46

Gassmann, P. (1977) *Der Episkopat in Gallien im 5. Jahrhundert.* Bonn

Gaudemet, J. and Basdevant, B. (eds.) (1989) *Les Canons des Conciles mérovingiens (SChrét. 353).* Paris

Gazda, E. K. (1981) 'A marble group of Ganymede and the eagle from the age of Augustine', in *Excavations at Carthage 1977 conducted by the University of Michigan* 6, ed. J. H. Humphrey. Ann Arbor (1981) 125–78

Geerard, M. (1974–87) *Clavis Patrum Graecorum.* 5 vols. Turnhout

Gelzer, T. (ed.) (1975) *Musaeus. Hero and Leander in Callimachus. Aetia, etc* (ed. C. A. Trypanis). Cambridge, MA

George, J. W. (1992) *Venantius Fortunatus: A Latin Poet in Merovingian Gaul.* Oxford

Gerstinger, H. (1970) *Codex Vindobonensis med. gr. 1 der Österreichischen Nationalbibliothek. Kommentarband zu der Faksimile.* Graz

Gilsenan, M. (1982) *Recognizing Islam: Religion and Society in the Modern Arab World.* New York

Glucker, C. A. M. (1987) *The City of Gaza in the Roman and Byzantine Periods.* Oxford

Glucker, J. (1978) *Antiochus and the Late Academy.* Göttingen

Goffart, W. (1988) *The Narrators of Barbarian History: Jordanes, Gregory of Tours, Bede and Paul the Deacon.* Princeton

Goodchild, R. G. (1976) 'The "Palace of the Dux"', in J. Humphrey (ed.), *Apollonia, The Port of Cyrene: Excavations by the University of Michigan, 1965–1967.* Supplements to *Libya Antiqua* 4: 245–65

Goubert, P. (1965) *Byzance avant l'Islam. Byzance et l'occident sous les successeurs de Justinien.* Vol. II, *Rome, Byzance et Carthage.* Paris

Gould, G. (1993) *The Desert Fathers on Monastic Community.* Oxford

Grabar, A. (1936) *L'empereur dans l'art byzantin.* Paris

Grabar, A. (1946) *Martyrium.* Paris

Grabar, A. (1958) *Les ampoules de Terre Sainte (Monza, Bobbio).* Paris

Greenslade, S. L. (1965) review of Jones, A. H. M., *JThS* n.s. 16: 220–4

Gregg, R. C. and Groh, D. E. (1981) *Early Arianism: A View of Salvation.* London

Grégoire, R. (1966) *Les homéliaires du Moyen Âge.* Rome

Gregory, T. E. (1979) *Vox Populi. Popular Opinion and Violence in the Religious Controversies of the Fifth Century A.D.* Columbus, OH

Gribomont, J. (1953) *Histoire du texte des Ascétiques de saint Basile* (Bibliothèque du Muséon 32). Louvain

Grillmeier, A. and Bacht, H. (1979) *Das Konzil von Chalkedon. Geschichte und Gegenwart* (5th edn). Würzburg

Grossman, P. (1990) 'Architecture', in K. A. Manafis (ed.), *Sinai: Treasures of the Monastery of St Catherine* (Athens) 29–39

Guenther, O. (ed.) (1895) *Collectio Avellana* (*CSEL* 35). Prague, Vienna, Leipzig

Guidi, I. (ed.) (1903, repr. 1955) *Chronica Minora* II (*CSCO* Ser. Syr. 3.4). Louvain

Guillou, A. and Durand, J. (eds.) (1994) *Byzance et les images.* Paris

Gutman, S., Yeivin, Z. and Netzer, E. (1981) 'Excavations in the synagogue at Horvat Susiya', in Levine (ed.) (1981)

Guy, J.-C. (1962) *Recherches sur la tradition grecque des Apophthegmata Patrum* (Subsidia hagiographica, 36). Brussels

Haas, C. (1993) 'Patriarch and people: Peter Mongus of Alexandria and Episcopal leadership in the late fifth century', *Journal of Early Christian Studies* 1: 297–316

Hachlili, R. (ed.) (1989) *Ancient Synagogues in Israel, Third–Seventh Century C.E.* (BAR International Series 499). Oxford

Hadot, I. (1978) *Le problème du néoplatonisme alexandrin: Hiéroclès et Simplicius.* Paris

Hadot, I. (1987a) 'Les introductions aux commentaires exégétiques chez les auteurs néoplatoniciens et les auteurs chrétiens', in M. Tardieu (ed.), *Les règles de l'interprétation* 99–122. Paris (= Hadot (1990b) 21–47)

Hadot, I. (ed.) (1987b) *Simplicius. Sa vie, son oeuvre, sa survie.* Berlin

Hadot, I. (1990a) 'The life and work of Simplicius in Greek and Arabic sources', in Sorabji (ed.) (1990) 275–303

Hadot, I. (1990b) *Simplicius. Commentaire sur les catégories* I. Leiden

Hadot, I. (1991) 'The role of the commentaries on Aristotle in the teaching of philosophy according to the prefaces of the Neoplatonic commentaries on the *Categories*', in H. Blumenthal and H. Robinson (eds.), *Aristotle and the Later Tradition* (Oxford) 175–89

Hajjar, J. (1962) *Le Synode Permanent (σύνοδος ἐνδημοῦσα) dans l'Église byzantine des origines au XIe siècle (OCA* 164). Rome

Halleux, A. de (1963) *Philoxène de Mabbog. Sa vie, ses écrits, sa théologie.* Louvain

Hallinger, K. (1957) 'Papst Gregor der Grosse und der heiliger Benedikt', in B. Steidle (ed.), *Commentationes in Regulam S. Benedicti* 231–319 (Studia Anselmiana 42). Rome

Harrauer, H. and Sijpesteijn, P. (1985) *Neue Texte aus dem antiken Unterricht.* Vienna

Harries, J. (1994) *Sidonius Apollinaris and the Fall of Rome, A.D. 407–485.* Oxford

Harrison, R. M. (1963) 'Churches and chapels in central Lycia', *AS* 13: 117–51

Harrison, R. M. (1989) *A Temple for Byzantium: The Discovery and Excavation of Anicia Juliana's Palace-Church in Istanbul.* London and Austin, TX

Harvey, S. A. (1988) 'The sense of a stylite', *VC* 42: 376–94

Harvey, S. A. (1998) 'The stylite's liturgy', *Journal of Early Christian Studies* 6: 523–39

Hasitzka, M. R. M. (1990) *Neue Texte und Dokumentation zam Koptischen Unterricht.* Vienna

Hawkins, E. J. W. and Mundell, M. C. (1973) 'The mosaics of the Monastery of Mar Samuel, Mar Simeon, and Mar Gabriel, near Kartmin', *DOP* 27: 279–96

Hefele, K. J. and Leclerq, H. (1907–) *Histoire des Conciles d'après les documents originaux.* Paris

Heinzelmann, M. (1976) *Bischofsherrschaft in Gallien. Zur Kontinuität römischer Führungsschichten vom 4. bis zum 7. Jahrhundert.* Munich

Hellemo, G. (1989) *Adventus Domini: Eschatological Thought in Fourth-Century Apses and Catechesis.* Leiden

Herbert, M. (1988) *Iona, Kells and Derry. The History and Hagiography of the Monastic Familia of Columba.* Oxford

Higham, N. J. (1994) *The English Conquest: Gildas and Britain in the Fifth Century.* Manchester

Hilgard, A. (ed.) (1889–1894) *Theodosii Alexandrini Canones.* Leipzig

Hillgarth, J. N. (1987) 'Modes of evangelization of western Europe in the seventh century', in Chatháin, P. Ní and Richter, M. (eds.), *Irland und die Christenheit* (Stuttgart) 311–31

Hirschfeld, Y. (1992) *The Judean Desert Monasteries in the Byzantine Period.* New Haven and London

Hirschle, M. (1979) *Sprachphilosophie und Namenmagie im Neuplatonismus.* Meisenheim am Glan

Hoffmann, P. (1994) 'Damascius', *Dictionnaire des philosophes antiques* 2: 541–93. Paris

Holtz, L. (1981) *Donat et la tradition de l'enseignment grammatical.* Paris

Holum, K. G. (1986) 'Andreas *philoktistes*: a proconsul of Byzantine Palestine', *Israel Exploration Journal* 36: 61–4

Holum, K. G. (1988) *King Herod's Dream: Caesarea on the Sea.* New York

Holze, H. (1992) *Erfahrung und Theologie im frühen Mönchtum.* Göttingen

Honigmann, E. (1951) *Évêques et évêchés monophysites d'Asie antérieure au VIe siècle (CSCO Subsidia* 2). Louvain

Horden, P. (1993) 'Responses to possession and insanity in the earlier Byzantine world', *Social History of Medicine* 6: 177–94

Howard-Johnston, J. and Hayward, P. (eds.) (1999) *The Cult of Saints in Late Antiquity and the Early Middle Ages*. Oxford

Hudson, P. J. (1989) 'Contributi archeologici alla storia dell' insediamento urbano veneto (IV–XI secolo)', in A. Castagnetti and G. M. Varanini (eds.), *Il Veneto nel medioevo*. 2 vols. Verona, II.338–9

Hughes, K. (1966) *The Church in Early Irish Society*. London

Hughes, K. (1987) *Church and Society in Ireland, A.D. 400–1200* (edited by D. Dumville). London

Huxley, G. W. (1959) *Anthemius of Tralles: A Study in Later Greek Geometry*. Cambridge, MA

Inan, J. and Alföldi-Rosenbaum, E. (1979) *Römische und frühbyzantinische Porträtplastik aus der Türkei. Neue Funde*. Mainz

Jalabert, L. and Mouterde, R. (1959) *Inscriptions grecques et latines de la Syrie* V. Paris

James, E. (tr.) (1985) *Gregory of Tours: Life of the Fathers*. Liverpool

Janin, R. (1964) *Constantinople byzantine*. 2nd edn. Paris

Janin, R. (1969) *Les Églises et les monastères* (Géographie ecclésiastique de l'empire byzantin, I, 3). 2nd edn. Paris

Janin, R. (1975) *Les Églises et les monastères des grands centres byzantins* (Géographie ecclésiastique de l'empire byzantin, I, 2). Paris

Janvier, Y. (1969), *La législation du bas-empire sur les édifices publics*. Aix-en-Provence

Jenal, G. (1995) *Italia Ascetica atque Monastica. Das Asketen- und Mönchtum in Italien von den Anfängen bis zur Zeit der Langobarden (ca. 150/250–604)* (Monographien zur Geschichte des Mittelalters, Bd 39, 1–2). Stuttgart

Johnson, A. C. and West, L. C. (1949) *Byzantine Egypt: Economic Studies* (Princeton University Studies in Papyrology 6). Princeton

Jones, A. H. M. (1960) 'Church finance in the fifth and sixth centuries', *JThS* n.s. 11: 84–94 (= Jones, *Roman Economy* 339–49)

Jones, C., Wainwright, G. and Yarnold, E. (eds.) (1986) *The Study of Christian Spirituality*. London

Kaplan, M. (1976) *Les propriétés de la couronne et de l'Église dans l'Empire byzantin (Ve–VIe siècles). Documents* (Byzantina Sorbonensia 2). Paris

Kaplan, S. (1984) *The Monastic Holy Man and the Evangelization of Early Solomonic Ethiopia*. Wiesbaden

Kasper, C. M. (1991) *Theologie und Askese. Die Spiritualität des Inselmönchtums von Lérins im 5. Jahrhundert* (Beiträge zur Geschichte des alten Mönchtums und des Benediktinertums, Bd 40). Münster

Kessler, H. L. (1988) 'On the state of medieval art history', *Art Bulletin* 70: 166–87

Khatchatrian, A. (1982) *Origine et typologie des baptistères paléochrétiens* (ed. F. M. Buhler). Paris

Kitzinger, E. (1940) *Early Medieval Art*. London

Kitzinger, E. (1954) 'The cult of images in the age before Iconoclasm', *DOP* 8: 83–150 (repr. in Kitzinger (1976))

Kitzinger, E. (1976) *The Art of Byzantium and the Medieval West: Selected Studies by E. Kitzinger* ed. W. E. Kleinbauer. Bloomington

Kleinbauer, W. E. (1972) 'The iconography and date of the mosaics of the rotunda of Hagios Georgios, Thessaloniki', *Viator* 3: 27ff.

Kleinbauer, W. E. (1973) 'The origin and functions of the aisled tetraconch churches in Syria and northern Mesopotamia', *DOP* 27: 91–114

Kleinbauer, W. E. (1992) *Early Christian and Byzantine Architecture: An Annotated Bibliography and Historiography.* Boston

Klingshirn, W. (1990) 'Caesarius of Arles', in Ferguson (ed.) (1990) 167–8

Klingshirn, W. E. (1994) *Caesarius of Arles: The Making of a Christian Community in Late Antique Gaul.* Cambridge

König, D. (1985) *Amt und Askese. Priesteramt und Mönchtum bei den lateinischen Kirchenvätern in der vorbenediktinischer Zeit* (Regulæ Benedicti Studia, Supplementa 12). Erzabtei St Ottilien

Kostof, S. (1965) *The Orthodox Baptistery of Ravenna.* New Haven

Kraeling, C. H. (1962) *Ptolemais, City of the Libyan Pentapolis.* Chicago

Krautheimer, R. (1980) *Rome. Profile of a City, 312–1308.* Princeton

Krautheimer, R. (1983) *Three Christian Capitals. Topography and Politics: Rome, Constantinople, Milan.* Berkeley and Los Angeles

Krautheimer, R. and others (1937–) *Corpus Basilicarum Romanarum.* Rome

Kropp, A. M. (1930) *Ausgewählte koptische Zaubertexte.* Brussels

Kugener, M. A. (ed.) (1907) *Zacharie le scholastique: Vie de Sévère, PO* 11.1. Paris (repr. Turnhout 1993)

Laga, C. (ed.) (1992) *Eustratii Presbyteri Vita Eutychii Patriarchae Constantinopolitani* (*CCSG* 25). Turnhout

Laing, L. (1990) *Celtic Britain and Ireland, A.D. 200–800: The Myth of the Dark Ages.* Dublin

Lamberz, E. (1987) 'Proklos und die Form des philosophischen Kommentars', in Pépin and Saffrey (eds.) (1987) 1–20

Lane Fox, R. (1997) 'The Life of Daniel', in M. J. Edwards and S. Swain (eds.), *Portraits. Biographical Representation in the Greek and Latin Literature of the Roman Empire* (Oxford) 175–225

Langgärtner, G. (1964) *Die Gallienpolitik des Papstes in 5. und 6. Jahrhundert. Eine Studie über den apostolischen Vikariat von Arles.* Theophaneia 16. Bonn

Lapidge, M. and Dumville, D. (eds.) (1984) *Gildas: New Approaches.* Woodbridge

Lassus, J. (1947) *Sanctuaires chrétiens de Syrie. Essai sur la genèse, la forme et l'usage liturgique des édifices de culte chrétiens en Syrie, du IIIe siècle à la conquête musulmane.* Paris

Lawless, G. (1990) *Augustine of Hippo and his Monastic Rule.* Oxford

Lawrence, A. W. (1983) 'A skeletal history of Byzantine fortification', *Annual of the British School at Athens* 78: 171–227

Lawrence, M. (1945) *The Sarcophagi of Ravenna.* New York

Le Moine, F. (1972) *Martianus Capella: A Literary Re-evaluation.* Munich

Leach, E. (1983) 'Melchisedech and the emperor: icons of subversion and orthodoxy', reprinted in E. Leach and D. A. Aycock (eds.), *Structuralist Interpretations of Biblical Myth* (Cambridge) 67–88

Leipoldt, J. (1903) *Schenute von Atripe und die Entstehung des national-ägyptischen Christentums. TU* 25: 1

Lemerle, P. (1971) *Le premier humanisme byzantin.* Paris (trs. as Lemerle, *Byzantine Humanism*)

Levine, L. I. (ed.) (1981) *Ancient Synagogues Revealed.* Jerusalem

Lloyd, A. C. (1987) 'Parhypostasis in Proclus', in G. Boss and G. Seel (eds.), *Proclus et son influence* (Zurich) 145–57

Lowden, J. (1990) 'Luxury and liturgy: the function of books', in R. Morris (ed.), *Church and People in Byzantium* (Birmingham) 263–80

Lowden, J. (1993) *The Octateuchs*. University Park and London

McCarthy, M. C. (1960) *The Rule for Nuns of St Caesarius of Arles*. Washington, DC

MacCormack, S. (1981) *Art and Ceremony in Late Antiquity*. Berkeley and London

MacCoull, L. S. B. (1987) 'Dioscorus of Aphrodito and John Philoponus', *Studia Patristica* 18: 163–68. Kalamazoo

McCready, W. D. (1989) *Signs of Sanctity: Miracles in the Thought of Gregory the Great*. Toronto

McGuckin, J. A. (1994) *St Cyril of Alexandria: The Christological Controversy. Its History, Theology, and Texts* (Supplements to *Vigiliae Christianae* 23). Leiden

McGuire, B. (1988) *Friendship and Community: The Monastic Experience, 350–1250*. Kalamazoo

Mackie, G. (1994) 'La Daurade: a royal mausoleum', *Cahiers Archéologiques* 42: 17–34

Macrides, R. and Magdalino, P. (1988) 'The architecture of *ekphrasis*: construction and context of Paul the Silentiary's *ekphrasis* of Hagia Sophia', *BMGS* 12: 47–82

Maguire, H. (1990) *Earth and Ocean*. University Park and London

Mahé, J. P. (1990) 'David l'Invincible dans la tradition arménienne', in Hadot (1990b) 189–207

Mainstone, R. J. (1988) *Hagia Sophia: Architecture, Structure and Liturgy of Justinian's Great Church*. London. Reissued London 1997

Majeska, G. (1984) *Russian Travelers to Constantinople in the Fourteenth and Fifteenth Centuries*. Washington, DC

Malbon, E. S. (1990) *The Iconography of the Sarcophagus of Junius Bassus*. Princeton

Manafis, K. A. (ed.) (1990) *Sinai: Treasures of the Monastery of Saint Catherine*. Athens

Mango, C. (1959) *The Brazen House: A Study of the Vestibule of the Imperial Palace of Constantinople*. Copenhagen

Mango, C. (1962) *Materials for the Study of the Mosaics of St Sophia at Istanbul*. Washington, DC

Mango, C. (1972) *The Art of the Byzantine Empire 312–1453* (Sources and Documents in the History of Art Series). Englewood Cliffs, NJ

Mango, C. (1977) 'Storia dell'arte', in A. Guillou (ed.), *La civiltà bizantina dal IV al IX secolo. Aspetti e problemi* (Bari) 285–350

Mango, C. (1980) *Byzantium: The Empire of New Rome*. London

Mango, C. (1984a) 'A Byzantine hagiographer at work', *Österreichische Akademie der Wissenschaften, philos.-hist. Kl. Sitzungsberichte* 432: 25–41

Mango, C. (1984b) *Byzantium and its Image*. Aldershot

Mango, C. (1986) 'The pilgrimage centre of St Michael at Germia', *JÖB* 36: 117–32

Mango, C., Dagron, D., with Greatrex, G. (eds.) (1995) *Constantinople and its Hinterland*. Aldershot

Mango, C., Vickers, M. and Francis, E. D. (1992) 'The palace of Lausus at Constantinople and its collection of ancient statues', *Journal of the History of Collections* 4: 89–98

Mango, M. Mundell (1986) *Silver from Early Byzantium*. Baltimore

Mango, M. Mundell (1984) *Artistic Patronage in the Roman Diocese of Oriens, AD 313–641*. Oxford D.Phil. thesis 1984. Oxford (in press)

Mansfeld, J. (1994) *Prolegomena. Questions to be Settled Before the Study of an Author or a Text*. Leiden

Marinus (1814) *Life of Proclus* ed. (1) J. F. Boissonade. Leipzig, 1814, reprinted 1966; (2) R. Masullo, with Italian translation and notes. Naples, 1985

Markus, R. (1985) 'Gregor I', *TRE* 14: 135–45

Markus, R. (1990) *The End of Ancient Christianity*. Cambridge

Martine, F. (ed.) (1968) *Vies des pères du Jura (SChrét.* 142). Paris

Masai, F. (1971) 'La *Vita patrum iurensium* et les débuts du monachisme à Saint-Maurice d'Agaune', in J. Authenrieth and F. Brunhölzl (eds.), *Festschrift Bernhard Bischoff zu seinem 65. Geburtstag* (Stuttgart) 43–69

Maspéro, J. (1931–43) *Fouilles exécutées à Baouit* I–II. Cairo

Mathews, T. F. (1971) *The Early Churches of Constantinople: Architecture and Liturgy*. University Park, PA

Mathews, T. F. (1993) *The Clash of the Gods: A Reinterpretation of Early Christian Art*. Princeton

Mathisen, R. W. (1989) *Ecclesiastical Factionalism and Religious Controversy in Fifth-Century Gaul*. Washington, DC

Mathisen, R. W. (1993) *Roman Aristocrats in Barbarian Gaul. Strategies for Survival in an Age of Transition*. Austin, TX

Mayr-Harting, H. (1991) *The Coming of Christianity to Anglo-Saxon England*. 3rd edn. London

Mazzarino, S. (1960) *Rapports du XIe Congrès International des Sciences Historiques* (Stockholm) 35 ff.

Megaw, A. H. S. and Hawkins, E. J. W. (1977) *The Church of the Panagia Kanakaria at Lythrankomi in Cyprus: Its Mosaics and Frescoes*. Washington, DC

Miller, T. S. (1984) 'Byzantine hospitals', *DOP* 38: 53–63

Miller, T. S. (1990) 'The Sampson Hospital of Constantinople', *BF* 15: 101–35

Molitor, R. (ed.) (1947) *Vir Dei Benedictus*. Münster

Momigliano, A. D. (1955) 'Cassiodorus and the Italian culture of his time', *PBA* 41: 207–45

Mommsen, Th. (ed.) (1894) *Cassiodori Senatoris Variae*. Berlin

Morey, C. R. (1942 and 1953) *Early Christian Art*. Princeton

Morin, G. (ed.) (1942) *Caesarii Opera Omnia*. Maredsous

Müller-Wiener, W. (1977) *Bildlexikon zur Topographie Istanbuls*. Tübingen

Munier, C. (1960) *Les* Statuta ecclesiae antiqua (Bibliothèque de l'Institut de Droit Canonique de l'Université de Strasbourg 5). Paris

Munier, C. (ed.) (1963a) *Statuta Ecclesiae Antiqua (CCSL* 148). Turnhout

Munier, C. (ed.) (1963b) *Concilia Galliae I. A.314–A.506, II. A.511–A.695 (CCSL* 98, 98A). Turnhout

Murphy, F.-X. and Sherwood, P. (1974) *Constantinople II et Constantinople III* (Histoire des conciles oecuméniques 3). Paris

Murray, C. (1977) 'Art and the Early Church', *JThS* n.s. 28: 305–45

Murray, R. (1975) *Symbols of Church and Kingdom: A Study in Early Syriac Tradition*. London and New York

Mynors, R. A. B. (ed.) (1937) *Cassiodori Institutiones*. Oxford

Mytum, H. C. (1992) *The Origins of Early Christian Ireland*. London and New York

Nau, F. (ed.) (1910) *Histoire de Saint Maurice, empereur des Romains (PO* v). Paris

Nau, F. (1913) *Revue de l'Orient chrétien* 18: 130

Navarra, L. (1990) 'Venantius Fortunatus', in Ferguson (ed.) (1990) 2, 862–3

Nielsen, I. (1990) *Thermae et Balnea: The Architecture and Cultural History of Roman Public Baths*. Aarhus

Nordström, C.-O. (1953) *Ravennastudien: Ideengeschichtliche und ikonographische Untersuchungen über die Mosaiken von Ravenna*. Stockholm

O'Connell, P. (1963) 'Equal representation from each patriarchate at Constantinople II?', *OCP* 29: 238–46

O'Donnell, J. (1979) *Cassiodorus*. Berkeley and Los Angeles

Onians, J. (1980) 'Abstraction and imagination in late antiquity', *Art History* 3: 1–24

Orlandi, J. and Ramos-Lisson, D. (1981) *Die Synoden auf der Iberischen Halbinsel bis zum Einbruch von Islam (711)* (Konziliengeschichte Reihe A: Darstellungen). Paderborn-Munich-Vienna-Zurich

Palmer, A. (1990) *Monk and Mason on the Tigris Frontier: The Early History of Tur 'Abdin* (University of Cambridge Oriental Publications 39). Cambridge

Papyri Greek and Egyptian: In Honour of Eric Gardiner Turner (1981). London

Patlagean, E. (1968) 'Ancienne hagiographie byzantine et histoire sociale', *Annales: ESC* 23: 106–26 (Eng. trans. Jane Hodgkin, 'Ancient Byzantine hagiography and social history', in S. Wilson (ed.) (1983) *Saints and their Cults* (Cambridge) 101–21)

Patrich, J. (1995) *Sabas, Leader of Palestinian Monasticism: A Comparative Study in Eastern Monasticism. Fourth to Seventh Centuries* (Dumbarton Oaks Studies 32). Washington, DC

Pelikan, J. (1990) *Imago Dei*. New Haven and London

Pépin, J. and Saffrey, H. D. (eds.) (1987) *Proclus, lecteur et interprète des anciens*. Paris

Peschlow, U. (1986). 'Eine wiedergewonnene byzant. Ehrensäule in Istanbul', in O. Feld and U. Peschlow (eds.), *Studien zur spätantiken und byzantinischen Kunst F. W. Deichmann gewidmet* 1 (Mainz)

Petersen, J. M. (1984) *The Dialogues of Gregory the Great in their Late Antique Cultural Background* (Studies and Texts 69). Toronto

Picard, C. (1982) 'The purpose of Adomnáns's *Vita Columbae*', *Peritia* 1: 160–77

Pietri, C. (1983) 'Frankreich I', *TRC* 11: 346–51

Pietri, L. (1985) 'Gregor von Tours', *TRE* 14: 184–8

Pizzaro, J. M. (1995) *Writing Ravenna: The Liber Pontificalis of Andreas Agnellus*. Michigan

Pontal, O. (1986) *Die Synoden im Merowingerreich* (Konziliengeschichte Reihe A: Darstellungen). Paderborn-Munich-Vienna-Zurich

Praechter, K. (1910) 'Richtungen und Schulen im Neuplatonismus', in *Genethliakon Carl Robert* (Berlin) 103–56

Praechter, K. (1913) 'Hierokles', *RE* VIII.2: 1479–87

Praechter, K. (1927) 'Simplikios', *RE* III.A.1: 204–13

Price, R. M. (tr.) (1991) *The Lives of the Monks of Palestine by Cyril of Scythopolis* (Cistercian Studies 114). Kalamazoo

Pricoco, S. (1967) 'Studi su Sidonio Apollinare', *Nuovo Didaskaleion* 15: 71–150

Pricoco, S. (1978) *L'Isola dei Santi. Il Cenobio di Lerino e le Origini del Monachesimo Gallico*. Rome

Pricoco, S. (1990) 'Sidonius Apollinaris', in Ferguson (ed.) (1990) 2, 778–9

Pricoco, S. (1993) 'Gli scritti agiografici in prosa di Venanzio Fortunato', in *Venanzio*

Fortunato tra Italia e Francia. Atti del Convegno Internazionale di Studi, Valdobbiadene 17 maggio 1990, Treviso 18–19 maggio 1990, ed. Giuseppe Marton (Treviso) 175–93

Prinz, F. (1965) *Frühes Mönchtum im Frankenreich. Kultur und Gesellschaft in Gallien, den Rheinlanden und Bayern am Beispiel der monastischen Entwicklung (4. bis 8. Jahrhundert)*. Munich and Vienna

Quibell, J. E. (1909–12) *Excavations at Saqqara* I–III. Cairo

Rabe, H. (ed.) (1931) *Prolegomenon Sylloge*. Leipzig

Recchia, V. (1990) 'Gregory the Great', in Ferguson (ed.) (1990) 1, 365–8

Reginald, G. (ed.) (1966) *Les homéliaires du Moyen Âge* (Rerum Ecclesiasticarum Documenta, series maior, Fontes 6). Rome

Regnault, L. (tr.) (1971) *Barsanuphe et Jean de Gaza: Correspondance*. Solesmes

Reydellet, M. (1993) 'Tradition et nouveauté dans les Carmina de Fortunat', in *Venanzio Fortunato tra Italia e Francia*. Atti del Convegno Internazionale di Studi, Valdobbiadene 17 maggio 1990, Treviso 18–19 maggio 1990, ed. Giuseppe Marton (Treviso) 81–98

Richards, J. (1980) *Consul of God: The Life and Times of Gregory the Great*. London-Boston-Henley

Riché, P. (1972) 'L'enseignement et la culture des laïcs dans l'occident pré-carolingien', *Settimane di Studi, Spoleto* 19: 231–51

Richter, M. (1982) 'Dionysius Exiguus', *TRE* 9: 1–4

Rommel, F. (ed.) and Morel, C. (tr.) (1992) *Grégoire le Grand, Règle Pastorale* (*SChrét.* 381–2). Paris

Rosán, L. J. (1949) *The Philosophy of Proclus*. New York

Roueché, C. (1991) 'Inscriptions and the later history of the theatre', in Smith and Erim (eds.) (1991) 99–108

Rouché, M. (1990) 'The definitions of philosophy and a new fragment of Stephanus the philosopher', *JÖB* 40: 107–28

Rousseau, P. (1975) 'Cassian, contemplation, and the coenobitic life', *JEH* 26: 113–26

Rousseau, P. (1995) 'Eccentrics and coenobites in the late Roman East', *BF* 21: 15–50 (= *Conformity and Non-Conformity in Byzantium*, ed. Lynda Garland)

Rousselle, A. (1990) *Croire et guérir. La foi en Gaule dans l'antiquité tardive*. Paris

Ruggini, L. Cracco (1981) 'Il miracolo nella cultura del tardo impero', in *Hagiographie, cultures et sociétés, IVe–XIIe siècles* (Paris) 161–204

Saffrey, H. D. (1975) 'Allusions antichrétiennes chez Proclus: le diadoque platonicien', *Revue des sciences philosophiques et théologiques* 59: 553–63

Saffrey, H. D. (1982) 'New objective links between the Pseudo-Dionysius and Proclus', in D. J. O'Meara (ed.), *Neoplatonism and Christian Thought* (Norfolk, VA) 64–74

Saffrey, H. D. (1990) 'How did Syrianus regard Aristotle?', in Sorabji (ed.) (1990) 173–9

Saffrey, H. D. and Westerink, L. G. (eds.) (1968, 1978) *Proclus. Théologie platonicienne* I, III. Paris

Saliou, C. (1994) *Les lois des bâtiments. Voisinage et habitat urbain dans l'empire romain. Recherches sur les rapports entre le droit et la construction privée du siècle d'Auguste au siècle de Justinien*. Beirut

Saller, S. J. (1941) *The Memorial of Moses on Mount Nebo.* Jerusalem

Scheller, R. W. (1963 and 1996) *A Survey of Medieval Model Books.* Haarlem

Scholz, S. (1992) *Transmigration und Translation. Studien zur Bistumswechsel der Bischöfe von der Spätantike bis zum hohen Mittelalter* (Kölner Historische Abhandlungen 37). Cologne-Weimar-Vienna

Schulz, H.-J. (1986) *The Byzantine Liturgy: Symbolic Structure and Faith Expression* (translated by M. J. O'Connell). New York

Schwartz, E. (ed.) (1927) 'Codex Vaticanus gr. 1431, eine anti-chalkedonische Sammlung aus der Zeit Kaisers Zenos', *Abh. der bayer. Akad. der Wiss., phil.-hist. Abt.* 32.6

Schwartz, E. (ed.) (1934) 'Publizistische Sammlungen zum acacianischen Schisma', *Abh. der bayer. Akad. der Wiss., phil.-hist. Abt.* n.s. 10.4

Sear, F. B. (1977) *Roman Wall and Vault Mosaics.* Heidelberg

Seiber, J. (1977) *The Urban Saint in Early Byzantine Social History* (BAR Supplementary Series 37). Oxford

Ševčenko, I. and Ševčenko, N. (eds.) (1984) *The Life of Nicholas of Sion.* Brookline, MA

Sheldon-Williams, I. P. (1967) 'The Greek Christian Platonist tradition from the Cappadocians to Maximus and Eriugena', in Armstrong (ed.) (1967) 421–533

Shelton, K. (1989) 'Roman aristocrats, Christian commissions: the Carrand diptych', in Clover and Humphreys (eds.) (1989) 105–27

Sheppard, A. (1982) 'Monad and dyad as cosmic principles in Syrianus', in H. J. Blumenthal and A. C. Lloyd (eds.), *Soul and the Structure of Being in late Neoplatonism* (Liverpool) 1–14

Sheppard, A. (1987) 'Proclus' philosophical method of exegesis: the use of Aristotle and the Stoics in the commentary on the *Cratylus*', in Pépin and Saffrey (eds.) (1987) 137–51

Shiel, J. (1990) 'Boethius' commentaries on Aristotle', in Sorabji (ed.) (1990) 349–72

Sieben, H. J. (1986) *Die Konzilsidee der alten Kirche* (Konziliengeschichte Reihe B: Untersuchungen). Paderborn-Munich-Vienna-Zurich

Small, A. M. and Buck, R. J. (1994) *The Excavations of San Giovanni di Ruoti, 1. The Villas and Their Environment.* Toronto

Smith, R. R. R. (1985) 'Roman portraits: honours, empresses, and late emperors', *JRS* 75: 209–21

Smith, R. R. R. (1990) 'Late Roman philosopher portraits from Aphrodisias' *JRS* 80: 127–55

Smith, R. R. R. (1991) 'Late Roman philosophers', in Smith and Erim (eds.) (1991) 144–58

Smith, R. R. R. and Erim, K. T. (eds.) (1991) *Aphrodisias Papers 2. The Theatre, a Sculptor's Workshop, Philosophers, and Coin-Types.* Ann Arbor

Sodini, J.-P. (1989) 'Le commerce des marbres à l'époque protobyzantine', in *Hommes et richesses* 1.162–86

Sodini, J.-P. (1994) 'Images sculptées et propagande impériale du IVe au VIe siècle: recherches récentes sur les colonnes honorifiques et les reliefs politiques à Byzance', in A. Guillou and J. Durand (eds.), *Byzance et les images* (Paris) 43–94

Sorabji, R. (ed.) (1987) *Philoponus and the Rejection of Aristotelian Science.* Ithaca, NY and London

Sorabji, R. (ed.) (1990) *Aristotle Transformed*. London

Spain, S. (1979) '"The Promised Blessing": the iconography of the mosaics of S. Maria Maggiore', *Art Bulletin* 61: 518–69

Speigl, J. (1984) 'Das Religionsgespräch mit den severianischen Bischöfen in Konstantinopel im Jahre 532', *Annuarium Historiae Conciliorum* 16: 264–85

Spieser, J.-M. (1984) *Thessalonique et ses monuments*. Paris

Stancliffe, C. (1983) *St Martin and his Hagiographer: History and Miracle in Sulpicius Severus*. Oxford

Steel, C. (1978) *The Changing Self: A Study on the Soul in Later Neoplatonism: Iamblichus, Damascius and Priscianus*. Brussels

Steel, C. (1987) 'Proclus et Aristote sur la causalité efficiente de l'intellect divin', in Pépin and Saffrey (eds.) (1987) 213–25

Stephens-Crawford, J. (1990) *The Byzantine Shops at Sardis*. Cambridge, MA and London

Stewart, C. (1991) *'Working the Earth of the Heart': The Messalian Controversy in History, Texts and Language*. Oxford

Stillwell, R. (ed.) (1938, 1941) *Antioch-on-the-Orontes*. II. *The Excavations 1933–1936*; III. *The Excavations 1937–1939*. Princeton

Stillwell, R. (1961) 'Houses of Antioch', *DOP* 15: 47–57

Straw, C. (1988) *Gregory the Great: Perfection in Imperfection* (The Transformation of the Classical Heritage 14). Berkeley and Los Angeles

Stroheker, K. F. (1948) *Der senatorische Adel im spätantiken Gallien*. Darmstadt

Studer, B. (1990) 'Leo I', *TRE* 20: 737–41

Studer, B. (1991) 'Leo the Great', in A. di Berardino (ed.), *Patrology IV. The Golden Age of Patristic Literature* (Westminster, MD) 589–612 (tr. from *Patrologia*, Casale (1978) III.557–78, with additional bibliography)

Summa, G. (1992) *Geistliche Unterscheidung bei Johannes Cassian*. Würzburg

Talbot Rice, D. (ed.) (1958) *The Great Palace of the Byzantine Emperors. Second Report*. Edinburgh

Tarán, L. (1978) *Anonymous Commentary on Aristotle's De Interpretatione*. Meisenheim am Glan

Tardieu, M. (1986) 'Sabiens coraniques et "Sabiens" de Harran', *Journal Asiatique* 274: 1–44

Tardieu, M. (1987) 'Les calendriers en usage à Harran d'après les sources arabes et le commentaire de Simplicius à la Physique d'Aristote', in Hadot (ed.) (1987b) 40–57. Berlin

Tardieu, M. (1990) *Les paysages reliques. Routes et haltes syriennes d'Isidore et Simplicius*. Louvain and Paris

Tate, G. (1992) *Les campagnes de la Syrie du Nord du IIe au VIIe siècle* I. Paris

Tchalenko, G. (1979) *Églises de village de la Syrie du nord*, Plates. Paris

Tchalenko, G. (1990) *Églises syriennes à bêma*. Paris

Teyssier, G. (1964) *Le baptême de Clovis*. Paris

Thélamon, F. (1981) *Païens et chrétiens au IVe siècle*. Paris

Theurillat, J.-M. (1954) *L'Abbaye de Saint-Maurice d'Agaune. Des origines à la réforme canoniale (515–830)*. Saint-Maurice

Thilo, G. and Hagen, H. (eds.) (1881–7) *Servii grammatici qui feruntur in Vergilii carmina commentarii*. Leipzig (= Berlin, 1891–7); repr. 1923–7

Thompson, E. A. (1986) *Who was Saint Patrick?* New York

Till, W. C. (1936) *Koptische Heiligen-und Märtyrerlegende: pt 2. ACO* 108. Rome

Till, W. C. (1960) 'Die koptischen Ostraka', *Österreichische Akademie der Wissenschaften, philos.-hist. Kl. Denkschrift* 78.1. Vienna

Tsafrir, Y. *et al.* (1992) 'The Bet Shean project (1989–1991)', *Excavations and Surveys in Israel* 11

Tsafrir, Y. and Foerster, G. (1997) 'Urbanism at Scythopolis-Bet Shean in the fourth to seventh centuries', *DOP* 51: 85–146

Tuilier, A. (1966) 'Le sens de l'adjectif οἰκουμενικός dans la tradition patristique et dans la tradition byzantine', *StPatr* 7: (TU 92) 412–24

Turner, V. and Turner, E. (1978) *Image and Pilgrimage in Christian Culture.* New York

Uthemann, K.-H. (1985) 'Stephanos von Alexandrien und die Konversion des Jakobiten Probos, des späteren Metropoliten von Chalkedon', in C. Laga, J. A. Munitiz, L. van Rompay (eds.), *After Chalcedon: Studies in Theology and Church History Offered to Prof. A. Van Roey for his 70th birthday* (Louvain) 381–99

Van Dam, R. (1988a) 'Images of St Martin in late Roman and early Merovingian Gaul', *Viator* 19: 1–27

Van Dam, R. (tr.) (1988b) *Gregory of Tours: Glory of the Confessors.* Liverpool

Van Dam, R. (1993) *Saints and their Miracles in Late Antique Gaul.* Princeton

Van Lantschoot, A. (1946) 'Fragments d'une homélie copte de Jean de Parallos', *Studi et Testi* 121: 296–326

Van Roey, A. (1961) 'Het dossier van Proba en Juhannan Barboer', *Scrinium Lovaniense* 24: 181–90

Van Roey, A. (1979) 'Les débuts de l'église jacobite', in A. Grillmeier and H. Bacht (eds.) (1979) II.339–60

Van Roey, A. (1982) 'La controverse trithéite depuis la condamnation de Conon et Eugène jusqu'à la conversion de l'évêque Élie', *Von Kanaan bis Kerala* (= FS J. P. M. van de Ploeg) (Alter Orient und Altes Testament 211) 487–97. Neukirchen

Van Roey, A. (1985) 'La controverse trithéite jusqu'à l'excommunication de Conon et d'Eugène (557–569)', *OLP* 16: 141–65

Van Roey, A. and Allen, P. (ed. and tr.) (1994) *Monophysite Texts of the Sixth Century* (*OLA* 56). Louvain

Van den Ven, P. (ed.) (1962) *La vie ancienne de St Symeon le Jeune,* 2 vols. (Subsidia Hagiographica 32). Brussels

Verheijen, L. (1967) *La Règle de Saint Augustin.* 2 vols. Paris

Verheijen, L. (1980) *Nouvelle approche de la règle de saint Augustin.* Abbaye de Bellefontaine

Verrycken, K. (ed.) (1990) 'The Metaphysics of Ammonius son of Hermeias', in Sorabji (ed.) (1990) 199–274

Volbach, W. F. (1976) *Elfenbeinarbeiten der Spätantik und des frühen Mittelalters* (3rd edn). Mainz

Vollmer, F. (ed.) (1914) *Poetae latini minores* 5. Leipzig

Von Simson, O. G. (1948) *Sacred Fortress: Byzantine Art and Statecraft in Ravenna.* Chicago

Vööbus, A. (1958, 1960) *History of Asceticism in the Syrian Orient.* 2 vols (*CSCO* 184, *Subsidia* 14; *CSCO* 197, *Subsidia* 17). Louvain

Vööbus, A. (1965) *History of the School of Nisibis* (*CSCO* 266). Louvain

Wallace-Hadrill, J. M. (1983) *The Frankish Church.* Oxford

Wallis, R. T. (1972) *Neoplatonism.* London

Walter, C. (1984) 'Expressionism and Hellenism', *REB* 42: 265–87

Walters, C. C. (1974) *Monastic Archaeology in Egypt.* Warminster

Walz, C. (ed.) (1832–6) *Rhetores Graeci.* Stuttgart-Tübingen

Ward-Perkins, B. (1978) 'L'abbandono degli edifici pubblici a Luni', *Centro di studi lunensi, Quaderni* 3: 33–46

Ward-Perkins, J. B. (1981) *Roman Imperial Architecture.* Harmondsworth

Weitzmann, K. (1976) *The Monastery of Saint Catherine at Mount Sinai: The Icons from the Sixth to the Tenth Century.* Princeton

Weitzmann, K. (1977) *Late Antique and Early Christian Book Illumination.* London

Weitzmann, K., Loerke, W. C., Kitzinger, E. and Buchthal, H. (1975) *The Place of Book Illumination in Byzantine Art.* Princeton

Westerink, L. G. (ed.) (1962) *Anonymous Prolegomena to Platonic Philosophy.* Amsterdam

Westerink, L. G. (1980) 'Philosophy and medicine in late antiquity', *Janus* 57: 169–77 (= *Texts and Studies in Neoplatonism and Byzantine Literature* (Amsterdam) 83–91

Westerink, L. G. (1990) 'The Alexandrian commentators and the introductions to their commentaries', in Sorabji (ed.) (1990) 325–48

Westerink, L. G. and Combès, J. (eds.) (1986, 1989) *Damascius. Traité des premiers principes.* I–II. Paris

Westerink, L. G. and Trouillard, J. (1990) *Prolégomènes à la philosophie de Platon.* Paris

Wharton, A. J. (1987) 'Ritual and reconstructed meaning: the Neonian Baptistery in Ravenna', *Art Bulletin*, 69: 358–75

Wickham, C. (1994) *Land and Power: Studies in Italian and European Social History.* London

Wickham, L. R. (1982a) 'Eucherius von Lyon', *TRE* 10: 522–6

Wickham, L. R. (1982b) 'Eutyches/Eutychianischer Streit', *TRE* 10: 558–65

Wickham, L. R. (1983) *Cyril of Alexandria: Select Letters* (Oxford Early Christian Texts). Oxford

Wickham, L. R. (1995) 'Aspects of clerical life in the early Byzantine Church in two scenes: Mopsuestia and Apamea', *JEH* 46: 3–18

Wildberg, C. (1988) *John Philoponus' Criticism of Aristotle's Theory of Aether.* Berlin and New York

Wilken, R. L. (1992) *The Land Called Holy: Palestine in Christian History and Thought.* New Haven and London

Wilson, N. G. (tr.) (1975) *Saint Basil on the Value of Greek Literature.* London

Wimbush, V. L. (ed.) (1990) *Ascetic Behavior in Greco-Roman Antiquity: A Sourcebook.* Minneapolis

Witakowski, W. (tr.) (1996) *Pseudo-Dionysius of Tel-Mahre. Chronicle, Part III.* Liverpool

Wolska-Conus, W. (1989) 'Stéphanos d'Athènes et Stéphanos d'Alexandrie. Essai d'identification et de biographie', *REB* 47: 5–89

Wood, I. N. (1981) 'A prelude to Columbanus: the monastic achievement in the Burgundian territories', in Clarke and Brennan (eds.) (1981) 3–32

Wortley, J. (tr.) (1992) *The Spiritual Meadow of John Moschus* (Cistercian Studies 139). Kalamazoo

Wouters, A. (1979) *The Grammatical Papyri from Graeco-Roman Egypt: Contributions to the Study of the 'Ars Grammatica' in Antiquity*. Brussels

Wright, D. H. (1993) *The Vatican Vergil: A Masterpiece of Late Antique Art*. Berkeley

Xydis, S. G. (1947) 'The chancel barrier, solea and ambo of Hagia Sophia', *Art Bulletin* 29: 1–24

Yegül, F. (1992) *Baths and Bathing in Classical Antiquity*. New York

Yeivin, Z. *et al.* (1992) 'The Bet Shean project', *Excavations and Surveys in Israel* 6

Zalateo, G. (1961) 'Papiri scolastici', *Aegyptus* 41: 160–235

Zettl, E. (1974) *Die Bestätigung des V. ökumenischen Konzils durch Papst Vigilius* (Antiquitas, Reihe 1, 20). Bonn

CONCLUSION

Brogiolo, G. P. (ed.) (1997) *Early Medieval Towns in the Western Mediterranean*, Ravello 22–24 September 1994 (Documenti di Archeologia 10), Società Archeologica Padana s.r.l.

Brown, P. R. L. (1967) 'The later Roman empire', *Economic History Review* 56, 2 ser., 20: 327–43 (= Brown, *Religion and Society* 46–73)

Brown, P. R. L. (1971) *The World of Late Antiquity*. London

Brown, P. R. L. (1974) '*Mohammed and Charlemagne* by Henri Pirenne', *Daedalus* 103: 25–33 (= Brown, *Society and the Holy* 63–79)

Brown, P. R. L. (1976) 'Eastern and western Christendom in late antiquity: a parting of the ways', in *The Orthodox Churches and the West*, Studies in Church History 13 (Oxford) 1–24 (= Brown, *Society and the Holy* 166–95)

Brown, P. R. L. (1992) *Power and Persuasion in Late Antiquity*. Madison

Cameron, Averil (1992) 'The language of images. The rise of icons and Christian representation', in D. Wood (ed.), *The Church and the Arts* (Studies in Church History 28) (Oxford) 1–42 (= Averil Cameron, *Changing Cultures* XII)

Cameron, Averil and King, G. R. D. (eds.) (1994) *The Byzantine and Early Islamic Near East* II: *Land Use and Settlement Patterns*. Princeton

Christie, N. and Loseby, S. T. (1996) *Towns in Transition: Urban Evolution in Late Antiquity and the Middle Ages*. Aldershot

Clark, G. (1993) *Women in Late Antiquity: Pagan and Christian Life-Styles*. Oxford

Consolino, F. E. (ed.) (1995) *Pagani e cristiani da Giuliano l'Apostat al Sacco di Roma*, Soveria Mannelli and Messina

Cormack, R. (1997) *Painting the Soul: Icons, Death Masks and Shrouds*. London

Croke, B. (1983) 'A.D. 476: the manufacture of a turning point', *Chiron* 13: 81–119

Dagron, G. (1981) 'Le saint, le savant, l'astrologue. Étude de thèmes hagiographiques à travers quelques recueils de "Questions et réponses" des Ve–VIIe siècles', in *Hagiographie, cultures et sociétés (IVe–VIIe s.)*, Études Augustiniennes. Paris (= G. Dagron, *La romanité chrétienne en Orient* (1984), London, IV)

Davies, N. (1996) *Europe: A History*. London

Elm, S. (1994) '*Virgins of God': The Making of Asceticism in Late Antiquity*. Oxford

Goffart, W. (1988) *The Narrators of Barbarian History: Jordanes, Gregory of Tours, Bede and Paul the Deacon*. Princeton

Hayes, J. (1972) *Late Roman Pottery: A Catalogue of Roman Fine Ware*. London (British School at Rome)

Heather, P. (1989) 'Cassiodorus and the rise of the Amals: genealogy and the Goths under Hun domination', *JRS* 79: 103–28

Hodges, R. and Whitehouse, D. (eds.) (1983) *Mohammed, Charlemagne and the Pirenne Thesis: Archaeology and the Origins of Europe.* London

Kazhdan, A. and Constable, G. (1982) *People and Power in Byzantium.* Washington, DC

Levine, L. I. (1981) *Ancient Synagogues Revealed.* Jerusalem

Lim, R. (1995) *Public Disputation, Power and Social Order in Late Antiquity.* Berkeley and Los Angeles

Mattioli, U. (ed.) (1992) *La donna nel pensiero cristiano antico.* Genoa

Momigliano, A. (1973) 'La caduta senza rumore di un impero nel 476 d.C', *Annali della Scuola Normale Superiore di Pisa,* ser. 3, vol. 3, fasc. 2: 397–418 (= *Sesto Contributo* I (Rome 1980) 160–79)

Momigliano, A. (ed.) (1963) *The Conflict between Paganism and Christianity.* Oxford

Piccirillo, M. (1993) *The Mosaics of Jordan* (ACOR Publications 1). Amman

Piganiol, A. (1947) *L'empire chrétien* (Histoire romaine IV.2). Paris

Pirenne, H. (1937) *Mohammed and Charlemagne,* Eng. trans. London

Rich, J. W. (ed.) (1992) *The City in Late Antiquity.* London

Ste Croix, G. E. M. de (1981) *The Class Struggle in the Ancient Greek World.* London

Tardieu, M. (1990) *Les paysages reliques. Routes et haltes syriennes d'Isidore à Simplicius.* Paris

Tate, G. (1992) *Les campagnes de la Syrie du Nord du IIe au VIe siècle* I. Paris

Walmsley, A. (1996) 'Byzantine Palestine and Arabia: urban prosperity in late antiquity', in Christie and Loseby (eds.) (1996) 126–58

Webster, L. and Brown, M. (eds.) (1997) *The Transformation of the Roman World AD 400–900.* London

Whittow, M. (1990) 'Ruling the late antique and early Byzantine city: a continuous history', *P&P* 129: 3–29

Whittow, M. (1996) *The Making of Orthodox Byzantium.* London

Wickham, C. (1988) 'Marx, Sherlock Holmes and the late Roman economy', *JRS* 78: 183–93

Wimbush, V. and Valantasis, R. (eds.) (1995) *Asceticism.* New York

INDEX

References in italics are to maps (by map number) and illustrations (by page number).

Arrangement of material within entries is predominantly alphabetical, though some entries begin with a chronologically-ordered section; all dates are A.D.

Footnotes are referred to only where the subject is not mentioned in the corresponding page of text.